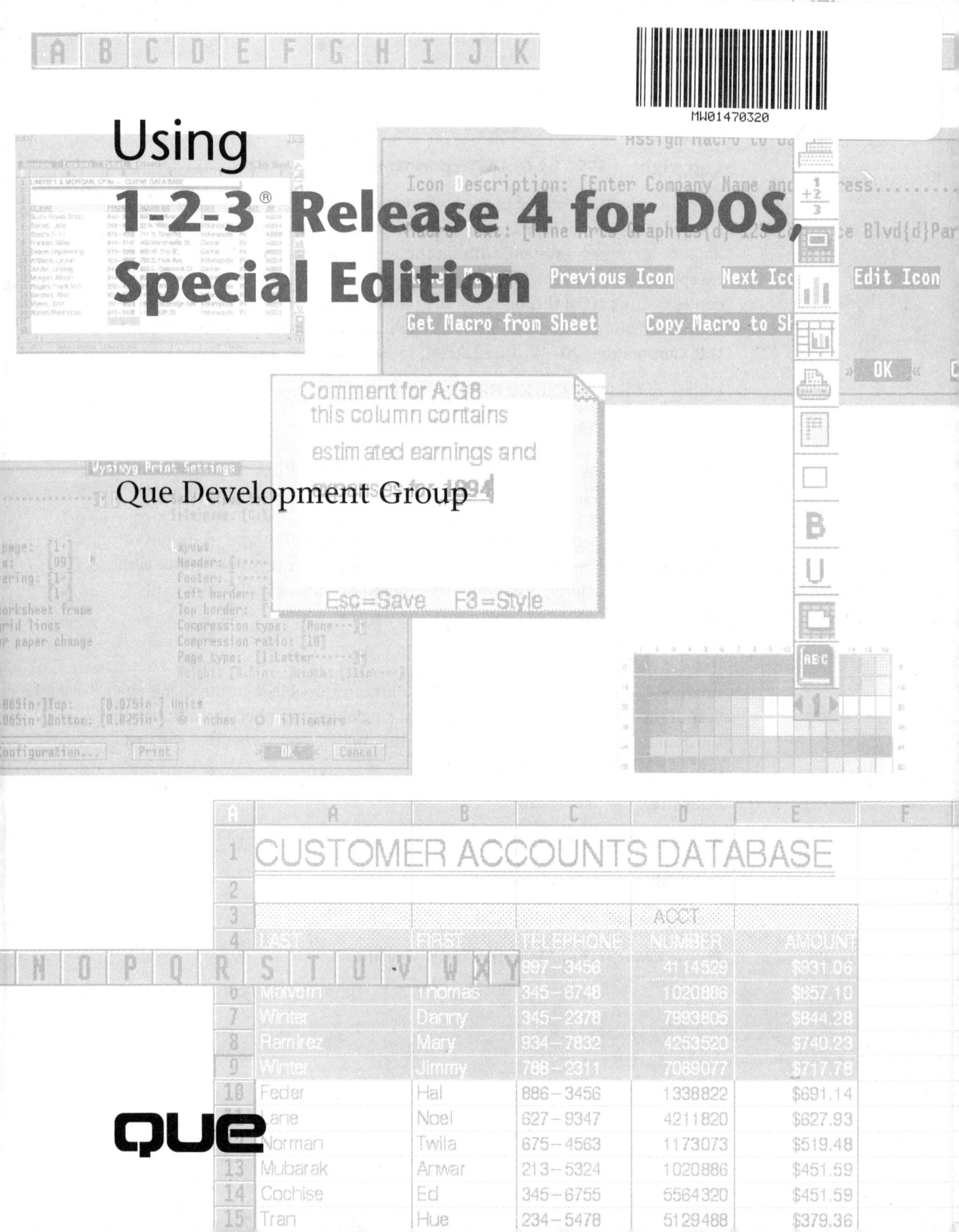

Using 1-2-3 Release 4 for DOS, Special Edition

Copyright © 1994 by Que® Corporation

All rights reserved. Printed in the United States of America. No part of this book may be used or reproduced in any form or by any means, or stored in a database or retrieval system, without the written permission of the publisher except in the case of brief quotations in critical articles and reviews. Making copies of any part of this book for any purpose other than your own personal use is a violation of United States copyright laws. For information, address Que Corporation, 201 W. 103rd Street, Indianapolis, IN, 46290.

Library of Congress Catalog Number: 94-66724

ISBN: 1-56529-629-x

This book is sold *as is*, without warranty of any kind, either express or implied, respecting the contents of this book, including but not limited to implied warranties for the book's quality, performance, merchantability, or fitness for any particular purpose. Neither Que Corporation nor its dealers or distributors shall be liable to the purchaser or any other person or entity with respect to any liability, loss, or damage caused directly or indirectly by this book.

96 95 94   6 5 4 3 2 1

Interpretation of the printing code: The rightmost double-digit number is the year of the book's printing; the rightmost single-digit number, the number of the book's printing. For example, a printing code of 94-1 shows that the first printing of the book occurred in 1994.

Publisher: David P. Ewing

Associate Publisher: Michael Miller

Publishing Director: Don Roche, Jr.

Managing Editor: Michael Cunningham

Product Marketing Manager: Greg Wiegand

Credits

Publishing Manager
Don Roche, Jr.

Acquisitions Editor
Thomas F. Godfrey III

Product Director
Joyce J. Nielsen

Production Editor
Lori Cates

Editors
Colleen Rainsberger
Kathy Simpson
Patrick Kanouse
Lynn Northrup
Andy Saff
Danielle Bird

Technical Editors
George Harding
Stephen Londergan
Michael Watson
Robert Holtz

Editorial Assistant
Jill Stanley

Acquisitions Assistant
Deborah Abshier

Book Designers
Amy Peppler-Adams
Paula Carroll

Cover Designer
Dan Armstrong

Production Team
Claudia Bell
Stephen Carlin
Karen Dodson
Joelynn Gifford
Dennis Clay Hager
Michael Hughes
Bob LaRoche
Steph Mineart
Tim Montgomery
G. Alan Palmore
Nanci Sears Perry
Dennis Sheehan
Tina Trettin
Susan VandeWalle
Johnna VanHoose
Mary Beth Wakefield
Donna Winter

Composed in *Stone Serif* and *MCPdigital* by Que Corporation

About the Authors

David Bradley is the Manager of Microcomputer Support at the Harvard Medical School. He has eight years experience in microcomputer support, training, and courseware development for a variety of training vendors in the Boston area. He also has worked as an independent training consultant for several firms in New England. David also served on the Advisory Board of the 1993 LotusWorld Conference in Boston.

Betty Brooks, owner of Records and Ranges, is an independent consultant specializing in spreadsheet and database applications written in Paradox PAL. She has been an active participant in computer user groups, especially HAL-PC (Houston Area League of PC Users) for more than 10 years. The HAL-PC User Journal's spreadsheet column, "Cells & Ranges," has been Betty's writing outlet for the past 8 1/2 years. After graduating from the School of Business at the University of Connecticut, she spent many years volunteering and car pooling while her son and daughter grew into independent adults who are now college students.

Shane Devenshire is a consultant specializing in project management and the scientific and business application of spreadsheets and graphics computer packages. He is a founding partner of the MAR&SHA Corporation, a computer consulting company providing application development, programming, and training in both the mainframe and personal computer areas. He has written over 100 computer-related articles for more than one dozen journals here and abroad, and has been a guest editor for *PC World* magazine. He also has been on the product review board of *INFO World*. He has three years of experience in the bio-tech arena, five years in business management, and 13 years in computer-related industries. Shane was a contributing author to Que's *Excel Professional Techniques*.

Linda A. Flanders is a Certified Public Accountant and holds a bachelor of science degree in Accounting from Indiana University. She has worked in public accounting for Arthur Andersen & Co., and private accounting for Mayflower Group, Inc., where she specialized in taxation. She currently operates a small individual tax practice. She is the author of Que's *Using Quicken Version 3 for Windows*, *Using Quicken Version 7 for DOS*, *Using QuickBooks for Windows*, and *Using Microsoft Money 2.0*.

Pat Freeland is a Design-Verification Engineer with Lotus Development Corporation and a former public-school teacher and software trainer. He has written articles for *Lotus* Magazine and written or contributed to several books on using computer software, including Que's *1-2-3 Release 4 for Windows QuickStart*. He lives with his wife, two children, and two dogs in Hingham, Massachusetts, near Boston.

Robert J. Perry is a Marketing Manager for Lotus Development Corporation. Perry has been with Lotus for more than 10 years and has held a variety of positions, including Product Manager for 1-2-3 for DOS Releases 3.1 and 3.1+. Rob also has been responsible for various other marketing efforts at Lotus, including international spreadsheet marketing, 1-2-3 upgrade programs, building a group responsible for performance and usability testing of 1-2-3, and marketing 1-2-3 for use on local area networks. Before joining Lotus in 1983, Perry was a Technical Consultant at Chase Econometrics/Interactive Data Corporation specializing in financial and econometric modeling applications. Perry has contributed to several of Que's *Using 1-2-3* books. He earned a bachelor of arts in Economics from the University of Virginia.

Brian Underdahl is an author and independent computer consultant based in Reno, NV. He is the author of Que's *Using Quattro Pro 5 for Windows*, Special Edition; and *Upgrading to MS-DOS 6*, among other titles. He was also a contributing author to many Que books, including *Using 1-2-3 Release 4 for Windows*, Special Edition; *Using 1-2-3 Release 2.4*, Special Edition; *1-2-3 Power Macros*; and other 1-2-3 and Symphony titles. Underdahl also has served as technical editor of several Que books.

Bob Voges is a Documentation Engineer for Lotus Development Corporation. He has worked for Lotus for nine years, teaching and writing about 1-2-3. Before joining Lotus, he worked for Arthur Andersen & Co., where he began using and teaching 1-2-3 when it first shipped in 1983. He has a degree in Accounting from Boston University and earned his Massachusetts CPA certificate in 1983.

Rick Winter is a Senior Partner at PRW Computer Services. He is President of Information Systems Trainers, a nonprofit organization of trainers in the Denver metro area. Rick has trained more than 2,600 adults on personal computers. Rick is a contributing author for Que's *Using Microsoft Office*, Special Edition; *Using Excel Version 5 for Windows*, Special Edition; *Using WordPerfect Version 6 for Windows*, and *Using PC Tools 8*. Rick won the Rocky Mountain Chapter Society for Technical Communication's Distinguished Award for his work on Que's *Excel for Windows SureSteps*. Rick has also written course manuals for Lotus 1-2-3, WordPerfect, Windows, Word, Excel, and Q&A.

Joyce J. Nielsen is a Senior Product Development Specialist for Que Corporation, where she focuses on the development of spreadsheet, database, and word processing books. Before joining Que five years ago, Nielsen worked as a Research Analyst for a shopping mall developer, where she began using 1-2-3 in 1984 to develop and document 1-2-3 business applications used nationwide. She is the author of *1-2-3 Release 4 for Windows Quick Reference*, *1-2-3 Release 2.4 Quick Reference*, *1-2-3 Release 3.4 Quick Reference*, and contributing author to many other Que titles, such as *Using 1-2-3 Release 4 for Windows*, Special Edition. Nielsen received a bachelor of science degree in Quantitative Business Analysis from Indiana University.

David P. Ewing is currently the President and Publisher of Que Corporation, a division of Macmillan Computer Publishing, which is the largest computer book publishing company in the world. David has been in computer book publishing since 1984, when he joined Que as a Staff Writer. Shortly after joining Que, he became a Product Development Specialist, focusing on the development of new 1-2-3 books, and continuing to write on such software topics as 1-2-3, Symphony, and Q&A. In 1985 (as Product Development Director), Ewing directed the expansion of the Que book line on topics such as WordPerfect, DOS, dBASE, Windows, Excel, and Word. In 1990, he became the President and Publisher of New Riders Publishing, a division of Macmillan Computer Publishing specializing in publishing books on AutoCAD, networking, and professional graphics software, and advanced books on MS-DOS, OS/2, and Windows. In 1993, Ewing returned to Que to focus on directing a publishing plan that would continue to bring the millions of dedicated Que customers high-quality books on the PC software and hardware used worldwide today.

Trademarks

All terms mentioned in this book that are known to be trademarks or service marks have been appropriately capitalized. Que cannot attest to the accuracy of this information. Use of a term in this book should not be regarded as affecting the validity of any trademark or service mark.

Lotus and 1-2-3 are registered trademarks of Lotus Development Corporation.

Screen Reproductions in this book were created using Collage Plus from Inner Media, Inc., Hollis, New Hampshire.

Acknowledgments

Using 1-2-3 Release 4 for DOS, Special Edition, is the result of the efforts of many talented and dedicated people. Que Corporation thanks the following people for their contributions to the revision of this book:

The authors: **David Bradley**, **Betty Brooks**, **Shane Devenshire**, **David Ewing**, **Linda Flanders**, **Pat Freeland**, **Joyce Nielsen**, **Rob Perry**, **Brian Underdahl**, **Bob Voges**, and **Rick Winter**, for adhering to our numerous instructions and guidelines, and for submitting high-quality material in record time.

Publishing Director **Don Roche, Jr.** and Product Director **Joyce Nielsen**, for greatly improving the overall outline and quality of this book, directing the authors, developing the text, and keeping this project on track through the development stage.

Acquisitions Editor **Tom Godfrey**, for assembling and managing the team of authors, and for helping to keep this book on schedule; Acquisitions Coordinator **Debbie Abshier**, for coordinating the technical editors on this project and keeping us informed of changes to the beta schedules.

Production Editor **Lori Cates** for her commitment to producing a high-quality book on a tight schedule. Editors **Danielle Bird**, **Patrick Kanouse**, **Lynn Northrup**, **Colleen Rainsberger**, **Andy Saff**, and **Kathy Simpson** for their editing skills, timeliness, and attention to detail.

Technical editors **George Harding**, **Bob Holtz**, **Steve Londergan**, and **Michael Watson** for their excellent technical review of this book.

Que President and Publisher, **David Ewing**, for contributing the Foreword and Introduction to this book.

Members of the Que Production team for their speed and flexibility, and their efforts in producing a high-quality text.

Contents at a Glance

Introduction	5	
The Basics	**29**	
1 What's New in Release 4 for DOS	31	
2 What Every 1-2-3 User Should Know	45	
3 Finding Solutions with Formulas and Functions	157	
4 Controlling Your Worksheet Display	233	
5 Using SmartIcons	249	

Presenting Data	**273**	
6 Making Your Worksheets Dazzle	275	
7 Attaching Comments to Worksheet Cells	345	
8 Printing Reports	357	

Organizing Your Work	**405**	
9 Working with Files	407	
10 Organizing Your Data with Multiple-Worksheet Files	457	
11 Consolidating Worksheet Data	475	
12 Creating and Using Templates	493	
13 Protecting Worksheet Data and Files	511	

Analyzing Your Data	**527**	
14 Analyzing Formulas with Auditor	529	
15 Using Functions To Analyze Data	541	
16 Finding Solutions with Solver	555	
17 Goal Seeking with Backsolver	591	
18 Tracking Multiple Sets of Data with Version Manager	601	

Working with Databases	**617**	
19 Creating Databases	619	
20 Sorting Your Data	631	
21 Finding Specific Data	643	
22 High-Level Database Techniques	667	

Graphing Your Data	**703**	
23 Creating Effective Graphs	705	
24 Creating Power Graphs	751	
25 Developing Business Presentations	797	

Automating with Macros — 827

26 Short Macros To Make Your
   Life Easier — 829
27 Advanced Macro Command
   Power Techniques — 863
28 Controlling 1-2-3 with Macros — 933

Sharing Data — 979

29 Sharing 1-2-3 Data with
   Windows Applications — 981
30 Sharing 1-2-3 Data with
   Databases — 1025
31 Sharing 1-2-3 Data with DOS
   Word Processors — 1041

Indexes — 1063

Index of Common Problems — 1065
Index — 1073

Contents

Foreword **1**

Introduction **5**
    A Quick Tour of This Book 6
        Conventions Used in This Book 11
    A Quick Tour of 1-2-3 13
        Understanding 1-2-3 Hardware Requirements
            and Options 13
        Using the Command Menus 14
        Using the Mouse with 1-2-3 14
        Learning the 1-2-3 Keyboard 16
        Learning the 1-2-3 Screen Display 22
    Conclusion 27

I The Basics   29

1 What's New in 1-2-3 Release 4 for DOS   31

    Improved Interface 31
    New Memory Model 35
    Auto-Backup Feature 35
    Column Fit to Widest Entry 35
    Cell Annotation 37
    SmartSheet Templates 37
    Tools Menu 38
    Version Manager 40
    Sending and Receiving Mail 42
    Spell Checker 43
    QuickStart 43

2 What Every 1-2-3 User Should Know   45

    Starting To Use 1-2-3 46
        Starting 1-2-3 46
        Starting Wyslwyg 47
        Exiting 1-2-3 49
    Moving Around the Worksheet 51
        Using the Keyboard to Move the Cell Pointer 51
        Using the Mouse to Move the Cell Pointer 51
        Using the Scroll Bar To Move the Cell Pointer 52
        Using the Basic Movement Keys 53

Using the 1-2-3 Help Features 60
    Finding On-Screen Help 60
    Using QuickStart 62
Choosing Commands from Command Menus 63
Entering and Editing Data 63
    Entering Data in the Worksheet 64
    Editing Data in a Worksheet 68
Filling Ranges with Data 70
    Filling Ranges with Numbers 70
    Using Formulas To Fill Ranges 71
    Filling Ranges with Dates or Times 72
Entering Basic Formulas 74
    Pointing to Cell References 74
    Using Operators in Numeric Formulas 75
    Using Operators in String Formulas 76
    Using Operators in Logical Formulas 78
    Correcting Errors in Formulas 78
    Addressing Cells 79
Working with Ranges 81
    Selecting Ranges 81
    Specifying a Range with Range Names 87
Copying and Moving Data 92
    Moving the Contents of Cells 92
    Copying the Contents of Cells 98
Finding and Replacing Data 112
Erasing Data 116
Inserting and Deleting Rows and Columns 117
    Inserting Rows and Columns 117
    Deleting Rows and Columns 119
Setting Column Widths 121
Setting Row Heights 124
Changing Text Alignment 125
    Aligning Labels 126
    Reformatting Paragraphs 127
    Setting and Clearing Text Attributes 130
    Changing Label Prefixes 130
Applying Wysiwyg Formatting 132
Using the Undo Feature 134
Saving and Retrieving Your Work 136
    Saving a 1-2-3 File 136
    Retrieving a 1-2-3 File 138
Clearing the Workspace 139
Printing Your Worksheet 140
    Checking the Printer Settings 140
    Specifying a Print Range 141
    Previewing the Print Range On-Screen 141
    Printing a Report 142
Creating Simple Graphs 143
    Selecting a Graph Type 147

Specifying Data Ranges 149
Using the QuickGraph Feature 154
Constructing the Default Line Graph 155
From Here… 156

3 Finding Solutions with Formulas and Functions 157

Entering Functions 159
Using the Mathematical Functions 161
Using General Mathematical Functions 161
Using Logarithmic Functions 165
Using Trigonometric Functions 167
Using Date and Time Functions 169
@D360—Dealing with 360-Day Years 170
@DATE—Converting Date Values to Serial Numbers 170
@DATEVALUE—Changing Date Strings to
Serial Numbers 172
@DAY, @MONTH, and @YEAR—Converting
Serial Numbers to Dates 173
@TIME—Converting Time Values to Serial Numbers 174
@TIMEVALUE—Converting Time Strings to
Serial Values 175
@HOUR, @MINUTE, and SECOND—Converting
Serial Numbers to Time Values 175
@NOW and @TODAY—Finding the current
Date and Time 176
Using the Financial and Accounting Functions 178
@IRR—Calculating Internal Rate of Return 179
@RATE—Calculating Compound Growth Rate 180
@PMT—Calculating Loan Payment Amounts 181
@NPV—Calculating Net Present Value 182
@PV—Calculating Present Value of an Annuity 183
@FV—Calculating Future Value 184
@TERM—Calculating the Term of an Investment 185
@CTERM—Calculating the Term of a
Compounding Investment 185
@SLN—Calculating Straight-Line Depreciation 185
@DDB—Calculating Double Declining-Balance
Depreciation 186
@SYD—Calculating Sum-of-the-Years'-Digits
Depreciation 187
@VDB—Calculating Variable Declining-Balance
Depreciation 187
Using the Statistical Functions 189
@AVG—Computing the Average of a List of Numbers 190
@COUNT—Counting Cell Entries 192
@MAX and @MIN—Finding Maximum and
Minimum Values 193

@STD and @STDS—Calculating the Standard
    Deviation 194
@VAR and @VARS—Calculating the Variance 195
@SUM—Totaling Values 196
@SUMPRODUCT—Multiplying Lists of Values 196
Using Database Functions 198
Using the Logical Functions 198
@IF—Creating Conditional Tests 199
@ISERR and @ISNA—Trapping Errors in
    Conditional Tests 203
@TRUE and @FALSE—Checking for Errors 204
@ISRANGE—Checking for a Range Name 204
@ISSTRING and @ISNUMBER—Checking the Cell's
    Aspect 205
Using the String Functions 206
@FIND—Locating One String Within Another 208
@MID—Extracting One String from Another 209
@LEFT and @RIGHT—Extracting Strings from
    Left and Right 210
@REPLACE—Replacing a String Within a String 210
@LENGTH—Computing the Length of a String 211
@EXACT—Comparing Strings 211
@LOWER, @UPPER, and @PROPER—Converting
    the Case of Strings 211
@REPEAT—Repeating Strings Within a Cell 212
@TRIM—Removing Blank Spaces from a String 213
@S and @N—Testing for Strings and Values 213
@STRING—Converting Values to Strings 214
@VALUE—Converting Strings to Values 215
@CLEAN—Removing Nonprintable Characters
    from Strings 215
@CHAR—Displaying LMBCS Characters 216
@CODE—Computing the LMBCS Code 216
Using the Special Functions 216
@?—Indicating Unknown Add-In Functions 217
@@—Referencing Cells Indirectly 218
@CELL and @CELLPOINTER—Checking Cell
    Attributes 219
@COORD—Creating a Cell Address 221
@CHOOSE—Selecting an Item from a List 222
@COLS, @ROWS, and @SHEETS—Finding the
    Dimensions of Ranges 223
@ERR and @NA—Trapping Errors 223
@INDEX—Retrieving Data from Specified Locations 224
@INFO—Getting System Information About the
    Current Session 225
Controlling Recalculation 226
Understanding Recalculation Methods 227

Understanding Circular References 228
Using Iteration To Solve Circular References 229
From Here... 231

4 Controlling Your Worksheet Display   233

Changing the Display Format 233
Splitting the Screen 234
Displaying a Graph in a Worksheet 237
Freezing Titles On-Screen 238
Setting Display Characteristics 241
    Changing the Display 242
    Zooming the Display 242
    Setting the Color Display 242
    Using Other Display Options 244
    Changing the Font-Directory 246
    Setting the Row Display 246
    Setting Default Display Values 246
From Here... 247

5 Using SmartIcons   249

Understanding SmartIcons 250
    Selecting SmartIcons by Using the Mouse 258
    Selecting SmartIcons by Using the Keyboard 258
    Hiding and Redisplaying the SmartIcon Palette 259
    Using the Version Manager, QuickGraph, and Sort
        SmartIcons 260
Customizing SmartIcons 261
    Using the Custom Palette 261
    Attaching Macros to SmartIcons 264
    Changing the Picture on a User SmartIcon 269
From Here... 271

II Presenting Data   273

6 Making Your Worksheets Dazzle   275

Setting Worksheet Global Defaults 276
Setting Range and Worksheet Global Formats 280
    The Available Formats 280
    The Contents Versus the Format of a Cell 283
Spell Checking Your Data 284
    Using the Spell Checker 285
    Adding and Deleting Words from the Personal
        Dictionary 288
Formatting Numbers 290
    General Format 296
    Fixed Format 297
    Comma (,) Format 297

        Currency Format 299
        Percent Format 300
        Scientific Format 301
        The +/– Format 302
        Date and Time Formats 303
        Text Format 309
        Hidden Format 311
        Label Format 312
        Automatic Format 312
        Parentheses Format 315
        Color Format 316
        International Formats 316
    Suppressing the Display of Zeros 317
    Justifying Text 318
    Formatting with the Wysiwyg Menu 320
        Understanding the Wysiwyg :Format Commands 320
        Understanding Fonts 321
        Using Boldface, Italics, and Underlining 329
        Changing Range Colors 330
        Drawing Lines and Boxes 330
        Adding Shading 332
        Using Formatting Sequences 333
    Managing Wysiwyg Formats 336
        Copying and Moving Formats 336
        Using Named Styles 337
        Importing Formats 340
        Exporting Formats 341
    From Here... 342

7 Attaching Comments to Worksheet Cells   345

    Appending Comments to Values and Formulas 346
    Using Notepads 346
        Attaching a Notepad to the Current Cell 348
        Editing a Notepad 349
        Changing a Notepad to an Icon 349
        Changing a Notepad to Full Size 350
        Hiding Notepads 351
        Copying and Moving Notepads 351
        Deleting Notepads 352
        Creating a Table of Notepads 352
        Formatting Text in a Notepad 353
    From Here... 356

8 Printing Reports   357

    Printing with /Print versus :Print 358
    Understanding the Default Print Settings 359
        Viewing the Current Printer Settings 360
        Modifying the Default Hardware-Specific Options 361
        Configuring the Printer 362

Using the :Print Commands 363
    Understanding the :Print Menu 363
    Specifying a Print Range 365
    Previewing On-Screen 367
    Printing a Short Report 367
    Printing Data and Graphics on a Single Page 368
    Printing Multiple-Page Reports 369
    Compressing the Printout 372
    Printing Three-Dimensional Print Ranges 373
    Printing Multiple Ranges 373
    Setting Up the Page 374
    Choosing the Print Orientation 379
    Specifying Other Print Settings 379
    Excluding Worksheet Areas from the Printout 380
Using the /Print Commands 381
    Understanding the /Print Menu 382
    Setting Defaults for the /Print Command 384
    Designing Reports 386
Enhancing Reports 390
    Improving the Layout 390
    Using Setup Strings 391
    Selecting Color 393
Controlling the Printer 393
    Choosing the Printer 393
    Controlling the Movement of the Paper 393
    Holding a Print Job 394
    Pausing the Printer 395
    Stopping the Printer 395
    Printing a Graph with Text 396
    Naming and Saving the Current Print Settings 397
    Clearing the Print Options 397
Printing to an Encoded File 398
Using Background Printing 399
    Loading the BPrint Utility 399
    Using /Print Background 401
    Using :Print Background 401
Preparing Output for Acceptance by Other Programs 401
Creating an Encapsulated PostScript (EPS) File 402
From Here… 403

III Organizing Your Work   405

9 Working with Files   407

Managing Active Files in Memory 408
Naming Files 409
    Displaying File Names 412
    Changing the Default Save Extension 413

Working with Disks 413
Changing Directories 414
    Changing the Default Directory 414
    Changing the Current Directory 415
Saving Files 416
Retrieving Files from Disk 421
    Using Wild Cards To Retrieve Files 424
    Retrieving Files from Subdirectories 425
    Retrieving a File Automatically 425
    Opening a New File in Memory 426
Managing Files with the Viewer 428
    Using the Viewer 428
    Understanding the Viewer Menu and Screen 430
    Navigating the Viewer 431
    Retrieving a File 432
    Changing the Display Sort Order 433
    Opening Files with the Viewer 433
    Linking Files with the Viewer 434
    Browsing Files with the Viewer 437
Erasing Files 437
Creating Lists and Tables of Files 440
Transferring Files 443
    Transferring Files with /File Import 443
    Transferring Files with the Translate Utility 446
    Using Earlier Versions of 1-2-3 and Symphony Files
        in Release 4 448
    Using External Databases 448
Accessing the Operating System 448
Using 1-2-3 on a Network 450
    Understanding File Sharing 450
    Getting a File's Reservation 452
    Preventing Changes to Worksheet Settings 453
    Updating Your Links 454
Sending and Receiving Mail Through cc:Mail 454
From Here… 456

10 Organizing Your Data with Multiple-Worksheet Files   457

Using Multiple-Worksheet Files 458
Referencing Cells in Multiple Worksheets 460
Working with Sheets in Multiple-Worksheet Files 461
    Inserting Worksheets 461
    Naming Worksheets 463
    Deleting Worksheets 464
    Hiding Worksheets 464
Displaying Multiple Worksheets 465
Moving Around Multiple Worksheets 467
Entering Formulas with Multiple-Worksheet Files 470

Formatting a Multiple-Worksheet File 471
    Formatting with 3-D Ranges 471
    Using GROUP Mode To Change All the
      Worksheets in a File 471
From Here... 474

11 Consolidating Worksheet Data   475

Extracting and Combining Data 476
    Extracting Information 476
    Combining Information from Other Files 481
Linking Files 487
    Entering Formulas That Link Files 488
    Managing Links 490
    Choosing Between Multiple-Worksheet Files
      and Linked Files 490
From Here... 492

12 Creating and Using Templates   493

Understanding the Contents of Templates 494
Using the SmartSheet Templates 494
    The Buy/Lease SmartSheet 495
    The Daily Planner SmartSheet 499
    The Expense Report SmartSheet 500
    The Investment Record SmartSheet 502
    The Statement of Net Worth SmartSheet 502
Managing Template Files 503
Creating Your Own Templates 504
Creating Other Useful Templates 507
From Here... 509

13 Protecting Worksheet Data and Files   511

Protecting Worksheet Data 512
    Protecting Cells from Change 512
    Restricting Data-Entry Options 514
Hiding Worksheet Data 516
Protecting Files with Passwords 519
Sealing Files 523
    Sealing a File To Prevent Tampering 523
    Protecting Files with Reservations 525
From Here... 525

IV Analyzing Your Data   527

14 Analyzing Formulas with Auditor   529

Starting and Using Auditor 529
Understanding the Auditor Menu 530
    Setting the Audit Range 531
    Changing the Way That Auditor Reports Results 532

Troubleshooting Formulas in a Worksheet 533
    Finding Formulas 534
    Finding Cells Used by a Formula (Precedents) 534
    Finding Formulas That Refer to a Cell (Dependents) 535
    Examining Recalculation Order 536
    Examining Circular References 537
    Resetting Auditor Options 538
From Here… 539

15 Using Functions To Analyze Data   541

Analyzing Database Information 541
    Calculating Simple Database Statistics 543
    Calculating Deviation and Variance 546
    Extracting a Value or Label 546
    Working with External Tables 548
Analyzing Information in a Table 549
    Looking Up Entries in a Table 549
    Retrieving Data from Specified Locations 551
From Here… 553

16 Finding Solutions with Solver   555

Understanding Solver 556
    What Types of Problems Can Solver Solve? 556
    How Does Solver Work? 557
Setting Up Your Problem 557
    Adjustable Cells: The Values Solver Can Change 558
    Constraints: The Limits to the Problem 559
    Optimal Cell: The Value To Maximize or Minimize 559
Solving a Problem 560
    Defining the Problem 561
    Examining Solver's Answers 563
Examples of Solver Problems 567
    Optimizing Production for Maximum Profit 567
    Allocating an Investment Portfolio 570
    Allocating an Advertising Budget 573
Using Solver Reports 577
    The Answer Report 578
    The How Solved Report 579
    The What-If Report 580
    The Differences Report 582
    The Inconsistent Constraints Report 583
    The Unused Constraints Report 585
    The Cells Used Report 586
Using Functions with Solver 587
Using Solver with Macros 588
From Here… 589

17 Goal Seeking with Backsolver — 591

Using Backsolver To Change a Single Variable 591
   Specifying the Goal 593
   Specifying the Variables 595
   Solving the Problem 595
Using Backsolver To Change Several Variables 596
   Specifying the Goal 597
   Specifying the Variables 598
   Solving the Problem 599
From Here… 600

18 Tracking Multiple Sets of Data with Version Manager — 601

Understanding Version Manager Basics 602
Working with Versions: The /Tools Version Menu 603
   Creating Versions 605
   Displaying Versions 608
   Updating Versions 609
   Deleting Versions 609
Working with Scenarios: The Manage-Scenario Menu 609
   Creating, Displaying, and Modifying Scenarios 610
   Deleting Scenarios 613
Using Version Manager To Share Data 614
Looking at Application Examples 614
   What-If Analysis 614
   Applications Requiring Frequent Updates
      or Iterations 615
   Applications with Several Contributors 615
From Here… 615

V Working with Databases — 617

19 Creating Databases — 619

Defining a Database 619
Designing a Database 621
Creating a Database 622
   Entering Field Names 623
   Entering Data 624
   Modifying a Database 626
From Here… 629

20 Sorting Your Data — 631

Sorting Database Records 631
   Using the One-Key Sort 633
   Using the Two-Key Sort 637
   Using the Extra-Key Sort 638

Contents

Determining the Sort Order 639
Restoring the Presort Order 640
From Here... 641

21 Finding Specific Data   643

Using Minimum Search Requirements 644
    Determining the Input Range 645
    Entering the Criteria Range 645
    Using the Find Command 647
Listing All Specified Records 650
    Defining the Output Range 650
    Executing the Extract Command 653
    Modifying Records 653
Extracting Unique Records 655
Deleting Specified Records 656
Handling More Complicated Criteria Ranges 657
    Using Wild Cards in Criteria Ranges 657
    Using Formulas in Criteria Ranges 658
    Setting Up AND Conditions 661
    Setting Up OR Conditions 662
    Using String Searches 663
    Using Special Operators 664
From Here... 666

22 High-Level Database Techniques   667

Performing What-If Analysis with Data Tables 667
    Understanding Data-Table Terms and Concepts 668
    Creating a One-Variable Data Table 669
    Creating a Two-Variable Data Table 671
    Creating a Three-Variable Data Table 674
    Creating a Labeled Data Table 677
Creating Frequency Distributions 687
Performing a Regression Analysis 688
Working with Matrices 693
Importing Data from Other Programs 695
From Here... 701

VI Graphing Your Data   703

23 Creating Effective Graphs   705

Choosing an Appropriate Graph Type 705
Building All Graph Types 706
    Line Graphs 707
    Bar Graphs 708
    Stack-Bar Graphs 710
    Area Graphs 711
    Mixed Graphs 712

Copying a Graph 772
Specifying Graph Settings 772
Using the Graphics Editor 773
Adding Objects 775
Selecting Objects 779
Editing Objects 780
Changing the Display of the Graphics Editing
  Window 786
Rearranging Objects 789
Transforming Objects 792
Printing Graphics Created with the Graphics Editor 795
From Here… 795

25 Developing Business Presentations — 797

Setting Up Your Worksheet Area for Presentations 798
Using the Row-and-Column Structure To Assist
  with Layout 798
Modifying the 1-2-3 Display for On-Screen
  Presentations 799
Developing Multiple-Page Presentations 800
Using 1-2-3 To Convey a Message 802
Following Guidelines for Presenting Text 802
Following Guidelines for Presenting Graphics 805
Using the Color Capabilities of 1-2-3 808
Using Color To Highlight Presentation Elements 809
Conveying Information with Selected Colors 809
Creating Alternative Color Schemes 810
Selecting Color Schemes for Black-and-White
  Printing 811
Selecting Color for Background, Text, and Graphics 812
Using Color To Guide the Audience 812
Emphasizing Text or Graphic Elements 813
Selecting the Appropriate Font 813
Using Special Symbols 814
Using Boldface and Italics 815
Using Lines, Boxes, and Shading 817
Using the :Graph Commands To Add Impact 819
Adding 1-2-3 Graphs 819
Adding Blank Graphs 820
Using Clip Art 820
Creating an Effective Background and Border
  for Presentations 821
Printing Slides from 1-2-3 822
Using Macros for Computer Presentations 823
A Macro for Changing Slides with the Enter Key 823
A Macro for Timing Slide Changes 824
From Here… 825

    Pie Graphs 713
    XY Graphs 716
    HLCO Graphs 718
Creating Graphs with the QuickGraph SmartIcon 720
Adding Descriptive Labels and Numbers................................ 720
    Using the Titles Option 721
    Adding Data Labels to a Graph 724
    Entering Labels Below the X-Axis............................... 726
    Using the Legend Option 727
Altering the Default Graph Display 728
    Selecting the Format for Data in Graphs................... 728
    Setting a Background Grid 729
Specifying Colors, Hatches, Line Styles, and Symbols 730
    Specifying Colors 731
    Specifying Hatches... 732
    Specifying Line Styles 734
    Specifying Symbol Styles 735
    Setting Text Attributes 736
Viewing Graphs 737
    Viewing Graphs from the Worksheet......................... 737
    Viewing Graphs in a Screen Window 737
    Viewing Graphs in Wysiwyg 738
    Viewing a Graph in Color 739
Saving Graphs and Graph Settings 739
    Saving Graphs on Disk 739
    Saving Graph Settings 740
Printing Graphs with the /Print Command 741
    Using the /Print Command 741
    Using the /Print [P,E] Options' Advanced
        Image Command 742
    Printing a Graph with Default Settings 744
    Printing a Graph with Customized Print Settings........... 745
    Saving Graph Print Settings 746
Including Graphs in Reports 746
From Here… 748

24 Creating Power Graphs   751

Modifying the Graph Axes 751
    Setting Minimum and Maximum Axis Values 754
    Formatting the Axis Numbers 755
    Changing the Axis Scale Indicator 756
    Specifying Axis Types 757
    Setting the Scale Number Exponent 758
    Specifying Scale Number Width 759
Adding a Second Y Scale 759
Using Other Features Menu Options 762
Enhancing Graphs with the :Graph Commands 768
    Adding a Graph 768
    Repositioning a Graph 771

VII Automating with Macros   827

26 Short Macros To Make Your Life Easier   829

Understanding Macros 830
    Creating Some Sample Macros 831
    Following Guidelines for Developing Macros 835
    Using Macro Key Names 838
    Planning the Macro Layout 842
    Documenting Macros 844
Creating Macros with the Record Feature 846
    Following Guidelines for Using the Record Feature 850
    Using Playback To Repeat Keystrokes 851
Naming and Running Macros 852
    Using Alt+*letter* Macros 852
    Using Macros with Descriptive Names 853
    Using Macros That Execute Automatically 853
Testing and Debugging Macros 855
    Using STEP and TRACE Modes 855
Protecting Macros 859
Assigning a Macro to a User SmartIcon 860
From Here… 862

27 Advanced Macro Command Power Techniques   863

    Why Use the Advanced Macro Commands? 864
What Are the Advanced Macro Commands? 864
Understanding Advanced Macro Command Syntax 865
Developing Programs with the Advanced Macro
    Commands 866
    Creating the Program 867
    Naming and Running the Program 867
    Debugging the Program 868
Listing the Advanced Macro Commands 869
    The ? Command 872
    The APPENDBELOW Command 873
    The APPENDRIGHT Command 874
    The BEEP Command 876
    The BLANK Command 877
    The BRANCH Command 877
    The BREAKOFF Command 879
    The BREAKON Command 880
    The CE or CLEARENTRY Command 880
    The CLOSE Command 880
    The CONTENTS Command 881
    The DEFINE Command 884
    The DISPATCH Command 885
    The FILESIZE Command 886
    The FOR and FORBREAK Commands 887

The FORM Command 889
The FORMBREAK Command 891
The FRAMEOFF Command 892
The FRAMEON Command 892
The GET Command 892
The GETLABEL Command 893
The GETNUMBER Command 894
The GETPOS Command 895
The GRAPHOFF Command 896
The GRAPHON Command 896
The IF Command 898
The INDICATE Command 900
The LET Command 901
The LOOK Command 903
The MENUBRANCH Command 905
The MENUCALL Command 906
The ONERROR Command 908
The OPEN Command 909
The PANELOFF Command 912
The PANELON Command 913
The PUT Command 913
The QUIT Command 915
The READ Command 916
The READLN Command 917
The RECALC and RECALCCOL Commands 918
The RESTART Command 920
The RETURN Command 922
The SETPOS Command 922
The {subroutine} Command 923
The SYSTEM Command 926
The WAIT Command 926
The WINDOWSOFF Command 928
The WINDOWSON Command 929
The WRITE Command 930
The WRITELN Command 930
The /x Commands 931
From Here… 932

28 Controlling 1-2-3 with Macros   933

Reviewing the Steps for Application Development 934
Developing a High-Level Overview 934
Breaking the Project into Logical, Manageable Units 936
Fleshing Out the Detail for Each Module 937
Developing Templates 939
Writing and Recording Program Modules 940
The Main Module 941
The Import Module 942

The DATA_WORKUP Module 947
The SLIDE_SHOW Module 953
The ROLLOVER Module 958
The OPENING Module 961
The WARNING and CHECK Modules 964
Automating the Monthly Update of the Budget Numbers 968
Debugging the Application 971
Documenting the Application 973
From Here… 977

VIII Sharing Data 979

29 Sharing 1-2-3 Data with Windows Applications 981

Using 1-2-3 Release 4 with Microsoft Windows 982
    Starting 1-2-3 from Microsoft Windows 982
    Operating 1-2-3 in Microsoft Windows 985
    Copying 1-2-3 Information to the Clipboard 986
Sharing Data with Windows Word Processors 989
    Preparing the 1-2-3 Worksheet 989
    Sharing 1-2-3 Data with Microsoft Word 6.0
        for Windows 990
    Sharing 1-2-3 Data with WordPerfect 6.0
        for Windows 999
    Sharing 1-2-3 Data with Ami Pro 3 1010
Sharing Data with Windows Spreadsheets 1018
    Sharing Data with 1-2-3 Release 4 for Windows 1018
    Sharing Data with Microsoft Excel 5 for Windows 1020
From Here… 1022

30 Sharing 1-2-3 Data with Databases 1025

Working with External Databases 1025
Understanding External Database Terminology 1027
Using an Existing External Table 1028
Listing External Tables 1030
Creating a New External Table 1031
    Duplicating an Existing Structure 1032
    Creating a New Structure 1034
Using Other Data External Commands 1036
    Controlling the External Database Updates 1036
    Sending Commands to the Database-Management
        Program 1037
    Using /Data External Other Translation 1038
Deleting an External Table 1038
Disconnecting 1-2-3 and the External Table 1039
From Here… 1040

31 Sharing 1-2-3 Data with DOS Word Processors 1041

Preparing the 1-2-3 Worksheet 1042
Sharing 1-2-3 Data with WordPerfect 6.0 for DOS 1042
    Importing 1-2-3 Data into a WordPerfect Document 1043
    Merging WordPerfect Documents with 1-2-3 Data 1049
    Importing a 1-2-3 Graph into a WordPerfect
        Document 1055
Sharing 1-2-3 Data with Microsoft Word 6.0 for DOS 1057
    Creating a Word Table from 1-2-3 Data 1057
    Creating a Link to Your 1-2-3 Data 1059
    Merging 1-2-3 Data with a Word Document 1059
    Importing a 1-2-3 Graph into a Word Document 1059
From Here… 1061

Indexes 1063

Index of Common Problems 1065

Index 1073

Foreword

by David Paul Ewing

President and Publisher of Que Corporation

In 1983, Que published the first edition of this book. In the months that followed the publication of that first edition, few of us realized how many millions of 1-2-3 users would depend on *Using 1-2-3* as their primary reference for learning and using 1-2-3 efficiently and productively. Now with the publication of this eleventh edition of *Using 1-2-3*, we are proud of the tradition that *Using 1-2-3* started worldwide. We recognize, however, that this edition of *Using 1-2-3* may be the last because Lotus Development Corporation has communicated its intention to focus future development efforts on new versions of the Windows release of 1-2-3 and possibly not develop another major upgrade of the DOS version. With the possibility of *Using 1-2-3 Release 4 for DOS,* Special Edition, being the last edition of the book, we thank all of you who made the success of *Using 1-2-3* possible—the millions of readers of previous editions as well as the new readers of *Using 1-2-3*.

I have had the very rewarding experience of having many different responsibilities in the development of many editions of this book, including Product Development Director, contributing author, and the Publisher of this edition. Through eleven editions and eleven years of work, I can proudly say that *Using 1-2-3 Release 4 for DOS,* Special Edition, represents the best, most comprehensive information available to users of 1-2-3. This book represents long hours of work from a team of expert authors and dedicated editors.

The experts who worked on this book include managers, consultants, trainers, authors of other best-selling computer books, and Lotus marketing, product design, and documentation professionals. They know firsthand the many ways people use 1-2-3 daily and are familiar with what you expect when turning to *Using 1-2-3 Release 4 for DOS,* Special Edition. They know how to answer your questions about 1-2-3 quickly, clearly, and completely. The authors of this book have used 1-2-3 and have taught others how to use 1-2-3 to build many types of applications—from accounting and general business applications to scientific applications. This experience, combined with the editorial expertise of the world's leading 1-2-3 publisher, brings you outstanding tutorial and reference information.

The authors of *Using 1-2-3 Release 4 for DOS*, Special Edition, wrote new sections and new chapters covering the new features of 1-2-3 Release 4 for DOS. If you have used a previous version of 1-2-3, you can easily find and learn what makes 1-2-3 Release 4 so different from earlier versions of 1-2-3. You learn more than what the new features of Release 4 are: *Using 1-2-3 Release 4 for DOS,* Special Edition, explains the exact benefits of the new features to your work. You learn, for example, that you can send and receive electronic mail messages without having to close your spreadsheet and quit the program. You learn also that 1-2-3 Release 4 can save you from the disaster of losing data with its new "Auto-Backup" feature. And if you need a professionally designed form using 1-2-3's Wysiwyg capabilities, *Using 1-2-3 Release 4 for DOS,* Special Edition, shows you what sample templates are available, such as the expense report and daily planner templates, to create professionally designed forms.

In addition to enhancements added to this book based on the new features of 1-2-3 Release 4, the design and overall structure of this book also have been greatly improved. User cautions and notes are emphasized with colored bars throughout the text, and tips are presented in the margins. Special cross-references within chapters enable you to follow alternative learning paths by providing quick access to related topics in other chapters. Within the text, the actual 1-2-3 Release 4 SmartIcons appear in the margin to highlight text that describes and uses the SmartIcons. To make it easier for you to solve problems as you work with 1-2-3, this book contains a special "Index of Common Problems." The inside back cover of *Using 1-2-3 Release 4 for DOS,* Special Edition, includes an Action Index, which enables you to quickly find information you need to complete common procedures.

Don Roche, the Publishing Director of this book, Joyce Nielsen, the Product Director, and the authors have also made this edition of *Using 1-2-3* easier to use. They have divided many of the long chapters from the previous edition into shorter chapters, giving you more logical chapter breaks and making it easier and faster to find information. Many chapters in this book also have been restructured to make them even easier to follow than in previous editions. The result of these efforts is a comprehensive tutorial and reference, written in the easy-to-follow style expected from Que books.

Because of these efforts, *Using 1-2-3 Release 4 for DOS*, Special Edition, is the best available comprehensive guide to 1-2-3 Release 4. Whether you are using 1-2-3 for inventory control, statistical analysis, or portfolio management, this book is designed for you. Like all previous editions of this title, *Using 1-2-3 Release 4 for DOS*, Special Edition, leads you step-by-step from worksheet basics to the advanced features of 1-2-3 Release 4. Whether you are a new user or an experienced user upgrading to Release 4, this book will occupy a prominent place next to your computer, as a valued reference to 1-2-3 Release 4.

As you use this eleventh edition of *Using 1-2-3*, write or call and let me know how Que can continue to serve you with the best tutorial and reference information available to computer users. And as you begin to learn other programs or decide to use the Windows version of 1-2-3, I invite you to try other excellent books published by the staff at Que.

Introduction

For both beginning and experienced users of 1-2-3, this introduction provides a road map to using this book and to the basics of 1-2-3 Release 4 for DOS. To help you find the information you need and understand the conventions of this book, turn to the section, "A Quick Tour of This Book." If you are a beginning user of 1-2-3, the section, "A Quick Tour of 1-2-3" provides the basics to help you get started. Whether you are a new or experienced user, use this introduction as a reference to the organization and conventions of *Using 1-2-3 Release 4 for DOS, Special Edition* and to the fundamentals of 1-2-3.

Using 1-2-3 Release 4 for DOS, Special Edition is written and organized to meet the needs of a wide range of readers, from those who have just started to use 1-2-3 to those who are experienced 1-2-3 Release 2.x and 3.x users who have upgraded to Release 4.

If you are just beginning to use 1-2-3, this book helps you learn the basics so that you can quickly begin using 1-2-3 for your needs. This introduction and chapters 2 through 5 in particular teach basic concepts for understanding 1-2-3: the commands, the differences between and organization of the two command menus in Release 4 (the 1-2-3 menu and the Wysiwyg menu), special uses of the keyboard and mouse, features of the 1-2-3 screen, SmartIcons, and methods for creating and modifying 1-2-3 worksheets.

> **Note**
>
> Release 4 and previous 1-2-3 versions often differ in the wording of prompts in menus. This book shows only the Release 4 version in the screens and in the text.

If you are an experienced 1-2-3 Release 2.x or 3.x user and have upgraded to Release 4, you learn about the new features of Release 4 and how to apply them as you develop worksheet applications. Chapter 1 presents an overview of the new features in 1-2-3 Release 4.

Whether you are a beginning 1-2-3 user or a user who has upgraded to Release 4, *Using 1-2-3 Release 4 for DOS*, Special Edition, provides the tips and techniques necessary to get the most from the program.

A Quick Tour of This Book

If you flip quickly through this book, you can get a better sense of its organization and layout. The book is organized to follow the natural flow of learning and using 1-2-3. *Using 1-2-3 Release 4 for DOS,* Special Edition also uses special conventions to help you identify different types of information and identify different elements of the 1-2-3 program, such as commands and special keys used by 1-2-3. The following sections describe the organization of this book and the conventions used within it.

Part I: The Basics

Chapter 1, "What's New in Release 4 for DOS," is a quick tour of the new features of the latest version of 1-2-3. If you used a previous version of 1-2-3, Chapter 1 shows you what to expect in the new release. Chapter 1 covers features in Release 4 that make using 1-2-3 easier. These features include the improved interface, the QuickStart introduction to Release 4, easier column width adjustment, and the Version Manager. The Version Manager enables you and your coworkers to create and view different sets of data for any named range in a worksheet.

Chapter 2, "What Every 1-2-3 User Should Know," is the overview of 1-2-3 fundamentals. If you are a new user of 1-2-3, this chapter gives you an easy-to-understand introduction to the basics. Chapter 2 covers the uses, features, and most frequent tasks users complete when developing 1-2-3 worksheets, including entering, editing, copying, and moving data. This chapter also introduces the general concepts for understanding 1-2-3 as a spreadsheet program and introduces the program's major uses: creating worksheets, databases, graphs, and using the Wysiwyg formatting features of the program.

Because so many 1-2-3 applications involve complex mathematical calculations, Chapter 3, "Finding Solutions with Formulas and Functions," covers the many different ways to create formulas. Chapter 3 also covers all types of functions available in Release 4: mathematical, date and time, financial and accounting, statistical, database, logical, string, and special functions.

Chapter 4, "Controlling Your Worksheet Display," introduces you to the many ways you can change the way worksheets and graphs can be displayed on your computer screen, from being able to view different sections of your worksheet on-screen at once to being able to display a graph directly on your worksheet.

Chapter 5, "Using SmartIcons," shows you how to begin using the SmartIcon feature of Release 4, a feature introduced in Release 2.4 and enhanced in later releases. You learn how to use the standard SmartIcons provided on multiple SmartIcon palettes, how to create a custom SmartIcon palette, and how to attach your macros and pictures to user-defined SmartIcons.

Part II: Presenting Data

Chapter 6, "Making Your Worksheets Dazzle," shows you how to change the way data appears on-screen, including the way 1-2-3 displays values, formulas, and text. You also learn how to use the Wysiwyg commands to highlight worksheet data with special elements such as boldface, italics, underlining, shading, boxes, and grids.

Chapter 7, "Adding Comments to Worksheet Cells," covers how to attach comments to values, formulas, or text. Chapter 7 also discusses the new capability in Release 4 of creating an electronic post-it note, called a *notepad*, that you attach to a worksheet cell. The chapter also explains how to hide, copy, delete, create a table of, and format text in notepads.

Chapter 8, "Printing Reports," shows you how to print a report immediately, print a file in the background while you work in the worksheet, or create a file to be read by another program. Chapter 8 explains the differences between the two Print command menus available in 1-2-3 Release 4—the **/P**rint menu and the **:P**rint menu. You also learn how to enhance a report by using other commands that change page layout, type size, character and line spacing, and that enable you to add elements such as headers and footers.

Part III: Organizing Your Work

Chapter 9, "Working with Files," covers commands for saving, erasing, and listing files, as well as commands for combining and extracting data from one or more files to other files, and opening more than one file in memory at a time. Chapter 9 also teaches you how to transfer files between different programs and how to use 1-2-3 in a multi-user environment. Chapter 9 concludes with information on how you send and receive electronic mail while working in 1-2-3 Release 4.

Chapter 10, "Organizing Your Data with Multiple-Worksheet Files," shows you how to create multiple-worksheet applications, including how to move from one worksheet to another in a multiple-worksheet file. The chapter also covers how to name worksheets using the New Sheet button in 1-2-3 Release 4 and how to insert, delete, and format worksheets.

Chapter 11, "Consolidating Worksheet Data," describes the techniques for extracting and combining data from other worksheet files and also shows how you can link data among separate worksheet files.

In Chapter 12, "Creating and Using Templates," you learn how to use SmartSheet templates that contain all the custom formatting for Wysiwyg on-screen design and for professionally designed printed forms. This chapter covers the SmartSheet templates included with 1-2-3 Release 4 as well as how to create templates for your specific needs.

Chapter 13, "Protecting Worksheet Data and Files," explains all the ways for ensuring both the security and confidentiality of worksheet data. Chapter 13 covers protecting specific data in the worksheet, protecting files, and limiting access to data and files.

Part IV: Analyzing Your Data

Chapter 14, "Analyzing Formulas with Auditor," contains information on using Auditor to analyze worksheet data. This chapter includes examples that show you how to use Auditor to identify and check worksheet formulas and locate circular references.

Chapter 15, "Using Functions To Analyze Data," covers the special database functions in 1-2-3 and the methods for analyzing information in a table. This chapter describes the purpose of each database function and shows how the functions are used in database applications.

Chapter 16, "Finding Solutions with Solver," shows you how to use Solver to find and evaluate solutions to "what-if" scenarios. Examples of Solver problems illustrate how the Solver is used in practical business situations. Chapter 16 also discusses the various Solver reports, and describes how you can use Solver with functions and macros.

Chapter 17, "Goal Seeking with Backsolver," discusses how to use the Backsolver utility, which enables you to find the values for variables based on a given goal value. Like Chapter 16, Chapter 17 presents examples to help you understand the power of Backsolver used in business applications.

In Chapter 18, "Tracking Multiple Sets of Data with Version Manager," you learn how to use the Version Manager capability of 1-2-3 Release 4 to manage and share data. You learn how to create and display different versions of data in a named range, and how to group versions together into scenarios.

Part V: Working with Databases

Chapter 19, "Creating Databases," introduces you to the advantages and limitations of 1-2-3's database. This chapter presents the essential concepts and methods for defining, designing, and creating a 1-2-3 database.

In Chapter 20, "Sorting Your Data," you learn how to use the data sort capability of 1-2-3 Release 4 when you want to sort data in a worksheet according to one, two, or more columns or data. Chapter 20 also explains how to restore worksheet data to its original order if you make a mistake when sorting or need a copy of the original data prior to sorting.

Chapter 21, "Finding Specific Data," shows you how to search a worksheet to find data. Chapter 21 covers the ways you can list, extract, and delete records in a 1-2-3 database. Also, the chapter explains the different methods for defining the criteria on which to conduct a search.

Chapter 22, "High-Level Database Techniques," covers the advanced data-management techniques available in 1-2-3 Release 4. Specifically, the chapter describes how to perform "what-if" analyses with data tables, create frequency distributions, perform regression analysis, and work with matrices.

Part VI: Graphing Your Data

Chapter 23, "Creating Effective Graphs," teaches you how to create graphs from worksheet data manually and automatically. This chapter introduces the graph types available with Release 4 and the options available to enhance the basic appearance and functionality of a graph. Chapter 23 also shows the different ways of viewing graphs on-screen and the methods for saving and printing graphs.

Chapter 24, "Creating Power Graphs," shows you how to modify graph axes and how to add a second Y scale to a graph. This chapter also shows you how to modify and embellish graphs through the :Graph commands on the Wysiwyg menu. You learn how to change the position of a graph on the page; adjust graph settings; add, modify, and rearrange text and geometric shapes; and change the size and rotation of objects displayed in graphs. Finally, Chapter 24 describes how to print graphs that are created through the :Graph command.

Chapter 25, "Developing Business Presentations," focuses on using spreadsheet publishing techniques to create computer, slide, and overhead presentations. Examples include how to combine text, graphics, and clip art effectively on a single page. The techniques used by professional page layout and graphics designers are included in sections covering the guidelines for presenting text and graphics.

Part VII: Automating with Macros

Chapter 26, "Short Macros To Make Your Life Easier," is an introduction to the powerful macro capabilities of 1-2-3. This chapter teaches you how to create, name, run, test, and debug macros. The chapter also covers such macro features as creating a macro by automatically recording keystrokes, naming macros with descriptive names, invoking macros from a menu, and assigning a macro to a SmartIcon.

Chapter 27, "Advanced Macro Command Power Techniques," explains the powerful advanced macro commands in 1-2-3 and includes a complete alphabetized reference of all advanced macro commands, along with examples of their use.

Chapter 28, "Controlling 1-2-3 with Macros," is an introduction to application development with 1-2-3 macros. In this chapter you learn how you can develop programs with 1-2-3 macros that will automate complex applications and even connect applications into automated business systems controlled complete through 1-2-3 macro capability.

Part VIII: Sharing Data

Chapter 29, "Sharing 1-2-3 Data with Windows Applications," describes the options available for running 1-2-3 Release 4 under the Windows operating environment. The chapter also explains the methods for sharing data among 1-2-3 Release 4 and Windows applications, such as Word, WordPerfect, Ami Pro, 1-2-3 for Windows, and Excel.

In Chapter 30, "Sharing 1-2-3 Data with Databases," you learn how to link a 1-2-3 worksheet to an external database table in a database program such as dBASE, Paradox, or FoxPro, and how to use and modify information from an external database table.

Chapter 31, "Sharing 1-2-3 Data with DOS Word Processors," presents the easiest, fail-safe techniques for Using 1-2-3 Release 4 for DOS data in word processors, such as the DOS versions of WordPerfect and Word.

Reference Card

In the back of this book is a tear-out reference card that lists 1-2-3 Release 4 shortcut keys and elements of the 1-2-3 Release 4 screen.

Conventions Used in This Book

Certain conventions are used in *Using 1-2-3 Release 4 for DOS*, Special Edition, to help you more easily use this book and understand 1-2-3's concepts. The following sections include examples of these conventions to help you distinguish among the different elements.

Special Typefaces and Representations

Special typefaces in *Using 1-2-3 Release 4 for DOS*, Special Edition, include the following:

Type	Meaning
italics	New terms or phrases when initially defined; function and advanced macro command syntax
boldface	Information you are asked to type, including the first character of menu options and the slash (/) and colon (:) that precede 1-2-3 and Wysiwyg commands, respectively
`special type`	Direct quotations of words that appear on-screen or in a figure; menu command prompts

Elements printed in uppercase include range names such as SALES, functions such as @FIND, mode and status indicators such as READY and END, and cell references such as A:B19. Also presented in uppercase letters are DOS commands such as CHKDSK and file names such as STATUS.WK3.

In most cases, keys are represented as they appear on the keyboard. The arrow keys usually are represented by name (for example, the *up-arrow key*). The Print Screen key is abbreviated PrtSc; Page Up is PgUp; Insert is Ins; and so on. On your keyboard, these key names may be spelled out or abbreviated differently.

When two keys appear together with a plus sign, such as Ctrl+Break, press and hold the first key as you press the second key. When two keys appear together without a plus sign, such as End Home, press and release the first key before you press the second key.

In the text, the first letter of each menu option from the 1-2-3 and Wysiwyg menus appears in boldface, such as **/R**ange **F**ormat **C**urrency and **:T**ext **E**dit.

> **Tip**
> This paragraph format suggests easier or alternative methods of executing a procedure.

The function keys, F1 through F10, are used for special situations in 1-2-3. In the text, the name of the function key is usually listed with the function key number, such as F7 (Query).

Note
This paragraph format indicates additional information that may help you avoid problems or that should be considered in using the described features.

Caution
This paragraph format warns the reader of hazardous procedures (for example, activities that delete files).

Margin Icons
Icons appear in the margin to indicate that the procedure described in the text includes instructions for using the appropriate SmartIcons in 1-2-3 Release 4.

Special Sections
Using 1-2-3 Release 4 for DOS, Special Edition, uses cross-references to help you access other parts of the book. Beside the relevant paragraphs, related tasks you may need to perform are listed in the margin by section name and page number.

In addition, troubleshooting sections are provided in most chapters to help you find solutions to common problems encountered with the 1-2-3 procedures covered in that section of the book.

Macro Conventions

Conventions that pertain to macros deserve special mention:

- Single-character macro names (Alt+*letter* combinations) appear with the backslash (\) and single-character name in lowercase: \a. The \ indicates that you press and hold the Alt key as you press the A key.

- Representations of direction keys such as {DOWN} and {NEXTSHEET}, function keys such as {CALC}, and editing keys such as {DEL} appear in uppercase letters and surrounded by braces.

- 1-2-3's advanced macro commands are enclosed within braces—such as {WINDOWSOFF} and {GETLABEL}—when used in a syntax line or within a macro; the same commands generally appear without braces in the text.

- The Enter key is represented by the tilde (~).

A Quick Tour of 1-2-3

If you are a beginning user of 1-2-3, the following section provides the basics to help you get started using the program. If you have used a prior release of 1-2-3, either 2.x or 3.x, you may want to review some of the information specific to Release 4, such as the hardware requirements and options described in the following section. Also, if you have not used a mouse with your computer programs, the section "Using the Mouse with 1-2-3" will get you started.

Understanding 1-2-3 Hardware Requirements and Options

1-2-3 Release 4 contains many features not included in previous versions and thereby places more demands on computer hardware and memory than any previous version of 1-2-3. Following are the specific hardware requirements for running 1-2-3 Release 4 (for a complete listing of supported computer monitors and printers, refer to the Lotus 1-2-3 Release 4 documentation):

14   Introduction

Published by:	Lotus Development Corporation
	55 Cambridge Parkway
	Cambridge, MA 02142
	1-800-343-5414 (U.S.)
	1-800-GO-LOTUS (Canada)
System requirements:	IBM-compatible 80286 PC or higher
Display:	EGA, VGA, or higher graphics card
Disk capacity:	6M minimum
Memory size:	2M RAM minimum
Operating system:	DOS Version 3.0 or later
Network operating systems supported:	Novell NetWare 386 Version 3.11
	Microsoft LAN Manager (OS/2) Version 2.1
	IBM LAN Server (OS/2) Version 3
	Banyan VINES Version 5.0
	DEC PATHWORKS Version 4.1
	NCR StarGroup Version 2.1a

Tip
The 1-2-3 main menu is available whenever you start 1-2-3. You access the 1-2-3 menu by pressing the / key or by moving the mouse into the control panel at the top of the screen. You access the Wysiwyg menu by pressing the : key. When the mouse pointer is in the control panel, you can use the right mouse button to toggle between the 1-2-3 main menu and the Wysiwyg main menu.

Using the Command Menus

The worksheet is the basis for all applications you create, modify, and print in 1-2-3. In the worksheet cells, you enter data in the form of text, numbers, and formulas. You perform operations on this data with two command menus in Release 4: the 1-2-3 main menu and the Wysiwyg main menu.

The 1-2-3 main menu enables you to format, copy, move, print, create a graph with, and perform database operations on this data. The Wysiwyg menu lets you enhance the look of text and numbers you enter as well as enhance the look of graphs you create.

The commands in the 1-2-3 main menu and Wysiwyg main menu provide access to many sublevels of commands. You use some commands frequently, such as those for creating or modifying a worksheet application. Other commands, such as specialized database commands, you may rarely or never use.

Using the Mouse with 1-2-3

To use a mouse with 1-2-3, you must load a mouse driver before you start 1-2-3. You can load the mouse driver by adding the driver to a batch file that starts 1-2-3 or by adding the driver to the AUTOEXEC.BAT file (the file that executes commands when you start the computer). Directions for using the mouse driver came with the documentation you received with your mouse.

The *mouse pointer* appears in the center of the screen when you start 1-2-3. Pressing the right and left mouse buttons enables you to select commands, switch between the 1-2-3 and Wysiwyg menus, move the cell pointer, select ranges, select SmartIcons, see the description of a SmartIcon, and change column widths and row heights. Before you use the mouse, take time to familiarize yourself with the mouse and mouse terminology in the following sections.

Understanding Mouse Terminology

The term *mouse pointer*, described in the preceding section, refers to an on-screen arrow that moves when you move the mouse. This section describes more mouse terms that you need to know.

To *point* means to move the mouse until the tip of the mouse pointer points at an item on-screen. If you are instructed to point to cell B5, for example, move the mouse until the tip of the arrow is *over* cell B5.

When you *click* the mouse, you press and immediately release one of the two buttons on the mouse. (If the mouse has three buttons, only the two outside buttons are active; you don't use the center button in 1-2-3.) Usually, you press a mouse button only after you point with the mouse. In this book, the term *click* in an expression such as "click the Save File SmartIcon" means to move the mouse pointer over the specified SmartIcon and quickly press and release the left mouse button.

The left button on the mouse acts as the Enter key. The right button has three functions. First, the right button acts as the Esc key; if you are typing a cell entry, for example, pressing the right button erases the text from the control panel and returns 1-2-3 to READY mode. The second function of the right mouse button is to switch between the 1-2-3 menu and the Wysiwyg menu. The third function of the right mouse button is to show a description of a SmartIcon at the top of the screen.

When you install 1-2-3, you can reverse the operations of the mouse buttons; you can make the right button act as the Enter button and the left button the Esc/switch button. If you are left-handed, reversing the buttons enables you to press the primary button with your left index finger and the secondary button with your left middle finger.

Click-and-drag is a combination of pointing, pressing, and moving the mouse. You usually use this method to highlight a range. To click-and-drag, follow these steps:

1. Move the mouse pointer to the desired beginning location, such as the top left corner of a range.

2. Hold down the left mouse button (this action anchors the cell pointer); don't release the button at this time.

3. Move the mouse to the desired ending location, such as the bottom right corner of a range, and release the mouse button. The desired range is highlighted.

To select a range from B5 through D10, for example, point to cell B5, press and hold down the left mouse button, drag the mouse pointer to cell D10, and release the mouse button.

Using the Mouse To Select Menu Commands

When you move the mouse pointer to the control panel, the 1-2-3 main menu or the Wysiwyg menu (whichever menu was active last) appears on-screen, as if you pressed the slash or colon key. Pressing the right mouse button with the mouse pointer in the control panel switches between the 1-2-3 and Wysiwyg menus.

Using the mouse to select a menu command is easy. First, activate a menu by moving the mouse pointer to the control panel. Then point to a menu command and press the left mouse button. You can use this technique to select all menu commands. Some commands require more information, often typed in a dialog box. For these commands, type the additional information; then press Enter, click OK, or click the mouse in the control panel to accept the entry.

Using the mouse can greatly increase your speed and productivity. If you used a previous version of 1-2-3, however, you may be more comfortable using the keyboard for now. Experiment with using the mouse, the keyboard, or a combination of both to find the method that works best for you.

Learning the 1-2-3 Keyboard

The enhanced keyboard is the standard keyboard on all new IBM personal computers and most compatibles. Some compatibles (particularly laptops) have different keyboards.

Keyboards are divided into four or five sections: the *alphanumeric keys* in the center, the *numeric keypad/direction keys* on the right, and the *function keys* on the left and/or across the top. The *special keys* can be in various locations. The *direction keys* are in a separate section on only the enhanced keyboard.

Most keys in the *alphanumeric* section match the keys on a typewriter, and most retain their usual functions in 1-2-3. Several alphanumeric keys, however, have functions unique to computer keyboards or to 1-2-3, and some don't even exist on typewriter keyboards.

The keys on the *numeric* keypad, on the right side of the keyboard, enter numbers or move the cell pointer or cursor.

The *function keys* perform special actions; you can use function keys, for example, to access 1-2-3's editing functions, to display graphs, and to summon Help information. Function keys lie across the top of the enhanced keyboard and on the left side of the other two keyboard types. Some enhanced keyboards have function keys across the top and on the left side of the keyboard.

The *special keys* are Del (Delete), Ins (Insert), Esc (Escape), Num Lock (Number Lock), Scroll Lock, Break, Pause, and PrtSc (Print Screen). Special keys perform certain specific actions and are located in different places on different keyboards.

Only the enhanced keyboard has a separate section for *direction keys*: the up arrow, down arrow, left arrow, right arrow, PgUp, PgDn, Home, and End keys. Use the enhanced keyboard's numeric keypad—a numeric keypad with direction keys—to enter numbers; use the keyboard's direction keys to move around the worksheet.

The Alphanumeric Keys

Although most alphanumeric keys have the same functions as on a typewriter, several keys have special functions in 1-2-3. Table I.1 lists these keys and their functions. The functions of these keys become clear when you use the keys in later chapters.

Table I.1 Alphanumeric Key Operation

Key	Function
. (period)	When used in a range address, separates the address of the cell at the beginning of the range from the address of the cell at the end of the range.
/ (slash)	Starts a command from READY mode. Used as the division sign when entering data or editing a formula in a cell.
< (less than)	Used in logical formulas. Also used as an alternative to the slash (/) to start a command from READY mode.
: (colon)	Starts a Wysiwyg command from READY mode when Wysiwyg is in memory.
Alt	Used with the function keys to provide different functions, or used with letter keys to invoke macros.
Backspace	During cell definition or editing, erases the preceding character. Cancels a range during some prompts that display the old range. Displays the previous help screen when using Help.
Caps Lock	Shifts the letter keys to uppercase.
Ctrl	Used with some function keys and other keys to change their functions.
Shift	Used with another key to shift the character produced. Used with a letter, produces an uppercase letter. Used with a number or symbol, produces the shifted character on the key. Used with the numeric keypad, produces a number.

The Numeric Keypad and the Direction Keys

You mainly use the keys in the numeric keypad for cell pointer and cursor movement. When Num Lock is off, these keys function as direction keys. When Num Lock is on, these keys act as number keys. You can use the Shift key to override Num Lock. If Num Lock is on, for example, you can hold down the Shift key while you press a key in the numeric keypad; the key you press functions as a direction key.

The functions of the direction keys and other special keys on the numeric keypad are discussed later in this introduction.

The Function Keys

The function keys, F1 through F10, are used for special actions in 1-2-3. These keys are located across the top of the enhanced keyboard and on the left side of the other two keyboards. (The enhanced keyboard has 12 function keys, but 1-2-3 uses only the first 10 keys.) You can use these keys alone or with the Alt or Ctrl key. Table I.2 lists the function keys and explains each key's action. In the first column of the table are the SmartIcons that apply to the actions of certain function keys.

Table I.2 Function Key Operation

SmartIcon (if applicable)	Key	Function
	F1 (Help)	Accesses the on-line Help utility.
	F2 (Edit)	Switches 1-2-3 to EDIT mode to change the current cell. Activates a dialog box, if one is displayed.
	F3 (Name)	Displays a list of names if a command or formula accepts a range name or a file name. Displays a list of functions after an @ (at sign) appears in a formula. Displays a list of macro key names and advanced macro commands after a left brace ({) appears in a label.
	F4 (Abs)	Changes a cell or range address from relative to absolute to mixed and back to relative. In READY mode, enables you to prespecify a range.
🚙	F5 (GoTo)	Moves the cell pointer to a specified cell, range, worksheet, or file.
	F6 (Window)	On split screens, moves the cell pointer to another window or worksheet.
	F7 (Query)	Repeats the last **/D**ata **Q**uery command.

(continues)

Table I.2 Continued

SmartIcon (if applicable)	Key	Function
	F8 (Table)	Repeats the last /Data Table command.
	F9 (Calc)	In READY mode, recalculates all worksheets in memory. Converts a formula you are entering or editing to the current value.
	F10 (Graph)	Displays the current graph, if one exists. If no current graph exists, creates and displays a graph of the data around the cell pointer.
	Alt+F1 (Compose)	Creates international characters you cannot type from the keyboard.
	Alt+F2 (Record)	Enables you to record and store up to the last 512 keystrokes in a cell or to repeat a series of commands.
	Alt+F3 (Run)	Runs a macro.
	Alt+F4 (Undo)	Reverses the last action.
	Alt+F6 (Zoom)	Enlarges a split window to full size. Also removes Graph and Print Settings sheets from the screen so that you can see worksheet data when you select commands.
	Alt+F7 (App1)	Starts an add-in program assigned to this key.
	Alt+F8 (App2)	Starts an add-in program assigned to this key.
	Alt+F9 (App3)	Starts an add-in program assigned to this key.
	Alt+F10 (Addin)	Accesses the Add-In menu.
	Ctrl+F9 (Display Icons)	Hides and redisplays the SmartIcon palette.
	Ctrl+F10 (Select Icons)	Enables you to select a SmartIcon with the keyboard.

The Special Keys

The special keys provide several important 1-2-3 functions. Some special keys, for example, cancel an action. Esc cancels a menu or an entry, for example, and Ctrl+Break cancels a macro. The Del key deletes the contents of the cell highlighted by the cell pointer or deletes a character when you edit a cell.

Some special keys change the actions of other keys. You can use the Ins key to change the mode from insert to overtype when you edit data in a cell. Num Lock changes the keys on the numeric keypad from direction keys to number keys. Scroll Lock changes how the arrow keys move the display. Table I.3 lists the special keys and each key's functions.

Table I.3 Special Key Operation

Key	Function
Ctrl+Break	Cancels a macro and returns 1-2-3 to READY mode.
Del	When you are editing, deletes the character at the cursor. In READY mode, deletes the contents of the cell highlighted by the cell pointer.
Esc	Cancels the current command menu and returns to the preceding menu. From the 1-2-3 main menu, returns to READY mode. Clears the edit line when you are entering or editing data in a cell. Cancels a range during some prompts that display the old range. Returns 1-2-3 to READY mode from the on-line Help utility.
Ins	Changes mode to overtype when you are editing a cell. Keystrokes replace characters at the cursor position. After you toggle Ins to return to insert mode, keystrokes again are inserted at the cursor position.
Num Lock	Shifts the actions of the numeric keypad from direction keys to numbers.
Pause	Pauses a macro, a recalculation, and some commands until you press a key.
PrtSc or Shift+PrtSc	Prints the current 1-2-3 screen, including worksheet and column letters, row numbers, and control panel information.
Scroll Lock	Scrolls the entire window when you use the arrow keys.

Learning the 1-2-3 Screen Display

The 1-2-3 worksheet is divided into three main parts: the *control panel* at the top of the screen, the *worksheet area* in the center of the screen, and the *status bar* at the bottom of the screen (see fig. I.1).

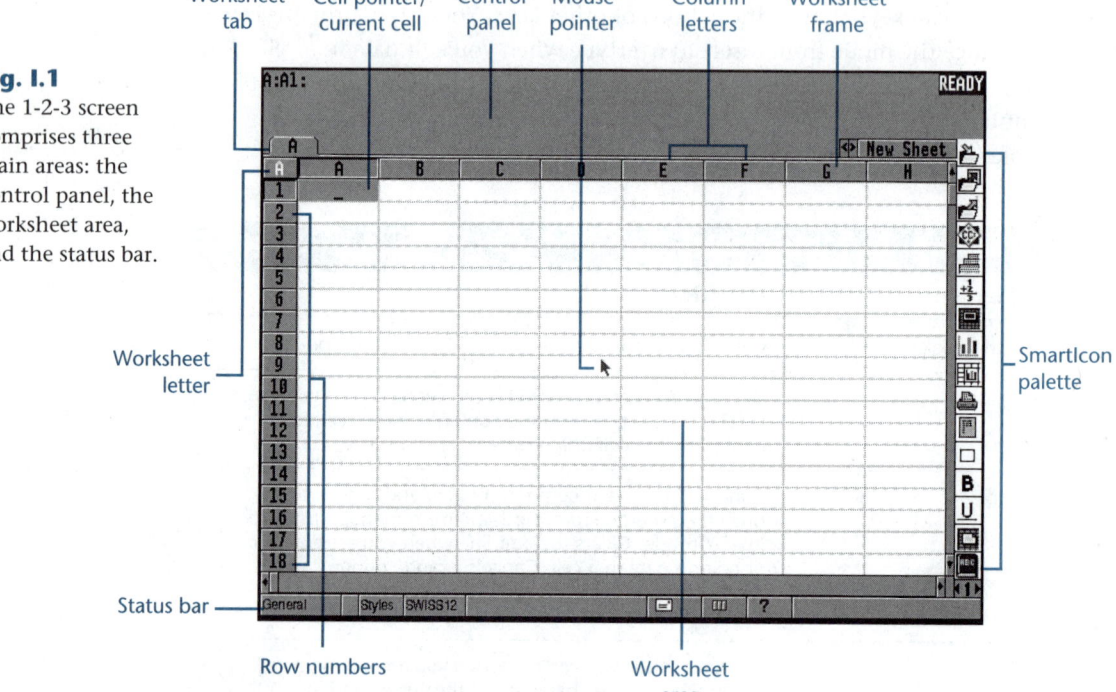

Fig. I.1
The 1-2-3 screen comprises three main areas: the control panel, the worksheet area, and the status bar.

The *worksheet frame* marks the worksheet area, and contains the worksheet letter, column letters (A through IV), and row numbers (1 through 8192). One or more *worksheet tabs*, which resemble file-folder tabs, appear just above the worksheet frame. Worksheet tabs enable you to name and easily move between several worksheets in a multiple-worksheet file.

The *cell pointer* marks the location of the current cell in the worksheet area. When you type data in the worksheet, the data appears in the cell marked by the cell pointer.

The Control Panel

The *control panel* is the area located above the worksheet frame containing the column letters. The first line of the control panel contains information about the current cell, including the address of the cell, the cell contents, and the cell's protection status (U if unprotected, PR if protected). The information in the first line also includes the format and column width if these attributes differ from the default settings (later chapters discuss these attributes). If Wysiwyg is active, the control panel also contains information that applies to Wysiwyg, such as row height, graph, and text formats.

The cell's *address* includes the worksheet letter, the column letter, and the row number (in that order); for example, A:D7 designates a cell in worksheet A, column D, row 7. If the file contains only one worksheet, the worksheet letter is always A.

When you use the command menus, the second line of the control panel lists the menu choices and the third line contains explanations of the current menu item (see fig. I.2) or the next hierarchical menu. When you move the mouse pointer from one item to the next in a command menu, the explanation on the third line of the control panel changes.

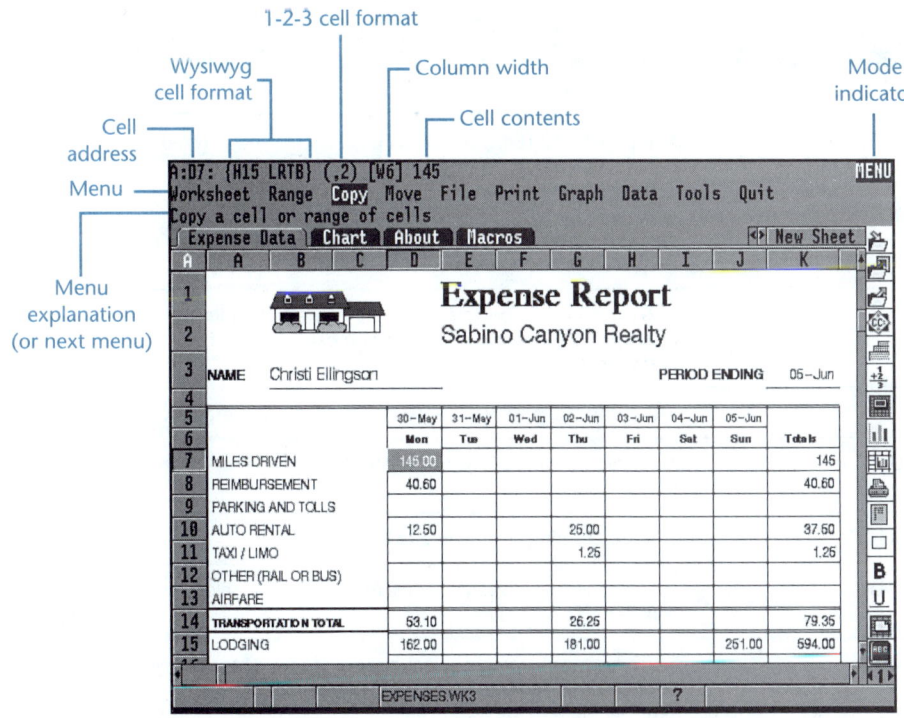

Fig. I.2

The control panel includes information about the current cell, the 1-2-3 (or Wysiwyg) main menu, and a menu explanation appearing just below the main menu.

If a command prompts you for information, the second line of the control panel displays the prompt. If a command prompts you for a file name, range name, graph name, or print settings name, the third line displays the beginning of a list of all names on file in this category.

The second line of the control panel also shows the data you are currently entering or editing in a cell of the worksheet. If you enter or edit data too long to display on one line, the control panel enlarges to accommodate the largest possible cell entry (512 characters). The worksheet area shrinks to make room for the expanded control panel.

The *mode indicator* is located in the top right corner of the control panel. This indicator tells you in which mode 1-2-3 currently is operating and what you can do next. When 1-2-3 awaits the next action, the mode indicator displayed is READY (refer to fig. I.2 for an example). Table I.4 lists the mode indicators and describes what each mode indicates.

Table I.4 Mode Indicators

Indicator	Description
EDIT	You pressed F2 (Edit) to edit a cell entry, or you entered data incorrectly.
ERROR	1-2-3 encountered an error, or you used Ctrl+Break to cancel a macro. Press Enter or Esc to clear the message in the status bar and return to READY mode.
FILES	1-2-3 prompted you to select a file name from a list of files. Type a file name or point to an existing file; then press Enter.
FIND	1-2-3 is in the process of a **/D**ata **Q**uery **F**ind operation.
HELP	The Help utility is active on-screen. Press Esc to return to the worksheet.
LABEL	You are entering a label in a cell.
MENU	A 1-2-3 menu is displayed on-screen for you to select commands.
NAMES	1-2-3 prompted you to select a range name, graph name, print setting, database driver, external database, or external table name and displayed a list of names. At the prompt, type an appropriate name and press Enter or use the mouse to click a name on the list.

Indicator	Description
POINT	1-2-3 prompted you to select a range or you used the direction keys to specify a range while entering a formula. Type the cell coordinates or the range name, or highlight the range by using the direction keys or the mouse; then press Enter.
READY	1-2-3 is waiting for the next entry or command.
STAT	1-2-3 is displaying a status screen.
VALUE	You are entering a number or a formula in a cell.
WAIT	1-2-3 is performing an activity. Don't proceed until the activity is complete and the WAIT indicator disappears.
WYSIWYG	A Wysiwyg menu is displayed on-screen for you to select commands.

The Worksheet Area

The *worksheet area* is the main portion of the screen that contains all of your worksheet data. In addition, the worksheet area includes the worksheet frame, the scroll bars, and the SmartIcon palette. The scroll bars, a new feature in Release 4, are discussed in Chapter 1, "What's New in Release 4 for DOS." SmartIcons and the SmartIcon palette are covered in Chapter 5, "Using SmartIcons."

The Status Bar

The appearance and functionality of the status bar have improved dramatically in 1-2-3 Release 4. Refer to Chapter 1, "What's New in Release 4 for DOS," for an explanation of these changes and a description of the buttons on the status bar. This section covers only the status indicators and error messages that appear in the status bar.

1-2-3 displays the *status indicators* near the right side of the status bar. These indicators give you information about the state of the 1-2-3 program. Table I.5 lists these indicators and describes the meanings of each indicator.

Table I.5 Status Indicators

Indicator	Description
CALC	Warns you that formula results in the file may not be current. Press Calc (F9) to perform a recalculation and clear the indicator.
CAP	You pressed Caps Lock. All letters you type appear as uppercase letters. Press Caps Lock again to turn off the indicator and type lowercase letters.
CIRC	The worksheet contains a circular reference. Use the /**W**orksheet **S**tatus command to find one of the cell addresses in the circular reference.
CMD	1-2-3 is running a macro.
END	You pressed the End key (to use with a direction key to move the cell pointer).
FILE	You pressed Ctrl+End (File). Combined with an arrow key, the File key moves across multiple files in memory.
GROUP	You selected /**W**orksheet **G**lobal **G**roup **E**nable to modify all worksheets in a file.
MEM	1-2-3 is running out of available memory.
NUM	You pressed Num Lock. The keys on the numeric keypad now act as number keys rather than direction keys. To use these keys as direction keys, press Num Lock again or hold down the Shift key while typing the numbers.
OVR	You pressed Ins while editing a cell, which switched 1-2-3 to overtype mode. Keystrokes replace whatever is at the cursor position. Press Ins again to return to insert mode, which inserts keystrokes at the cursor position.
PRT	1-2-3 is printing to a printer or a file.
RO	The current file is read-only. You can save the file only under a different name. Applies to files used on a network or multi-user system. Sometimes appears if you run out of memory while reading a file.
SCROLL	You pressed Scroll Lock. When you use an arrow key, the entire window moves opposite the direction of the arrow. To use the arrow keys to move the cursor from cell to cell, press Scroll Lock again.
STEP	You turned on single-step mode for macros.
ZOOM	You used /**W**orksheet **W**indow to split the screen into multiple windows and then pressed Alt+F6 to enlarge the current window to fill the entire screen. To return the display to multiple windows, press Alt+F6 again.

If 1-2-3 encounters an error, the mode indicator changes to ERROR and an error message appears at the left end of the status bar. Many situations can result in errors. You may have specified an invalid cell address or range name in response to a prompt, for example, or tried to retrieve a file that doesn't exist. In most cases, you can press F1 (Help) while the error message appears if you need detailed information on correcting the problem; press Esc to return to the worksheet. Press Esc or Enter to clear the error and return to READY mode.

Conclusion

With this introduction to *Using 1-2-3 Release 4 for DOS*, Special Edition and to the basics of 1-2-3, you're now ready to explore and use as a reference those sections you'll need as you create, change, and expand 1-2-3 worksheets and graphs. Whether you're learning a feature of 1-2-3 for the first time or turning to a section in this book for reference, *Using 1-2-3 Release 4 for DOS*, Special Edition is the best tutorial and reference on 1-2-3 Release 4 available!

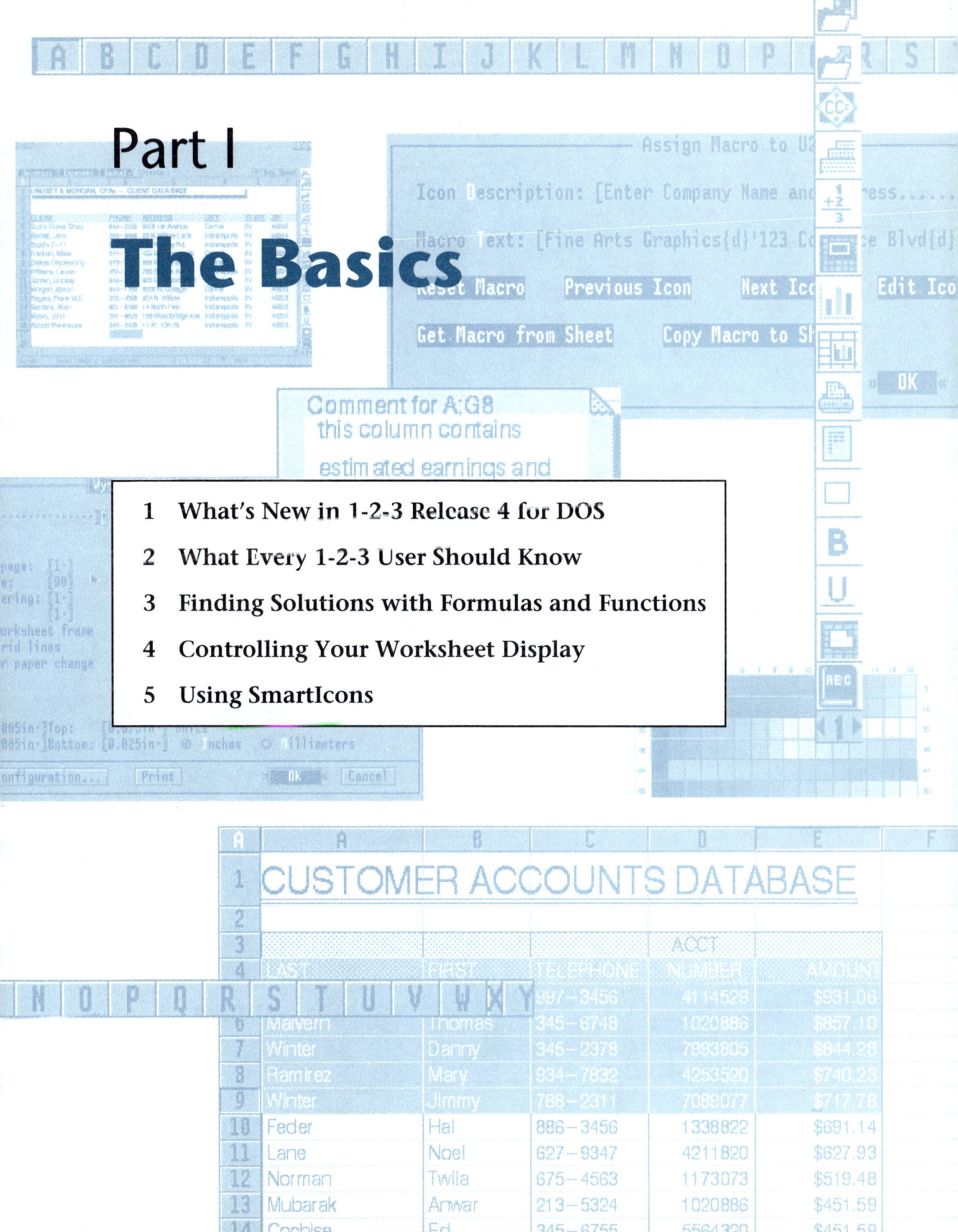

Part I
The Basics

1 What's New in 1-2-3 Release 4 for DOS
2 What Every 1-2-3 User Should Know
3 Finding Solutions with Formulas and Functions
4 Controlling Your Worksheet Display
5 Using SmartIcons

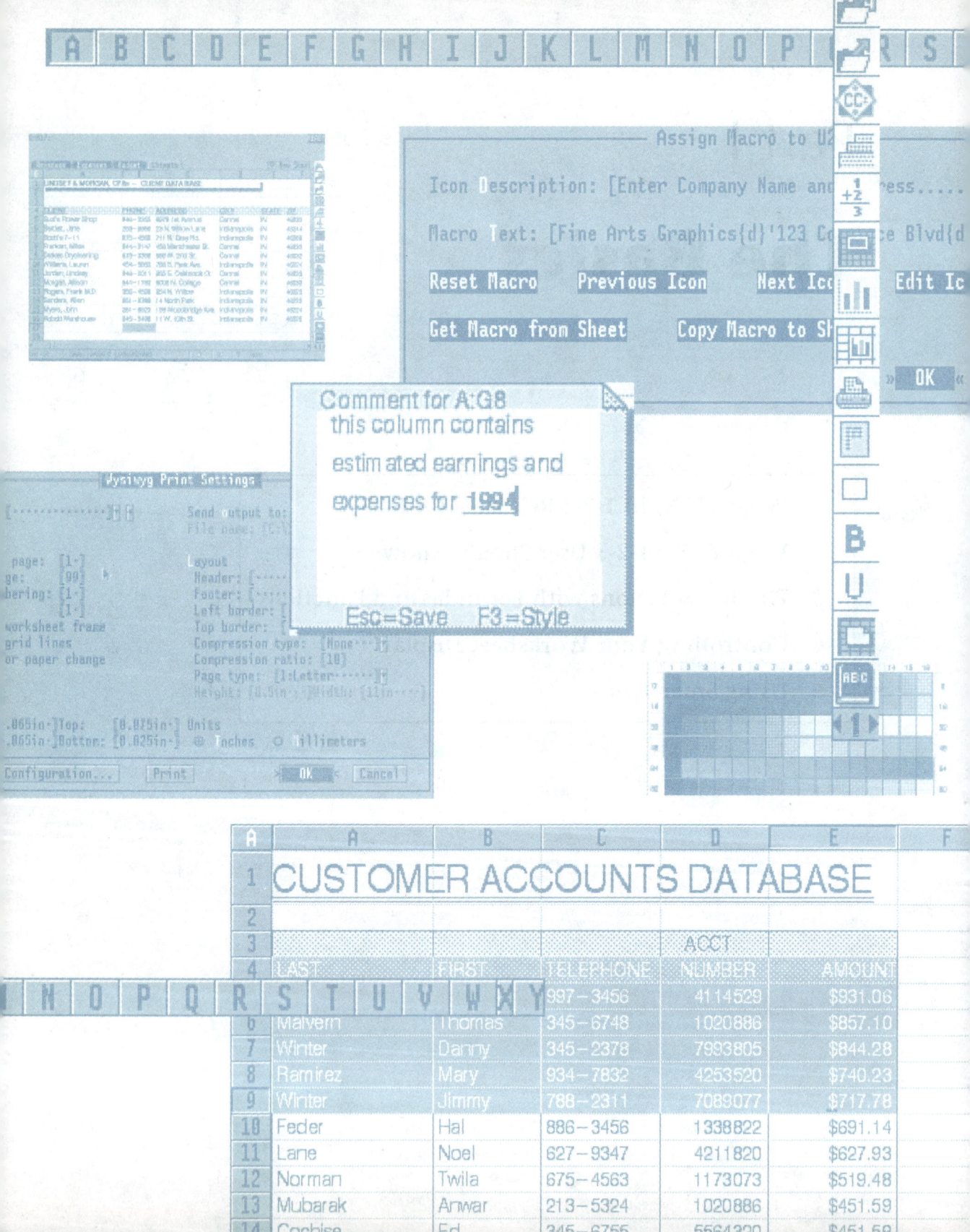

Chapter 1

What's New in 1-2-3 Release 4 for DOS

1-2-3 Release 4 for DOS is a powerful combination of old and new. This new version of the most popular spreadsheet program combines the familiarity of the existing 1-2-3 for DOS versions with exciting new features that make the program much easier to use. Whether you've used 1-2-3 Release 2.x or 1-2-3 Release 3.x, you'll find Release 4 is a logical step up for DOS spreadsheet fans.

> **Note**
>
> Although 1-2-3 Release 4 for DOS is intended to replace both the 2.x and 3.x versions of 1-2-3 for DOS, you must have at least an 80286 processor, 2M of RAM, 6M of available hard disk space, and an EGA or higher monitor to install Release 4.

This chapter is the place to start if you want a quick overview of the new features in 1-2-3 Release 4 for DOS. You can use this chapter to learn how Release 4 differs from your old, familiar 1-2-3 version. If you're already familiar with 1-2-3 basics, you can use this chapter as a guide, allowing you to quickly pick out the items you haven't encountered before, so that you can concentrate on the later chapters that cover these features in depth.

Improved Interface

Whether you're a long-time 1-2-3 DOS spreadsheet user or new to 1-2-3, you'll find that the appearance of 1-2-3 Release 4 for DOS is easy to understand and use. This new appearance, or *user interface*, makes it easy to

32 Chapter 1—What's New in 1-2-3 Release 4 for DOS

use 1-2-3 Release 4 for DOS for everyday business and personal tasks. By borrowing some of the best features from Windows programs, the new interface becomes very intuitive.

Figure 1.1 shows some of the new elements in the 1-2-3 Release 4 for DOS screen.

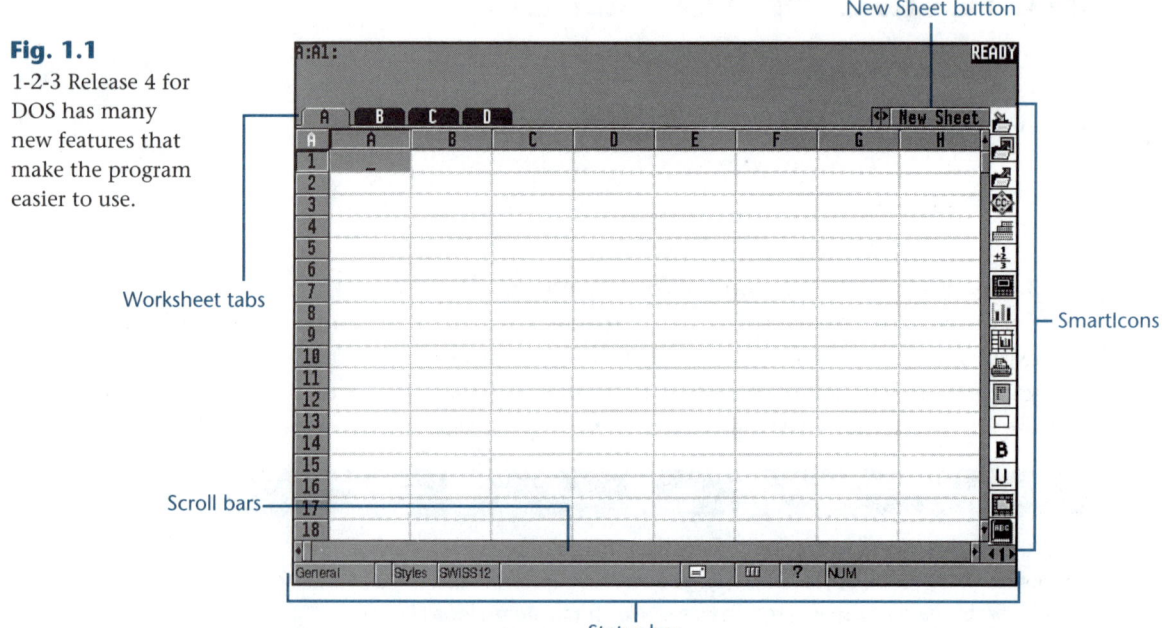

Fig. 1.1
1-2-3 Release 4 for DOS has many new features that make the program easier to use.

Worksheet tabs enable you to quickly navigate between worksheet pages—whether you are using a three-dimensional worksheet or have simply opened several worksheets at the same time—by simply clicking the appropriate worksheet tab. You can name worksheet tabs to make it easier to remember where to find your data, much as you probably label the dividers in a file cabinet. Labeling a set of worksheets as "Sales," "Expenses," and "Budgets" makes things much easier. Worksheet tabs also give you a quick, highly visual method of determining whether a worksheet has more than one page. You can simply look to see if there's more than one worksheet tab displayed, and you'll know instantly whether more worksheet pages exist.

The New Sheet button provides a quick way to add more worksheets to a model. Clicking this button is the equivalent of choosing the **/W**orksheet **I**nsert **S**heet **A**fter **1** command. Now that adding new worksheets is so easy, you won't have any excuse for not taking advantage of the three-dimensional power of 1-2-3 Release 4 for DOS. See Chapter 10, "Organizing Your Data with Multiple-Worksheet Files," for more information about using multiple worksheets and the New Sheet button.

The SmartIcons provide even more shortcut methods of performing common worksheet tasks. For example, the SmartIcon at the top of the SmartIcon palette saves the current worksheet with a single click of the left mouse button. 1-2-3 Release 4 for DOS offers seven predefined SmartIcon palettes and one user-definable SmartIcon palette. See Chapter 5, "Using SmartIcons," for more information about using SmartIcons.

The horizontal and vertical scroll bars (below and to the right of the spreadsheet) enable you to quickly navigate large worksheets. You can click the up- or down-arrows at the ends of the vertical scroll bar to move vertically, or the right- or left-arrows at the ends of the horizontal scroll bar to move horizontally. To move more quickly, point to the box in the scroll bar and drag it until the correct row or column is displayed. For more information about the scroll bars and moving around the 1-2-3 worksheet, see Chapter 2, "What Every 1-2-3 User Should Know."

Tip
Point to a SmartIcon and hold down the right mouse button for a description of the SmartIcon.

The status bar (which displays at the bottom of the 1-2-3 screen) has several purposes. The most obvious is to display messages, such as the numeric format, style, and font of the current selection, the status indicators, and the current date and time or row height and column width. As useful as this information may be, you'll probably find the additional function of the status bar even more useful. The 1-2-3 Release 4 for DOS status bar doesn't just provide a static display of information, it also enables you to quickly change numeric formatting, apply styles, and control the use of different typefaces in your worksheet (see figure 1.2). See Chapter 6, "Making Your Worksheets Dazzle," for more information on using the status bar formatting, style, and typeface options.

The status bar also provides access to e-mail and the 1-2-3 Help system, and allows you to select the SmartIcon palette.

34 Chapter 1—What's New in 1-2-3 Release 4 for DOS

A final feature of the improved interface is the use of dialog boxes, such as the one shown in figure 1.3, to present information in a comprehensive format. You can view and modify several related settings in a typical dialog box.

Fig. 1.2
The status bar provides shortcut methods of applying formats, styles, and typefaces.

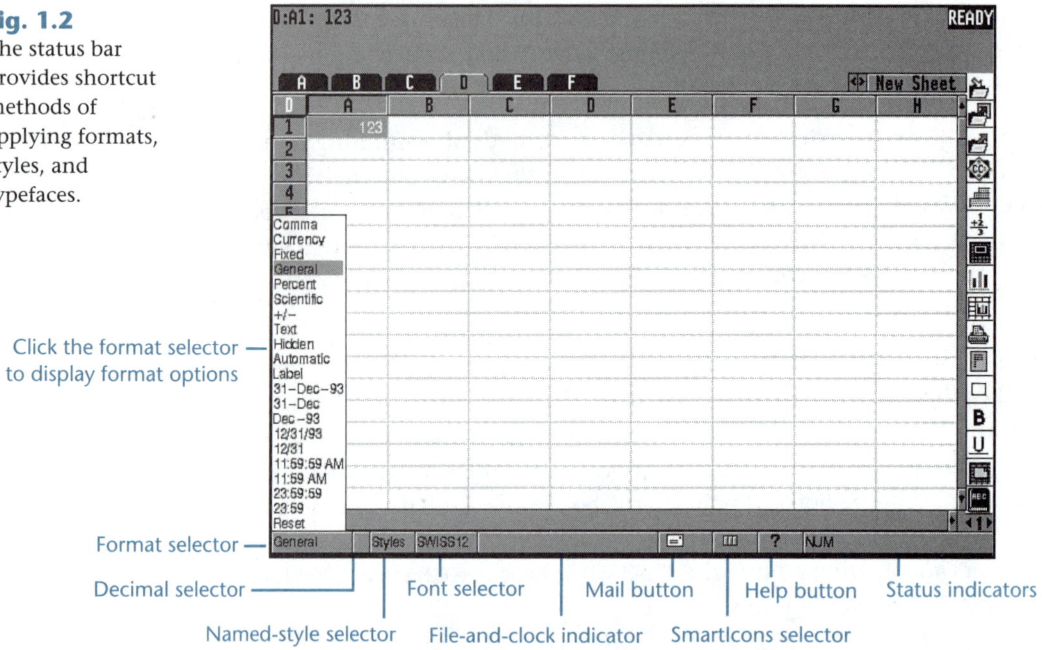

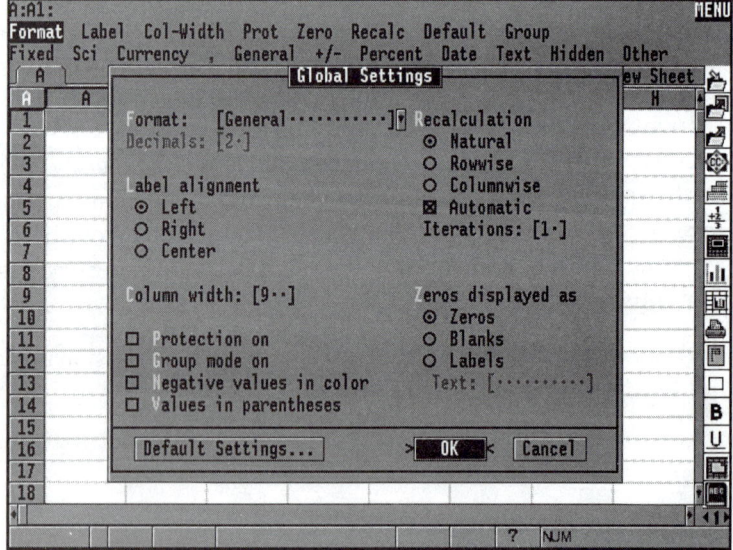

Fig. 1.3
Dialog boxes make it easier to view and modify related settings.

New Memory Model

1-2-3 Release 4 for DOS is the first version of 1-2-3 that supports any type of memory that may be available in your PC. In addition to conventional memory, 1-2-3 Release 4 for DOS can use EMS (expanded) memory, XMS (extended) memory, and virtual memory (using your hard disk to simulate additional RAM). In fact, 1-2-3 Release 4 for DOS can use up to 64M of memory, combining the available types on your system. Whether you upgrade to 1-2-3 Release 4 for DOS from Release 2.x or from Release 3.x, you'll find it's unnecessary to modify your existing system configuration.

Auto-Backup Feature

Everyone knows they should save their work periodically, but how often do you remember to save your 1-2-3 files? It's just too much trouble to interrupt your work just to save the worksheet, so most people wait until they're done working to save everything. This can be a dangerous practice, because a power failure, an incorrect command, or even a simple distraction are the only things necessary to cause hours of work to be lost in an instant.

The new 1-2-3 Release 4 for DOS auto-backup feature enables you to specify a time interval (up to 60 minutes) after which your work is automatically saved. If a problem occurs and you have the auto-backup feature enabled, the most work you'll lose is as much as you've done since the last automatic backup. Figure 1.4 shows the Default Settings dialog box you use to set the auto-backup time interval. See Chapter 2, "What Every 1-2-3 User Should Know," for more information on saving your work and using the auto-backup feature.

Column Fit to Widest Entry

Another new 1-2-3 Release 4 for DOS feature solves a sometimes annoying problem. In past DOS versions of 1-2-3, you had to set column widths manually, adjusting those widths to the correct number of character spaces to display your data properly. If you didn't make a column wide enough, numbers and formula results displayed as asterisks (*), and labels either spilled over into the next column to the right or were truncated, depending on the contents of the cell to the right.

36 Chapter 1—What's New in 1-2-3 Release 4 for DOS

Fig. 1.4
Set the auto-backup interval to save your work automatically.

Auto-backup option

Tip
If you want to automatically fit the column width to the size of numeric data, but want to allow a label to spill over into the next column, double-click the column letter after you've entered the numeric data but before you enter the label.

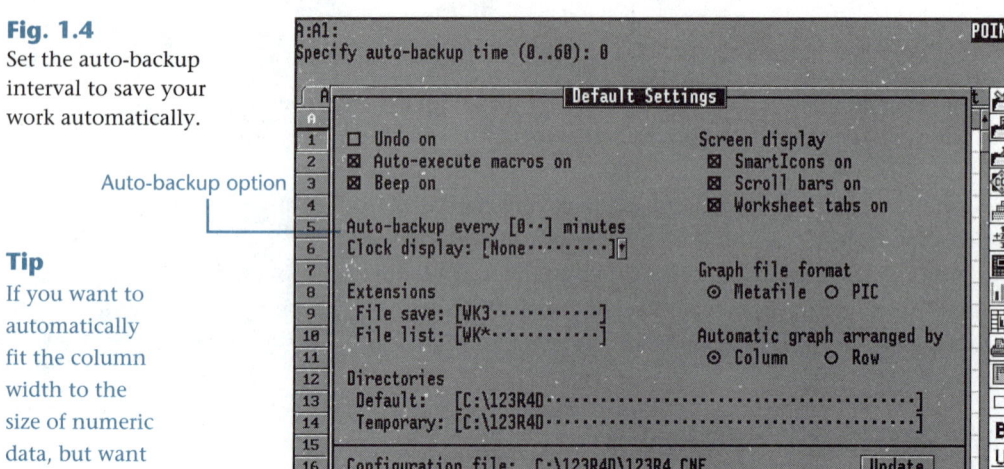

Now you can use the **/W**orksheet **C**olumn **F**it-Widest command to automatically adjust a column's width so that all data fits within the column width. You can also use the mouse shortcut, double-clicking the column letter, to quickly apply this handy command. Figure 1.5 shows how this command was used to adjust the width of column B to automatically fit all of the data. See Chapter 2, "What Every 1-2-3 User Should Know," for more information on setting column widths to fit your data.

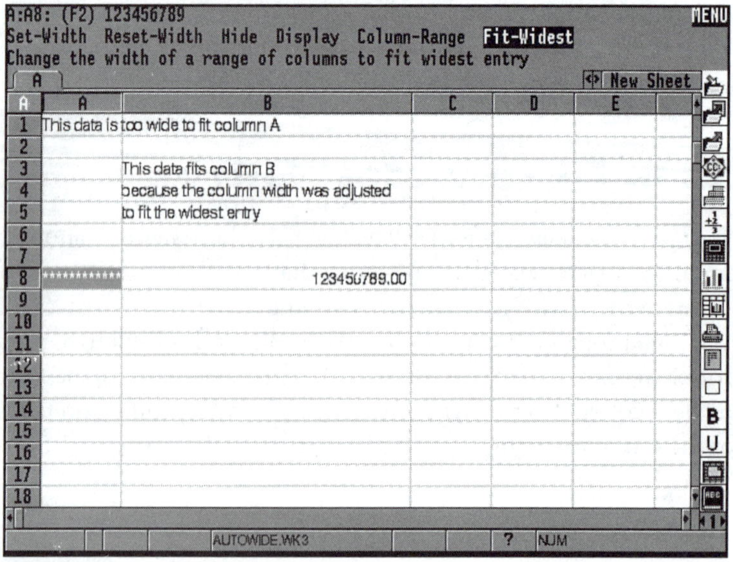

Fig. 1.5
Use the /**W**orksheet **C**olumn **F**it-Widest command to fit the data width into a column.

Cell Annotation

One of the most difficult things about 1-2-3 worksheets is trying to understand the assumptions someone used in creating formulas and macros. Good documentation in worksheets is almost as rare as flawless diamonds; both can be found, but neither is very common.

One reason for this poor documentation has been that it was difficult to create notes or annotations in a worksheet. In 1-2-3 Release 4 for DOS, this has changed with the addition of the new cell annotation feature (/**T**ools **N**ote **A**dd). You can now easily attach a note of up to 512 characters to any cell in a worksheet (see figure 1.6). When you create your complicated masterpiece formula, you can now add a note explaining the logic behind your formula. See Chapter 7, "Attaching Comments to Worksheet Cells," for more information on adding annotations to worksheet cells.

Tip

Use /**T**ools **N**ote **T**able to create a single list of all cell annotations in a worksheet file.

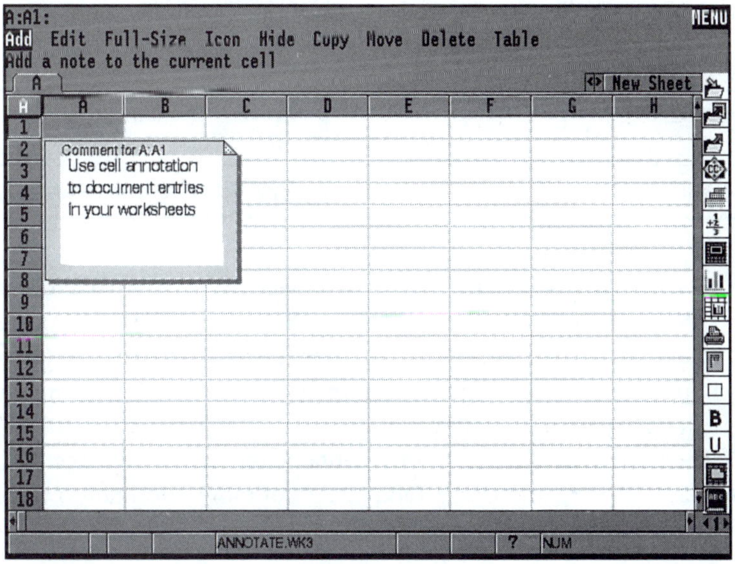

Fig. 1.6

Use /**T**ools **N**ote **A**dd or the Cell Annotation SmartIcon to document your worksheets.

SmartSheet Templates

It's always nice to have an expert's help, especially when it comes to making financial decisions. 1-2-3 is an ideal tool for performing the often-complex calculations necessary when making these decisions, but you still must do the work of developing the model worksheet. Such a model is often called a *template*, because it serves as the basis on which you can build the scenarios you examine while making your decisions.

In the past, 1-2-3 users could build their own models, buy a template someone else developed, or try to copy a model shown in a publication. Each of these approaches had its own problems, including possible errors or high cost. 1-2-3 Release 4 for DOS, however, includes several *SmartSheets*—sample templates you can immediately use either without change or as the basis for more complex models.

Table 1.1 summarizes the SmartSheet sample templates included with 1-2-3 Release 4 for DOS.

Table 1.1   SmartSheet Sample Templates

Template	Description
BUYLEASE.WK3	Analyzes whether it is better to buy or to lease an automobile.
DLYPLNNR.WK3	Prints a daily planner template.
EXPREPRT.WK3	Creates a standard expense report.
INVSTREC.WK3	Serves as a review and inventory of your investments.
STMTWRTH.WK3	Creates a personal net worth statement.

Tip
If you modify a SmartSheet sample template, save your modified version using a new name so that you can preserve the original version.

Figure 1.7 shows the BUYLEASE.WK3 SmartSheet sample template. Like all of the SmartSheet sample templates, this template includes several worksheet pages. One page, labeled *SmartSheet*, contains the actual model and formulas. A second page, labeled *About*, provides a brief description of the template, along with an explanation telling you how to use the macros included in the model. The third page, labeled *Macros*, contains the model's macros. See Chapter 12, "Creating and Using Templates," for more information about using the SmartSheet sample templates.

Tools Menu

1-2-3 has always been a powerful program with many built-in features. Almost from its inception, however, people have been devising methods of enhancing the program's capabilities. Many different types of add-in programs have been created, each designed to provide capabilities beyond those of the basic spreadsheet. When add-ins first became available, most were the products of third-party vendors, and you purchased them separately from 1-2-3. In recent years, however, Lotus has provided a large number of specialized add-ins along with 1-2-3 itself. For example, the Solver and Backsolver add-ins, which you can use to simplify the tasks of finding solutions to complex problems, were first developed as third-party add-in programs, but today Lotus provides these tools with every copy of 1-2-3.

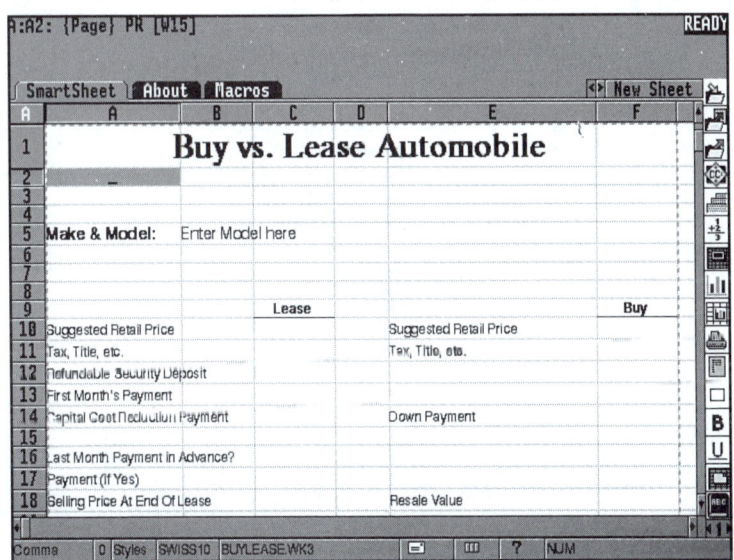

Fig. 1.7
1-2-3 Release 4 for DOS includes several useful SmartSheet sample templates like this one.

One of the problems with add-ins, however, is that each add-in you use requires its own allotment of memory in order to function. Often this memory requirement is high, making it difficult, if not impossible, to use more than a few add-in tools at one time. This is especially true if you are using a large, complex model that also requires considerable memory.

The various tools that extend 1-2-3 can cause memory problems, especially if you try to use several of these tools at the same time. 1-2-3 Release 4 for DOS offers a new solution to these memory problems with the new **T**ools menu. The new **T**ools menu provides a simple method of accessing both the add-ins familiar from previous 1-2-3 DOS versions, and the new tools included in Release 4. Table 1.2 summarizes the options on the new **T**ools menu.

Table 1.2 Tools Menu Options

Option	Description	Chapters
Wysiwyg	Starts the Wysiwyg add-in, allowing you to enhance the appearance and printing of your worksheets.	2, 4, 6, 8, 23
Version	Starts the Version Manager, enabling you to create and manage multiple scenarios in a single worksheet.	18
Spell	Starts the Spell Checker, which verifies correct spelling in your worksheets.	6
Note	Enables you to create a notepad in order to annotate worksheet cells.	7
E-Mail	Starts cc:Mail, enabling you to exchange electronic mail with other cc:Mail users.	9
Analyze	Enables you to start the Auditor, Backsolver, or Solver add-ins. These tools help you find worksheet errors as well as solve complex problems.	14, 16, 17
Config-Addins	Enables you to load, unload, and control add-in programs, whether they are included with 1-2-3 or purchased separately from a third-party vendor.	14
Macro	Enables you to record, run, play back, and debug macros.	26, 27, 28
DOS	Enables you to temporarily invoke the DOS command line and perform simple tasks such as formatting diskettes, copying files, and creating directories.	9

The **T**ools menu provides a convenient place to find many of the powerful enhancements to 1-2-3 Release 4 for DOS. Many of these enhancements are introduced throughout this chapter. See Chapter 2, "What Every 1-2-3 User Should Know," for more information about using 1-2-3 menus.

Version Manager

1-2-3 is a wonderful tool for creating what-if scenarios, but by itself it has a severe limitation. If you want to examine several possible scenarios, you have to create and save many different versions of the same model. Otherwise, only the most recent set of conditions is saved, and you must rekey your data if you want to re-examine one of the other possible outcomes.

Version Manager (see figure 1.8) is a powerful new tool in 1-2-3 Release 4 for DOS designed to make examining multiple scenarios an easy task. When you use Version Manager, you save each of the different sets of data in a single worksheet. These named data sets can then be quickly recalled whenever you want to re-examine one of the proposed outcomes.

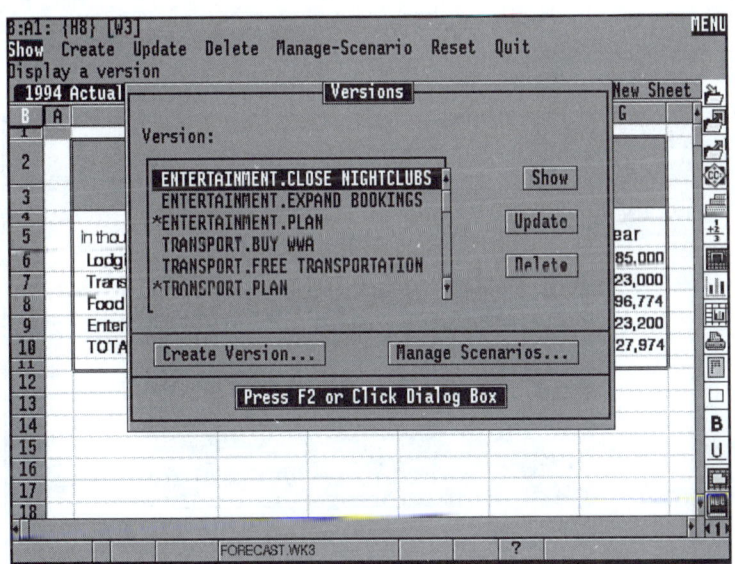

Fig. 1.8
Use Version Manager to experiment with multiple what-if scenarios.

Multiple what-if scenarios are quite useful for such tasks as predicting outcomes based on incomplete information. Suppose, for example, you need to predict the potential profits for a new business location. You can't predict the exact level of business you'll do, but you can probably estimate a range of possibilities. Using multiple what-if scenarios, you can see what your profits might be given the worst case, the best case, and some moderate instances between these two. See Chapter 18, "Tracking Multiple Sets of Data with Version Manager," for more detailed information on using Version Manager.

Sending and Receiving Mail

Electronic mail (or e-mail), is one of the fastest methods of sharing information between different computers. Most business computers, especially in larger organizations, are connected to other computers by a network or through some other means. It's becoming more important for application programs such as 1-2-3 to be *mail-enabled*, allowing their users to share data conveniently.

 1-2-3 Release 4 for DOS offers the E-Mail option on the **T**ools menu (see figure 1.9), which allows users of cc:Mail Release 4.02 (or later) for DOS to share worksheets electronically.

Fig. 1.9
Use /Tools E-Mail to share 1-2-3 worksheets using cc:Mail.

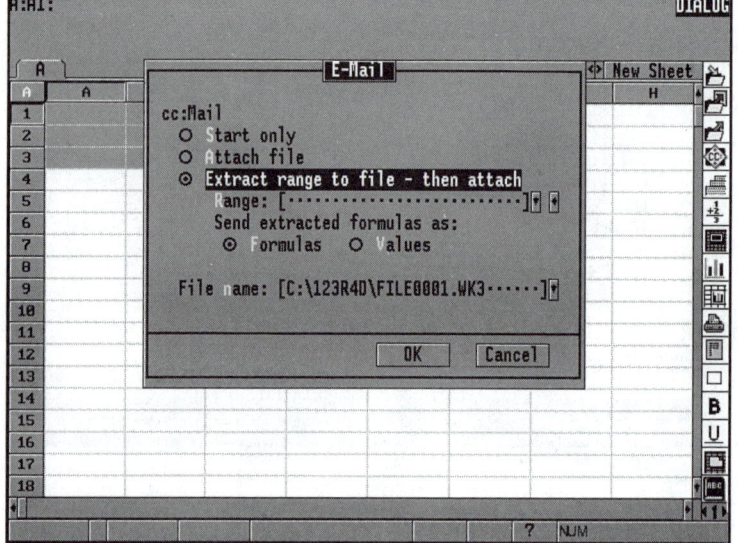

E-mail is not only one of the fastest methods of sharing information, but it can also be one of the most convenient. When you send an e-mail message, the recipient does not have to be immediately available, but can receive the message at a more convenient time. This makes e-mail especially convenient when you're working with other people who don't necessarily work the same schedule as you, or who are located in a different time zone. Business travelers can often increase their efficiency by using e-mail to access information when they need it, not when someone is available to provide it. See Chapter 9, "Working with Files," for more detailed information on using e-mail with 1-2-3 Release 4 for DOS.

Spell Checker

Typing and spelling errors are a common problem for most PC users. Whether you misspell or duplicate words, your worksheet's appearance is degraded by such errors. Even worse, spelling errors in macros can cause your macros to fail or even do damage to your carefully designed models. It's important to catch these errors before they have a chance to cause problems or make you look incompetent.

The 1-2-3 Release 4 for DOS spell checker (see figure 1.10) enables you to quickly examine your worksheets for misspelled or duplicated words. You can check a single cell, a range of cells, a chart, a single worksheet, or an entire file. See Chapter 6, "Making Your Worksheets Dazzle," for more information on using the spell checker.

Tip
Use the spell checker to look for misspelled macro keywords before running new macro programs.

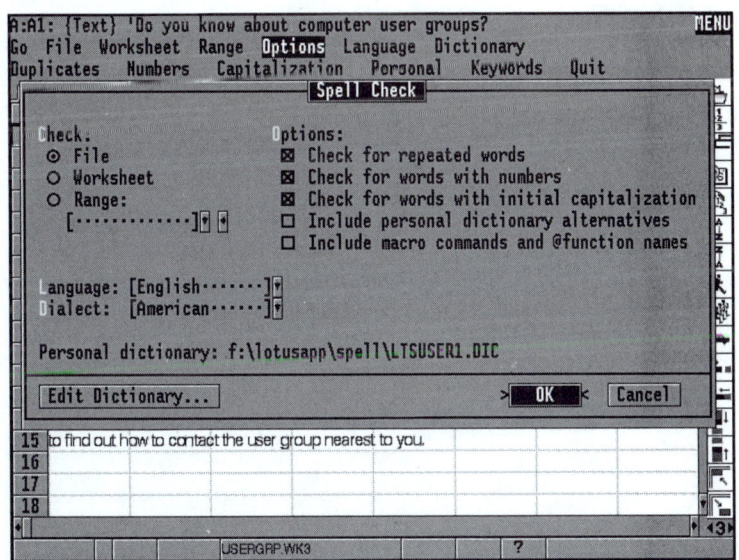

Fig. 1.10
Use the spell checker to be certain that your worksheets do not contain misspelled or duplicated words.

QuickStart

With all the new features in 1-2-3 Release 4 for DOS, you might wonder how you'll ever learn to use all of them. Don't worry: there's a new QuickStart tutorial program designed just for you. When you use the QuickStart, you'll become familiar with 1-2-3 Release 4 for DOS in just a few minutes.

The QuickStart is separate from 1-2-3, so you must exit from 1-2-3 before starting the QuickStart. Change to the QSTART directory and enter the command **QSTART** to run the QuickStart tutorial. Figure 1.11 shows the QuickStart menu, which you see after a few introductory screens.

Fig. 1.11
Use the new QuickStart to learn about the new features in 1-2-3 Release 4 for DOS.

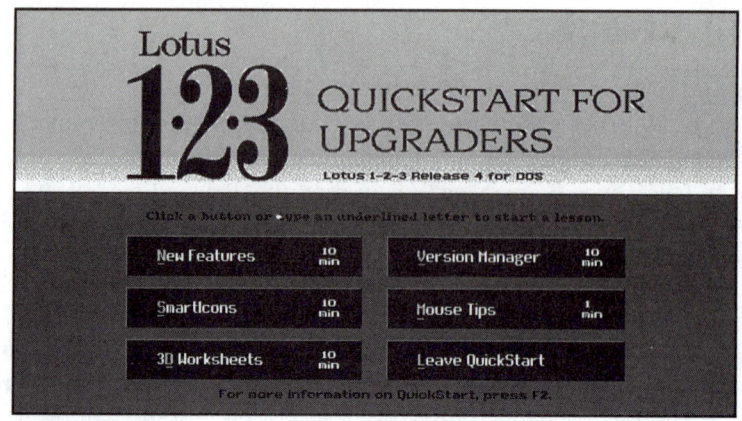

> **Troubleshooting**
>
> *I cannot load some of the new features of 1-2-3 Release 4 for DOS.*
>
> Be sure you install all of the optional components. If you tried to save disk space by not installing some of the options, you won't be able to use those options.
>
> *I can't find the QuickStart tutorial on the 1-2-3 menu.*
>
> The QuickStart tutorial is a separate program that you must run from the DOS command line. Exit from 1-2-3 Release 4 for DOS, change to the QSTART directory, and enter the command **QSTART** to run the QuickStart tutorial.

Chapter 2
What Every 1-2-3 User Should Know

Chapter 1, "What's New in Release 4 for DOS," introduced Lotus 1-2-3 and discussed the program's power and versatility. This chapter starts you out in 1-2-3 and helps you develop the skills necessary to fully use the program's many features. If you are new to spreadsheet software, you learn how to use a spreadsheet program for data analysis. If you are familiar with electronic spreadsheets but new to 1-2-3 or to Release 4, you can find information to help you understand the features of 1-2-3 Release 4.

> **Note**
>
> Users who are familiar with 1-2-3 but not with Release 4 may find some of the introductory material in this chapter too basic. To use a 1-2-3 worksheet immediately, skip this chapter and go on to Chapter 3, "Finding Solutions with Formulas and Functions."

The 1-2-3 spreadsheet is known as a *worksheet*. This chapter familiarizes you with the worksheet and teaches you how to perform several actions that alter the worksheet, such as entering and editing data. The chapter also covers the Undo feature, which enables you to reverse changes made in error.

The basic 1-2-3 worksheet is a two-dimensional grid of columns and rows that can be expanded to a three-dimensional array of multiple-worksheet files. In this chapter, you learn how to use a two-dimensional worksheet. See Chapter 10, "Organizing Your Data with Multiple-Worksheet Files," to learn how to build three-dimensional worksheets, which are useful tools for consolidating information. (You can link worksheets, for example, by writing formulas in one worksheet that refer to cells in another worksheet.) When you must work with large amounts of data or data from different sources, multiple-worksheet files enable you to work with several worksheets at the same time.

The primary purpose of 1-2-3 is to enable you to perform *data analysis*—to manipulate and analyze data, numbers, and formulas. Because the worksheet also reports the results of an analysis, you need a way to organize this material. This chapter demonstrates how to use *labels*—titles, headings, names, comments, descriptions, and other entries—to make your final worksheet clear and easy to follow.

In this chapter, you learn how to do the following:

- Start and exit 1-2-3 and Wysiwyg
- Move around the worksheet
- Enter and edit data
- Enter basic formulas
- Select, copy, move, and erase data
- Insert and delete rows and columns
- Save and retrieve worksheets
- Print a worksheet
- Create graphs

Tip
If you name a worksheet file AUTO123.WK3, 1-2-3 retrieves this file each time you start the program. The AUTO123.WK3 file must be in the 1-2-3 default directory (the directory specified with **/W**orksheet **G**lobal **D**efault **D**ir).

Starting To Use 1-2-3

Before you start to use 1-2-3, the program must be installed on your computer. If you chose the default installation, the 1-2-3 program is in the directory \123R4D. (For 1-2-3 Releases 3.0, 3.1, and 3.1+, the directory name is \123R3. For 1-2-3 Release 3.4, the directory name is \123R34.)

Starting 1-2-3

To start 1-2-3 from the operating system, follow these steps:

1. If 1-2-3 is installed on drive C and drive C isn't the current drive, type **C:** and press Enter. (If you installed 1-2-3 on drive D, E, or another drive, substitute the appropriate drive letter in this step.)

2. To make \123R4D the active directory, type **CD\123R4D** and press Enter. (If you installed 1-2-3 in a different directory, substitute that directory name for 123R4D.)

3. Type **123** and press Enter to start 1-2-3.

After you start 1-2-3, the registration screen appears for a few seconds while the program loads. A blank worksheet appears, and you can start using 1-2-3.

To retrieve a specific file at the same time you start 1-2-3 from the operating system, you can type **123**, followed by a space, a hyphen (-), the letter **w**, and the file name—for example, **123 -wFILENAME**. If the file isn't in the 1-2-3 default directory, include the directory name with the file name. (Chapter 9, "Working with Files," explains how to change the 1-2-3 default directory.) To retrieve the file SALES.WK3 from a nondefault directory—C:\DATA, for example—type the following command at the operating-system prompt and then press Enter:

123 -wC:\DATA\SALES

In this example, if the 1-2-3 default directory is C:\DATA, simply type the following and press Enter:

123 -wSALES

> **Note**
>
> You can start 1-2-3 from the Lotus 1-2-3 Access Menu or from the operating system. (Most users start 1-2-3 from the operating system because this method is easier, faster, and uses less memory.) To start 1-2-3 from the Access Menu, type **LOTUS** at the C:\123R4D prompt. Then select 1-2-3 and press Enter.

Starting Wysiwyg

1-2-3 Releases 3.4 and 4 start with Wysiwyg loaded and invoked in graphics display mode. When the mouse pointer is in the control panel, clicking the right mouse button switches between the 1-2-3 main menu and the Wyslwyg menu. To take advantage of the Wysiwyg features of Release 3.1 or 3.1+, however, you first must load the Wysiwyg add-in into memory. You must perform this procedure each time you start 1-2-3, unless you set 1-2-3 to load and invoke Wysiwyg automatically. Users of Release 3.1 or 3.1+ who want to learn how to set up their system to invoke Wysiwyg on startup can skip to the section titled "Starting Wysiwyg Automatically."

▶ "Formatting with the Wysiwyg Menu," p. 320

▶ "Managing Wysiwyg Formats," p. 336

Starting Wysiwyg Manually

When you load Wysiwyg manually, you can attach the Wysiwyg add-in to one of three function keys. Attaching an add-in to a function key means that you can *invoke* the add-in (bring up the add-in menu) by pressing the Alt key and a function key. This procedure isn't recommended for Wysiwyg, however, because you need to press only **:** (the colon key) to invoke the add-in.

To load Wysiwyg manually, follow these steps:

1. Hold down the Alt key and press F10. The Add-In menu appears in the control panel.

2. Choose **L**oad (the first option in the menu) by pressing **L** or by pressing Enter (because **L**oad is highlighted). A list of add-in files appears.

3. Choose the file named WYSIWYG.PLC by highlighting the file name and pressing Enter. 1-2-3 displays another menu to request a key assignment for the add-in.

4. Choose **N**o-Key by pressing **N** or pressing Enter if **N**o-Key is highlighted. (If you want to attach Wysiwyg to a function key, choose **1** (Alt+F7), **2** (Alt+F8), or **3** (Alt+F9) by typing the number or by highlighting the number and then pressing Enter.) After you make the selection, the worksheet appears with Wysiwyg loaded.

5. Choose **Q**uit to leave the Add-In menu.

Starting Wysiwyg Automatically

Loading Wysiwyg each time you start 1-2-3 is time-consuming. You can save time by configuring 1-2-3 to load Wysiwyg automatically. To set up 1-2-3 to invoke Wysiwyg automatically, follow these steps:

1. Press Alt+F10 (Addin) to access the Add-In menu.

2. Choose **S**ettings **S**ystem by typing **SS** or by highlighting each option and then pressing Enter. 1-2-3 displays the System Add-Ins dialog box with a list of the add-in files that are set to automatically load.

3. Choose **S**et by typing **S**. 1-2-3 displays the available add-in files in the control panel.

4. Highlight WYSIWYG.PLC and press Enter. 1-2-3 adds WYSIWYG to the System Add-Ins dialog box.

5. Next, choose **Y**es (to start the application automatically when 1-2-3 reads Wysiwyg into memory).

6. Choose **N**o-Key if you don't want to attach Wysiwyg to a function key (see the steps in the preceding section for a discussion of this option).

7. Choose **U**pdate **Q**uit.

After you execute this procedure, the 1-2-3 worksheet loads with Wysiwyg each time you start 1-2-3.

Exiting 1-2-3

To exit 1-2-3, you use the 1-2-3 main menu. Press the slash (/) key; the 1-2-3 main menu appears across the top of the worksheet (see fig. 2.1). Choose the **Q**uit option from this menu to exit the worksheet and return to the operating system.

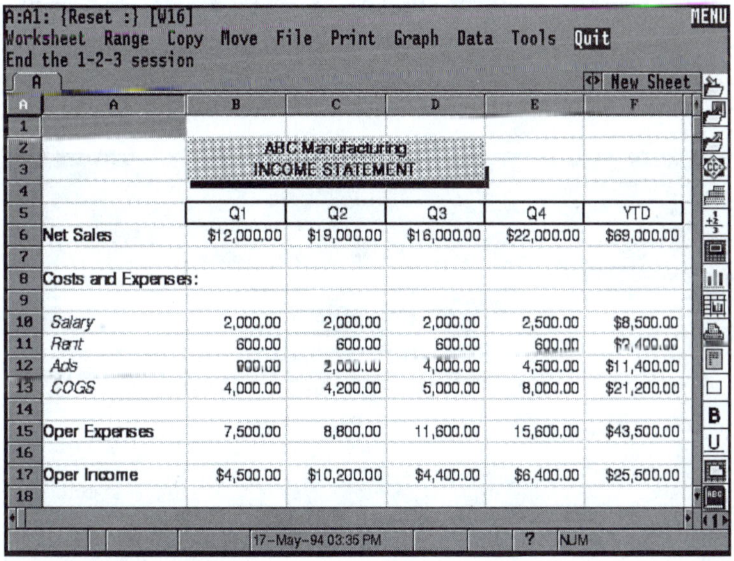

Fig. 2.1
The 1-2-3 main menu.

When you choose **Q**uit from the 1-2-3 main menu, 1-2-3 prompts you to verify that you want to exit the program; **N**o is the default answer. When you exit 1-2-3, you lose all changes made to the current worksheet file and any temporary settings that you didn't save. To verify that you want to exit, choose **Y**es (see fig. 2.2). If you made changes to your worksheet without saving your worksheet file, 1-2-3 prompts you a second time to verify this choice before you exit (see fig. 2.3).

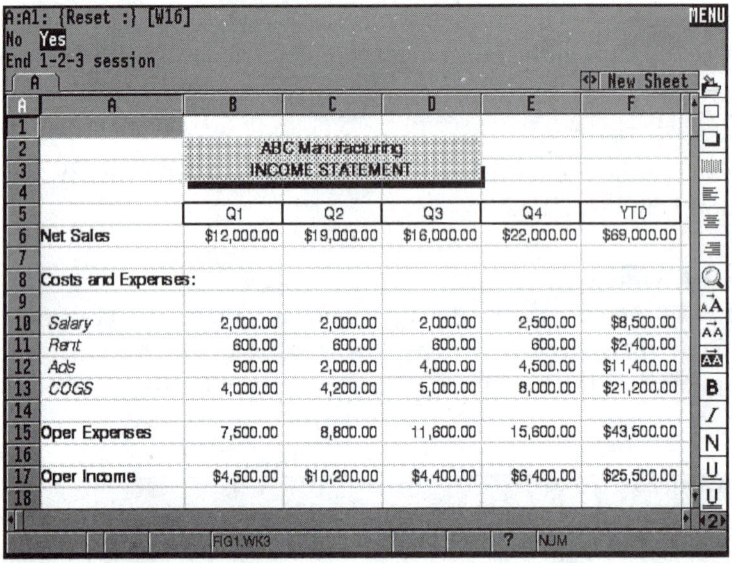

Fig. 2.2
1-2-3 displays a confirmation prompt before you exit the program.

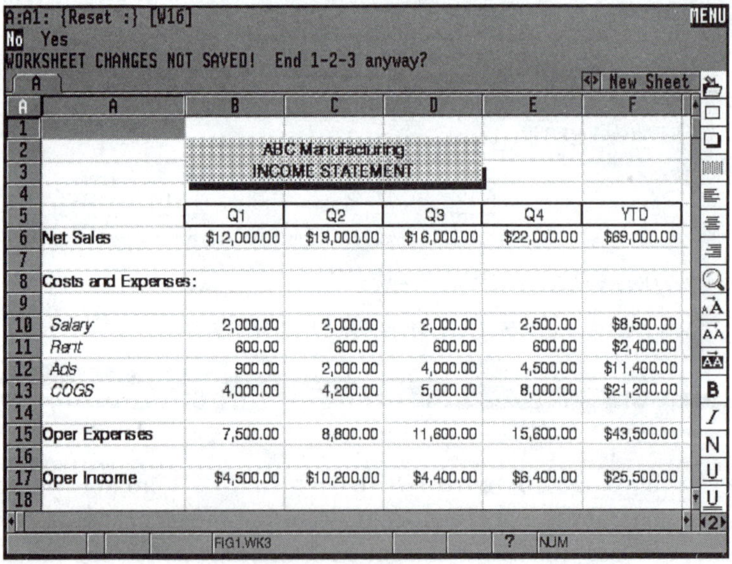

Fig. 2.3
1-2-3 prompts you to save worksheet changes before leaving the program.

If you want to save files before exiting 1-2-3, choose **N**o to cancel the **/Q**uit command. (The commands for saving files are introduced later in this chapter and covered in detail in Chapter 9, "Working with Files.") To exit 1-2-3 without saving the files, choose **Y**es.

Moving Around the Worksheet

You move around the worksheet by moving the *cell pointer*; you move the cell pointer by using the mouse, the direction keys, or the scroll bar. Characters within the cell pointer appear in reverse video on the highlighted background. All data typed in the worksheet goes into the cell at the location of the cell pointer. The *cursor* is the line that appears in the control panel when you type or edit data in a cell. The cursor indicates the position of the next character you type. Within a command menu, you use the *menu pointer* to highlight, or select, a command.

Tip
You can use the Wysiwyg **:D**is-play **O**ptions **C**ell-Pointer **O**utline command to change the default solid cell pointer to an outline.

Because you can enter data only at the location of the cell pointer, you must know how to move the cell pointer to the location you want before you enter data. Because you can display only a small part of the worksheet at a time, you also must know how to use the cell pointer to bring different parts of the worksheet on-screen. You control the cell pointer with the keyboard keys or the mouse.

The following sections discuss how to move the cell pointer around one worksheet. In Chapter 10, "Organizing Your Data with Multiple-Worksheet Files," you learn how to move around multiple-worksheet files and multiple files.

Using the Keyboard to Move the Cell Pointer

Many of the same direction keys move the cell pointer or the cursor, depending on the current mode. This section discusses cell-pointer movement. Cursor movement is covered in a later section of this chapter. Menu-pointer movement is discussed in the introduction of this book (in the section titled "Using the Command Menus").

◄ "Learning the 1-2-3 Keyboard," p. 16

When 1-2-3 is in READY or POINT mode, the direction keys move the cell pointer. In LABEL or VALUE mode, using the direction keys ends the entry and returns 1-2-3 to READY mode, where the direction keys again move the cell pointer. In EDIT mode, some direction keys move the cursor in the control panel; other direction keys end the edit session and return 1-2-3 to READY mode, where the direction keys again move the cell pointer. In MENU mode, the direction keys move the menu pointer to menu commands.

Using the Mouse to Move the Cell Pointer

You can use the mouse to move the cell pointer in READY or POINT mode. In VALUE mode, clicking the mouse button ends the entry and returns 1-2-3 to READY mode. The mouse does not function when 1-2-3 is in LABEL or EDIT

◄ "Using the Mouse with 1-2-3," p. 14

52 Chapter 2—What Every 1-2-3 User Should Know

mode. In MENU mode, you can use the mouse to move the menu pointer to menu commands.

The simplest technique for moving the cell pointer with the mouse is to point to a cell and click the mouse button. You also can move the cell pointer by using the mouse in conjunction with the SmartIcons on the right side of the worksheet. The SmartIcon palette contains four arrows that point in four directions (see fig. 2.4).

Fig. 2.4
The Right, Left, Up, and Down arrow SmartIcons.

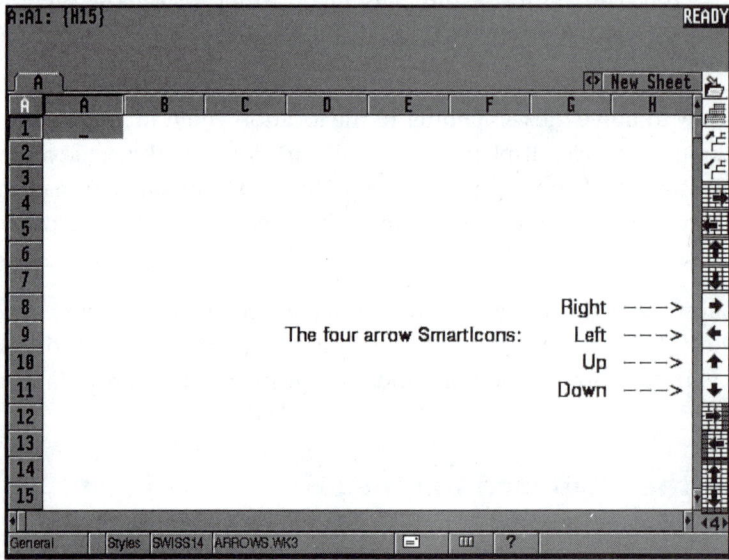

Clicking an arrow SmartIcon moves the cell pointer one cell in the direction of the arrow. If you hold down the left mouse button, the cell pointer keeps moving in the direction of the arrow. If you want to move the cell pointer to a cell not shown on-screen, point to the appropriate arrow SmartIcon and hold down the left mouse button until the worksheet starts to scroll. When you reach the row or column you want, release the mouse button.

Using the Scroll Bar To Move the Cell Pointer

You can move the cell pointer right, left, up, or down by using 1-2-3 Release 4's new *scroll bars* (see fig. 2.5). The scroll bar on the right side of the worksheet (vertical scroll bar) moves the cell pointer up or down; the scroll bar at the bottom of the worksheet (horizontal scroll bar) moves the cell pointer right or left. To use the scroll bar to move the cell pointer, click the appropriate arrow. To move one cell to the right, for example, click the right arrow once. To move two cells to the right, click the right arrow twice.

Moving Around the Worksheet

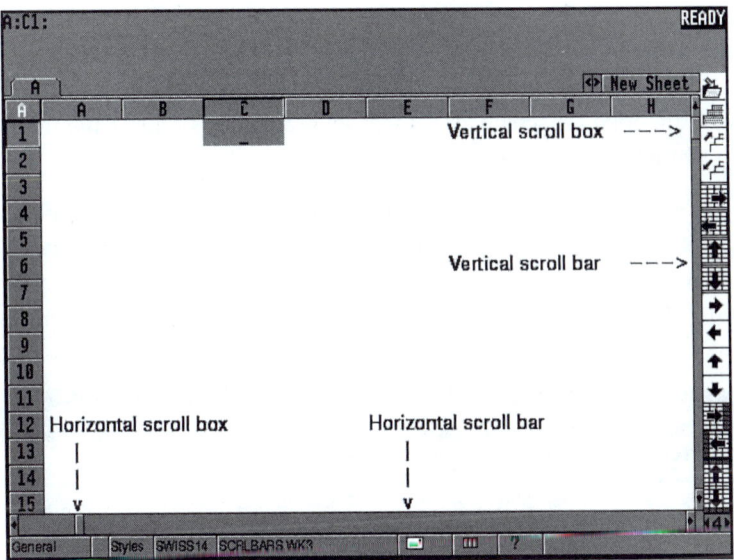

Fig. 2.5
Using the scroll bar to move the cell pointer.

Within each scroll bar, 1-2-3 displays a *vertical scroll box* and a *horizontal scroll box* that indicate the relative position of the cell pointer within the worksheet (see fig. 2.5). As you move the cell pointer through the worksheet, the scroll boxes move within the scroll bar. If you move the cell pointer to the right, for example, the horizontal scroll box moves to the right.

You also can use the scroll boxes to scroll the worksheet right, left, up, or down. To scroll the worksheet by using a scroll box, follow these steps:

1. Place the mouse pointer on the scroll box.

2. Press and hold down the left mouse button as you *drag* (move) the scroll box right, left, up, or down.

Using the Basic Movement Keys

Four direction keys that move the cell pointer are located on the numeric keypad and in a separate keypad on the enhanced keyboard. The cell pointer moves in the direction of the arrow on the direction key. If you press and hold down the direction key, the cell pointer continues to move in the direction of that key's arrow. When the cell pointer reaches the edge of the screen, the worksheet continues to scroll. If you try to move past the edge of the worksheet (beyond row 8,192, for example), 1-2-3 beeps.

You use other keys to move the cell pointer one screen at a time. Press PgUp or PgDn to move up or down one screen. Press Ctrl+right arrow or Tab to move one screen to the right; press Ctrl+left arrow or Shift+Tab (hold down the Shift key and press Tab) to move one screen to the left. The size of a one-screen move depends on the display driver in your system and how many windows are open on-screen. 1-2-3 windows are discussed in Chapter 4, "Controlling Your Worksheet Display."

Table 2.1 summarizes the actions of the direction keys within a single worksheet. The Home key moves the cell pointer to the *home position*—usually cell A1. The other keys listed in table 2.1 are discussed in the sections following the table. The first column shows the associated SmartIcon.

Table 2.1 Direction-Key Operation Within One Worksheet

SmartIcon	Key	Function
	→	Moves the cell pointer right one cell
	←	Moves the cell pointer left one cell
	↑	Moves the cell pointer up one cell
	↓	Moves the cell pointer down one cell
	Ctrl+ → or Tab	Moves the cell pointer right one screen
	Ctrl+ ← or Shift+Tab	Moves the cell pointer left one screen
	PgUp	Moves the cell pointer up one screen
	PgDn	Moves the cell pointer down one screen
	Home	Moves the cell pointer to the home position, usually cell A1 (locked titles may change the home position; see Chapter 4 for details)
	End Home	Moves the cell pointer to the bottom right corner of the active area
	End ←	Moves the cell pointer left to the next cell that contains data
	End →	Moves the cell pointer right to the next cell that contains data
	End ↑	Moves the cell pointer up to the next cell that contains data

SmartIcon	Key	Function
	End ↓	Moves the cell pointer down to the next cell that contains data
	F5 (GoTo)	Prompts for a cell address or range name; then moves the cell pointer to that cell
	Scroll Lock ←	Moves the worksheet right one column
	Scroll Lock →	Moves the worksheet left one column
	Scroll Lock ↑	Moves the worksheet down one row
	Scroll Lock ↓	Moves the worksheet up one row

> **Note**
>
> You may have to experiment with the Scroll Lock key before you become accustomed to the way this key works. The operation *seems* backward; with Scroll Lock on, when you press the left-arrow key the worksheet moves one column to the right.

Scrolling the Worksheet

The Scroll Lock key toggles the scroll function on and off. When you press the Scroll Lock key, you activate the scroll function, and the SCROLL status indicator appears in the status bar.

When you press an arrow key with Scroll Lock on, the cell pointer stays in the current cell and the entire window moves opposite the direction of the arrow key. If you continue pressing the arrow key when the cell pointer reaches the edge of the display, the cell pointer moves to the next cell as the entire window scrolls. Whenever the SCROLL status indicator is on, you can press the Scroll Lock key again to turn off Scroll Lock.

You also can use the Scroll Left, Scroll Right, Scroll Up, and Scroll Down SmartIcons to scroll the worksheet (see fig. 2.6). The Scroll Left SmartIcon, for example, functions similarly to pressing Scroll Lock and then pressing the left-arrow key.

56 Chapter 2—What Every 1-2-3 User Should Know

Fig. 2.6
The SmartIcons used to scroll the worksheet right, left, up, and down.

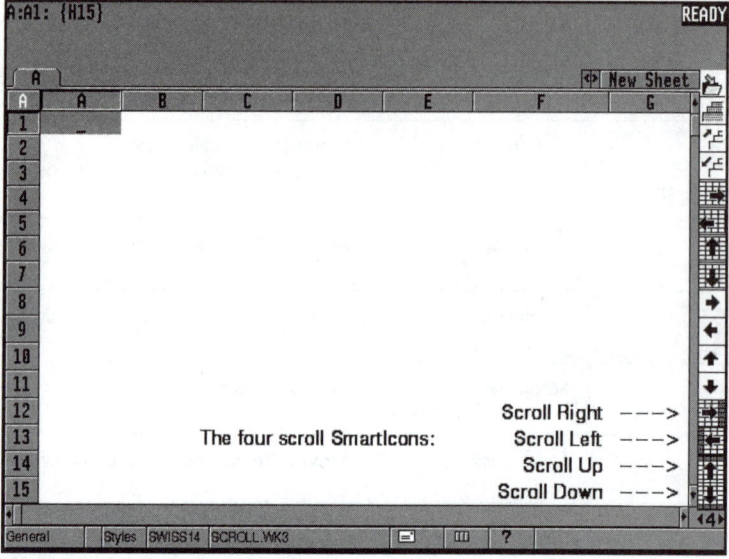

Troubleshooting

The cell pointer doesn't move in the way I expect.

Scroll Lock may have been turned on accidentally. Check for the SCROLL indicator in the status bar to determine whether Scroll Lock is on. If the indicator appears, press the Scroll Lock key to make it disappear.

When I press the arrow keys, 1-2-3 beeps and will not move the cell pointer in the worksheet.

The 1-2-3 menu may be active. When the 1-2-3 menu is active, the arrow keys on the keyboard highlight the options in the menu instead of moving the cell pointer in the worksheet. If you did not press the slash (/) key to activate the menu, the mouse pointer may be positioned in the control panel, which also activates the menu.

Using the End Key

Tip
Use the End key with an arrow key to move directly to the end of a list of data.

The End key has a special function in 1-2-3. When you press and release End, the END status indicator appears in the status bar. If you then click one of the arrow SmartIcons with the mouse or press one of the arrow keys, the cell pointer moves in the direction of the arrow or arrow key to the next cell that contains data. The cell pointer stops in a cell containing data, if such a cell exists. If no cells in the direction of the arrow or arrow key contain data, the cell pointer stops at the edge of the worksheet.

Figure 2.7 shows the cell pointer in cell A3. The END status indicator in the status bar shows that the user has pressed the End key. If the user now clicks the Down SmartIcon or presses the down-arrow key, the cell pointer moves down and stops at the last cell containing data in this column. In this case, the cell pointer moves to cell A8, as shown in figure 2.8. If you press End and then click the Right SmartIcon or press the right-arrow key, the cell pointer moves to the last cell containing data in the current row. Here, the cell pointer moves to cell E8, as shown in figure 2.9.

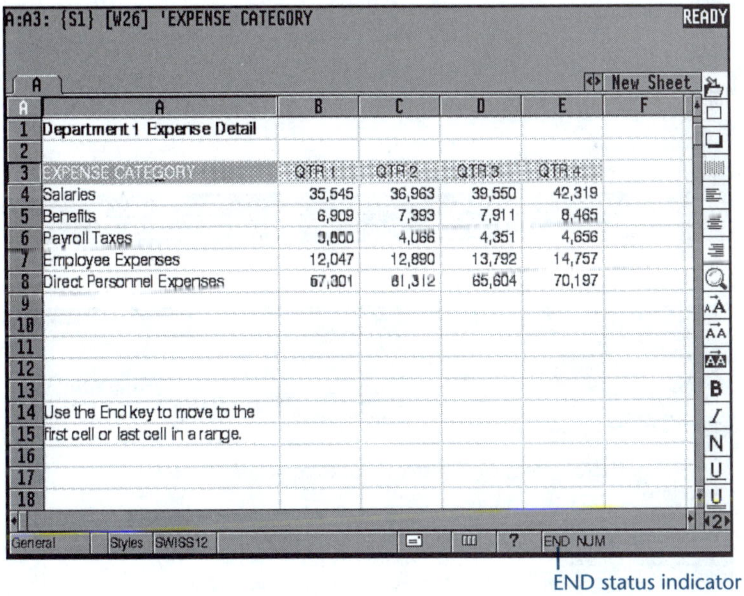

Fig. 2.7
The END key status indicator appears in the status bar.

END status indicator

The End key works the same way with the left- and up-arrow SmartIcons and the left- and up-arrow keys. From cell A3 in figure 2.8, pressing End+down arrow or pressing End and clicking the Left SmartIcon moves the cell pointer to cell A8. After you press End, the END indicator stays on only until you click an arrow SmartIcon, press a direction key, or press the End key again. If you press End accidentally, press End again to turn off the END status indicator.

If you press End and then Home, the cell pointer moves to the bottom right corner of the active area. The *active area* includes all rows and all columns containing data or cell formats. If you press End and then Home in figure 2.9, the cell pointer moves to cell E15 (see fig. 2.10). 1-2-3 considers this blank cell to be the end of the active area because column E contains an entry, as does row 17 (in cell A17).

Tip
Use End Home to find the end of the active area if you want to add a section to your worksheet without interfering with any existing data.

Fig. 2.8

The cell pointer moves down to the last cell containing data.

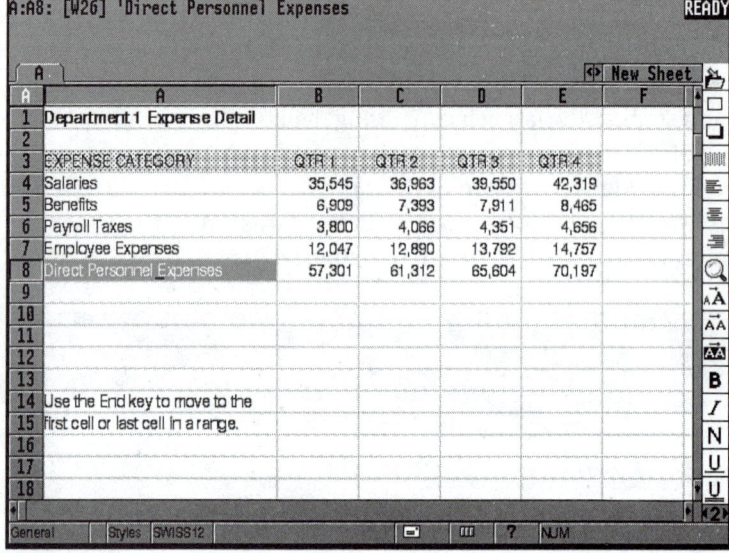

Fig. 2.9

The cell pointer moves right to the last cell containing data.

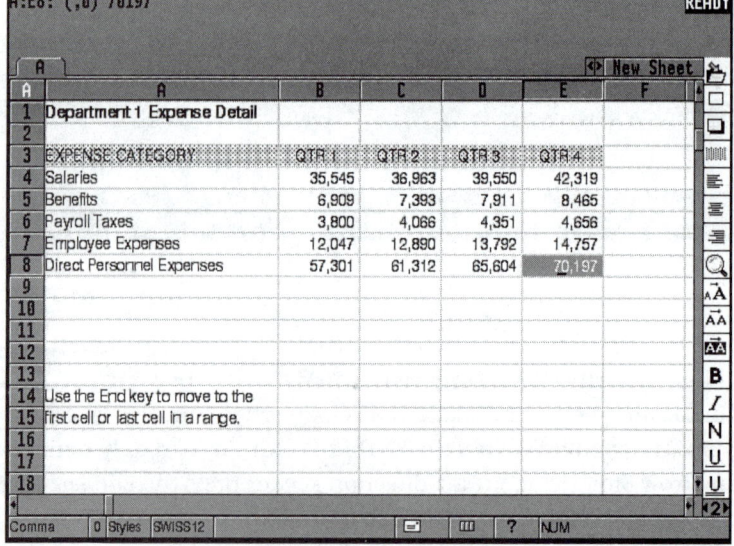

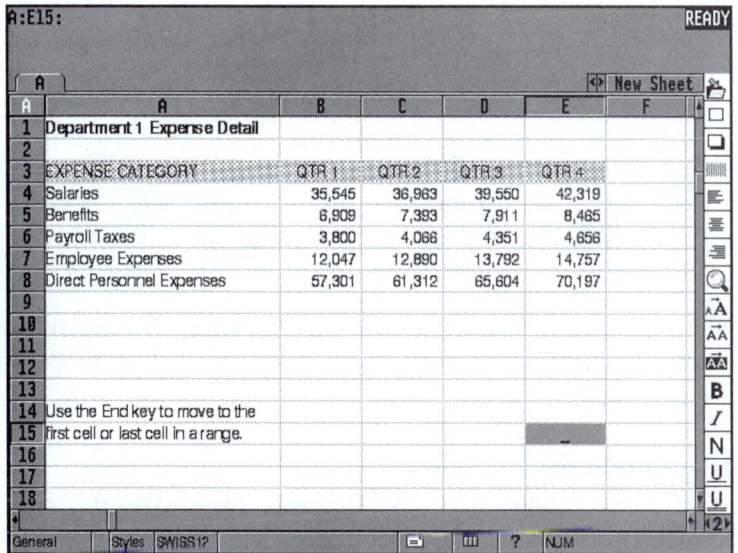

Fig. 2.10
Pressing End Home moves the cell pointer to the bottom right corner of the active area.

Using the GoTo (F5) Key

You can use the GoTo (F5) key to jump to any cell in the worksheet. When you press F5 (GoTo), 1-2-3 prompts you for an address. After you type the cell address and press Enter, the cell pointer moves to that address.

If you have a large worksheet, you may have to hold down the mouse button or a direction key for a long time to move from one part of the worksheet to another. With the GoTo (F5) key, you can move quickly across large parts of the worksheet.

You may not remember the addresses for every part of a large worksheet and therefore have problems using GoTo. To avoid these problems, you can list commonly used addresses in a separate worksheet and then press Ctrl+PgUp to access the other worksheet and view the addresses. You also can use range names with GoTo so that you don't need to remember cell addresses. A *range name* is a distinctive name you assign to a cell or range of cells. If the worksheet lists profits in cell B56, for example, you can give cell B56 the range name PROFIT. Range names are easier to remember than cell addresses. If you include range names in a worksheet, you can press F5 (GoTo) and then type the range name rather than the cell address. If the range name refers to more than one cell, the cell pointer moves to the top left corner of the range. For more explanation of using ranges and range names, refer to the section "Working with Ranges" later in this chapter.

Tip
After you press F5 (GoTo), you also can press F3 (Name) to display a list of range names from which you can select the desired range name. (If you press F3 twice, you get a full-screen listing of the range names.) Highlight the desired range name and press Enter.

Using the 1-2-3 Help Features

1-2-3 incorporates three features that provide help to users: the on-screen Help utility, and interactive and online QuickStart lessons.

1-2-3 provides context-sensitive Help information at the touch of a key. If you are performing a 1-2-3 operation, you can press the Help (F1) key or click the Help button at any time to summon one or more screens that contain explanations and advice on what to do next.

QuickStart, a new feature in 1-2-3, is an interactive, online introduction to the new features in Release 4. The QuickStart is particularly helpful to users of 1-2-3 Releases 2 and 3.x.

Finding On-Screen Help

Press Help (F1) at any time to access online Help. If you access Help while in READY mode, the Help Index appears (see fig. 2.11). The Help Index includes categories of help that 1-2-3 provides. Choose a category in the Help Index to access the list of topics within the category.

Fig. 2.11
The 1-2-3 Help Index screen.

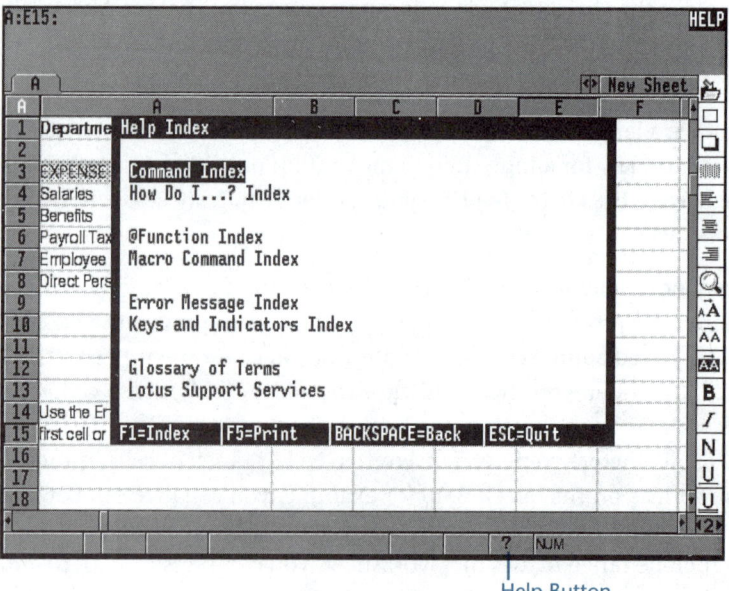

Help Button

You also can click the Help button in the status bar to access the online Help system.

You can access the Help system even while executing a command or editing a cell. Help is context-sensitive. If you are executing a particular command when you press F1 (Help) or click the Help button, 1-2-3 shows a Help screen for that command (see fig. 2.12).

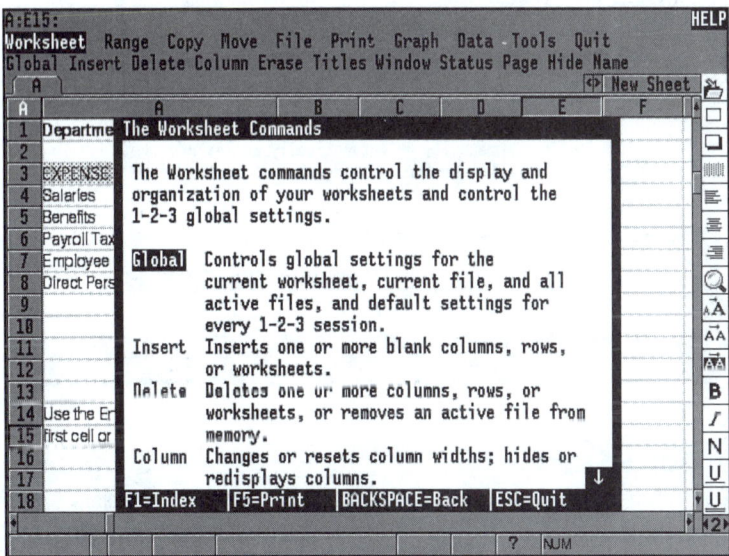

Fig. 2.12

A context-sensitive Help screen that explains the /Worksheet commands.

Certain parts of the Help screen identify additional help topics. 1-2-3 displays these topics in boldface on a monochrome monitor or in red on a color monitor. For more information about a topic, highlight the topic and press Enter or click the topic. Options that take you to the Help Index or to additional topics appear at the bottom of the screen at all times.

A function-key bar at the bottom of the Help screen shows the keys that you can use from this screen. Press the F1 key to return to the Help Index screen. Press F5 to print the current Help topic. Press the Backspace key to view a previous Help screen. Press the Esc key to return to the 1-2-3 worksheet when you finish consulting Help. You also can use the mouse to click the appropriate command at the bottom of the Help screen. For example, click F5=Print to print the current Help topic.

If you are working from the Wysiwyg command menu, pressing F1 brings up the Wysiwyg command Help screen, shown in figure 2.13. This Help facility is separate from the 1-2-3 Help screens. To get help on a Wysiwyg feature, therefore, you first must display the Wysiwyg menu.

Fig. 2.13
The Wysiwyg Help screen for the :Worksheet commands.

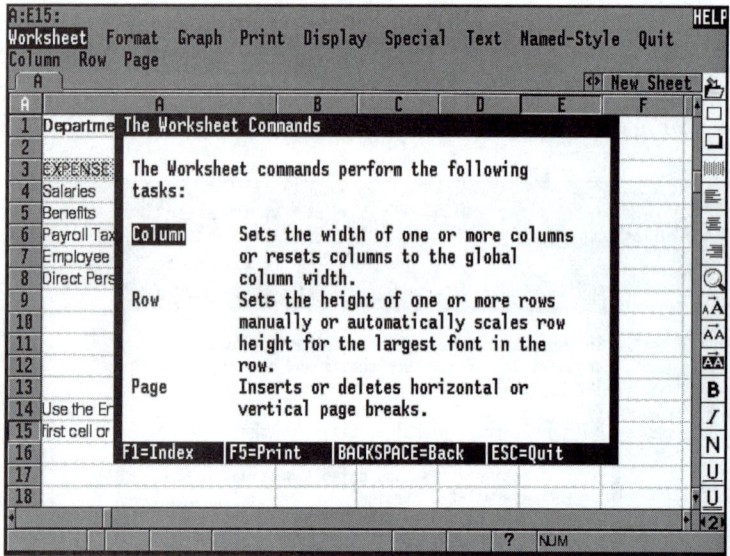

Using QuickStart

Release 4 includes a new feature called QuickStart that shows users of previous versions of 1-2-3 what's new in this release. QuickStart is an interactive online lesson on the new features of Release 4.

> **Note**
>
> You cannot use QuickStart while you are using 1-2-3. QuickStart is not an add-in file, but a separate program file within the \123R4D directory.

To use QuickStart, follow these steps:

1. Exit 1-2-3, if necessary.

2. If 1-2-3 is installed on drive C and drive C isn't the current drive, type **C:** and press Enter. (If you installed 1-2-3 on drive D, E, or another drive, substitute the appropriate drive letter in this step.)

3. Type **CD\123R4D\QSTART** and press Enter.

4. Type **QSTART** and press Enter.

Choosing Commands from Command Menus

You execute 1-2-3 commands through a series of menus. To access the 1-2-3 menu, which appears in the second line of the control panel, press the slash key (/) from READY mode. To access the Wysiwyg menu, press the colon (:) key from READY mode. When the 1-2-3 menu is on-screen, the mode indicator changes to MENU. When Wysiwyg is loaded and the Wysiwyg menu is on-screen, the mode indicator changes to WYSIWYG. To use the mouse to access these menus, just move the mouse pointer into the control panel; one of the menus appears. To toggle between the 1-2-3 and Wysiwyg menus, click the right mouse button.

When you first access a menu, the **W**orksheet command is highlighted. Most commands in the main menu lead to additional menus. You can determine the active menu by looking at the rest of the commands in the menu or by observing the mode indicator. Below the menu options, in the third line of the control panel, you see either an explanation of the highlighted menu option or a list of the options in the next menu.

To choose a menu option, use the direction keys to highlight an option and then press Enter, use the mouse to click the option, or type the first letter of the menu option (for example, to choose **W**orksheet, type **W**).

As you choose commands from the menus, you may make an occasional error. To correct an error, press Esc or click the right mouse button to return to the preceding menu. If you press Esc or click the right mouse button from the 1-2-3 or Wysiwyg main menu, you clear the menu and return to READY mode. If you press Ctrl+Break from any menu, you go directly to READY mode.

Entering and Editing Data

Now that you know how to start 1-2-3 and navigate the worksheet, you're ready to build a worksheet by entering data in cells. After you build your worksheet, you can edit the data within the worksheet at any time. The sections that follow show you how to enter labels and numbers in cells and how to edit that data.

Entering Data in the Worksheet

To enter data in a cell, move the cell pointer to the cell, type the entry, and then press Enter. When you type, the entry appears in the second line of the control panel (the *edit line*). When you press Enter, the entry appears in the current cell in the worksheet and also in the first line of the control panel. If you enter data in a cell that already contains information, the new data replaces the earlier entry.

If you plan to enter data in more than one cell, you don't need to press Enter and then move the cell pointer to the next cell. You can type the entry in the cell and move the cell pointer with one operation. Simply click an arrow SmartIcon or press one of the direction keys—such as the arrow keys, Tab, Shift+Tab, PgUp, or PgDn—after typing the entry.

The two kinds of cell entries are labels and values. A *label* is a text entry. A *value* is a number or a formula. 1-2-3 determines the kind of cell entry from the first character that you type. 1-2-3 treats your entry as a value (a number or a formula) if you begin with one of the following numeric characters:

    0 1 2 3 4 5 6 7 8 9 + – . (@ # $

If you begin by typing any other character, 1-2-3 treats the entry as a label. As soon as you type the first character, the mode indicator changes from READY to VALUE or LABEL.

Entering Labels

Labels can help make the numbers and formulas in worksheets more understandable. You can use labels to create headings for columns or rows of data or to enter explanatory text in a worksheet. The labels in figure 2.14, for example, explain what the figures in each column and row represent.

Because a label is a text entry, labels can contain any string of characters and can be up to 512 characters long. You can use labels for titles, headings, explanations, and notes—all of which help make your worksheet more readable.

When you enter a label, 1-2-3 adds a *label prefix* at the beginning of the cell entry. The label prefix isn't visible in the worksheet but is visible in the control panel (notice the control panel in fig. 2.14). 1-2-3 uses the label prefix to identify the entry as a label and to determine how the label is displayed and printed.

Entering and Editing Data 65

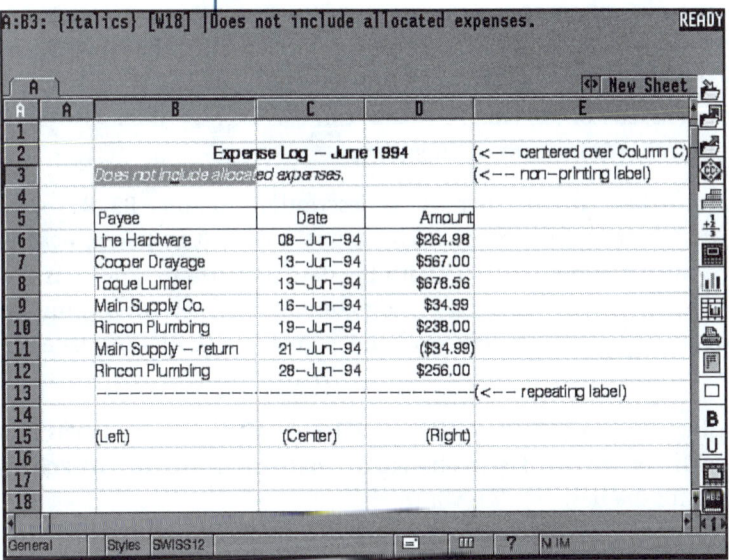

Fig. 2.14
Examples of different types of labels.

> **Note**
>
> 1-2-3 alone doesn't correctly center or right-align text that overflows a cell. If you have Wysiwyg in memory, however, you can correct this problem by preceding a label entry with a double caret (^^) to center the entry, or a double set of quotation marks ("") to justify the entry. The label in cell C2 of figure 2.14 uses the double caret to center the report title over the Date column.

The following table describes the label prefixes.

Prefix	Meaning
'	Left-aligned (the default setting)
"	Right-aligned
^	Centered
\	Repeating
|	Left-aligned and nonprinting, if located in the first column of a print range
^^	Centered in Wysiwyg, if text overflows the current cell
""	Right-aligned in Wysiwyg, if text overflows the current cell

Unless you change the default label prefix with **/W**orksheet **G**lobal **L**abel [**L**eft, **R**ight, **C**enter] or format a range of cells with **/R**ange **L**abel [**L**eft, **R**ight, **C**enter], 1-2-3 uses the apostrophe (') to left-align the label. To assign a different label prefix to a single cell or a few cells, you can type the prefix as the first character of the label. You also can use the Left Align, Center Align, and Right Align SmartIcons to align labels.

A column of descriptions, such as the descriptions in range B5..B14 shown in figure 2.14, usually looks best left-aligned—the default text alignment. As a practice, align column headings with the data they describe, such as the Payee column heading in cell B5. Use right-aligned labels for column headings over columns of numbers or formulas, such as the Amount label in cell D5.

The dashed lines in row 13 are repeating labels. The repeating labels fill the entire width of the cell. If you change the column width, the label changes length to fill the new column width.

The text in cell B3 of figure 2.14 has a nonprinting label prefix (|). The label is left-aligned in the display but doesn't print if the print range starts in the same column as the label. In this example, if the print range starts in cell B2, the text in cell B3 doesn't print. If the print range starts in A2, the text prints. Chapter 8, "Printing Reports," discusses printing and nonprinting labels in greater detail.

Tip
Wysiwyg enables you to create solid lines in a worksheet. A solid line looks more professional than a dashed line (see the line below row 5 in figure 2.14).

To display a label-prefix character as the first character of a label, type a label prefix and then type the character you want to display. If you type \015 in a cell, for example, the cell displays 015015015015015 as a repeating label. To display \015, you first must type a label prefix (in this case, an apostrophe) and then \015 (type '\015).

You must type a label prefix if the first character of the label is a numeric character (such as a street address). If you don't type a label prefix, when you type the numeric character 1-2-3 switches to VALUE mode and expects a valid number or formula (you often encounter this problem when you type a street address). If the label happens to be a valid formula, 1-2-3 evaluates the formula. If the formula is invalid, 1-2-3 refuses to accept the entry and switches to EDIT mode. (EDIT mode is explained in the section "Editing Data in a Worksheet" later in this chapter.) To create the label 5.25/3.5, for example, you must type a label prefix to precede the label. If you don't, 1-2-3 treats the entry as a formula and displays the result of 5.25 divided by 3.5 (1.5).

If a label is longer than the cell width, the label spills out of the cell and across the cells to the right, provided that those cells are empty (see cell B3 in fig. 2.14). The cell display can continue in the next window to the right, provided that all those cells are empty.

1-2-3 includes several commands that can change many label prefixes simultaneously. Chapter 6, "Making Your Worksheets Dazzle," discusses these commands in detail.

Entering Numbers

To enter a valid number, you can type 0 through 9 and certain other characters, as described in the following table. (The Displayed and Stored column of the table shows how the example appears with the default column width of nine characters and the Wysiwyg default font, 12-point Swiss.)

Character	Example	Displayed and Stored	Description
+ (plus)	+123	123	If the number is preceded by a plus sign, 1-2-3 doesn't store the plus sign.
– (minus)	–123	–123	If the number is preceded by a minus sign, 1-2-3 stores the number as a negative number.
( ) parentheses	(123)	–123	If the number is in parentheses, 1-2-3 stores the number as a negative number, displays the number preceded by a minus sign, and drops the parentheses.
$ (dollar sign)	$123	123	If the number is preceded by a dollar sign, 1-2-3 doesn't store the dollar sign.
. (period)	123.24	123.24	You can include one decimal point, which 1-2-3 stores with the number.
, (comma)	123,456,789	123456789	Three digits must follow each comma; 1-2-3 doesn't store the commas.
% (percent)	123%	1.23	If the number is followed by a percent sign, 1-2-3 divides the number by 100 and drops the percent sign.

1-2-3 stores only 18 digits of any number. If you enter a number with more than 17 digits, 1-2-3 rounds the number after the 18th digit. When displaying numbers on-screen, 1-2-3 stores the complete number (to 18 digits) but displays only what fits in the cell. If the cell uses the default **G**eneral format and the integer part of the number fits within the cell width, 1-2-3 rounds the decimal characters that don't fit. If the integer part of the number doesn't fit in the cell, 1-2-3 displays the number by using *scientific* (exponential) *notation*. The following table shows examples of how 1-2-3 stores and displays numbers.

Entry	Stored	Displayed
123E3	123000	123000
123E30	1.23E+30	1.23E+30
123E–4	0.0123	0.0123
1.23E–30	1.23E–30	1.23E–30
12345678998765432198	12345678998765432200	1.2E+19
123456789987654321987	1.23456789987654322E+20	1.2E+20

If the cell uses a format other than **G**eneral or if the cell width is too narrow to display the number in scientific notation, 1-2-3 displays asterisks. Chapter 6, "Making Your Worksheets Dazzle," describes cell formats in detail.

Editing Data in a Worksheet

You sometimes need to change data that you entered in a cell. You may have misspelled a word in a label, for example, or created an incorrect formula. You can change existing entries by using the keyboard and mouse with the 1-2-3 menu or the Wysiwyg menu.

You replace the contents of a cell by typing a new entry. The new entry replaces the entire old entry. You also can edit the contents of the cell. To edit a cell's contents, move the cell pointer to the cell and press F2 (Edit) to switch to EDIT mode. If you try to enter an invalid formula, 1-2-3 automatically switches to EDIT mode.

If the cell entry can fit on one line, 1-2-3 displays the entry on the second line in the control panel. If the entry is too large to display on one line, the entire worksheet area drops down to enlarge the entry area to display a full 512-character entry.

Table 2.2 describes the action of keys in EDIT mode. While 1-2-3 is in EDIT mode, a cursor is in the edit line of the control panel. You use the keys in table 2.2 to move the cursor. When you edit the cell, the contents of the cell (as displayed in the first line of the control panel and in the worksheet) don't change. The cell contents change only when you click the control panel or press Enter to complete the edit. Keep in mind that you cannot use the mouse to move the cursor while you are in EDIT mode.

Table 2.2 Key Actions in EDIT Mode

Key	Action
←	Moves the cursor one character to the left
→	Moves the cursor one character to the right
↑	If the entry fits on one line, completes the edit and moves the cell pointer up one row; if the entry is on more than one line, moves the cursor up one line in the entry
↓	If the entry fits on one line, completes the edit and moves the cell pointer down one row; if the entry is on more than one line, moves the cursor down one line in the entry
Ctrl+← or Shift+Tab	Moves the cursor left five characters
Ctrl+→ or Tab	Moves the cursor right five characters
Home	Moves the cursor to the beginning of the entry
End	Moves the cursor to the end of the entry
Backspace	Deletes the character to the left of the cursor
Del	Deletes the character at the cursor location
Ins	Toggles between Insert and Overtype mode
Esc	Clears the edit line; when pressed again, abandons changes and returns to READY mode
F2 (Edit)	Switches to VALUE or LABEL mode
Enter	Completes the edit

If you press Esc or click the right mouse button while in EDIT mode, you clear the edit area. If you then click the right mouse button or press Esc or Enter in a blank edit area, you don't erase the cell; instead, you cancel the edit, and the cell reverts to the way it was before you pressed F2 (Edit).

Filling Ranges with Data

A *range* is a rectangular group of cells and is defined by the cell addresses of two opposite corners, separated by two periods. A range can be a single cell or a group of cells. (You learn about ranges in more detail in "Working with Ranges" later in this chapter.)

When entering data in a worksheet, you sometimes need to fill a range of cells with a series of numbers. For example, you may have a column set up that numbers the rows in your worksheet. In this case, you would enter values in numerical order, starting at 1 and going up to the number of rows in your worksheet (maximum of 8,192). Ordinarily, filling in the cells with these numbers would be repetitive and time-consuming. But you can use **/D**ata **F**ill to fill a range of cells with a series of numbers (in the form of numbers, formulas, or functions), dates, or times that increase or decrease by a specified amount.

Filling Ranges with Numbers

To fill a range of cells with numbers, follow these steps:

1. Choose **/D**ata **F**ill or click the Data Fill SmartIcon. 1-2-3 prompts you for the range of cells that you want to fill.

2. Specify the range by typing the addresses of the corners of the range or by highlighting the cells in the range in POINT mode using the arrow keys or the mouse.

3. Press Enter.

4. 1-2-3 then asks for the Start number that you want to use to fill the range. If you're counting the number of rows in a report, for example, enter **1** as the start number.

5. Press Enter again. 1-2-3 asks for the *Step* (incremental) *value* to add to the preceding value. If you enter **1** as the step value, 1-2-3 adds 1 to the preceding cell entry in the range and adds the result in the next cell.

6. Finally, 1-2-3 prompts you for the Stop value of the numbers in the range. For the stop value, 1-2-3 defaults to 8,192. The **/D**ata **F**ill command, however, fills only the specified range and doesn't fill cells beyond the end of the range.

7. Press Enter to fill the range with the sequence of numbers that you specified.

1-2-3 fills the range top to bottom, left to right. 1-2-3 fills the first cell with the start value and fills each subsequent cell with the value in the preceding cell plus the increment or the step value. This filling stops when 1-2-3 reaches the stop value or the end of the fill range, whichever comes first.

Note

Use /**D**ata **F**ill to enter a sequence of year numbers for a five-year forecast. Enter the start value of 1994, the step value of 1, and the ending value of 1998. A disadvantage of using the /**D**ata **F**ill command for year numbers is that you cannot center or left-justify the numbers after you create them. These numbers always are right-justified. If you want centered or left-justified year numbers, type the numbers as labels instead of using this command.

You can use /**D**ata **F**ill to quickly create a column of interest rates for use in financial functions. Figure 2.15 shows a worksheet in which the interest rates were entered in Column B with the /**D**ata **F**ill command.

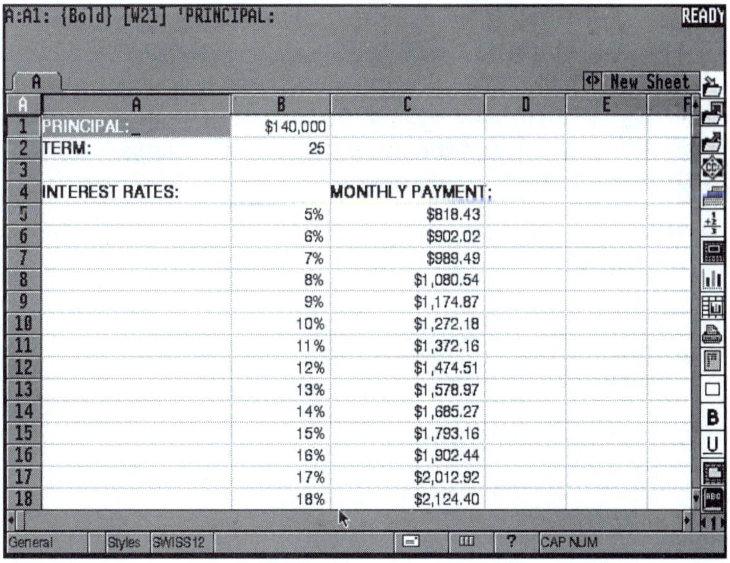

A	A	B	C
1	PRINCIPAL:	$140,000	
2	TERM:	25	
3			
4	INTEREST RATES:		MONTHLY PAYMENT:
5		5%	$818.43
6		6%	$902.02
7		7%	$989.49
8		8%	$1,080.54
9		9%	$1,174.87
10		10%	$1,272.18
11		11%	$1,372.16
12		12%	$1,474.51
13		13%	$1,578.97
14		14%	$1,685.27
15		15%	$1,793.16
16		16%	$1,902.44
17		17%	$2,012.92
18		18%	$2,124.40

Fig. 2.15
Using /**D**ata **F**ill to fill a range of interest rates.

Using Formulas To Fill Ranges

Rather than use regular numbers for the start, step (incremental), and stop values, you can use formulas and functions. If you want to fill a range of cells with incrementing dates, first set the range, and then use a date as the start value (for example, 1/1/95). You also can use a cell formula, such as +E4, for the incremental value. E4 may contain the increment 10, for example, to enable increments of 10. You can use a formula—+E4*100, for example—as the step value. This step value is determined by multiplying the number in cell E4 by 100.

You also can use a cell formula for the stop value. If the stop date is in a cell, for example, you can reference the cell rather than type the stop date. 1-2-3 provides many combinations of commands that make /**D**ata **F**ill a flexible and useful command.

You learn more about entering formulas in 1-2-3 in the section "Entering Basic Formulas" later in this chapter.

Filling Ranges with Dates or Times

The /**D**ata **F**ill command also enables you to fill a worksheet range with a sequence of dates or times without using values, formulas, or functions. You specify the starting and stopping values and the increment between values.

▶ "Date and Time Formats," p. 303

To fill a range with dates or times, first use the /**R**ange **F**ormat **O**ther **A**utomatic command (or one of the date or time formats, if you prefer). Next, choose /**D**ata **F**ill and specify the worksheet range that you want to fill. Then enter the start value. To fill a range with dates, enter a start date in any 1-2-3 date format. If you enter a date without the day or the year, 1-2-3 assumes the first day of the month and the current year. To fill a range with times, enter a start time in a 1-2-3 time format.

Next, you must specify the increment. For dates, enter a value n, followed by a letter to indicate the increment unit:

d to increment by n days

w to increment by n weeks

m to increment by n months

q to increment by n quarters

y to increment by n years

For times, enter a value n, followed by one of the following increment units:

s to increment by n seconds

min to increment by n minutes

h to increment by n hours

Next, enter a stop value. Remember that a date is a 5-digit number, so you must change the stop value (because the default is 8,192). Enter the stop value either as a value (e.g., **99999**, which surely is larger than the start date you enter) or in a valid date or time format. For negative increments, the stop value must be smaller than the start value.

To fill a range with a sequence of half-hour times, for example, choose **/D**ata **F**ill and enter the range **C1..C10**. For the start value, type **1:00**; for the increment, enter **30min**; and for the stop value, enter **6:00**.

To fill a range with a sequence of biweekly dates, choose **/D**ata **F**ill and enter the range **F1..F10**. Type **01-Jan** for the start value, **2w** for the increment, and **07-May** for the stop value.

After you fill a range formatted as **A**utomatic with a date or time, 1-2-3 formats the range with the same format you use to specify the start and stop date or time. Figure 2.16 shows the result of using **/D**ata **F**ill with dates and times.

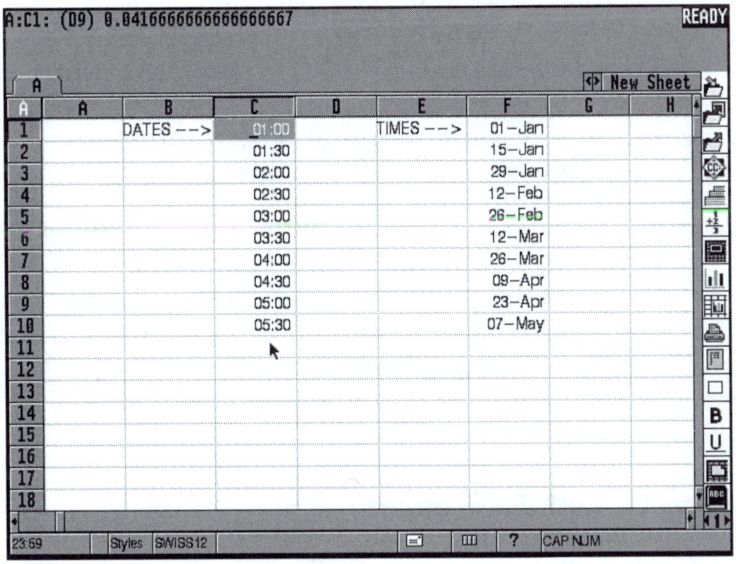

Fig. 2.16
Filling a range with dates and times.

Notice that when you fill a range with times, 1-2-3 may put in the last cell of the fill range a time that differs slightly from the stop value you specified. A slight loss of accuracy occasionally occurs when 1-2-3 converts between the binary numbers it uses internally and the decimal numbers used for times. To prevent this problem, specify a stop value of less than one increment larger than the desired stop value. If the increment is 10 minutes, for example, and you want the last cell in the range to contain 10:30, specify a stop value between 10:30 and 10:40, such as **10:35**.

Entering Basic Formulas

The real power of 1-2-3 comes from its capability to perform calculations with formulas. In fact, the formulas you enter make 1-2-3 an electronic worksheet—not just a computerized method of assembling data for reports. When you enter a formula in a worksheet, 1-2-3 calculates the result of the formula. When you add or change data, you don't need to figure out the effects of the changes; 1-2-3 performs these recalculations. This automatic recalculation capability is a powerful feature of the 1-2-3 electronic worksheet.

1-2-3 recognizes three kinds of formulas: numeric, string, and logical. *Numeric formulas* operate on numbers, other numeric formulas, and numeric functions. *String formulas* operate on labels, other string formulas, and string functions. *Logical formulas* are true/false tests that can test numeric or string values. Like labels, a formula can be up to 512 characters long. This chapter covers each kind of formula. Chapter 3, "Finding Solutions with Formulas and Functions," discusses functions in detail. (*Functions* are built-in formulas that enable you to take advantage of 1-2-3's analytical capabilities.)

When a formula operates on numbers in a cell, such as the formula 8+26, the formula uses 1-2-3 only as a calculator. A more useful formula uses *cell references* (specified cell addresses) in the calculation. The formula in cell F1 of figure 2.17 is 1+B1+C1+D1+E1. The control panel shows the formula, and the worksheet shows the result of the calculation (184 in this example). If you change any numbers in the cells referenced by the formula, the result in cell F1 changes.

Tip
You can use the mouse to point to a cell without moving the cell pointer. Move the mouse pointer to the desired cell and double-click the cell. This action enters that cell address in the formula.

Pointing to Cell References

You can type each address in the formula 1+B1+C1+D1+E1, but a faster way to enter a cell reference exists. When 1-2-3 expects a cell address, you can use the mouse, the direction keys, or the arrow SmartIcons to move the cell pointer and *point* to the cell. After you start entering a formula, if you move the cell pointer, 1-2-3 changes to POINT mode and the current address appears in the formula in the control panel.

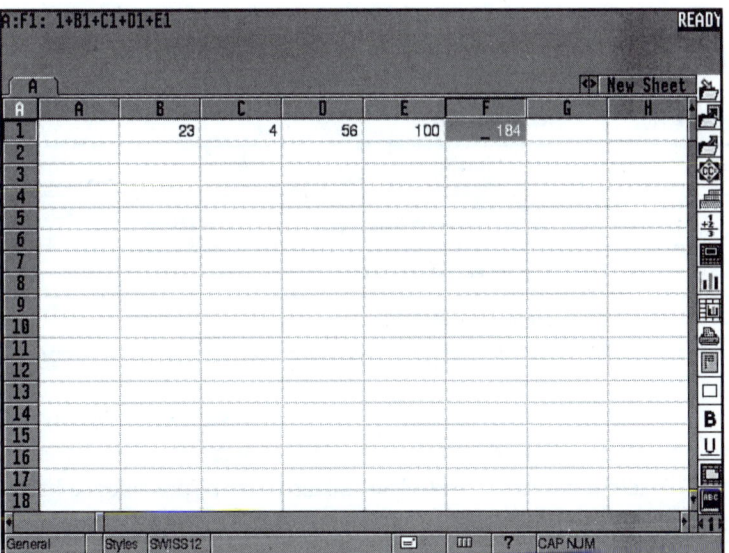

Fig. 2.17
1-2-3 performs a calculation based on the formula in cell F1.

Move the cell pointer to the first cell you want to reference in the formula. If this location marks the end of the formula, press Enter. If the formula acts on other cells, type the next operator and specify the next cell. Continue this process until you finish specifying cells and operators; then press Enter.

You easily can type an incorrect address in a formula. Pointing to cells is faster and more accurate than typing, so experienced 1-2-3 users rarely type addresses. The only situation in which typing an address is easier than pointing to the cell is when the cell reference is far from the current cell and you happen to remember the cell address. If you enter a formula in cell Z238, for example, and you want to refer to cell H23, typing **+H23** may be faster than pointing to cell H23.

Using Operators in Numeric Formulas

A *formula* is an instruction to 1-2-3 to perform a calculation. You use *operators* to specify the calculations that 1-2-3 performs. The numeric operators are addition, subtraction, multiplication, division, and *exponentiation* (raising a number to a power). The formula in figure 2.17 uses the plus sign, which is the *addition operator*. The simplest numeric formula uses just the plus sign and a cell reference to repeat the value in another cell.

When evaluating a formula, 1-2-3 calculates terms within the formula in a specified sequence or in the *order of precedence*. The order of precedence represents the order in which 1-2-3 performs operations in a formula as it reads

Tip
You can mix-and-match cell reference methods, typing some addresses and pointing to others.

the formula from left to right. The following table shows the arithmetic operators, in order of precedence.

Operator	Meaning
^	Exponentiation
+, –	Identification of value as positive or negative
*, /	Multiplication, division
+, –	Addition, subtraction

If a formula uses all these operators, 1-2-3 calculates exponentiation operations first and then works down the list. If two operators are equal in precedence, 1-2-3 calculates from left to right. This order of precedence has a critical effect on the result of many formulas. You can override the order by using parentheses; 1-2-3 always evaluates operations in a set of parentheses first.

The examples in the following table show how 1-2-3 uses the order of precedence to evaluate complex formulas.

Formula	Evaluation	Result
5+3*2	5+(3*2)	11
(5+3)*2	(5+3)*2	16
–3^2*2	–(3^2)*2	–18
–3^(2*2)	–(3^(2*2))	–81
5+4*8/4–3	5+((4*8)/4)–3	10
5+4*8/(4–3)	5+((4*8)/(4–3))	37
(5+4)*8/(4–3)	((5+4)*8)/(4–3)	72
(5+4)*8/4–3	(((5+4)*8)/4)–3	15
5+3*4^2/6–2*3^4	5+(3*((4^2)/6))–(2*(3^4))	–149

Using Operators in String Formulas

The rules for using string formulas differ from the rules for using numeric formulas. A *string* is either a label or a string formula. 1-2-3 uses only two string-formula operators: the plus sign (+) to repeat another string, and the ampersand (&) to join (*concatenate*) two or more strings.

The simplest string formula uses only the plus sign and a cell reference to repeat the string in another cell. In figure 2.18, the formula in cell A7 is +A3. Although similar to a numeric formula, the formula in cell A7 is a string formula because this formula refers to a cell with a string.

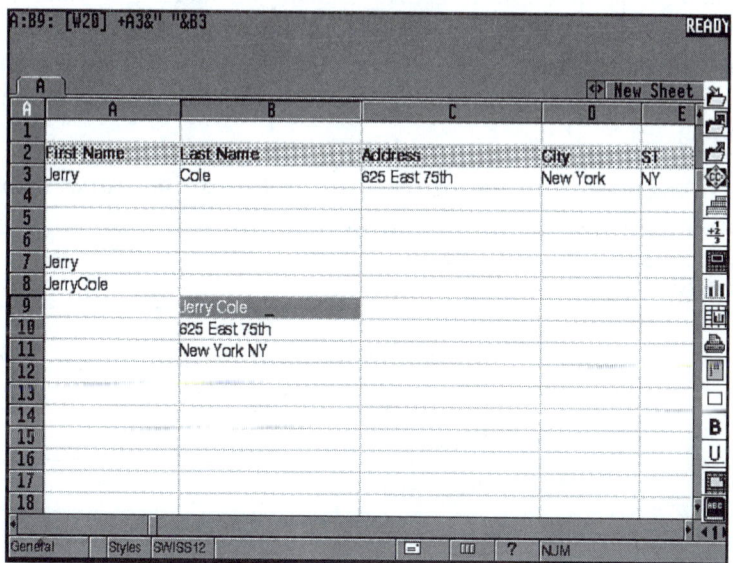

Fig. 2.18
Using string formulas to repeat or concatenate strings.

The string-concatenation operator is the ampersand (&). The formula in cell A8 of figure 2.18 is +A3&B3. The first operator in a string formula must be a plus sign; all other operators in the formula must be ampersands. If you don't use the ampersand and you use any numeric operators, 1-2-3 treats the formula as a numeric formula; if you use any numeric operators after the plus sign at the beginning, 1-2-3 considers the formula to be invalid. The formulas +A3&B3+C3 and +A3+B3&C3, for example, are invalid. When you enter an invalid formula, 1-2-3 switches to EDIT mode.

A cell that contains a label has a numeric value of zero. If you enter the formula **+A3+B3** in the worksheet shown in figure 2.18, 1-2-3 treats the formula as a numeric formula and evaluates to 0.

In figure 2.18, the names run together in cell A8. You can place a space between the first and last names, however, by adding another string formula. To insert a space into a string formula, enclose the inserted space in quotation marks (" "). The formula in cell B9 is +A3&" "&B3. The formula in cell B11 is +D3&" "&E3.

You can write more complex string formulas with string functions, as detailed in Chapter 3, "Finding Solutions with Formulas and Functions."

Using Operators in Logical Formulas

Logical formulas are true/false tests that compare two values and evaluate to 1 if the test is true and 0 if the test is false. Logical formulas are used mainly in database criteria ranges; Chapters 3, "Finding Solutions with Formulas and Functions," and Chapter 21, "Finding Specific Data," discuss these formulas in greater detail.

The following table shows the logical operators. Figure 2.19, following the table, shows examples of logical formulas.

Operator	Meaning
=	Equal to
>	Greater than
<	Less than
>=	Greater than or equal to
<=	Less than or equal to
<>	Not equal
#NOT#	Reverses the results of a test (changes the result from true to false or from false to true)
#OR#	Logical OR to join two tests; the result is true if *either* test is true
#AND#	Logical AND to join two tests; the result is true if *both* tests are true

Correcting Errors in Formulas

If you inadvertently enter a formula that 1-2-3 cannot evaluate, the program beeps, switches to EDIT mode, and moves the cursor to the first place in the formula where 1-2-3 encountered an error. You cannot enter an invalid formula in a worksheet. For more information about changing a cell in EDIT mode, refer to "Editing Data in a Worksheet" earlier in this chapter.

Common errors that make a formula invalid are missing or extra parentheses and mixed numeric and string operators. Other common errors are misspelled function names and incorrect arguments in functions (discussed in Chapter 3, "Finding Solutions with Formulas and Functions"). The following table shows some common errors.

Entering Basic Formulas 79

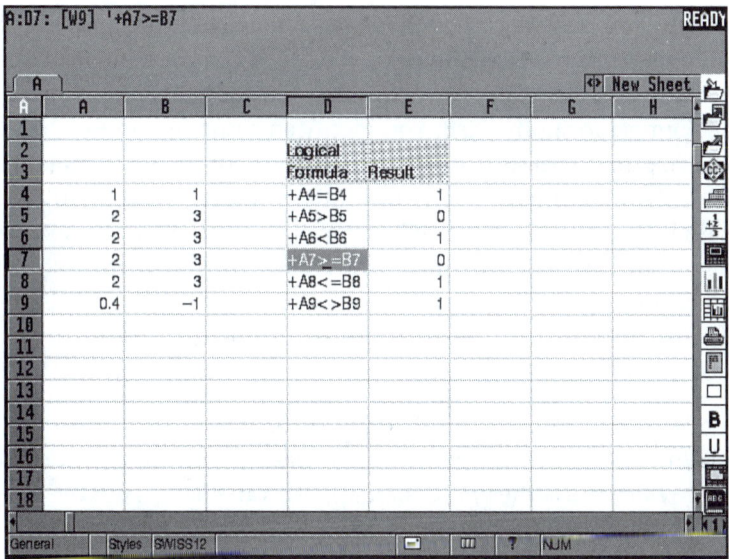

Fig. 2.19
Logical formulas evaluate to 1 if true or 0 if false.

Formula	Error
+A1+A2&A3	Mixed numeric and string operators
+A1/(A2–A3	Missing right parenthesis
@SIM(A1..A3)	Misspelled @SUM function

▶ "Starting and Using the Auditor," p. 529

When 1-2-3 encounters an error in your work, you may not know what's wrong or how to fix the formula. You may want to use the Help feature to check the format of a function. Before you can do anything else, however, you must clear the error. If you press Esc or the right mouse button, you erase the entire entry. If you press Esc or right-click again, you return to READY mode, but you lose the entire formula.

To fix the formula, follow the procedures in the section "Editing Data in a Worksheet" earlier in this chapter. You also may want to use the Help utility to check the format of a function, or you can use the Auditor add-in to help correct errors in your formulas.

Tip
If you don't know how to correct the formula, convert it to a label by typing an apostrophe as the prefix. When you find the error, make the correction and change the label back to a formula by removing the prefix.

Addressing Cells

Usually, when you copy a formula from one cell to another cell, the cell references adjust. If you use the **/C**opy command to copy the formula +B1+C1+D1+E1 from cell F1 to cell F2, the cell references change to +B2+C2+D2+E2. This automatic change of cell references is *relative addressing*.

Occasionally, you may want the cell reference to remain the same, even if the formula moves to another cell. In these cases, you can use absolute addresses in your formula. An *absolute address* in a formula doesn't change when you copy the formula to another cell. You specify an absolute address when you type a dollar sign ($) before the column and row address in a formula. The address +$A$1, for example, is absolute. If this address is in cell C10 and you copy the address to cell E19, the cell reference remains +$A$1. To specify an absolute cell address in POINT mode, press the F4 (Abs) key. You also can make a reference to a cell in a specific worksheet absolute. The reference +$A:$A$1 refers to cell A1 in worksheet A, no matter to what cell or worksheet you copy the address.

Besides relative and absolute cell addresses, 1-2-3 uses *mixed addresses*. In a mixed address, part of the address is relative and part is absolute. The reference +A$1 is a mixed address; the column letter can change, but the row number cannot change.

Whether a cell reference is relative, absolute, or mixed doesn't affect how 1-2-3 calculates the formula. This kind of addressing matters only when you copy the formula to another cell. Copying and cell addressing are covered in detail in the section "Copying the Contents of Cells" later in this chapter.

Troubleshooting

I entered a formula in a cell, and the formula is displayed in the cell instead of the calculated results.

If a formula begins with the characters of the cell, such as B1, 1-2-3 assumes that you are entering a label and doesn't perform a calculation. To enter a cell reference in a formula, you must type a plus sign before the cell reference (+B1) so that 1-2-3 identifies the entry as a formula and not a label.

Asterisks (*****) appear in a cell where a value should be.

If a cell is too narrow to display a number in its entirety, 1-2-3 displays asterisks to fill the cell. You must change the column width to accommodate the value entry. Choose the **/W**orksheet **C**olumn **S**et-Width command or double-click the column-letter to adjust the column width to the largest entry in the column.

1-2-3 converted a date to a number.

1-2-3 converts dates to numbers when they are entered in cells formatted in a numeric format (**G**eneral, **C**urrency, and so on). Change the format of the cell to a date format by choosing **/R**ange **F**ormat **D**ate.

> *Nothing happens when I use the Alt+F4 (Undo) command or click the Undo SmartIcon.*
>
> For the Undo command to undo your changes, you must choose the command immediately following the action you performed.
>
> *The formulas in my worksheet result in errors when I delete a row or column.*
>
> Deleting cells, rows, or columns that contain information used by formulas can cause errors. Because the cell and its contents no longer exist, formulas that used that cell cannot find a cell to reference. These cells produce ERR.
>
> *1-2-3 adds decimals to every value I enter in a cell.*
>
> The cell is formatted for a decimal value. To change the format of a cell, choose **/R**ange **F**ormat and then choose another format.

Working with Ranges

Many 1-2-3 commands act on one or more ranges of cells and prompt you to select the range(s) on which the command should be performed. A range can be a single cell (for example, A:G3..A:G3 in fig. 2.20) or more than one cell (B:B5..B:E5, also in fig. 2.20).

Selecting Ranges

To select a range made up of a single cell, simply move to that cell. (Earlier in this chapter, in "Moving Around the Worksheet," you learned how to move from cell to cell by using the mouse, keyboard keys, and scroll bar.)

To select a range that consists of more than one cell, you must define the cell addresses of two opposite corners in the range and separate those addresses with two periods. A range can be part of a row (B:B5..B:E5), part of a column (A:B2..A:B5), or a rectangle that spans multiple rows and columns (C:A1..C:G5), all as shown in figure 2.20. A range also can span multiple worksheets (A:J1..B:J5). A range can span an entire worksheet or file, but a range cannot span multiple files. In 1-2-3, you can define only one range at a time.

You can respond to a prompt for a range in several ways, each of which is convenient in certain circumstances. To specify a range, you can use any of the following methods:

82 Chapter 2—What Every 1-2-3 User Should Know

Fig. 2.20
Examples of cell ranges in 1-2-3 worksheets.

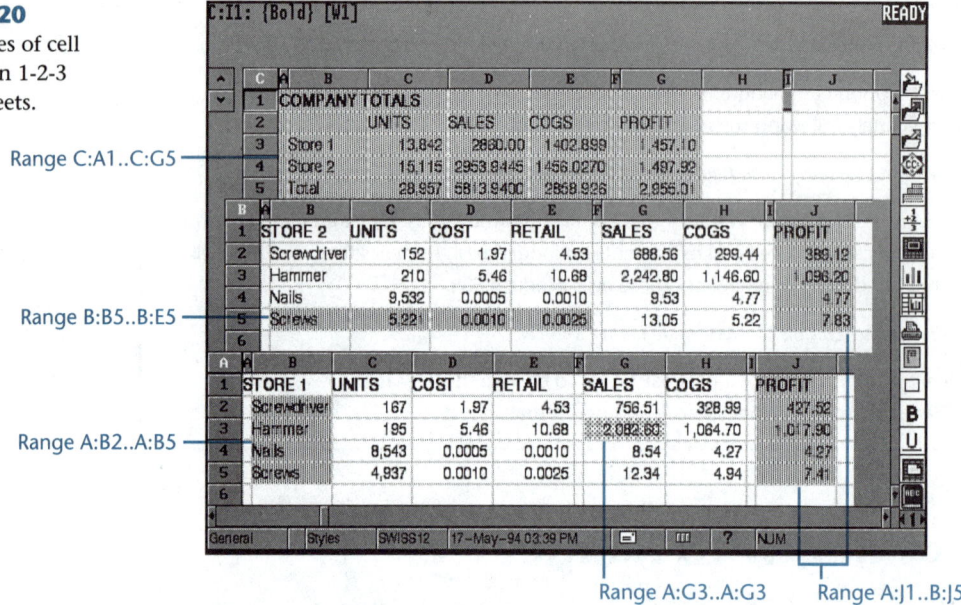

Range C:A1..C:G5
Range B:B5..B:E5
Range A:B2..A:B5
Range A:G3..A:G3
Range A:J1..B:J5

> **Note**
>
> Experienced 1-2-3 users rarely type cell addresses. Instead, these users employ one of the following alternative methods: specifying a range in POINT mode, preselecting a range with the F4 key or the mouse, or typing or selecting an existing range name.

■ Type the addresses of the corners of the range.

Tip
1-2-3 always stores a range with two periods to separate the addresses, but you need to type only one period.

You can specify a range by first typing the address of the top left corner, then one or two periods, and finally the address of the bottom right corner. If the range is only one cell, you can type only the cell address (A5 rather than A5..A5). To specify a range in the current worksheet, you can leave off the worksheet letter. If you want to specify a range in another worksheet or in multiple worksheets, however, you need to include the worksheet letter for each corner.

To specify the range A1..G5 in worksheet C shown in figure 2.20, you would type A1..G5 or A1.G5 or G5..A1 or G5.A1. You also could use the other two opposite corners: A5..G1 or G1..A5. In all cases, 1-2-3 stores the range as A1..G5.

- Highlight the cells in the range in POINT mode by using the arrow keys or the mouse. (This is the most common technique.)

Usually, pointing and highlighting is faster and easier than typing the range addresses, and because you can see the range as you specify it, you make fewer errors pointing than typing (see fig. 2.21).

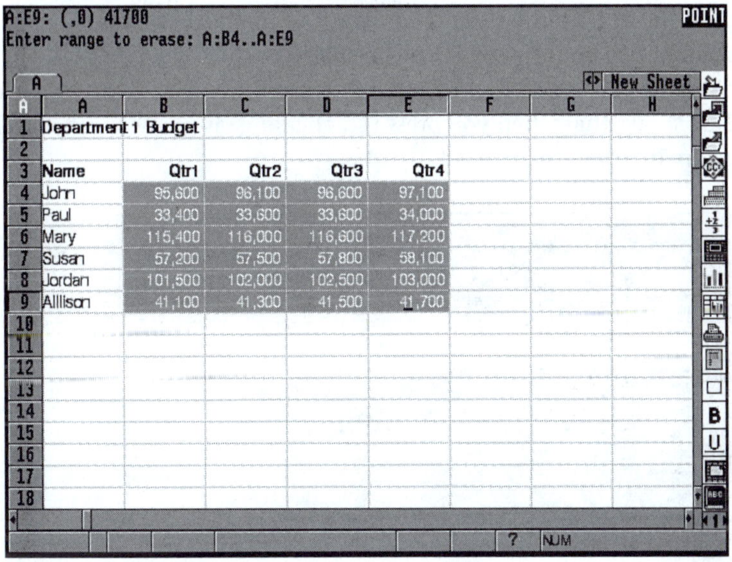

Fig. 2.21
Highlighting a range by moving the cell pointer.

When you issue a command, such as **/R**ange **E**rase, 1-2-3 prompts you for the range on which you want it to act. The default range in the control panel is the current location of the cell pointer; the single cell appears as a one-cell range. When the prompt shows a single cell as a one-cell range, the cell is referred to as *anchored*. Most 1-2-3 commands use a one-cell range as the default range. When the cell is anchored, as you *drag* (move the mouse while holding the left mouse button) or use the direction keys to move the cell pointer from the anchored cell, the range becomes highlighted. Figure 2.21 shows the screen after you drag the cell pointer from A:B4 to A:E9 and release the left mouse button.

Use the End key when you highlight ranges from the keyboard. The End key moves to the border of a range of occupied and unoccupied cells. To highlight the range from A:B4..A:E9 in figure 2.21, you can press End down arrow and End right arrow. Without the End key, you have to press the right-arrow key three times and the down-arrow key five times. In this example, A:E9 also is the last cell in the worksheet.

Starting from the anchored position at A:B4..A:B4, you can press End and then Home to move to the last cell in the worksheet and highlight the range A:B4..A:E9.

You can click the right mouse button, press Esc, or press Backspace to clear an anchored or incorrectly highlighted range. The highlight collapses to the anchored cell only, and the anchor is removed. If you press Esc or click the right mouse button, the range becomes unanchored and the cell pointer remains at the top left corner of the old range. Figure 2.22 shows an existing print range (A:A3..A:E9). Figure 2.23 shows that when you press Esc, the range is unanchored and the cell pointer returns to A:A3.

Fig. 2.22
Choosing the /**P**rint **P**rinter **R**ange command shows that the range was defined as A:A3..A:E9.

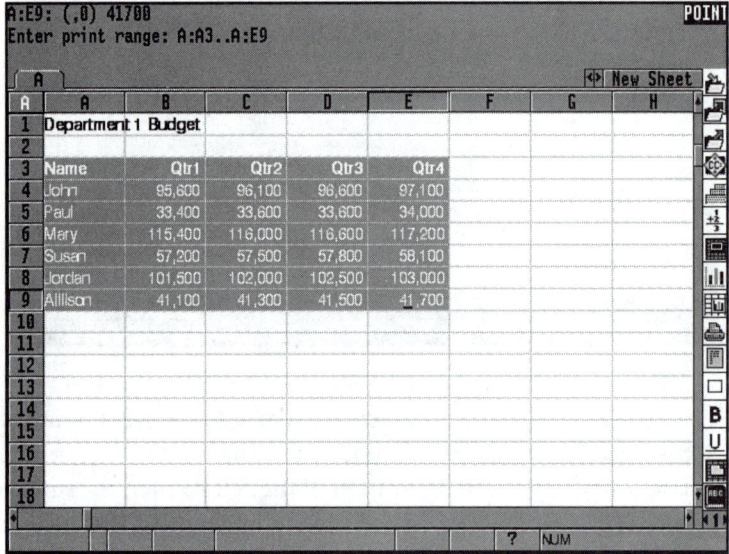

If a range is highlighted at a prompt and you press Backspace, however, the cell pointer returns to the position it occupied before you issued the /**P**rint **P**rinter **R**ange command, rather than to the top left corner of the old highlighted range (see fig. 2.24).

> **Note**
>
> When you use other commands, however—including /**D**ata, /**G**raph, /**P**rint, and /**R**ange **S**earch from the 1-2-3 menu and **:G**raph and **:P**rint from the Wysiwyg menu—1-2-3 doesn't start the range at the current location of the cell pointer. Therefore, at the Enter range prompt, the control panel shows the current cell address as a single address, and the cell pointer isn't anchored.

Working with Ranges

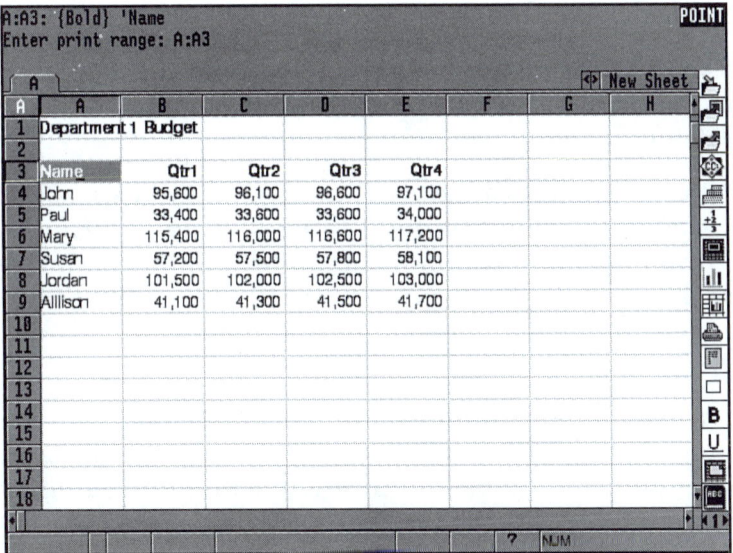

Fig. 2.23
When you press Esc in figure 2.22, the range shrinks to A:A3.

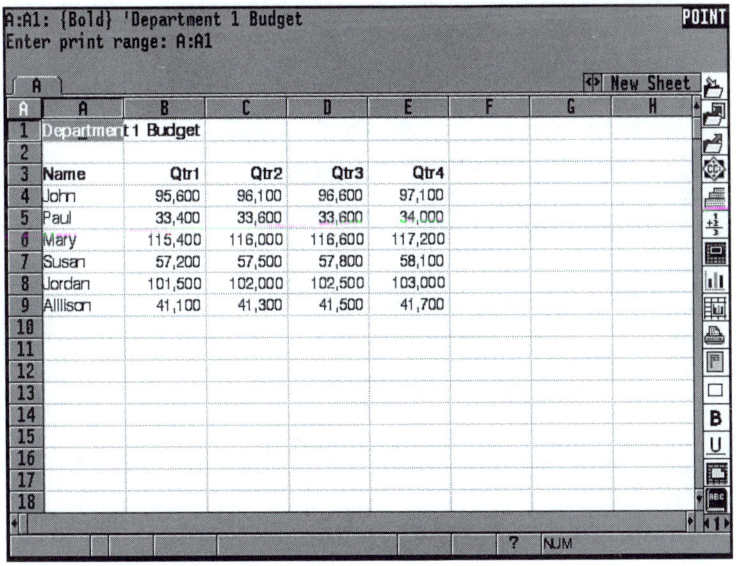

Fig. 2.24
When you press Backspace in figure 2.23, the range shrinks to A:A1.

Whether you press Esc or Backspace, you then can move the cell pointer to the corner of the new range. Type a period (.) to anchor the range; then move to the opposite corner to select the new range.

86   Chapter 2—What Every 1-2-3 User Should Know

- Preselect the range with the F4 key or by clicking the mouse.

If you have enabled Wysiwyg, you can select the range to be affected by the command before you issue it. This technique is known as *preselecting a range*.

Preselecting a range enables you to issue several Wysiwyg formatting commands that affect the range. The range that you preselect remains selected. To change the font of some numbers and then outline the cells, for example, you can preselect the range and perform both commands.

You can preselect a range with the keyboard by moving the cell pointer to the beginning of the range and pressing F4. The mode indicator changes from READY to POINT, and an anchored range address appears in the control panel. Using the arrow keys, select the range. Figure 2.25 shows the screen when you are preselecting the range A:A3..A:E9. After selecting the desired range, press Enter to accept the range setting.

Fig. 2.25
Preselecting the range A:A3..A:E9.

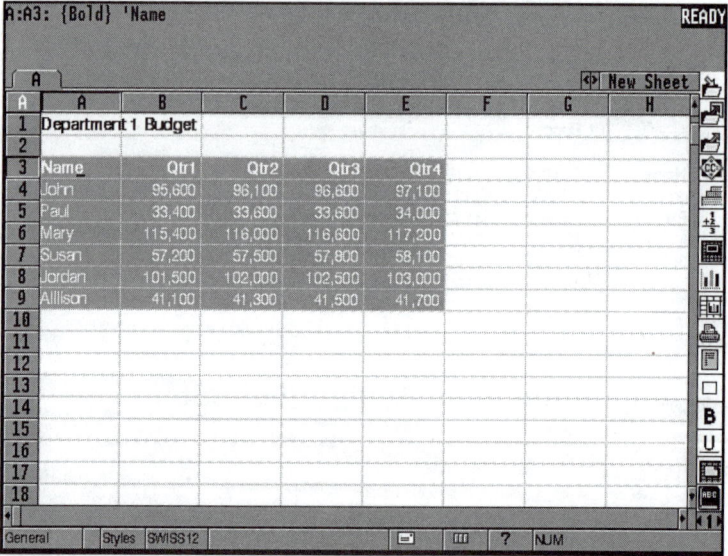

You also can use the mouse to preselect a range by moving the cell pointer to the corner cell of the range and then holding down the left mouse button. 1-2-3 enters POINT mode. Drag the cell pointer to highlight the range and then release the mouse button. You don't need to press Enter; releasing the mouse button completes the selection. After you select the range, you can begin issuing commands that affect the preselected range.

- If you assigned a range name, type the name, or press F3 (Name) and point to the name. Naming ranges is explained in the next section.

Specifying a Range with Range Names

The final method of specifying a range at the prompt involves giving the range a name. Range names, which should describe the file, can include up to 15 characters and can be used in formulas and commands. When 1-2-3 expects a cell or range address, you can specify a range name. Two ways to specify a range name are available: you can type the range name, or you can press F3 (Name) and point to the range name.

Using range names has several advantages. Range names are easier to remember than addresses. Using a range name is at times faster than pointing to a range in another part of the worksheet. Range names also make formulas easier to understand. If you see the range name QTR1 in a formula, for example, you may remember that the entry represents "Quarter 1" (see fig. 2.26).

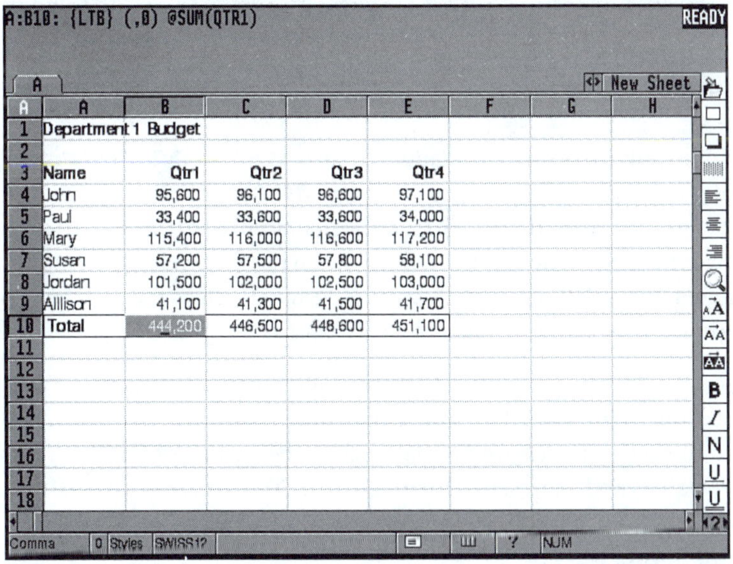

Fig. 2.26
Using a range name in a formula.

If more than one file exists in memory, 1-2-3 displays a list of range names in the current file and also a list of the other files in memory. To select a range name in another file, first select the file name to see the display of range names in that file. Then select the range name in that file.

Chapter 2—What Every 1-2-3 User Should Know

When you press F3 (Name), the third line of the control panel lists the first four range names in alphabetical order. Use the mouse or arrow keys to point to the correct range name; then either click the left mouse button or press Enter. If you have many range names, press F3 (Name) again; 1-2-3 displays a full screen of range names (see fig. 2.27).

Fig. 2.27
A full-screen listing of range names, with other open files listed in angle brackets.

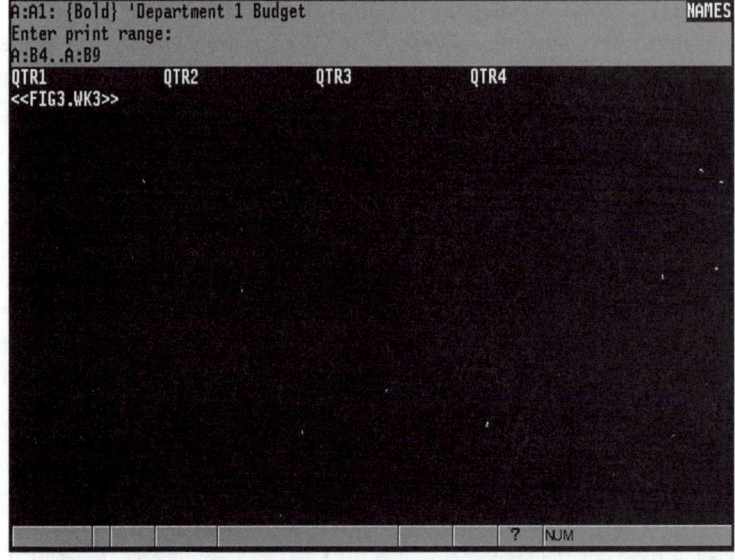

Tip
Range names make great bookmarks in your worksheet. Use the F5 (GoTo) key and type the range name, or press F5 (GoTo) and F3 (Name) twice to see a full-screen list of range names.

▶ "Using the One-Key Sort," p. 633

If a prompt calls for a single cell address, such as with **/D**ata **S**ort **P**rimary-Key or GoTo (F5), 1-2-3 can specify a range whether you type an English name or a cell address. If you type a range name that applies to a multiple-cell range, 1-2-3 uses the top left corner of the range. If you type a nonexistent range name, 1-2-3 displays an error message. To clear the error and try again, press Esc or Enter, or click the right mouse button.

Because a single cell is considered to be a valid range, you can name a single cell as a range. When 1-2-3 expects a cell address, you can type the address, point to the cell, type the single-cell range name, or press F3 (Name) for a list of range names and then select the name from the list.

Creating Range Names

To create range names, use the **/R**ange **N**ame **C**reate or **/R**ange **N**ame **L**abels command to assign names to individual cells or ranges. To create range names with the **/R**ange **N**ame **C**reate command, follow these steps:

1. Move to the top left corner of the range you want to name.
2. Choose **/R**ange **N**ame **C**reate.
3. Type the name at the `Enter name to create` prompt and then, using the left mouse button, click anywhere in the control panel or press Enter. 1-2-3 displays the `Enter range` prompt.
4. If you type a new range name, 1-2-3 shows the current cell as an anchored range. Highlight the range or type the address or addresses of the cell or range; then click the mouse or press Enter.

    If you type an existing range name, 1-2-3 highlights the existing range. Use the arrow keys to extend or contract the range.

    To specify a new range, press Backspace to cancel the existing range; the cell pointer returns to the cell that it occupied before you issued the command. (Clicking the right mouse button or pressing Esc cancels the range but leaves the cell pointer in the top left corner of the range, except for single-cell ranges.) Then specify the new range.
5. To complete the operation, click the mouse or press Enter.

Range names can include up to 15 characters, and the names don't need to be case-sensitive. Although you can type or refer to the name in any combination of uppercase and lowercase letters, 1-2-3 stores all range names as uppercase letters.

Following are a few rules and precautions for naming ranges:

- Don't use spaces or special characters, except for the underscore character (_), in range names. If you use special characters, you may confuse 1-2-3 when you use the name in formulas.

- Don't start the name with a number. You can use numbers in the rest of the range name, but you cannot use a range name that starts with a number as part of a formula.

- Don't use range names that also are cell addresses (such as P2), key names (such as GoTo), function names (such as @SUM), or advanced macro command keyword names (such as BRANCH). If you use a cell address as a range name and then type the range name, 1-2-3 uses the cell address.

90 Chapter 2—What Every 1-2-3 User Should Know

You also can create range names with the **/R**ange **N**ame **L**abels command. Use this command to assign range names to many individual cells at one time.

> **Note**
>
> You can use **/R**ange **N**ame **L**abels to assign range names to single-cell ranges only.

When using **/R**ange **N**ame **L**abels, use labels already typed in the worksheet as range names for adjacent cells. In figure 2.28, for example, you can use the labels in cells B4..B16 to name the cells with ad-budget data (C4..C16). Because you want to name the cells to the right of the labels, use **/R**ange **N**ame **L**abels **R**ight. Specify a range of B4..B16, and click the left mouse button or press Enter. Now cell C4 has the range name JAN, cell C5 has the range name FEB, and so on.

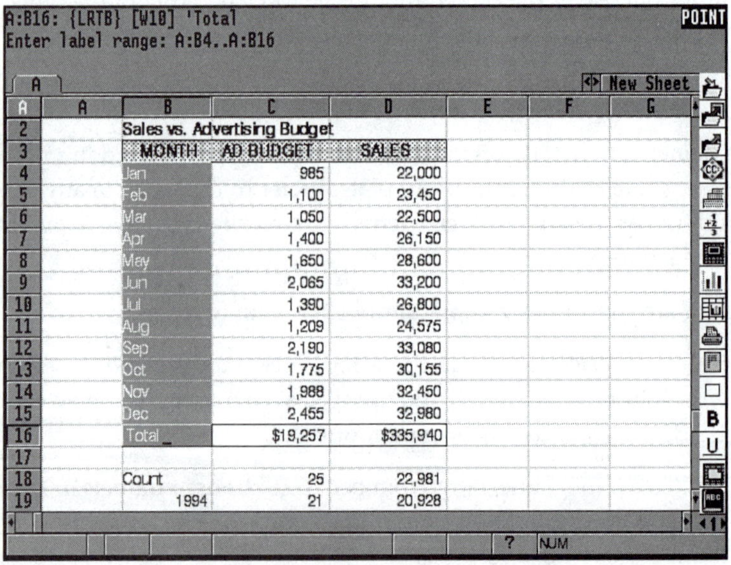

Fig. 2.28
Use **/R**ange **N**ame **L**abels **R**ight to name all cells to the right of the labels.

	B	C	D
2	Sales vs. Advertising Budget		
3	MONTH	AD BUDGET	SALES
4	Jan	985	22,000
5	Feb	1,100	23,450
6	Mar	1,050	22,500
7	Apr	1,400	26,150
8	May	1,650	28,600
9	Jun	2,065	33,200
10	Jul	1,390	26,800
11	Aug	1,209	24,575
12	Sep	2,190	33,080
13	Oct	1,775	30,155
14	Nov	1,988	32,450
15	Dec	2,455	32,980
16	Total	$19,257	$335,940
17			
18	Count	25	22,981
19	1994	21	20,928

The other options with **/R**ange **N**ame **L**abels are **L**eft, **D**own, and **U**p. These options assign range names only to labels in the range you specify. If you specify the range B2..B19 in figure 2.28, 1-2-3 ignores the blank cell in B17 and the number in B19. The first 15 characters in the label in B2 become the range name for C2: `Sales vs. Adver`. If you include blank cells, numbers, or formulas in a **/R**ange **N**ame **L**abels range, no harm occurs. Don't include other labels, however, or you end up with unwanted range names.

Adding Notes About Ranges

After you create a range name, you can append a note with **/R**ange **N**ame **N**otation **C**reate. First, select the range name to be annotated; then type a note of up to 512 characters. Use this feature to explain the meaning of the range or how the range is used. You also can use this command to change an existing note. You can list these notes with **/R**ange **N**ame **N**otation **T**able.

Listing All Range Names and Notes

1-2-3 includes two commands that can create a table of named ranges in your worksheet. **/R**ange **N**ame **T**able creates a list of range names and addresses. **/R**ange **N**ame **N**ote **T**able creates a list of range names, addresses, and notes. Using these commands is the only way to see your range-name notes (see fig. 2.29). This table is part of the documentation for the worksheet file and can be placed in a worksheet separate from the actual data.

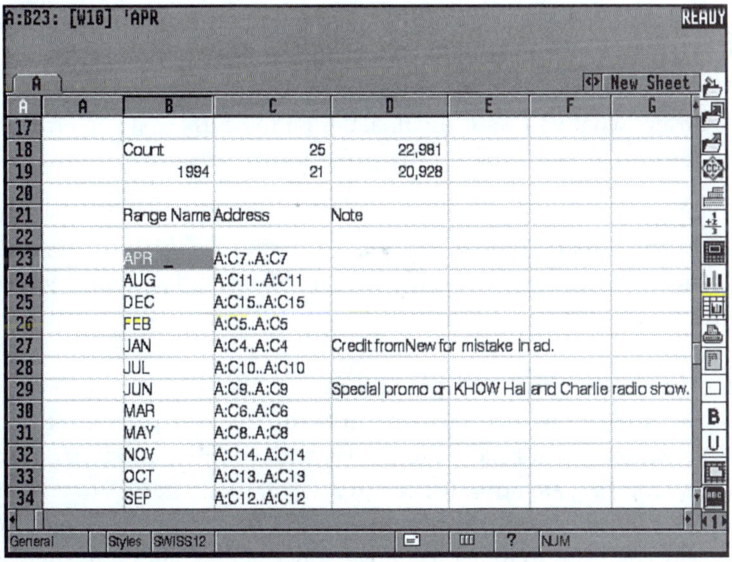

Fig. 2.29
A table of range names, addresses, and notes, created with **/R**ange **N**ame **N**ote **T**able.

To delete an unwanted range name, use **/R**ange **N**ame **D**elete. You also can use **/R**ange **N**ame **R**eset, but this command immediately deletes all the range names in the file.

Tip
If you have Undo enabled, and you accidentally choose **/R**ange **N**ame **R**eset, you can get your range names back by using Alt+F4 (Undo) or clicking the Undo SmartIcon.

> **Caution**
> The command **/R**ange **N**ame **R**eset immediately deletes all the range names in a file.

Copying and Moving Data

▶ "Extracting and Combining Data," p. 476

▶ "Copying and Moving Formats," p. 336

When you build worksheets, you often enter data and formulas in one part of the worksheet and later want to move the information elsewhere. Using the /Move command, you can move a cell or range to another part of the same worksheet or to a different worksheet in the same file. You cannot, however, move a range from one file to another file.

In a typical file, most formulas are duplicated many times. Fortunately, if you need the same number, label, or formula in several places in a file, you can enter the information once and then copy the repeating data many times.

In the following sections, you learn how to make your work in 1-2-3 more efficient by moving and copying data within worksheets in the same file.

Moving the Contents of Cells

Use /Move to move other data out of the way so that you can add to a list, a report, or a database. You also use /Move to rearrange a report so that it will print in the exact format you want. When you start to lay out a report, you may be unsure what you want the final design to be. By trial and error, by moving the data around, you get the report format you want.

When you move a range, you also move the format and protection status of these cells, but you don't move the column width. The original cells still exist after you move the contents, but the cells are blank, and all protection and formatting is removed.

Moving the Contents of a Single Cell

Figure 2.30 shows 12 numbers in column D and the average of these numbers in C18. These cells are formatted to display with commas and zero decimal places. The numbers are unprotected. To move the sum in C18 to D18, move the cell pointer to C18 and start the /Move command. Move FROM prompts you for cells you want to move. To move only cell C18, click anywhere in the control panel or press Enter. The next prompt, Move TO, asks where to move the cells. Move the cell pointer to D18, and click anywhere in the control panel, double-click the mouse, or press Enter. Figure 2.31 shows the result: the formula that was in C18 now is in D18.

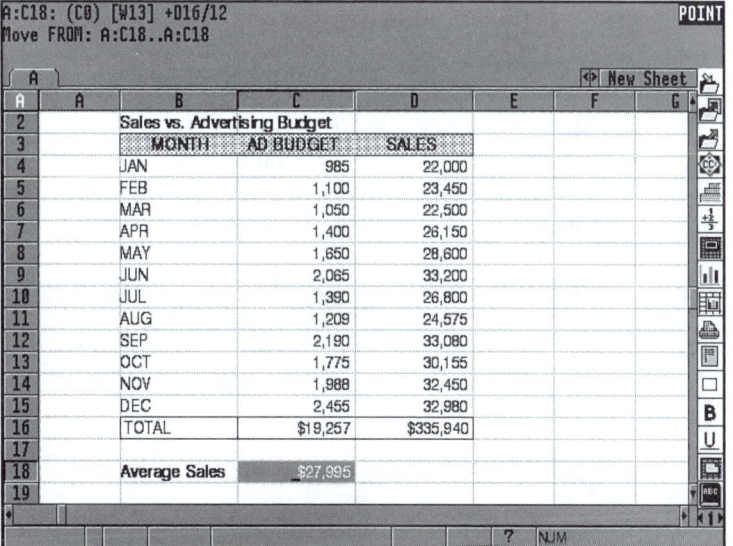

Fig. 2.30
Specifying the cell to be moved.

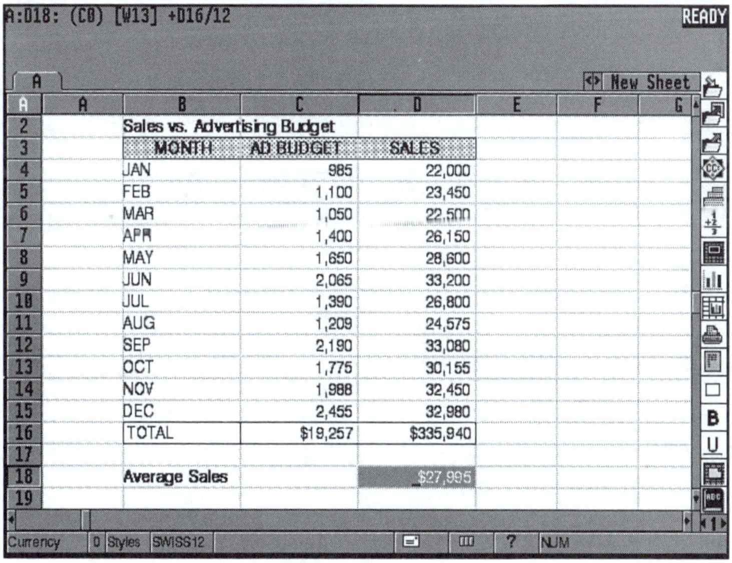

Fig. 2.31
Moving the contents of cell C18 in figure 2.30 to cell D18.

Moving the Contents of a Range

To move a range, move the cell pointer to the top left corner of the range and choose **/M**ove. At the Move FROM prompt, highlight the range of cells to be moved, as shown in figure 2.32. This prompt starts with the address of the cell pointer as an anchored range. When you move the cell pointer,

94   Chapter 2—What Every 1-2-3 User Should Know

you highlight the range from the original location of the cell pointer to the corner where you place the cell pointer. Click the mouse or press Enter to lock in this source range. At the Move TO prompt, move the cell pointer to the top- left corner of the new location (the destination or target range), and click the mouse or press Enter. Like all commands that prompt for ranges, the /**M**ove command can accept typed addresses, highlighted ranges, or range names. Figure 2.33 shows the range D3..D16 from figure 2.32 moved to C3.

Fig. 2.32
Specifying a range of cells to be moved.

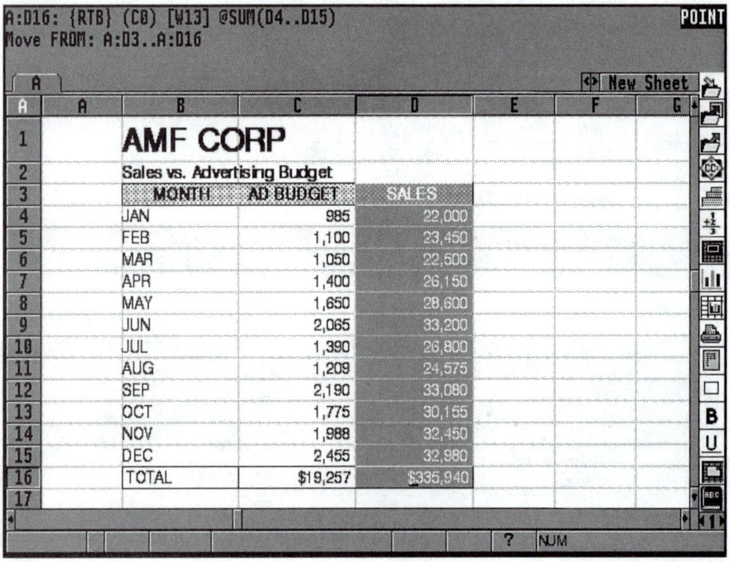

MONTH	AD BUDGET	SALES
JAN	985	22,000
FEB	1,100	23,450
MAR	1,050	22,500
APR	1,400	26,150
MAY	1,650	28,600
JUN	2,065	33,200
JUL	1,390	26,800
AUG	1,209	24,575
SEP	2,190	33,080
OCT	1,775	30,155
NOV	1,988	32,450
DEC	2,455	32,980
TOTAL	$19,257	$335,940

Tip
Moved data retains its original format. When moved, a cell that contains data with a large font causes 1-2-3 to adjust the row of the target cell to accommodate the incoming font.

In figure 2.33, the formats of the cells moved with the contents. The protection status, if any, also moved. The original cells in column D remain but no longer contain data or formatting.

1-2-3's address-adjusting capability is an important feature of /**M**ove. When you move data, all formulas that refer to this data adjust the cell references to refer to the new location.

If formulas refer to cells in the destination range before the move, the references change to ERR. In figure 2.34, for example, assume that you want to replace the data in D3..D16 with the data in C3..C16. Figure 2.35 shows the result if you move C3..C16 to D3..D16. The formula in D18 changes from @AVG(D4..D15) to @AVG(ERR).

Copying and Moving Data 95

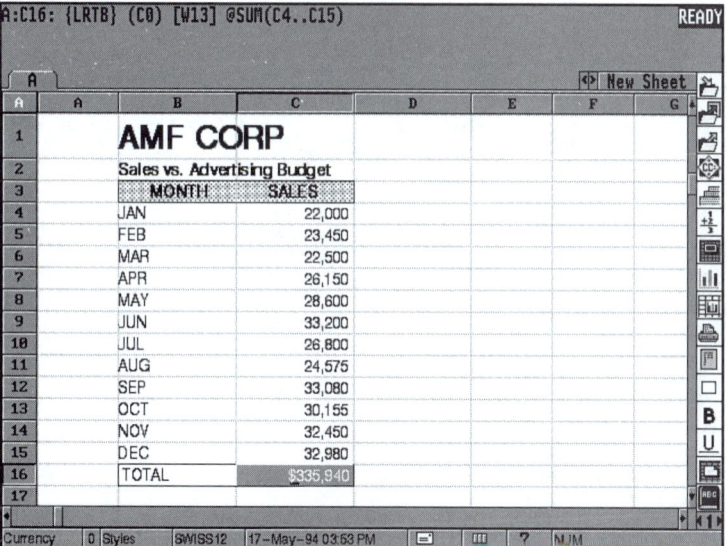

Fig. 2.33
The formula adjusts after you move the cells with numbers.

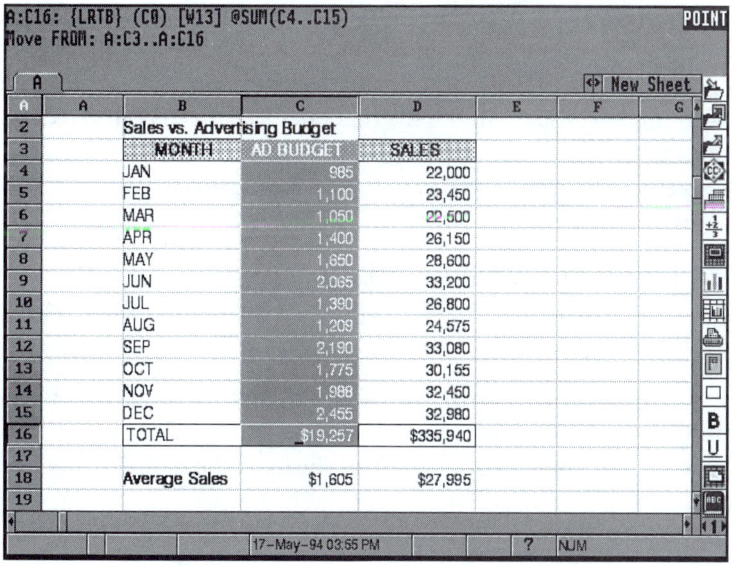

Fig. 2.34
The worksheet before data is moved.

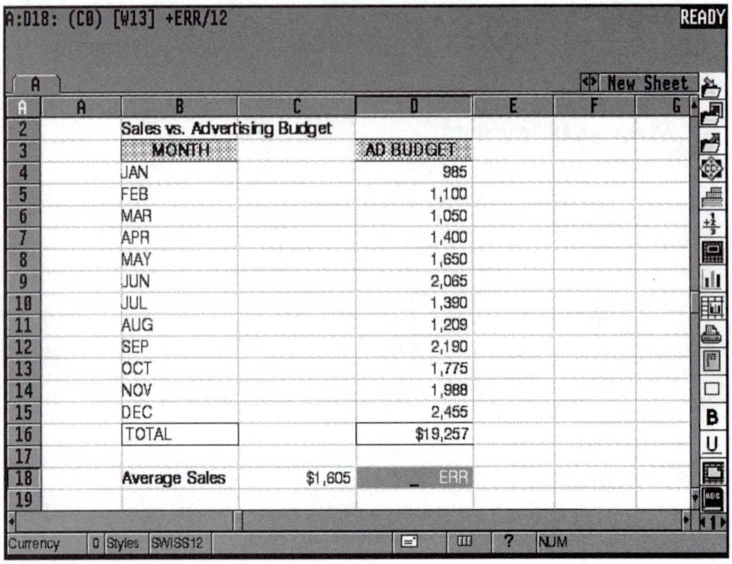

96 Chapter 2—What Every 1-2-3 User Should Know

Fig. 2.35
1-2-3 displays ERR when data is moved into cells referenced by a formula.

	A	B	C	D
2	Sales vs. Advertising Budget			
3	MONTH			AD BUDGET
4	JAN			985
5	FEB			1,100
6	MAR			1,050
7	APR			1,400
8	MAY			1,650
9	JUN			2,065
10	JUL			1,390
11	AUG			1,209
12	SEP			2,190
13	OCT			1,775
14	NOV			1,988
15	DEC			2,455
16	TOTAL			$19,257
17				
18	Average Sales		$1,605	ERR

Cell: A:D18: (C0) [W13] +ERR/12

Tip
Use the Auditor add-in before moving data to determine whether any other formulas in the worksheet depend on cells in the selected area.

Unless you immediately press Alt+F4 to Undo the move (if the Undo feature is active), or retrieve a previous version of the worksheet, this change is permanent and you must reenter the formula in cell D18. You can have hundreds of formulas throughout the file that refer to the cells D4..D15, and every formula must be corrected. Because of this potentially undesirable result, be careful with /**M**ove; you can destroy a worksheet if you use /**M**ove incorrectly.

The correct way to replace the data in D3..D15 with the data in C3..C15 is to copy C3..C15 to D3..D15 with /**C**opy and then use /**R**ange **E**rase on range C3..C15 (refer to fig. 2.35).

You can move ranges of any size; you also can move ranges between worksheets. If you build a large model, starting with one worksheet, you can move parts of the model to different worksheets as the model grows (see figs. 2.36 and 2.37).

Copying and Moving Data

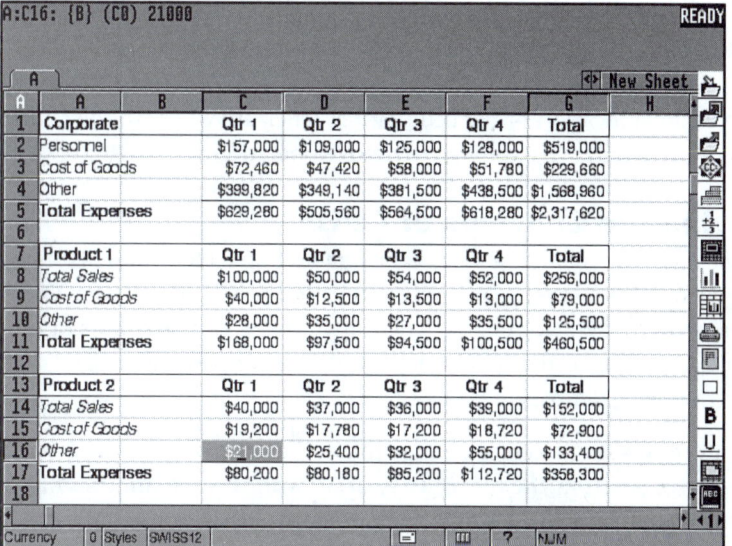

Fig. 2.36
The worksheet before data is moved to other worksheets.

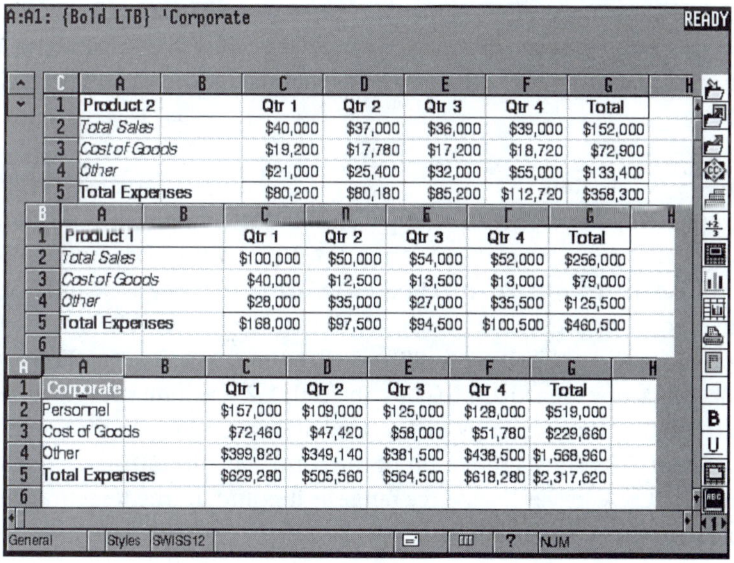

Fig. 2.37
Each product now appears in a separate worksheet.

The cell pointer doesn't need to be at the top of the range when you start the /Move command. The Move SmartIcon, however, assumes that you selected the source cell or range, and 1-2-3 immediately prompts you for the target range. Sometimes, however, starting a move at the destination range is easier. At the Move FROM prompt, click the right mouse button or press Esc to unanchor the range. Place the cell pointer at one corner of the range that you want to move. Drag the cell pointer to highlight the range, or press the period key (.) to anchor the range and use the arrow keys to highlight the range. Then click the mouse or press Enter. At the Move TO prompt, 1-2-3 moves back to the original location of the cell pointer. Click anywhere in the control panel or press Enter to complete the move operation.

Copying the Contents of Cells

/**M**ove rearranges data in a file. /**C**opy makes duplicate copies of a range in a file or a copy from one file to another file. You probably will use /**C**opy more than any other 1-2-3 command. The Copy process can be simple or quite complicated. This section begins with simple examples and progresses to more complex examples.

You can copy a single cell or a range to another part of the worksheet, to another worksheet in the file, or to another worksheet in another file. When you copy, you can make a single copy or many copies at the same time. When you copy a range, you also copy the format and protection status, but you don't copy the column width. The original cells remain unchanged when the copy process is complete. When you copy, the duplicate cells overwrite all data that existed in the destination range before the copy operation. You lose the destination range's data as well as that data's format and protection status.

Copying a Single Cell

The simplest copy operation is to copy a label or number from one cell to another. Figure 2.38 shows the number 123. To copy this data from A1 to B2, move the cell pointer to A1 and choose /**C**opy. At the Copy FROM prompt, click the mouse or press Enter to specify the one-cell range A1. At the Copy TO prompt, move the cell pointer to B2 and click the mouse or press Enter. (If you click the Copy SmartIcon to copy the cell, 1-2-3 assumes that you selected the cell or range to copy and immediately prompts you for the target range.) Figure 2.39 shows the result of the copy operation. Unlike the /**M**ove command, /**C**opy leaves the source range as it is and, in the target range, produces another copy of the data.

Copying and Moving Data   99

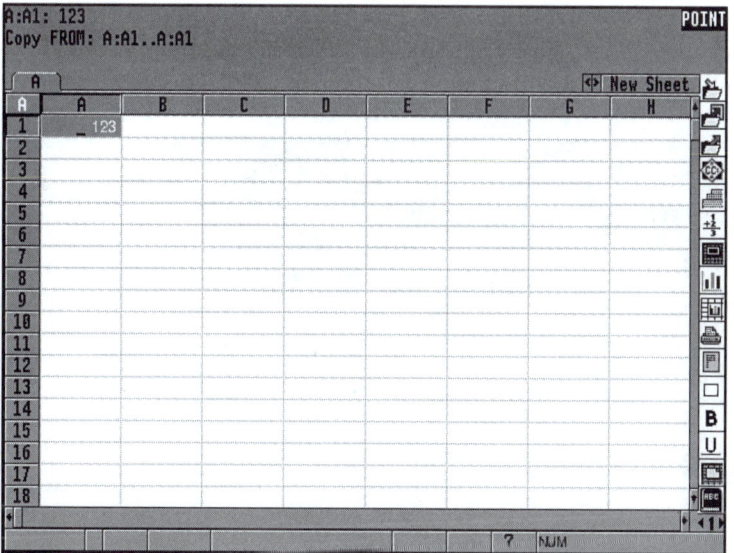

Fig. 2.38
Data to be copied in cell A1.

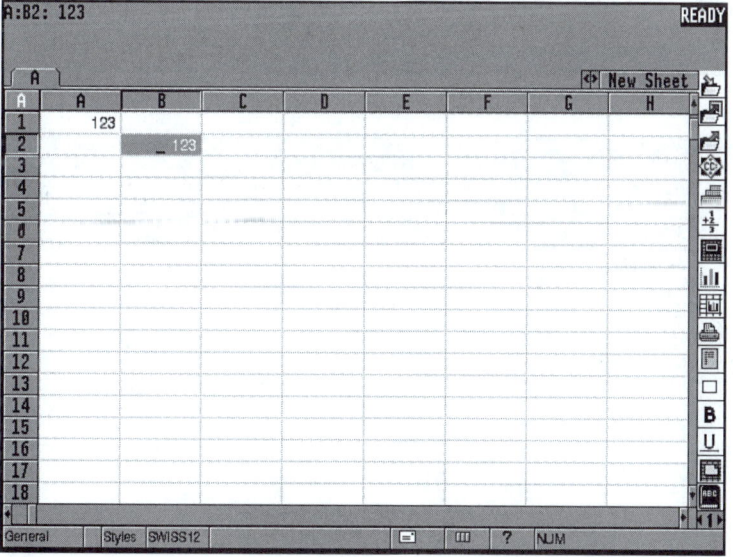

Fig. 2.39
The copied data in cell B2.

Copying One Cell's Contents Several Times

In figure 2.39, one cell was copied one time. You can duplicate a cell's contents many times in one copy operation. You can use the single cell's data in figure 2.38 and copy the data to many cells. The Enter range to copy FROM range still is A1. At the Copy TO prompt, move the cell pointer to B2, drag the cell pointer to highlight through G2; or press the period (.) to anchor the cell, use the right-arrow key to highlight through G2, and then press Enter (see fig. 2.40). The number in A1 copies to the range B2..G2 (see fig. 2.41).

Fig. 2.40
Copying from a single cell to a range.

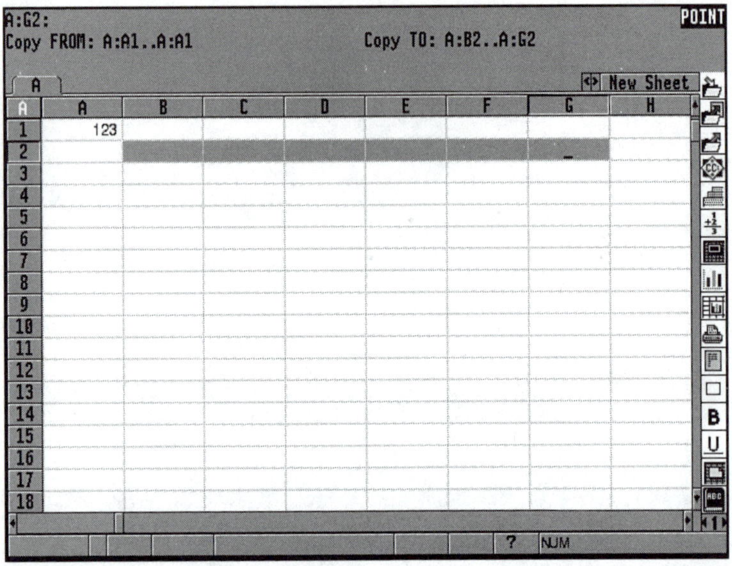

Fig. 2.41
The worksheet after the copy operation.

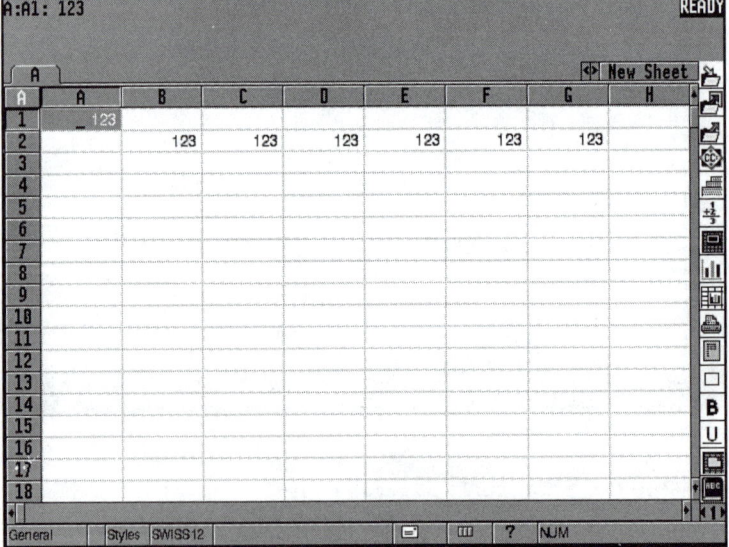

Copying One Cell's Contents to a Range of Cells

You can copy a single cell to a range in the same worksheet or a range that spans multiple worksheets. To copy the same data in figure 2.38 to a rectangular range, move to A1, select /Copy, and press Enter. When you copy a single cell, you can include the source cell in the target range. If you want to copy A1 to G1 and down to G10, include A1 in the Copy TO range as shown in figure 2.42. As a rule, the first cell in the source range can be the same cell as the first cell of the target range. Figure 2.43 shows the result of the copy operation.

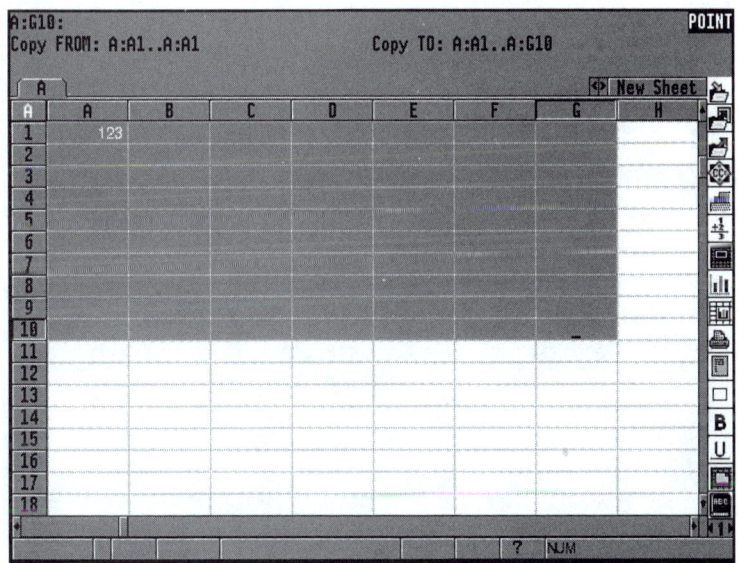

Fig. 2.42
The target range can include the source range.

You can copy a single cell to multiple worksheets. Again, use the data in A1 shown in figure 2.38. Because the copy operation includes row 1, column A, and cell A1 in each worksheet, the target range contains the source cell, as shown in the preceding example. With the cell pointer in cell A:A1, choose /Copy and press Enter. At the Copy TO prompt, move the cell pointer to cell A:G1 and down to cell A:G5. Click the Next Worksheet SmartIcon or press Ctrl+PgUp to copy this same range through to the next worksheet. In that worksheet, click the Next Worksheet SmartIcon or press Ctrl+PgUp twice to extend the range to A:C1..C:G5 (see fig. 2.44). The result of the copy operation includes cell A:A1, which is both the source cell and part of the target range (see fig. 2.45).

▶ "Using Multiple-Worksheet Files," p. 458

Fig. 2.43
The worksheet after the copy operation.

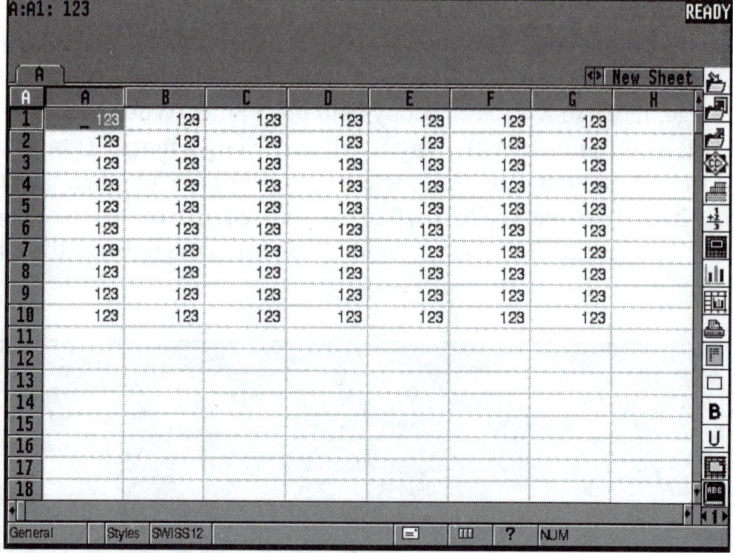

Fig. 2.44
The target range across multiple worksheets.

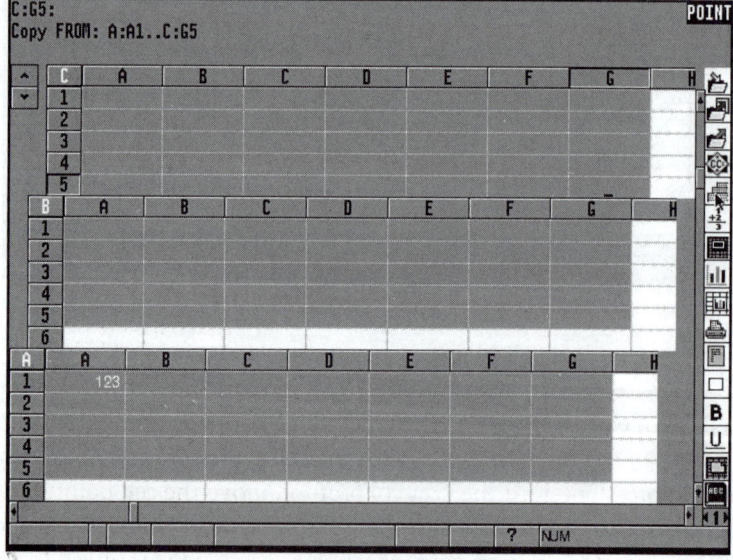

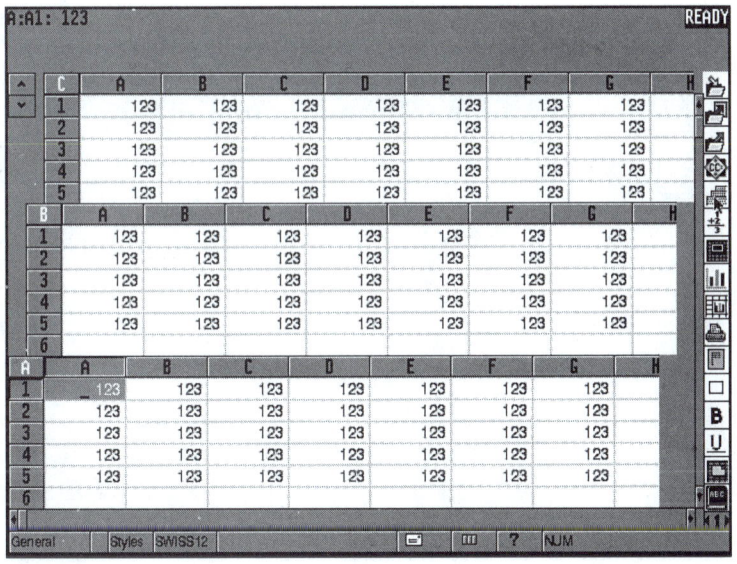

Fig. 2.45
The worksheet after the copy operation.

Copying the Contents of a Range

In previous examples, one cell at a time was copied. You can copy a row, a column, or a range of cells to several locations. In figure 2.46, suppose that you want to copy data in the range A1..F1 to rows 3 through 15. Move to A1 and choose /Copy. The Copy FROM prompt shows a one-cell range anchored at A1 (A:A1..A:A1). Highlight the range from A:A1 to A:F1 and press Enter. At the Copy TO prompt, highlight A:A3 through A:A15, as shown in figure 2.46. Press Enter to complete the copy operation.

In this example, a range across a row is copied a number of times down a column. Notice that the target range is down column A; this action highlights only the first cell into which each copy goes. 1-2-3 remembers the size of each copy and the contents of the cells in the source range, and then fills in the cells of the target range accordingly. Figure 2.47 shows the result. You also can perform the reverse procedure by copying a column range to multiple rows.

The Copy Cell to Range SmartIcon duplicates the contents of the current cell in a highlighted range to all other cells in the range. This feature provides a fast way to copy a formula along cells in a row or column.

When you copy a range, you copy the numeric format (such as **P**ercent) and protection status. However, you don't copy all Wysiwyg formatting. To copy Wysiwyg formats such as lines, use the Copy Formats SmartIcon or the **:S**pecial **C**opy command.

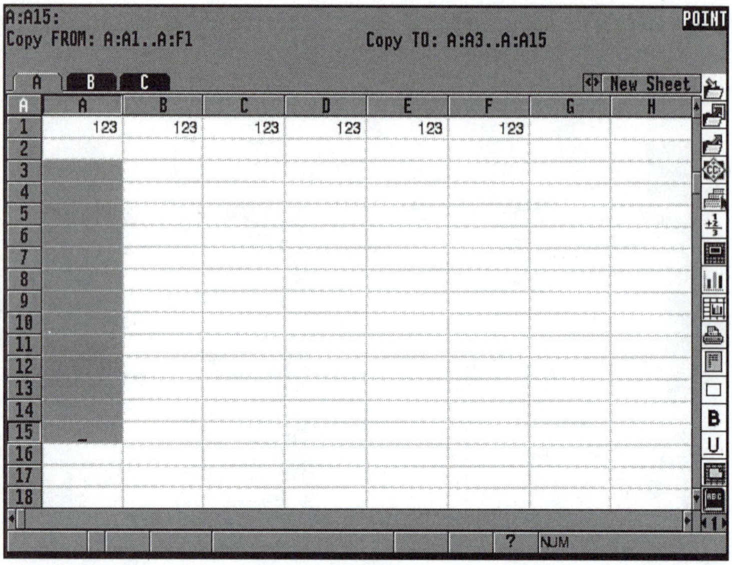

Fig. 2.46
The target range includes the first cell in multiple rows.

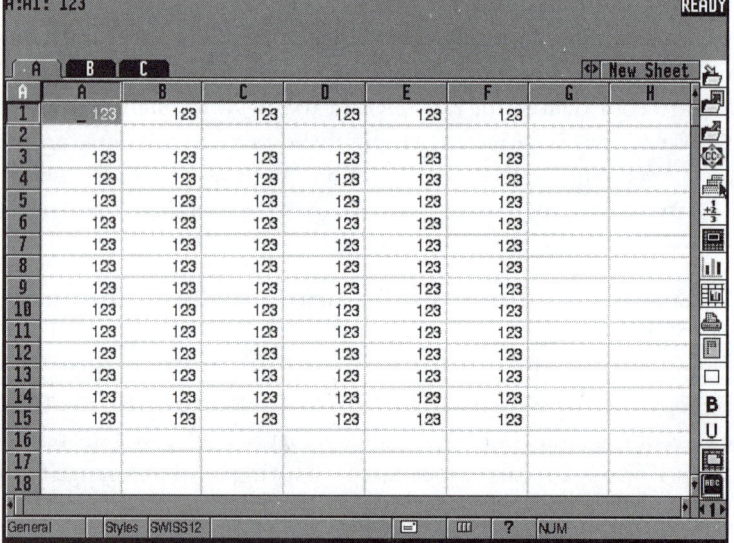

Fig. 2.47
The worksheet after the copy operation.

Copying a Formula with Relative Addressing

The true power of /Copy appears when you copy a formula. The formula in B10 of figure 2.48 is @SUM(B4..B9). When you copy B10 to C10, the formula in C10 is @SUM(C4..C9), as shown in figure 2.49. This concept, known as *relative addressing*, is very important in 1-2-3. When you copy a formula, 1-2-3 adjusts the new formula so that the related cell references are in the same relative locations as in the original formula.

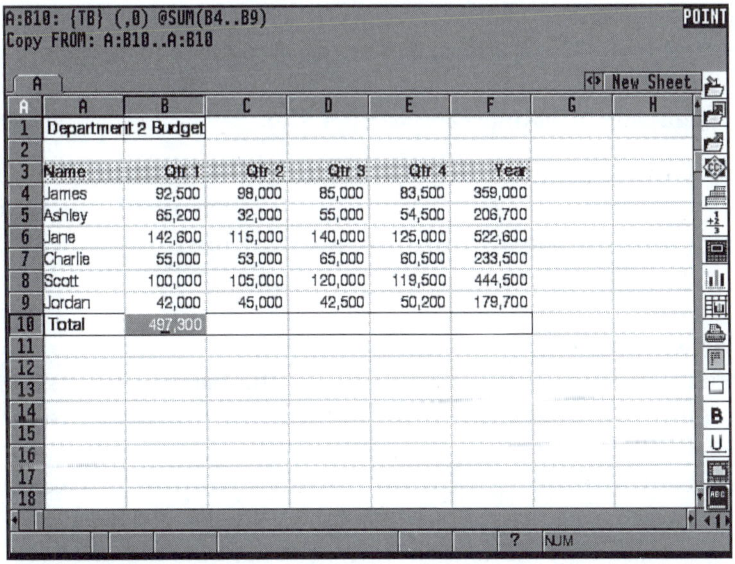

Fig. 2.48
The cell to be copied contains a formula that refers to cells above.

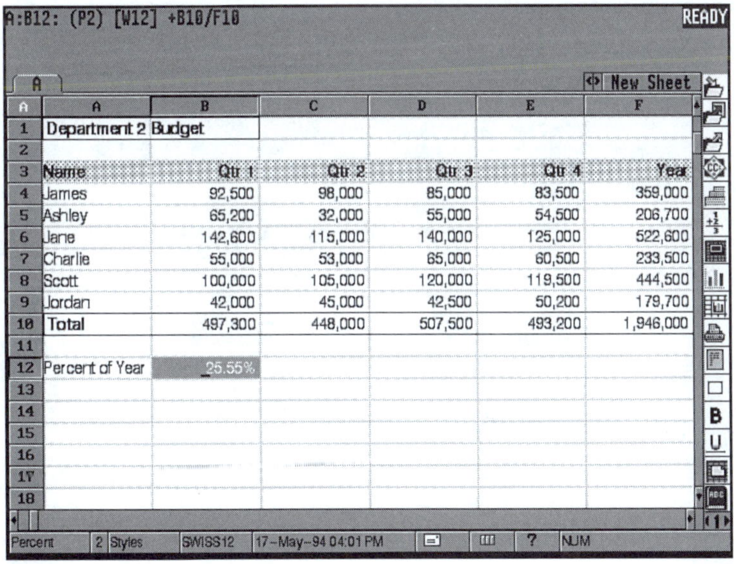

Fig. 2.49
The copy operation adjusts to the new location and refers to the cells above the new location of the formula.

The best way to understand relative addressing is to understand how 1-2-3 actually stores addresses in formulas. The formula in B10 of figure 2.48 is @SUM(B4..B9). In other words, this formula means "sum the contents of all the cells in the range from B4 to B9." But this definition isn't how 1-2-3 really stores this formula. To 1-2-3, the formula is "sum the contents of all the cells in the range from the cell 6 rows above this cell to the cell 1 row above this cell." When you copy this formula to C10, 1-2-3 uses the same relative formula but displays the formula as @SUM(C4..C9).

When you copy a formula, you usually want the addresses to adjust automatically. Sometimes, however, you don't want addresses to adjust, or you want only part of an address to adjust. These situations are examined separately in the following sections.

Copying a Formula with Absolute Addressing

The formula in B12 of figure 2.49 is +B10/F10. This figure represents the first quarter's budget as a percentage of the year. If you copy this formula to C12, you get +C10/G10, as shown in figure 2.50. The budget for the first quarter, C10, is correct. The G10 reference, however, is incorrect; G10 is a blank cell that evaluates to 0, and you get ERR in C12 (any number divided by zero is an error). When you copy the formula in B12, you want the address F10 to copy as an *absolute address;* you don't want the F10 reference to change when you copy the formula to C12.

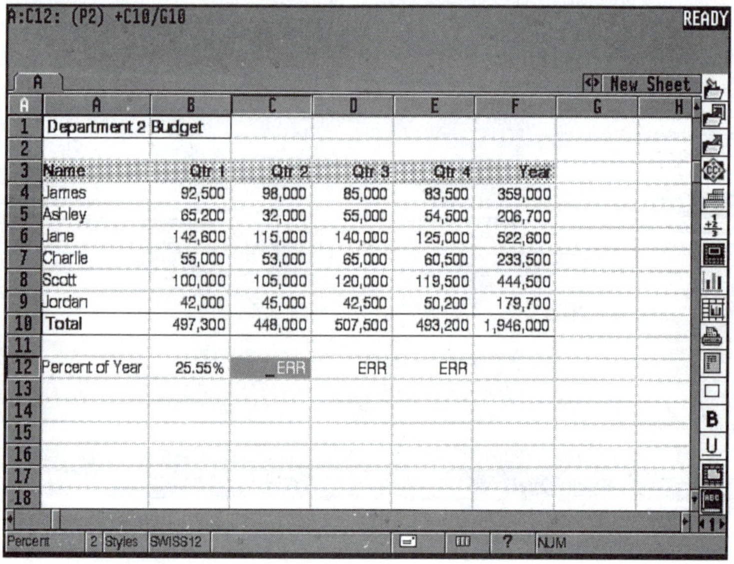

Fig. 2.50
When you copy a formula with relative addressing, an ERR sometimes results.

If you need absolute references, you should specify absolute addresses while you write a formula. To specify an absolute address, type a dollar sign (**$**) before each part of the address that you want to remain *absolutely* the same. The formula in B12 should be +B10/$F$10. When you copy this formula to C12, the formula becomes +C10/$F$10 (see fig. 2.51).

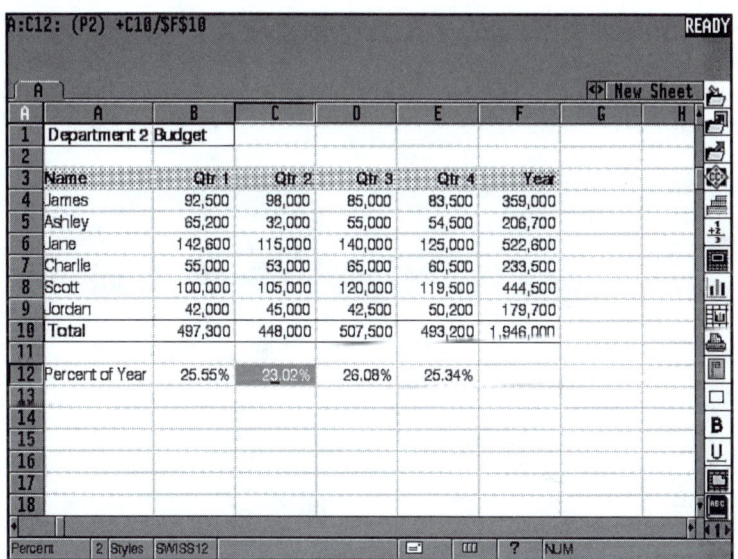

Fig. 2.51
An absolute address ($F$10) that remained unchanged when copied.

While you point to addresses in a formula, you can make these addresses absolute. As you point to a cell to be included in a formula, press F4 (Abs) to make the address absolute. After you create a formula, if you forgot to make an address absolute, press F2 (Edit) to access EDIT mode, move the cursor in the control panel to the address you want to make absolute, and then press F4.

If you want to change an absolute reference (with dollar signs) back to a relative reference, press F2 (Edit), move the cursor to the reference, and then press F4 (Abs) repeatedly until the dollar signs disappear. Click the left mouse button or press Enter to accept the formula.

Another kind of addressing is mixed addressing. *Mixed addressing*, which combines relative addressing with absolute addressing, is covered in the following section.

Tip
Rather than type the dollar sign, you can press F4 (Abs) after you type the address; the address changes to absolute.

Copying with Mixed Addressing

Figure 2.52 shows a sales-forecast worksheet. The discount in B1 is referred to in the formula to estimate sales for product 1 in January. Because this discount remains for all products for all months, the reference to the discount is absolute

108   Chapter 2—What Every 1-2-3 User Should Know

in the formula in C7. Each product has an individual unit price (in B5, B10, and B15). Although you want the row reference of B5 in the formula in C7 to change when you copy C7 to product 2 and product 3, you don't want the column to change. A mixed reference is a reference in which at least one portion of an address (row, column, or sheet) is relative and another portion of the address is absolute. The reference to B5 in the formula in C7 has an absolute column and relative row ($B5). The complete formula in C7, +C6*$A:$B5*(1-$B$1), has one relative reference (C6), a mixed reference ($A:$B5), and an absolute reference ($B$1). When this formula is copied to D12, the result is +D11*$A:$B10*(1-$B$1).

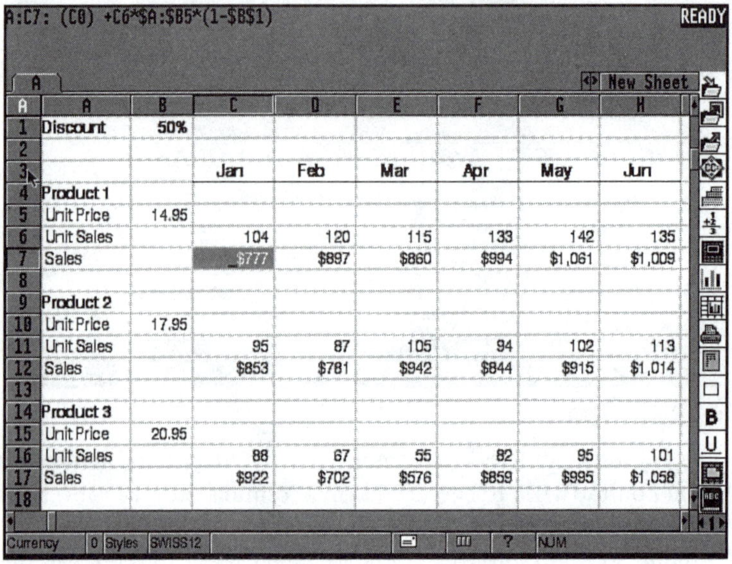

Fig. 2.52
The mixed-reference formula appears in the control panel of this sales-forecast worksheet.

To make an address mixed without typing the dollar signs, press the F4 (Abs) key. The first time you press F4, the address becomes absolute. As you press F4 repeatedly, though, the address cycles through the possible mixed-address combinations and then changes the address to relative. To obtain the address ($B5) shown in figure 2.52, press F4 three times.

Table 2.3 shows the complete list of relative, absolute, and mixed addresses.

Table 2.3 Using F4 (Abs) To Change Address Type

Number of Times To Press F4 (Abs)	Result	Explanation
1	$A:$B$1	Completely absolute
2	$A:B$1	Absolute worksheet and row
3	$A:$B1	Absolute worksheet and column
4	$A:B1	Absolute worksheet
5	A:$B$1	Absolute column and row
6	A:B$1	Absolute row
7	A:$B1	Absolute column
8	A:B1	Returns to relative

When you work with multiple worksheets, you have three parts of the address to consider, which leaves the eight possibilities shown in table 2.3 for cell addressing. When you first press F4 (Abs), the worksheet is absolute. Often, you don't want the worksheet to be absolute. Consider the worksheet shown in figure 2.52. The term $A:$B5 in cell C7 forces the $B5 reference to always look at worksheet A. If you plan to expand this model to multiple worksheets, you want each worksheet to reference the price range and discount for that worksheet. You want the worksheet letter to change relative to the new worksheet; you therefore want a term of A:$B5 and not the original $A:$B5. Here, the correct formula in C7 is +A:C6*A:$B5*(1−A:$B$1). To get the A:$B5 in the formula correct, press F4 (Abs) seven times.

▶ "Using Multiple-Worksheet Files," p. 458

Using Range Names with /Copy

As with all commands that prompt for a range, the /Copy command accepts range names. You can use range names for the source range, the target range, or both. At the prompt, type the range name, or press the F3 (Name) key and point to the range name. Unfortunately, you cannot use range names with mixed addresses in 1-2-3.

To specify an absolute address for a range, type or select the range name and press F4.(Abs). When you press F4 (Abs) with a range name, you cycle between relative and absolute only. You cannot specify a range name and make the range name a mixed address; you must use the actual cell addresses for a mixed address.

Converting Formulas to Values

/**R**ange **V**alue is a special kind of copy command. When you use /**R**ange **V**alue on a cell that contains a label or a number, this command works exactly like /**C**opy. When you use /**R**ange **V**alue on a cell that contains a formula, however, 1-2-3 copies the current value rather than the formula.

You use /**R**ange **V**alue to freeze the values of formulas so that they don't change. Figure 2.53 shows a worksheet that contains income statements for the current year and the past three years. After the results for the current year (1994) are complete, you may want to copy the values to column F and title the column 1995. You then could maintain the formulas in the current-year column that are linked to other cells in the worksheet for the next year. To convert the formulas in column B to numbers, move to B3, choose /**R**ange **V**alue, highlight B3 through B18, press Enter, move to F3, and press Enter. In this example, the title in F3 was edited to show 1995 (see fig. 2.54).

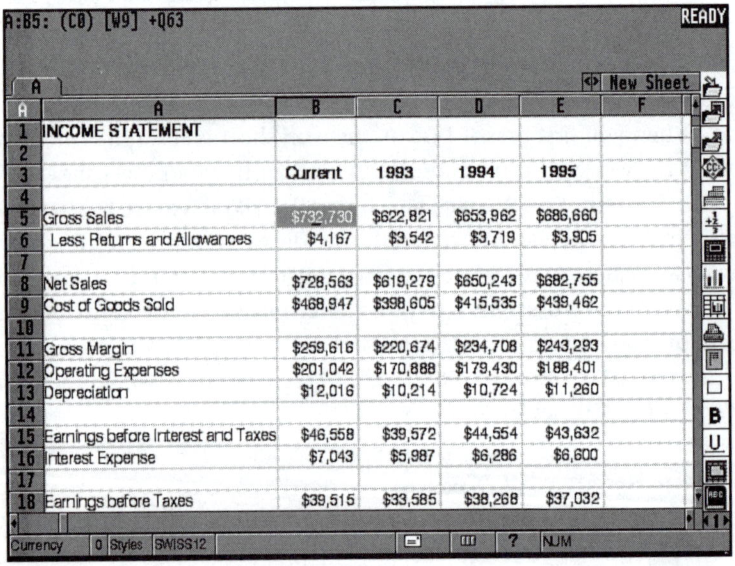

A:B5: (C0) [W9] +Q63 READY

	A	B	C	D	E	F
1	INCOME STATEMENT					
2						
3		Current	1993	1994	1995	
4						
5	Gross Sales	$732,730	$622,821	$653,962	$686,660	
6	Less: Returns and Allowances	$4,167	$3,542	$3,719	$3,905	
7						
8	Net Sales	$728,563	$619,279	$650,243	$682,755	
9	Cost of Goods Sold	$468,947	$398,605	$415,535	$439,462	
10						
11	Gross Margin	$259,616	$220,674	$234,708	$243,293	
12	Operating Expenses	$201,042	$170,888	$179,430	$188,401	
13	Depreciation	$12,016	$10,214	$10,724	$11,260	
14						
15	Earnings before Interest and Taxes	$46,558	$39,572	$44,554	$43,632	
16	Interest Expense	$7,043	$5,987	$6,286	$6,600	
17						
18	Earnings before Taxes	$39,515	$33,585	$38,268	$37,032	

Fig. 2.53
A worksheet before a /**R**ange **V**alue operation.

One danger you can encounter when using /**R**ange **V**alue occurs if you set /**W**orksheet **G**lobal **R**ecalculation to **M**anual. If you use /**R**ange **V**alue on a formula that is not current, you freeze the old value. This problem isn't a major difficulty if the value is placed in a cell other than the cell that holds the formula. To correct this mistake, press F9 (Calc) to update the formula and then perform the /**R**ange **V**alue operation again.

Tip
To change a formula in a single cell to a number, place the cell pointer in the cell, press F2 (Edit), and then press F9 (Calc). 1-2-3 converts formulas in the edit line to a value. Finally, press Enter to insert the result into the cell.

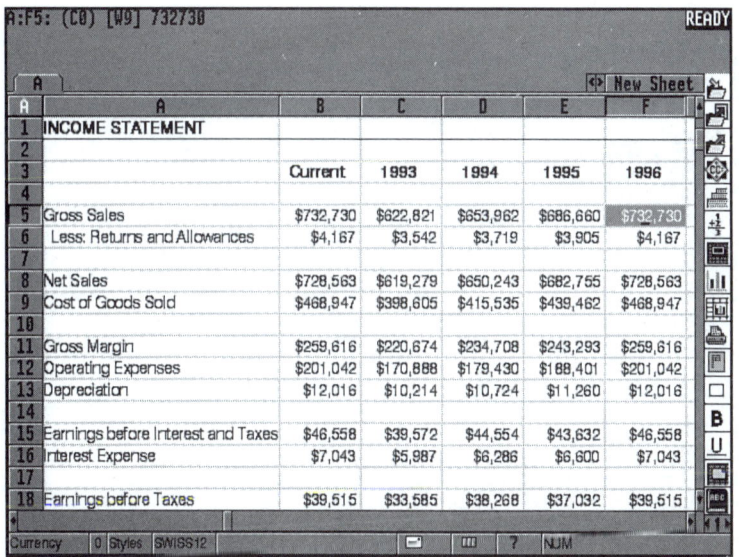

Fig. 2.54
The income-statement worksheet, after locking in 1996 values with /Range Value.

If you convert a formula that isn't current to a number and then copy the value to the cell that contains the formula, however, you lose the formula, and the resulting number also is wrong. To correct this mistake, press Alt+F4 (Undo). If Undo is disabled, you must reenter the formula in the cell. This procedure works for ranges and for individual cells. If the CALC indicator appears in the status bar, you need to calculate the worksheet. Press F9 before you use /Range Value.

Transposing Data

/Range Trans (Transpose) is another special kind of copy command. /Range Trans converts rows to columns and columns to rows, and changes formulas to values at the same time. In figure 2.55, range B9..G14 shows the result of executing /Range Trans from A2..F7 to B9. The rows and columns are transposed.

As with /Range Value, /Range Trans can freeze incorrect values if recalculation is set to manual. Make sure that you turn off the CALC indicator before you transpose a range.

112 Chapter 2—What Every 1-2-3 User Should Know

Fig. 2.55
A table after using /**R**ange **T**rans to transpose the rows and columns.

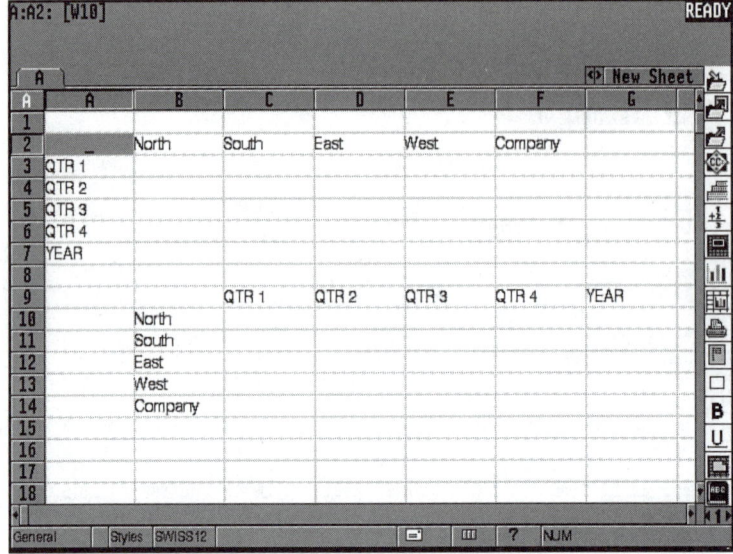

Finding and Replacing Data

/**R**ange **S**earch searches a range of cells to find a string of characters in labels and formulas. You also can execute a search operation by clicking the Search SmartIcon. This feature works much like the search-and-replace feature in many word processing programs.

Tip
Because an incorrect search-and-replace operation can destroy a file, always save the file to disk first.

Suppose that you have a list of department names as labels, and you want to shorten the labels from *Department* to *Dept*. To search for and replace the labels, choose /**R**ange **S**earch and then follow these steps:

1. At the Enter range to search prompt, highlight the range you want to search. Specify A3..A10 (see fig. 2.56). Then click anywhere in the control panel or press Enter.

2. Type **department** as the search string; then click anywhere in the control panel or press Enter.

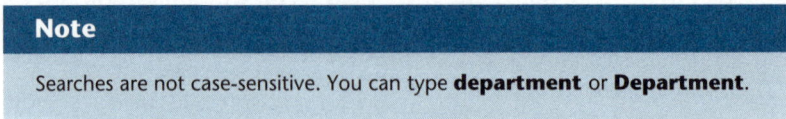

Searches are not case-sensitive. You can type **department** or **Department**.

3. At the resulting menu, indicate whether you want to search **F**ormulas, **L**abels, or **B**oth. For this example, choose **L**abels.

Finding and Replacing Data 113

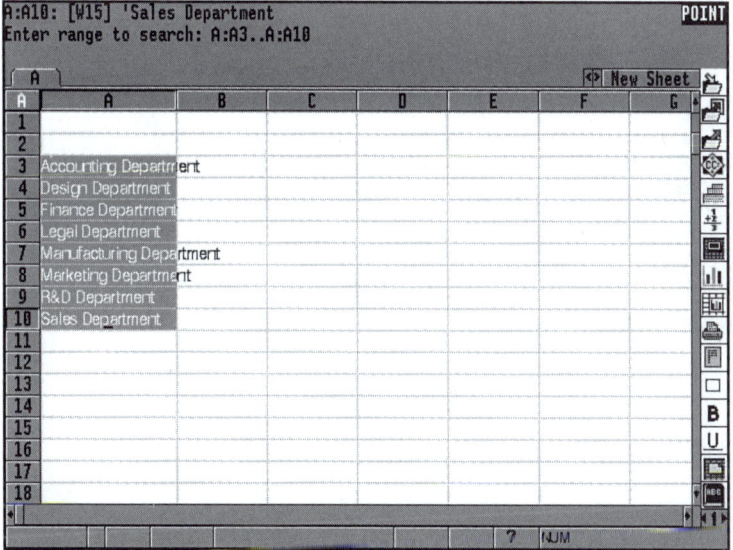

Fig. 2.56
Specifying a column of labels as a search range.

4. In the **F**ind or **R**eplace menu, choose **R**eplace.

5. Type **Dept** as the replacement string; then click anywhere in the control panel or press Enter.

> **Note**
>
> Replacement strings are case-sensitive, so you must type the capital *D*.

6. The cell pointer moves to the first cell that contains a matching string (A3), highlights the found string, and displays a replacement menu. For this example, choose **R**eplace (see fig. 2.57).

The following list describes how to use the options in the replacement menu:

- Choose **R**eplace to replace the search string with the replacement string in this cell and then move to the next matching cell.

> **Note**
>
> Before choosing the **A**ll option, choose **R**eplace for the first cell and ensure that the change is correct. If the change is correct, choose **A**ll to replace the rest of the matching cells. If you make an error on the first **R**eplace, choose **Q**uit and redo the command.

▶ "@INDEX—Retrieving Data from Specified Locations," p. 224

▶ "Looking Up Entries in a Table," p. 549

▶ "Using Minimum Search Requirements," p. 644

Fig. 2.57
The **/R**ange **S**earch menu after **R**eplace is chosen.

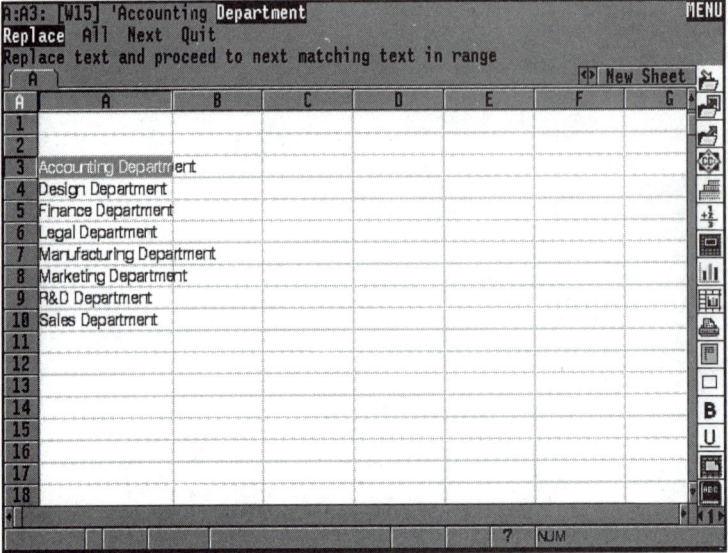

- Choose **A**ll to replace the search string with the replacement string in all matching cells in the range.

- Choose **N**ext to skip—without changing—the current cell and move to the next matching cell.

- Choose **Q**uit to stop the search-and-replace operation and return to READY mode.

Figure 2.58 shows the result of the preceding series of steps. Case isn't used with a search string—*department* matches *Department*, for example—but case is important in the replacement string (*Dept*).

If you choose **F**ind rather than **R**eplace in the preceding example, the cell pointer moves to the first cell in the range that contains a matching string, and a menu appears with the options **N**ext or **Q**uit. Choose **N**ext to find the next occurrence or **Q**uit to return to READY mode. If no more matching strings exist, 1-2-3 stops and displays an error message. At the end of a **R**eplace operation, the cell pointer appears in the last cell replaced.

You also can use **/R**ange **S**earch to modify formulas. If you have many formulas that round to two decimal places, such as @ROUND(A1*B1,2), you can change the formulas to round to four decimal places by using a search string of ,2) and a replace string of ,4).

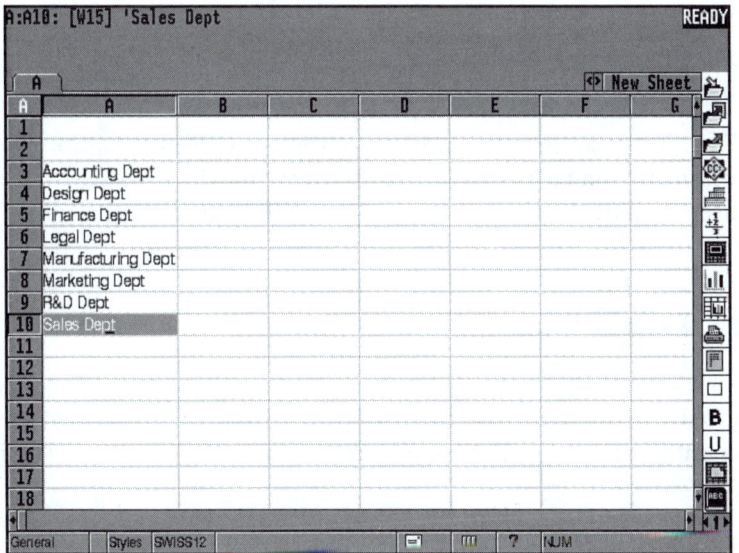

Fig. 2.58
The result of the /**R**ange **S**earch operation.

> **Caution**
> Be careful when you replace numbers in formulas. If you try to replace 2 with 4 in the preceding example, the formula @ROUND(A2*B2,2) becomes @ROUND(A4*B4,4).

If a replacement makes a formula invalid, 1-2-3 cancels the replacement and returns to READY mode, with the cell pointer in the cell containing the formula that could not be replaced.

Remember the following tips when you use 1-2-3's search-and-replace feature:

- If you confine your search to a given range, you can accelerate the search, and you're less likely to accidentally replace strings that you want to leave undisturbed.

- The search string can consist of more than a single word. In fact, the string can be as long as 512 characters and can contain many words.

- The string you are searching for is not case-sensitive. 1-2-3 finds any string that matches the characters you type, regardless of whether you type the string in uppercase, lowercase, or a combination of uppercase and lowercase.

- Unlike the search string, the replacement string is case-sensitive. The substitution consists of precisely what you type, in keeping with your use of uppercase and lowercase.

- The **/R**ange **S**earch command doesn't search hidden columns. The command can be used, however, to search individual cells that have been formatted with the **/R**ange **F**ormat **H**idden command.

Erasing Data

You can erase parts or all of your work in several ways. All data that you erase is removed from the worksheet in memory, but erasing doesn't affect the files on disk until you use the **/F**ile commands (explained in Chapter 9, "Working with Files").

You can erase part of your work in memory in two ways. If you erase a cell or range of cells, you remove all the contents of the cell(s). If you delete the contents of a cell or cells by deleting the column or row where the cells preside, however, you remove not only the contents but also the deleted cells from the worksheet.

 Use the **/R**ange **E**rase command or the Delete SmartIcon to erase sections of a file in memory. You can erase a single cell, a range within one worksheet, or a range that spans multiple worksheets in one file. You cannot, however, use one **/R**ange **E**rase command to erase cells in more than one file.

When you erase a range, you lose only the contents of the range. Characteristics such as format, protection status, and column width remain.

After you choose **/R**ange **E**rase, 1-2-3 prompts you for the range to be erased. Highlight a range or type a range name; then click anywhere in the control panel or press Enter. You also can press F3 (Name) to display a list of range names. To erase the current cell or a preselected range, move to the cell and press Del.

To learn how to erase the contents of cells by deleting columns and rows, see the section "Deleting Rows and Columns" later in this chapter.

Inserting and Deleting Rows and Columns

You can change the layout of a worksheet by inserting or deleting rows and columns. The following sections show you how to use the **/W**orksheet **I**nsert **R**ow and **/W**orksheet **I**nsert **C**olumn commands to insert rows and columns and the **/W**orksheet **D**elete **R**ow and **/W**orksheet **D**elete **C**olumn commands to delete rows and columns.

Inserting Rows and Columns

You can insert rows and columns anywhere in a worksheet. Insert rows with **/W**orksheet **I**nsert **R**ow and columns with **/W**orksheet **I**nsert **C**olumn, or use the Insert Row and Insert Column SmartIcons. You can insert one or more rows or columns at one time. At the `Enter row insert range` prompt, highlight the number of rows you want to insert and then click the mouse or press Enter. At the `Enter column insert range` prompt, highlight the number of columns you want to insert and then click the mouse or press Enter.

> **Note**
>
> When you insert rows or columns, 1-2-3 adjusts all addresses in formulas and range names.

When you insert columns, the column that contains the cell pointer and all the columns to the right of the cell pointer move to the right. When you insert rows, the row that includes the cell pointer and all the rows below the cell pointer move down. 1-2-3 adjusts all addresses (both relative and absolute) in formulas and range names. Suppose that you want to insert a row between rows 3 and 4 of the worksheet shown in figure 2.59. Place the cell pointer in row 4 and choose **/W**orksheet **I**nsert **R**ow; then press Enter. 1-2-3 inserts one row into the worksheet (see fig. 2.60).

If you insert a row or column within a range, the range expands to accommodate the new rows or columns. In figure 2.59, the formula in C5 is @SUM(C2..C4). In figure 2.60, the formula is pushed to C6 to make room for the inserted row. The formula now reads @SUM(C2..C5) in the control panel, and includes the rows in the old range and the inserted row.

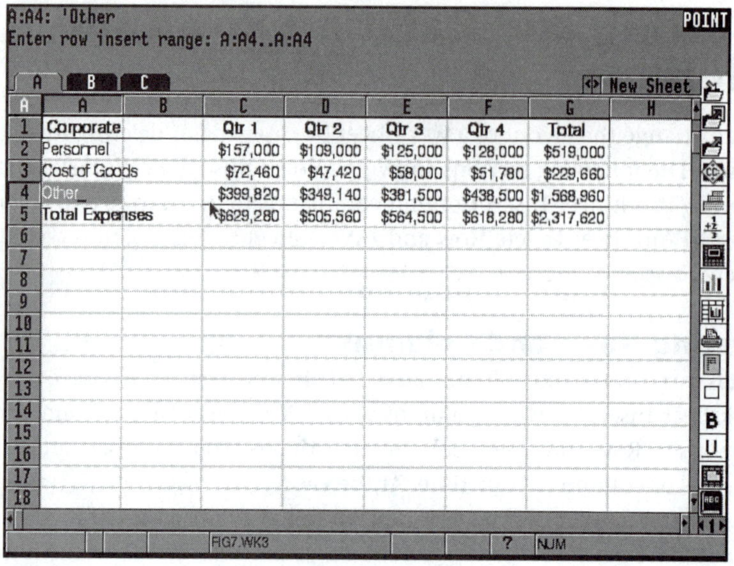

Chapter 2—What Every 1-2-3 User Should Know

Fig. 2.59
Specifying the location of the row to be inserted.

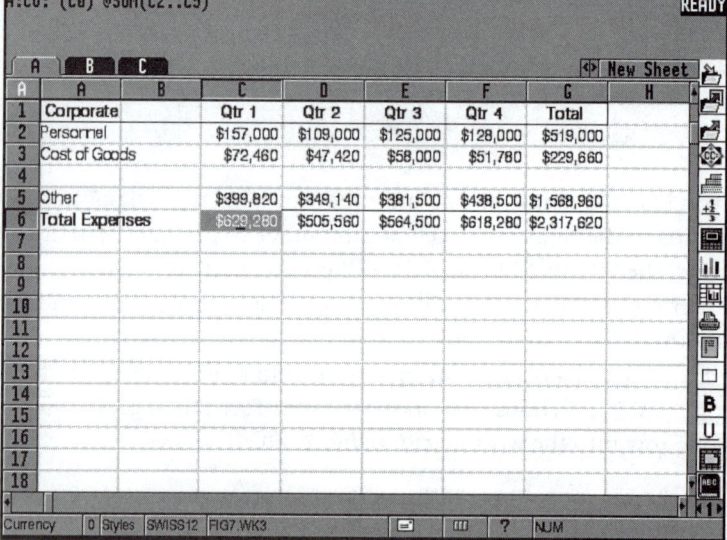

Fig. 2.60
Cell addresses in formulas automatically adjust after row insertion.

> **Caution**
> Inserting or deleting columns and rows can affect both macros and formulas.

Deleting Rows and Columns

Deleting rows and columns is not the same as erasing a range of cells in a row or column. After you erase a range, the blank cells remain. By contrast, when you delete rows or columns, 1-2-3 deletes the entire row or column and updates the remaining addresses in the worksheet to reflect the removal.

To delete a row, move the cell pointer to the row you want to delete and choose **/W**orksheet **D**elete **R**ow. 1-2-3 prompts you for the range of rows to be deleted. To delete one row, point to any cell in the row; then double-click or press Enter. To delete more than one row, highlight the rows you want to delete; then click the mouse or press Enter. You need to highlight only one cell in each row—not the entire row (see fig. 2.61). You also can delete a row by moving the cell pointer to the row and then clicking the Delete Row SmartIcon. To delete multiple rows, select the rows and then click the Delete Row SmartIcon.

Tip
To prevent data loss or formula corrections, always save the worksheet file before deleting rows or columns.

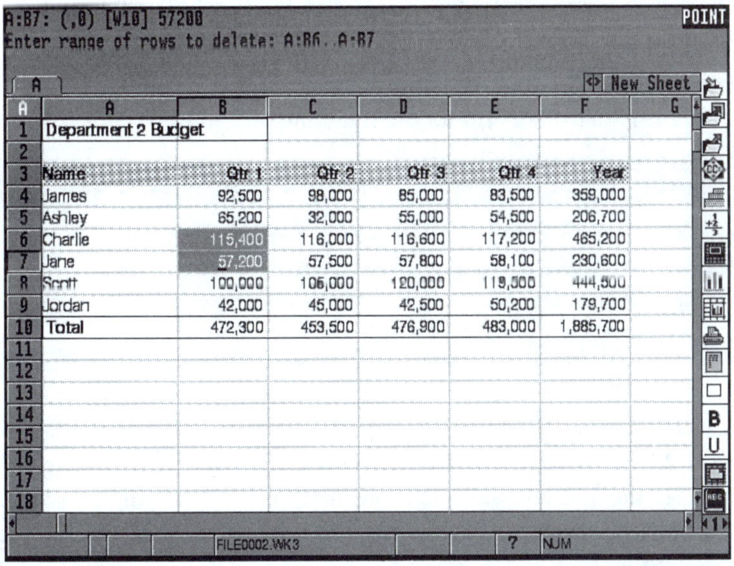

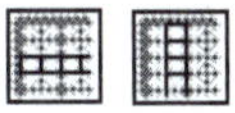

Fig. 2.61
Highlighting rows to be deleted.

When you click the left mouse button or press Enter, 1-2-3 deletes the rows that contain highlighted cells and moves the rest of the worksheet up (see fig. 2.62). 1-2-3 also adjusts all addresses, range names, and formulas (including absolute addresses).

Fig. 2.62
The worksheet after rows are deleted.

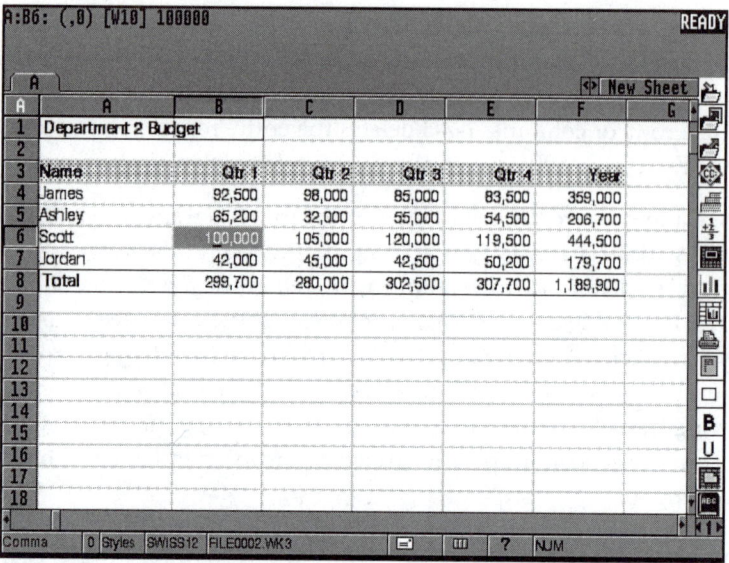

To delete columns, use the **/W**orksheet **D**elete **C**olumn command or the Delete Column SmartIcon and follow the same procedure.

> **Note**
>
> You can use the Auditor add-in to list or highlight formulas that are dependent on cell locations in the rows or columns marked for deletion. This technique prevents accidental deletion of cells referenced by other cells. See Chapter 14, "Analyzing Formulas with Auditor," for more information on the Auditor add-in.

If you delete rows or columns that are part of a range name or a range in a formula, 1-2-3 adjusts this range to reflect the deletion. If the deleted rows or columns contain cells referenced by formulas in the remaining part of the worksheet, the references change to ERR and the formulas become invalid—a serious consequence of the deletion (see fig. 2.63). Affected formulas need not be visible on-screen; formulas anywhere in the file are affected by an incorrect deletion. Formulas in other worksheets that you linked to the deleted rows or columns also are affected.

> **Caution**
>
> If you delete the rows or columns in a worksheet that contains formulas that refer to deleted cells, ERR can occur anywhere in the worksheet.

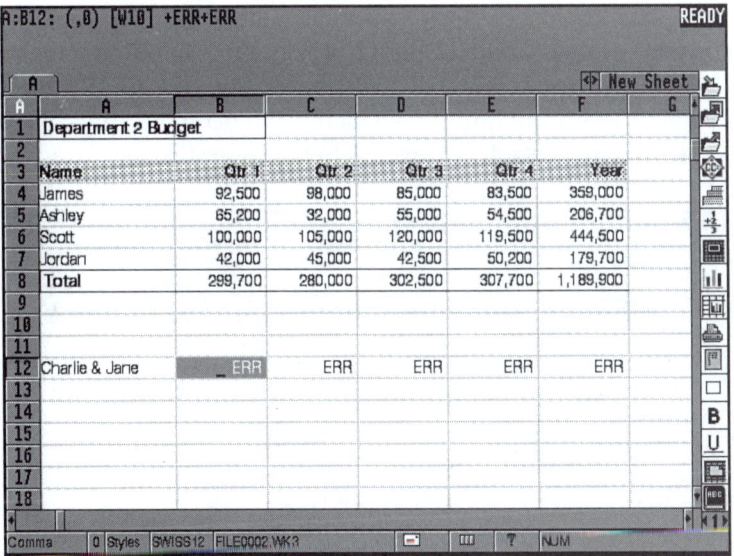

Fig. 2.63
Formulas that reference deleted cells display ERR.

If you accidentally delete the wrong part of the worksheet, you can press Alt+F4 (Undo) or click the Undo SmartIcon to restore the deleted columns or rows if Undo is enabled.

Setting Column Widths

When you start a new worksheet, all columns are nine characters wide. You can change this default column width and the width of each individual column to accommodate the data. If columns are too narrow, 1-2-3 retains the numbers and labels in the cells but displays formatted numbers as asterisks or in scientific format and truncates labels (if the adjacent cell to the right is used). If columns are too wide, you cannot see or print much information. 1-2-3 Release 4 includes a new command that enables you to adjust the width of a column in a worksheet to accommodate the largest entry in a selected range.

> **Note**
> A column width changed by /**W**orksheet **C**olumn displays a column-width notation (for example, [W12]) in the control panel when a cell in the column is highlighted.

122   Chapter 2—What Every 1-2-3 User Should Know

Figure 2.64 shows a worksheet with a default column width of 4 and an individual column width of 10 for column A. The number in cell J8 is too wide for the column and displays as a row of asterisks. The label in A5 is too long for the column width and is truncated by the number in B5. Any column width other than the default is displayed in the control panel.

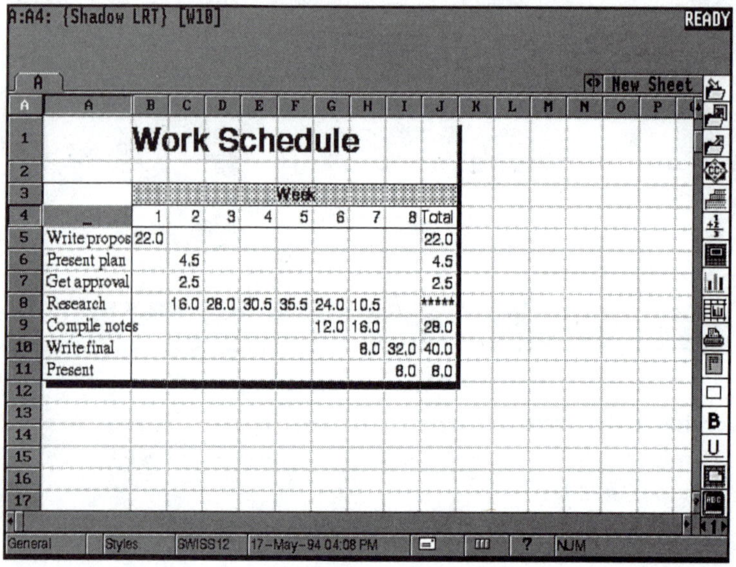

Fig. 2.64

A worksheet with a global column width of 4 and an individual column width of 10 for column A.

Tip

You also can set the width of a column using /**W**orksheet **C**olumn **S**et-Width or :**W**orksheet **C**olumn **S**et-Width and entering a number between 1 and 240 or using the right- and left-arrow keys to change the column-width value.

Whether a number can fit into a cell depends on both the column width and the format. Usually, a number's width must be one character less than the column width. Some negative numbers display with parentheses, which require two extra characters of column width. If a number displays as a row of asterisks, change the column width, the format, or both.

To set the width of one column, move the cell pointer to the column letter cell (A, B, C, D, and so on) in the top frame of the worksheet and point to the vertical line that marks the right side of a particular column. When you hold down the left mouse button, the pointer changes to a double-headed arrow pointing right and left, as shown in figure 2.65. To increase a column's width, move the mouse to the right while holding down the left mouse button. To decrease the width of the column, move the pointer to the left while holding down the left mouse button.

To adjust the column width to fit the largest entry within a range, choose /**W**orksheet **C**olumn **F**it-Widest. You also can adjust the width of a column to fit the largest entry by double-clicking the column-letter cell.

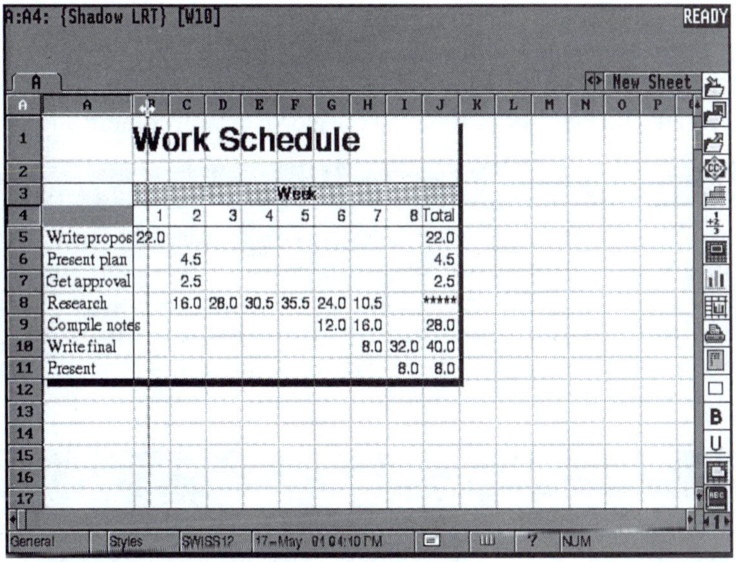

Fig. 2.65
The cell pointer changes to a double-headed arrow when you change a column width with the mouse.

To use the 1-2-3 menu to change column widths for more than one column at a time, use **/W**orksheet **G**lobal **C**ol-Width or **/W**orksheet **C**olumn **C**olumn-Range **S**et-Width.

To change the column widths for an entire worksheet, choose **/W**orksheet **G**lobal **C**ol-Width. At the prompt, type a number between 1 and 240. Then press Enter or click anywhere in the control panel.

To change multiple columns' widths but not the default setting, choose **/W**orksheet **C**olumn **C**olumn-Range **S**et-Width. At the first prompt, highlight the range of columns to be set, type the new column width, and then press Enter or click anywhere in the control panel.

/Worksheet **C**olumn **C**olumn-Range **S**et-Width works only on contiguous columns. You also can choose **:W**orksheet **C**olumn **S**et-Width from the Wysiwyg menu to change the widths of a contiguous group of columns.

> **Note**
>
> An individual column-width setting overrides the global column width. If you change the global column width shown in figure 2.64, the width of column A doesn't change because you set the width of column A individually.

124 Chapter 2—What Every 1-2-3 User Should Know

Use **/W**orksheet **C**olumn **R**eset-Width or **:W**orksheet **C**olumn **R**eset-Width to reset individual column widths to the global default. The **/W**orksheet **C**olumn **C**olumn-Range **R**eset-Width or **:W**orksheet **C**olumn **R**eset-Width commands reset a range of columns to the global default column width.

> **Note**
>
> If the worksheet window is split when you change column widths, the column width applies only to the current window. When you clear a split window with **/W**orksheet **W**indow **C**lear, 1-2-3 saves the column widths in the top or left window. All column widths in the bottom or right window are lost. (To learn how to split a worksheet window, see Chapter 4, "Controlling Your Worksheet Display.")

> **Note**
>
> Column widths and global column widths apply only to the current worksheet unless you turn on GROUP mode with **/W**orksheet **G**lobal **G**roup. In GROUP mode, all worksheets in the file change column widths at the same time. To learn how to work with more than one worksheet, see Chapter 10, "Organizing Your Data with Multiple-Worksheet Files."

▶ "Formatting with the Wysiwyg Menu," p. 320

Setting Row Heights

The Wysiwyg features of 1-2-3 Releases 3.1, 3.1+, 3.4, and 4 make viewing a variety of type fonts on-screen possible (see fig. 2.66). Many fonts, however, are too large to fit in a normal-size cell. By default, 1-2-3 adjusts the height of a row to compensate for the size of the font. With Wysiwyg attached, you can adjust the row height.

Tip
You also can use **:W**orksheet **R**ow **S**et-Height to change the row height by selecting the row(s) and typing a number between 1 and 240.

To adjust the height of a single row, move the cell pointer to the row-number cell at the left border of the worksheet and point to the horizontal line that marks the bottom of a particular row. When you click and hold down the left mouse button, a double-headed arrow appears, pointing up and down (see fig. 2.66). To increase the row height, drag the arrow down; to decrease the row height, drag the arrow up.

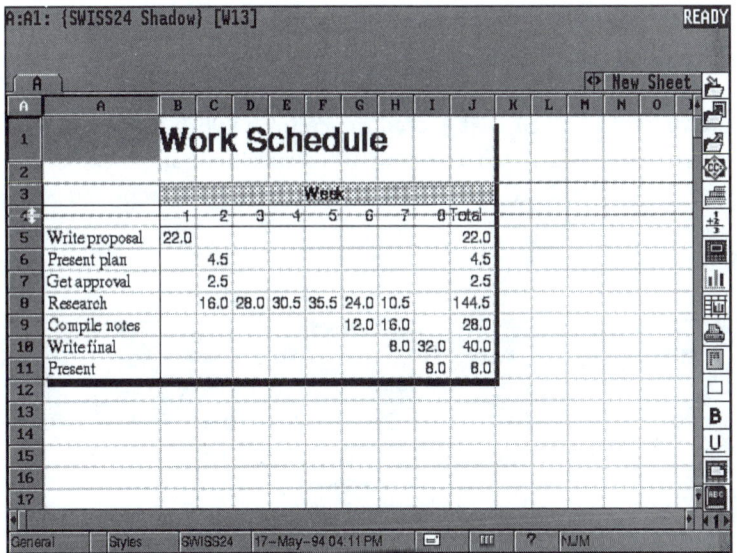

Fig. 2.66
The cell pointer changes to a double-headed arrow when you change the height of a row with the mouse.

> **Note**
>
> If you use **:W**orksheet **R**ow **S**et-Height to set the height of a row or rows, 1-2-3 doesn't adjust the height automatically when you change the font size for the row. To make the row sizes adjust automatically again, choose **:W**orksheet **R**ow **A**uto and then select the rows you want to reset.

Changing Text Alignment

Many people use 1-2-3 to type short letters and memos. Typing and editing even a simple document in any spreadsheet program, however, was far more cumbersome than typing and editing the same document in a word processing program—until the advent of Wysiwyg. You can use Wysiwyg's **:T**ext commands to align a label over a defined worksheet range, center a title at the top of a worksheet table, and adjust a column of long labels to fit in a designated range.

Aligning Labels

Wysiwyg's **:T**ext **A**lign command is an enhanced version of 1-2-3's **/R**ange **L**abel command. The **/R**ange **L**abel command aligns a label within the current column width; labels that exceed the column width are left-aligned. The **:T**ext **A**lign command aligns a label within a specified range. You therefore can align a label across a range of cells so that the label is centered over all the worksheet data. Figure 2.67 shows titles entered in range A1..A7 and centered over range A1..H7.

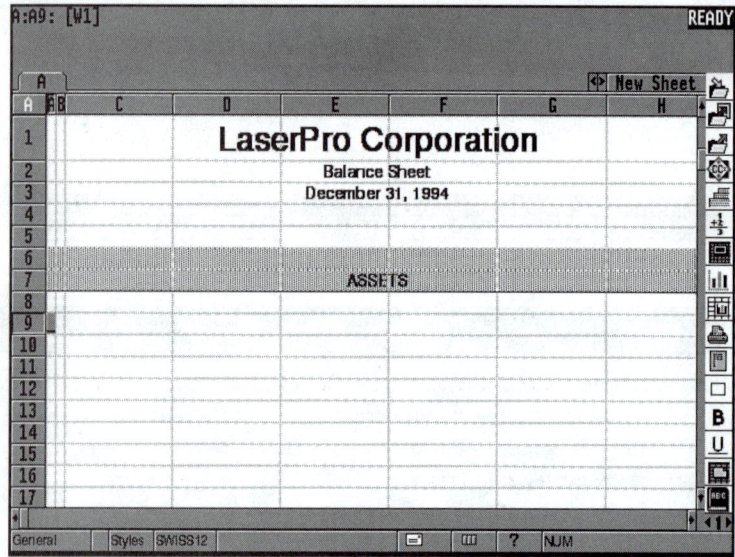

Fig. 2.67
Centering a report heading with **:T**ext **A**lign.

You can align text in a text range by clicking the Align Text SmartIcon. The choice of alignment (**L**eft, **R**ight, **C**enter, or **E**ven) depends on the current alignment setting.

After you choose **:T**ext **A**lign, Wysiwyg offers four options: **L**eft, **R**ight, **C**enter, and **E**ven. **L**eft is the default alignment; **R**ight aligns the label at the right edge of the far-right cell in the text range; **C**enter aligns the text in the middle of the range; and **E**ven stretches, or fully justifies, the text between the left and right edges of the text range (spaces are inserted between words for smoothing). Figure 2.68 shows examples of each kind of alignment.

After you make the alignment selection, the program prompts you for a text range. Highlight the rows for which you want to change the alignment. To align the text in the current range, simply highlight the first column of the range. The text range for the **E**ven-aligned paragraph in figure 2.68, for example, is C15..F18. To align the text in a wider range, highlight the entire width of the text range.

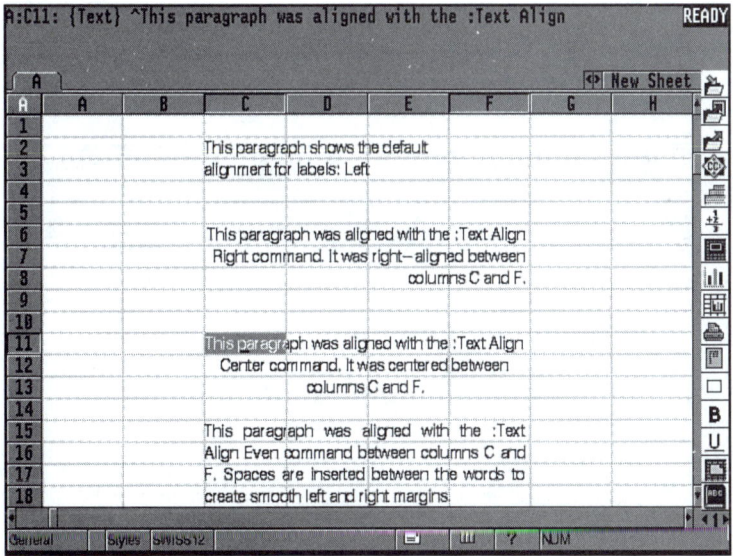

Fig. 2.68
The four kinds of alignment: **L**eft, **R**ight, **C**enter, and **E**ven.

The following table describes the symbols Wysiwyg uses to identify each kind of alignment.

Symbol	Description
'	Left
"	Right
^	Center
|	Even

Notice that the first three symbols in the table correspond to the label-alignment symbols inserted with the **/R**ange **L**abel command. The symbols have different functions, however, when the cell shows the {Text} attribute. You can insert these symbols when you are working in 1-2-3's EDIT mode and the cell has the {Text} attribute. When you edit in Wysiwyg's text editor, the control panel displays the alignment of the current line (Left-Aligned, Right-Aligned, Centered, or Justified).

Reformatting Paragraphs

An advantage of using the text editor is that you can easily correct typing mistakes, reword a passage, or insert more text. After you start editing and formatting, however, you may notice that paragraphs no longer align correctly.

Some lines, for example, may be too short. In the first paragraph in figure 2.69, words were deleted. The second paragraph illustrates how the same text readjusts after the **:T**ext **R**eformat command is issued.

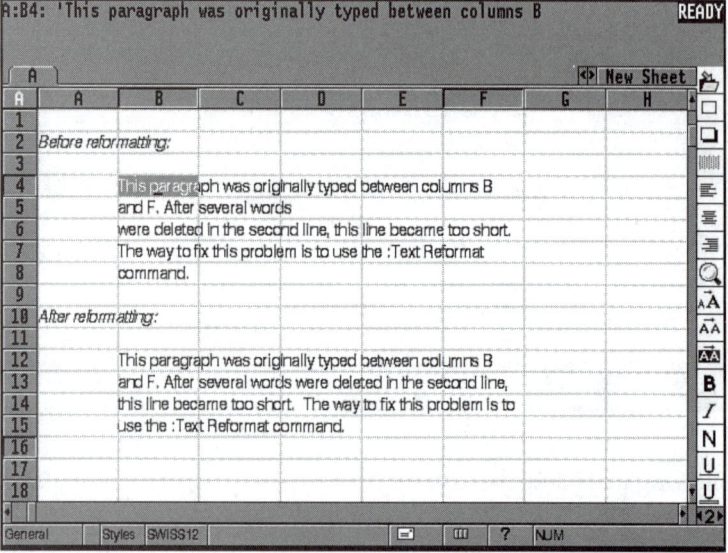

Fig. 2.69
Edited text, reformatted with the :Text Reformat command (shown before and after reformatting).

Because **:T**ext **R**eformat is similar to 1-2-3's **/R**ange **J**ustify command, you often can use the two commands interchangeably. The main difference between these commands is that **/R**ange **J**ustify ignores Wysiwyg alignment and consequently left-aligns during the reformatting process. **:T**ext **R**eformat, however, retains the Wysiwyg alignment during reformatting.

You must invoke the **:T**ext **R**eformat command from READY mode. (If you are using the text editor, press Esc to return to READY mode.) If you didn't prespecify the text range and the cell pointer currently is in a cell formatted as text, the entire text range now is highlighted. If this range is acceptable, press Enter to readjust the text. To indicate a different range, press Esc or Backspace and then highlight the width and length of the range you want. This method of indicating the range works only if you are increasing the size of the text range. To make a text range smaller, use the **:T**ext **C**lear command to remove the text attribute from cells that you no longer want to include in the text range.

:Text **R**eformat adjusts the text within each paragraph—when necessary, by bringing up text from subsequent lines—to fit the specified range. This command doesn't combine text from separate paragraphs.

Another reason to use the **:T**ext **R**eformat command is to align text in a different number of columns. Suppose that the text range currently spans four columns, and you want the range to go across six columns. To make longer lines of text, include these extra columns in the reformat range.

Shortening lines of text requires a different process. If the reformat range contains fewer columns than the text range, nothing happens when you reformat; 1-2-3 ignores the command. Wysiwyg doesn't reformat the range because all columns in the text range contain the {Text} attribute. In figure 2.70, for example, all cells in range B4..F6 have the {Text} attribute. You must remove this attribute from the extra columns before you can reformat.

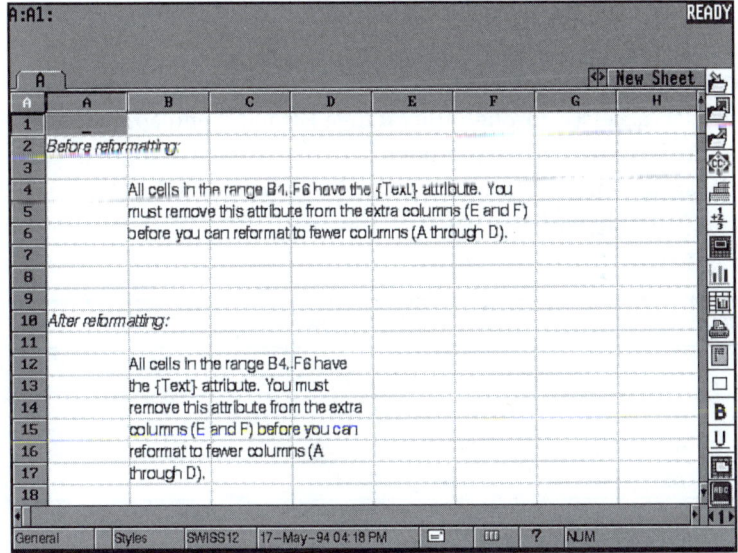

Fig. 2.70

A text range that includes too many columns, shown before and after reformatting.

To reformat the range in figure 2.70 to columns B through D, you must use **:T**ext **C**lear to eliminate the {Text} attribute from columns E and F.

Another consideration in reformatting to include fewer columns is that the new text range is longer than the current range (it uses more rows). When specifying the range for the reformatting operation, you must include additional blank rows at the bottom of the range; otherwise, the message Text range full appears. Press Esc to clear the error message, reissue the **:T**ext **R**eformat command, and specify a longer range.

Setting and Clearing Text Attributes

The final commands in the :**T**ext menu are **S**et and **C**lear. The **S**et command assigns the {Text} attribute to a cell or range. Because the **A**lign, **E**dit, and **R**eformat commands of the :**T**ext menu assign the {Text} attribute, you may need to use the **C**lear option often to clear text ranges.

Tip
Use :**T**ext **S**et if you accidentally clear the {Text} attribute from a cell—for example, with the :**T**ext **C**lear or :**F**ormat **R**eset command.

Another reason to define a text range with :**T**ext **S**et is that you can use the mouse to invoke the text editor. If you have a mouse, you don't need to use the :**T**ext **E**dit command. After you define a text range with :**T**ext **S**et or another :**T**ext command, you can place the mouse pointer anywhere in the text and double-click. The cursor moves to the beginning of the text range in the row where you double-clicked. To exit the text editor and return to READY mode, click the right mouse button.

Changing Label Prefixes

Most formats accessed through the /**R**ange **F**ormat menu apply to numeric data. Almost all numeric data formats have one thing in common: the numbers appear right-aligned in the cell. Labels, however, can be aligned in different ways. Label alignment is based on the label prefix. The following table shows several label prefixes.

Prefix	Alignment
'	Left
"	Right
^	Center
\	Repeating
|	Nonprinting

If you want a label to be a repeating or nonprinting label, you must precede the label with the appropriate label prefix when you enter the label. If you enter a label with another prefix and later want to change the label to a repeating or nonprinting label, you must edit the cell, delete the old prefix, and then enter the new one. Refer to the section "Entering Labels" in this chapter for more information on entering labels in 1-2-3.

You can, however, change the label alignment of a cell or range of cells to left, right, or center by using the **/R**ange **L**abel command or the **:T**ext **A**lign command (discussed in the section "Aligning Labels" earlier in this chapter). You also can change the default label prefix that 1-2-3 adds to your label when you enter a label without a prefix.

Any time you enter a label without adding a label prefix, 1-2-3 adds the default label prefix. For a new worksheet file, the default is left-aligned ('). You can change this default by choosing **/W**orksheet **G**lobal **L**abel. Changing the default has no effect on existing labels; they retain their prefixes. This method is different from how 1-2-3 handles formats. When you change the global format, you change all cells that have not been range-formatted.

To change the label prefix of existing labels, use **/R**ange **L**abel. Choose **L**eft, **R**ight, or **C**enter, and specify the range of cells to be affected. Using these commands usually is faster than typing individual label prefixes as you enter labels.

Figure 2.71 shows left-aligned column headings that don't line up with the data. Figure 2.72 shows these headings after **/R**ange **L**abel **R**ight is selected.

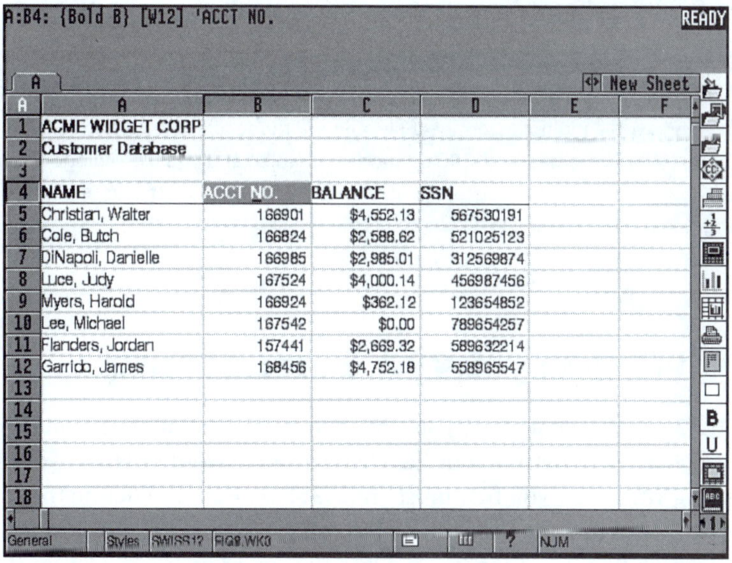

Fig. 2.71
Left-aligned column headings that don't line up with the column's numeric data.

Fig. 2.72
Using the /**R**ange **L**abel **R**ight command to align column headings with the data in the column.

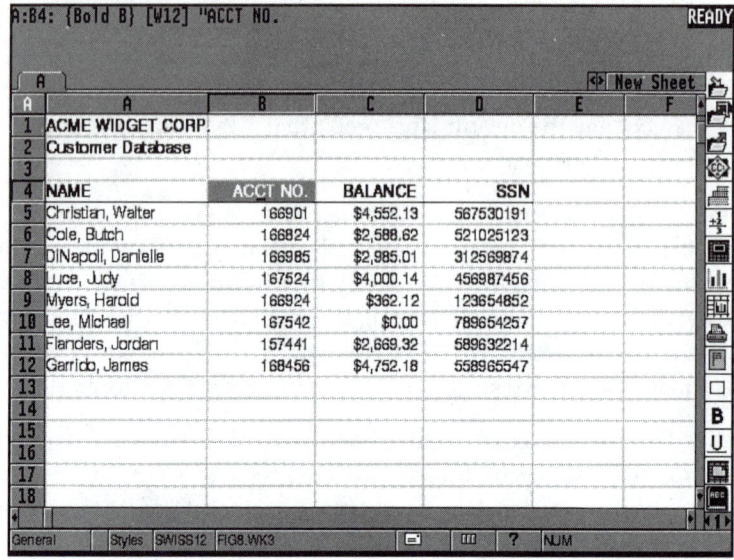

Right-alignment starts a label one position from the extreme right edge of the column (reserved for a percent sign or right parenthesis). Right-aligned labels match the alignment of numeric data.

> **Note**
>
> If you work with a multiple-worksheet file, GROUP mode affects the /**R**ange **L**abel and **:T**ext **A**lign commands. If GROUP mode is enabled and you use /**R**ange **L**abel or **:T**ext **A**lign to change the label prefix in a range in one worksheet, the label prefix changes in the same range in all worksheets in the file.

Applying Wysiwyg Formatting

With 1-2-3's Wysiwyg feature, you can change the format of individual characters, such as by underlining or italicizing a single word or letter. To add formatting attributes, you first must choose **:T**ext **E**dit and define the text range. Be sure to include the entire width of the long labels, not just the column in which you typed the labels. Place the cursor just to the left of the first character you want to format, and press F3 (Name) to display the following menu of attributes in the control panel:

Font **B**old **I**talics **U**nderline **C**olor + – **O**utline **N**ormal

The first five attributes (**F**ont, **B**old, **I**talics, **U**nderline, and **C**olor) should be familiar. The other attributes are unique to the F3 key in the text editor. The + option superscripts the text; the – option subscripts the text; **O**utline traces the outsides of the letters, leaving the insides hollow; and the **N**ormal option removes formatting. Figure 2.73 shows examples of these attributes.

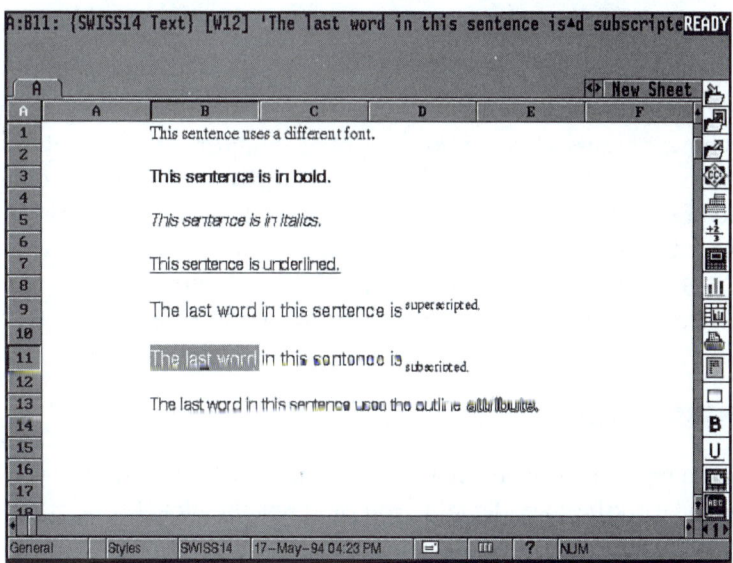

Fig. 2.73
The format attributes that you can add to individual characters with the text editor.

You also can change the attributes of characters by highlighting the cell or range of cells that contain the data that you want to change and then clicking the appropriate SmartIcon. To boldface characters in a cell, for example, highlight the cell and click the Bold SmartIcon.

If superscripted or subscripted text is cut off at the top or bottom of its row on-screen, you can increase the row height. To learn how to specify the height of a row, refer to "Setting Row Heights" earlier in this chapter.

After you choose the attribute you want, all text from the right of the cursor through the end of the line assumes this attribute. The next step is to indicate where you want the attribute to stop (for example, at the end of a word). Place the cursor to the right of the final character you want to format and press F3 (Name). Choose **N**ormal or select a different attribute.

> **Note**
>
> Character formatting isn't limited to existing text; you also can apply attributes as you type new text in the text editor. Press F3 (Name) and choose the format(s) you want before you begin typing. Then type the text. When you want to discontinue an attribute, press F3 and choose **N**ormal.

Because some attributes change the size of characters, you may notice that paragraphs no longer are aligned after you change the formatting. When misalignment occurs, choose **:T**ext **R**eformat to adjust the paragraphs. Because the **:T**ext **R**eformat command remembers the text range, you don't need to prespecify the range when you want to reformat paragraphs. Be sure to leave extra space at the bottom of the range, however, to avoid the Text range full error when reformatting. (For additional information on reformatting, refer to "Reformatting Paragraphs" earlier in this chapter.)

Using the Undo Feature

When you type an entry or edit a cell, you change the worksheet. If you change the worksheet accidentally, you can press the Alt+F4 (Undo) key to reverse the last change. If you type over an existing entry, for example, you can undo the new entry and restore the old one. When you choose commands from the 1-2-3 menu or the Wysiwyg menu, you usually change the worksheet. Often, you can press Undo to reverse the changes you made with the command menus.

 You also can click the Undo SmartIcon to reverse the last change you made in a worksheet.

Because the Undo feature is disabled by default, you must use commands to enable Undo. To turn on the Undo feature, choose **/W**orksheet **G**lobal **D**efault **O**ther **U**ndo **E**nable. To make this change permanent, choose **/W**orksheet **G**lobal **D**efault **U**pdate. When Undo is enabled, 1-2-3 must remember the last action that changed the worksheet. Undo therefore requires memory, in amounts that vary according to the action that Undo must remember. You can disable Undo on your system with **/W**orksheet **G**lobal **D**efault **O**ther **U**ndo **D**isable if you run low on memory.

When you press Alt+F4 (Undo), a menu appears that offers two options: **N**o and **Y**es. You must press **Y** to undo the last change. For the exercises in this book, when you are asked to undo or press the Undo key, remember that you also must press **Y**.

Undo is a useful and powerful command, but Undo also is tricky and can surprise you, so use it carefully. 1-2-3 remembers the last change to the worksheet and reverses this change when you press Alt+F4 (Undo).

You must understand what 1-2-3 considers to be a change. A *change* occurs between the time 1-2-3 is in READY mode and the next time 1-2-3 is in READY mode. Suppose that you press F2 (Edit) to change a cell in EDIT mode. You can make any number of changes to the cell, and then press Enter to save the changes and return to READY mode. If you then press Alt+F4 (Undo), 1-2-3 returns the worksheet to its condition during the last READY mode. Here, Undo returns the cell to its pre-edit condition.

Remember that you can undo only the last change; if you make an error, use Undo immediately or the old data may be lost. If you undo but then decide to restore a change, you cannot undo the undo. If you press Undo at the wrong time and undo an entry, you cannot recover the entry.

If you press Alt+F4 (Undo) after a command, you undo all the effects of the command. With some commands, such as **/P**rint (Chapter 8); **/G**raph (chapters 23 through 25); and **/D**ata (chapters 19 through 22), you can execute many commands before you return to READY mode. If you press Undo at this time, you reverse all the commands executed since the last time 1-2-3 was in READY mode. Suppose that you type an entry in cell K33, press Enter, and then press Home. The cell pointer moves to A1. If you press Undo now, you undo the press of the Home key and the entry in cell K33.

A change can refer to either a change to one or more cells or a change to command settings. To print a report, for example, you must specify a print range. Specifying a command setting doesn't change data in the worksheet—only the last setting. If you press Alt+F4 (Undo) the next time you are in READY mode, you undo the print range you specified.

Some commands don't change any cells or settings. Examples of these kinds of commands are **/F**ile **S**ave, **/F**ile **X**tract, **/F**ile **E**rase, and **/P**rint **P**rinter **P**age. If you type an entry in a cell, save the file, and then press Undo, you undo the last change, which is the cell entry.

The more extensive a change, the more memory 1-2-3 needs to remember the status of the worksheet before the change. If you don't have enough memory to save the status before the change, 1-2-3 pauses and presents the following menu:

>**P**roceed **D**isable **Q**uit

Choose **P**roceed to disable Undo temporarily and complete the command. Undo is re-enabled as soon as 1-2-3 completes the command. Choose **D**isable to disable Undo and complete the command. Undo remains disabled until you quit and restart 1-2-3 or enable Undo again with **/W**orksheet **G**lobal **D**efault **O**ther **U**ndo **E**nable.

To cancel the command in progress, choose **Q**uit. You don't quit 1-2-3; you just return to READY mode. The command may have been partially completed before 1-2-3 ran out of memory. If you copy a range multiple times, run out of memory, and choose **Q**uit, for example, 1-2-3 may have copied the source range to part of the target range you specified. Check all work carefully to determine the effect of the last command.

Usually, you choose **P**roceed. Be sure that you want to perform the command, however, because you cannot undo it. If you executed the command in error, choose **Q**uit and then immediately undo whatever the command changed. If you see this menu often and the menu is slowing your work, choose **D**isable. Although you prevent the menu from stopping you again, you also cannot use the Undo feature.

Saving and Retrieving Your Work

A file that you create exists only in the computer's memory. When you use **/Q**uit to exit 1-2-3 and return to the operating system, you lose all work if you did not first save the work as a file. When you save a file, you copy the file in memory to a disk and give the file a name. The file then exists not just in memory but as a duplicate file on disk. You can retrieve a saved file after you quit 1-2-3 or turn off the computer. When you edit a file, the changes are made only in the computer's memory until you save the new version of the file to disk.

You find more information about file operations in Chapter 9, "Working with Files," where you learn how to read, use, save, and retrieve multiple files in memory at the same time. For now, you can learn to save your work by using the **/F**ile **S**ave command. This chapter covers saving only one file in memory and retrieving a file.

Saving a 1-2-3 File

To save the 1-2-3 worksheet file in which you've been working, first choose **/F**ile **S**ave from the 1-2-3 menu or click the Save File SmartIcon, located at the top of each SmartIcon palette. If you have only one file in memory, 1-2-3 prompts you for the name of the file to be saved, and displays a default path and file name for the file. If you have never saved the file before, 1-2-3 displays the `Enter name of file to save` prompt and assigns a default file name, such as FILE0001.WK3. Don't use this name; type a more meaningful file name, such as DEPT1BUD (a budget file for Department 1). For information on saving when more than one file is open in memory, see Chapter 9, "Working with Files."

▶ "Saving Files," p. 416

▶ "Naming Files," p. 409

▶ "Managing Files with the Viewer," p. 428

If you previously saved the file, 1-2-3 displays the name you supplied, such as DEPT1BUD.WK3, as the default file name (see fig. 2.74). To save the file again and keep the same name, press Enter or click anywhere in the control panel.

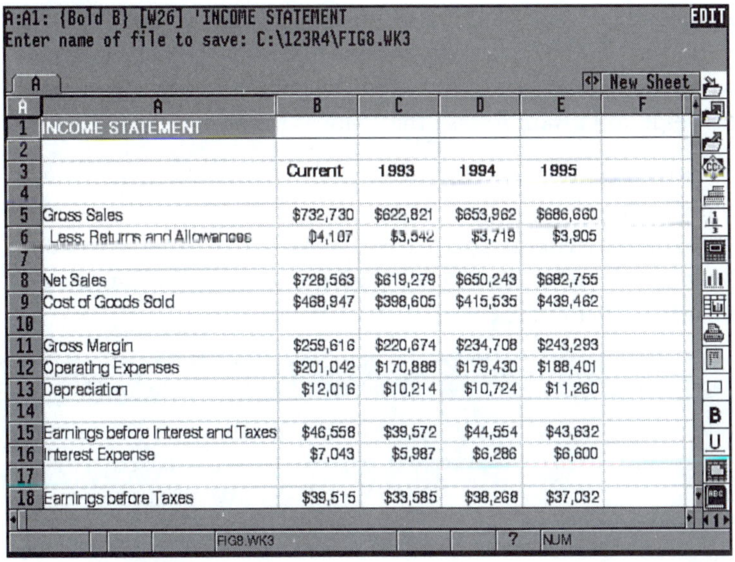

Fig. 2.74
Saving a file with the default file name (the name used the last time the file was saved).

To give the file a different name when you save it, type the new file name. The file name you type replaces the existing name. If the file already exists on the disk, 1-2-3 displays the following three-option menu:

Cancel **R**eplace **B**ackup

Choose **R**eplace to write over the preceding file. When you choose **R**eplace, however, you lose the preceding file. If you make an error in a file and then save the file with the same name and choose **R**eplace, the preceding file is gone.

Choose **C**ancel to abort the /**F**ile **S**ave operation. If you type a file name that matches another file name, **C**ancel the command so that you don't lose the other file.

138 Chapter 2—What Every 1-2-3 User Should Know

Tip
Choose **B**ackup to keep a backup copy of the preceding version of your file.

If you choose **B**ackup, 1-2-3 renames the existing file on disk with a BAK extension and then saves the new file. When you choose this option, you have both the new file and the preceding file on disk.

Retrieving a 1-2-3 File

Two commands read a file from disk into memory: **/F**ile **R**etrieve and **/F**ile **O**pen. **/F**ile **R**etrieve replaces the current file with the new file. If you just started 1-2-3, or if only a blank worksheet is in memory, use this command. You also can retrieve a file by clicking the File Retrieve SmartIcon.

If you changed the current file in memory and you choose **/F**ile **R**etrieve without saving the changes, 1-2-3 prompts you to verify that you want to retrieve another file to replace the current file. **N**o is the default answer. Choose **N**o if you want to return to the **/F**ile menu to save the current file. Choose **Y**es if don't want to save the changes in the current file.

The **/F**ile **O**pen command also reads a file from disk into memory; however, it does not replace the current file in memory. **/F**ile **O**pen keeps open the file(s) currently in memory and opens additional files. After you choose **/F**ile **O**pen, choose **B**efore or **A**fter to tell 1-2-3 to place the file that you are retrieving before or after the current file.

> **Note**
>
> 1-2-3 enables you to open several files at the same time. With **/F**ile **O**pen, you can open files until you run out of memory or until a total of 256 worksheets are in memory.

▶ "Retrieving Files from Disk," p. 421

▶ "Changing Directories," p. 414

Both retrieval commands prompt you for the name of the file that you want to retrieve, and both commands list the files in the current directory. You can type the file name or point to the file in the list in the control panel. If several files are in the directory, you can press F3 (Name) to display a full screen of file names, as shown in figure 2.75.

Files are listed in alphabetical order, reading from left to right. When a file name is highlighted, 1-2-3 displays (below the prompt) the date and time when the file was created and the size of the file. To retrieve a file, highlight the file name and press Enter.

Clearing the Workspace

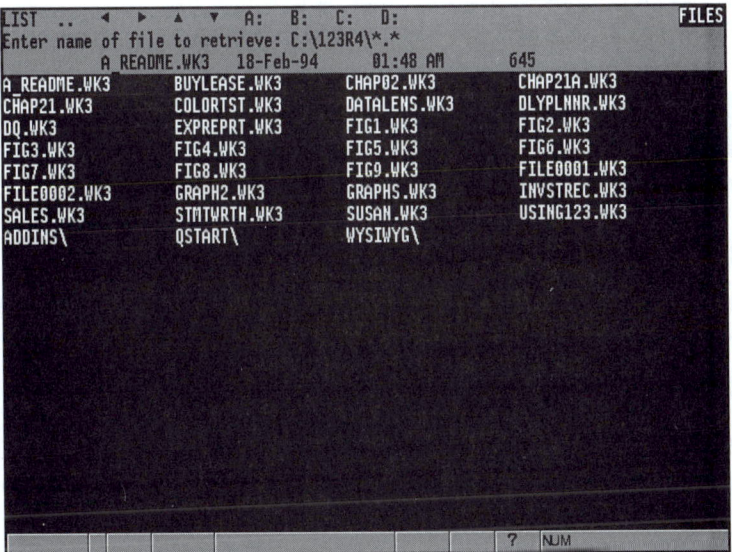

Fig. 2.75
Press F3 (Name) to display a full screen of file names.

Clearing the Workspace

You can clear all files from memory with **/W**orksheet **E**rase **Y**es. The command deletes all worksheets and files from memory, not just a single worksheet. This command's name, which some people find confusing, is a holdover from previous versions of 1-2-3, which allowed only one file and one worksheet in memory at one time. **/W**orksheet **E**rase **Y**es also restores all the global default settings. The effect is the same as if you quit and then restarted 1-2-3 from the operating system. Note that if you select **/W**orksheet **E**rase and you have not saved the current worksheet, 1-2-3 prompts you to save the worksheet before you erase it from memory.

Tip
Use **/F**ile **S**ave before you use **/W**orksheet **E**rase. If Undo is disabled, you can retrieve the saved file without losing data.

> **Caution**
> **/W**orksheet **E**rase **Y**es deletes all files in memory, not just the current worksheet.

When you finish working with multiple files in memory, you can use **/W**orksheet **E**rase **Y**es to clear all the files from memory. You then can retrieve another file or read in another worksheet system.

Printing Your Worksheet

1-2-3 provides two commands for printing: **/P**rint through the main menu and **:P**rint through the Wysiwyg menu. You can use both commands to print worksheets. To use 1-2-3's full capability for creating professional-looking output, however, you should use the **:P**rint command for most printing. The Wysiwyg **:P**rint command gives you better-looking printed text than **/P**rint. For first drafts of reports, you can use either command.

This section provides a brief overview of printing worksheets with **:P**rint. For a more detailed explanation and to learn how to use **/P**rint, see Chapter 9, "Printing Reports."

Checking the Printer Settings

Before you begin printing, you should check the printer settings in 1-2-3 to make sure that they are appropriate for the printer that you are using. When you install 1-2-3, you select the printer or printers that you will be using to print worksheets. 1-2-3 automatically enters the default printer settings based on the printer selections that you make during installation.

To check the printer settings, choose **/W**orksheet **G**lobal **D**efault **P**rinter to display the Default Printer Settings dialog box, shown in figure 2.76. Review the settings in this dialog box to make sure that they are accurate. If you need to make changes, click the dialog box or press F2 (Edit) and make the necessary changes in the appropriate fields. When you finish making changes, click OK or press Enter.

Fig. 2.76
Check the Default Printer Settings dialog box to make sure that your printer settings are correct.

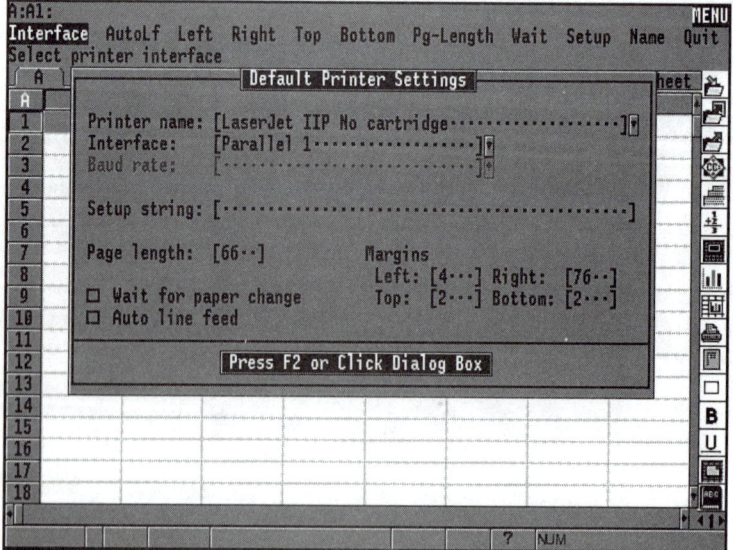

Specifying a Print Range

After you have entered and formatted data in your worksheet, you can print any part of the worksheet. You may want to print the entire worksheet or only a range within the worksheet. Before you print, you must set the print range. To specify a print range, choose **:P**rint **R**ange **S**et; then type the range address, the range name, or use the arrow keys or the mouse to highlight the range that you want to print (see fig. 2.77).

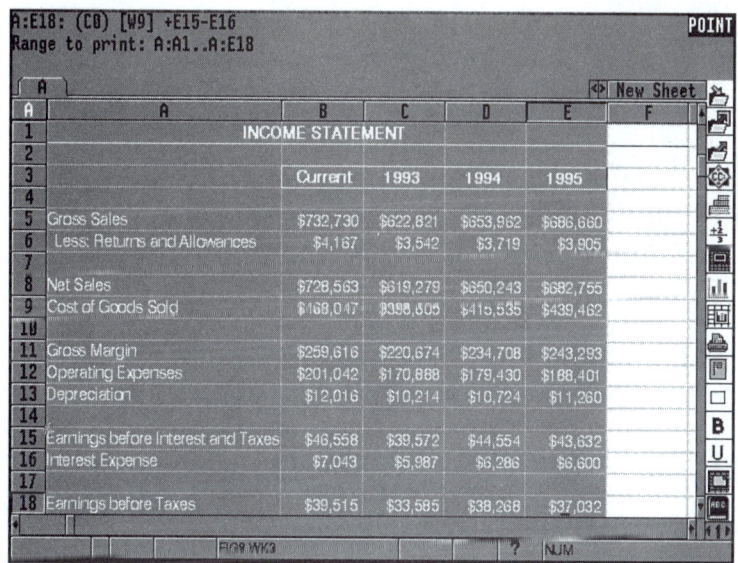

Fig. 2.77
Specifying a print range with the **:P**rint **R**ange **S**et command.

Previewing the Print Range On-Screen

The **:P**rint **P**review option gives you an idea of what a worksheet will look like when it is printed. This option displays a print range one page at a time. Press any key to display subsequent pages and to return to the **:P**rint menu. Although you probably will not be able to read every character on-screen, you can see the overall page layout and page breaks. For easy previewing of a print range, click the Print Preview SmartIcon. Figure 2.78 shows an example of a previewed page on-screen.

Fig. 2.78
Previewing a print range on-screen.

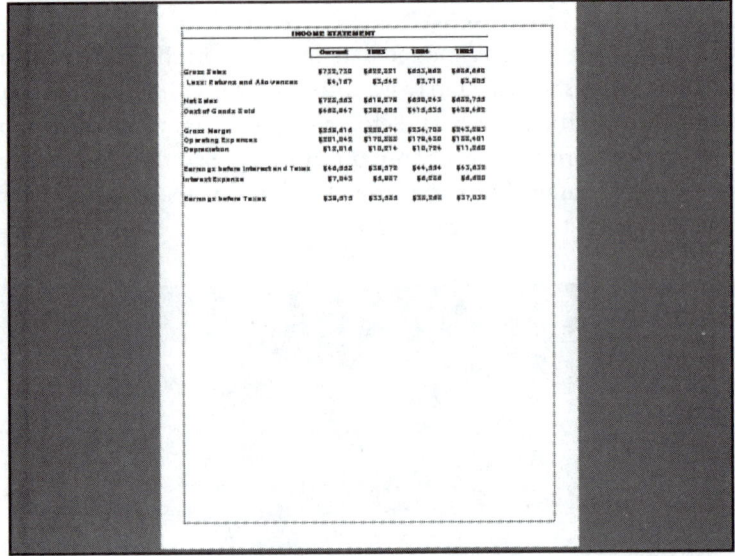

Printing a Report

After you specify the range that you want to print, choose **G**o from the **:P**rint menu to print the report. If the selected range exceeds the width and length of the page, 1-2-3 prints the left part of the range from top to bottom and then prints the right part of the range from top to bottom until the entire range is printed. The dashed lines on-screen show where the page breaks occur.

Figure 2.77 shows the selected range to be printed, and figure 2.79 shows the resulting report.

Fig. 2.79
The printed report.

INCOME STATEMENT				
	Current	1993	1994	1995
Gross Sales	$732,730	$622,821	$653,962	$686,660
Less: Returns and Allowances	$4,167	$3,542	$3,719	$3,905
Net Sales	$728,563	$619,279	$650,243	$682,755
Cost of Goods Sold	$468,947	$398,605	$415,535	$439,462
Gross Margin	$259,616	$220,674	$234,708	$243,293
Operating Expenses	$201,042	$170,888	$179,430	$188,401
Depreciation	$12,016	$10,214	$10,724	$11,260
Earnings before Interest and Taxes	$46,558	$39,572	$44,554	$43,632
Interest Expense	$7,043	$5,987	$6,286	$6,600
Earnings before Taxes	$39,515	$33,585	$38,268	$37,032

After you choose **G**o, you can choose **Q**uit to return to READY mode.

You also can use the Print SmartIcon to print a selected range. Simply click the Print SmartIcon; 1-2-3 prints the range.

Creating Simple Graphs

A basic graph requires only a small amount of data, such as that shown in the sales worksheet in figure 2.80. The first step in creating a graph is to decide which numeric data to plot and which data (numeric or label) to use to enhance the graph. In figure 2.80, time-period labels are listed across row 6. Category identifiers are located in column A. The numeric information in rows 8 through 11 is suitable for graphing as data points.

1-2-3 includes two graph menus: the 1-2-3 **/G**raph menu and the Wysiwyg **:G**raph menu. The two menus serve different purposes. The **/G**raph commands are used to create a new graph and to modify the basic settings of the graph, such as the graph type, graph axes, and legends. The **:G**raph commands enable you to add the graph to the worksheet and to customize it with additional text and drawings. You also can use the **:G**raph commands to place a blank drawing area in the worksheet for creating freehand drawings.

This section explains how to use the **/G**raph commands to create a simple graph. Refer to Chapter 23, "Creating Effective Graphs," and Chapter 24, "Creating Power Graphs," to learn more about the **/G**raph commands. To learn how to use the **:G**raph commands, refer to Chapter 25, "Developing Business Presentations."

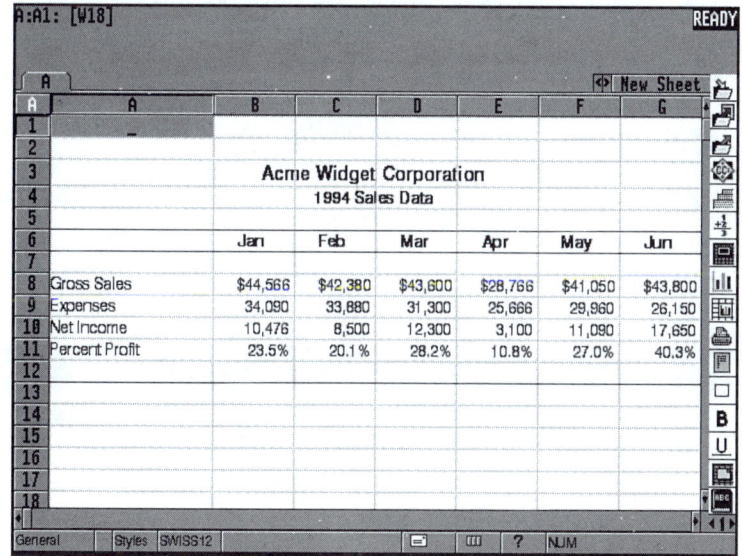

Fig. 2.80
A basic worksheet to be graphed.

144 Chapter 2—What Every 1-2-3 User Should Know

To create a graph from this worksheet, choose **/G**raph from the 1-2-3 main menu. The following **/G**raph menu appears:

Type **X A B C D E F R**eset **V**iew **S**ave **O**ptions **N**ame **G**roup **Q**uit

When you choose **/G**raph, 1-2-3 also displays the Graph Settings dialog box (see fig. 2.81). The settings sheet displays the options set for a graph, including data ranges and graph type. You can create a basic graph by choosing two options from the main **/G**raph menu. You must indicate which **T**ype of graph you want (unless you want the default **L**ine graph), and you must define at least one data series from the choices **A**, **B**, **C**, **D**, **E**, and **F**. After you specify these two options, you can choose **V**iew to display the graph.

Fig. 2.81
The **/G**raph menu and the Graph Settings dialog box.

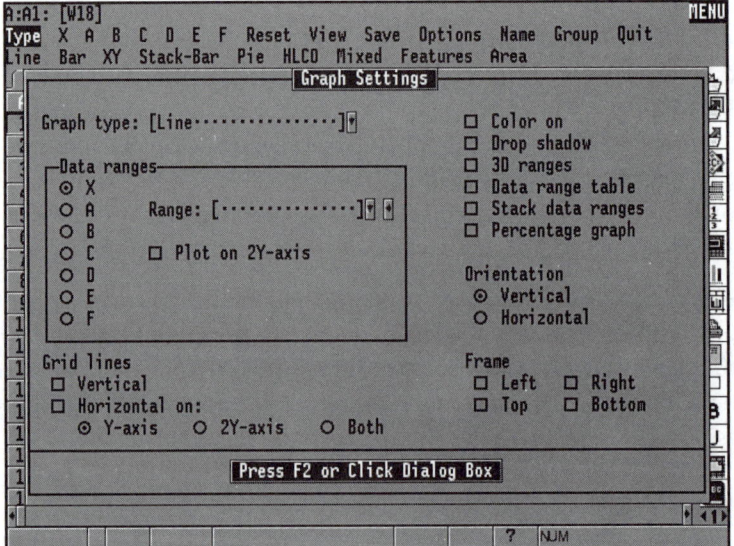

A, **B**, **C**, **D**, **E**, and **F** are data ranges plotted along the y-axis (the vertical axis). 1-2-3 can plot as many as six sets of data in a single graph. **X** defines the range for labels along the x-axis (the horizontal axis). Units of time (for example, months or years) usually are displayed on this axis. The **X** range defaults to a sequence of numbers, starting at 1 and increasing to number each data point in the range.

> **Note**
> To return to the worksheet when a graph is displayed, press any key.

To create a basic graph from the worksheet shown in figure 2.80, issue the following command sequences (after each range specification, press Enter):

/Graph **T**ype **B**ar

A A:B8..A:G8 (Gross Sales: data range A)

B A:B9..A:G9 (Expenses: data range B)

View

The result is a basic graph that depicts relationships between numbers or trends over time (see fig. 2.82).

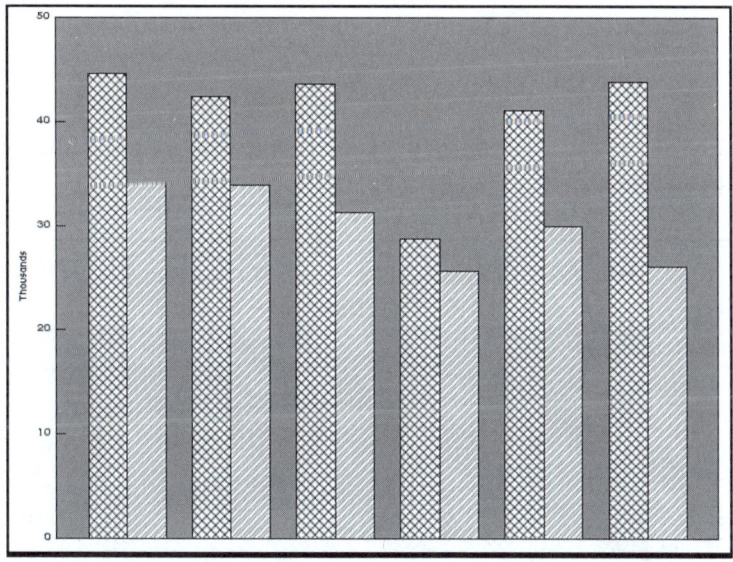

Fig. 2.82
A basic 1-2-3 graph.

In figure 2.82, the six sets of bars represent monthly data. The bars are graphed in order from left to right, starting with the January data. Within each set of bars, the left bar represents the Gross Sales figure and the right bar represents the corresponding Expenses figure. The graph doesn't give you this information, however, and therefore isn't yet complete.

1-2-3 has many options you can use to improve the appearance of your graphs and to produce labeled, final-quality output suitable for business presentations. (These options are explained in detail in Chapter 23, "Creating Effective Graphs.") To add more information to the sample graph and to improve its appearance, choose the following commands from the **/G**raph menu (press Enter after each range or text specification):

146 Chapter 2—What Every 1-2-3 User Should Know

> **X A:B6..A:G6** (monthly headings below x-axis)
>
> **O**ptions **T**itles **F**irst **ACME WIDGET CORP**.
>
> **T**itles **S**econd **1994 Sales Data, Jan - June**
>
> **T**itles **X**-Axis **East Coast Operations**
>
> **T**itles **Y**-Axis **Dollars**
>
> **L**egend **A Gross Sales**
>
> **L**egend **B Expenses**
>
> **G**rid **H**orizontal
>
> **S**cale **Y**-Scale **F**ormat **C**urrency **0** (decimal places)
>
> **Q**uit **Q**uit **V**iew

Figure 2.83 shows the resulting graph. Even people who are unfamiliar with the data can understand an enhanced graph such as this.

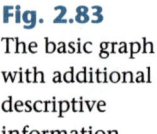
Fig. 2.83
The basic graph with additional descriptive information.

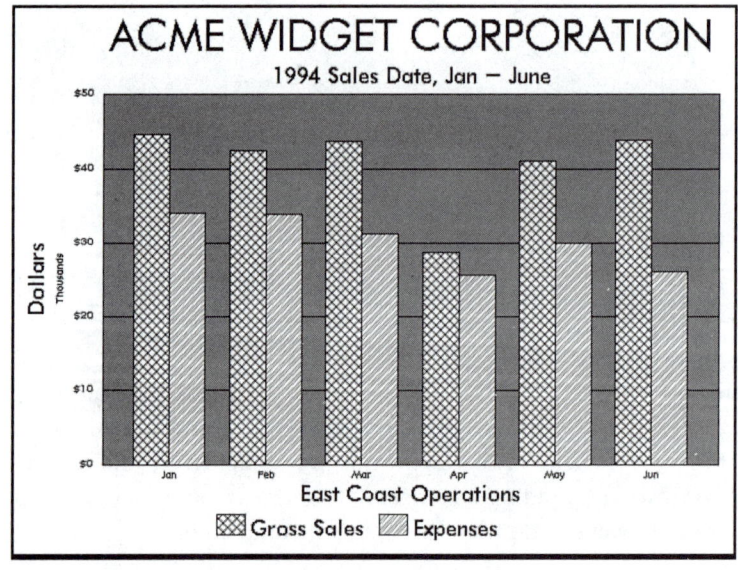

Selecting a Graph Type

The **T**ype option in the **/G**raph menu enables you to choose one of the 1-2-3 graph types. Choosing **T**ype displays the following menu:

Line **B**ar **X**Y **S**tack-Bar **P**ie **H**LCO **M**ixed **F**eatures **A**rea

All these options (except the **F**eatures option) set the listed graph type and automatically return 1-2-3 to the **/G**raph menu. The **F**eatures option displays an additional menu that contains a variety of options for the selected graph type (see Chapter 23, "Creating Effective Graphs"). The combination of the eight basic graph types and the **F**eatures option gives you extensive flexibility in designing a graph.

All the major 1-2-3 graph types except the pie graph display x- and y-axes. Line, bar, stacked-bar, HLCO (high-low-close-open), mixed, and area graphs display numbers along the y-axis based on the range of the data being graphed. The x-axis of these graph types can display labels centered on the x-axis tick marks. The XY graph displays numbers on both axes. The eight graph types can present different types or amounts of data, or present different information about the data.

Line graphs show trends through a large number of data points. You can enter as many as six sets of data within ranges. 1-2-3 creates one graph line for each range; each point on a line represents one value in the range. The data points in each data range are marked by a unique symbol and/or color when graphed (see table 2.4).

Bar graphs, like line graphs, show trends and relationships among data, but this graph type is best used with fewer data points than in a line graph. Again, you can enter as many as six data ranges. 1-2-3 creates one set of bars for each range with each bar representing one value in the range. On a monochrome monitor, the bars for each data range are displayed with unique shading. On a color monitor, the bars are displayed with a unique color (limited by the number of colors possible on your hardware). Shading and screen colors are summarized in table 2.4.

XY graphs (also called *scatter graphs*) show the relationship between the data in the X range and other ranges specified. XY graphs often are used in conjunction with regression analysis. 1-2-3 creates one set of points for each dependent variable range. The data points for each data range are marked by a unique symbol when graphed. The symbols are the same as the **L**ine symbols shown in table 2.4.

A **S**tack-Bar graph is used when the specified ranges sum to a meaningful result. (For example, bars for profit and costs stacked on top of each other can show total revenue.) In a stacked-bar graph, multiple data ranges are stacked on top of each other, with the A range on the bottom. To use this graph type, follow the bar-graph instructions.

Only one data range series is entered to create a **P**ie graph. For each value in the range, 1-2-3 creates a pie *slice*. The **X** range describes each pie slice. (The **B** and **C** ranges control other graph attributes, such as shading, placement of pie slices, and display of labels.) A pie graph shows the relative properties or shares of each value in a range.

The **H**LCO (high-low-close-open) graph often is called a *stock-market graph*, but also can be used to show data points that represent a range of observations for a given period. The **A**, **B**, **C**, and **D** ranges specify (respectively) the high, low, closing, and opening values. The **E** range is used for the bars in the bottom portion of the graph, and the **F** range is used for the single graph line.

The **M**ixed graph is useful for combining different types of data—such as actual values and percentages—in the same graph. Mixed graphs combine bars and lines in a single graph. These graphs often use both the left and the right y-axes.

Area graphs are used to show trends in data over time, with the emphasis on totals. Area graphs use the **X** data range as the x-axis labels and the **A** through **F** ranges as the lines in the graph.

Table 2.4 shows each data range with the corresponding default assignments for line symbols, bar shading, and color.

Table 2.4 Graph Symbols and Shading

Data Range	Line-Graph Symbols	Bar-Graph B&W Shading	On-Screen Color
A	■		Red
B	◆		Green
C	▲		Blue
D	☐		Yellow
E	◇		Magenta
F	△		Light blue

Specifying Data Ranges

The data to be graphed must be present in the current worksheet, either as values or as the result of formula calculations. You also can use labels in the worksheet or add text with the **:G**raph **E**dit command (explained in Chapter 24, "Creating Power Graphs").

> **Note**
>
> Don't confuse the process of specifying data points (which are numeric) with adding text descriptions such as titles.

A graph *data range* consists of a rectangular range of numbers. As mentioned earlier, you must specify at least one data range in the currently displayed worksheet. If the range contains labels or blank cells, 1-2-3 gives these cells a value of zero.

If the data is in adjacent rows or columns, you can use 1-2-3's automatic graph feature to assign the data ranges. Otherwise, you must assign the data ranges manually, as described in the next section.

Specifying Data Ranges Manually

To specify a graph data range, first choose **A**, **B**, **C**, **D**, **E**, or **F** from the **/G**raph menu and then specify the range just as you do any other 1-2-3 range: by entering cell addresses or a range name, or by using the mouse or arrow keys in POINT mode.

The **X** data-range option is used for numeric data only with the XY graph type. For the other graph types (except pie), this option is used to specify x-axis labels.

Specifying Data Ranges Automatically

In some circumstances, 1-2-3 can automatically perform some or all of the work of specifying data ranges for a graph. An *automatic graph* creates an entire graph with a single keystroke. A *graph group* enables you to specify multiple-graph data ranges in one step. The following sections describe these 1-2-3 features, which can be great time-savers.

Creating Automatic Graphs. 1-2-3's automatic-graph feature enables you to create certain types of graphs with a single keystroke. For an automatic graph, the position of the cell pointer—not the settings of the **/G**raph **X** and **/G**raph

150 Chapter 2—What Every 1-2-3 User Should Know

A through **F** options—determines which data is included in the graph. To create an automatic graph, make sure that your worksheet meets the following two conditions:

- No current graph exists. (You can clear the **/G**raph **X** and **A** through **F** settings with the **/G**raph **R**eset **R**anges command.)

- The cell pointer is in a section of the worksheet that can be interpreted as an automatic graph range (explained in this section).

If these conditions are satisfied, displaying an automatic graph requires only that you position the cell pointer anywhere within the worksheet data range and press Graph (F10) or choose **/G**raph **V**iew.

The following list describes the criteria for an automatic-graph range (many common arrangements of data in a worksheet meet these conditions):

- An automatic-graph range must contain data that can be divided—by rows or columns—into the X and the A through F ranges for the graph.

- An automatic-graph range must be separated from other data in the worksheet by at least two blank rows and columns.

- The data in an automatic-graph range must be arranged by columns or rows with the X data range first, the A data range second, the B data range third, and so on. The first row or column in the range can contain labels.

1-2-3 divides an automatic-graph range into rows or columns, depending on the setting of the **/W**orksheet **G**lobal **D**efault **G**raph command. Use **R**owwise when each data range is located in a row; use **C**olumnwise when each data range is in a column. The type of graph created depends on the setting of **/G**raph **T**ype; if no setting has been specified, 1-2-3 creates the default graph type (**L**ine). 1-2-3 makes data assignments as follows:

- The first column or row containing numbers is used as the A data range. (XY graphs use this column or row for the X data range.) Adjacent columns or rows are used for additional data ranges, in order from left to right or top to bottom. Labels in these ranges are treated as zeros.

■ For all graph types except XY, a column or row of labels *preceding* the first numeric data range is used as the X data range. This range must contain only labels. If no such column or row exists, no X range assignment is made.

An automatic graph makes use of all current **/G**raph menu selections, such as **T**ype, **F**eatures, and **O**ptions. The only part of an automatic graph that is "automatic" is the assignment of data ranges. After an automatic graph exists, you can treat it as you would any other graph—naming it, saving it, printing it, and so on.

Consider the worksheet shown in figure 2.84. The data in the range A:A2..A:D6 is a valid automatic-graph range. If **/W**orksheet **G**lobal **D**efault **G**raph **C**olumnwise is in effect (the default setting) and you chose **/G**raph **T**ype **B**ar, positioning the cell pointer anywhere in the range A:A2..A:D6 and pressing Graph (F10) displays the graph shown in figure 2.85. The other data ranges in figure 2.84 aren't valid automatic-graph ranges because they aren't separated from other worksheet data by at least two rows or columns.

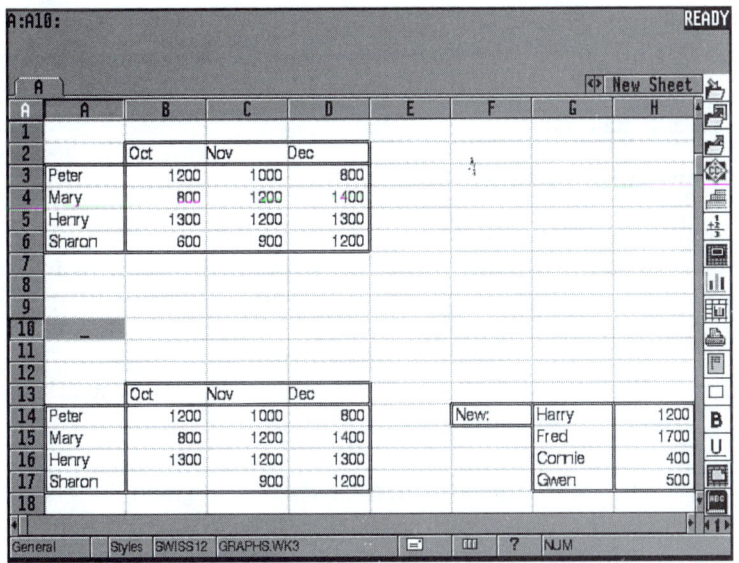

Fig. 2.84
Valid and invalid automatic-graph ranges.

Fig. 2.85
The graph created with 1-2-3's automatic-graph capability.

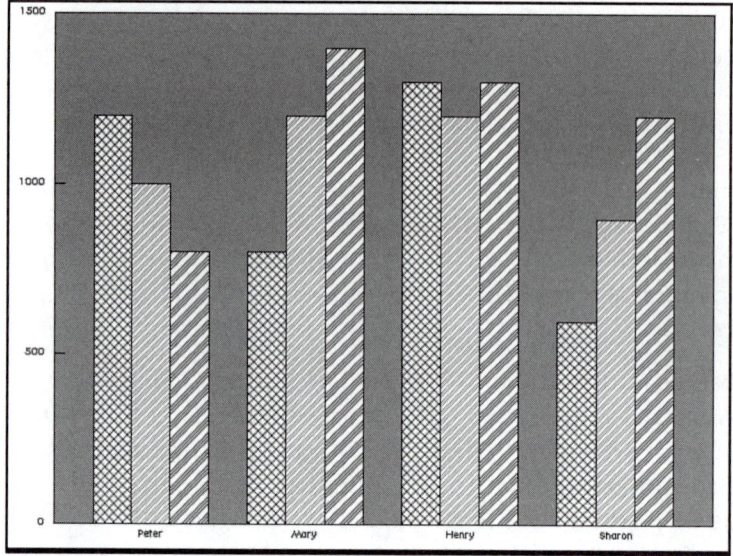

Using /Graph Group. You also can use the /Graph Group command when graph data ranges are in adjacent worksheet rows or columns. /Graph Group can save a significant number of keystrokes. The Group option enables you to specify all graph data ranges—X and A through F—in one operation. The procedure is as follows:

1. Choose /Graph Group.

2. Indicate the rectangular range to be divided into data ranges. You can enter cell addresses, enter a range name, or use the mouse or arrow keys in POINT mode. This range shouldn't include the data-range descriptions (that is, the legends).

3. Choose Columnwise or Rowwise to indicate whether the data ranges are located in columns or rows.

Consider the small worksheet shown in figure 2.86. To graph this data as rows in a bar graph, you first must set /Graph Type to Bar. In this figure, /Graph Group has been selected, and POINT mode is being used to indicate range A:B2..A:D5. When prompted, choose Rowwise, followed by View; the graph shown in figure 2.87 appears.

Creating Simple Graphs   153

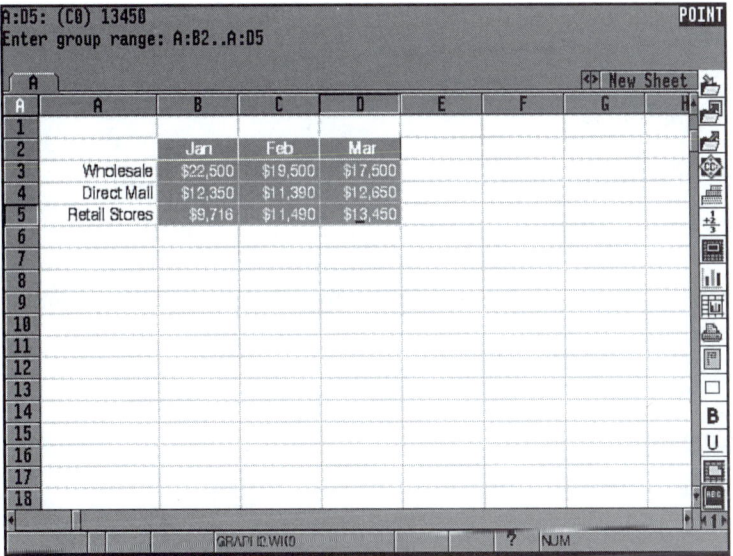

Fig. 2.86
A group range selected for graphing.

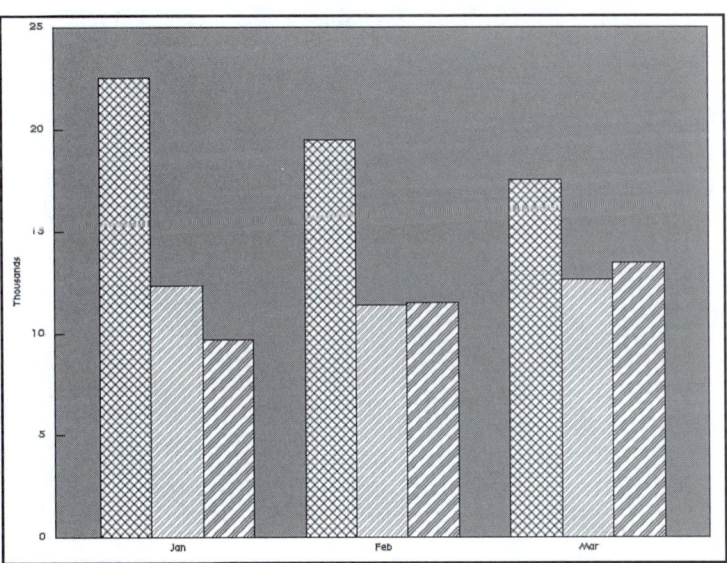

Fig. 2.87
A rowwise graph created from data shown in figure 2.86.

1-2-3 made the following data-range assignments automatically:

X A:B2..A:D2

A A:B3..A:D3

B A:B4..A:D4

C A:B5..A:D5

You can graph the same data as columns by using the following command sequence:

/Graph **G**roup A:A3..A:D5

Columnwise

View

Figure 2.88 shows the result.

Fig. 2.88
Group data graphed columnwise.

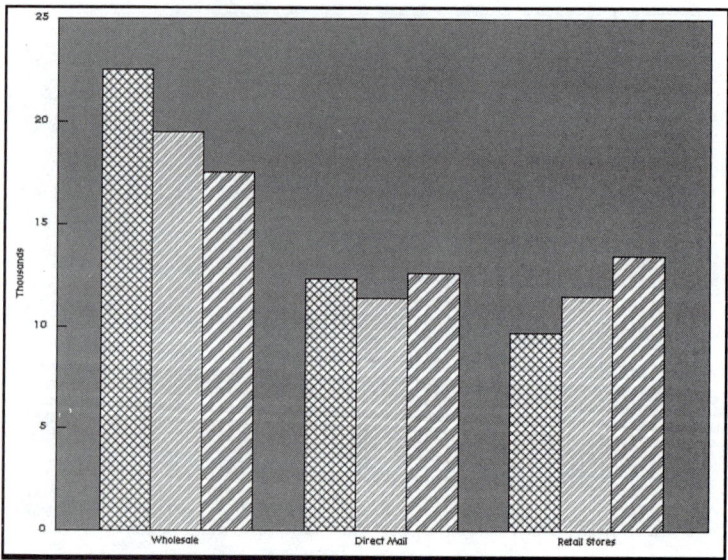

Using the QuickGraph Feature

 The QuickGraph feature works much like the **/G**raph **G**roup **C**olumnwise command. To use the QuickGraph feature, preselect the range of data for the graph and then click the QuickGraph SmartIcon. 1-2-3 displays the Quick-Graph Settings dialog box (see fig. 2.89), which is preset for a columnwise bar graph unless the default settings have been changed. Columns in the range correspond to the X through F ranges. Use the mouse or the keyboard to change the graph type or options as necessary or to select a rowwise graph. Click OK or press Enter to display the graph. The graph appears in full-screen view, as it would if you chose **V**iew from the **/G**raph menu. Press any key to return to READY mode.

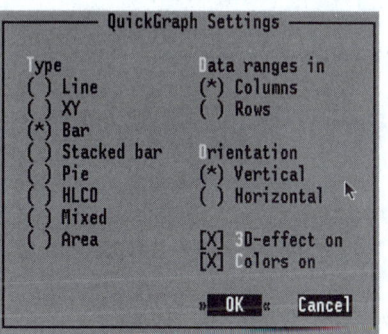

Fig. 2.89

The QuickGraph Settings dialog box appears when you click the QuickGraph SmartIcon.

Constructing the Default Line Graph

After you specify the type of graph you want and the location of the data, producing a graph is easy. Using the sales data shown in figure 2.80, you easily can create a line graph of the January through June amounts.

From 1-2-3's main menu, choose **/G**raph to access the **G**raph menu. Ordinarily, the next step is to choose **T**ype. If you want to create a line graph, however, you don't need to make a selection, because **L**ine is the default type.

The next step is to specify the data range(s). You first want to graph the Gross Sales amounts in row 8. To enter the first data range, choose **A** from the main **/G**raph menu, and respond to the prompt for a range by typing **A:B8..A:G8**. You also can use the mouse or arrow keys in POINT mode to specify the range or enter the range name (if one has been assigned).

By specifying the type of graph and the location of data to plot, you have completed the minimum requirements for creating a graph manually. If you choose **V**iew, you see a graph similar to the one shown in figure 2.90.

Although *you* know what this graph represents, it doesn't mean much to anyone else. The six data points corresponding to the figures for January through June have been plotted, but the points haven't been labeled to indicate what they represent, and the graph axes aren't labeled (except for the Thousands indicator on the y-axis). Notice also that the y-axis origin on this initial graph isn't zero, which makes the April decrease seem larger than it really is. To learn how to improve the appearance of graphs, see Chapter 23, "Creating Effective Graphs."

Fig. 2.90
A basic 1-2-3 line graph.

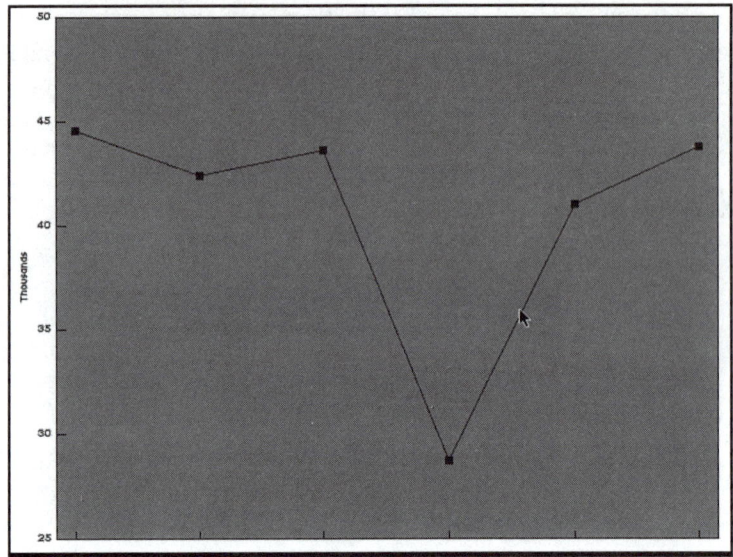

From Here...

For information related to the techniques you learned in this chapter, review the following chapters of this book:

- Chapter 3, "Finding Solutions with Formulas and Functions." This chapter shows you how to use 1-2-3's built-in functions to create complex calculations.

- Chapter 4, "Controlling Your Worksheet Display." Chapter 4 shows you how to change the way 1-2-3 displays worksheets on-screen.

- Chapter 6, "Making Your Worksheets Dazzle." In this chapter, you learn how to enhance the format of your worksheet.

- Chapter 8, "Printing Reports." Chapter 8 explains printing in more depth. You learn how to enhance reports by improving the layout, choosing fonts and colors, changing the line spacing, and so on.

- Chapter 10, "Organizing Your Data with Multiple-Worksheet Files." This chapter shows you how to move around and work in more than one worksheet at a time.

- Chapter 23, "Creating Effective Graphs." In Chapter 23, you learn more about the available graph types. You also learn how to add labels, alter the default graph display, specify colors and hatches, set text attributes, and save graphs.

Chapter 3
Finding Solutions with Formulas and Functions

This chapter describes the basic steps for using 1-2-3 functions and then provides discussions and examples of specific functions. In this chapter, you learn how to do the following:

- Enter functions in a formula
- Use the mathematical, date and time, financial, accounting, statistical, logical, and string functions
- Use functions that provide information about cell or range contents or about worksheet location
- Control the way 1-2-3 calculates your worksheet

In addition to the worksheet formulas you can create, you can take advantage of a variety of ready-made formulas provided by 1-2-3. These built-in formulas—called *functions*—enable you to take advantage of 1-2-3's analytical capability. You can use functions by themselves, in formulas with mathematical operators, or in macros and advanced macro command programs to calculate results and solve problems.

1-2-3 provides you with functions in the following categories:

- Mathematical
- Date and time
- Financial and accounting
- Statistical

- Database
- Logical
- String
- Special

The *general mathematical, logarithmic, and trigonometric functions* are useful in engineering and scientific applications. These functions are also handy for performing a variety of standard arithmetic operations, such as rounding values or calculating square roots.

The *date and time functions* convert dates, such as November 26, 1995, and times, such as 6:00 p.m., to serial numbers. (1-2-3 assigns a serial number to each of the 73,050 days from January 1, 1900 through December 31, 2099. The serial number 5, for example, corresponds to January 5, 1900, and the serial number 34588 corresponds to September 11, 1994.) You then can use the serial numbers to perform date and time arithmetic. These functions are useful when dates and times affect calculations and logic in worksheets.

The *financial and accounting functions* perform a variety of business-related calculations. These calculations include discounting cash flows, calculating depreciation, and analyzing the return on investments. These functions help you perform investment analysis and a variety of accounting tasks, including finding the value of depreciable assets.

A set of *statistical and database statistical functions* rounds out the data analysis capabilities of 1-2-3. These functions perform all the standard statistical calculations on data in a worksheet or in a 1-2-3 database. You can find minimum and maximum values, calculate averages, and compute standard deviations and variances. (In some cases, the database statistical functions are considered a separate function type; in practice, however, they are used as specialized versions of the statistical functions and are applied to 1-2-3 databases.)

Database functions perform, in one simple formula, calculations that would otherwise require several mathematical processes. Among other uses, these functions can find the number of items in a list, sum the items, and find the minimum, maximum, standard deviation, variance, and average of the items. The database functions are covered in Chapter 15, "Using Functions To Analyze Data."

With the *logical functions*, you can add standard Boolean logic to worksheets and use the logic either alone or as part of other worksheet formulas. Essentially, each of the logical functions can test whether a condition—one that you have defined or one of 1-2-3's predefined conditions—is true or false. These logical tests are important for using functions that make decisions; the function or its result acts one way or another, depending on a condition elsewhere in the worksheet.

Another set of 1-2-3 functions is the *string functions*, which manipulate text. You can use string functions to repeat text characters, to convert letters in a string to upper- or lowercase, to change strings into numbers, and to change numbers into strings. String functions also can be important when you convert data for use by other programs, such as word processing mailing lists.

Finally, the *special functions* deal with the worksheet. One special function, for example, returns information about specific cells. Other special functions count the number of rows, columns, or worksheets in a range.

Entering Functions

To enter a 1-2-3 function into a worksheet, follow this four-step process:

1. With 1-2-3 in either READY, VALUE, or EDIT mode, type the @ sign to tell 1-2-3 that you want to enter a function. (If you are already in the middle of entering a label, 1-2-3 treats an @ sign like any other character.)

2. Type the function name.

3. If the function requires arguments, type an open parenthesis, type the argument or arguments (separate two or more arguments with commas), and type a close parenthesis.

4. Press Enter.

An example of a function is @AVG. If you type the function **@AVG(1,2,3)**, 1-2-3 returns the calculated result 2, which is the average of the three numbers 1, 2, and 3.

All functions begin with (and are identified by) the @ character. In effect, by typing @ you tell 1-2-3 that you are entering a function.

The next step is to enter the name of the function. 1-2-3 helps you remember the name of the appropriate function by using easy-to-remember abbreviations for frequently used functions. The function to calculate the average, a statistical function, for example, is @AVG; the function to calculate the internal rate of return, a financial function, is @IRR; and the function to round numbers, a mathematical function, is @ROUND.

Tip
To get help from 1-2-3 in selecting a function, type the @ symbol, and then press F3 (Name) twice. 1-2-3 shows a full-screen display of all functions. To select a function from the list, highlight the function, and press Enter or click the function with the mouse.

After typing @ and the function name, enter any of the arguments or inputs the function needs to perform its calculations. You place a function's arguments inside parentheses that immediately follow the function's name. If the function has multiple arguments, you separate them with commas. You also can use a semicolon to separate function arguments; 1-2-3 automatically converts semicolons to commas.

Entering functions is straightforward. Suppose that you want to calculate the average monthly revenue from four products. To calculate the result, type the following:

@AVG(1000,5000,6000,8000)

1-2-3 returns 5000, which is the average of the numbers entered as arguments. Again, the function begins with the @ character, followed by the function name AVG, and the function's arguments are included inside parentheses and separated by commas.

In the preceding example, the arguments use actual numeric values. You also can use cell addresses and range names as arguments. If you store, for example, the monthly revenue values of these products or the formulas that produce these revenue values in worksheet cells B1, B6, B11, and B16, you can type the following function:

@AVG(B1,B6,B11,B16)

Or if you name each of the four cells that contain the revenue values or formulas with each product's name or product number, you can type the following function:

@AVG(PART12,PART14,PART21,PART22)

If the values you want to average are in adjacent cells (for example, B1, B2, B3, and B4) you can average the values by using the range of cells as the argument for the @AVG function: @AVG(B1..B4). If you assign a range name, such as REVENUES, to the range B1..B4, you can use that name as the argument, as in the following example:

@AVG(REVENUES)

Some functions do not require arguments or inputs, so you don't use parentheses. The mathematical function @PI, for example, returns the value of π (approximately 3.1415926536). The @RAND function produces a random number between 0 and 1.

◄ "Selecting Ranges," p. 81

▶ "Printing a Listing of Cell Contents," p. 387

> **Troubleshooting**
>
> *1-2-3 displays text when a function is entered in a cell.*
>
> 1-2-3 does not recognize a function unless it is preceded by the @ symbol. If you enter SUM(D3..K3), for example, 1-2-3 thinks that this entry is text. To correct the problem, edit the cell by pressing Edit (F2) and then Home to move the cursor to the beginning of the function. Delete the label prefix, insert the @ symbol, and then press Enter.
>
> *1-2-3 will not accept the entry of a function into a cell.*
>
> 1-2-3 has detected an error in the way the function was entered. When an error is detected in a formula with a function, 1-2-3 switches to EDIT mode and positions the cursor nearest to the part of the formula with the error if it knows what the error is. You can then make the necessary change to the formula and press Enter.
>
> If 1-2-3 cannot detect the error, the cursor is positioned at the end of the formula.

Using the Mathematical Functions

1-2-3's mathematical functions perform most common and some specialized mathematical operations. The operations you can perform include general mathematical, logarithmic, and trigonometric calculations.

Using General Mathematical Functions

1-2-3 offers six general mathematical functions. Table 3.1 summarizes these functions.

Table 3.1 General Mathematical Functions

Function	Description
@ABS(*number* or *cell_reference*)	Computes the absolute value of the argument
@INT(*number* or *cell_reference*)	Computes the integer portions of a specified number
@MOD(*number,divisor*)	Computes the remainder, or modulus, of a division operation
@ROUND(*number* or *cell_reference, precision*)	Rounds a number to a specified precision

(continues)

162 Chapter 3—Finding Solutions with Formulas and Functions

Table 3.1 Continued

Function	Description
@RAND	Generates a random number between 0 and 1
@SQRT(number or cell_reference)	Computes the square root of a number

@ABS—Computing Absolute Value

The @ABS function calculates the absolute value of a number. Use the following syntax for this function:

@ABS(*number* or *cell_reference*)

The @ABS function has one argument, which can be either a numeric value or a cell reference to a numeric value. The result of @ABS is the positive value of its argument. @ABS converts a negative value into its corresponding positive value. @ABS has no effect on positive values.

In figure 3.1, formulas in column E show the amount by which each test score in column C deviates from the average of the test scores. Whether a score is higher or lower doesn't matter. The object is to find those scores that differ greatly from the average. The formula in cell E5 is @ABS(:$C$13–C5), subtracting the value in cell C5 from the value in cell C13 and removing the minus sign if there is one. This shows the "raw" difference between the two values.

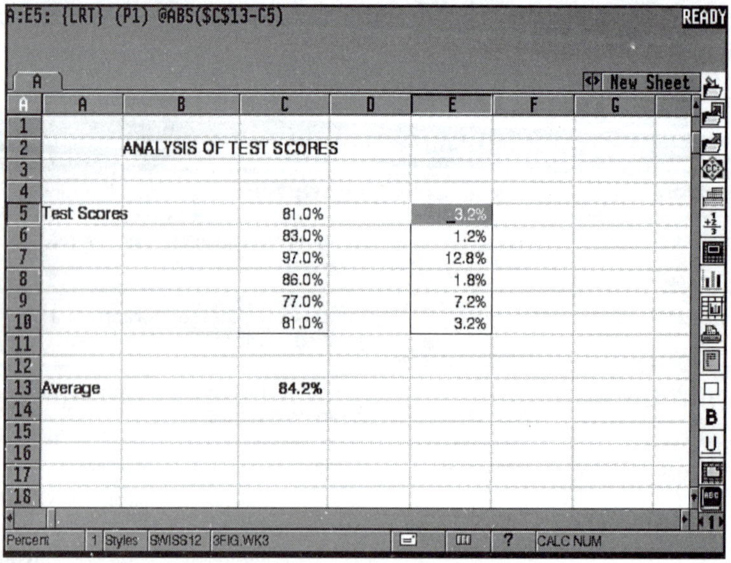

Fig. 3.1
@ABS returns the positive value of both positive and negative numbers.

@INT—Computing the Integer

The @INT function converts a decimal number into an integer, or whole number. @INT doesn't round the number but strips off the decimal portion of the number, if any. @INT uses the following syntax:

@INT(*number* or *cell_reference*)

@INT has one argument, which can be either a numeric value or a cell reference to a numeric value. @INT(3.1) returns 3, but @INT(3.9) also returns 3.

@INT is useful for computations in which the decimal portion of a number is irrelevant or insignificant. Suppose that you have $1,000 to invest in XYZ company and that shares of XYZ sell for $17 each. You divide 1,000 by 17 to compute the total number of shares that can be purchased. 1,000 divided by 17 is approximately 58.824. Because you cannot purchase a fractional share, you can use @INT to truncate the decimal portion. In figure 3.2, cell E6 uses @INT(E3/E4) to compute the number of shares you can buy with $1,000, (which is 58 shares). Cell E7 multiplies cell E4 by cell E6 to compute the cost of 58 shares, which is $986.

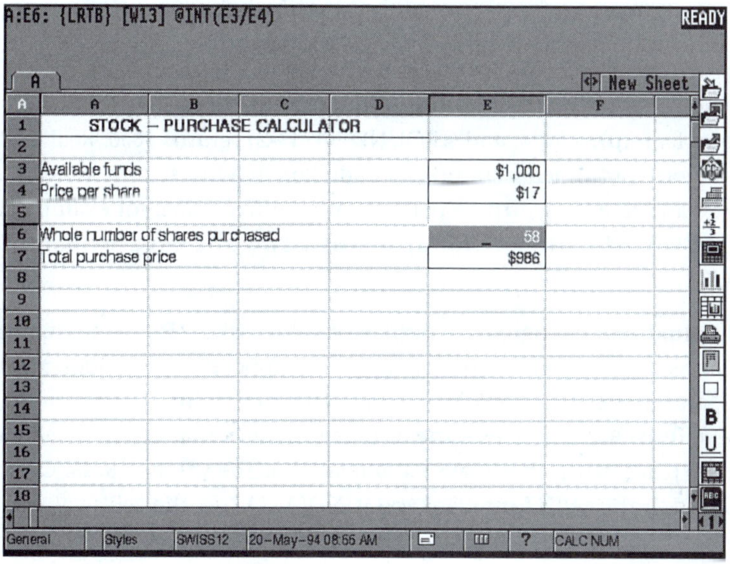

Fig. 3.2
@INT drops the fractional portion of a number.

@MOD—Finding the Modulus or Remainder

The @MOD function computes the remainder, or *modulus*, that results when one number is divided by another. For example, 25 divided by 4 leaves a remainder of 1, so @MOD(25,4) returns 1.

@MOD uses two arguments that can be either numeric values or cell references. The @MOD function uses the following syntax:

@MOD(*number,divisor*)

The sign of the *number* argument determines the sign of the function's result. @MOD(–25,4) returns -1, but @MOD(25,–4) returns 1. The argument returns ERR if the *divisor* argument is zero.

@ROUND—Rounding Numbers

The @ROUND function rounds values to a precision you specify. The function uses two arguments: the value you want to round and the precision you want to use in the rounding. @ROUND uses the following syntax:

@ROUND(*number* or *cell_reference,precision*)

The *precision* argument determines the number of decimal places and can be a numeric value between –100 and +100. A value of 0 rounds the number to the nearest integer. @ROUND(3.1,0) returns 3; @ROUND(3.9,0) returns 4. Use positive precision values to specify digits to the right of the decimal place; use 1 to round to the nearest 10th, 2 to round to the nearest 100th, and so on.

Use negative values to specify places to the left of the decimal place; –1 rounds to the nearest 10, –2 rounds to the nearest 100. @ROUND(3471,–1), for example, returns 3470, and @ROUND(3471,–2) returns 3500. Real estate prices are often rounded to hundreds of dollars. If a house now sells for $201,500 and may be worth 15 percent more in five years, for example, the formula @ROUND(201500*1.15,–2) returns $231,700—a more useful figure than $231,725.

Keep in mind that changing the display of values with **/R**ange **F**ormat is not the same as rounding values with @ROUND. Suppose a cell divides cell A1 by cell A2, and that cell A1 contains 25 and cell A2 contains 4. The formula +A1/A2 returns 6.25. If you set the display format of that cell to **F**ixed with **1** decimal place, the cell displays 6.3 but still has the value of 6.25. On the other hand, if the cell's formula is @ROUND(A1/A2,1), the cell's value really is 6.3.

This discrepancy can cause errors of thousands of dollars in worksheets that calculate mortgage tables. To prevent such errors, use @ROUND to round the results of intermediate formulas before totaling the formulas.

@RAND—Producing Random Numbers

You use the @RAND function to generate random numbers. The function requires no arguments and uses the following syntax:

   @RAND

@RAND returns a randomly generated number between 0 and 1, to a precision of 17 decimal places. If you want a random number greater than 1, multiply the @RAND function by the maximum random number you want. If you want a random number within a range of numbers, use a formula similar to the following:

   +10+@RAND*20

In the preceding example, the random numbers generated are greater than 10 and less than 20. If you need random integers, enclose random number calculations in an @INT function. New random numbers are generated each time you recalculate. To see the results from new random numbers, press F9 (Calc).

@SQRT—Calculating the Square Root

The @SQRT function calculates the square root of a positive number. The function uses one argument, the number whose square root you want to find. @SQRT uses the following syntax:

   @SQRT(*number* or *cell_reference*)

The value must be either a nonnegative numeric value or a cell reference to such a value. If the argument is a negative value, the function returns ERR.

   @SQRT(4) returns 2.

   @SQRT(C15), where cell C15 contains the value 2, returns approximately 1.414.

   @SQRT(DATA1), where DATA1 is the name of a cell that is empty, contains a character string, or contains the value 0, returns 0.

   @SQRT(C15), where cell C15 contains a negative number, returns ERR.

Using Logarithmic Functions

1-2-3 has three logarithmic functions—@LOG, @EXP, and @LN. Each of these functions has one argument, which can be a numeric value or a cell reference to a numeric value. Table 3.2 lists and describes these functions.

Table 3.2 Logarithmic Functions

Function	Description
@LOG(*number* or *cell_reference*)	Calculates the common, or base 10, logarithm of a specified number
@EXP(*number* or *cell_reference*)	Computes the number *e* raised to the power of the argument
@LN(*number* or *cell_reference*)	Calculates the natural logarithm of a specified number

@LOG—Computing Logarithms

The @LOG function computes the base 10 logarithm. @LOG uses the following syntax:

@LOG(*number* or *cell_reference*)

If you use a negative value with this function, the function returns ERR.

@LOG(*x*) answers the question "To what power do I raise 10 to get the value *x*?" @LOG(1000) returns 3 because raising 10 to the third power results in 1000. Logs of values between 1000 and the next whole power of 10 (10,000) are 3 plus a fractional portion. @LOG(9873) returns approximately `3.994449`. @LOG(10000) returns `4`.

@EXP—Finding Powers of *e*

The @EXP function raises the natural number *e* (approximately 2.718282) to a power. Use the following syntax:

@EXP(*number* or *cell_reference*)

@EXP(10), for example, returns e to the 10th power, or approximately `22026.46579`.

If you use a number higher than 230 as the argument, 1-2-3 computes an undisplayable result and fills the cell with asterisks. 1-2-3 stores the result of this computation internally, however, and other formulas can refer to the cell that displays the asterisks. If you use a number higher than 460 as the argument, @EXP computes a number too large for 1-2-3 to store.

@LN—Computing Natural Logarithms

@LN is similar to @LOG, except that it computes the natural, or base *e*, logarithm (approximately 2.718282). @LN uses the following syntax:

@LN(*number* or *cell_reference*)

@LN(*x*) answers the question "To what power is *e* raised to get *x*?" @LN(10), for example, returns 2.302585093. *e* to the power of 2.302585093 returns 10. If you use a negative argument with @LN, 1-2-3 returns ERR.

Using Trigonometric Functions

1-2-3 provides eight trigonometric functions for engineering and scientific applications. Table 3.3 lists the functions, their arguments, and the operations they perform.

Table 3.3 Trigonometric Functions

Function	Description
@PI	Calculates the value of π
@COS(*angle*)	Calculates the cosine, given an angle in radians
@SIN(*angle*)	Calculates the sine, given an angle in radians
@TAN(*angle*)	Calculates the tangent, given an angle in radians
@ACOS(*angle*)	Calculates the arccosine, given an angle in radians
@ASIN(*angle*)	Calculates the arcsine, given an angle in radians
@ATAN(*angle*)	Calculates the arctangent, given an angle in radians
@ATAN2(*number1*,*number2*)	Calculates the four-quadrant arctangent

@PI—Computing Pi

The @PI function results in the value of π. The function uses no arguments. Its syntax is simply @PI.

@PI returns the value 3.14159265358979324. Use @PI to calculate the areas of circles and the volumes of spheres. In addition, @PI converts angle measurements in degrees to angle measurements in radians.

@COS, @SIN, and @TAN—Computing Trigonometric Functions

The @COS, @SIN, and @TAN functions calculate the cosine, sine, and tangent, respectively, for an angle. Each function uses one argument—an angle measured in radians. Use the following syntaxes for the functions:

@COS(*angle*)

@SIN(*angle*)

@TAN(*angle*)

Be sure to convert angle measurements into radians before you use these functions. Because 2*π radians are in 360 degrees, you can calculate radian angles by multiplying the number of degrees by @PI and dividing by 180.

@ACOS, @ASIN, @ATAN, and @ATAN2—Computing Inverse Trigonometric Functions

The @ACOS, @ASIN, @ATAN, and @ATAN2 functions calculate the arccosine, the arcsine, the arctangent, and the four-quadrant arctangent, respectively. @ACOS computes the inverse of cosine; @ASIN computes the inverse of sine—a radian angle between $-\pi/2$ and $\pi/2$ (between –90 and +90 degrees). @ATAN computes the inverse of tangent—a radian angle between $-\pi/2$ and $\pi/2$ (between –90 and +90 degrees). @ATAN2 calculates the four-quadrant arc-tangent, using the ratio of its two arguments.

@ACOS and @ASIN each use one argument in the following syntaxes:

@ACOS(*angle*)

@ASIN(*angle*)

Because all cosine and sine values lie between –1 and 1, @ACOS and @ASIN work only with values between –1 and 1. Either function returns ERR if you use an argument outside this range. @ASIN returns angles between $-\pi/2$ and $+\pi/2$, whereas @ACOS returns angles between 0 and $\pi/2$.

Like @ACOS and @ASIN, the @ATAN function uses one argument. @ATAN can use any number and returns a value between $-\pi/2$ and $+\pi/2$. The syntax of @ATAN is the following:

@ATAN(*angle*)

@ATAN2 computes the angle whose tangent is specified by the ratio *number2/ number1*—the two arguments. At least one of the arguments must be a number other than zero. @ATAN2 returns radian angles between $-\pi$ and $+\pi$. Use the following syntax for @ATAN2:

@ATAN2(*number1,number2*)

Using Date and Time Functions

1-2-3's date and time functions convert dates, such as November 26, 1995, and times, such as 6:00 p.m., to serial numbers. You then can use the serial numbers in date arithmetic and time arithmetic, valuable tools when dates and times affect worksheet calculations and logic.

As you review the examples of 1-2-3's date and time functions, you will develop a better appreciation of their potential contributions to applications. The date and time functions available in 1-2-3 are summarized in table 3.4.

Table 3.4 Date and Time Functions

Function	Description
@D360(date1,date2)	Calculates the number of days between two dates, based on a 360-day year
@DATE(year,month,day)	Calculates the serial number that represents the described date
@DATEVALUE(date_string)	Converts a date expressed as a quoted string into a serial number
@DAY(date)	Extracts the day number from a serial number
@MONTH(date)	Extracts the month number from a serial number
@YEAR(date)	Extracts the year number from a serial number
@TIME(hour,minute,second)	Calculates the serial number representing the described time
@TIMEVALUE(time_string)	Converts a time expressed as a string into a serial number
@HOUR(time)	Extracts the hour number from a serial number
@MINUTE(time)	Extracts the minute number from a serial number
@SECOND(time)	Extracts the seconds from a serial number
@NOW	Calculates the serial date and time from the current system date and time
@TODAY	Calculates the serial number for the current system date

@D360—Dealing with 360-Day Years

The @D360 function calculates the number of days between two dates, based on a 360-day year. Both date arguments must be expressed as valid serial numbers; otherwise, the function returns ERR. @D360 uses the following syntax:

@D360(*date1,date2*)

The @D360 function proves helpful in cases where interest calculations are made by using a 360-day year. In figure 3.3, cell B12 uses @D360 to compute the days between the deposit and withdrawal of a sum for which interest is compounded daily.

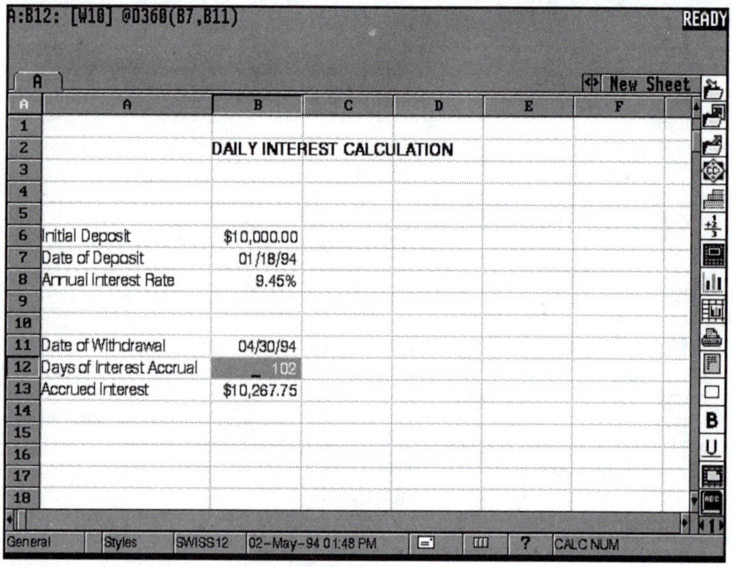

Fig. 3.3
@D360 computes the days between two dates based on a 360-day year.

	A	B
2	DAILY INTEREST CALCULATION	
6	Initial Deposit	$10,000.00
7	Date of Deposit	01/18/94
8	Annual Interest Rate	9.45%
11	Date of Withdrawal	04/30/94
12	Days of Interest Accrual	102
13	Accrued Interest	$10,267.75

Cell reference: A:B12: [W10] @D360(B7,B11)

@DATE—Converting Date Values to Serial Numbers

The first step in using dates in arithmetic operations is to convert the dates to serial numbers. You can then use the numbers in addition, subtraction, multiplication, and division operations. Probably the most frequently used date function is @DATE. This function converts three values, representing a year, a month, and a day, into a serial date number. @DATE uses the following syntax:

@DATE(*year,month,day*)

Each argument is an expression that 1-2-3 can treat as a value—a number, a reference to a cell containing a number, or a formula that evaluates to a number. @DATE(95,3,10) returns the serial value of March 10, 1995 as 34768.

@DATE returns ERR if the values of its arguments don't comprise a valid date. @DATE(95,4,31), for example, returns ERR because April has 30 days. So does @DATE(95,2,29) because 1995 is not a leap year. The year value must be between 0 and 199 (the number 100 represents the year 2000, 101 represents 2001, and so on). The month number must be between 1 and 12. The day number must be a number appropriate for the year and month numbers. If any of these values has a fractional portion, 1-2-3 just uses the integer portion; @DATE(95.75,5.01,31.3) is the same as @DATE(95,5,31).

To view the actual date that a certain number represents, assign one of the date formats to its cell. If a cell contains either the formula @DATE(95,3,10) or the value 34768, and its format is **Date 1**, the cell displays 10-Mar-95 (provided the cell is in a column wide enough to display this date format). If Wysiwyg is not attached or 1-2-3 is in TEXT mode, the column must be at least 10 characters wide to display the date in this format. In Wysiwyg the minimum width necessary to display this date format depends on the font used. The **/R**ange **F**ormat commands and the various **D**ate and **T**ime formats available are discussed in detail in Chapter 6, "Making Your Worksheets Dazzle."

> **Caution**
>
> All serial values for dates from March 1, 1900 to the end of the next century are off by 1.

1-2-3 assigns serial numbers between 1 and 73050 to the dates from January 1, 1900 through December 31, 2099. January 1, 1900, has a serial value of 1; January 2, 1900, has a serial value of 2; and so on. In a sense, most of those numbers are wrong. 1-2-3 treats February 29, 1900, as a valid date, even though 1900 wasn't a leap year. In reality, March 1, 1900, is the 60th day of the period beginning with January 1, 1900, but if a cell contains the number 60 and has the **Date 1** format, it displays 29-Feb-00. The number 61 is displayed as 01-Mar-00. All serial values for dates from March 1, 1900, to the end of the next century are off by 1.

In practice, this miscalculation shouldn't cause you any trouble. If you subtract one day from another, you get the correct number of days between the two dates, except in the unlikely event that only one of the dates occurs before March 1, 1900.

In figure 3.4, the formula in cell C15 computes two serial values based on values elsewhere in the worksheet and subtracts the earlier one from the later one to determine the number of elapsed days.

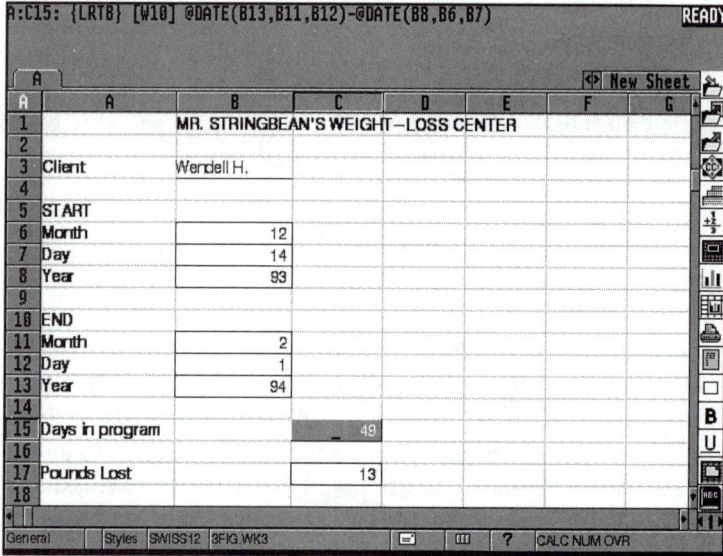

Fig. 3.4
The @DATE function, used to calculate elapsed days.

Although @DATE is useful for computing serial dates from year, month, and day values, it's not really the easiest way to enter a date into a worksheet. Release 3.4 and 4 turn entries into date values automatically where appropriate and possible. If you type the characters **3/10/95**, 1-2-3 turns the entry into the value 34768 when you press Enter. Unless the cell already has a date format (or the **A**utomatic format), the cell initially will display the value 34768 rather than the date.

@DATEVALUE—Changing Date Strings to Serial Numbers

@DATEVALUE converts a text string that resembles a date to a serial value. Its syntax is

@DATEVALUE(*date_string*)

Date_string can be a string in quotes, a reference to a cell that contains a label or string-returning formula, or an expression that evaluates to a character string. The string must resemble one of the date formats that 1-2-3 displays.

The following date formats all return the date serial number 34768:

@DATEVALUE("3/10/95")

@DATEVALUE("10-Mar-95")

@DATEVALUE(B15)   (if cell B15 contains the label '3/10/95 or '10-Mar-95)

@DATEVALUE("3/10")   (if the year of the computer's system date is 1995)

@DATEVALUE("10-Mar")   (if the year of the computer's system date is 1995)

You also can use just the month and year in the format MM-YY to get the serial value of the first day of the month. The formula **@DATEVALUE("Mar95")** returns the value 34768, the serial value of March 1, 1995.

> **Note**
>
> The 10-Mar-95 format always works, but the 3/10/95 format works only if 1-2-3 is configured so that **I**nternational **D**ate formats display dates as MM/DD/YY. If you have changed 1-2-3 to use DD/MM/YY (using the **/W**orksheet **G**lobal **D**efault **O**ther **I**nternational **D**ate commands), you must type **@DATEVALUE("3/10/95")** to get the serial value 34768.

You can use @DATEVALUE to convert dates imported into 1-2-3 as text strings to their date-value equivalents.

@DAY, @MONTH, and @YEAR—Converting Serial Numbers to Dates

The @DAY, @MONTH, and @YEAR functions extract the day, month, and year values from serial date values. These functions use the following respective syntaxes:

@DAY(*date*)

@MONTH(*date*)

@YEAR(*date*)

Date can be any number from 1 to 73050 or any expression that evaluates to such a number.

@DAY extracts the day-of-the-month number from a date value. If you use the serial value of 34768 (for March 10, 1995) with @DAY(34768), for example, it returns 10.

@MONTH extracts the month number. @MONTH(34768) returns 3.

@YEAR extracts the year number. @YEAR(34768) returns 95. For dates in the 21st century, @YEAR returns numbers between 100 and 199. @YEAR(36526) returns 100 (36526 is the serial value of January 1, 2000).

@TIME—Converting Time Values to Serial Numbers

Just as 1-2-3 represents dates as numbers from 1 to 73050, it represents times as numbers between 0 (inclusive) and 1 (exclusive). The value 0 represents midnight. The value .25 represents 6:00 a.m. because 6:00 a.m. is one-quarter of the way through a 24-hour day. The value .5 represents noon, and the value .75 represents 6:00 p.m. 12:01 a.m. has a time value of approximately .000694. 11:59 p.m. has a time value of approximately .9993.

The @TIME function produces a serial number for a specified time of day. @TIME uses the following syntax:

@TIME(*hour,minute,second*)

Use the 24-hour system when specifying the hour. Use @TIME(6,0,0), for example, for the serial value of 6:00 a.m. and use @TIME(18,0,0) for the serial value of 6:00 p.m.

When entering an @TIME formula, be aware that the *hour* number must be between 0 and 23, and both the *minute* and *second* number must be between 0 and 59. Finally, although 1-2-3 accepts numeric arguments that contain integers and decimals, it uses only the integer portion.

After you have used @TIME to compute a serial value, you can make 1-2-3 display the value as a time by applying a TIME format to its cell. If you type **@TIME(15,13,20)** in a cell, for example, the formula returns 0.634259259. If you select **/R**ange **F**ormat **D**ate **T**ime **1**, specify that cell and widen its column to at least 12 characters, the cell displays 03:13:20 PM. (The **/R**ange **F**ormat commands and the various **D**ate and **T**ime formats available are discussed in detail in Chapter 6, "Making Your Worksheets Dazzle.")

@TIMEVALUE—Converting Time Strings to Serial Values

Like @DATEVALUE, the @TIMEVALUE function converts character strings to serial values. Its syntax is

@TIMEVALUE(*time_string*)

The *time_string* argument can be text in quotes or an expression that evaluates to a character string. The character string must resemble one of the time formats that 1-2-3 displays. The following examples all return the serial value .75:

@TIMEVALUE("6:00:00 PM")

@TIMEVALUE("18:00:00")

@TIMEVALUE(B15)   (where B15 contains the label '6:00:00 PM or '18:00:00)

@TIMEVALUE("6:00 PM")

@TIMEVALUE("18:00")

> **Note**
>
> If you use 24-hour times in these strings, you should use colons only if 1-2-3 is set to display international times as HH:MM:SS. If you reconfigure 1-2-3 so that it displays international times as, for example, HH.MM.SS, use periods in the *time_string* argument of @TIMEVALUE—for example, type **@TIMEVALUE("18.00.00")**.

@HOUR, @MINUTE, and @SECOND—Converting Serial Numbers to Time Values

With the @HOUR, @MINUTE, and @SECOND functions, you can extract the hour value, the minute value, and the second value from serial numbers. These functions use the following syntax, respectively:

@HOUR(*time*)

@MINUTE(*time*)

@SECOND(*time*)

The *time* argument can be any positive value. These functions only consider the fractional portion of the value.

Consider the number 0.29458333, the serial value of 7:04:12 AM. @HOUR extracts the hours portion of that number: @HOUR(0.29458333) returns 7. The result of the @HOUR function is based on 24-hour time; @HOUR(0.79448333) returns 19. @MINUTE extracts the minutes portion: @MINUTE(0.29458333) returns 4. @SECOND extracts the seconds portion: @SECOND(0.29458333) returns 12.

@NOW and @TODAY—Finding the Current Date and Time

1-2-3 provides two functions, @NOW and @TODAY, that return values from the computer's system clock. @TODAY is the simpler of the two; it returns an integer that represents the current date. If the date is March 10, 1995 (and the system clock is set correctly), @TODAY returns 34768. As with the @DATE function, you can display this value as a date by assigning a date format to its cell.

You can combine @TODAY with other date functions. If the computer's system date is a date in 1995, for example, @YEAR(@TODAY) returns 95.

After you enter a formula by using the @TODAY function, the formula reflects the system date as of the time you enter it. If you have /**W**orksheet **G**lobal **R**ecalc set to **M**anual, a formula using @TODAY doesn't change to the new date automatically if the system clock reaches midnight; instead, it changes when you either recalculate the worksheet or edit the cell that contains the @TODAY function. (If /**W**orksheet **G**lobal **R**ecalc is set to **A**utomatic, however, the formula changes to reflect a new day when you change a cell in any active worksheet file.)

If you retrieve a worksheet that contains a formula using @TODAY, the formula will not reflect the current date initially. If /**W**orksheet **G**lobal **R**ecalc is set to **A**utomatic, the formula adjusts when you change any cell in the worksheet. If /**W**orksheet **G**lobal **R**ecalc is set to **M**anual, you must recalculate the worksheet to update the formula using @TODAY.

@NOW returns the exact time, as well as the date, of the system clock. @NOW requires no arguments. At exactly noon on March 10, 1995, the value of @NOW is 34768.5. At five seconds after noon on that date, @NOW returns 34768.500057870. As with the @TIME function, you can display the value of @NOW as a time by assigning a time format to its cell.

You can combine @NOW with other time functions. @HOUR(@NOW), for example, returns the current hour value of the system clock.

The value of @NOW changes all the time, of course, but the displayed result doesn't change to reflect the current time until you recalculate the worksheet (if **/W**orksheet **G**lobal **R**ecalc is set to **M**anual) or until you change another cell (if **/W**orksheet **G**lobal **R**ecalc is set to **A**utomatic).

In some ways, @TODAY and @NOW are interchangeable. @MONTH(@TODAY) and @MONTH(@NOW), for example, both return the month value of the system clock. In some cases, however, you must use @NOW, particularly with other time functions. @HOUR(@TODAY) always returns 0 because @TODAY returns an integer. You must use @HOUR(@NOW) rather than @HOUR(@TODAY). In other cases, @TODAY is preferable. To compute the number of days between the current date and an earlier date, use @TODAY-@DATE(92,11,3). @NOW-@DATE(92,11,3) returns a number with a fractional portion. When @NOW-@DATE(92,11,3) is in a cell with the **F**ixed **0** format and the current time is later than noon, the formula displays too high a number.

You can use @TODAY and @NOW to time-stamp a worksheet. Selecting **/R**ange **V**alue freezes the formulas into unchanging values. Figure 3.5 shows a time-stamped worksheet. Cells C4 and E4 have the **D**ate **1** and **T**ime **2** formats, respectively. After entering new values in cells C12 and C13, type **@TODAY** in cell C4 and **@NOW** in cell E4. Then select **/R**ange **V**alue, specify range C4..E4 as the FROM range, and specify cell C4 as the TO range.

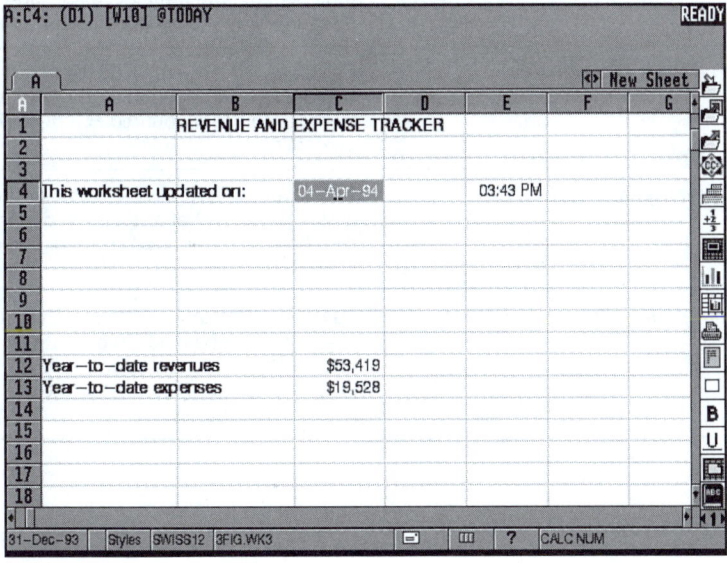

Fig. 3.5
Using @TODAY and @NOW to time-stamp a worksheet.

Chapter 3—Finding Solutions with Formulas and Functions

▶ "Setting Range and Worksheet Global Formats," p. 280

▶ "Date and Time Formats," p. 303

▶ "Automatic Format," p. 312

Using the Financial and Accounting Functions

1-2-3 provides 12 financial and accounting functions that calculate cash flow discounts, loan amortizations, and asset depreciations. The 1-2-3 financial functions include two functions that calculate return on investment (@IRR and @RATE); one, loan payments (@PMT); two, present value (@NPV and @PV); one, future value (@FV); two, compound growth (@TERM and @CTERM); and four, asset depreciation (@SLN, @DDB, @SYD, and @VDB). Table 3.5 summarizes the financial and accounting functions available in 1-2-3.

Table 3.5 Financial and Accounting Functions

Function	Description
@IRR(*guess,cashflows*)	Calculates the internal rate of return on an investment
@RATE(*future_value,present_value,term*)	Calculates the periodic return required to increase the present-value investment to the size of the future value in the length of time indicated (*term*)
@PMT(*principal,interest,term*)	Calculates the loan payment amount
@NPV(*interest,cashflows*)	Calculates the present value (today's value) of a stream of cash flows of uneven amounts, but at evenly spaced time periods, when the payments are discounted by the periodic interest rate
@PV(*payment,interest,term*)	Calculates the present value (today's value) a stream of periodic cash flows of even payments discounted at a periodic interest rate
@FV(*payment,interest,term*)	Calculates the future value (value at the end of payments) of a stream of periodic cash flows compounded at the periodic interest rate
@TERM(*payment,interest,future_value*)	Calculates the number of times an equal payment must be made in order to accumulate the future value when payments are compounded at the periodic interest rate

Function	Description
@CTERM(*interest,future_value, present_value*)	Calculates the number of periods required for the present-value amount to grow to a future-value amount given a periodic interest rate
@SLN(*cost,salvage,life*)	Calculates straight-line depreciation
@DDB(*cost,salvage,life,period*)	Calculates double declining-balance depreciation for a given period
@SYD(*cost,salvage,life,period*)	Calculates sum-of-the-years'-digits depreciation
@VDB(*cost,salvage,life,start, end,[depreciation],[switch]*)	Calculates the depreciation in a period, using a variable-rate declining-balance method

@IRR—Calculating Internal Rate of Return

The @IRR function calculates the internal rate of return on an investment. @IRR uses the following syntax:

@IRR(*guess,cashflows*)

The *guess* argument is a guess at the interest rate. You generally use a value between 0 and 1. *Cashflows* is a worksheet range containing the initial investment and the returns. Enter the investment as a negative value in the top left cell of the range. Fill the remaining cells of the range with positive values representing the amounts you expect the investment to return. 1-2-3 ignores empty cells in the range of cash flows and treats cells containing labels as zeros.

You should start the calculation with a guessed interest rate that is as accurate as possible. From this guess, 1-2-3 attempts to converge to a correct interest rate, with .0000001 precision within 20 iterations. If the program cannot do so, the @IRR function returns ERR. If this error message occurs, enter another guess.

Figure 3.6 shows the @IRR function calculating the internal rate of return on an investment with uneven cash flows. Here the investor puts up $100,000 to back a real estate development. The development is not expected to return any money for the first two years but to start paying back in the third year. The @IRR function in cell C17 indicates that if the investment pays as expected it will have an effective interest rate of 17.70 percent.

Fig. 3.6
Calculating the internal rate of return with the @IRR function.

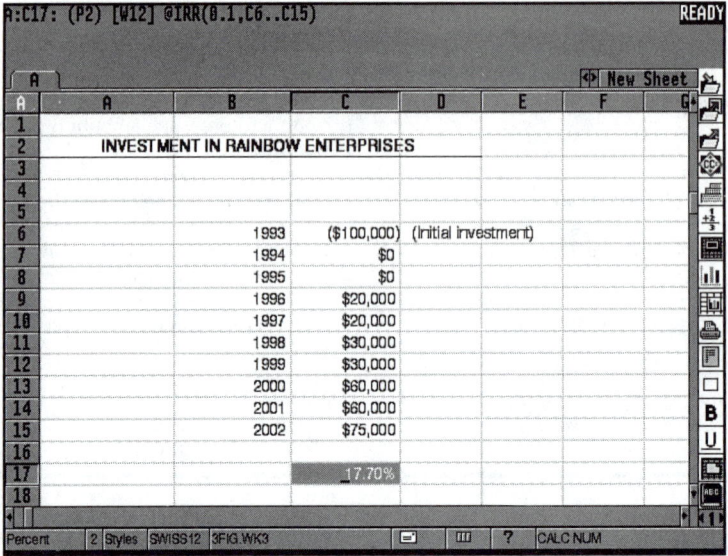

> **Caution**
>
> Be aware that the internal-rate-of-return method (the concept itself, not 1-2-3's @IRR function) is based on a complex mathematical approach that in some cases has many possible solutions. Many financial professionals advise putting no trust in the results of IRR calculations.
>
> One serious problem with the @IRR method is that it tends to overestimate a positive rate of return from the investment and fails to account for the additional outside capital that's often injected into an investment over its lifespan. This overestimation occurs because the @IRR method assumes that positive cash flows are reinvested at the same rate of return earned by the total investment. Actually, a small return rarely can be reinvested at the same high rate as that of a large investment. This situation is especially true in the analysis of large fixed assets and land investments.
>
> An alternative and more accurate method of evaluating investments is to calculate an investment's net present value. You use 1-2-3's @NPV function to perform net present-value analysis, discussed later in this chapter.

@RATE—Calculating Compound Growth Rate

The @RATE function calculates the compound growth rate for an initial investment that grows to a specified future value over a specified number of periods. The rate is the periodic interest rate and not necessarily an annual rate. @RATE uses the following syntax:

@RATE(*future_value,present_value,term*)

You can use @RATE to determine, for example, the yield of a zero-coupon bond sold at a discount of its face value. Suppose that for $350 you can purchase a zero-coupon bond with a $1,000 face value, maturing on the last day of 2003. Assuming that the current date is in January 1994, what is the implied annual interest rate? The answer, as shown in figure 3.7, is 11.10 percent.

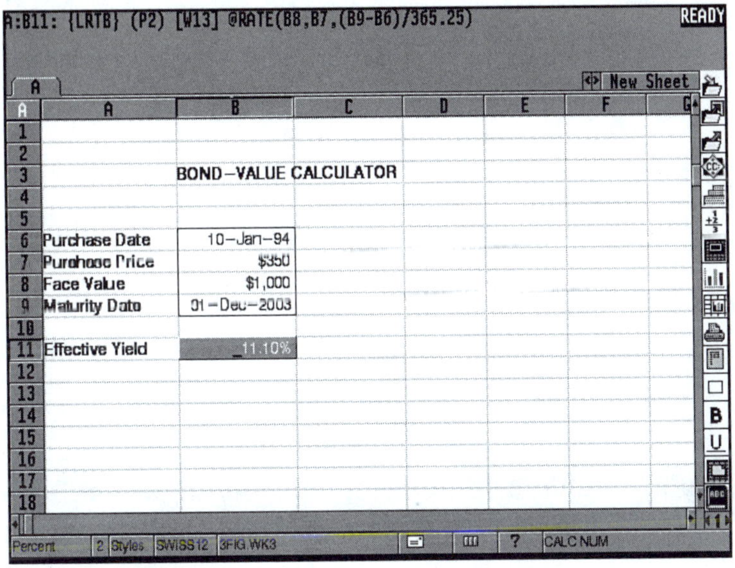

Fig. 3.7
The @RATE function computes the effective interest rate of an investment.

@PMT—Calculating Loan Payment Amounts

You use the @PMT function to calculate the periodic payments necessary to pay the entire principal on an amortizing loan. This function uses the following syntax:

@PMT(*principal,interest,term*)

Figure 3.8 shows the @PMT function being used to calculate the monthly car payment on a $32,000 car loan. The loan is repaid over 60 months, and the loan rate is 1 percent (12 percent divided by 12 periods per year).

@PMT assumes that payments are to be made at the end of each period—an ordinary annuity. You can modify the calculated result of the @PMT function if payments are to be made at the beginning of the period—an annuity due. The modified syntax for the function is

@PMT(*principal,interest,term*)/(1+*interest*)

In figure 3.8, cell C15 contains the following formula:

@PMT(B8,B9/12,B10)/(1+B9/12)

Fig. 3.8
The @PMT function calculates loan payments.

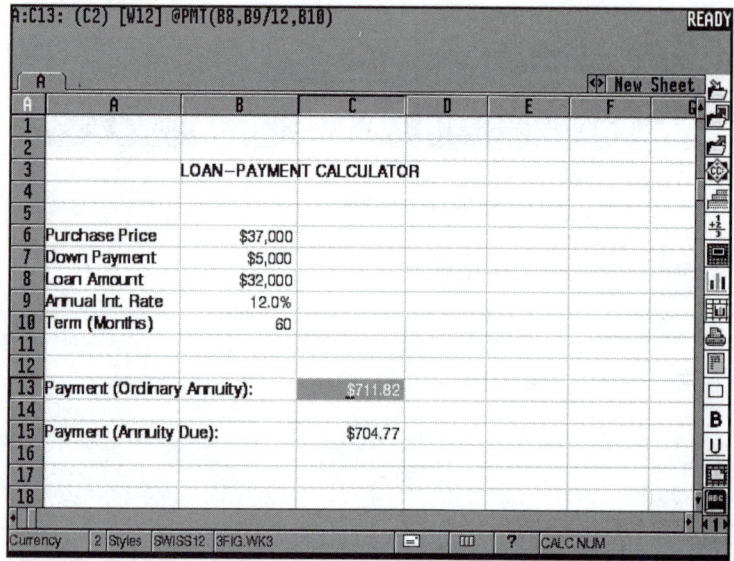

Whether you are calculating ordinary annuities or annuities due, you need to keep two important guidelines in mind. First, calibrate the interest rate to the frequency of payments. If you make monthly payments, enter the interest rate as a monthly rate and enter the number of months in which you will be making payments as the term. If you make the payment once a year, use the annual interest rate as the interest argument and enter as the term the number of years in which you will be making payments.

@NPV—Calculating Net Present Value

The @NPV calculates the present value of a series of unequal cash flows. (Present value is the concept that a sum of money received in the future is worth less than the same sum received immediately.) The syntax of this function is

@NPV(*interest,cashflows*)

Interest is the rate of return you could get on an investment of comparable risk. *Cashflows* is a reference to a range containing the cashflow amounts.

Figure 3.9 shows how you can use @NPV to calculate the present value of a stream of varying cash flows.

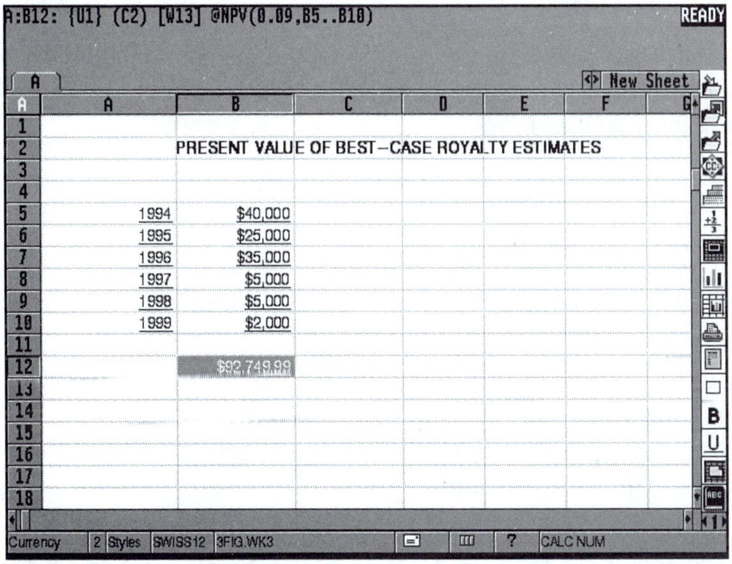

Fig. 3.9
Calculating the present value of future cash flows with the @NPV function.

The name of the @NPV function, *Net Present Value*, isn't entirely accurate. Net present value, as distinguished from present value, is the present value of a stream of cash flows less the investment required to earn the cash flows. @NPV is really a function for computing the present value of uneven flows, whereas @PV (discussed in the next section) computes the present value of equal cash flows. To compute the net present value of a series of unequal numbers in a range, use the following syntax:

@NPV(*interest,cashflows*)–*investment*

@PV—Calculating Present Value of an Annuity

@PV calculates the present value of an amount to be received at a regular interval over a period of time. It uses the following syntax:

@PV(*payment,interest,term*)

Suppose that you win a lawsuit and the other party offers to pay $900 per month for the next year in lieu of an immediate payment of $10,000 (the amount you were awarded). That way, he reasons, you will get $10,800 rather than $10,000. But, is $10,800 spread out over a year really worth more than $10,000? If you can invest money at a rate of 8.5 percent, use the formula @PV(900,.085/12,12) to find the present value of your opponent's offer. The answer is $10,318.76; his offer is slightly better for you than an immediate payment of $10,000.

@PV assumes that payments arrive at the ends of periods. To adjust the formula for an annuity-due situation, where the first payment arrives immediately, use the following form:

@PV(*payment,interest,term*)*(1+*interest*)

@FV—Calculating Future Value

The @FV function calculates what a current amount will grow to, based on an interest rate and number of years you specify. @FV uses this syntax:

@FV(*payment,interest,term*)

Figure 3.10 shows a worksheet that uses @FV to determine the value of a vacation fund in two years' time.

Fig. 3.10
@FV calculates the future value of a fund to which you make regular, equal deposits.

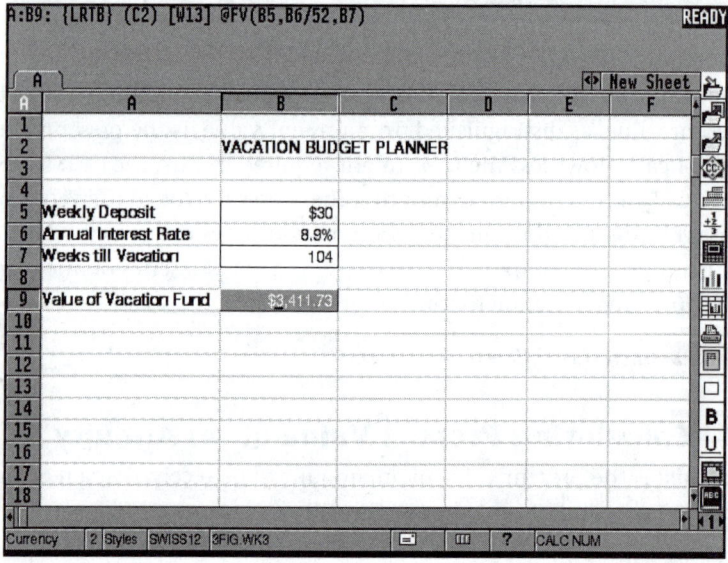

To adjust the @FV function for an annuity-due situation, use this variation:

@FV(*payment,interest,term*)*(1+*interest*)

@TERM—Calculating the Term of an Investment

The @TERM function calculates the number of periods required to accumulate a specified future value by making equal payments into an interest-bearing account at the end of each period. This number of periods is the term for an ordinary annuity. The @TERM function uses the following syntax:

@TERM(*payment,interest,future_value*)

Suppose that you want to determine the number of months required to accumulate $5,000 by making a monthly payment of $50 into an account that pays 8 percent annual interest compounded monthly (0.67 percent per month). The formula @TERM(50,0.08/12,5000) gives you the answer: approximately 76.9 months.

To calculate the term for an annuity-due situation, in which payments are made at the beginnings of periods, use the following form:

@TERM(*payment,Interest,future_value*/(1+*interest*))

@CTERM—Calculating the Term of a Compounding Investment

The @CTERM function calculates the number of periods required for a one-time investment, earning a specified interest rate, to grow to a specified future value. The @CTERM function uses the following syntax:

@CTERM(*interest,future_value,present_value*)

Suppose that you want to determine how many years $2,000 must be invested in an IRA at 10 percent interest to grow to $10,000. Figure 3.11 shows how to use the @CTERM function to determine the answer of just under 17 years.

@SLN—Calculating Straight-Line Depreciation

The @SLN function calculates straight-line depreciation, given the asset's cost, salvage value, and depreciable life. The @SLN function uses the following syntax:

@SLN(*cost,salvage,life*)

@SLN calculates the simplest kind of depreciation, in which an asset loses the same amount of its value each year. Suppose that you have purchased a machine for $5,000 that has a useful life of three years and a salvage value estimated to be 10 percent of the purchase price ($500) at the end of its useful life. It will lose, therefore, one-third of $4,500 each year. You can calculate the depreciation amount with the formula @SLN(5000,500,3), which returns $1,500.

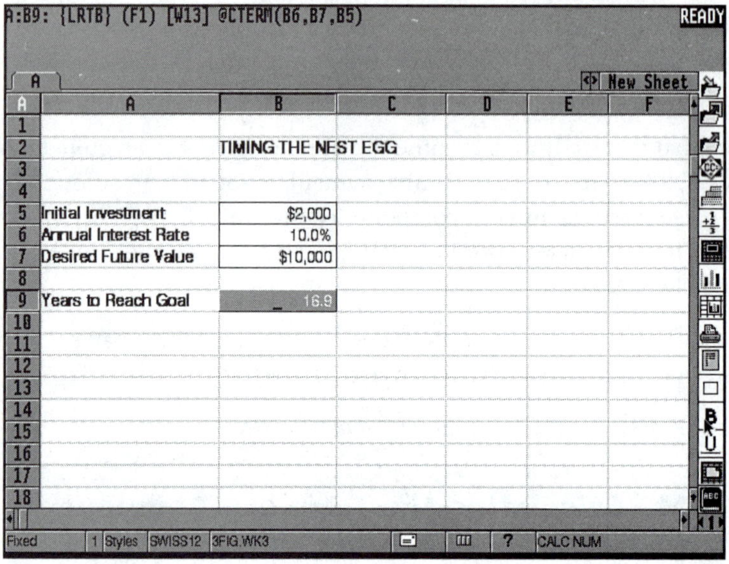

Fig. 3.11
@CTERM computes the time required to grow a one-time investment.

@DDB—Calculating Double Declining-Balance Depreciation

The @DDB function calculates depreciation by using the double declining-balance method, with depreciation ending when the book value equals the salvage value. The double declining-balance method accelerates depreciation so that greater depreciation expense occurs in the earlier periods rather than in the later ones. Book value in any period is the purchase price less the total depreciation in all previous periods. @DDB uses the following syntax:

@DDB(*cost,salvage,life,period*)

Figure 3.12 shows a worksheet in which the depreciation amounts for a computer are calculated for each year of the computer's useful life.

If an asset has a small salvage value, the @DDB function may not fully depreciate the asset in the final period. You can solve this problem using the @VDB (variable declining balance) function, discussed later in this chapter.

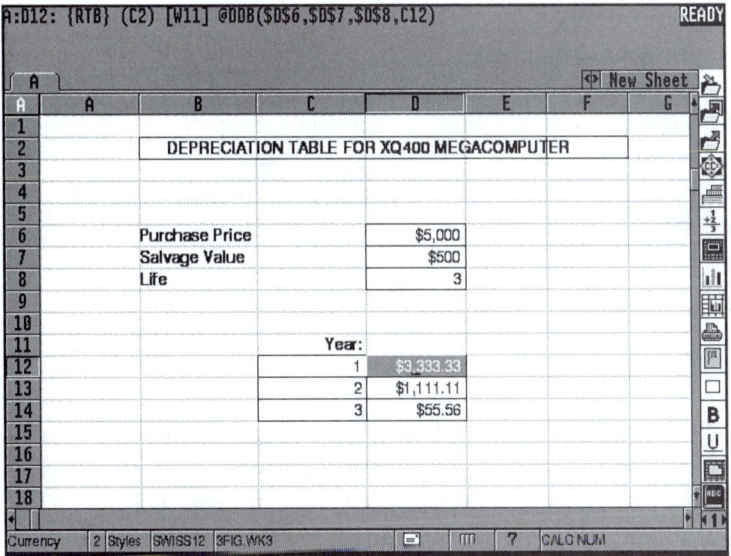

Fig. 3.12
Using @DDB to compute an asset's depreciation.

@SYD—Calculating Sum-of-the-Years'-Digits Depreciation

The @SYD function calculates depreciation by the sum-of-the-years'-digits method. Similar to the double declining-balance method, this method accelerates depreciation so that earlier periods of the item's life reflect greater depreciation than do later periods. @SYD uses the following syntax:

@SYD(*cost,salvage,life,period*)

Although @SYD depreciates assets more in earlier years, the rate of decrease from one year to the next is slower than with @DDB. If @SYD formulas were used in figure 3.12, the depreciation amounts would be $2,250, $1,500, and $750.

@VDB—Calculating Variable Declining-Balance Depreciation

The @VDB function calculates depreciation by using a variable-rate declining-balance method. The variable-rate depreciation method gives you accelerated depreciation during the early part of the term. If you do not specify a depreciation rate, 1-2-3 uses 200 percent to produce double declining-balance depreciation.

Chapter 3—Finding Solutions with Formulas and Functions

Normally, @VDB automatically switches from accelerated depreciation to straight-line depreciation when it is most advantageous, but you can set a switch in the @VDB argument if you do not want automatic switchover to straight-line depreciation. The start period and end period correspond to the beginning and end of the asset's life, respectively, relative to the fiscal period. To find the first year's depreciation of an asset purchased at the beginning of the third quarter of the fiscal year, for example, the start period would be zero and the end period would be .50 (half of the year).

The @VDB function uses the following syntax:

@VDB(cost,salvage,life,start,end,[depreciation],[switch])

Figure 3.13 shows how the @VDB function can calculate depreciation on an asset with an original purchase price of $5,000, a depreciable life of three years, and an estimated salvage value of $500 when that asset was placed into service at the beginning of the third quarter of the first fiscal year. The optional percent argument is set at 150 percent.

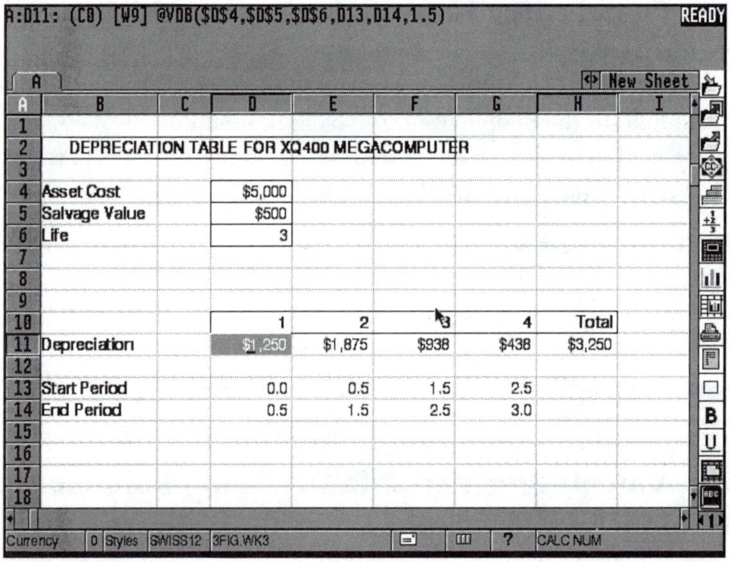

Fig. 3.13
Using @VDB to compute an asset's depreciation with your choice of declining-balance rate.

An easy way to enter the start and end period for each fiscal year is to create a table, as shown in figure 3.13. After entering the initial start and end periods for the first year, you can use a formula to calculate the subsequent years' start and end periods. Or you can use 1-2-3's **/D**ata **F**ill command to enter the values for you. Either way, this method eliminates the need for you to type the start and end period's decimal fractions required to calculate the depreciation for that year.

Using the Statistical Functions

◄ "Filling Ranges with Data," p. 70

1-2-3 provides 10 statistical functions. Table 3.6 lists the functions, their arguments, and the statistical operations they perform.

Table 3.6 Statistical Functions	
Function	**Description**
@AVG(*list*)	Calculates the average of a list of values
@COUNT(*list*)	Counts the number of cells that contain entries
@MAX(*list*)	Returns the maximum value in a list of values
@MIN(*list*)	Returns the minimum value in a list of values
@STD(*list*)	Calculates the population standard deviation of a list of values
@STDS(*list*)	Calculates the sample population standard deviation of a list of values
@SUM(*list*)	Sums a list of values
@SUMPRODUCT(*range1,range2*)	Multiplies cells in *range1* by corresponding cells in *range2* and sums the values
@VAR(*list*)	Calculates the population variance of a list of values
@VARS(*list*)	Calculates the sample population variance of a list of values

Each of the statistical functions except @SUMPRODUCT uses the *list* argument. This argument can take several forms:

- A range
- Two or more ranges separated by commas
- Two or more cell references separated by commas

- Two or more numbers separated by commas
- Any combination of the preceding

The following list includes some examples:

@SUM(1,2,3,4)

@SUM(B1,B2,B3,B4)

@SUM(B1..B4)

@SUM(B1..B2,B3..B4)

@SUM(B1..B2,4)

@SUM(B1..B2,B4,4)

Although these examples use the @SUM function (which totals the values included as arguments), the principles that these examples illustrate apply equally to each of the statistical functions (except @SUMPRODUCT).

Note that some of the statistical functions perform differently when you specify cells individually rather than in ranges. The functions that perform differently in this case include @AVG, @MAX, @MIN, @STD, @STDS, @VAR, and @VARS. When you specify a range of cells, 1-2-3 ignores empty cells within the specified range. When you specify cells individually, however, 1-2-3 takes empty cells into consideration for the particular functions mentioned.

Suppose that you are looking for the minimum value in a range that includes an empty cell and cells containing the entries 1, 2, and 3; in this case, 1-2-3 returns the value 1 as the minimum value. If you specify an individual cell that is empty, along with cells containing the entries 1, 2, and 3, however, 1-2-3 returns the value 0 as the minimum.

Tip
When you specify cells as part of a range or individually, remember that 1-2-3 treats cells containing labels as zeros.

1-2-3 makes this distinction because empty cells actually contain zeros, although they are invisible. 1-2-3 assumes that if you go to the extra effort of actually specifying an individual cell (even if it is empty), you must want it included in the calculation.

@AVG—Computing the Average of a List of Numbers

The @AVG function computes the average of a set of values by summing the values in a list and dividing the result by the number of entries in the list. Use the following syntax for @AVG:

@AVG(*list*)

As noted earlier, the *list* argument can consist of values, cell addresses, cell names, cell ranges, range names, or a combination of these. Figure 3.14 shows an example of the @AVG function calculating the average price per share of an imaginary company's stock. In the figure, the function's argument is the range C5..C15. The formula in cell F6 adds up the values in that range and divides the result by 9, the number of entries in that range, and ignores the empty cells in the range.

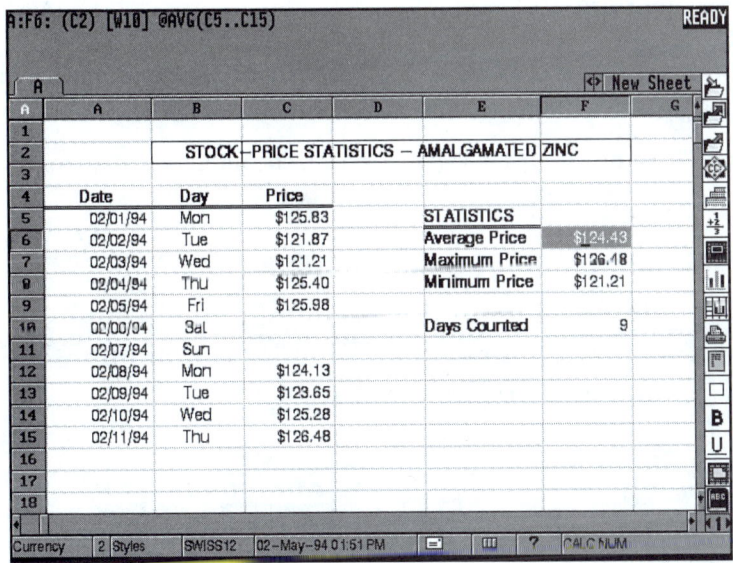

Fig. 3.14
The @AVG function averages the values of entries in a range.

Although @AVG supports the various possible list arguments listed in the general discussion of statistical functions, you should use multicell ranges. That is, @AVG(B10..B16,B20..B25) is okay, but @AVG(B10..B15,B17) is risky. @AVG uses a denominator of 1 for a one-cell range, even if the range is empty. If all the cells in the range B10..B15 and in cell B17 contain values, @AVG(B10..B15,B17) sums the values in the cells and divides by 7. If you erase cell B17, however, @AVG still divides the sum of values by 7. To avoid this problem, just use range references, even if you use two addresses to signify one cell, as in @AVG(B10..B15,B17..B17).

Note that the formula in cell F6 of figure 3.14 divides the sum of range C5..C15 by 9 because cells C10 and C11 are empty. If these cells contained labels, the summing part of the @AVG function would treat the labels as zeros, but the counting part would count the labels as entries and the formula would give an erroneous average by dividing the sum by 11.

@COUNT—Counting Cell Entries

The @COUNT function totals the number of cells that contain entries of any kind, including labels, label-prefix characters, or the values ERR and NA. Use the following syntax for @COUNT:

@COUNT(*list*)

The *list* argument can be values, cell addresses, cell names, cell ranges, range names, or a combination of these.

In figure 3.15, the formula in cell F10 returns the number of days for which stock prices are recorded.

Fig. 3.15
The @COUNT function returns the number of entries in a range.

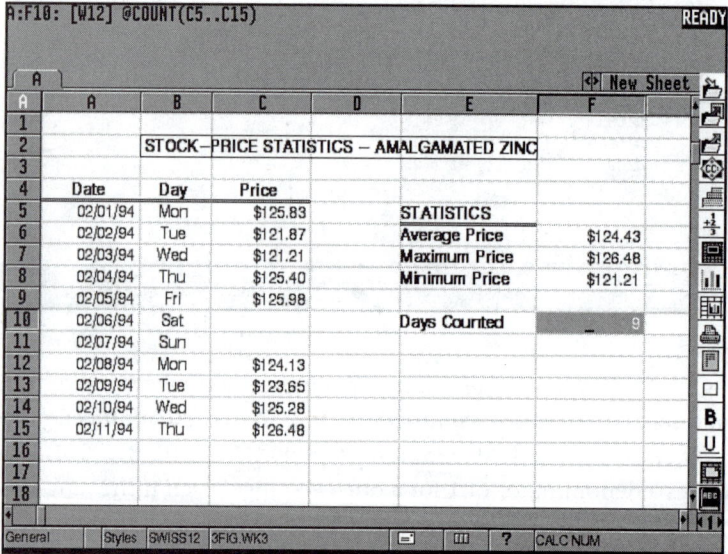

@COUNT always counts a single cell as 1. @COUNT(B17), for example, returns 1 whether cell B17 contains an entry or not. @COUNT(B17..B17), however, returns 0 if cell B17 is empty. @COUNT(B10..B15,B17) always returns one more than the number of entries in range B10..B15. But @COUNT(B10..B15,B17..B17) returns an accurate count of the entries in those ranges. Use only multicell range references with @COUNT.

@MAX and @MIN—Finding Maximum and Minimum Values

The @MAX function finds the largest value included in the *list* argument; the @MIN function finds the smallest value included in the *list* argument. The functions use the following syntax:

@MAX(*list*)

@MIN(*list*)

In figure 3.16, cell F7 returns the highest stock price in range C5..C15. The formula right below cell F7 uses the same range reference but uses the @MIN function to return the lowest price.

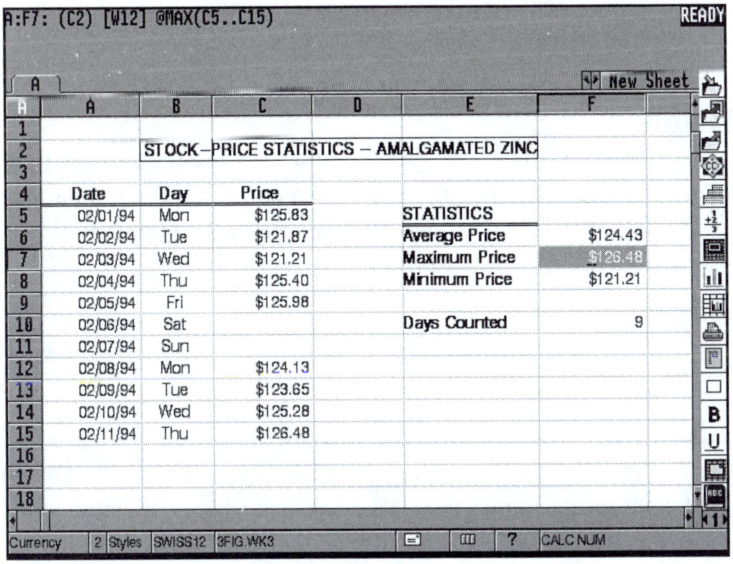

Fig. 3.16
The @MAX function returns the highest value in a range.

A less familiar use of the @MAX and @MIN functions is the setting of ceilings and floors for values. Suppose a library imposes a 10 cent-per-day overdue fine but never fines more than $5.00. If the number of days a book is overdue is in a worksheet cell named DAYS, you can compute the fine with the formula @MIN(DAYS*0.1,5). This formula returns the number of days 5, 10¢, or $5.00, whichever is less. For another example, suppose that a company charges 5 percent of an item's price for shipping but never charges less than $5.00 for shipping. The formula @MAX(PUR_PRICE*0.05,5) returns the appropriate amount.

> **Troubleshooting**
>
> *The @MIN function returns a value of zero in a range that does not contain zero.*
>
> You may have included a cell with a label in the range that you performed the @MIN function on. The @MIN function ignores empty cells but treats labels as zeros. If the range appears to consist only of values but actually contains any labels—including spaces—1-2-3 returns 0. Watch out for invisible spaces or numbers entered as labels when using @MIN.
>
> *The @MAX function returns a value of zero in a range that contains negative numbers.*
>
> The @MAX function also ignores empty cells but treats labels as zeros. If the range contains only negative values but contains a label, the label is treated as a zero, and is therefore the maximum value in the range.

@STD and @STDS—Calculating the Standard Deviation

@STD computes the standard deviation of a set of values, assuming that the values represent the entire population. @STDS computes the standard deviation assuming that the values represent a sample of the population. Use the following syntax for these functions:

@STD(*list*)

@STDS(*list*)

Essentially, the standard deviation is a measure of how individual values vary from the average of the other values in the list. Figure 3.17 shows the results of taking two 10-unit samples from automated machines designed to fill boxes with 100 paper clips each. Machine B comes closer to consistently dispensing 100 paper clips into a box than machine A does; machine B also has the lower standard deviation, as computed by the @STDS formula in cell E17. (If all the values in range E6..E15 are 100, @STDS returns 0.)

Standard deviation is often a better measure than the average for determining how close values come to a desired value. In the case of figure 3.17, the average would favor machine A; the average of the values in column B is exactly 100, while the average of the values in column E is 99.9. Yet machine B clearly does a better job of creating 100-piece boxes of paper clips.

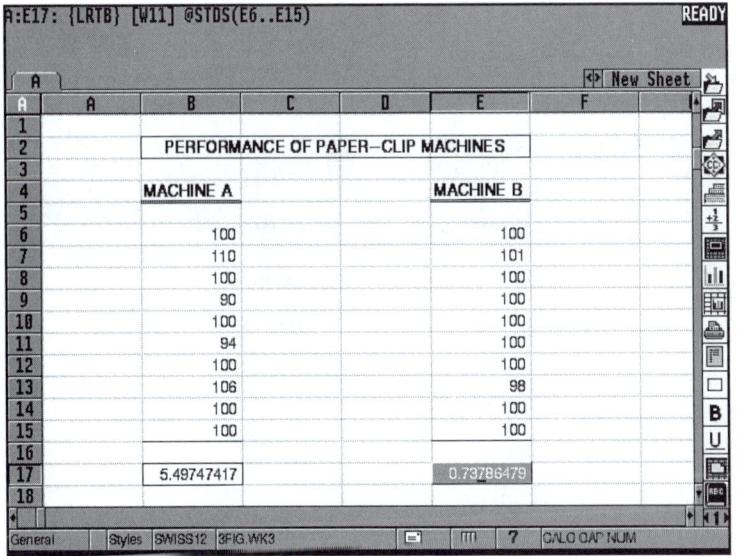

Fig. 3.17
@STDS computes the standard deviation of a sample.

Use @STDS with samples of data. A *sample* is a randomly selected set of numbers that represents the larger set of data from which the sample is selected. The larger set is commonly known as the population. Working with samples is usually more practical than recording a measure of every unit in a population that may have thousands or millions of members. But sometimes you can work with complete sets of data. You could use @STD, for example, to compute the standard deviation of the heights of fifth-graders in a small school district.

@VAR and @VARS—Calculating the Variance

The variance, like the standard deviation, is a measure of dispersion around an average. The @VAR function calculates the variance for a population; @VARS computes the variance of a sample. These functions use the following syntax:

@VAR(*list*)

@VARS(*list*)

Variation is simply the square of standard deviation. Figure 3.18 shows how @VARS is used to evaluate the paper-clip machines. The results in row 17 are larger than their counterpart in figure 3.17, but comparing variation to variation leads to the same conclusion as comparing standard deviation to standard deviation: that machine B (with the lower variation) is more accurate than machine A.

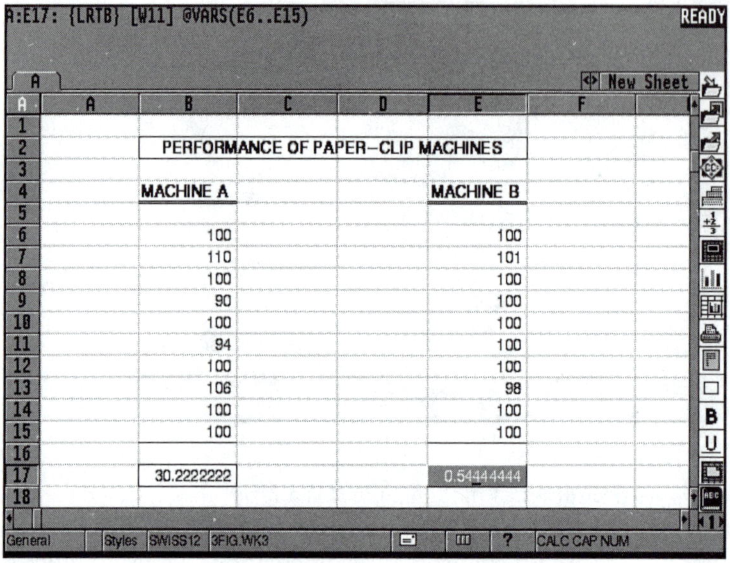

Fig. 3.18
Computing the variation of a sample of data using the @VARS function.

	A	B	C	D	E	F
1						
2		PERFORMANCE OF PAPER–CLIP MACHINES				
3						
4		MACHINE A			MACHINE B	
5						
6		100			100	
7		110			101	
8		100			100	
9		90			100	
10		100			100	
11		94			100	
12		100			100	
13		106			98	
14		100			100	
15		100			100	
16						
17		30.2222222			0.5444444	
18						

For explanations of the terms population and sample, refer to the earlier discussion of the @STD and @STDS functions.

@SUM—Totaling Values

The @SUM function provides a convenient way to add up a list of values. Of all the statistical functions that 1-2-3 provides, @SUM is the one you probably use most often. @SUM uses the following syntax:

@SUM(*list*)

Figure 3.19 shows the results of the @SUM function.

@SUMPRODUCT—Multiplying Lists of Values

The @SUMPRODUCT function gets its name because it multiplies pairs of values and sums the products. The syntax for @SUMPRODUCT is the following:

@SUMPRODUCT(*range1,range2*)

Range1 and *range2* must be references to contiguous ranges, and both ranges must have the same dimensions. You can use @SUMPRODUCT to calculate the value of an inventory; every per-unit price is multiplied by a corresponding on-hand amount, and the results are summed. Figure 3.20 demonstrates the @SUMPRODUCT function.

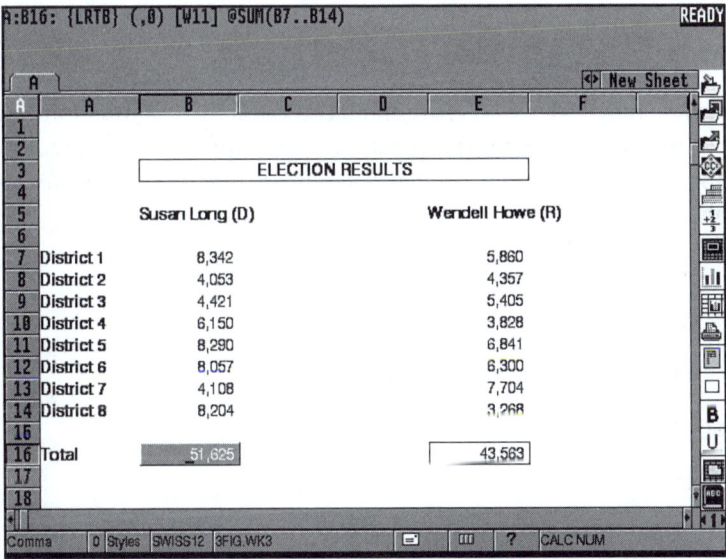

Fig. 3.19
The @SUM function totals the values in a range.

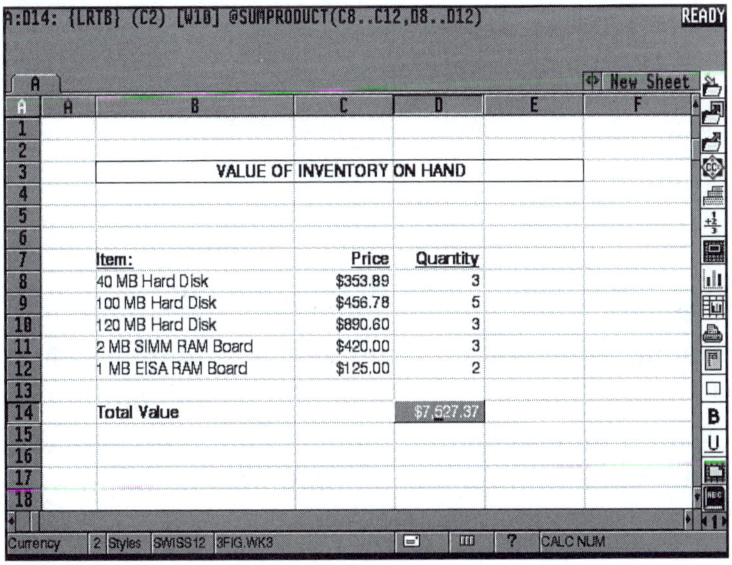

Fig. 3.20
@SUMPRODUCT multiplies pairs of values from two ranges and sums the results.

Some statistical applications require computing a value called the *sum of the squares*; every value in a set is squared (multiplied by itself) and the results are added together. @SUMPRODUCT computes the sum of the squares when you use the same range reference twice. @SUMPRODUCT(B8..B19,B8..B19) multiplies every value in range B8..B19 by itself and totals the results.

Using Database Functions

The database functions of 1-2-3 are similar to the statistical functions, except that they return statistics for specific items taken from a database range. The following database functions are described in Chapter 15, "Using Functions To Analyze Data":

- @DSUM
- @DMAX
- @DMIN
- @DAVG
- @DCOUNT
- @DSTD
- @DSTDS
- @DVAR
- @DVARS
- @DGET
- @DQUERY

Using the Logical Functions

The logical functions enable you to use Boolean logic within worksheets. Most of the logical functions test whether a condition is true or false.

For most logical functions, both the test and the answer the function returns based on the test are built into the function. The @ISSTRING function is a good example because it tests whether the argument is a string and returns 1 if the test is true or a 0 if the test is false. The @IF function, on the other hand, enables you to specify the condition to test.

The eight logical functions that 1-2-3 provides are summarized in table 3.7. In the text that follows, the logical functions are described in order of complexity.

Table 3.7 Logical Functions

Function	Description
@IF(*test,true,false*)	Tests the condition and returns one result if the condition is true and another result if the condition is false
@ISERR(*cell_reference*)	Tests whether the argument results in ERR
@ISNA(*cell_reference*)	Tests whether the argument results in NA (Not Available)
@TRUE	Equals 1, the logical value for true
@FALSE	Equals 0, the logical value for false
@ISRANGE(*cell_reference*)	Tests whether the argument is a defined range
@ISSTRING(*cell_reference*)	Tests whether the argument is a string
@ISNUMBER(*cell_reference*)	Tests whether the argument is a number

@IF—Creating Conditional Tests

The @IF function represents a powerful tool—one you can use to manipulate text within worksheets and to affect calculations. You can use the @IF function, for example, to test the condition "Is the inventory on hand below 1,000 units?" and then return one value or string if the answer to the question is true or another value or string if the answer is false. The @IF function uses the following syntax:

@IF(*test,true,false*)

The function evaluates the expression specified for *test*. If the expression is true, the function returns the value of the *true* argument. Otherwise, the function returns the value of the *false* argument.

In the discussion of the @ABS function, earlier in this chapter, that function was used to find the amount by which individual members of a set of values

Chapter 3—Finding Solutions with Formulas and Functions

differ from the average of that set of values. In figure 3.21, @IF was used to expand on that concept. The formulas in column E return the message Note variation only if the individual score varies from the average by more than 10 percent. The formula in cell E7 uses @ABS(C$13–C7)>0.1 as its *test* argument. In the case of cell C7, that expression is true, so cell E7 returns its *true* argument, the string Note variation. Other formulas in range E5..E10 also compare cell C13 to the test scores in their respective rows. Because in all the other cases, the test expression is false, these formulas return their *false* argument, an empty character string.

Fig. 3.21
The @IF function returns a message only when a certain condition is met.

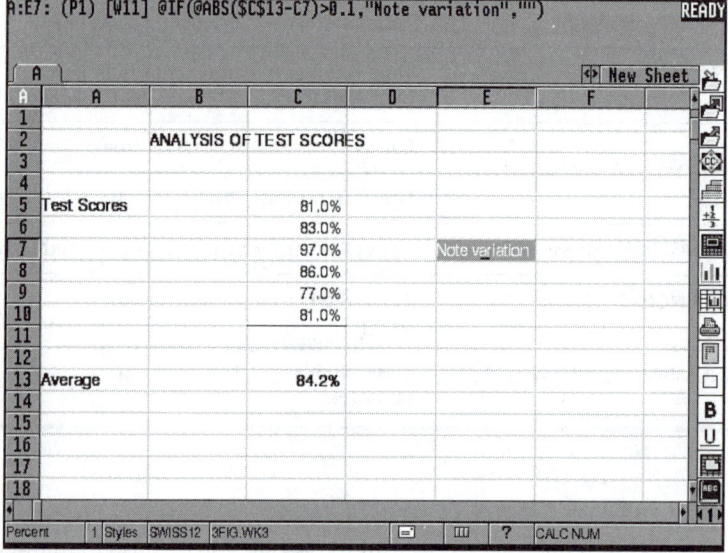

The @IF function can use six operators when testing conditions. These operators are summarized in table 3.8.

Table 3.8 Logical Test Operators

Operator	Description
<	Less than
<=	Less than or equal to
=	Equal to
>=	Greater than or equal to

Operator	Description
>	Greater than
<>	Not equal to

In addition, you can do complex conditional tests by using @IF functions with logical operators that test multiple conditions in one @IF function. These complex operators are summarized in table 3.9.

Table 3.9 Complex Operators

Operator	Description
#AND#	Used to test two conditions, both of which must be true in order for the entire test to be true
#NOT#	Used to test that a condition is not true
#OR#	Used to test two conditions; if either condition is true, the entire test condition is true

The *test* argument can compare two values with an equal sign or an inequality sign (<, >, <=, <>, and so on). The *test* argument can combine tests with the operators #AND# and #OR#. Figure 3.22 shows a worksheet that reflects the fact that the shipping charge is waived for preferred customers or for customers who place orders larger than $100. In cell D8 of figure 3.22, these two conditions are defined mathematically and connected with the #OR# operator. As you can see from the results in column D, only one of the conditions needs to be true for the formula to return its *true* argument, 0.

Figure 3.23 reflects a scenario where a customer must be preferred and place a large order to qualify for the waiver. Cell D8 connects the expression B8="y" and C8>=100 with the operator #AND#. Both conditions must be true for the formula to return its *true* argument.

You can actually use @IF expressions as the true or false arguments of @IF formulas. Formulas based on the @IF function can become very complex, resembling complete programs in a single cell. We could accomplish the task of the formula in cell D8 of figure 3.23 with the following nested @IF formula:

@IF(B8="y",@IF(C8>=100,0,10),10)

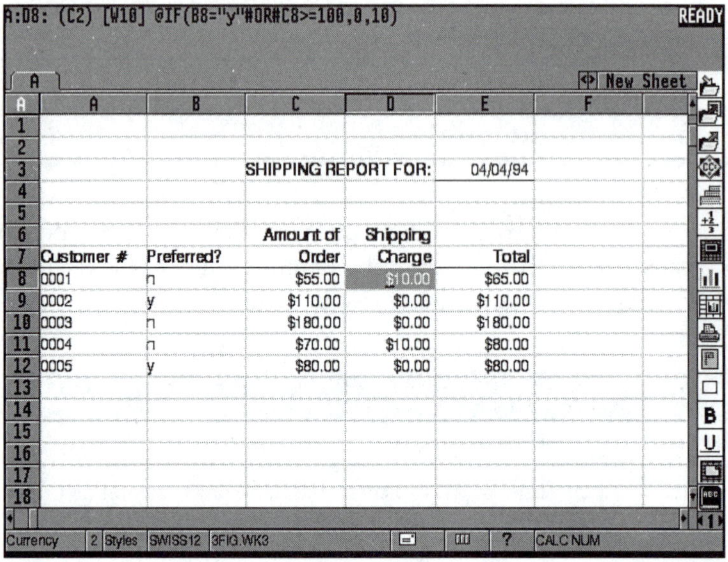

Fig. 3.22
Using #OR# to select a value when one of two conditions is met.

Fig. 3.23
Using #AND# to select a value when two conditions are met.

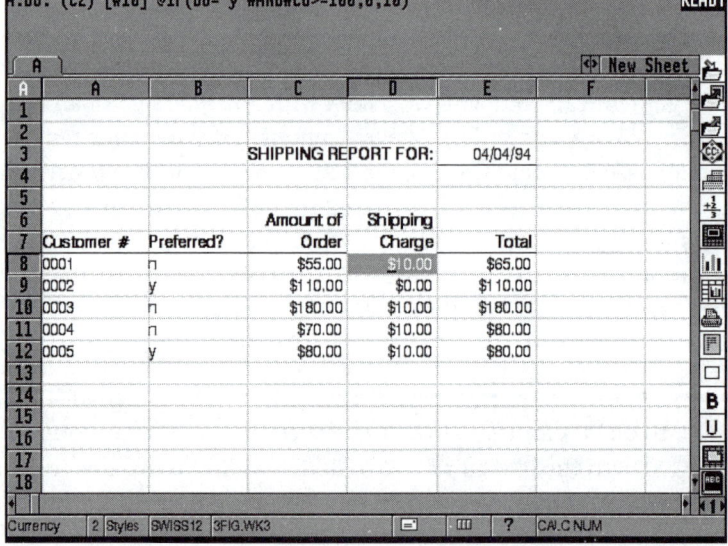

In this formula, if the first *test* argument is true, the formula proceeds to a second test. If that test is also true, the formula returns the *true* argument of the second @IF expression, 0. If the second test is false, the formula returns the *false* argument of the second @IF (10). Finally, if the result of the original test is false, the formula skips the second @IF and returns the *false* argument of the first @IF, which is also 10.

This technique, called *nesting IF statements*, enables you to construct sophisticated logical tests and operations in 1-2-3 worksheets.

@ISERR and @ISNA—Trapping Errors in Conditional Tests

The @ISERR function tests whether the argument equals ERR. If the test is true, the function returns the value 1; if the test is false, the function returns the value 0. @ISERR uses the following syntax:

@ISERR(*cell_reference*)

This function is helpful because it can be used to trap errors produced in one location that can cause more drastic results in other locations. Figure 3.24 shows how to use @ISERR to trap a possible division-by-zero error that could cause many other cells in the worksheet to return ERR.

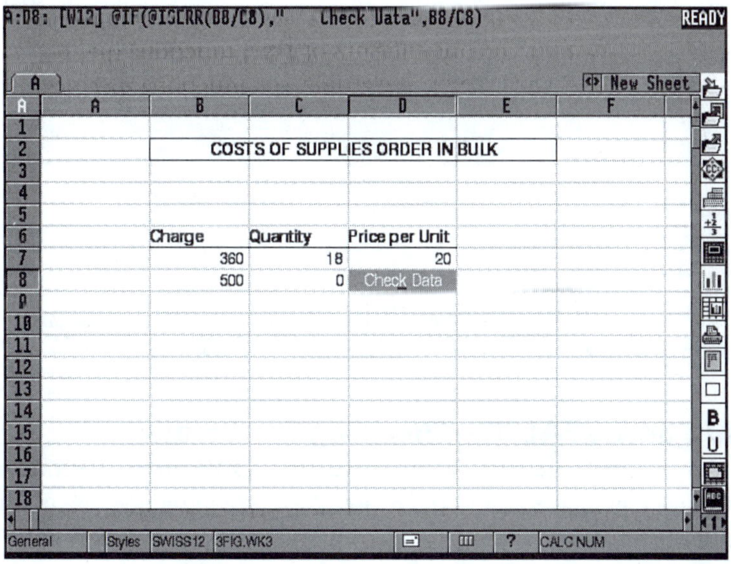

Fig. 3.24
@ISERR returns a message when a computation results in ERR.

The @ISNA function works similarly to @ISERR. @ISNA tests whether the argument you include is equal to NA (Not Available). If the test is true, the function returns the value 1; if the test is false, the function returns the value 0. The @ISNA function uses the following syntax:

@ISNA(*cell_reference*)

You can use the @ISNA function to trap NA values in worksheets that use the @NA function. The @NA function, which represents "Not Available," is discussed in the section "Using Special Functions" later in this chapter.

Figure 3.25 shows @ISNA used to detect missing data. Each formula in column E returns the value of @NA. The sum of a range that includes even one NA is NA, so the formula in cell D11 tests to see if the expression @SUM(E6..E9) is NA. If this is true, the formula returns the message `Missing data`. Otherwise, the formula returns the sum of range E6..E9.

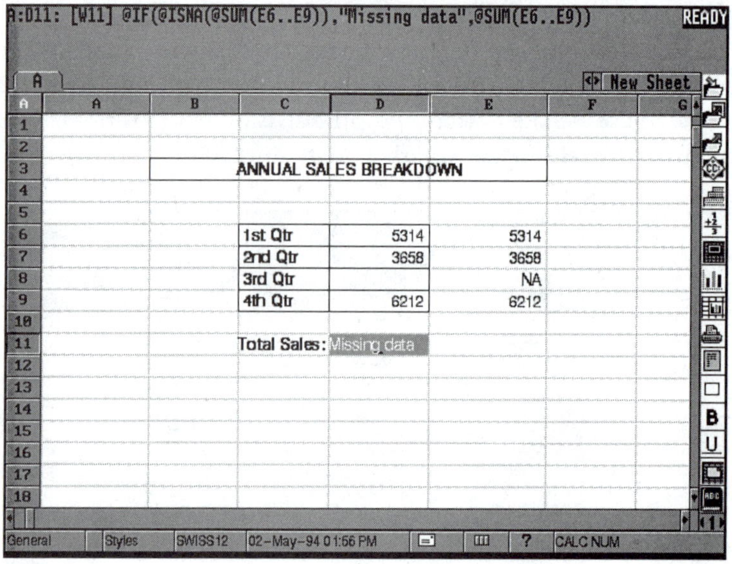

Fig. 3.25
@ISNA can flag the absence of data in a range.

@TRUE and @FALSE—Checking for Errors

You use the @TRUE and @FALSE functions to check for errors. Neither function requires arguments, but both are useful for providing documentation for formulas and advanced macro commands. The @TRUE function returns the value `1`, the Boolean logical value for true. The @FALSE function returns the value `0`, the Boolean logical value for false.

@ISRANGE—Checking for a Range Name

@ISRANGE determines whether a character string refers to a valid range. If so, the function returns the value 1; otherwise, the function returns the value 0. @ISRANGE uses the following syntax:

@ISRANGE(*cell_reference*)

You use this function most often to determine whether a named range exists or is defined. @ISRANGE(B10..B15) returns 1. @ISRANGE(B10..15) returns 0. If you assign the range name TAXDATA to a worksheet range, @ISRANGE(TAXDATA) returns 1. If you haven't assigned the range name TAXDATA to a worksheet range, however, or if TAXDATA becomes corrupted or the TAXDATA range name is undefined by the **/R**ange **N**ame **U**ndefine command, @ISRANGE(TAXDATA) returns 0.

@ISSTRING and @ISNUMBER—Checking the Cell's Aspect

Two functions that help you determine the type of value stored in a cell are @ISSTRING and @ISNUMBER. They often are used with @IF to check for data entry errors (numbers entered in the place of text or text entered in the place of numbers). For @ISNUMBER, use the following syntax:

@ISNUMBER(*cell_reference*)

If the argument is a number, the numeric value of the function is 1 (true). If the argument is a string, the numeric value of the function is 0 (false); even the null string ("") causes the numeric value of the function to be 0. @ISNUMBER considers an empty cell and the results of @NA and @ERR to be values.

Use @ISNUMBER to prevent a formula from returning misleading results if a cell it refers to only appears to contain a number. If you think, for example, a user may type a label such as **'4%** in a cell named MARKUP, you can use the following formula:

@IF(@ISNUMBER(MARKUP),COST*(1+MARKUP),"Markup must be a value")

If the cell named MARKUP is empty or contains a number or number-returning formula, the @ISNUMBER expression is true and the formula returns the marked-up value. If MARKUP contains a label or string-returning formula, the formula returns the message Markup must be a value.

Again, @ISNUMBER cannot distinguish between a cell containing a value and an empty cell; to accomplish that, use @CELL, described later in this chapter.

The @ISSTRING function works in nearly the same way as @ISNUMBER, determining whether a cell contains a label or string-returning formula. In either of these conditions, @ISSTRING returns 1. Otherwise, it returns 0, even when a cell is empty.

Tip
Use @ISRANGE and @@ to determine if the entry stored in a cell can be treated as a range. If cell B30 contains the label A1..A12, for example, @ISRANGE(@@(B30)) returns 1.

The syntax of @ISSTRING is

@ISSTRING(*cell_reference*)

Use @ISSTRING to prevent a string-concatenation formula from returning ERR, as in the following example:

@IF(@ISSTRING(ZIPCODE),+"ZC"&ZIPCODE,"")

If the cell named ZIPCODE contains a label or string-returning formula, the @ISSTRING expression is true and the formula concatenates the string in ZIPCODE with the letters ZC. Otherwise, the formula returns an empty string.

Using the String Functions

1-2-3 offers 19 string functions that provide significant power to manipulate text strings.

Strings are labels or portions of labels. More specifically, strings are data consisting of characters (alphabetic, numeric, blank, and special) enclosed in quotation marks; the label "total" is a string. The functions specifically designated as string functions are one category of 1-2-3 functions that take advantage of the power and flexibility of strings. Logical, error-trapping, and special functions can use strings as well as values. The string functions, however, are specifically designated to manipulate strings. Table 3.10 summarizes the string functions available in 1-2-3.

Table 3.10   String Functions

Function	Description
@FIND(*search_string, string, start_number*)	Locates the start position of one string within another string
@MID(*string, start_number, number*)	Extracts a string of a specified number of characters from the middle of another string, beginning at the starting position
@LEFT(*string, number*)	Extracts the leftmost specified number of characters from the string
@RIGHT(*string, number*)	Extracts the rightmost specified number of characters from the string

Using the String Functions

Function	Description
@REPLACE(*original_string, start_number, length, replacement_string*)	Replaces a number of characters in the original string with new string characters, starting at the character identified by the start position
@LENGTH(*string*)	Returns the number of characters in the string
@EXACT(*string1,string2*)	Returns 1 (true) if *string1* and *string2* are exact matches; otherwise, returns 0 (false)
@LOWER(*string*)	Converts all characters in the string to lowercase
@UPPER(*string*)	Converts all characters in the string to uppercase
@PROPER(*string*)	Converts the first character in each word in the string to uppercase and converts the remaining characters to lowercase
@REPEAT(*string,number*)	Copies the string the specified number of times in a cell
@TRIM(*string*)	Removes blank spaces from the string
@S(*range*)	Returns as a label the contents of the cell in the top left corner of a range
@N(*range*)	Returns as a value the contents of the cell in the top left corner of a range
@STRING(*numeric_value, decimal_places*)	Converts a value to a string showing the specified number of decimal places
@VALUE(*string*)	Converts a string to a value
@CLEAN(*string*)	Removes certain nonprintable characters from the string
@CHAR(*number*)	Converts a code number into an ASCII/LMBCS character
@CODE(*string*)	Converts the first character in the string into an ASCII/LMBCS code

> **Note**
>
> You can link strings to other strings by using the concatenation operator (&). The discussion of the individual string functions in this section shows several examples of the use of the concatenation operator. Keep in mind that you cannot link strings to cells that contain numeric values or that are empty. If you try, 1-2-3 returns ERR. Use @STRING if you want to concatenate a number with text.

Avoid mixing data types in string functions. For example, some functions produce strings, but other functions produce numeric results. If a function's result is not of the data type you need, use the @STRING and @VALUE functions to convert a numeric value to a string value or a string value to a numeric value.

> **Caution**
>
> Some of the string functions return or require a position number. The numbering scheme for positioning characters in a string begins with zero and continues to the number corresponding to the last character in the label. The prefix before a label is not counted for numeric positioning. Negative position numbers are not allowed.

@FIND—Locating One String Within Another

The @FIND function locates the starting position of one string within another string. The @FIND function uses the following syntax:

@FIND(*search_string*,*string*,*start_number*)

You can use @FIND, for example, to determine at what position the blank space occurs within the string *Jim Johnson*; the following formula returns 3:

@FIND(" ","Jim Johnson",0)

The *search_string* argument is the string you want to locate. The *string* argument defines the string to be searched. The search string is " " in this example. The string "Jim Johnson" is being searched. The *start_number* is the position number in the string where you want to start the search. Remember, the first character of a string is zero. If you wanted to disregard the first character of the string being searched, use the following formula:

@FIND(" ","Jim Johnson",1)

Although these examples show a search for the single blank-space character, @FIND also will find the location of multiple character strings, such as *Calif*, within longer strings.

> **Caution**
>
> @FIND performs only exact searches; uppercase and lowercase are significant.

When @FIND cannot find a match, the result is ERR.

@MID—Extracting One String from Another

Whereas @FIND helps you locate one string within another, the @MID function extracts one string from within another. @MID uses the following syntax:

@MID(*string,start_number,number*)

The *start_number* argument is a number representing the character position in the string where you want to begin extracting characters. The *number* argument, which indicates the length of the string, is the number of characters to extract. To extract the first four characters from the string "Jennifer Davidson", use the following formula:

@MID("Jennifer Davidson",0,4)

This formula returns Jenn because it extracts the string starting in position 0 (the first character) and continuing for a length of four characters.

You also can extract the first four letters of a string with the @LEFT function (discussed in the following section). But @MID, as its name implies, extracts characters from the middle of a string. To get the first three characters of Jennifer Davidson's last name, type the following formula:

@MID("Jennifer Davidson",5,3)

This formula returns Dav, the three characters beginning at character number 5.

You can use @MID with @FIND to extract the first few characters of last names from a variety of first-name/last-name strings. Use the following formula:

@MID(FULLNAME,@FIND(" ",FULLNAME,0)+1,3)

(Assume that FULLNAME is the name of a cell containing a name as one label.) This formula uses @FIND to determine the position number of the first space in the string and then returns the three characters starting one position after that space.

@LEFT and @RIGHT—Extracting Strings from Left and Right

The @LEFT and @RIGHT functions are variations of @MID. They extract characters from one end or the other of a string. These functions require the following syntaxes:

@LEFT(*string,number*)

@RIGHT(*string,number*)

The *number* argument is the number of characters to be extracted. If you want to extract the ZIP code from the string Cincinnati, Ohio 45243, for example, use the following function statement:

@RIGHT("Cincinnati, Ohio 45243",5)

@LEFT works the same way as @RIGHT except that @LEFT extracts from the beginning of a string. You can use the following statement to extract the city from the preceding statement:

@LEFT("Cincinnati, Ohio 45243",10)

You also can use @LEFT together with @FIND to determine the number of characters that precede the first comma. Suppose that a cell named FULLCITY contains the label Cincinnati, Ohio 45243. The following formula finds the text that precedes the first comma in that label:

@LEFT(FULLCITY,@FIND(",",FULLCITY,0))

@REPLACE—Replacing a String Within a String

The @REPLACE function replaces one group of characters in a string with another group of characters. @REPLACE is a valuable tool for correcting a frequently incorrect text entry without retyping the entry. Use the following syntax for @REPLACE:

@REPLACE(*original_string,start_number,length,replacement_string*)

The *start_number* argument indicates the position where 1-2-3 begins removing characters in the *original_string*. The *length* argument shows how many characters to remove, and *replacement_string* contains the new characters to replace the removed ones. @REPLACE numbers the character positions in a string, starting with zero and continuing to the end of the string (up to 239 positions).

@LENGTH—Computing the Length of a String

The @LENGTH function calculates the length of a string. @LENGTH uses the following syntax:

@LENGTH(*string*)

@LENGTH is frequently used to calculate the length of a string being extracted from another string. This function can also be used to check for data-entry errors. The function returns ERR as the length of numeric values, number-returning formulas, or empty cells.

@EXACT—Comparing Strings

The @EXACT function compares two strings, returning the value 1 (true) for strings that are exactly the same or returning the value 0 (false) for strings that are different. @EXACT uses the following syntax:

@EXACT(*string1,string2*)

Comparing strings with @EXACT differs from comparing strings with an equal sign. Consider the following formula:

@IF(A1=A2,"They match","They don't match")

If A1 and A2 both contain the name JONES, this formula returns the message They match. But this also holds true if A1 contains JONES and A2 contains Jones. Two strings are said to be equal if they contain all the same letters.

Now consider this formula:

@IF(@EXACT(A1,A2),"They match","They don't match")

This formula returns They don't match unless cells A1 and A2 contain the same label, capitalized exactly the same way.

@LOWER, @UPPER, and @PROPER—Converting the Case of Strings

1-2-3 offers three different functions for converting the case of a string value:

@LOWER(*string*)   Converts all letters in a string to lowercase.

@UPPER(*string*)   Converts all letters in a string to uppercase.

@PROPER(*string*)   Capitalizes the first letter in each word of a label. (Words are defined as groups of letters separated by spaces or other non-letters.) @PROPER sets the remaining letters in each word to lowercase.

Here are some examples of these functions:

@LOWER("David Letterman") returns `david letterman`

@UPPER("David Letterman") returns `DAVID LETTERMAN`

@PROPER("david letterman") returns `David Letterman`

> **Caution**
>
> The @PROPER function capitalizes every letter that follows anything that isn't a letter. Here are two examples where @PROPER provides unwanted results:
>
> @PROPER("Kelsey's Bar") returns `Kelsey'S Bar`
>
> @PROPER("1st qtr") returns `1St Qtr`

The three functions, @LOWER, @UPPER, and @PROPER, work with string values or references to strings. Used with a reference to a cell containing a value or an empty cell, they return ERR.

You can use @LOWER, @UPPER, or @PROPER to modify the contents of a database so that all entries in a field appear with the same capitalization. This technique produces reports that appear consistent. Capitalization also will affect sorting order. Uppercase and lowercase letters do not sort together. To ensure that data with different capitalization sorts together, first create a column, using one of the functions that references the data, and then sort on this new column.

@REPEAT—Repeating Strings Within a Cell

The @REPEAT function repeats strings a specified number of times, much like the backslash (\) repeats strings to fill a cell. But @REPEAT has some distinct advantages over the backslash. When you use the backslash to repeat a string, 1-2-3 fills the column to the exact column width. By using @REPEAT, you can repeat the string the precise number of times you want. If the result is wider than the cell width, the result is displayed in empty adjacent cells to the right. @REPEAT uses the following syntax:

@REPEAT(*string*,*number*)

The *number* argument indicates the number of times you want to repeat a string in a cell. If you want to repeat the string "-**-" three times, for example, you can type **@REPEAT("-**-",3)** as the formula. The string "-**--**--**-" is the result. This string follows 1-2-3's rule for long labels. That is, the string is displayed beyond the right boundary of the column, provided that no entry is in the cell to the right.

@TRIM—Removing Blank Spaces from a String

The @TRIM function eliminates spaces from the beginning and end of a string and converts multiple spaces to single spaces. Use the following syntax for @TRIM:

@TRIM(*string*)

The following example returns I hate loose text:

@TRIM(" I   hate   loose   text ")

In some cases, importing data from non-1-2-3 sources creates labels padded with leading or trailing spaces. Use @TRIM to remove these extraneous spaces.

@S and @N—Testing for Strings and Values

The @S and @N functions convert cell contents into string values or numeric values, respectively. They use the following syntaxes:

@S(*range*)

@N(*range*)

When *range* is larger than one cell, these functions operate on the entry at the top left corner of range.

Think of @S as returning the string located at *range*, if there is one. If cell B12 contains a label or string-returning formula, @S(B12) returns that string. But if cell B12 is blank or contains a value, @S(B12) returns a null string, the equivalent of just entering a label prefix in a cell.

Use @S to concatenate the contents of a cell with another string conditionally. Assuming that there is a cell named CITY1, the following example may return City: Milwaukee or City: Phoenix or just City: if CITY1 is empty or contains a number:

    +"City: "&@S(CITY1)

@N returns the number at a location if there is one. Otherwise, it returns 0. The formula @N(B12) is a bit like +B12. If cell B12 contains a number, @N(B12) returns that number, as does +B12. If cell B12 is empty, @N(B12) returns 0. But if cell B12 contains a label or string-returning formula, @N(B12) returns 0, whereas +B12 echoes that string. Use @N when calculations must treat character strings as 0.

@STRING—Converting Values to Strings

The @STRING function converts a number to its text-string equivalent so that you can work with the number as text. You can use @STRING to convert a number to text and then concatenate the result into a text sentence.

Use the following syntax for @STRING:

    @STRING(*numeric_value,decimal_places*)

1-2-3 uses the **F**ixed format for the @STRING function and left-justifies the resulting text-string. The *decimal_places* argument represents the number of decimal places to be included in the string and must be greater than or equal to zero and less than 16 (1-2-3 ignores any fractional portion of this value). 1-2-3 rounds the resulting textual number to match the number of decimal places you specify. Note that @STRING ignores all numeric formats you placed on the cell and operates on just the numeric contents of the cell.

If cell H15 contains the value 8438.295, the following holds true. @STRING(H15,0) returns the character string 8438. Again, the format of cell H15 has no bearing on the result of @STRING. @STRING does not produce strings with commas, dollar signs, or other formatting. The following example returns 8438.3:

    @STRING(H15,1)

Suppose that you have devised a worksheet model that gives meaningless results if the value in cell B10 is higher than the value in cell H15. You can embed a message to the user in an area near cell B10 by entering the following formula:

    +"Entry in cell B10 cannot be greater than "&@STRING(H15,0)

@VALUE—Converting Strings to Values

The @VALUE function converts a string that resembles a number to a value. The following is its syntax:

@VALUE(*string*)

The *string* argument can contain numerals, a dollar sign at the beginning or a percent sign at the end, up to one decimal point, or commas, if they are at appropriate places. The *string* argument also can use a slash to indicate fractions. If the string does not resemble a value, the function returns ERR. The following list gives examples of the @VALUE function:

@VALUE("438") returns the number 438.

@VALUE("$438.72") returns the number 438.72. The dollar sign only appears in the result if the cell is formatted for currency.

@VALUE("4,365") returns the value 4365.

> **Note**
>
> A comma appears in the result only if the cell is formatted to display values with commas.
>
> @VALUE("43,65") returns ERR
>
> @VALUE("5%") returns the value 0.05
>
> @VALUE("3/4") returns the value 0.75
>
> @VALUE("4 3/4") returns the value 4.75

@CLEAN—Removing Nonprintable Characters from Strings

Sometimes when you import strings with **/F**ile **I**mport, particularly with a modem, the strings contain nonprintable characters. The @CLEAN function removes many nonprintable characters from the strings. @CLEAN uses the following syntax:

@CLEAN(*string*)

The argument used with @CLEAN must be a string value or a cell reference to a cell containing a string value.

Tip
@CLEAN removes nonprintable characters from data imported into a 1-2-3 worksheet from other sources.

@CHAR—Displaying LMBCS Characters

The @CHAR function produces on-screen the LMBCS equivalent of a number which specifies that character. @CHAR uses the following syntax:

@CHAR(*number*)

@CHAR(184), for example, produces a copyright symbol.

@CODE—Computing the LMBCS Code

The @CODE function performs the opposite action of @CHAR. Whereas @CHAR takes a number and returns the LMBCS, @CODE returns the LMBCS code of the first character in a string. @CODE uses the following syntax:

@CODE(*string*)

Suppose that you want to find the LMBCS code for the letter A. You type **@CODE("A")** in a cell, and 1-2-3 returns the number 65. If you type **@CODE("Aardvark")** in a cell, 1-2-3 still returns 65, the code of the first character in the string.

Using the Special Functions

The 16 special functions provide information about cell or range contents or about worksheet location. @CELL, @CELLPOINTER, and @COORD are three of 1-2-3's most powerful special functions and have many different capabilities. @CELL and @CELLPOINTER can return up to 58 different characteristics of a cell. These characteristics are known as attributes. @COORD specifies a cell address as absolute, relative, or mixed. @NA and @ERR trap errors that may otherwise appear in a worksheet. With @ROWS, @COLS, and @SHEETS, you can determine the size of a range. The @@ function enables you to reference a cell indirectly through another cell within the worksheet. With @CHOOSE, @HLOOKUP, @VLOOKUP, and @INDEX, you can use specified keys in the functions' arguments to look up values in tables or lists. @INFO retrieves system-related information. @? and @SOLVER are new functions in 1-2-3 Release 4 that relate to add-in functions and Solver (an add-in program).

The @HLOOKUP and @VLOOKUP functions are explained in detail in Chapter 15, "Using Functions To Analyze Data." Refer to Chapter 16, "Finding Solutions with Solver," to learn about the @SOLVER function.

Table 3.11 lists 1-2-3's special functions.

Table 3.11 Special Functions

Function	Description
@?(not entered in worksheet)	1-2-3 returns this function name when an add-in function is used that has not been read into memory
@@(*cell_reference*)	Returns the contents of the cell referenced by the cell address in the argument
@CELL(*attribute,range*)	Returns the designated attribute for the cell in the top left corner of the referenced range
@CELLPOINTER(*attribute*)	Returns the designated attribute for the current cell
@COORD(*worksheet, column,row,absolute*)	Constructs a cell address from values corresponding to worksheets, rows, and columns
@CHOOSE(*offset,list*)	Locates in a list the entry that is offset a specified amount from the beginning of the list
@COLS(*range*)	Computes the number of columns in a range
@ROWS(*range*)	Computes the number of rows in a range
@SHEETS(*range*)	Computes the number of worksheets in a range
@ERR	Displays ERR in the cell
@NA	Displays NA in the cell
@HLOOKUP(*key,range, row_offset*)	Locates the specified key in a lookup table and returns a value from that row of the range
@VLOOKUP(*key,range, column_offset*)	Locates the specified key in a lookup table and returns a value from that column of the range
@INDEX(*range,column, row,[worksheet]*)	Returns the contents of a cell specified by the intersection of a row and column within a range on a designated worksheet
@INFO(*attribute*)	Retrieves system information
@SOLVER(*query-string*)	Returns a value that indicates the status of the Solver add-in program (when added in memory)

@?—Indicating Unknown Add-In Functions

New to 1-2-3 Release 4 is the @? function that is used to indicate unknown functions from add-in programs. When you retrieve a file that contains an @function that 1-2-3 does not recognize, the @function name is translated to @? and returns the result **NA** in the worksheet. 1-2-3 uses the @? function internally; you cannot enter @? in a worksheet.

@@—Referencing Cells Indirectly

The @@ function provides a way of indirectly referencing one cell through the contents of another cell. @@ uses the following syntax:

@@(*cell_reference*)

Simple examples show how the @@ function works. If cell A1 contains the label A2, and cell A2 contains the number 5, the function @@(A1) returns the value 5. If the label in cell A1 is changed to B10, and cell B10 contains the label `hi there`, the function @@(A1) returns the string value `hi there`.

The argument of the @@ function must be a cell reference of a cell containing an address or the name of a single cell. This address is an indirect address. Similarly, the cell referenced by the argument of the @@ function must contain a label, string formula, or reference to another cell that results in a string value that is a cell reference.

The @@ function is useful primarily in cases where several formulas have the same argument, and the argument must be changed from time to time during the course of the application. 1-2-3 enables you to specify the argument of each formula through a common indirect address. In figure 3.26, the payment formulas in column D refer indirectly to one of three interest rates in cells C5, C6, and C7. Because the PMT formulas use @@(C$10) as the interest-rate argument, you can make all three formulas in column D reflect one of the three interest rates just by changing the label in cell C10.

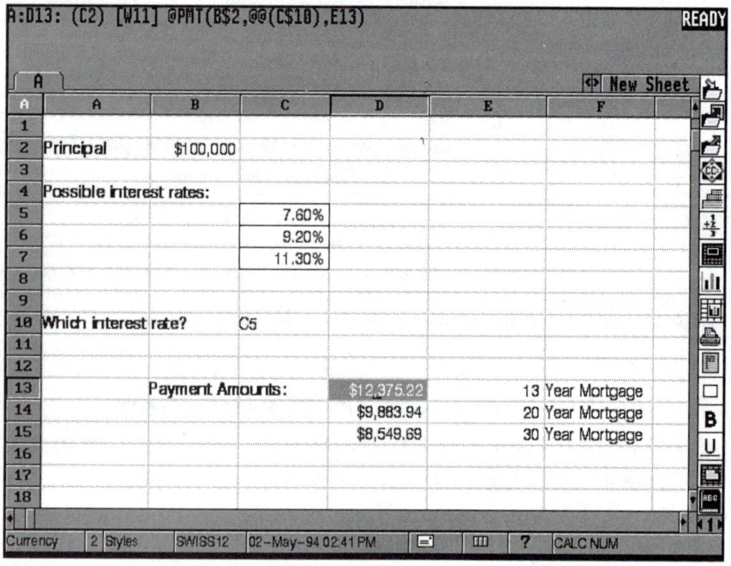

Fig. 3.26
The @@ function indirectly references one cell through another cell.

@CELL and @CELLPOINTER—Checking Cell Attributes

The @CELL and @CELLPOINTER functions provide an efficient way to determine the nature of a cell because these functions return up to 58 different cell characteristics, such as a cell's number or value, color, and width. @CELL and @CELLPOINTER are used primarily in macros and advanced macro command programs (see Chapters 14 and 15). Use the following syntaxes for @CELL and @CELLPOINTER:

@CELL(*attribute,range*)

@CELLPOINTER(*attribute*)

Because you want to examine a cell's attributes, both functions have *attribute* as a string argument. @CELL, however, also requires the specification of a range; @CELLPOINTER works with the current cell.

The following examples illustrate how the @CELL function can be used to examine some cell attributes:

- @CELL("address",SALES)

    If the range named SALES is C187..E187, returns the character string $C$187. This statement is convenient for listing the top left corner of a range's address in the worksheet.

- @CELL("prefix",C195..C195)

    If cell C195 contains the label 'Chicago, returns ' (indicating left alignment). If cell C195 is blank or contains a value or formula, however, the function returns an empty string.

- @CELL("format",A10)

    Returns the format of cell A10 as a text string, using the same notation as that used on the worksheet. A **C**urrency format with **2** decimal places, for example, appears as C2.

- @CELL("width",B12..B12)

    Returns the width of column B.

The *attribute* argument is text and must be enclosed in quotation marks. If a range of cells is specified, the returned value refers to the top left cell in the range.

Table 3.12 lists the full set of attributes that can be examined with @CELL and @CELLPOINTER.

Chapter 3—Finding Solutions with Formulas and Functions

Table 3.12 Attributes Used with @CELL and @CELLPOINTER

Attribute	What the Function Returns
"address"	The abbreviated absolute cell address
"col"	Column letter, from 1 to 256
"color"	1 - Cell is formatted for color 0 - Cell is not formatted for color
"contents"	Cell contents
"filename"	Name of file that contains the cell
"format"	**F**ixed decimal, F0 to F15 **S**cientific, S0 to S15 **C**urrency, C0 to C15 **,** (comma), ,0 to ,15 **G** for General **+** for +/- **P**ercent, P0 to P15 **D**ate/Time, D1 to D9 **A**utomatic, A **T**ext, T **L**abel, L **H**idden, H Color, - Parentheses ( )
"prefix"	Same as label prefixes; blank if no label
"protect"	1 if protected; 0 if not
"row"	Row number, 1 to 8192
"sheet"	Worksheet letter, 1 to 256
"type"	b for a blank cell, v for a cell that contains a value or a formula (including a string-returning formula), or l (lower case L) for a cell that contains a label
"width"	Column width

The @CELLPOINTER function works well within @IF functions to test whether data entered into a cell is numeric or text. @CELL and @CELLPOINTER are frequently used within macros to examine the current contents or format of cells. Then {IF} macros can use the results to change the worksheet accordingly.

> **Note**
>
> The difference between @CELL and @CELLPOINTER is important. The @CELL function examines the string attribute of a cell you designate in a range format, such as A1..A1. If you use a single range format, such as A1, 1-2-3 changes to the range format (A1..A1) and returns the attribute of the single-cell range. If you define a range larger than a single cell, 1-2-3 evaluates the cell in the top left corner of the range.

The @CELLPOINTER function operates on the current cell—the cell where the cell pointer was positioned when the worksheet was last recalculated. The result remains the same until you enter a value or press Calc (F9) if the worksheet is in automatic recalculation mode or until you press Calc (F9) in manual calculation mode.

To determine the address of the current cell, for example, you can type **@CELLPOINTER("address")** in cell B22. If recalculation is set to automatic, the value displayed in that cell is displayed as the absolute address $B$22. This same address remains displayed until you recalculate the worksheet by making an entry elsewhere in the worksheet or by pressing Calc (F9). The address that appears in cell B22 changes to reflect the position of the cell pointer when the worksheet was recalculated. If recalculation is set to manual, you can change the address only by pressing Calc (F9).

@COORD—Creating a Cell Address

You use @COORD to convert a number in a worksheet, column, and row to a cell address. @COORD uses the following syntax:

@COORD(*worksheet,column,row,absolute*)

The *worksheet* argument is a number between 1 and 256. Worksheet A is 1, worksheet B is 2, and so on. The *column* number is also a number between 1 and 256. Column A is 1, column B is 2, and so on. The *row* number is a number between 1 and 8,192. The *absolute* argument is a number between 1 and 8 that determines where the resulting address contains dollar signs. Table 3.13 shows the results of using different absolute values.

Table 3.13 Values of Absolute

Value	Worksheet	Column	Row	Example
1	Absolute	Absolute	Absolute	$A:$A$1
2	Absolute	Relative	Absolute	$A:A$1
3	Absolute	Absolute	Relative	$A:$A1
4	Absolute	Relative	Relative	$A:A1
5	Relative	Absolute	Absolute	A:$A$1
6	Relative	Relative	Absolute	A:A$1
7	Relative	Absolute	Relative	A:$A1
8	Relative	Relative	Relative	A:A1

@CHOOSE—Selecting an Item from a List

The @CHOOSE function uses position to select an item from a list. The syntax of the function is

@CHOOSE(*offset,list*)

The function selects the item in the specified position, or *offset*, in the *list*. Keep in mind that positions in the list are numbered starting with 0. The first position is 0, the second is 1, the third is 2, and so on.

Earlier you learned that the formula @MONTH(@TODAY) returns the month number of the current date. You can use @CHOOSE to convert that value into the name of the month. Because month numbers range from 1 to 12, and the numbers of the @CHOOSE list arguments start with 0, subtract 1 from the current month value. To get the name of the current month, use the following formula:

@CHOOSE(@MONTH(@TODAY)-1,"January","February","March", "April","May","June","July","August","September","October", "November","December")

@COLS, @ROWS, and @SHEETS—Finding the Dimensions of Ranges

The @COLS, @ROWS, and @SHEETS functions describe the dimensions of ranges. Use the following syntaxes for these functions:

@COLS(*range*)

@ROWS(*range*)

@SHEETS(*range*)

Suppose that you want first to determine the number of columns in a range called PRICE_TABLES, which has the cell coordinates A:D4..C:G50, and then to display that value in the current cell. To calculate the number of columns, you type **@COLS(PRICE_TABLES)**; this returns 4. Similarly, you can type **@ROWS(PRICE_TABLES)** to display the number of rows in the range, 47, and **@SHEETS(PRICE_TABLES)** to display the number of worksheets in the range, 0.

If you adjust the coordinates of the range name PRICE_TABLES, or add new columns, rows, or sheets within that range, the results of @COLS, @ROWS, and @SHEETS adjust accordingly.

@COLS, @ROWS, and @SHEETS are useful within macros to determine the size of a range. After the size of a range is determined, you can create, for example, a {FOR} loop. The loop uses the result of an @ROWS expression as its stop value to have the macro to perform an operation on each row in a range.

If you specify a single cell (such as C3) as the argument for the @COLS, @ROWS, or @SHEETS function, 1-2-3 changes the argument to range format (C3..C3) and returns the value 1 for the function.

@ERR and @NA—Trapping Errors

If you create templates for other users, you may want to use @NA or @ERR to screen out unacceptable values for cell entries. Suppose that you are developing a checkbook-balancing macro in which checks with values less than or equal to zero are unacceptable. One way to indicate the unacceptability of these checks is to use @ERR to signal that fact. You can use the following version of the @IF function:

@IF(B9<=0,@ERR,B9)

This statement translated into English says: "If the amount in cell B9 is less than or equal to zero, display ERR on-screen; otherwise, use the amount in cell B9." This formula provides a quick way to discover an unacceptable condition in the worksheet; you may, however, find that writing a formula displaying an explicit message is often a more useful procedure. For example, you can replace the preceding formula with the following formula:

@IF(B9<=0,"Enter positive amounts",B9)

If necessary, you can use @NA to indicate that data is missing. Suppose that formulas in a worksheet can return misleading results if no value is entered in cell B15. You can use the formula @IF(@CELL("type",B15)="v",B15,@NA) to start a cascade of NAs throughout the worksheet. This procedure demonstrates clearly that an important factor in the worksheet's calculations is missing.

@INDEX—Retrieving Data from Specified Locations

@INDEX, a data-management function, is similar to the table-lookup functions described earlier, but @INDEX has some unique features. @INDEX uses the following syntax:

@INDEX(*range,column,row,[worksheet]*)

Like @HLOOKUP and @VLOOKUP, @INDEX finds a value within a table. But unlike the lookup functions, @INDEX does not compare a key value against values in the first row or column of the table: @INDEX requires you to indicate the column offset and row offset of the range from which you want to retrieve data. If the range spans several worksheets, you also may indicate a worksheet number.

Figure 3.27 shows a worksheet using @INDEX. A mail-order company uses a shipping charge based on shipping zones and the number of packages shipped. Because these factors can be indicated by numbers, you can arrange the various charges in a table and access them by a column number, which corresponds to a shipping-zone number, and a row number, which corresponds to a number of packages.

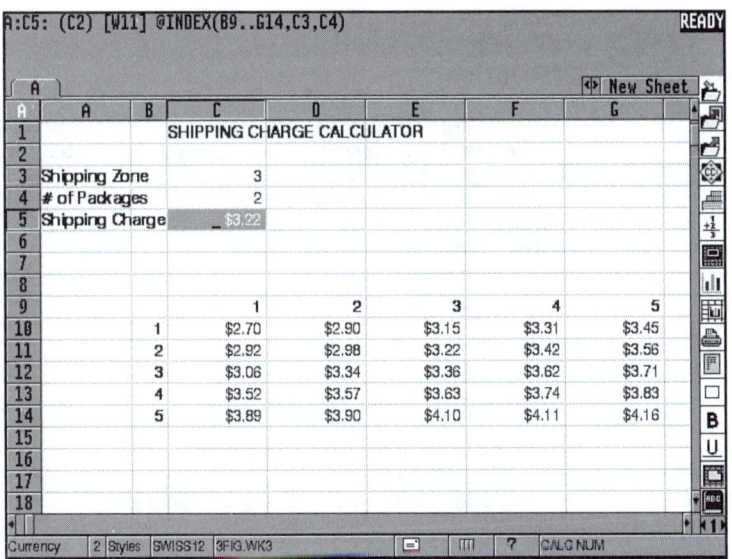

Fig. 3.27
Using @INDEX to find the value at a specific column and row within a range.

@INFO—Getting System Information About the Current Session

The @INFO function accesses system information about the current 1-2-3 session. Table 3.14 summarizes the attributes you can check by using @INFO.

Table 3.14 @INFO Session Attributes

Attribute	Description
"directory"	Returns the current directory path
"memavail"	Returns the memory available
"mode"	Returns a numeric code indicating one of these modes: 0 = WAIT mode 1 = READY mode 2 = LABEL mode 3 = MENU mode 4 = VALUE mode 5 = POINT mode 6 = EDIT mode 10 = HELP mode 99 = All other modes (such as those set by the {INDICATE} command)
"numfile"	Returns the number of currently open files

(continues)

Table 3.14 Continued

Attribute	Description
"origin"	Returns the cell address of the cell appearing at the top left corner of the screen. If the screen is split into two windows, returns the address of the top left corner of the active window
"osreturncode"	Returns the value returned by the most recent **/S**ystem or {SYSTEM} command
"osversion"	Returns the current operating system description
"recalc"	Returns the current recalculation setting
"release"	Returns the 1-2-3 release number
"system"	Returns the name of the operating system
"totmem"	Returns the total amount of memory (amount used plus amount available)

If the current directory is the root directory of a disk in the A: drive, for example, this formula returns the string `A:\`:

@INFO("directory")

If recalculation is currently manual, the following formula returns the string `Manual`.

@INFO("recalc")

If 1-2-3 is currently in POINT mode, the following formula returns the value 5.

@INFO("mode")

Controlling Recalculation

When a value in a file changes, 1-2-3 recalculates all other cells dependent on the changed value. This feature essentially makes 1-2-3 an electronic worksheet. 1-2-3 provides a number of recalculation options for various circumstances. This section covers how you can control the way 1-2-3 updates the file while you are changing it.

Understanding Recalculation Methods

Usually, 1-2-3 recalculates the file whenever a cell changes. This feature is *automatic recalculation*. Some of the previous versions of 1-2-3 took a long time to recalculate large worksheets. With Release 3.4 and 4, however, recalculation is optimal and in the background.

Optimal recalculation means that the only cells recalculated are cells that contain formulas that refer to the changed cell. If you change a cell in a large file, and the cell is used in only one formula, only the one formula is recalculated. Therefore, recalculation is accelerated.

Background recalculation means that you can continue working while 1-2-3 recalculates the file. You may have many numbers to add or change, and each can affect hundreds of calculations in the file. As you enter each number, 1-2-3 starts recalculating, but you still can enter numbers in the worksheet. As long as you change cells faster than 1-2-3 can recalculate the file, the CALC indicator stays on in the status line at the bottom of the display. When 1-2-3 completes the recalculation, the CALC indicator disappears.

Because of these recalculation schemes, recalculation is best left in the default, **A**utomatic mode. You can use **/W**orksheet **G**lobal **R**ecalc **M**anual, however, to tell 1-2-3 not to recalculate the worksheet when you make a change. To force a recalculation, press the Calc (F9) key or click the Recalculate SmartIcon. Pressing F9 produces a foreground calculation. Until the recalculation is complete, the mode indicator is set to WAIT, and you cannot use 1-2-3.

Automatic recalculation can slow macro execution because the recalculation is done in the background. If you use macros, you may want to include commands in the macro to set the recalculation to manual while the macro executes and then reset recalculation to automatic before the macro ends. 1-2-3 makes special considerations for macros when recalculation is manual. These considerations are covered in Chapter 26, "Short Macros To Make Your Life Easier."

During recalculation, 1-2-3 determines which formulas depend on which cells and sets up a recalculation order to ensure the correct answer. This process is known as the *natural order of recalculation*. Older spreadsheet programs designed before 1-2-3 didn't use this approach and at times required many successive recalculations before arriving at the right answer in all cells.

228 Chapter 3—Finding Solutions with Formulas and Functions

The early spreadsheet programs only recalculated either columnwise or rowwise. Columnwise recalculation starts in cell A1 and calculates the cells down column A, then down column B, and so on. Rowwise recalculation starts in cell A1 and calculates the cells across row 1, then across row 2, and so on. **C**olumnwise and **R**owwise are options in the **/W**orksheet **G**lobal **R**ecalc menu but, as a rule, ignore these options and leave recalculation on **N**atural.

Understanding Circular References

When a *circular reference* occurs, the natural order of recalculation doesn't ensure the correct answer for all cells. A circular reference is a formula that depends, either directly or indirectly, on its own value. Usually, a circular reference is an error that you should eliminate immediately. Whenever 1-2-3 performs a recalculation and finds a circular reference, the CIRC indicator appears in the status line at the bottom of the display. Figure 3.28 shows an erroneous circular reference in which the @SUM function includes itself. In this example, the sum of cells B2 through B10 (444200) is added to itself, which makes 888,400. Every time you press F9 (Calc) or edit the worksheet, 444,200 is added to the formula.

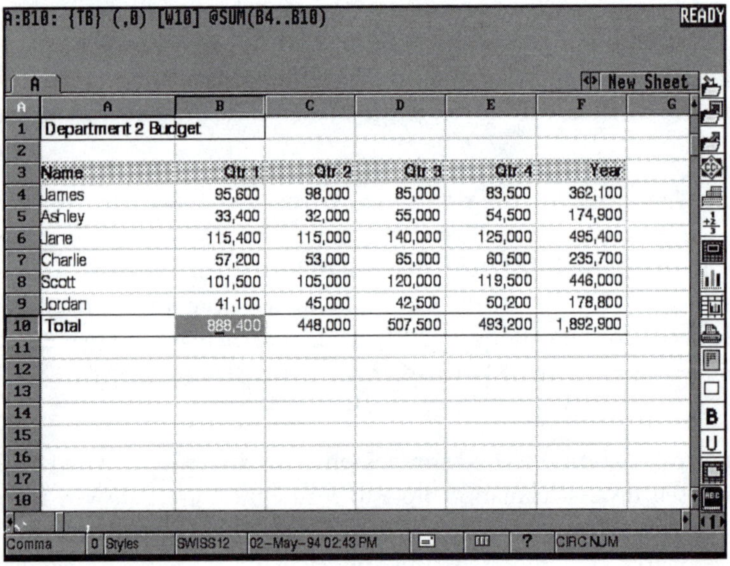

Fig. 3.28
A circular reference that produces the CIRC indicator.

	A	B	C	D	E	F
1	Department 2 Budget					
2						
3	Name	Qtr 1	Qtr 2	Qtr 3	Qtr 4	Year
4	James	95,600	98,000	85,000	83,500	362,100
5	Ashley	33,400	32,000	55,000	54,500	174,900
6	Jane	115,400	115,000	140,000	125,000	495,400
7	Charlie	57,200	53,000	65,000	60,500	235,700
8	Scott	101,500	105,000	120,000	119,500	446,000
9	Jordan	41,100	45,000	42,500	50,200	178,800
10	Total	888,400	448,000	507,500	493,200	1,892,900

When the CIRC indicator appears and you don't know why, use **/W**orksheet **S**tatus to display the Worksheet Status settings sheet (see fig. 3.29). This display points out the cell that caused the circular reference, and you can fix the error. Occasionally, the source of the problem may not be obvious, and you may have to check every cell to which the formula cell refers.

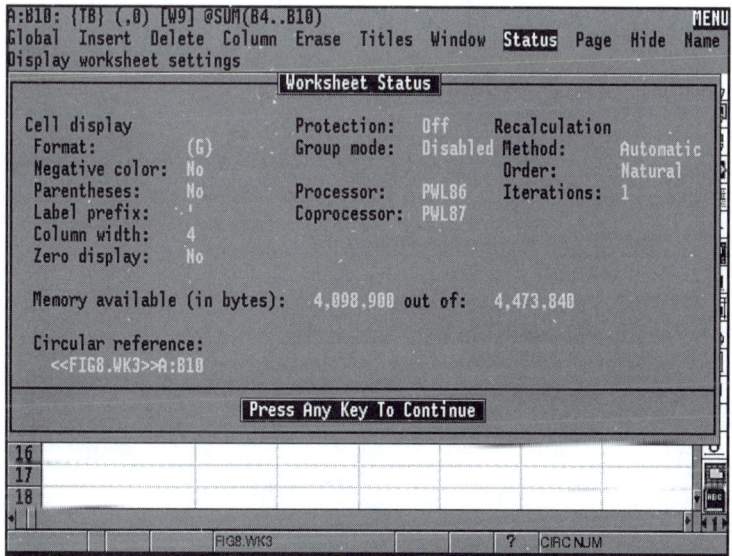

Fig. 3.29
The location of a circular reference displayed in the Worksheet Status settings sheet.

Another aid for finding circular references is the Auditor add-in. Auditor checks formulas in the worksheet. If you select **C**ircs from the Auditor menu, Auditor displays a cell address for each circular reference. When you select a cell, Auditor describes the path of the circular reference and displays the formulas involved. Auditor also provides other useful data about formulas in the worksheet. Detailed information about the Auditor add-in appears in Chapter 14, "Analyzing Formulas with Auditor."

Tip
Use /**W**orksheet **S**tatus to find the location of a circular reference.

> **Note**
>
> Auditor identifies all circular references in a worksheet; the /**W**orksheet **S**tatus command displays only the last circular reference created. If multiple circular references exist, using Auditor is the quickest and safest way to identify the cells involved in the circular reference.

Using Iteration To Solve Circular References

Occasionally, you may want to create a circular reference. Figure 3.30 shows a worksheet with a deliberate circular reference. In this example, a company sets aside 10 percent of the net profit for employee bonuses. The bonuses, however, represent an expense that reduces net profit. The formula in C5 shows that the amount of bonuses is net profit in D5 times .1, or 10 percent, but net profit is profit before bonuses minus bonuses (B5-C5). The value of Employee Bonuses depends on the value of Net Profit, and the value of Net Profit depends on the value of Employee Bonuses. In figure 3.30, C5 depends on D5 and D5 depends on C5.

Fig. 3.30
A worksheet with a deliberate circular reference.

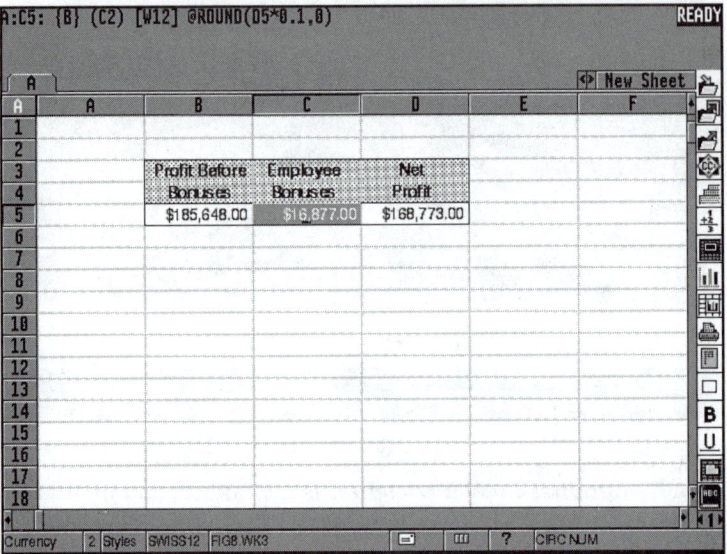

Each time you recalculate the worksheet, the answers change by a smaller amount when you use a legitimate circular reference. Eventually, the changes become insignificant. This decrease in change is known as *convergence*. Note that the erroneous circular reference in figure 3.29 never converges, and the @SUM result grows larger every time you recalculate.

The worksheet in figure 3.30 needs five recalculations before the changes become less than a dollar. After you establish this number (by pressing the F9 (Calc) key and watching the effect on the formulas), you can set 1-2-3 to recalculate the worksheet five times for every recalculation. Select **/W**orksheet **G**lobal **R**ecalc **I**teration, press **5**, and then click anywhere in the control panel or press Enter. Usually, you can handle a converging circular reference with a macro.

From Here...

You may want to review the following chapters for more information on the functions that you learned:

- Chapter 4, "Controlling Your Worksheet Display," shows you how to change the way a worksheet is displayed so that it's easier to enter formulas and functions in various parts of a worksheet.

- Chapter 6, "Making Your Worksheets Dazzle," covers formatting cells to display values that formulas and functions return and suppressing the display of zeros in a worksheet.

- Chapter 7, "Attaching Comments to Worksheet Cells," describes how to add comments to values and formulas.

- Chapter 13, "Protecting Worksheet Data and Files," shows you how to protect the formulas stored in cells so that they cannot be altered.

- Chapter 15, "Using Functions To Analyze Data," tells you how to use the database functions (like @DSTD, @DVAR, @DQUERY, @HLOOKUP, @HVLOOKUP, and so on).

Chapter 4

Controlling Your Worksheet Display

You can change the way you view the worksheets in memory in a number of ways. You can change the display format to view more rows and columns at one time. You can split the screen into two windows either vertically or horizontally, and you can view parts of three worksheets at once in perspective, a three-dimensional view. These options give you the ability to see different parts of your work at the same time.

In this chapter, you learn how to do the following:

- Change the way the worksheet is displayed
- Split the screen
- Display a graph within a worksheet
- Freeze worksheet titles
- Set display characteristics

Changing the Display Format

When you work with large databases, reports, or tables of data, you cannot see all the data at one time. Depending on the monitor hardware, you can change the display to view more columns and rows of data at the same time. The more data you can see at one time, the more easily you can compare different months or different departments.

Besides the standard 80-character by 25-line (80x25) display, many monitor and graphic card combinations give you a choice of other formats. You choose these display formats when you install 1-2-3. If your system has a Hercules Monochrome Graphics Card, you can choose an 80x25 or 90x43 display. With an EGA card, you can choose an 80x25 or 80x43 display. With a VGA card, you can choose an 80x25, 80x43, or 80x60 display.

> **Note**
>
> If you have a monochrome display adapter (no graphics), a Color Graphics Adapter, or EGA with only 64K of video memory, you can display data only in the 80x25 format.

If the display hardware gives a choice of formats, you can choose two of these formats at installation. This setup enables you to switch formats from within 1-2-3. Your first format choice is marked with a 1 and becomes the primary display.

This preferred display appears when you first load 1-2-3. The second format becomes the secondary display. If you want to display a worksheet with more columns than the default, use the /**W**orksheet **W**indow **D**isplay **2** command.

You may want to do most of your work in standard 80x25 format, because this format is both the sharpest and the easiest on the eyes. When you want to see more of the worksheet at one time, however, switch to the higher-density secondary display format. To return to the primary 80x25 display, use /**W**orksheet **W**indow **D**isplay **1**.

Another way to vary the display is to use the **:D**isplay **R**ows and the **:D**isplay **Z**oom commands. These commands are discussed in a later section in this chapter.

Splitting the Screen

You can split the screen either horizontally or vertically into two windows by using /**W**orksheet **W**indow **H**orizontal or /**W**orksheet **W**indow **V**ertical. These commands are useful when you are using large, single-worksheet applications, enabling you to see different parts of the worksheet at the same time.

In the worksheet in figure 4.1, for example, you can split the screen horizontally when you want to see the assumptions on one half of the screen and the 1995 Budget results on the other half of the screen. With a split screen, you can change data in one window to see how the totals change in the other window. This capability is well-suited for *what-if* analysis. If you change the capacity, for example, from 6% shown in cell E5 to 1%, the profit of $12.8 million changes to a loss of $3.7 million (see fig. 4.2).

You also may find a split screen helpful when you write macros. You can

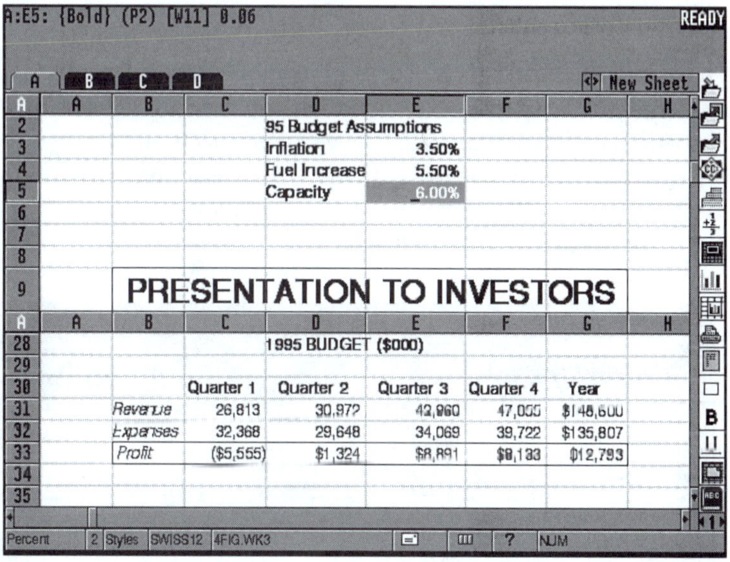

Fig. 4.1
Two different parts of a worksheet, displayed in two horizontal windows.

write the macro in one window and see the data that the macro alters in the other window. Macros are covered in Chapter 26, "Short Macros To Make Your Life Easier," and Chapter 27, "Advanced Macro Command Power Techniques."

Because the window splits at the position of the cell pointer, be sure that you first move the cell pointer to the desired position before splitting the screen. When you split the screen horizontally, the upper window includes the rows above the cell pointer. (The cell pointer moves to the upper window when you execute the command.) In figure 4.1, the cell pointer was in row 11 when the window was split. Rows 1 through 10 became the upper window. The lower window was scrolled to display the 1995 Budget table.

As you move to the right in the worksheet shown in figure 4.1, both windows scroll together. If you move the cell pointer past column H, both windows scroll so that you can see column I. In this example, you don't want synchronized scrolling of data. To stop synchronized scrolling, select **/W**orksheet **W**indow **U**nsync. To restore synchronized scrolling, select **/W**orksheet **W**indow **S**ync.

Tip
When you want two windows to scroll separately, use **/W**orksheet **W**indow **U**nsync.

When you split the screen vertically, the left window includes the columns to the immediate left of the cell pointer but doesn't include the cell pointer's column. (The cell pointer moves to the left window when you execute the command.) To display columns A through D, for example, move the cell pointer to column E and select **/W**orksheet **W**indow **V**ertical.

If you have multiple worksheets or files in memory, you can use the split screen to display different worksheets. When you use Ctrl+PgUp, Ctrl+PgDn, or the other direction keys to move between worksheets and files, you affect only the current window. The file in figure 4.2, for example, has multiple worksheets. With the cell pointer in the lower window, if you press Ctrl+PgUp, the lower window displays 1994 Actual data.

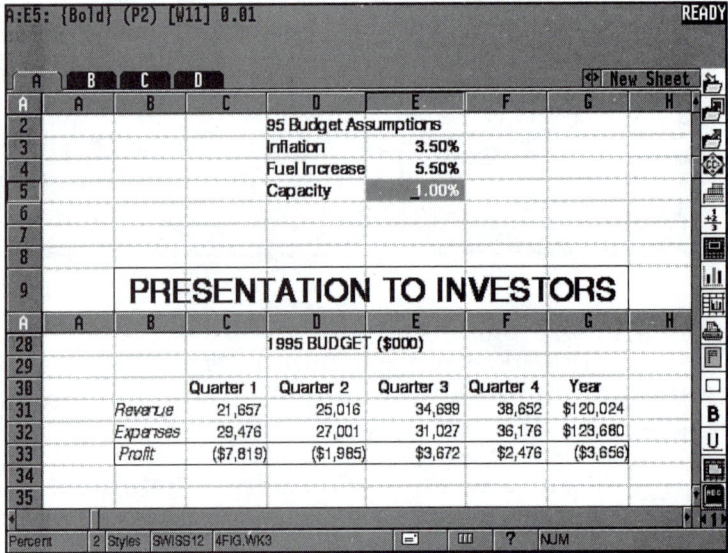

Fig. 4.2
Splitting the screen with multiple worksheets.

To move between windows, click in the desired window or use the Window (F6) key. To clear a split screen, select **/W**orksheet **W**indow **C**lear. No matter which window you are in, the cell pointer moves to either the left or the upper window when you clear a split screen.

You also can divide the screen by using **/W**orksheet **W**indow **P**erspective, which displays three worksheets as if all three worksheets were stacked up on a desk. This command always presents three worksheets. If fewer than three worksheets exist in memory, you see blank worksheets. In perspective view, each window displays a separate worksheet.

You can have either a split screen or a perspective view, but not both at the same time. To go from one option to the other, first use **/W**orksheet **W**indow **C**lear; then choose the other window option. To move between the windows in perspective mode, click in a window, use Ctrl+PgUp or Ctrl+PgDn, use the Next Worksheet or Previous Worksheet SmartIcons, or press the Window (F6) key.

If you want to make the current window (the one with the cell pointer) go to full screen, press the Alt+F6 (Zoom) key. The ZOOM status indicator appears in the status bar at the bottom of the display. To return to the separate windows, press Alt+F6 again. You can use Zoom for windows that are split horizontally or vertically or in perspective mode.

Tip
Use Zoom (Alt+F6) to enlarge a window to full-screen size.

Caution
When you use the Alt+F6 (Zoom) key, the tabs that designate the worksheet within which you are working disappear. The worksheet name, however, does appear in the intersection of the row and column cells at the upper left corner of the worksheet.

▶ "Using Multiple Worksheet Files," p. 458

Displaying a Graph in a Worksheet

The **/W**orksheet **W**indow **G**raph command applies only when you work with graphs. Use **/W**orksheet **W**indow **G**raph to split the screen into a data window and a graph window. The graph changes as you change the data in the worksheet. Figure 4.3 shows a display with a graph window. You cannot use **/W**orksheet **W**indow **G**raph with a Color Graphics Adapter (CGA) because of the CGA's low resolution. Chapter 23, "Creating Effective Graphs," covers graphing in detail.

Tip
Select **/W**orksheet **W**indow **G**raph as you create a graph. You can watch the graph change as you change the data.

To remove the graph from the worksheet, select **/W**orksheet **W**indow **C**lear.

Troubleshooting
1-2-3 beeps when I attempt to split the screen.

The cell pointer was positioned in column A when you tried to split the screen vertically. Because there is nothing to the left of the cell pointer, 1-2-3 cannot split the worksheet.

(continues)

> (continued)
>
> Or, the cell pointer was positioned in row 1 when you tried to split the screen horizontally. Because there is nothing above the cell pointer, 1-2-3 cannot split the worksheet.
>
> To split the screen, move the cell pointer closer to the middle of the worksheet before you attempt to split the screen again.
>
> *The graph window that's displayed in the worksheet is too narrow to interpret.*
>
> When you selected **/W**orksheet **W**indow **G**raph, the cell pointer was in column A in the worksheet. Position the cell pointer in the middle of the worksheet before displaying the graph window.

Fig. 4.3
The screen split into a data window and a graph window.

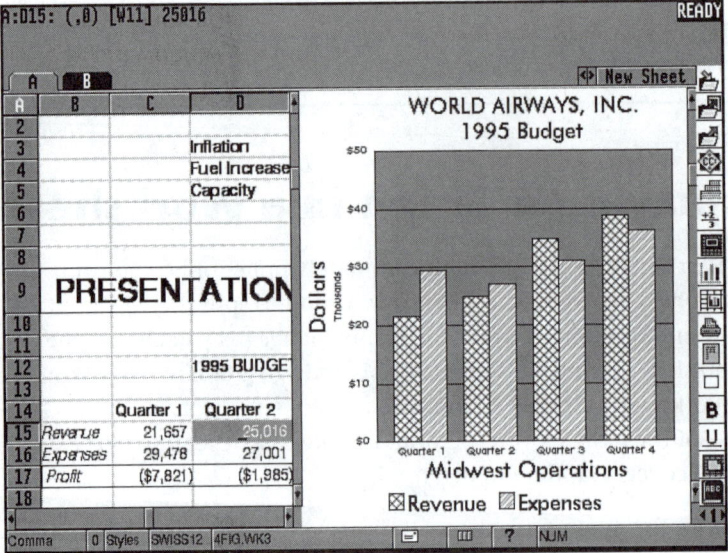

Freezing Titles On-Screen

Most worksheets are larger than you can display on-screen at one time (see fig. 4.4). As you move the cell pointer, you scroll the display. New data appears at one edge of the display while the data at the other edge scrolls out of sight. This scrolling becomes a problem when titles at the top of the worksheet and descriptions at the left also scroll off the screen; you no longer can tell what labels apply to each cell (see fig. 4.5).

Freezing Titles On-Screen   239

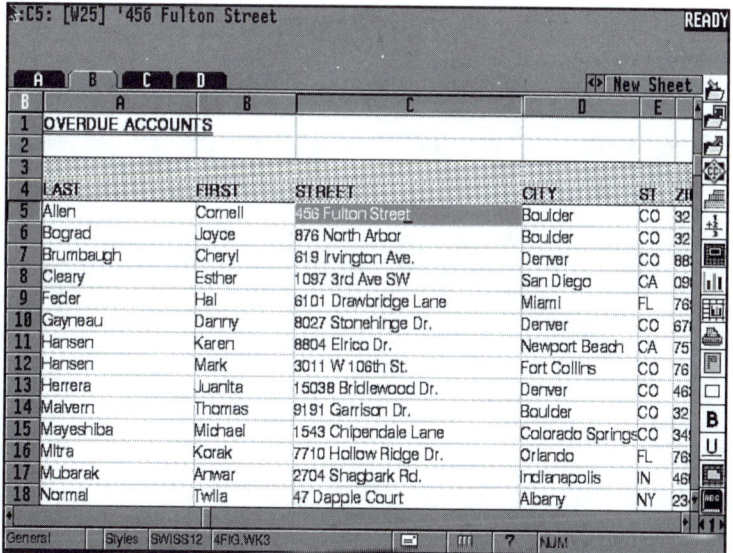

Fig. 4.4
Part of the data visible in the worksheet.

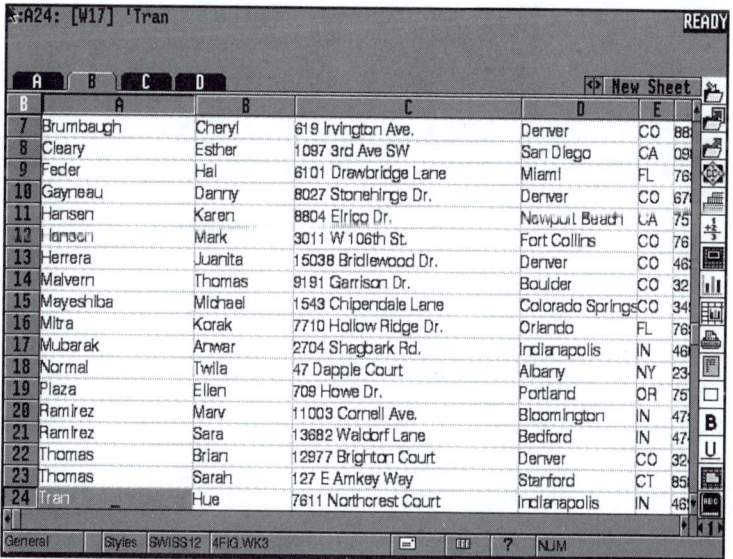

Fig. 4.5
The titles scrolled off the screen.

Use the **/W**orksheet **T**itles command to prevent titles from scrolling off the screen. To lock (or freeze) titles, follow these steps:

1. Position the display so that the titles to freeze are at the top and left of the display.

2. Move the cell pointer to the first row below the titles and the first column to the right of the titles. In figure 4.4, the titles are in rows 1 through 4 and columns A and B; the cell pointer is in C5.

3. Select **/W**orksheet **T**itles **B**oth to lock both horizontal and vertical titles (see fig. 4.6).

Fig. 4.6
Locked titles on-screen (rows 1 through 4 and columns A and B).

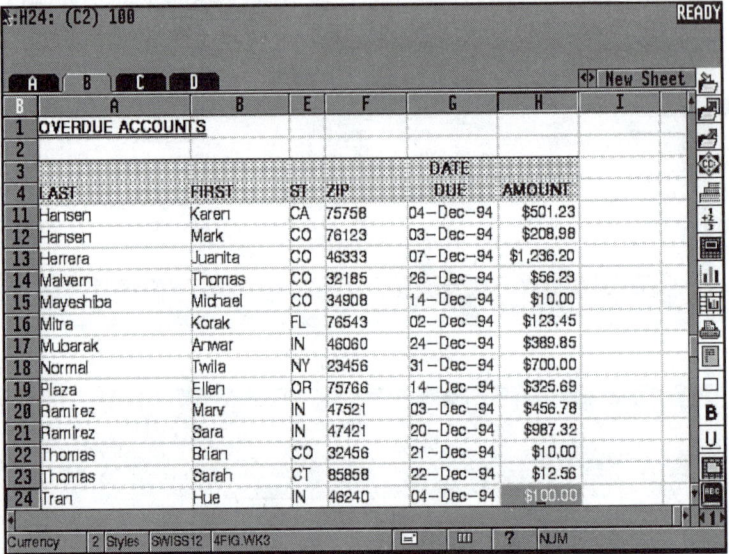

With locked titles, pressing Home moves the cell pointer to the position following the titles, not to cell A1. In figure 4.4, the Home position is C5. You cannot use the mouse or the direction keys to move into the titles area, but you can use the GoTo (F5) key. When you use GoTo to move to a cell in the titles area, the title rows and columns display twice (see fig. 4.7). This double set of titles can confuse you. You also can move into the titles area in POINT mode (for example, when using the **/C**opy command) and see the same double display as in figure 4.7.

You can lock just the rows at the top of the screen with **/W**orksheet **T**itles **H**orizontal or just the columns at the left with **/W**orksheet **T**itles **V**ertical.

To change the locked titles, just move the cell pointer to the first row below the new titles and the first column to the right of the new titles and select **/W**orksheet **T**itles **H**orizontal or **/W**orksheet **T**itles **V**ertical. Use **/W**orksheet **T**itles **C**lear to cancel the locked titles so that you can move freely in the titles area.

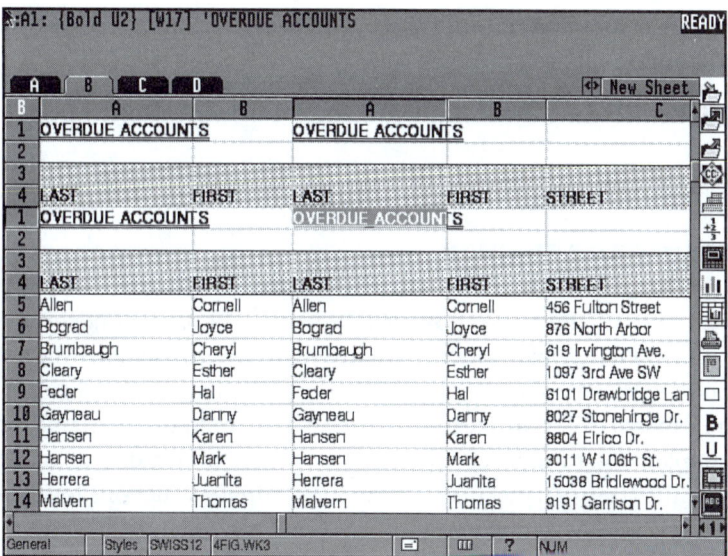

Fig. 4.7
Double display of titles with the cell pointer in the titles area.

With a split screen, locking titles affects the current (active) window. With a multiple-worksheet file, locking titles affects only the current worksheet unless you are in GROUP mode.

Setting Display Characteristics

Although a major advantage provided by Wysiwyg is the capability of producing professional-quality printed documents, you also can use Wysiwyg to change the screen display to suit your needs. You can make text, numbers, and graphics on-screen look similar to the way they appear when printed. You also can change the screen to create computer slide presentations or to simplify the process for creating and changing a worksheet application.

With Wysiwyg, you can change many characteristics of the screen; you can set the screen colors, for example, display the worksheet in graphics display mode ("what-you-see-is-what-you-get") or in text display mode (the standard 1-2-3 display), display gridlines between worksheet columns and rows, change the brightness of the screen, and specify a cell pointer style.

You also can change the size of the characters on-screen. You can reduce the characters so that you can see more of the worksheet at the same time or magnify the characters to see small fonts more clearly. The **:D**isplay commands don't affect the report printout; rather, these commands change how

▶ "Printing Multiple-Page Reports," p. 369

▶ "Setting Up the Page," p. 374

◀ "Using the GoTo (F5) Key," p. 59

the worksheet looks on-screen. When you select **:D**isplay, the following menu of options appears:

Mode   **Z**oom   **C**olors   **O**ptions   **F**ont   **D**irectory   **R**ows   **D**efault   **Q**uit

The following sections describe each option on the **:D**isplay menu.

Changing the Display

With the **:D**isplay **M**ode command, you can choose between the **G**raphics and **T**ext options and between **B**&**W** (black-and-white, or monochrome) and **C**olor. In graphics display mode, formatting on-screen resembles the final printout. Only in graphics display mode can you change the color of various screen elements (the worksheet background, text, cell pointer, frame, or grid, for example). You cannot see formatting on-screen in text display mode, although the control panel displays the formatting instructions for the current cell if Wysiwyg is in memory.

If you use a color monitor, you may want to use **B**&**W** mode occasionally to see how the worksheet looks when printed on a black-and-white printer.

Zooming the Display

The **:D**isplay **Z**oom command enables you to choose from **T**iny, **S**mall, **N**ormal, **L**arge, and **H**uge (standard character display settings) and **M**anual (specific character display reduction or enlargement, with a range of 25 to 400 percent of the normal size). Figure 4.8 shows **T**iny magnification; figure 4.9 shows **H**uge. The zoom feature does not work in text display mode. You also can use the Zoom SmartIcon to cycle through the magnification sizes.

Setting the Color Display

Tip
You can switch the background from white to black if you prefer a dark background on your screen.

The **C**olors option of the **:D**isplay command specifies the colors for the following parts of the screen: background, text (characters), unprotected cells, the cell pointer, grid lines, the worksheet frame, negative numbers, lines, and drop shadows. Wysiwyg can use the following eight colors: black, white, red, green, dark blue, cyan, yellow, and magenta.

Usually, the screen colors you select don't affect the printed report. If you use a color printer, however, the negative values, lines, and drop shadows print in the colors you specify (if your printer supports these colors).

The **R**eplace option on the **:D**isplay **C**olors menu defines the palette setting for each color. To adjust a color, choose **:D**isplay **C**olors **R**eplace, select the color, and enter a number between 0 and 63. Each number represents a different color. Experiment by entering different numbers, pressing the left- and right-arrow keys, or the plus (+) or minus (–) key to adjust the color until you find the desired color. The color in the worksheet adjusts to match the new setting. To make the color change permanent, use the **:D**isplay **D**efault **U**pdate command. Note that the name of your new color is not changed; if you reset Black to Yellow, it will still be labeled *Black*.

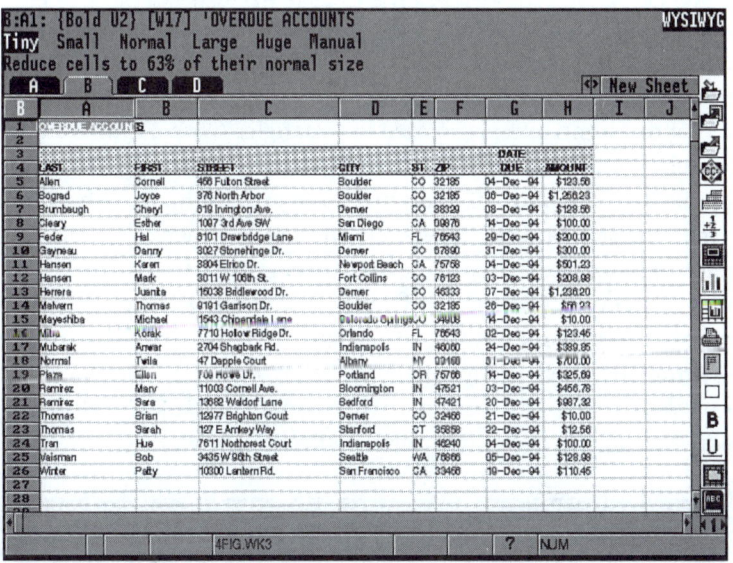

Fig. 4.8
A worksheet zoomed to the **T**iny magnification size.

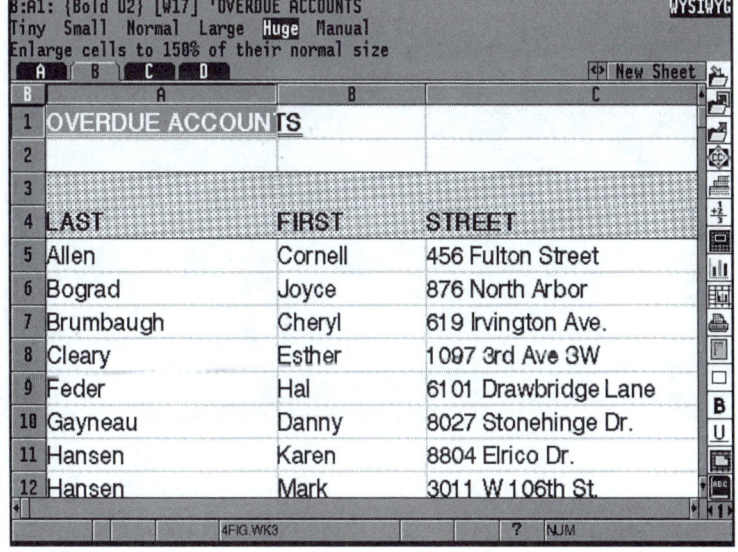

Fig. 4.9
A worksheet zoomed to the **H**uge magnification size.

Using Other Display Options

With the **:D**isplay **O**ptions command, you can set options for the following screen aspects: **F**rame, **G**rid, **P**age-Breaks, **C**ell-Pointer, and **I**ntensity. The following sections describe these options.

Setting the Frame Display

The **F**rame option of the **:D**isplay **O**ptions command controls how the worksheet frame (column letters and row numbers) displays. The default frame display is **R**elief. **R**elief displays a sculpted worksheet frame (this option also changes all uses of the color cyan to gray). **E**nhanced displays row numbers and column letters centered in rectangles (with a cyan frame). The **1**-2-3 frame is similar to the frame you see in 1-2-3 without Wysiwyg attached. The **S**pecial option displays measurements in the worksheet frame rather than the standard column letters and row numbers. You can display **C**haracters, **I**nches, **M**etric (centimeters), or **P**oints/Picas. The **I**nches frame is shown in figure 4.10. Because 1-2-3 depends so heavily on cell coordinates, you probably don't want to work with a **S**pecial frame setting all the time. These settings are most useful when you are laying out and balancing elements on your screen—for example, when setting up tables, positioning graphics, centering text, or outlining sections of your worksheet.

Fig. 4.10
Inches displayed in the worksheet frame.

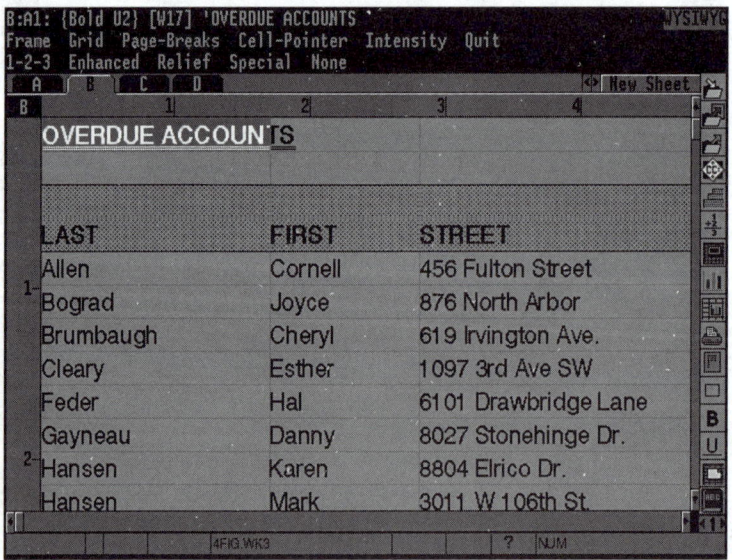

The final **F**rame option, **N**one, turns off the display of the frame. You may want to use this option in macros when you don't need to see column letters or row numbers on-screen—for example, when the macro displays an information screen. The macro option is also handy when you use 1-2-3 to project screen shows from a PC.

Using :Display Options Grid

The **G**rid option on the **:D**isplay **O**ptions menu controls the display of dotted lines (grid lines) between columns and rows. Figure 4.11 shows grid lines turned off. With grid lines displayed, your electronic worksheet more closely resembles accounting ledger paper. You also can use this option to determine the addresses of the cells displayed on-screen. Many of the figures in this book were created with grid lines displayed.

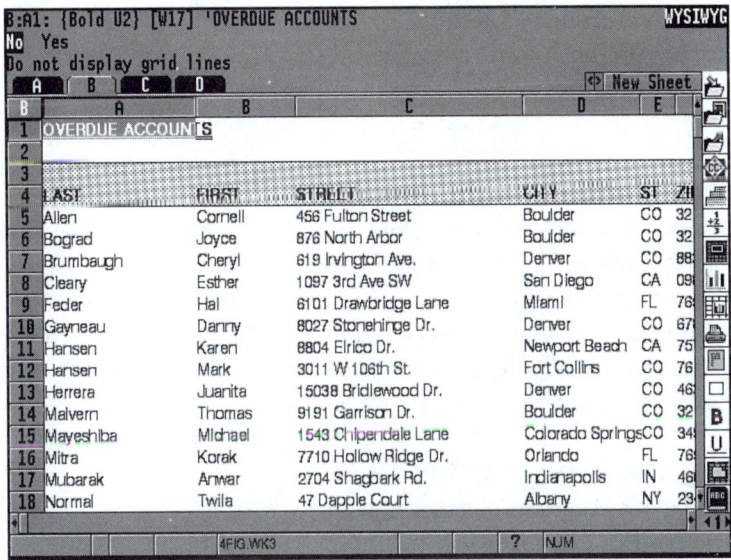

Fig. 4.11

Eliminating grid lines around cells in the worksheet.

Turning on the grid with **:D**isplay **O**ptions **G**rid **Y**es doesn't mean that the grid appears on your printed report. To print the grid, use the **:P**rint **S**ettings **G**rid **Y**es command.

Displaying Page-Breaks

With the **P**age-Breaks option of the **:D**isplay **O**ptions command, you control whether the dashed-print borders that represent page breaks are displayed on-screen. These borders usually display when you define a print range with **:P**rint **R**ange **S**et and when you insert page breaks with **:W**orksheet **P**age. To turn off the display of page breaks, select **:D**isplay **O**ptions **P**age-Breaks **N**o. Even if page breaks aren't displayed, 1-2-3 uses the page breaks when you print the report through Wysiwyg.

Setting the Cell-Pointer Display

The **C**ell-Pointer option of the **:D**isplay **O**ptions command controls the style of the cell pointer; you choose between **S**olid or **O**utline. You can display the cell pointer as a solid rectangular bar (the default) or as an outline around the cell. This option also controls how ranges are highlighted. With the **O**utline style, the highlighted range is not actually highlighted, but is enclosed in an outline border. Unless you choose background, grid, and cell-pointer colors that are distinguishably different, the cell pointer is more difficult to see in **O**utline style, especially when the grid is turned on. If you plan to do much cell formatting, however, you should use the outline cell pointer; it shows the formats in the cell more clearly than does the solid cell pointer.

Changing the Intensity Settings

The **:D**isplay **O**ptions **I**ntensity command provides two intensity settings: **N**ormal (the default) and **H**igh. For a brighter screen, change the screen intensity to **H**igh.

Changing the Font-Directory

The **:D**isplay **F**ont-Directory command indicates the directory in which the screen and print fonts are located. When the Install program creates the Bitstream soft fonts, the files are stored in the WYSIWYG directory, a subdirectory of the directory that contains the 1-2-3 program files. If you move these fonts to another directory or if you want to use fonts located in another directory, enter the path in the **F**ont-Directory option.

Setting the Row Display

The **:D**isplay **R**ows option specifies how many worksheet rows are displayed on-screen. Enter a value between 16 and 60. This option applies only when the screen is in graphics display mode (select **:D**isplay **M**ode **G**raphics).

Setting Default Display Values

The settings you change on the **:D**isplay menu are temporary, are valid for only the current 1-2-3 session, and are lost when you quit the program. To save the **:D**isplay settings permanently, select **:D**isplay **D**efault **U**pdate. The current settings then become active every time you use 1-2-3 and Wysiwyg. To cancel the current display settings and return to the default values, select **:D**isplay **D**efault **R**estore.

From Here...

For more information relating to the worksheet display, you may want to review the following chapters:

- Chapter 6, "Making Your Worksheets Dazzle." This chapter shows you how to use the :**F**ormat commands in the Wysiwyg menu to change the way data appears in your worksheet.

- Chapter 23, "Creating Effective Graphs." In this chapter, you learn how to set the graph criteria that 1-2-3 uses to display graphs in a worksheet.

Chapter 5
Using SmartIcons

SmartIcons are a graphical technique for making software easier to use. The SmartIcons provided with 1-2-3 Release 4 for DOS offer instant access to the most commonly used 1-2-3 commands and procedures.

Icons are small graphics or pictures. The *SmartIcons* in Release 4 represent 1-2-3 actions or commands. To execute a 1-2-3 command, point to a SmartIcon with the mouse pointer and click the mouse. Rather than choose **:F**ormat **B**old **S**et to apply boldfacing to a selected range, for example, you can click the Bold SmartIcon to produce the same result. You also can access SmartIcons by using the keyboard, but SmartIcons are of greatest benefit to mouse users.

1-2-3 Release 4 provides SmartIcons for most commands and procedures you perform frequently, from copying ranges and inserting worksheets to creating and printing graphs. SmartIcons also are available for some of the more complicated tasks you perform less frequently, such as circling data in a highlighted range—a procedure that otherwise involves choosing three commands from the Wysiwyg menu.

Note

The SmartIcons are installed in your system along with 1-2-3 and Wysiwyg during the 1-2-3 Release 4 installation procedure. 1-2-3 attaches the SmartIcons each time you use 1-2-3. If the SmartIcons don't appear on-screen because you previously detached the Wysiwyg add-in, see Chapter 2, "What Every 1-2-3 User Should Know," for instructions on reattaching the Wysiwyg add-in.

This chapter shows you how to perform the following procedures:

- Use SmartIcons with the mouse and keyboard
- Hide and redisplay the SmartIcon palette

- Add, delete, and rearrange SmartIcons in the custom palette
- Attach macros to SmartIcons
- Change the picture on a user SmartIcon

Understanding SmartIcons

SmartIcons appear on the right side of the 1-2-3 screen, in several *palettes*, or collections of SmartIcons (see fig. 5.1). The total number of palettes depends on the resolution of your graphics monitor and graphics-card adapter.

Fig. 5.1
The SmartIcon palette appears at the right side of the screen when Wysiwyg is attached.

The SmartIcon palette

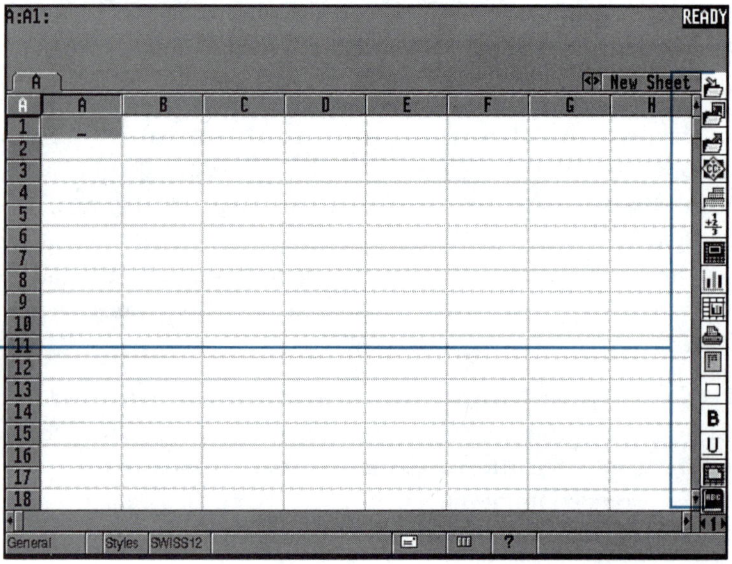

Tip
When you start 1-2-3, the last SmartIcon palette displayed in the preceding 1-2-3 session appears on-screen. To start 1-2-3 with a specific SmartIcon palette as the current palette, you must exit 1-2-3 with this palette displayed on-screen.

To view a description of a SmartIcon, point to the SmartIcon with the mouse pointer, and then press and hold down the right mouse button. A brief description of the function of this SmartIcon appears in the 1-2-3 control panel.

The current SmartIcon palette number appears at the bottom of the SmartIcon palette. On either side of the number, you see an arrow. You can click these arrows to switch between SmartIcon palettes. Click the right arrow to move to the next palette, or click the left arrow to move to the preceding palette.

Clicking the left arrow in the first palette displays the last SmartIcon palette. If you click the right arrow in the last palette, the first palette appears.

Table 5.1 shows and briefly describes the functions of all the 1-2-3 SmartIcons. Chapter references in the Description column indicate the chapter in this book that describes these SmartIcons in detail. (The 12 user SmartIcons and the SmartIcons that enable you to modify the custom palette are discussed in following sections of this chapter.) The related SmartIcon appears in the margin beside the sections that discuss individual SmartIcons in this and other chapters.

Table 5.1 The 1-2-3 Release 4 SmartIcons

SmartIcon	Description
Save File	Saves the current worksheet; functions similarly to the **/F**ile **S**ave command (see Chapter 9).
Retrieve File	Replaces the current file on-screen with a file on disk; functions similarly to the **/F**ile **R**etrieve command (see Chapter 9).
Open File	Reads a file into memory after the current file; functions similarly to the **/F**ile **O**pen **A**fter command (see Chapter 9).
cc:Mail	Sends a cc:Mail message; functions similarly to **/T**ools **E**-Mail. You must have the cc:Mail software installed on your computer to use this SmartIcon (see Chapter 9).
Perspective View	Displays worksheets in perspective view, starting with the current sheet; click this SmartIcon a second time to restore the screen to single-sheet display. Functions similarly to the **/W**orksheet **W**indow **P**erspective command (see Chapter 4).
@SUM	Sums the values in all cells immediately above or to the left of the current cell or cells with an @SUM function. Sums only values to the left if no values are in the cells immediately above the current cell. Does not sum values across spaces. Highlighting some values and blank spaces below or to the right of the values generates the sum of only the highlighted values (see Chapter 3).
Version	Enables you to work with versions and scenarios; functions similarly to **/T**ools **V**ersion (see Chapter 18).
QuickGraph	Displays the QuickGraph dialog box and enables you to graph the current range; functions similarly to **/G**raph **G**roup or **/G**raph **V**iew (see Chapter 23).

(continues)

Table 5.1 Continued

SmartIcon	Description
Add Graph	Adds the current graph to the worksheet in selected cells; functions similarly to **:G**raph **A**dd **C**urrent (see Chapter 23).
Print	Prints the current print range or the highlighted range; functions similarly to **:P**rint (see Chapter 8).
Print Preview	Previews the print range or highlighted range; functions similarly to **:P**rint **P**review (see Chapter 8).
Outline	Applies an outline to the highlighted range. Each click of the SmartIcon cycles to the next outline style: single, double, wide, or none. Functions similarly to **:F**ormat **L**ines **O**utline (see Chapter 6).
Bold	Adds or removes boldfacing to cell contents in the highlighted range; functions similarly to **:F**ormat **B**old **S**et or **:F**ormat **B**old **C**lear (see Chapter 6).
Single Underline	Adds or removes single underlining to cell contents in the highlighted range; functions similarly to **:F**ormat **U**nderline **S**ingle or **:F**ormat **U**nderline **C**lear (see Chapter 6).
Comment	Enables you to add a comment box (notepad) to the cell; functions similarly to **/T**ools **N**ote (see Chapter 7).
Spell Check	Checks spelling in the worksheet or highlighted range; functions similarly to **/T**ools **S**pell (see Chapter 6).
Drop Shadow	Adds a drop shadow to a highlighted range or removes an existing drop shadow; functions similarly to **:F**ormat **L**ines **S**hadow **S**et and **:F**ormat **L**ines **S**hadow **C**lear (see Chapter 6).
Shading	Adds shading to the highlighted range. Each click of the SmartIcon cycles to the next shading style: light, dark, solid, or none. Functions similarly to **:F**ormat **S**hade (see Chapter 6).
Left Align	Aligns text in highlighted cells at the left side of the cell; functions similarly to **/R**ange **L**abel **L**eft (see Chapter 2).
Center Align	Aligns text in highlighted cells in the center of the cell; functions similarly to **/R**ange **L**abel **C**enter (see Chapter 2).

Understanding SmartIcons 253

SmartIcon	Description
Right Align	Aligns text in highlighted cells at right side of cell; functions similarly to **/R**ange **L**abel **R**ight (see Chapter 2).
Zoom	Changes the screen-display size of the worksheet, each click on the icon cycles through large, huge, tiny, small, normal; functions similarly to **:D**isplay **Z**oom (see Chapter 4).
Font	Applies a font to the highlighted range. Each click of the SmartIcon cycles to the next font of the eight fonts listed in **:F**ormat **F**ont (see Chapter 6).
Text Color	Applies color to the contents of a cell. Each click of the SmartIcon cycles through red, green, dark-blue, cyan, yellow, magenta, or normal, listed in **:F**ormat **C**olor **T**ext (see Chapter 6).
Background Color	Applies color to the background of a cell. Each click of the SmartIcon cycles through red, green, dark-blue, cyan, yellow, magenta, and normal, listed in **:F**ormat **C**olor **B**ackground (see Chapter 6).
Italics	Adds or removes italics to cell contents in the highlighted range; functions similarly to **:F**ormat **I**talics **S**et or **:F**ormat **I**talics **C**lear (see Chapter 6).
Normal Format	Removes all Wysiwyg formatting from highlighted range; functions similarly to **:F**ormat **R**eset (see Chapter 6).
Double Underline	Adds or removes double underlining; functions similarly to **:F**ormat **U**nderline **D**ouble (see Chapter 6).
3d @Sum	Sums values in cells directly behind the current cell(s) in a 3-D file, using @SUM (see Chapter 11).
Insert Date	Enters today's date in the current cell or uses the current date/time format (see Chapter 6).
Data Fill	Fills the highlighted range with a sequence of values; functions similarly to **/D**ata **F**ill (see Chapter 2).
Ascending Sort	Displays the QuickSort dialog box and enables you to sort data in ascending order, using the current cell as a key; functions similarly to **/D**ata **S**ort (see Chapter 20).
Descending Sort	Displays the QuickSort dialog box and enables you to sort data in descending order, using the current cell as a key; functions similarly to **/D**ata **S**ort (see Chapter 20).

(continues)

Table 5.1 Continued

SmartIcon	Description
STEP Mode	Turns on STEP mode; functions similarly to /**T**ools **M**acro **S**tep or to pressing Alt+F2 and choosing **S**tep (see Chapter 26).
Run Macro	Selects and runs a macro; functions similarly to /**T**ools **M**acro **R**un (see Chapter 26).
GoTo	Moves cell pointer to a cell or named range you specify; functions similarly to pressing F5 (Goto) (see Chapter 2).
End Right	Moves the cell pointer right to a filled cell that is an intersection between a filled and an empty cell; functions similarly to pressing End → (see Chapter 2).
End Left	Moves the cell pointer left to a filled cell that is an intersection between a filled and an empty cell; functions similarly to pressing End ← (see Chapter 2).
End Down	Moves the cell pointer down to a filled cell that is an intersection between a filled and an empty cell; functions similarly to pressing End ↓ (see Chapter 2).
End Up	Moves the cell pointer up to a filled cell that is an intersection between a filled and an empty cell; functions similarly to pressing End ↑ (see Chapter 2).
Home	Moves the cell pointer to the home position (usually cell A1); functions similarly to the Home key (see Chapter 2).
End Home	Moves cell pointer to the bottom right corner of the sheet; functions similarly to pressing End Home (see Chapter 2).
Next Worksheet	Moves cell pointer to the next worksheet; functions similarly to pressing Ctrl+PgUp (see Chapter 10).
Previous Worksheet	Moves cell pointer to the previous sheet; functions similarly to pressing Ctrl+PgDn (see Chapter 10).
Page Right	Moves cell pointer one screen to the right; functions similarly to pressing Tab (see Chapter 2).
Page Left	Moves cell pointer one screen to the left; functions similarly to pressing Shift+Tab (see Chapter 2).

SmartIcon	Description
Page Up	Moves cell pointer up one screen; functions similarly to pressing PgUp (see Chapter 2).
Page Down	Moves cell pointer down one screen; functions similarly to pressing PgDn (see Chapter 2).
Right	Moves cell pointer one cell to the right; functions similarly to pressing the → key (see Chapter 2).
Left	Moves cell pointer one cell to the left; functions similarly to pressing the ← key (see Chapter 2).
Up	Moves cell pointer up one cell; functions similarly to pressing the ↑ key (see Chapter 2).
Down	Moves cell pointer down one cell; functions similarly to pressing the ↓ key (see Chapter 2).
Scroll Right	Moves the display one column to the right; functions similarly to pressing the → key with Scroll Lock on (see Chapter 2).
Scroll Left	Moves the display one column to the left; functions similarly to pressing the ← key with Scroll Lock on (see Chapter 2).
Scroll Up	Moves the display up one row; functions similarly to pressing the ↑ key with Scroll Lock on (see Chapter 2).
Scroll Down	Moves the display down one row; functions similarly to pressing the ↓ key with Scroll Lock on (see Chapter 2).
New File	Starts a new file after the current file; functions similarly to /**F**ile **N**ew **A**fter (see Chapter 9).
Find/Replace	Finds or replaces characters in labels and formulas in a range; functions similarly to /**R**ange **S**earch **B**oth (see Chapter 2).
Copy	Copies the highlighted range; functions similarly to /**C**opy (see Chapter 2).
Move	Moves the highlighted range; functions similarly to /**M**ove (see Chapter 2).
Undo	Undoes the most recent action if Undo is enabled; similar to pressing Alt+F4 (see Chapter 2).
Delete	Erases the contents of the current cell or highlighted range; functions similarly to /**R**ange **E**rase or the Del key (see Chapter 2).

(continues)

Table 5.1 Continued

SmartIcon	Description
Copy Cell to Range	Copies the contents of the current cell to all cells in the highlighted range; functions similarly to **/C**opy (see Chapter 2).
Insert Row	Inserts a row at the current cell-pointer location; functions similarly to **/W**orksheet **I**nsert **R**ow (see Chapter 2).
Insert Column	Inserts a column at the current cell-pointer location; functions similarly to **/W**orksheet **I**nsert **C**olumn (see Chapter 2).
Delete Row	Displays a confirmation box before deleting the current or selected rows; functions similarly to **/W**orksheet **D**elete **R**ow (see Chapter 2).
Delete Column	Displays a confirmation box before deleting the current or selected columns; functions similarly to **/W**orksheet **D**elete **C**olumn (see Chapter 2).
Delete Worksheet	Displays a confirmation box before deleting selected worksheets; functions similarly to **/W**orksheet **D**elete **S**heet (see Chapter 10).
Insert Worksheet	Inserts a worksheet after the current sheet; functions similarly to **/W**orksheet **I**nsert **S**heet (see Chapter 10).
Currency 2	Applies or removes Currency format with two decimal places; functions similarly to **/R**ange **F**ormat **C**urrency **2** (see Chapter 6).
Comma 0	Applies or removes Comma format with zero decimal places; functions similarly to **/R**ange **F**ormat **,** (comma) **0** (see Chapter 6).
Percent 2	Applies or removes percent format with two decimal places; functions similarly to **/R**ange **F**ormat **P**ercent **2** (see Chapter 6).
Horizontal Page Break	Inserts a horizontal (row) page break; functions similarly to **:W**orksheet **P**age **R**ow (see Chapter 8).
Vertical Page Break	Inserts a vertical (column) page break; functions similarly to **:W**orksheet **P**age **C**olumn (see Chapter 8).
View Graph	Displays the current graph; functions similarly to **/G**raph **V**iew or the F10 (Graph) key (see Chapter 23).

Understanding SmartIcons 257

SmartIcon	Description
Edit Text	Enters text-edit mode in selected range; functions similarly to :**T**ext **E**dit (see Chapter 2).
Text Align	Changes the text alignment in a range of cells; functions similarly to :**T**ext **A**lign (see Chapter 2).
Circle Range	Circles or removes circle from the highlighted cell or range; functions similarly to :**G**raph **A**dd **B**lank, :**G**raph **E**dit **A**dd **E**llipse, and :**G**raph **S**ettings **O**paque **N**o (see Chapter 24).
Copy Formats	Copies the Wysiwyg formats so that they can be applied to another range; functions similarly to :**S**pecial **C**opy (see Chapter 6).
Recalculate	Recalculates formulas; functions similarly to the F9 (Calc) key (see Chapter 3).
Attach Macro to Icon	Enables you to attach a macro to a user SmartIcon, also enables you to change the picture on a SmartIcon (see "Attaching Macros to SmartIcons" and "Changing the Picture on a User SmartIcon" later in this chapter).
Add Icon	Adds a SmartIcon to the custom palette (see "Adding SmartIcons to the Custom Palette" later in this chapter).
Remove Icon	Removes a SmartIcon from the custom palette (see "Removing SmartIcons from the Custom Palette" later in this chapter).
Rearrange Icons	Rearranges SmartIcons on the custom palette in the order you specify (see "Rearranging SmartIcons in the Custom Palette" later in this chapter).
User SmartIcon #1	
User SmartIcon #2	
User SmartIcon #3	
User SmartIcon #4	
User SmartIcon #5	

(continues)

Table 5.1 Continued

SmartIcon	Description
U6	User SmartIcon #6
U7	User SmartIcon #7
U8	User SmartIcon #8
U9	User SmartIcon #9
U10	User SmartIcon #10
U11	User SmartIcon #11
U12	User SmartIcon #12

Selecting SmartIcons by Using the Mouse

SmartIcons are designed for use with the mouse. To select a SmartIcon, position the mouse pointer on the SmartIcon and click the left mouse button.

> **Note**
>
> The best way to use most SmartIcons is with preselected ranges. To learn more about preselecting ranges in 1-2-3, see Chapter 2, "What Every 1-2-3 User Should Know."

Selecting SmartIcons by Using the Keyboard

Although SmartIcons are easiest to use with a mouse, keyboard users also can use SmartIcons. To select a SmartIcon by using the keyboard, follow these steps:

1. Press Ctrl+F10 (Select Icons). This action highlights the first SmartIcon in the current palette.

   When a SmartIcon is highlighted, the SmartIcon description appears in the third line of the control panel, just above the worksheet frame (see fig. 5.2). Notice that the selected SmartIcon is shaded.

Understanding SmartIcons   259

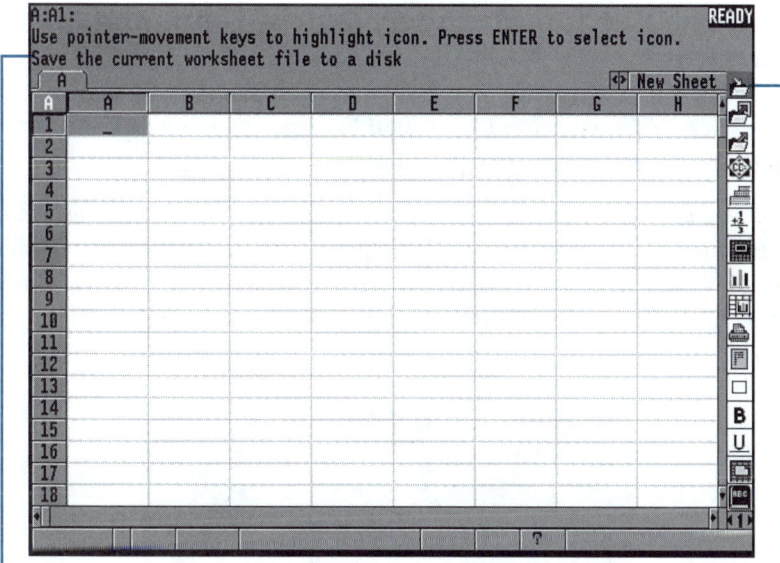

Fig. 5.2
The appearance of the screen when you use the keyboard to highlight a SmartIcon.

SmartIcon description   Selected SmartIcon

2. Press ↑ or ↓ to move the highlight in the current palette to another SmartIcon.

   Press Home to move the highlight to the first SmartIcon in the current palette. Press End to move the highlight to the last SmartIcon in the current palette. To move to the next or the preceding SmartIcon palette, press ← or →.

3. When you have highlighted the SmartIcon you want to select, press Enter.

Hiding and Redisplaying the SmartIcon Palette

Occasionally, you may want to remove the SmartIcon palette from the screen. When presenting a computer slide show, for example, you may prefer to remove the SmartIcon palette so that the palette doesn't divert the attention of the audience.

To hide the SmartIcon palette, click the *SmartIcons selector*, which is located in the status bar in the third section from the right. To redisplay the SmartIcons, click the SmartIcons selector again. (This feature works as a toggle.)

Keyboard users can hide and redisplay the SmartIcon palette by pressing Ctrl+F9 (Display Icons). This key combination also works as a toggle.

Using the Version Manager, QuickGraph, and Sort SmartIcons

Most of the SmartIcons select and complete a command with only one mouse click. When you click the Version Manager, QuickGraph, and Sort SmartIcons, however, dialog boxes appear.

 When you click the Version Manager SmartIcon, the Version Manager menu and the dialog box shown in figure 5.3 appear, enabling you to create and manage versions and scenarios. (For more information about the Version Manager, see Chapter 18, "Tracking Multiple Sets of Data with Version Manager.")

Fig. 5.3
This dialog box appears when you click the Version Manager SmartIcon.

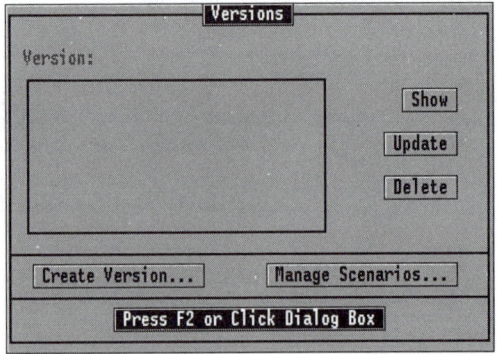

 Using the QuickGraph Settings dialog box (see fig. 5.4), you can choose among several options, including the type of graph, whether data ranges for a graph are arranged in columns or rows in the worksheet, whether the graph is displayed in landscape or portrait orientation, and whether the graph will be displayed in 3-D and in colors.

Fig. 5.4
The QuickGraph Settings dialog box gives you several choices about how the graph will be displayed.

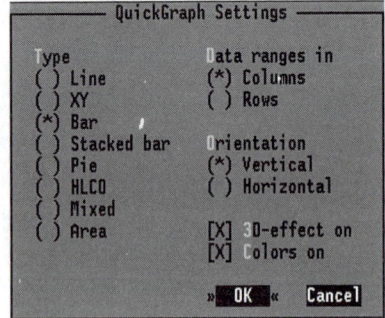

The Ascending Sort and Descending Sort SmartIcons invoke dialog boxes. To use the Sort SmartIcons, place the cell pointer in the column you want to sort. After you click a Sort SmartIcon, 1-2-3 determines the range to sort by searching in all directions for the next blank row or column in the worksheet. Before sorting the table, the QuickSort dialog box displays the sort range and the key field for confirmation (see fig. 5.5). Click OK or press Enter to confirm the dialog box; click Cancel or press Esc to return to the worksheet.

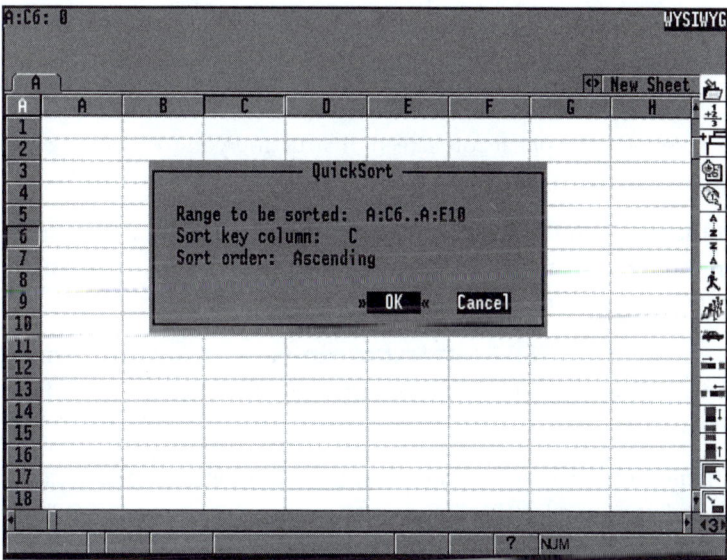

Fig. 5.5
The QuickSort dialog box appears when you click either of the two Sort SmartIcons.

Customizing SmartIcons

You can customize SmartIcons in two ways. You can add SmartIcons to the custom palette so that the most-used SmartIcons are available in the same palette, or you can create any of 12 user SmartIcons, to which you can attach macros that you also create. The macros you attach to user SmartIcons enable you to perform procedures not available through the other SmartIcons. You also can add user SmartIcons to the custom palette.

Using the Custom Palette

The first SmartIcon palette is the *custom palette* (refer to fig. 5.1). Although many SmartIcons that you use frequently already appear in the custom palette, you can add, remove, or rearrange SmartIcons in this palette. You cannot modify the SmartIcons that appear in other palettes. To add, remove, or

262 Chapter 5—Using SmartIcons

rearrange SmartIcons in the custom palette, use the Add Icon, Remove Icon, and Rearrange Icon SmartIcons. The following sections discuss these SmartIcons.

Adding SmartIcons to the Custom Palette

To add SmartIcons to the custom palette, switch SmartIcon palettes until you see the Add Icon SmartIcon. This special SmartIcon adds other SmartIcons to the custom palette.

To add a SmartIcon to the custom palette, follow these steps:

1. Select the Add Icon SmartIcon.

   A message box appears on-screen, instructing you to select the SmartIcon you want to add to the custom palette.

2. If the SmartIcon you want to add to the custom palette does not appear in the current palette, click the arrows at the bottom of the SmartIcon palette to move to the palette that contains this SmartIcon.

   If you want to add the Left Text Align SmartIcon to the custom palette, for example, move to the palette that contains the Left Text Align SmartIcon.

3. Highlight the SmartIcon you want to add to the custom palette and press Enter, or click this SmartIcon.

   To add the Left Text Align SmartIcon to the custom palette, for example, highlight this SmartIcon and press Enter, or click this SmartIcon.

The SmartIcon you added appears at the bottom of the custom palette. If the custom palette was full before you added a SmartIcon, the added SmartIcon replaces the bottom SmartIcon.

> **Note**
>
> All SmartIcons in the custom palette also exist in other palettes. If you replace (or delete) existing SmartIcons in the custom palette, you can access these SmartIcons in other palettes.

Removing SmartIcons from the Custom Palette

The procedure for removing SmartIcons from the custom palette is similar to the procedure for adding SmartIcons. First, switch SmartIcon palettes until you see the Remove Icon SmartIcon. (The palette in which you find the Remove Icon varies, depending on your display.)

To remove a SmartIcon from the custom palette, follow these steps:

1. Select the Remove Icon SmartIcon.

    The program displays the custom palette; a message box instructing you to select the SmartIcon you want to remove from the custom palette also appears on-screen.

2. Highlight the SmartIcon you want to remove from the custom palette and press Enter, or click this SmartIcon.

    To remove the Open File SmartIcon from the custom palette, for example, highlight this SmartIcon and press Enter, or click this SmartIcon.

The SmartIcon you selected no longer appears in the custom palette. (You can access the removed SmartIcon from another palette, however.) The remaining SmartIcons in the custom palette move up to fill the empty space.

Rearranging SmartIcons in the Custom Palette

At times, you may want to rearrange the order of the SmartIcons in the custom palette. For example, you may want to position the SmartIcons you frequently use, such as the Print and Print Preview SmartIcons, at the top of the custom palette.

To change the order of the SmartIcons in the custom palette, follow these steps:

1. Click the Rearrange Icon SmartIcon.

    The program displays the custom palette; a message box also appears on-screen, instructing you to select the SmartIcon you want to move in the custom palette.

2. Highlight the SmartIcon you want to move in the custom palette and press Enter, or click this SmartIcon.

    If you want to move the Print SmartIcon, for example, highlight this SmartIcon and press Enter, or click this SmartIcon.

    1-2-3 removes the SmartIcon from the custom palette and replaces it with a shaded box.

3. Highlight the SmartIcon in the location where you want the SmartIcon you are moving to appear and press Enter, or click the SmartIcon.

The program places the SmartIcon in its new location and adjusts the location of other SmartIcons in the custom palette.

Attaching Macros to SmartIcons

A powerful feature of Release 4 is the capability to attach 1-2-3 macros to SmartIcons. These programmable SmartIcons are known as *user SmartIcons*. You can program the 12 user SmartIcons to perform commonly used tasks or to make various 1-2-3 procedures easier.

The user SmartIcons, labeled U1 through U12, are located in the last SmartIcon palette (see fig. 5.6). You can add user SmartIcons to the custom palette, and you can change the appearance of user SmartIcons.

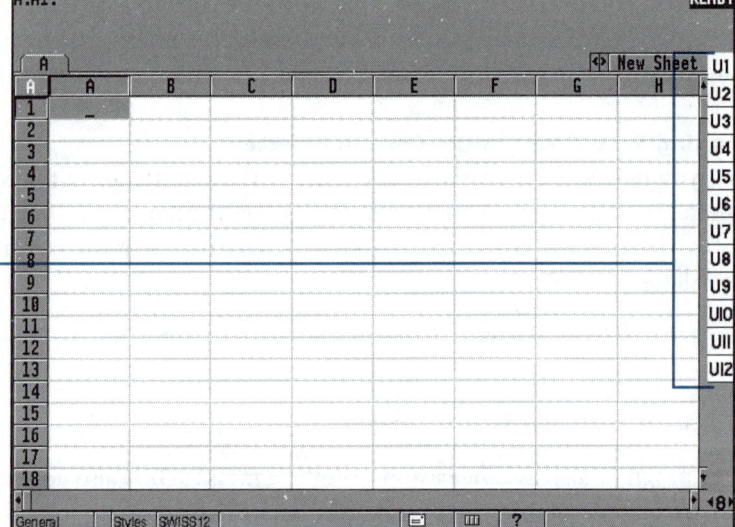

Fig. 5.6
The user SmartIcons are located in the last palette.

The User SmartIcon palette

To attach a macro to a user SmartIcon, follow these steps:

1. Select the Attach Macro to Icon SmartIcon.

   The Assign Macro to U*n* dialog box appears (see fig. 5.7). *n* is a number from 1 through 12, representing one of the user SmartIcons labeled U1 through U12.

Customizing SmartIcons **265**

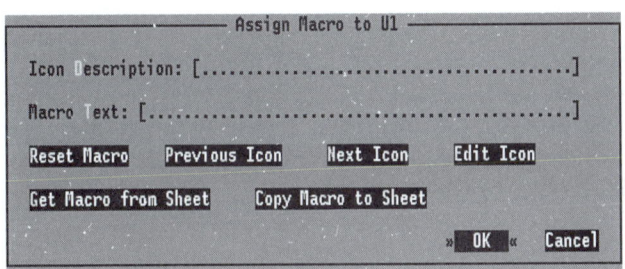

Fig. 5.7
The Assign Macro to U1 dialog box.

2. To select the user SmartIcon number to which you want to assign a macro, select **P**revious Icon or **N**ext Icon until the number of the desired user SmartIcon appears in the title of the dialog box.

3. Select the Icon **D**escription text box, and type a description to appear when the SmartIcon is selected.

   For this example, select Icon **D**escription and type **Enter Company Name and Address** (see fig. 5.8). This text describes a macro that enters a company's name and address when you select the SmartIcon to which the macro is attached.

   A SmartIcon description, which can be up to 72 characters long, appears in the control panel when you point to the SmartIcon with the mouse pointer and then press and hold down the right mouse button.

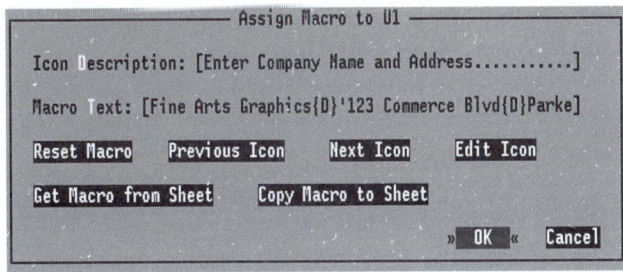

Fig. 5.8
The completed Assign Macro to U1 dialog box.

4. Select Macro **T**ext, and type the macro in the text box. (You can type up to 512 characters of macro text in this text box.) When you finish, press Enter.

   For this example, select Macro **T**ext and type the following text in the text box; then press Enter:

Fine Arts Graphics{D}'123 Commerce Blvd{D}Parker, CO 80134~

266 Chapter 5—Using SmartIcons

> **Note**
>
> To copy the macro text directly from a worksheet that contains one or more macros, select **G**et Macro from Sheet. Then specify the cell or range that contains the macro and press Enter. The macro remains in the worksheet after you select **G**et Macro from Sheet.

5. To assign the macro to the selected user SmartIcon, click OK. 1-2-3 returns to READY mode. The macro now is attached to the user SmartIcon and runs whenever you click this SmartIcon.

To clear the information in the text boxes of the Assign Macro to U*n* dialog box, select **R**eset Macro. Selecting this option enables you to start over if you make a mistake when you type the macro text or if you select the wrong macro from the worksheet.

To cancel all changes you made in the Assign Macro to U*n* dialog box and return to READY mode, select Cancel.

> **Note**
>
> The **E**dit Icon and **C**opy Macro to Sheet dialog-box options are discussed in following sections of this chapter.

Clearing a Macro from a User SmartIcon

If you no longer use a macro that you attached to a user SmartIcon, you can clear the macro from the SmartIcon. This procedure enables you to attach a different macro to this SmartIcon.

To clear a macro from a user SmartIcon, follow these steps:

1. Select the Attach Macro to Icon SmartIcon to display the Assign Macro to U*n* dialog box.

2. Select **P**revious Icon or **N**ext Icon until the number of the desired user SmartIcon appears in the title bar of the dialog box.

3. To clear the macro from the specified user SmartIcon, select **R**eset Macro in the Attach Macro to U*n* dialog box.

4. Click OK to save this change and return to READY mode.

The macro no longer is attached to the selected SmartIcon. You now can attach a different macro to this SmartIcon.

Customizing SmartIcons

> **Troubleshooting**
>
> *You added too many icons to the custom palette, and now some original icons are missing.*
>
> The icons you no longer see are part of other palettes. You can move them back to the custom palette or switch to other palettes when you need them.
>
> *You edited a macro in the worksheet, but clicking the User icon to which it was assigned still works the way it did before the edit.*
>
> Use the Assign Macro to Icon icon and choose Get Macro From Sheet to assign the latest version of the edited macro to the icon.
>
> *The Undo SmartIcon doesn't work.*
>
> Be sure to use **/W**orksheet **G**lobal **D**efault **O**ther **U**ndo **E**nable to turn on Undo. Then choose **U**pdate to make the change permanent.

Modifying a User SmartIcon

You also can modify a user SmartIcon without retyping the entire macro text.

To modify a user SmartIcon, follow these steps:

1. Select the Attach Macro to Icon SmartIcon to display the Assign Macro to U*n* dialog box.

2. Select **P**revious Icon or **N**ext Icon until the number of the desired user SmartIcon appears in the title bar of the dialog box.

3. Select Macro **T**ext and edit the macro text that appears in the text box. You also can select Icon **D**escription and edit the text of the icon description.

4. Click OK to save the changes and return to READY mode.

Editing the Macro Text

An easy way to edit long macro text is to copy the text to the worksheet, edit the text in the worksheet, and then copy the text back to the Macro **T**ext box in the Assign Macro to U*n* dialog box.

To copy the macro text to the worksheet, follow these steps:

1. Select the Attach Macro to Icon SmartIcon to display the Assign Macro to U*n* dialog box.

268 Chapter 5—Using SmartIcons

2. Select **P**revious Icon or **N**ext Icon until the number of the desired user SmartIcon appears in the title of the dialog box.

3. Select **C**opy Macro to Sheet.

4. At the Copy macro to cell prompt in the control panel, highlight the cell to which you want to copy the macro text and press Enter (or double-click the target cell).

> **Note**
>
> If you select a cell that contains data, a confirmation box appears. Click OK to overwrite the existing data or Cancel to return to the Assign Macro to U*n* dialog box.

For this example, highlight cell A1 and press Enter (or double-click cell A1).

The text from the Macro **T**ext box appears in the worksheet, and the Assign Macro to U*n* dialog box appears (see fig. 5.9). Click OK to return to READY mode so that you can edit the macro.

Fig. 5.9
The macro in cell A1 after being copied from the Assign Macro to U*n* dialog box.

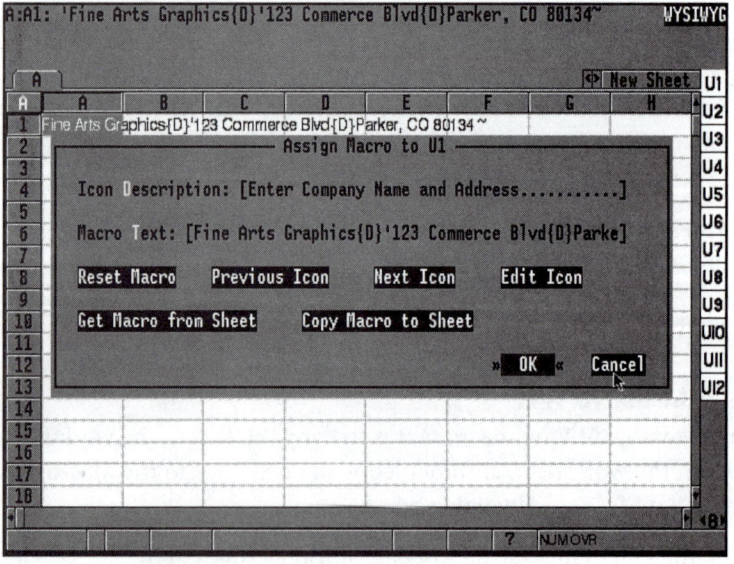

5. Edit the macro by using the editing keys.

6. After you edit the macro, select the Attach Macro to Icon SmartIcon.

7. To copy the revised macro to the Macro **T**ext box in the Assign Macro to U*n* dialog box, select **G**et Macro from Sheet. Then highlight the location of the macro in the worksheet and press Enter.

▶ "Understanding Macros," p. 830

8. To assign the revised macro to the selected user SmartIcon, click OK. 1-2-3 returns to READY mode. The macro now is attached to the user SmartIcon and runs whenever you select this SmartIcon.

▶ "Assigning a Macro to a User SmartIcon," p. 860

Changing the Picture on a User SmartIcon

1-2-3 enables you to customize the pictures on the user SmartIcons so that you can more easily remember the purpose of these SmartIcons.

To change the picture on a user SmartIcon, follow these steps:

1. Select the Attach Macro to Icon SmartIcon to display the Assign Macro to U*n* dialog box.

2. Select **Pr**evious Icon or **N**ext Icon until the number of the desired user SmartIcon appears in the title bar of the dialog box.

3. Select **E**dit Icon. The Icon Editor dialog box appears (see fig. 5.10). The picture on the current user SmartIcon appears in a drawing grid.

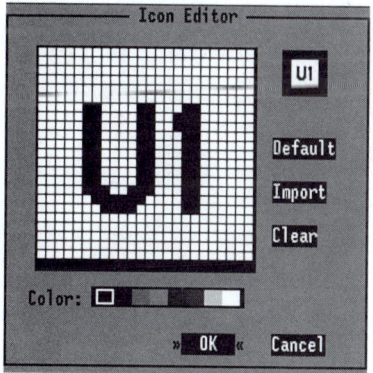

Fig. 5.10
The Icon Editor dialog box (before any changes are made).

4. Select **C**lear to erase the current graphic from the grid.

5. If you want the picture on the SmartIcon to be a color other than black, select the color you prefer from the Color box. (You must select the color before you draw the graphic.)

6. Use the mouse to draw any picture that you want to represent the user SmartIcon. Click a grid box to apply the selected color to that box.

270 Chapter 5—Using SmartIcons

> **Note**
>
> You must click each grid box individually to apply the selected color. Dragging the mouse over the boxes doesn't fill these boxes with the selected color.

In figure 5.11, the grid box in the Icon Editor displays the letters *FA*. Because the macro for this user SmartIcon enters the name and address of Fine Arts Graphics, the letters *FA* remind the user that this SmartIcon runs the macro that enters the company's name and address.

> **Note**
>
> You also can select **I**mport and specify the file name of an existing graphic you want to import as the new representation of the user SmartIcon.

Fig. 5.11
The new design for the user-defined SmartIcon.

Tip
Select the Add Icon SmartIcon to add the modified user SmartIcon to the custom palette. You can attach macros to all 12 user SmartIcons, which you then can add to the custom palette for better accessibility.

7. Click OK. The new picture you created (or imported) appears in the user SmartIcon palette in place of the preceding version of the SmartIcon.

You now can click this SmartIcon to run the macro associated with the SmartIcon. For this example, you first should position the cell pointer where you want the company name and address to appear. Figure 5.12 shows the result of clicking the *FA* user SmartIcon.

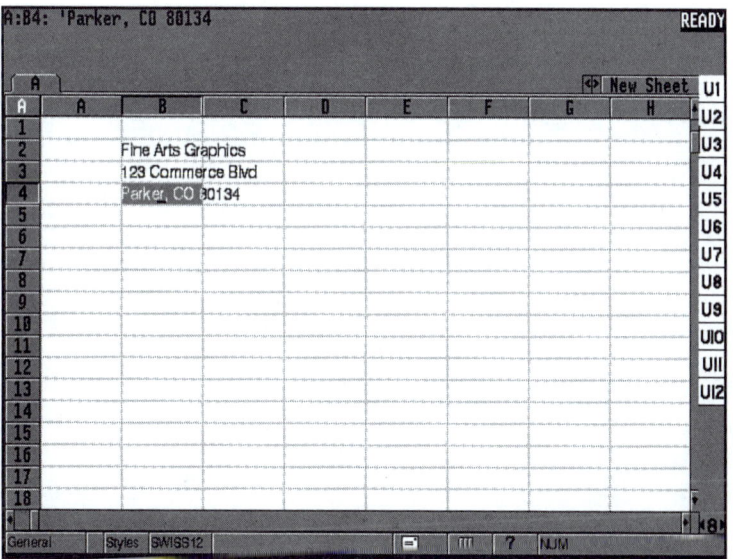

Fig. 5.12
The result of clicking the *FA* user icon.

From Here...

For more information relating to SmartIcons, you may want to review the following chapter of this book:

- Chapter 26, "Short Macros To Make Your Life Easier." This chapter contains essential information for automating tasks. You will learn techniques for writing simple macros, which you then can attach to user-defined SmartIcons.

Part II
Presenting Data

6 Making Your Worksheets Dazzle

7 Attaching Comments to Worksheet Cells

8 Printing Reports

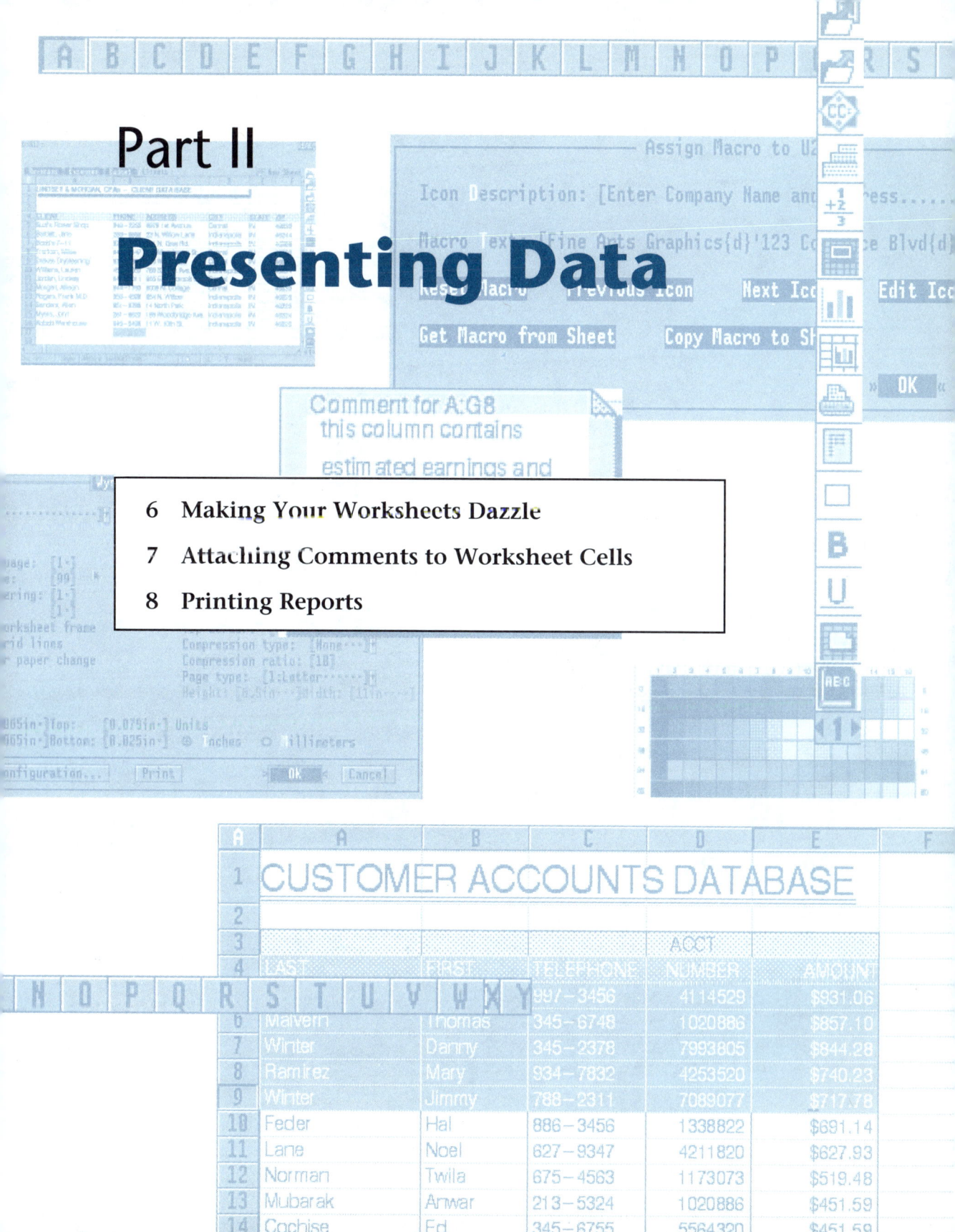

Chapter 6

Making Your Worksheets Dazzle

Manipulating data is only the first step in using an electronic spreadsheet program such as 1-2-3. Making the results clear and easy to understand can be just as important as calculating the correct answer. In this chapter, you learn to use the tools that control the on-screen appearance of data within cells. Changing the way data appears is called *formatting*. When you format data, you change *only* the way the data appears, not the value of the data itself.

1-2-3 provides three types of formatting commands: the Wysiwyg **:F**ormat commands, which affect the appearance of individual cells; the **/R**ange commands, which also affect the appearance of individual cells or designated groups of cells; and the **/W**orksheet **G**lobal commands, which affect the appearance of an entire worksheet or file. You use these formatting commands to customize the appearance of the data that 1-2-3 displays on-screen. Formatting options also are available when you print reports. Those printing capabilities are discussed in Chapter 8, "Printing Reports."

Although not a full-featured desktop publishing program, Wysiwyg may be all you need to perform many desktop publishing tasks that involve 1-2-3 reports and graphs. By using the Wysiwyg **:F**ormat commands, you can produce printed 1-2-3 reports that incorporate various type fonts, lines, shadings, and other formatting features (such as boldface, underlining, and italics). To add further impact, you can use the **:G**raph menu commands to add clip art and graphs.

▶ "Using the **:G**raph Commands To Add Impact," p. 819

Chapter 6—Making Your Worksheets Dazzle

This chapter shows you how to perform the following formatting operations:

- Set worksheet global default settings
- Set range and worksheet global formats
- Check the spelling of your data
- Use the format commands to change how cells appear
- Justify long labels across columns
- Suppress the display of zeros within cells
- Replace fonts
- Create font libraries
- Draw lines and boxes
- Manage formats and styles
- Add shading

Setting Worksheet Global Defaults

You can configure 1-2-3 to define how the program operates or how the screen appears. Some configuration settings must be specified when you run the Install program. You specify the type of monitor and printers connected to the computer, for example, when you install 1-2-3. Other settings can be changed as you work in 1-2-3. /**W**orksheet **G**lobal **D**efault is the main command used to change these settings from within 1-2-3. Table 6.1 describes the menu options that appear when you choose this command. Figure 6.1 shows the screen as it appears when you select /**W**orksheet **G**lobal **D**efault.

Table 6.1 The /Worksheet Global Default Menu

Menu Item	Description
Printer	Changes the printer defaults (see Chapter 8, "Printing Reports")
Dir	Changes the default directory (see Chapter 9, "Working with Files")
Status	Displays the current /**W**orksheet **G**lobal **D**efault settings in a dialog box (see fig. 6.2)
Update	Updates changes made to the current default settings so that these new settings become the defaults the next time you start 1-2-3

Setting Worksheet Global Defaults

Menu Item	Description
Other	Accesses the **O**ther menu commands: **I**nternational, **H**elp, **C**lock, **U**ndo, and **B**eep (see the following table of **/W**orksheet **G**lobal **D**efault **O**ther menu items)
Graph	Changes the graphing defaults (see Chapter 23, "Creating Effective Graphs")
Temp	Sets the directory in which 1-2-3 saves temporary files used during operation
Ext	Changes the default file extension (see Chapter 9, "Working with Files")
Autoexec	Controls macros that execute when you retrieve a file (see Chapter 28, "Controlling 1-2-3 with Macros")
Quit	Exits the **/W**orksheet **G**lobal **D**efault menu

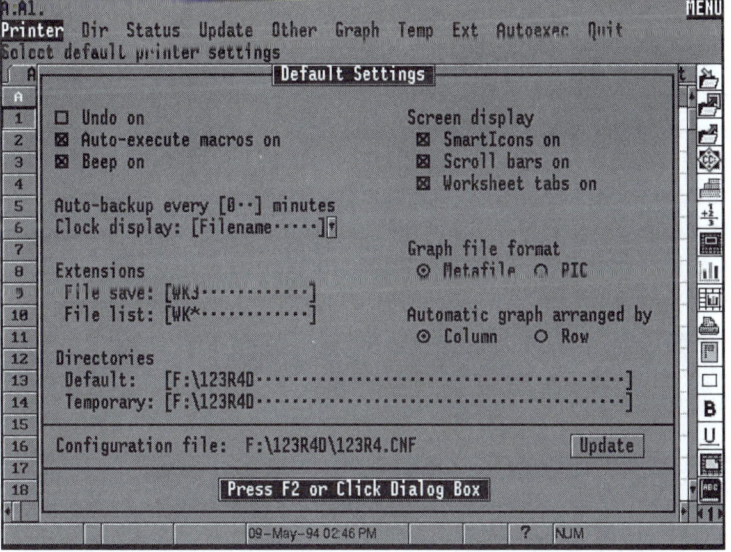

Fig. 6.1
The **/W**orksheet **G**lobal **D**efault screen and dialog box.

The **O**ther command in the **/W**orksheet **G**lobal **D**efault menu accesses the additional commands described in the following table:

Menu Item	Description
International	Accesses the **I**nternational menu, which provides additional formatting options (see "International Formats" later in this chapter).

(continues)

278   Chapter 6—Making Your Worksheets Dazzle

Menu Item	Description
Help	**H**elp is always **R**emovable in Releases 3.1, 3.1+, 3.4, and 4 but should be retained for compatibility with Release 2.x macros.
Clock	Accesses the **C**lock menu, which changes the default file and clock indicator at the bottom of the screen in the status bar. The options are **S**tandard, **I**nternational, **N**one, **C**lock, and **F**ilename. The **S**tandard and **I**nternational options determine the style of time used in the status-bar display. The other options determine whether the status bar should show the file name and clock, only the clock, or nothing.
Undo	Activates the Undo feature (see Chapter 2, "What Every 1-2-3 User Should Know").
Beep	Used to turn on and off the beep that 1-2-3 Releases 3.x and 4 normally sound when you make an error. Turn off the beep by choosing **N**o; turn the beep back on by selecting **Y**es.
Auto-Backup	Automatically backs up the active files.
Display	Accesses the **D**isplay menu, which contains options for displaying or hiding the SmartIcons, as well as the options **S**croll-Bars, **T**abs, **D**ialog Boxes, and **Q**uit.

> **Tip**
> You may want to turn off the beep when it might disturb others, such as in a library, or when you demonstrate a 1-2-3 system to others (that way, pressing a key in error isn't as obvious).

To see the current status of the global default settings, choose /**W**orksheet **G**lobal **D**efault **S**tatus; the /**W**orksheet **G**lobal **D**efault **S**tatus screen appears (see fig. 6.2). Any changes you make in any of these settings are effective only until you exit 1-2-3. The next time you start 1-2-3, these settings revert to their original values. To update the changed default settings, choose /**W**orksheet **G**lobal **D**efault **U**pdate. This command updates a configuration file that 1-2-3 uses to determine the default values for these settings, making the changes the new defaults.

Caution
If you don't **U**pdate the configuration file before you exit 1-2-3, you lose all the global default changes.

Note
The dialog box makes it much easier to see all your defaults at one time, instead of going through each menu option to bring the particular feature to the control panel for inspection. Whenever a dialog box is on-screen, you can move the mouse pointer to the option you want to change and click the check box for the option to change

it. First, however, you must be in EDIT mode. Using the mouse in the dialog box can be faster and easier than using the menu options, especially when you want to change multiple options.

To get into EDIT mode for the dialog box, press the F2 (Edit) key or click anywhere in the dialog box. Double-clicking an option check box also works. The dialog box changes somewhat when you are in EDIT mode; OK and Cancel buttons appear at the bottom of all dialog boxes in EDIT mode.

You can use the dialog box without the mouse by pressing the F2 (Edit) key and then pressing the Alt key in combination with the highlighted letter next to the option you want to change. You also can use the Tab key to move the cell pointer around to the different options. Remember to click the OK button to leave the dialog box when you finish making changes. Also don't forget to use the **U**pdate option if you want to make the changes permanent.

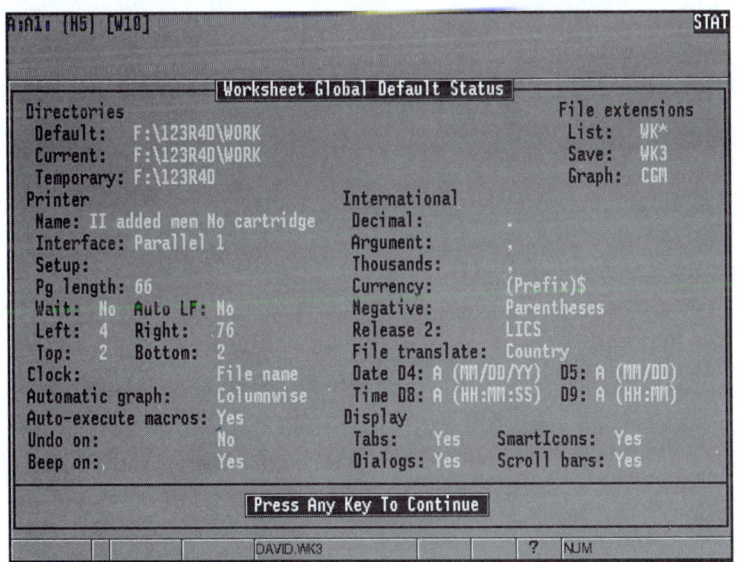

Fig. 6.2
The /**W**orksheet **G**lobal **D**efault **S**tatus screen and dialog box.

Use the /**W**orksheet **S**tatus command to view information such as the amount of memory currently available; the processor installed in the computer, the current recalculation method; default formats, label prefix, and column width for the current worksheet; and whether the current worksheet is using global protection (see fig. 6.3). This status screen is used mainly to check the amount of memory available and to locate circular references.

◀ "Controlling Recalculation," p. 226

▶ "Examining Circular References," p. 537

Fig. 6.3
The /**W**orksheet **S**tatus screen and dialog box.

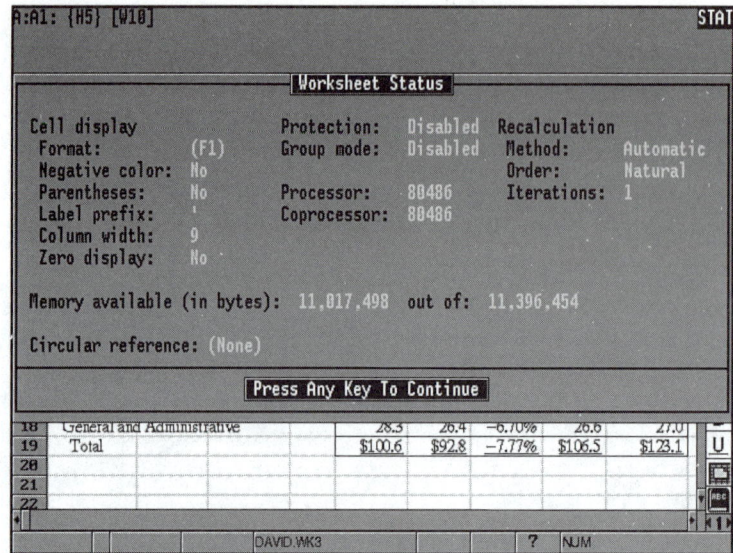

Setting Range and Worksheet Global Formats

Data contained in a worksheet cell has two characteristics: *content* and *format*. Although not the same, these two characteristics are related. The contents of the current cell are displayed in the control panel when you highlight that cell; the formatted display of the cell's contents appears in the worksheet itself (see fig. 6.4).

A cell may contain a formula, such as +D5 in cell F5, but the *current value* of the formula is what actually appears in the cell. 1-2-3 therefore displays the formula in F5 as 1,2345.12. Other factors, such as column width, can affect how a cell appears, but the cell format is the most important factor in a cell's on-screen appearance in a worksheet.

The Available Formats

You can display data in a cell in several different formats. Table 6.2 lists the formats available in the 1-2-3 /**R**ange **F**ormat and /**W**orksheet **G**lobal **F**ormat menus. Additional formats are available from the Wysiwyg **:F**ormat menu, which is discussed in the "Formatting with the Wysiwyg Menu" section of this chapter.

Setting Range and Worksheet Global Formats 281

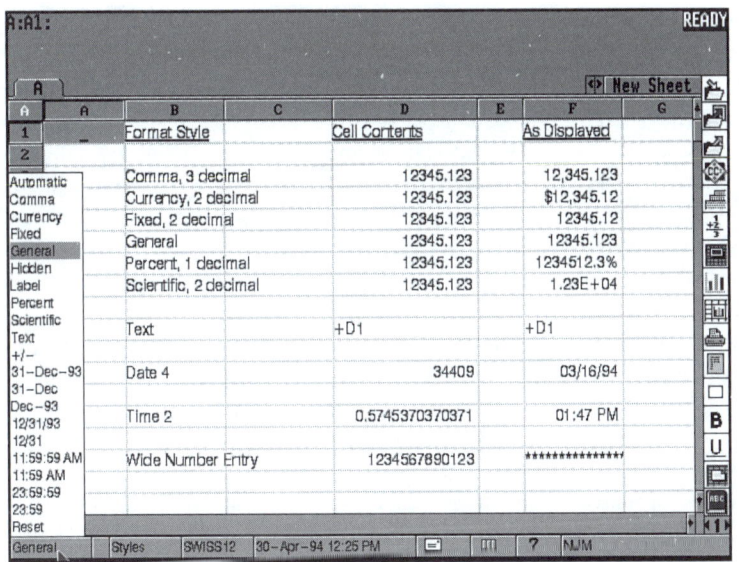

Fig. 6.4
A worksheet showing the indicated formats with the format status bar accessed.

Table 6.2 Display Formats

Format	Example	Application
Fixed	1234.50	Numeric data
Sci (scientific)	1.2345E+03	Numeric data
Currency	₡1,234.50	Numeric data
, (comma)	1,234.50	Numeric data
General	1234.5	Numeric data
+/−	+++++	Numeric data
Percent	35.4%	Numeric data
Date	10/10/93	Special date serial numbers
Time	06:23 AM	Special time fractions
Text	+C6	All formulas
Hidden	No display	All data
Automatic	1,234.50	Blank cells before data is entered
Color	-1,234.50	Negative numeric data appears in color
Label	57 Main St.	Blank cells before labels are entered
Parentheses	(1,234.50)	Numeric data

> **Note**
>
> Most of the formats available in the 1-2-3 /**R**ange **F**ormat and /**W**orksheet **G**lobal **F**ormat menus apply only to numeric data (numeric formulas and numbers). If you format a label as **F**ixed or **C**urrency, for example, the format has no effect on how the label appears. A few formats, such as **H**idden, can apply to labels and string formulas. Figure 6.4 shows examples of some of the possible formats. The labels in column B indicate the type of format displayed in column F.

The formats available in the Wysiwyg **:F**ormat menu apply to both numeric data and labels. If you format a cell or range of cells with a particular Wysiwyg font, for example, the contents of the cell (or cells) appear in that font, whether these contents consist of numbers or labels.

Regardless of its format, numeric data always is right-aligned when displayed in a cell (refer to fig. 6.4). The result of a string (text) formula always appears left-aligned in a cell, even if the formula refers to a label with a different alignment.

◀ "Setting Column Widths," p. 121

The width of a cell is controlled by its column-width setting. If the column isn't wide enough to display a long numeric entry, asterisks fill the cell (refer to the last entry in column F in fig. 6.4). To display the data itself, you must change either the format of the data in the cell or the column width.

In 1-2-3 text mode (Wysiwyg mode is turned off), the numeric entry in a cell always must be *one digit less* than the cell's column width for the entry to fit into that cell. The farthest-right digit in a cell's numeric entry always appears in the second position from the right of the cell border. The extreme-right position in the cell always is reserved for a percent sign or right parenthesis, even if these characters aren't part of the number in that particular cell. If the column width of a cell is 9, for example, the formatted number (not counting any percent sign or right parenthesis) must fit into only 8 positions. Negative numbers appear in a cell display either with a minus sign or in parentheses; a negative number must be an additional digit smaller than the column width for the number to fit within a cell. To fit within a column width of 9, therefore, a negative number must fill only 7 positions in the cell.

1-2-3 graphics mode (Wysiwyg mode is turned on) reserves the extreme-right position within a cell for a right parenthesis but not for a percent sign. The exact number of characters or digits that actually fit within a particular column width, however, depends on the font used in formatting the cell's data. With a column width of 9, the 12-point nonproportional Courier font always displays 9 characters, but the 12-point proportional Swiss font displays 6 to

24 characters (depending on which characters are used). Refer to table 6.7 for more information explaining terms, such as proportional, serif, and sans serif.

The Contents Versus the Format of a Cell

Remember that *formatting* alters only how data *appears*; the data itself isn't changed by its format. The number 1234, for example, can appear as 1,234, $1,234.00, 123400% and many other combinations, depending on how the number is formatted. Wysiwyg even formats data to appear in any font and in any color. Regardless of how the number appears, however, it remains the same number.

In some formats, a number containing a decimal is rounded to the nearest whole number. If you format 1234.5 in **F**ixed format with **0** decimal places, for example, the number appears on-screen as 1235, but the actual value of 1234.5 is used in formulas derived from that value. In figure 6.5, the total in cell F13 appears to be an addition error. The actual value of the formula in F11 is 96.7189. The display, however, shows 96.7 because the data is formatted as **F**ixed with **1** decimal places. The value of the formula in F12 actually is 4.0491, but the display shows 4.0. The value of the sum in F13 is 100.7680, but the display shows 100.8. Therefore, these values appear as 96.7 + 4.0 = 100.8—an apparent error in the sum resulting from the format's rounding of the value displayed in the Totals cell.

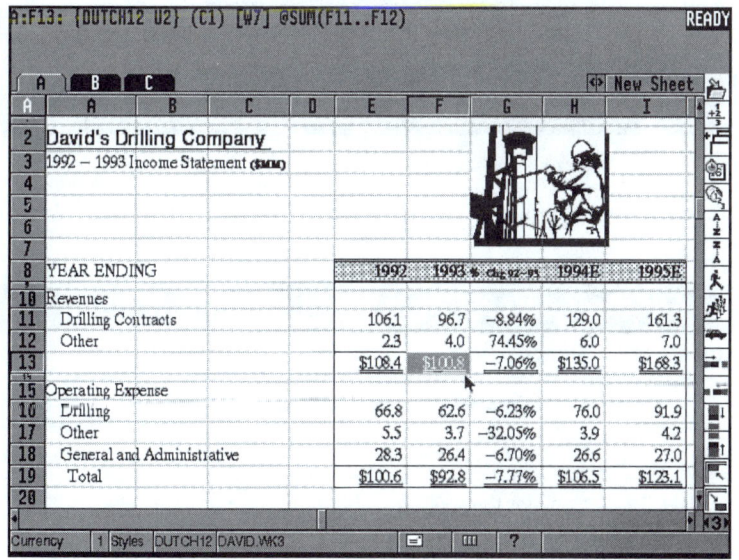

Fig. 6.5

An apparent summation error caused by rounding from the format type and number of decimal places.

284   Chapter 6—Making Your Worksheets Dazzle

◀ "@ROUND— Rounding Numbers," p. 164

To prevent such rounding errors, you must round the *actual values* of the formulas in figure 6.5, not just the displayed values. To round the value of a formula, use the @ROUND function.

Spell Checking Your Data

A feature that many people have wanted to use in their worksheets is a spell checker. This feature has been added to 1-2-3 Release 4 for DOS. To start the spell checker, click the spell checker SmartIcon or type /**T**ools **S**pell to access the Spell Check dialog box (see fig. 6.6).

Fig. 6.6
The dialog box and screen that appear when you choose /**T**ools **S**pell or click the Spell Checker SmartIcon. The **O**ptions menu option is highlighted to show the **O**ptions submenu below it.

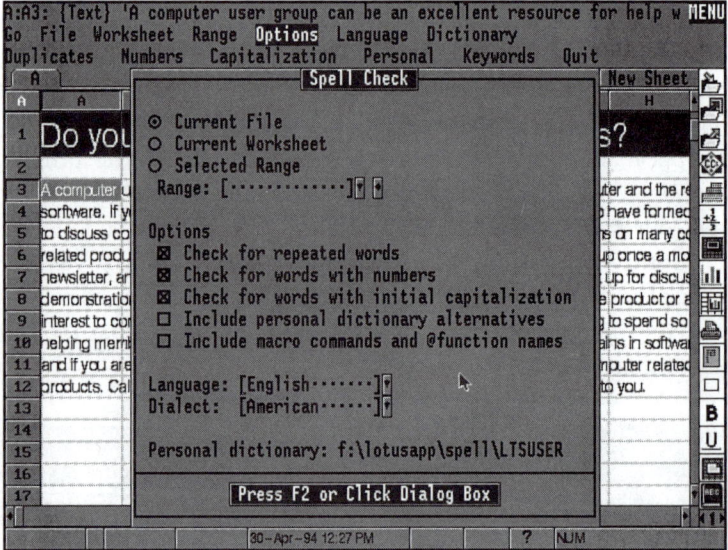

Table 6.3 describes the options in the /**T**ools **S**pell menu.

Table 6.3 The Spell Checker Menu

Menu Item	Description
Go	Starts the spell checking procedure.
File	Checks the spelling of the entire file.
Worksheet	Confines the spell checking to the current worksheet.
Range	Confines the spell checking to the range of cells you indicate.

Menu Item	Description
Options	Accesses the **O**ptions menu.
Language	Permits the choice of an **E**nglish, **S**panish, or **F**rench dictionary. If you choose **E**nglish, you also can choose the dialect (**A**merican or **B**ritish).
Dictionary	Enables you to add words to or delete words from your personal dictionary or to tell 1-2-3 where your personal dictionary is located. This dictionary can be shared with other Lotus applications if you have any that use a spell checker.

The following table describes the choices in the **/T**ools **S**pell **O**ptions menu.

Menu	Description
Duplicates	Checks for repeated words
Numbers	Checks for words with numbers
Capitalization	Checks for words with initial capitalization
Personal	Includes personal-dictionary alternatives in the spell check
Keywords	Includes macro commands and function names in the spell check
Quit	Returns to the **S**pell menu

Using the Spell Checker

When the Spell Check dialog box and **/T**ools **S**pell menu are on-screen, you need to tell 1-2-3 what you want to do. For example, if you are ready to spell check the entire file (the default option), you can accept all the defaults on-screen and choose **G**o to start the spell-checking procedure. If you need to change any of the defaults, choose options from the menu as described in table 6.3; or press F2 (or click on the dialog box) and then select the options you want to change. See figure 6.7 for an example of the Spell Check dialog box in EDIT mode.

If, for example, you need to spell check only part of the worksheet, select the **R**ange menu option. If you prefer to use your mouse, you can click the left mouse button while pointing to the **R**ange radio button in the dialog box. After selecting the **R**ange option, you are prompted for the range to spell check. You can type the cell location of the range or highlight the selected range by using your direction keys to highlight the range or holding down the left mouse button while highlighting the range. After indicating the selected range, press Enter.

Fig. 6.7
The Spell Check dialog box in EDIT mode.

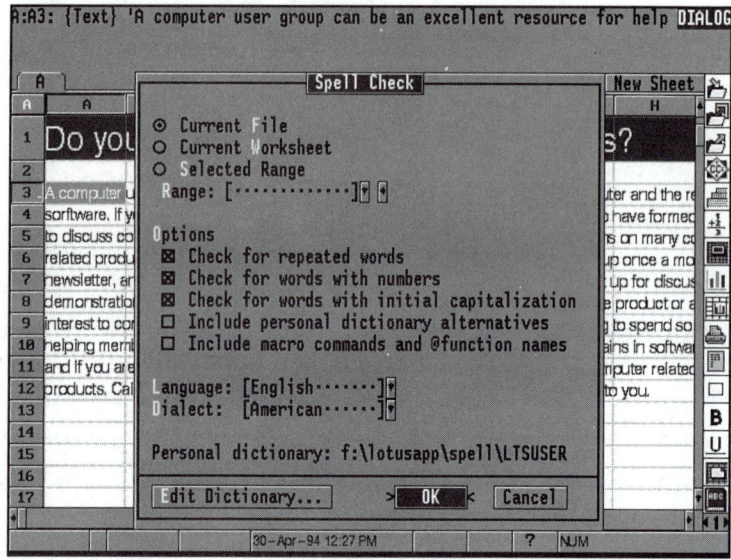

When you finish changing options, choose **G**o from the menu to start the spell check. If you are in the dialog box edit mode, click the left button while the mouse pointer is on the OK button in the dialog box and then select the **G**o menu option. After making changes in the options, you can select the **Q**uit menu option to leave the /**T**ools **S**pell menu if there is no spell checking needed.

When 1-2-3's spell checker finds an error, the top line of the screen shows the cell contents with the incorrectly spelled word highlighted. A menu appears with the following choices:

   Guess **E**dit **S**kip-This **I**gnore-All **Q**uit

Figure 6.8 shows an example of what the screen will look like when an incorrectly spelled word is found. Notice in the control panel that the incorrectly spelled word is highlighted in the context of the cell contents. If you choose the **G**uess option, the spell checker displays a list of guesses about the correct word (see fig. 6.9). Highlight the correct spelling option and press Enter.

After you correct the spelling and press Enter to continue, you see the options **A**ll and **T**his. If you choose the **A**ll option, you are telling the spell checker to use the corrected spelling anywhere else it finds the same incorrect word. If you want the spell checker to substitute the corrected spelling only in the current location, choose **T**his.

If the spell checker cannot find a replacement word, the space after the `Replace with:` prompt is blank. Refer to figure 6.9 to see an example of this prompt with the correctly spelled word following the prompt. If there are no suggested words, you should press the Esc key to return to the **G**uess menu. You now decide whether you need to edit or ignore the word. If you know the correct spelling of the word, choose **E**dit, type the correct spelling, and press Enter to put the correction in place. There will be times when you have a correctly spelled word that is not in the dictionary, and the spell checker will stop to indicate these words as incorrect. Use the other options, such as **S**kip or **I**gnore, when appropriate to continue the spell check in these circumstances.

Other options in the /**T**ools **S**pell **G**uess menu enable you to **S**kip that instance of the word, or to **I**gnore all instances of the word, or to **Q**uit the spell check.

When the spell checker finishes checking, 1-2-3 returns to READY mode. The spreadsheet is ready for you to continue your work.

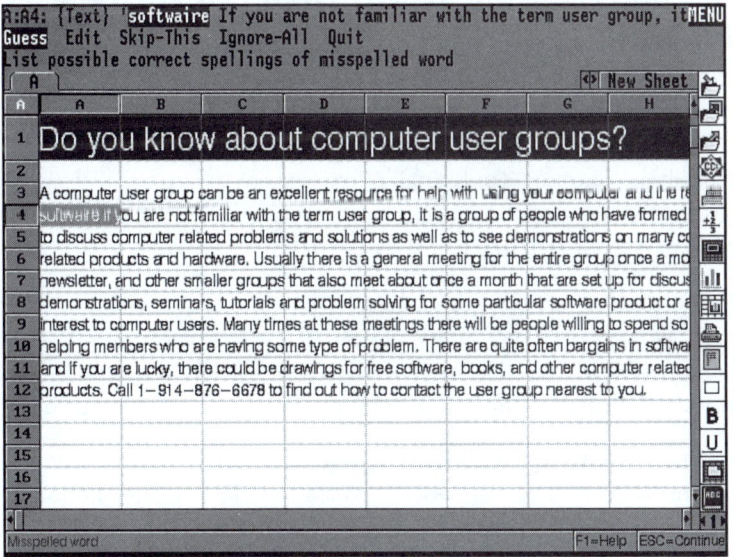

Fig. 6.8
The screen as it looks when 1-2-3 finds a spelling error.

Fig. 6.9

The screen in which the spell checker gives its best guess about the correct spelling when the **G**uess option is selected.

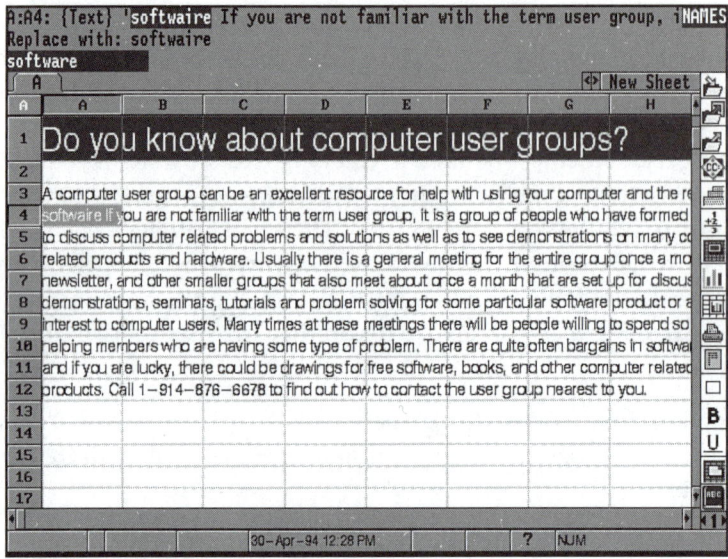

Adding and Deleting Words from the Personal Dictionary

Your worksheet may contain some specialized words that are correct but that the spell checker flags as incorrect because they are not in the dictionary. It is a good idea to add these words to your personal dictionary if you are going to use them often. Choose **/T**ools **S**pell **D**ictionary to get into the dictionary editing session. When the dictionary-editing session begins, you are prompted to **A**dd or **D**elete a word (see fig. 6.10).

To delete a word, choose **D**elete and then press the F3 (Name) key to display a screen of words in the dictionary. Highlight the word you want to delete and then press Enter. Be sure that you do want to delete the word, because 1-2-3 does not display a warning prompt to enable you to change your mind.

To **A**dd a new word, choose the **A**dd option, type the word when prompted, and then press Enter. The new word is added to your personal dictionary exactly the way you typed it.

If you already are in the **/T**ools **S**pell menu and prefer to use the Spell Check dialog box, click the dialog box or press the F2 key to get into the Spell Check dialog box for making changes. A new button, Edit Dictionary..., appears at the bottom of the dialog box along with the OK and Cancel buttons. (To see how these buttons appear on-screen, refer to fig. 6.7.) Click the Edit Dictionary... button to begin your dictionary-editing session. The Personal Dictionary dialog box appears (see fig. 6.11).

Spell Checking Your Data   **289**

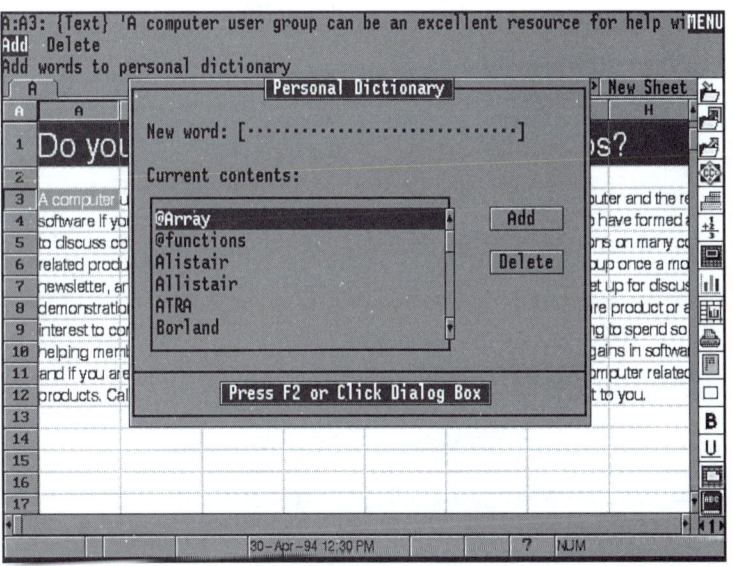

Fig. 6.10
The /**T**ools **S**pell **D**ictionary [**A**dd, **D**elete] screen.

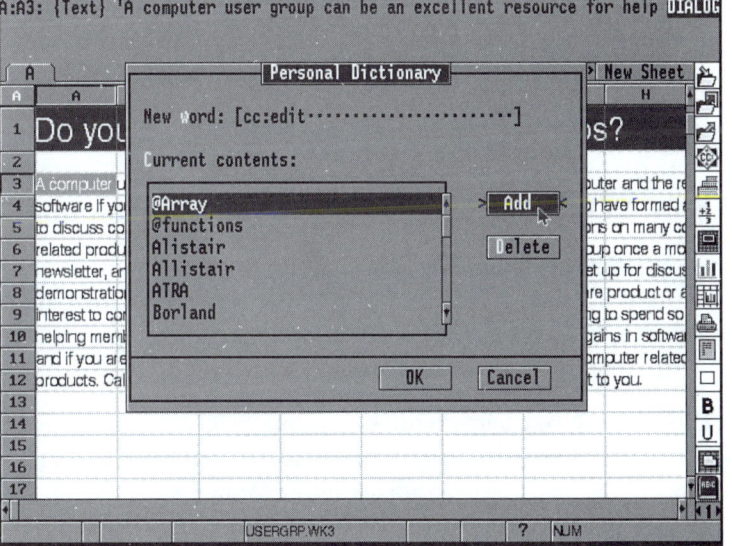

Fig. 6.11
The Personal Dictionary dialog box.

To add a new word to the dictionary, follow these steps:

1. Click the New **W**ord box or press W.

2. Type the word you want to add, and then press Enter.

3. At this point, you will notice that the Add button is highlighted. Press Enter again or click the Add button to enter the new word into the personal dictionary.

4. When you finish adding words to your personal dictionary, click the OK button and then press Esc to return to the Spell Check dialog box.

To delete a word from the dictionary, follow these steps:

1. Click the **C**urrent Contents box or press C to display a list of the words that currently are in the dictionary.

2. Highlight the word you want to delete.

3. Click the Delete button or press Enter.

4. When you finish deleting words from your personal dictionary, click the OK button and then press Esc to return to the Spell Check dialog box.

The Cancel button in the Personal Dictionary dialog box will not undo any changes you made in the dictionary during the editing session. When you click the OK or Cancel button, the menu mode reappears. You need to press Exc to return to the **/T**ools **S**pell **D**ictionary menu. Press Esc again to return to the **/T**ools **S**pell menu prompt.

Formatting Numbers

To change the format of a cell or range of cells, use the **/R**ange **F**ormat command in the 1-2-3 main menu (see fig. 6.12). Choose one of the formats or choose **O**ther to see additional formatting options (see fig. 6.13). The formats listed in these menus are known as *range formats*.

If you choose the **F**ixed, **S**ci (scientific), comma (,), **C**urrency, or **P**ercent range format, 1-2-3 prompts you (in the second line of the control panel) for the number of decimal places to appear in the format (see fig. 6.14). Whenever this prompt appears, a default value of 2 decimal places follows the prompt. Press Enter to accept the default, or enter a different number ranging from 0 to 15 and then press Enter.

Formatting Numbers 291

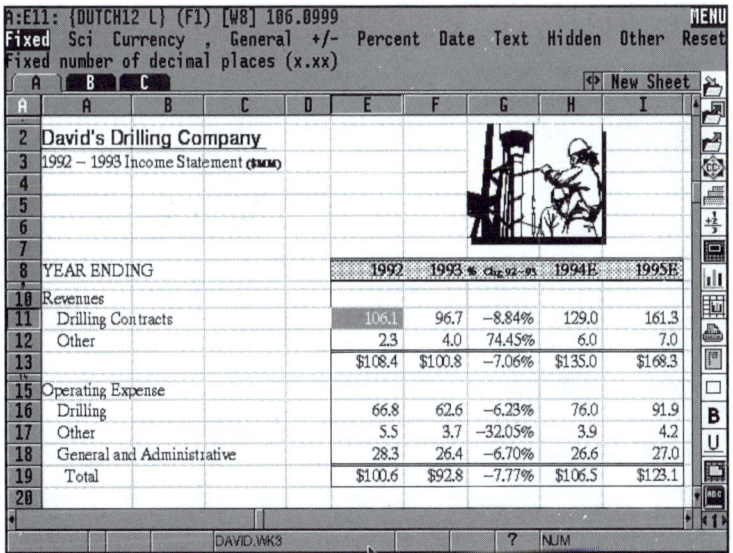

Fig. 6.12
The /Range Format menu.

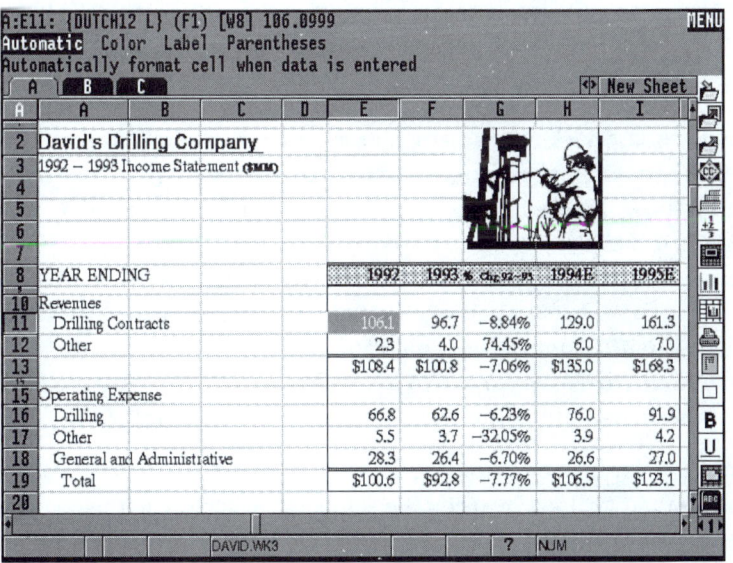

Fig. 6.13
The /Range Format Other menu.

> **Note**
> To select comma format with the keyboard, press the comma key (,).

Fig. 6.14

The control-panel prompt to enter the number of decimal places.

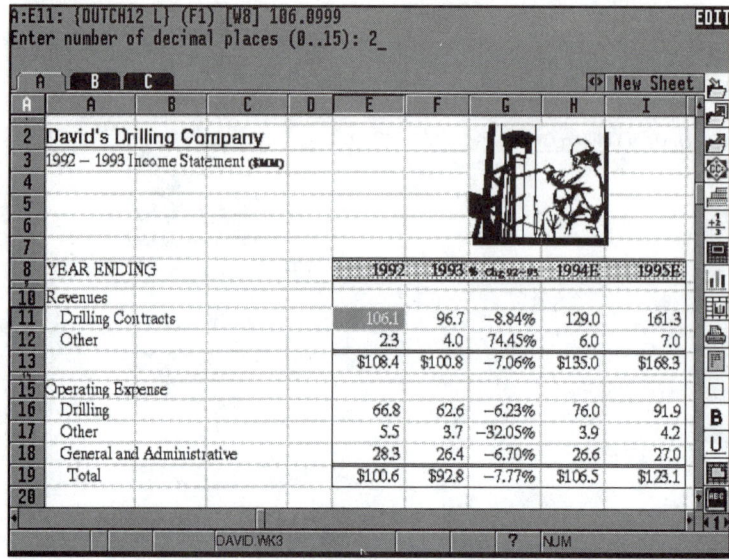

The **D**ate and **T**ime formats access additional menus that are discussed later in this chapter in the section "Date and Time Formats." (The **T**ime format itself is accessed from the **D**ate menu.)

After you choose a format and any options (such as decimal places), the program prompts you for the range of cells to be formatted. Highlight the range and press Enter. Figure 6.14 shows the result of choosing **/R**ange **F**ormat **F**ixed with **1** decimal place and selecting the range E11..E19 to be formatted. An abbreviation of the selected format appears in the first line of the control panel if the current cell is part of a formatted range. In figure 6.14, the abbreviation (F1) in the control panel indicates that cell E11 (the highlighted cell) has been formatted as **F**ixed with **1** decimal place. If the highlighted cell has no range format, no format indicator appears in the control panel.

When you are using your mouse in 1-2-3, it sometimes is quicker and easier to make format changes by using the status bar. Click the left part of the status bar, called the *format selector*, to invoke the format menu. If no format has been applied to the selected cell or range of cells, the format selector displays the default global format.

Figure 6.15 illustrates how to use the format selector to change the format type. Figure 6.16 shows how to use the decimal-place selector (in the status bar to the right of the format selector) to select the number of decimal places for the selected format type.

Formatting Numbers **293**

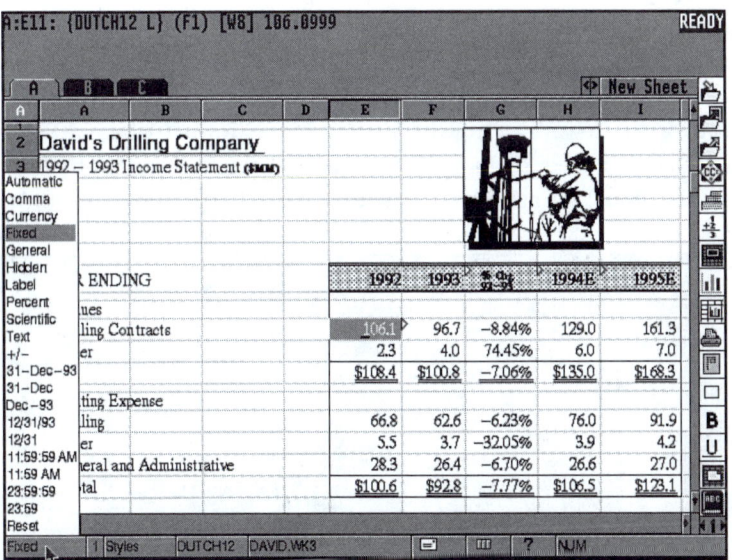

Fig. 6.15
The format selector with Fixed format highlighted.

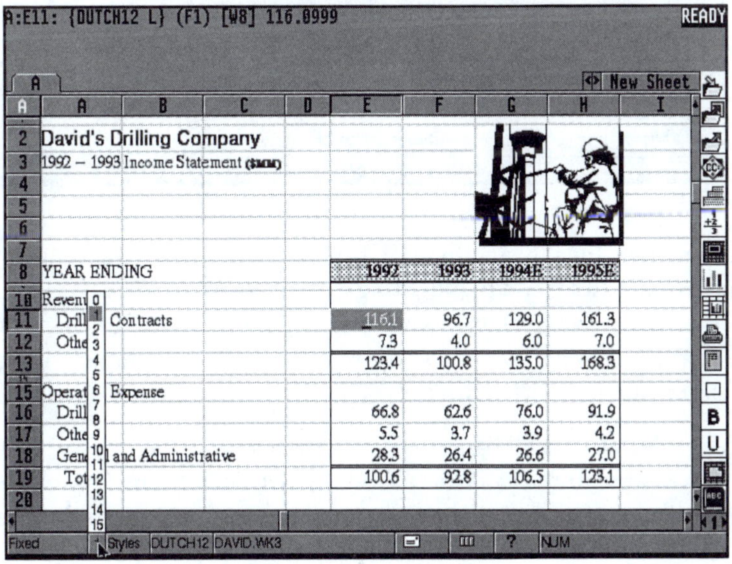

Fig. 6.16
The decimal-place selector with 1 highlighted.

If you start a new worksheet, no cells in that worksheet contain any range formats. If a cell doesn't have a range format, that cell uses the global format specified by /**W**orksheet **G**lobal **F**ormat. After you change a cell's format with the /**R**ange **F**ormat commands, that cell's format will not change if you change the global format type. Only cells without specific formats change when the global format is changed.

294 Chapter 6—Making Your Worksheets Dazzle

When you start a new worksheet, the default global format for that file is **G**eneral. To change the global format of the worksheet, choose **/W**orksheet **G**lobal **F**ormat to access the Global Settings dialog box (see fig. 6.17). Notice that the format doesn't change to the new global format where **/R**ange **F**ormat has been used to change cell formats. These cells retain their range format; the global format affects only cells with no specific range format.

Fig. 6.17
The Global Settings dialog box.

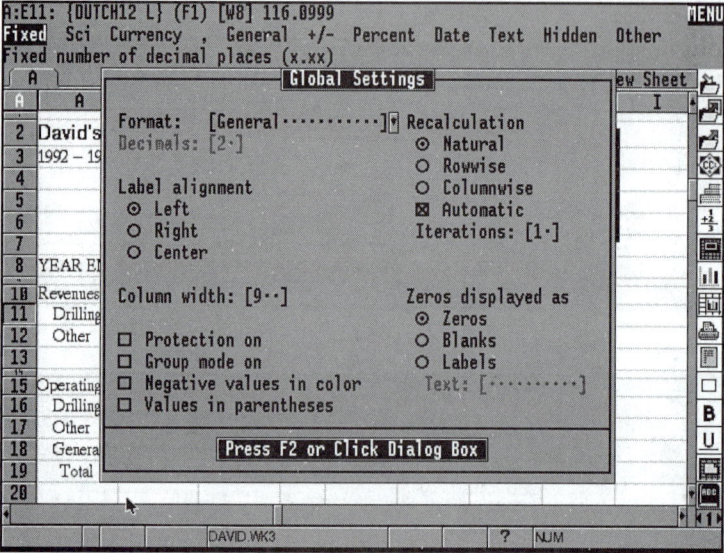

You can remove the range formatting from a cell or range by choosing **/R**ange **F**ormat **R**eset and highlighting that cell or range of cells. The cell or range then takes on the global formatting of the worksheet. To change the range format of a cell or range, choose the **/R**ange **F**ormat command again and select a different format for the cell or range.

When you decide on a global format for a worksheet, select the format that you expect to use in the worksheet most frequently. Then use **/R**ange **F**ormat to format ranges that require different formats. Most worksheets look best if several different formats are used to match the data contained in specific cells or ranges. Figure 6.18 shows a worksheet with a Fixed (1) global format and **C**urrency and **P**ercent range formats. (This worksheet also contains Wysiwyg shading and lines; Wysiwyg formatting is discussed later in this chapter in the section "Formatting with the Wysiwyg Menu.")

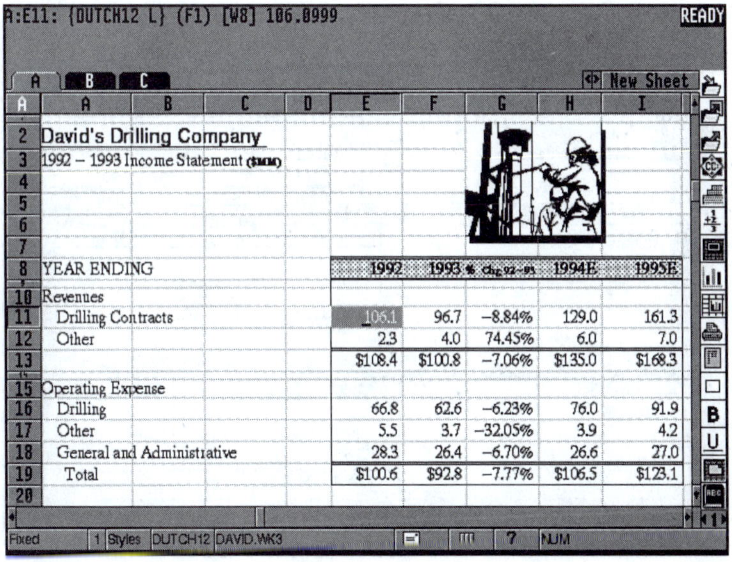

Fig. 6.18
A worksheet with Fixed (1) global format and Currency and Percent range formats.

/**W**orksheet **G**lobal **F**ormat applies only to the current worksheet. If you use /**W**orksheet **G**lobal **F**ormat to change the global format of a worksheet in a file containing multiple worksheets, you change the format of only the current worksheet. To give all the worksheets in the file the same global format, you must turn on GROUP mode by choosing /**W**orksheet **G**lobal **G**roup. If every worksheet in the file has the same layout, such as the worksheets in the file shown in figure 6.19, using GROUP mode ensures that changes made in one worksheet affect all worksheets. If each worksheet in the file has a different layout (when separate worksheets are used for input areas, notes and assumptions, reports, and macros, for example), turn off GROUP mode to format each worksheet separately.

GROUP mode also affects the /**R**ange **F**ormat and Wysiwyg **:F**ormat commands. If GROUP mode is enabled, formatting a range in one worksheet formats the same range in all worksheets in the file. Figure 6.19 shows the effect of choosing /**R**ange **F**ormat **P**ercent with **2** decimal places for the range A:G11..A:G19 when GROUP mode is enabled. Although the specified range covers only cells in worksheet A, the same range in the other worksheets in the file also changes format.

The following sections describe the 1-2-3 format options in detail. Choose /**W**orksheet **G**lobal **F**ormat or /**R**ange **F**ormat to access these formatting options. If you did not choose the /**W**orksheet **G**lobal **D**efault **U**pdate option after the /**W**orksheet **G**lobal **F**ormat changes, the change applies only to the current session, not to subsequent 1-2-3 sessions.

Fig. 6.19
In GROUP mode, formatting a range changes all worksheets in the file.

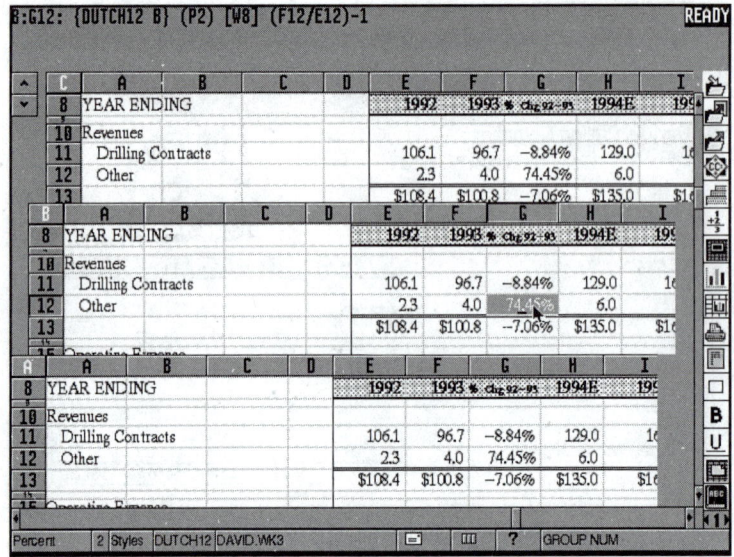

General Format

General format, the default setting for all new worksheets, displays only the number itself in cells that contain values. Negative numbers are preceded by a minus sign. Numbers containing decimal digits also contain a decimal point. If a number contains too many digits to the right of the decimal to fit within the cell's column width, the decimal portion is rounded to the nearest whole number. If the number is too large or too small to appear in the cell normally, the number is displayed in **S**ci (scientific) format (123400000 appears as 1.2E+08, for example, and 0.0000000012 as 1.2E-09). Negative numbers in **S**ci format are displayed with a leading minus sign (such as -123).

The following table shows several examples of **G**eneral formatting in cells with a column width of 9 and a **:F**ormat **F**ont format of 12-point Dutch.

Typed Entry	Cell Format	Display Result
123.46	(G)	123.46
-123.36	(G)	-123.36
1.2345678912	(G)	1.234568
150000000	(G)	1.5E+08
-.00000002638	(G)	-2.6E-08

> **Note**
>
> The abbreviation (G) appears in the control panel for cells formatted with /Range Format General.

Fixed Format

Use **F**ixed format to line up a column of numbers at the decimal point. 1-2-3 displays in the worksheet the fixed number of decimal places (0 to 15) that you specify. If the actual number contains more decimal digits than are allowed in the format you specify, the displayed number is rounded to the specified number of decimals in the cell, but the value used for calculation stays the same as that of the original number.

The following table shows several examples of **F**ixed formatting in cells with a column width of 9 and a **:F**ormat **F**ont format of 12-point Dutch.

Typed Entry	Cell Format	Display Result
123.46	(F0)	123
123.46	(F1)	123.5
–123.46	(F2)	–123.46
123.46	(F4)	123.4600
–123.46	(F4)	–123.4600
12345678	(F2)	************

In all cases, the complete value entered in the cell is used in calculations. Negative numbers appear with a leading minus sign, as shown in the third and fifth entries in the preceding table.

> **Note**
>
> The abbreviation (F*n*) appears in the control panel for cells that have been formatted with **/R**ange **F**ormat **F**ixed. *n* represents the number of decimal places.

Comma (,) Format

As is true of **F**ixed format, comma (,) format displays data with a fixed number of decimal places (0 to 15). The format also separates thousands, millions, and greater numbers with commas. Positive numbers less than 1,000, however, appear identically in **F**ixed and comma format. Comma format is used most frequently in displays of financial data.

After selecting the cells to be formatted, you can apply comma (**,**) **0** format to the range by clicking the Comma 0 SmartIcon.

If a number contains more decimal digits than are permitted in the comma format you specify, 1-2-3 rounds the number to the nearest whole number, just as it does in **F**ixed format. The full value of the number originally entered in the cell is used in calculations.

Use comma format rather than **F**ixed format to display large numbers. A number formatted with comma format and zero decimal places, such as 12,300,000, is easier to read than 12300000. Comma-formatted negative numbers appear in parentheses within cells—for example, –1234 formatted with 0 decimal places appears as (1,234).

You can change the default setting, however, so that comma-formatted negative numbers appear with a leading minus sign rather than in parentheses. To make this change, choose **/W**orksheet **G**lobal **D**efault **O**ther **I**nternational **N**egative **S**ign. After you change the default setting, –1234 appears as -1,234. To reinstate parentheses as the default for comma-formatted negative numbers, choose **/W**orksheet **G**lobal **D**efault **O**ther **I**nternational **N**egative **P**arentheses. Be aware that this default setting applies to 1-2-3 as a whole, not just to the current worksheet or file; changing the default changes how negative numbers with the comma format appear in every file you create with 1-2-3. If you did not choose the **/W**orksheet **G**lobal **D**efault **U**pdate option, the change applies only to the current session, not to subsequent 1-2-3 sessions.

> **Note**
>
> The abbreviation (**,**n) appears in the control panel for cells that have been formatted with **/R**ange **F**ormat **,** (comma). *n* represents the number of decimal places specified.

The following table shows several examples of comma format in cells with a column width of 9 and a **:F**ormat **F**ont format of 12-point Dutch.

Typed Entry	Cell Format	Display Result
123.46	(,0)	123
1234.6	(,2)	1,234.60

Typed Entry	Cell Format	Display Result
−1234.6	(,0)	(1,235)
		−1,235 (with a default minus sign)
−1234567	(,2)	************

Currency Format

Currency format functions similarly to comma (,) format but adds a leading dollar sign to the displayed number. You can specify up to 15 decimal places for Currency format. Because of the dollar sign, you must add an extra position to the column width of a cell in which you intend to display a number in Currency format; if you don't add the additional position to the column width, the Currency-formatted number cannot fit within the cell. Negative numbers are handled in Currency format the same as in comma format, appearing in parentheses rather than with a leading minus sign.

After selecting a range of cells to be formatted, you can apply Currency 2 format to the numbers in those cells by clicking the Currency 2 SmartIcon.

The dollar sign ($) is the default currency symbol in 1-2-3, but you can change this default if you need to use a different type of currency. Choose /Worksheet Global Default Other International Currency to specify a different currency symbol and to specify whether that symbol is a prefix or a suffix to the number. Be aware that this default setting applies to 1-2-3 as a whole, not just to the current worksheet or file; changing the default currency symbol for one file changes the default for all files you create with 1-2-3. If you did not choose the /Worksheet Global Default Update option, the change applies only to the current session, not to subsequent 1-2-3 sessions.

Suppose that you create a file in which you use the Currency-format default setting for U.S. dollars, and you save that file. You later create a file in which you must use the British pound (£). You can change the default currency symbol to the British-pound symbol by choosing the /Worksheet Global Default Other International Currency command. When the prompt Currency symbol: $ appears, press Backspace to remove the dollar sign, and then substitute the British pound sign by pressing Alt+F1 (Compose) and typing L=. (Refer to your Lotus 1-2-3 Release 4 documentation for more information on specifying Lotus Multibyte Character Set [LMBCS] characters such as the pound symbol.) Then press Enter and choose Prefix. The new file now displays the British-pound symbol for all Currency-formatted numbers. You must remember, however, that this change in the currency symbol affects all

1-2-3 files on a computer, not just the new one. When you retrieve another file, any cells formatted as **C**urrency display the British-pound symbol as the currency symbol, even if those cells originally were formatted with the dollar sign. If you did not choose the **/W**orksheet **G**lobal **D**efault **U**pdate option after using the **/W**orksheet **G**lobal menu options, the change applies only to the current session, not to subsequent 1-2-3 sessions.

> **Note**
>
> The abbreviation (Cn) appears in the control panel for cells formatted with **/R**ange **F**ormat **C**urrency. *n* represents the number of decimal places selected.

The following table shows several examples of **C**urrency format in cells with a column width of 9 and a **:F**ormat **F**ont format of 12-point Dutch.

Typed Entry	Cell Format	Display Result
123	(C2)	$123.00 £123.00 (using the pound symbol as the default)
–123.124	(C2)	($123.12) –$123.12 (using a default minus sign)
1234.12	(C0)	$1,234
–123456.12	(C2)	************

Percent Format

The **P**ercent format shows numbers in cells as percentages. As with the other types of formats, you must specify the number of decimal places that can appear in a percentage, from 0 to 15. The number displayed in a **P**ercent-formatted cell is the value of the cell multiplied by 100, followed by a percent sign (%). If the number contains more decimal digits than the format you specify allows, 1-2-3 rounds the number displayed to the nearest decimal position or whole number that fits.

After selecting a range of cells to be formatted, you can apply a **P**ercent 2 format to the numbers in those cells by clicking the Percent 2 SmartIcon.

Notice that the number of decimal places you specify are the decimal places that appear in that number as a percentage, not in the value you enter into the cell. The number in the cell appears as if the value you entered was multiplied by 100, but the actual value of the cell is unchanged. To display 50% in a cell, therefore, you must enter **.5** and format the cell for **P**ercent with **0** decimal places. If you enter **50** and format the cell **P**ercent with **0** decimal places, 5000% appears in the cell instead.

> **Note**
>
> The abbreviation (P*n*) appears in the control panel for cells formatted with **/R**ange **F**ormat **P**ercent. *n* represents the number of decimal places specified.

The following table shows several examples of **P**ercent format in cells with a column width of 9 and a **:F**ormat **F**ont format of 12-point Dutch.

Typed Entry	Cell Format	Display Result
.3	(P2)	30.00%
-.3528	(P2)	-35.28%
30	(P0)	3000%
30	(P4)	************

Scientific Format

Use **S**ci (scientific) format to display very large or very small numbers. Very large and very small numbers usually contain a few significant digits and many zeros as placeholders to tell you how large or how small the number is.

A number in scientific notation has two parts: a mantissa and an exponent. The *mantissa* is a number, ranging from 1 to 10, that contains the significant digits. The *exponent* tells you how many places to move the decimal point to get the actual value of the number. You specify the number of decimal places for the mantissa (0 to 15). If the number has more significant digits than the format you specify allows, 1-2-3 rounds the number displayed.

1230000000000 appears as 1.23E+12 in **S**ci format with **2** decimal places. E+12 signifies that you must move the decimal point 12 places to the right to get the actual number. 0.000000000237 appears as 2.4E-10 in **S**ci format with **1** decimal place. E-10 means that you must move the decimal point 10 places to the left to get the actual number. As previously noted, any number too large to display in a cell in **G**eneral format appears in **S**ci format instead.

Note

The abbreviation (S*n*) appears in the control panel for cells formatted with **/R**ange **F**ormat **S**ci. *n* represents the number of decimal places.

The following table shows several examples of **S**ci format in cells with a column width of 9 and a **:F**ormat **F**ont format of 12-point Dutch.

Typed Entry	Cell Format	Display Result
1632116750000	(S2)	1.63E+12
1632116750000	(S0)	2E+12
−1632116750000	(S1)	−1.6E+12
−1632116750000	(S4)	************
−.00000000012	(S0)	−1E−10

The +/− Format

The +/− format creates a horizontal bar chart in the specified cell based on the actual value in the cell. A positive number appears as a row of plus signs; a negative number appears as a row of minus signs; and a zero (or any other number less than 1, but greater than −1) appears as a period. The number of pluses or minuses can be no wider than the cell.

This format was devised to create imitation bar charts in spreadsheet programs that had no graphing capability. The format has little use today.

Note

The abbreviation (+) appears in the control panel for cells formatted with **/R**ange **F**ormat **+/−**.

If you display cells with this format and you are using **:F**ormat **F**ont to change the appearance of cells, use a nonproportional font (such as Courier) for cells formatted with **/R**ange **F**ormat **+/−**. Using a proportional font causes minus signs to appear as a solid bar on-screen. Using the nonproportional font gives each minus sign its own position, distinguishing one minus sign from another. For more explanation on the types of fonts available, refer to table 6.7.

The following table shows several examples of **+/–** format in cells with a column width of 9 and a **:F**ormat **F**ont format of 12-point Courier, which is a nonproportional font.

Typed Entry	Cell Format	Display Result
6	(+)	++++++
4.9	(+)	++++
–3	(+)	---
0	(+)	.
17.2	(+)	**********
.95	(+)	.

Date and Time Formats

All the formats mentioned so far deal with regular numeric values. **D**ate and **T**ime formats, however, are used mainly when you work with date and time calculations or time functions. These functions are covered more fully in Chapter 3, "Finding Solutions with Formulas and Functions."

Choose **/R**ange **F**ormat **D**ate or **/W**orksheet **G**lobal **F**ormat **D**ate for the five **D**ate format options or a **T**ime format. The menu for **/R**ange **F**ormat **D**ate or **/W**orksheet **G**lobal **F**ormat **D**ate is as follows:

    1 (DD-MMM-YY) **2** (DD-MMM) **3** (MMM-YY) **4** (Long Int'l) **5** (Short Int'l) **Time**

Choose **/R**ange **F**ormat **D**ate **T**ime or **/W**orksheet **G**lobal **F**ormat **D**ate **T**ime for the four **T**ime format options that follow:

    1 (HH:MM:SS AM/PM) **2** (HH:MM AM/PM) **3** (Long Int'l) **4** (Short Int'l)

Date Formats

If you use date functions, 1-2-3 stores the date as a serial number representing the number of days elapsed since January 1, 1900. The serial date number for January 1, 1900, is 1. The serial date number for January 15, 1994, is 34349. The latest date that 1-2-3 can handle is December 31, 2099, represented by the serial number 73050. If the number is less than 1 or greater than 73050, a **D**ate format appears as asterisks; in Wysiwyg, however, the cell appears

Tip
The format selector in the status bar (refer to fig. 6.15) displays examples of all the available date and time formats, making it quicker and easier to select the desired format.

blank. **D**ate formats ignore any fraction. For example, 34349.99 with format **D4** (long international) appears as 01/15/94. The fraction represents the time, a fractional portion of a 24-hour clock.

Don't be concerned about which serial date number refers to which date. 1-2-3 can format the serial date number to appear as a text date.

> **Caution**
>
> All the date serial numbers starting with March 1, 1900, are off by one day. The calendar inside 1-2-3 treats 1900 as a leap year; it isn't. A date serial number of 60, for example, appears as 02/29/00—a date that doesn't exist. Unless you compare dates before February 28, 1900, with dates after February 28, 1900, this error has no effect on worksheets. Dates may be off by one day, however, if you export data to a database program.

If you choose /**R**ange **F**ormat **D**ate, the **D**ate menu appears. Five **D**ate formats can format serial numbers to appear as dates. Table 6.4 lists these formats. Long international (**D4**) and short international (**D5**) each have four different formats. The defaults are those that are most common in the United States. If you prefer one of the other international **D**ate formats, use /**W**orksheet **G**lobal **D**efault **O**ther **I**nternational **D**ate and then choose a format (**A** through **D**).

Table 6.4 Date Formats

Menu Item	Format	Description	Example
1	(D1)	Day-Month-Year DD-MMM-YY	15-Jan-94
2	(D2)	Day-Month DD-MMM	15-Jan
3	(D3)	Month-Year MMM-YY	Jan-94
4	(D4) A B C D	Long International* MM/DD/YY DD/MM/YY DD.MM.YY YY-MM-DD	 01/15/94 15/01/94 15.01.94 94-01-15

Menu Item	Format	Description	Example
5	(D5)	Short International*	
	A	MM/DD	01/15
	B	DD/MM	15/01
	C	DD.MM	15.01
	D	MM-DD	01-15

* Use the **/W**orksheet **G**lobal **D**efault **O**ther **I**nternational **D**ate command to choose one of the international formats (**A**, **B**, **C**, or **D**).

You can insert the current date (formatted as **D4**) in a cell by clicking the Insert Date SmartIcon.

You can enter date serial numbers without using date functions. You simply enter what appears as a date, and 1-2-3 converts what you enter to a serial date number. This method often is the fastest way to enter dates. You can enter a date in either **Date 4** format (**1/15/94**) or **Date 1** format (**15-Jan-94**); 1-2-3 converts the entry to the date serial number (34349). If you enter the date **15-Jan** (the **Date 2** format), 1-2-3 assumes that you are referring to a date in the current year. If the internal clock in the computer says that the current year is 1994, **15-Jan** converts to 34349—the date serial number for January 15, 1994. If you enter **15-Jan** during 1990, you get 32888—the date serial number for January 15, 1990. If, however, you are entering the formula 1 divided by 15 divided by 94, which looks like the date 1/15/94, you must enter the formula with a value prefix—for example, **+1/15/94**.

Either the global format or the range format must be a **D**ate format for a number to appear in a cell as a date. You can use **/R**ange **F**ormat to format the cell before you enter the date in the cell or after you enter a serial number. If you expect to enter dates in certain cells, format the blank cells with a **D**ate format. Then the date serial numbers (such as 34349) don't appear in the cells; only the formatted dates appear (Jan-94), although if the current cell is a date cell, the serial number will appear in the control panel.

You cannot enter dates as date serial numbers by using any date format other than **Date 1**, **Date 2**, or **Date 4**. If you enter a date in **Date 3** format (for example, **Jan-94**), 1-2-3 treats the entry as a label. If you enter a date in **Date 5** format (for example, **1/15**), 1-2-3 treats that date as a formula and converts the date to a number (in this case, 0.066667).

> **Note**
>
> The abbreviation (Dn) appears in the control panel for cells formatted with **/R**ange **F**ormat **D**ate. *n* represents the **D**ate format selection (**1** through **5**) in the **F**ormat **D**ate menu.

The following table shows several examples of **D**ate format in cells with a column width of 9 and a **:F**ormat **F**ont format of 12-point Dutch.

Typed Entry	Cell Format	Display Result	Cell Contents
10/12/94	(D1)	************	34619
10/12/94	(D2)	12-Oct	34619
10/12/94	(D3)	Oct-94	34619
10/12/94	(D4)	10/12/94	34619
10/12/94	(D5)	10/12	34619
15	(D4)	01/15/00	15
34349	(D4)	01/15/94	34349
34349.4538	(D4)	01/15/94	34349.4538
–33984	any date format	************	–34349
12-Oct-94	(D4)	10/12/94	34619
12-oct (during 1994)	(D4)	10/12/94	34619
Oct-94	any date format	Oct-94	'Oct-94
10/12	any date format	************	0.8333333333333333

The following table shows several examples of **D**ate **1** format in cells with a column width of 10 and a **:F**ormat **F**ont format of 12-point Dutch. (**D**ate **1** format cannot appear in a cell with a default column width of 9 and this font.)

Typed Entry	Cell Format	Display Result	Cell Contents
10/12/94	(D1)	12-Oct-94	34619
12-Oct-94	(D1)	12-Oct-94	34619
12-oct (during 1994)	(D1)	12-Oct-94	34619

Time Formats

1-2-3 maintains times in a special format known as *time fractions*. You can format time fractions so that they appear as a time of day.

If you enter a time, 1-2-3 stores the time as a decimal fraction (0 to 1) that represents a fraction of the 24-hour clock. The time fraction for 3 a.m., for example, is 0.125; the time fraction for noon is 0.5; and the time fraction for 6 p.m. is 0.75. You can ignore the actual fractions and leave the displaying of the fraction as a time to 1-2-3.

You can enter a time fraction without using time functions. To do so, enter what appears to be a time; 1-2-3 converts what you enter to a time fraction. You can enter a time in any **T**ime format, using regular time (a.m./p.m.) or 24-hour military time. The use of seconds is optional.

If you enter **6:23**, **6:23:00**, **6:23AM**, or **6:23:00 am**, 1-2-3 converts the entry to the time fraction 0.265972. (Actually, 1-2-3 stores fractions with up to 19 significant digits, but only six to eight digits are shown in these examples.) If you enter **6:23:57** or **6:23:57 AM**, 1-2-3 converts the entry to the time fraction 0.266632. If you enter **6:23 pm** or **18:23**, 1-2-3 converts the entry to the time fraction 0.765972.

You don't need to enter **AM** at the end of times before noon. For times after noon, however, enter **PM** or enter the hour (12 to 23). The AM or PM can be in uppercase or lowercase letters and can follow a space after the time.

If you choose **/R**ange **F**ormat **D**ate **T**ime, the **T**ime menu appears. 1-2-3 includes four **T**ime formats that show fractions as times. Table 6.5 lists these formats. Long International and Short International each have four different formats. The defaults are those that are most common in the United States. If you prefer one of the other international time formats, choose **/W**orksheet **G**lobal **D**efault **O**ther **I**nternational **T**ime and then choose one of the four format options (**A** through **D**).

Table 6.5 Time Formats

Menu Choice	Format	Description	Example
1	(D6)	Hour:Minute:Second HH:MM:SS AM/PM	06:23:57 PM
2	(D7)	Hour:Minute HH:MM AM/PM	06:23 PM

(continues)

Table 6.5 Continued

Menu Choice	Format	Description	Example
3	(D8)	Long International*	
	A	HH:MM:SS	18:23:57
	B	HH.MM.SS	18.23.57
	C	HH,MM,SS	18,23,57
	D	HHhMMmSSs	18h23m57s
4	(D9)	Short International*	
	A	HH:MM	18:23
	B	HH.MM	18.23
	C	HH,MM	18,23
	D	HHhMMm	18h23m

* Use the **/W**orksheet **G**lobal **D**efault **O**ther **I**nternational **T**ime command to choose one of the international formats (**A**, **B**, **C**, or **D**).

Either the global format or the range format must be a **T**ime format for a number to appear in a cell as a time. You can use **/R**ange **F**ormat to format a cell either before or after you enter the time in the cell. If you enter the time in a cell formatted with **G**eneral format, however, the appearance of the time fraction can be confusing until you format the cell with the **T**ime format. If you expect to enter times in certain cells, format them with a **T**ime format while they are blank. Then, when you enter the times into the cells, the formatted times appear, not the time fractions.

If a time serial number is greater than 1, **T**ime formats ignore the integer portion. Therefore, the time serial number 34254.75 with format **D7** (Time **2** or Lotus standard short form) appears as 06:00 PM. Negative numbers represent the fraction of a day before midnight; –0.75 (or –34254.75) is the same as 0.25 and appears as 06:00 AM. The time –0.125 is the same as 0.875 and appears as 9:00 PM.

> **Note**
>
> The abbreviation (Dn) appears in the control panel for cells range-formatted with **/R**ange **F**ormat **D**ate **T**ime. *n* represents the **T**ime format selection (**6** through **9**).

1-2-3 identifies **T**ime formats in a confusing way. If you choose **D**ate **T**ime **1**, 1-2-3 shows (D6) in the control panel, not (T1). **D**ate **T**ime **2** shows (D7), **D**ate **T**ime **3** shows (D8), and **D**ate **T**ime **4** shows (D9).

Formatting Numbers 309

The following table shows several examples of **T**ime format in cells with a column width of 9 and a **:**F**ormat **F**ont format of 12-point Dutch.

Typed Entry	Cell Format	Display Result	Cell Contents
6:23 AM	(D6)	************	0.265972
6:23 AM	(D7)	06:23 AM	0.265972
6:23	(D8)	06:23:00	0.265972
6:23	(D9)	06:23	0.265972
6:23:57	(D7)	06:23 AM	0.266632
6:23:57	(D8)	06:23:57	0.266632
6:23 pm	(D7)	06:23 PM	0.765972
6:23:57 pm	(D8)	18:23:57	0.766632
18:23	(D7)	06:23 PM	0.765972
2	(D7)	12:00 AM	2
−.25	(D7)	06:00 PM	−.25

The following table shows several examples of **T**ime **1** (D6) format in cells with a column width of 12 and a **:**F**ormat **F**ont format of 12-point Dutch. (**T**ime **1** format cannot appear in a cell with a default column width of 9 and this font.)

Typed Entry	Cell Format	Display Result	Cell Contents
6:23	(D6)	06:23:00 AM	0.265972
6:23:57	(D6)	06:23:57 AM	0.266632
18:23:57	(D6)	06:23:57 PM	0.766632

Text Format

Use **T**ext format to display both numeric and string formulas in a cell instead of current values. Numbers formatted for **T**ext appear in **G**eneral format. If the formula being displayed in **T**ext format is too long to appear within the column width, the formula is *truncated*, or shortened, and doesn't appear across the blank cells to the right as a long label does. If you attach a note to the number or formula in a cell, the note also appears in that cell (if the column is wide enough).

The entries shown in column D of figure 6.20 are formatted as **Text**. The labels are unaffected. The numbers in D3..D16 appear in **G**eneral format. The formula in D10 has a note attached and appears with the note left-aligned. The formula and note in D10 appear instead of the current value of the formula.

Fig. 6.20
Examples of **T**ext-formatted cells in column D of a worksheet.

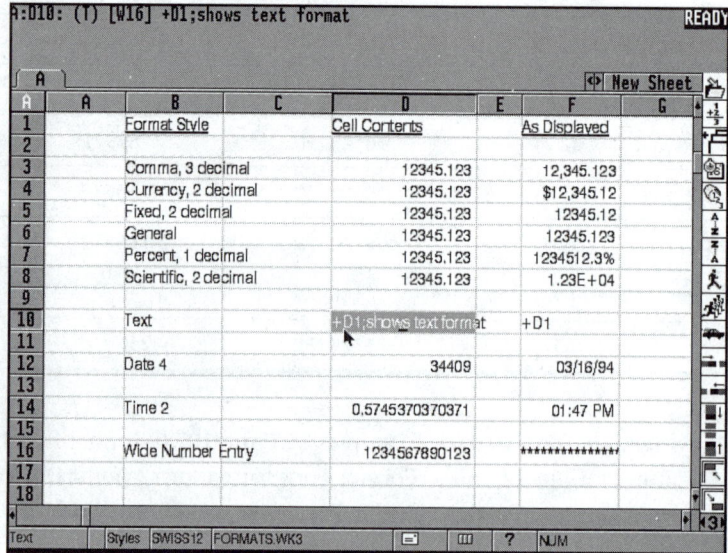

Text format can be used for criteria ranges with **/D**ata **Q**uery commands, which are covered in Chapter 21, "Finding Specific Data." You also can use **T**ext format when you enter or debug complex formulas. You can temporarily change the format of a formula to **T**ext so you can view the formula in one cell as you build a similar formula in another cell. You may need to temporarily widen the column containing the original formula as you do this.

> **Note**
> The abbreviation (T) appears in the control panel for cells formatted with **/R**ange **F**ormat **T**ext.

Formatting Numbers   311

Hidden Format

A cell formatted as **H**idden appears blank regardless of what the cell contains. You can use this format for intermediate calculations or sensitive formulas that you don't want to display in a cell. If the cell is protected and global protection is enabled, the contents of a hidden cell don't appear in the control panel when you move the cell pointer to that cell. In other cases, you can see the contents of the cell with hidden formatting in the control panel.

You cannot use **H**idden format to hide data completely, however. If you can change the format or the protection status of the cell, you can view the contents of the cell, so don't rely on **H**idden format to hide sensitive information. If the file isn't sealed, you can use one of the /**R**ange **F**ormat commands to change or reset the format, and the contents of the cell become visible.

▶ "Hiding Worksheet Data," p. 516

▶ "Sealing Files," p. 523

In the worksheet shown in figure 6.21, the numbers in cells G10..G13 have been hidden with **H**idden format.

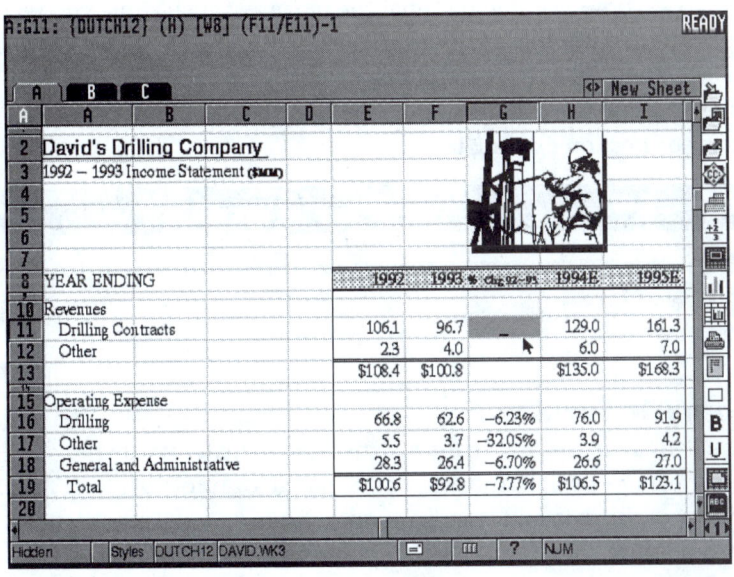

Fig. 6.21
The appearance of a worksheet after **H**idden formatting was used in cells G10..G13.

> **Note**
> The abbreviation (H) appears in the control panel for cells formatted with /**R**ange **F**ormat **H**idden.

Label Format

You can use **/R**ange **F**ormat **O**ther **L**abel to assign **L**abel format to a cell. You can use this format in blank cells to make typing labels easier. All entries in cells formatted as **L**abel are considered to be labels, and 1-2-3 precedes the entry with the default label prefix. This step facilitates typing labels that appear as numbers and entering formulas that begin with a numeric character.

Suppose that you type **57 Main Street** in a cell and press Enter. 1-2-3 considers the entry to be an invalid numeric entry (because the entry includes letters) and switches to EDIT mode. You must precede the entry with a label prefix, such as an apostrophe (').

Suppose, on the other hand, that you type **10/15** in a cell and press Enter. 1-2-3 considers **10/15** to be a formula, so it converts that value to a number and displays `0.666667`. To convert this entry to a label, you must reenter the label with a label prefix, such as a caret (^).

In both cases, however, if you format the range as **L**abel before you type the entry, 1-2-3 precedes the entry with a label prefix, and the entry becomes a text label. If you change existing numeric entries to **L**abel format, those entries don't become labels; the numbers appear in **G**eneral format. **L**abel format has no effect on existing labels.

> **Note**
>
> The abbreviation (L) appears in the control panel for cells formatted as **/R**ange **F**ormat **O**ther **L**abel.

Automatic Format

/Range **F**ormat **O**ther **A**utomatic assigns **A**utomatic formatting to a cell. If you enter data in a cell that has been formatted as **A**utomatic, 1-2-3 analyzes the format of the data and selects a format. Table 6.6 lists examples of **A**utomatic formatting.

The first column of the table lists the data that you enter in a cell formatted as **A**utomatic. After you complete the entry, 1-2-3 analyzes the data and stores that data in the cell with the format shown in the second column. This format is displayed in the control panel. The third and fourth columns show how 1-2-3 stores the data (to 10 places) and how the data appears in the worksheet. (This table assumes a column width of 10.)

Formatting Numbers   **313**

Table 6.6 Automatic Formatting Examples

Data Typed	Data Format	Stored Data	Data Displayed
57 Main	(L)	'57 Main	57 Main
@SUM(xxxx	(L)	'@SUM(xxxx	@SUM(xxxx
258	(F0)	258	258
258.46	(F2)	258.46	258.46
258.00	(F2)	258	258.00
1,258	(,0)	1258	1,258
1,258.69	(,2)	1258.69	1,258.69
0,087.00	(,2)	87	87.00
$258.00	(C2)	258	$258.00
25%	(P0)	0.25	25%
2.50%	(P2)	0.025	2.50%
1.2E4	(S1)	12000	1.2E+04
2.587E–16	(S3)	2.587E-16	2.587E-16
25.87E117	(L)	25.87E117	25.87E-117
15-jan-94	(D1)	34349	15-Jan-94
15-jan	(D2)	34349*	15-Jan
jan-94	(L)	'jan-94	jan-94
1/15/94	(D4)	34349	01/15/94
10/15	(A)	0.6666666667	0.6666667
6:23:57 am	(D6)	0.2666319444	06:23:57 AM
6:23:57	(D8)	0.2666319444	06:23:57
6:23:57 pm	(D6)	0.7666319444	06:23:57 PM
6:23 am	(D7)	0.2659722222	06:23 AM
6:23	(D9)	0.2659722222	06:23
6:23 PM	(D7)	0.7659722222	06:23 PM

(continues)

Table 6.6 Continued

Data Typed	Data Format	Stored Data	Data Displayed
18:23:57	(D8)	0.7666319444	018:23:57
18:23	(D9)	0.7659722222	18:23

If the current year is 1994.

After you enter a number in a cell and 1-2-3 applies an **Automatic** format, this format stays with the cell. You can use **/Range Format**, however, to change the format of a cell after the cell has been formatted as **Automatic**. **Automatic** format works for only the first item entered in a cell after the cell is formatted. The format doesn't change when a number with a different format is entered in the cell.

1-2-3 normally treats as invalid an entry in a cell that isn't formatted as **Automatic** if it starts with a number, @ sign, + sign, – sign, # sign, $ sign, or a parenthesis. Consider the entries **57 Main Street** and **@SUM(ABCD**. If you type one of these entries in a cell and press Enter, 1-2-3 switches to EDIT mode for correcting the entry. If you are using **Automatic** format in the cell, however, 1-2-3 precedes the entry with a label prefix and considers the entry to be a label. The $ sign preceding an entry causes 1-2-3 to treat the entry as a range name and transforms the entry into a formula by placing a + sign in front of the $ sign.

If you enter a number containing decimal places in a cell formatted as **Automatic**, 1-2-3 formats the number with the same amount of decimal places. If you use no other formatting characters, 1-2-3 uses **Fixed** format. If you enter **123.4**, 1-2-3 assigns to the cell the format **Fixed** with **1** decimal place (F1). If you enter **123.40**, for example, 1-2-3 drops the last zero when displaying the number in the control panel but assigns the format **Fixed** with **2** decimal places (F2).

If you precede the number entered in a cell formatted as **Automatic** with a dollar sign (or another one-character currency symbol specified by using **/Worksheet Global Default Other International Currency**), 1-2-3 formats the cell as **Currency**. If you enter a number with commas, 1-2-3 doesn't store the commas but formats the cell with comma (,) format. If you follow the number with a percent sign (%), 1-2-3 drops the percent sign, divides the number by 100, and then formats the cell with **Percent** format. (Ordinarily, if you enter a number with a percent sign, 1-2-3 divides the number by 100 and displays the result in the cell.)

If the number entered in a cell that has been formatted as **A**utomatic appears to be the long **D**ate or **T**ime format, 1-2-3 uses that **D**ate format. 1-2-3 doesn't recognize the short **D**ate formats **D**ate **3**: MMM-YY or **D**ate **5**: MM/DD (refer to table 6.3).

If you enter a formula in a cell, the format stays **A**utomatic. If you enter a number in the cell later, 1-2-3 applies an appropriate format. If the cell contains a numeric formula and you convert the formula to a number by using the F2 (Edit) key, 1-2-3 applies a format at that time.

> **Note**
>
> The abbreviation (A) appears in the control panel for cells formatted with **/R**ange **F**ormat **O**ther **A**utomatic. After you first enter data in the cell, the abbreviation changes to match the entry's format.

Parentheses Format

Parentheses format is used to enclose numbers in parentheses. In certain situations, you may want a number to appear in parentheses, but you don't want to enter the number as a negative number. In such a case, use **/R**ange **F**ormat **O**ther **P**arentheses **Y**es. You can combine this format with the other formats. Use **/R**ange **F**ormat **O**ther **P**arentheses **N**o to remove the parentheses.

/Worksheet **G**lobal **F**ormat **O**ther **P**arentheses **Y**es places parentheses around all numbers in the default format only. The command doesn't affect numbers with separate range formats or labels. Use **/W**orksheet **G**lobal **F**ormat **O**ther **P**arentheses **N**o to remove the parentheses from all numeric cells with the default format.

> **Caution**
>
> Use the **P**arentheses format with care; it can cause confusion, especially when used in conjunction with negative numbers. In **P**arentheses format, for example, 456 appears as (456), which is how −456 appears when parentheses are used in place of the minus sign. If you apply this format to a negative number, however, the number still appears as a negative. In **G**eneral format, for example, −1234 appears as (−1234). In comma (,) format with **2** decimal places, −1234 appears as ((1,234.00)). The double set of parentheses is confusing.

> **Note**
>
> The abbreviation (()) appears in the control panel for cells formatted with **/R**ange **F**ormat **O**ther **P**arentheses, in addition to any other format indicators. If you also assign the **C**urrency **2** format to a cell formatted with **P**arentheses, for example, the abbreviation appears as (C2()).

Color Format

Tip
Use **/R**ange **F**ormat **O**ther **C**olor **R**eset to turn off the color display of negative numbers.

You can use **/R**ange **F**ormat **O**ther **C**olor **N**egative to display negative numbers in color on a color monitor or in boldface on a monochrome monitor. This method is a handy way to make negative numbers stand out from regular numbers in a worksheet. The minus sign or parentheses appear as part of the number as well. As is true of all formatting options, you can use this option in the entire worksheet or only in a specified range.

> **Note**
>
> The abbreviation (-) appears in the control panel for cells formatted with **/R**ange **F**ormat **O**ther **C**olor **N**egative, in addition to any other format indicators. If you also assign the **C**urrency **2** format to a cell formatted with **N**egative, for example, the abbreviation appears as (C2-).

International Formats

You can change the display of some **D**ate and **T**ime formats, as well as the characters 1-2-3 uses for currency, the decimal point, and the thousands separator. Because different countries follow different formatting standards, these different standards are called *international formatting options*. If you work with U.S. dollars in the United States, you can retain the standard 1-2-3 defaults and ignore these options. If you need to use a different formatting standard, however, choose the **/W**orksheet **G**lobal **D**efault **O**ther **I**nternational command to access the following menu:

Punctuation **C**urrency **D**ate **T**ime **N**egative **R**elease-2 **F**ile-Translation **Q**uit

After you change the formatting defaults, choose **/W**orksheet **G**lobal **D**efault **U**pdate to save the changes.

Choose **D**ate and **T**ime from this menu, for example, to change the international **D**ate and **T**ime formats. (The different format options are listed in tables 6.4 and 6.5 earlier in this chapter.) Choose **C**urrency to change the currency symbol from the dollar sign ($) to another symbol and to specify whether the symbol is a prefix or suffix. You even can use multiple characters and special Lotus Multibyte Character Set (LMBCS) characters to enter characters such as the British pound (£).

Choose **P**unctuation to change the characters used for the decimal point, the argument separator, and the thousands separator. Eight different combinations, such as the default of (.,,), are available. Choose **N**egative to specify how negative numbers appear in the comma and **C**urrency formats. (The default is **P**arentheses, but you can change the default to a minus sign.)

Suppressing the Display of Zeros

You can use the **/W**orksheet **G**lobal **Z**ero command to change the appearance of cells that contain the number zero or formulas that evaluate to zero. To hide zeros completely, choose **/W**orksheet **G**lobal **Z**ero **Y**es. The zero cells now appear blank.

This feature can be useful when you are working with worksheets in which zeros represent missing or meaningless information. Blanking these cells can improve the appearance of the worksheet. This procedure can cause confusion, however, if you or other users aren't sure whether the cell is blank because you forgot to enter the data or because you suppressed the display of zeros.

You also can display a label of your choice instead of the zero or a blank cell. Choose **/W**orksheet **G**lobal **Z**ero **L**abel, and enter the label you want to appear in place of the zero. Common labels include none, zero, and NA or N/A (not available). Figure 6.22 shows a worksheet with **/W**orksheet **G**lobal **Z**ero **L**abel set to display no change.

Choose **/W**orksheet **G**lobal **Z**ero **N**o to cancel this option and display zeros as zeros again.

If you are working with a multiple-worksheet file, GROUP mode affects the **/W**orksheet **G**lobal **Z**ero command. If GROUP mode is disabled, the command affects only the current worksheet. If GROUP mode is enabled, the command affects all worksheets in the file.

Fig. 6.22
Worksheet with zeros displayed as *no change*.

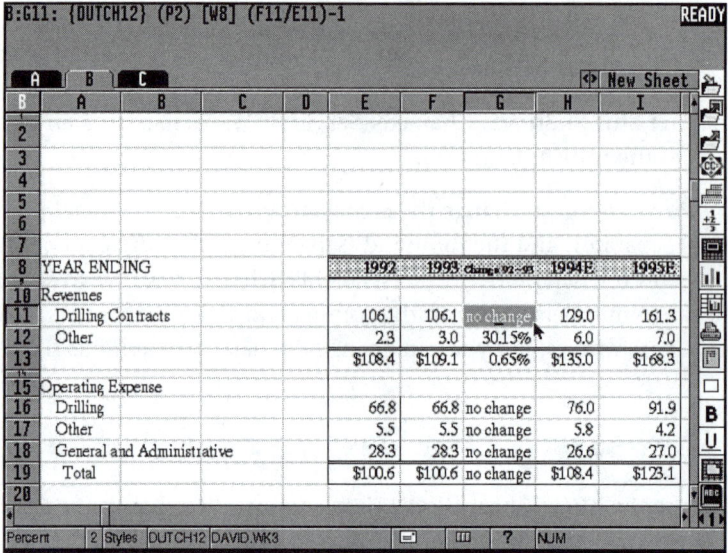

Justifying Text

At times, you may want to include in a worksheet several lines (or even a paragraph) to explain a table, graph, or report. If you choose the **:T**ext **E**dit command from the Wysiwyg menu, 1-2-3 even provides word-wrap features similar to those in most word processing programs. Otherwise, the text you enter doesn't wrap and is placed in the current cell when you press Enter. You can enter one line of text in each cell, but typing and editing paragraphs this way is slow and imprecise. The result may look something like the ragged text shown in figure 6.23.

You can justify labels by choosing the **/R**ange **J**ustify command from the 1-2-3 main menu or by choosing the **:T**ext **R**eformat command from the Wysiwyg menu.

Enter text in one cell or in multiple cells running down a column, as shown in figure 6.23, and then choose **/R**ange **J**ustify to arrange the text. At the Enter justify range: prompt, highlight the rows that contain the labels and include any additional rows into which the labels can expand. Highlight across the columns to show how wide each label can be. After you press Enter, 1-2-3 rearranges the text to fit the area you highlighted (see fig. 6.24). 1-2-3 wraps labels only at spaces and then eliminates the spaces. If all or parts of two labels are combined into one label, 1-2-3 adds a space. If you add more text, you can choose **/R**ange **J**ustify again to rejustify the text.

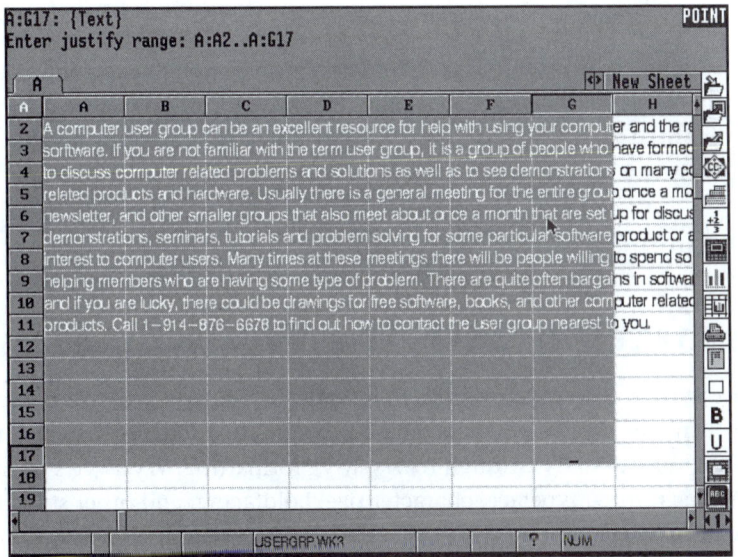

Fig. 6.23
A column of long labels for a note is difficult to align.

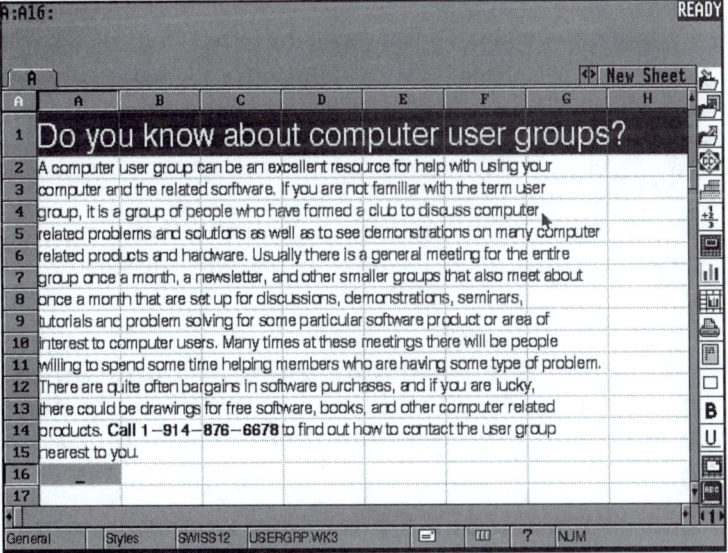

Fig. 6.24
A series of long labels after **/R**ange **J**ustify is selected.

You cannot justify more than one column of labels at a time. 1-2-3 stops justifying when it reaches a blank or numeric cell in the first column. All the labels must be in the first column of the highlighted range.

To justify labels with **/R**ange **J**ustify, follow these steps:

1. Move the cell pointer to the first cell in the range of text.

2. Choose /**R**ange **J**ustify.

3. Highlight the rows that contain labels; leave enough extra rows below the labels for the labels to expand into when they are justified. Highlight the number of columns to show how wide each label can be (refer to fig. 6.23).

◄ "Entering and Editing Data," p. 63

4. Press Enter to complete the justification (refer to fig. 6.24).

Formatting with the Wysiwyg Menu

The heart of Wysiwyg's power lies in its capability to add professional formatting touches to your worksheets. The 1-2-3 formats—numeric display and label alignment—carry through to Wysiwyg formatting. Wysiwyg's formats govern the printed typeface, character size, boldfacing, and other stylistic features, such as lines and shading.

Wysiwyg's additional formats provide many ways to enhance the appearance of printed text. To assign a Wysiwyg format to a cell or range, choose the Wysiwyg **:F**ormat command. To determine the format of a cell, move the cell pointer to the cell. The format appears at the top of the screen, next to the current cell address. If you use Wysiwyg in graphics display mode (the default), you can actually see the formatting on-screen, in the cells that contain the formatted text.

1-2-3 offers many SmartIcons that you can click rather than use the Wysiwyg menu. These SmartIcons will be identified in the following sections as the particular format types are discussed.

Understanding the Wysiwyg :Format Commands

You change the format of a cell or range of cells by choosing the **:F**ormat command from the Wysiwyg menu. The commands in the **:F**ormat menu are as follows:

Tip
GROUP mode affects the **:F**ormat command. If GROUP mode is enabled and you format a range in one worksheet, the same range is formatted in all worksheets in the file.

   Font **B**old **I**talics **U**nderline **C**olor **L**ines **S**hade **R**eset **Q**uit

These format commands affect the way data appears on-screen and in printed reports.

If the current cell has a format, the name of the format (or an abbreviation) appears in the control panel. One cell can contain several formats. In figure 6.25, {SWISS14 Bold U1} appears in the control panel to indicate that cell A2 has been formatted as **B**old and **U**nderline **S**ingle. If the cell has no format, no format indicator appears in the control panel.

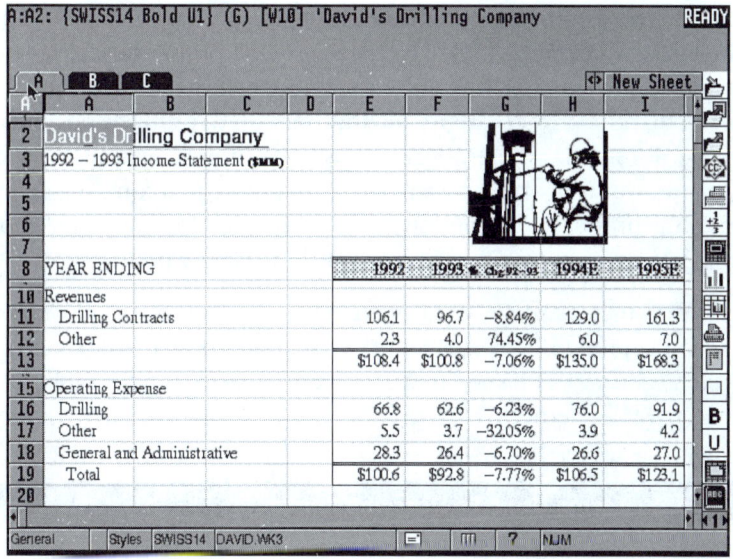

Fig. 6.25
Cell A2's multiple formats appear in the control panel.

When you start a new file, its cells aren't formatted. If a cell has no format, the cell appears in the current default font.

The **:F**ormat **R**eset command removes Wysiwyg formatting from a specified range but doesn't remove any data from the range. You also can click the Normal Format SmartIcon to clear Wysiwyg formatting from a specified range.

The remaining **:F**ormat options are discussed in the following sections.

Understanding Fonts

Most of Wysiwyg's formatting effects result from the use of different fonts. In Wysiwyg, a *font* is a particular typeface (for example, Swiss) set in a particular point size. A *point*, a printer's unit of measure, is 1/72 inch (an inch contains 72 points). The larger the point size, the larger the type. The number of fonts available to you depends on your printer. Wysiwyg can use any font that your printer is capable of printing.

> **Note**
>
> If a printer provides additional fonts, those fonts also are available to Wysiwyg. The Hewlett-Packard LaserJet-series printers, for example, come with two built-in fonts (Courier and Line Printer), and you can buy dozens of cartridges to access additional fonts.

Wysiwyg comes with four soft fonts from Bitstream: Swiss, Dutch, Courier, and XSymbol. A *soft font* is a file on disk that tells a printer how to create the font. Soft fonts are sent to the printer's memory before the document is printed so that the printer can use the information to print the document. If you have a dot-matrix printer, Wysiwyg uses the printer's graphics mode to produce these fonts. If you have a laser printer, these four fonts are downloaded to the printer when you use them. The printer may not have enough memory, however, for many different fonts or for larger point sizes.

The soft fonts included with Wysiwyg represent four of the most common types of fonts: proportional sans serif (Swiss), proportional serif (Dutch), fixed-pitch (Courier), and special-effects characters (XSymbol). Table 6.7 defines some of these terms.

Table 6.7   Terms Used To Describe Fonts

Term	Definition
Proportional	Characterizes a font in which the actual width of each character determines how much space the character occupies when printed
Fixed-pitch	Characterizes a font in which each printed character occupies the same amount of space regardless of character width
Serif	Characterizes a font that has short curlicues, or decorative "tails," at the ends of many characters' main strokes
Sans serif	Characterizes a font without the tails or curlicues; it just has straight edges

The XSymbol font contains special characters, such as arrows and circled numbers. Figure 6.26 shows different letters and numbers formatted with the XSymbol font. If you enter a lowercase *a* in a cell and format the cell with the XSymbol font, for example, a right-pointing arrow appears. These special characters sometimes are referred to as *dingbats*.

Some laser printers have a restricted amount of memory. In general, the larger the point size of a font, the more memory the font takes in the printer's memory. When you download soft fonts to a laser printer, the printer stores the fonts in its memory for use during the printing process. If you get an `Out of memory` message when you print, the printer doesn't have enough memory to support the font set you downloaded. Try replacing the large fonts with smaller fonts or using an internal or cartridge font.

Formatting with the Wysiwyg Menu   **323**

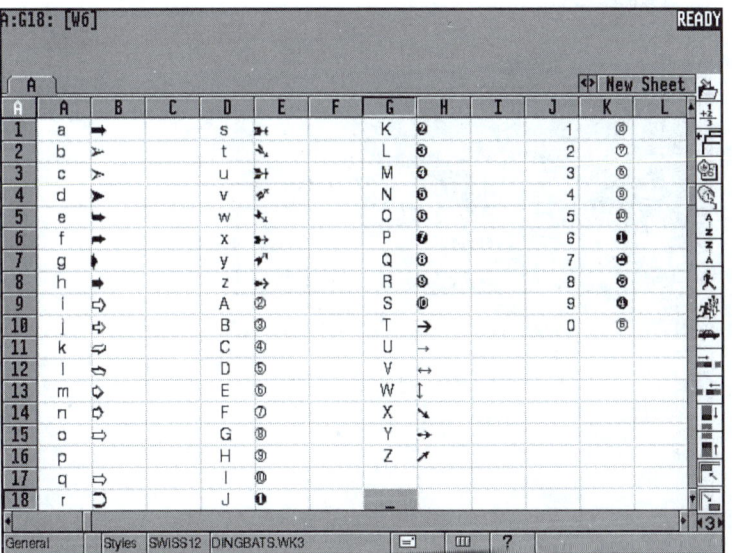

Fig. 6.26
Examples of the XSymbol font characters (dingbats).

Using Fonts

Each worksheet can use up to eight different fonts. These eight fonts are stored in a *font set*. The font list displayed in figure 6.27 is the default font set, which you display by clicking the font selector in the status bar. The list is composed primarily of Swiss and Dutch fonts. The same list is shown in figure 6.28 but you access the list by selecting the :Format Font menu options. Figure 6.29 shows examples of the default fonts as they would appear on-screen.

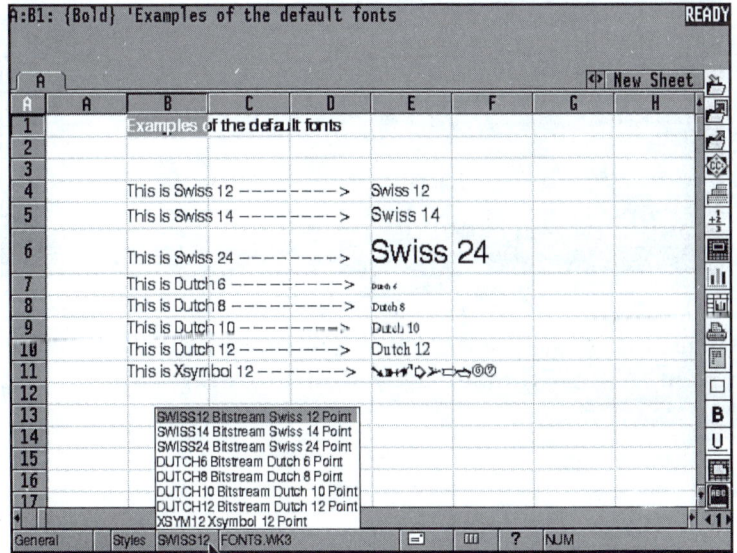

Fig. 6.27
The font selector with the default font set offered in Wysiwyg displayed.

324 Chapter 6—Making Your Worksheets Dazzle

Fig. 6.28
The default font set offered in Wysiwyg, displayed by choosing **:**Format **F**ont.

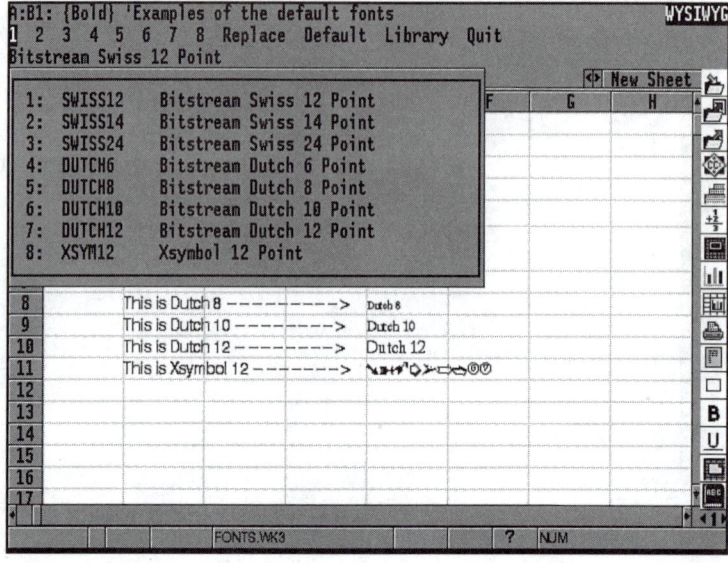

Fig. 6.29
Examples of the default fonts.

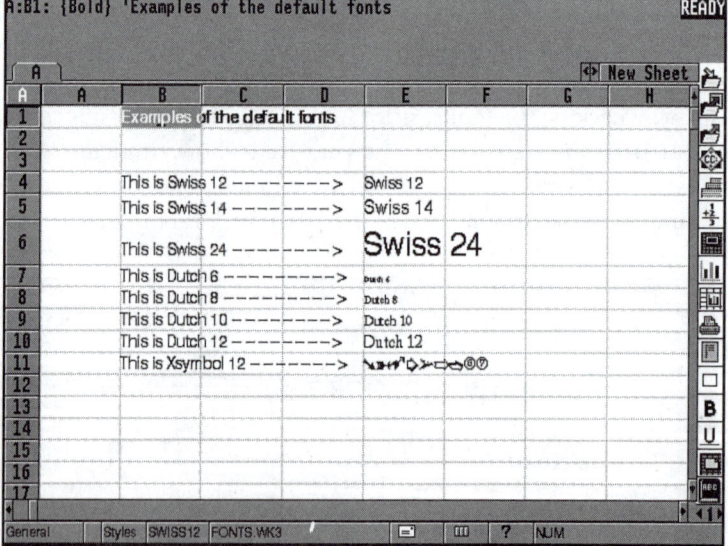

 You can use the Font/Size SmartIcon to cycle through the eight fonts in the current font set. Highlight the range you want to change before clicking the Font/Size SmartIcon.

> **Note**
>
> If necessary, Wysiwyg adjusts the height of the row to conform to the tallest point size used.

Use the **F**ont formats to change the typeface and size of text and numbers that appear on-screen. As figure 6.28 shows, a number is assigned to each font. You select a font by selecting its corresponding number from the **F**ont menu. After you select a number, you are prompted to highlight a range (see fig. 6.30). Figure 6.31 shows the result of formatting range A:A10..A:A19 with the Bitstream Dutch 12-Point font.

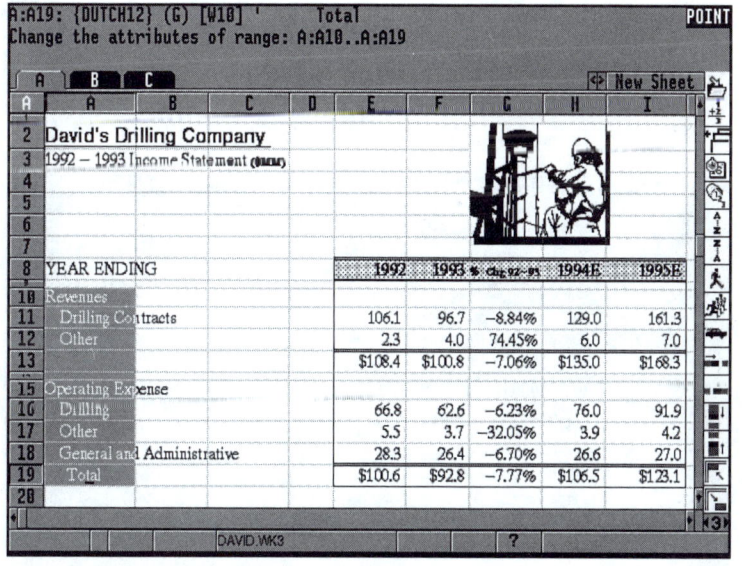

Fig. 6.30
The prompt to specify a range with **:F**ormat **F**ont.

After selecting cells to format, you can cycle through the available fonts in the current font set by clicking the Font/Size SmartIcon.

Replacing Fonts

You aren't limited to the eight fonts listed in the **F**ont menu; you can replace any font by choosing **R**eplace from the **F**ont menu. When you choose **R**eplace, the font numbers appear in the menu. If you select one of the numbers in the menu, another menu appears, listing four typefaces and **O**ther (see fig. 6.32). If you select a typeface, you are prompted for a point size (3 to 72).

326   Chapter 6—Making Your Worksheets Dazzle

Fig. 6.31
The highlighted cells show the area formatted with Dutch 12.

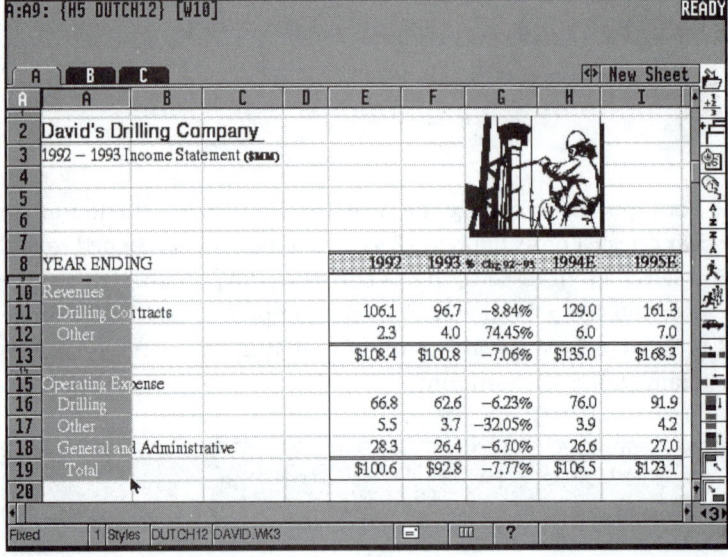

Fig. 6.32
The :Format Font Replace menu after a number is selected.

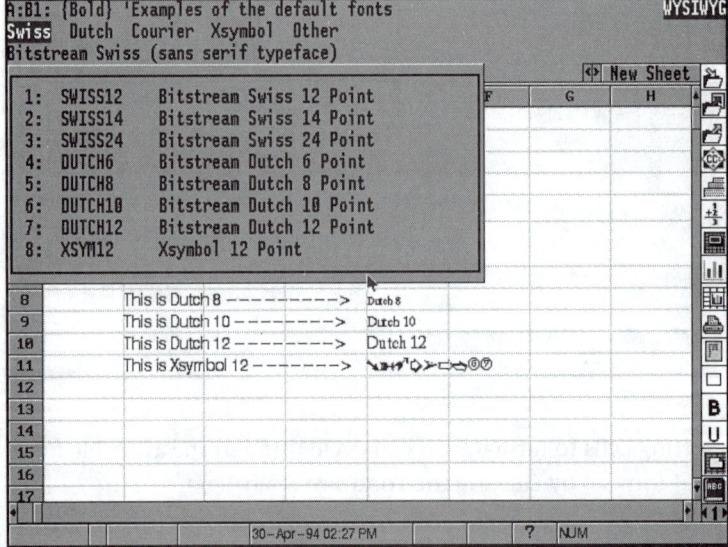

> **Note**
>
> If a font that you want to use isn't in the default font set, you can substitute that font for any of the default fonts. Because you are limited to eight fonts per worksheet, you must replace one of the existing fonts in the list; you cannot add fonts to the list.

If you choose **O**ther, a full-page list of typefaces appears, as shown in figure 6.33. After you select a typeface, you are prompted for a point size (3 to 72). Type the point size and then press Enter to complete the replacement. The next time you select a font, the new font appears in the list with the number that was assigned to the old font. To switch back to the old font set, choose **D**efault **R**estore from the **F**ont menu. To make the new font set the default set, choose **D**efault **U**pdate.

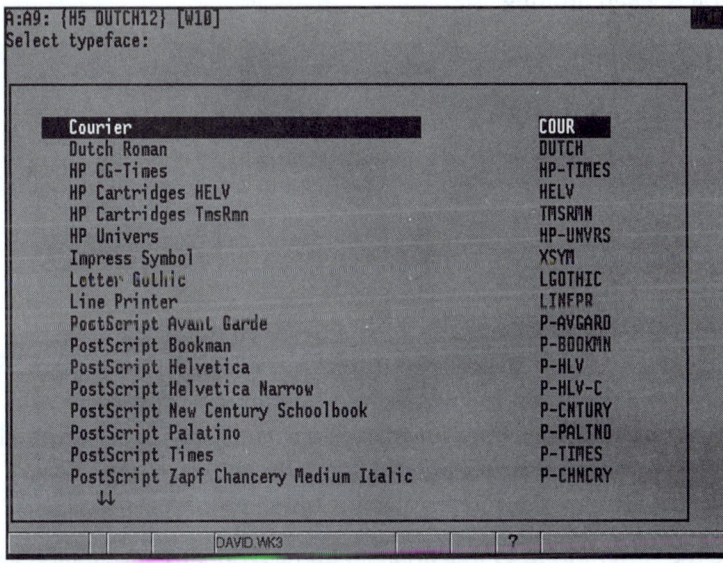

Fig. 6.33
A full-screen list of typefaces appears when you choose **:**Format **F**ont **R**eplace **O**ther.

> **Note**
>
> Although 1-2-3 prompts you to enter a size between 3 and 72 points, not all point sizes are available. The Line Printer font, for example, comes in only one size: 8-point. If you choose a size that isn't available in a certain typeface, Wysiwyg substitutes a similar typeface in the size you specified (for example, Courier 10-point in place of the nonexistent Line Printer 10-point).

To use the new font, select its number in the **:F**ormat **F**ont menu. Then highlight the range to which you want to apply the font and press Enter. If you prefer, you can highlight the range, click the font selector in the status bar, highlight the font, and click the left mouse button to complete the selection.

When you replace fonts, any worksheet cells formatted with that particular font change. Suppose that you use **:**Format **F**ont **R**eplace to replace 12-point

▶ "Manipulating a Notepad," p. 346

Swiss with 10-point Courier. All worksheet cells previously formatted as SWISS12 are reformatted as COURIER10.

As mentioned previously, font 1 is assigned to all cells. Thus, when you replace font 1 with a different font, all cells (except for the ones assigned to other font numbers) change to the new font 1. You don't need to choose **:F**ormat **F**ont **1** and highlight a range to change to the new font 1. 1-2-3 always will apply this font to the notes in the notepads and to the headers and footers when printing.

> **Note**
>
> If you change the font size for an existing paragraph of text, you may find that the text occupies more or fewer columns. To correct the spacing of the text, use the **:T**ext **R**eformat command. This command is similar to 1-2-3's **/R**ange **J**ustify command, which word-wraps text within the range you define.

Tip
Save in a font library those font sets that you are likely to use with other worksheets.

Tip
If you frequently retrieve the same font library, make that library the default font set. To do so, retrieve the font library that is to become the default and choose **:F**ormat **F**ont **D**efault **U**pdate.

Creating Font Libraries

If you use **:F**ormat **F**ont **R**eplace to customize the font list for the current worksheet, you may want to save the font set for use with another worksheet file. The font set can be named and saved in a *font library* to be used again in any other worksheet. Creating a font library relieves you of the chore of choosing the **:F**ormat **F**ont **R**eplace command in each worksheet.

To save the current font set in a library, choose **:F**ormat **F**ont **L**ibrary **S**ave. Wysiwyg prompts you to enter a file name. Type a file name of up to eight characters and press Enter. 1-2-3 saves the file with the extension AF3.

When you want to use a font library, choose **:F**ormat **F**ont **L**ibrary **R**etrieve. Wysiwyg displays a list of library files with the AF3 extension. Highlight the name of the library you want to use; then press Enter. The eight fonts saved in this library appear in the font box, and you can use any of these fonts in the current worksheet.

If you know that you want to use the fonts stored in another file but you haven't saved them to a library, you still can use those fonts in the current file. Choose the **:S**pecial **I**mport **F**onts command, as described in "Importing Formats" later in this chapter.

To delete a font library, choose **:F**ormat **F**ont **L**ibrary **E**rase and enter the name at the prompt or select the name in the list that appears.

Using Boldface, Italics, and Underlining

Font formats are only one type of formatting you can apply to a cell or a range. You also can apply boldface, italics, and underline attributes (see the label *David's Drilling Company* in cell A2 of fig. 6.25). You can use boldface, underlining, or italics to enhance column headings, totals, or other ranges you want to emphasize.

To boldface a range, choose **:F**ormat **B**old **S**et and indicate the range to which you want to apply the attribute. Choose **:F**ormat **I**talics **S**et to italicize a range. Boldface text appears darker on-screen; italicized text slants to the right. The first line of the control panel indicates the attribute: {Bold} or {Italics}. You can cancel boldface and italics by choosing the **:F**ormat **B**old **C**lear and **:F**ormat **I**talics **C**lear commands.

After selecting cells to be formatted, you can apply the boldface attribute by clicking the Bold SmartIcon or apply the italics attribute by clicking the Italics SmartIcon. The Bold SmartIcon acts as a toggle between bold and not bold. The Italics SmartIcon also acts as a toggle for the italics attribute.

Use the Wysiwyg underline formatting option instead of the 1-2-3 repeating label to create underlines. In 1-2-3 text mode, you must type \- to create a single underline and \= to produce a double underline. This method has several disadvantages. First, you must enter these labels in blank cells, consuming valuable worksheet space. Second, the underlines aren't solid and don't look professional.

Tip
Use the Wysiwyg **:F**ormat **U**nderline command to create professional-looking underlines in a worksheet.

Wysiwyg solves these problems by offering true underlining—the same as in word processing programs. You don't use blank rows for the underlines; underlines are solid and appear directly below existing cell entries, not in separate cells.

The **U**nderline option in the **:F**ormat menu offers three types of underlining: **S**ingle, **D**ouble, and **W**ide. The **S**ingle underline option can be used at the bottom of a column of numbers (above a total). This option underlines only the characters in the cell, not the full width of the cell. If the single underline isn't long enough, use the **:F**ormat **L**ines **B**ottom command (for details, see "Drawing Lines and Boxes" later in this chapter). You are most likely to use the **S**ingle option only when the last number in the column is the longest number. The **D**ouble option is ideal for double-underlining grand totals. To get a thicker line, choose the **W**ide underline option. You can cancel underlining by choosing the **:F**ormat **U**nderline **C**lear command.

After selecting cells to be formatted, you can apply the underline attribute by clicking the Single Underline SmartIcon; you can apply the double-underline attribute by clicking the Double Underline SmartIcon.

Changing Range Colors

If you have a color printer, such as the Hewlett-Packard PaintJet, you may want to enhance printouts by using different colors. You can print up to seven colors if your printer has that capability. To change the color of a range, choose **:F**ormat **C**olor. The following menu appears:

Text **B**ackground **N**egative **R**everse **Q**uit

The **T**ext option defines the color of the characters in the range, whereas **B**ackground refers to the color behind the characters. To change the colors of labels and numbers in a range, choose **T**ext. A menu with six color options plus **N**ormal (the default color) appears. These options are as follows:

Normal **R**ed **G**reen **D**ark-Blue **C**yan **Y**ellow **M**agenta

If you select a color, the prompt Change the attributes of range appears. Highlight the range and press Enter.

After selecting cells to be formatted, you can cycle through the available text colors by clicking the Text Color SmartIcon.

You change the background color of a range in a similar way. You can change the color of negative numbers in a range to red by selecting **N**egative and then choosing **R**ed. The only color options that exist for negative numbers are the default color (**N**ormal) and **R**ed. After selecting **N**ormal or **R**ed, highlight the range and press Enter.

After selecting cells to be formatted, you can cycle through the available background colors by clicking the Background Color SmartIcon.

◄ "Changing the Display Format," p. 233

To reverse the colors of data and background in a range, choose **R**everse from the **C**olor menu, highlight the range, and press Enter. For any color-menu options to take effect, you must be in **G**raphics and **C**olor modes (chosen from the **:D**isplay **M**ode menu).

Drawing Lines and Boxes

You can make a worksheet appear more professional by adding horizontal or vertical lines and creating boxes. Use line formats to replace the hyphenated lines that appear in many worksheets created with older versions of 1-2-3 and to enhance the overall appearance of worksheets and printed reports.

The **:F**ormat **L**ines command places lines around any part of a cell or range. You can choose the options **O**utline, **L**eft, **R**ight, **T**op, **B**ottom, and **A**ll. The **O**utline option draws lines around the entire range, forming a single box. The

Left, Right, Top, and Bottom options draw a line along the appropriate side of each selected cell in the range. If you choose the All option, 1-2-3 draws lines around each cell in the range, boxing each cell. Choosing All is the equivalent of choosing Left, Right, Top, *and* Bottom for each cell in the range. Figure 6.34 shows a format of :Format Lines All (the worksheet grid has been removed for clarity).

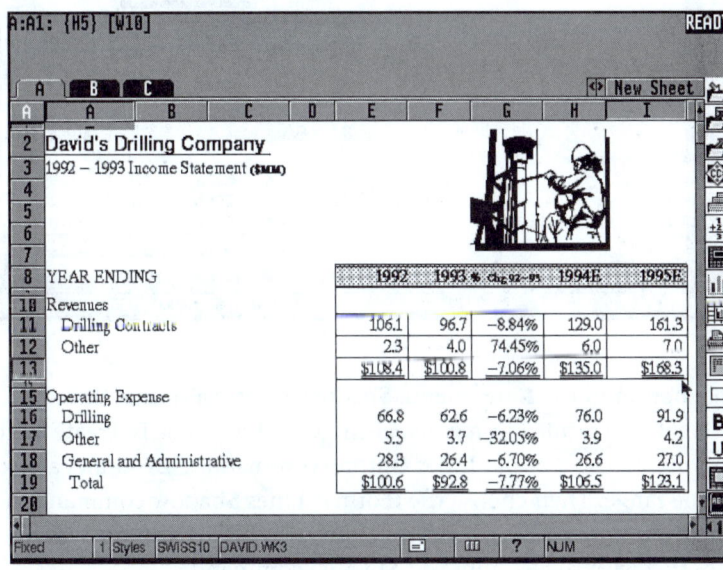

Fig. 6.34
The :Format Lines All command outlines each cell in the range A:E11..A:I13.

After selecting cells that you want to outline, you can outline the range by clicking the Outline SmartIcon.

If you choose one of the options in the Lines menu, 1-2-3 draws a single thin line in the specified range. Wysiwyg offers two other line styles: Double and Wide. To draw a double line, choose :Format Lines Double and then specify the line location (Outline, Left, Right, Top, Bottom, or All). To double-underline the range that includes the totals shown in figure 6.34, for example, choose :Format Underline Double, highlight the range (E13..I13), and press Enter (see fig. 6.35). The difference between the double underline and the double bottom is that the double underline places the double lines under the cell contents, whereas the double bottom places the double lines across the entire cell width.

The :Format Lines Wide command creates a thicker line. If you need even thicker lines, you can use the :Format Shade Solid option. (See the following section for details.)

Fig. 6.35
A worksheet with double underlines under the totals. This worksheet also shows shading in cells E8..I8 and a drop shadow and outline around the picture in cells G2..H6.

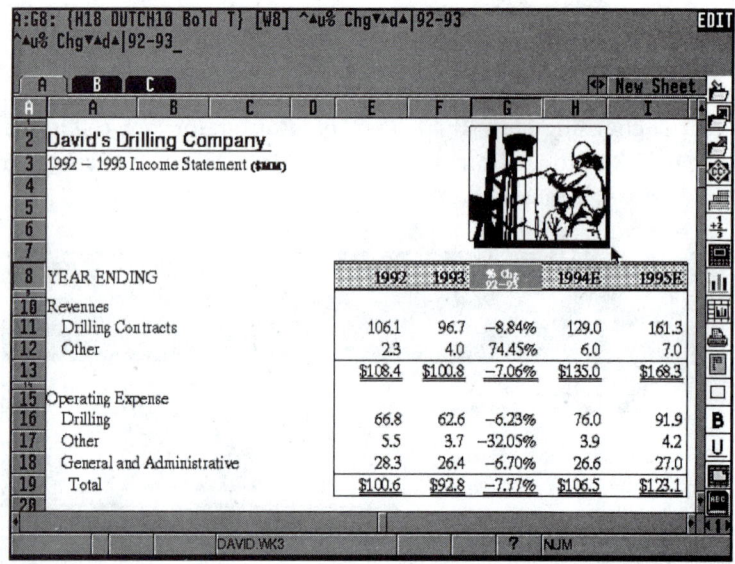

The final option in the **L**ines menu, **S**hadow, creates a special three-dimensional effect called a *drop shadow* (refer to fig. 6.35). To create a drop shadow, choose the **:F**ormat **L**ines **O**utline command; 1-2-3 draws a box around the range. Then choose the **:F**ormat **L**ines **S**hadow command in the same range. In figure 6.35, the drop shadow was placed around a picture that was imported with the **:G**raph **A**dd **M**etafile command.

 You also can create a drop shadow by using a SmartIcon. After selecting the cells to which you want to apply a drop shadow, click the Shadow SmartIcon.

To clear any kind of single-, double-, or wide-line format, choose **C**lear from the **:F**ormat **L**ines menu, and then choose **O**utline, **L**eft, **R**ight, **T**op, **B**ottom, or **A**ll. Finally, highlight the range and press Enter.

Adding Shading

The **:F**ormat **S**hade command highlights important areas in the worksheet, such as totals or the largest and smallest amounts in a table. If you choose **S**hade from the **:F**ormat menu, the following four options appear:

Light **D**ark **S**olid **C**lear

> **Note**
>
> You can create thick horizontal and vertical lines by using the **S**olid shade in blank cells. You cannot see the cell contents if you assign **S**olid to cells that contain data. This method is a good way to hide data that you don't want others to see.

> If you want to create a white-on-black effect, use **S**olid shading and change the text color to **W**hite or some other light color.

The column headings in cells E8..I8 shown in figure 6.35 stand out because of the background shading. Shades can be **L**ight (as in fig. 6.35), **D**ark, or **S**olid (black). If you shade a range, you also may want to format labels and numbers in the range in boldface to create more contrast. Whereas light and dark shading highlight data in a range, solid shading actually obscures data unless you choose a color for the data by using **:F**ormat **C**olor **T**ext. If you choose a color, the data appears in the selected color on top of the solid shading. To clear shading from a range, choose **:F**ormat **S**hade **C**lear.

After selecting the cells you want to shade, you can cycle through the shading types by clicking the Shading SmartIcon.

Using Formatting Sequences

The **:F**ormat menu options format cells and ranges. To format individual characters within a cell, you can use formatting sequences. *Formatting sequences* are codes that you enter as you enter or edit text in the control panel; when you press Enter, the actual formatting appears in the cell.

The code to insert when you begin a formatting sequence is Ctrl+A (for *attribute*). An upright triangle appears. You then enter the one- or two-character code for the attribute. Table 6.8 lists these codes. Be sure to use the exact uppercase or lowercase characters listed in the table. To end the formatting sequence, press Ctrl+N and an upside-down triangle appears.

Table 6.8   Attribute Codes

Code	Description	Code	Description
b	Bold	1c	Default color
i	Italics	2c	Red
u	Superscript	3c	Green
d	Subscript	4c	Dark blue
o	Outline	5c	Cyan
t	Thick filled	6c	Yellow

(continues)

Table 6.8 Continued

Code	Description	Code	Description
x	Flip x-axis	7c	Magenta
y	Flip y-axis	8c	Reverse colors
1_	Single underline	1g to 6g	Graying
2_	Double underline	1k to 127k	Kerning (positive)
3_	Wide underline	–1k to –127k	Kerning (negative)
4_	Box around characters		
5_	Strikethrough characters		
1F	Font 1	!	Hidden text
2F	Font 2			Word wrap
3F	Font 3	1r to 3r	Rotate 90, 180 , or 270 degrees
4F	Font 4		
5F	Font 5		
6F	Font 6		
7F	Font 7		
8F	Font 8		

To specify multiple attributes, press Ctrl+A and type the first attribute code, followed by Ctrl+A and the second code, and so on. To boldface and italicize a word, for example, press Ctrl+A and type **b**, and then press Ctrl+A and type **i**. At the end of the word, press Ctrl+N to cancel all formatting sequences for the following text. If you want to cancel only one of the attributes, press Ctrl+E followed by the attribute code you want to discontinue (for example, **i** for italics).

Two attributes are interesting in that they enable you to enter text that will not appear on-screen (!) or force text to start at the left side of the cell (|).

The exclamation mark (!) is the attribute that you use to enter text that will not appear on-screen. This method is handy for attaching a note to text in a cell. To see how this attribute works, type **Using <Ctrl+A>!1-2-3** and press Enter. Only the word *Using* appears on-screen, although the entire cell contents appear in the control panel.

The word-wrap attribute (| — vertical bar) is a little more difficult to use, because when this attribute is used by itself, the text following it will overwrite the previous text in that cell. This attribute is best used for forcing word wrapping. To see how the word-wrap attribute works, type the following and then press Enter:

<Ctrl+A>uUsing<Ctrl+N><Ctrl+A>d <Ctrl+A>| 1-2-3

> **Note**
>
> To see the entry, you may need to change the height of the row and the size of the font.

The word-wrap attribute takes some experimentation, but it is fun to use. Following is another interesting use for it:

1. Use <Ctrl+A>o to begin the outline attribute for the words you want to enter in the cell, type in the cell entry such as **Using 1-2-3**, and then end the outline attribute by pressing <Ctrl+N>.

2. Start the word-wrap attribute along with a color attribute by using <Ctrl+A>2c to start the red color attribute followed by <Ctrl+A>| to start the word-wrap attribute.

3. Type the same cell entry (**Using 1-2-3**) again, then press Enter. You should see red words outlined in black.

Many times, you need to use kerning (the k attribute) to get the words in the cell to align correctly. Kerning is the way that the space between letters in a word can be moved closer together or further apart. For instance, the outlined words might not line up exactly with the colored words because of the difference in spacing between the letters used by the different font attributes. Type the following in one cell, press Enter, and then experiment until the words look aligned on your screen:

<Ctrl+A>1oUsing 1-2-3 <Ctrl+N><Ctrl+A>2k<Ctrl+A>3c<Ctrl+A>|Using 1-2-3

Remember to place spaces between the words *Using* and *1-2-3*. If you don't, you will find that you have problems with the spacing. If the words do not align correctly on top of each other, try using different amounts of kerning. Notice that the attribute 2k was used before the second *Using 1-2-3*. This attribute moves the colored lettering a little to the right. You can use the numbers 1 to 127 (both positive and negative) to specify the amount of kerning you need. The font size and other attributes affect how well the word-wrap technique works.

Refer to figure 6.35 and look at the control panel, which shows that cell G8 is in EDIT mode. The control panel also shows the codes for making the words "% Chg" use the superscript attribute and then word-wrapping the "92-93" part of the cell entry, which also is formatted with the subscript attribute. Figure 6.37, later in this chapter, shows cell G8 without shading to display the word-wrapped cell entry.

Managing Wysiwyg Formats

Because formatting is the heart of Wysiwyg, the program offers several commands for dealing with the formats assigned to cells. You can copy and move formats—not the cell contents, but the formats associated with the cell. You can assign a name to the set of formatting instructions in a cell and then apply this format to any range. You also can save *all* the formats associated with the file and apply them to another file.

Copying and Moving Formats

If one cell or range should be formatted the same way as another cell or range, you can use the **:S**pecial **C**opy command to copy the formatting instructions (not the data) to a different part of the same worksheet or to another worksheet in the same file. Figure 6.36 shows the result of using **:S**pecial **C**opy to copy the Wysiwyg formatting from E8..I8 to E15..I15.

Fig. 6.36
Copying formats (not data) to a range by using **:S**pecial **C**opy.

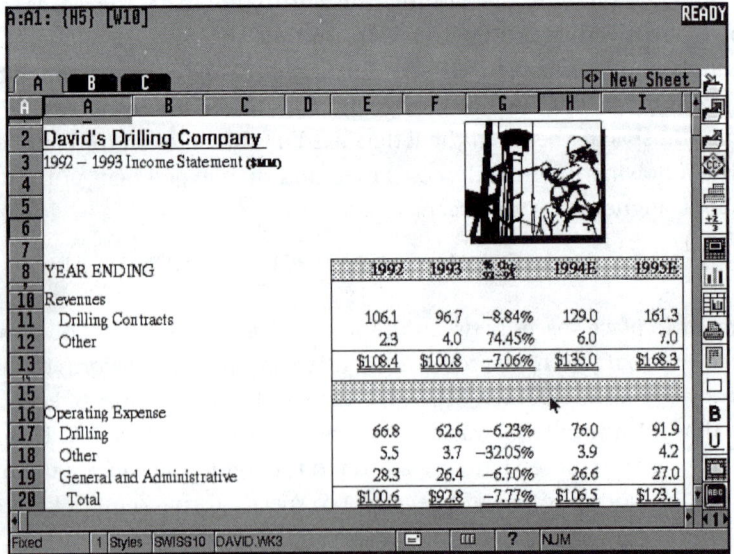

As you can see in figure 6.36, the command copies only formats, not cell contents. 1-2-3's **/C**opy command copies cell contents *and* formats (assuming that Wysiwyg is attached). The formats that you can copy with **:S**pecial **C**opy include the font, boldface, italics, underline, shading, color, and lines.

You also can select a range and then click the Copy Formats SmartIcon to copy the range's Wysiwyg formatting.

If you use Wysiwyg's **:S**pecial **C**opy command, 1-2-3 prompts you to enter the range from which you want to copy attributes (the cell or cells containing the formatting) and the range to which you want to copy the attributes (the target cell or cells). You can copy formats between any active worksheets or files. To copy a format from one file to another, choose **/F**ile **O**pen to retrieve each file before using **:S**pecial **C**opy. Use the direction keys or the Next Worksheet/Previous Worksheet SmartIcons to indicate ranges in other files.

Use **:S**pecial **M**ove to move the formats (not the data) to a different part of the same worksheet or to another worksheet in the same file. **:S**pecial **M**ove simultaneously resets all source-range formats to the default settings. The source range is set to font 1, and all special formatting (boldface, italics, underline, shading, lines, and colors) is cleared. Like **:S**pecial **C**opy, this command doesn't affect the contents of either the source or the target range.

Because the command resets source-range formats, use the command carefully. In some cases, using **:S**pecial **C**opy and resetting source-range formats with **:F**ormat may be safer.

Like **:S**pecial **M**ove, 1-2-3's **/M**ove command reverts the source range to the default format settings. **/M**ove moves the cell contents, however, as well as the format.

Using Named Styles

Another way to apply a format from one cell to another is to create and use named styles. You may want to create named styles for the formats you use frequently. Suppose that a worksheet contains 10 subheadings, and you want all of them to be 14-point Swiss bold with a heavy shade. To simplify the formatting process and to ensure consistency, you can name this particular formatting style SUB and then apply this style to all the subheadings.

Another advantage to using named styles is that you can make format changes rapidly. If you decide that you want the subheadings to have a light instead of a heavy shade, you need to change the format of only one cell.

One option in the Wysiwyg menu, **:N**amed-Style, facilitates formatting ranges with certain combinations of formats. Suppose that every time you

Tip
Release 4 has seven default named styles. You can create named styles for the formats you use frequently and replace any of the default styles, or you can use style 8, which is the custom style.

338 Chapter 6—Making Your Worksheets Dazzle

have a row of totals, you format the row with boldface, double underline, and light shading. To apply these formats, you begin by choosing **:N**amed-Style; the menu shown at the top of the screen in figure 6.37 appears. You then choose **D**efine, and a menu containing eight styles appears (see fig. 6.38).

Fig. 6.37
The **:N**amed-Style menu.

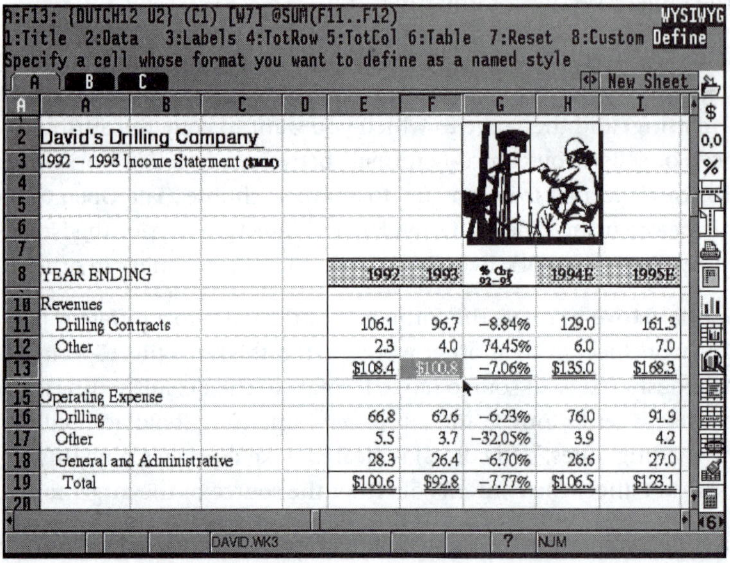

Fig. 6.38
The **:N**amed-Style **D**efine menu.

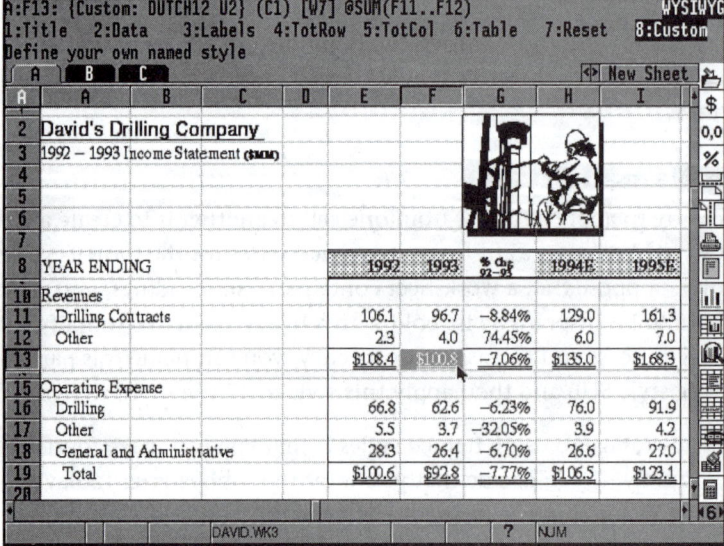

If you haven't defined any styles yet, the styles listed are the defaults. To define a style named Totals, choose one of the numbered styles from the menu, such as the **8**:Custom option. When the prompt Cell defining the style: appears, point to the cell containing the desired style. In this case, you can point to any totals cell in row 13 or enter a cell name, such as A:F13. (If you place the cell pointer in an appropriate cell before choosing **:N**amed-Style, the cell address appears after the prompt; you don't need to enter the cell address manually.) After you type the cell address, press Enter. The Style name: prompt appears. Enter a name such as **Totals** (the name can't be more than six characters). At the next prompt, Style description:, enter a description of the style, such as **Double Underline Totals**. This style now is available in the **:N**amed-Style menu. The description you entered appears in the third line of the control panel (see fig. 6.39).

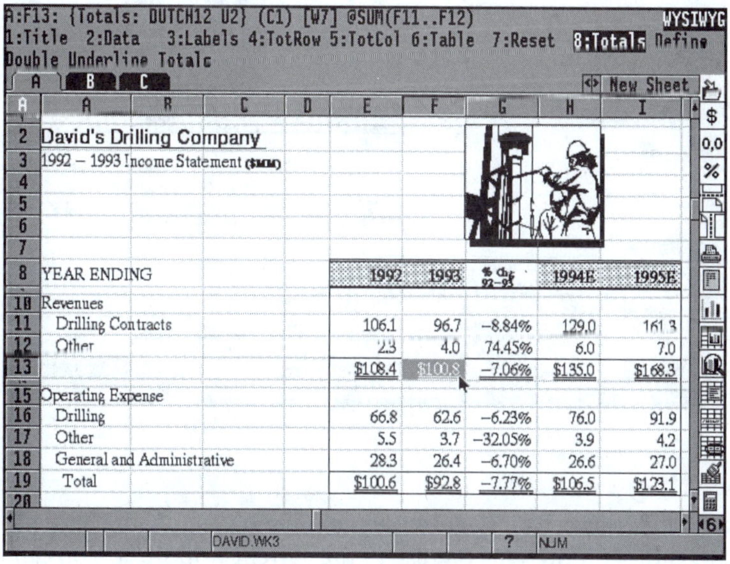

Fig. 6.39
A named style called Totals added to the **:N**amed-Style menu.

Use a named style whenever you want to format a cell or a range of cells in that style. To format a range with the named style Totals, for example, choose **:N**amed-Style **8**:Totals. Then highlight the range and press Enter. The control panel shows the format in braces (refer to fig. 6.39).

Using named styles facilitates making global formatting changes. Changing the format of an existing style requires only two simple steps. First, go to any cell formatted with the style you want to change, and modify the format. The cell no longer is associated with the named style. Now you must redefine the style. The second step, therefore, is to use the **:N**amed-Style **D**efine command

340 Chapter 6—Making Your Worksheets Dazzle

to assign the same style number and name to the cell, changing the description of the style if necessary. Now all cells with that style name reflect the format change.

The status bar contains the style selector, which you can click the left mouse button on to display the list of named styles (see fig. 6.40). Move to the cell or highlight the range to which you want to apply formatting, and then select the named style you want to use from the style selector. 1-2-3 applies the named style to the selected cell or cells.

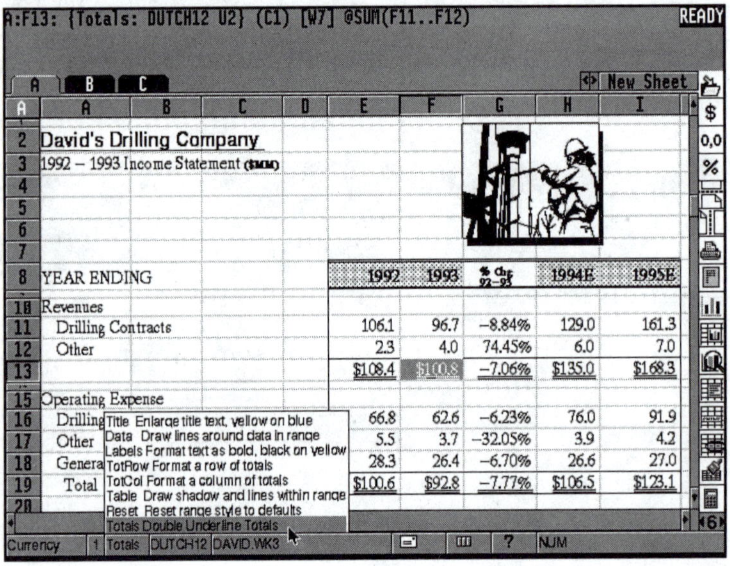

Fig. 6.40
The style-selector list, showing the new custom style named Totals.

Importing Formats

You can use Wysiwyg's **:S**pecial **I**mport command to apply the formats contained in another format file on disk to the current worksheet. You can import the following types of formatting: the font set, graphs, named styles, or all formatting.

The Wysiwyg **:S**pecial **I**mport command is similar to 1-2-3's **/F**ile **C**ombine **C**opy, but the Wysiwyg command imports only formatting and printing instructions, not data. If a series of files have identical structures (for example, a series of budget worksheets), you can eliminate the need to format each worksheet; simply import all the formatting. If you want to use a set of fonts or named styles contained in another file, you can copy only those settings.

To import formats from another file, choose **:S**pecial **I**mport and then choose one of the options listed in the following table.

Option	Description
All	Copies individual cell formats; the font set; named styles; graphics; and print range, orientation, bin, settings, and layout
Named-Styles	Replaces the styles in the current file with the styles in the specified format file
Fonts	Replaces the font set in the current file with the font set in the specified format file (similar to **:F**ormat **F**ont **L**ibrary **R**etrieve)
Graphs	Places graphs in the same location and with the same enhancements as in the specified format file

1-2-3 prompts you to enter the name of the format file from which you want to import a format. You can import from Wysiwyg, Impress, or Allways format files. Wysiwyg displays a list of files that have the FM extension (either Wysiwyg FM3 files or Impress FMT files). You can import from an Allways file by including the ALL extension when you type the file name.

The **:S**pecial **I**mport **A**ll command strips all formatting from the current worksheet and replaces the formats with imported ones. The imported formats appear in the same locations in the current worksheet as they appear in the imported worksheet. If the two worksheets aren't organized identically, formats may appear in unexpected places. You may be able to fix minor problems by using **:S**pecial **M**ove to move imported cell formats that don't match the current file. The best procedure, however, is to organize the current worksheet identically to the worksheet from which you are importing formats.

If you don't like the result of importing the formats from another file, you can undo the formats by pressing Alt+F4 Undo key and choosing **Y**es (if Undo is enabled).

Exporting Formats

If you use the **/F**ile **S**ave command with Wysiwyg attached, two files are stored: the 1-2-3 worksheet file (WK3 extension) and the Wysiwyg format file (FM3 extension). If you want to save only the format file, use the **:S**pecial **E**xport option. This command creates a file on disk that contains the current file's formatting, graphing, and printing instructions. The exported file can be a Wysiwyg FM3 file, an Impress FMT file, or an Allways ALL file. The file contains individual cell formats; the current font set; named styles; graph placement and enhancements (but not the actual graphs); and the print range, settings, orientation, and layout.

One possible use of the :**S**pecial **E**xport command is to create a format file that can be used in Impress or Allways. Be aware that if the file contains formatting commands that are unavailable in Allways, you cannot save those formats in the ALL file. Allways doesn't feature double or wide lines, for example, so these formats aren't stored in the ALL file.

Troubleshooting

A worksheet that someone else created looks different on my computer than it did on his.

If the worksheet uses fonts that you do not have installed on your computer, the worksheet will look different; when the program cannot find a certain font, it substitutes one that is as close as possible to the unavailable font. If you used the extended set of fonts during installation of 1-2-3, you will have all the fonts shipped by Lotus.

I have other versions of 1-2-3 for DOS installed on my machine. Is it possible for all of them to use the same set of fonts?

Yes. Choose :**D**isplay **F**ont-Directory, and type the directory path to the fonts you want to use. Do this in all your 1-2-3 programs, and then you will be able to delete unused fonts from unused directories. Remember to choose :**D**isplay **D**efault **U**pdate to save the new font and directory settings in the Wysiwyg configuration file; otherwise, the next time you start 1-2-3, the program will revert to the default settings in that file.

The titles at the top of my worksheet never look centered.

Highlight the row of cells across which you want to center the title, and then click the Align Across Columns SmartIcon. If you later change the column widths, you need to repeat this procedure.

From Here...

For more information related to making your data look good, refer to the following chapters:

- Chapter 8, "Printing Reports." This chapter covers how to set up a good-looking report and then print by using commands in the /**P**rint menu (for text display mode) and the :**P**rint menu (for Wysiwyg).

- Chapter 23, "Creating Effective Graphs." This chapter covers the basics of creating graphs from your worksheet data, adding colors and labels, printing graphs, and including a graph in a report.

- Chapter 25, "Developing Business Presentations." This chapter covers using the **:G**raph commands to set up your worksheet for presentations.

Chapter 7

Attaching Comments to Worksheet Cells

There are several ways to add comments and notes to supplement the data on the worksheet, thus giving further information to anyone looking at the worksheet. Adding comments and notes is particularly useful for documenting complicated formulas that may not be especially easy to decipher at a later time. For example, the data in a cell might include some assumptions that are not readily apparent at first and you want to be sure to document those assumptions.

New in Release 4 is the ability to attach comments to cells using *notepads*. You can enhance the text in these notepads with some types of style attributes to make them stand out and look attractive. This chapter shows you how to use different procedures to create comments and notes, and attach them to cells. It also shows you how to format and manipulate notes.

In this chapter, you learn how to do the following:

- Add comments to values and formulas
- Add a notepad
- Edit a notepad
- Change the type of notepad display
- Copy, move, or delete notepads
- Create a table of notepads and their contents
- Change the style of the notepad contents

Appending Comments to Values and Formulas

You can append a note to a cell that contains a value; the note can explain a number or a formula. 1-2-3 displays the note in the control panel but not in the worksheet (see fig. 7.1). Immediately after the number or formula, type a semicolon (;) and then the note. Don't add a space between the semicolon and the first character of the note. Remember that you are limited to the 512-character length for the entire cell entry, which includes the formula and the note. If you need to add a longer note, you should instead use the new notepad feature (see the next section for more details).

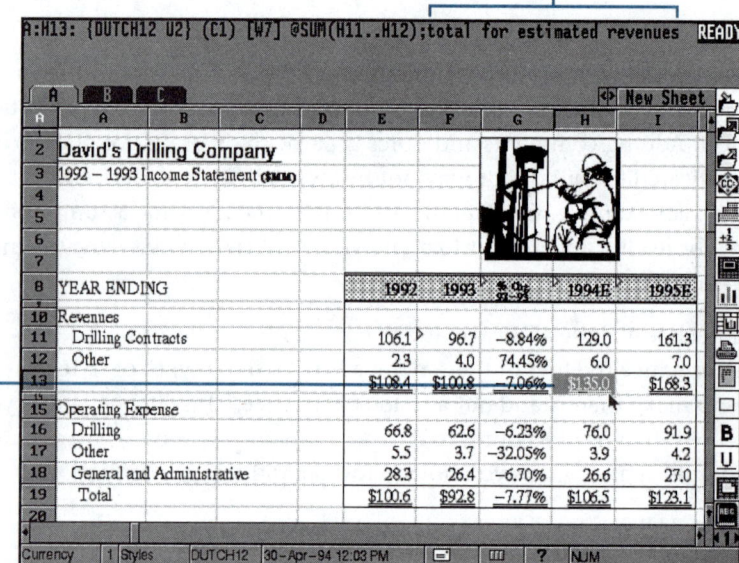

A comment appended to a formula

Fig. 7.1
Cell H13 shows a formula with a comment appended to it.

Only the formula result appears in the worksheet

Using Notepads

One of the helpful new features added to 1-2-3 is the ability to add notes to the worksheet by creating *notepads*. If you have any complex formulas or other data that need extra documentation, the notepads are useful, especially because they allow up to 512 characters. When you use the technique described in the previous section (in which you put the comment after a semicolon at the end of the formula), the size limit for the cell note is the number of characters left after the number of characters used in the formula. In other words, the limit is 512 characters minus the length of the formula.

A notepad can be displayed under the cell to which it is attached, displayed as an icon, or hidden. Figure 7.2 shows an example of the notepad as it appears under cell G8, the cell to which the note was attached. This view of the screen also shows how the screen appears if you use the **F**ull size option from the /**T**ools **N**otepad menu. The notes always appear full size unless you use the **I**con or **H**idden options to change their appearance on the screen. Of course, they must be full size for you to edit and create them.

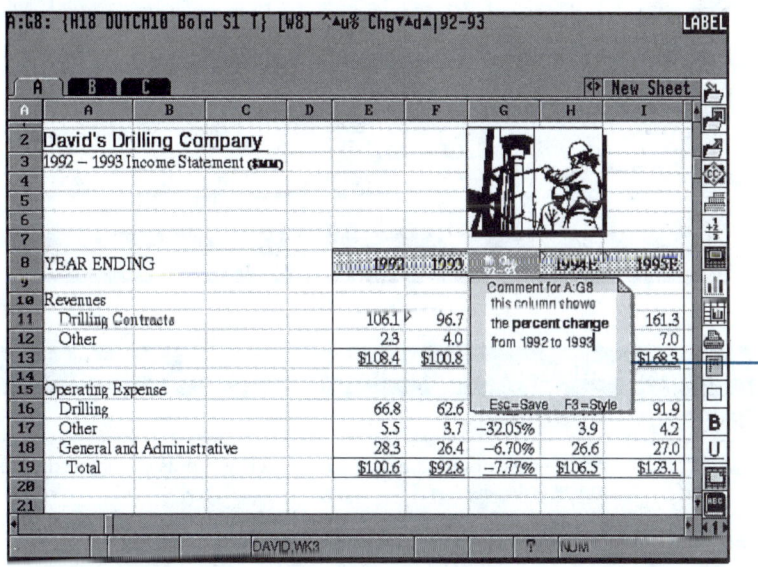

Fig. 7.2
Cell G8 has a notepad attached to it. Notice how the frame of the attached notepad indicates which cell it is attached to.

A notepad attached to cell G8

If you choose the **I**con option under the /**T**ools **N**otepad menu, the screen looks like figure 7.3. Note the small triangle on the left side of cell G8, which is the notepad icon. There is also an option to **H**ide all or some of the notepads, which leaves you with a clean worksheet with no notepads or icons showing.

Choose /**T**ools **N**otepad to access the command options for using notepads. These commands are described in Table 7.1. In following sections, you learn how to use these commands.

Tip
The /**T**ools **N**otepad commands are available in a sealed file, but if the current cell is protected, you can't access those commands.

348 Chapter 7—Attaching Comments to Worksheet Cells

Fig. 7.3
The notepad icon appears as a triangle on the left side of cell G8.

Notepad icon

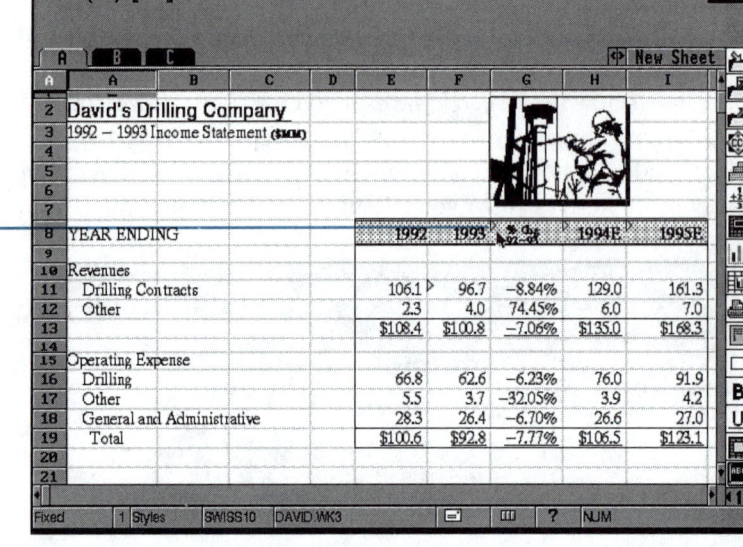

Table 7.1	Options on the /Tools Notepad Menu
Option	**Description**
Add	Adds a new notepad to the current cell and puts you into edit mode in the notepad
Edit	Allows you to chose a notepad or iconized notepad to edit
Full size	Displays all the notes or a selected range of notes in notepad form
Icon	Displays all the notes or a selected range of notes in icon form
Hide	Hides all notes or a selected range of notes
Copy	Copies a note or a selected range of notes to a new location
Move	Moves a note or a selected range of notes to a new location
Delete	Deletes a note or range of notes
Table	Creates a table of notes in the current file at the location you indicate

Attaching a Notepad to the Current Cell

  Select **/T**ools **N**otepad **A**dd or click the Notepad SmartIcon when your cell pointer is on a cell that you want to annotate with information in a notepad. A blank notepad, 18 characters by 5 rows in size and located below the related cell, appears on-screen. You then can type anything you want, up to 512 characters. When you are finished typing the information, press Esc to leave the notepad. The notepads are saved with the worksheet when you select **/F**ile **S**ave. You can format the information in the notepad in many ways. For more information about formatting the text in a notepad, see the section "Formatting Text in a Notepad" later in this chapter.

Lotus has also added the ability to convert the semicolon text comment following a numerical entry to a notepad. If you try to add a notepad to a cell with a comment, you see the prompt `Use semicolon text to create note?` You can then select either **Y**es or **N**o. Selecting **Y**es creates a notepad with the semicolon text entered into the notepad, with the cursor ready for text editing. The semicolon text remains after the cell entry, too.

Editing a Notepad

When you need to make changes to a notepad that is already present on the worksheet, you can use the **/T**ools **N**otepad **E**dit menu options. Because 1-2-3 does not prompt you for which cell to edit, you must move to the cell attached to the note you want to edit before invoking the command. When you are finished editing the notepad, press the Esc key to return to the worksheet. While you are editing a notepad, you can use the F3 (Style) key to invoke a special style menu for enhancing the text. For more information about formatting the text in the notepad, refer to the section "Formatting Text in a Notepad" later in this chapter. You can also double-click the left mouse button on the full size notepad or the icon to place the notepad into full size and EDIT mode.

Changing a Notepad to an Icon

The easiest way to indicate where notepads are attached to cells without the notepads being full size and obscuring other cells on the screen is to use the **/T**ools **N**otepad **I**con menu option. After you select the **I**con option, another menu appears. You can choose the **R**ange option to select just a part of the worksheet and change the notepads to icons or use the **A**ll option to change all the notepads in the worksheet to icons. Refer to figure 7.3 to see the notepad icon.

The icon indicates there is a notepad attached to a cell, but you can't read the contents of the note without changing the notepad to full size. Click the left mouse button on the icon and the notepad becomes full size—ready for reading. Double-clicking the icon changes the current cell's notepad to full size and places it into edit mode. You also can use the menu to change to

Tip
If you use **/F**ile **X**tract to extract a range of a worksheet that included cells with notepads attached, the notepads also are extracted. Using a linking formula to a cell with a notepad attached does not link the notepad, however.

Tip
If you run the spell checker after entering all the information into your notepads, it checks the contents of all notepads whether they are full-size, hidden, or appear as icons.

◄ "Editing Data in a Worksheet," p. 68

◄ "Spell Checking Your Data," p. 284

Tip

If you have zoomed your display down to a smaller size, you may find it difficult to see the notepad icons. You can use the **:Dis**play **Z**oom **L**arge **Q**uit command to make the screen larger and the icons easier to see. If you prefer, you can click the left mouse button on the Change Display Size SmartIcon to cycle through the display sizes.

full size. This is discussed in the next section, "Changing a Notepad to Full size." You can also click the left mouse button on the full size notepad to make it become an icon in the cell. Double-clicking the full size notepad places it into EDIT mode, just the same as double-clicking the icon.

Changing a Notepad to Full size

Most of the time, you will want to hide your notepads or have them reduced to an icon so that they don't obscure worksheet data. If you want to read the contents of iconized notes, select **/T**ools **N**otepad **F**ull size or double-click the icon. After choosing the **F**ull size option in the menu, you can choose to change all the notes attached in one particular area of the worksheet by using the **R**ange option. Or you can use the **A**ll option to display in full size all of the attached notes in the worksheet.

If there are several attached notes in a worksheet, you may want to use the **R**ange option so that you can select just part of the worksheet at a time to display the notes. When the notes are attached to cells close together, one note overlaps the other note. See figure 7.4 for an example of how overlapping notes appear. As you can see, you can read only the top note. There is one other alternative, which allows you to read the notes without hiding them. Change the column widths of the columns with the overlapping notes so that they are each wide enough to completely display the note. Remember the original column widths so that you can change the columns back after reading the notes if the wider columns are unacceptable for general use.

Fig. 7.4

Four notepads in nearby cells overlap each other when the notepads are full size.

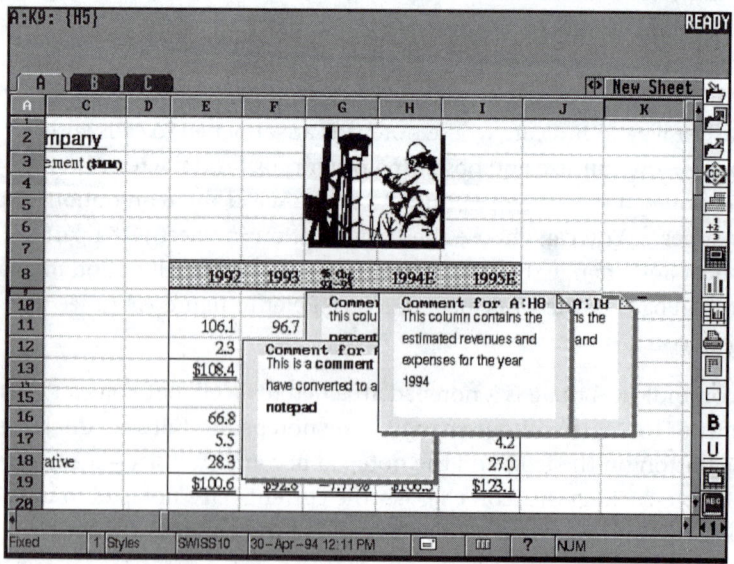

The **A**ll option is useful when there are not many notepads close together or when you want to see where all the hidden notepads are located. If you want to read the overlapping notepads, you can either hide some of them or select the desired notepad and go into edit mode by typing **/T**ools **N**otepad **E**dit when your cell pointer is on the cell to which the notepad is attached.

Hiding Notepads

For a clean-looking worksheet without any indication of attached notepads, select the **/T**ools **N**otepad **H**ide command. If you want to hide only a selected area of the worksheet's notepads, select the **R**ange option from the resulting menu and highlight the part of the worksheet where you want to hide the attached notepads. To hide all the notepads in the entire worksheet, select the **A**ll option. When the notepads are hidden, there is no indication as to which cells have notes attached to them. The only way to find the notepads is to use the **/T**ools **N**otepad **F**ull size menu option or create a table of notepads and their contents, which is discussed in the section "Creating a Table of Notepads" later in this chapter.

Copying and Moving Notepads

Sometimes it is necessary to copy or move a notepad to another cell on the current worksheet or to another worksheet that is open. You can copy or move the notepads by following these steps:

1. Choose the **/T**ools **N**otepad [**C**opy or **M**ove] menu option.

2. You are then prompted for the range from which to copy or move the notepads. For example, the prompt for copying is `Copy notes FROM:` followed by the current cell pointer location.

3. Type the cell address(es) or highlight the range and then press Enter.

4. Next, you are prompted for the range to copy or move to. For example, the prompt for copying is `Copy notes TO:` followed by the current cell pointer location, which is the same location as was prompted in the `FROM:` range.

5. Move to the target cell or range and type the cell address(es) or highlight the range where you want to have the new notepads appear. Remember that you must highlight or give the cell addresses of a range starting in the top left corner of the area, and it must be a contiguous area.

After the notepad is copied or moved, the cell reference at the top of the notepad changes to indicate the new location.

Deleting Notepads

In order to delete a notepad, select **/T**ools **N**otepad **D**elete. If you need to delete only the current cell, select the **R**ange option from the main menu. The current cell pointer location appears. Press Enter to accept that range. Deleting a selected area of notepads on the worksheet is also done by choosing the **R**ange option, then specifying the range, and pressing Enter. To delete all the notepads on the worksheet, select the **A**ll menu option and all the notepads are deleted.

> **Caution**
>
> Be sure that deleting the notepad is really what you want to do before doing it. There is no warning prompt to allow you to cancel the operation after you select **/T**ools **N**otepad **D**elete [**R**ange or **A**ll]. If you have the Undo feature enabled, you can click the Undo SmartIcon or press the Alt+F4 (Undo) key to cancel the deletion immediately after performing it.

◄ "Using the Undo Feature," p. 134

Creating a Table of Notepads

The **/T**ools **N**otepad **T**able command enables you to create a two-column table on a selected range of the worksheet. This table shows a listing of all the cell locations where a notepad is attached and the text of each of those notepads. When prompted for the target location of the table, choose a blank area of the worksheet. See figure 7.5 for an example of what the table looks like when notes are on the worksheet.

> **Note**
>
> This table of notepad contents is a good example of the type of documentation to put on a separate sheet in the file. It is always a good safeguard to create a special sheet or two for documentation of things such as macros, tables of range names, assumptions for the data, or any other helpful supporting information you want to include in the file. Many times a worksheet is easy to understand when it is created, but it becomes difficult to remember all the assumptions, macros, and range names used to create the worksheet when it has been put aside for a while. This type of documentation is even more important if you are creating the worksheet for other users who are not familiar with the structure of the worksheet and its assumptions.

Using Notepads 353

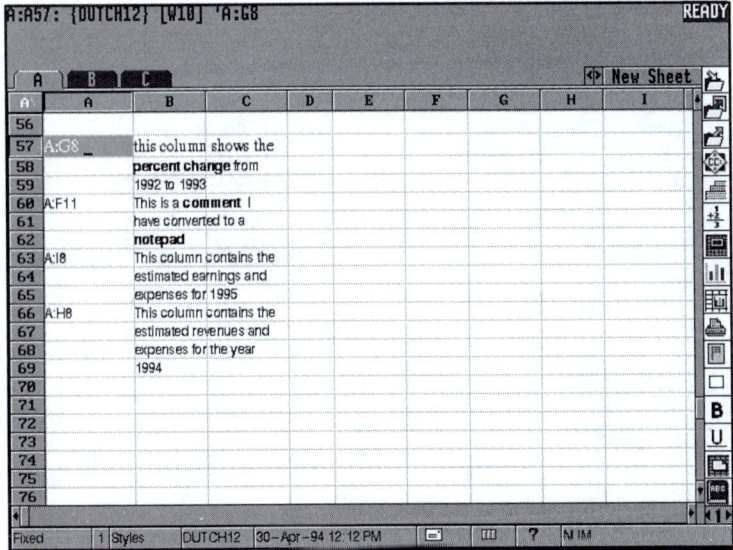

Fig. 7.5
The /**T**ools
Notepad **T**able
command creates a
table like the one
on this screen in
cells A57..B69.

Formatting Text in a Notepad

After you have placed a notepad on-screen and started typing whatever information you want, you may want to enhance the text in some way. You can do this by pressing the F3 key to access the special style menu for the notepad. Figure 7.6 shows what your screen should look like with the style menu. You must place the cursor before the data you want to enhance. For example, in figure 7.6, the cursor is in back of the "1994". The styles for underline and bold were invoked for the "1994" when the cursor was in front of it and then the "1994" was typed.

The style menu contains the following choices:

Bold **I**talics **U**nderline **C**olor + − **O**utline **N**ormal

You use the **B**old, **I**talics, and **U**nderline menu choices to give the subsequent text those particular attributes. You can make these style selections before entering the text. Or, after typing the text, you can place the cursor in front of the text you want to enhance and press F3 to make the style menu appear. If you choose the **C**olor option, the following menu appears:

Normal **R**ed **G**reen **D**ark-Blue **C**yan **Y**ellow **M**agenta

The **N**ormal menu option on the **C**olor menu changes the current color to the default text color of the cell. After you select a color, the subsequent text you type is in the new color.

Fig. 7.6
When you press the F3 key while editing a notepad, the style menu appears on-screen.

The notepad style menu

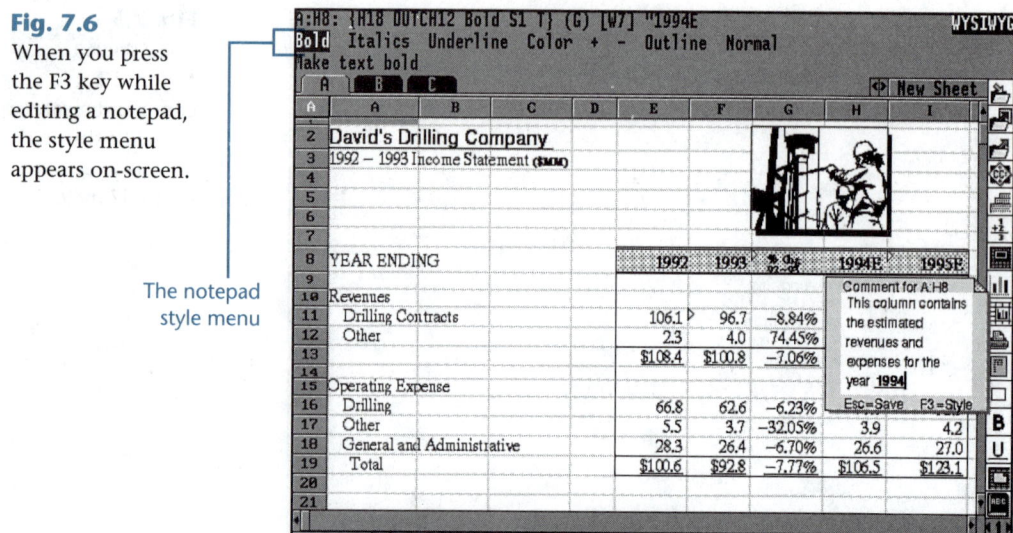

> **Note**
> If you prefer, you can use the Ctrl+A key sequence to add attributes to the text being typed into the notepad. All the attributes listed in Chapter 6 in the section titled "Using Formatting Sequences" work in the notepad text-editing mode. Unlike in a regular cell, no little triangle shows up to indicate the beginning and end of the attributes. Use the Ctrl+N key sequence to end the attribute. Most of the common attributes are available in the F3 style menu, but there are some others that you might want to use by implementing the formatting sequence method.

The + menu option on the style menu changes the subsequent text to superscript and the – option changes the subsequent text to subscript. This is useful if you are entering information about a formula and want to depict the formula in scientific notation. It also makes text more difficult to read, so don't overuse these styles.

The **O**utline menu option changes the subsequent text to an outline font. This is a nice way to emphasize an important point; as with the superscript and subscripts, however, you should not overuse it.

To try out a sample notepad and change some of the styles, follow these steps:

1. Type "**1994** in cell H8 and press Enter. (Using the opening quotation marks right-justifies the text.)
2. Select **/T**ools **N**otepad **A**dd while keeping your cell pointer on cell H8.
3. Type **this column contains**, and then press F3.
4. Choose **C**olor **R**ed.
5. Type **estimated**, and then press F3.
6. Choose **C**olor **N**ormal.
7. Type **earnings and expenses for**, and then press F3.
8. Choose **B**old.
9. Press F3.
10. Choose **U**nderline, and type **1994.**
11. Press Esc. In the notepad, the word estimated appears in red and the number 1994 appears in boldface and underlined.

Refer to figure 7.6 to see what this looks like on-screen.

> ### Troubleshooting
>
> *My notepad displays text in a font that's too small to read.*
>
> Notepads use the default font (Font 1 in the font listing that appears when you choose **:F**ormat **F**ont). If you need to increase the size of the font in the notepad, choose **:F**ont **R**eplace **1** while in READY mode, then choose a font type and larger point size. Remember that any cells on the worksheet that rely on the default font because they have not been given a different font also will change to the new font size and type.
>
> *When I tried to access the **/T**ools **N**otepad menu, it did not allow me to use it.*
>
> The notepad feature of 1-2-3 Release 4 for DOS works only when you are in Wysiwyg mode. In other words, if you try to access the notepads while in text mode, you can't see or edit the notepads. If you create a table of the notepads and their contents by selecting the **/T**ools **N**otepad **T**able menu options and creating the table in a blank area of the worksheet, you can see this table in text mode, although you can't do anything using the **/T**ools **N**otepad menu options.
>
> (continues)

> (continued)
>
> *I know I have notepads attached to cells in my worksheet, but I can't see any when I retrieve the file.*
>
> You most likely saved your worksheet with all the notepads hidden. Try selecting the **/T**ools **N**otepad [**F**ull size or **I**con] [**R**ange or **A**ll] menu options to either display notepads as full size or as icons. Because you don't know where the notepads may be, you should choose the **A**ll option rather than the **R**ange option after choosing to display the notepads as **F**ull size or **I**cons.
>
> If you still do not find any notepads, chances are that you forgot to save the file after adding the notepads to the worksheet, or you used the **/T**ools **N**otepad **D**elete menu options and saved the file in that state. There is no way to get the lost notepads back at this point unless you have a backup copy of the file.

From Here...

For information relating to making your data look good, refer to the following chapters of this book:

- Chapter 6, "Making Your Worksheets Dazzle." This chapter discusses how to format the data in your worksheet, and to use the Wysiwyg menu to create a polished-looking worksheet with graphics, shading, lines, and different fonts and attributes. This chapter also covers using the spell checker.

- Chapter 8, "Printing Reports." This chapter covers more detailed information on how to take your worksheet from the screen to the printer and have it look good.

- Chapter 9, "Working with Files." This chapter helps you learn more about saving, creating, and managing files and directories. It also discusses creating lists and tables of files.

Chapter 8
Printing Reports

1-2-3 is a powerful tool for developing and manipulating tabular information. You can enter and edit data on worksheets and database files on-screen, as well as store the data on disk. But to report and share data, you need it in printed form—as an income forecast, a budget analysis, or a detailed reorder list, for example.

1-2-3 Release 4 offers two ways to print worksheet data. You can use the /**P**rint **P**rinter command to print directly from 1-2-3 to the printer. This command is the only available choice if you aren't currently using Wysiwyg. If you are using the Wysiwyg add-in, you also can use the Wysiwyg **:P**rint command. When you start 1-2-3 Release 4, it automatically attaches and loads Wysiwyg.

This chapter shows you how to complete the following tasks:

- ■ Print a single-page report
- ■ Print a multiple-page report
- ■ Print multiple ranges
- ■ Adjust the page layout
- ■ Change page layout and printer control defaults
- ■ Print worksheet formulas
- ■ Use the background print capability

Printing with /Print Versus :Print

Both the **/P**rint and the **:P**rint commands print worksheets and graphs. To use 1-2-3's full capabilities for creating professional-looking output, however, you should select the **:P**rint command for most printing. Therefore, this chapter focuses first on using the **:P**rint command. Printing commands and features available only through the **/P**rint menu are discussed in detail in the section titled "Using the /Print Commands" later in this chapter.

▶ "Including Graphs in Reports," p. 746

▶ "Adding a Graph," p. 768

How do you know when to use **/P**rint and when to use **:P**rint? If you use the graph or formatting options in Wysiwyg to enhance a worksheet, you must use Wysiwyg's **:P**rint command; the **/P**rint command doesn't print formats applied with the **:F**ormat command. If you use **:F**ormat **B**old to boldface a row of column headings, for example, you must use **:P**rint to see the boldface on the printed report. If you have used the **:G**raph **A**dd command to insert a graph into a worksheet range, you must print the inserted graph with **:P**rint.

Compare a report printed with the 1-2-3 **/P**rint command (see fig. 8.1) and the same report formatted and printed with the Wysiwyg **:P**rint command (see fig. 8.2).

Fig. 8.1

A report printed with the 1-2-3 /Print command.

```
EnviroTech Corporation
Monthly Activity
Year To Date

   Income
              January  February   March     April      May     Totals
   Surveys   $34,500   $32,000   $41,000   $43,000   $40,000  $190,500
   Consultin  25,000    16,000    20,000    18,500    12,000   $91,500
   Mapping    24,500    26,200    29,000    22,600    23,000  $125,300
   Legal      11,200    14,400    15,000    15,200    14,900   $70,700
   Reports    11,600    10,500    11,000    11,400    11,560   $56,060
   Drilling   62,000    52,300    42,000    30,000    45,000  $231,300
   Totals   $168,800  $151,400  $158,000  $140,700  $146,460  $765,360

   Expenditures
              January  February   March     April      May     Totals
   Travel     $4,500    $6,200    $1,900    $2,500    $3,300   $18,400
   Software      500     1,900     1,800       200       300    $4,700
   Hardware    1,200     5,000       300     1,200         0    $7,700
   Labor      12,000    12,000    14,000    15,000    12,000   $65,000
   Heavy Eqp  20,000    20,000    20,000    20,000    20,000  $100,000
   Leases     15,000    15,000    15,000    15,000    15,000   $75,000
   Salaries   50,000    52,000    49,000    46,000    49,000  $246,000
   Totals   $103,200  $112,100  $102,000   $99,900   $99,600  $516,800
```

EnviroTech Corporation
Monthly Activity
Year To Date

Income

	January	February	March	April	May	Totals
Surveys	$34,500	$32,000	$41,000	$43,000	$40,000	$190,500
Consulting	25,000	16,000	20,000	18,500	12,000	$91,500
Mapping	24,500	26,200	29,000	22,600	23,000	$125,300
Legal	11,200	14,400	15,000	15,200	14,900	$70,700
Reports	11,600	10,500	11,000	11,400	11,560	$56,060
Drilling	62,000	52,300	42,000	30,000	45,000	$231,300
Totals	$168,800	$151,400	$158,000	$140,700	$146,460	$765,360

Expenditures

	January	February	March	April	May	Totals
Travel	$4,500	$6,200	$1,900	$2,500	$3,300	$18,400
Software	500	1,900	1,800	200	300	$4,700
Hardware	1,200	5,000	300	1,200	0	$7,700
Labor	12,000	12,000	14,000	15,000	12,000	$65,000
Heavy Eqpt	20,000	20,000	20,000	20,000	20,000	$100,000
Leases	15,000	15,000	15,000	15,000	15,000	$75,000
Salaries	50,000	52,000	49,000	46,000	49,000	$246,000
Totals	$103,200	$112,100	$102,000	$99,900	$99,600	$516,800

Fig. 8.2
The same report formatted and printed with the Wysiwyg :Print command.

If the worksheet hasn't been formatted with the :Format or other Wysiwyg commands, you may print the report with either the 1-2-3 or Wysiwyg Print command. Feel free to use either /Print or :Print for first drafts that you haven't formatted with Wysiwyg and for simple internal reports that don't need fancy formatting. Even if you don't need high-quality printed pages, however, the Wysiwyg :Print command gives you better-looking printed text than /Print.

The /Print command, however, does offer a fast draft printing capability. The /Print command also offers the /Print [Printer,File,Encoded,Background] Options Other Unformatted command for removing page breaks, headers, and footers from a printout. :Print has no equivalent command.

Understanding the Default Print Settings

To minimize the keystrokes necessary for a basic print operation, 1-2-3 provides default settings that match the printing requirements of most users. Many of these defaults don't apply to the :Print command.

360 Chapter 8—Printing Reports

By default **:P**rint measures the page in inches. The default page is 8 1/2-by-11-inch continuous-feed paper with 1/2-inch right and left margins, a 1/2-inch top margin, and a slightly larger bottom margin (.55 inches). Wysiwyg uses proportional fonts, which makes it impractical to measure the width of the page based on printed characters.

The **/P**rint command measures the page in line and text characters per line. The default page produced by **/P**rint has 72 text characters per line with 56 lines per page on 8 1/2-by-11-inch continuous-feed paper.

Viewing the Current Printer Settings

Figure 8.3 shows the default settings for the **:P**rint command. If you select a different page size, change the margins, create a header or footer, designate print borders, or change the compression, and then choose Default Update, the new settings you chose become the default layout settings for all future print jobs.

The print settings are at the left side of the status screen. The two settings containing hardware-specific information, the printer Name and Interface settings, affect both the **:P**rint and the **/P**rint commands.

Several settings apply only to the **/P**rint command. The margins and page length settings show page layout information. The Wait option displays the setting for continuous-feed paper. The Setup string option displays the setup string (if one has been selected). (See the section titled "Using Setup Strings" later in this chapter.)

Tip

The default printer for the **:P**rint and **/P**rint commands is the first parallel printer installed. You should always check the current settings before printing; another user may have changed them.

Fig. 8.3
The 1-2-3 Release 4 **:P**rint **L**ayout **S**tatus dialog box.

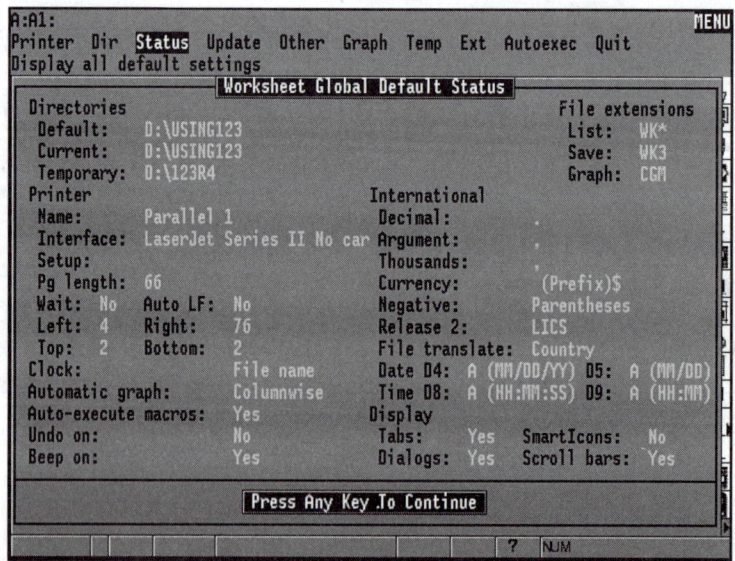

Modifying the Default Hardware-Specific Options

If you want to change any of the print settings shown in the default status sheet, you invoke the **/W**orksheet **G**lobal **D**efault **P**rinter command. Only two options, **I**nterface and **N**ame, affect the **:P**rint command. The other settings are explained later in this chapter, in the section titled "Setting Defaults for the **/P**rint Command."

The **I**nterface option specifies one of the following connections between the computer and the printer:

1 Parallel 1 (the default)

2 Serial 1

3 Parallel 2

4 Serial 2

5 Output Device LPT1

6 Output Device LPT2

7 Output Device LPT3

8 Output Device COM1

9 Output Device COM2

Choices 5 through 9 are necessary only if the computer is connected to a local area network (LAN). If you select either of the serial port options (**2** or **4**), another menu appears. From that menu, you must specify one of the following baud rates (data transmission speeds):

1 110 baud

2 150 baud

3 300 baud

4 600 baud

5 1200 baud

6 2400 baud

7 4800 baud

8 9600 baud

9 19200 baud

362   Chapter 8—Printing Reports

Tip
A 1200-baud rate equals approximately 120 characters per second.

The baud rate that you select must match the printer's baud rate setting. In addition, the printer must be configured for 8 data bits, 1 stop bit (2 stop bits at 110 baud), and no parity. Check the printer manual for information about the interface and baud rate settings, as well as other print settings.

The menu that appears after you select **N**ame depends on the printers you selected during the initial installation of 1-2-3 Release 4. If you installed 1-2-3 to print on two different printers (for example, an Epson printer at your desk and an HP LaserJet printer connected to a network print server), selecting **N**ame produces a menu that offers option **1** (the Epson printer) and option **2** (the HP LaserJet printer). To print to the Epson, select **1**; to print to the LaserJet, select **2**. In this example, you also need to change the interface selection from Parallel 1 to a network address such as LPT2. To change the interface selection to LPT2, select **/W**orksheet **G**lobal **D**efault **P**rinter **I**nterface **6**.

Tip
Remember, **/W**orksheet **G**lobal **D**efault **P**rinter settings remain in effect only for the current work session. Use the **/W**orksheet **G**lobal **D**efault **U**pdate command to save the changes permanently.

> **Troubleshooting**
>
> **/W**orksheet **G**lobal **D**efault **P**rinter **N**ame and **I**nterface do not work in some worksheets.
>
> You may have used **/P**rint **P**rinter **O**ptions **D**evice or **:P**rint **C**onfig to choose a printer or interface. This unique setting is saved with the file and overrides the default settings. Use **/P**rint **P**rinter **C**lear **D**evice to restore default hardware settings.

Configuring the Printer

Before you print, select **:P**rint and check the status sheet to make sure that Wysiwyg is set to work with the printer. Not all the options on the **:P**rint **C**onfig menu apply to all printers. An Epson RX-80, for example, doesn't have cartridges or bins and cannot print with the landscape orientation.

The following table describes the **:P**rint **C**onfig options.

Menu Item	Description
Printer	The printer to be used. When multiple printers have been selected in the Install program, you can select the **P**rinter option to specify which printer you want to use.
Interface	The printer port to which the printer is attached (Parallel 1, Serial 1, Parallel 2, Serial 2, or one of the following output devices: LPT1, LPT2, LPT3, COM1, or COM2).
1st-Cart	The primary printer cartridge.

Menu Item	Description
2nd-Cart	The secondary cartridge. You can buy separate cartridges or cards with additional fonts for some printers. The HP LaserJet, for example, offers a B cartridge that includes 14-point Helvetica and 8-point and 10-point Times Roman.
Orientation	The orientation of the page to be printed: **P**ortrait (vertical) or **L**andscape (horizontal). This setting is saved in the current worksheet's format file.
Resolution	The print quality: **F**inal or **D**raft. The **D**raft resolution prints faster but with poorer quality. Not all printers have two print qualities.
Bin	The paper feeding method. **C**ontinuous (for perforated paper) is the default. Use **S**ingle-Sheet for laser printers and other single-sheet feed printers. You also can use multiple paper trays or feed paper manually with this option. (If you feed paper manually, you also may want to select **:P**rint **S**ettings **W**ait to pause between pages.) This setting is saved in the current worksheet's format file.

The following sections describe how to use the **:P**rint commands and the capabilities of a printer to meet a variety of printing needs.

Using the :Print Commands

This section shows you how to print reports quickly and easily by using a minimum of commands on the **:P**rint menu. You learn how to print a short report and then a multiple-page report. In the next section, you learn how to include headers and footers in reports, how to print borders on each page, and how to include the worksheet frame in printouts.

Understanding the :Print Menu

As discussed earlier, you must use the **:P**rint command to print worksheet enhancements added with Wysiwyg commands. This section discusses the capabilities of the **:P**rint command and how you can use it to create high-quality printed reports.

When you select **:P**rint, a full-screen dialog box appears (see fig. 8.4). With a quick glance, you can immediately see the current print settings. The page layout is at the right side of the dialog box, the margins are along the bottom, and the print settings at the left. The worksheet is hidden when the

364 Chapter 8—Printing Reports

dialog box is displayed but the **I**nfo command on the **:P**rint menu lets you temporarily hide the dialog box so you can see your work. Select **I**nfo again to redisplay the dialog box.

Fig. 8.4
The **:P**rint menu dialog box showing the default settings.

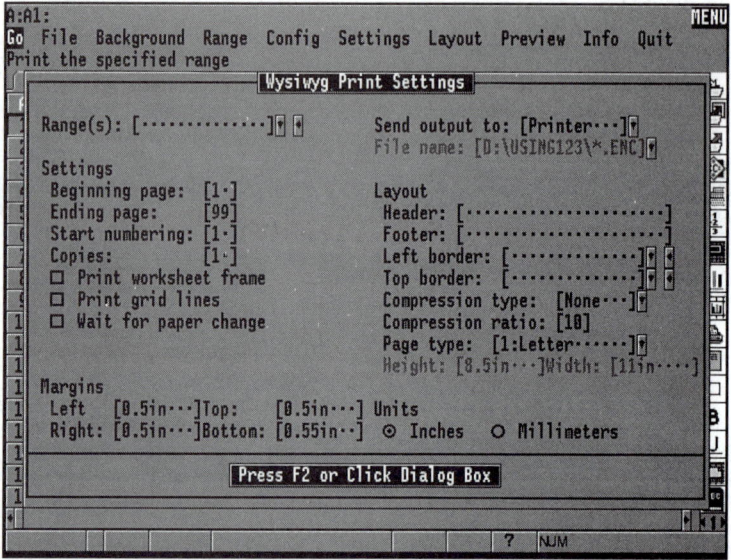

The **:P**rint command includes commands to set the print range, control the attributes of the printer, modify the page layout, and print in different ways. Table 8.1 describes the commands on the **:P**rint menu.

Tip
You also can use F6 (Window) as a toggle to hide the dialog box and redisplay the worksheet.

Table 8.1 :Print Menu Options

Menu Item	Description
Go	Prints the designated range to the current printer.
File	Creates a file containing print control codes (encoded file) for printing later.
Background	Creates an encoded file and sends it to the BPrint utility (see the section "Using Background Printing").
Range	Indicates the section(s) of the worksheet to be printed.
Config	Provides commands for setting the current printer and controlling capabilities, such as paper bins and orientation.
Settings	Sets page numbers, number of copies, and other controls for the printout.

Menu Item	Description
Layout	Sets page layout options, including margins and headers and footers.
Preview	Displays an on-screen preview of the specified print range as it will look on paper.
Info	Shows the worksheet by hiding the print dialog box. **I**nfo is the same as F6 (Window).
Quit	Returns to READY mode.

Specifying a Print Range

Before you print, you must set the print range in the command you are going to use. The **:P**rint **R**ange **S**et command is equivalent to the **/P**rint **P**rinter **R**ange command. If you use the **/P**rint command to enter a print range, however, it isn't transferred to Wysiwyg and vice versa.

To specify a print range, select **:P**rint **R**ange **S**et; then type the range, type a 1-2-3 range name, or use the direction keys or the mouse to highlight the range (see fig. 8.5). If you are specifying a multiple-worksheet print range, you can press Ctrl+PgUp or Ctrl+PgDn as you highlight the range. Printing ranges from multiple worksheets is explained later in this chapter, in the section titled "Printing Three-Dimensional Print Ranges."

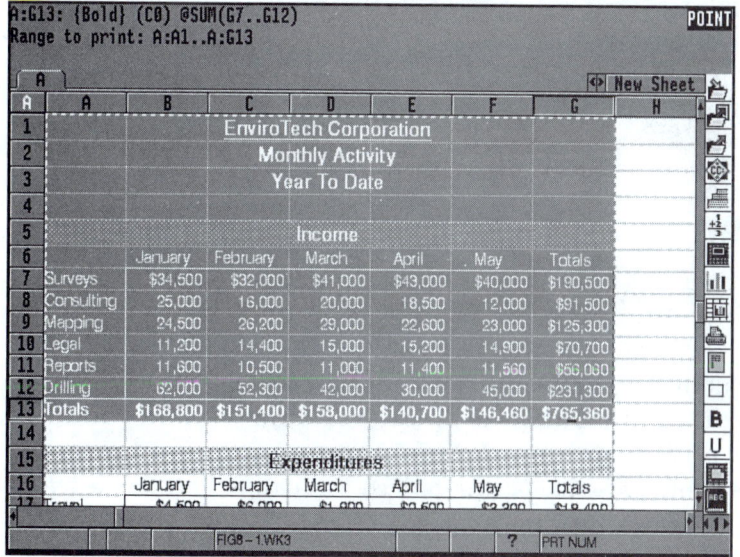

Fig. 8.5
Specifying a range with the **:P**rint **R**ange **S**et command.

366 Chapter 8—Printing Reports

Tip
To select the entire worksheet as the print range, press Home. Then press period (.) to anchor the range, and press End Home. Press Enter to finish specifying the range.

To enter a range name, either type the range name or press F3 (Name) to select from a list of range names. The print range can include ranges in other worksheets in the same file but not ranges in other open files.

After you define the print range, 1-2-3 places dashed borders around the area. To see these dashed lines, either select **Q**uit from the **:P**rint menu, select **I**nfo, or press F6 (Window); 1-2-3 then displays the worksheet. If the print area includes more than one page, dashed lines appear around each page (see fig. 8.6). You can insert breaks to change the page breaks (see the section "Printing Multiple-Page Reports" later in this chapter).

You also can select the range to print before choosing **:P**rint **R**ange. To use the keyboard to preselect the range, place the cell pointer in the upper left cell in the range, press F4 (Abs), and use the direction keys to highlight to the lower right corner of the desired range. To preselect the range using the mouse, click and drag the cell pointer. When you use **:P**rint **R**ange **S**et, 1-2-3 automatically highlights the selected range; press Enter to accept it.

Fig. 8.6
Dotted lines mark a print range specified with the **:P**rint command.

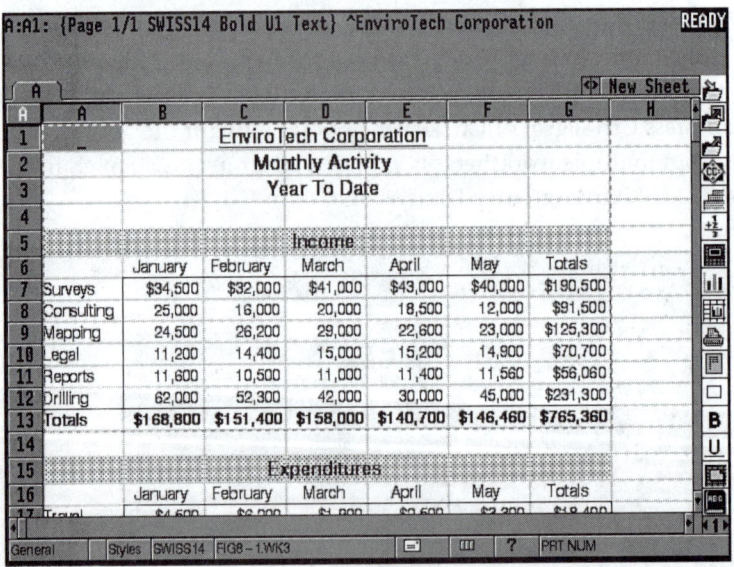

To print the range, select **G**o from the **:P**rint menu. If the selected range exceeds the width and length of the page, 1-2-3 prints the left part of the range from top to bottom and then prints the right part of the range from top to bottom until the entire range is printed. The dashed lines on the screen let you know where the page breaks occur.

1-2-3 Release 4 includes a SmartIcon for easy printing of 1-2-3 worksheets. Because the SmartIcons are only available when Wysiwyg is loaded, the Print SmartIcon uses the Wysiwyg **:P**rint command. To print with the SmartIcon, use the mouse or the keyboard to preselect a range and then simply click the Print SmartIcon. Using the current printer settings, the printer automatically prints the selected range.

Previewing On-Screen

The **:P**rint **P**review option gives you an idea of what a worksheet will look like when it is printed. This option displays a print range, one page at a time. Press any key to display subsequent pages and to return to the **:P**rint menu. Although you probably cannot read every character on-screen, you can see the overall page layout and page breaks.

1-2-3 Release 4 also includes a SmartIcon for easy previewing of a print range. To preview a specified print range, select **:P**rint **P**review or click the Print Preview SmartIcon. Figure 8.7 shows an example of a previewed page.

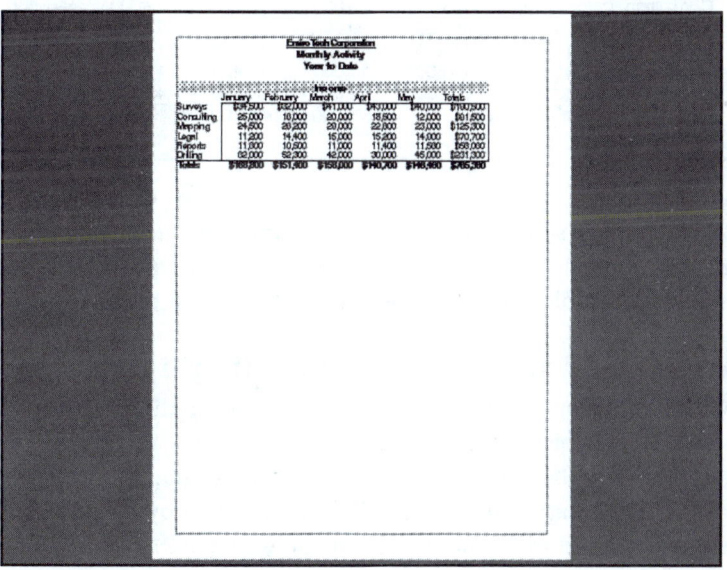

Fig. 8.7
An on-screen preview of a worksheet printout.

Printing a Short Report

When the defaults and the printer are already set up, printing a single-page report usually involves only a few steps. Once you determine that the default settings are correct, follow these steps to print the worksheet:

1. Select **:P**rint.
2. Choose **R**ange **S**et to select the worksheet area you want to print.
3. Check that the printer is on-line and that the paper is correctly positioned at the top of a page.
4. Select **G**o to begin printing.

Figure 8.7 shows a preview of the range designated to be printed; figure 8.8 shows the resulting report. After you select **G**o, you can select **Q**uit to return to READY mode.

Fig. 8.8
The printed short report.

```
                    EnviroTech Corporation
                       Monthly Activity
                        Year To Date

                              Income
               January  February    March     April      May      Totals
Surveys        $34,500   $32,000   $41,000   $43,000   $40,000   $190,500
Consulting      25,000    16,000    20,000    18,500    12,000    $91,500
Mapping         24,500    26,200    29,000    22,600    23,000   $125,300
Legal           11,200    14,400    15,000    15,200    14,900    $70,700
Reports         11,600    10,500    11,000    11,400    11,560    $56,060
Drilling        62,000    52,300    42,000    30,000    45,000   $231,300
Totals        $168,800  $151,400  $158,000  $140,700  $146,460   $765,360
```

For many reports, a single, two-dimensional range (one rectangular region in a single worksheet) is all you need. You can specify multiple ranges, however, for a single print job. This technique is discussed later in the chapter.

Printing Data and Graphics on a Single Page

▶ "Including Graphs in Reports," p. 746

The **:G**raph **A**dd command allows you to place a graph directly on the worksheet (see Chapter 23, "Creating Effective Graphs"). To print the graph that is on the worksheet, you must include the entire graph range in the print range. You can print worksheet data and graphics by including both the graph and worksheet in the same print range (see fig. 8.9). Figure 8.10 shows the printed version of this range.

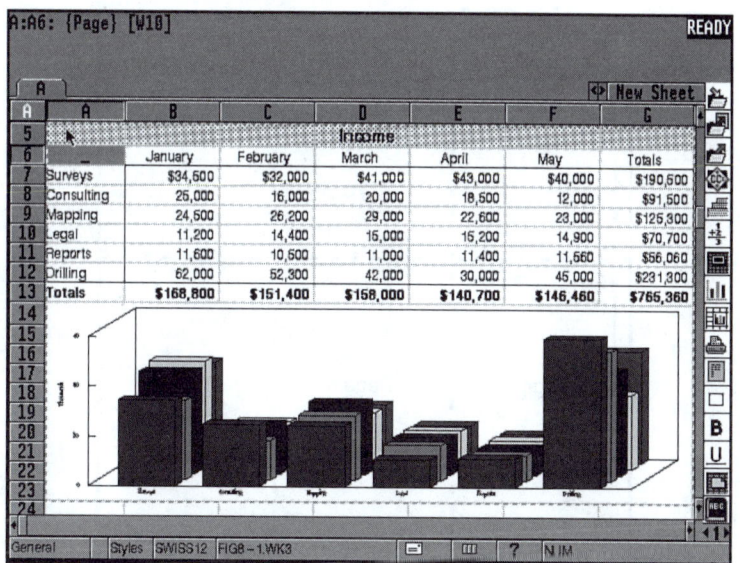

Fig. 8.9
A print range that includes worksheet data and an embedded graphic.

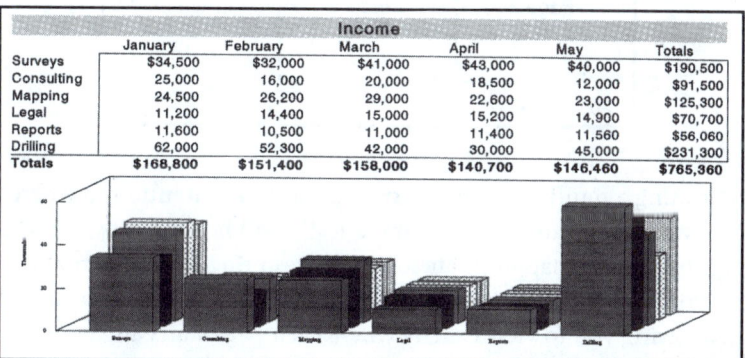

Fig. 8.10
A graph printed in report data.

Printing Multiple-Page Reports

If a print range contains more rows or columns than can fit on a single page, 1-2-3 automatically prints the report on multiple pages. Figure 8.11 shows how 1-2-3 breaks a print range (from cells A1 through X150) into pages.

370 Chapter 8—Printing Reports

Fig. 8.11
A large print range is automatically printed on multiple pages.

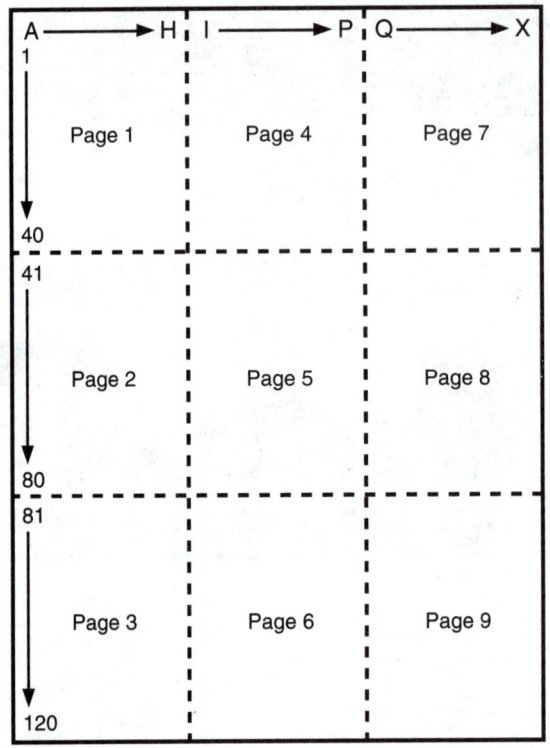

▶ "Using Multiple-Worksheet Files," p. 458

When printing a multiple-page report, you must pay attention to where 1-2-3 splits the worksheet into pages, both vertically and horizontally. 1-2-3 sometimes splits pages at inappropriate locations, resulting in reports that are hard to read. Print ranges set with the **:P**rint command display page breaks on-screen, allowing you to view exactly where each page starts and ends. By checking these visible page breaks, you can address any pagination problems before printing on paper.

Using Horizontal Page Breaks
After filling the area between the top and bottom margins, 1-2-3 automatically inserts horizontal page breaks between worksheet rows; the row just before a horizontal page break is printed at the bottom of one page, and the row just below the break is printed at the top of the next page. The **:P**rint command prints 51 lines formatted with the default Wysiwyg font. Using a different font size affects the number of lines printed on a page. Frequently, you will want to override 1-2-3's choice of page breaks. To improve the readability of the report, you can insert a horizontal page break into the worksheet.

To insert a page break using 1-2-3 commands, first move the cell pointer to the first column in the print range and then to the row in which you want the new page to begin. Use the **:Worksheet Page Row** command to start a new page at the top of the row in which the cell pointer is located. The dotted lines in figure 8.12 show the page break on-screen. To remove the page break, use the **:Worksheet Page Delete** command.

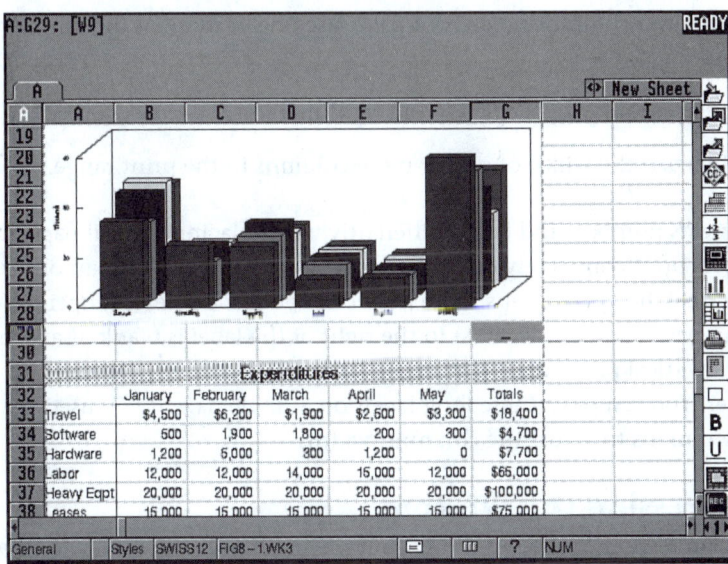

Fig. 8.12
A page break inserted with the **:Worksheet Page Row** command.

Using Vertical Page Breaks

1-2-3 always places vertical page breaks between worksheet columns. The number of columns that print across a page is determined by the widths of the worksheet columns, the width of the page, and the fonts used in the worksheet. During printing, the column that extends past the right margin is made the first column on the next page.

The 1-2-3 default settings print eight columns per page. A range that includes more (or wider) columns prints on multiple pages. Vertical page breaks are also visible on-screen.

To select the first column for a new page, use the **:Worksheet Page** command. Move the cell pointer to the column that you want to start the new page; then select **:Worksheet Page Column**. The page break line appears at the left side of the column where the cell pointer is located.

To increase the number of columns that print on a page, use one or more of the following options:

- Decrease the size of the side margins. (Use the :Print Layout Margins command.)
- Decrease the width of one or more columns in the print range.

To print fewer columns on a given page, use one or more of the following options:

- Increase the size of the left and right margins.
- Increase the width of one or more columns in the print range.

◀ "Setting Column Widths," p. 121

1-2-3 treats numbers and labels differently when placing vertical page breaks. Numbers print completely on a single page because they can span only one cell. A label, however, spans more than one cell if the label is longer than the column width and if the cell(s) to the right of the label is blank. If a label spans a vertical page break, part of the label prints on one page and part on another. You can print these long labels on a single page if you used the preceding options to adjust the columns' widths.

Compressing the Printout

The **C**ompression option on the **L**ayout menu offers an ideal way to fit a large worksheet onto one page. Rather than guess at the font size or column widths needed to print a report on a single page, you can use the **:P**rint Layout **C**ompression **A**utomatic command. The **:P**rint command then determines how much the font size needs to be reduced. A worksheet cannot be reduced to less than 15 percent of its original size. If a print range is too large for the maximum reduction 1-2-3 allows, the worksheet will print on multiple pages.

Compressed type doesn't look any different on-screen. The dashed lines around the print range accurately reflect the page breaks. **:P**rint still uses all manual page breaks that you have entered with **:W**orksheet **P**age for pagination. If you don't want these page breaks in the compressed printout, delete them before printing. To view the compressed page before it prints, use the **:P**rint **P**review command.

The **C**ompression command also offers a **M**anual option; you can enter a reduction or enlargement percentage. To reduce the type, enter a number greater than or equal to 15 but less than 100. To spread the type across and down the page, enter a number greater than 100.

To remove the automatic or manual compression factors you have entered, use the **:P**rint **L**ayout **C**ompression **N**one command.

Printing Three-Dimensional Print Ranges

For many reports, a single two-dimensional print range, like those used in the preceding examples, is all you need. You can create a print job, however, that includes more than one two-dimensional range in one or more worksheets, one or more three-dimensional ranges, or a combination of these.

You specify a three-dimensional print range just as you specify a two-dimensional range—by entering cell addresses or an assigned range name or by pointing. When pointing, remember that Ctrl+PgUp and Ctrl+PgDn are used to move up and down through active worksheets. You also can click the Next Worksheet and Previous Worksheet SmartIcons to specify multiple-worksheet print ranges. Figure 8.13 shows a worksheet with a three-dimensional print range selected.

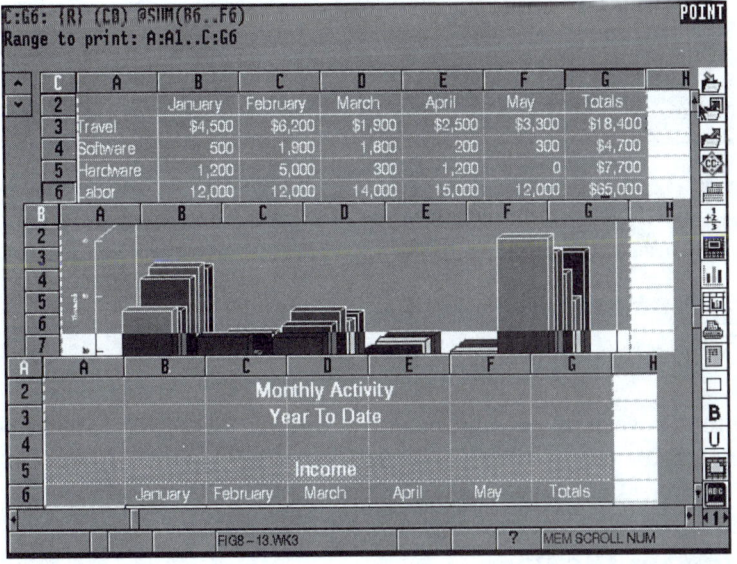

Fig. 8.13
A worksheet with a three-dimensional print range selected.

Printing Multiple Ranges

It also is possible to enter multiple print ranges in a single **:P**rint **R**ange **S**et command. Enter the address or name for each range as you would enter a single print range but with an argument separator between the ranges. Use either the semicolon (;) or the comma (,) as an argument separator. Each range is enclosed in the dashed borders. Notice that the inner edges of the print ranges have smaller dashes than the outer edges. The smaller dashes indicate that the print range continues and isn't the beginning or end of a page. Figure 8.14 shows two specified ranges. The first range is surrounded by the dotted lines, and the second range is highlighted.

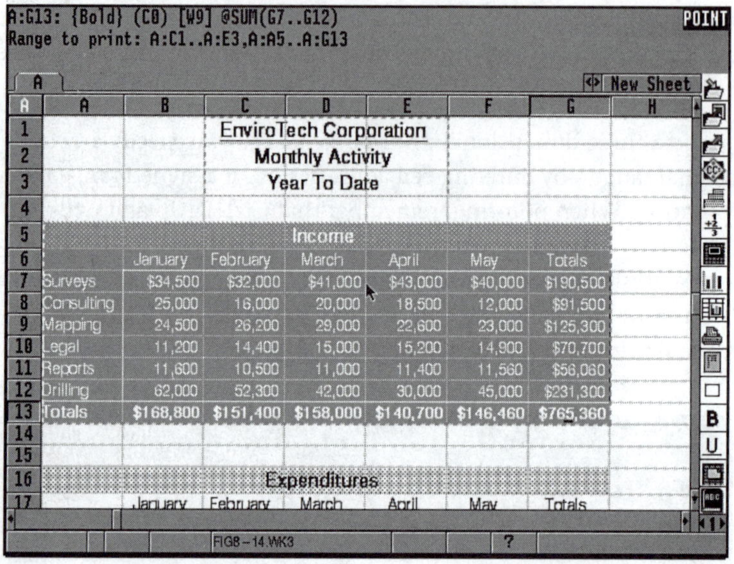

Fig. 8.14
Multiple print ranges specified with the **:P**rint menu.

Tip
If you frequently use the same set of ranges, use named ranges for easier input.

You can specify any combination of two- and three-dimensional ranges. The following examples are valid multiple print ranges:

   A:A1..A:H10;B:C5..B:E12;C:C1..C:D5

   A:A1..C:D10;A:F10..D:H20;C:C1..C:H10

In a print job, each range prints below the last, in the order specified when you entered the ranges. If you prefer to have each range on a separate page, insert page breaks at the bottom of each range.

Setting Up the Page

Use the **:P**rint **L**ayout command to fine-tune the page layout. Figure 8.15 shows the **:P**rint **L**ayout menu and the Wysiwyg Print Dialog box. All the Layout settings are located in the upper half of the screen. Although many of these layout options are in both the **:P**rint and the **/P**rint commands, they apply only to the command in which they are set. Headers, footers, margins, and borders that you enter with **/P**rint don't transfer into the **:P**rint command. The following sections explain how to use the various options on the Layout menu.

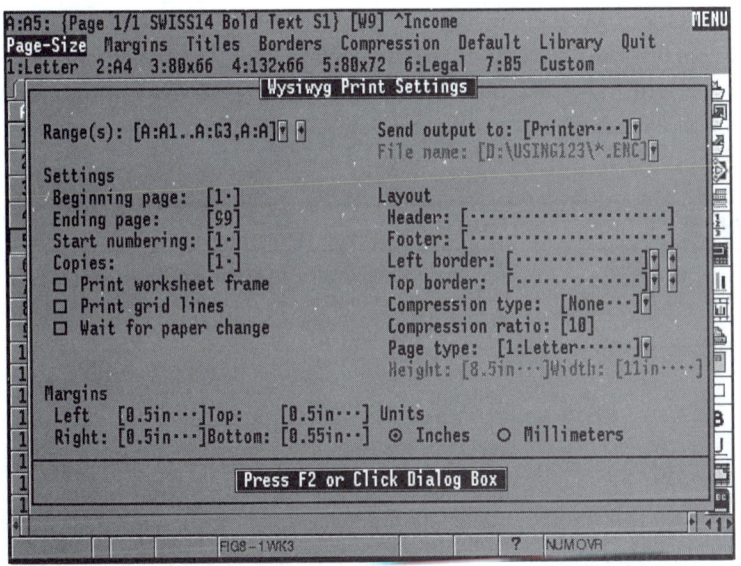

Fig. 8.15
The :Print Layout menu shown above the :Print dialog box.

Defining the Page Layout

The default page size is standard letter size (8 1/2 inches by 11 inches). You can use **:P**rint **L**ayout **P**age-Size to select from several predetermined sizes, or, if the paper size doesn't fall in any of the predefined dimensions, select **Cu**stom. The **C**ustom option lets you define the page width and page length as any size you need. Enter the size in either inches or millimeters. The current unit of measurement appears in the lower right corner of the **L**ayout screen. To change to a different unit of measurement, type **mm** (millimeters) or **in** (inches) after the number.

The **:P**rint **L**ayout **M**argins option is similar to the **/P**rint command but with several important differences. In the **:P**rint command, all margins are entered in inches, millimeters, or centimeters. If you enter a number in centimeters (for example, **1cm**), it is automatically converted into millimeters (10mm). In **/P**rint the right and left margins represent numbers of characters, and the top and bottom margins represent lines.

Specifying Headers and Footers

The **:P**rint **L**ayout **T**itles command allows you to set headers and footers for the printed pages. A header is a one-line title at the top of every page; a footer is a line that prints at the bottom of each page. You don't see headers or footers on-screen with Wysiwyg unless you preview the print range with **:P**rint **P**review.

1-2-3 provides special characters you can include in a header or footer. These characters print the page number, the current date, or the contents of a worksheet cell. 1-2-3 also provides special characters to control the positioning of text within a header or footer. The following table lists these special characters.

Character	Function
#	Automatically prints page numbers, starting with 1 by default. This character can be overridden by the **:P**rint **S**ettings **S**tart-Number command.
@	Automatically inserts the current system date (in the form 25-Jun-95).
|	Separates the header area into three areas, left-justified, centered, and right-justified. If this character isn't present, the entire header or footer is left-justified. Text to the right of the first | is centered. Text to the right of a second | is right-justified.
\	When followed by a cell address or range name, this character fills the header or footer with the contents of the indicated cell.

Figure 8.16 shows a header created using these special characters. The date appears on the left, the company name is centered on the page, and the page number appears on the right. To add this header, select **:P**rint **L**ayout **T**itles. At the prompt, type the following string and then press Enter:

```
@¦EnviroTech¦Page - #
```

Whenever the print range is too large to fit on a single page, 1-2-3 places the header on each succeeding page and increases the page number by one.

◄ "Using Formatting Sequences," p. 333

You can format headers and footers set with the **:P**rint command by including formatting sequences in the text string. To print an entire header in boldface, for example, press Ctrl+A to begin the formatting sequence, type **b** for boldface, and then type the rest of the header.

Wysiwyg reserves three lines on the printout for each header and footer. Remember to add these extra lines when you calculate the number of lines of text to place on a printed page. Unlike the **/P**rint command, **:P**rint doesn't reserve lines for titles if you don't have any titles. To delete headers or footers, use the **:P**rint **L**ayout **T**itles **C**lear command.

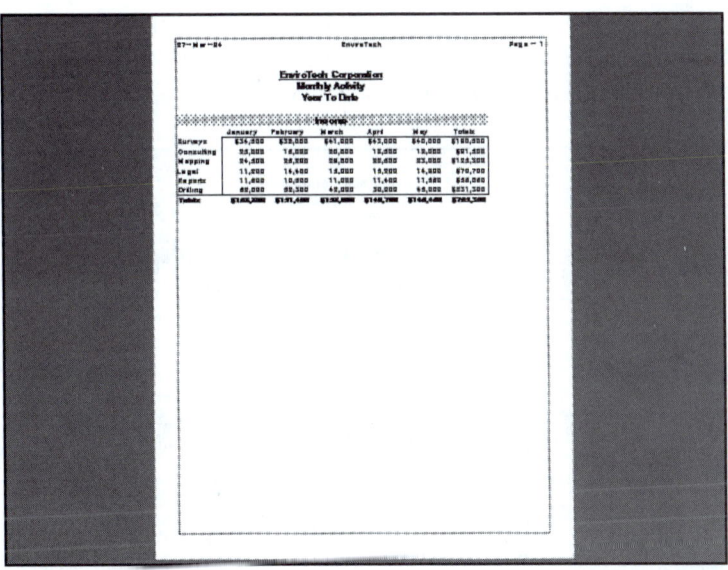

Fig. 8.16
A header that includes the date, the company name, and the page number.

Specifying Print Borders

When a range of data continues beyond the first page, it can be difficult after the first page to tell which row or column a given bit of data is in. To make a report easier to understand, 1-2-3 makes it possible to specify certain rows and/or columns to be printed on every page as print borders.

Designate columns and rows to be *borders* with the **:P**rint **L**ayout **B**orders command. (This command functions the same as the **/P**rint **P**rinter **O**ptions **B**orders command.) The **L**eft command allows you to choose one or more columns to appear at the left margin of every page. The **B**orders **T**op command designates one or more rows of labels that print at the top of every page, identifying the columns on the page. Setting borders in a printout is analogous to freezing titles in the worksheet: **B**orders **L**eft produces a border like a frozen vertical title display, and **B**orders **T**op produces a border like a frozen horizontal title display.

Tip
Remember that the print range and the border range must not include any of the same cells, or the borders will print twice. To cancel borders, select **:P**rint **L**ayout **B**orders **C**lear.

Printing the Worksheet Frame

In addition to printing worksheet borders, you can include the worksheet frame in the printout (the row numbers located on the left of the screen and the column letters located at the top).

To include the worksheet frame (vertical row numbers and horizontal column letters) on each page of the printed report, select **:P**rint **S**ettings **F**rame **Y**es. Each page then includes the worksheet frame (see fig. 8.17). To turn off the frame, select **:Print Settings Frame No**. The **Frame** option is particularly useful during worksheet development when you want printouts to show the location of data and formulas within a large worksheet.

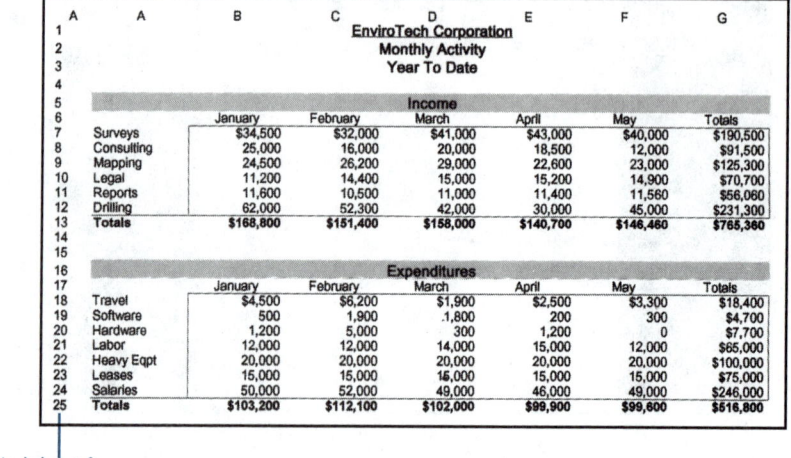

Fig. 8.17
The worksheet frame printed with a report.

Worksheet frame

Saving and Restoring Layout Settings

The **:Print Layout Default** and **Layout Library** commands can modify all the layout settings at once. To clear any print layout changes you have made and return all the layout settings to the default values, select **:Print Layout Default Restore**. If you are constantly changing the layout settings to the same values, consider changing the default settings permanently to those currently displayed by using **:Print Layout Default Update**. All worksheets you create in the future will automatically start with these modified layout values.

Use **:Print Layout Library** to save the layout settings to a disk file. If you need certain combinations of layout settings for different types of worksheets, you can save each group of settings and then retrieve them to use later with any worksheet.

To save the current page-layout settings in a library file, use **:Print Layout Library Save** and specify a file name. 1-2-3 gives the file the extension AL3. When you want to use the settings with another worksheet, use **:Print Layout Library Retrieve**. If you no longer need a library file, delete it by using **:Print Layout Library Erase**.

Choosing the Print Orientation

One way to deal with a print range that is too wide to fit on a page is to use Print Compression to squeeze a range onto a page. An alternative to Print Compression is the **:P**rint **C**onfig **O**rientation command. With this command you can specify whether the output is printed in **L**andscape or **P**ortrait mode. In **P**ortrait mode (the default), the lines of text are printed on the paper in the usual manner; the shorter side of the page is at the top and bottom. In **L**andscape mode, the page is horizontal, and the lines of text are printed sideways on the page (see fig. 8.18). Landscape printing is useful for fitting wide worksheets onto single pages. The **:P**rint command can print text in landscape orientation on most dot-matrix and laser printers. To print using landscape orientation, use **:P**rint **C**onfig **O**rientation **L**andscape.

Fig. 8.18
Printing in landscape orientation, using the **:P**rint command.

Specifying Other Print Settings

Use the **:P**rint **S**ettings command to control page numbering, ranges of pages to print, the number of copies to print, print pausing, and the printing of the worksheet grid or frame. The **:P**rint **S**ettings menu offers the options listed in the following chart.

Menu Item	Description
Begin and **E**nd	Prints the specified page numbers. Normally, Wysiwyg prints the entire range specified in **:P**rint **R**ange **S**et. If you want to print only selected pages in the range (for instance, only the ones that changed from a previous printing), set the **B**egin and **E**nd options accordingly.

(continues)

Menu Item	Description
Start-Number	Specifies the first page number to be printed in a title. The page number is inserted where the # symbol appears in the header or footer. If you are printing a document from several different worksheets, for example, use this option to specify the first page number of each subdocument so that the page numbers are continuous. The default setting is 1.
Copies	Prints the specified number of copies. The default setting is 1.
Wait	Pauses the printer between pages. The default setting is **N**o. If you want to feed individual sheets into the printer, select **Y**es to pause the printer before each new page. Use this option if you selected the **M**anual option for **:P**rint **C**onfig **B**in. If you set **W**ait to **Y**es, the message Insert next sheet of paper and select Resume appears at the bottom of the screen before you print each page.
Grid	Produces a printout that looks like ledger paper, with dotted lines enclosing every cell on the printout. This option prints grid lines throughout the printout. If you want to enclose only part of a printout in a grid, use **:F**ormat **L**ines **A**ll and specify a range.
Frame	Prints the column letters at the top of each page and the row numbers to the left of the print range if the **F**rame setting is on. Use this option for draft copies.
Reset	Restores the default **:P**rint settings for the document.
Quit	Leaves the **:P**rint **S**ettings menu.

Excluding Worksheet Areas from the Printout

Although you can print only rectangular blocks from the worksheet, you can suppress the display of cell contents within the range. You can eliminate one or more rows, exclude one or more columns, or remove from view a segment that occupies only part of a row or column. When printed with the default settings, each of the examples discussed here prints on one page.

To avoid printing some worksheet rows, set multiple print ranges in the **:P**rint command. See the earlier section "Printing Multiple Ranges" for more information on this technique.

You can use the **/W**orksheet **C**olumn **H**ide command to indicate columns that you don't want displayed on-screen. If these marked columns are included in a print range, they won't appear on the printout.

To restore the columns, select **/W**orksheet **C**olumn **D**isplay. When the hidden columns (marked with an asterisk) reappear on-screen, you can specify which column or columns to display by highlighting them and pressing Enter.

If you want to hide only part of a row or column, or an area that spans one or more rows and columns, you can use the **/R**ange **F**ormat **H**idden command to hide the data in the ranges.

▶ "Hiding Worksheet Data," p. 516

You also can hide a row by including two pipe symbols (||) in the leftmost cell of the print range. The entire row will be eliminated from the printed result.

> **Note**
> Hiding columns completely removes the column from view. For instance, if you hide column B, column A appears next to column C. However, using the Hidden format only hides the cell contents of the formatted range, but the empty column remains visible.

Using the /Print Commands

The **/P**rint command offers most of the same functions the **:P**rint command offers but doesn't offer the printing formats applied to the worksheet. For this reason, you will probably use the **:P**rint command most frequently. **/P**rint commands do meet some specific needs, however, that the **:P**rint command doesn't. This section gives an overview of the **/P**rint commands and focuses on capabilities that aren't included with the **:P**rint menu.

The **/P**rint menu is one of the most complex menus in 1-2-3. The menu is complex because 1-2-3 gives you considerable control over the design of printed output—from simple one-page reports to longer reports that incorporate data from many worksheets and that include sophisticated graphs. The **/P**rint **O**ptions menu offers additional commands that you can use to design and enhance reports, to control the printer, and to set headers and footers, margins, and page length.

▶ "Printing Graphs with the /Print Command," p. 741

Although earlier versions of 1-2-3 required the use of a separate program to print graphs, you now can print graphs from both the **/P**rint and **:P**rint menus. For more information about printing graphs, see "Printing a Graph with Text" later in this chapter.

▶ "Including Graphs in Reports," p. 746

Understanding the /Print Menu

You must start any **/P**rint command sequence from the 1-2-3 command menu. After choosing **/P**rint, you must select one of the first four options: **P**rinter, **F**ile, **E**ncoded, or **B**ackground. You use the next three options—**S**uspend, **R**esume, and **C**ancel—only when a print job is in progress. These options are covered later in the chapter. The seventh option, **Q**uit, returns you to READY mode.

To send a report directly to the current printer, select **P**rinter. (See "Choosing the Printer" later in this chapter for details on how to specify a printer.)

To create a text file on disk, select **F**ile. A text file can contain data but no graphs or special printer codes. You can print a text file from the operating system prompt, or you can use a text file with other programs, such as a word processing program.

You can create a file to be printed later in the **E**ncoded option. The section "Printing to an Encoded File" describes this option in detail.

The **B**ackground option allows you to continue working while a file is printing. This option is explained in more detail in the section "Using Background Printing."

If you select **F**ile, **E**ncoded, or **B**ackground, you must respond to the prompt for a file name by typing a name that contains up to eight characters. Although you don't need to add a file extension because 1-2-3 automatically assigns the PRN (print file) or ENC (encoded file) extension, you can specify a different extension if you want.

Throughout this section, this menu is referred to as the **/P**rint [**P,F,E,B**] menu. The notation **/P**rint [**P,F,E,B**] indicates that options on this menu are available when you select **/P**rint **P**rinter, **/P**rint **F**ile, **/P**rint **E**ncoded, or **/P**rint **B**ackground.

After choosing a destination, 1-2-3 displays the **/P**rint dialog box (see fig. 8.19). This dialog box displays all the settings for the **/P**rint command.

The following table shows the options offered by the **/P**rint [**P,F,E,B**] menu.

Menu Item	Description
Range	Indicates the section(s) of the worksheet to be printed.
Line	Advances the paper in the printer by one line.
Page	Advances the paper in the printer to the top of the next page.

Menu Item	Description
Options	Changes default print settings and offers a number of print enhancements.
Clear	Erases some or all of the previously entered print settings.
Align	Signals that the paper in the printer is set to the beginning of a page.
Go	Starts printing.
Image	Selects a graph to print.
Hold	Returns to READY mode without closing the current print job.
Quit	Exits from the **P**rint menu and closes the current print job.

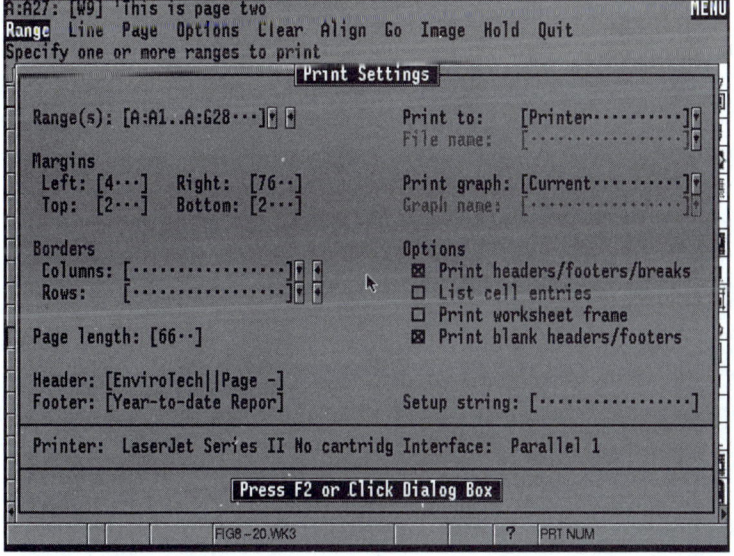

Fig. 8.19
The /**P**rint dialog box.

In 1-2-3, the most frequently used commands are usually on the left side of a menu. In any print command sequence, you start with /**P**rint; branch to **P**rinter, **F**ile, **E**ncoded, or **B**ackground; and then proceed to the next menu. Regardless of which branch you select, you must specify a **R**ange to print, select **G**o to begin printing, and then select **Q**uit or press Esc twice to return to the worksheet. All other selections are optional.

Although you aren't required to select **A**lign, you should do so before you start a new print job. Selecting **A**lign ensures that printing begins at the top of all succeeding pages after the first page. Make sure that you reposition the printer paper and use the **A**lign command whenever you have aborted a print job.

You use **P**age to move the paper to the top of the next page. **P**age also can be used to eject a blank page, making it easier for you to tear off the last page of a report.

Setting Defaults for the /Print Command

As discussed earlier in the chapter, the **/W**orksheet **G**lobal **D**efault **P**rinter command sets the defaults for printing. Two menu choices, **I**nterface and **N**ame, affect both the **/P**rint and the **:P**rint commands. The other commands set the defaults for only the **/P**rint command. This section discusses these other settings.

The AutoLf setting specifies the printer's end-of-line procedure. **Y**es indicates that the paper is automatically advanced one line when the printer receives a carriage return; **N**o means that a line is *not* automatically advanced when the printer receives a carriage return. With most printers, you should leave AutoLf in its default setting of **N**o. To determine whether the setting is correct, you can print a range of two or more rows. If the output is double-spaced or if the paper doesn't advance between lines, just change AutoLf to the opposite setting.

For laying out pages for printing, you must consider the length and width of the paper in the printer and the left, right, top, and bottom margins. The **/P**rint command controls these settings through lines and text characters, not inches or centimeters.

The key measurements are the number of lines that print on one page (lines per inch), and the number of characters per line. The default page length is 66 lines, for 11-inch-long paper and a printer output of 6 lines per inch. The page length for laser printers should be set to 60 lines. The default line length is 80 characters (1/4 inch at either edge of the paper isn't available for printing) for 8 1/2-inch-wide paper and a printer output of 10 characters per inch. Because of 1-2-3's default margin settings (2-line margins at the top and bottom, and 4-character margins at the right and left), the full page width and length aren't used. To maximize the amount of information per printed page, set the top, bottom, and left margins to 0; set the right margin to the maximum (1000).

The options on the **/W**orksheet **G**lobal **D**efault **P**rinter menu determine default page-layout characteristics.

Menu Item	Description	Setting Range	Default Setting
Left	Default left margin	0..1000	4
Right	Default right margin	0..1000	76
Top	Default top margin	0..240	2
Bottom	Default bottom margin	0..240	2
Pg-Length	Default lines per page	1..1000	66

Both the left and right margins refer to the number of characters from the left edge of the paper. To calculate the width of the report, subtract the left margin setting (4) from the right margin setting (76). The report is printed with 72 characters per line.

The easiest way to see how many lines appear on a printed page with the **/P**rint command is to use **/D**ata **F**ill to fill column A from row 1 to row 100. Use **/P**rint to print that filled range. The last number printed at the bottom of the first page is the number of rows that will be printed on each page.

The number of lines printed on a page is determined by the number of lines 1-2-3 uses for margins and titles. If you are using all default settings, the actual number of worksheet lines (or rows) that print is usually 56. 1-2-3 reserves two lines for the top and bottom margins (a total of four lines) and reserves three lines each for the header and footer, one line for text, and two lines to separate the title from the regular page data (a total of six lines). The lines are reserved for the header and footer even if you don't supply a header or footer (unless you select **/P**rint [**P**,**F**,**E**,**B**] **O**ptions **O**ther **B**lank-Header **S**uppress). Because the default page length is 66, you subtract 10 lines reserved for the margins, header, and footer to get 56 lines printed. (For more information about including headers and footers in printed reports, refer to "Creating Headers and Footers" on the following page.)

The final three options for default printer settings control the way paper is fed to the printer (**W**ait), printer codes (**S**etup), and the specific printer you use (**N**ame).

If you are using continuous-feed paper or a sheet-feeder bin, don't change the **W**ait option's default setting of **N**o. If you are hand-feeding single sheets of paper, select **Y**es to change the default setting; printing pauses at the end of each page so that you can insert a new sheet of paper. After you insert the page, select **/P**rint **R**esume to continue printing.

The default setting for **S**etup is no setup string. No special printer-control features, such as italic or double-striking, are in effect. (For more information about setup strings, see the section "Using Setup Strings" later in this chapter.)

Remember that if you use the **/W**orksheet **G**lobal **D**efault **P**rinter command to change print settings, the new settings remain in effect for the current work session. For 1-2-3 to use the new settings as the default settings, you must use the **/W**orksheet **G**lobal **D**efault **U**pdate command to save the changes permanently.

Designing Reports

As indicated earlier in the chapter, you can use the **/W**orksheet **G**lobal **D**efault **P**rinter command to change the default print settings. 1-2-3 provides, however, another method for changing the print settings. You can use the **/P**rint [**P,F,E,B**] **O**ptions menu. The **M**argins, **S**etup, and **P**g-Length options override the settings in **/W**orksheet **G**lobal **D**efault **P**rinter. The **H**eader, **F**ooter, and **B**orders settings are unique to this menu; they are provided to help you improve the readability of reports. Two selections, **O**ther and **N**ame, lead to other menus containing a number of options for designing reports and naming and saving the current settings. All these menu items are discussed in this section.

One menu item—**A**dvanced—leads to additional menus with options for enhancing worksheets for printing and for controlling the printer. These **A**dvanced options are discussed later in the chapter in the section "Enhancing Reports."

The print settings you select are saved with the worksheet file when you use **/F**ile **S**ave. When you retrieve the file, the settings are still in effect. You also can save sets of printer options with the **N**ame command, discussed in the section "Naming and Saving the Current Print Settings."

Creating Headers and Footers

On each page printed by the **/P**rint command, 1-2-3 reserves three lines for a header and an additional three lines for a footer. You can either retain the six lines (regardless of whether you use them) or eliminate all six lines by selecting **O**ther **B**lank-Header **S**uppress from the **/P**rint [**P,F,E,B**] **O**ptions menu. This option is discussed later in the chapter.

The header text, printed on the first line after the current top-margin lines, is followed by two blank header lines (for spacing). The footer text line is printed above the current bottom-margin line; above it are two blank footer lines (for spacing).

Both the **H**eader or **F**ooter options can specify up to 512 characters of text on one line. Portions of the header or footer can be positioned at the left, right, or center of the page. The length of the header or footer, however, cannot exceed the page width.

You can use the **/P**rint [**P,F,E,B**], **O**ptions **H**eader or **F**ooter command to enter the text string. The special characters described earlier for date, page number, and spacing also work in the **/P**rint command.

Specifying Formatted or Unformatted Output

Selecting **U**nformatted from the **/P**rint [**P,F,E,B**] **O**ptions **O**ther menu suppresses the printing of headers, footers, and page breaks. Unformatted output is often appropriate when you are using **/P**rint **F**ile to create a data file to be imported by another program, such as a word processing program. You select **F**ormatted to turn the headers, footers, and page breaks back on.

Using the Blank-Header Option

Whether or not you create a header or footer, 1-2-3 reserves three blank lines at the top and at the bottom of each page for a header and footer. The **B**lank-Header option from the **/P**rint [**P,F,E,B**] **O**ptions **O**ther menu allows you to eliminate these six lines when no header or footer has been specified. (You cannot suppress blank lines at only the top or only the bottom of the page.) With the **S**uppress option, 1-2-3 can print six more lines of data per page. Selecting **B**lank-Header **P**rint reinstates the six blank lines.

Printing a Listing of Cell Contents

To print cell contents instead of cell values, select **C**ell-Formulas from the **/P**rint [**P,F,E,B**] **O**ptions **O**ther menu. Choosing **C**ell-Formulas produces a printout that consists of one line for each cell in the print range. The line shows the cell's width and format (if different from the default), protection status, and contents. By subsequently selecting **A**s-Displayed, you restore the default setting that prints the range as it appears on-screen.

Chapter 8—Printing Reports

> **Note**
>
> Developing and debugging a complex worksheet can take days of hard work. You should safeguard all work, of course, by making backup disk copies of important files. For both backup and reference purposes, you also can make regular printouts of a worksheet's cell contents, including formulas and formatting information.

Figure 8.20 shows a partial printout of **C**ell-Formulas from the worksheet in figure 8.14. Notice that within the specified print range, all the cells in the first row are listed before the cells in the next row.

Fig. 8.20
A listing of cell contents produced with the **C**ell-Formulas option.

```
A:A1: {Page 1/2 SWISS14 Bold U1 Text} [W10] ^EnviroTech Corporation
A:A2: {Page SWISS14 Bold Text} [W10] ^Monthly Activity
A:A3: {Page SWISS14 Bold Text} [W10] ^Year To Date
A:A5: {Page SWISS14 Bold Text S1} [W10] ^Income
A:B6: [W9] ^January
A:C6: [W9] ^February
A:D6: [W9] ^March
A:E6: [W9] ^April
A:F6: [W9] ^May
A:G6: [W9] ^Totals
A:A7: {Page} [W10] 'Surveys
A:B7: {LT} (C0) [W9] 34500
A:C7: {T} (C0) [W9] 32000
A:D7: {T} (C0) [W9] 41000
A:E7: {T} (C0) [W9] 43000
A:F7: {T} (C0) [W9] 40000
A:G7: {RT} (C0) [W9] @SUM(B7..F7)
A:A8: {Page} [W10] 'Consulting
A:B8: {L} (,0) [W9] 25000
A:C8: (,0) [W9] 16000
A:D8: (,0) [W9] 20000
A:E8: (,0) [W9] 18500
A:F8: (,0) [W9] 12000
A:G8: {R} (C0) [W9] @SUM(B8..F8)
A:A9: {Page} [W10] 'Mapping
A:B9: {L} (,0) [W9] 24500
A:C9: (,0) [W9] 26200
A:D9: (,0) [W9] 29000
A:E9: (,0) [W9] 22600
A:F9: (,0) [W9] 23000
A:G9: {R} (C0) [W9] @SUM(B9..F9)
A:A10: {Page} [W10] 'Legal
A:B10: {L} (,0) [W9] 11200
A:C10: (,0) [W9] 14400
A:D10: (,0) [W9] 15000
A:E10: (,0) [W9] 15200
A:F10: (,0) [W9] 14900
A:G10: {R} (C0) [W9] @SUM(B10..F10)
A:A11: {Page} [W10] 'Reports
A:B11: {L} (,0) [W9] 11600
A:C11: (,0) [W9] 10500
A:D11: (,0) [W9] 11000
A:E11: (,0) [W9] 11400
A:F11: (,0) [W9] 11560
A:G11: {R} (C0) [W9] @SUM(B11..F11)
A:A12: {Page B} [W10] 'Drilling
A:B12: {LB} (,0) [W9] 62000
A:C12: {B} (,0) [W9] 52300
A:D12: {B} (,0) [W9] 42000
A:E12: {B} (,0) [W9] 30000
A:F12: {B} (,0) [W9] 45000
A:G12: {RB} (C0) [W9] @SUM(B12..F12)
A:A13: {Page Bold} (C2) [W10] 'Totals
A:B13: {Bold} (C0) [W9] @SUM(B7..B12)
A:C13: {Bold} (C0) [W9] @SUM(C7..C12)
```

The information within parentheses indicates a range format established independently of the global format in effect. The (C0) in cell B7, for example, indicates that the cell was formatted using a **/R**ange **F**ormat command and **C**urrency, with zero decimal places. Information within square brackets indicates a column width set independently of the global column width in effect. The [W10] in cell A2, for example, indicates that column G was set specifically to be 10 characters wide. The {LT} in cell B7 means lines have been placed at the left and top of that cell.

Cell contents are printed after the information for range format and column width. The formula in cell B13, for example, results in $168,800 for January Totals.

Setting the Page Layout
To change the page layout of the current worksheet, you use the **/P**rint [**P,F,E,B**] **O**ptions menu. If you want to change the margins, select **M**argins and then select **L**eft, **R**ight, **T**op, **B**ottom, or **N**one from the menu. The following table indicates the message for each menu item.

Menu Item	Message
Left	Set left margin (0..1000):*xx*
Right	Set right margin (0..1000):*xx*
Top	Set top margin (0..240):*xx*
Bottom	Set bottom margin (0..240):*xx*
None	Clear all margin settings

The numbers in parentheses are the minimum and maximum for each margin setting. The *xx* at the end of each line denotes the current setting that you can change. Selecting **N**one sets the left, top, and bottom margins to 0 and the right margin to 1000. Before you make any changes, review the section "Understanding the Default Print Settings" at the beginning of this chapter.

Be sure that you set left and right margins that are consistent with the width of the paper and the established pitch (characters per inch). The right margin must be greater than the left margin. Make sure also that the settings for the top and bottom margins are consistent with the paper's length and the established number of lines per inch.

The specified page length must not be less than the top margin *plus* the header lines *plus* one line of data *plus* the footer lines *plus* the bottom margin—unless you use /**P**rint [**P,F,E,B**] **O**ptions **O**ther **U**nformatted to suppress all formatting. To maximize the output on every printed page of a large worksheet, you can combine the **U**nformatted option with commands that condense printing and increase the number of lines per inch.

Enhancing Reports

Now that you have examined the **:P**rint and the /**P**rint menu options for designing reports, you should become familiar with the menu options for enhancing printed reports. The /**P**rint [**P,E,B**] **O**ptions **A**dvanced menu offers a number of enhancements. These same enhancements also are available through the **:F**ormat command. The Wysiwyg add-in offers the additional advantage of allowing you to see enhancements on the worksheet exactly as they will appear on the printed page. Wysiwyg also offers greater flexibility in formatting with fonts and colors. See Chapter 6, "Making Your Worksheets Dazzle," for complete information on the formatting capabilities in Wysiwyg.

Improving the Layout

With the /**P**rint [**P,E,B**] **O**ptions **A**dvanced **L**ayout menu, you can specify the *pitch* (character spacing), line spacing, and orientation of printed pages. These options customize the layout of reports.

Changing the Pitch

The *pitch* affects character size and, thus, the number of characters printed on each line. The choices available with the **P**itch option are **S**tandard, **C**ompressed, and **E**xpanded. Again, the actual effect of each of these options depends on the printer. Typical pitch settings are 5 characters per inch (cpi) for **E**xpanded, 10 cpi for **S**tandard, and 17 cpi for **C**ompressed. You don't see the pitch change on-screen. However, you can see the pitch change on-screen while in Wysiwyg.

Changing Line Spacing

The **L**ine-Spacing options are **S**tandard (the default) and **C**ompressed. Like pitch, the line spacing with each of these options depends on the printer. For many printers, **S**tandard spacing is six lines per inch, and **C**ompressed spacing is eight lines per inch. Changing line spacing also affects the number of lines printed on each page.

Selecting Fonts

With the **/P**rint **[P,E,B] O**ptions **A**dvanced **F**onts option, you can specify the fonts, or type styles, used to print different sections of each page.

The **/P**rint command offers eight different fonts, numbered as follows:

1. Normal serif
2. Bold serif
3. Italic serif
4. Bold italic serif
5. Normal sans serif
6. Bold sans serif
7. Italic sans serif
8. Bold Italic sans serif

> **Tip**
> Fonts are much easier to set and print when selected with the **:F**ormat command.

The number of fonts available to you depends on the printer. Some printers have all eight fonts, and other printers have only one or two.

You can specify different fonts for different areas of the report. After selecting **O**ptions **A**dvanced **F**onts, select one of the following: **R**ange, **H**eader/Footer, **B**order, or **F**rame. 1-2-3 then displays the numbers 1 through 8, corresponding to the preceding fonts. Select the desired font. Selecting **Q**uit returns you to the **O**ptions **A**dvanced menu.

Using Setup Strings

A *setup string* is a code that you send to the printer to change the way portions of the worksheet print, such as compressing the print, underlining, or boldfacing. In 1-2-3, you type a setup string consisting of one or more backslashes (\), followed by a three-digit decimal number corresponding to the desired code. Some codes have multiple strings (for example, \027\069). Because different printers use different codes, you need to refer to the printer manual (look for such topics as "escape codes" or "printer control codes"). A setup string has a maximum length of 512 characters.

Setup strings aren't necessary in Wysiwyg because you can specify print characteristics by choosing menu options for any range of cells. You can select **:F**ormat **B**old or **:F**ormat **U**nderline, for example, and then highlight a range. The Wysiwyg **:F**ormat menu makes setting attributes very easy. Setup strings now are necessary only for using specific capabilities of the printer that aren't directly supported by 1-2-3.

You can use one of the following methods to send a setup string from 1-2-3 to the printer:

- Use the /Print [P,E,B] Options Setup command to create a setup string. 1-2-3 sends the setup string to the printer at the start of every print job. The setup string also is saved with the worksheet and used the next time you retrieve the worksheet file.

- Use the /Worksheet Global Default Printer Setup command to create a default setup string which would take effect whenever you use the /Print command in 1-2-3. After typing the setup string, select Update from the /Worksheet Global Default menu to make the new setup string a permanent default. The Options Setup string can be combined with or can override the default setup string, depending on the setup strings used.

- Embed one or more setup strings in the worksheet itself. To use this method, you type two vertical bars (||) and the setup string in the first cell of a blank row in the print range. Because an embedded setup string is sent to the printer only when printing reaches the row that contains the setup string, a setup string can be used to affect only portions of a report. The setup string affects the entire width of all worksheet rows below the row in which the setup string is located. A second setup string can change or cancel the effect of the first string.

To remove a setup string, select **S**etup from the **/P**rint [**P,F,E,B**] **O**ptions menu, press Esc, and then press Enter. Removing a printer code from the **S**etup option, however, doesn't cancel the code in the printer. Even though you have removed the setup string, the printer remembers the last received code until the code's string is canceled. To cancel the previous setup string sent to the printer, you can either turn off the printer or enter a reset code in the **S**etup option. The reset code for a LaserJet printer, for example, is \027E. The printer manual should list the reset and other codes for a printer.

> **Note**
>
> A printer code entered in the **S**etup option affects all output from the current print operation.

Selecting Color

With the **C**olor option on the **/P**rint **P**rinter **O**ptions **A**dvanced menu, you can select from as many as eight colors, depending on the printer, for printed reports. Headers, footers, and the print range are printed in the selected color. If negative numbers are displayed on-screen in red (in other words, if you have selected **/W**orksheet **G**lobal **F**ormat **O**ther **C**olor **N**egative), those numbers are printed in red also, if possible.

◀ "Setting Range and Worksheet Global Formats," p. 280

Controlling the Printer

Some of the print commands deal directly with controlling the printer hardware. You need to understand these commands so that you can create printed reports efficiently.

Choosing the Printer

/Print [**P,F,E,B**] **O**ptions **A**dvanced **D**evice selects the **N**ame and the **I**nterface of the printer to be used. You select **D**evice **N**ame to select from the list of printers selected during the Install procedure. Next, you select **D**evice **I**nterface to indicate the port to which the printer is attached. If the port is a serial port, you also must specify the baud rate.

Controlling the Movement of the Paper

If you print a range containing fewer lines than the default page length, the paper doesn't advance automatically to the top of the next page. If you print a range containing more lines than the default page length, 1-2-3 automatically inserts page breaks between pages, but the paper doesn't advance to the top of the next page after the last page has printed. In both cases, the next print job begins wherever the preceding operation ended.

If you want to advance to a new page after printing less than a full page, select **/P**rint **P**rinter **P**age. Whenever you issue this command, the printer advances to the start of the next page.

To print an existing footer on the last page of a report, use the **P**age command at the end of the printing session. If you select the **Q**uit command from the **P**rint menu without issuing the **P**age command, this final footer doesn't print. If this happens, reissue the **/P**rint **P**rinter command and select **P**age, and the footer prints when the page ejects.

If you want to advance the paper one line at a time (for example, to separate several ranges that fit on one printed page), use the **/P**rint **P**rinter **L**ine command.

When you are using a dot-matrix printer and continuous-feed paper, 1-2-3 must know the position of the perforations between pages if the printed output is to be positioned properly on the paper. The top of a page is initially marked by the print head's position when you turn on the printer and load 1-2-3. At the start of each work session, be sure that the paper is positioned so that the print head is at the top of the page; then turn on the printer.

As printing progresses, both the printer and 1-2-3 maintain internal line counters that indicate the print head's current position on the page. If these two pointers get "out of sync," you are likely to get output that is printed on top of the perforations and blank lines in the middle of pages. If this problem occurs, take the following steps:

1. Turn off the printer.

2. Advance the paper manually until the print head is at the top of a page; then turn the printer back on.

3. Select **A**lign from the **/P**rint **P**rinter menu.

Note that the **A**lign command resets 1-2-3's page number counter. If you are including page numbers in a report, you may want to skip the third step.

To avoid internal line counters becoming "out of sync," don't advance the paper manually—use the **P**age or **L**ine commands. Any lines you advance manually aren't counted by 1-2-3, causing page breaks to appear in unwanted places. To prevent this problem, you should check that the paper is set at the top of the page and then select **A**lign before you select **G**o.

Holding a Print Job

To keep the current print job open and return to 1-2-3 READY mode after you have selected **G**o, select **/P**rint **P**rinter **H**old. In READY mode, you can perform a number of tasks, including the following:

- Importing new data into the worksheet

- Changing column widths, cell formats, or other aspects of the worksheet display

- Modifying **/W**orksheet **G**lobal settings

After finishing the tasks in READY mode, you can return to the **/P**rint [**P**,**F**,**E**,**B**] menu and continue creating the same print job. If you return to READY mode by any means other than **H**old, the current print job closes and is sent to the printer.

Note that **H**old doesn't affect the printer itself. If a print job is in progress—actually printing—the **H**old option doesn't stop the printer. To pause or stop the printer, use **/P**rint **S**uspend or **/P**rint **C**ancel.

Pausing the Printer

You can temporarily pause the printer by invoking the **/P**rint **S**uspend command. Printing pauses as soon as the printer's internal buffer empties. Don't turn the printer off, or you will lose part of the report! You may lose only a few lines or several pages, depending on the printer. Use **/P**rint **S**uspend to perform such tasks as refilling the paper bin or changing the ribbon.

/Print **R**esume restarts printing that was paused in one of the following ways:

- You invoked a **/P**rint **S**uspend command.

- You selected **/P**rint **P**rinter **O**ptions **A**dvanced **W**ait **Y**es or **/W**orksheet **G**lobal **D**efault **P**rinter **W**ait **Y**es, and the printer is at the end of a page, waiting for another sheet of paper.

- A printer error has occurred. After correcting the error, you can invoke **/P**rint **R**esume to clear the error message and resume printing.

Select **W**ait **Y**es if you are hand-feeding paper to the printer; 1-2-3 stops sending data to the printer at the end of each page. The printer pauses, enabling you to insert a new sheet of paper. Selecting **R**esume then continues printing with the next page. This option is different from **S**uspend, which temporarily pauses printing under user control, and from **C**ancel, which permanently ends all print jobs.

Stopping the Printer

After starting one or more print jobs, you may realize that you have made an error in the worksheet data or print settings and that you need to correct the error before the report is printed. Selecting **/P**rint **C**ancel stops the current print job whether in (**/P**rint **P**rinter) or in Wysiwyg (**:P**rint), and removes any other print jobs from the queue. Once you have canceled the current print jobs, you cannot restart them; you must reissue the necessary commands if you decide to print later.

When you select **/P**rint **C**ancel, printing may not stop immediately if the printer has an internal print buffer or if a software print spooler has been installed. Turning off the printer for a few seconds clears the printer buffer.

If printing resumes when you turn the printer back on, a print spooler probably is installed. Refer to the print spooler documentation for instructions on how to flush it.

The **/P**rint **C**ancel command resets 1-2-3's page and line counters to 1. If the printer stops in the middle of a page, you need to take one of the following steps to realign the paper:

- Turn off the printer, advance the paper manually to the top of the page, turn the printer back on, and select **/P**rint **P**rinter **A**lign.

- With the printer on, use **/P**rint **P**rinter **L**ine to advance the paper, one line at a time, to the top of the next page; and then select **A**lign.

> **Note**
>
> You cannot select one print job among several to be canceled; you must cancel all print jobs or none.

Printing a Graph with Text

You can include a 1-2-3 graph in a report by placing the graph on a separate page or on a page containing text. (Graph printing is covered in detail in Chapter 23, "Creating Effective Graphs.") You can use three methods to print a graph as part of a report:

Tip
You can modify a graph's size, rotation, or density with the **/P**rint [**P,E,B**] **O**ptions **A**dvanced **I**mage menu or the **:G**raph **S**ettings **R**ange or the **:G**raph **E**dit menus. (See Chapter 24, "Creating Power Graphs.")

- Use the Wysiwyg **:G**raph **A**dd command to indicate the worksheet range in which you want the graph to print. See Chapter 25, "Developing Business Presentations," for details.

- In 1-2-3, print the text portion of the report without form-feeding the page. Then select **I**mage from the **/P**rint [**P,F,E,B**] menu, specify the graph to print, and select **G**o again. The selected graph prints immediately after the text.

- After specifying the worksheet range to print but before pressing Enter, type a range separator (; or ,) and an asterisk followed by the name of the graph to print. Following is an example of a print range:

    B1..H20;*PROFITS;K10..N15

This range prints the text in cells B1..H20, followed by the graph named PROFITS, and the text in cells K10..N15.

Naming and Saving the Current Print Settings

1-2-3 can save all current print settings under a unique name, recall the settings with that name, and reuse the settings without requiring you to specify them individually. To do so, select **/P**rint [**P**,**F**,**E**,**B**] **O**ptions **N**ame. The following table lists the options.

Menu Item	Description
Create	Assigns a name to the current print settings. You select this command; then enter a name in response to the prompt. The name can contain up to 15 characters and can include any combination of letters, numbers, and symbols—except for two "less than" symbols (<<). If you type a print-settings name already in use, the current settings replace the original settings associated with that name.
Delete	Deletes a print-settings name. You select this command; then select the print-settings name to delete.
Reset	Deletes all print-settings names from the current file.
Table	Creates a list of all print-setting names in the current file. You select this command; then position the cell pointer at the worksheet location where you want the table to appear. The table occupies one column and as many rows as print-settings names.
Use	Makes current the print settings associated with a particular print-settings name.

Clearing the Print Options

With **/P**rint **P**rinter **C**lear, you can eliminate all or some of the **P**rint options you chose earlier. When you select **C**lear, the following menu appears:

    All **R**ange **B**orders **F**ormat **I**mage **D**evice

You can select **A**ll to clear every **P**rint option, including the print range, or you can be more specific by using one of the choices in the following table.

Menu Item	Description
Range	Clears existing print range specifications.
Borders	Cancels **C**olumns and **R**ows specified as borders.
Format	Eliminates **M**argins, **P**g-Length, and **S**etup string settings.
Image	Clears graphs selected for printing.
Device	Returns device name and interface to defaults.

Printing to an Encoded File

You also can create a disk file that includes instructions on printing by selecting **E**ncoded. An encoded file can contain data, graphs, and printer codes for 1-2-3 print options such as fonts, colors, and line spacing. An encoded file can be printed from the operating system prompt but cannot be used to transfer data to another program.

To create the encoded file, select **:P**rint **F**ile or **/P**rint **E**ncoded. 1-2-3 prompts you for a file name and provides the extension ENC (for encoded) if you don't provide one.

You can use an encoded file to print at another time or from another computer while preserving all the special print options available in 1-2-3. When you create an encoded file, be sure that the printer you select is the one you eventually use to print the file. An encoded file contains printer codes that control special printer features, such as fonts and line spacing. Because these codes are printer-specific, an encoded file created for one printer may not print correctly on another printer. The printer control codes embedded in the encoded file ensure that the final output looks the same as output printed directly from 1-2-3.

To print an encoded file, use the operating system COPY command with the /B option. The following command prints the file SALES.ENC, located in directory C:\DATA, on the printer connected to the port LPT1 (usually the default printer port):

```
COPY C:\DATA\SALES.ENC/B LPT1:
```

You can create an encoded file if you want to print the worksheet on a remote printer connected to a computer that doesn't have 1-2-3 and Wysiwyg. The print file you create contains all the necessary data and formatting instructions so that it can be printed from DOS. Before you print to a file, however, make sure that the following conditions are met:

- The final destination printer is selected under **:P**rint **C**onfig **P**rinter.
- The fonts you have chosen for the worksheet are available on the final destination printer.
- The print range is selected.

Using Background Printing

With 1-2-3 Release 4, you can print reports and continue working in 1-2-3 while waiting for a report to finish printing. This capability is called *background printing*.

When you enter a special command at the operating system prompt, background printing creates or uses an existing encoded file and prints that file through a utility print program stored in the computer's memory. With background printing you can begin printing directly from the operating system prompt or from the **/P**rint command in 1-2-3.

Printing in the background works from both **/P**rint and **:P**rint. In each case, you must first load the BPrint utility from DOS before entering 1-2-3 (see the next section), and you must specify a temporary file name for the print queue.

Loading the BPrint Utility

To use the background printing capability, first load the BPrint utility from the operating system prompt. The first time BPrint is loaded, it remains resident in memory. You then can execute the BPrint command with different arguments to manage the print jobs currently in the queue.

Load BPrint by entering the following:

[*path*]BPRINT[*argument1...argument2...argumentN*]

[*path*] specifies the drive in which the BPrint program (BPRINT.EXE) is stored.

A sample BPRINT command might look like this:

```
c:\123r4\BPRINT -T -PA
```

You can use the following arguments to specify items such as the printer port and names of all files you want to print. You also can use arguments to pause, continue, or stop printing. BPrint arguments don't need to follow a particular order.

Argument	Description
filename	Specifies the file or files you want to print. These files include encoded files (ENC) or text files.
-p=*number*	Specifies the parallel printer port, followed by the equal sign (=) and then a 1, indicating port 1 (the default), or a 2, indicating port 2. After you specify a particular port, you can't change that port without first clearing the BPrint program from memory and starting BPrint with the different port.
-s=*number*	Specifies the serial printer port, followed by the equal sign (=) and number 1 or 2.
-pa	Instructs the BPrint program to pause printing.
-r	Restarts printing after printing is paused with the -pa argument.
-c *filename*	Cancels printing of the file you enter after -c. This argument doesn't cancel printing currently in process.
-t	Stops all printing currently in process and data waiting in queue to print.

If 1-2-3 Release 4 is installed in the directory C:\123R34, for example, enter the command **C:\123R34\BPRINT** to load the background print utility.

Because the BPrint program is a terminate-and-stay-resident program (TSR), keep the following tips and cautions in mind when using BPrint:

- If you are running other TSR programs, begin the other programs before you start BPrint to avoid BPrint's conflicting with the others. If you are working in 1-2-3 and want to use BPrint by temporarily leaving 1-2-3 and returning to the system prompt, save the 1-2-3 worksheet file before leaving 1-2-3.

- BPrint doesn't work if you have loaded the DOS program PRINT.COM.

- If you are working on a network, you must start the networking program before starting BPrint. You cannot use BPrint to print to a network printer. BPrint supports only printers connected directly to the PC.

- Finally, using BPrint with Windows requires that you use the PIF file that starts 1-2-3 to run BPrint. See the Windows documentation for information about creating a PIF file.

Using /Print Background

To use the **/P**rint command to print in the background, follow these steps:

1. Select **/P**rint **B**ackground and enter a file name for the encoded file that 1-2-3 creates for the background printing operation. You can use an existing file name for an encoded file, but remember that new settings overwrite the existing file.

2. Specify the print range and any other print settings you want to include (for example, margin settings, borders, and headers).

3. Select **A**lign and then **G**o.

4. Select **Q**uit to exit the menu. 1-2-3 will start printing in the background.

Using :Print Background

To print in the background with the **:P**rint command, follow these steps:

1. Select **:P**rint **R**ange **S**et and enter the worksheet range to print.

2. Specify any necessary configuration or layout settings for the printout.

3. Select **B**ackground and enter a file name for the encoded file that 1-2-3 creates for the background printing operation. Once again, you can use an existing file name for the encoded file, but remember that new settings overwrite the existing file.

To pause, continue, or stop the print job in process, select **/S**ystem from the 1-2-3 main menu and enter BPrint with the appropriate argument. Remember to save the worksheet file you are working on before using the **/S**ystem command. You can return to 1-2-3 and the worksheet by typing **EXIT** at the system prompt.

> **Tip**
> Remember to save the worksheet file on which you are working before using the **/S**ystem command in case an error occurs in DOS that locks the system and you can't return to 1-2-3.

Preparing Output for Acceptance by Other Programs

Many word processing programs and other software packages accept ASCII text files—the kind created by 1-2-3's **/P**rint **F**ile option. You can maximize chances of successfully exporting 1-2-3 files to other programs if you use several **/P**rint command sequences to eliminate unwanted formatting from the output.

Tip
Many spreadsheet programs can import 1-2-3 data directly. For these types of programs, you don't need to print the 1-2-3 worksheet to a PRN file.

You begin by selecting **/P**rint **F**ile to direct output to an ASCII PRN file. After specifying a file name and the **R**ange to print, select **O**ptions **O**ther **U**nformatted. Selecting **U**nformatted removes all headers, footers, and page breaks from the output.

You then set the left margin to 0 and the right margin to 255. Don't worry about worksheet lines shorter than 255 characters; the line ends after the last printed character, not at 255.

Next, you select **Q**uit to leave the **O**ptions menu. Then create the PRN file on disk by selecting **G**o. Select **Q**uit to exit the **/P**rint **F**ile menu. You should then follow the instructions provided with the word processing program or other software package to import the specially prepared 1-2-3 disk file.

Refer also to the word processing manual for more information about ASCII or text file retrieval. Before retrieving the PRN file, be sure that all word processing margins are set as wide as or wider than the print range. After retrieving the PRN file, use a search-and-replace command to remove unwanted hard carriage returns at the end of lines.

To restore the default printing settings for headers, footers, and page breaks, issue the **/P**rint **P**rinter **O**ptions **O**ther **F**ormatted command. Ordinarily, you select **F**ormatted for printing to the printer or an encoded (ENC) file and **U**nformatted for printing to a PRN file.

Creating an Encapsulated PostScript (EPS) File

Tip
EPS files can be embedded in many popular word processing programs, such as Ami Pro.

1-2-3 Release 4 can create encapsulated PostScript (EPS) files for use with PostScript printers. Many word processing and graphics programs can import these files. To create an EPS file, you must install the encapsulated PostScript printer driver with the 1-2-3 Install program.

To print to an EPS file, select the encapsulated PostScript printer driver with the **:P**rint **C**onfig **P**rinter command. Then print to a file with the **:P**rint **F**ile command and specify a file name. 1-2-3 automatically adds the EPS extension.

The EPS file can contain only a single page of printed output. Use a print range that will print on a single page, or use **:P**rint **L**ayout **C**onfig **A**utomatic to size the range properly.

> **Troubleshooting**
>
> *When I issue a print command (/**P**rint or :**P**rint), nothing prints and I get an error message.*
>
> Be sure the printer is connected by cable to the computer. Then be sure that the printer is on, has paper, and is on-line.
>
> *When I use /**P**rint to print a multiple-page report, gaps appear in the middle of the pages.*
>
> Choose **A**lign before choosing **G**o to indicate to the printer that it should start at the top of a new sheet of paper.
>
> *Wysiwyg enhancements don't print.*
>
> Use the :**P**rint commands when you want to print Wysiwyg enhancements. The /**P**rint commands print a plain, unenhanced copy.
>
> *A header created with :**P**rint **L**ayout **T**itles contains page numbers, but they are not the numbers I would like the page to have.*
>
> Use :**P**rint **S**ettings **S**tart-Number to set the number for the first page you are printing in the current print job.
>
> *Rows or columns I designated as print borders appear twice in the printout.*
>
> Do not include print borders in a print range. If the borders are within the print range, they will print twice: once as borders and again as part of the print range.

From Here...

For information relating directly to printing, you may want to review the following chapters of this book:

- Chapter 6, "Making Your Worksheets Dazzle," to learn more about Wysiwyg formatting options that are available when you print reports.

- Chapter 23, "Creating Effective Graphs," for information on creating and printing 1-2-3 graphs.

- Chapter 25, "Developing Business Presentations," to learn more about how to create and print presentations and reports with graphs.

Part III
Organizing Your Work

9   Working with Files

10 Organizing Your Data with Multiple-Worksheet Files

11 Consolidating Worksheet Data

12 Creating and Using Templates

13 Protecting Worksheet Data and Files

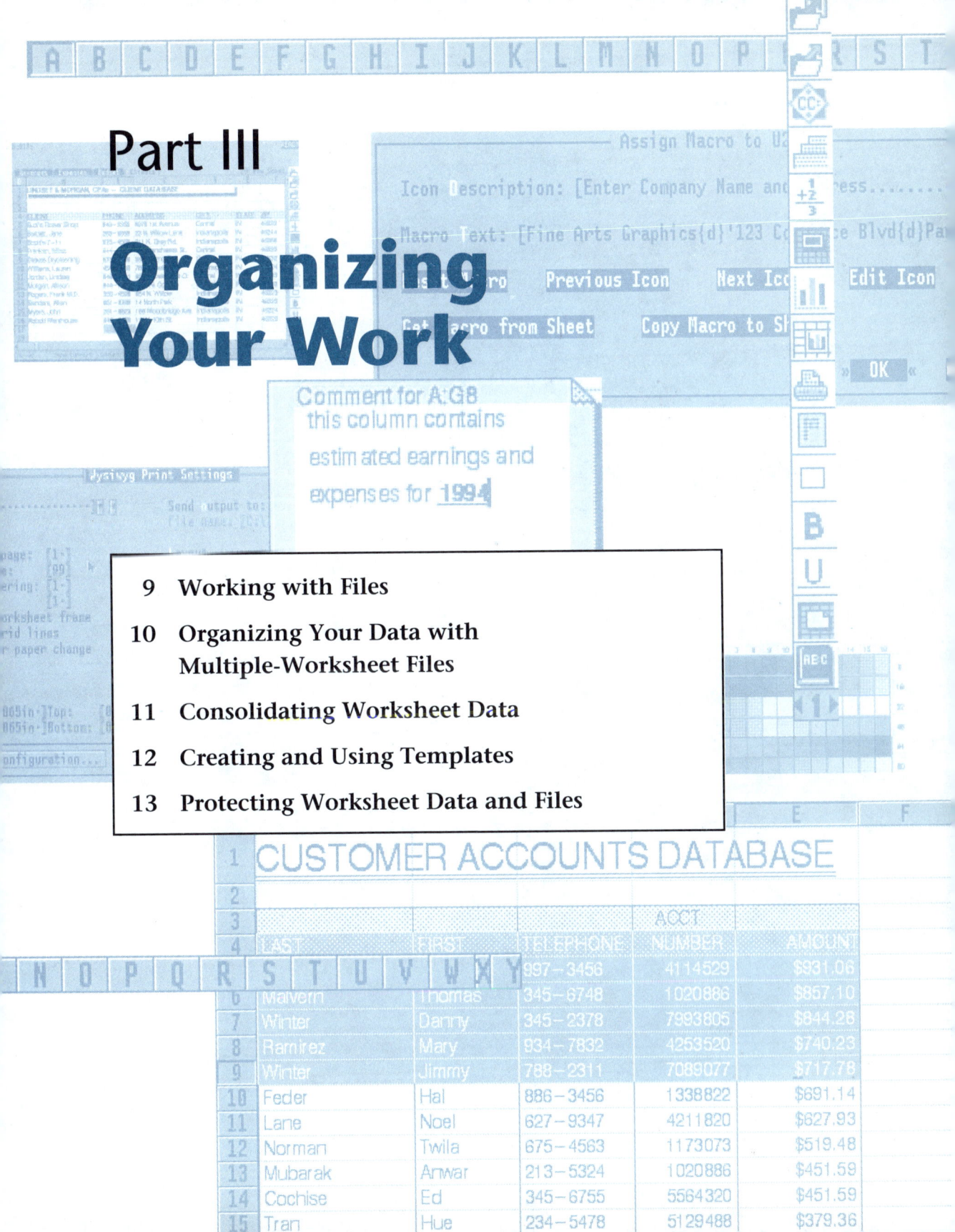

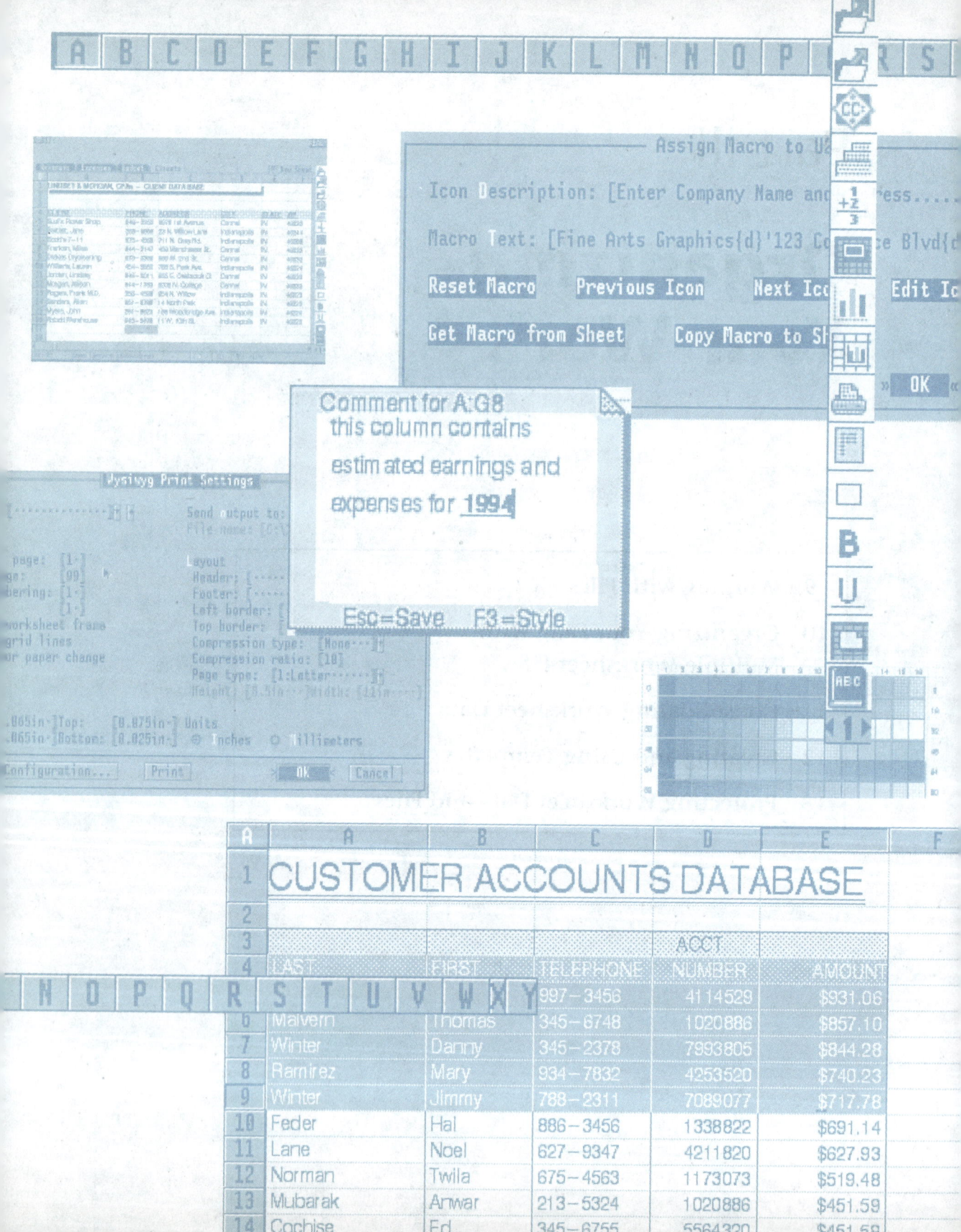

Chapter 9

Working with Files

When you start 1-2-3, you begin with a blank worksheet file and build a worksheet in the computer's memory. To keep a worksheet, you save the worksheet—with a file name—on disk. In 1-2-3, a file can consist of one worksheet (the simplest kind of file) or multiple worksheets. When you want to use the saved file on disk, you can retrieve or open the file. Saving and retrieving are a small subset of the procedures you use to manage files.

The commands available when you choose **/F**ile from 1-2-3's main menu provide a wide range of file-management and file-modification functions. Some commands, such as **/F**ile **E**rase and **/F**ile **L**ist, are similar to operating-system commands. Other commands are related to specific 1-2-3 tasks and applications. Through the **/F**ile menu, for example, you can combine data from several files, extract data from one file and put it in another file, and open more than one file in memory at a time. You also can set a file "reservation" status so that only one user at a time is permitted to write information to and update the file (when the file is located on a shared network drive). The Viewer enables you to see or retrieve the contents of disk worksheet files and to create links between files. An additional command in the **/T**ools menu, **D**OS, enables you to issue file-management and other commands from the DOS prompt without ending your 1-2-3 session.

▶ "Extracting and Combining Data," p. 476

▶ "Linking Files," p. 487

In this chapter, you learn how to do the following:

- Name files
- Change directories
- Save files to disk
- Retrieve files from disk
- Use the Viewer to see the contents of files

- Erase files from disk
- Transfer files between programs
- Access DOS without quitting 1-2-3
- Use 1-2-3 in a network environment

Managing Active Files in Memory

In 1-2-3, the word *file* refers to two types of files: disk-based files and RAM files. A *disk-based file* stores computer information magnetically for the long term. A *RAM file* is in temporary memory. When you build or change files in temporary memory and then exit 1-2-3, the information is lost unless you saved it as a disk-based file. Because a file can be composed of worksheets, a Lotus 1-2-3 file also is called a worksheet file.

◀ "Saving and Retrieving Your Work," p. 136

▶ "Using Multiple-Worksheet Files," p. 458

In 1-2-3 Releases 4 and 3.x, a single file can contain one or more worksheets. When you save a file to disk, you save all the file's worksheets together. When you read a file from disk, you read into memory all the file's worksheets.

Reading a file from disk produces a copy of the disk file in the computer's memory. The file that you see on-screen is in memory, not on the disk. When you change the file in memory, the file still exists unchanged on disk. When you save a file, you store on disk a copy of the file from the computer's memory. To manage files on disk, you also must understand how to manage files in memory.

The computer's memory is your work area. Files in memory are called *active files*. When you choose **/F**ile **R**etrieve, you replace the current file in memory with another file from the disk. The current file is the file that contains the cell pointer. When you choose **/F**ile **N**ew, you create a new workspace for an additional file, and the new file becomes the current file. When you choose **/F**ile **O**pen, you read an additional file into memory. **/F**ile **N**ew and **/F**ile **O**pen do not remove the current file in memory, as **/F**ile **R**etrieve does.

◀ "Exiting 1-2-3," p. 49

◀ "Clearing the Workspace," p. 139

When you choose **/Q**uit or **/W**orksheet **E**rase, you lose all active files in memory. Choose **/W**orksheet **D**elete **F**ile to remove a single active file from memory.

> **Caution**
>
> Be careful about using **/Q**uit, **/W**orksheet **E**rase, and **/W**orksheet **D**elete **F**ile. If you make changes to your file and do not save the file, the changes will not be saved. **/Q**uit and **/W**orksheet **E**rase warn you that changes are not saved, but **/W**orksheet **D**elete **F**ile does not warn you that your changes will be lost.

> **Note**
>
> **/W**orksheet **D**elete **F**ile and **/W**orksheet **E**rase do not affect files on disk. These commands only remove the files from memory. If you save a file before removing it from memory, you get a copy of that file the next time you retrieve it. If you make changes in a file and don't save it to disk with **/F**ile **S**ave, the changes are lost if you delete the file or replace it in memory.

> **Caution**
>
> There are many horror stories about lost files. One of the first rules of computing is to save files—and save them often. You also should have a backup procedure that will save at least one extra copy of your important files somewhere away from your computer. Keep copies of very important files in a different location.

Naming Files

The rules for file names depend on the operating system you use. This book assumes that you use a version of MS-DOS or PC DOS. In DOS format, file names consist of a *root name* (one to eight characters) and an optional *file extension* (one to three characters). The extension usually identifies the file type. For example, files in 1-2-3 Releases 4 and 3.x have the file extension WK3; therefore, a file named BUDGET.WK3 is a file saved in 1-2-3 Release 3, 3.1, 3.1+, 3.4, or 4. Many software products, including 1-2-3, automatically attach the file extension; you type the root name, and 1-2-3 adds the WK3 file extension.

A file name in DOS can contain letters, numbers, and the following characters:

~ ! @ $ % ^ & ( ) – _ { } # '

Spaces aren't allowed. Notice that DOS saves all letters in uppercase.

> **Note**
>
> For file names, use only letters, numbers, hyphens (-), and underline characters (_). Other characters may work now but may not work in later versions of DOS or other operating systems. The characters # and ', for example, work with current versions of DOS but not with OS/2; future versions of DOS may make these and other characters invalid in file names.

Good file-naming techniques can make using 1-2-3 much easier, especially when you work with a large number of files. Use a file name that helps you remember the contents of the file. The file name BUD95, for example, can indicate that the file contains the 1995 budget. You also can use version numbers in file names, such as BUD95R2.WK3 and BUD95R3.WK3, so you can return to previous versions of your work. The file name INCSOUTH can indicate that the file contains income data for the South division.

1-2-3 creates many types of files: worksheet files, backup worksheet files, graph files, and ASCII files. The following table describes the extensions that 1-2-3 Release 4 uses for various types of files.

Extension	Description
WK3	Release 4 and 3.x worksheet files
FM3	Wysiwyg format file (the root name of the format file is the same as the root name of the corresponding WK3 worksheet file)
BAK	Backup worksheet files
FMB	Backup Wysiwyg format files
PRN	Print-image text files with no special characters; commonly called *ASCII files*
ENC	Encoded print-image files with graphics and/or formatting characters specific to one printer
PIC	Files in Lotus graph-image format
CGM	Files in graphic metafile graph-image format (the default format when you create a 1-2-3 graph)
AL3	Print-layout libraries
AF3	Font libraries

1-2-3 also can read worksheets with the extensions described in the following table.

Extension	Description
WK1	Release 2, 2.01, 2.2, 2.3, and 2.4 worksheet files
WKS	Release 1A worksheet files
WRK	Symphony Release 1 and 1.01 worksheet files
WR1	Symphony Release 1.1, 1.2, 2, 2.2, and 3.0 worksheet files

Although you can override these standard extensions and type your own, this practice isn't recommended. When you choose most file commands, 1-2-3 assumes that you want to see the existing files with WK* extensions, and the program lists these files in the control panel. The asterisk (*) means "all characters"; WK* designates such extensions as WK3, WK1, and WKS. If you create a file with an extension that doesn't start with WK, 1-2-3 doesn't list that file name as a default. To read a file with a nonstandard extension, you must type the complete file name and extension. You also can use wild cards to list files with nonstandard extensions. For example, *.XYZ lists all files with the extension XYZ.

> **Note**
>
> Save a file with a nonstandard extension if you don't want the file to appear when 1-2-3 lists the worksheet files. The nonstandard extension "hides" the file from any list of worksheet files. For example, you may want to hide a file containing employee salaries. When you want to retrieve the file, type the entire file name and extension. To further protect the file, use a password when you save.

If you save a file with a WK1 extension, 1-2-3 saves the Release 4 file in Release 2.x format, and the file then can be read by 1-2-3 Release 2.x. For this reason, you may choose to override the default WK3 extension. This arrangement works only if the file contains one worksheet; you cannot save a 1-2-3 Release 4 or 3.x multiple-worksheet file with a WK1 extension. Because Release 2.x doesn't work with multiple-worksheet files, attempting to save a multiple-worksheet Release 4 file with a WK1 extension results in the following error message:

    Incompatibility with previous versions of 1-2-3

412 Chapter 9—Working with Files

1-2-3 doesn't save the file. Only functions or macro commands available in Release 2.x are saved in the file. If the file contains functions or macro commands that are specific to Release 4, 1-2-3 beeps and displays the error message `Incompatible worksheet information lost during saving` when you save the file with the WK1 extension. The file is saved, but all Release 4-specific functions and macro commands appear as `N/A` when you retrieve the file in 1-2-3 Release 2.x.

Tip
If you share files with users who have Release 2.x, save the files with a WK1 extension. You may lose some new 1-2-3 features, but you can exchange the files.

If you want to get information from other file formats, you may have to use the Lotus Translate utility, choose **/F**ile **I**mport, or use the program that created the file and save the file in a different format. If you need to use a Lotus 1-2-3 Release 4 for Windows file format (WK4 extension), for example, you can use Lotus Translate to convert the file to WK3 format. You generally can tell the file format by looking at the extension. For more information, see "Transferring Files" later in this chapter.

Displaying File Names

When you retrieve, open, import, or combine files, Lotus 1-2-3 presents a list of worksheet files. To change the file list's default extension (WK*), follow these steps:

1. Choose **/W**orksheet **G**lobal **D**efault **E**xt **L**ist. Lotus displays the prompt `Enter default extension of the files to list:` and also displays the current extension.

2. If necessary, press Backspace to delete the current extension and type the new extension.

   To list only Release 4 and 3.x worksheets, for example, type **WK3**.
   To list 1-2-3 and Symphony worksheet files, type **W***.

3. Press Enter to complete the entry.

4. Choose **U**pdate if you want this change to be permanent (to be in effect after you exit and later return to 1-2-3).

5. To return to the worksheet, choose **Q**uit.

> **Note**
> You also can override the extension setting when a file list displays. To change the list, press Esc during a file-list prompt, type *. and the extension you want, and press Enter.

Changing the Default Save Extension

If you often exchange files between 1-2-3 Release 2.x and 1-2-3 Release 4, and if you don't use any Release 4 features, functions, or macros that aren't included in 1-2-3 Release 2.x, you can change the default file save extension to WK1.

To change the default extension, follow these steps:

1. Choose **/W**orksheet **G**lobal **D**efault **E**xt **S**ave. Lotus displays the prompt `Enter default extension of the files to save:` and also displays the current extension.

2. If necessary, press Backspace to delete the current extension and type the new extension. To save files in Release 2.x format, for example, type **WK1**.

3. Press Enter to complete the entry.

4. Choose **U**pdate if you want this change to be permanent (to be in effect after you exit and later return to 1-2-3).

5. To return to the worksheet, choose **Q**uit.

> **Note**
>
> You also can override the default save extension when you are prompted for a file name. When you type the file name, simply include the extension.

Working with Disks

When you save a file, in addition to a file name, you must supply the location where the file will reside. This location includes a disk reference and a directory reference.

To refer to a disk, type a letter followed by a colon. Floppy disks generally are referred to as A: and B:. Hard disks within your personal computer generally are referred to as C: and D:. If you are connected to a network or have other storage devices attached to your computer—for example, a CD-ROM drive, removable disk cartridges, or optical disks—you may have additional drive letters available (D: to Z:).

If you have a mouse loaded, the available drive letters appear in the top line of the control panel when you choose **/F**ile **R**etrieve or **/F**ile **L**ist.

> **Note**
>
> When you use multiple drives, each drive has its own current directory (see the following section, "Changing Directories"). If you switch back and forth between drives, Lotus 1-2-3 remembers the current directory for each drive. When you are prompted for a directory, type the directory letter and colon without the directory name (for example, **H:**); 1-2-3 uses the default directory on the drive. Do not include a backslash after the colon.

Changing Directories

Because you store so many files on a hard disk, the disk usually is divided into several directories (also called subdirectories). Each directory can be further subdivided into other directories. The set of directories leading from the *root directory* (generally, C:\) to the directory that contains a file you want is called the *path* or *directory path*.

◄ "Setting Worksheet Global Defaults," p. 276

You can change the path, indicating the location where the file will reside, at three different times. With **/W**orksheet **G**lobal **D**efault **D**ir, you can set the default directory—the directory where Lotus 1-2-3 first looks every time you load 1-2-3. The current directory overrides the default directory but is not saved as the default when you exit 1-2-3. You set the current directory with **/F**ile **D**ir. Your third choice is to change the directory each time you list or choose a file.

Changing the Default Directory

To change the default directory, follow these steps:

1. Choose **/W**orksheet **G**lobal **D**efault **D**ir. The `Default directory:` prompt appears with the current directory.

   Figure 9.1 shows the original default path name C:\123R4D (your computer may show a different drive letter).

2. If necessary, press Esc to clear the existing path, or press Backspace to delete part of the path name.

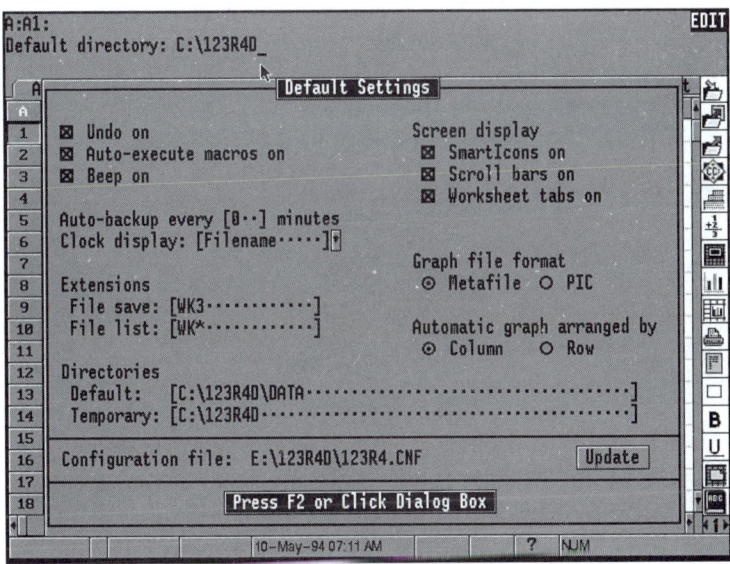

Fig. 9.1
The Default Settings dialog box displays the default-directory prompt and the sample default directory C:\123R4D.

3. Type the path to the directory that contains the files you use most often; then press Enter.

4. To save the new path permanently, choose **U**pdate.

5. To return to the worksheet, choose **Q**uit.

> **Note**
>
> Unless you choose **U**pdate in step 4, there really is no difference between changing the default directory and changing the current directory, as shown in the following section.

Changing the Current Directory

To change the current directory, follow these steps:

1. Choose **/F**ile **D**ir. 1-2-3 displays the Enter current directory: prompt and the current directory path.

2. Type the new path.

   You can ignore the current path and type a new one; as soon as you type a character, the old path clears. To edit the existing path, use the End, left-arrow, right-arrow, Del, and Backspace keys (see fig. 9.2).

Fig. 9.2
Changing the current directory to C:\123R4D\DATA.

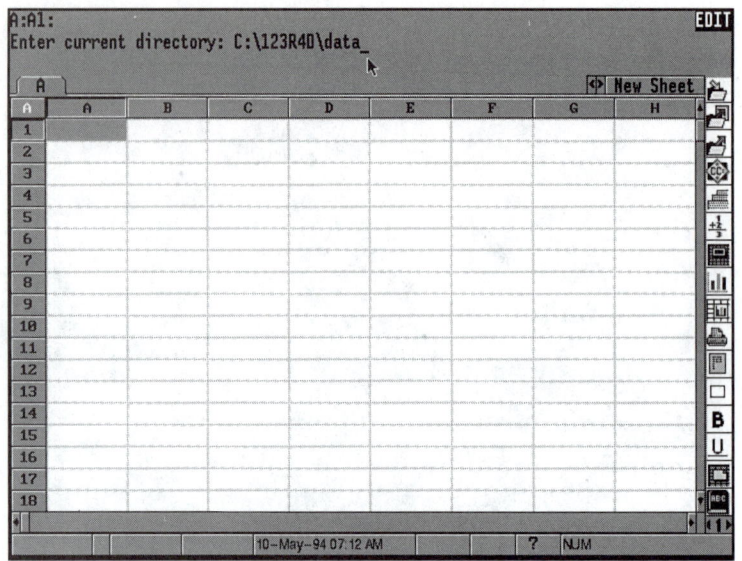

3. When you finish, press Enter.

When you perform any /File command except /File View, such as /File Retrieve, 1-2-3 uses the current directory and displays the current path. Unless you specify a different directory by using /File Dir, the current directory is the default directory, as identified by /Worksheet Global Default Dir.

> **Note**
>
> When you use /File View, the command uses the last directory accessed by the Viewer.

Saving Files

The /File Save command stores on disk a copy of one or all active files in memory, including all the formats, names, and settings. You also can execute a save command by clicking the Save File SmartIcon.

> **Note**
>
> Although the description for the Save SmartIcon (accessed by using the right mouse button to click the icon) says that the SmartIcon will save the current worksheet, all files in memory will be saved when you choose the Save SmartIcon.

▶ "Saving Graphs and Graph Settings," p. 739

To save a file, follow these steps:

1. Choose **/F**ile **S**ave.

2. If you have more than one file open, the prompt [ALL MODIFIED FILES] appears. If you want to save all files, press Enter and go to step 4. If you want to save only the current file, press Esc and go to step 3.

3. Type, edit, or accept the current file name, and press Enter.

> **Note**
>
> If you use the Save File SmartIcon and you previously saved the file, you will not be prompted for a file name; go directly to step 4.

4. If the file already exists, Lotus displays a menu containing three options.

    Choose **C**ancel to do nothing.

    Choose **R**eplace to replace the old file on disk.

    Choose **B**ackup to save the old file with a BAK extension and copy the file in memory to the disk.

When you save a file for the first time, the file has no name. 1-2-3 supplies the default file name FILE0001.WK3 (see fig. 9.3). If this file name already exists in the current directory, 1-2-3 uses FILE0002.WK3, then FILE0003.WK3, and so on.

Rather than accept the default file name, you should type a more meaningful name. You don't need to erase the default name; when you begin to type a new name, 1-2-3 clears the default name but leaves the path. Figure 9.4 shows the control panel after you type the letter **b** as the first character of the file name BUDGET. After you type the file name, press Enter.

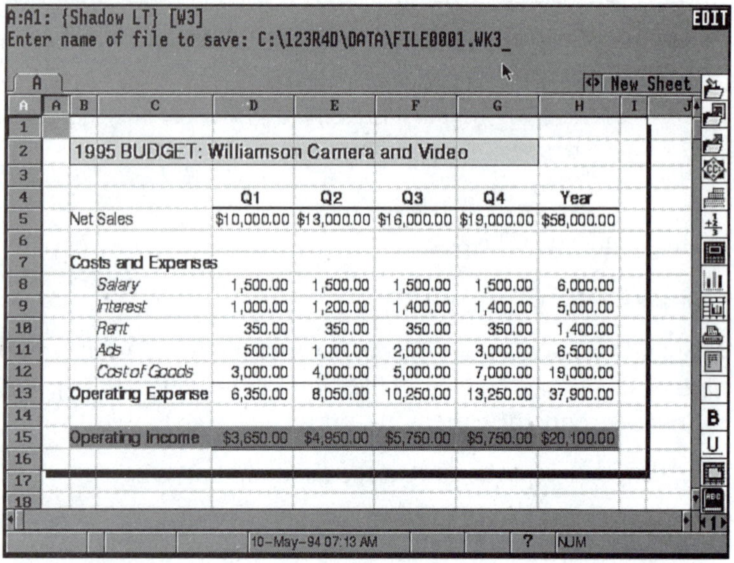

Fig. 9.3
1-2-3 supplies the default file name FILE0001.WK3.

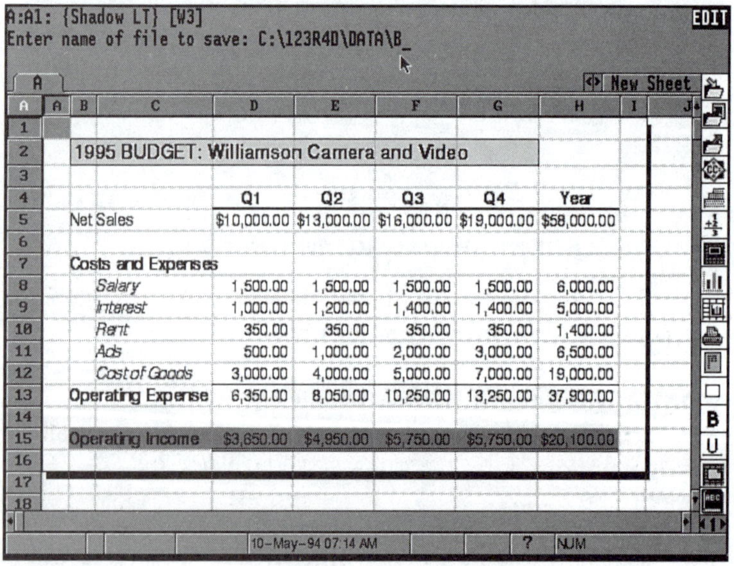

Fig. 9.4
1-2-3 clears the default file name when you type a character.

When you resave a file, 1-2-3 supplies the existing name as the default. If you change the BUD95.WK3 file, for example, and then choose /File Save, the control panel displays the existing path and file name for the file (see fig. 9.5). To save the file under the same name, press Enter.

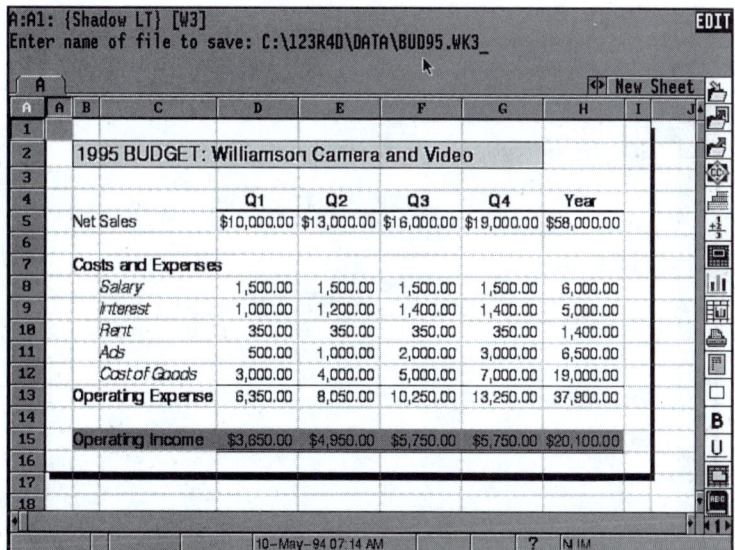

Fig. 9.5
When you save BUD95.WK3 again, 1-2-3 supplies the existing name as the default.

To save the file under a different name, type the new name and press Enter. You don't need to clear the default name; when you begin to type a new name, 1-2-3 clears the default name but leaves the path.

To change the existing name slightly, use the arrow keys, Backspace, and Del to erase part of the old name; then type any additional characters. To change the name BUD95 to BUD95R1, for example, use the left-arrow key to move the cursor after the *5 in BUD95*, type **R1**, and then press Enter. Renaming different versions of the same worksheet is a good way to keep several backup copies accessible while you build a worksheet. If you discover a catastrophic error after you save the file, you can return to an earlier version of the file.

If you try to save a file under an existing name, 1-2-3 presents three options when you choose **/F**ile **S**ave: **C**ancel, **R**eplace, and **B**ackup (see fig. 9.6). If you don't want to write over the old file on disk, choose **C**ancel to cancel the command; then save the file under a different name. If you want to write over the old file, choose **R**eplace. 1-2-3 overwrites the old file with the same name, and you lose the old file permanently.

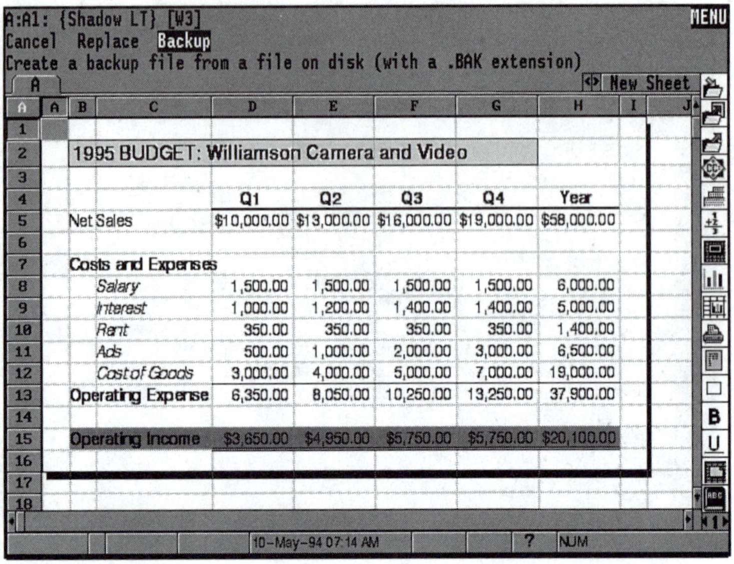

Fig. 9.6
The menu that appears when you try to save a file under an existing name.

> **Caution**
>
> When you choose **R**eplace, 1-2-3 first deletes the old file from the disk. If you see a `Disk full` message while saving a file, you must save the file on another disk or erase some existing files to make room on the current disk. If 1-2-3 doesn't succeed in saving the file and you quit 1-2-3, you lose the new version in memory *and* the old version on disk.

Tip
If you have plenty of disk space, choose the **B**ackup option. If you choose the **B**ackup option, you always have a backup copy of the file.

If you want to save a file under an existing name but not lose the old file on disk, choose **B**ackup. **B**ackup renames the old file with a BAK extension and then saves the new file under the same file name, with a WK3 extension or the default extention specified with **/W**orksheet **G**lobal **D**efault **E**xt **S**ave. You then have both files on disk.

The **B**ackup option saves only one file as a backup. If you save the file again and choose **B**ackup, 1-2-3 deletes the current backup file, renames the WK3 file with a BAK extension, and saves the new file with a WK3 extension. If you want to keep the old file with a BAK extension, you must copy the file to a different disk or directory, or rename the file.

You now can automatically back up your files with 1-2-3 Release 4. Choose **/W**orksheet **G**lobal **D**efault **O**ther **A**uto-Backup. Specify a number from 1 through 60, indicating the number of minutes between backups. To turn the feature off, type **0** (which is the default setting). If you use this feature, 1-2-3 will overwrite any backup created with **/F**ile **S**ave **B**ackup.

Troubleshooting

I cannot save a file.

Check the following things:

- Did you use legal file characters? Make sure that you type up to eight characters, with no spaces. Do not include periods (let 1-2-3 provide a WK3 extension).

- If you are saving to a floppy disk, make sure that the disk is in the drive and that the disk is not copy-protected.

- If all else fails, try a different file name.

I try to save a file, but I get a `Disk full` *message in the status bar.*

Try one or more of the following things:

- Use **/F**ile **E**rase and remove some files.

- If you are saving to a floppy disk (drive A: or B:), use a new disk.

- When you use **/F**ile **S**ave, save to a different disk drive.

- If necessary, choose **/T**ools **D**OS and use FORMAT to format a new disk. Before you format, make sure that the disk contains no files. Also make sure that you return directly to 1-2-3 to save the file.

Retrieving Files from Disk

Two commands read a file from disk into memory: **/F**ile **R**etrieve and **/F**ile **O**pen. **/F**ile **R**etrieve replaces the current file with the new file. If you just started 1-2-3, or if only a blank worksheet is in memory, use this command. You also can execute a retrieve command by clicking the Retrieve File SmartIcon. The Viewer also enables you to retrieve and open files. See "Managing Files with the Viewer" later in this chapter.

To replace the current file in memory with a different file, follow these steps:

1. Choose **/F**ile **R**etrieve.

2. If the current file in memory has changed since your last save, 1-2-3 displays the prompt WORKSHEET CHANGES NOT SAVED! Retrieve file

422 Chapter 9—Working with Files

anyway? Choose **N**o to start over, save the file, and return to step 1. Choose **Y**es to delete the changes in memory and retrieve a new file.

> **Note**
>
> If you use the Retrieve SmartIcon, you will not be warned that changes are not saved.

Tip

If your file contains links to other files, choose **/F**ile **A**dmin **L**ink-**R**efresh to ensure that all formulas are updated.

3. If necessary, change the path and type the file name, or press F3 (Name) to display a full-screen list from which you can select the file name.

4. Press Enter.

The **/F**ile **O**pen command also reads a file from disk into memory. Unlike **/F**ile **R**etrieve, this command doesn't replace the current file in memory. **/F**ile **O**pen keeps open the file(s) that are currently in memory and opens additional files.

To read an additional file from disk into memory, follow these steps:

1. Choose **/F**ile **O**pen.

2. Choose **B**efore to retrieve the file in front of the current file or **A**fter to retrieve the file behind the current file.

3. If necessary, change the path and type the file name, or press F3 (Name) to display a full-screen list from which you can select the file name.

4. Press Enter.

Tip

One benefit of 1-2-3 Release 4 is its capability to open and work with several files at the same time.

After you choose **/F**ile **O**pen, choose **B**efore or **A**fter to tell 1-2-3 to put the file before or after the current file. In perspective view, *before* means toward the bottom of the screen, and *after* means toward the top. In figure 9.7, 1994 BUDGET is after 1995 BUDGET and before 1993 BUDGET.

Each worksheet in figure 9.7 displays the letter *A* in the top-left corner of the frame. This visual cue reminds you that 1-2-3 is displaying three files—not three worksheets in a single file.

You can easily move the cell pointer among files when more than one file is in memory. Press Ctrl+PgUp to move the cell pointer up to the next file and Ctrl+PgDn to move the cell pointer down to the preceding file. You also can move among files by clicking the Next Worksheet and Previous Worksheet SmartIcons.

Retrieving Files from Disk   **423**

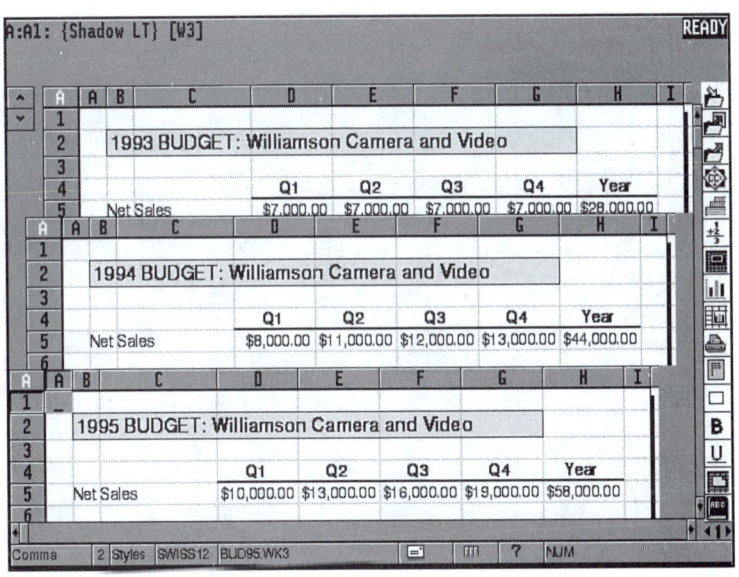

Fig. 9.7
Three files in perspective view.

/**F**ile **R**etrieve and /**F**ile **O**pen prompt you for the name of a file to be read into memory. Both commands list the files in the current directory at the prompt that requests the file name. You can type the file name or highlight the file name in the control-panel list. If the directory contains several files, you can press F3 (Name) or click List to see a full-screen display of file names, as shown in figure 9.8. (The mouse indicators appear on-screen only if you have a mouse driver loaded.)

▶ "Moving Around Multiple-Worksheets," p. 467

Files are listed in alphabetic order, reading from left to right. Notice that the name of the highlighted file, the date and time the file was created, and the size of the file appear below the prompt. Highlight the file you want to retrieve; then press Enter.

All 1-2-3 Release 3.1, 3.1+, 3.4, and 4 files have Wysiwyg formatting capabilities when Wysiwyg is loaded. When you read into memory a WK3 file with Wysiwyg formatting, 1-2-3 also reads into memory the formatting information from the Wysiwyg format file (this file has the same file name as the WK3 file and the extension FM3). 1-2-3 Releases 2.3 and 2.4 also have Wysiwyg formatting and printing capabilities through the Wysiwyg add-in. 1-2-3 Release 2.2 only has Wysiwyg printing capabilities derived from the Allways add-in. When reading into memory a WK1 file with Wysiwyg or Allways formatting, 1-2-3 reads into memory the formatting information from an Impress-format file (extension FMT) or Allways-format file (extension ALL).

Tip
To see a list of open files and go to an open file in memory, press F5 (Go To) and then press F3 (Name) twice.

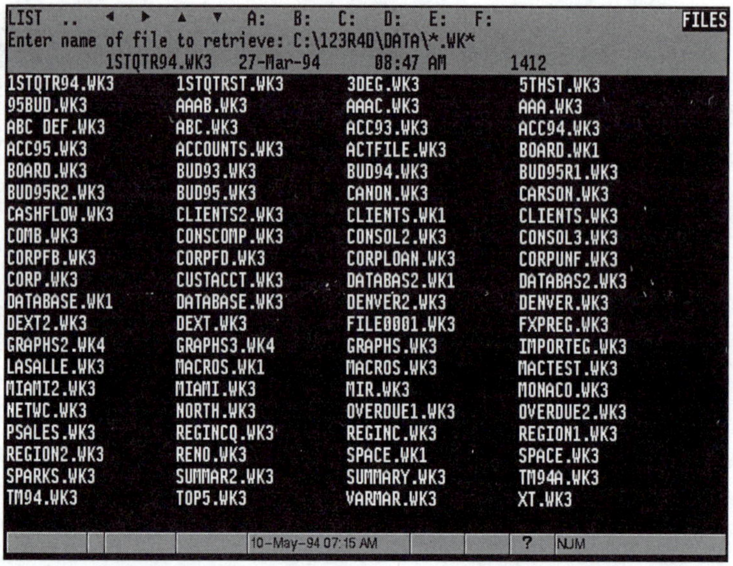

Fig. 9.8

Press F3 (Name) to show a full-screen list of file names whenever 1-2-3 prompts you for a file name.

```
LIST   ..  ◄  ►  ▲  ▼   A:   B:   C:   D:   E:   F:              FILES
Enter name of file to retrieve: C:\123R4D\DATA\*.WK*
         1STQTR94.WK3    27-Mar-94       08:47 AM      1412
1STQTR94.WK3    1STQTRST.WK3    3DEG.WK3        5THST.WK3
95BUD.WK3       AAAB.WK3        AAAC.WK3        AAA.WK3
ABC_DEF.WK3     ABC.WK3         ACC93.WK3       ACC94.WK3
ACC95.WK3       ACCOUNTS.WK3    ACTFILE.WK3     BOARD.WK1
BOARD.WK3       BUD93.WK3       BUD94.WK3       BUD95R1.WK3
BUD95R2.WK3     BUD95.WK3       CANON.WK3       CARSON.WK3
CASHFLOW.WK3    CLIENTS2.WK3    CLIENTS.WK1     CLIENTS.WK3
COMB.WK3        CONSCOMP.WK3    CONSOL2.WK3     CONSOL3.WK3
CORPFB.WK3      CORPFD.WK3      CORPLOAN.WK3    CORPUNF.WK3
CORP.WK3        CUSTACCT.WK3    DATABAS2.WK1    DATABAS2.WK3
DATABASE.WK1    DATABASE.WK3    DENVER2.WK3     DENVER.WK3
DEXT2.WK3       DEXT.WK3        FILE0001.WK3    FXPREG.WK3
GRAPHS2.WK4     GRAPHS3.WK4     GRAPHS.WK3      IMPORTEG.WK3
LASALLE.WK3     MACROS.WK1      MACROS.WK3      MACTEST.WK3
MIAMI2.WK3      MIAMI.WK3       MIR.WK3         MONACO.WK3
NETWC.WK3       NORTH.WK3       OVERDUE1.WK3    OVERDUE2.WK3
PSALES.WK3      REGINCQ.WK3     REGINC.WK3      REGION1.WK3
REGION2.WK3     RENO.WK3        SPACE.WK1       SPACE.WK3
SPARKS.WK3      SUMMAR2.WK3     SUMMARY.WK3     TM94A.WK3
TM94.WK3        TOP5.WK3        VARMAR.WK3      XT.WK3

                       10-May-94 07:15 AM          ?     NUM
```

> **Note**
>
> You can retrieve a file automatically when you load 1-2-3. First, make sure that the directory containing the file is the default directory. At the DOS prompt, type **123** and press the space bar once. Type a hyphen (-), the letter **w**, and the name of the file. Then press Enter. Typing the following, for example, automatically retrieves the file named BUDGET when the 1-2-3 program loads:
>
>   123 -wBUDGET

Using Wild Cards To Retrieve Files

When 1-2-3 prompts you for a file name, you can include the asterisk (*) and the question mark (?) as wild cards in the file name. *Wild cards* are characters that enable you to make one file name match several files. The ? wild-card character matches any single character in the name; the * wild-card character matches any number of characters.

When you use wild cards in response to a file-name prompt, 1-2-3 lists only the files whose names match the wild-card pattern; 1-2-3 doesn't actually execute the command (unless you choose /File List). If you use wild cards after you choose /File Retrieve, /File Open, /File Combine, or /File Import, for example, 1-2-3 doesn't try to read a file but lists only the files that match the wild-card pattern.

Suppose that you type **BUD??** at the prompt shown in figure 9.8. 1-2-3 lists all file names that start with BUD, followed by any two characters—such as BUD93, BUD94, and BUD95 (not BUD95R1 and BUD95R2) If you type **ACC***, 1-2-3 lists all file names that start with ACC—such as ACC93, ACC94, ACC95, and ACCOUNTS.

> **Note**
>
> The asterisk (*) wild card works only for characters that *follow* a given character or characters—not for characters that *precede* a given character or characters. ***S**, for example, doesn't find all files that end with the letter *S*.

Retrieving Files from Subdirectories

As mentioned earlier, when 1-2-3 prompts you for a file name, the program lists the complete path. If you are working on a file named BUDGET and you choose **/**File **S**ave, the current directory and file name (for example, C:\123R4D\DATA\BUDGET.WK3) appears at the prompt.

To change the current directory, choose **/**File **D**ir. To retrieve or save a file in another directory without changing the current directory, press Esc two or three times to clear the old path; then type the new path. You also can edit the existing path in the prompt.

When 1-2-3 lists the files in the current directory, the program lists any subdirectories in the current directory, placing a backslash (\) after each directory's name. To read a file in one of the subdirectories, move the menu pointer to the subdirectory name and press Enter. 1-2-3 then lists the files and any subdirectories in that subdirectory. To list the files in the parent directory (the directory above the one displayed), press Backspace; 1-2-3 lists the files and subdirectories in the parent directory. You can move up and down the directory structure this way until you find the directory and file you want.

For more information about directory structure and file management, consult Que Corporation's *Using MS-DOS 6.2*, Special Edition, or your operating-system documentation.

Tip
Change the default drive by choosing **/**File **D**ir and specifying the desired drive. To change the drive permanently, choose **/W**orksheet **G**lobal **D**efault **D**ir, type the drive letter, and choose **U**pdate.

Retrieving a File Automatically

When you start 1-2-3, a blank worksheet appears. If you save a file in the default directory under the name AUTO123, however, 1-2-3 retrieves that file automatically when you start 1-2-3. This capability is especially useful if you work with macro-driven worksheet files. You can use the AUTO123 file, for example, to provide the first menu of a macro-driven system or a menu of other files to retrieve. The file extension can be WK1 or WK3; if you have AUTO123.WK1 and AUTO123.WK3 in the same directory, however, Release 4 retrieves AUTO123.WK3.

Opening a New File in Memory

In 1-2-3 Releases 4 and 3.x, you can start a new file without clearing existing files from memory. /**F**ile **N**ew creates a new, blank file in the computer's memory. You also can execute the /**F**ile **N**ew command by clicking the New File SmartIcon.

◀ "Understanding the Default Print Settings," p. 359

◀ "Setting Display Characteristics," p. 241

The newly created file uses the settings from the current Wysiwyg session for the default font set, named styles, **:P**rint **C**onfig, **:P**rint **L**ayout, and **:P**rint **S**ettings. /**F**ile **N**ew doesn't affect the **:D**isplay settings for the current Wysiwyg session if Wysiwyg is active. Any files that are active before you issue this command remain active after you insert the new file. As with /**F**ile **O**pen, /**F**ile **N**ew enables you to work with more than one active file in memory.

After you choose /**F**ile **N**ew, choose **B**efore or **A**fter to insert the blank worksheet file before or after the current file. When you start a new file, 1-2-3 prompts you for a file name, offers a default file name such as FILE0001.WK3, and then writes the blank file to disk. When you use the File New SmartIcon, 1-2-3 inserts the new file after the current file.

Figure 9.9 shows the workspace from figure 9.7 when the cell pointer was in 1995 BUDGET and the /**F**ile **N**ew **A**fter command was issued to create a new file. (Because the file is new, it is blank.) Notice that 1993 BUDGET has dropped out of view (although it still is in memory), and that 1995 BUDGET, 1994 BUDGET, and the new file are displayed.

◀ "Clearing the Workspace," p. 139

To build a new worksheet file and remove all other files and worksheets, use the /**W**orksheet **E**rase command to clear the workspace. This command clears all files in memory, not just the current file. 1-2-3 asks you to confirm **N**o or **Y**es before it clears the workspace. If you changed any active files since you last saved them, 1-2-3 warns you with another **N**o or **Y**es menu. To save the changes, choose **N**o and save the file; then choose /**W**orksheet **E**rase **Y**es again.

Retrieving Files from Disk **427**

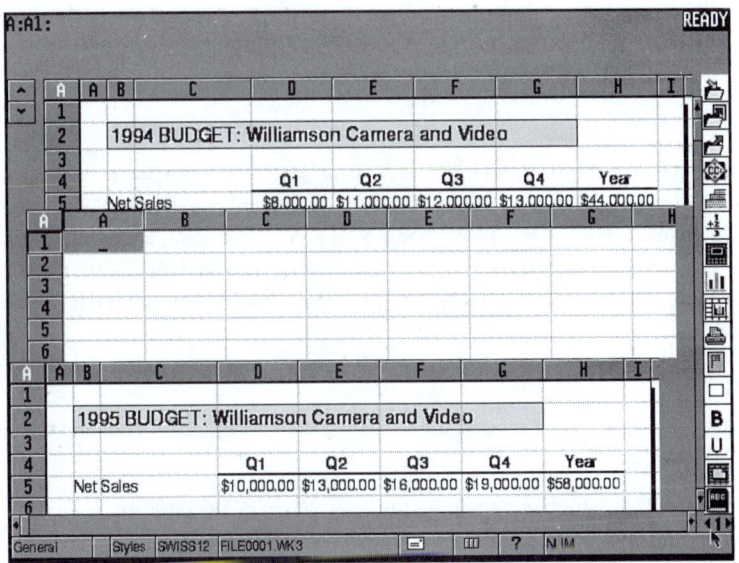

Fig. 9.9
A new file opened after the current file in memory.

> **Troubleshooting**
>
> *When I try to retrieve my file, it is not listed.*
>
> When you saved the file, did you include an extension rather than let 1-2-3 attach its own .WK3 extension? If so, when you choose **/F**ile **R**etrieve, type ***.*** to list all files.
>
> Another possibility is that the file is not in the current directory. Use **/F**ile **D**ir to change the directory.
>
> *I don't remember the name of my file or where it's located.*
>
> Use **/F**ile **V**iew **R**etrieve to look for and retrieve the file.
>
> If you know the approximate date when you last saved the file or the approximate size of the file, you can sort the list of the files shown in the Viewer by date. You also can choose **/T**ools **D**OS and use the DOS command DIR with different switches, as follows:
>
> | Command | Description |
> | --- | --- |
> | DIR /on | Sorts by name |
> | DIR /od | Sorts by date and time |
> | DIR /os | Sorts by size |
>
> *(continues)*

> (continued)
>
> You also can use the DOS command DIR *filename*/s to look for the file in all subdirectories.
>
> If you have a word processing program that can search text, use that program. In WordPerfect 5.1, for example, press F5 (File List) and type the directory where the file exists. In the File Manager screen, choose **F**ind **E**ntire Document, and type a phrase that is in the 1-2-3 file. To print the resulting file list, press Shift+F7 (Print). Do not try to retrieve the file through WordPerfect; return to 1-2-3 and look at your files in the list.
>
> *I can't retrieve a listed file.*
>
> Make sure that you are retrieving the file with a WK3 extension and not an FM3 or other extension.
>
> Also look at the status bar. If the message `File already exists in memory` appears, the file already is open. Press F5 (Go To) and then F3 (Name) to see a list of your open files.

Managing Files with the Viewer

If you can't remember the file name or aren't sure what's in the file, you can use the Viewer. The 1-2-3 Release 4 Viewer displays a file before you retrieve it, makes file linking much easier, and enables you to browse worksheet and text files. This section shows you how to use the Viewer to perform the following tasks:

- View and retrieve worksheet files
- View and open additional worksheet files
- Create worksheet linking formulas
- Browse worksheet and text files

Using the Viewer

In Lotus 1-2-3 Release 3.4, users accessed the Viewer as an add-in by pressing Alt+F10 (Addin) and choosing **I**nvoke. Lotus Release 4 integrates the Viewer with the /**F**ile menu.

To use the Viewer, follow these steps:

1. Choose /**F**ile **V**iew. The resulting menu has four choices, as shown in figure 9.10.

Managing Files with the Viewer   429

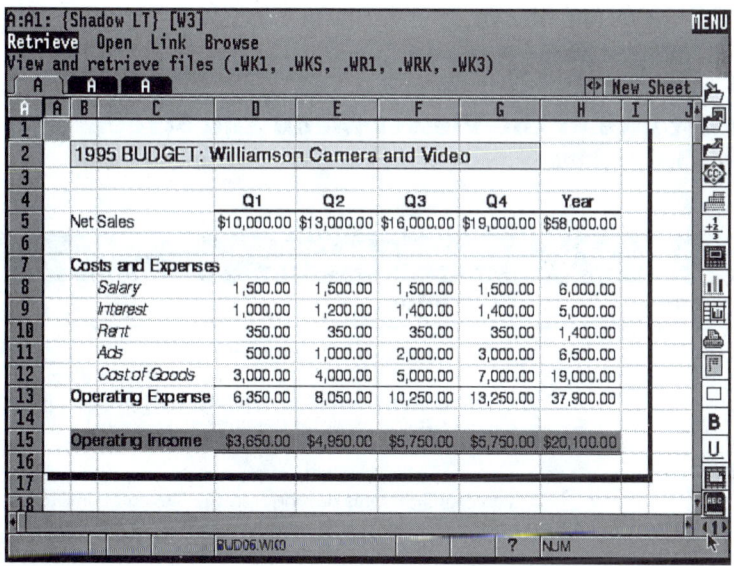

Fig. 9.10
The /**F**ile **V**iew menu gives you four choices.

2. Do one of the following things:

    ■ To preview and retrieve a file in the location of the current file, choose **R**etrieve.

    ■ To open an additional file without closing other files, choose **O**pen.

    ■ To create a formula that links a previewed file to the current worksheet, choose **L**ink.

    ■ To preview a file only, choose **B**rowse.

    After you choose one of these commands, you enter the Viewer.

3. Move to the desired file in the list of files on the left side of the screen. Lotus 1-2-3 and Symphony files appear on the right side of the screen. If you use Browse, all files are displayed.

4. If you chose **L**ink in Step 2, press the right-arrow key to enter worksheet view and move to the first cell of the range to which you want to link, press period (.) and highlight the range.

5. Press Enter.

    If you chose **B**rowse in Step 2, you return to 1-2-3. If you chose **R**etrieve or **O**pen, the file appears on-screen. If you chose **L**ink, you create a formula linking to the desired worksheet.

Chapter 9—Working with Files

The following section describes the Viewer menu choices and the Viewer screen in more detail.

Understanding the Viewer Menu and Screen

Table 9.1 describes the four commands in the Viewer menu.

Table 9.1	The Viewer Menu Commands
Command	**Description**
Retrieve	Reads a worksheet file into memory
Open	Opens a worksheet file in memory; you specify whether the file goes **B**efore or **A**fter the current worksheet
Link	Enters one or more linking formulas in the current worksheet; you highlight cells or ranges in the files to be linked
Browse	Displays the contents of worksheet and text files; doesn't retrieve, open, or link to files being browsed

After you choose a Viewer command, 1-2-3 removes the worksheet from the screen and displays the Viewer screen (see fig. 9.11). The directory names appear in angle brackets—for example, <FINANCES>.

Table 9.2 describes the elements of the Viewer screen.

Table 9.2	The Viewer Screen Elements
Screen Element	**Description**
Status bar	Displays prompts and an indicator showing whether the highlight is in the List window or the View window
Directory path	Lists the path of the highlighted (current) directory
List window	Displays a list of file names in the highlighted (current) directory
View window	Displays the contents of the file highlighted in the List window and a count of the number of worksheets
Information line	Shows the worksheet in the file being displayed, the file name, the date and time the file was last saved, and the size of the file (in bytes)
Key bar	Displays a list of available Viewer function keys

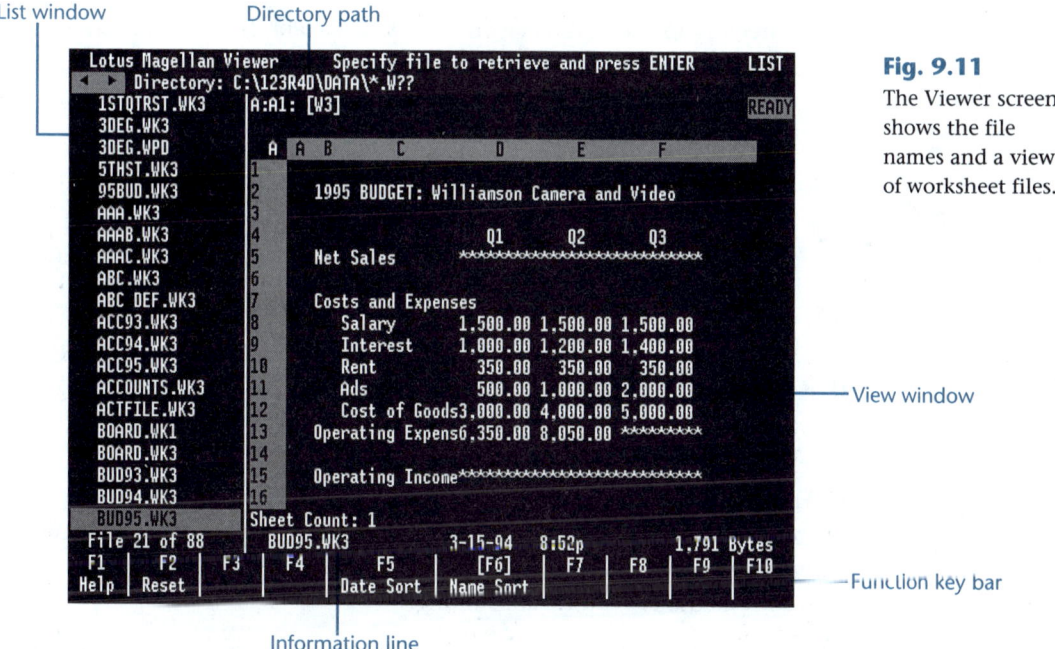

Fig. 9.11
The Viewer screen shows the file names and a view of worksheet files.

Navigating the Viewer

The Viewer screen displays different directories, files, or portions of files when you move the highlight on the Viewer screen. You use the same direction keys with all Viewer commands; you cannot use a mouse with the Viewer. You can use all the direction keys to move the highlight around. Use the up-arrow and down-arrow keys, for example, to move the highlight up or down one or more lines, regardless of whether the highlight is in the List window or the View window. If the file is a multiple-worksheet file, you can press Ctrl+PgUp and Ctrl+PgDn to move to the different sheets in the file.

When you start the Viewer, the current 1-2-3 directory is displayed. To change the directory, follow these steps:

1. Make sure that the highlight is in the List window. If the highlight is in the View window, press the left-arrow key one or more times to move the highlight to the List window.

2. In the List window, use the direction keys to move the highlight to the desired directory.

3. Press the left-arrow key to move the highlight to the parent directory of the displayed directory. To change from the C:\123R4D\DATA

directory to the C:\123R4D directory, for example, press the left-arrow key when the <DATA> directory is highlighted in the List window. If the root directory is the current directory, pressing the left-arrow key displays a list of available disk drives.

4. Press the right-arrow key to make a highlighted directory current. If the current directory is C:\123R4D, for example, highlight <DATA> and press the right-arrow key to make the C:\123R4D\DATA directory current.

5. To reset the Viewer to the original directory, press the F2 (Reset) key.

Retrieving a File

As your collection of worksheet files grows, remembering which file serves which purpose may become increasingly difficult. Is MYREC95.WK3 or MYFILE95.WK3 the business-expense worksheet for 1995? Without the Viewer add-in, you can keep written records documenting each worksheet's purpose or try retrieving each worksheet in turn until you find the correct one. Both methods are time-consuming.

The Viewer's **R**etrieve command displays the contents of worksheet files as you scroll through the list of files in the current Viewer directory. The major advantage to retrieving with the Viewer instead of **/F**ile **R**etrieve is that you can display the file contents before retrieving, to ensure that you have the desired file.

The Viewer displays each worksheet as it appears in READY mode, without Wysiwyg attached. Graphs, special fonts, and cell formatting aren't displayed. Figure 9.11 shows how the Viewer displays a typical worksheet file.

When you choose **/F**ile **V**iew **R**etrieve and your current file's changes have not been saved, 1-2-3 displays the prompt WORKSHEET CHANGES NOT SAVED! Retrieve file anyway? Choose **N**o to return to READY mode; then save the worksheet file with **/F**ile **S**ave. If you choose **Y**es, the Viewer replaces the current worksheet file without saving it.

◄ "Moving Around the Worksheet," p. 51

When a file is displayed in the View window but the window doesn't show the area of the file you want to see, press the right-arrow key to move the highlight from the List window to the View window. With the highlight in the View window, scroll through the file, using the same direction keys you use to navigate a worksheet in 1-2-3.

To retrieve a worksheet file, press Enter while the file name is highlighted in the List window and the worksheet contents are displayed in the View window.

> **Note**
>
> If you are scrolling through the worksheet in the View window, you don't need to return to the List window before pressing Enter to retrieve the file.

Suppose that the file you're viewing isn't the correct file. To view and select another file, move the highlight back to the List window by pressing the left-arrow key when the highlight is in column A of the displayed worksheet. Depending on the worksheet structure, you may need to use several keystrokes to move the highlight to column A. You may be able to save keystrokes by using the Home key to move the highlight to column A and then pressing the left-arrow key to move the highlight to the List window.

Changing the Display Sort Order

By default, the Viewer displays file names in alphabetical order, but the add-in also can list files by using a date sort. You can see the date of each file in the list by looking at the information line near the bottom of the screen. Suppose that you have several hundred worksheet files, but all you know about the file you want to use is that someone in the office updated that file within the past week. To change the display so that the Viewer shows the newest files at the top of the list, press F5 (Date Sort).

To return to alphabetical order, press F6 (Name Sort). The Viewer continues to use the last sort-order setting you selected until you remove the add-in from memory.

Opening Files with the Viewer

In 1-2-3 Releases 4 and 3.x, you can have multiple files loaded in memory at the same time. When you open a worksheet file, any worksheet files that are already in memory remain open and available for use.

The /**F**ile **V**iew **O**pen command functions much like the /**F**ile **V**iew **R**etrieve command discussed in the preceding section. Instead of warning you if the current worksheet has been modified, however, **O**pen prompts you with two choices: **B**efore and **A**fter. The **B**efore option reads a file into memory in front of the current file; **A**fter reads a file into memory behind the current file. After you choose **B**efore or **A**fter, the **V**iewer **O**pen screen appears, and you choose the file to open.

▶ "Moving Around Multiple-Worksheets," p. 467

434 Chapter 9—Working with Files

 When you open a new file, 1-2-3 moves the cell pointer to the new file. To see both open files, choose **/W**orksheet **W**indow **P**erspective. 1-2-3 displays a three-dimensional perspective view of the open worksheets, as shown in figure 9.12.

Fig. 9.12
Two open worksheets displayed in perspective view.

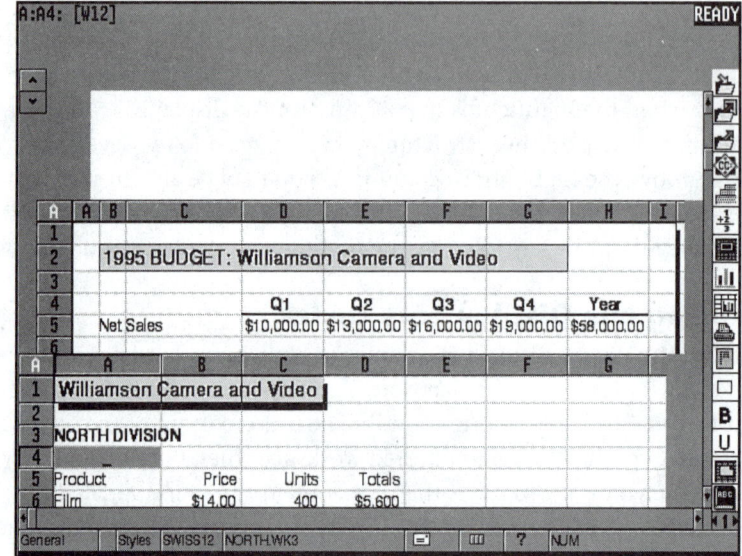

Linking Files with the Viewer

▶ "Extracting and Combining Data," p. 476

▶ "Linking Files," p. 487

Using links between 1-2-3 worksheet files, you can consolidate data from several files automatically. Before file linking was available, consolidating data was difficult at best. You could use the **/F**ile **C**ombine command and automate the process with macros, but this method can be dangerous; errors can result if changes in the worksheet insert or delete rows or columns, for example.

The process of linking formulas between files offers many advantages over **/F**ile **C**ombine. The file links are updated automatically when you retrieve the master file; you don't need to perform a manual or macro-driven **/F**ile **C**ombine operation to ensure that you are using the latest data. Because file linking uses formulas, if you rearrange the master worksheet, the links remain updated.

A disadvantage of file-linking formulas is the complexity of the formulas. You must specify the file name of the source file and the desired source-cell address or range name. The Viewer add-in makes creating linking formulas much easier because with the Viewer you can highlight the cell or address in another file.

Suppose that you run a chain of small discount computer stores located in Reno, Sparks, and Carson City, Nevada. Separate worksheet files contain the sales results for the three stores. The sales manager decides to run a contest, with prizes for the store with the best performance in each department. The sales manager wants a single report that compares each store's results, not three separate worksheets. A consolidation worksheet can show the combined results for all stores (see fig. 9.13).

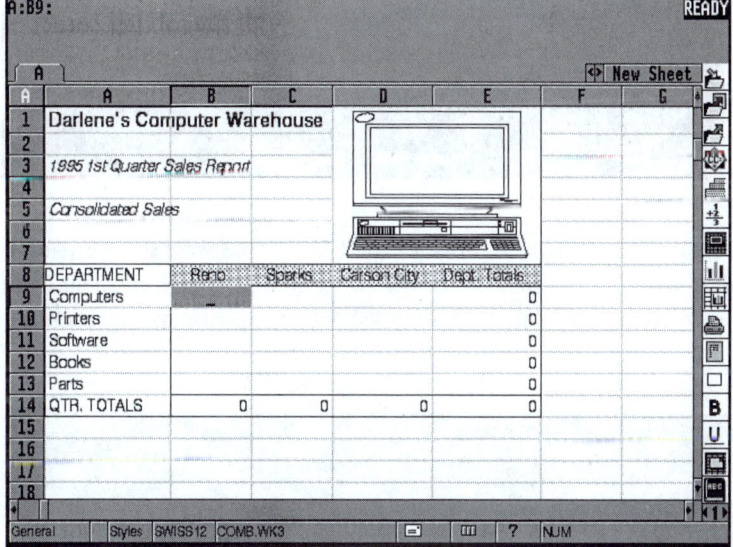

Fig. 9.13
A consolidation worksheet before formula links are added.

To consolidate the data, you can use the Viewer. Place the cell pointer in cell A:B9—the first cell to contain a linking formula. Choose the Viewer with /**F**ile **V**iew **L**ink. Because you consolidate data for the Reno store first, move the highlight in the List window to RENO.WK3. With the file name highlighted, press the right-arrow key to move the highlight to the View window. Move the highlight to the beginning of the range you want to link (cell A:B9). Press the period key (.) to anchor the range, and move the highlight down until you have highlighted cells A:B9..A:B13 (see fig. 9.14). Press Enter to complete the selection and enter the linking formulas in the consolidation worksheet.

Fig. 9.14
In the View window, select the cells to be linked to the current worksheet.

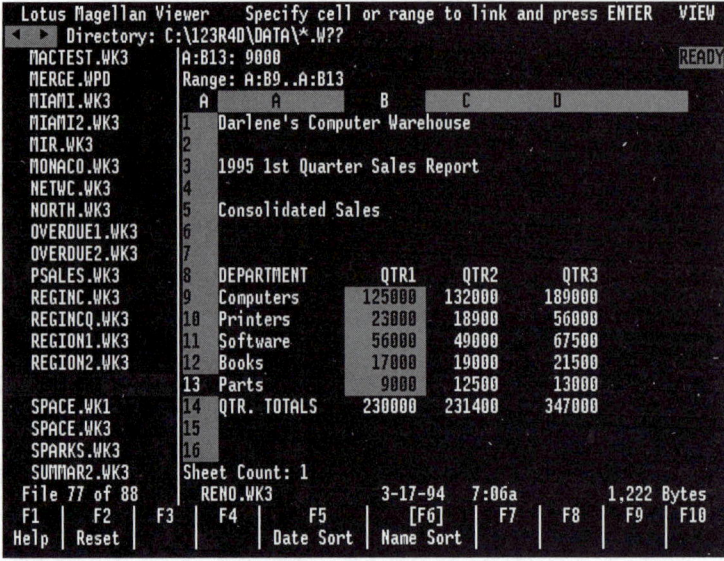

Each cell in the highlighted range of the RENO.WK3 worksheet creates a formula starting in the first cell of the consolidated sales worksheet. Figure 9.15 shows the consolidated sales worksheet with formulas in cells A:B9 to A:B13.

Fig. 9.15
The consolidated worksheet shows the linking formula in cell A:B9.

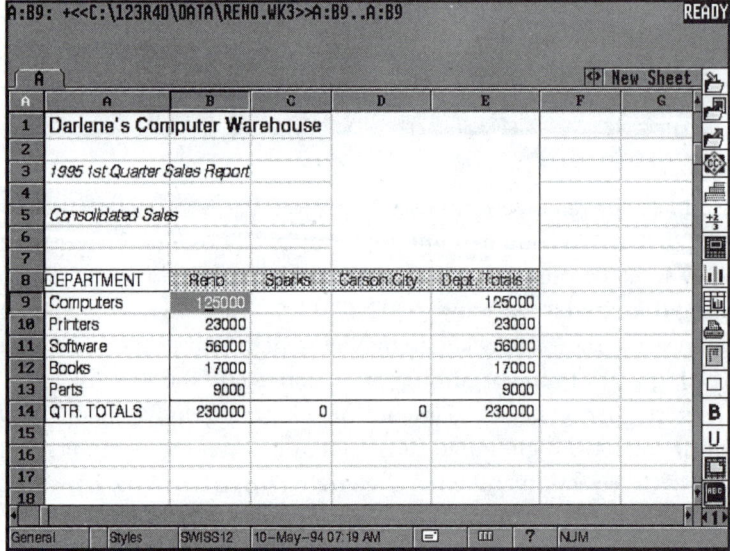

Continue the linking process by moving the cell pointer in the master worksheet to the next cell where you want to start a series of linking formulas (cell A:C9), and use the Viewer to create links to SPARKS.WK3. Finally, move the cell pointer to cell A:D5 and create the links to CARSON.WK3.

In figure 9.15, the cell pointer is in A:B9, the cell contents line shows the linked formula:

    +<<C:\123R4D\DATA\RENO.WK3>>A:B9..A:B9

The Viewer created this formula and can create similar ones in the range A:B9..A:D13—a total 15 linking formulas. You can see the advantage of using the Viewer to create file links rather than typing these formulas.

Browsing Files with the Viewer

The Viewer's **B**rowse command enables you to look at 1-2-3 and Symphony worksheet and text files. **B**rowse is for viewing only; you cannot retrieve, open, or link to the file displayed in the View window.

The **B**rowse command is handy for examining text files before you issue a **/F**ile **I**mport **T**ext or **/F**ile **I**mport **N**umbers command. With **B**rowse, you can verify that you are importing the correct file.

Browse displays 1-2-3 and Symphony worksheet files as they would appear if you retrieved the file; the command treats all other files as text files. As a result, if you **B**rowse program files, you see unintelligible characters and the text of any messages contained in the file.

Erasing Files

Every time you save a file, you use space on your computer's hard disk. If you don't erase unneeded files from the hard disk occasionally, you may run out of disk space. Even if you still have disk space available, you may have a difficult time finding the files you want to read if the disk contains many obsolete files. Before you erase old files, however, you may want to save them to a floppy disk in case you ever need them again.

Tip
To see available space on your hard disk, choose **/T**ools **D**OS to temporarily exit to DOS. Type **DIR** and press Enter. The number of bytes available appears after the file list.

> **Caution**
>
> Always keep a backup copy of your files on a floppy disk. If you erase a file from your hard disk, or if the disk crashes or fails, you can recover a copy of the file from the floppy disk.

438 Chapter 9—Working with Files

When you choose /**W**orksheet **D**elete **F**ile, you clear the file from memory but don't erase the file from the disk; you still can retrieve or open the file. To erase an unneeded file from disk, choose /**F**ile **E**rase. This command removes the file from the disk and frees the disk space for other files. You can erase only one file at a time. You also can use the DOS ERASE or DEL command to erase files on disk.

If you accidentally erase a file and haven't saved other files to the hard disk, you may be able to recover the erased file by using a special utility program. After you have written to the disk, however, the erased file's space on the disk may have been replaced by new data.

◄ "Setting Worksheet Global Defaults," p. 276

When you choose /**F**ile **E**rase, 1-2-3 displays the menu shown in figure 9.16. Use this menu to specify the type of file you want to erase. If you choose **W**orksheet, 1-2-3 lists all files in the current directory that have WK* extensions (unless you change the default with /**W**orksheet **G**lobal **D**efault **E**xt **L**ist). If you choose **P**rint, 1-2-3 lists all files in the current directory that have PRN extensions. Choosing **G**raph produces a list of all files in the current directory that have CGM extensions (unless you change the default by choosing /**W**orksheet **G**lobal **D**efault **G**raph **P**IC). Choosing **O**ther produces a list of all files in the current directory (in this case, *other* files means *all* files).

Fig. 9.16
The /**F**ile **E**rase menu enables you to choose **W**orksheet (*.WK?) and other options.

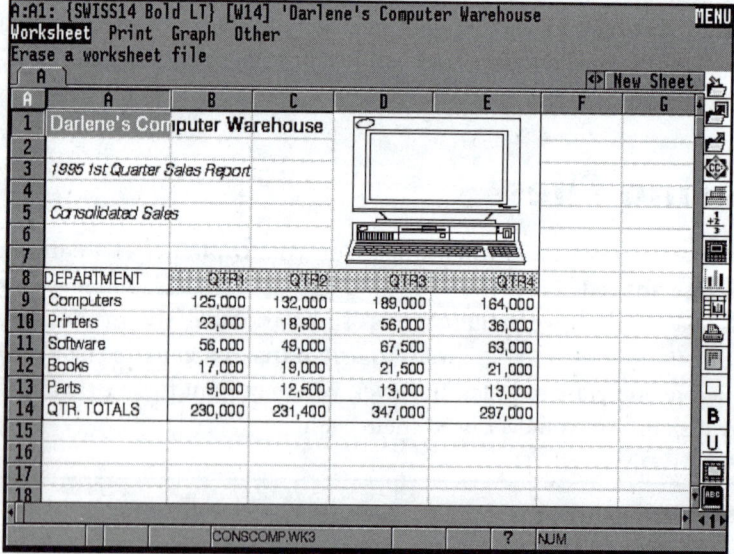

To list a different set of files, choose any of the options in the /**F**ile **E**rase menu; then press F2 (Edit) and change the file specification. To list all worksheet files that start with BUDGET, for example, type **BUDGET*.WK***. To list all backup worksheet files, type ***.BAK**.

> ▶ "Protecting Files with Passwords," p. 519

Caution

If you specify a password-protected file, 1-2-3 doesn't prompt you to provide the password when you erase the file.

You cannot erase a worksheet file from disk if that file currently is in memory. When the file that you want to erase is listed, highlight the file name and press Enter. Choose **Y**es to confirm that you want to erase the file. 1-2-3 erases the file.

Note

To erase multiple files simultaneously, choose /**T**ools **D**OS to suspend 1-2-3 and temporarily exit to DOS. Type **CD** and the name of the desired directory (for example, **CD\123R4D\DATA**); then press Enter. Use the DIR command to list the files in the directory (for example, type **DIR *.BAK**). To delete files, type **DEL**, followed by the file specification (using wild-card characters if desired); to delete all backup files, for example, type **DEL *.BAK**. To return to 1-2-3 after deleting the files, change back to the directory where you were working, type **EXIT**, and press Enter.

When you select a file to erase, 1-2-3 also erases the corresponding Wysiwyg-format file (with the extension FM3), Impress-format file (extension FMT), or Allways-format file (extension ALL), if one exists.

Troubleshooting

I accidentally erased the wrong file, and I really need it back.

Immediately—before you save any more files or write anything to the disk—find a copy of PC Tools (or another software-management package) and look up the instructions for undeleting a file.

Choose /**T**ools **D**OS to access the DOS prompt, and then use the DOS UNDELETE command—for example, UNDELETE *filename*. To see a list of deleted files, type **UNDELETE /list**. Warning: UNDELETE is available only with DOS Version 5 and higher. (So don't make any mistakes if you have an earlier version of DOS.)

(continues)

> (continued)
>
> If you don't have a software-management package, or if this procedure doesn't work, type the file again. (This is not what you wanted to hear, but you may have no choice.)
>
> *I've gotten into DOS by using /Tools DOS and have used DOS commands, but I can't get back to my worksheet.*
>
> Type **EXIT** and press Enter. When you first go to DOS, the prompt tells you this. As soon as you move past the first screen, however, you will not see the EXIT message again.
>
> In some cases, when you launch another program while you are in DOS, you will not be able to return to 1-2-3. You need to reboot your computer (turn it off and then on again) and start 1-2-3 again. If you did not save your file before you used **/T**ools **D**OS, the file will be lost.

Creating Lists and Tables of Files

If you work with many files, you may forget the names of certain files or the times they were last updated. 1-2-3 provides commands to help you keep track of the files you have on disk. You can list the files or save a table of files in your worksheet. In addition, you can list the files that are active in memory. This capability is handy if you work with many files in memory at the same time.

To see a list of files, choose **/F**ile **L**ist. The menu shown in figure 9.17 appears. The **W**orksheet, **P**rint, **G**raph, and **O**ther options provide the same lists that they provide in the **/F**ile **E**rase menu (described in "Erasing Files" earlier in this chapter). The **A**ctive option lists all files currently in memory. **L**inked lists all files referenced in formulas in the current file.

Figure 9.18 shows a list of files currently in memory, generated by choosing the **A**ctive option. When the pointer is on the file name, the third line of the screen shows the file name, date and time the file was last saved, and the size of the file (in bytes). The fifth entry indicates how many worksheets the file contains. The list also indicates whether an active file has been modified since the last time it was saved. (MOD means modified; UNMOD means unmodified.) If the file does not have a reservation or is unnamed, another entry, RO (Read Only), appears next to MOD or UNMOD.

Creating Lists and Tables of Files   **441**

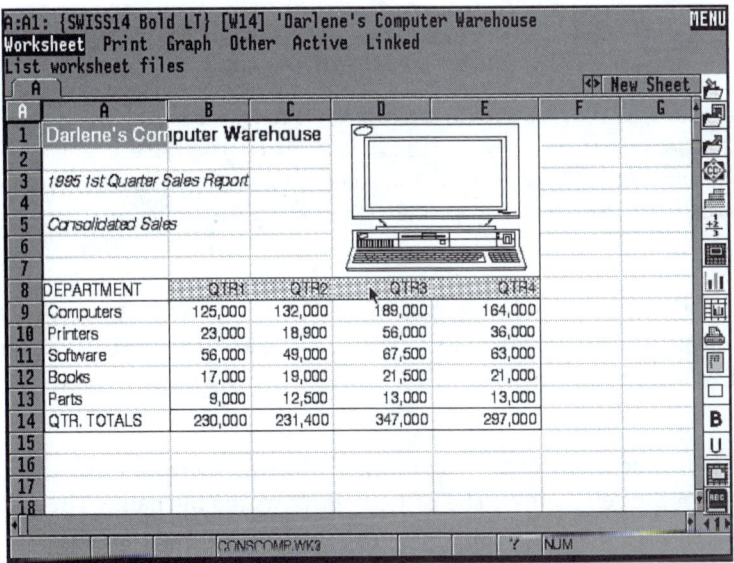

Fig. 9.17
The /File List menu enables you to specify the file types you want to display.

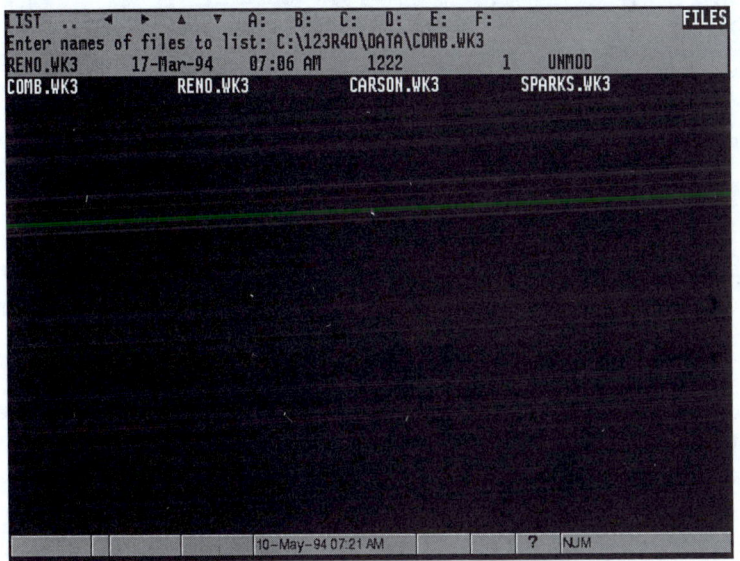

Fig. 9.18
The active file list shows the names of files in memory. To find information about a file, move to the file name.

> **Note**
>
> After working with several files at the same time, you may be confused about which ones have been changed. Use the **/F**ile **L**ist **A**ctive command to find out whether a file has been changed since being opened. Highlight each file name; a name with the designation MOD has been modified. This action can prevent you from deleting an unsaved file from memory with the **/W**orksheet **D**elete **F**ile command.

To place a file list in your worksheet as a table, choose **/F**ile **A**dmin **T**able. 1-2-3 displays the same menu for this command as for the **/F**ile **L**ist command: **W**orksheet, **P**rint, **G**raph, **O**ther, **A**ctive, and **L**inked (refer to fig. 9.17).

When you choose one of these options, 1-2-3 creates a table starting at the position of the cell pointer. The first column lists the file name. The second column lists the date. The third column lists the time that the file was saved. The fourth column lists the size of the file (in bytes).

> **Note**
>
> To display the columns in the list, format the second column with **/R**ange **F**ormat **D**ate, format the third column with **/R**ange **F**ormat **D**ate **T**ime, and format the fourth column with **/R**ange **F**ormat **,** (comma).

Tip
Use **/W**orksheet **C**olumn **F**it-Widest to set the size of your columns, if necessary.

If you choose any of the **/F**ile **A**dmin **T**able options, 1-2-3 displays these four columns with unformatted data for dates, times, and file sizes. Figure 9.19 shows the information after formatting the numbers, changing the column width, and formatting with Wysiwyg commands. If you choose **L**inked, the file name includes the complete path. When you choose **A**ctive, you get three additional columns. The fifth column lists the number of worksheets in the file. The sixth column shows 0 if you haven't modified the file since the last save operation and 1 if you have modified the file. The seventh column shows 1 to indicate that you have the reservation and can save the file. The seventh column shows 0 if the file is shared on a network, if the file is on your local hard disk but you have released the reservation, or if the file is marked read-only and you don't have the file reservation.

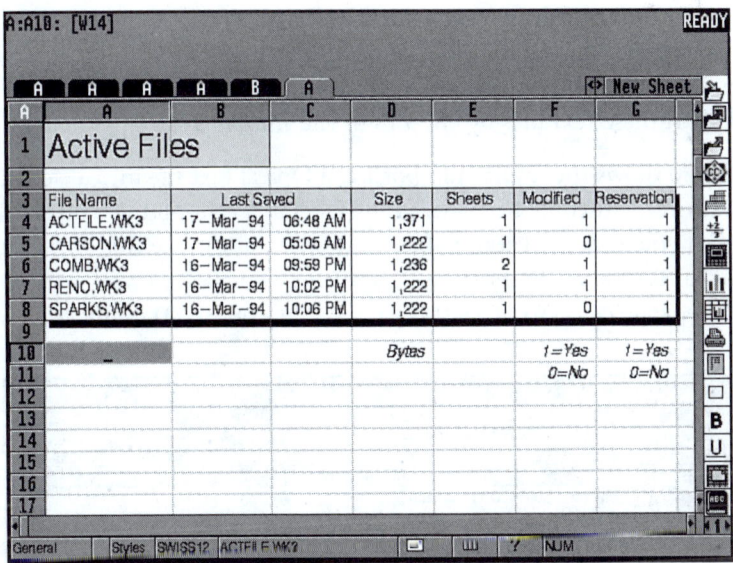

Fig. 9.19
The /File Admin Table Active command produces a list and information about files in memory.

Transferring Files

1-2-3 Release 4 provides several ways to pass data between 1-2-3 and other programs. This section describes these methods. The simplest file format is straight text (*ASCII* format). Most programs—including spreadsheet programs, word processing packages, and database management systems—can create text files.

◀ "Preparing Output for Acceptance by Other Programs," p. 401

To create a text file in 1-2-3, choose **/P**rint **F**ile. To read a text file into a worksheet, choose **/F**ile **I**mport, as described in the following section.

Transferring Files with /File Import

/File **I**mport is a special type of file-combining operation. Like **/F**ile **C**ombine, **/F**ile Import imports the information into the current worksheet, starting at the position of the cell pointer. Any existing data in these cells is overwritten. When you choose **/F**ile **I**mport, 1-2-3 lists the files with PRN extensions in the current directory. To list files that have another extension—TXT, for example—type the appropriate characters (such as ***.TXT**) and press Enter.

▶ "Extracting and Combining Data," p. 476

▶ "Importing Data from Other Programs," p. 695

Importing Unstructured Text Files

The typical text file contains lines of data, each line ending with a carriage return. Except for the carriage returns, these text files have no structure. You import these text files by choosing **/F**ile **I**mport **T**ext.

Figure 9.20 shows the result of importing a typical text file into a worksheet. Each line in the text file becomes a long label in a cell. All the data is in column A. If you import a list of names or simply want to see this data, you are finished at this point. In most cases, however, you want to work with this data in separate cells. To make this data usable, choose **/D**ata **P**arse.

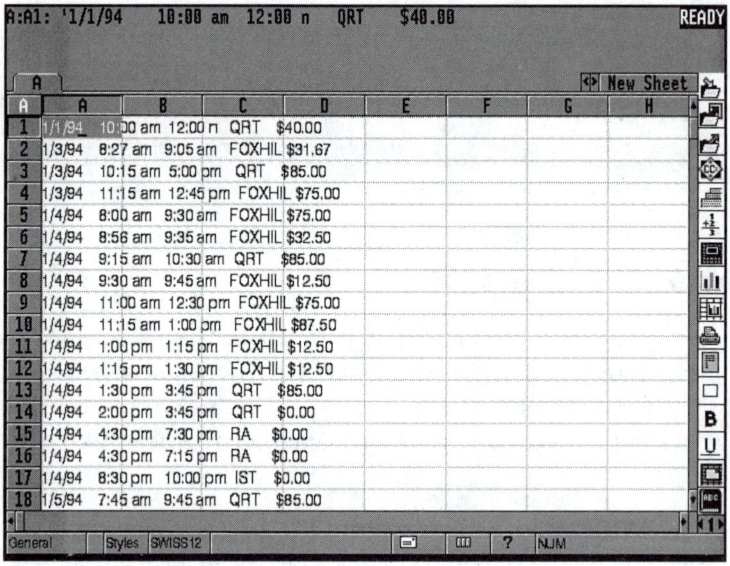

Fig. 9.20
An unstructured text file, imported as long labels with **/F**ile **I**mport **T**ext.

Tip
When you save text files in a different program for importing into 1-2-3, use the extension PRN. Then, when you use **/F**ile **I**mport **T**ext or **N**umbers, the files will be listed.

When you import data extracted from a database, the columns of data may not line up because of 1-2-3's default font. Change the font with **:F**ormat **F**ont **R**eplace, and choose a Courier (fixed-space) font.

Importing Delimited Files

Some ASCII files are in a special format that enables them to be imported into separate cells without being parsed. This special format is called the *delimited format*. A delimited file contains a delimiter between each field, and labels are enclosed in quotation marks. The *delimiter* can be a space, comma, colon, or semicolon. If the labels aren't enclosed in quotation marks, they are ignored, and only the numbers are imported.

To import a delimited file, choose **/F**ile **I**mport **N**umbers. Despite its name, this command really means "file import delimited." Figure 9.21 shows an example of a delimited file. Figure 9.22 shows the result after you choose **/F**ile **I**mport **N**umbers.

◀ "Understanding Fonts," p. 321

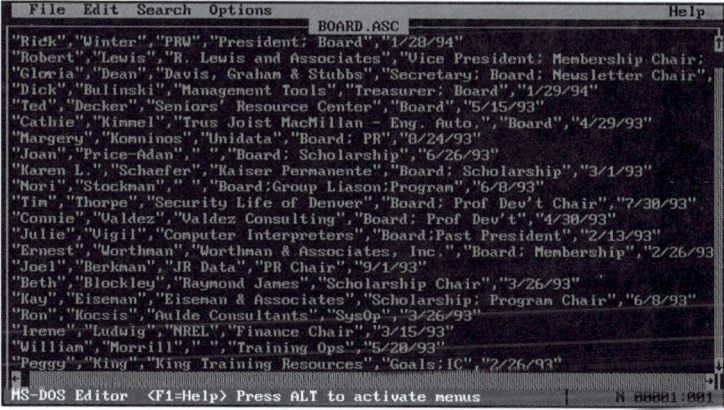

Fig. 9.21
A delimited ASCII file shows quotes around text and commas separating the fields in the DOS editor.

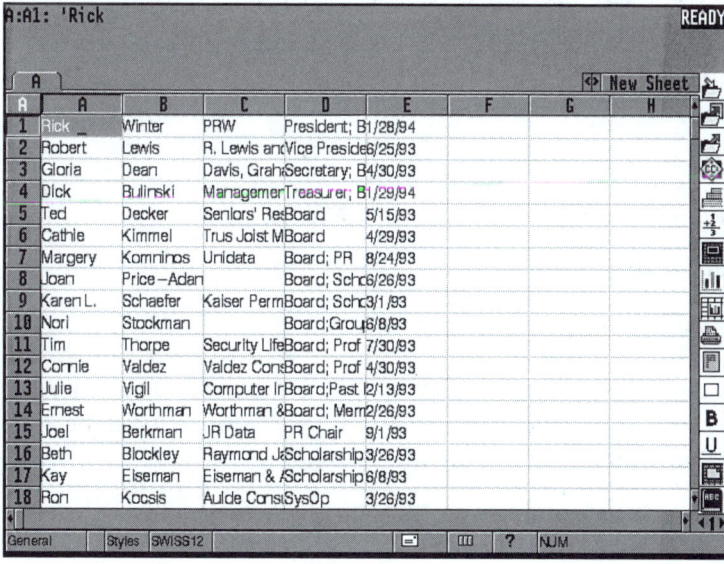

Fig. 9.22
The delimited ASCII file after you import it with **/F**ile **I**mport **N**umbers. You must change column widths to see the entire text in each column.

Transferring Files with the Translate Utility

The Translate utility is a separate program from the 1-2-3 spreadsheet program. Translate converts files so that they can be read by another program. You can convert files to 1-2-3 Release 4 for DOS format from the following formats:

- 1-2-3 Release 4 for Windows
- dBASE II, III, and III Plus
- Enable 2.0
- Multiplan 4.2 and Multiplan with SYLK format
- SuperCalc 4
- Products that use the DIF format

You can convert files from 1-2-3 Release 4 for DOS to the following formats:

- 1-2-3 Releases 1A, 2, 2.01, 2.2, 2.3, and 2.4
- 1-2-3 Release 4 for Windows
- Symphony Releases 1, 1.01, 1.1, 1.2, 2, 2.2, and 3.0
- dBASE II, III, and III Plus
- Enable 2.0
- Multiplan 4.2 and Multiplan with SYLK format
- SuperCalc 4
- Products that use the DIF format

When you convert 1-2-3 Release 4 for DOS files to the formats of earlier versions of 1-2-3 or Symphony, you may lose some information if the Release 4 file uses any features that are unique to Release 4.

To use the Translate utility, type **TRANS** from the operating-system prompt or choose **T**ranslate from the Lotus 1-2-3 Access menu (accessed by typing **LOTUS** at the DOS prompt). Use the menu pointer in Translate to choose the format or program from which you want to translate; then choose the format or program to which you want to translate (see fig. 9.23). Finally, choose the file that you want to translate. Type the name of the output file to be created by Translate, and press Enter.

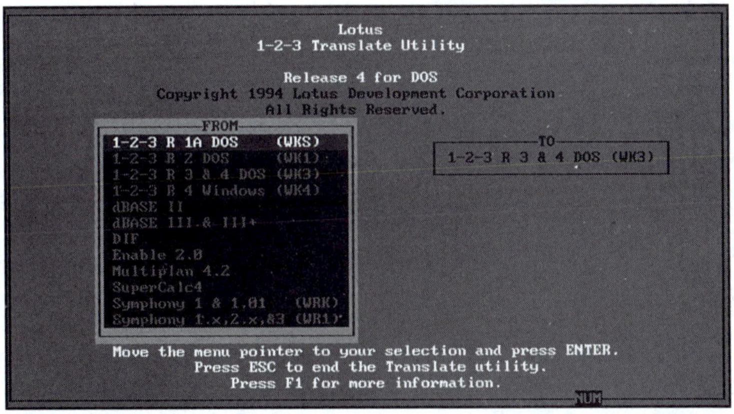

Fig. 9.23
On the left side of the screen, move the selection bar up or down to see the formats from which you can transfer. The formats to which you can transfer change, depending on the highlighted FROM choice.

When you translate from 1-2-3 Release 4, you can translate one worksheet or all worksheets (into separate files).

> **Note**
>
> The database *input range* consists of one row of field headings (the first row in the database), followed immediately by the first record (the second row in the database). You cannot include blank rows between the headings and the data. Usually, your 1-2-3 worksheet file contains information in addition to the database. You specify the input range for the database by choosing **/R**ange **N**ame **C**reate in 1-2-3 and naming the input range. Be sure to save the file before exiting 1-2-3 and starting the Translate utility.

When you translate to dBASE format, you can translate the entire file or only a named range. When you translate a file to dBASE format, the range that you translate (or the entire file, if you choose that option) must consist of the database input range only. If you are translating from a database format to 1-2-3, you can use the **/D**ata **E**xternal command to link to or copy a portion of the data.

▶ "Working with External Databases," p. 1025

Tip
In a multiple-worksheet file, all the worksheets are translated into separate files. The last letter of the file name indicates the original worksheet letter.

> **Note**
>
> Use the command **TRANWKS** *FILE*.**WK3** *FILE*.**WK1** **-l** **-a** from the DOS prompt to translate Release 4 files to Release 2.x format. Because Release 4 has new functions and arguments and offers file-linking range formulas, you must use the **-a** flag to translate files from WK3 format to WK1 format. The **-a** flag changes new functions and arguments to add-in functions and converts file-linking formulas to @@ functions. If you don't include this flag, these elements become labels. Use the **-l** flag to indicate the worksheet file (**-ld** would translate worksheet D).

Using Earlier Versions of 1-2-3 and Symphony Files in Release 4

1-2-3 Release 4 can read files created by all previous releases of 1-2-3 and Symphony. Simply choose **/F**ile **R**etrieve or **/F**ile **O**pen and then specify the complete file name and extension; you don't need to use Translate. The Translate menu (refer to fig. 9.23) contains an option that translates files to 1-2-3 Release 4 format from previous releases of 1-2-3 and Symphony; if you choose one of these formats, however, you get a message indicating that you don't need to translate the file.

1-2-3 Release 4 can write files in 1-2-3 Release 2.x format if you haven't used any features unique to Release 4. Choose **/F**ile **S**ave and specify a file name with a WK1 extension. Symphony Releases 1.1, 1.2, 2, 2.2, and 3.0 also can read WK1 files.

You cannot save a file in 1-2-3 Release 2.x format if the file contains multiple worksheets or is sealed. Functions that are new in 1-2-3 Release 4 or that contain new arguments are treated like 1-2-3 Release 2.x add-in functions. New functions or those that contain new arguments evaluate to NA in the worksheet. Formats and settings that are new in Release 4, as well as notes, are lost. Labels longer than 240 characters are truncated. Formulas longer than 240 characters remain in the cell, but the cell cannot be edited in 1-2-3 Release 2.x or Symphony.

To create a file in 1-2-3 Release 4 that can be read by 1-2-3 Release 1A or Symphony Releases 1 or 1.01, you must use Translate.

Using External Databases

▶ "Working with External Databases," p. 1025

You can read and create dBASE III files in a 1-2-3 worksheet. Lotus provides a special driver program that enables you to access and create dBASE III files by using **/D**ata **E**xternal commands. Other vendors of database management programs supply their own drivers that enable 1-2-3 to access and create files for their programs. If you use a database management program and want to share files with 1-2-3, contact the vendor to learn whether such a driver is available.

Accessing the Operating System

In this chapter, you have learned how to use many different 1-2-3 commands to build and modify worksheet files. At times, however, you may need to perform a function that requires you to use the operating system or another program. Suppose that you want to save a file on a floppy disk, but you have no formatted disks available. In this case, you want to use the DOS FORMAT command. Another possible situation is that, while you are working in 1-2-3, you are asked to print a copy of a letter you created in a word processing program.

In these situations, you can save your files and use **/Q**uit to exit 1-2-3. When you finish the other task, you can restart 1-2-3 and retrieve the file. However, you may not need to use **/Q**uit; 1-2-3 offers a faster alternative.

> **Note**
>
> The **/T**ools **D**OS command was **/S**ystem in previous versions of 1-2-3. After you choose the command, however, its function is identical.

Use the **/T**ools **D**OS command to temporarily suspend 1-2-3 and access the operating system (DOS). When in DOS, you can copy files, format floppy disks, and execute other system functions; if you have enough memory available, you can even execute another program. To return to 1-2-3, type **EXIT** and press Enter. You return to 1-2-3 with the same worksheet status as when you left; the same worksheet files are in memory, and the cell pointer is in the same place. Window settings and any other defaults also remain undisturbed.

▶ "The SYSTEM Command," p. 926

You also can use the {SYSTEM} macro command to invoke DOS from your 1-2-3 macros.

> **Note**
>
> If not enough memory is available, 1-2-3 cannot invoke the operating system. You can recover some memory if you save your files and erase your worksheets, but clearing memory defeats the purpose of the **/T**ools **D**OS command.

Always save your files before you use **/T**ools **D**OS. If you execute any *memory-resident program* (a program that remains in memory while you run other programs), you may not be able to reenter 1-2-3. Examples of memory-resident programs include SideKick and SideKick Plus from Borland International, Lotus Magellan, the DOS MODE and PRINT commands, and print spoolers. If you don't save your files and later find that you cannot reenter 1-2-3, you lose all your work.

If you use the DOS Shell program (included with DOS versions 4 through 6) or a graphical operating environment such as Microsoft Windows, the **/T**ools **D**OS command doesn't return to the shell or environment. Instead, **/T**ools **D**OS provides access to the DOS command-line interface (the DOS prompt). If you are unfamiliar with the DOS prompt, avoid using the **/T**ools **D**OS command.

> **Note**
>
> If you want to disable the **/T**ools **D**OS command, type **123 -o** when you start 1-2-3. This command also disables the {SYSTEM} macro command.

Using 1-2-3 on a Network

In a networked environment, two or more people can try to access or update the same 1-2-3 file simultaneously. The network administrator sets up shared directories so that some files can be shared and some cannot. (You don't need to worry about the files on a network server that only you can read.)

The **/F**ile **A**dmin commands control reservations for sharing worksheet files, creating tables of information about files, sealing some settings in worksheet files, and recalculating all formulas in active files. The following sections describe the commands that perform these tasks.

Understanding File Sharing

Programs handle the problems of multiple access in several ways. With a database management system such as dBASE III Plus, the program controls access; many users can access the database at the same time. With most programs, such as word processing packages, the network administrator makes sure that these files are identified as *nonsharable*, meaning that only one person at a time can access the file. If you are working with a word processing file, for example, no one else can read the file until you close it. Then the file is available to the next person who wants it.

1-2-3 uses reservations to handle file sharing. For the 1-2-3 file-reservation system to work properly, your work group must use 1-2-3 Release 2.2, 2.3, 2.4, 3, 3.1, 3.1+, 3.4, 3.4a, or 4; 1-2-3 Networker; or another product that supports file sharing. If you attempt to share data files without these types of software, you may experience data loss.

You shouldn't use a program other than 1-2-3 Release 4 to modify a file for which you have a reservation. This strategy prevents loss of data or, as is possible in some environments, equipment failure.

When attempting to read a shared file created in 1-2-3 Release 1A or 2 format without the WK* extension (for example, Symphony WR1 files), 1-2-3 Release 4 reads the file into memory and renames it in memory with the WK3 extension. If no WK3 file with that name exists, 1-2-3 gets a reservation for the new file. If a file with that name exists, however, 1-2-3 gives read-only status to the file in memory and displays the RO status indicator with an error message. To save the file, you must choose **/F**ile **S**ave and give the file a new name.

If you try to read a file from disk while another user is reading that file or saving it to disk, 1-2-3 displays the WAIT indicator. The WAIT indicator remains on-screen until the first user completes the process of reading or saving the file. An error message appears if 1-2-3 cannot read or save the file within one wait cycle. You can use Ctrl+Break to interrupt the wait cycle and return 1-2-3 to the position the program was in before you tried to read or save the file.

If you create or save a shared file and then release the reservation or exit 1-2-3, another user may get the file's reservation and save changes. Such a file change and save by another user alters the file before you can read it into memory again. To determine when changes were saved to a file, you can choose **/F**ile **L**ist (explained in "Creating Lists and Tables of Files" earlier in this chapter).

> **Caution**
>
> If you make changes to a file without a reservation and decide to save the changes in a file with a different name, don't copy your file over the original file after the reservation for the original file is available. By doing so, you may inadvertently overwrite another user's work.

If you need to access a file for read-only purposes and the file has an **A**utomatic reservation setting in memory, release the reservation so that another user can get the reservation.

Getting a File's Reservation

To prevent concurrent updates of the same shared file, 1-2-3 provides a **R**eservation option. Only one user at a time can have a file's reservation. The reservation status, therefore, is "available" or "unavailable."

Before reading a file into memory, 1-2-3 checks the reservation status and acts accordingly. If the reservation is available and the reservation setting is **A**utomatic, 1-2-3 reads the file into memory with its reservation. If the reservation isn't available and the reservation setting is **A**utomatic, 1-2-3 displays a **Y**es/**N**o menu and the following prompt:

```
Retrieve the file without a reservation?
```

If you choose **Y**es, you can access the file in read-only status. In other words, you can look at the file, but changes you make aren't saved in the file with the original file name.

The RO status indicator at the bottom of the screen warns you that you cannot save the file under its current name (see fig. 9.24). If you want to save the file, you must give it a different name.

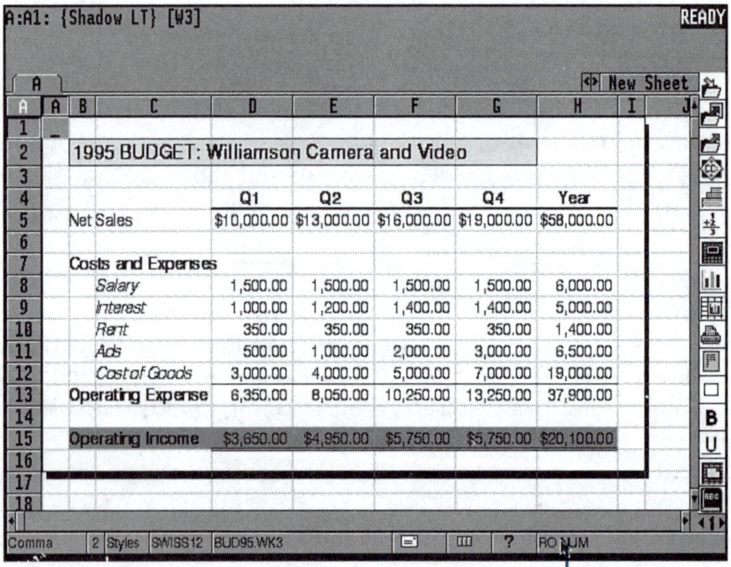

Fig. 9.24
The RO status indicator displays on the right side of the status bar.

RO status indicator

Network users can assign read-only status to a file, or a network file may be in a read-only network directory. If either situation occurs, you cannot get a reservation for a file of this type, even if no other user has the reservation. In network situations such as these, the network commands take precedence over the 1-2-3 reservation status.

If you have the reservation for a file, you keep the reservation until you remove the file (under the same name) from your worksheet. You can remove the file by choosing **/Q**uit, **/W**orksheet **E**rase, **/W**orksheet **D**elete **F**ile, or **/F**ile **R**etrieve. You can release the reservation with **/F**ile **S**ave if you save the file under a different name. You also can release the reservation by choosing **/F**ile **A**dmin **R**eservation **R**elease; after you execute this command, the file remains in memory, but you cannot save the file with the original name.

This reservation system also works manually. If many people can read a file but only one person can update it, you can assign the reservation manually. Choose **/F**ile **A**dmin **R**eservation **S**etting **M**anual so that the first person to read a file doesn't get the reservation. Everyone who reads the file has read-only access until one person gets the reservation with **/F**ile **A**dmin **R**eservation **G**et. In general, using manual reservation settings is a bad idea, because you cannot ensure that only authorized people get the reservation. The network administrator may be able to set up restricted access for those people who can read but shouldn't write to a file.

/File **A**dmin **R**eservation **S**etting **A**utomatic sets the file's reservation so that the first person to read the file into memory gets the reservation; **M**anual sets the file reservation so that no one automatically gets the reservation and the user must choose **/F**ile **A**dmin **R**eservation **G**et. To make the setting permanent, save the file. The **/F**ile **A**dmin **T**able **A**ctive command (mentioned in "Creating Lists and Tables of Files" earlier in this chapter) creates a table of information about files in memory. The seventh column displays 1 if you have the file's reservation and 0 if you don't.

Preventing Changes to Worksheet Settings

The **/F**ile **A**dmin **S**eal **F**ile command seals the current file with a password so that no one can change certain properties of the file without knowing the password. If you use this command to seal the current file, you can prevent changes to some graph, print, range, and worksheet settings.

▶ "Sealing Files," p. 523

The **/F**ile **A**dmin **S**eal **R**eservation-Settings command seals the reservation setting with a password so that no one can change the reservation without

Tip
For maximum protection for a file, seal the file with protection enabled (**/W**orksheet **G**lobal **P**rot **E**nable) and with a password.

knowing the password. This command prevents changes to the reservation setting of a file.

After you choose **/F**ile **A**dmin **S**eal **F**ile or **/F**ile **A**dmin **S**eal **R**eservation-Settings, 1-2-3 prompts you for a password. Type a password, and then verify the password just as you do when you password-protect a file with **/F**ile **S**ave. After a file is sealed with a password, the only way to unseal it is to choose **/F**ile **A**dmin **S**eal **D**isable and provide the correct password.

> **Caution**
> Use a password you won't forget because you won't be able to unseal the file without it.

> **Caution**
> Don't forget to save your file after you use a **/F**ile **A**dmin **S**eal command. Your changes will not take effect unless you choose **/F**ile **S**ave after you seal the file.

Updating Your Links

▶ "Linking Data," p. 487

When you have a file that contains links to other files, 1-2-3 updates these formulas when you read the file and choose **/F**ile **A**dmin **L**ink-Refresh. Although executing the **/F**ile **A**dmin **L**ink-Refresh command requires only choosing the command and pressing Enter, you may need to insert into your files a note that reminds you to update files when necessary.

Sending and Receiving Mail Through cc:Mail

If you have cc:Mail Release 4.02 for DOS installed on your computer or are mapped to a network drive containing cc:Mail, you can read a message or send a message, your file, or a range from your file. To access cc:Mail, choose **/T**ools **E**-Mail or click the cc:Mail SmartIcon. As shown in figure 9.25, you have three options in the menu: **S**tart, **F**ile, and **R**ange. Do one of the following things:

- Choose **S**tart to begin cc:Mail so you can send and receive messages.

- Choose **F**ile and type a file name as an electronic-mail message.

Sending and Receiving Mail Through cc:Mail

■ Choose **R**ange, indicate whether you want to include **F**ormulas or convert formulas to **V**alues, and type the file name and range to extract as an electronic-mail message.

> **Note**
>
> When you use **/T**ools **E**-Mail **F**ile, 1-2-3 prompts you with the name of the active file. If you have multiple files active, 1-2-3 prompts you for all files. You can press Backspace and select only one of the active files.

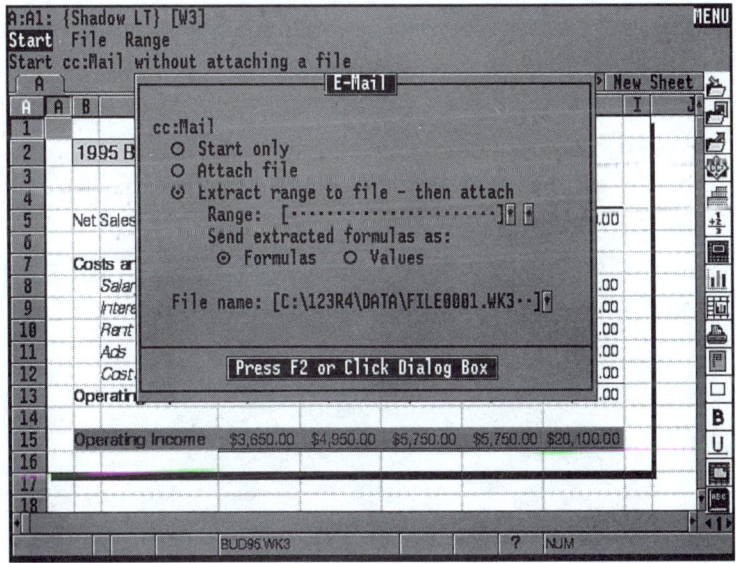

Fig. 9.25
To enter cc:Mail, choose **/T**ools **E**-Mail or click the cc:Mail SmartIcon. The E-Mail menu gives you three options.

When you press Enter, you launch your e-mail package. Address the letter, indicate the subject, and send the message in the normal way. When you exit e-mail, you return to 1-2-3.

While you are in 1-2-3, you can start cc:Mail by clicking the envelope icon in the status bar. This is equivalent to choosing **/T**ools **E**-Mail **S**tart. The envelope icon also shows how many messages you have waiting.

> **Note**
>
> To see the number of messages you have, you need to run 123TSR.EXE before starting 1-2-3.

From Here...

As you work with files, you may want to look at the following chapters:

- Chapter 10, "Organizing Your Data with Multiple-Worksheet Files." This chapter deals with working with 3-D files.

- Chapter 11, "Consolidating Worksheet Data." This chapter deals with combining and linking information from one file to your current file.

- Chapter 13, "Protecting Worksheet Data and Files." This chapter shows you how to protect your worksheet from unwanted changes.

- Chapter 29, "Sharing 1-2-3 Data with Windows Applications." This chapter shows you how to copy and use information within 1-2-3 files to Windows applications.

- Chapter 30, "Sharing 1-2-3 Data with Databases." This chapter shows you how to use the **/D**ata **E**xternal command to link your 1-2-3 files to database management programs.

- Chapter 31, "Sharing 1-2-3 Data with DOS Word Processors." This chapter shows you how to copy and use information within 1-2-3 files to word processing applications.

Chapter 10

Organizing Your Data with Multiple-Worksheet Files

When you work with a 1-2-3 file, it contains at least one worksheet. Starting with Release 3, Lotus added the capability of having more than one worksheet or "page" per file. Depending on your computer's memory and the size of your file, you can have as many as 256 worksheets in a file. The first sheet is labeled A, the second sheet B, and so on up to IV. With Release 4, you can also name the sheets and use the mouse to click the worksheet tab to quickly navigate to the worksheet.

The following sections cover creating and naming multiple worksheets, moving around multiple worksheets, entering data and formulas with multiple worksheets, and also formatting multiple worksheets.

In this chapter, you learn the following about multiple-worksheet files:

- Referencing cells
- Inserting, deleting, and hiding sheets
- Naming sheets
- Moving around multiple sheets
- Creating formulas and functions
- Formatting

Using Multiple-Worksheet Files

Using multiple worksheets creates, in effect, a set of separate worksheets for a large file. Usually, you use multiple-worksheet files in two basic situations, described as follows:

▶ "Extracting and Combining Data," p. 476

- *Multiple-worksheet files are ideal for consolidations.* Use multiple-worksheet files for consolidations that contain separate parts, such as products, countries, or projects. If you need worksheets for many departments in a single company, for example, a multiple-worksheet file enables you to build a separate, identical worksheet for each department. The individual worksheets are smaller, less confusing, and easier to use than a single large worksheet containing all the data for every department. You can make one worksheet a consolidation worksheet that combines the data from the individual department worksheets; you can put a formula in a cell in one worksheet that refers to cells in other worksheets.

▶ "Designing a Database," p. 621

▶ "Including Graphs in Reports," p. 746

▶ "Understanding Macros," p. 830

- *You can use multiple-worksheet files to place separate sections of an application in separate worksheets.* You might want to put your input data such as invoices on one worksheet and then summaries of the data (such as by date, by employee, or by client) on different worksheets. You may want to put graphs on separate sheets. If you work with database functions and commands, you may want to put the input range on one sheet, the criteria range on another, the output range on another, and data tables on other sheets. Generally, it is a good idea to put assumptions on one sheet, notes on another sheet, and macros on another sheet.

An important advantage of using multiple worksheets is that you can change one worksheet in a file without risking accidental changes to the other worksheets. If an entire file consists of one worksheet, however, inserting or deleting a row or column in one area can accidentally destroy part of another area that shares the same row or column. You can design multiple-worksheet files so that inserting and deleting rows and columns anywhere in the file doesn't affect other parts of the file. Accidentally overwriting formulas that are part of input areas is another common error you can avoid by using multiple worksheets, which enable you to separate input areas and formulas.

Although you may want to separate your work on different sheets to avoid accidentally deleting data, you may also want to set up your worksheets so that any formatting or deleting rows or columns works on all worksheets in the file at the same time. You can choose to segregate worksheets or choose the GROUP mode to have changes appear on all worksheets at the same time. See "Formatting a Multiple-Worksheet File" later in this chapter.

Table 10.1 describes some commands and keystrokes related to multiple worksheets, and indicates whether a SmartIcon exists to help you with the task.

Table 10.1 Commands and SmartIcons Related to Multiple Worksheets

Command	SmartIcon	Action
/**F**ile **N**ew		Opens and adds a new, blank file to memory; doesn't replace existing files in memory
/**F**ile **O**pen		Reads and adds a file from disk to memory; doesn't replace existing files in memory
/**W**orksheet **D**elete **F**ile		Removes an active file from memory when more than one file is in memory at the same time
/**W**orksheet **D**elete **S**heet		Deletes one or more existing worksheets from the current file
/**W**orksheet **G**lobal **G**roup **E**nable		Changes the scope of many /**W**orksheet commands, such as **I**nsert, **G**lobal **F**ormat, and **G**lobal **C**ol-Width, and Wysiwyg formatting so that they affect all worksheets in the file, not just the current worksheet
/**W**orksheet **I**nsert **S**heet		Adds one or more new worksheets to the current file
/**W**orksheet **W**indow **P**erspective		Displays three worksheets at a time in perspective view
F6		Switches between windows
Alt+F6		In perspective view, toggles between three sheets and one sheet
Ctrl+PgUp		Moves to the next worksheet
Ctrl+PgDn		Moves to the previous worksheet
Ctrl+Home		Moves to the first cell in the first worksheet
F5		Goes to the specified cell or range
		Sums a 3-D range

Referencing Cells in Multiple Worksheets

If you've used 1-2-3 for a while, especially any Release 2.x version, you are familiar with the standard cell reference of column followed by row. For example, the cell in the third column and fifth row is C5. You need to use cell references when using the F5 (GoTo) key, defining ranges during many commands, and creating formulas. Even if you have used Release 3.x or 4 for a while, you may be using just the column and row reference because you have been working on a single worksheet.

After you start using the multiple-worksheet feature, you need to use the sheet reference. The sheet reference starts with A and goes through IV, just as do column references. The complete cell reference includes the sheet letter, a colon (:), a column letter, and a row number. B:C5 stands for the cell on the second sheet, third column, and fifth row. The range A:A1..C:E5 includes the block A1..E5 on sheets A, B, and C.

A multiple-worksheet cell reference works like any other cell reference. You can use F5 (GoTo) and type **D:A5** to move to that cell. You can use **/R**ange **F**ormat **C**urrency and choose A:B20..E:F20 to format the row on the five sheets (A through E) with dollar signs. You can also create the formula @SUM(A:B5..D:B5) to sum the B5 cells on sheets A through D.

◄ "Learning the 1-2-3 Screen Display," p. 22

You can see the sheet reference in three places on the screen as shown in figure 10.1. The cell contents line of the control panel shows the sheet reference of the current cell along with the column and row reference. In the worksheet frame, the sheet letter of the current worksheet shows above the row numbers and to the left of column letters. Finally, Release 4 has added worksheet tabs that show sheet letters. You can click on the tab to move to the sheet you want. You can also name the tabs for easier reference (see "Naming Worksheets" later in this chapter). Figure 10.1 also shows other screen features relating to multiple worksheets.

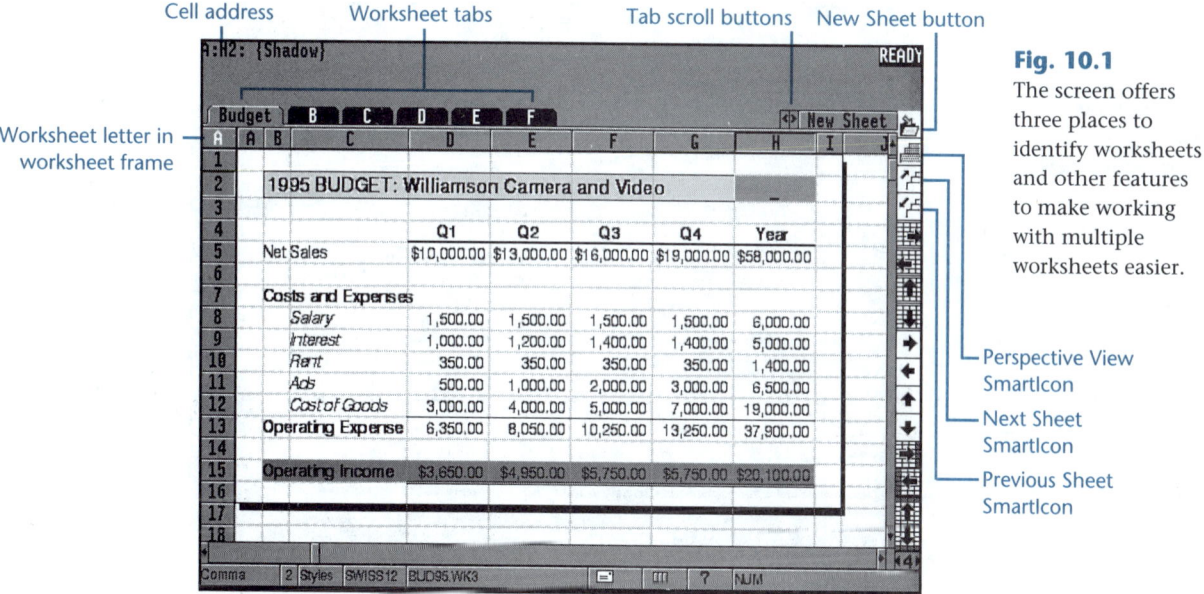

Fig. 10.1
The screen offers three places to identify worksheets and other features to make working with multiple worksheets easier.

Working with Sheets in Multiple-Worksheet Files

Worksheets and columns have much in common. Both are identified with a letter and both can go up to IV (256 columns or sheets). To add columns or sheets in a multiple-worksheet file, you use the /**W**orksheet **I**nsert command. To delete columns or sheets, you also start with the similar column command: /**W**orksheet **D**elete. Also, like the /**W**orksheet **C**olumn **H**ide command, you can hide sheets, but you use /**W**orksheet **H**ide.

Inserting Worksheets

You can create multiple-worksheet files just by inserting more worksheets into the current file. To insert one sheet at a time, you can click the New Sheet button or the Insert Worksheet SmartIcon. To insert one or more new worksheets in a file, select /**W**orksheet **I**nsert **S**heet. 1-2-3 then prompts you to insert the new worksheets either **B**efore or **A**fter the current worksheet. Usually, you select **A**fter to insert the new worksheet(s) behind the current worksheet. Then type the number of worksheets you want to insert and press Enter. Figure 10.2 shows a file before a worksheet is inserted. Figure 10.3 shows the same file after a new worksheet is inserted after worksheet B.

Fig. 10.2
The cell pointer is in worksheet A of a multiple-worksheet file in perspective view.

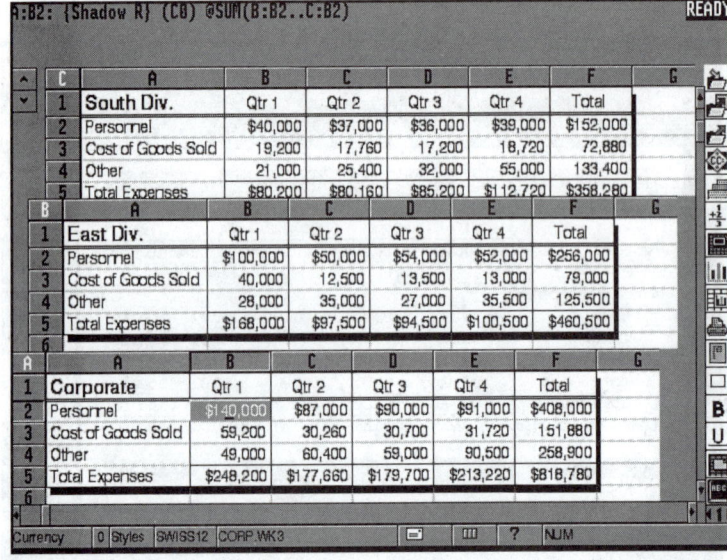

Fig. 10.3
When you select /**W**orksheet **I**nsert **S**heet **A**fter, a new blank worksheet B appears after worksheet A.

New sheet

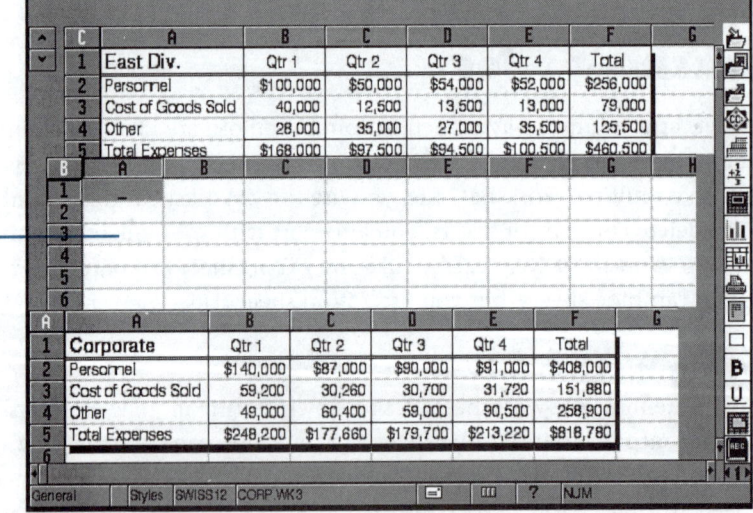

If you introduce worksheets in the middle of a multiple-worksheet file, all the worksheets behind the new ones receive new worksheet letters. As in figure 10.2, if you insert a new worksheet after worksheet A, and worksheet B already exists, the new worksheet becomes B, and the old worksheet B becomes C. 1-2-3 adjusts all addresses and formulas. If you insert a worksheet within a range that spans more than one worksheet, the range expands to accommodate the new worksheet.

> **Caution**
>
> Inserting or deleting worksheets can affect both macros and formulas.

Naming Worksheets

1-2-3 Release 4 now shows worksheet tabs above the worksheet frame. You can turn the tabs on or off with **/W**orksheet **G**lobal **D**efault **O**ther **D**isplay **T**abs. By default, the first worksheet tab is A and the next is B. In other words, the tab matches the worksheet letter of the sheet in the current cell reference and on the worksheet frame.

To move to another worksheet, you can click the worksheet tab. If you cannot see all the tabs, click the tab scroll buttons to see more tabs on the screen.

You can also name the worksheet tabs for easier reference. Move to the worksheet you want to name or edit the name of. Double-click the tab or choose **/W**orksheet **N**ame. At the Enter name: prompt, type a worksheet name of up to 15 characters and press Enter. Figure 10.4 shows a worksheet with named tabs.

> **Note**
>
> When you are in perspective view, 1-2-3 does not display worksheet tabs. If you want to return a worksheet tab to the worksheet letter, choose **/W**orksheet **N**ame and delete the entire name. Worksheet names are not like range names; you cannot use the F5 key to go to a worksheet name or use worksheet names when formatting.

Fig. 10.4

After you choose /**W**orksheet **N**ame, type the name of the worksheet.

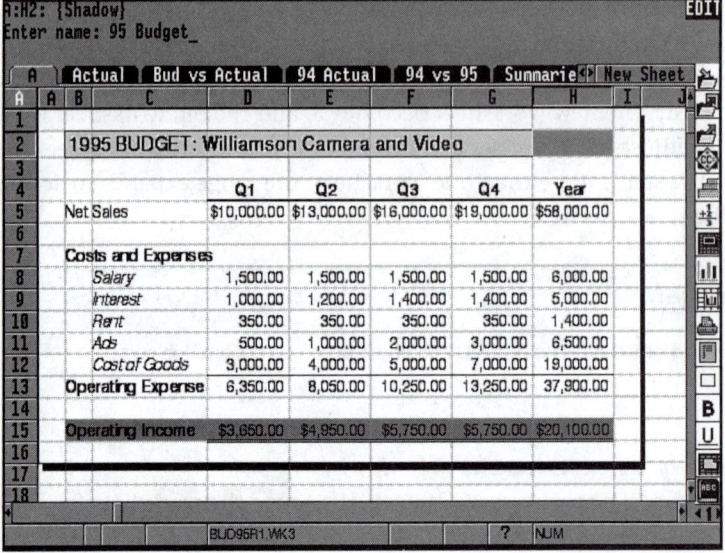

Deleting Worksheets

If the file has multiple worksheets, you can delete an entire worksheet the same way you delete a row or a column. If you want to delete the sheet where the cell pointer is, click the Delete Worksheet SmartIcon and choose OK to confirm the deletion.

You can also use menu commands to delete sheets. Position the cell pointer in the first or last worksheet to delete. Select /**W**orksheet **D**elete **S**heet and use Ctrl+PgUp or Ctrl+PgDn or the Next Worksheet or Previous Worksheet SmartIcons to move the cell pointer to each worksheet to be deleted. After you have highlighted a cell in each worksheet to be deleted, press Enter or click anywhere in the control panel. You cannot delete all the worksheets from a file; at least one worksheet must remain after the deletion. If you try to delete all worksheets in a file, you see an error message and no worksheets are deleted.

Hiding Worksheets

Instead of deleting a worksheet, you may simply want to hide the sheet from view. If you do not want to display a worksheet, use /**W**orksheet **H**ide **E**nable. You are prompted for the worksheets to hide. Anchor the cell reference and use the cell-movement keys mentioned in "Moving Around Multiple Worksheets" to highlight one cell in each sheet to hide. You can also type a range reference such as B:A1..D:A1 to hide sheets B through D. To unhide the sheets, use /**W**orksheet **H**ide **D**isable.

> **Note**
>
> After you hide worksheets, when you choose commands that request a range, the hidden worksheets display with an asterisk (*) in the worksheet letter of the worksheet frame. You can copy, format, or use other features with the hidden worksheets, but the worksheets return to their hidden state after you finish the command.

You may want to hide unnecessary detail from your view so that you can quickly move to the displayed sheets. For example, you may have monthly, quarterly, and annual sheets in a file. To see only monthly and annual sheets, you could hide the monthly detail sheets. If you have employees who should only input information and not change macros or summary sheets, you may want to hide all non-input sheets. If the employees know the **/W**orksheet **H**ide **D**isable command, or use operations like **/C**opy and **/M**ove they can see information on hidden worksheets if they want.

▶ "Sealing Files," p. 523

Displaying Multiple Worksheets

1-2-3 provides options that alter the display of your worksheet(s). The default screen display is a single window that shows part of one worksheet. The worksheet shown in figure 10.5 displays one sheet of a multiple-worksheet file.

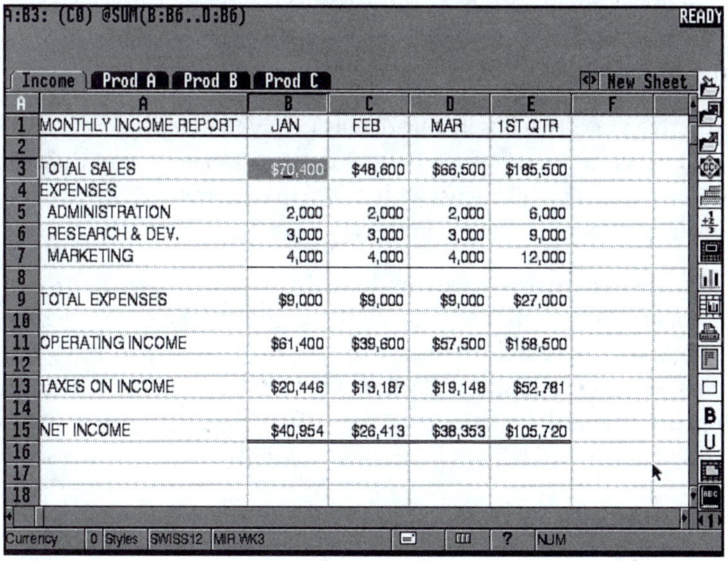

Fig. 10.5
One sheet of a multiple-worksheet file is currently displayed.

466 Chapter 10—Organizing Your Data with Multiple-Worksheet Files

In figure 10.6, the 1-2-3 screen is in perspective view. *Perspective view* can display parts of up to three worksheets at one time. Click the Perspective Window SmartIcon or choose /**W**orksheet **W**indow **P**erspective. While you are in perspective mode, press Alt+F6 (Zoom) to change the view to one worksheet. Press Alt+F6 (Zoom) again to toggle back to three worksheets. To turn off perspective view, choose /**W**orksheet **W**indow **C**lear.

Fig. 10.6
Choose /**W**orksheet **W**indow **P**erspective to turn on perspective view.

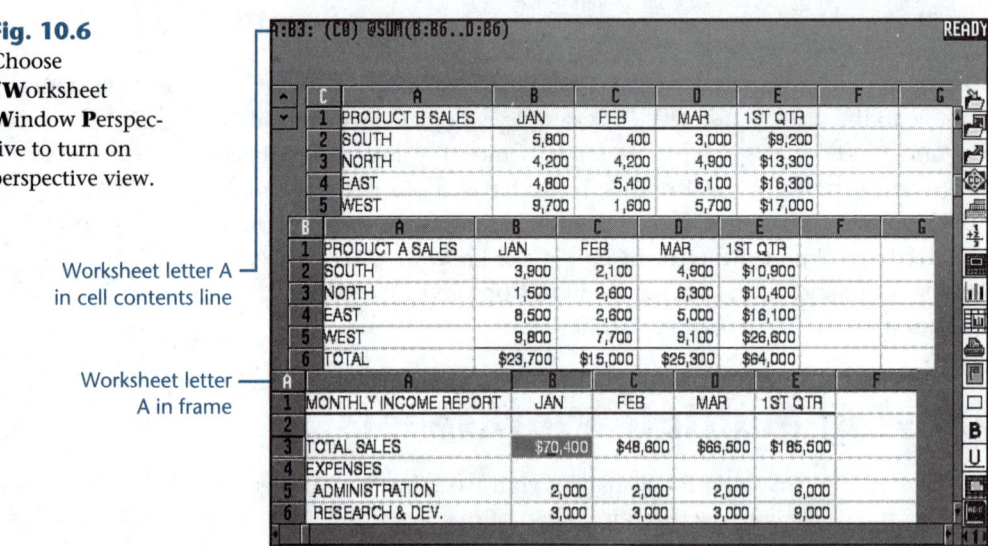

Worksheet letter A in cell contents line

Worksheet letter A in frame

If you use the window options to display more than one worksheet at a time, the current worksheet is the worksheet displaying the cell pointer. In figure 10.6, the current worksheet is A and the current cell is A:B3.

In perspective view, two observable details help you determine the current worksheet in figure 10.6: the cell pointer is in worksheet A, and the cell address in the control panel begins with A. If a file has more than three worksheets, you cannot display all the worksheets at one time.

◀ "Splitting the Screen," p. 234

While you are in perspective view and use the right or left arrows, PgUp, PgDn, Tab, and Shift+Tab, normally all three worksheets scroll together. If you want to keep the columns of two of the worksheets static and scroll the current sheet, use /**W**orksheet **W**indow **U**nsync. To return to synchronized scrolling, use /**W**orksheet **W**indow **S**ync. When you are in perspective view, the worksheet tabs and tab scroll buttons no longer display on the screen.

> **Note**
>
> If you want to see only two different worksheets, use **/W**orksheet **W**indow **V**ertical or **H**orizontal. After the worksheet is split, press Ctrl+PgUp or Ctrl+PgDn to move one of the views to a different sheet in the file.

> **Troubleshooting**
>
> *I try to use perspective view and the bottom two worksheets have no frame and are blank.*
>
> You are displaying a file with only one worksheet. If you want to add more worksheets, use **/W**orksheet **I**nsert **S**heet.
>
> *I can't get to perspective view even though only one worksheet is on-screen and I use /Worksheet Window Perspective.*
>
> Check the right side of your status line. If you are in zoom mode, you already have chosen perspective mode. Press Alt+F6 to return to displaying three worksheets.

Moving Around Multiple Worksheets

You can move around multiple worksheets or files with the mouse in a number of different ways. Figure 10.7 shows some of the elements of the screen used for navigating multiple worksheets. To move around the multiple worksheets, do the following:

- Click the Next Worksheet SmartIcon to move to the next worksheet or file.

- Click the Previous Worksheet SmartIcon to move to the previous worksheet or file.

- If you display three worksheets in perspective view, point to a cell in a worksheet or file and click the mouse to move to that worksheet or file.

- In perspective view, click the Previous Worksheet or Next Worksheet button to the left of the last visible sheet.

Fig. 10.7
The mouse offers many alternatives for moving around on multiple worksheets.

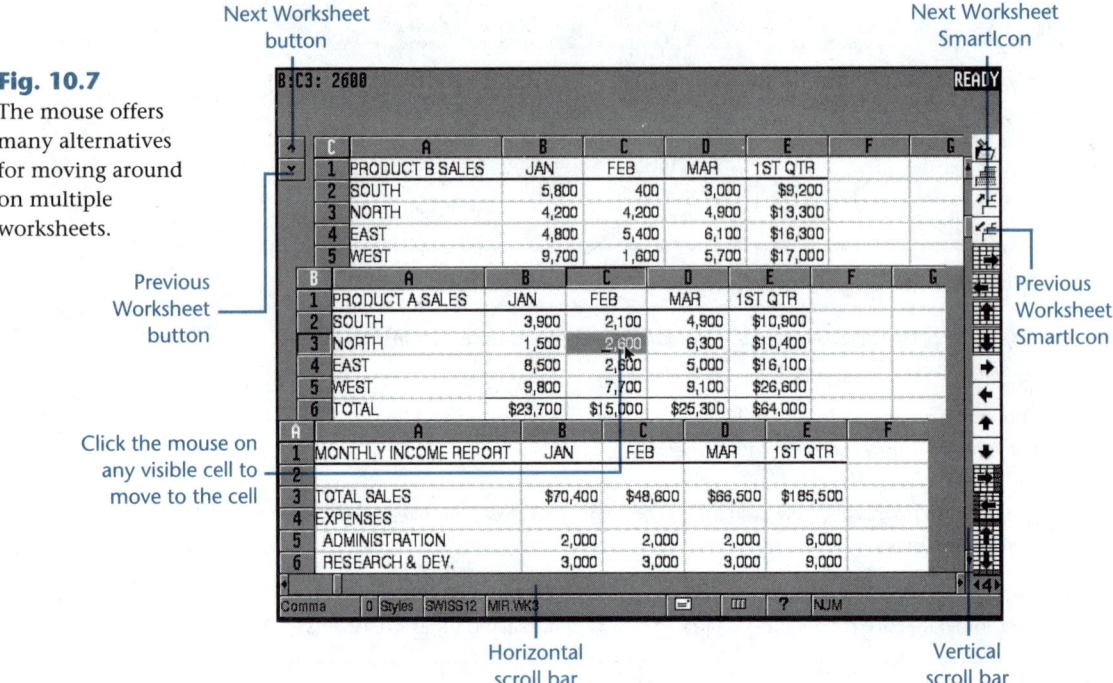

Table 10.2 shows keys that you use when working with multiple-worksheet files and multiple files in memory. The most important key combinations in table 10.2 are Ctrl+PgUp (to move to the next worksheet), Ctrl+PgDn (to move to the previous worksheet), and Ctrl+Home (to move to cell A:A1).

Table 10.2 Direction Key Operation with Multiple Worksheets

Key	Description
Ctrl+PgUp	Moves the cell pointer to the next worksheet
Ctrl+PgDn	Moves the cell pointer to the previous worksheet
Ctrl+Home	Moves the cell pointer to the home position in the first worksheet in the file (usually A:A1)
End Ctrl+Home	Moves the cell pointer to the end of the active area in the last worksheet in the file
End Ctrl+PgUp or End Ctrl+PgDn	Moves the cell pointer through the worksheets to the next cell containing data (the intersection between a blank cell and a cell containing data)

Key	Description
F5 (GoTo)	Prompts for a cell address or range name and then moves the cell pointer directly to this cell (which can be in another worksheet or file)
F6 (Window)	If the screen is split, moves the cell pointer to the next window (which can contain another worksheet or file)
Alt+F6 (Zoom)	In perspective view, toggles between viewing one worksheet and three worksheets

Figure 10.7 shows a multiple-worksheet file. Worksheet A is the consolidation worksheet. Worksheet B contains the detail data for sales for Product A, and worksheet C contains the detail data for Product B. Worksheet D (not in view) contains sales for Product C. Point to cell B:B3 and press the left mouse button. You also can press Ctrl+PgUp or click the Next Worksheet SmartIcon to move the cell pointer from A:B3 to B:B3.

◀ "Creating Range Names," p. 87

You can use GoTo (F5) to move within multiple worksheets. If you press GoTo and then type a cell address that includes only the column and row, the cell pointer moves to this address in the current worksheet. Include a worksheet letter in the cell address to move the cell pointer to another worksheet in the file. To move the cell pointer to C:A1 in the file in figure 10.7, press GoTo (F5), type **C:A1**, and press Enter.

To move the cell pointer to the current cell in worksheet B, press GoTo (F5), type **B:**, and then press Enter. 1-2-3 remembers a current cell for every worksheet in memory. In some cases, 1-2-3 returns to the cell pointer's last location in a worksheet. If you are in cell B:C3 in figure 10.7 and press GoTo (F5) to go to A:C6, the cell pointer jumps to C6 in worksheet A but remembers the last location in worksheet B. If you then press GoTo (F5) to go to worksheet B, the cell pointer returns to cell C3 in worksheet B.

When you use the window options, such as the perspective view used in figure 10.7, you can synchronize or unsynchronize the current cells in each worksheet. When *synchronized*, the current location of the cell pointer determines the current cell for all worksheets on-screen. If you are in cell A:B3 and press GoTo to go to B:C15, for example, the cell pointer jumps to C15 in worksheet B. C15 becomes the current cell. If you then press GoTo (F5) to go to worksheet A, the cell pointer moves to cell C15 in worksheet A.

Tip
Because multiple-worksheet files can get large, you may want to name ranges to use as "bookmarks" to navigate around the worksheet or use with range or print commands. Use **/R**ange **N**ame **C**reate to name the range. After you've named a range, you can use GoTo (F5), type the range name, and press Enter to go to the range name.

Tip
If you want to reference cells only on the current worksheet of a multiple-worksheet file, you can ignore the sheet reference when typing formulas or functions.

> **Troubleshooting**
>
> *I'm on sheet C, but when I press Ctrl+PgUp, I can't move to sheet B.*
>
> Use Ctrl+PgDn. If you picture your multiple-worksheet file with sheets stacked in front of each other, Ctrl+PgUp is used to move to worksheets in the direction of your computer (from sheet A to B to C, and so on). Ctrl+PgDn is used to move toward you (from C to B to A).
>
> *I know I have a sheet B, but when I try to go to it, I get ERROR in the mode indicator.*
>
> The worksheet may be hidden. Use **/W**orksheet **H**ide **D**isable to unhide the worksheet. It is also possible that you have more than one file in memory. Check the status line to see the name of the current file.

Entering Formulas with Multiple-Worksheet Files

◀ "Entering Basic Formulas," p. 74

◀ "Entering Functions," p. 159

A formula can refer to cells in other worksheets if the formula includes the worksheet letter in the address. If the cell pointer is in A:A1, to refer to cell C4 in worksheet B, type **+B:C4**. To point to a cell in another worksheet, press **+**, use the mouse to click the Next Worksheet and Previous Worksheet SmartIcons to move to the other worksheet, use the direction keys Ctrl+PgUp and Ctrl+PgDn to move to the cell in the other worksheet, or click cell B:C4 if you are in perspective mode.

To see how to use three-dimensional files for consolidations, see figure 10.8. The formula in A:C2 is @SUM(B:C2..C:C2). This formula sums the sales data in the other two worksheets. Similar formulas in the range A:C2..A:FC4 sum the data for the other quarters and for costs. Writing formulas by using multiple-worksheet files is similar to writing formulas for a single worksheet. When you write formulas for multiple-worksheet files, however, you must include the worksheet letter when you use an address in another worksheet.

If you have values in worksheets directly behind the current worksheet, the Sum 3-D Range SmartIcon sums the same cell through the worksheets (see fig. 10.8). For example, suppose you have entries in B:B20 through E:B20. When you move to A:B20 and click the Sum 3-D Range SmartIcon, 1-2-3 creates the formula @SUM(B:B20..E:B20). In order for this to work, you cannot have a blank cell in the range to sum.

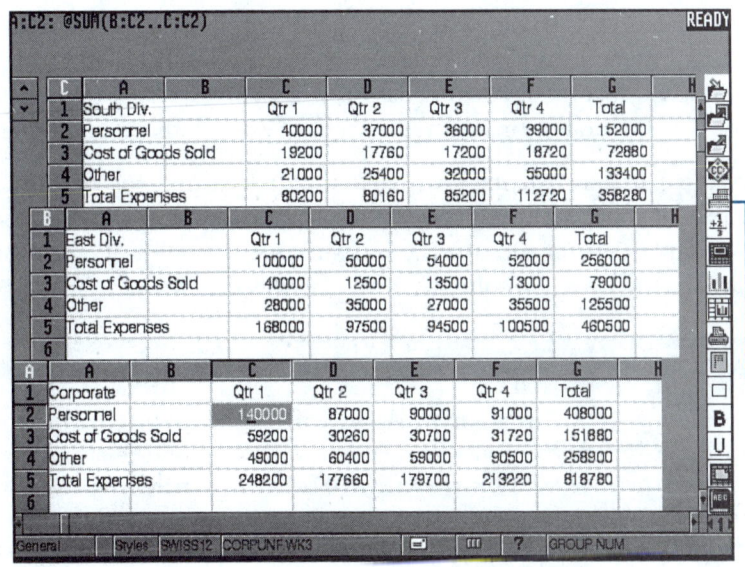

Fig. 10.8
The cell contents line of this cell shows that the sum formula references a multiple worksheet range that includes cells on sheets B and C.

Click on the Sum 3-D Range button to sum cells behind the current one

Formatting a Multiple-Worksheet File

When formatting a multiple-worksheet file, you have two options. You can format worksheets using the movement keys to highlight 3-D ranges. You can also format one worksheet and have all other worksheets in the file formatted the same way.

Formatting with 3-D Ranges

Formatting multiple-worksheet files is no different than formatting a single worksheet file. When prompted for a range, type the range including multiple-worksheet references or use the multiple-worksheet movement keys and SmartIcons to select the range. As with a single worksheet, you can also select the range first and then choose the format commands. To pre-select a range, press F4, highlight the range, and press Enter. The range appears highlighted. You can then use multiple commands to format the same range.

Using GROUP Mode To Change All the Worksheets in a File

In normal mode, each worksheet is formatted separately. If you want to format more than one sheet of the worksheet, you include multiple sheets in the range.

Tip
If you're formatting a multiple-worksheet range and all cells in every sheet are not empty, you can use the End key to move through the worksheet. Press End, Ctrl+PgUp to move to the last sheet with a non-empty cell in the range. Press End, Ctrl+PgDn to move to the cell on the first sheet.

Chapter 10—Organizing Your Data with Multiple-Worksheet Files

In some instances, you will want identical formatting for all worksheets in a file. These instances usually include consolidation worksheets or worksheets with the same data for different divisions, parts, employees, or clients. You can use GROUP mode to make the same changes on all sheets of the file.

◄ "Inserting and Deleting Rows and Columns," p. 117

For example, usually deleting rows or columns affects only the current worksheet. If you have multiple worksheets in the file, have GROUP mode enabled, and delete (or add) rows or columns in one worksheet, you delete (or add) the same rows or columns in all worksheets in the file.

> **Caution**
>
> Be careful with GROUP mode. Unless your worksheets contain all the same kinds of information, you probably won't want to turn on GROUP mode. For example, as soon as you turn on GROUP mode, cells in all sheets of the worksheet file take on the formatting of the current worksheet. If the cell pointer is on sheet A and you have currency format in cell A:B20 when you turn on GROUP mode, every B20 cell in the other worksheets will format as currency (even if they were originally formatted as percent or commas). Turning off GROUP mode does not reverse the changes.

Choose **/W**orksheet **G**lobal **G**roup **E**nable to turn on GROUP mode. The GROUP status indicator appears on the status line (see fig. 10.9). If you now delete the column highlighted in figure 10.9, you delete the same column in all worksheets in the file (see fig. 10.10). To turn off GROUP mode, choose **/W**orksheet **G**lobal **G**roup **D**isable.

Fig. 10.9
The GROUP mode indicator means that any formatting, including deleting, will affect all worksheets of the file.

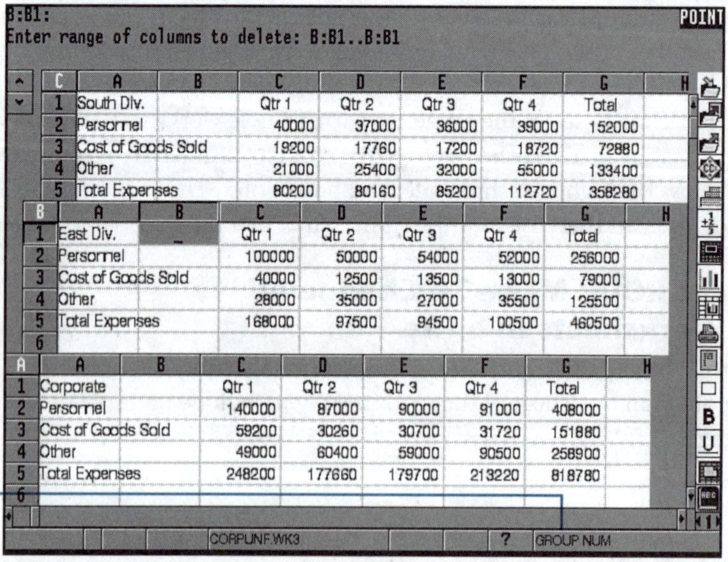

GROUP mode indicator

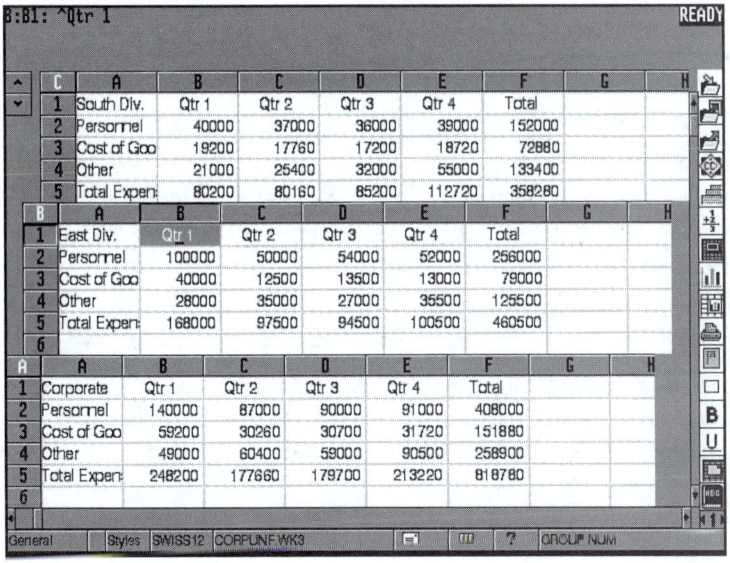

Fig. 10.10
After choosing the column to delete on worksheet B, the column disappears from all worksheets in the file.

GROUP mode applies to all commands that affect the status of a worksheet. Normally, a **/W**orksheet **G**lobal command affects just the current worksheet. In GROUP mode, **/W**orksheet **G**lobal commands affect all sheets in a file. When you turn on GROUP mode, the following commands affect all worksheets when you apply a change to one worksheet, and the formatting settings of all worksheets take on the settings of the current worksheet:

/**R**ange [**F**ormat, **L**abel, **P**rot, **U**nprot]

/**W**orksheet **C**olumn

/**W**orksheet **G**lobal [**C**ol-Width, **F**ormat, **L**abel, **P**rot, **Z**ero]

/**W**orksheet **I**nsert [**C**olumn, **R**ow]

/**W**orksheet **D**elete [**C**olumn, **R**ow]

/**W**orksheet **T**itles

:**F**ormat

:**N**amed-**S**tyle

:**T**ext

:**W**orksheet [**P**age, **C**olumn, **R**ow]

> **Troubleshooting**
>
> *I forgot about my macros and I turned on GROUP mode. When I deleted rows on one sheet, my macros got messed up.*
>
> This is a prime example of why you should be careful with GROUP mode. If you saved your file before starting GROUP mode, you can retrieve the file. If undo is enabled and you haven't done anything else, press Alt+F4 (Undo) to undo the last change. If you have a backup file, you may have to return to that file.
>
> *What if I want to format part of my file so that every worksheet is formatted the same way, yet other parts of the file format corresponding cells on sheets differently?*
>
> If you haven't formatted the worksheet at all, turn on GROUP mode, use the common formatting, turn off GROUP mode, and then do other formatting. Another option is to highlight the 3-D range for each formatting command when you are not in GROUP mode.

From Here...

Some of the features of 1-2-3 lend themselves well to working with multiple worksheets. Look at the following chapters to see these features:

- Chapter 9, "Working with Files." This chapter covers how to save, name, retrieve, and manage files.

- Chapter 11, "Consolidating Worksheet Data." This chapter deals with combining and linking information from one file to your current file. Combining and linking information from separate files is an alternative to using multiple-worksheet files.

- Chapter 19, "Creating Databases." Databases enable you to find and summarize information in a worksheet table. Database procedures work well with segregating your files on separate worksheets.

- Chapter 26, "Short Macros To Make Your Life Easier." Macros automate working with worksheets. The need for a protected location for macros makes multiple worksheets ideal.

Chapter 11

Consolidating Worksheet Data

The preceding chapter, "Organizing your Data with Multiple-Worksheet Files," showed how to create one file with more than one worksheet. One of the uses of multiple-worksheet files is the ability to consolidate information. Each worksheet in a file can contain data about company divisions, products, or time periods. You can use one worksheet to sum up the information from the other sheets.

You have other choices to consolidate information. Instead of having one large worksheet, you can create smaller files and use the data from each to create a summary file. If each person is responsible for a different file, using separate files is more advantageous than using a single multiple-worksheet file. With separate files, each person can work on his own piece of the project. If the information were in one file, the second person to open the file would not be able to save changes.

Another reason to use separate files rather than a multiple-worksheet file is a size and memory issue. If your multiple-worksheet file becomes extremely large, you may not be able to open the file on some computers because of memory limitations. Also, navigating the large file may be cumbersome, and time spent opening, saving, and recalculating the file may be unreasonable.

If you decide to work in separate files but need to use the data from multiple files, you have several options:

- You can load the files you need in memory with **/F**ile **O**pen and copy the information between files with **/C**opy.

- You can save a portion of your current file to a file on disk with **/F**ile **X**tract.

- You can copy values or formulas from a file on disk to your current file with **/F**ile **C**ombine.

- You can create formulas that link cells between files.

◄ "Opening a New File in Memory," p. 426

◄ "Using Multiple-Worksheet Files," p. 471

In this chapter, you learn about the following:

- Creating a new file (extracting) with formulas or values of an existing file

- Merging (combining) data from an existing file to the current file

- Copying or subtracting values from a file on disk to the current file

- Creating formulas and functions that link values from files on disk

Extracting and Combining Data

With the **/F**ile **X**tract command, you can take part of the data from a file and use that data to create another, smaller file. You may have a large budget file, for example, containing information from many departments. For each department, you can create an input file that contains only the data for that department.

You then may want to reverse the procedure; you may have many departmental input files and want to combine them into one file for company-wide analysis and reporting. You can use the **/F**ile **C**ombine command to combine data from other files into the current file.

The following sections describe the **/F**ile **X**tract and **/F**ile **C**ombine commands.

Extracting Information

The **/F**ile **X**tract command enables you to save as a separate file a range from the current file. You can use this command to save part of a file before making changes, to break a large file into smaller files that can be read by a computer with less memory, to show only relevant requested information to someone else, to pass information to another file, to create small snapshots of a file in time, and so on.

The extracted range can be a single cell or a two-dimensional or three-dimensional range. The new file contains the following information from the extracted range: the cell contents, including cell format and protection status; all range names in the file; and all file settings such as column widths, window options, print ranges, and graph options. The new file doesn't contain any Wysiwyg formatting.

To extract part of a worksheet, choose **/F**ile **X**tract and select **F**ormulas or **V**alues. When you select **F**ormulas, cells containing formulas are copied into the extracted file as formulas. When you select **V**alues, cells containing formulas are copied into the extracted file as values. 1-2-3 then prompts for a file name for the new (extracted) file, offering the default name FILE0001.WK3 (unless this name exists on disk or in memory). Type a file name and press Enter; then specify the range to extract and press Enter. To specify the range, you can type addresses, highlight the range, type a range name, or press Name (F3) and select a range name. If another file exists with the specified name, 1-2-3 displays the **C**ancel/**R**eplace/**B**ackup menu.

◀ "Specifying a Range with Range Names," p. 87

◀ "Saving Files," p. 416

Extracting Values

When you extract values, the extracted file contains the current value of any formulas in the extract range. For example, suppose the original file contains the formula @SUM(B21..B26). When you extract values, the new file contains the results of the formula rather than a corresponding formula. The **/R**ange **V**alue command also converts formulas to values, but within the same file.

◀ "Using /Range Value to Convert Formulas to Values," p. 110

> **Caution**
>
> If recalculation is set to manual and the CALC indicator is on, press Calc (F9) to calculate the worksheet before you extract a range; otherwise, you may inadvertently extract old values.

Suppose the department manager wants to see the top five customers. You can show her your spreadsheet with all customers or sort your list of customers with **/D**ata **S**ort and then extract just the top five.

The extracted range can be anywhere in the current file (in fig. 11.1, the range is A:A4..A:E9). The top left corner of the extracted range becomes cell A:A1 in the new file (see fig. 11.2).

▶ "Using the One-Key Sort," p. 633

> **Note**
>
> Although the range to be extracted must be in the current file, the range can extend over multiple worksheets; the resulting extracted file also contains multiple worksheets.

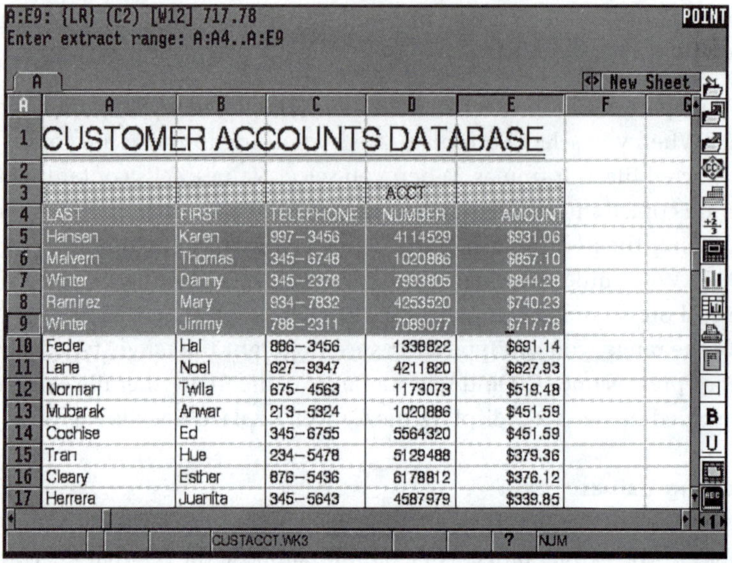

478   Chapter 11—Consolidating Worksheet Data

Fig. 11.1
After you choose /**F**ile **X**tract and define the file name, highlight the range to extract.

Fig. 11.2
The extracted range starts in cell A:A1 of the new file. Notice that the Wysiwyg formatting isn't extracted to the new file but the column width and currency format is.

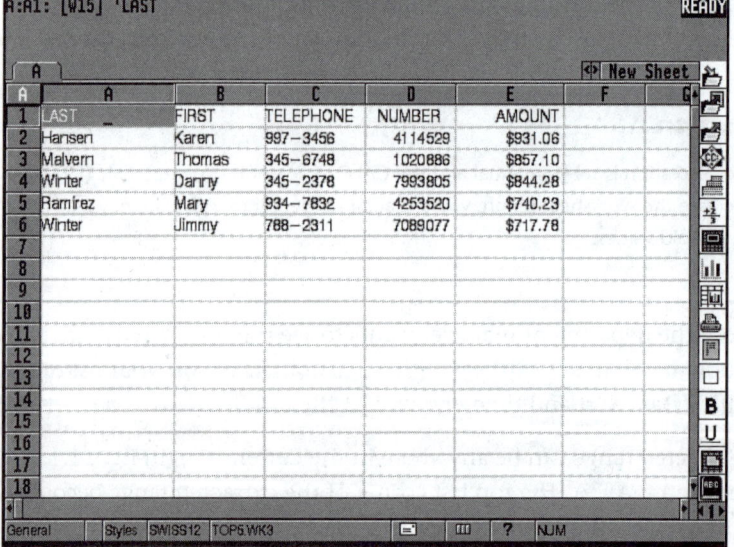

Figure 11.3 shows a cash flow worksheet with profit center monthly totals in cells B27 through D27. The monthly totals calculate by using the @SUM function. When you select /**F**ile **X**tract **V**alues, 1-2-3 converts any cells that contain formulas to the corresponding values in the extracted file. Figure 11.4 shows the results of extracting the range A20..D27 with the **V**alues option. The formulas are converted to values, and the Wysiwyg formatting in the original file isn't extracted.

Extracting and Combining Data   479

> **Note**
> 1-2-3 adjusts range names when extracting. If cell A20 has the range name TOTAL and you extract cells A10..A20, the range name TOTAL in the extracted file refers to cell A10. Because the extracted data always begins in cell A1, A10..A20 in the original file becomes A1..A10 in the new file.

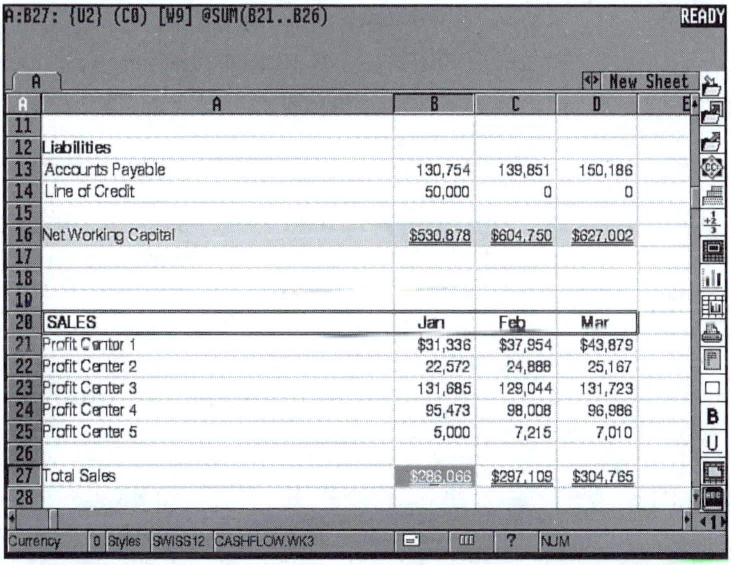

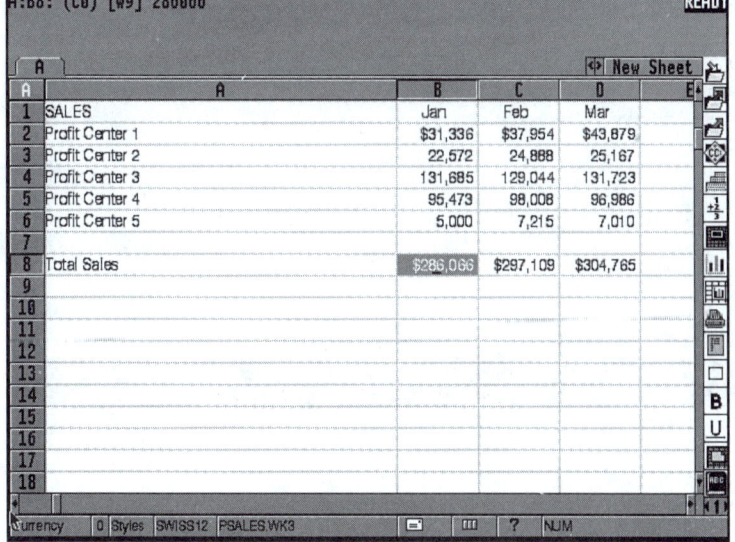

Fig. 11.3
The sales portion of the CASHFLOW.WK3 worksheet shows the formula @SUM(B21..B26) in B27 to sum up the sales for the five profit centers for January.

Fig. 11.4
When the range A20..D27 is extracted to the new file PSALES.WK3, the Total Sales for January cell, now B8, shows the value 286,066.

Extracting Formulas

Tip
Extract with the Formulas option only if the numbers referenced by the formulas are included in the extract range or if you want to create a template in which you will enter the numbers later.

In some cases, you will want to include the formulas from the original worksheet in the extracted worksheet. Although the cell references of the formulas may change, the formulas will refer to the same data. You should extract formulas only when the formulas in the extract range refer solely to other cells in the extract range.

> **Caution**
> If you try to extract formulas that refer to cells not included in the extract range, the formulas may produce unexpected results and lead you to incorrect worksheets. Use /File Xtract Values in these cases.

Figure 11.5 shows a file created with **/F**ile **X**tract **F**ormulas from the file in figure 11.3. The extract range (A:A16..A:D16) contains formulas referring to cells in ranges earlier on the spreadsheet. For example, the formula in B16 is @SUM(B8..B10)-@SUM(B13..B14). Figure 11.5 shows the same formula and the resulting problem. Because the numbers in the range B8..B14 weren't in the extract range, the @SUM formulas in the extract file sum blank cells, which have a numeric value of zero (0).

Fig. 11.5
The sum formula in the extracted file refers to empty cells at the end of the worksheet, showing a result of 0.

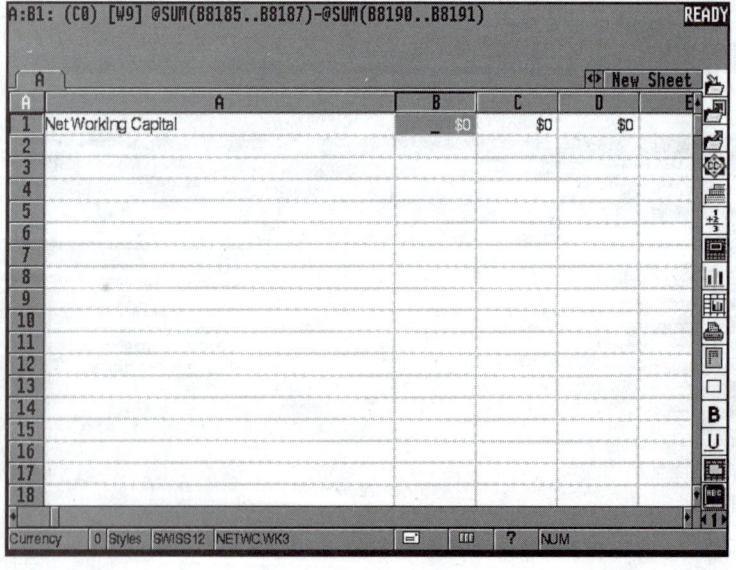

Relative addressing affects extracted formulas in the same way it affects formulas copied in a worksheet. If cell A20 contains the formula @SUM(A10..A19) and you extract the range A10..A20, the formula in the extract file changes to @SUM(A1..A9). Because extracted data always begins in cell A:A1, the extracted numbers are in A1..A9 and the extracted formula is in cell A10.

◀ "Copying a Formula with Relative Addressing," p. 104

Caution
When you extract formulas, the formulas adjust even if they are absolute. The resulting formulas are absolute but have new addresses.

Combining Information from Other Files

Combining information from other files is the opposite of extracting information. When you extract (/**F**ile **X**tract), you take information from the current file in memory and put it onto a file on disk. When you combine, you take information from a file on disk and put it into the current file in memory.

You can combine information from one or more files into the current file. Depending on your needs, you can combine information with formulas or with the /**F**ile **C**ombine command.

Instead of combining, you can create a formula that can include links to cells in other files. Linked worksheets and formulas are described later in this chapter.

You also may not want to update the file automatically every time you open the file. You may want to update the consolidation only once a month, when all the new detail data is available. The rest of the time, you may use the consolidation file for "what-if" analysis, using the previous month's data.

When you want manual control over when and how you update a file with data from other files, select /**F**ile **C**ombine. This command combines the cell contents of all or part of another file into the current file, starting at the location of the cell pointer.

/**F**ile **C**ombine offers three options: **C**opy, **A**dd, and **S**ubtract. **C**opy replaces data in the current file with data from another file or copies data from another file into the current file. **A**dd sums the values of the cells in another file with the values of the cells in the current file. **S**ubtract subtracts the data in another file from the data in the current file. The /**F**ile **C**ombine command, like the /**F**ile **X**tract command, doesn't transfer Wysiwyg formatting.

Tip
In certain situations, you may not want to use linked files for consolidations. If you use formulas that link many external files, for example, each time you retrieve the consolidation file 1-2-3 must read parts of each linked file to update the linked formulas. This process may take too long.

Chapter 11—Consolidating Worksheet Data

Each **/F**ile **C**ombine option displays the menu choices **E**ntire-File and **N**amed/Specified-Range. The range can be a single cell, a two-dimensional range, or a three-dimensional range. You can specify range addresses, but you should use range names if possible. Because you cannot see the external file from which the data is coming, you can easily make an error by specifying range addresses.

When you use **/F**ile **C**ombine, blank cells in the external file are ignored. Cells with data in the external file update the corresponding cells in the current file.

Copying Data from Other Files

The example in this section uses **/F**ile **C**ombine **C**opy to update the Corporate Flyers Regional Income Report with the latest quarterly division amounts from the REGINCQ.WK3 worksheet (see fig. 11.6). In the receiving worksheet (CORPFB.WK3 in this example), move the cell pointer to the top left corner of the range to receive the combined data (cell B4 in fig. 11.7). Because **/F**ile **C**ombine **C**opy begins combining data into the current worksheet at the cell pointer location, you must move the cell pointer to the correct cell location *before* you select **/F**ile **C**ombine **C**opy, or you may accidentally overwrite data.

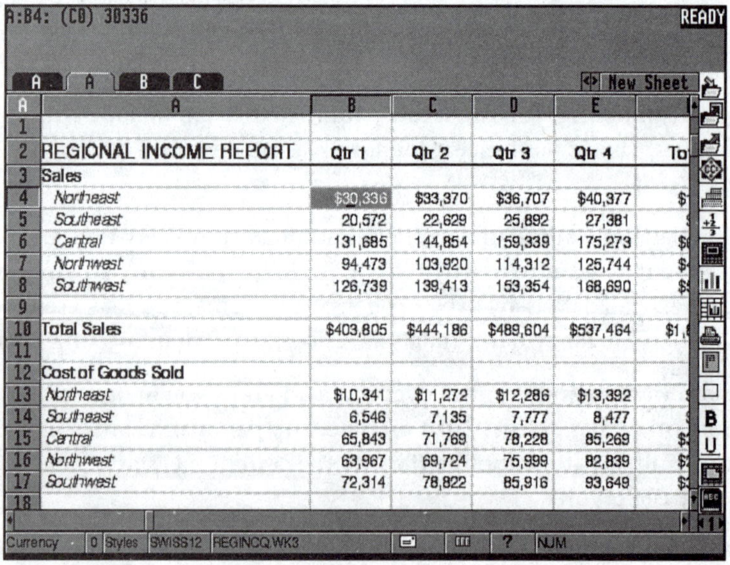

Fig. 11.6
The data to copy will come from the regional income sheet for the first quarter starting in cell A:B4.

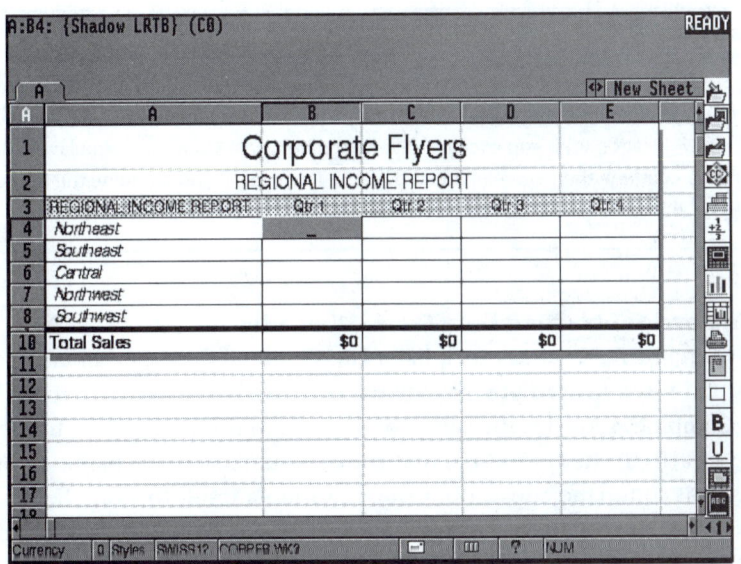

Fig. 11.7
Move the cell pointer to the first cell to receive the data (in this case, B4 on the CORPFB.WK3 worksheet).

Select /**F**ile **C**ombine **C**opy; then indicate whether you want to combine the entire file or only a range. For this example, you choose **N**amed/Specified-Range, specify the range A:B4..A:B8, and press Enter. Finally, you specify the external file. Figure 11.8 shows the updated file. The numbers in the external file are values, not formulas. The values in the external file replaced the values in the current file.

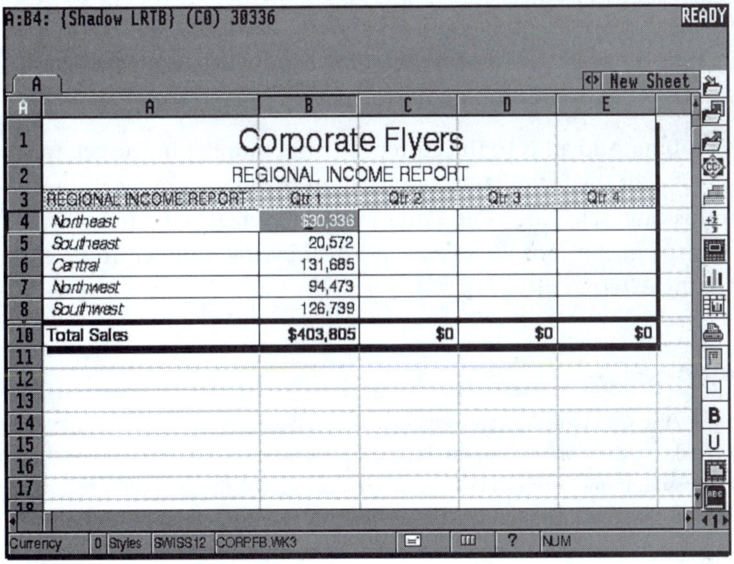

Fig. 11.8
The updated CORPFB.WK3 file shows values from the REGINCQ.WK3 file.

Tip
If you need to combine from a file that includes formulas rather than values, first make sure that the receiving file cells are empty (with **/R**ange **E**rase if necessary). Then use **/F**ile **C**ombine **A**dd rather than **C**opy. The resulting cell will contain values rather than formulas.

Tip
If you distribute files to the branches, you may want to protect the worksheet with **/W**orksheet **G**lobal **P**rot and then unprotect the data entry area with **/R**ange **U**nprot to ensure consistency between the files.

> **Caution**
>
> Be careful when you use **/F**ile **C**ombine **C**opy to combine incoming files that contain formulas. Addresses in formulas—even if they are absolute—adjust automatically to their new location after you execute **/F**ile **C**ombine **C**opy. Combine formulas only if you also combine the data referenced by those formulas; if you combine the formulas without the data, the results are meaningless or incorrect.

Adding and Subtracting Data From Other Files

/File **C**ombine **A**dd works much like **/F**ile **C**ombine **C**opy but differs in some important ways. Instead of replacing the contents of cells in the current file, **/F**ile **C**ombine **A**dd adds the values of the cells in the external file to the values of cells in the current file that contain numbers or are blank. In other words, this command adds a number or a formula result to a number or a blank cell. If the cell in the current file contains a formula or a label, **/F**ile **C**ombine **A**dd doesn't change the formula, its result, or the label.

/File **C**ombine **S**ubtract is similar to **/F**ile **C**ombine **A**dd except that you subtract rather than add; with this single exception, all the following material about **/F**ile **C**ombine **A**dd applies to **/F**ile **C**ombine **S**ubtract as well.

Suppose a bank wants to total figures from all its branches. Each bank sends monthly report worksheets for consolidation at the corporate headquarters. Figure 11.9 shows the corporate consolidation worksheet after January's consolidation. Figure 11.10 shows three separate files with Breakdown of Loan Activity for three of the branches for February's activity. The example in this section adds the loan activity for each of the branches to the consolidation worksheet, using **/F**ile **C**ombine **A**dd.

/File **C**ombine **A**dd adds to the current file the number in the cell (or the current value of the formula) for each cell in the extract range of the external file. In this case, selecting **/F**ile **C**ombine **A**dd increases the number of loans for each type in the consolidation worksheet by the number in the extract range of the external file.

> **Caution**
>
> Because **/F**ile **C**ombine **A**dd converts formulas in the external file to current values before adding them to the current file, the values must be correct to obtain the correct result. If the external file is set to manual recalculation and the CALC indicator appears in that file, incorrect data may be added when you select **/F**ile **C**ombine. To ensure that the values are correct, open the external file, press Calc (F9) to recalculate all values, save and close the file, and then select **/F**ile **C**ombine **A**dd.

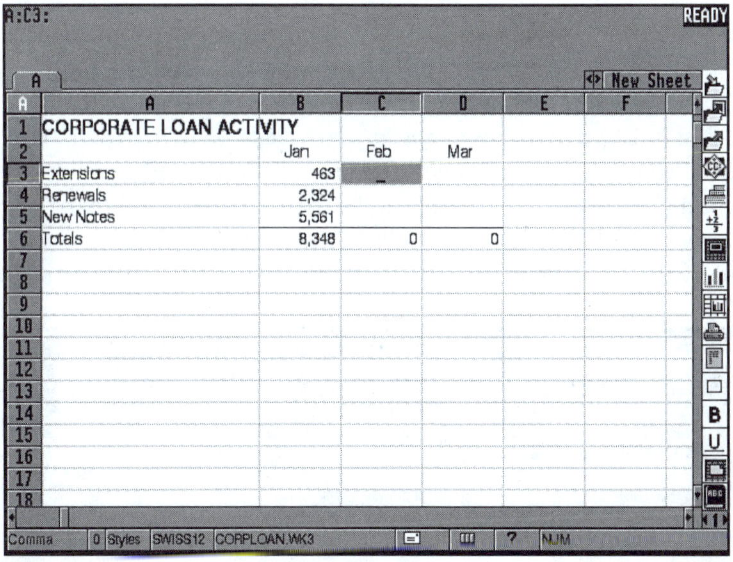

Extracting and Combining Data 485

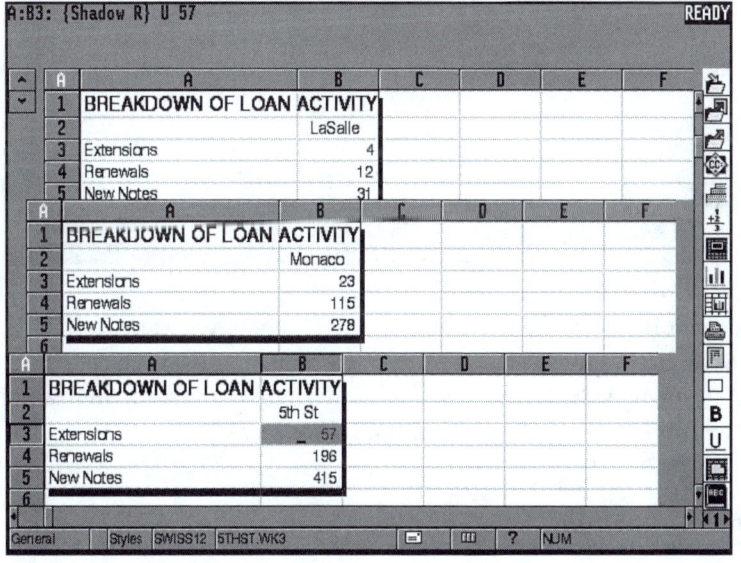

Fig. 11.9
The worksheet CORPLOAN.WK3 consolidated the data for January and is ready for February's data.

Fig. 11.10
Three of the bank's branches sent their monthly worksheets.

You can use /File Combine Add to add to one worksheet the totals from one input file or several input files. This process creates a consolidation worksheet by accumulating the total units from each branch. In this example, do the following:

1. Select /File Combine Add.

2. Select Named/Specified-Range.

486 Chapter 11—Consolidating Worksheet Data

3. Specify the range OUTPUT or B3..B5, and press Enter.

4. Specify the file containing the data for the Monaco branch.

When you finish, repeat these steps for the LaSalle branch. Figure 11.11 shows the consolidated worksheet after the LaSalle and Monaco branches were combined; notice that in cell C3 the total number of February Extensions now is 27 (4+23). The other cells in the range C3..C5 also have increased by the amounts in the corresponding cells in the source worksheet.

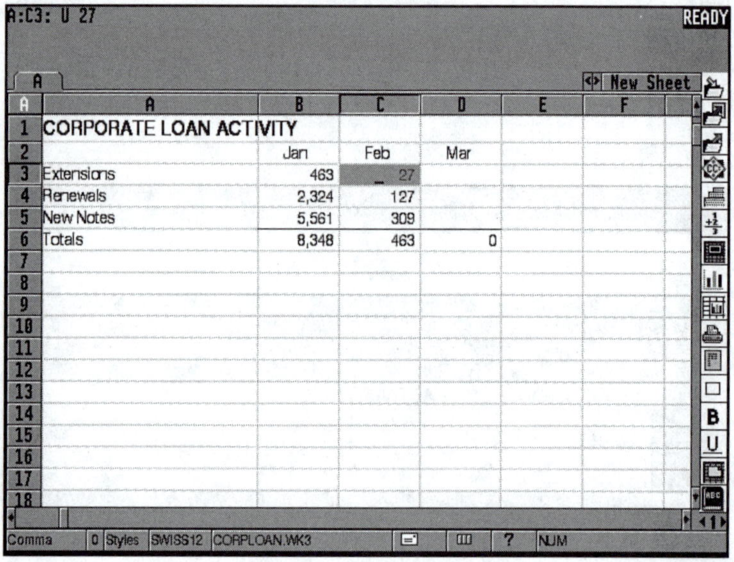

Fig. 11.11
After using /File Combine Add twice (with LASALLE.WK3 and MONACO.WK3), the consolidated worksheet CORPLOAN.WK3 displays the total from each of the branch results.

◄ "Specifying a Range with Range Names," p. 87

► "Protecting Worksheet Data," p. 512

► "Understanding Macros," p. 830

If you want to exclude units from a specific branch, you can select /File Combine Subtract to subtract the units for that branch after you have consolidated all the branch worksheets. You can use this command, for example, to subtract from the total the units of the largest branch.

> **Troubleshooting**
>
> *I'm doing a lot of file combining and I can never remember the cell references I'm supposed to combine or where I'm at in the process.*
>
> Use range names in the source files so that you don't have to remember references. If you do the process repeatedly, consider creating a macro for the process.

> *I do a lot of file combining with a lot of different users. My problem is that some of the users insert or delete rows and ruin my cell references.*
>
> Use range names so that specific cell references are not as important. You may also want to consider protecting the worksheet with **/W**orksheet **G**lobal **P**rot **E**nable. In the area where your users are supposed to input data, choose **/R**ange **U**nprot. To make sure the user cannot undo the protection, choose **/F**ile **A**dmin **S**eal **F**ile and seal the file with a password. Finally, don't give the users the password to unseal the file.
>
> *I accidentally chose /File Combine Copy rather than /File Combine Add and my total is now wrong.*
>
> Don't forget to save your file before you combine files. If you have Undo enabled (**/W**orksheet **G**lobal **D**efault **O**ther **U**ndo **E**nable) before you start the combine, you can press Alt+F4 to undo the last combine.
>
> *I accidentally repeated the last /File Combine Add twice.*
>
> If you don't have Undo enabled, use **/F**ile **C**ombine **S**ubtract and choose the same range to remove the last values added.

Tip
Before you combine files, it may be helpful to name the range from each file on disk the same thing. In this example, all branch files contain the range OUTPUT.

Linking Files

Using **/F**ile **C**ombine is only one way to summarize the information from different files. You can put a formula in a cell in one worksheet that refers to cells in worksheets in another file. This procedure is known as *file linking* or *creating file links*.

This capability enables you to consolidate data from separate files and update the latest results continually. Suppose that you must consolidate data from separate departments or divisions of a company. Each department's data is in a separate file. The consolidation file can use formulas to combine data from each separate file. The process also works in reverse. You can create a central database file and also separate files to distribute to each department. The individual department files can contain formulas that refer to data in the central database file.

Linking has some advantages over combining files. Some of the advantages are

- You can see any updated results at any time just by retrieving the file.

- You can see where the data came from and if you made a mistake by looking at the linking formulas.

Chapter 11—Consolidating Worksheet Data

◀ "Using Multiple-Worksheet Files," p. 458

You could also create one large file with multiple worksheets; however, using linked files rather than one large file offers several advantages, as described in the following list:

- You can use file linking to build large worksheet systems too large to fit into memory at the same time. If the current worksheet contains links to other worksheets, for example, these other worksheets don't need to be in memory for the links to function properly.

- You can link files from different sources.

- You can more easily build formulas in one file that refer to cells in another file (if both files are in memory at the same time).

Entering Formulas That Link Files

A formula can refer to cells in other files. This method of using multiple worksheets in different files is known as *file linking*. Figure 11.12 shows three files in memory. The formula in A:B3 in CONSOL2 refers to cell A:B3 in REGION1 and cell A:B3 in REGION2. The powerful feature of file linking enables you to consolidate data from separate files automatically.

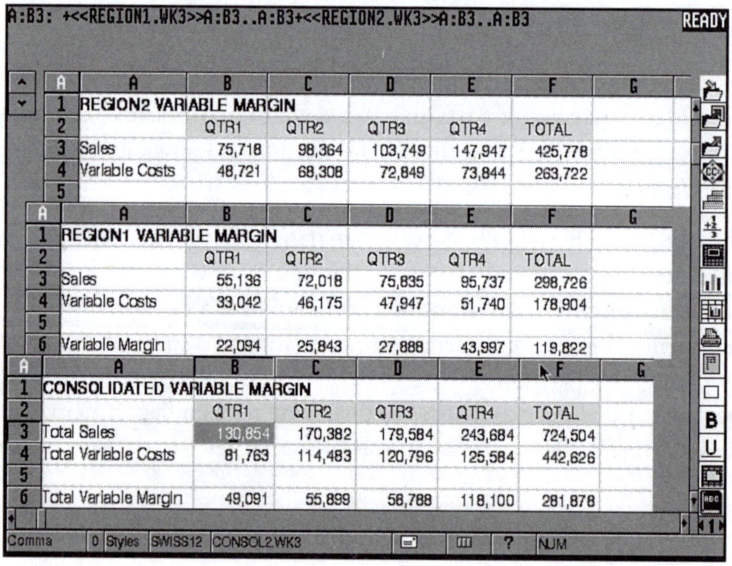

Fig. 11.12
The formula in the control panel shows data from REGION1 and REGION2 worksheets added together in A:B3 of the CONSOL2.WK3 worksheet.

You can use file linking on a network or other multiuser environment. If you believe another user may have updated one or more linked files since you last read the file that contains the links, use **/F**ile **A**dmin **L**ink-Refresh to update the formulas.

When you write a formula that refers to a cell in another file in memory, you can point to this cell as though the cell were a worksheet in the same file. 1-2-3 includes the path and file name as part of the cell reference. If the file isn't in memory, you must type the entire cell reference, including the file name and extension inside double angle brackets, as in the following example:

+<<REGION1.WK3>>A:B3

If the file is in another directory, you must include the entire path, as in the following example:

+<<C:\123R4D\DATA\REGION1.WK3>>A:B3

As you can see, a formula that links files can be quite long. A good practice is, when you build a formula that refers to a cell or a range in another file, try to have this file in memory so that you can point to the cells instead of typing the complete address. After you build the formulas, you don't need all the linked files in memory at the same time.

◄ "Linking Files with Viewer," p. 434

If the file is not in memory, even writing the formula is difficult because you have to remember the location of the file, the file name, and the cell contents. You can also use **/F**ile **V**iew **L**ink to move to the file and cell for the linked file.

When you work with linked files, 1-2-3 can read the referenced cells from each linked file and recalculate each linked formula. 1-2-3 doesn't read the linked files into memory. Therefore, you can build large consolidation models that update automatically without running out of memory.

You can read the CONSOL2 file in figure 11.12 without reading the REGION1 and REGION2 files. You can use the following formula to accomplish this:

+<<REGION1.WK3>>A:B3..A:B3+<<REGION2.WK3>>A:B3..A:B3

Tip
Because formulas are longer and more complex with multiple worksheets and files, try to use POINT mode or **/F**ile **V**iew **L**ink when you enter a formula.

You could create a formula for cells B3 through E4 in the CONSOL2 worksheet. However, relative copying works with files as well as with cells. You can copy the formula in B3 with **/C**opy. The Copy FROM range is B3 and the Copy TO range is B3..E4.

◄ "Copying a Formula with Relative Addressing," p. 104

The formulas on the previous worksheets assume that you are adding data. You can also subtract, multiply, and divide linked cell references just as you do with any other cell reference. Figure 11.13 shows that you can use linked references in functions as well. The contents line shows the @SUM function in B3 on the operating expenses worksheet. The function indicates to sum

Chapter 11—Consolidating Worksheet Data

the range from A:B5..A:B9 on the MIAMI.WK3 worksheet. As with formulas, it is easier to load the file to link in memory and then use the Ctrl+PgUp, Ctrl+PgDn, or other movement keys or SmartIcons to point to cells within the function.

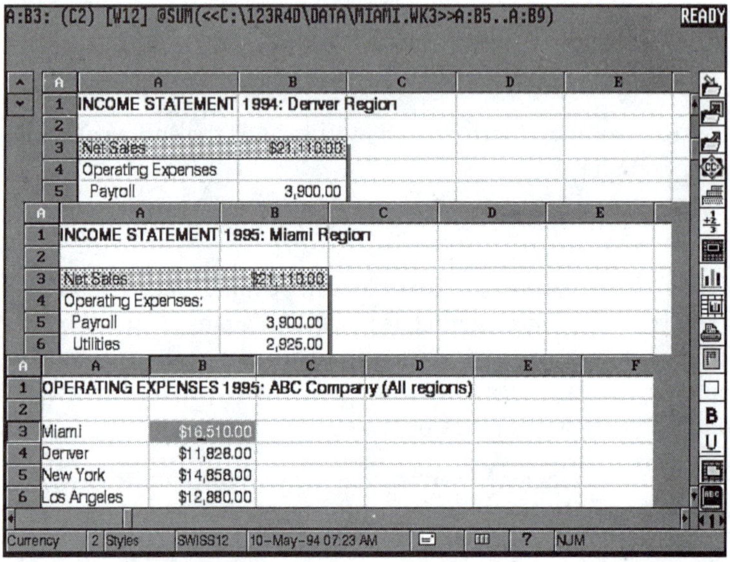

Fig. 11.13
Three worksheets in perspective view show the DENVER.WK3, MIAMI.WK3, and SUMMARY.WK3 files. The function in the contents line shows summing up a range on a different file.

◀ "Creating Lists and Tables of Files," p. 440

◀ "Finding and Replacing Data," p. 112

Tip
If the linked files are moved or renamed, ERR is displayed in the cells if 1-2-3 cannot find the files. Instead of redoing all the formulas, however, you can use /**R**ange **S**earch and replace the incorrect file name or location with the new location.

Managing Links

If you have many links to different files, it may be difficult to tell which files will affect your file. You can see an on-screen list of linked files or document your worksheet with a table of linked files. To see an on-screen list of linked files, choose /**F**ile **L**ist **L**inked. To add the list to your document, position your cell pointer in an empty area of the file (an empty worksheet works well) and choose /**F**ile **A**dmin **T**able **L**inked. You will have to format the columns to display the values, but both /**F**ile **L**ist **L**inked and /**F**ile **A**dmin **T**able **L**inked show the name of the file, the last date and time saved, and the size of the file.

Choosing Between Multiple-Worksheet Files and Linked Files

Chapter 10, "Organizing Your Data with Multiple-Worksheet Files," showed a consolidation using multiple-worksheet files. This chapter also showed consolidation, but by using linked files. The specific circumstances of each application determine the best consolidation method. If each worksheet is updated by a different person, using separate files is the best choice. If each file is so large that you don't have enough memory to put them all into one file, you must use separate files.

If you have many regions but each regional worksheet is small, use a single, multiple-worksheet file. Summing a range of any size in a multiple-worksheet file is easy. Ranges cannot include multiple files, however, so you must write long formulas with individual cell addresses, as shown in figure 11.12. A formula can be no more than 512 characters long. You usually exceed this amount with a formula that includes 16 or more files. Another consideration is recalculation time. Separate linked files may take longer to recalculate than multiple-worksheet files, especially if the files are on different disks.

> **Tip**
> Use separate worksheet files if the worksheets are updated by different people or if the worksheets are too large to fit together in memory.
>
> ◀ "Managing Active Files in Memory," p. 408
>
> ◀ "Opening a New File in Memory," p. 426

Troubleshooting

When I look at my linked file, I see ERR in some of the cells that should be linked.

Double-check the formulas in those cells. Does the file still exist, and is it in the right location? You can edit the links or search for all occurrences of the file name with **/R**ange **S**earch and replace them with the correct path and file name.

If you know that the link reference is correct, retrieve the source file. Check the file for errors. If you delete a row or column that refers to a cell referenced in a formula, the formula itself may present an error.

Also, if a linked source file has a password, you get an ERR reference in the linked cell.

I'm trying to link to files from Release 2, Release 3, and Release 4. What do I have to do differently?

For files with an extension of WK3, you do not have to include the extension in the link reference. However, for Release 2 files, you need to include the WK1 extension in the link reference.

I'm trying to create a long formula to link multiple files but I only get so far (the edit line shows about eight lines for the formula) and then the program beeps at me when I try to add more.

A formula can only be up to 512 characters. If you link many references to one cell, try creating simpler formulas and then summing up the simpler formulas. Another option may be to use the **/F**ile **C**ombine feature.

I'm tired of typing these long references for file combining. Isn't there an easier way?

Use **/F**ile **O**pen and open the source file. Then use your cell pointer and Ctrl+PgUp or Ctrl+PgDn to move to the cell reference in a different file. If you're limited with memory, open only one source file at a time.

> **Tip**
> If memory and recalculation time aren't an issue and you don't have to distribute parts of the file to others, multiple-worksheet files usually are easier to build and update than separate linked files.

From Here...

This chapter showed you how to add data from one file to another. You can use /File Xtract to copy a portion of the current file to a file on disk. You can use /File Combine to copy or add data from a file on disk to the current file. You can also link files and use the cell references to create formulas. If you want to work with more than one file, you may want to read some of the other chapters in this book:

- Chapter 10, "Organizing Your Data with Multiple-Worksheet Files." This chapter deals with working with 3-D files.

- Chapter 29, "Sharing 1-2-3 Data with Windows Applications." This chapter shows you how to copy and use information within 1-2-3 files to Windows applications.

- Chapter 30, "Sharing 1-2-3 Data with Databases." This chapter shows you how to use the /Data External feature to link your 1-2-3 files to database-management programs.

- Chapter 31, "Sharing 1-2-3 Data with DOS Word Processors." This chapter shows you how to copy and use information within 1-2-3 files to word processing applications.

Chapter 12

Creating and Using Templates

Simply stated, *templates* are skeleton files. They are saved to disk as a framework for future spreadsheets you regularly use. Every time you fill in a printed form such as a bill or an employment application, you are using a template. The templates described in this chapter are more useful than printed forms because they are available on disk rather than on paper.

Using templates can make your job much easier. Regardless of what you do with 1-2-3, it's likely you'll find a use for at least one template.

Take the time to create a series of templates, each the basic framework for the types of spreadsheets you use frequently. You'll find yourself spending much less valuable time reinventing the wheel. In organizations in which many people are required to produce similar documents, such as expense reports, inventories or schedules, templates save considerable time.

Templates not only save time, but they also guarantee consistency by providing the same format for a given spreadsheet and help you avoid the inevitable mistakes that result from repeatedly performing the same tasks.

With 1-2-3 Release 4 for DOS you received a series of templates, called SmartSheets, which you can tailor to your personal or company needs. Later in this chapter, you see some possibilities for additional templates you may want to create.

In this chapter, you learn

- The uses and contents of templates
- How to use the SmartSheet Templates

494 Chapter 12—Creating and Using Templates

- How to manage template files
- Ideas for additional templates

Understanding the Contents of Templates

Templates are 1-2-3 worksheets, not separate types of files as exist in some word processing programs. They can contain data, formatting, formulas, macros, or any combination of these elements. A simple memo template may contain only a bit of text, some minor formatting, and no macros. On the other hand, a complex template provided for inventory control might contain formulas to process data and macros to automate some of the tasks involved in preparing the form. The section of this chapter called "Creating Your Own Templates" contains complete descriptions and suggestions about the elements of a template.

Using the SmartSheet Templates

Tip
When you install 1-2-3 Release 4 for DOS, you have several choices including Sample Files. Select Sample Files to include the SmartSheets with the program when it is transferred to your hard disk.

Several useful templates are included with the 1-2-3 Release 4 for DOS program. Not only are they useful for work you need to do, but they also give you some ideas and elements for templates you may want to create. You could copy the Save macro, for instance, or the entire sheet of macros in one of the SmartSheets to a template file you create.

The SmartSheets include templates for comparing the costs of buying versus leasing a car, creating a daily planner, preparing expense reports, maintaining investment records, and compiling statements of personal worth.

> **Note**
>
> Use **/F**ile **R**etrieve to retrieve the SmartSheet templates from the directory where you installed 1-2-3. It is a good idea to get into the habit of saving and retrieving your spreadsheet files from a different directory than the one in which you have installed the program files. Create a separate directory on your hard disk, then use **/W**orksheet **G**lobal **D**efault **D**irectory, enter the new directory name, and use **U**pdate to designate that directory as the place where you will store your working files. Finally, use the DOS COPY command to copy the template files from the program directory to this new directory. To protect your template files from being accidentally overwritten, you might want to put them in a directory separate from other spreadsheets.

The Buy/Lease SmartSheet

Considering the increasing popularity of leasing a car versus buying one, BUYLEASE.WK3 provides a way for you to determine which alternative is best for you (see fig. 12.1).

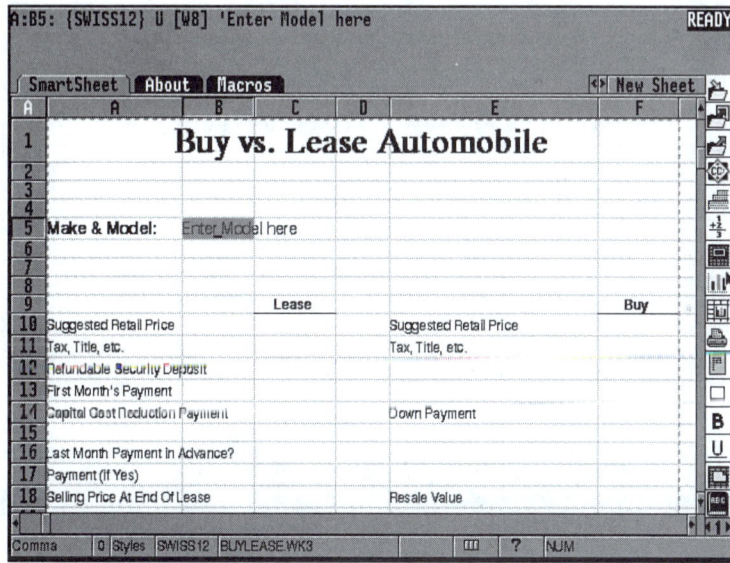

Fig. 12.1
The blank BUYLEASE.WK3 template file.

This template contains three named sheets, SmartSheet, About, and Macros. The cell pointer is in cell A1 of SmartSheet, the sheet where you enter the data. The second sheet, named About, contains information the creator of the file wanted you to know. Click the tab of the sheet named About to see the information, which includes a description of the macros (see fig. 12.2). The third sheet contains the macros. Unless you want to change or study them, you do not need to go to that sheet (see fig. 12.3).

Four macros are associated with these templates. Macros are covered later in this book in Chapter 26, "Short Macros To Make Your Life Easier," but here is a brief description of the use of the macros in the BUYLEASE.WK3 template.

- The save macro, Alt+S, saves the template with data you have entered after it prompts you for a new name so that you don't overwrite the original template file. Press Alt+S; then at the prompt at the top of the screen, type a unique file name and press Enter. Typing the unique file name is necessary only the first time you use the macro with a new file. If you use the macro again in the same worksheet, it is saved with the same file name; you do not have to enter a new name.

496   Chapter 12—Creating and Using Templates

Fig. 12.2
The sheet labeled "About" contains information about the template.

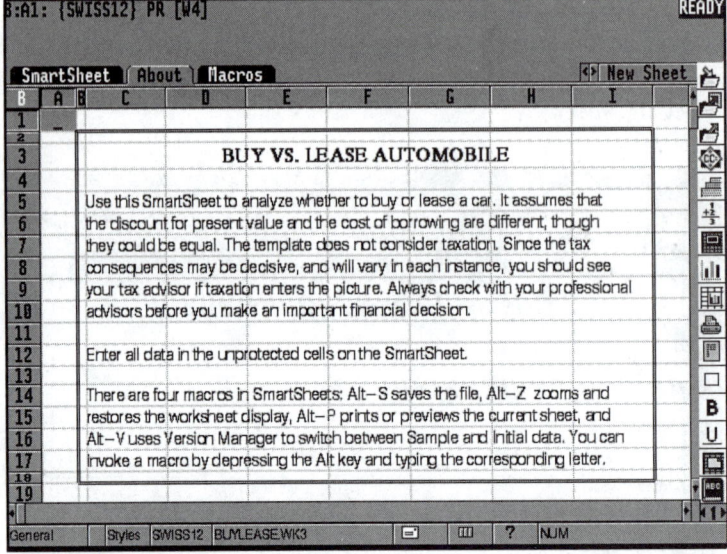

Fig. 12.3
The "Macro" sheet contains the four macros for the template.

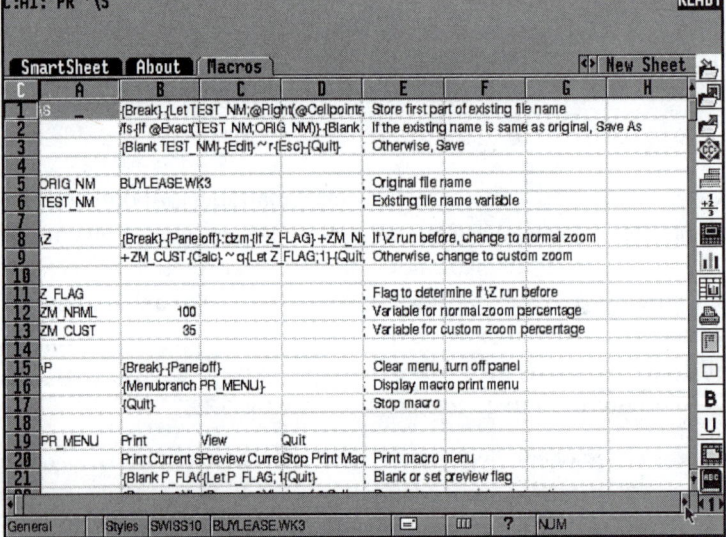

- The zoom macro, Alt+Z, decreases the size of all cells so that you can see more of the worksheet on-screen to get a bird's-eye view of the worksheet. Press Alt+Z again to restore the original view of your work.

- The print macro, Alt+P, enables you to print the worksheet or view (preview) it. When you press Alt+P, a menu appears at the top of the screen from which you can choose **P**rint or **V**iew. Pressing the first letter of the choice selects that choice. **Q**uit dismisses the macro without printing or displaying the worksheet.

> **Troubleshooting**
>
> *I can't print my spreadsheet because my printer doesn't print in landscape.*
>
> Some of the template macros are set to print landscape (the wider side of the paper is at the top and bottom of the printout). If this is a problem, you could use the **:P**rint menu to print the sheet manually. You might also want to use **:P**rint **L**ayout **C**ompression to fit the printout to the page, or **:W**orksheet **P**age **C**olumn to put a page break between columns where you want a page break. You can also edit the macro, changing the macro to print portrait, and inserting a page break or changing compression.

- The Version Manager macro, Alt+V, also presents a menu at the top of the screen. If you choose **S**ample, the data you have already entered will be replaced by the information in a version created with sample data to illustrate the way you should use the worksheet. Thus, it is best to use this macro before you start to enter data. Press Alt+V and select **I**nitial to clear the sample data from the screen and provide blank cells for you to use for data entry. To learn about creating and using versions and scenarios, see Chapter 18, "Tracking Multiple Sets of Data with Version Manager."

To use the template, move to the proper cell and begin data entry. You can enter data only in unprotected cells. If you try to enter data into a protected cell, you hear a beep, the mode indicator contains the word ERROR, and the status bar contains the error message `Protected Cell—Press F1 (Help)`. Press Esc to clear the error, and then move to an unprotected cell to continue entering data.

> **Note**
>
> If you are using a color monitor, you can tell which cells are unprotected if they have data in them. The data is blue. Protected cells contain black data. If the cell is empty or if you are using a monochrome monitor, you can tell the protection status of the current cell by looking in the control panel. If protection is enabled, you will see an uppercase U after the cell address meaning that the cell is unprotected; you can enter data in it. PR means the cell is protected; you cannot enter, delete, or overwrite data in that cell.

498   Chapter 12—Creating and Using Templates

Notice as you enter data in some cells that data appears elsewhere. Those other cells are protected and contain formulas that wait for you to enter data and then display the results of their calculations.

The "Last Month Payment in Advance?" item requires a Yes or No answer (see fig. 12.4); formulas elsewhere look only at the first letter of the word you type, so be sure it is a Y or an N, upper- or lowercase. Some cells in the Buy column contain formulas that will use the data you entered in the Lease column so that you don't have to enter the data in two places.

Fig. 12.4
The lower part of the SmartSheet section of the Buy/Lease template.

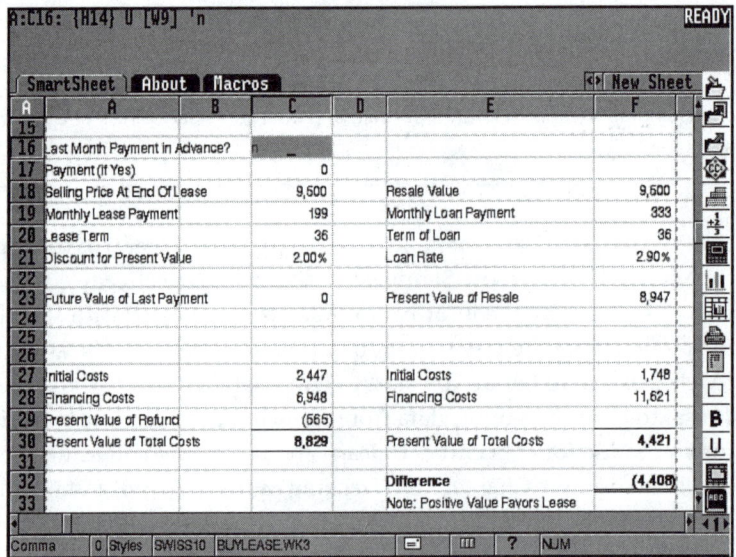

In most cells, the information you enter is data you have read in the newspaper or heard from the car dealer. One cell requires a guess. It is the cell labeled "Discount for Present Value," which is your estimate of the rate at which the amount you used for a required last payment would grow if it were invested instead of being used for the payment. If you entered Yes in the "Last Month Payment in Advance" cell and a percent figure in the "Discount for Present Value" cell, the future value of the current payment appears in the "Future Value of Last Payment" cell.

After you have entered all data in the proper cells, you can look at the comparison of the costs for leasing and buying in the lower part of the sheet named SmartSheet. If the number in the "Difference" cell is in parentheses, it is negative. It is better to lease than to buy when the value in that cell is positive.

To do a lease/buy comparison for a different car, save the current document, then retrieve the template and enter new data.

The Daily Planner SmartSheet

The file DLYPLNNR.WK3 is a template for a daily schedule. Before you can create a schedule, you need to enter the date in the appropriate cells below the information box on the sheet named About. Enter the year in two or four digits (dates after 2000 must be four digits), the number of the month, and the day in the proper cells.

Return to the sheet named SmartSheet and note that the template contains information for the date you entered. Figure 12.5 shows the template for June 15, 1994 with some appointments entered to give you an idea of how to use the template.

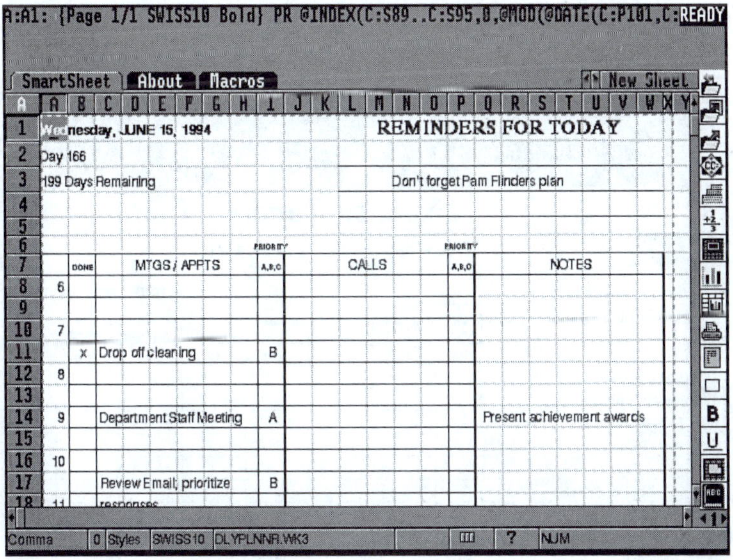

Fig. 12.5
The Daily Planner SmartSheet with sample data supplied by the template's creator.

You may want to enter any recurrent events, such as daily staff meetings, into the template to make them a permanent part of the template. Doing so eliminates the necessity of typing them into every daily plan. Then resave the original template. Use the /**F**ile **S**ave command rather than the Alt+S macro because you will be saving the template under its original name. The Alt+S macro prompts you for a new file name.

The best way to use this template is to print a sheet for each day as far into the future as you want to plan, and then bind them into a notebook. If you want to use a smaller notebook for your planner sheets, change the paper size in the **:P**rint **L**ayout **P**age-Size menu. To make the change of page size permanent, be sure to save the new setting with the original template so that it is automatically used each time you update and print a schedule.

> **Note**
>
> As described in the About sheet, the same four macros used in the car lease/buy template are used in the daily planner template and in all other SmartSheets.

The Expense Report SmartSheet

Figure 12.6 shows the expense report SmartSheet, EXPREPRT.WK3, with sample data entered to show you how and where to enter data. Naturally, you will want to delete most of the data and replace such entries as the name and the company name with your own information.

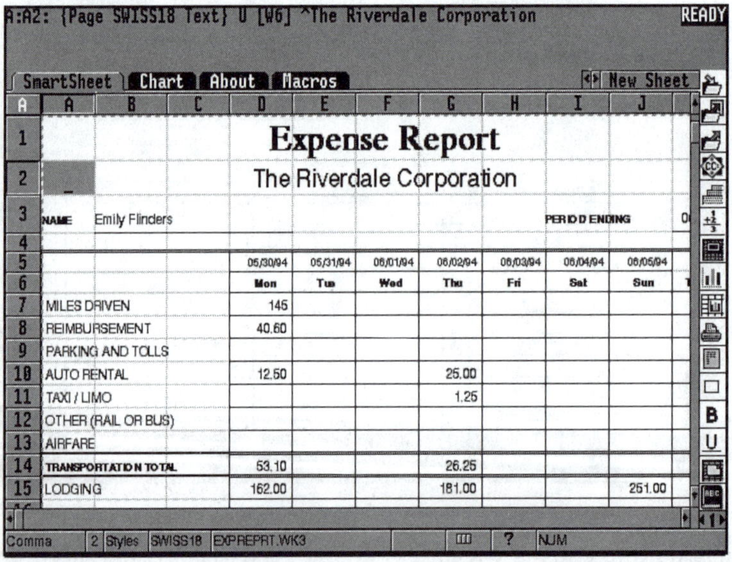

Fig. 12.6
The Expense Report SmartSheet with the data you see when you retrieve it.

> **Note**
>
> The company name appears to be in cells in the middle of the row, but this is not the case. Notice in figure 12.4 that the cell pointer is in cell A2. The control panel shows that the company name is in that cell but centered across row B with the **:T**ext **A**lign command. To change the company name, you need to edit cell B2—deleting the existing text and entering your own.

On the About sheet below the information box is a cell in which you may need to change the rate at which your company reimburses employees for mileage. The figure is used in a formula in cell D8 in the report itself.

Although this procedure is covered in more detail in Chapter 13, "Protecting Worksheet Data and Files," you may find it helpful to know how to disable the protection feature temporarily to make it possible to make changes to protected cells. For instance, you may need to use two or more lines for the name and address of your company. Use **/W**orksheet **G**lobal **P**rotection **D**isable to turn off protection. Now you can change any cell in the sheet, insert rows and columns, delete unwanted text, or edit formulas. Use **/W**orksheet **G**lobal **P**rotection **E**nable to turn protection back on.

> **Caution**
>
> Be careful when making changes to the template in previously protected cells. As added insurance against ruining the original, it is a good idea to make a copy of the template in another directory or with a different file name. If you make a mistake, retrieve the template file without saving and start again. Also, be sure any data you add in newly inserted rows or columns is included in the existing formulas.

Figure 12.7 shows the graph sheet included with the expense report, for those who want to see their expenses in graphic form. It is a stacked-bar graph of each of the seven days represented in the SmartSheet. As you enter data in the SmartSheet, the graph automatically updates.

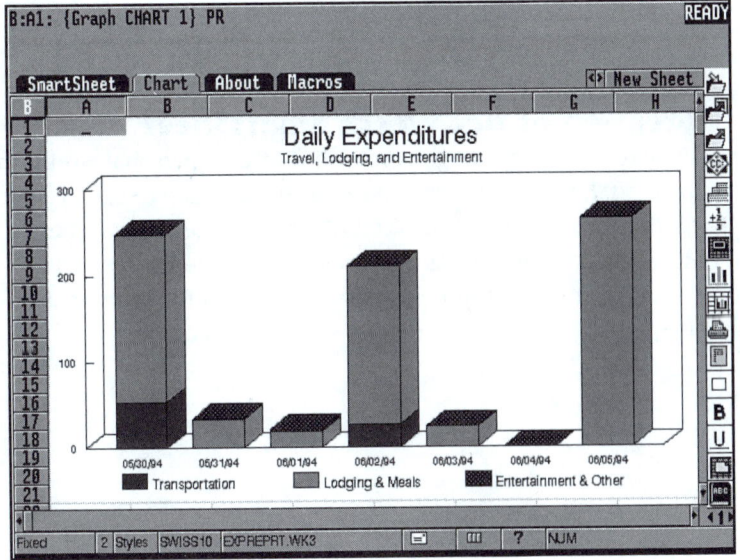

Fig. 12.7

The "Chart" sheet, which is included with the Expense Report template.

The Investment Record SmartSheet

This relatively simple template, INVSTREC.WK3, shown in figure 12.8 as a print preview, allows you to enter records of your assets. You might argue that there is no need for a template; you could simply fill in the form and your work is done. The reason the form is a template is that the data you enter starting in column H is for current valuations of assets. Therefore, you may want to enter and save a list of your assets in the original template itself, then retrieve the template to do periodic updates of the current worth. After doing updates, use the Alt+S macro to save the work under different file names.

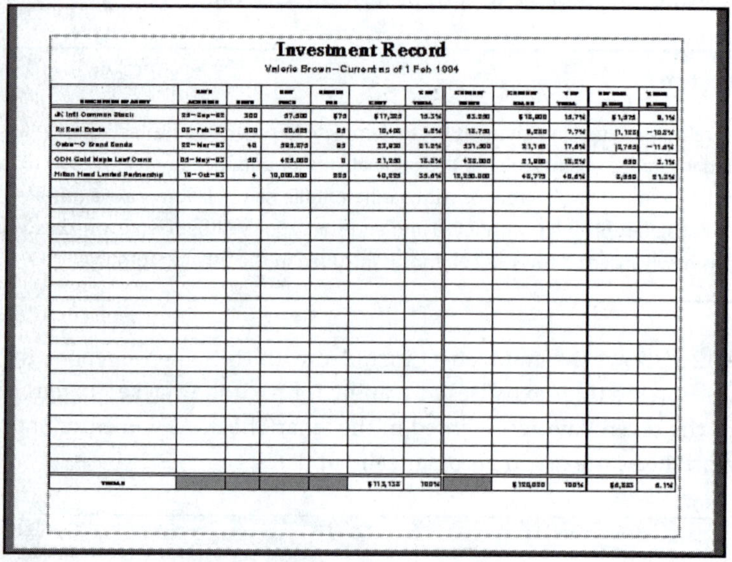

Fig. 12.8
The print preview of the Investment Record SmartSheet.

Tip
You might want to protect additional cells to which you added data that you want to be permanent. See Chapter 13 for details about protecting cells and ranges.

The Statement of Net Worth SmartSheet

Periodically, when you want to get a snapshot of your personal worth, the Net Worth SmartSheet, STMTWRTH.WK3, is the template to use (see fig. 12.9). Enter the correct name(s) into cell A2 and change any assets to more appropriate labels as necessary. As mentioned earlier, you may need to disable protection and insert more rows to make room for additional information.

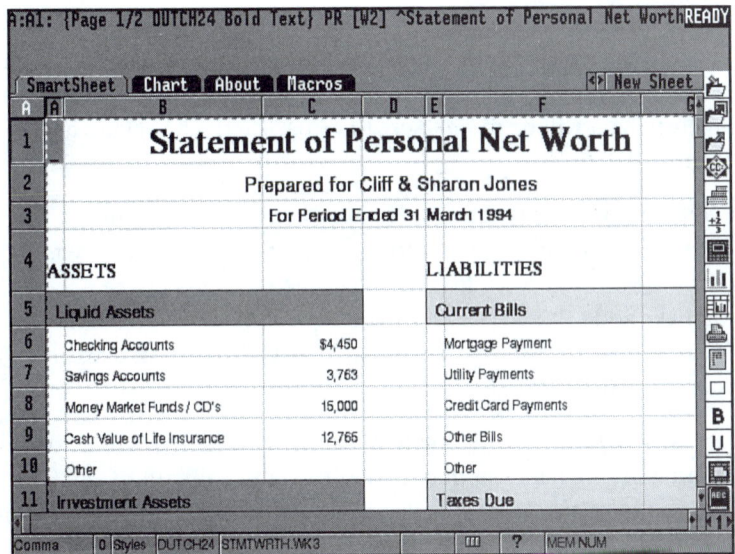

Fig. 12.9
This is the Net Worth SmartSheet with sample data.

> **Troubleshooting**
>
> *I saved a worksheet using the template file name.*
>
> Save the current file (which has the file name of the template) using a different file name. Retrieve the file with the template file name, delete all data, and save the file using the original template name.
>
> *I want to add data and additional information to the original template, but I get beeped and am told that the cell is protected.*
>
> Disable protection, add data, enable protection, and save the template using /**F**ile **S**ave (Enter). Replace to keep the original file name.

Managing Template Files

To be sure that the template is easy to retrieve, save it to the default directory. As mentioned in the preceding section, it is a good idea to create and use a directory other than the program directory for your template and data files.

Consider using a similar naming convention for all template files so that they are immediately identifiable as templates. One example is using TP as the first two letters in all template files. Then, if you decide to "clean house" in your data directory, you will be more likely to recognize the templates as files you don't want to delete.

Tip
Use the DOS ATTRIB command to make the template files read-only and thus prevent their accidental erasure. Use ATTRIB +R TP*.WK3 to make all template files read-only (assuming that all template files begin with TP).

When you are ready to save the file, remember that it is a template, and therefore you should not save it with the original file name after you have added data. Using /**F**ile **S**ave **R**eplace is *not* the way to save a template file after you have added data. The first working file you create from the template, if saved with the original file name, replaces the blank template. The next time you retrieve the template, it will be full of old data.

Keep a backup copy of your template file either in a different directory or under a different file name so that if you do accidentally fill in and save the template, you have another copy. (Don't forget to rename the filled-in file you accidentally saved under the template name, so that when you copy your backup template into the current directory, your work is not lost.)

Creating Your Own Templates

Now that you understand the value and usefulness of templates, you may want to consider creating some templates of your own for your use or that of fellow employees.

The following are some suggestions for creating templates.

- Use separate sheets for data, macros, and supporting information. This keeps the types of data separate, reduces clutter, and helps prevent a user from accidentally changing valuable information.

- Use /**W**orksheet **H**ide **E**nable to conceal the sheets in your file that the user does not need to see.

- Protect all cells in which users will not be entering data so that they can't inadvertently delete, change, or overwrite useful formulas or information. (See Chapter 13 for information about using protection.)

- Set the print range and print configuration settings such as page size or margins in the template and save it so that you don't have to set them every time you create a new file.

- After creating the template, preview or print it so that you are sure the printed version is legible and arranged the way you want it to be.

- Remember to save each sheet created from the template under a separate file name so that you don't overwrite the original template file.

- Consider copying the macros from the SmartSheets you received with the program to your own templates. The save macro is useful for guaranteeing that a user will not inadvertently save new work over the existing file name.

- Use macros to automate the tasks users will perform with the template. See Chapter 26, "Short Macros To Make Your Life Easier," for information about creating and using macros. Macros perform the same purpose as the template itself: to standardize, prevent mistakes, and eliminate repetition.

Invoking a macro with one or two keystrokes certainly saves work and time, but it also guarantees that anyone performing tasks such as saving, printing, or entering data does it correctly and completely.

It is worthwhile to include in a template macros that do the following:

Save a file under a new file name.

Print a preset range.

Change print settings (allowing the user to print multiple copies, a different print range, or use a different printer, for example).

Insert a row or a column.

Add protection to a cell.

Turn off global protection.

Prompt the user for information in cells where information is required.

- Consider using an autoexec macro. See Chapter 26, "Short Macros To Make Your Life Easier" for information about writing a macro that automatically executes when a user retrieves a file. The macro could prompt users for important initial information or allow them to make choices from a menu before they start adding data.

- Be sure the data in the template is only that which you want to appear on every document created from the template. It makes sense to expect users to add data to a form, but expecting them to find extra data that doesn't belong there and delete it is providing an opportunity for unnecessary mistakes. The formulas you write may include cells containing data the user should have deleted.

- Set the Wysiwyg and numeric formats for each cell, and the overall arrangement of the elements of the document before you distribute the template to ensure consistency and to reduce the amount of redundant work.

- Use formulas to process the data users will enter later. Don't be bothered by the fact that some formulas may return ERR or 0 if they refer to empty cells. As soon as a user enters data in the cells, the formulas will return correct information.

    Using a formula as simple as @TODAY or @NOW places the current date in a cell with no effort on the part of the user.

    > **Note**
    >
    > If you don't want to see the zeros returned by formulas, use **/W**orksheet **G**lobal **Z**ero **Y**es to suppress the display of zeros. You can also use **/W**orksheet **G**lobal **Z**ero **L**abel to place text in cells where a zero would otherwise appear. Use a brief instruction or the label "formula" to show that a formula currently returning zero is in that cell. Using a label reminds users that there is a formula there and prevents accidental erasure.

- Use named ranges in formulas and macros so that data entered in any columns or rows added to a range is more likely to be included in the formula or macro.

- Save the template with the cell pointer in the cell or range you want the user to see first when retrieving the template. You guarantee users will see instructions, for instance, if the cell pointer is saved in a range of instructions. If there is a cell into which you want to be sure they enter data, save the cell pointer in that cell with instructions in a nearby cell.

- Save the template to the default directory with the name AUTO123.WK3 if you want the template file to be retrieved automatically when users start the program. The first file they see after starting 1-2-3 is a template for a task they must do before proceeding to other work.

Creating Other Useful Templates

In the figures that follow are several examples of templates you might find useful. Naturally, you will want to tailor the style and relevant data to your own needs.

Figure 12.10 shows a memo template. This template is simple, but it's better than random slips of paper being passed around the office.

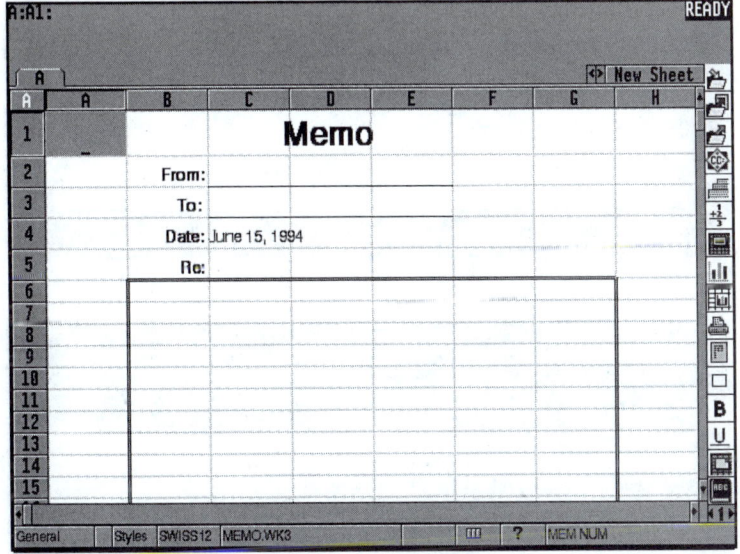

Fig. 12.10
A simple memo template.

In the outline template in figure 12.11, the narrowed columns allow the user to place letters and numbers for the elements of the outline. The existing letters/numbers show what goes in each column, and a macro allows the insertion of rows. Another macro also allows the user to apply boldface and a larger font to the first level of the outline.

Narrowed columns, the use of **:Format Lines** to place outlines or bottom lines in cells where the user enters data, and the absence of the grid are features of the employee form in figure 12.12. Requiring a prospective employee to fill it out online is one way of determining just how computer-literate a person is. Naturally, you could print this form for paper applications.

Fig. 12.11
A sample outline template with narrowed columns.

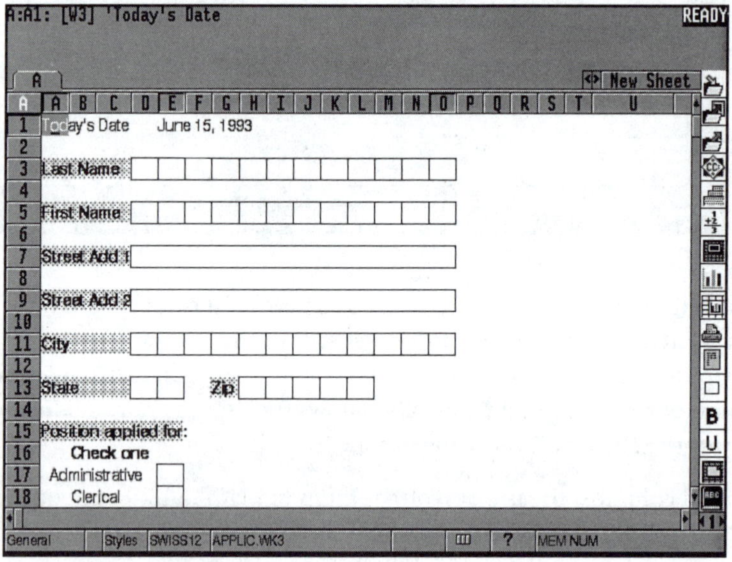

Fig. 12.12
An employee application, useful as an online or paper form.

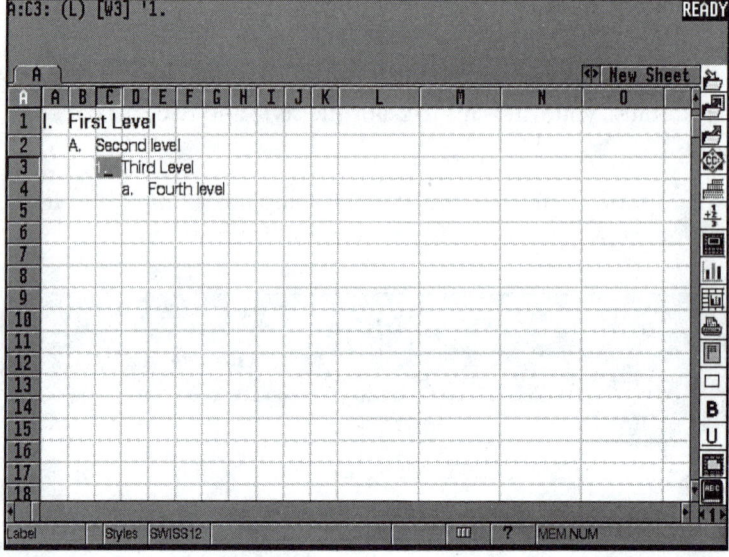

An invoice template (see fig. 12.13) is much more professional than store-bought blanks, and it is neater and quicker to use because the math is all done automatically by formulas.

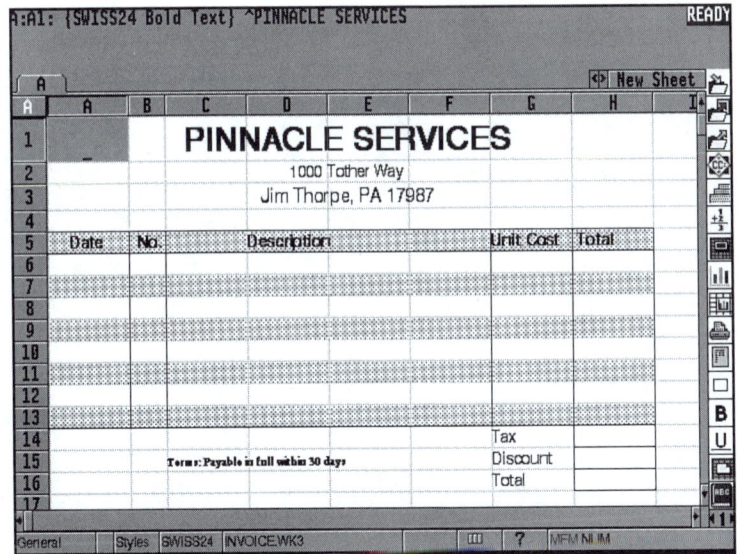

Fig. 12.13
An invoice with formulas to do the totals.

From Here...

To create professional templates, there are several topics you may want to learn more about. Refer to the following chapters:

- Chapter 6, "Making Your Worksheets Dazzle." Read this chapter to learn about creative uses of Wysiwyg formatting to make a more attractive template. Using named styles allows you to apply the same formats to similar cells.

- Chapter 13, "Protecting Worksheet Data and Files." This chapter shows you how to prevent accidental damage to permanent parts of a template.

- Chapter 26, "Short Macros To Make Your Life Easier." This chapter contains essential information for automating tasks.

Chapter 13

Protecting Worksheet Data and Files

Your 1-2-3 worksheet data and files probably represent a large investment of your time and may have considerable monetary value, too. Protecting your investment in 1-2-3 worksheets is a sensible precaution, similar to the one you probably take to protect your home: locking the door when you leave. Likewise, you can take measures to lock your 1-2-3 worksheets to prevent someone from accidentally damaging them, or even from purposely corrupting or stealing them.

Protecting 1-2-3 worksheet data and files isn't difficult. You can apply several different levels of protection, depending upon your needs. You simply may need to prevent accidental erasure of formulas or important data; you may need to prevent others from viewing data while still providing access to a worksheet file; or you may need to prevent unauthorized people from even retrieving a worksheet file.

This chapter covers the following important data protection issues:

- Protecting worksheet data from accidental erasure
- Hiding worksheet data
- Password-protecting worksheet files
- Protecting worksheet files on a network

Protecting Worksheet Data

A typical 1-2-3 file contains numbers, labels, formulas, macros, and at least one worksheet. When you first build a file, you can lay out worksheets for an entire year. A budget model, for example, may contain all the labels and formulas for a yearly budget. After you build this file, you don't want the labels and formulas to change. You may want to change the assumptions many times, however, as you receive new data and feedback from management.

Parts of a file may hold confidential data, such as salaries or cost factors. 1-2-3 includes a variety of features that protect this kind of data from accidental or deliberate change.

Protecting Cells from Change

Most worksheets contain formulas and labels that don't change over time. Other areas of the worksheet contain data that constantly changes. You can protect the cells that you don't want changed and still allow changes to other cells by using two related commands. **/R**ange **U**nprot marks the cells that can be changed; **/W**orksheet **G**lobal **P**rot **E**nable turns on protection for all other cells.

Tip
Don't enable global protection until you finish building your worksheet model.

You must set 1-2-3 to use the cell-protection feature. When you build a new worksheet, protection is disabled, and all cells in the worksheet are accessible. To turn on the protection feature, use **/W**orksheet **G**lobal **P**rot **E**nable. After you issue this command, all cells in the worksheet are protected, and the symbol PR appears in the control panel whenever the current cell is protected. If you enable protection and try to change a protected cell, 1-2-3 displays an error message and doesn't make the change (see fig. 13.1).

To remove global worksheet protection from cells you want to change, choose **/R**ange **U**nprot. At the Enter range to unprotect prompt, highlight the range of cells you want to unprotect. The letter U appears in the control panel whenever the current cell is unprotected. Unprotected cells that contain data generally appear in a different color or intensity (you can change the colors with **:D**isplay **C**olors **U**nprot).

An unprotected range of cells can be protected again with **/R**ange **P**rot. You can protect or unprotect ranges with global protection enabled or disabled. Usually, when you build a new worksheet, you leave global protection disabled. When you finish the worksheet, and you think that all the formulas and labels are correct, you can unprotect the data-input areas and enable global protection.

Protecting Worksheet Data

Indicates current cell is protected

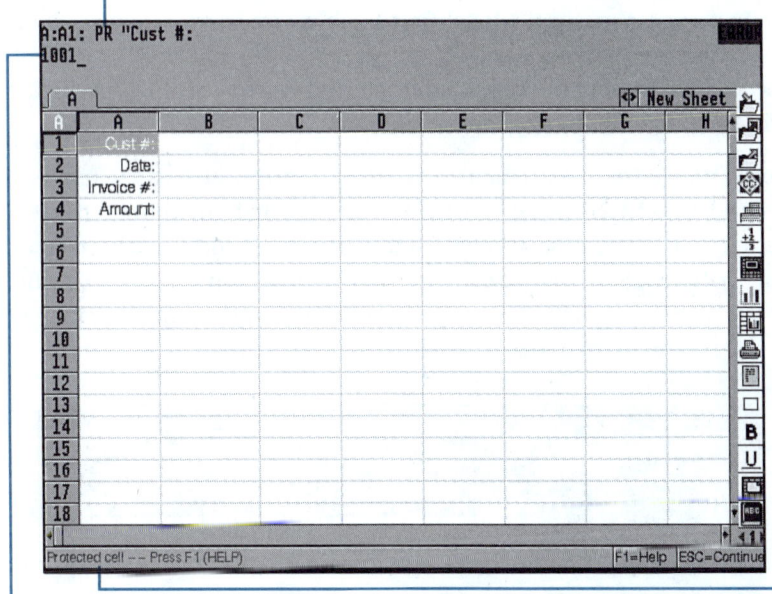

Fig. 13.1
Use global protection to prevent changes to worksheet cells.

Attempted cell entry

Error message

/**W**orksheet **G**lobal **P**rot affects only the current worksheet in a multiple-worksheet file. You can enable global protection for some worksheets in a file and disable global protection for other worksheets in the same file. If you are in GROUP mode, however, you change the global protection status of all worksheets at the same time. When you enable GROUP mode, all worksheets change to the global-protection status of the current worksheet.

◀ "Formatting a Multiple-Worksheet File," p. 471

If you need to change a protected cell, you can unprotect the cell, make the change, and then protect the cell again. You also can disable global protection, change the cell or cells, and then enable protection again. Because of this flexible feature of /**W**orksheet **G**lobal **P**rot, 1-2-3's protection features protect only against accidental change, not against deliberate alteration of the worksheet by an unauthorized person. To prevent unauthorized tampering, you must seal the file, as explained in "Sealing Files" later in this chapter.

Tip
To protect all worksheets in a multiple-worksheet file, enable GROUP mode with /**W**orksheet **G**lobal **G**roup Enable.

Caution
Unless a file is sealed, protection doesn't stop other users from deliberately tampering with the file.

Restricting Data-Entry Options

When you use /**W**orksheet **G**lobal **P**rot **E**nable, you restrict changes to cells that are not protected by /**R**ange **U**nprotect. You can add another level of protection—restricting the cell pointer to unprotected cells in a specified range—by using the /**R**ange **I**nput command.

You use /**R**ange **I**nput with data-entry areas or forms, such as the range shown in figure 13.2. The range B1..B4 is unprotected; the other cells are protected. You usually use /**R**ange **I**nput when you build worksheets in which other people will enter data. In this example, you want people who enter the data to see the entire range A1..B4, but you want them to move the cell pointer only in the range B1..B4.

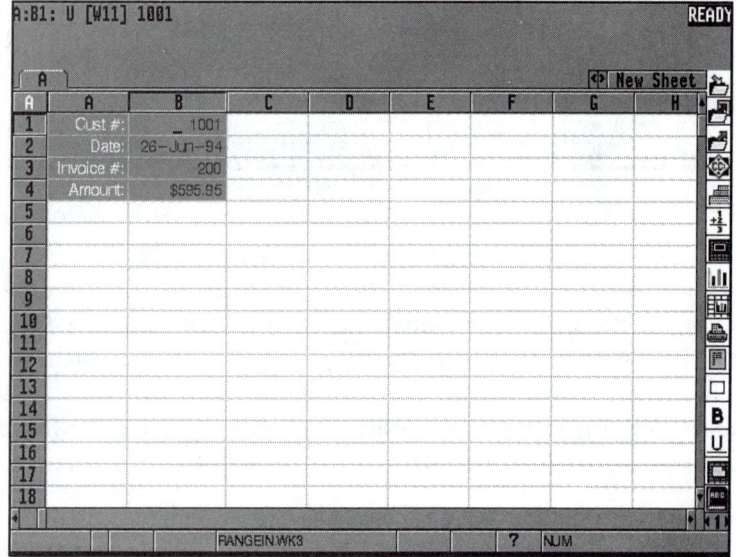

Fig. 13.2
Use /**R**ange **I**nput to restrict data input to unprotected cells in a range.

When you select /**R**ange **I**nput, the `Enter data-input range` prompt appears unless you already have a cell range selected. If necessary, specify the input range; then click anywhere in the control panel or press Enter. In figure 13.2, the data-input range is A1..B4. 1-2-3 positions the display at the beginning of the data-input range and moves the cell pointer to the first unprotected cell in the range (here, B1).

Note

Make certain that the range you specify for the /**R**ange **I**nput command includes any columns containing descriptive text (for example, column A in figure 13.2). 1-2-3 displays the top left cell of the input range in the top left corner of the screen, so if

> you do not include in the input range the column that contains the descriptive text, 1-2-3 will not display that column.

While **/R**ange **I**nput is active, you can move the cell pointer only to unprotected cells in the input range. If you press Home, the cell pointer moves to B1; press End to go to B4. If you are in B4 and press the down-arrow key or the right-arrow key, you *wrap* to B1. In cell B1, if you press the up-arrow key or the left-arrow key, the cell pointer moves to B4.

When **/R**ange **I**nput is active, you can type entries and edit any unprotected cells, but you cannot execute commands. If you press the slash key (/), you enter the slash character in a cell. To deactivate **/R**ange **I**nput, press Enter or Esc in READY mode. The cell pointer returns to its former position (before **/R**ange **I**nput was activated).

> **Caution**
>
> Don't move the mouse pointer into the control panel while **/R**ange **I**nput is active, because this action enters the slash character (/) in the active cell.

/Range **I**nput almost always is executed by a macro as part of a data-entry system. The advanced macro command FORM provides another way to create and use data-entry forms.

▶ "The FORM Command," p. 889

> **Troubleshooting**
>
> *Nothing happens when I choose **/R**ange **P**rot.*
>
> The **/R**ange **P**rot command is effective only after the **/W**orksheet **G**lobal **P**rot **E**nable command is issued.
>
> *When I choose **/R**ange **I**nput, the screen display changes, and I can't see which data I'm supposed to input.*
>
> The **/R**ange **I**nput command places the top left corner of the input range in the top left corner of the screen. Be sure that you include the descriptive cells in the input range and that you leave those cells unprotected.
>
> *When I press Enter to complete an entry, the **/R**ange **I**nput command ends, and the cell pointer moves outside the input range.*
>
> Pressing either the Enter or Esc key ends the **/R**ange **I**nput command. You may want to consider using the FORM macro command to create a more user-friendly routine for data input.

Hiding Worksheet Data

Occasionally, you may want to do more than just stop other users from changing data or formulas; you want to prevent unauthorized people from even seeing the information. You can hide cells, columns, and worksheets so that the data isn't visible.

To hide a cell or range of cells, use **/R**ange **F**ormat **H**idden. Hidden cells appear in the worksheet as blank cells. If protection is disabled, however, the contents of a hidden cell appear in the control panel when the cell pointer is in that cell (see fig. 13.3).

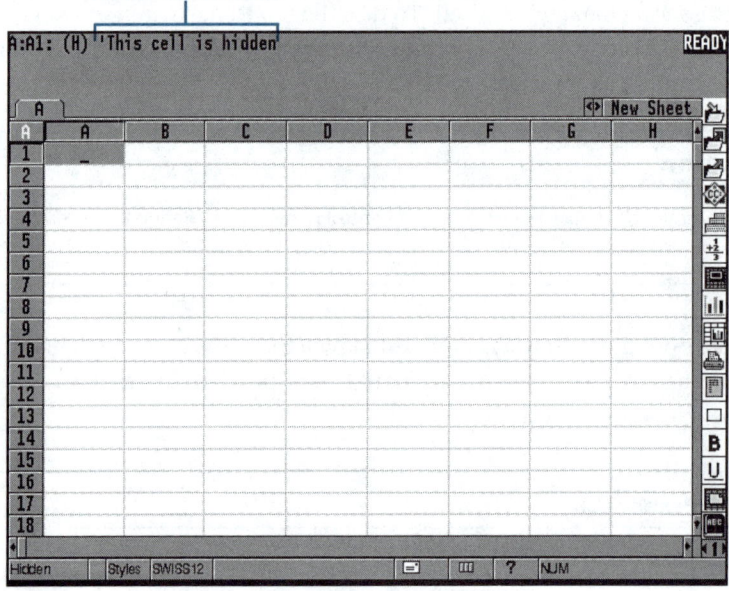

Fig. 13.3
The contents of hidden cells appear in the control panel if global protection is disabled.

If you move the cell pointer to a hidden cell while global protection is enabled, the cell contents don't appear in the control panel. To redisplay the cell contents in the worksheet, change the format of the cell to a range format other than hidden. (See Chapter 6, "Making Your Worksheets Dazzle," for more information on changing formats.) You also can use **/R**ange **F**ormat **R**eset to reset the cell to the global format.

> **Caution**
>
> You cannot use the hidden format to hide data completely. Even if cells are hidden, global protection is enabled, and the file is sealed, a user still can determine the contents of hidden cells. To view the value of a hidden cell, select an unprotected cell in the worksheet and enter a formula that refers to the hidden cell (such as **+A1** in cell B2 of fig. 13.4).

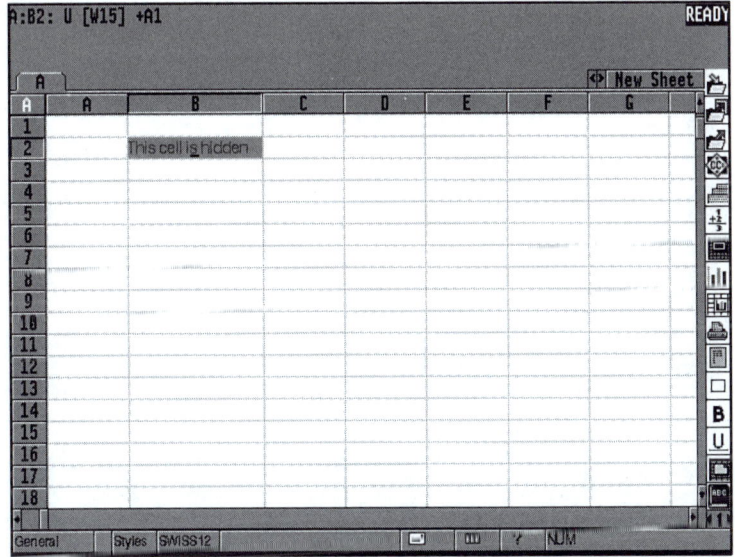

Fig. 13.4

Even in a sealed and globally protected worksheet, you can use a formula to view hidden-cell contents.

To hide complete columns, choose **/W**orksheet **C**olumn **H**ide and highlight the columns you want to hide. You need to highlight only one cell in each column. A hidden column doesn't display in the window but retains the column letter. Figure 13.5 shows a worksheet in which some columns are about to be hidden. Figure 13.6 shows the worksheet after the columns are hidden. Notice that in the column borders, column letters C, D, E, and F are skipped. The columns still are present but don't display, and you cannot move the cell pointer to these columns.

When you print a range that contains hidden columns, the hidden columns don't print. Although you can use hidden columns to change the appearance of the display and printouts, this technique isn't an effective way to hide sensitive information. In POINT mode, 1-2-3 displays the hidden columns so that you can include in ranges any cells in hidden columns. This situation is true even if the file is sealed, as described in a following section, "Sealing Files."

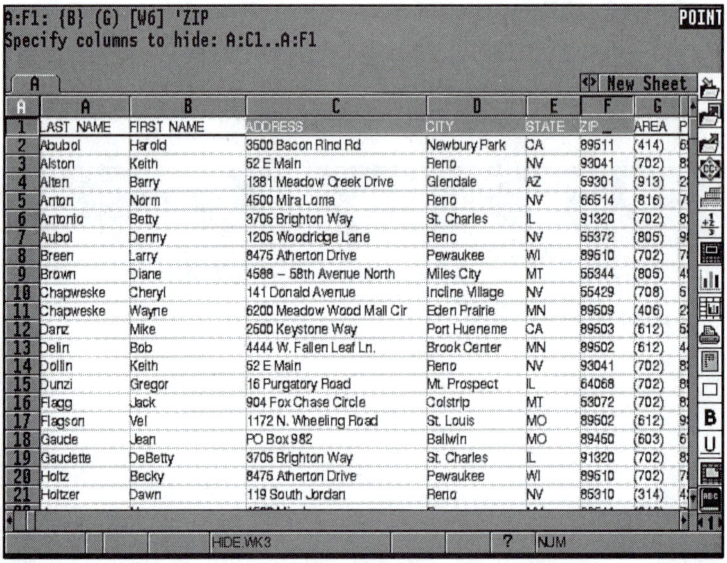

Fig. 13.5
Specify the columns to hide by using /**W**orksheet **C**olumn **H**ide.

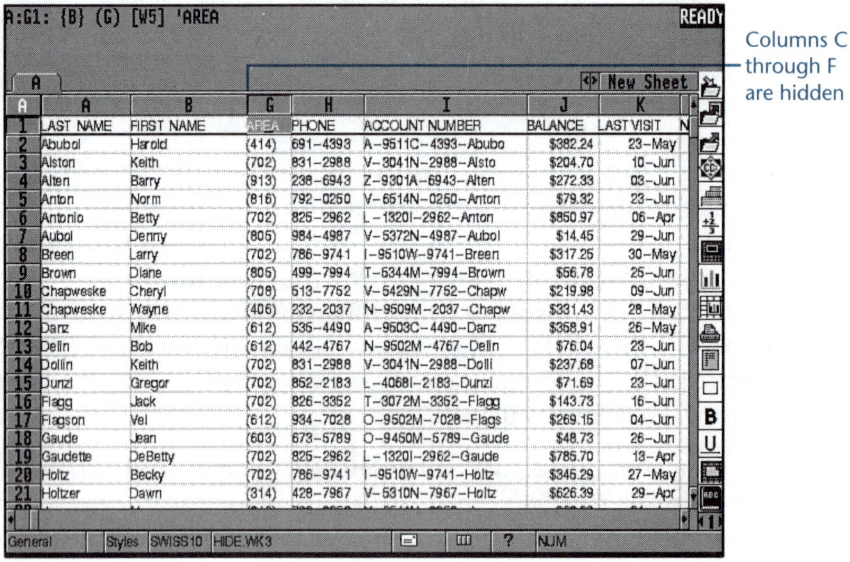

Fig. 13.6
Hidden columns do not appear on-screen or in printed reports.

Columns C through F are hidden

Tip
To make hidden worksheets less obvious, assign a name to each worksheet in a file. This arrangement eliminates missing worksheet letters, which indicate hidden worksheets.

To hide a worksheet in a multiple-worksheet file, choose /**W**orksheet **H**ide **E**nable and highlight the worksheets you want to hide. The worksheets and all the data still exist, but you cannot move the cell pointer to a hidden worksheet. Figure 13.7 shows a worksheet file in which one worksheet is hidden.

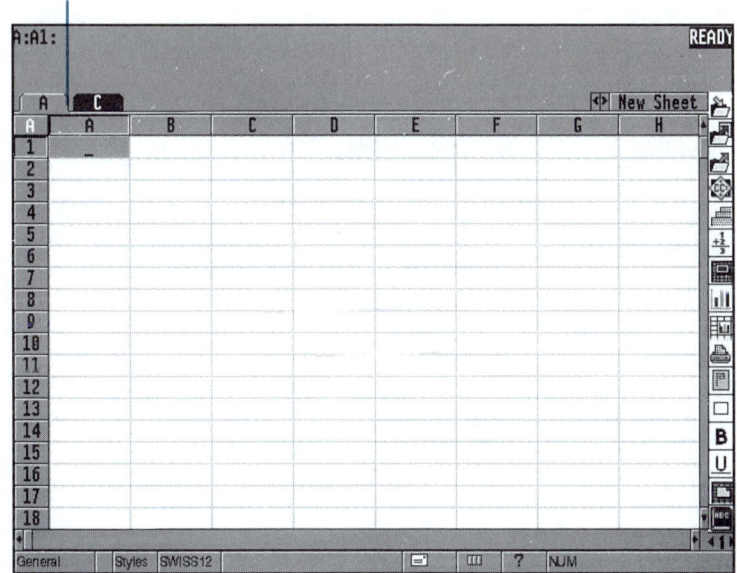

Fig. 13.7
Use /**W**orksheet **H**ide **E**nable to hide an entire worksheet.

Protecting Files with Passwords

Sometimes, hiding worksheet data isn't enough. You may need to use a higher level of protection—*password protection*—to prevent unauthorized users from even accessing a 1-2-3 file. This security measure, which prevents file access by users who don't know the password, is the best way to protect sensitive data such as payroll or personnel files.

You can protect worksheet files by using passwords. When a file is password-protected, no one can read the file without supplying the password. This restriction applies to /**F**ile **R**etrieve, /**F**ile **O**pen, and /**F**ile **C**ombine operations and to the Translate Utility (from the Lotus 1-2-3 Access Menu).

You password-protect a file when you specify the file name during a /**F**ile **S**ave or /**F**ile **X**tract operation. Type the file name, press the space bar once,

Chapter 13—Protecting Worksheet Data and Files

type **p**, and then press Enter. The letter *p* tells 1-2-3 to password-protect the file (see fig. 13.8). 1-2-3 prompts you to type a password of up to 15 characters.

> **Caution**
>
> Passwords are case-sensitive. Be sure to check the Caps Lock indicator before assigning a password so that you know whether you are entering letters in uppercase or lowercase, because 1-2-3 does not display the password you enter.

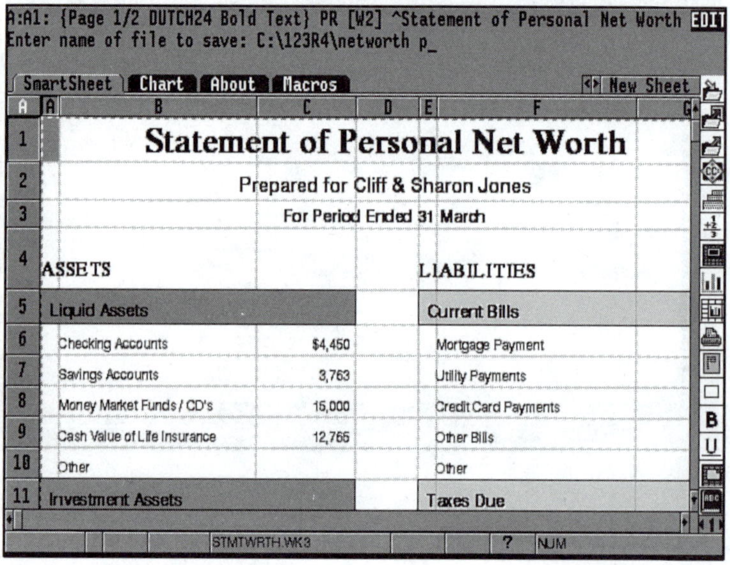

Fig. 13.8
To password-protect a file, add a **p** after the file name when you save the file.

After you type the password, 1-2-3 prompts you to type the password again. To provide additional security, 1-2-3 displays asterisks (*) on-screen in place of the characters when you type your password. If both entries are identical, the file is saved in a special format, and no one can access the file without typing the password. If the two passwords don't match, an error message appears, and you must type the password again.

Unlike a file name, a password can contain spaces and is case-sensitive. Lowercase letters in passwords don't match the corresponding uppercase letters, so BUDGET95 and budget95 aren't the same password.

> **Note**
>
> Password protection of your 1-2-3 files provides true security only if you use it properly. Don't use passwords that are too easy to guess, and don't keep a list of passwords. Computer-security experts know that the best places to look for passwords are in your desk drawer and on a stick-up note on your monitor.

When you choose either **/F**ile **R**etrieve, **/F**ile **O**pen, or **/F**ile **C**ombine with a password-protected file, 1-2-3 prompts you for the password. 1-2-3 accesses the file only if you type the correct password. If you don't type the correct password, 1-2-3 displays an error message (see fig. 13.9). In figure 13.9, the Help (F1) key was pressed to display a more detailed error message.

> **Caution**
>
> If a file is password-protected, any links to that file appear as ERR unless the file is in memory. The link formulas aren't invalid; they appear as ERR due to the password protection for the linked file. After you open the linked file and supply the password, 1-2-3 updates the linked cells from ERR to the correct value.

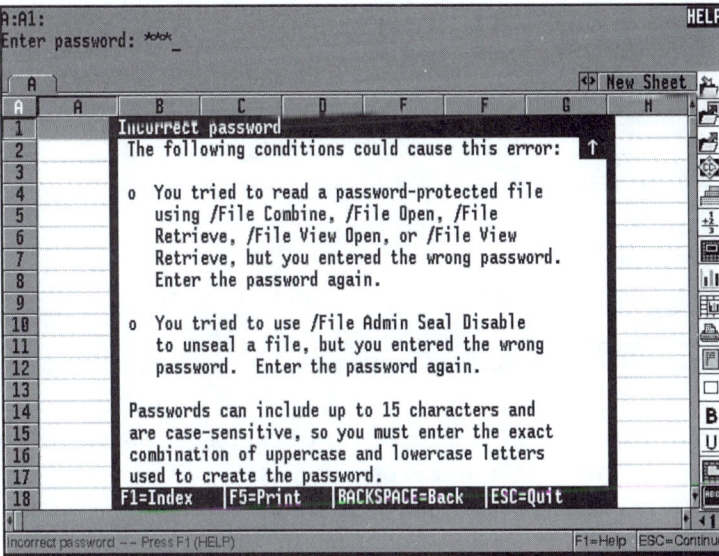

Fig. 13.9

If you type an incorrect password, 1-2-3 will not open a password-protected file.

When you resave a file that has been saved with a password, 1-2-3 displays the message [PASSWORD PROTECTED] after the file name (see fig. 13.10). To save the file with the same password, press Enter. To delete the password, press Backspace once to clear the [PASSWORD PROTECTED] message; then press Enter and select **R**eplace. To change the password, press Backspace once to clear the [PASSWORD PROTECTED] message; then press the space bar once, type **p**, press Enter, and assign a new password.

> **Caution**
>
> If you forget the password, you cannot access the file—*ever*. Write down the password and put it in a safe place (for example, your office safe) other than a desk drawer. Be certain that at least two responsible people know the passwords for any files that are vital to your business.

Fig. 13.10
When you resave a password-protected file, the [PASSWORD PROTECTED] message is displayed.

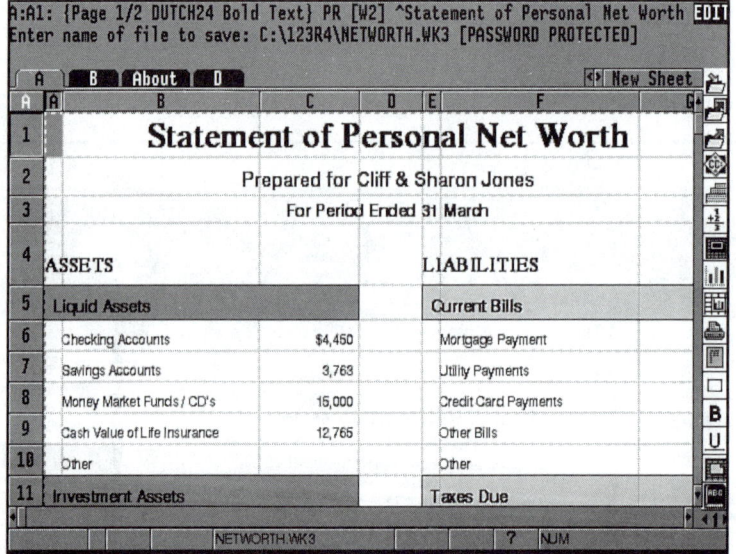

If you have several files in memory when you choose /**F**ile **S**ave, 1-2-3 displays [ALL MODIFIED FILES] instead of a file name. To save one of the files and add, delete, or change its password, press Esc or Edit (F2) to change the prompt to the current file name. You then can proceed as explained earlier.

> **Troubleshooting**
>
> *I typed a file's password but can't retrieve one of my important files.*
>
> Passwords can be dangerous, especially because you can't be sure exactly what you're typing when you enter a password. Try pressing the Caps Lock key before you enter the password. If you accidentally pressed Caps Lock before you saved the file, you may be entering the password with uppercase and lowercase characters reversed.
>
> *How can I make certain we can access our important files even if the person who knows the password leaves the company?*
>
> You might try instituting a policy of saving backup copies of important files on diskettes that you store in a locked safe. Don't use passwords when saving the backup copies.

Sealing Files

Protecting 1-2-3 files on a network requires different methods from those that you use on a stand-alone PC. On a network, you may need to share files, or you may want to prevent other users from accessing certain files. In some cases, several users may need to access the same data simultaneously, so you need a way to ensure that such access doesn't corrupt the files.

Sealing a File To Prevent Tampering

The **/F**ile **A**dmin **S**eal **F**ile command provides the maximum protection for a file that other people may use. Even someone who is knowledgeable about 1-2-3 cannot tamper with a sealed file. You can be sure that the protected formulas and labels, the formats, and the worksheet and range settings remain unchanged. Remember, though, that sealing a file does not prevent access to the file's data, even if that data is hidden.

To prevent other users from tampering with a file, enable global protection with **/W**orksheet **G**lobal **P**rot **E**nable. Then choose **/R**ange **U**nprot and unprotect the cells that you want to make available for changes. To use a password to seal the file, choose **/F**ile **A**dmin **S**eal **F**ile. At the Enter password prompt, type a password of up to 15 characters and press Enter. 1-2-3 prompts you to verify the password.

Tip
Seal a shared file to protect the data against tampering.

> **Caution**
>
> If you lose the password, you cannot unseal the file or change the password.

After you seal the file, no one can change the protection status or global protection without the password, or change protected cells' format or contents by editing, erasing, or deleting. If you need to change the file, first unseal the file with **/F**ile **A**dmin **S**eal **D**isable. 1-2-3 prompts you for the password. Passwords are case-sensitive; a lowercase letter does not match an uppercase letter. You should write down and keep the password in a safe place.

When you choose **/F**ile **A**dmin **S**eal, the following commands are sealed and cannot be used to change the file:

/File **A**dmin **R**eservation **S**etting

/File **X**tract

/Graph **N**ame [**C**reate, **D**elete, **R**eset]

/Print [**P**rinter, **F**ile, **E**ncoded, **B**ackground] **O**ptions **N**ame [**C**reate, **D**elete, **R**eset]

/Range [**F**ormat, **L**abel, **J**ustify, **P**rot, **U**nprot]

/Range **N**ame [**C**reate, **D**elete, **L**abels, **R**eset, **U**ndefine]

/Range **N**ame N**o**te [**C**reate, **D**elete, **R**eset]

/Worksheet **C**olumn [**H**ide, **D**isplay]

/Worksheet **G**lobal [**C**ol-Width, **F**ormat, **G**roup, **L**abel, **P**rot, **Z**ero]

:Format [**B**old, **I**talics, **U**nderline, **C**olor, **L**ines, **S**hade, **R**eset]

:Format Font [**1-8**]

:Named-Style

:Special [**C**opy, **M**ove, **I**mport]

:Text

:Worksheet [**C**olumn, **R**ow]

Protecting Files with Reservations

To ensure that network users who share your data files cannot write over your work, 1-2-3 provides controls called *reservations*. A reservation provides the user a guarantee that other network users cannot make changes to a file and save the file with the same file name.

To obtain a file reservation, choose **/F**ile **A**dmin **R**eservation **G**et. (On a network, 1-2-3 automatically provides the file reservation to the first person who retrieves the file if the **/F**ile **A**dmin **R**eservation **S**etting is **A**utomatic—the default setting—rather than **M**anual.) When you have the file reservation, you can save your changes in the file under the existing file name.

If someone else has the reservation and hasn't released it with the **/F**ile **A**dmin **R**eservation **R**elease command, 1-2-3 displays the message `The worksheet file is already reserved; you cannot make changes`. Anyone who has the file open without the reservation sees the read-only indicator (`RO`) at the bottom of the screen. Because the file is read-only, you cannot save changes to the file unless you use a new name for the file.

From Here...

For information relating to protecting worksheet data and files, you may want to review the following chapters of this book:

- Chapter 6, "Making Your Worksheets Dazzle." This chapter shows you how to apply range and global formats.

- Chapter 9, "Working with Files." This chapter shows you how to save and retrieve your work.

- Chapter 10, "Organizing Your Data with Multiple-Worksheet Files." This chapter shows you how to name worksheets and how to use multiple-worksheet files.

Part IV

Analyzing Your Data

14 Analyzing Formulas with Auditor

15 Using Functions To Analyze Data

16 Finding Solutions with Solver

17 Goal Seeking with Backsolver

18 Tracking Multiple Sets of Data with Version Manager

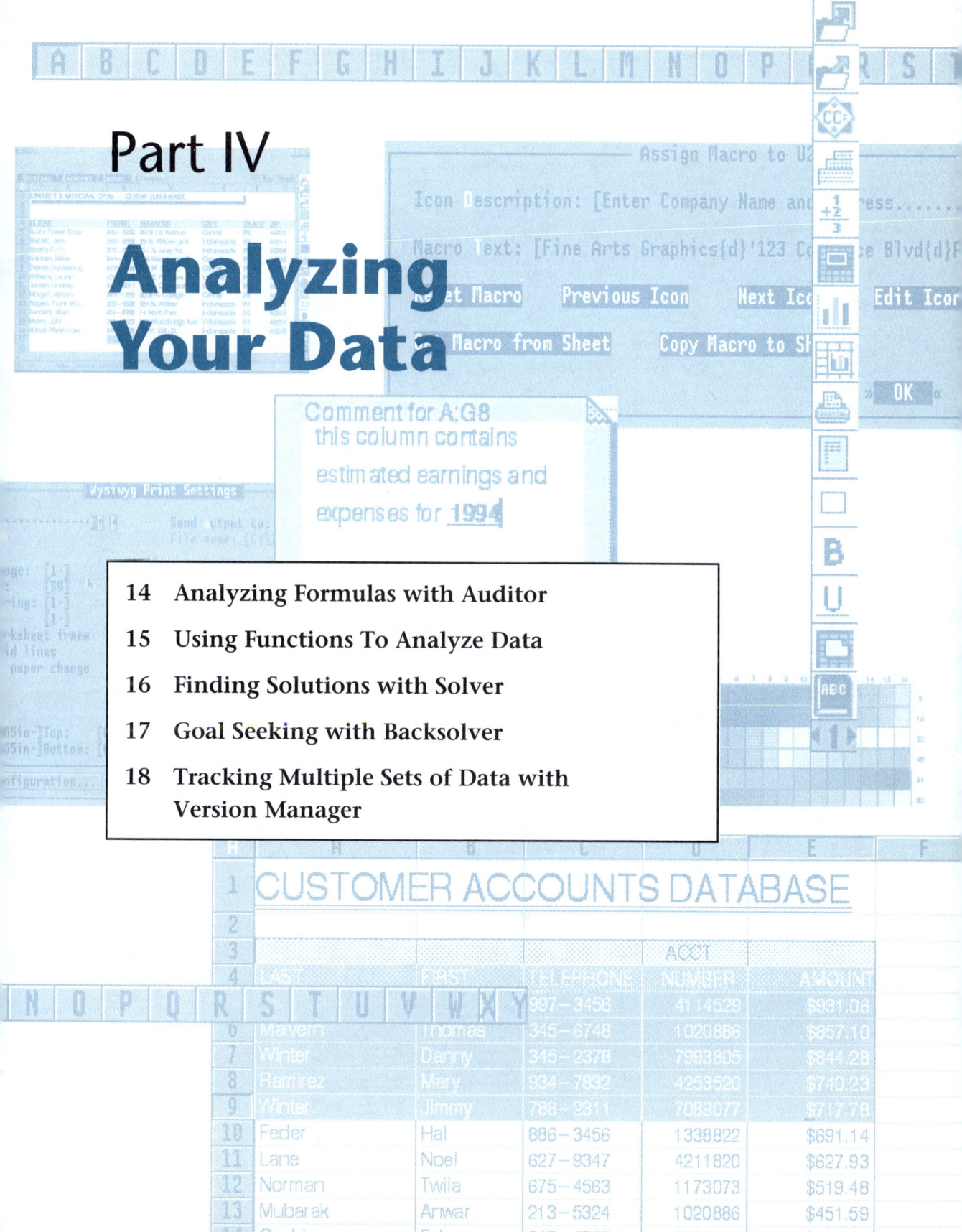

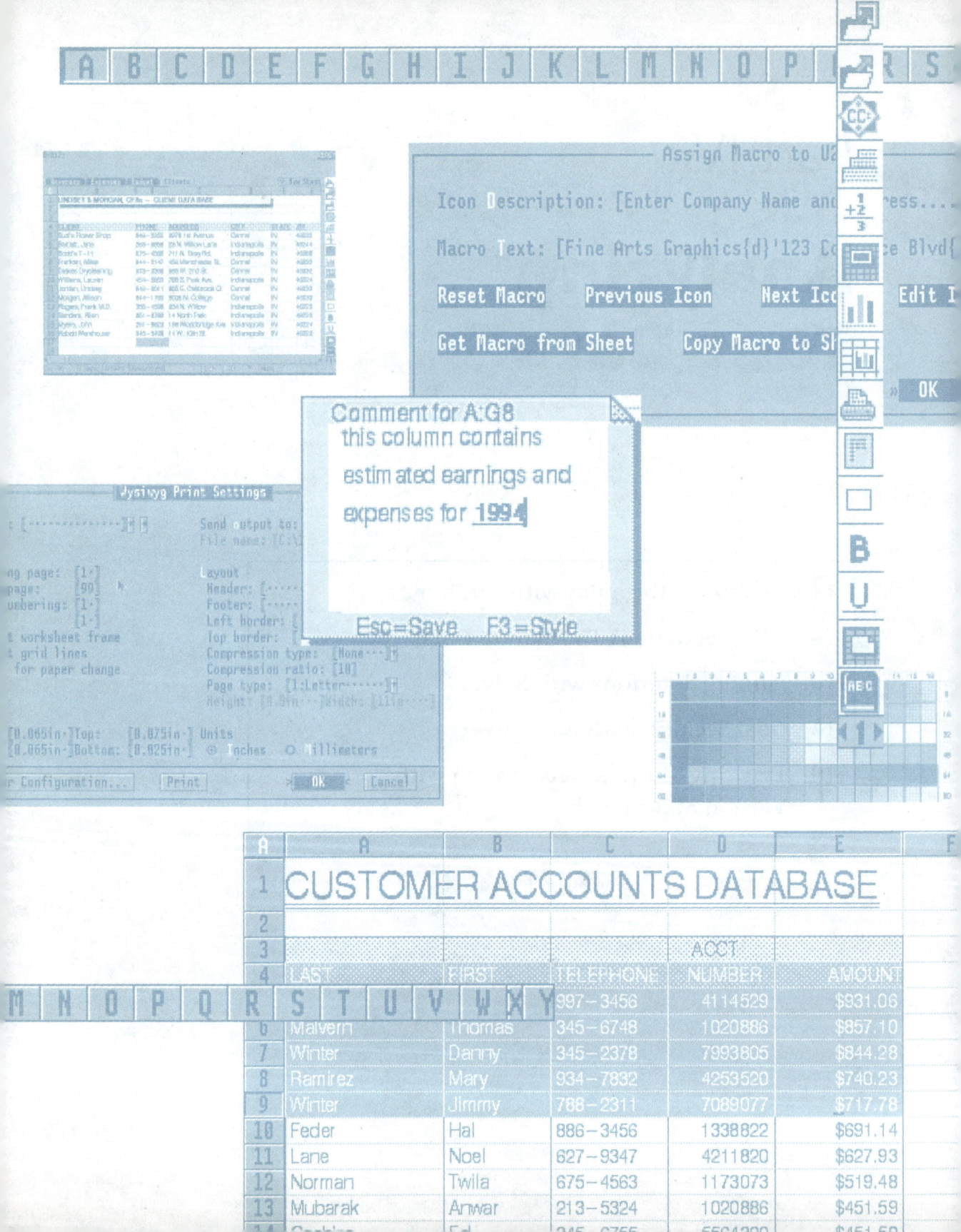

Chapter 14

Analyzing Formulas with Auditor

1-2-3 Release 4 includes several tools that help you analyze your data. One of these tools, Auditor, can be very handy, especially when you are working with large worksheets. You can use Auditor to find and analyze the formulas in a worksheet and to help verify the accuracy of data.

Auditor is particularly useful when you want to fine-tune or debug formulas. You can use Auditor to ensure that formulas refer to the proper cells. You can also use the tool to find and correct circular references, and to determine the recalculation order that 1-2-3 uses within an audit range.

This chapter shows you how to use Auditor to do the following:

- Highlight all formulas in a worksheet
- Find all cells that supply data to a formula
- Find all formulas that rely on a particular cell
- Trace the path of circular references
- Check the order of recalculation

Starting and Using Auditor

To start Auditor, first load the worksheet that you want to analyze, then select /**T**ools **A**nalyze **A**uditor. 1-2-3 displays the Auditor menu and the Auditor Settings box (shown in fig. 14.1). The box indicates the audit mode and the range (see "Setting the Audit Range").

Fig. 14.1
Use the Auditor menu and the Auditor Settings box to find information about formulas in your worksheet files.

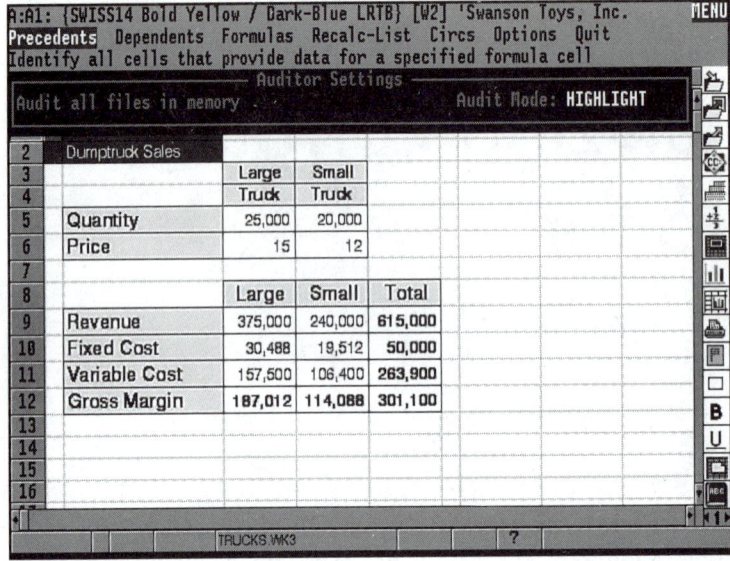

The Auditor menu lists the five types of audits that you can perform on your worksheet: **P**recedents, **D**ependents, **F**ormulas, **R**ecalc-List, and **C**ircs. (See table 14.1 for a description of each type.) For example, **F**ormulas finds all the cells on the worksheet that contain formulas.

The **O**ptions command enables you to change the range that you want Auditor to analyze or the way that you want Auditor to report results. To exit Auditor and return to 1-2-3 READY mode, select **Q**uit from the Auditor menu.

Understanding the Auditor Menu

The Auditor menu contains seven options. Table 14.1 describes each option.

Table 14.1	Auditor Menu Selections
Menu Item	**Description**
Precedents	Finds all cells in the audit range that supply data to a formula
Dependents	Finds all formulas in the audit range that depend on a specified cell
Formulas	Identifies all cells in the audit range that contain formulas

Menu Item	Description
Recalc-List	Shows the path that 1-2-3 follows when recalculating the worksheet
Circs	Lists all cells involved in a circular reference
Options	Modifies or resets the audit range and audit mode
Quit	Exits Auditor and returns to 1-2-3

Setting the Audit Range

The *audit range* specifies the area that you want Auditor to analyze. By default, Auditor assumes that you want to analyze the entire area of all worksheet files in memory—that is, every cell from cell A:A1 to cell IV:IV8192 of every open file.

Auditor indicates the current audit range on the left side of the Auditor Settings box. In figure 14.1, for example, the box indicates that the audit range consists of all files in memory. The right side of the Auditor Settings box is the mode indicator, which displays the current audit mode. For example, the audit mode indicated in figure 14.1 is HIGHLIGHT. (The audit mode is discussed in more detail in the section "Changing the Way That Auditor Reports Results.")

Sometimes you may want to fine-tune a small section of a large worksheet. For example, after checking the worksheet, you might make just a few changes in a certain area. In such instances, you can specify a smaller audit range, even if the cells refer to other formulas or cells outside the specified range.

To change the audit range, select **O**ptions **A**udit-Range from the Auditor menu. Auditor highlights the current audit range in the worksheet and changes to POINT mode. Press Esc to unanchor the range, and then highlight a new range. After highlighting the correct range of cells, press Enter. Auditor indicates the new range in the Auditor Settings box.

If you want to change the audit range, you can edit the current range in the control panel. Select **O**ptions **A**udit-Range, and then press F2 (Edit). Auditor displays a cursor at the end of the address of the audit range in the edit line. Edit the address as necessary and press Enter to accept the new range.

Tip
The Auditor Settings box covers part of the worksheet. So, whenever you highlight a range, you should watch the addresses in the control panel, to make sure that you are highlighting the correct range.

Changing the Way That Auditor Reports Results

To make it as easy as possible for you to view the results of an operation, Auditor offers you three different ways to display the information. The various ways are called *audit modes*.

By default, Auditor uses HIGHLIGHT mode, which highlights all the worksheet cells that match a command you select. On a color monitor, the cells appear in a different color; on a monochrome monitor, they appear in a high-intensity format. HIGHLIGHT mode works well for small worksheets. However, if your worksheet is large, Auditor may not be capable of displaying all the highlighted cells on one screen, so that you have to scroll through the worksheet to see all matching cells.

To make it easier to use Auditor with large worksheets, you should choose one of the other audit modes. Using LIST mode, you can create a list of matching cells in a separate range of the worksheet. TRACE mode lets you move a highlight through the worksheet and display one matching cell at a time.

To change the audit mode, select **H**ighlight, **L**ist, or **T**race from the **O**ptions menu.

> **Note**
>
> If you use Auditor a second time in the same worksheet, Auditor doesn't remove existing highlights automatically. To remove highlights, select **O**ptions **R**eset **H**ighlight before using Auditor again in the same worksheet.

If you select **O**ptions **T**RACE and then select an Auditor command, Auditor highlights the first cell that matches the command and displays a menu that offers the options **F**orward, **B**ackward, and **Q**uit. Each time you select **F**orward, Auditor traces through the worksheet to find the next matching cell. Each time you select **B**ackward, you move to the preceding cell that matches.

When you are using Auditor on TRACE mode, the mode indicator in the top right corner of the screen displays the Auditor command that you selected. If you choose **P**recedents, for example, the mode indicator displays PRECEDENTS. You can refer to this feature if you forget which Auditor command you selected.

When the list has no more matching cells in the direction that you selected, Auditor beeps instead of moving the cell pointer. After viewing the matching cells, select **Q**uit to return to the Auditor main menu.

Use the same procedure to change the audit mode to LIST. The LIST mode differs from TRACE in that it prompts for a target range in which to copy the list of matching cell addresses and their contents. Figure 14.2 shows a list of precedents for cell A:D12.

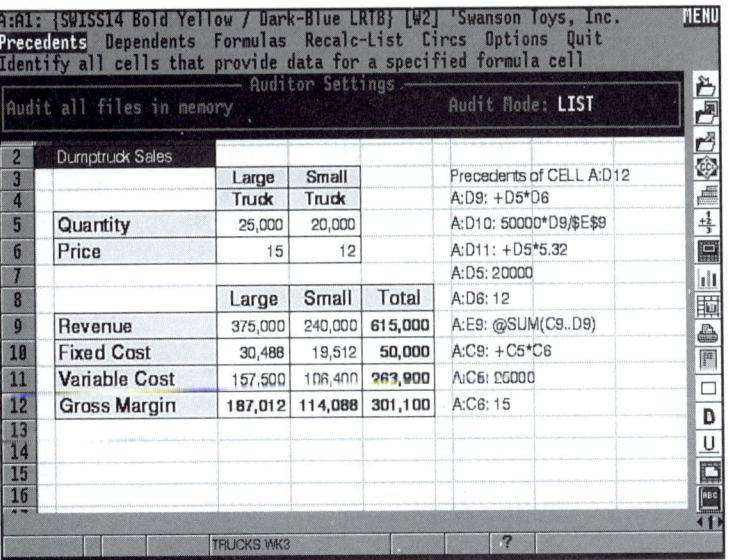

Fig. 14.2
When you use Auditor in LIST mode, it lists in the worksheet the information it finds—in this case, a list of precedent cells for a formula.

Note

When using LIST mode, make sure that you specify an empty target range. Although Auditor doesn't write over existing data, you cannot complete the command until you specify an empty range. If you specify a range that contains data, or a single cell in a column that contains data below the specified cell, Auditor displays an error message and forces you to respecify the range. If you specify a single cell as the target range, Auditor expands the range downward in the same column as far as necessary.

Tip
If you turned off the beep with the /**W**orksheet **G**lobal **D**efault **O**ther **B**eep **N**o command, Auditor fails to beep when it finds no matching cells. If you want Auditor to beep, make sure that you turn the beep back on when you use Auditor.

Troubleshooting Formulas in a Worksheet

Auditor provides five different kinds of information about formulas in a worksheet. Within the specified audit range, you can use Auditor to find the precedent cells of a formula, the formulas that depend on a cell, or all cells

534 Chapter 14—Analyzing Formulas with Auditor

that contain formulas. Auditor can also provide information about circular references or the recalculation sequence in all active files.

Finding Formulas

◄ "Entering Basic Formulas," p. 74

◄ "Protecting Cells from Change," p. 512

To find all the cells in a worksheet that contain formulas, select the **F**ormulas command on the Auditor main menu. Auditor then displays the results, using the audit mode (HIGHLIGHT, LIST, or TRACE) currently indicated in the Audit Settings box's mode indicator. (See "Changing the Way That Auditor Reports Results.")

If the current audit mode is HIGHLIGHT, Auditor highlights all the cells on the worksheet that contain formulas. If you want to move around in the worksheet and examine or edit the formulas in the highlighted cells, you must exit the Auditor menu (select **Q**uit).

Tip

Before sharing a worksheet with coworkers, use Auditor to highlight all the formulas. Then make sure all formulas are protected so that they cannot be written over. (See Chapter 9, "Working with Files," for information on data-protection strategies.)

As you examine these cells, you may notice an error in one of the formulas. If you edit the cell to correct the mistake, the highlight remains unless the correction involves a change in the worksheet (such as moving cells, inserting or deleting rows or columns, or redefining range names). In such cases, Auditor removes all highlights. To highlight the formula cells again, select **/T**ools **A**nalyze **A**uditor, and select **F**ormulas again.

If the audit mode is LIST, Auditor places in the worksheet a list of all formulas contained in the audit range.

Finding Cells Used by a Formula (Precedents)

To better understand a formula, you can use Auditor to find the formula's *precedents*. Each cell that the formula uses is one of the formula's precedents. You cannot always determine a formula's precedents by examining the formula. For example, the formula +B10-B11 seems to use only cells B10 and B11, but if B10 contains the formula @SUM(Z1..Z100), then all the cells in the range Z1 through Z100 are precedents of the formula.

Finding a formula's precedents can be valuable in many situations, such as the following:

- When you're trying to understand a worksheet that a coworker created
- When debugging a formula that returns an incorrect result
- When debugging a formula that returns ERR

To find all the cells that supply information to a particular formula, select the **P**recedents option from the Auditor menu. Auditor prompts you for the cell location of the formula. Point to the cell or type the cell address, and then press Enter. After finding all cells that the formula uses, Auditor displays the results in the specified audit mode (HIGHLIGHT, LIST, or TRACE).

Finding Formulas That Refer to a Cell (Dependents)

Dependent formulas are those that may be affected by a change that you make in another cell. Using Auditor to find dependent formulas can help you avoid making a serious mistake in a worksheet. For example, if Auditor points out that a formula in another area of the worksheet depends on a value in a cell, you know that you must avoid erasing that value.

To find all dependent formulas, use the **D**ependents option on the Auditor menu. This command finds all formulas in the audit range that depend on a specific cell. When you select **D**ependents, Auditor prompts you for the source cell. Point to the cell or type the address of the cell whose value you want to change, and then press Enter. Auditor uses the current audit mode (HIGHLIGHT, LIST, or TRACE) to report any formulas that depend on the cell's information.

For example, suppose that you want to find all formulas that depend on cell A:B9 in the sample worksheet. After selecting **D**ependents, specify cell A:B9. Auditor then displays all the formulas that depend directly or indirectly on the value in cell A:B9 for calculations (see fig. 14.3). In this example, the audit mode is LIST.

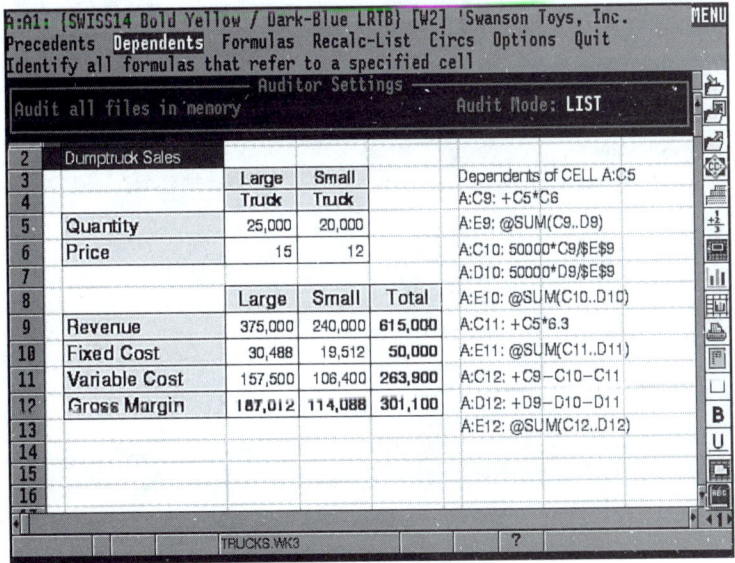

Fig. 14.3

Using Auditor in LIST mode to list the formulas that depend on a specified cell.

Examining Recalculation Order

◄ "Controlling Recalculation," p. 226

For some worksheets, the order that 1-2-3 uses to recalculate the worksheet is important. As discussed in Chapter 3, you can use **/W**orksheet **G**lobal **R**ecalc to set the recalculation order to one of the following: **N**atural, **C**olumnwise, or **R**owwise. You also can change the recalculation method to either **A**utomatic, **M**anual, or **I**teration.

During recalculation, 1-2-3 may skip around the worksheet. With natural recalculation, for example, 1-2-3 begins by determining the dependencies among the worksheet's formulas. If no formulas depend on other formulas, 1-2-3 begins recalculating formula cells starting at the top left corner of the first worksheet. However, if a formula refers to another formula cell, 1-2-3 performs the calculation in the referenced formula first.

To determine the recalculation order that 1-2-3 uses, change the audit mode to TRACE or LIST, then select **R**ecalc-List from the Auditor main menu. If you select TRACE for the audit mode, Auditor highlights the first cell that 1-2-3 calculates in the audit range. Select **F**orward to move to the next cell to be recalculated. To move back through the cells, select **B**ackward. Select **Q**uit to exit the TRACE display and return to the Auditor main menu. If you select LIST for the audit mode, Auditor copies the list of formula cells from the worksheet, in the order that the cells are to be recalculated (see fig. 14.4).

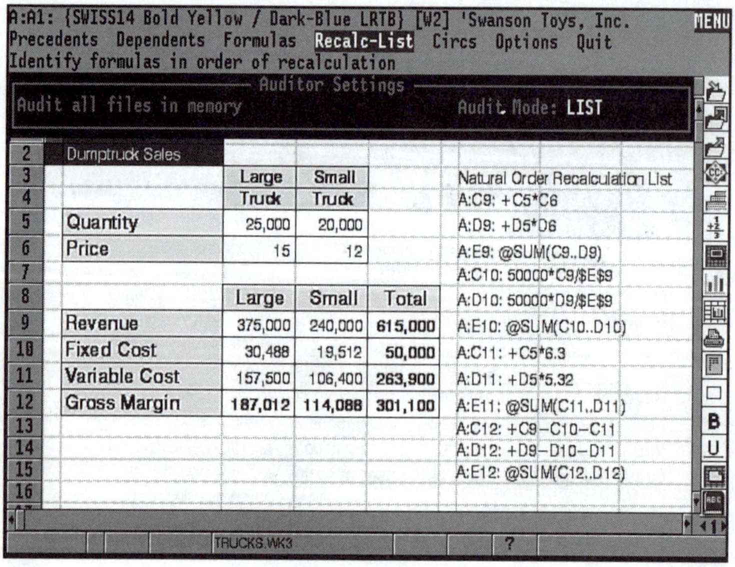

Fig. 14.4
Using the **R**ecalc-List command in LIST mode to display the formula recalculation order.

> **Note**
>
> Before using Auditor to determine recalculation order, select **/W**orksheet **G**lobal to make sure that **R**ecalc is set to **N**atural. If recalculation is set to rowwise or columnwise, you need not use Auditor to determine the recalculation order; 1-2-3 starts recalculating in cell A:A1 of the first active file, and proceeds row by row or column by column through every worksheet in every active file.

> **Note**
>
> Unlike other Auditor options, **R**ecalc-List isn't limited to the audit range, so the list that the command generates can use up much of a worksheet's space. Consider using three-dimensional worksheets and specifying a report range in a blank worksheet.

Examining Circular References

In 1-2-3 worksheets, circular references are among the most complicated and difficult errors to correct. In rare cases, you intentionally create circular references to perform calculations, but the CIRC indicator, which appears in the status bar at the bottom of the screen, usually is an unwelcome surprise.

Circular references in formulas are hard to find because these errors often result from an indirect reference that seems reasonable. Suppose that you want to make the number of sales staff hired contingent on a company's net income. You reason that if net income is too far in the red (negative numbers), you may need to increase the number of sales staff to bring in more revenue. Because the number of sales staff depends on net profit, net profit depends on sales, and sales depends on the number of sales staff, you have a circular reference.

More often, however, circular references result from an error made when entering or editing a formula. In figure 14.5, for example, the formula in cell A:C12 reads as follows:

    +C9–C10–C12

The **C**ircs command on the **A**uditor main menu helps you determine why a formula (such as the one just described) causes a circular reference. If you select **C**ircs with LIST as the audit mode, Auditor displays a list of the cells involved with a circular reference.

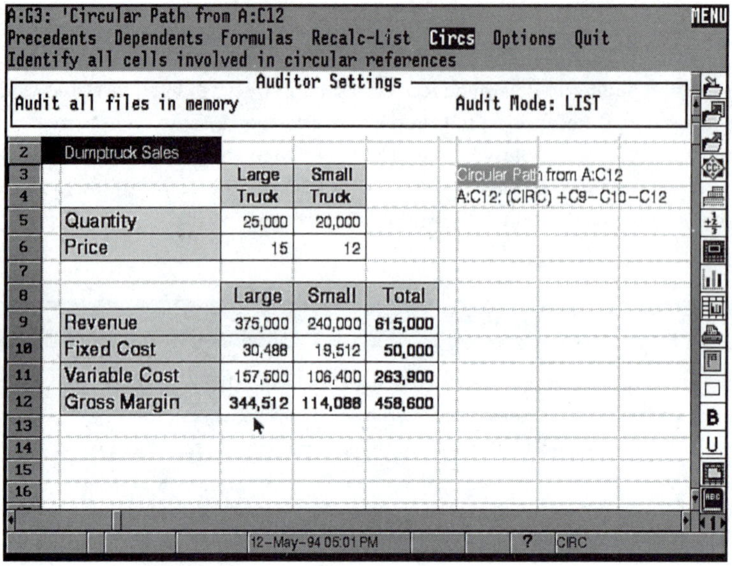

Fig. 14.5

The formula in cell A:C12 refers to cell A:C12, causing a circular reference. Use the **C**ircs command in LIST mode to display a list of all cells involved in a circular reference.

Tip

When you select /**W**orksheet **S**tatus, 1-2-3 shows a single circular reference. If several exist in the worksheet, the last one created is displayed. Auditor's **C**ircs report is much more comprehensive, so use this feature for a complete report of all circular reference problems in a worksheet.

The worksheet may have more than one circular reference. If it does, then when you select the **C**ircs command, 1-2-3 will display a menu listing one cell from each circular reference. Select one of the cells in that menu list and press Enter. Auditor highlights or lists all cells involved in that circular reference.

Resetting Auditor Options

After using Auditor to correct one worksheet, you may want to check other worksheets. Before retrieving another worksheet, reset the audit range and audit mode as necessary. If you highlighted a range of cells by selecting **O**ptions **H**ighlight and then **P**recedents, **D**ependents, or **F**ormulas, you may want to remove the highlighting from those cells.

To reset the audit range and audit mode, select **O**ptions **R**eset **O**ptions. Auditor resets the audit range to `Audit all files in memory` and the audit mode to HIGHLIGHT. (These changes appear in the Auditor Settings box.) Select **Q**uit to return to the Auditor main menu.

To remove the existing highlights (or color) from cells in the worksheet, select **O**ptions **R**eset **H**ighlight from the Auditor main menu. Select **Q**uit twice to return to the worksheet and the READY mode.

From Here...

For information relating to using Auditor, you may want to review the following chapters of this book:

- Chapter 2, "What Every 1-2-3 User Should Know," shows you the easiest techniques for setting up a worksheet, and introduces the basics of creating formulas.

- Chapter 3, "Finding Solutions with Formulas and Functions," gives you more information about creating and troubleshooting formulas and about using 1-2-3's built-in functions.

Chapter 15

Using Functions To Analyze Data

1-2-3 Release 4 provides more than 100 built-in formulas, called *functions*, that enable you to take advantage of 1-2-3's analytical capability. You can use these functions to calculate results and solve problems in formulas with mathematical operators or in macros and advanced macro-command programs. Several of these functions are especially useful for analyzing data in a table or a database range in your worksheet.

In this chapter, you learn to

- Use the database functions to analyze information in a database range
- Use the @VLOOKUP, @HLOOKUP, and @INDEX functions to analyze information in a table

◀ "Entering Basic Formulas," p. 74

◀ "Entering Functions," p. 159

◀ "Using the Statistical Functions," p. 189

Analyzing Database Information

Using the 11 database functions of 1-2-3, you can generate statistics for specific items taken from a database range. Table 15.1 describes the database functions.

Chapter 15—Using Functions To Analyze Data

Tip
Because 1-2-3 counts offset numbers beginning with 0 instead of 1, it's easy to make a mistake when specifying the offset column. To avoid making mistakes with offset numbers, always use field names enclosed in quotation marks when you use database functions.

▶ "Creating a Database," p. 622

▶ "Listing All Specified Records," p. 650

▶ "Handling More Complicated Criteria Ranges," p. 657

Table 15.1 Database Functions

Function	Description
@DSUM	Sums the values of items in a field that match the specified criteria
@DMAX	Gives the maximum value of items in a field that match the specified criteria
@DMIN	Gives the minimum value of items in a field that match the specified criteria
@DAVG	Gives the average value of items in a field that match the specified criteria
@DCOUNT	Gives the number of items in a field that match the specified criteria
@DSTD	Gives the standard deviation of items in a field that match the specified criteria
@DSTDS	Gives the sample standard deviation of values in a field that match the specified criteria
@DVAR	Gives the variance of items in a field that match the specified criteria
@DVARS	Gives the sample variance of values in a field that match the specified criteria
@DGET	Extracts an item that matches the specified criteria from a field in a database
@DQUERY	Sends a command to an external database-management program

The general syntax of these functions follows:

@*database_function*(*input_range*,*offset*,*criteria_range*)

The only function that varies from this syntax is @DQUERY, which is discussed later in this section.

The *input_range* and *criteria_range* arguments are the same as those that the /**D**ata **Q**uery command uses. The *input_range* argument specifies the database or part of a database to be scanned, and the *criteria_range* argument specifies the records to be selected. The *offset* argument indicates which field to select from the database records. The *offset* value must be either zero or a positive integer. A value of 0 indicates the first column in the database, a value of 1 indicates the second column, and so on. The *offset* argument can also be the name of a field enclosed in quotation marks. For example, to sum the values from a database's Salary field, use the text `"Salary"` as the *offset* argument.

For example, figure 15.1 shows a worksheet with a small database. The range name DATABASE has been assigned to range A6..D11. Note that database ranges must include, in the top row, a unique field name for each field. Range D1..D2 contains a criteria range that directs 1-2-3 to select only records in which Chicago appears in the Location field when performing database operations. The name CRITRANGE is assigned to this range. Notice that cell D1 contains a field name from the database. The characters in this label must match those in the label in cell C6 exactly. (The case of the letters in these labels does not have to match, although it does in this example.) If you used the **/D**ata **Q**uery **E**xtract commands and specified this criteria range, 1-2-3 would copy only the third and fifth records to the output range. Similarly, the examples that follow show formulas in which only the third and fifth records figure into the calculations.

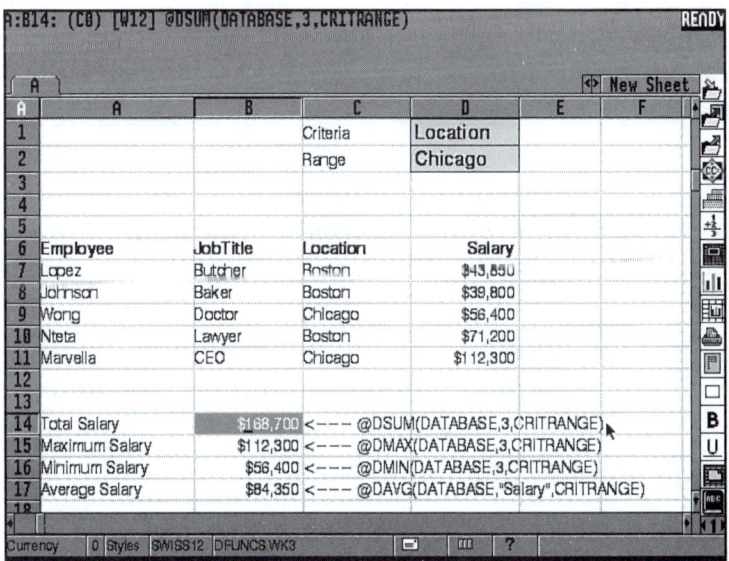

Fig. 15.1
A sample database illustrating the use of database functions.

Calculating Simple Database Statistics

@DSUM adds up the values in a database field, selecting only those records that match a specified criteria range. In figure 15.1, the formula in cell B14 specifies DATABASE as the criteria range, 3 as the column from which to sum values, and CRITRANGE as the criteria range by which it selects records. This formula returns the sum of the salaries for the two employees located in Chicago.

Chapter 15—Using Functions To Analyze Data

@DMAX finds the highest of the values in a database field that accompany records specified by a criteria range. In figure 15.2, @DMAX has found the highest value in cell B15.

Fig. 15.2
@DMAX finds the highest value in the specified field for selected records.

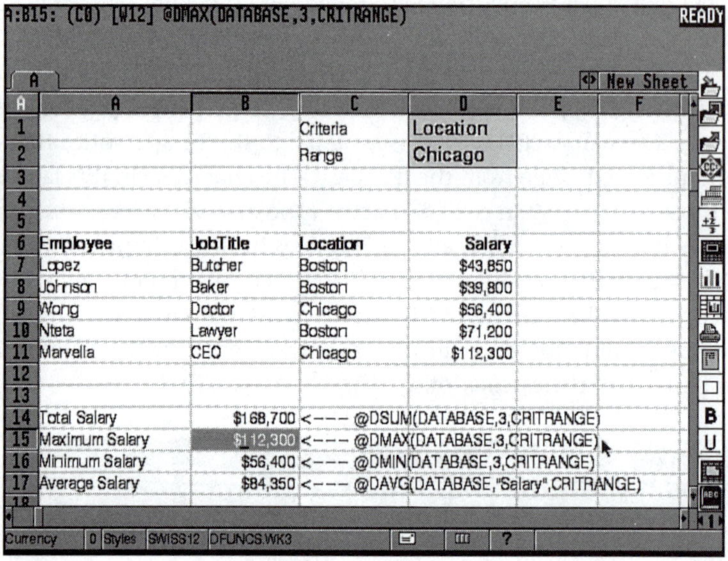

	A	B	C	D	E	F
1			Criteria	Location		
2			Range	Chicago		
3						
4						
5						
6	Employee	JobTitle	Location	Salary		
7	Lopez	Butcher	Boston	$43,850		
8	Johnson	Baker	Boston	$39,800		
9	Wong	Doctor	Chicago	$56,400		
10	Nteta	Lawyer	Boston	$71,200		
11	Marvella	CEO	Chicago	$112,300		
12						
13						
14	Total Salary	$168,700	<--- @DSUM(DATABASE,3,CRITRANGE)			
15	Maximum Salary	$112,300	<--- @DMAX(DATABASE,3,CRITRANGE)			
16	Minimum Salary	$56,400	<--- @DMIN(DATABASE,3,CRITRANGE)			
17	Average Salary	$84,350	<--- @DAVG(DATABASE,"Salary",CRITRANGE)			

@DMIN returns the lowest of the values in a database field that accompany records specified by a criteria range. In figure 15.2, the arguments in cell B16 are identical to the arguments in the highlighted cell B15, but the function used is @DMIN.

@DAVG returns the average of the values in a database field that accompany records specified by a criteria range. Figure 15.3 demonstrates @DAVG. Notice that in this example, the column is specified by its name, `"Salary"`. When you use a field name in a database function, enclose the field name in quotation marks. The characters inside the quotation marks must match the field name from the database exactly, but the case does not matter.

@DCOUNT returns the number of nonblank entries in a database field that match a specified criteria. Figure 15.4 shows the database from the preceding figures but with the salary omitted from one of the Chicago records. The formula in cell B14 refers to a criteria range that specifies the Location field and counts the number of Chicago entries in that field, returning a value of 2; however, if you change the formula to

@DCOUNT(DATABASE,"salary",CRITRANGE)

the formula returns 1, even though two records have Chicago in the Location field; now only one Chicago record contains an entry in the Salary field.

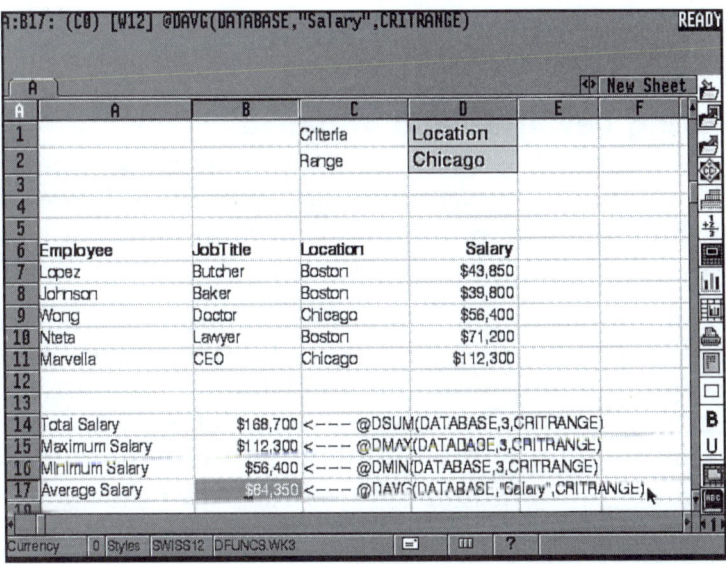

Fig. 15.3
@DAVG finds the average of the values in a specified field for selected records.

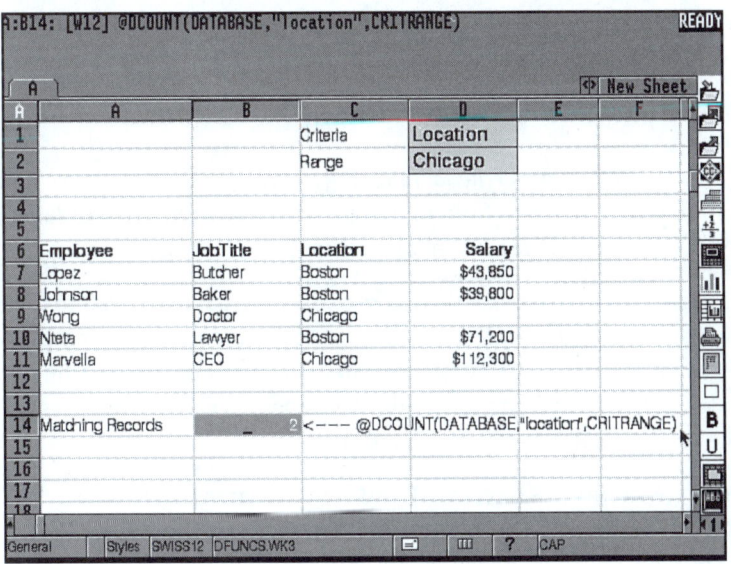

Fig. 15.4
@DCOUNT counts the number of records that match a specified criteria in the database.

Although @DSUM, @DMAX, @DMIN, and @DAVG usually refer only to fields that contain values, @DCOUNT can count the entries in any field. Unless you specifically want a value, however, such as the number of nonblank Salary fields among the Chicago records, you should specify in @DCOUNT an offset argument that also is one of the fields named in the criteria range.

Calculating Deviation and Variance

◄ "Using the Statistical Functions," p. 189

Use @DSTD and @DSTDS to extract from a database the values that accompany selected records and to compute the standard deviation of those values. Use @DVAR and @DVARS to extract from a database the values that accompany selected records and to compute the variance of those values.

Standard deviation and variance are both measures of how much individual values in a population or sample vary from the average value in the population or sample. Variance is the square of standard deviation. Use @DSTD and @DVAR to calculate standard deviation and variance when you have data for an entire population. Use @DSTDS and @DVARS to calculate standard deviation and variance when you have data for a sample of data from a larger population.

Extracting a Value or Label

The database function @DGET extracts a value or label from a field in the database. The syntax for @DGET is as follows:

@DGET(*input_range*,*offset*,*criteria_range*)

The *input_range*, *offset*, and *criteria_range* arguments are used in the same manner as in the other database functions. @DGET returns the value or label in the specified field of the record that matches the specified criteria.

@DGET returns ERR unless exactly one record in the database matches exactly the criteria range. Figure 15.5 shows how @DGET can retrieve an employee's job title when you enter the employee's name in a criteria range. The formula returns Butcher; however, if you change the label in cell D2 from Lopez to Wong, the result in cell B14 changes to Doctor.

If you change the entries in cells D1 and D2 to Location and Boston, the formula in cell B14 returns ERR. You are effectively asking the formula what the job title is when Location is Boston. Because three different answers to that question are possible, the function returns ERR.

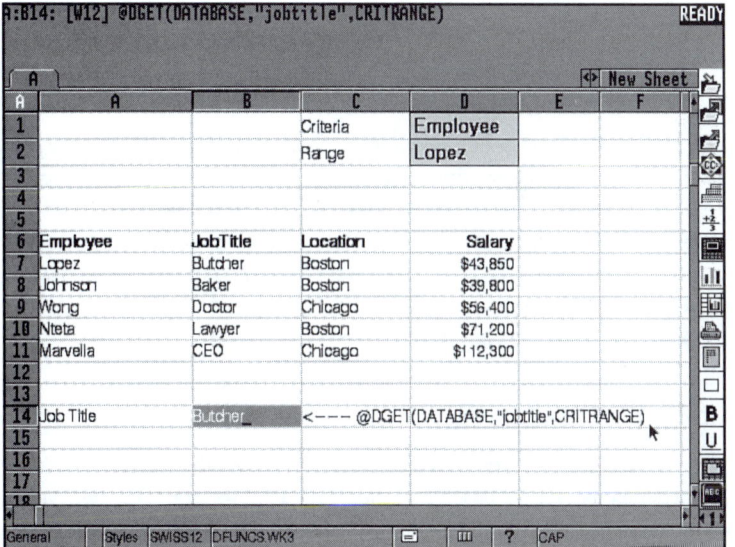

Fig. 15.5
@DGET extracts information from a unique record.

Troubleshooting

One of the database functions other than @DGET or @DQUERY returns ERR.

One of the following conditions might be causing the problem:

- You specified the input range incorrectly. Check to see whether the range that you specified as the *input_range* argument includes the entire database range, including field names.

- You specified the *offset* argument incorrectly. If you specified a numeric offset, make sure that the number you used is a valid offset for the size of your input range. For example, if your input range contains four columns, the valid offset numbers are 0, 1, 2, and 3. Specifying another number causes the function to return ERR. If you specified a field name as the offset, make sure that the field name is enclosed in quotes, and check to see whether you spelled the field name exactly as it is spelled in the input range.

- The criteria range is specified incorrectly. Make sure that the range that you specified as the *criteria_range* includes at least two rows and that the top row contains field names from the database.

(continues)

> (continued)
>
> *The @DGET function returns ERR.*
>
> First check for the conditions described for the other functions. If you have specified the input range, offset, and criteria range correctly, then either no records in the input range match the criteria or more than one record matches. To check for this, enter the @DCOUNT function in another cell, using the same arguments that you used in the @DGET function. If @DCOUNT returns a number other than 1, @DGET returns ERR. If you modify your criteria until @DCOUNT returns 1, @DGET should return an appropriate value.
>
> *One of the database functions other than @DQUERY returns an incorrect or unexpected result other than ERR.*
>
> First check the previously discussed conditions to ensure that you have correctly specified the input range, offset, and criteria range. If you specified these arguments correctly, then the criteria that you entered in the criteria range may be incorrect. You can test for this problem by using either the **/D**ata **Q**uery **F**ind or the **/D**ata **Q**uery **E**xtract command, specifying the same input range and criteria range that you used in the database function. Make sure that the records the **F**ind or **E**xtract command generates are the ones you expected would match your criteria. If not, enter a new criteria. For more information about specifying criteria, see the section "Handling More Complicated Criteria Ranges" in Chapter 21, "Finding Specific Data."

Working with External Tables

▶ "Working with External Databases," p. 1025

@DQUERY sends commands to an external database. This function differs from most of the others in that it doesn't return a piece of useful information. To enter formulas, you use @DQUERY in a criteria range before using a **/D**ata **Q**uery command with an internal table.

Use this syntax for the @DQUERY function:

@DQUERY(*external_function,argument1,argument2,...*)

Suppose that you are working with an external database that includes a LastName field, and that the database management program you're using has a function called LIKE that performs phonetic matches. That is, it can use `LIKE("Smith")` to find records with last names such as Smith, Smyth, and Smythe. To use this function in the external database, you create a criteria range that includes the LastName field and then type the formula

@DQUERY("LIKE","SMITH") in that field. This formula returns LIKE, but, when you issue query commands, the formula tells the external database program to use its LIKE function and to use SMITH as its argument. In order for the @DQUERY function in this example to be of any use, you must have established a connection to an external database, and the database must support the LIKE function.

Analyzing Information in a Table

The database functions are useful for analyzing information that is organized into a database range. Three other functions—@HLOOKUP, @VLOOKUP, and @INDEX—can look up entries in a table regardless of whether the table is organized as a database range.

Looking Up Entries in a Table

The @HLOOKUP and @VLOOKUP functions retrieve a string or value from a table, based on a specified key that is used to find the information. The operation and format of the two functions are essentially the same except that @HLOOKUP looks through horizontal tables (hence the *H* in the function's name) and @VLOOKUP looks through vertical tables (the source of the *V* in its name).

These functions use the following syntaxes, respectively:

@HLOOKUP(*key,range,row_offset*)

@VLOOKUP(*key,range,column_offset*)

If you use numeric keys, make sure that the key values ascend in order. If keys are labels, you can list the keys in any order.

If you use numeric keys, @HLOOKUP and @VLOOKUP actually search for the largest value that is less than or equal to the key. If the function doesn't find an exact match, the function selects the largest value that is less than the numeric key.

The *range* argument specifies the area that makes up the entire lookup table. The *offset* argument, which is always a number, specifies which row or column contains the data that you are looking up. A 0 indicates the leftmost column or the top row of the range (which is also the lookup column or lookup row), a 1 indicates the second column or row of the range, and so on. When you specify an offset number, it cannot be negative or exceed the number of columns or rows that the table contains.

550 Chapter 15—Using Functions To Analyze Data

> **Note**
>
> Because 1-2-3 counts offset numbers beginning with 0 rather than 1, you can easily make a mistake when specifying the offset column or row. To make sure that you use the correct offset number when you use @VLOOKUP and @HLOOKUP, think of the offset number as being a number of columns *away from* the lookup column or a number of rows *away from* the lookup row.

Figure 15.6 shows an @VLOOKUP formula that looks for the label entered in cell B14 in the left column of range A6..D11. After finding the label, the formula returns the name of the capital from the cell that is one column to the right of the label. Cells C17 and C18 contain almost identical formulas, except that their offset numbers are 2 and 3, respectively.

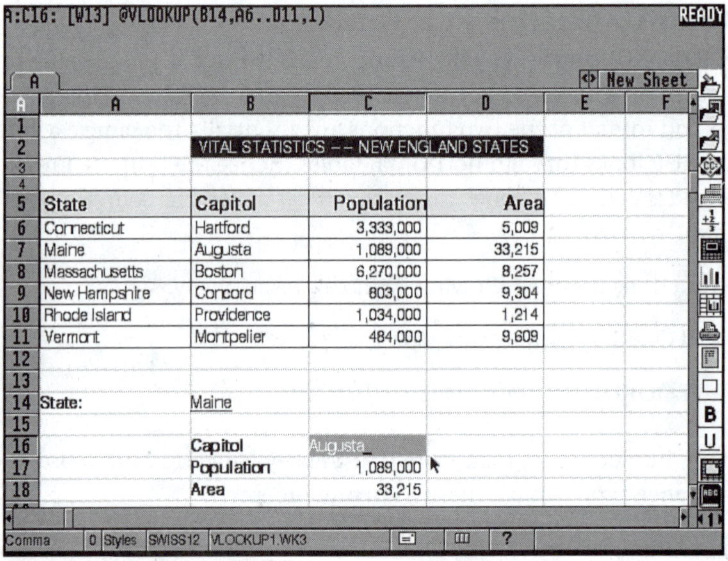

Fig. 15.6
Using @VLOOKUP to find data that accompanies a lookup label.

	A	B	C	D
1				
2		VITAL STATISTICS -- NEW ENGLAND STATES		
3				
4				
5	State	Capitol	Population	Area
6	Connecticut	Hartford	3,333,000	5,009
7	Maine	Augusta	1,089,000	33,215
8	Massachusetts	Boston	6,270,000	8,257
9	New Hampshire	Concord	803,000	9,304
10	Rhode Island	Providence	1,034,000	1,214
11	Vermont	Montpelier	484,000	9,609
12				
13				
14	State:		Maine	
15				
16		Capitol	Augusta	
17		Population	1,089,000	
18		Area	33,215	

A:C16: [W13] @VLOOKUP(B14,A6..D11,1)

The formulas in range C16..C18 return ERR if the label entered in cell B14 doesn't match one of the states in column A exactly. Case matters here. For example, if you type **MASSACHUSETTS** in cell B14, the @VLOOKUP formulas return ERR.

Figure 15.7 shows @VLOOKUP used with values. In this example, an exact match is not necessary, but the values in the lookup column must be arranged in ascending order. To determine the bonus, @VLOOKUP examines each value in range A7..A11 from top to bottom. If @VLOOKUP finds a match for the value in cell C15, it stops; however, if it finds a value that's greater than the value in cell C15, it goes back up one row. That is, @VLOOKUP finds the highest value that does not exceed the value in cell C15. The formula then finds the appropriate value and returns the number that is one cell to the right of that value. This formula also multiplies that percentage by the value in cell C15 to compute the dollar amount of the bonus.

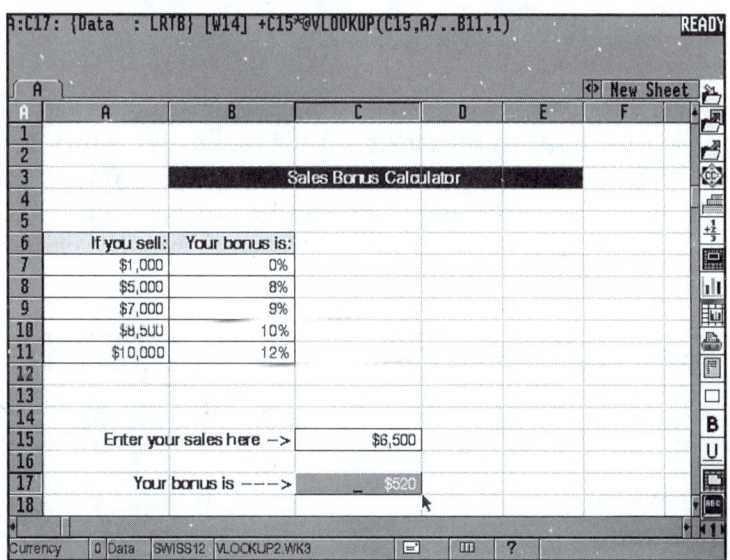

Fig. 15.7
Using @VLOOKUP with an ascending list of values.

Retrieving Data from Specified Locations

@INDEX, a data-management function, is similar to the table-lookup functions described earlier, but has some unique features.

The function uses the following syntax:

@INDEX(*range,column-offset,row-offset,[worksheet-offset]*)

Like @HLOOKUP and @VLOOKUP, @INDEX finds a value within a table. But unlike the lookup functions, @INDEX does not compare a key value to the values in the first row or column of the table. Instead, when you use @INDEX, you must indicate the column offset and row offset of the range from which you want to retrieve data. You also can indicate a worksheet number.

552 Chapter 15—Using Functions To Analyze Data

> **Note**
>
> Because 1-2-3 counts offset numbers beginning with 0 instead of 1, it's easy to make a mistake when specifying the offset column or row. To make sure you use the correct offset numbers when you use @INDEX, specify a range that includes the column and row headings of your table in addition to the data that you want to look up. Then row 1 is the first row that contains data, and column 1 is the first column that contains data.

Figure 15.8 shows a worksheet that uses @INDEX. A mail-order company uses a shipping charge based on shipping zones and the number of packages shipped. Because these factors can be indicated by numbers, you can arrange the various charges in a table and access them by a column number (which corresponds to a shipping-zone number) and a row number (which corresponds to a number of packages).

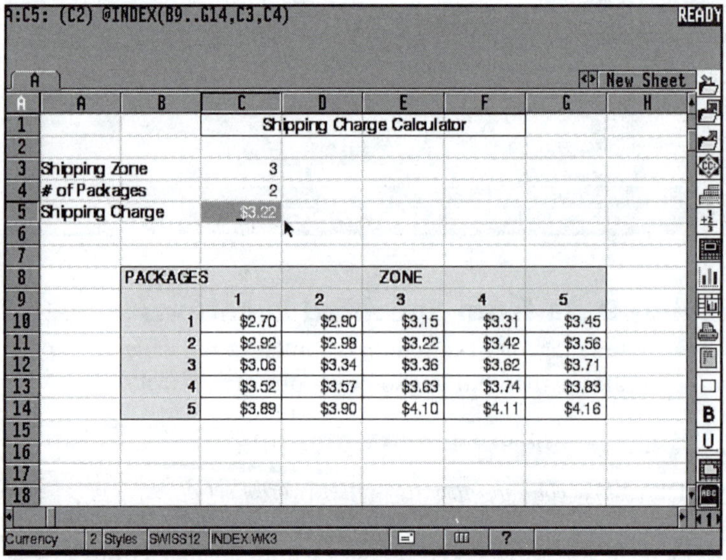

Fig. 15.8
Using @INDEX to find the value at a specific column and row within a range.

From Here...

For information that relates directly to using functions to analyze your data, you may want to review the following chapters of this book:

- Chapter 2, "What Every 1-2-3 User Should Know," shows you the easiest techniques for setting up a worksheet and introduces the basics of creating formulas.

- Chapter 3, "Finding Solutions with Formulas and Functions," gives you more information about creating and troubleshooting formulas and about using 1-2-3's built-in functions.

- Chapter 19, "Creating Databases," explains how to design and create databases. After you create a database, return to this chapter to find out how to use the database functions to analyze the information in your database.

- Chapter 21, "Finding Specific Data," describes how to set up criteria ranges to find data in your database. You also need to use criteria ranges to use the database functions.

Chapter 16

Finding Solutions with Solver

One of the most powerful analytical tools included in 1-2-3 Release 4 is Solver, which lets you solve and analyze problems in your worksheets. Solver provides an easy way to find several solutions to a problem, based on various assumptions. Solver is especially useful when you are working with *what-if scenarios*, in which you try different combinations of values for several variables in a complex problem.

For example, suppose that you want to determine the best product mix based on production capacity. You can use Solver to perform a what-if analysis that maximizes bottom-line profits by determining the optimal production ratio for each product.

Solver analyzes data in a problem and finds a set of possible answers. Depending on the problem, Solver may find no answer, one answer, or several answers. Solver is both easy to use and powerful enough to solve very complex problems. To help you make the best use of the answers it finds, Solver can produce several different reports that give information about its answers.

In this chapter, you learn

- How Solver works and what kind of problems it can solve
- How to set up and solve a problem using Solver
- How to use Solver to solve several specific kinds of business problems
- How to use the reports that Solver can create

Understanding Solver

Understanding what Solver can do and how it works will help you make better use of Solver to solve your business problems. This section describes the kinds of problems Solver is good at solving and the methods Solver uses to solve problems.

What Types of Problems Can Solver Solve?

Solver solves problems that you can describe using mathematical relationships. In other words, if you can describe the problem using formulas in a worksheet, Solver can probably solve it.

For example, Solver can solve all of the following problems:

- Find out the most profitable combination of different products to manufacture in a factory with limited production capacity.

- Find how much you can afford to spend on a house with different combinations of down payment, interest rate, and mortgage term.

- Find out different ways to allocate your advertising budget to reach as many potential customers as possible.

You could solve problems such as these by inserting different amounts for each of the variables and comparing the results until you find values that produce answers that meet your needs. Using this manual method is time-consuming and frustrating, however, because you must guess at possible answers, saving each set of answers for comparison later. Solver finds several answers, keeps track of each answer it finds, and displays any answer on demand.

Solver can also determine the best answer from the set of all possible answers (the "optimal answer") or from the set of all answers it found (the "best answer"). With its report capability, Solver can also show how it found each of its answers.

Solver uses the formulas that you enter in the worksheet to solve the problem. You don't need to know a special modeling language to use Solver; you simply enter formulas in a worksheet.

How Does Solver Work?

Solver can use several different methods to solve problems. You can think of these methods as being in two groups: symbolic and numeric.

The symbolic methods that Solver uses depend on mathematical rules that you may be familiar with, such as the rules of algebra. For example, Solver knows that if A + B = C, then C – B = A.

In terms of a real business problem, this means that if your shoe factory can operate 16 hours a day and you are spending 12 hours a day making running shoes, Solver "knows" that you can spend at most 4 hours a day making other kinds of shoes.

Or to look at it in terms of formulas in a worksheet, if cell F10 contains the formula +F6+F8, Solver can figure out that if the formula in cell F10 results in 16, and cell F8 contains the value 12, cell F6 must contain the value 4.

Numeric methods are similar to the trial-and-error method. Solver tries substituting many different combinations of values into a problem and keeps the combinations that solve the problem. Sometimes, when using numeric methods, Solver requires that you supply guesses for some values in a problem and then uses your guesses as starting points for its trial-and-error process.

Solver first tries symbolic methods to solve a problem. If symbolic methods don't solve the problem, Solver turns to numeric methods.

Setting Up Your Problem

You usually don't need to create a new worksheet just to solve a problem using Solver. You can use Solver to solve problems that are already set up in your existing worksheets, just by adding a few formulas.

For example, you might already have a worksheet to calculate the profit that results from manufacturing a particular mix of running shoes and hiking boots. In figure 16.1, cell D11 contains the profit that results from making the number of running shoes in cell B4 and the number of hiking boots in cell C4.

Fig. 16.1
A worksheet to calculate the profit from manufacturing shoes.

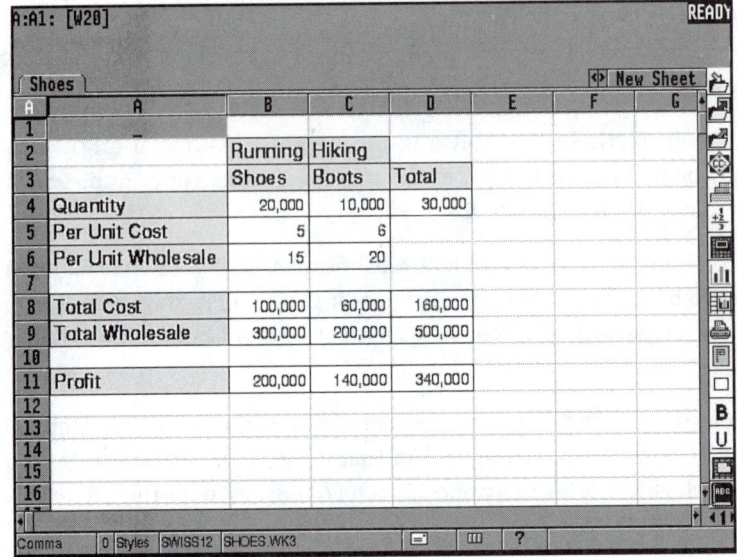

Adjustable Cells: The Values Solver Can Change

Suppose you want Solver to tell you how many running shoes and hiking boots to manufacture to make the largest possible profit. The first thing you need to tell Solver is which cells in the worksheet it should change to arrive at solutions to the problem.

In this case, you don't want Solver to change any of the cells that contain formulas that are used to calculate profit; you just want it to change the numbers of the two kinds of shoes that you make. Cells containing values that Solver can change are called *adjustable cells*. Adjustable cells must be blank or contain only values, never text or formulas. The adjustable cells in figure 16.1 are B4 and C4.

To find the largest possible profit, all Solver needs to do is put the largest possible values in the adjustable cells, B4 and C4, to yield the largest possible profit in cell D11. Because the largest possible value is infinity, you should make an infinite number of running shoes and an infinite number of hiking boots, thus making an infinite profit. Obviously, this answer doesn't make sense. There's something missing.

Constraints: The Limits to the Problem

In reality, the number of shoes you can make and sell is always limited somehow. For example, your factory may be able to make only 50,000 pairs of shoes per year. You might also know, based on past sales, that at least two-thirds of your sales are always running shoes, no matter how many of each kind of shoe you make. You need to consider these limits in any solution to the problem. What is missing from the problem is an expression of these limits that restrict the possible solutions to the problem.

To describe the limits of your problem in a way that Solver can understand, you use *logical formulas*. A logical formula is a formula that contains a logical operator and that results in either 1 (True) or 0 (False).

In this example, the limits are that you can make at most 50,000 pairs of shoes and that at least two-thirds of the shoes you make should be running shoes. You can express these limits using logical formulas.

Because the number of shoes is in cell D4, you can express the first limit with the formula +D4<=50000, which reads "D4 is less than or equal to 50000." This formula results in 1 if the value in cell D4 is less than or equal to 50000; otherwise, it results in 0.

To express the second limit, you could use the formula +B4>=(2/3*D4), which reads "B4 is greater than or equal to two-thirds times D4." A simpler formula that also works is +B4>=2*C4—"B4 is greater than or equal to two times C4." Notice that if B4 is at least two times C4, B4 is always at least two-thirds of D4 because D4 is equal to the sum of B4 and C4.

Logical formulas that are used to express the limits of a problem are called *constraints*; the cells containing them are called *constraint cells*.

Figure 16.2 shows the example worksheet with the constraints entered in cells A14 and A15. Both constraints are currently true, which means that the values in the worksheet represent one possible answer to the problem.

◀ "Entering Basic Formulas," p. 74

◀ "Formatting Numbers," p. 290

Tip
To display the constraint formulas rather than their results, highlight the constraint cells; then select /**R**ange Format **T**ext and press Enter. 1-2-3 displays the logical constraint formulas (see fig. 16.2).

Optimal Cell: The Value To Maximize or Minimize

In some problems, you want Solver to find solutions that result in the highest (or sometimes the lowest) value for a particular cell. In this example, you want a solution that results in the highest value for profit in cell D11. A cell that contains a value that you want Solver to maximize or minimize is called an *optimal cell*. A problem can have at most one optimal cell; some problems have no optimal cell. If a problem has an optimal cell, you can ask Solver to find the highest possible value or the lowest possible value for the optimal cell.

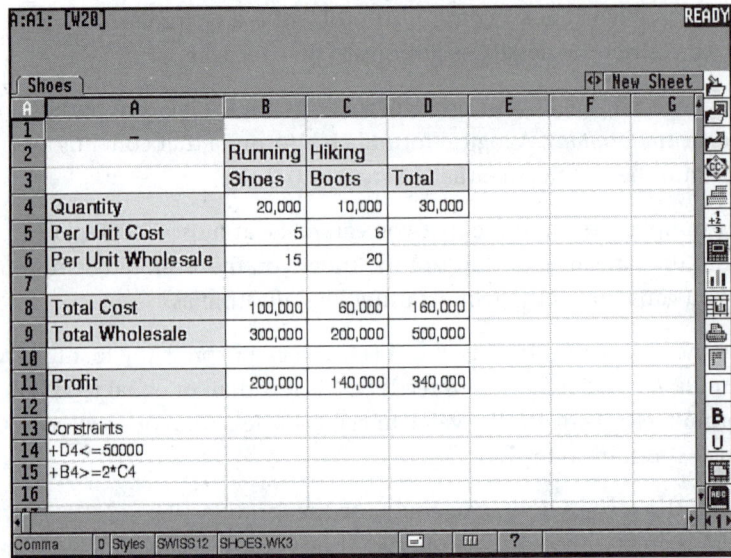

Fig. 16.2
The shoes worksheet with constraint formulas entered.

In this example, cell D11 is the optimal cell, and you want Solver to find the highest value, or to *maximize* the value of the optimal cell.

The example worksheet now contains everything that Solver needs to solve the problem: a problem expressed with formulas in a worksheet, adjustable cells containing values that Solver can change, constraints that express the limits of the problem, and an (optional) optimal cell that Solver should maximize.

Solving a Problem

After you set up your problem and enter constraints, you can use Solver to find solutions to the problem.

To begin, select **/T**ools **A**nalyze **S**olver. (The Tools menu is new in 1-2-3 Release 4 for DOS.) The first time you start Solver in a 1-2-3 session, there may be a pause while 1-2-3 loads the Solver add-in.

After you select **/T**ools **A**nalyze **S**olver, the Solver menu appears. The following sections describe how to define the problem and examine Solver's answers.

Defining the Problem

The first thing you need to do is define your problem, so select **/T**ools **A**nalyze **S**olve **D**efine. The **D**efine menu appears (see fig. 16.3).

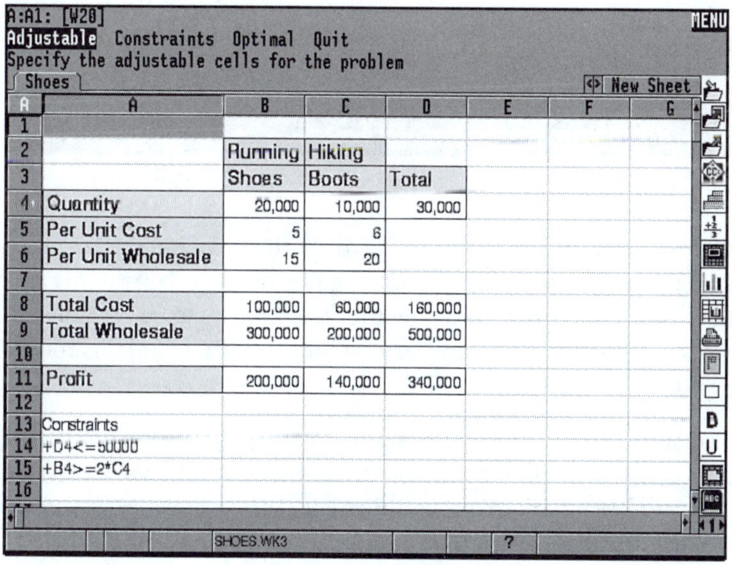

Fig. 16.3
The **/T**ools **A**nalyze **S**olve **D**efine menu.

Before you solve a problem, you must define the adjustable cells and constraint cells. Optionally, you can define the optimal cell.

In this problem, the adjustable cells are the cells that contain the quantities of the two kinds of shoes, cells A:B4..A:C4. Changing (or "adjusting") the values in these cells changes the value of profit in cell A:D11. To define the adjustable cells, select **A**djustable from the **S**olver **D**efine menu and specify the range that contains the adjustable cells. Figure 16.4 shows the adjustable cells being defined.

Fig. 16.4
Specifying the adjustable cells for the shoe problem.

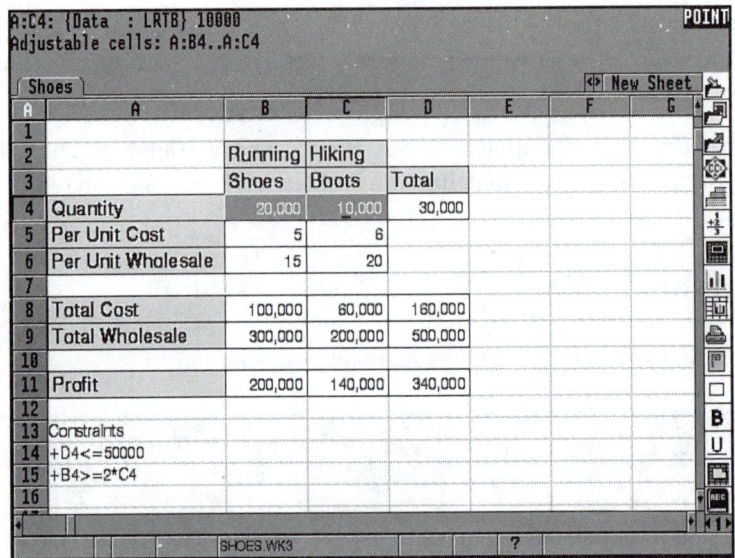

The constraint cells in any Solver problem are the cells that contain the logical formulas that define the constraints. In this case, the constraints are entered in cells A:A14..A:A15. To define the constraint cells, select **C**onstraints from the **S**olver **D**efine menu and specify the range that contains the constraint cells.

The optimal cell in this problem is the cell that contains total profit, cell A:D11. To define the optimal cell, select **O**ptimal from the **S**olver **D**efine menu. Solver displays another menu that lets you select whether you want Solver to maximize or minimize the value in the optimal cell. In this example, select **X** Maximize and then specify the cell containing the value you want Solver to maximize.

After defining the problem, select **Q**uit to return to the Solver menu; then select **S**olve **P**roblem to begin searching for the best answer (see fig. 16.5).

Solver displays a message in the status bar at the bottom of the screen, informing you of progress made as it uses various techniques to find answers that satisfy all the constraints. If the constraints you set are valid, Solver should find at least one answer (see fig. 16.6).

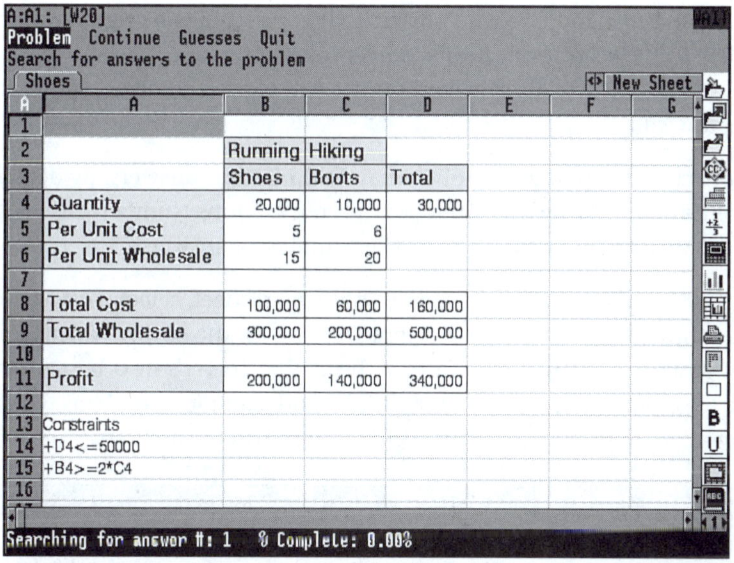

Fig. 16.5 Solving the shoe problem.

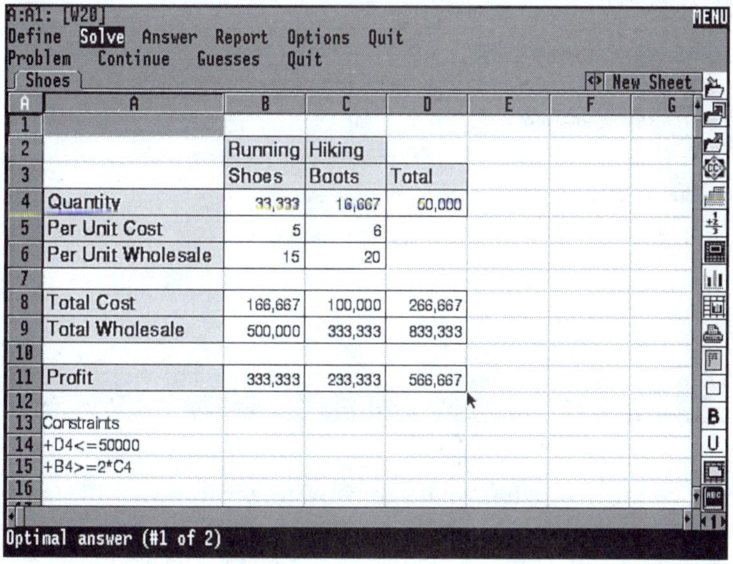

Fig. 16.6 Solver found two answers to the shoe problem.

Examining Solver's Answers

For the simple problem presented here, Solver "finds" only two answers: an optimal answer that produces the highest possible value for profit under the given constraints, and a second answer that consists of the original values that were in the worksheet. Really, Solver found only one new answer, but because the worksheet already contained a valid answer, Solver reports that answer as well.

For more complex problems, Solver may find multiple answers. By default, Solver finds up to 10 answers, but you can use **O**ptions **N**umber-Answers to instruct Solver to find a larger or smaller number of answers.

To display Solver's additional answers in the worksheet, select **A**nswer **N**ext to cycle through the answers. As figure 16.6 shows, the optimal answer increases profit to $566,667. Figure 16.7 shows that Solver's next best answer gives a total profit of only $340,000. With more complex problems, you may see several more solutions as you cycle through Solver's answers.

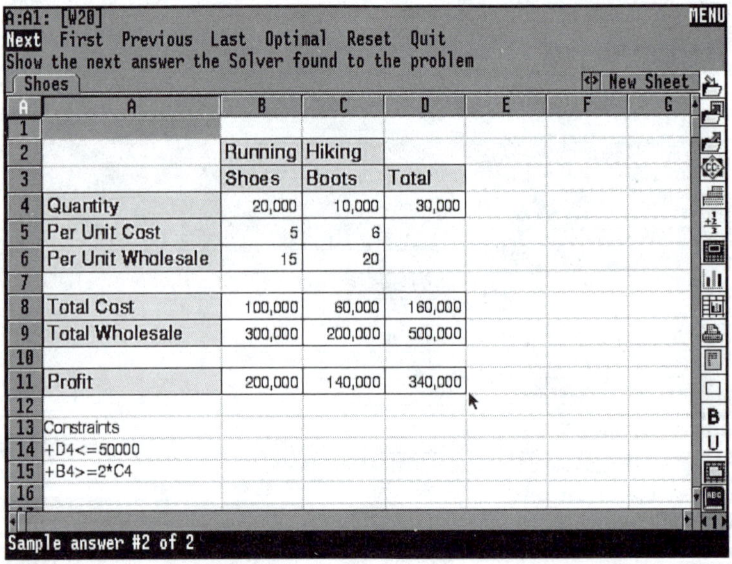

Fig. 16.7
Showing the next answer Solver found.

Tip
After Solver finds an answer that it reports is the best answer, select **S**olve **C**ontinue to have Solver find more answers. Depending on the problem, Solver may be able to find a better answer than the one it initially reported as the best answer.

Instead of cycling through the different answers, you can view the optimal answer or the best answer found by selecting **O**ptimal from the Solver Answer menu. Select **R**eset to view the original values in the worksheet at any time as you cycle through the answers.

In some cases, the default number of solutions doesn't produce an optimal answer, but Solver hasn't exhausted all possibilities. To have Solver seek additional answers, select **S**olve **C**ontinue. Solver attempts to find an additional set of answers (up to the **N**umber-Answers setting).

Supplying Guesses

Sometimes Solver cannot solve a problem as initially stated because the problem is too complex or because Solver lacks pertinent information to establish starting values for the adjustable cells. In such cases, the following message appears:

    Guesses required

Before Solver can proceed, you must supply a new starting value for one or more of the adjustable cells. Select **S**olve **G**uesses **G**uess to specify a new value for the currently highlighted adjustable cell. To specify a new value for a different adjustable cell, select **S**olve **G**uesses **N**ext and cycle through the adjustable cells until the correct cell is highlighted. Then select **S**olve **G**uesses **G**uess to specify a new value for the adjustable cell.

After you specify new starting values for the adjustable cells, select **S**olve **G**uesses **S**olve to tell Solver to attempt another solution. Solver discards the previous attempts if the new values lead to a successful solution.

> **Tip**
> If Solver cannot find answers for a problem, it is usually because of inconsistent constraints. Select **R**eport **I**nconsistent **T**able to create a report listing inconsistent constraints. See "Using Solver Reports" later in this chapter for more information.

Understanding Best and Optimal Answers

Solver differentiates between best and optimal answers. If you specify an optimal cell to maximize or minimize, and Solver uses the rules of algebra to find answers to a problem, Solver can find an optimal answer. If you specify an optimal cell and Solver doesn't solve the problem algebraically, it finds a best answer. An optimal answer is determined mathematically to be the highest or lowest possible answer, depending on whether you selected **X** Maximize or **N** Minimize. Solver finds a best answer when it cannot verify whether the answer found is the best of all possible answers. The best answer is always the highest or lowest answer that Solver found, but Solver cannot determine definitively that it is the highest or lowest possible answer.

> **Tip**
> To save all the answers to a problem in one place, select **R**eport **A**nswer to create an Answer Table report in a separate worksheet file. See "Using Solver Reports" for more information.

Displaying Attempted Answers

If Solver cannot find an answer that satisfies all constraints, the add-in displays attempted answers. An attempted answer is really a partial answer because at least one of the constraint formulas doesn't evaluate to True.

Selecting an Answer

By selecting **Q**uit on the Solver menu, you can exit Solver. Before selecting **Q**uit, decide which of the answers you want to keep in the worksheet. Be sure to save the worksheet after leaving Solver if you want to retain the solution. You can keep alternate solutions in separate worksheets of the same file or in separate files if you prefer.

◄ "Saving Files," p. 416

Chapter 16—Finding Solutions with Solver

Tip
Another way to save all the answers Solver finds is to save the worksheet file immediately after solving. The next time you open the file, select **/T**ools **A**nalyze **S**olver and Solver finds the same answers.

1-2-3 doesn't remove the alternate answers immediately when you leave Solver. Alternate answers are removed when 1-2-3 recalculates the worksheet; you can restart Solver and recover all previous solutions if the worksheet hasn't been recalculated. Changing the worksheet eliminates previous solutions.

Troubleshooting

Solver finds fewer answers than I specified.

If Solver finds fewer answers than you specified, there are no more possible answers.

Solver finds more answers than I specified.

If Solver finds more answers than you specified, it found more than one answer simultaneously.

Solver uses negative values for adjustable cells that shouldn't be negative.

If Solver finds answers that contain negative values for adjustable cells that should not be negative, add new constraints specifying that the adjustable cells must be at least 0.

Solver reports a roundoff error.

If Solver reports roundoff errors and one or more constraint appears not to be satisfied, treat the answer as if the constraint were satisfied. Roundoff errors are caused by slight differences between calculations that Solver performs and the calculations in the worksheet, and they usually occur only in problems with very small or very large numbers.

Solver runs out of memory, or takes too long to solve a problem.

If Solver runs out of memory while solving a problem or takes an unusually long time to solve a problem, try one or more of the following:

Using **/T**ools **A**nalyze **A**uditor, find the formulas that are precedents for the optimal cell. For each formula cell that is a precedent for the optimal cell, find out whether it depends on any adjustable cells. If it doesn't, change it to a constant by using **/R**ange **V**alue, or by pressing F2 (Edit), F9 (Calc), and then Enter. Chapter 14, "Analyzing Formulas with Auditor," describes how to use Auditor to find precedents and dependents.

If possible, eliminate unnecessary adjustable cells, constraint cells, and cells that contain functions other than @SUM and @AVG.

Examples of Solver Problems

The following sections contain three examples that show how to set up and solve some different kinds of business problems. These examples are

- Optimizing Production for Maximum Profit
- Allocating an Investment Portfolio
- Allocating an Advertising Budget

Optimizing Production for Maximum Profit

Determining the best mix of products to optimize a company's profits can be a difficult problem. The example used earlier in this chapter demonstrated a simple problem in optimizing production, but this kind of problem can easily become much more complex. Many factors can be involved, including production capacity, relative costs of production, warehousing costs, and so on. The following example demonstrates how to set up and solve a more complex production optimization problem.

Figure 16.8 shows a sample worksheet that details how a small shirt factory calculates its production levels and profits.

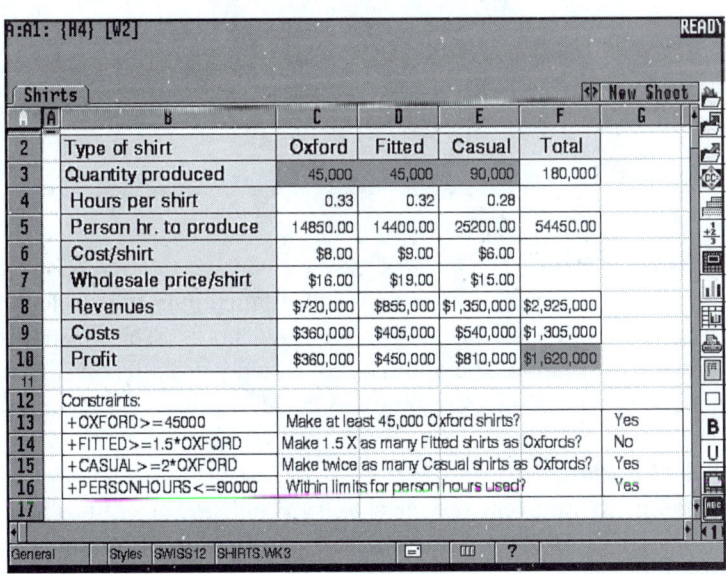

Fig. 16.8
The worksheet for the shirt production problem.

The company makes three kinds of shirts—oxfords, fitted shirts, and casual shirts—and wants to determine how many of each kind of shirt to produce each year. Each kind of shirt costs a different amount to make, sells for a different price, and requires a different number of labor hours to produce. Fitted shirts cost the most but are the most profitable; however, the company sells the most casual shirts. Oxford shirts are the least profitable, but the company must make a certain number of oxfords to fulfill contractual obligations.

Constraints of the Problem

The constraints for this problem are as follows: First, the company must make 45,000 oxford shirts to meet contractual obligations with certain customers. The company also knows that if it meets those obligations, those customers will also buy 50 percent more fitted shirts than oxford shirts, and twice as many casual shirts as oxfords. Finally, there is a limit of 90,000 available labor hours in the shirt factory. These constraints are expressed by formulas in cells A:B13..A:B16.

> **Note**
>
> To make the constraint formulas more readable, use the **/R**ange **N**ame **C**reate command to name the adjustable cells, the optimal cell, and any other cells that are referred to in the constraint formulas. You can also make your worksheet easier to understand if you write out the constraints as sentences next to the constraint cells. Finally, use the @IF function to create formulas that show whether each constraint is satisfied. For example, the formula in cell A:G13 of figure 16.8 is @IF(B13," Yes"," No").

Defining the Problem

In figure 16.8, the adjustable cells are the cells that contain the production quantities of the different kinds of shirts, cells A:C3..A:E3. The constraint cells are cells A:B13..A:B16. The optimal cell, which you want Solver to maximize, is the cell that contains the Total Profit, cell A:F10.

Solving the Problem

After you define the problem and select **S**olve **P**roblem, Solver finds four answers. Answer 1, the optimal answer, is shown in figure 16.9, and results in a total profit of $2,756,250 by making 45,000 oxford shirts, 67,500 fitted shirts, and 191,250 casual shirts.

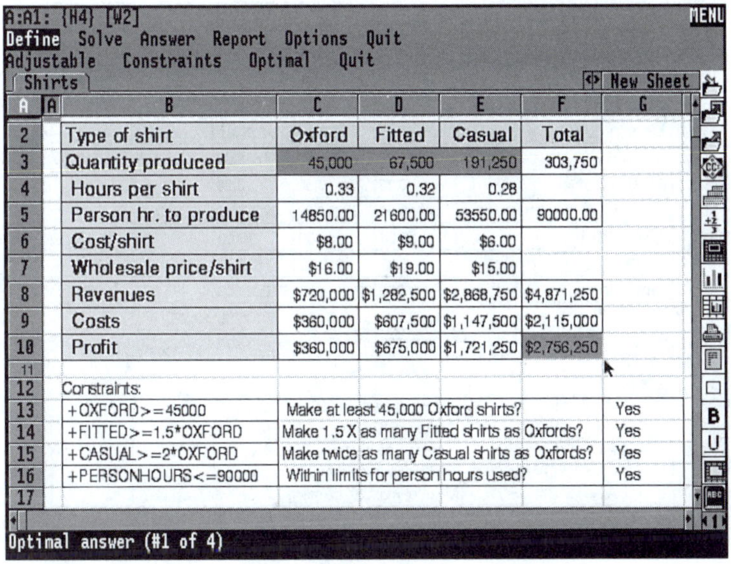

Fig. 16.9
The optimal answer to the shirt production problem.

	Oxford	Fitted	Casual	Total
Type of shirt				
Quantity produced	45,000	67,500	191,250	303,750
Hours per shirt	0.33	0.32	0.28	
Person hr. to produce	14850.00	21600.00	53550.00	90000.00
Cost/shirt	$8.00	$9.00	$6.00	
Wholesale price/shirt	$16.00	$19.00	$15.00	
Revenues	$720,000	$1,282,500	$2,868,750	$4,871,250
Costs	$360,000	$607,500	$1,147,500	$2,115,000
Profit	$360,000	$675,000	$1,721,250	$2,756,250

Constraints:
+OXFORD>=45000	Make at least 45,000 Oxford shirts?	Yes
+FITTED>=1.5*OXFORD	Make 1.5 X as many Fitted shirts as Oxfords?	Yes
+CASUAL>=2*OXFORD	Make twice as many Casual shirts as Oxfords?	Yes
+PERSONHOURS<=90000	Within limits for person hours used?	Yes

Optimal answer (#1 of 4)

Modifying the Problem—Adding a Constraint

Remember that Solver's answers are only as good as the information you provide. The company may not be able to sell more than four times as many casual shirts as oxford shirts (the optimal answer in fig. 16.9). Use care in determining the problem definition. In this example, you might add a constraint stating that the number of casual shirts must be at most three times as many as the number of oxford shirts. The resulting optimal solution from the added constraint is shown in figure 16.10.

Notice that in the optimal solution, the constraint in cell A:B17 appears not to be satisfied (cell A:G17 reads No) and the following message appears:

    Optimal answer (#1 of 6) Minor roundoff

But the number of casual shirts, 135,000, is no more than three times the number of oxfords, 45,000, so the constraint in cell A:B17 should be satisfied.

Messages such as this one sometimes occur when a constraint cell appears false after rounding off to five decimal places (Roundoff) or 16 decimal places (Minor roundoff). You can ignore errors such as this, and treat the answer as you would any other; for all practical purposes, the answer meets all the constraints.

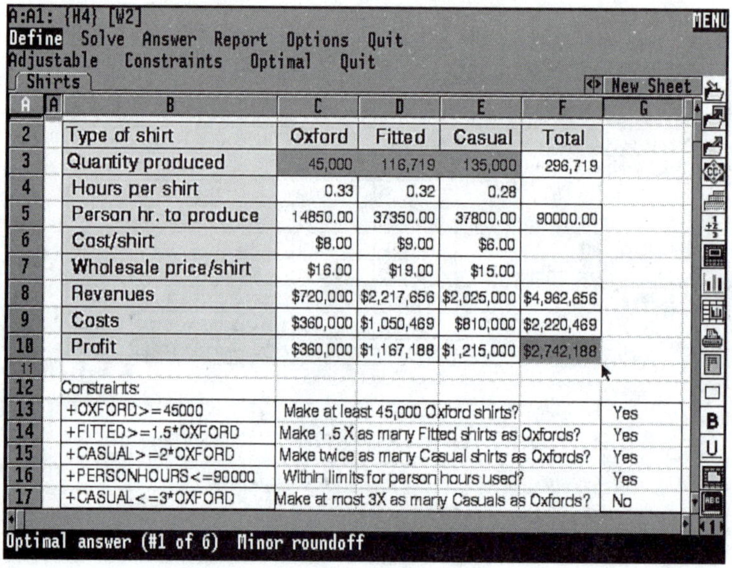

Fig. 16.10
The new optimal answer to the modified problem.

```
A:A1: {H4} [W2]                                                    MENU
Define Solve Answer Report Options Quit
Adjustable  Constraints  Optimal  Quit
  Shirts                                                    New Sheet
  A   B                    C          D          E          F        G
  2   Type of shirt        Oxford     Fitted     Casual     Total
  3   Quantity produced    45,000     116,719    135,000    296,719
  4   Hours per shirt      0.33       0.32       0.28
  5   Person hr. to produce 14850.00  37350.00   37800.00   90000.00
  6   Cost/shirt           $8.00      $9.00      $6.00
  7   Wholesale price/shirt $16.00    $19.00     $15.00
  8   Revenues             $720,000   $2,217,656 $2,025,000 $4,962,656
  9   Costs                $360,000   $1,050,469 $810,000   $2,220,469
 10   Profit               $360,000   $1,167,188 $1,215,000 $2,742,188
 11
 12   Constraints:
 13   +OXFORD>=45000        Make at least 45,000 Oxford shirts?       Yes
 14   +FITTED>=1.5*OXFORD   Make 1.5 X as many Fitted shirts as Oxfords? Yes
 15   +CASUAL>=2*OXFORD     Make twice as many Casual shirts as Oxfords? Yes
 16   +PERSONHOURS<=90000   Within limits for person hours used?       Yes
 17   +CASUAL<=3*OXFORD     Make at most 3X as many Casuals as Oxfords? No
Optimal answer (#1 of 6)  Minor roundoff
```

Allocating an Investment Portfolio

Another type of problem with which Solver can be very helpful is determining how to choose between different investments to meet different goals. Investment goals can be very simple—"maximize profit"—or much more complex—"maximize profit while maintaining an acceptable level of risk and meeting recommended diversification guidelines." The following example demonstrates one approach to using Solver to help make investment decisions.

Figure 16.11 shows a sample worksheet that an investor might use to decide how to allocate a $20,000 investment among four different mutual funds. Each fund has a different investment goal, a different five-year return percentage, and a different risk rating.

Constraints of the Problem

The investor wants to allocate her investment among the funds so as to meet certain goals for diversification, income, and risk level. These goals are expressed in the constraints in cells A:A9..A:A16 of figure 16.11; they include minimum investment percentages for all four funds, maximum percentages for two of the funds, a maximum acceptable level of risk, and a minimum percentage return.

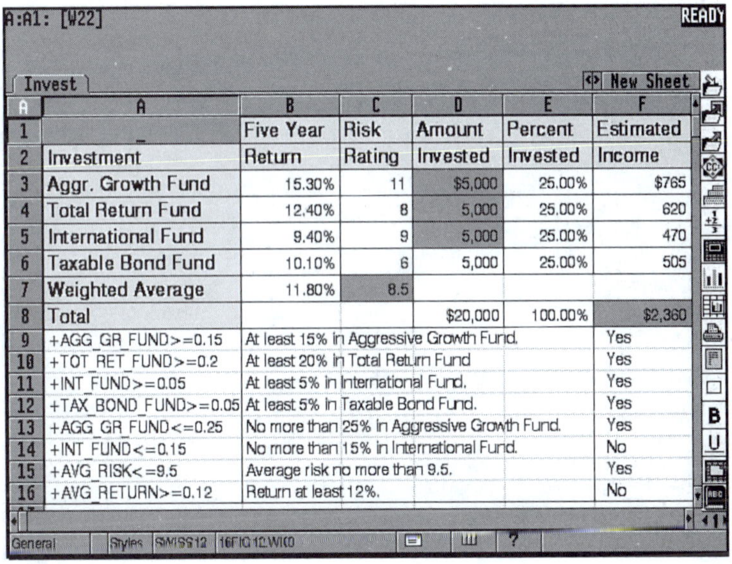

Fig. 16.11
The worksheet for the investment portfolio problem.

	A	B	C	D	E	F
1		Five Year Return	Risk Rating	Amount Invested	Percent Invested	Estimated Income
2	Investment					
3	Aggr. Growth Fund	15.30%	11	$5,000	25.00%	$765
4	Total Return Fund	12.40%	8	5,000	25.00%	620
5	International Fund	9.40%	9	5,000	25.00%	470
6	Taxable Bond Fund	10.10%	6	5,000	25.00%	505
7	Weighted Average	11.80%	8.5			
8	Total			$20,000	100.00%	$2,360
9	+AGG_GR_FUND>=0.15	At least 15% in Aggressive Growth Fund.			Yes	
10	+TOT_RET_FUND>=0.2	At least 20% in Total Return Fund			Yes	
11	+INT_FUND>=0.05	At least 5% in International Fund.			Yes	
12	+TAX_BOND_FUND>=0.05	At least 5% in Taxable Bond Fund.			Yes	
13	+AGG_GR_FUND<=0.25	No more than 25% in Aggressive Growth Fund.			Yes	
14	+INT_FUND<=0.15	No more than 15% in International Fund.			No	
15	+AVG_RISK<=9.5	Average risk no more than 9.5.			Yes	
16	+AVG_RETURN>=0.12	Return at least 12%.			No	

Defining the Problem

In figure 16.11, the adjustable cells are the cells that contain the amounts invested in the Aggressive Growth, Total Return, and International funds, cells A:D3..A:D5. Any amounts left over are invested in the Taxable Bond fund. The constraint cells are cells A:A9..A:A16. The optimal cell, which you want Solver to maximize, is the cell that contains Total Estimated Income, cell A:F8.

Solving the Problem

After you define the problem and select **S**olve **P**roblem, Solver finds eight answers. Answer 1, the optimal answer, is shown in figure 16.12 and results in a total estimated income of $2,572 by investing $5,000 in the Aggressive Growth fund, $13,000 in the Total Return Fund, and $1,000 in each of the other two funds.

Modifying the Problem—Changing the Optimal Cell

When you specify an optimal cell, Solver tries to find an answer that maximizes or minimizes the value of that cell, and reports its answers in rank order based on the value in the optimal cell. Changing the optimal cell may change the answers that Solver finds, or it may simply change the order in which Solver ranks the answers it finds.

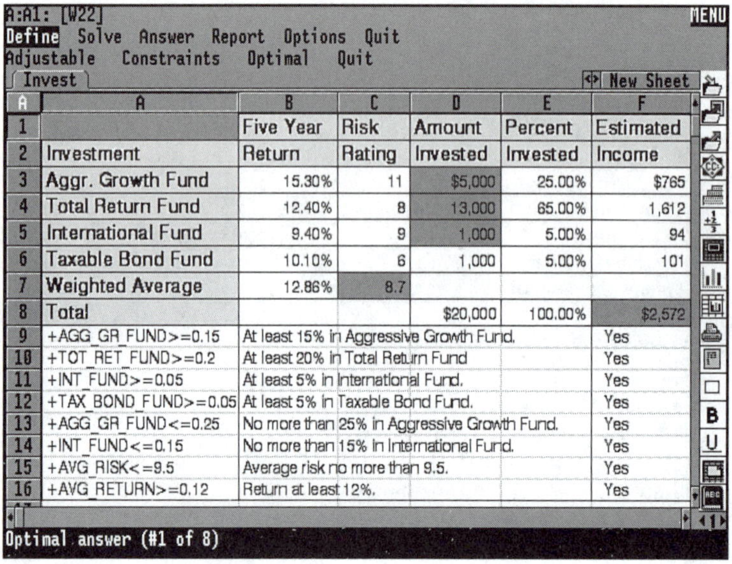

Fig. 16.12
The optimal answer for the investment portfolio problem, maximizing income.

```
A:A1: [W22]                                                    MENU
Define  Solve  Answer  Report  Options  Quit
Adjustable     Constraints    Optimal   Quit
  Invest                                          New Sheet
   A          A              B       C       D        E         F
   1                      Five Year  Risk  Amount  Percent  Estimated
   2     Investment       Return     Rating Invested Invested Income
   3     Aggr. Growth Fund  15.30%    11    $5,000   25.00%    $765
   4     Total Return Fund  12.40%     8   13,000    65.00%   1,612
   5     International Fund  9.40%     9    1,000     5.00%      94
   6     Taxable Bond Fund  10.10%     6    1,000     5.00%     101
   7     Weighted Average   12.86%    8.7
   8     Total                              $20,000  100.00%  $2,572
   9    +AGG_GR_FUND>=0.15   At least 15% in Aggressive Growth Fund.   Yes
  10    +TOT_RET_FUND>=0.2   At least 20% in Total Return Fund         Yes
  11    +INT_FUND>=0.05      At least 5% in International Fund.        Yes
  12    +TAX_BOND_FUND>=0.05 At least 5% in Taxable Bond Fund.         Yes
  13    +AGG_GR_FUND<=0.25   No more than 25% in Aggressive Growth Fund. Yes
  14    +INT_FUND<=0.15      No more than 15% in International Fund.   Yes
  15    +AVG_RISK<=9.5       Average risk no more than 9.5.            Yes
  16    +AVG_RETURN>=0.12    Return at least 12%.                      Yes

Optimal answer (#1 of 8)
```

For example, suppose another investor wanted to invest the same amount of money, in the same four funds, with the same guidelines for diversification, risk, and income but with an overall goal of minimizing risk rather than maximizing income. Changing the optimal cell to the cell that contains the weighted average risk rating, cell A:C7, and selecting **N** Minimize instead of **X** Maximize, restates the problem to meet this goal. Figure 16.13 shows the resulting optimal answer. In this case, Solver found the same eight answers but presented them in a different order.

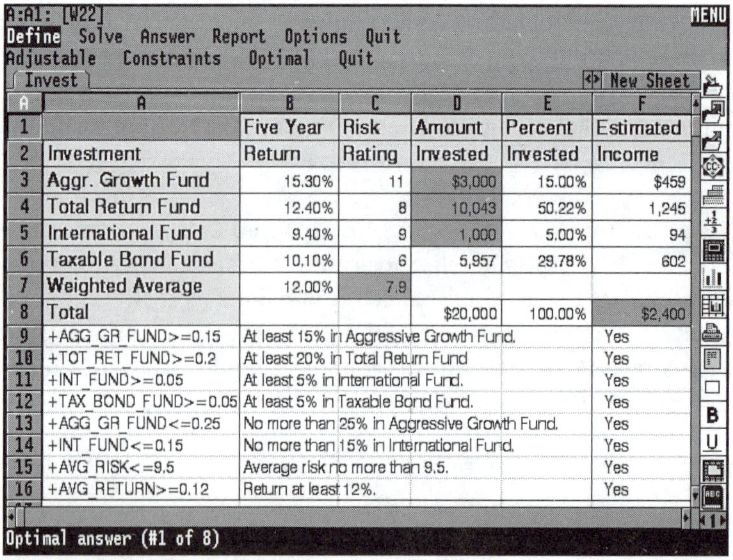

Fig. 16.13
The optimal answer for the investment portfolio problem, minimizing risk.

```
A:A1: [W22]                                                    MENU
Define  Solve  Answer  Report  Options  Quit
Adjustable     Constraints    Optimal   Quit
  Invest                                          New Sheet
   A          A              B       C       D        E         F
   1                      Five Year  Risk  Amount  Percent  Estimated
   2     Investment       Return     Rating Invested Invested Income
   3     Aggr. Growth Fund  15.30%    11    $3,000   15.00%    $459
   4     Total Return Fund  12.40%     8   10,043    50.22%   1,245
   5     International Fund  9.40%     9    1,000     5.00%      94
   6     Taxable Bond Fund  10.10%     6    5,957    29.78%     602
   7     Weighted Average   12.00%    7.9
   8     Total                              $20,000  100.00%  $2,400
   9    +AGG_GR_FUND>=0.15   At least 15% in Aggressive Growth Fund.   Yes
  10    +TOT_RET_FUND>=0.2   At least 20% in Total Return Fund         Yes
  11    +INT_FUND>=0.05      At least 5% in International Fund.        Yes
  12    +TAX_BOND_FUND>=0.05 At least 5% in Taxable Bond Fund.         Yes
  13    +AGG_GR_FUND<=0.25   No more than 25% in Aggressive Growth Fund. Yes
  14    +INT_FUND<=0.15      No more than 15% in International Fund.   Yes
  15    +AVG_RISK<=9.5       Average risk no more than 9.5.            Yes
  16    +AVG_RETURN>=0.12    Return at least 12%.                      Yes

Optimal answer (#1 of 8)
```

Allocating an Advertising Budget

A third example of a problem that Solver can help you solve is deciding how to spend an advertising budget. This example, like the others, illustrates the principle that the quality of Solver's answers depends on the quality of its information. The better your worksheet models the real world, the more valid Solver's answers are.

Figure 16.14 shows a sample worksheet that you could use to decide how to allocate a $1,000,000 advertising budget to television, radio, and newspaper ads. The key information in this model is the cost and effectiveness of each ad. Cost is easy to measure, but effectiveness is more difficult. The model attempts to measure effectiveness by calculating the number of people that see each type of ad (estimated exposure) and the sales that result from each exposure (estimated sales/exposure). Initially, the model uses a simple formula to measure effectiveness; it multiplies the number of ads by a different constant for each type of ad to determine the number of exposures and then multiplies the number of exposures by a second constant to determine the resulting sales.

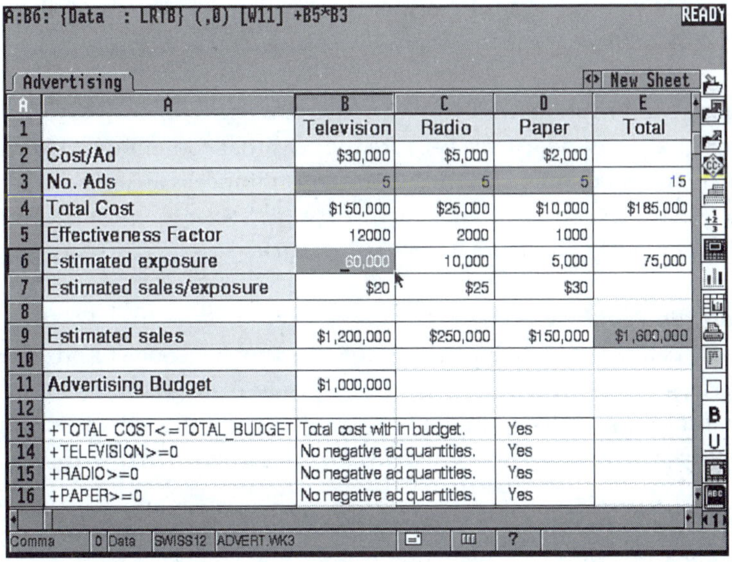

Fig. 16.14 The worksheet for the advertising budget problem.

Constraints of the Problem

The limits for this problem are very simple: the total cost must be within budget, and the number of each type of ad must be at least 0. The first limit is expressed by the formula in cell A:A13. The second limit is expressed by the three formulas in cells A:A14..A:A16. This second limit deserves more explanation because it may seem unnecessary at first. After all, how could you possibly have a negative number of ads?

Remember that Solver is simply performing some mathematical operations on the formulas in the worksheet; Solver doesn't really "understand" the problem in any meaningful way. As far as Solver is concerned, a negative number of ads might be perfectly reasonable—especially if it results in a higher value for the optimal cell. However, if you don't provide some lower limit to the number of each type of ad in this problem, Solver displays the following message when you select **S**olve **P**roblem:

```
Cannot find an optimal answer -- the optimal cell is unbounded
```

The reason this message appears is that without the constraints in cells A:A14..A:A16, Solver can force the value of the optimal cell to be arbitrarily high, just by substituting larger and larger quantities for the most effective type of ad, and offsetting them with negative quantities for the other types of ads so as to stay within the budget. There really is no limit to the value of the optimal cell. So, in order to force Solver to consider only realistic possibilities in which the number of ads is positive, you need to add the constraints in cells A:A14..A:A16.

Defining the Problem
In figure 16.14, the adjustable cells are the cells that contain the quantities for each type of ad, cells A:B3..A:D3. The constraint cells are cells A:A13..A:A16. The optimal cell, which you want Solver to maximize, is the cell that contains Total Estimated Sales, cell A:E9.

Solving the Problem
After you define the problem and select **S**olve **P**roblem, Solver finds five answers. Answer 1, the optimal answer, is shown in figure 16.15, and results in total estimated sales of $15 million by spending the entire advertising budget on newspaper ads. If that answer seems too simple, it is—and so is the model.

Modifying the Problem—Changing the Model's Assumptions
Because the advertising problem uses simple linear formulas to model the effectiveness of the different types of ads, it oversimplifies real-world relationships that are much more complex.

Examples of Solver Problems 575

```
A:B6: {Data : LRTB} (,0) [W11] +B5*B3                          MENU
Define Solve Answer Report Options Quit
Adjustable Constraints Optimal Quit
  Advertising                                    <> New Sheet
     A              |    B    |   C   |    D     |    E
  1                 |Television|Radio |  Paper   |  Total
  2  Cost/Ad        | $30,000 |$5,000 |  $2,000  |
  3  No. Ads        |    0    |   0   |   500    |   500
  4  Total Cost     |   $0    |  $0   |$1,000,000|$1,000,000
  5  Effectiveness Factor| 12000 | 2000 |  1000  |
  6  Estimated exposure  |   0   |   0  | 500,000 | 500,000
  7  Estimated sales/exposure| $20 | $25 |   $30  |
  8
  9  Estimated sales |   $0    |  $0   |$15,000,000|$15,000,000
 10
 11 Advertising Budget|$1,000,000|
 12
 13 +TOTAL_COST<=TOTAL_BUDGET|Total cost within budget.|Yes
 14 +TELEVISION>=0   |No negative ad quantities.|Yes
 15 +RADIO>=0        |No negative ad quantities.|Yes
 16 +PAPER>=0        |No negative ad quantities.|Yes
Optimal answer (#1 of 5)
```

Fig. 16.15
The optimal answer to the advertising budget problem.

One way to make the model more realistic is to introduce the concept of *diminishing returns*—the idea that the benefit from each additional ad decreases as the total number of ads increases. An easy way to model diminishing returns is by using the @LN function, which calculates the natural logarithm of its argument. Natural logarithms are often used to model real-world behaviors that follow the law of diminishing returns.

The revised model is shown in figure 16.16. The formula for calculating estimated exposure has been revised to use the natural logarithm of the number of ads. First, the number of ads is adjusted by adding 1. This correction is necessary when using natural logarithms so that zero ads result in zero exposures. The natural logarithm of the adjusted number of ads is then multiplied by a constant to calculate the number of exposures. Note that the constants in this version of the model are much larger than the constants in the simple model; this is to compensate for the effect of using the natural logarithm. If you use this approach, be careful to choose constants that give reasonable results.

◀ "Using the Mathematical Functions," p. 161

Figure 16.17 shows the best answer that Solver finds using this more complex model. Total sales in this answer are significantly lower than in the first model. More importantly, this model results in an answer that seems to make more sense: that the best strategy involves a combination of all three types of ads.

Fig. 16.16 The advertising budget problem, modified to reflect diminishing returns.

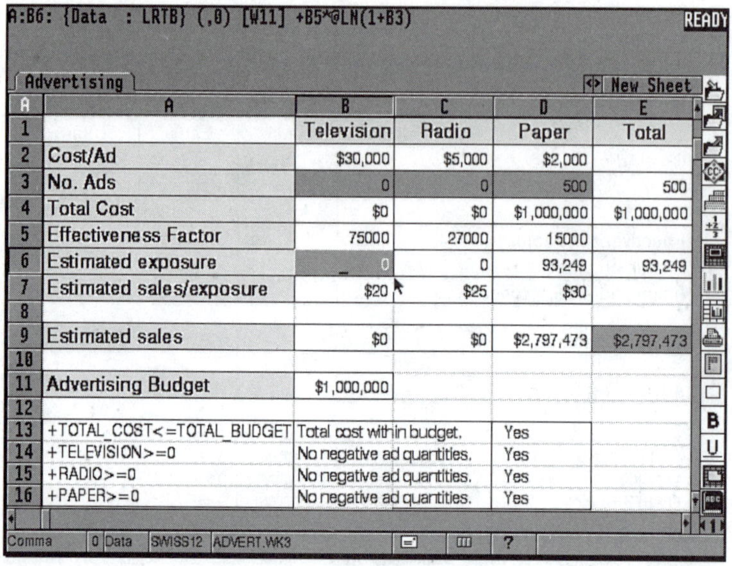

A:B6: {Data : LRTB} (,0) [W11] +B5*@LN(1+B3) READY

Advertising — New Sheet

A	A	B	C	D	E
1		Television	Radio	Paper	Total
2	Cost/Ad	$30,000	$5,000	$2,000	
3	No. Ads	0	0	500	500
4	Total Cost	$0	$0	$1,000,000	$1,000,000
5	Effectiveness Factor	75000	27000	15000	
6	Estimated exposure	0	0	93,249	93,249
7	Estimated sales/exposure	$20	$25	$30	
8					
9	Estimated sales	$0	$0	$2,797,473	$2,797,473
10					
11	Advertising Budget	$1,000,000			
12					
13	+TOTAL_COST<=TOTAL_BUDGET	Total cost within budget.		Yes	
14	+TELEVISION>=0	No negative ad quantities.		Yes	
15	+RADIO>=0	No negative ad quantities.		Yes	
16	+PAPER>=0	No negative ad quantities.		Yes	

Comma 0 Data SWISS12 ADVERT.WK3 ?

Fig. 16.17 The best answer found for the modified advertising budget problem.

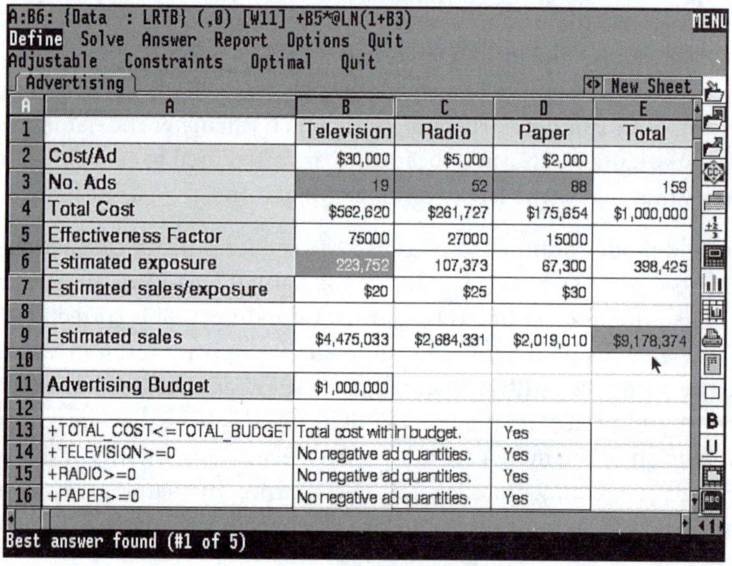

A:B6: {Data : LRTB} (,0) [W11] +B5*@LN(1+B3) MENU
Define Solve Answer Report Options Quit
Adjustable Constraints Optimal Quit

Advertising — New Sheet

A	A	B	C	D	E
1		Television	Radio	Paper	Total
2	Cost/Ad	$30,000	$5,000	$2,000	
3	No. Ads	19	52	88	159
4	Total Cost	$562,620	$261,727	$175,654	$1,000,000
5	Effectiveness Factor	75000	27000	15000	
6	Estimated exposure	223,752	107,373	67,300	398,425
7	Estimated sales/exposure	$20	$25	$30	
8					
9	Estimated sales	$4,475,033	$2,684,331	$2,019,010	$9,178,374
10					
11	Advertising Budget	$1,000,000			
12					
13	+TOTAL_COST<=TOTAL_BUDGET	Total cost within budget.		Yes	
14	+TELEVISION>=0	No negative ad quantities.		Yes	
15	+RADIO>=0	No negative ad quantities.		Yes	
16	+PAPER>=0	No negative ad quantities.		Yes	

Best answer found (#1 of 5)

Notice that Solver describes this answer as the best answer found, not as the optimal answer. This is because Solver cannot determine whether this answer is truly the best possible answer for the model. To have Solver find more answers, choose **S**olve **C**ontinue. In this case, Solver is unable to find more answers, so the best answer found is probably the best answer possible, or the optimal answer.

Using Solver Reports

1-2-3 can create the following types of reports on the answers found by Solver:

- Answer
- How Solved
- What-If
- Differences
- Inconsistent Constraints
- Unused Constraints
- Cells Used

You can view most of these reports in two report formats. *Table format* shows the report in a table in a separate worksheet. *Cell format* shows information about one cell at a time in a display window. Figure 16.18 shows the Solver **R**eport menu. The following sections describe each of these report types.

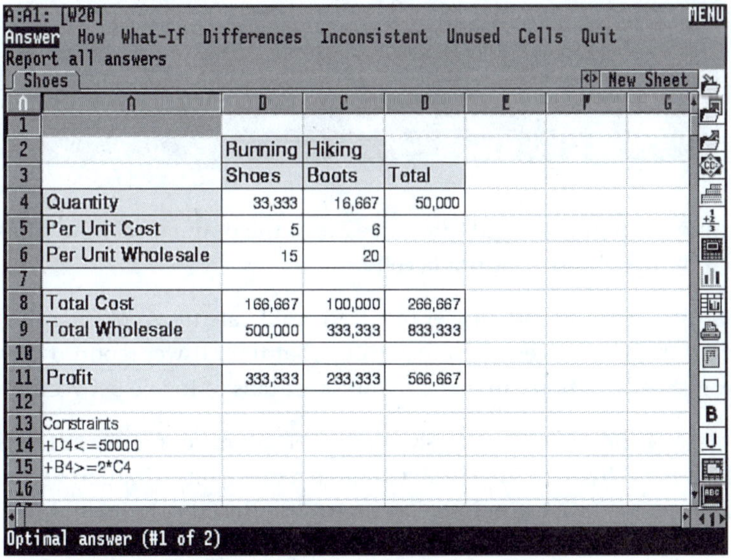

Fig. 16.18
The /**T**ools **A**nalyze **S**olve **R**eport menu.

578 Chapter 16—Finding Solutions with Solver

The Answer Report

◄ "Managing Active Files in Memory," p. 408

Selecting the **R**eport **A**nswer command causes Solver to create a new worksheet file named ANSWER??.WK3, containing an overview of all answers. The ?? in the file name is replaced with a number supplied by Solver; for example, the first Answer report is named ANSWER01.WK3. The report number increases by 1 for each subsequent Answer report. Solver stores the file in the default drive and directory. Figures 16.19 shows all but the last few rows of the Answer report for the shoe production example.

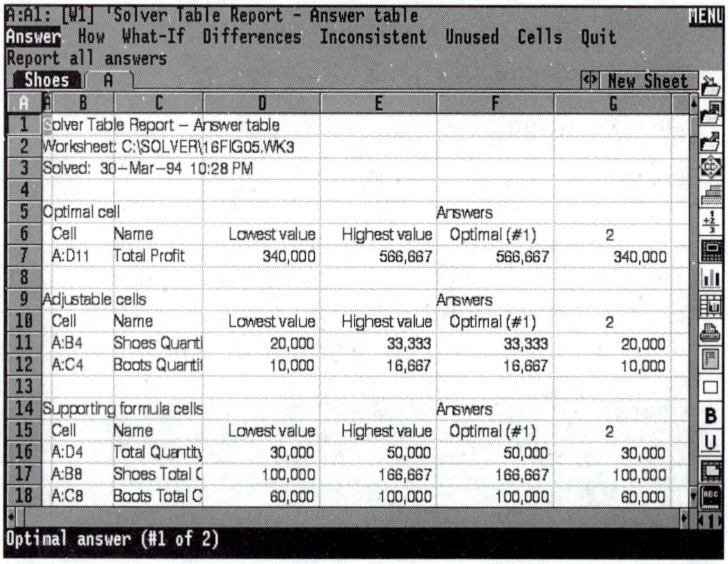

Fig. 16.19
The Answer Table report for the shoe production problem.

The Answer report is divided into three areas: the optimal cell, the adjustable cells, and the supporting formula cells.

Because Solver places the Answer report in a separate file (replacing the current worksheet on-screen), you may think that the Answer report overwrote the worksheet, but you can use the worksheet tabs to toggle between the files.

Column B of the Answer report shows the cell addresses for all cells in the problem. If a cell used in the problem has a range name, Column C contains the range name. If not, Column C contains the closest column and row labels (displayed in the same case as in the worksheet). This naming convention can lead to duplicate names for different cells if the closest row and column labels are the same for both cells.

Columns D and E of the Answer report show the lowest and highest values for all cells across the set of answers found. 1-2-3 begins displaying the answers in column F.

The optimal cell row in the Answer report (row 7 in fig. 16.19) shows that the expected profit on shoe production varies from a high of $566,667 for the optimal answer to a low of $340,000 for the second answer. Rows 11 and 12 contain information about the adjustable cells, and rows 16 through 22 contain information about the supporting formula cells for the problem.

The How Solved Report

1-2-3 displays the How Solved report only in Table format. Figures 16.20 and 16.21 show the How Solved report for this example.

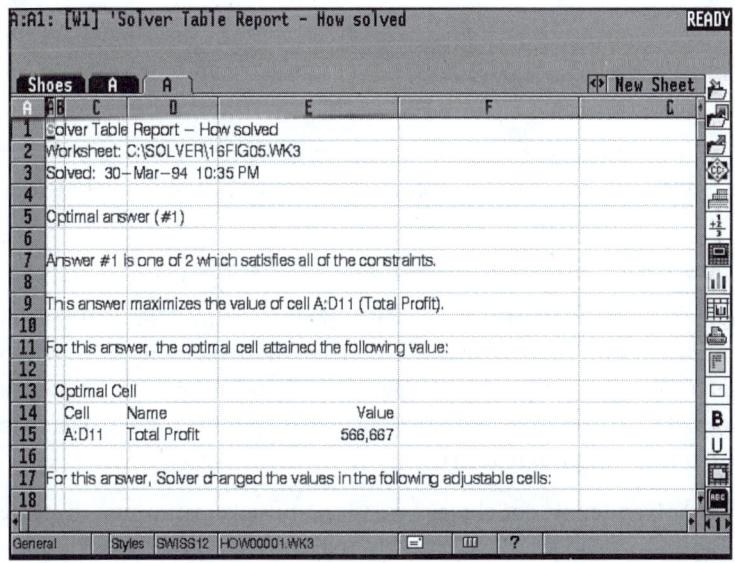

Fig. 16.20
The first part of the How Solved report for the shoe production problem.

Selecting the **R**eport **H**ow command causes Solver to create a new worksheet file named HOW?????.WK3, containing a breakdown of how the problem was solved. The ????? in the file name is replaced with a number supplied by Solver; for example, the first Answer report is named HOW00001.WK3. The report number increases by 1 for each subsequent How Solved report. Solver stores the file in the default drive and directory.

Fig. 16.21
The second part of the How Solved report for the shoe production problem.

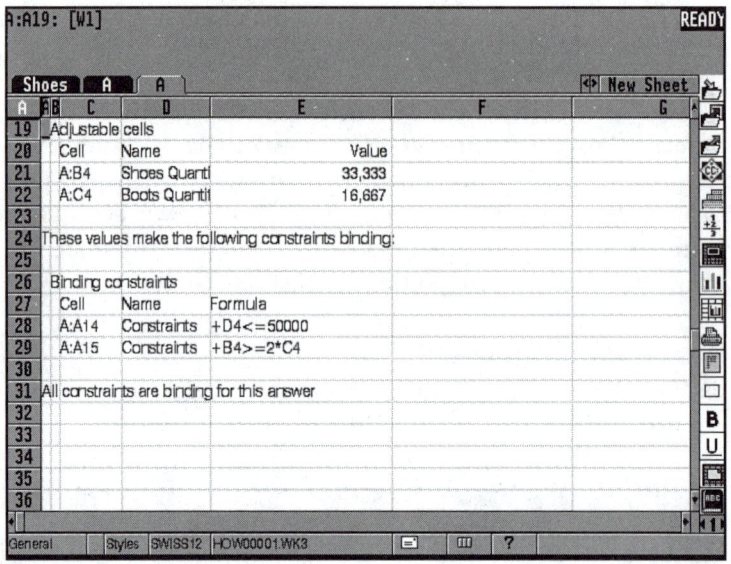

This report is for the first answer, the maximized profit on shoe production. Solver reports this result to the user by displaying the following message in row 9:

```
This answer maximizes the value of cell A:D11 (Total Profit)
```

Solver displays the highest value attained by the optimal cell and the corresponding values for the adjustable cells. The following group of rows reports on the *binding constraints*, which actively bind a solution. In this problem, there were two constraints, both of which were binding, or actively restricted the search for the optimal answer.

The How Solved report concludes by listing unused constraints, showing how these constraints can be transformed to make them binding for the current solution. There were no binding constraints for this answer.

The What-If Report

The What-If report notes the range of values an adjustable cell can assume in the current answer and for any other answer (with all constraints in the current answer still evaluating to True). This report applies to the answer displayed in the worksheet before invoking the **S**olver **R**eport command.

The what-if range for the current answer assumes that no other adjustable cells change. The range for limits is occasionally approximate so that at least one constraint doesn't evaluate to True; you can fix this problem by modifying the limit slightly in the direction that makes the constraint True.

You can display the What-If report in both **C**ell and **T**able formats. When you select the **R**eport **W**hat-If **T**able command from the **S**olver menu, Solver creates a new worksheet file containing a table that shows the highest and lowest values for all adjustable cells. As figure 16.22 shows, the What-If table displays all adjustable cells in one report.

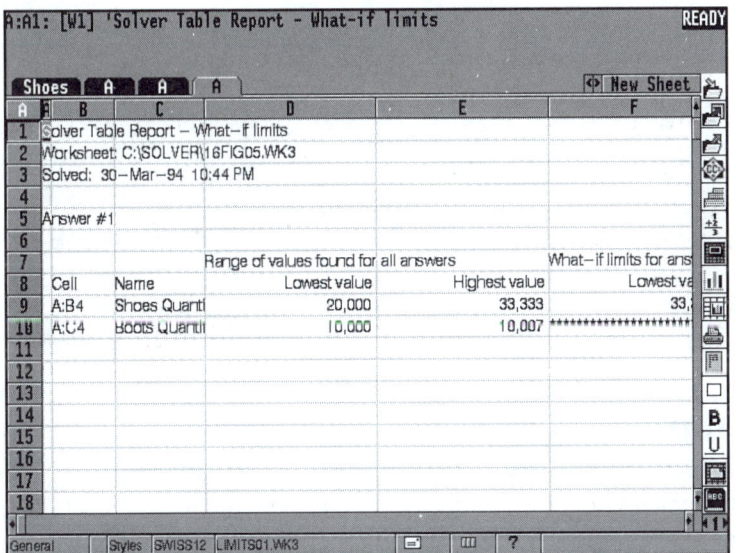

Fig. 16.22
The What-If Limits report for the shoe production problem.

Selecting the **R**eport **W**hat-If command causes Solver to create a new worksheet file named LIMITS??.WK3, containing a what-if limits analysis. Solver replaces the ?? in the file name with a number supplied by Solver; for example, the first What-If report is named LIMITS01.WK3. The report number increases by 1 for each subsequent How report. Solver stores the file in the default drive and directory.

If you want to see a single adjustable cell (perhaps because the problem contains a large number of adjustable cells), the What-If cell report shown in figure 16.23 may be a better choice for you. (For this answer, changing the quantity of running shoes in either direction without changing the quantity of hiking boots makes at least one constraint false; therefore, the report shows a what-if limit for Answer #1 of 33,333 to 33,333.) The **R**eport **W**hat-If **C**ell command doesn't create a new worksheet file. After viewing the What-If cell report box, select **N**ext to view the next adjustable cell or **Q**uit to return to the Solver menu.

Fig. 16.23

The What-If Limits report in Cell format.

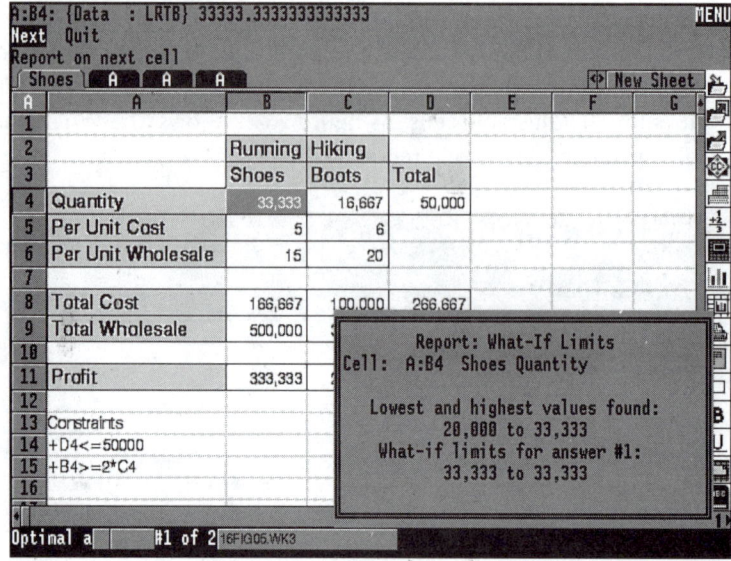

The Differences Report

The Differences report shows how answers compare with each other. The report compares only two solutions at a time, but you can contrast different pairs of answers by repeatedly invoking the report, specifying a new pair each time.

To see the Differences report, select **R**eport **D**ifferences from the Solver menu. Select **C**ell or **T**able, depending on whether you want to view the differences between the values in one cell or in a complete report format. Solver asks you to specify which two answers you want to compare and requests the minimum size of differences to report. The default (0) displays all differences. After reviewing an initial Differences report, you may want to screen the differences by setting the minimum difference to a value greater than 0.

If you specify **T**able format, Solver generates the DIFFS???.WK3 worksheet file, replacing ??? with 001 for the first Differences report. The report number is increased by 1 each time a Differences report is generated with the same default drive and directory. Figure 16.24 shows the Differences report in **T**able format.

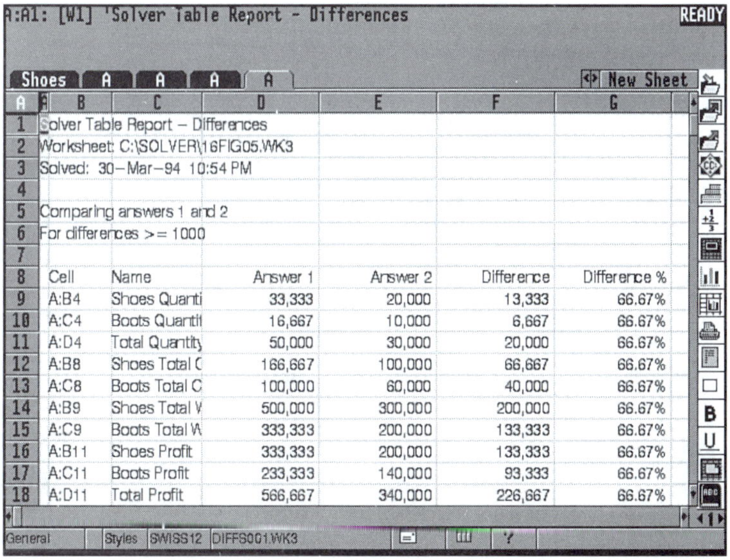
A:A1: [W1] 'Solver Table Report - Differences
READY
Shoes A A A A
New Sheet
Solver Table Report – Differences
Worksheet: C:\SOLVER\16FIG05.WK3
Solved: 30–Mar–94 10:54 PM
Comparing answers 1 and 2
For differences >= 1000
Cell Name Answer 1 Answer 2 Difference Difference %
A:B4 Shoes Quanti 33,333 20,000 13,333 66.67%
A:C4 Boots Quantit 16,667 10,000 6,667 66.67%
A:D4 Total Quantity 50,000 30,000 20,000 66.67%
A:B8 Shoes Total C 166,667 100,000 66,667 66.67%
A:C8 Boots Total C 100,000 60,000 40,000 66.67%
A:B9 Shoes Total V 500,000 300,000 200,000 66.67%
A:C9 Boots Total W 333,333 200,000 133,333 66.67%
A:B11 Shoes Profit 333,333 200,000 133,333 66.67%
A:C11 Boots Profit 233,333 140,000 93,333 66.67%
A:D11 Total Profit 566,667 340,000 226,667 66.67%
General Styles SWISS12 DIFFS001.WK3

Fig. 16.24
The Differences report for the shoe production problem.

If you requested **C**ell format for the Differences report, the Solver cell report box appears, displayed in the same manner as the What-If cell report box (see fig. 16.23). By repeatedly selecting the **N**ext command, you can view the cells that contribute to the result shown in the worksheet.

The Inconsistent Constraints Report

Sometimes, constraints are mutually exclusive; if one constraint is True, the other constraint must be False. Solver calls mutually exclusive constraints *inconsistent constraints*. Suppose that a new constraint in the shoe example specifies that total profit must be at least $750,000. If you make this change in the worksheet and solve the problem (making sure that you redefine the constraints to include the new constraint), Solver reports that no answers were found, but one attempt with inconsistent constraints was tried. The `+D4<=50000` constraint in cell A:A14 is the constraint that has not been satisfied for this attempt (see fig. 16.25).

The Inconsistent Constraints report provides a definitive way of determining which constraints are inconsistent. Figure 16.26 shows the result of selecting this report in a worksheet without inconsistent constraints (see the prompt at the bottom of the screen). Figure 16.27 shows the result of issuing the **S**olver **R**eport **I**nconsistent **T**able command after modifying the constraints to make them inconsistent.

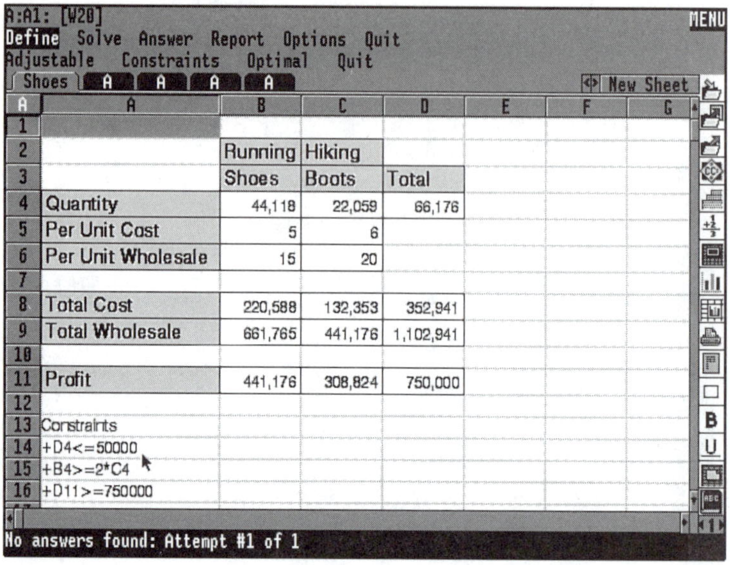

Fig. 16.25
A problem that cannot be solved because of inconsistent constraints.

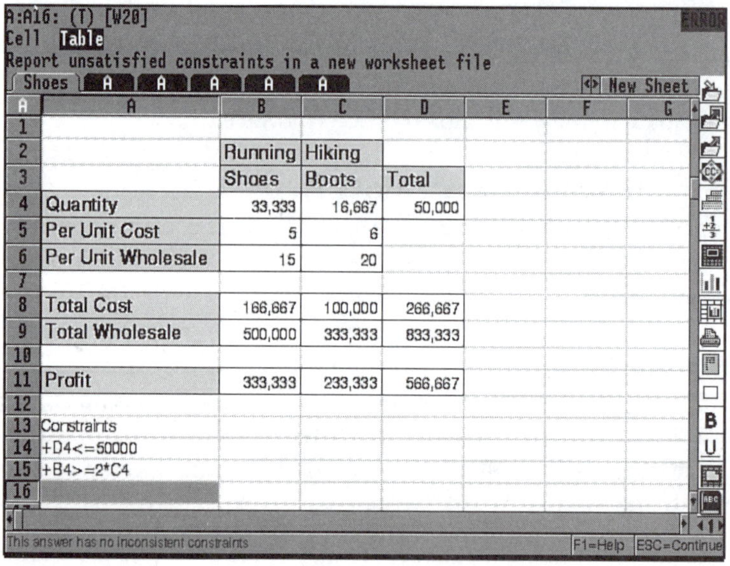

Fig. 16.26
Trying to select the Inconsistent Constraints report in a problem with no inconsistent constraints.

As figure 16.27 shows, Solver indicates which constraints weren't satisfied and notes what changes are necessary before those constraints can be satisfied. Because Solver cannot determine which constraints you can modify in a "real-world" situation, you may have to examine other possibilities to determine which constraints to change.

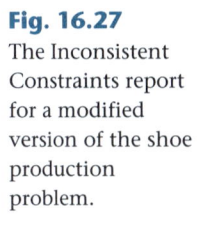

Fig. 16.27
The Inconsistent Constraints report for a modified version of the shoe production problem.

If you specify **T**able format, Solver generates the INCONS??.WK3 worksheet file, replacing ?? with 01 for the first Inconsistent constraints report. Solver increases the report number by 1 each time an Inconsistent constraints report is generated with the same default drive and directory.

The Unused Constraints Report

Constraints may bind some answers, but not others. In some situations, knowing which constraints don't bind or limit a solution may be helpful. If you select **R**eport **U**nused **T**able, Solver generates an UNUSED??.WK3 worksheet file, listing the unused constraints for the current answer. You can select **R**eport **U**nused **C**ell to report unused constraints one cell at a time.

Suppose that you revised the new constraint from the previous example to state that total profit must equal at least $300,000. If you make this change in the worksheet and solve the problem, Solver finds three answers. The Unused Constraints report in figure 16.28 shows that for the optimal answer, the new constraint had no effect on the solution found by Solver. Row 8 indicates that the constraint requiring that the profit be at least $300,000 isn't binding for this answer because the profit is substantially higher than that amount. The Unused Constraints report shows how to transform the constraint to make it binding (add $266,666.67 to the amount).

Fig. 16.28
The Unused Constraints report for the shoe production problem.

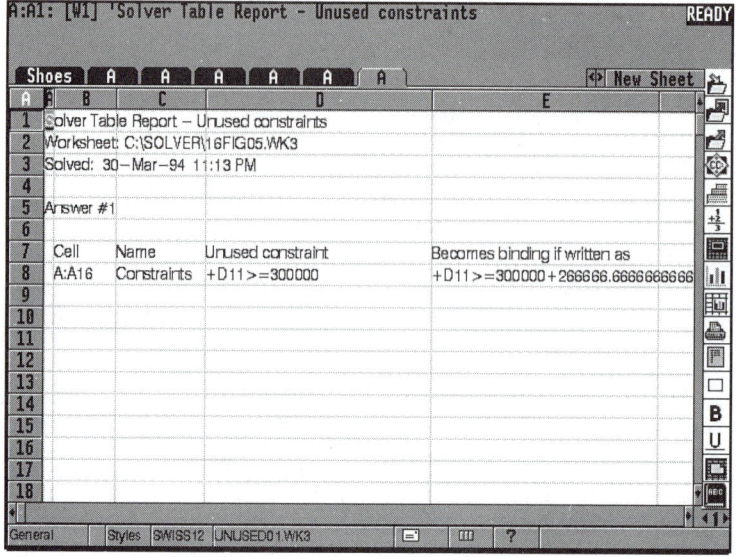

The Cells Used Report

The Cells Used report provides a summary of the cells used in a Solver problem, including all adjustable, constraint, and optimal cells. Figure 16.29 shows the report in **T**able format. The Cells Used report can be displayed also in **C**ell format.

Fig. 16.29
The Cells Used report for the shoe production problem.

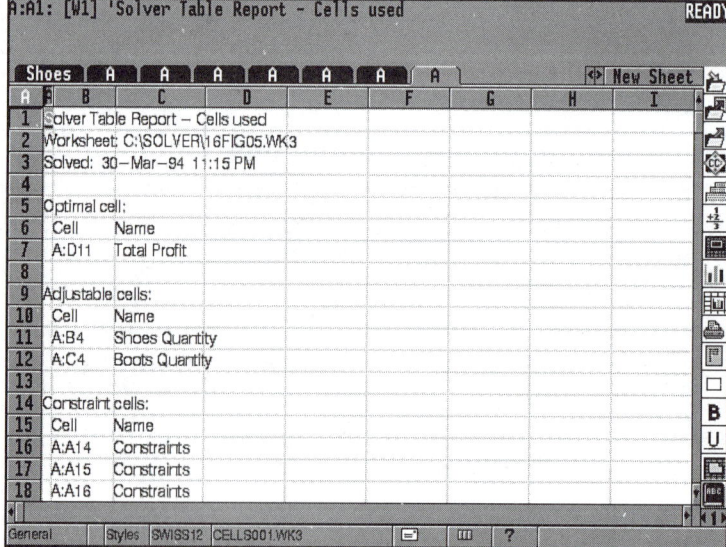

For each cell used in solving the problem, the Cells Used report indicates the type of cell (adjustable, constraint, or optimal); the cell's address; and the cell's range name or, if the cell has no range name, the closest row and column labels.

If you specify **T**able format, Solver generates the CELLS???.WK3 worksheet file, replacing ??? with 001 for the first Cells Used report. Solver increases the report number by 1 each time a Cells Used report is generated with the same default drive and directory.

If you use cell format rather than table format, two menu commands appear. The **N**ext command advances from the cell shown in the display box to the next cell. The progression starts with the first adjustable cell and moves through all remaining adjustable cells before advancing to the first constraint cell. After noting the constraint cells, Solver highlights the optimal cell before starting the cycle again with the first adjustable cell. Select **Q**uit to return to the Solver **R**eport menu.

Using Functions with Solver

You can use 1-2-3 functions in the cell formulas that Solver uses to determine solutions if you follow these basic rules:

- Functions in problem cells must use only numbers as arguments. Problem cells cannot contain functions requiring strings, date or time values, or values from a database. You can use @AVG in a Solver problem cell because @AVG uses only numbers to determine a numeric average, but you cannot use @TRIM or @DAVG because these functions require a string argument and a value from a database, respectively.

- Functions in problem cells must return numbers. In problem cells, you cannot use any functions returning a string (such as @STRING), a date or time value (such as @DATE), or a value from a database (such as @DQUERY). You can use functions returning Boolean values (such as @ERR and @ISNA), however, because 1-2-3 Release 4 considers Boolean values to be regular numbers.

Remember that these rules apply only to problem cells containing functions. Because Solver uses only the problem cells to find solutions, other cells in the worksheet can use any functions or formulas.

The following list shows the functions you can use in Solver problem cells (see Chapter 3, "Finding Solutions with Formulas and Functions," for information on using these functions in formulas):

@ABS	@ACOS	@ASIN	@ATAN	@ATAN2
@AVG	@CHOOSE	@COLS	@COS	@COUNT
@CTERM	@DDB	@EXP	@FALSE	@FV
@HLOOKUP	@IF	@INDEX	@INT	@IRR
@ISNUMBER	@LN	@LOG	@MAX	@MIN
@MOD	@NPV	@PI	@PMT	@PV
@RATE	@ROUND	@ROWS	@SHEETS	@SIN
@SLN	@SQRT	@STD	@STDS	@SUM
@SUMPRODUCT	@SYD	@TAN	@TERM	@TRUE
@VAR	@VARS	@VDB	@VLOOKUP	

> **Troubleshooting**
>
> *Solver runs out of memory or takes too long to solve a problem that contains functions.*
>
> Avoid adding or multiplying functions together in a Solver problem. If possible, avoid using any of the following functions: @CHOOSE, @HLOOKUP, @IF, @INDEX, @INT, @MOD, @ROUND, and @VLOOKUP. If you cannot avoid using @HLOOKUP, @VLOOKUP, or @INDEX, do not use large ranges for the range argument. Also, avoid using large ranges with statistical functions.
>
> Try to avoid nesting functions inside one another, especially @IF. If Solver cannot solve a problem that uses nested functions, rewrite the formulas that contain the nested functions so that each function is in a different cell.

Using Solver with Macros

The Solver add-in adds a new function called @SOLVER to 1-2-3. This function is used with macros to determine the state of Solver. Following is the syntax for @SOLVER:

```
@SOLVER("query_string")
```

@SOLVER has eight possible arguments you can use as the *query_string*, as shown in table 16.1.

Table 16.1 @SOLVER Arguments

Argument	Value Returned	Description
"consistent"	1	All constraints met
	2	At least one constraint not met
	ERR	No answer in file
"done "	1	Solver finished
	2	Solver in progress
	3	Problem not yet solved
"moreanswers "	1	No more answers exist
	2	Solve Continue may produce additional answers
	ERR	Problem not yet solved
"needguess "	1	No guesses needed
	2	Guesses needed
	ERR	No answer in file
"numanswers "	x	x number of answers found
	ERR	Problem not yet solved
"optimal "	1	Optimal answer found
	2	Best answer found
	3	No binding constraints
	4	No optimal cell defined or no answer found
	ERR	Problem not yet solved
"progress "	x	x fraction of problem solved
	ERR	Problem not yet solved
"result"	1	One or more answers found
	2	Answers not found but Solver can display attempts
	ERR	Problem not yet solved

Chapter 27, "Advanced Macro Command Power Techniques," provides more information on using functions with 1-2-3 macros.

From Here...

For information relating directly to using Solver, you may want to review the following chapters of this book:

- Chapter 2, "What Every 1-2-3 User Should Know," shows you the easiest techniques for setting up a worksheet and introduces the basics of creating formulas.

- Chapter 3, "Finding Solutions with Formulas and Functions," gives you more information about creating and troubleshooting formulas and about using 1-2-3's built-in functions.

- Chapter 17, "Goal Seeking with Backsolver," shows you how to use Backsolver to change variables in a worksheet to meet a specific goal in one formula cell.

Chapter 17
Goal Seeking with Backsolver

IV

Analyzing Your Data

Like Solver, Backsolver helps find answers to questions about various mathematical alternatives. However, as its name indicates, Backsolver works back from a goal that you specify, offering different values for the given variables. Backsolver offers a quick and efficient way to make preliminary estimates for the variables in any "what-if" problem.

When you use Backsolver, 1-2-3 changes the values of one or more adjustable cells to make one formula cell equal to a specified value. If you specify more than one adjustable cell, Backsolver changes all the adjustable cells by the same percentage.

This chapter shows you how to

- Use Backsolver to change a single value so that you can determine how much you can borrow.

- Use Backsolver to change several values so that you can adjust an expense budget to meet a profitability goal.

Using Backsolver To Change a Single Variable

Figure 17.1 shows a "what-if" problem that Backsolver can help you solve. In this example, the worksheet shows that you can repay a loan of $50,000 at 10 percent interest in 12 months with a monthly payment of $4,395.79. But suppose that you can pay $5,000 per month. How much more money can you borrow, assuming the same term and interest rate?

◀ "Using Financial and Accounting Functions," p. 178

Fig. 17.1
A worksheet that calculates a loan payment.

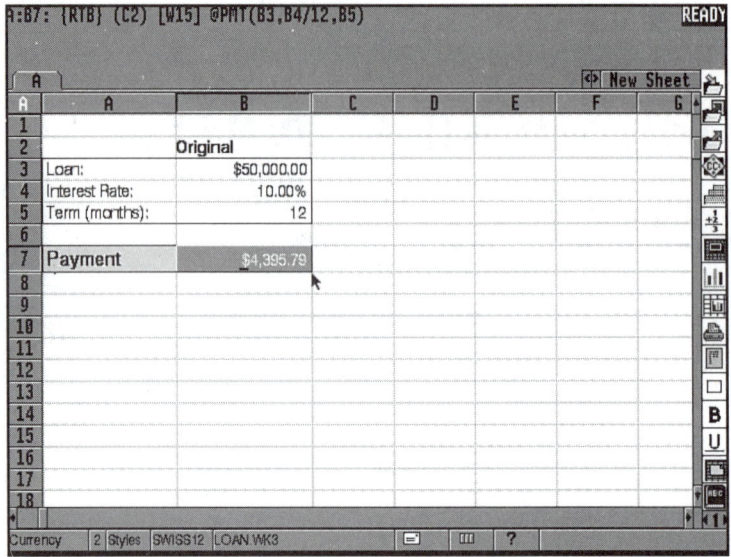

Backsolver changes the data in the worksheet, so you should save the worksheet before starting. If the Undo feature is active, you can reverse changes made by Backsolver by pressing Undo (Alt+F4) immediately after you finish using Backsolver.

> **Note**
> When you solve a problem with Backsolver, it changes data in the worksheet. You can easily avoid problems by using the **/T**ools **V**ersion feature (described in Chapter 18, "Tracking Multiple Sets of Data with Version Manager") to save the problem cells as a range version before you use Backsolver. Not only do the original worksheet figures remain intact in the range version, but you can also compare Backsolver's solution to the original answers.

To use Backsolver, select **/T**ools **A**nalyze **B**acksolver. Figure 17.2 shows the screen that results. Note the Backsolver menu at the top of the screen.

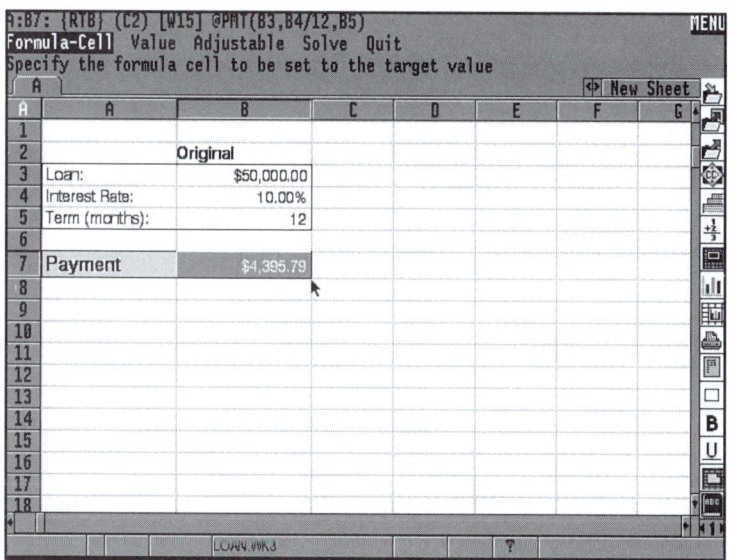

Fig. 17.2
The Backsolver menu.

Before Backsolver can solve a problem, you must specify the following:

- The cell that contains the formula to which you want to return a specific value

- The desired value

- The cells that contain the variables that you want to change to achieve the desired result

Specifying the Goal

First, you specify the goal that you want to meet: the cell that contains the formula to which you want to return a specified value, and the value that you want the formula to return.

Begin this process by selecting **F**ormula-Cell from the Backsolver menu. Backsolver prompts you to specify the range address of the formula (see fig. 17.3). Specify the range or cell, and then press Enter to return to the Backsolver main menu.

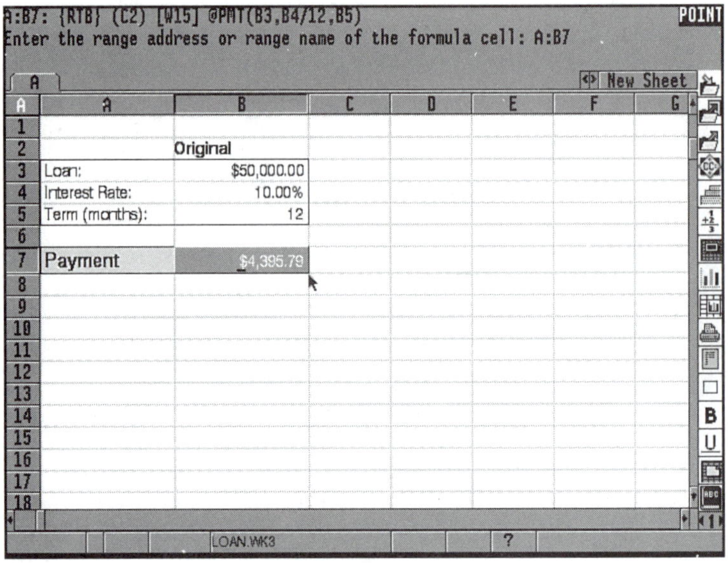

594 Chapter 17—Goal Seeking with Backsolver

Fig. 17.3
Specifying A:B7 as the address of the formula cell.

```
A:B7: {RTB} (C2) [W15] @PMT(B3,B4/12,B5)                    POINT
Enter the range address or range name of the formula cell: A:B7
```

	A	B	C	D	E	F	G
1							
2		Original					
3	Loan:	$50,000.00					
4	Interest Rate:	10.00%					
5	Term (months):	12					
6							
7	Payment	$4,395.79					

LOAN.WK3

Select **V**alue, specify the desired value that you want the formula to attain, and then press Enter. In figure 17.4, the specified value is $5,000—the maximum monthly payment.

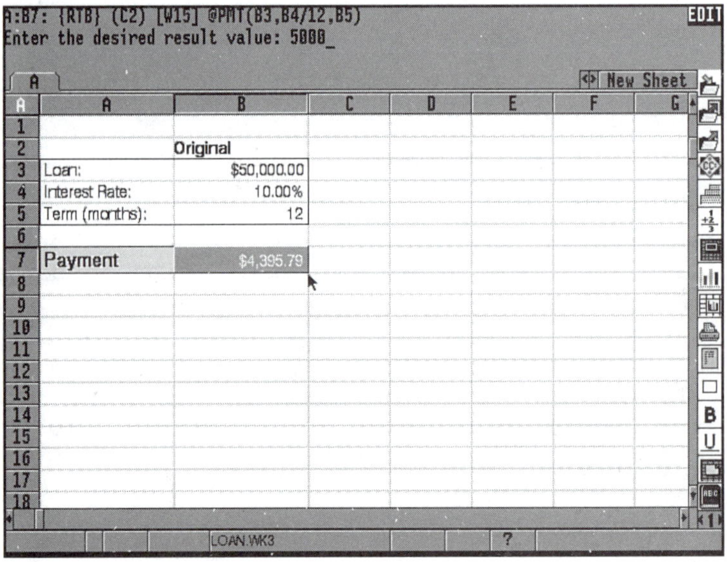

Fig. 17.4
Entering 5000 as the desired value for the formula cell.

```
A:B7: {RTB} (C2) [W15] @PMT(B3,B4/12,B5)                    EDIT
Enter the desired result value: 5000_
```

	A	B	C	D	E	F	G
1							
2		Original					
3	Loan:	$50,000.00					
4	Interest Rate:	10.00%					
5	Term (months):	12					
6							
7	Payment	$4,395.79					

LOAN.WK3

Specifying the Variables

Backsolver can change one or more values to achieve the specified goal. In this example, only one value needs to be adjusted: the loan amount in cell A:B3. Select **A**djustable from the Backsolver menu and specify the adjustable cell. In this example, the adjustable cell is A:B3 (see fig. 17.5). Then press Enter.

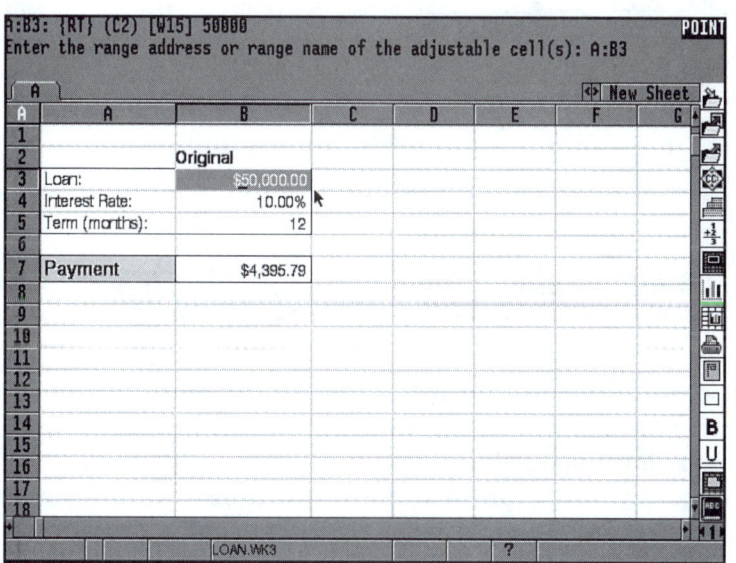

Fig. 17.5
Specifying A:B3 as the address of the adjustable cell.

Solving the Problem

When you select **S**olve from the Backsolver menu, Backsolver changes the value in the adjustable cell so that the formula cell returns the desired amount. Figure 17.6 shows the sample worksheet after Backsolver solves the problem by changing the value in cell A:B3 to $56,872.54. If all other values in the problem remain constant, you can borrow a maximum of $56,872.54.

Tip
If you enable Undo while working with Backsolver, you can restore the original values by pressing Undo (Alt+F4) and selecting **Y**es.

596   Chapter 17—Goal Seeking with Backsolver

Fig. 17.6
The worksheet after selecting Solve from the Backsolver menu. The largest loan you can afford is $56,872.54.

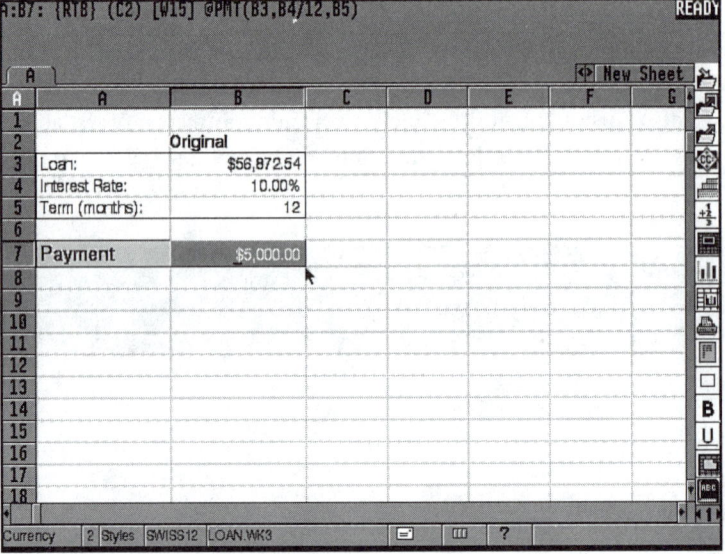

If Backsolver cannot find a solution that adjusts the value of the formula to the desired amount, an error message appears describing the problem. If Backsolver cannot find a value that adjusts the value of the formula to the desired figure, you may want to use Solver to determine reasonable estimates.

Using Backsolver To Change Several Variables

In the previous example, Backsolver changed the value in only one cell, the loan amount, to meet the goal of setting the loan payment amount to $5,000. Backsolver can also change the values in several cells to meet a goal. When you specify several adjustable cells, Backsolver meets your specified goal by increasing or decreasing the value in each cell proportionally.

This capability is useful when you need to change a particular value by adjusting several other values by the same proportion. For example, suppose that you are planning a budget and you need to reduce all expenses to meet a profitability goal. Figure 17.7 shows a worksheet that a small company might use to figure its expense budget.

You want to increase profitability to 20 percent by reducing expenses. Backsolver can help you find a good starting point for your budget by adjusting all three types of expense by the same percentage to yield a profitability of 20 percent.

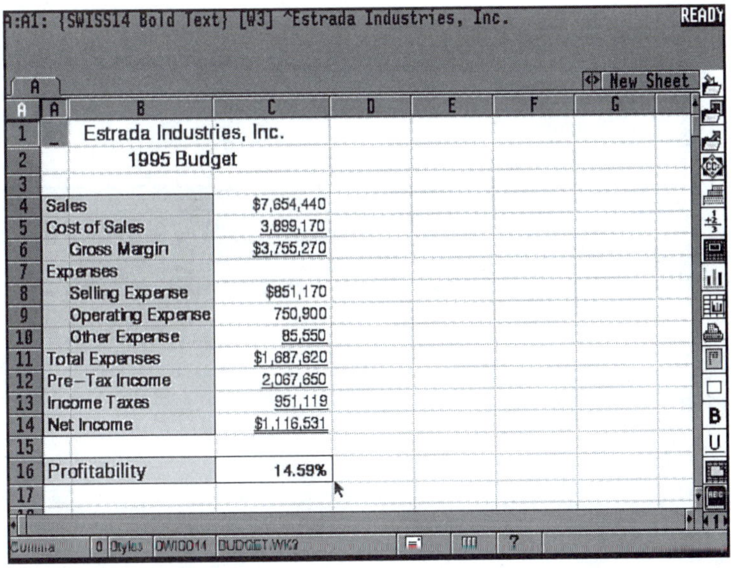

Fig. 17.7
The 1995 budget worksheet for Estrada Industries, Inc.

Specifying the Goal

Again, you begin by specifying the cell that contains the formula to which you want to return a specified value, and the value that you want the formula to return. For this problem, you specify the cell that displays the profitability value, cell A:C16, as the formula cell, as shown in figure 17.8.

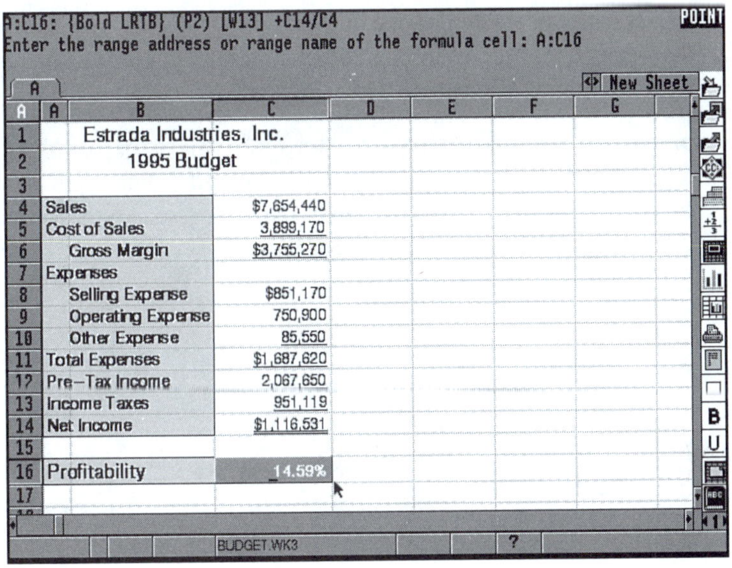

Fig. 17.8
Specifying cell A:C16 as the formula cell.

The value that you want the formula to attain is 20 percent, as shown in figure 17.9. Notice that you can specify 20 percent directly, as a percentage. 1-2-3 recognizes the percent symbol and automatically converts the amount to 0.2, the correct decimal value.

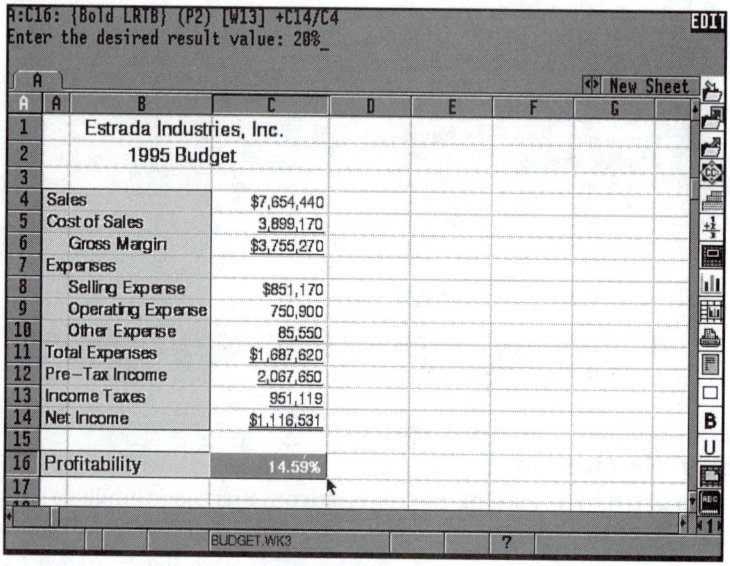

Fig. 17.9
Entering 20% as the desired value for the formula cell.

Specifying the Variables

Remember that Backsolver can change one or more values to achieve a specified goal. If you specify more than one adjustable cell, Backsolver changes each cell by the same percentage.

In this example, you want Backsolver to change the values for Selling Expense in cell A:C8, Operating Expense in cell A:C9, and Other Expense in cell A:C10. Select **A**djustable from the Backsolver menu and specify the adjustable cells A:C8..A:C10 (see fig. 17.10). Then press Enter.

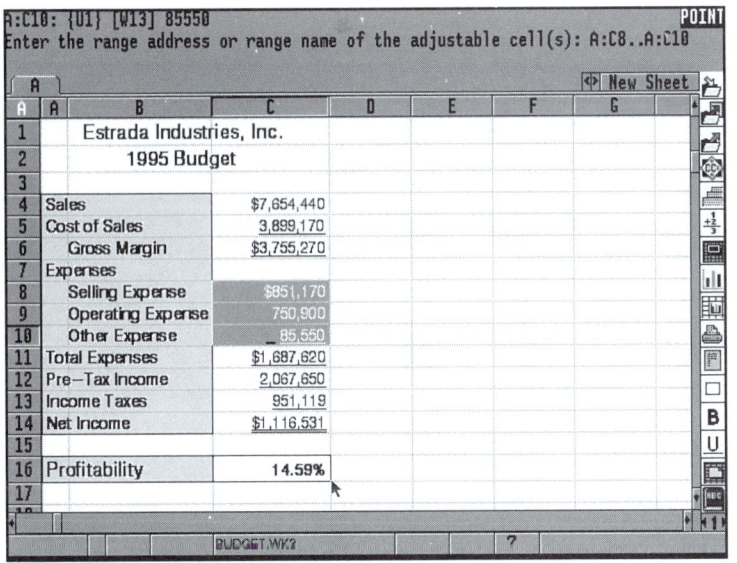

Fig. 17.10
Specifying the range A:C8 through A:C10 as the adjustable cell range.

Solving the Problem

When you select **S**olve from the Backsolver menu, Backsolver changes the value in each adjustable cell by the same percentage so that the formula cell returns the desired amount. Figure 17.11 shows the sample worksheet after Backsolver solves the problem by changing the values in cells A:C8 through A:C10 to $464,160; 409,480; and 46,652 respectively. By comparing these amounts with the original expense amounts in figure 17.10, you can see that Backsolver multiplied each of the original expense amounts by 0.5453, or approximately 55 percent, to arrive at the new amounts. This is the same as subtracting 45 percent from each of the original amounts. If you can reduce expenses by 45 percent, you can meet your profitability goal of 20 percent.

Troubleshooting

Backsolver reports an invalid formula cell.

Make sure that the cell you specified as the formula cell contains a formula.

Backsolver reports that it could not find a solution.

The cell you specified as the formula cell must depend, directly or indirectly, on the cell(s) you specified as the adjustable cells. To test this, change the values in the adjustable cells and make sure that the value in the formula cell changes. If Backsolver still cannot find a solution, perhaps the formula in the formula cell cannot be solved by changing the adjustable cells you specified. Check your formula carefully to make sure that it is correct.

Fig. 17.11

The completed budget worksheet. Expenses have been reduced by 45%, producing the desired 20% profitability.

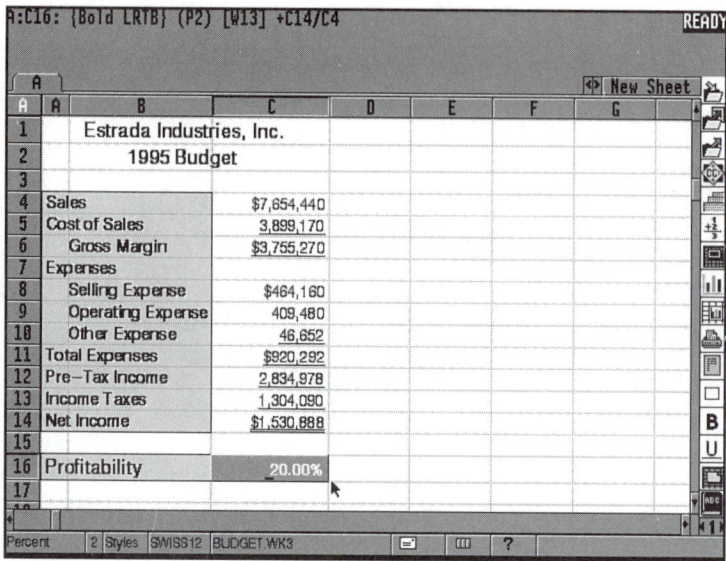

From Here...

For information related directly to using Backsolver, you may want to review the following chapters:

- Chapter 2, "What Every 1-2-3 User Should Know," shows you the easiest techniques for setting up a worksheet and introduces the basics of creating formulas.

- Chapter 3, "Finding Solutions with Formulas and Functions," provides more information about creating and troubleshooting formulas and about using 1-2-3's built-in functions.

- Chapter 16, "Finding Solutions with Solver," describes how to use Solver to find multiple solutions to complex "what-if" problems.

Chapter 18

Tracking Multiple Sets of Data with Version Manager

Version Manager is a new tool in 1-2-3 Release 4 that provides easy-to-use "what-if" analytical power. This power enables you to create and view different sets of data for any named range. For example, you can create high and low projections for a range named SALES and compare their effects on other items in the application. Each different set of data that you create is called a *version*.

To make it easier to manage versions, you also can group versions of different ranges together to create *scenarios*. For example, you can group the high-sales projection with the low-expenses projection so that you can easily display them together.

Version Manager also makes it easier for you to share data with coworkers. Different people can enter versions in the same range of a worksheet file without writing over each other's data.

In this chapter, you learn to do the following:

- Manage and share data with Version Manager
- Create and display different versions of data in a named range
- Group versions together into scenarios

Understanding Version Manager Basics

Prior to Release 4, if you wanted to keep track of different versions of data in the same range, you could do so by saving different versions of the entire file. For example, you could save several versions of the first-quarter expense budget, naming the files Q1EXP1.WK3, Q1EXP2.WK3, and so on. Alternatively, you could save the different assumptions on separate worksheets within a single file. With Version Manager, you can store these different sets of data in a single worksheet by creating different versions of named ranges.

Before getting into the details of Version Manager, you should understand some terms used throughout this chapter. This section reviews some terms with which you may already be familiar and introduces some new terms.

You can create different sets of data only for named ranges. A *range* is a single cell or a block of adjoining cells. For example, A:A1..A:A1 is a range consisting of a single cell; A:B1..A:C5 is a range consisting of a block of adjoining cells; A:C10..C:E15 is a 3-D range consisting of a block of adjoining cells in adjoining worksheets.

A *named range* is a range to which you have assigned a name. A range name can be up to 15 characters long. For example, you can assign the name REVENUES to the range A:B5..A:E5 and the name EXPENSES to the range A:B10..A:E10. You use **/R**ange **N**ame **C**reate to assign a name to a range and then use **/T**ools **V**ersion **C**reate to create a version of the range.

When you create different sets of data for a single named range, you assign each set a name, such as HIGH SALES or LOW SALES. Each named set of data for a named range is called a *version* of that range. When you create a version of a named range, Version Manager stores the current contents of the range.

For example, in a range named REVENUES, you can enter the values 500, 400, 300, and 200 and then use Version Manager to create a version with the name HIGH SALES. You then can enter the values 50, 40, 30, and 20 in the same named range and create a second version with the name LOW SALES. Both versions of the named range are stored in memory, and you can use Version Manager to display either version. When you save the file, 1-2-3 saves both versions of the named range as part of the worksheet file.

You can create versions for any named range in a file. For example, if you want to compare different combinations of revenues and expenses, you can create several different versions of the range named EXPENSES and use Version Manager to display the different combinations.

After you create versions, you can treat selected versions of different named ranges as a group. A named group of versions is called a *scenario*. For example, you can group the HIGH SALES version of the REVENUES range with the LOW EXPENSES version of the EXPENSES range to create a scenario named BEST CASE. You can also create a WORST CASE scenario that contains the LOW SALES version of REVENUES and the HIGH EXPENSES version of EXPENSES. To create a scenario, you use **/T**ools **V**ersion **M**anage-Scenario **C**reate.

Working with Versions: The /Tools Version Menu

You use the **/T**ools **V**ersion menu to create, show, update, and delete versions. In this section, you learn how to create and use versions of named ranges in a revenue plan worksheet.

Figure 18.1 shows the 1995 Revenue Forecast worksheet for Resorts International. This company hopes to diversify its revenue sources by increasing total nonlodging revenues in 1995. You can use Version Manager to explore the results of different strategies for reaching this goal.

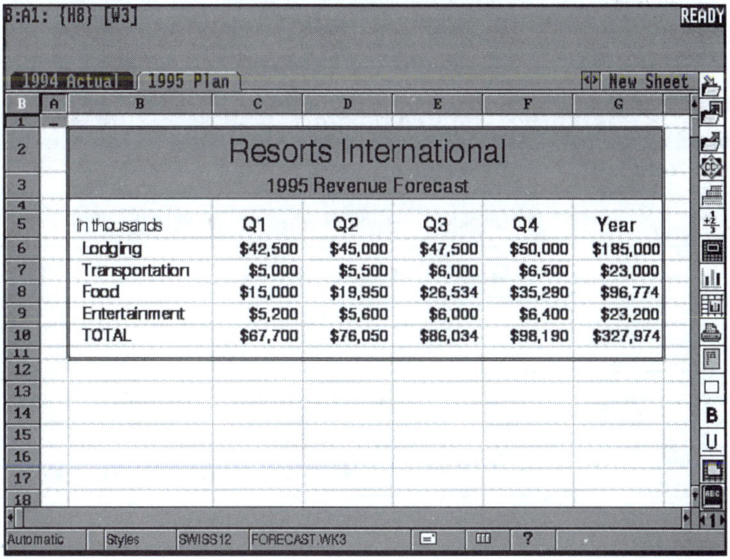

Fig. 18.1
The 1995 Revenue Forecast worksheet for Resorts International.

604 Chapter 18—Tracking Multiple Sets of Data with Version Manager

Figure 18.2 shows the **/T**ools **V**ersion menu and the Versions dialog box. The **/T**ools **V**ersion menu has seven commands. The asterisk at the beginning of a version name indicates a version that is currently displayed in the worksheet. Table 18.1 describes what each command on the **/T**ools **V**ersion menu does.

Fig. 18.2

Use the **/T**ools **V**ersion menu and the Versions dialog box to work with different versions of the data in your worksheet files.

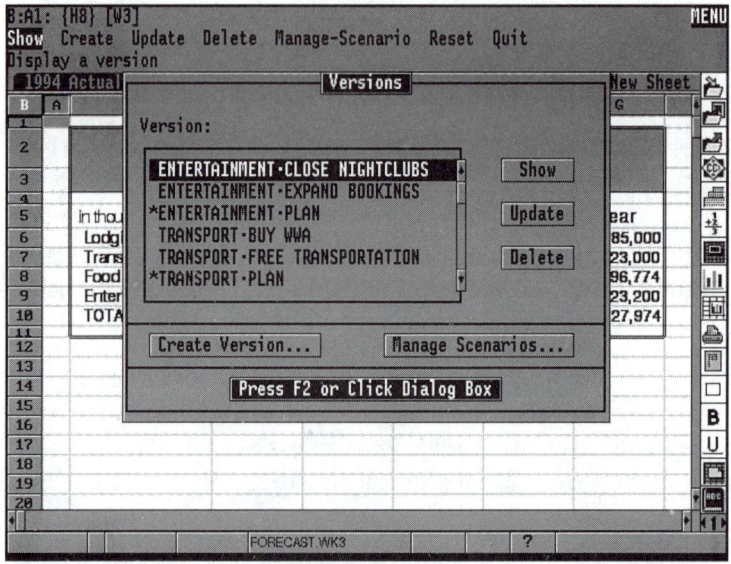

Table 18.1	/Tools Version Commands
Menu Item	**Description**
Show	Displays a version of a named range in the worksheet
Create	Creates a version of a named range
Update	Updates a version of a named range with the current data in that range
Delete	Deletes a version of a named range
Manage-Scenario	Displays the **M**anage-Scenario menu, which presents commands that enable you to work with scenarios
Reset	Deletes all versions of a named range
Quit	Returns the worksheet to READY mode

Creating Versions

The first step in creating a version of a range is to name the range. To do so, you use the **/R**ange **N**ame **C**reate command. You can create versions of named ranges only. Figure 18.3 shows a range name table for the Revenue Forecast worksheet. The names ENTERTAINMENT, LODGING, and TRANSPORT have been assigned to the ranges B:C9..B:F9, B:C6..B:F6, and B:C7..B:F7, respectively.

◀ "Entering and Editing Data," p. 63

◀ "Creating Range Names," p. 88

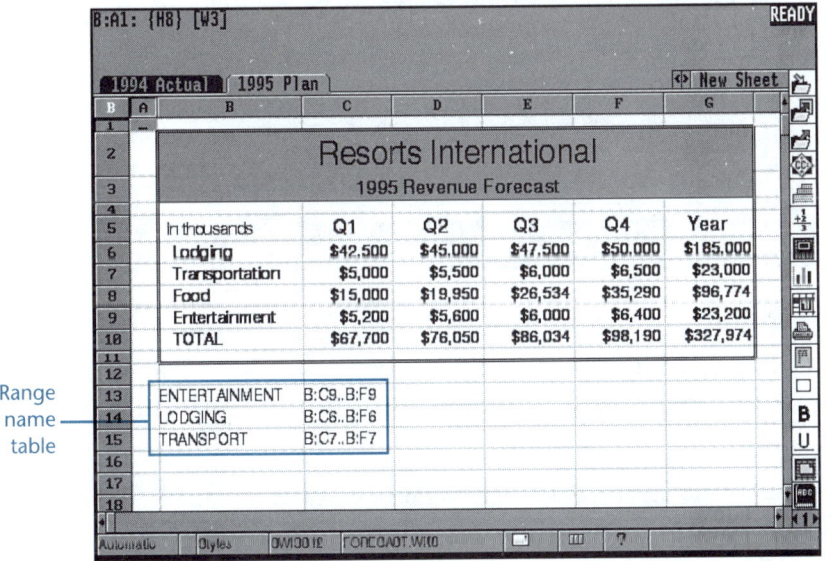

Fig. 18.3
A range name table for the Revenue Forecast worksheet. Use versions to maintain different sets of data for the ENTERTAINMENT, LODGING, and TRANSPORT ranges.

The next step is to enter the data for the version. If the range already contains data that you want to preserve, begin by creating a version that contains the data currently stored in the range. This action saves that data so that you don't lose it when you enter different sets of data for the range.

For example, to explore different assumptions about lodging revenues, begin by creating a version that contains the data currently stored in the LODGING range.

To create a version, select **/T**ools **V**ersion **C**reate. 1-2-3 prompts you to select a range, and displays a menu of named ranges. Select the range for which you want to create a version, then enter a name for the version. In the example, you would select the range LODGING, then type **plan** as the name for the version, as shown in figure 18.4.

Fig. 18.4
Use the /**T**ools **V**ersion **C**reate command to create the PLAN version of the LODGING range.

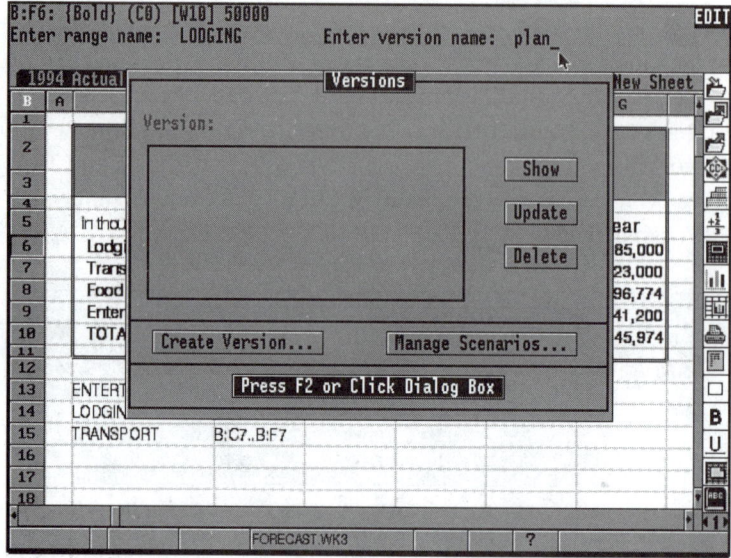

Range names can be up to 15 characters long, should not contain spaces or special characters, and are not case-sensitive. Version names can be up to 32 characters long, may contain spaces or special characters, and are not case-sensitive.

To create a second version of a range, begin by entering into the worksheet the data for the new version. Then select /**T**ools **V**ersion **C**reate to create the second version, and specify the range name and version name. Figure 18.5 shows the screen during the creation of a second version (GOOD YEAR) of the LODGING range.

After you create a version of a range, the name of the version appears in the Versions dialog box whenever you select /**T**ools **V**ersion. Version Manager displays the name of each version preceded by the name of the range and a raised dot. For example, the PLAN version of the LODGING range appears in the Versions dialog box as LODGING•PLAN. Figure 18.6 shows how the Versions dialog box appears after the creation of two versions of the LODGING range and two versions of the ENTERTAINMENT range.

Working with Versions: The /Tools Version Menu

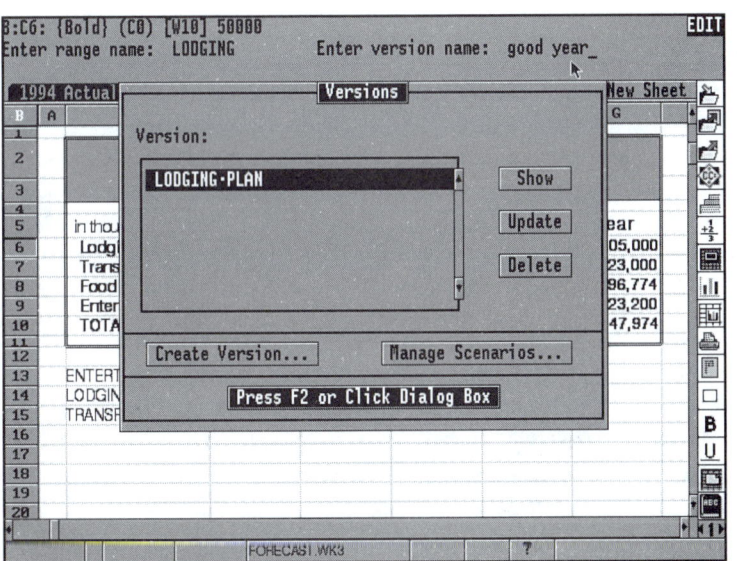

Fig. 18.5
Creating a second version of the LODGING range.

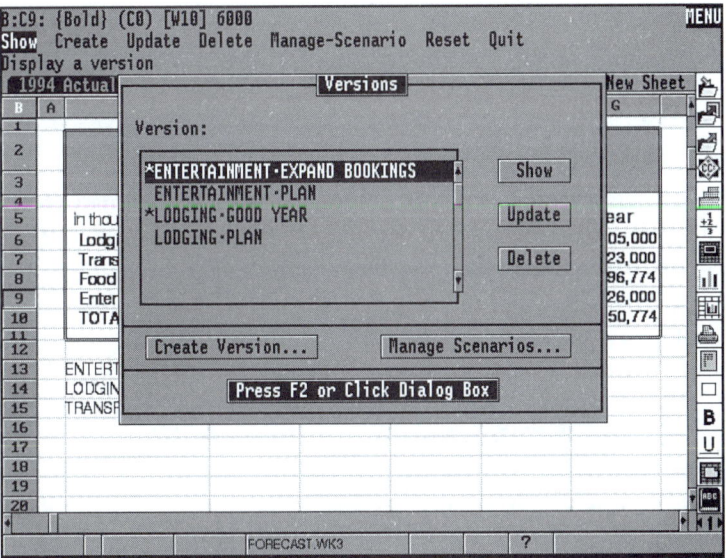

Fig. 18.6
The Versions dialog box, showing two versions of the ENTERTAINMENT range and two versions of the LODGING range. Asterisks indicate the versions that are currently displayed in the worksheet.

> **Note**
>
> Avoid creating versions for ranges that overlap. For example, the ranges A:A1..A:D2 and A:B2..A:C15 both contain the cells A:B2 and A:C2. If you create versions for overlapping ranges, only one version's data appears in the cells that overlap. If you create a scenario that includes versions in overlapping ranges, only one version's data appears in the cells that overlap. For example, if RANGE1 were A:A1..A:D2, RANGE2 were A:B2..A:C15, and you created a scenario that included the best-case version of RANGE1 and the worst-case version of RANGE2, only the values from one of those versions could appear in cells A:B2 and A:C2.

> **Note**
>
> A version can contain anything that you can enter in a cell, including values, labels, formulas, functions, or macros. By creating versions that contain formulas, you can perform complex "what-if" analyses. For example, you can save one version of a projected sales range that contains formulas that calculate the increase in sales based on projected economic trends, and another that uses a different method to project the increase. With Version Manager, you can quickly compare and test the results of different assumptions and their effects on other data in your worksheet.

Displaying Versions

After you create several versions of a range, you can display the versions in the worksheet. To display a version of a range in the worksheet, select /**T**ools **V**ersion **S**how and specify the range name and the version name. 1-2-3 places the data for that version of the range into the worksheet, replacing any data already there.

> **Caution**
>
> If you select /**T**ools **V**ersion **S**how and specify a version of a range, and that range currently contains data that you have not saved as a version, 1-2-3 displays the following prompt:
>
>   Data in the range has changed. Write over data in the range?
>
> If you select **Y**es from the menu that appears, 1-2-3 places the data for the version into the worksheet, and the data that was previously in the range is lost. To avoid losing the data, select **N**o, then select /**T**ools **V**ersion **C**reate to save the data in a new version.

In the Resorts International example, you can create several versions of the LODGING range, the TRANSPORT range, the FOOD range, and the ENTERTAINMENT range. Then you can use Version Manager to display the versions in the worksheet in different combinations, and examine the effects of the revenue mix.

Updating Versions

After you create a version, you may want to change the data for the version. For example, if your Lodging revenue forecast changes, you might want to modify the FORECAST version of the LODGING range so that it contains the data from the new forecast. (Alternatively, you could use the new data to create a new version, which you might name FORECAST1, for example.)

To change the data in a version, enter the new data for the version into the range in the worksheet. Then select **/T**ools **V**ersion **U**pdate, specify the name of the range, and specify the name of the version that includes the data that you want to change. 1-2-3 replaces the data in the version with the data in the worksheet.

Tip
To change a version's name, create a second version with the same data, but with a new name, and then delete the original version.

> **Caution**
>
> When you update a version, you replace the original data stored in the version with the data currently in the worksheet.

Deleting Versions

To delete a version, select **/T**ools **V**ersion **D**elete, specify the range name, and specify the version name. To delete all versions of a range, select **/T**ools **V**ersion **R**eset and specify the range name.

Tip
To delete a named range that contains versions, you must delete all versions of the range first. Use **/T**ools **V**ersion **R**eset to delete all versions of the range, then use **/R**ange **N**ame **D**elete to delete the range.

Working with Scenarios: The Manage-Scenario Menu

In addition to letting you create different versions of the data in a range, Version Manager also lets you group versions together into scenarios, making it easier to work with particular groups of versions.

To create, show, modify, and delete scenarios, you use the **/T**ools **V**ersion **M**anage-Scenario menu. In this section, you learn how to create and use scenarios in the revenue plan worksheet.

610 Chapter 18—Tracking Multiple Sets of Data with Version Manager

Figure 18.7 shows the /**T**ools **V**ersion **M**anage-Scenario menu and the Manage Scenarios dialog box. The /**T**ools **V**ersion **M**anage-Scenario menu has six commands. Table 18.2 describes what each of these commands does.

Fig. 18.7
The /**T**ools **V**ersion **M**anage-Scenario menu and the Manage Scenarios dialog box. The BIG ON TRANSPORTATION scenario includes the CLOSE NIGHTCLUBS version of the ENTERTAINMENT range, the PLAN version of the LODGING range, and the BUY WWA version of the TRANSPORT range.

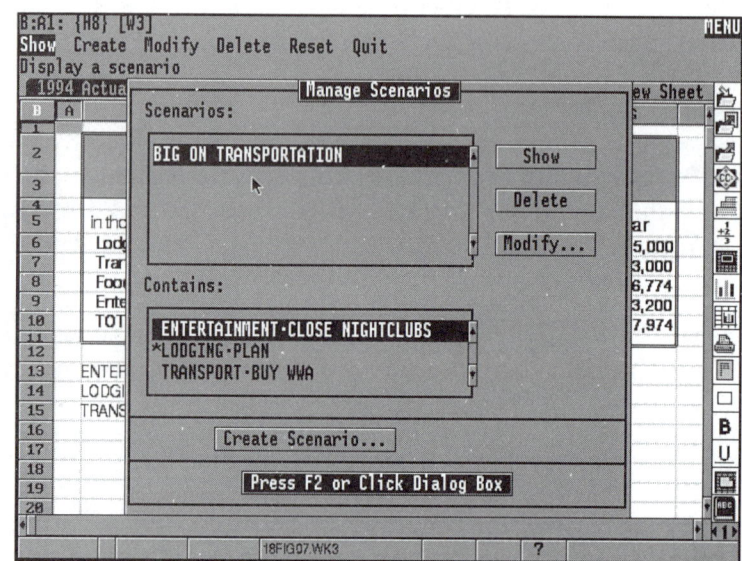

Table 18.2	/**T**ools **V**ersion **M**anage-Scenario Commands
Menu Item	**Description**
Show	Displays a scenario in the worksheet
Create	Creates a scenario
Modify	Adds or removes versions in a scenario
Delete	Deletes a scenario
Reset	Deletes all scenarios in the active file
Quit	Returns the worksheet to READY mode

Creating, Displaying, and Modifying Scenarios

A scenario is a named group of versions. Use scenarios when you want to group a particular set of versions together. You may want to display all the PLAN versions in the worksheet and then display all the versions that contain your most optimistic estimates. You can do this easily by creating a scenario named Plan that includes all the versions named PLAN, and creating a second scenario named My Best Guess that contains those versions that have the most optimistic projections.

To create a scenario, select **/T**ools **V**ersion **M**anage-Scenario **C**reate. When you select **M**anage-Scenario, the Manage Scenarios dialog box appears. When you select **C**reate, 1-2-3 prompts you to enter a scenario name, as shown in figure 18.8.

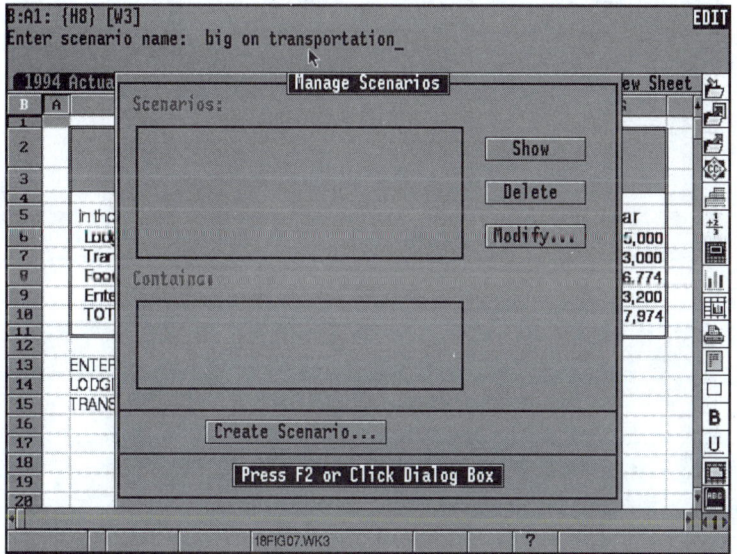

Fig. 18.8
When you select **/T**ools **V**ersion **M**anage-Scenario **C**reate, 1-2-3 prompts you to enter a scenario name.

After you enter the scenario name, 1-2-3 creates an empty scenario with the name you entered and displays the menu in figure 18.9. To finish creating the scenario, select **A**dd from this menu to add versions to the scenario. If you change your mind about which versions to include in the scenario, select **R**emove to remove a version or **M**odify to select a different version of a particular range.

Figure 18.10 shows the Manage Scenarios dialog box after you have created a scenario called BIG ON TRANSPORTATION, consisting of the CLOSE NIGHT-CLUBS version of ENTERTAINMENT, the PLAN version of LODGING, and the BUY WWA version of TRANSPORT. The asterisk next to LODGING.PLAN indicates that the version is currently displayed in the worksheet.

Fig. 18.9

When you first create a scenario, it is empty. To add versions to the scenario, use the **A**dd command on the menu that appears.

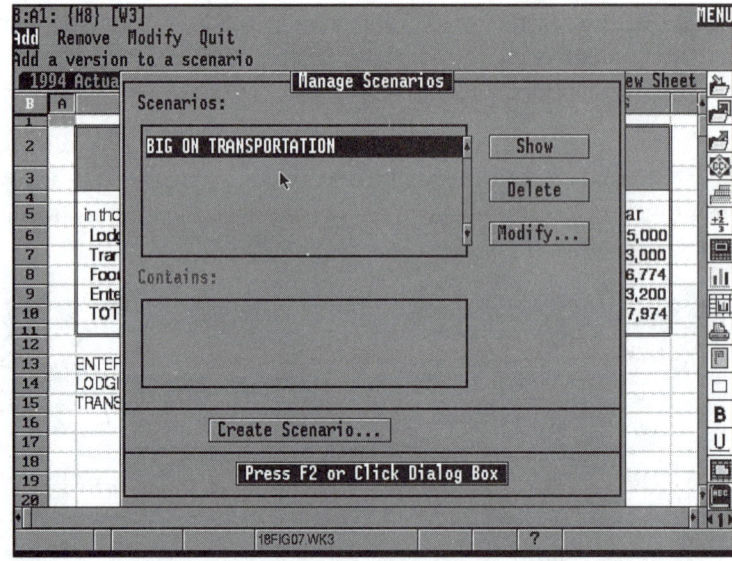

Fig. 18.10

The completed Manage Scenarios dialog box for BIG ON TRANSPOR-TATION.

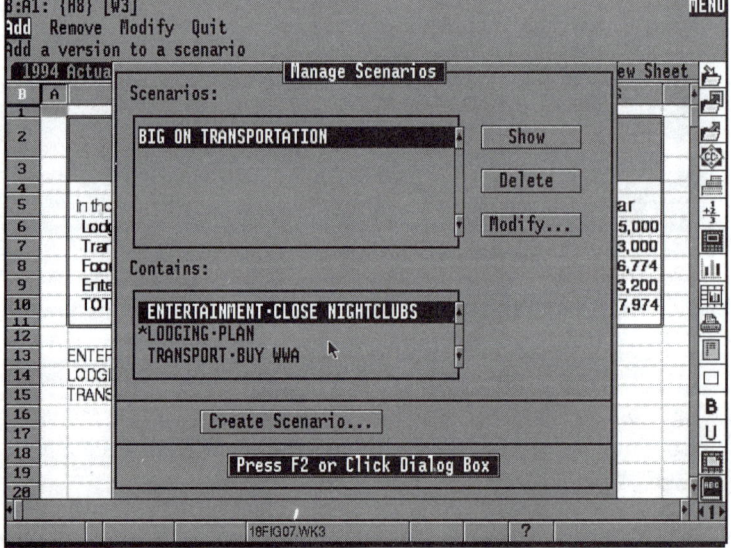

A scenario can contain only one version of any named range. For example, you cannot create a scenario that contains two versions of the SALES range (because you can display only one version of the range at a time).

To display a scenario in the worksheet, select **/T**ools **V**ersion **M**anage-Scenario **S**how and specify the scenario name.

Caution

If you select **/T**ools **V**ersion **M**anage-Scenario **S**how and specify a scenario that contains a version of a range that currently contains data that has not been saved as a version, 1-2-3 displays the following prompt:

    Data in at least one range has changed. Write over data in the
    range?

If you select **Y**es from the menu that appears, 1-2-3 places the data for the version into the worksheet, and the data that was previously in the range is lost. To avoid losing the data, select **N**o, then select **/T**ools **V**ersion **C**reate to save the data in a new version.

To change the versions included in the scenario, select **/T**ools **V**ersion **M**anage-Scenario **M**odify and specify the scenario name. The Manage Scenario dialog box and menu appear (see fig. 18.11). From the resulting menu, you can add, remove, or modify versions in the scenario you specified.

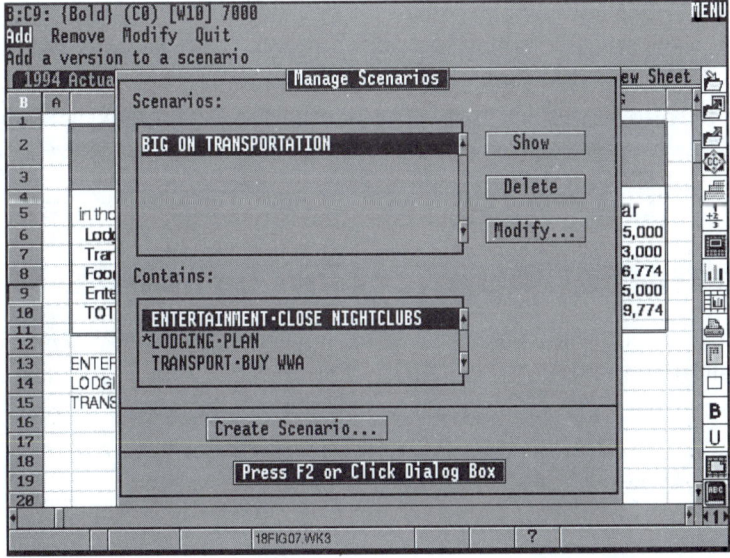

Fig. 18.11
The Manage Scenarios dialog box and menu.

Deleting Scenarios

To delete a scenario, select **/T**ools **V**ersion **M**anage-Scenario **D**elete and specify the scenario name by typing it or by selecting it from the list that appears in the control panel. To delete all scenarios in the active file, select **/T**ools **V**ersion **M**anage-Scenario **R**eset.

Using Version Manager To Share Data

Tip
If you use Version Manager to share data with other users, each user can store comments about his or her version by adding comments to the values and formulas in the version.

In addition to letting you create and maintain different versions of data in your own worksheets, Version Manager makes it easier than ever to share data with other 1-2-3 users. Several users can enter versions in the same file without writing over each other's data. If each user includes his or her initials as part of the version name, you should always be able to determine who entered which version.

If you have a local area network, you can share data by keeping a file on a network file server. Users can add versions to the same file. For example, different people can enter revenue forecasts based on their individual expertise. Coworkers can review each other's versions, and perhaps create new versions based on someone else's ideas.

If you don't have access to a network, you can still use Version Manager to share data. Simply pass around a copy of a worksheet file and let each person add versions to it.

◀ "Adding Comments to Values and Formulas," p. 346

◀ "Using 1-2-3 on a Network," p. 450

◀ "Protecting Worksheet Data," p. 512

◀ "Sealing Files," p. 523

Whenever you share a file, whether on a network or not, you may want to unprotect the ranges in which you want others to create versions and then seal the file with a password. This arrangement prevents other people from rearranging the file but lets them create versions in the unprotected ranges. Sealing the file also prevents other users from changing protected versions or from seeing hidden versions.

Looking at Application Examples

Now that you know the mechanics of using Version Manager, you may have an application in mind that would benefit from Version Manager's features, or you may need some additional ideas for how to put Version Manager to use in your environment. The following sections give you some ideas for different ways to use Version Manager.

What-If Analysis

One of the most obvious uses for Version Manager is in "what-if" analyses. For example, suppose that your child is considering several colleges and financial aid packages. After you create named ranges for Tuition and Financial Aid, you can then create versions in each range for all the options.

Or, suppose that you manage a "cafeteria-style" benefits plan, in which employees choose from different options in each benefit category. For each benefit category, you can create versions that contain different selections of options.

Applications Requiring Frequent Updates or Iterations

Many spreadsheet applications go through several updates or iterations before being published as a finished report. For example, departmental expense budgets can go through several rounds of review and update before being approved and consolidated into the company budget. You can use Version Manager to save each round of updates without losing earlier data or having to save several files. You can also create customized reports to measure the effects of the changes by comparing the results of placing different versions in the worksheet.

Applications with Several Contributors

Some applications require contributions from several people. For example, a marketing forecast may require input from several product-line and marketing managers. Version Manager supports this kind of application by tracking all changes that you or your coworkers make to a worksheet. You can manage this process by using a single copy of a worksheet that you pass from one person to the next, or by putting the worksheet file on a network server from which everyone can access the file.

From Here...

For information relating directly to using Version Manager, you may want to review the following chapters of this book:

- Chapter 2, "What Every 1-2-3 User Should Know," shows you the easiest techniques for setting up a worksheet and introduces the basics of creating formulas.

- Chapter 3, "Finding Solutions with Formulas and Functions," gives you more information about creating and troubleshooting formulas and about using 1-2-3's built-in functions.

- Chapter 16, "Finding Solutions with Solver," explains how to use Solver to find multiple solutions to complex business problems. Using Solver and Version Manager together, you can quickly solve business problems, save multiple solutions in a worksheet as versions, and perform complex what-if analysis.

- Chapter 22, "High-Level Database Techniques," teaches you how to use data tables, another powerful tool for what-if analysis.

Part V

Working with Databases

19	Creating Databases
20	Sorting Your Data
21	Finding Specific Data
22	High-Level Database Techniques

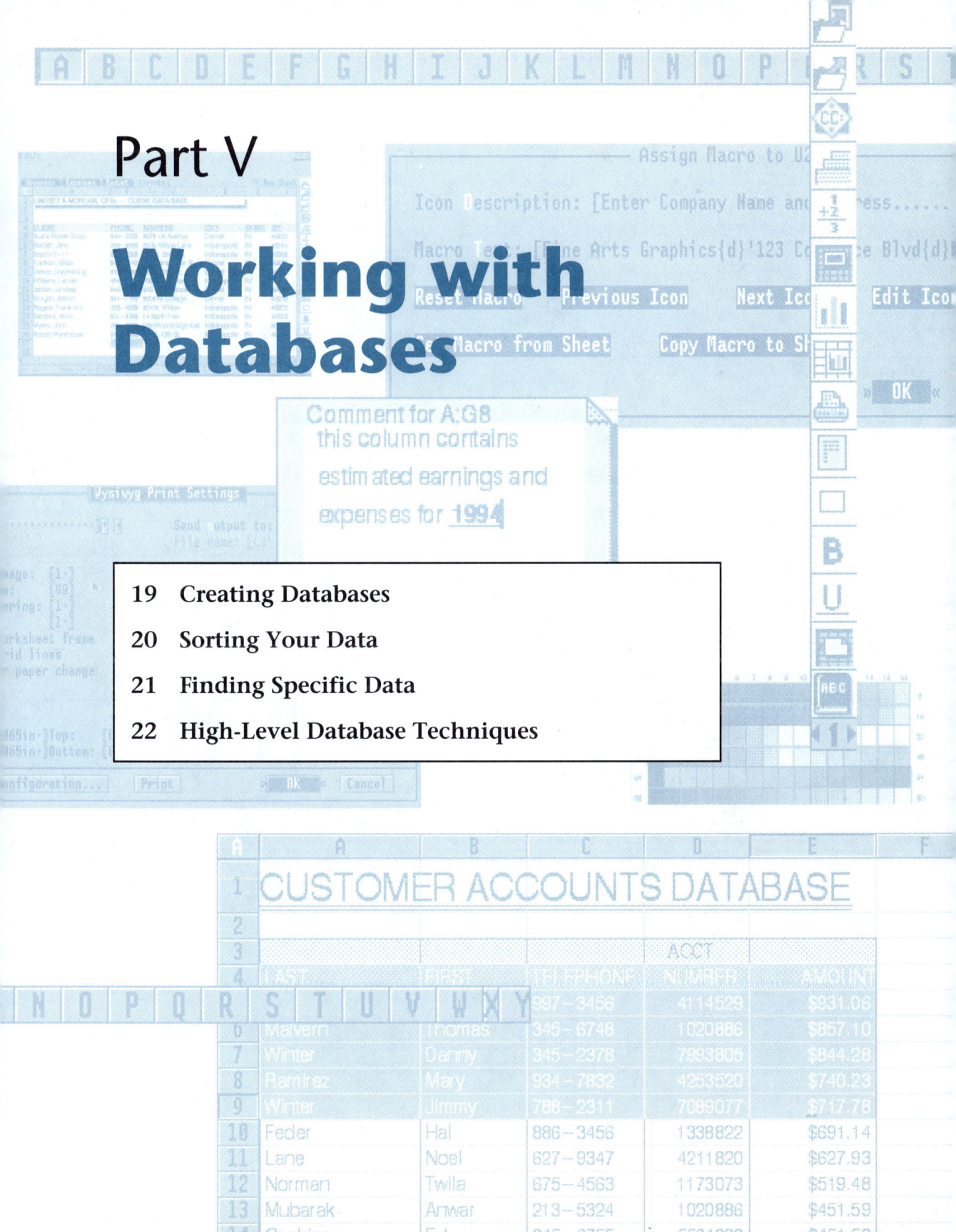

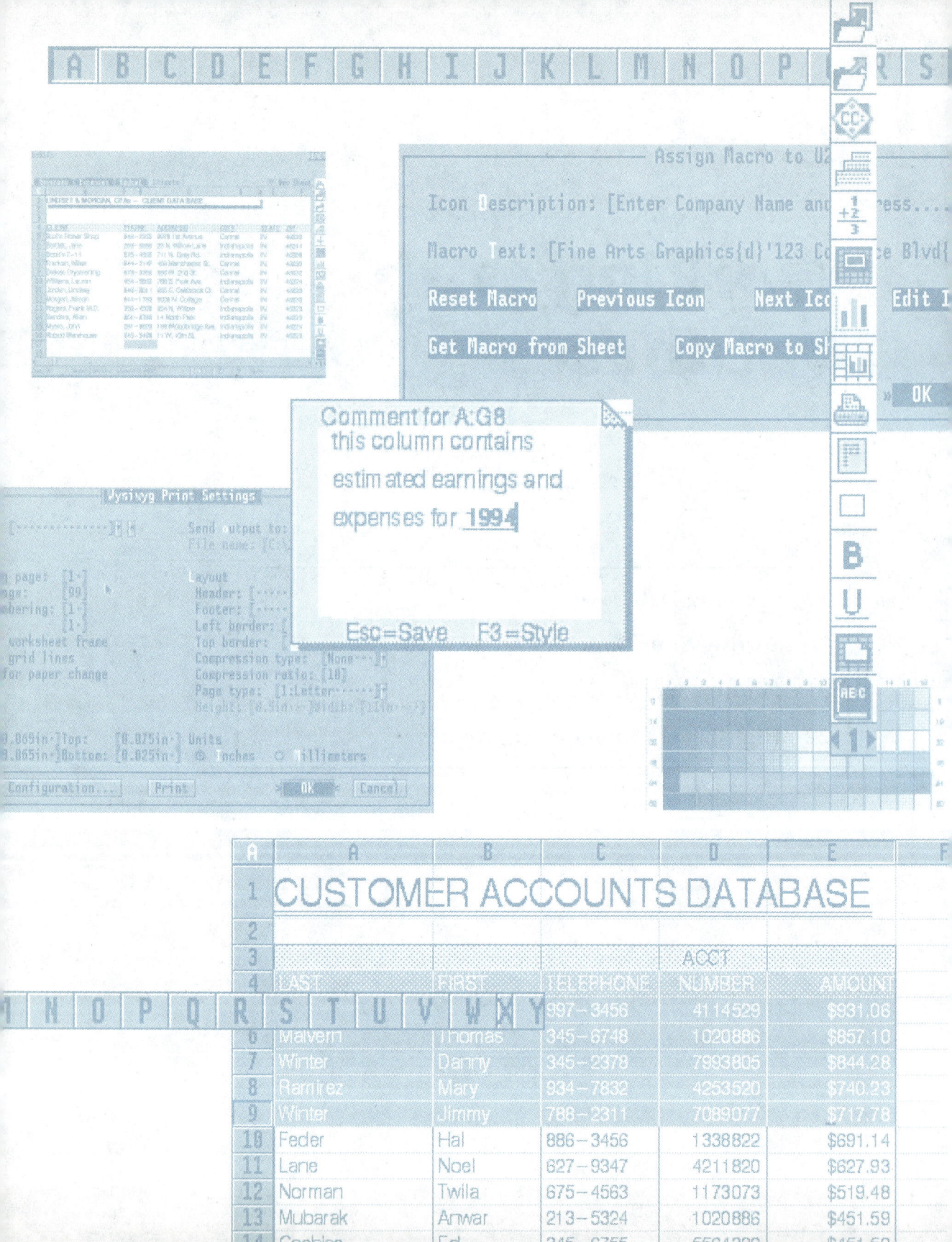

Chapter 19

Creating Databases

In addition to the electronic spreadsheet and business graphics, 1-2-3 has a third capability: data management. These three elements, along with 1-2-3's virtual memory capability, provide a powerful software package for 1-2-3 users. *Virtual memory* is a technique that enables 1-2-3 to use files that are too large to fit in main memory. Virtual memory creates a *temporary* file (also known as a swap file) on the hard disk as an extension to main memory.

Release 4 provides many strong database features, including some of the relational enhancements and large database capabilities found in products such as dBASE.

The database functionality of 1-2-3 Release 4 is easy to use because data management is integrated with worksheet and graphics functions. The commands to add, modify, and delete items in a database are the same commands that you already use to manipulate cells or groups of cells within a worksheet. Creating graphs from ranges in a database is as easy as creating graphs in a worksheet.

This chapter shows you how to

- Understand the advantages and limitations of 1-2-3's database
- Design a database
- Create, modify, and maintain data records

Defining a Database

A *database* is a collection of related information—data organized so that you can list, sort, or search its contents. A database can contain all kinds of information, from addresses to tax-deductible expenditures. A telephone book is one kind of database; personal address books, personal checkbooks, and Rolodex files also are common databases.

Usually, you work with three kinds of database organizations in 1-2-3. The simplest of these database organizations is a single database contained in a single worksheet. You use this organization in most of the examples in this chapter and the following two chapters, and also in most real-world applications. You also can work with multiple databases in 1-2-3, with each database occupying a different portion of one worksheet. Finally, with 1-2-3's three-dimensional capabilities, you can work with multiple databases on two or more worksheets. Note that a single database table, however, cannot span worksheets.

Databases are made of fields and records. A *field*, or single data item, is the smallest unit in a database. If you develop an information base of companies with which you do business, for example, you can include the following six pieces, or fields, of information about each company:

Name

Address

City

State

ZIP

Phone

A *record* is a collection of associated fields. Each of the six fields in the preceding example represents one record about one company. In 1-2-3, a field is a single cell, and a record is a row of cells within a database.

For a database to be useful, you must have access to the information the database holds. Retrieval of information usually involves key fields. A database *key field* is a field on which you base a list, sort, or search operation. You can use the ZIP field, for example, as a key field to sort the data in the company database and to assign contact representatives to specific geographic areas.

Designing a Database

A 1-2-3 database resides within the worksheet's row-and-column format. Figure 19.1 shows the general organization of a 1-2-3 database. Labels, or *field names*, that describe the data items appear as column headings. Information about each data item (field) occupies a cell in the appropriate column. In figure 19.1, cell A5 represents data (Suzi's Flower Shop) for the first field (CLIENT) in the database's first record.

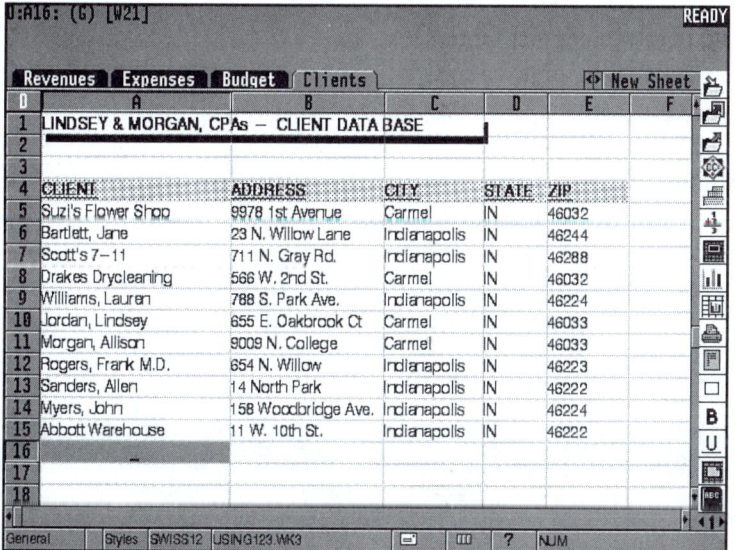

Fig. 19.1

Organizing a client database in a 1-2-3 worksheet.

In theory, the maximum number of records you can include in a 1-2-3 database corresponds to the maximum number of rows in the worksheet (8,192 rows minus 1 row for the field names). Realistically, however, your computer system's available memory determines the number of records you can include in a specific database.

When you estimate the maximum database size you can use on your computer, remember that you must accommodate the maximum output you expect from extract operations (you learn about extract operations in Chapter 21, "Finding Specific Data"). You also can split a large 1-2-3 database into separate database tables on different worksheet levels—if you don't need to sort or search all the data as a unit. You can separate a telephone list database, for example, by name (A through M in one file; N through Z in another) or area code.

You access the menu of **/D**ata commands from the 1-2-3 command menu. Because all the options (**W**orksheet, **R**ange, **C**opy, **M**ove, **F**ile, **P**rint, and **G**raph) that precede **D**ata on the main menu work as well on databases as they do on worksheets, the power of 1-2-3 is at your fingertips.

You also can use 1-2-3's file-translation capabilities (see Chapter 9, "Working with Files") or 1-2-3's **/D**ata **E**xternal command (see Chapter 30, "Sharing 1-2-3 Data with Databases") to access database files created with other products.

When you select **/D**ata from the 1-2-3 command menu, the following options appear in the control panel's second line:

Fill **T**able **S**ort **Q**uery **D**istribution **M**atrix **R**egression **P**arse **E**xternal

The **S**ort and **Q**uery (search) options are true data-management operations. (These options are described in Chapters 20 and 21.) You use most of the other options (**F**ill, **T**able, **D**istribution, **M**atrix, **R**egression, and **P**arse) for data-creation and data-manipulation operations. (Refer to Chapter 22 to learn how to use these options.) You use the **E**xternal option to access database files created with other database programs. (Chapter 30 shows you how to use this option.)

> **Note**
>
> Now with 1-2-3 Release 4, you can assign names to your worksheets within a file. So if you create your database on a separate sheet, identify your database by assigning a name to the sheet. Notice in figure 19.1 that the database worksheet is named "Clients." To name a worksheet, use the **/W**orksheet **N**ame command or double-click the worksheet tab. Then type the name that you want to assign to the worksheet, using up to 15 characters.

Tip
If you add a database to a file—for example, if you add a client database to a budget file—insert a new sheet and create the database on the new sheet. If you put the database on a separate sheet, you eliminate the possibility of the database or database operations interfering with the budget data.

Creating a Database

You can create a database as a new worksheet file or as part of an existing worksheet. If you decide to build a database as part of an existing worksheet, choose a worksheet area that you don't need for other uses. Select an area large enough to accommodate the number of records you plan to enter during the current session and in the future. Better yet, add another worksheet to the current file. Adding another worksheet prevents the database and an existing worksheet from interfering with each other.

To add a worksheet to the current file, use the /**W**orksheet **I**nsert **S**heet command. You can add the worksheet before or after the current worksheet. You can also add a worksheet by clicking the New Sheet button. When you use the New Sheet button to add a worksheet, 1-2-3 adds the worksheet after the current worksheet.

After you add the database worksheet, disable GROUP mode by selecting /**W**orksheet **G**lobal **G**roup **D**isable. Disabling GROUP mode prevents column-width settings and row or column insertions (or deletions) in one worksheet from applying to the other worksheet. Click the worksheet tab that you want to work in, or use Ctrl+PgUp or Ctrl+PgDn to move between the worksheets. Use /**W**orksheet **W**indow **P**erspective to arrange multiple worksheets together on-screen.

You create a database by specifying field names across a row and then entering the appropriate data in the cells below the field names (see fig. 19.2). You enter database information exactly as you enter any information into a worksheet; the critical step in creating a useful database is choosing fields properly.

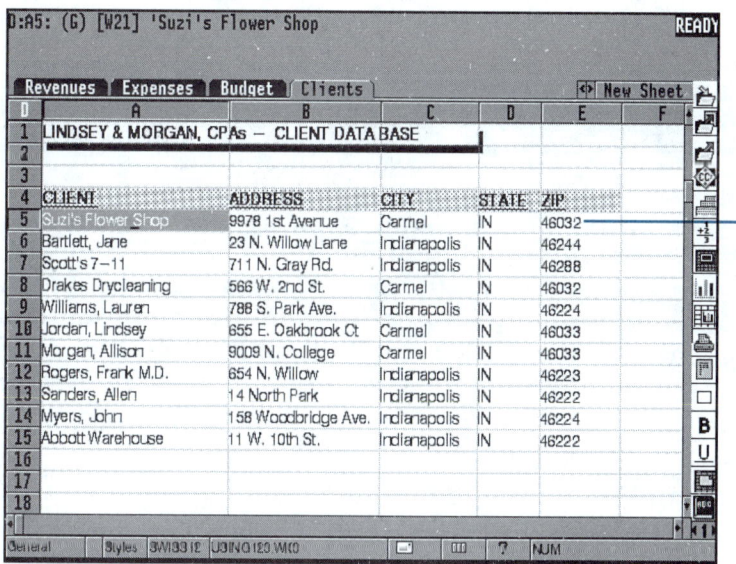

Fig. 19.2
The first record (row) in a client database.

The first database record

Entering Field Names

1-2-3's data-retrieval techniques rely on locating data by field names. You may want to write down the output you expect from the database before you create the field names. If you want 1-2-3 to locate data based on account numbers, for example, you must include an account number field.

You can use the following field names for a client mailing list database:

Client

Address

City

State

ZIP

When you enter each field name, adjust the column width to accommodate the information for the field. The default column width of 9, for example, is rarely wide enough to accommodate addresses.

> **Caution**
>
> You can make a common error in setting up the database if you choose a field name (and enter data) without thinking about the output you want from that field. Suppose that you want to find database records based on last names. If you have a single name field, rather than a first name field and a last name field, you must create a complex formula to find records based on the last name.

> **Note**
>
> To get maximum flexibility when working with dates in a database, enter each date as a value. If you enter the dates as labels, you cannot perform a math-based search for all dates within a specified period of time or before a certain date. If you enter a date as a label, you can search only for this specific date—just as you search for the last name, Smith. You don't need to use the @DATE function to enter dates; Release 4 recognizes the simpler *MM/DD/YY* form as a date entry. Remember that you enter dates as values formatted to appear as dates.

Entering Data

After planning the database, you are ready to build it. To understand how this process works, create a Client database as a new database in a blank worksheet. Enter the field names across a single row (A4..E4 in figure 19.2).

Keep in mind that all field names must be unique; any repetition of names confuses 1-2-3 when you search or sort the database. The field names also must be labels, not values. You can, however, include numeric labels by entering a label prefix before the value. For example, if you need numeric field names, such as 1994, 1995, and so on, or department numbers, such as 400 or 500, enter the field names as labels, as in '1994, ^1995, "400, '500.

Although you can use more than one row for the field names, 1-2-3 uses only the labels that appear in the bottom row as the field name. In the database in figure 19.2, if you type **STREET** in cell B3, the second field name in the Client database remains ADDRESS, and doesn't change to STREET ADDRESS.

To control the manner in which 1-2-3 displays cells on-screen, you use the program's **/R**ange **F**ormat and **/W**orksheet **C**olumn **S**et-Width options. In figure 19.2, notice that the column widths on the worksheet vary (from 7 to 21 characters).

> **Note**
>
> 1-2-3 Release 4 includes a new menu choice that allows you to adjust the width of a column in a worksheet to accommodate the largest entry in a selected range. To adjust the column width, select **/W**orksheet **C**olumn **F**it-Widest. You can also adjust the width of a column to fit the largest entry by double-clicking the top of the column.

After you enter the field names and alter the column widths, you can add records to the database. To enter the first record, move the cell pointer to the row directly below the first field name and then enter the data across the row. To enter the first record shown in figure 19.2, for example, type these entries in the following cells:

A5: **Suzi's Flower Shop**

B5: **'9978 1st Avenue**

C5: **Carmel**

D5: **IN**

E5: **'46032**

Notice that you enter the contents of the ADDRESS and ZIP fields as labels by typing a ' label character. You enter ZIP codes as labels because some ZIP codes begin with zero. If you enter a ZIP code that starts with zero as a number, 1-2-3 drops the zero and then the ZIP code is incorrect.

Several examples in this and the following two chapters use this sample client database to illustrate the results of using the **/D**ata commands. In this example, the fields fit on a single screen. In many databases, however, you track more data items.

Tip
If the database data looks crowded, insert blank columns to change the spacing between fields. If a field with right-aligned numeric entries precedes a field that contains left-aligned label entries, the two fields may run together on-screen and in print.

626 Chapter 19—Creating Databases

> **Note**
> As your database sets larger, you can freeze the field names at the top of the worksheet so that they are always displayed and you can easily see into which field you are entering data. Freeze the field names with the **/W**orksheet **T**itles command.

◀ "Naming Worksheets," p. 463

◀ "Entering Data into the Worksheet," p. 64

◀ "Setting Column Widths," p. 121

◀ "Freezing Titles On-Screen," p. 238

> **Troubleshooting**
>
> *The number of records being entered in the database is so extensive that the field row scrolls off the screen.*
>
> As you are entering a large number of rows in 1-2-3, or in this case a large number of records in a database, the rows that appear at the top of the screen scroll off the screen as you move down the worksheet. This makes it difficult, however, to see which field you are entering data in. To prevent this problem, simply freeze the field row as the horizontal title row. To freeze the field row, place the cell pointer in the first record row and select **/W**orksheet **T**itles **H**orizontal. 1-2-3 keeps the field row on-screen at all times. To clear the title row, select **/W**orksheet **T**itles **C**lear.
>
> *The completed database is missing an important field.*
>
> When you were designing your database, you probably forgot to include this field in a column. If the placement of the field is not important, you can simply add another field at the end of the database. If placement is important, just insert another column for the field by placing the cell pointer in the column that you want to appear immediately to the right of the new field, and then clicking the Insert Column SmartIcon.

Modifying a Database

After you enter the data into the database, you use many standard 1-2-3 commands to maintain the accuracy of the database. To add and delete records in a database, use the same commands for inserting and deleting rows that you use in a 1-2-3 worksheet. Because records correspond to rows, you begin inserting a record by selecting **/W**orksheet **I**nsert **R**ow or by clicking the Insert Row SmartIcon. You then fill in the various fields in the rows with the appropriate data. Figure 19.3 shows a record being inserted in the middle of a database. Instead of inserting a record in the middle of a database, however, you can add new records at the end of the database and then use 1-2-3's sorting capabilities, which are illustrated in the following section, to rearrange the order of database records.

To delete records, move the cell pointer to the row or rows you want to delete and select **/W**orksheet **D**elete **R**ow, or click the Delete Row SmartIcon. If you aren't using Undo (Alt+F4), be extremely careful when you choose the records to delete. If you want to remove only inactive records, use the **/D**ata **Q**uery **E**xtract command to store the extracted inactive records in a separate file before you delete the records (a procedure that is explained in Chapter 21).

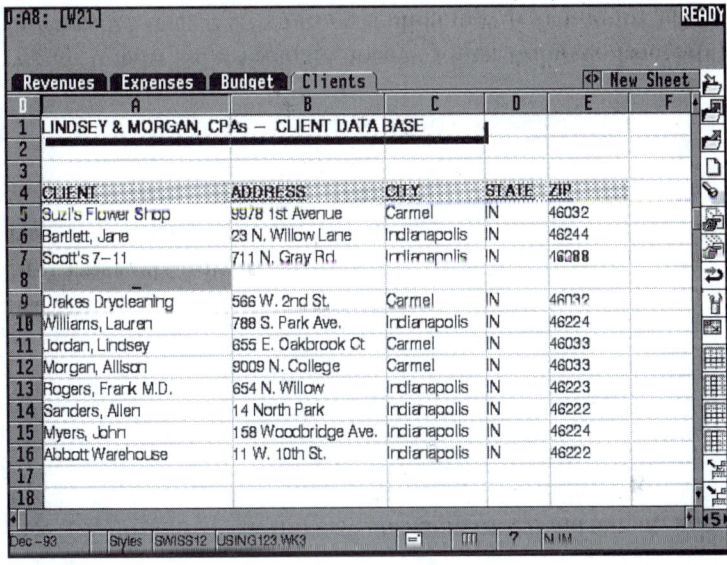

Fig. 19.3
Insert a record into a database by clicking the Insert Row SmartIcon.

> **Caution**
>
> If the database is in a multilevel worksheet file, use **/W**orksheet **G**lobal **G**roup **D**isable to ensure that when you insert or delete rows or columns in one worksheet, 1-2-3 doesn't insert or delete these rows or columns in other worksheets.

You modify fields in a database the same way you modify the contents of cells in any other application. As you learned in Chapter 2, "What Every 1-2-3 User Should Know," you change the cell contents by either retyping the cell entry or using Edit (F2) and then editing the entry.

You can add a new field to a database by inserting a new column. To add a new column to a database, place the cell pointer anywhere within the column that you want to appear immediately to the right of the new column. (1-2-3 inserts columns to the left of the current column.) You issue the

/Worksheet **I**nsert **C**olumn command or click the Insert Column SmartIcon to insert a new column. You then can enter the field name and information for each record in the new column. For example, to insert a PHONE field between the CLIENT and ADDRESS fields, as shown in figure 19.4, place the cell pointer on any cell in the ADDRESS column. Then issue the **/W**orksheet **I**nsert **C**olumn command or click the Insert Column SmartIcon and type the new field name (**PHONE** in cell B3).

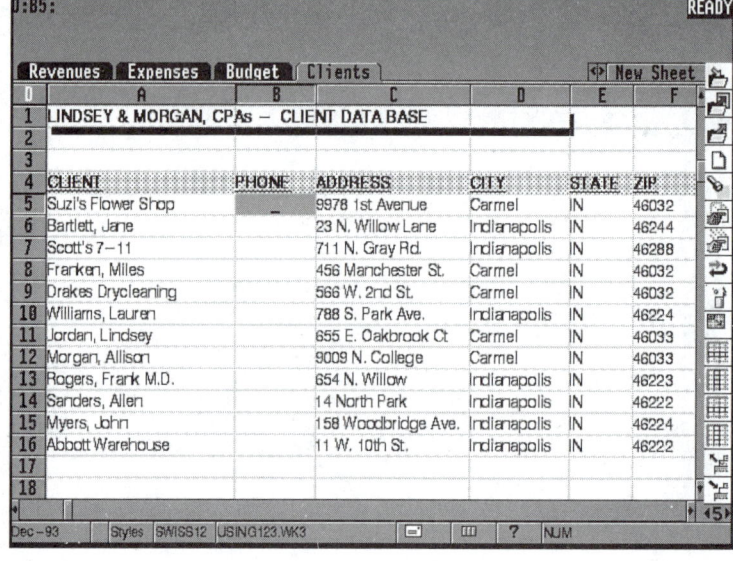

Fig. 19.4
Insert a new column for the PHONE field by placing the cell pointer in the ADDRESS field and clicking the Insert Column SmartIcon.

◀ "Editing Data in a Worksheet," p. 68

◀ "Erasing Data," p. 116

◀ "Inserting and Deleting Rows and Columns," p. 117

◀ "Setting Column Widths," p. 121

To delete a field, place the cell pointer anywhere in the column you want to remove; then select the **/W**orksheet **D**elete **C**olumn command or click the Delete Column SmartIcon.

All other commands, such as the commands for moving cells, copying cells, and formatting cells, work the same way in both database and worksheet applications.

From Here...

For more information relating to using databases in 1-2-3, you may want to review the following chapters of this book:

- Chapter 20, "Sorting Your Data." This chapter shows you how to sort the records in your database.

- Chapter 21, "Finding Specific Data." In this chapter, you learn how to search your database to find records that relate to specific criteria.

- Chapter 22, "High-Level Database Techniques." This chapter shows you how to be a power user of databases by creating frequency distributions, performing regression analyses, and so on.

Chapter 20

Sorting Your Data

In Chapter 19, "Creating Databases," you learned about 1-2-3's database capabilities and how to design and create a database in a worksheet. A database is of little use, however, unless you can sort and retrieve necessary data. In this chapter, you learn how to change the order of the records in a database based on the criteria (fields) that you select. (Chapter 21 shows you how to retrieve specific data in a database.) For example, you can sort your client database alphabetically (by client name) in either ascending or descending order.

This chapter shows you how to

- Sort records in a database based on a primary key (field), a secondary key, and an extra key

- Determine how 1-2-3 will sort data based on the collating sequence that you select

- Restore the original order of records in a database

Sorting Database Records

1-2-3's data-management capability enables you to change the order of records by sorting these records according to the contents of the fields. You can use the /Data Sort command only with a worksheet database, not with an external database. Selecting /Data Sort produces the following menu:

    Data-Range **P**rimary-Key **S**econdary-Key **E**xtra-Key **R**eset **G**o **Q**uit

The first step in sorting the database is to specify a *data range*. This range must include all the records to sort and all the fields in each record. (If you are unfamiliar with how to designate or name ranges, refer to Chapter 2.)

In figure 20.1, the Client database covers the range from A5..F16. This range, which doesn't include the field name row, is the range you specify as the **D**ata-Range when sorting.

Fig. 20.1
The records in the Client database appear as they are entered until you issue the /**D**ata **S**ort command.

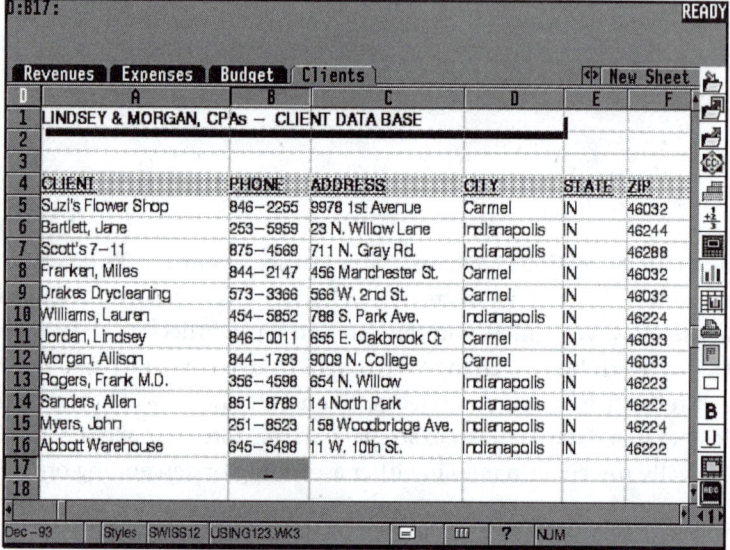

> **Caution**
>
> If you don't include all fields when sorting, you destroy the integrity of the database because parts of one record end up with parts of other records. Make sure, too, that the **D**ata-Range doesn't include the field name row; otherwise, 1-2-3 sorts the field name row with the records.

The **D**ata-Range doesn't need to include the entire database. If part of the database already has the desired organization, or if you don't want to sort all the records, you can sort only a portion of the database.

After selecting the **D**ata-Range, you must specify the keys for the sort. The *key* is the field 1-2-3 uses to determine the sort order of the records. The field with the highest precedence is the **P**rimary-Key, and the field with the next-highest precedence is the **S**econdary-Key. You may designate the CITY field in figure 20.1, for example, as the primary (first) key to use when sorting.

If two or more records have the same value in the primary-key field (the same STATE), you can select a secondary key; you may want to sort records with the same CITY alphabetically by CLIENT. You can use the **E**xtra-Key option to further define the sort precedence. You must set a **P**rimary-Key, but the **S**econdary-Key and **E**xtra-Key are optional.

When you type a primary or secondary key entry, 1-2-3 prompts you to indicate, by choosing either **A** or **D**, whether the sort is in ascending or descending order. Ascending order sorts labels from A to Z and numbers from lowest to highest. Descending order sorts labels from Z to A and numbers from highest to lowest.

After you specify the range to sort, specify the sort key(s) on which to base the reordering of the records, and indicate whether the sort order—based on the sort key—is ascending or descending, you select **G**o to execute the command. For safety, use **/F**ile **S**ave before performing the sort so that you can retrieve the original database if something goes wrong with the sort operation. To begin the sort, select **/D**ata **S**ort **G**o to sort the records.

Using the One-Key Sort

One of the simplest examples of a database sorted according to a primary key (often referred to as a *single-key* database) is the white pages of a telephone book. All records in the white pages are sorted in ascending alphabetical order, with the last name used as the primary key.

You can use 1-2-3's sorting capability to reorder records alphabetically on a field within a database. For example, in figure 20.1, the CITY field can be sorted alphabetically. To specify the range of data to be sorted, select **/D**ata **S**ort **D**ata-Range. When 1-2-3 prompts for a range to sort, type **A5..F16** or highlight this range of cells. After you specify the range, the **/D**ata **S**ort menu returns to the screen.

> **Tip**
> Use **/F**ile **S**ave before sorting the database, in case you later need to restore the original order. Another way to restore the original order is to number the records before sorting. (See the section "Restoring the Presort Order" later in this chapter for more information.)

> **Note**
> The **/D**ata **S**ort menu remains displayed and active until you select **Q**uit. This is helpful because you don't have to specify **/D**ata **S**ort at the beginning of each command in the sorting process.

Chapter 20—Sorting Your Data

> **Note**
>
> Because you can preselect ranges in 1-2-3, you can select the range to sort (**D**ata-Range) before you select the **/D**ata **S**ort **D**ata-Range command. To preselect a range, position the mouse pointer on the top left cell of the range, press and hold the left mouse button, and drag the mouse pointer to the bottom right cell of the range. After the range is highlighted, release the mouse button. You also can preselect a range by pressing F4 and then using the direction keys to highlight the range. Press Enter after the range is highlighted. 1-2-3 remembers this range unless you press Esc or move the cell pointer. When you select **/D**ata **S**ort **D**ata-Range, 1-2-3 automatically assigns the preselected range as the **D**ata-Range.

After choosing **D**ata-Range, select **P**rimary-Key and then type or point to the address of any cell in the column that contains the primary-key field. Type **D5** (for CITY), for example, as the **P**rimary-Key. 1-2-3 then asks you to choose a sort order (ascending or descending). Here, choose **A** for ascending order and press Enter. Finally, select **G**o from the menu to execute the sort. Figure 20.2 shows the database, sorted in ascending order by city.

Fig. 20.2

Sorting the database in ascending order by the CITY field.

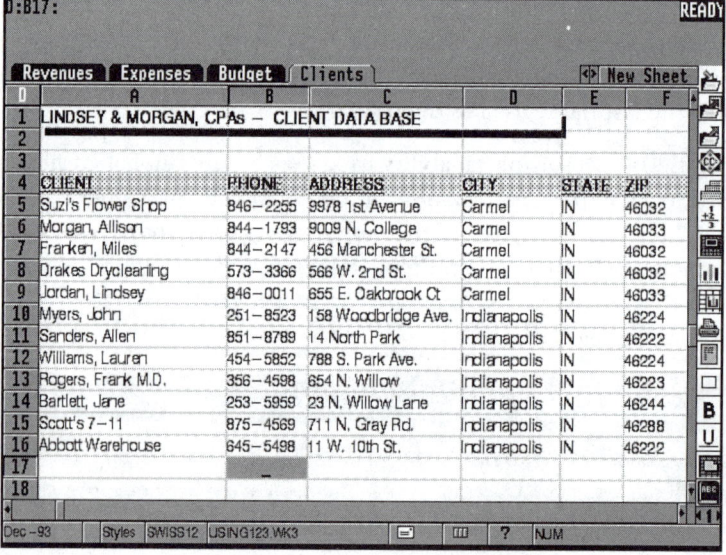

To arrange the database in a different order, such as descending by CLIENT, select /**D**ata **S**ort **P**rimary-Key. Notice that the CITY field remains selected; point to cell A5 (for CLIENT) and press Enter. Type **D** for descending, press Enter, and then select **G**o (see fig. 20.3). Here, you don't need to select the **D**ata-Range again (which 1-2-3 remembers) because you added no records.

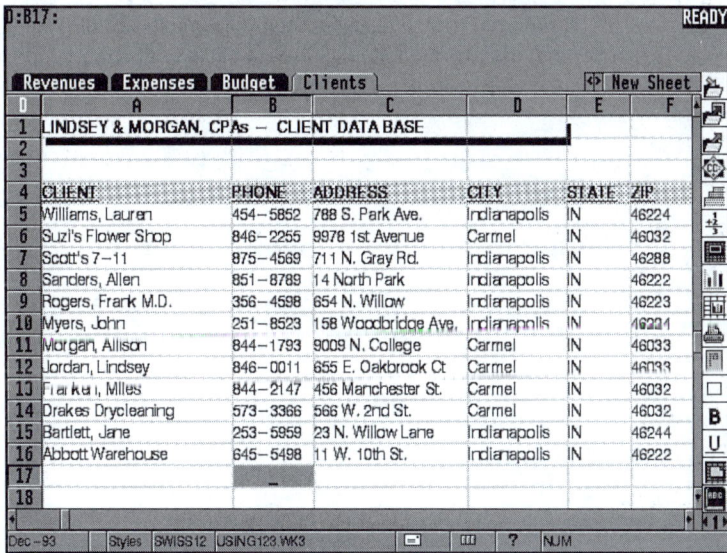

Fig. 20.3
Sorting the database in descending order by the CLIENT field.

You can execute a quick sort by highlighting the data range and clicking the Ascending Sort SmartIcon or the Descending Sort SmartIcon. If you highlight the range from left to right, 1-2-3 uses the extreme left column of the data range as the primary key. If you highlight the range from right to left, 1-2-3 uses the extreme right column of the data range as the primary key.

If you click either the Ascending Sort SmartIcon or the Descending Sort SmartIcon, a dialog box appears, indicating the range to be sorted, the key column, and the sort order. Figure 20.4 shows the appearance of the QuickSort dialog box after you highlight the range A5..F16 and then click the Ascending Sort SmartIcon.

Fig. 20.4
The QuickSort dialog box appears when you click the Ascending or Descending Sort SmartIcons.

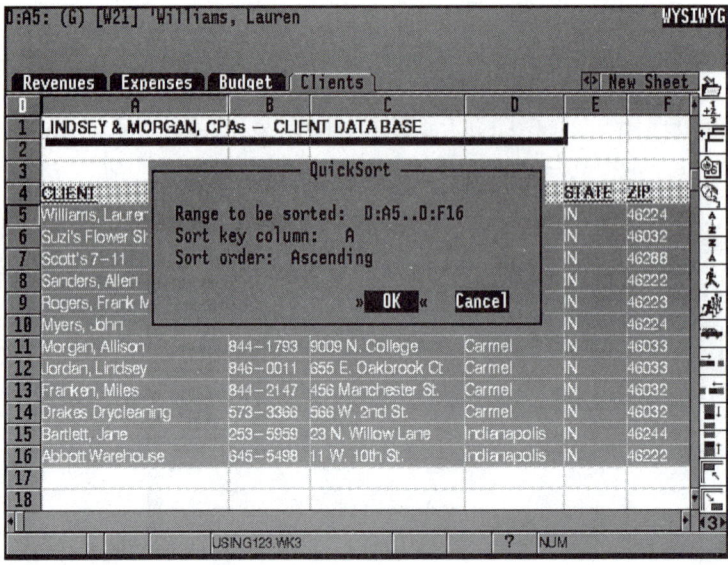

After you select OK, the database is sorted alphabetically by the CLIENT field, as shown in figure 20.5.

Fig. 20.5
Sorting the database by CLIENT, using the one-key sort.

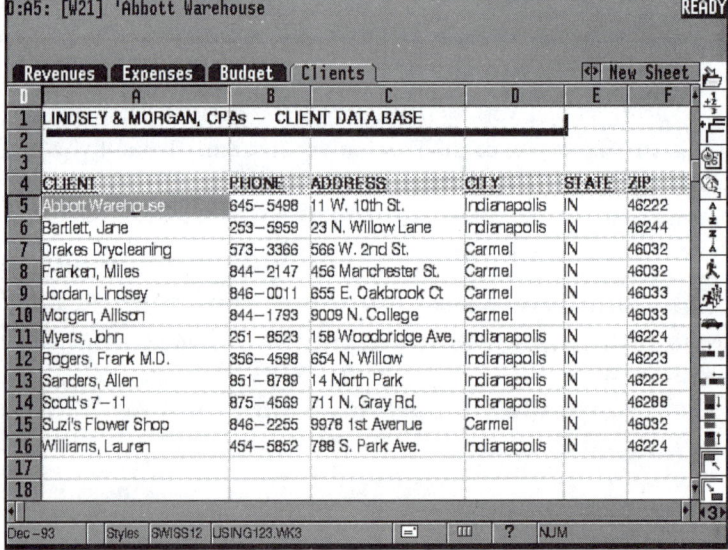

Although you cannot set up multiple-key sorts by using the Sort SmartIcons, the Ascending Sort and the Descending Sort SmartIcons are excellent tools for performing quick, one-key sorts.

You can add a record to a sorted database without inserting a row to place the new record in the proper sorted position; just add the new record to the bottom of the current database, expand the **D**ata-Range, and then sort the database again, using the desired sort key.

Using the Two-Key Sort

A two-key sort uses both a primary and a secondary sort key. The yellow pages of the telephone book, for example, sorts records first according to business type—the primary key, and then by business name—the secondary key. The secondary key determines the sort order when two or more records contain identical values in the primary-key field.

To simulate a two-key sort—first sorting by one key and then sorting by another key within the first sort order—select **/D**ata **S**ort **D**ata-Range. Note that the **D**ata-Range still is set. Select **P**rimary-Key; the CLIENT field still is selected as the **P**rimary-Key, so you must respecify the primary key as D5 (for CITY) and choose **A** for Ascending. Then select **S**econdary-Key; type **A5** (for CLIENT); choose **A** for the Ascending sort order. Figure 20.6 shows the results of issuing the **G**o command after you specify the two-key sort.

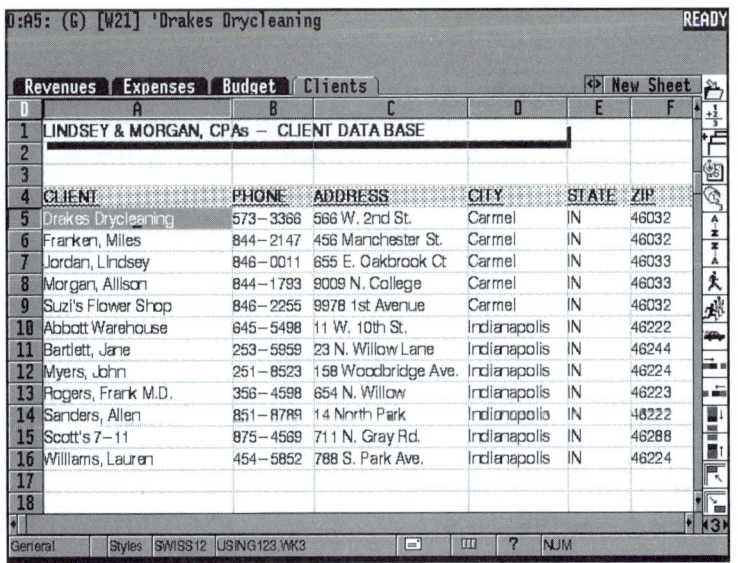

Fig. 20.6
Sorting the database by the CITY and CLIENT fields, using the two-key sort.

As figure 20.6 illustrates, records now are sorted and grouped alphabetically by CITY (Carmel, Indianapolis) and then sorted alphabetically by CLIENT within each CITY (for example, in Carmel, Drakes Drycleaning comes first, then Miles Franken, followed by Lindsey Jordan, and so on). After you determine whether to use a primary or secondary sort key, request a reasonable sort. You probably don't want to sort, for example, first by CITY and then by STATE within CITY.

Using the Extra-Key Sort

The Extra-Key option can specify up to 253 sort keys to use besides the primary and secondary sort keys. You use these extra keys to determine the sort order when two or more records contain identical values in both the primary- and secondary-key fields. The extra keys are numbered from 1 through 253 and are applied in numeric order. Use **E**xtra-Key **1** to break ties in the secondary-key field, **E**xtra-Key **2** to break ties in extra-key field 1, and so on.

To assign an extra key, use the same technique you use to assign primary and secondary keys. Select **E**xtra-Key from the **/D**ata **S**ort menu; then enter the number (1 through 253) of the extra key. Next, enter the field (column) to be used for the extra key, followed by the sort order (**A** or **D**).

Troubleshooting

After sorting the database, the field row shows up within the records.

1-2-3 sorts all rows included in the **D**ata-**R**ange. If you included the field row in the **D**ata-**R**ange, it gets sorted as if it is a record in the database. 1-2-3 arranges the database either in ascending or descending order, depending on which you choose. The field row therefore is placed within the database in its appropriate order.

After adding new records, the database is out of order.

When you add new records to a database, 1-2-3 does not automatically sort them into their proper order. You must re-sort the database to get the new records in the appropriate positions.

After sorting the database, the records aren't sorted the way I intended.

You may have chosen the wrong primary or secondary sort key when you performed the **/D**ata **S**ort operation. To undo the sort, press Alt+F4 immediately after you sort the database. You cannot use the Undo option, however, if you've performed other operations in 1-2-3. If you can't use Undo, choose the **/F**ile **R**etrieve command to close the current worksheet (but don't save your changes); then retrieve it again.

> **Note**
>
> The **/D**ata **S**ort **R**eset command resets the **D**ata-Range and all sort keys. To reset an extra sort key without resetting the **D**ata-Range or all the sort keys, assign the extra sort key's number to the data field used by a higher sort key. To cancel **E**xtra-Key **2**, for example, select **/D**ata **S**ort **E**xtra-Key, type **2**, and specify the column used by **E**xtra-Key **1**. To cancel **E**xtra-Key **1**, assign this key to the data field used by the **S**econdary-Key.

Determining the Sort Order

When you installed 1-2-3, you established a collating-sequence setting. This setting determines certain aspects of the sort order. The three options for this setting are Numbers First, Numbers Last, and ASCII. Table 20.1 shows the effects of each setting. (The table shows the effects of an ascending order sort; selecting descending order reverses the orders shown.)

Table 20.1 Collating Sequences for Ascending Order

Collating Sequence	Sort Order
Numbers First	Blank cells
	Labels that begin with numbers in numerical order
	Labels that begin with letters in alphabetical order
	Labels that begin with other characters in ASCII value order
	Values
Numbers Last	Blank cells
	Labels that begin with letters in alphabetical order
	Labels that begin with numbers in numerical order
	Labels that begin with other characters in ASCII value order
	Values
ASCII	Blank cells
	All labels in ASCII value order
	Values

For Numbers First and Numbers Last, 1-2-3 ignores capitalization. For ASCII, uppercase letters precede lowercase letters (*Drakes* comes before *benson*, for example).

Problems can arise when you specify numbers as labels, because 1-2-3 sorts from left to right, one character at a time. If you sort the company database in ascending order according to ADDRESS, for example, the result of the sort looks like figure 20.7.

Fig. 20.7
1-2-3 sorts numbers in label fields (such as the ADDRESS field) one character at a time.

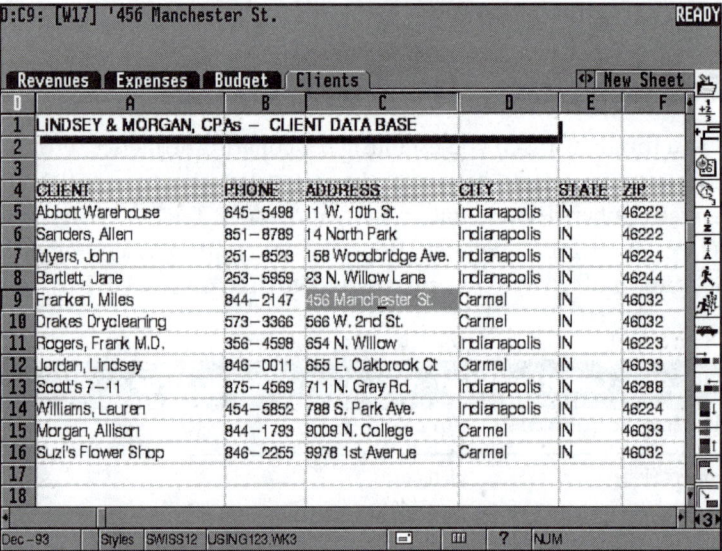

Although you may expect the records to be sorted in ascending order on the ADDRESS field, notice that the 158 in row 7 appears before the 23 in row 8. This problem occurs because 1-2-3 sorts the numbers one character at a time when sorting labels; therefore, 158 actually is considered to be 1 for sorting purposes, and 23 is considered to be 2.

Restoring the Presort Order

If you sort the database on the ADDRESS field, you cannot restore the records to the original order (refer to fig. 20.5) unless you have Undo enabled. If you add a record number column to the database before a sort, however, you can reorder the records on any field and then restore the original order by sorting again on the record number field. Use the **/D**ata **F**ill command to automatically enter record numbers before sorting the database. In figure 20.8, a record number column is added to the database.

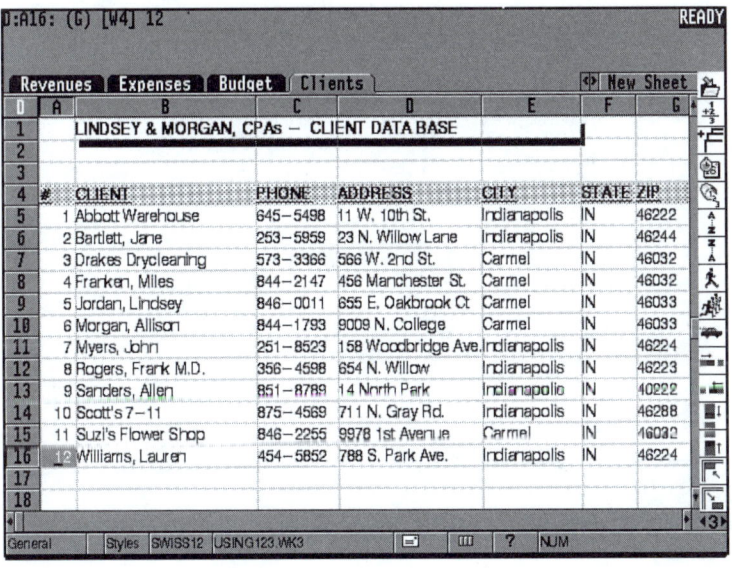

Fig. 20.8
Adding a record number field makes it easy to restore the presort order of a database.

◀ "Filling Ranges with Data," p. 70

From Here...

For more information relating to using databases in 1-2-3, you may want to review the following major sections of this book:

■ Chapter 21, "Finding Specific Data." In this chapter, you learn how to search your database to find records that relate to specific criteria.

■ Chapter 22, "High-Level Database Techniques." This chapter shows you how to be a power user of databases, creating frequency distributions, performing regression analyses, and so on.

Chapter 21

Finding Specific Data

If you read the previous chapter, you learned how to use the **/D**ata **S**ort option to reorganize information in the database by sorting records according to key fields. In this chapter, you learn how to use **/D**ata **Q**uery, the menu's other data management command, to search for records. You can either locate and then edit the record in the database, or you can extract or delete the records. You can use the **/D**ata **Q**uery commands with a 1-2-3 database or with an external table. In the latter case, you first must use the **/D**ata **E**xternal **U**se command (discussed in Chapter 30, "Sharing 1-2-3 Data with Databases") to establish a connection to the external table. Looking for records that meet certain conditions is the easiest form of searching a 1-2-3 database.

To determine which companies in Indiana are in a company database, for example, you can use a search operation to find records with IN as the value in the STATE field. You also can extract all records with an Indiana address and then print just the extracted records.

1-2-3's search operations also can look for only the first occurrence of a specified field value to develop a unique list of field entries. You can search the STATE field to extract a list of the different states, or you can delete all inventory records of a state.

In this chapter, you learn to do the following:

- Search for specific records in a database
- Extract records to another area (output range) in the worksheet
- Modify and delete records in a database
- Perform database searches based on wild-card, formula, AND condition, and special operator entries

Using Minimum Search Requirements

To initiate a search operation in a database, you select the appropriate operation from the **/D**ata **Q**uery menu.

The ten options of the **/D**ata **Q**uery menu perform the search functions described in the following table.

Menu Item	Description
Input	Gives the location of search area; must be specified in all **Q**uery operations.
Criteria	Gives the locations of search conditions; must be specified in all **Q**uery operations.
Output	Specifies a range where a **Q**uery command copies records or parts of records to an area outside the database. Necessary only when you select a **Q**uery command that copies records or parts of records to an area outside the database (**E**xtract, **U**nique, or **M**odify).
Find	Moves down through a database and places the cell pointer on records that match given criteria. You can enter or edit data in the records as you move the cell pointer through the records.
Extract	In a specified area of the worksheet, creates copies of all or some of the fields in records that match the given criteria.
Unique	Similar to **E**xtract, but recognizes that some field contents in the database may duplicate other cell entries in the same fields. Eliminates duplicates as entries are copied to the output range.
Del	Deletes from a database all records that match the given criteria and shifts the remaining records to fill the resulting gaps.
Modify	Either inserts or replaces records in the input range with records from the output range. Use this command to add new records to a data table or to extract, modify, and then reinsert records in a database.
Reset	Removes all previous search-related ranges so that you can specify a different search location and conditions.
Quit	Returns 1-2-3 to READY mode.

To perform a **Q**uery operation, you must specify both an input range and a criteria range, and select one of four search options. Before you can issue an **E**xtract, **U**nique, or **M**odify command, you also must specify an output range.

Determining the Input Range

The input range for the **/D**ata **Q**uery command is the range of records you want to search. In the company database shown in figure 21.1, specifying an input range of A4..F9 defines the entire database as the search area. Although you usually use the entire database as the input range, you can specify a portion of the database as the input range.

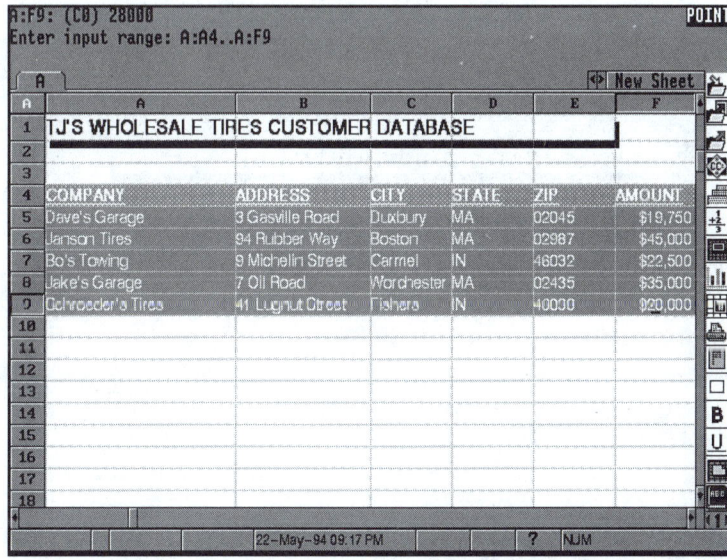

Fig. 21.1
Specifying the input range of the database.

Whether you search all or only a part of a database, you must include the field-name row in the input range. (Remember that you must not include field names in a sort operation.) If field names occupy space on more than one row, specify only the bottom row to start the input range. In the company database, because row 4 contains the field names, you start the input range with row 4 (by entering **A4..F9**).

Select **/D**ata **Q**uery **I**nput, and specify the range by typing the cell addresses, by pointing to the cell addresses, or by typing a range name. You need not specify the range again unless the search area changes. To search more than one database, enter the ranges one after the other, separated by a comma.

Tip
The input range can contain a single database or multiple-worksheet and/or external databases.

Entering the Criteria Range

If you want 1-2-3 to search for records that meet certain criteria, you must enter the criteria in terms that 1-2-3 understands. Suppose that you want to identify all records in the database from Indiana. These records contain IN in the STATE field. After the database is on-screen and 1-2-3 is in READY mode, type **STATE** in cell A12 and **IN** in cell A13 (refer to fig. 21.2). These two cells contain the criteria range for the search. If desired, you can type **Criteria Range** in cell A11 to document that A12 and A13 contain the criteria range, although this step isn't really necessary. (In practice, you place the criteria range to one side of, not below, the database range. The criteria range is below the database range here to allow the entire operation to appear on-screen.)

Fig. 21.2
Adding a criteria range to the database.

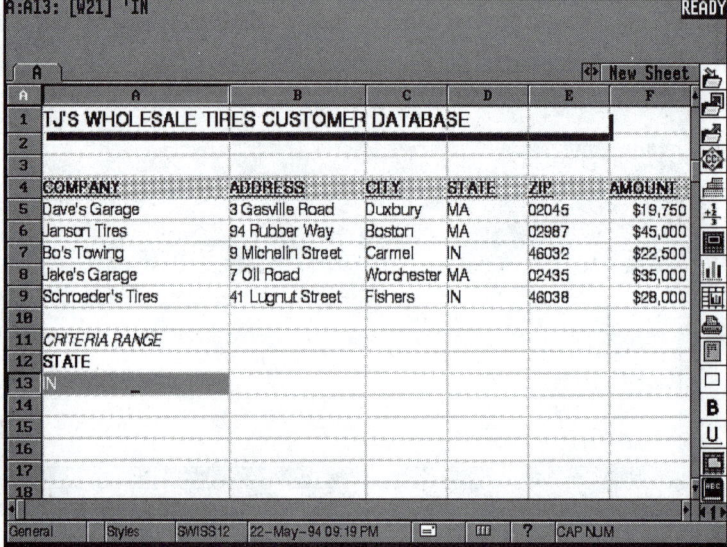

Select **/D**ata **Q**uery, and specify A4..F9 as the input range. The **Q**uery menu appears in the control panel after you enter the input range. Select **C**riteria, and then type or point to the range A12..A13 as the location of the search condition. The **Q**uery menu again returns to the screen.

You can use numbers, labels, or formulas as criteria. A criteria range can include up to 256 fields in at least two rows. The first row in the criteria range must contain the field names of the search criteria, such as STATE in row 12 of figure 21.2. The rows below the unique field names in the criteria range contain the actual criteria, such as IN in row 13. The field names of the input range and the criteria range must match exactly.

> **Caution**
>
> **/D**ata **Q**uery commands work only if the field names in the input range and the criteria range match exactly. To ensure that the field names in the input range and the criteria range are exactly the same, copy the field names from the input range to the criteria range.

By entering criteria in the worksheet and by specifying the input and criteria ranges, you complete the minimum steps needed to execute a **F**ind or **D**el command.

Using the Find Command

After you select **F**ind from the **/D**ata **Q**uery menu, a highlighted bar rests on the first record (in the input range) that meets the conditions you specified in the criteria range. In this example, the highlighted bar rests on the first field of the first record that includes IN in the STATE field—the third record in the database (see fig. 21.3).

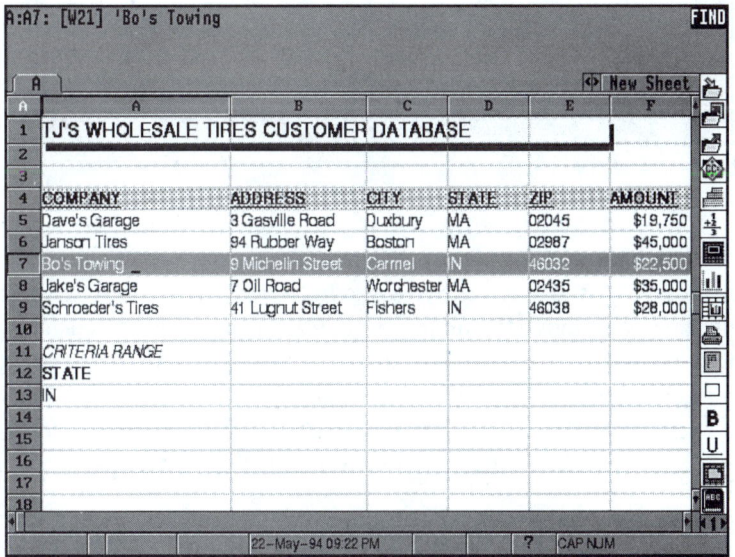

Fig. 21.3
The initial record highlighted in the **F**ind operation.

648   Chapter 21—Finding Specific Data

By using the down-arrow key, you can move the highlight to the next record that meets the criteria. Continue pressing the down-arrow key until the last record that meets the criteria is highlighted. Figure 21.4 shows the second and last record that meets the highlighted criteria after the down-arrow key is pressed. Notice that the mode indicator changes from READY to FIND during the search.

Fig. 21.4
The final record highlighted in the Find operation.

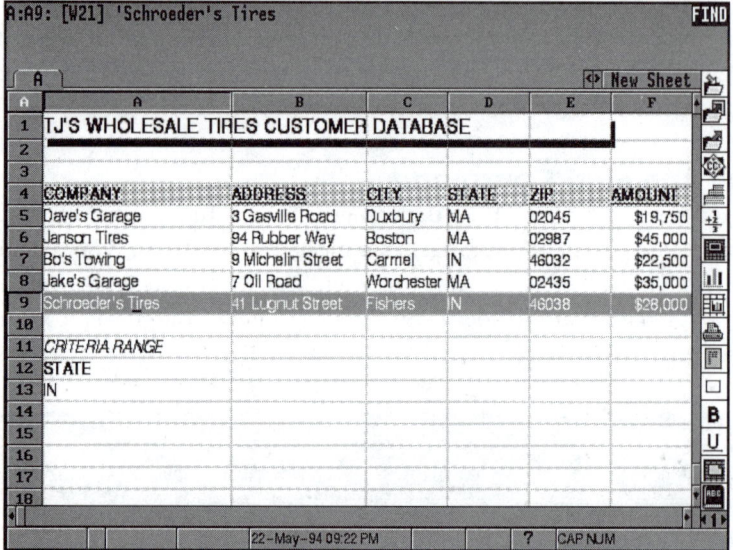

You use the down- and up-arrow keys to place the highlighted bar on the next and previous records that meet the search criteria. You can use the Home and End keys to reach the first and last matching records. The right- and left-arrow keys move the highlight to different fields in the current record. You can enter new values or use the Edit (F2) key to update the current values in any field; however, if you change the record in a manner so that the field no longer satisfies the Find criteria and then move away from this record, you cannot return to the record during the Find operation.

Suppose that you need to change the amount of money Schroeder's Tires owes you. You aren't sure how to spell *Schroeder's*, but you know the business is in Indiana. You search for records with the STATE of IN and locate Schroeder's Tires. To change the value in the AMOUNT field, press the right-arrow key five times to move the cell pointer to the AMOUNT column (see fig. 21.5). The entire record remains highlighted but, as the control panel in figure 21.6 shows, the current cell is A:F9.

Using Minimum Search Requirements   649

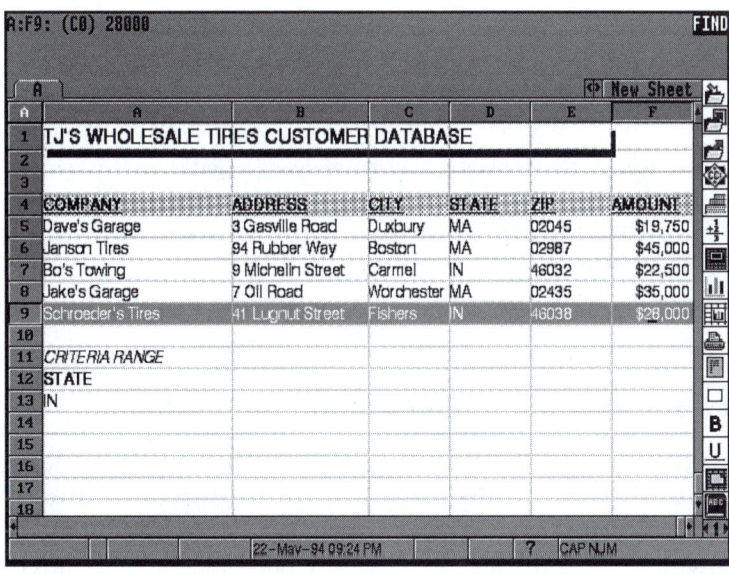

Fig. 21.5
The cell pointer moved to the last field of the current record.

Press F2 to edit the highlighted cell and change the AMOUNT value to **7500**. Figure 21.6 shows the changed record. Notice that you still are in FIND mode.

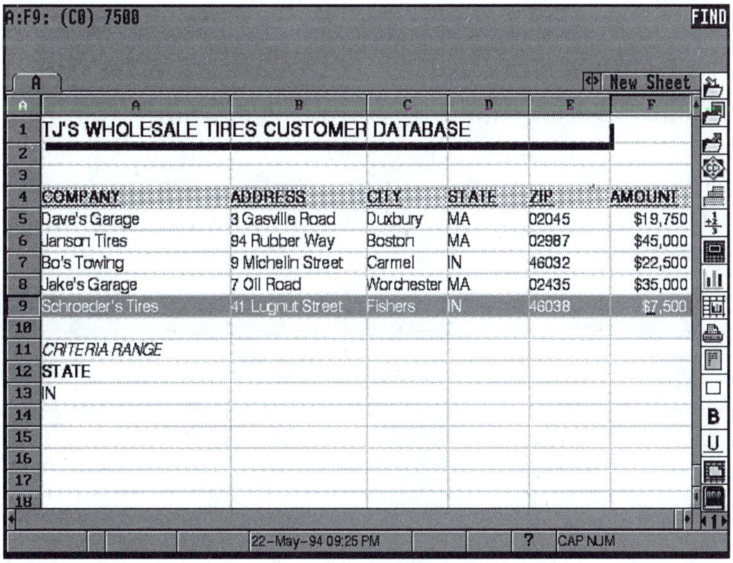

Fig. 21.6
The AMOUNT value changed to $7,500 for Schroeder's Tires.

To end the **F**ind operation and return to the **/D**ata **Q**uery menu, press Enter or Esc. To return directly to READY mode, press Ctrl+Break.

> **Troubleshooting**
>
> *The highlighted field in a record cannot be edited.*
>
> If you want to edit fields in a highlighted record during a Find operation, use the arrow keys to move the cell pointer to the field that you want to change and then press F2 to activate the Edit mode so that you can edit the field. After editing, press Enter to return to Find mode.

Listing All Specified Records

The **F**ind command has limited use, especially in a large database, because the command must scroll through the entire file if you want to view each record that meets the specified criteria. As an alternative, you can use the **/D**ata **Q**uery **E**xtract command to copy to an output range all records that meet the conditions. You then can view, print, or even use the **/F**ile **X**tract command on the extracted records contained in the output range.

Defining the Output Range

Tip
To avoid mismatch errors, use the **/C**opy command to copy the database field names in the criteria and output ranges.

Choose a blank area in the worksheet as the output range to receive records copied in an **E**xtract operation. Designate the range to the right of, or below, the database. In the first row of the output range, type or copy the field names of only the fields whose contents you want to extract. You don't have to include all the field names. Also, the field names don't have to appear in the same order as in the database, although the field names used in both the criteria and output ranges must match the corresponding field names in the input range exactly.

> **Note**
>
> Because Releases 3.1, 3.1+, 3.4, and 4.0 incorporate Wysiwyg publishing features, these versions of 1-2-3 match field names in input and output ranges differently than do earlier versions. Previous releases include field-name label prefixes as criteria for matching. Early 1-2-3 releases, for example, don't match a centered database field name with the corresponding left-justified field name. Releases 3.1, 3.1+, 3.4, and 4.0, however, ignore the field name label prefixes when matching field names.

Select **/D**ata **Q**uery **O**utput and then type or point to the range location of the output area. You can create an open-ended extract area by entering only the field-name row as the range, or you can set the exact size of the extract area.

To limit the size of the extract area, enter the upper-left and lower-right cell coordinates of the entire output range. The first row in the specified range must contain the field names; the remaining rows must accommodate the maximum number of records you expect to receive from the **E**xtract operation. Use this method when you want to retain additional data located below the extract area. In figure 21.7, for example, naming A15..F18 as the output range limits incoming records to three (one row for field names and three record rows). If you don't leave sufficient room in the fixed-length output area, the extract operation aborts and the message Too many records appears on-screen.

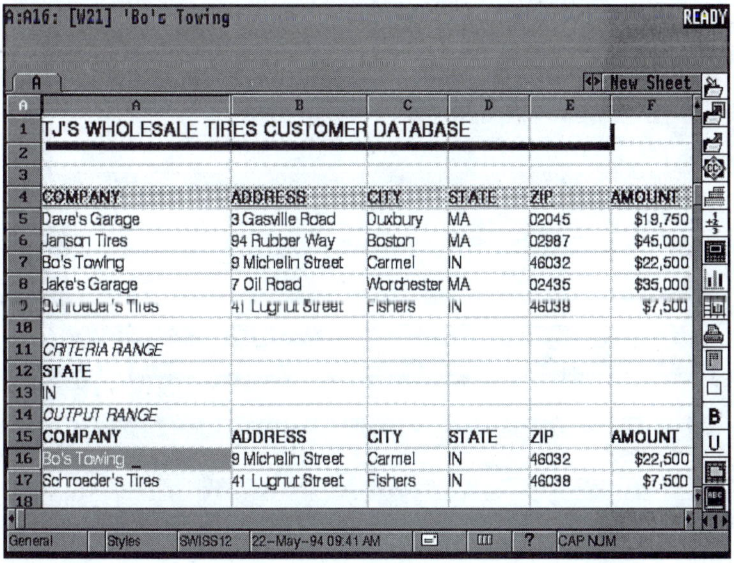

Fig. 21.7
A successful **E**xtract operation.

To create an open-ended extract range that doesn't limit the number of incoming records, specify as the output range only the row that contains the output field names. By naming A15..F15 as the output range, you define the area to receive records from an **E**xtract operation without limiting the number of records (see fig. 21.7).

An **E**xtract operation first removes all existing data from the output range. If you use only the field-name row to specify the output area, 1-2-3 destroys all data below this row to make room for the unknown number of incoming extracted records. Before you issue the **E**xtract command, make sure that you don't need any data contained below the output range.

Because Release 3 and later version files can have multiple worksheets, the best way to work with these database capabilities is to place the input range, the criteria range, and the output range on separate worksheets. If the database ranges are on different worksheets, you eliminate possible conflicts when adding data to the input range or extracting records to the output range. Figure 21.8 shows a multiple worksheet database set up in perspective view. You can see the input range in worksheet A, the criteria range in worksheet B, and the output range in worksheet C.

Fig. 21.8
Setting up a three-dimensional database.

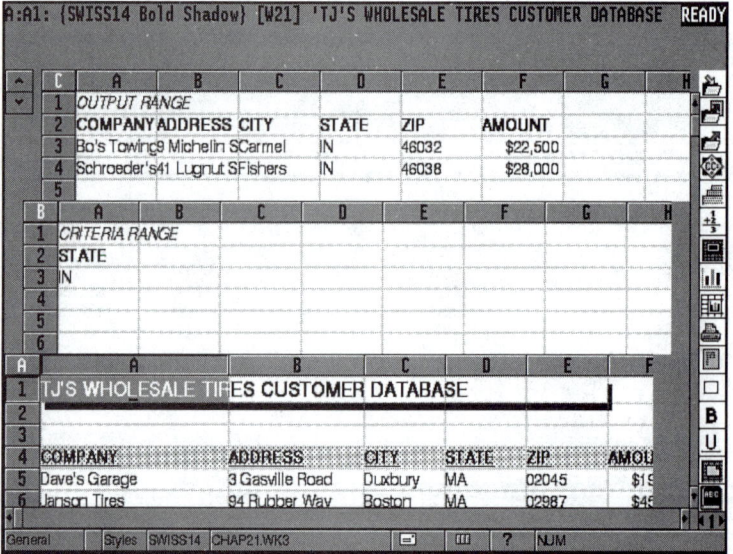

> **Caution**
>
> If you create an open-ended extract area, 1-2-3 eliminates all data below the output field names, down to row 8192 (the last row in the worksheet), after you select **/D**ata **Q**uery **E**xtract.

Executing the Extract Command

To execute an **E**xtract command, you must type the search conditions in the worksheet; copy the output field names in the worksheet; and set the input, criteria, and output ranges from the **/D**ata **Q**uery menu.

The input and criteria ranges are established in the company database example that we've been working with so far. To establish the output range, select **/D**ata **Q**uery **O**utput and type or point to the range A15..F15. Then select **/D**ata **Q**uery **E**xtract. The operation extracts the two records with Indiana companies.

You don't have to extract entire records or maintain the order of field names within the extracted records. You can create an extract list that contains only the COMPANY and AMOUNT fields, as the following section that details **/D**ata **Q**uery **M**odify shows.

Modifying Records

You can use the **/D**ata **Q**uery **M**odify command to extract records for modification and then return the modified records as new records or replacements of the original versions. You also can place the modified records in an output range located in another worksheet or external table.

The first steps in using **/D**ata **Q**uery **M**odify are exactly like the steps in using **/D**ata **Q**uery **E**xtract. You first specify input, criteria and output ranges and then you select **/D**ata **Q**uery **M**odify **E**xtract to extract the matching records to the output range. The **/D**ata **Q**uery **M**odify **E**xtract command records the original location of each extracted record so that you later can reinsert the record correctly after editing. Don't add or delete rows in the output range, however, or 1-2-3 cannot replace the records correctly.

> **Note**
>
> After you extract the records that you want to modify using the **/D**ata **Q**uery **M**odify **E**xtract command, press Ctrl+Break to return to READY mode. You can then make changes to the records in the output range.

After you edit the records, select **/D**ata **Q**uery **M**odify **R**eplace or **/D**ata **Q**uery **M**odify **I**nsert. If you select **R**eplace, the original records in the input range are replaced by the edited versions from the output range. If you select **I**nsert, the records from the output range are appended at the end of the input range, and the original records remain in place. In either case, 1-2-3 doesn't delete the records in the output range.

Tip
You can specify an output range in another worksheet or in an external table by using the **/D**ata **Q**uery **E**xtract command.

Tip
You can guard against destroying existing data in the current worksheet by using the three-dimensional worksheet features of Release 3 and later versions to extract data to another worksheet.

654   Chapter 21—Finding Specific Data

> ### Troubleshooting
>
> *1-2-3 does not replace the records in the database with the modified records that you entered.*
>
> You may have used **/D**ata **Q**uery **E**xtract to extract the records that you want to change to the output range. When you use **/D**ata **Q**uery **E**xtract, 1-2-3 does not record the original location of extracted records and therefore cannot replace the original records with the modified records. Instead, use **/D**ata **Q**uery **M**odify **E**xtract to extract the records that you want to change.

Figures 21.9 and 21.10 show an example of using **/D**ata **Q**uery **M**odify. In this example, you change the amount owed by the companies located in Indiana. You use an output range that contains only the COMPANY and AMOUNT fields. In figure 21.9, you use **/D**ata **Q**uery **M**odify **E**xtract to extract the records for Indiana companies and then change the AMOUNT values. As figure 21.10 shows, the **/D**ata **Q**uery **M**odify **R**eplace command replaces the original values in the input range with the updated numbers.

Fig. 21.9
Extracting information in the database by using **/D**ata **Q**uery **M**odify **E**xtract.

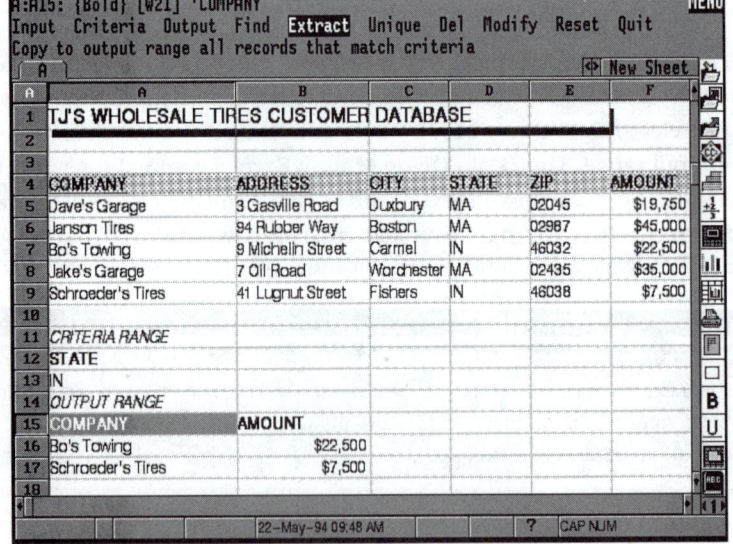

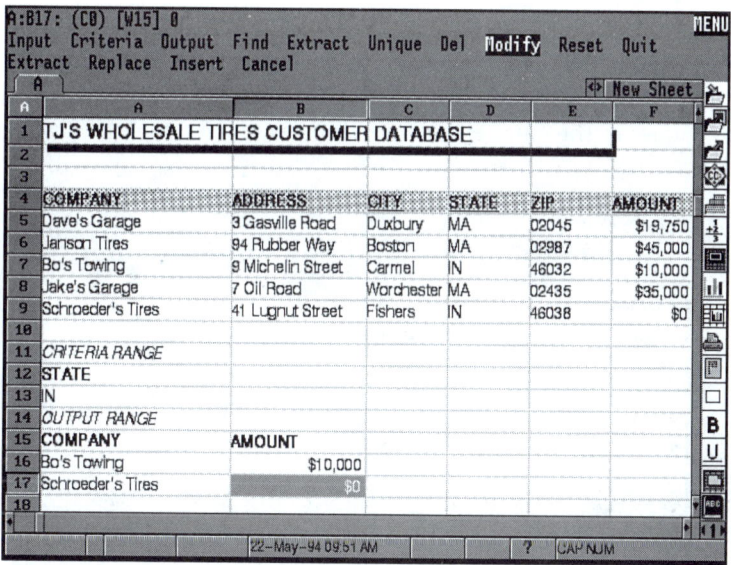

Fig. 21.10
Replacing database information by using /**D**ata **Q**uery **M**odify **R**eplace.

◄ "Editing Data in a Worksheet," p. 68

> **Caution**
>
> After you perform a /**D**ata **Q**uery **M**odify **E**xtract, you *must* select /**D**ata **Q**uery **M**odify **R**eplace before you perform any worksheet operations that alter the database data. If you select /**D**ata **Q**uery **M**odify **E**xtract and then erase data in the worksheet, for example, you receive the message Error replacing extracted records after you select /**D**ata **Q**uery **M**odify **R**eplace. If you alter the structure of the database or change database data, 1-2-3 breaks the connection to the records established when a /**D**ata **Q**uery **M**odify **E**xtract is performed. This connection enables 1-2-3 to know where to put records when you select /**D**ata **Q**uery **M**odify **R**eplace.

Extracting Unique Records

You can produce (in the output range) a copy of the first occurrence only of a record that meets a specified criterion by issuing the /**D**ata **Q**uery **U**nique command. Ordinarily, you use the **U**nique command to copy into the output area only a small portion of each record that meets the criteria. To create a list of the states in the database, for example, set up an output range that includes only the STATE field (cell A16 in fig. 21.11). To search all records,

656 Chapter 21—Finding Specific Data

leave blank the row below the field-name row in the criteria range. You must, however, include the blank row when you define the criteria range. Then set the output range at A16 and select **/D**ata **Q**uery **U**nique to produce a list of the three states in the database.

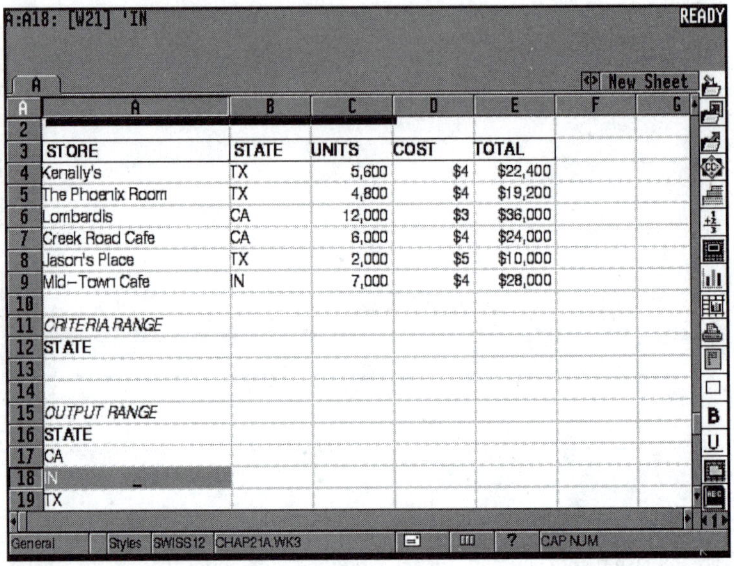

Fig. 21.11
The result of a
/Data **Q**uery
Unique command.

	A	B	C	D	E
3	STORE	STATE	UNITS	COST	TOTAL
4	Kenally's	TX	5,600	$4	$22,400
5	The Phoenix Room	TX	4,800	$4	$19,200
6	Lombardis	CA	12,000	$3	$36,000
7	Creek Road Cafe	CA	6,000	$4	$24,000
8	Jason's Place	TX	2,000	$5	$10,000
9	Mid-Town Cafe	IN	7,000	$4	$28,000
10					
11	CRITERIA RANGE				
12	STATE				
13					
14					
15	OUTPUT RANGE				
16	STATE				
17	CA				
18	IN				
19	TX				

As another example, if you have a large mailing-list database, you can produce a list of ZIP codes to assist in preparing mailings. To produce this list, specify in the output area only the field name ZIP, leave blank the row under ZIP in the criteria range, and execute the **/D**ata **Q**uery **U**nique command.

As with **/D**ata **Q**uery **E**xtract and **/D**ata **Q**uery **M**odify **E**xtract, you can specify as the output range an external table where 1-2-3 is to place the results of a **/D**ata **Q**uery **U**nique operation.

Deleting Specified Records

The **/D**ata **Q**uery **D**el enables you to delete all records that meet a specified criterion. As you learned in Chapter 2, "What Every 1-2-3 User Should Know," you can use the **/W**orksheet **D**elete **R**ow command or the Delete Row SmartIcon to remove rows from a worksheet. If you want a fast alternative to this one-by-one approach, use the **/D**ata **Q**uery **D**el command to remove unwanted records from the database files. Before you select **D**el from the **Q**uery menu, specify the range of records 1-2-3 is to search (input range) and the conditions for the deletion (criteria).

Suppose that you want to remove all records of companies in Indiana by using the criterion IN in the STATE field. Then issue the **/D**ata **Q**uery **D**el command to delete the rows and remove all records for states that match IN for Indiana. The remaining records group together, and the input range adjusts.

> **Caution**
>
> Use extreme caution when you issue the **/D**ata **Q**uery **D**el command. To give you the opportunity to change your mind, 1-2-3 displays the following menu, with the left (the least dangerous) command highlighted:
>
> **C**ancel **D**elete
>
> Choose **C**ancel to abort the **D**el command. Select **D**elete to verify that you want to execute the delete operation.

Although the **/D**ata **Q**uery **D**el command doesn't display the exact rows to delete, you can guard against deleting the wrong records by first saving the file or by using the **/D**ata **Q**uery **F**ind (or **/D**ata **Q**uery **E**xtract) command to examine the records before you perform the delete operation.

> **Tip**
> Use **/D**ata **Q**uery **E**xtract before you execute a **/D**ata **Q**uery **D**el command. If the extracted records are the ones you want to delete, you know the delete criteria are correct and you then can perform the **/D**ata **Q**uery **D**el command.

Handling More Complicated Criteria Ranges

Besides searching for an *exact match* to a single label field, 1-2-3 enables you to conduct a wide variety of record searches. You can perform searches on exact matches to numeric fields, on partial matches of field contents, on fields that meet formula conditions, on fields that meet several conditions, and on fields that meet either one condition or another. The following section focuses on some variations of queries on single fields.

Using Wild Cards in Criteria Ranges

You can use 1-2-3's wild cards for matching labels in database operations. The characters ?, *, and ~ have special meaning in the criteria range. The question mark (?) instructs 1-2-3 to accept any character in this specific position; you can use this character only to locate fields of the same length. The asterisk (*) tells 1-2-3 to accept all characters that follow; you can use this character on field contents of unequal length. By placing a tilde symbol (~) at the beginning of a label, you tell 1-2-3 to accept all values except the values that follow. Table 21.1 shows how you can use wild cards in search operations.

Table 21.1 Using Wild Cards in Search Operations

Type	To Find
N?	Any two-character label starting with the letter N, such as NC, NJ, and NY.
BO?L?	A five-character label such as BOWLE or BOLLI, but not a shorter label like BOWL or longer label like BOWLEY.
BO?L*	A four-or-more character label such as BOWLE, BOWL, BOLLESON, and BOELING.
SAN*	A three-or-more character label starting with SAN and followed by any number of characters, such as SANTA BARBARA and SAN FRANCISCO.
SAN *	A four-or-more character label starting with SAN followed by a space, and then followed by any number of characters—such as SAN FRANCISCO—but not SANTA BARBARA.
~N*	Strings that don't begin with the letter N.

> **Caution**
>
> The * wild card matches all characters after a single character or characters but doesn't match characters *before* a single character or characters. Using the criteria *s, for example, to find all matches in a field that end with the letter *s* doesn't work.

Use the ? and * wild-card characters when you are unsure of the spelling or when you need to match several slightly different records. Always check the results by using **/D**ata **Q**uery **F**ind or **/D**ata **Q**uery **E**xtract before you use wild cards in a **D**el command. If you aren't careful, you may remove more records than you intend.

> **Note**
>
> To get an exact case-sensitive match, use @EXACT. The criterion *Tyler*, for example, finds TYLER, tyler, Tyler, and so on. If you want to find only the uppercase instances of Tyler, use **@EXACT(B4,"TYLER")** (where B4 is the first cell underneath the field name). This criterion returns only instances of TYLER. You cannot use wild-card characters with this technique, because 1-2-3 matches the search string exactly.

Using Formulas in Criteria Ranges

To set up formulas that query numeric or label fields in the database, you can use the following relational operators:

Handling More Complicated Criteria Ranges

Operator	Meaning
>	Greater than
>=	Greater than or equal to
<	Less than
<=	Less than or equal to
=	Equal to
<>	Not equal to

Create a formula that references the first field entry in the numeric column you want to search. 1-2-3 tests the formula on each cell, and follows down the column until the program reaches the end of the specified input range.

You can use a formula, for example, to extract the records that have a UNITS entry with a value of less than 6000. First, type '**<6000** in cell A13 (see fig. 21.12).

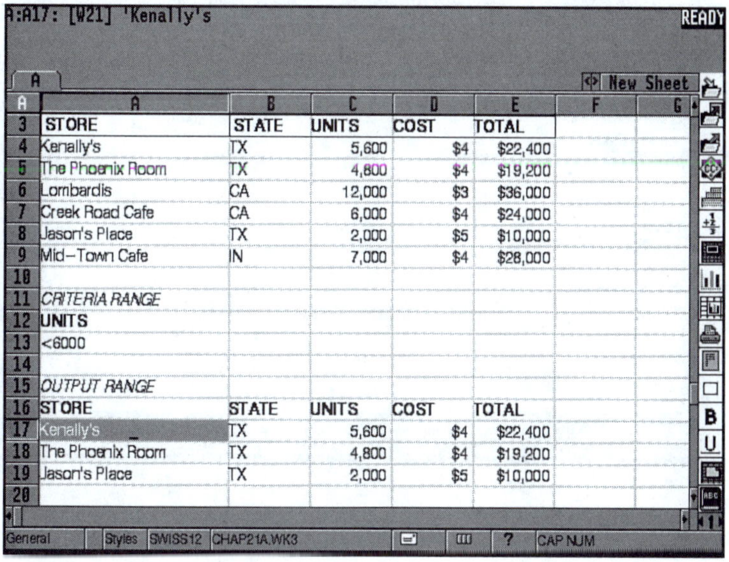

Fig. 21.12
Using a relational formula condition to extract records.

After you correctly specify the input, criteria, and output ranges, executing an **Extract** operation produces three records for which the value in UNITS is less than 6000.

660 Chapter 21—Finding Specific Data

Tip
To find blank cells in the database, use +B4="" (where B4 is the first cell beneath the field name). For the sample database, this search string finds all records with no entry in the STATE field.

> **Note**
>
> Release 3.4 and 4 enable you to use a shorthand syntax for criteria formulas—type the formula as '<6000 rather than the longhand version of +C5<6000 (which is used in other versions of 1-2-3). Because pressing the < key is an alternative method for displaying the 1-2-3 main menu, you must type a label prefix before you enter the formula in this format.

To reference cells outside the database, you must use formulas that include absolute cell addressing. For addressing information, see Chapter 2, "What Every 1-2-3 User Should Know." Suppose that you want to extract all records that have a TOTAL entry with a value less than $20,000. You can type the number **20000** in cell C13, and then enter the formula **+E4<$C$13** in the criteria range. You must use an absolute reference to cell C13. Figure 21.13 shows the result of the extract.

Fig. 21.13
Criteria referencing a cell outside the database.

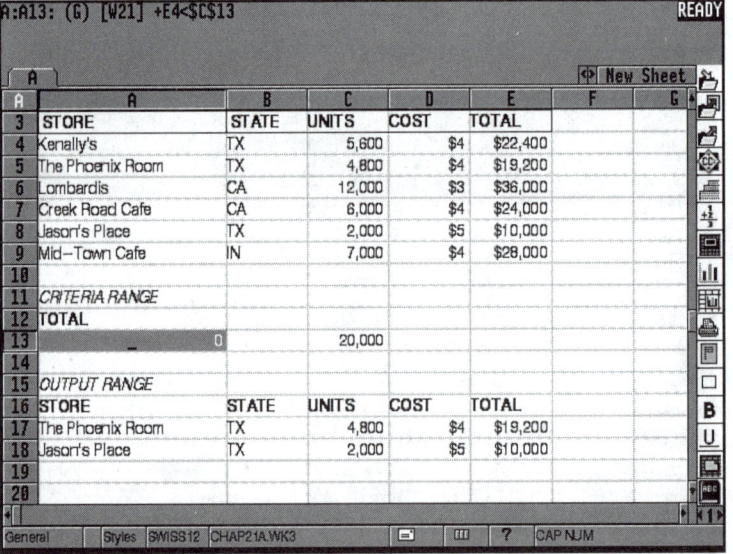

◀ "Entering Basic Formulas," p. 74

◀ "Finding and Replacing Data," p. 112

An advantage to using this method is that you can extract records quickly that have a TOTAL-column entry with a value less than another value, such as $15,000. Just enter **15000** in cell C13 (the cell referenced by the formula in the criteria), and perform the **/D**ata **Q**uery **E**xtract command again. You also can press Query (F7). The Query key (F7) repeats the most recent query operation (**E**xtract, in this example) and eliminates the need to select **/D**ata **Q**uery **E**xtract.

Setting Up AND Conditions

Now that you know how to base a **F**ind or **E**xtract operation on only one criterion, you can advance to using multiple criteria for queries. You can set up multiple criteria as AND conditions (in which *all* the criteria must be met) or as OR conditions (in which any *one* criterion must be met). Searching a music department's library for sheet music that requires drums AND trumpets, for example, probably produces fewer selections than a search for music that requires drums OR trumpets.

You indicate two or more criteria, *all* of which must be met, by specifying the conditions on the criteria row immediately below the field names. First, however, you must add another field to the criteria range. Use **/C**opy to copy the UNITS field name from C3 to B12. You must adjust the size of the criteria range by using the **/D**ata **Q**uery **C**riteria command and by typing **A12..B13** or by highlighting this range of cells. Now you can add the desired criteria to the criteria range.

For this example, if you want only the records for companies not located in Texas and with units above 6000, in cell A13 type the formula **+B4<>"TX"**. Then, in cell B13, type the criteria formula **+C4>6000**. Next, issue a **/D**ata **Q**uery **E**xtract command; 1-2-3 extracts the two records in the database that meet both conditions. The results should resemble the screen shown in figure 21.14.

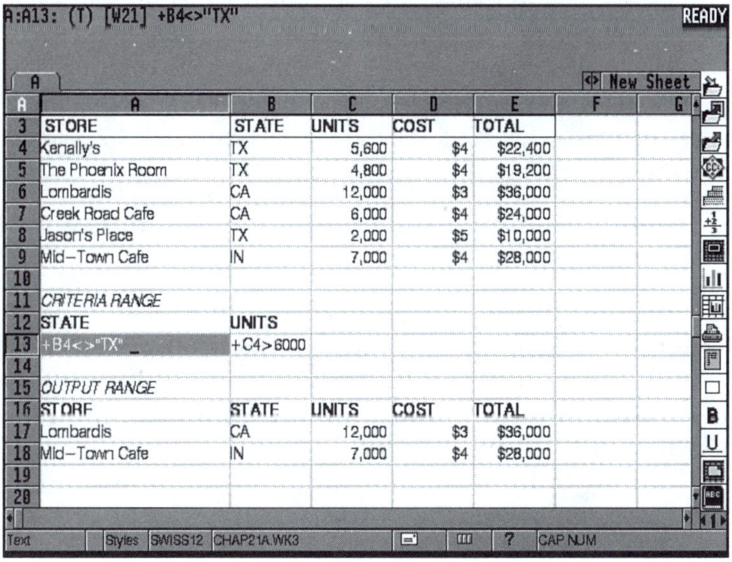

Fig. 21.14

Setting up a two-field logical AND search.

The figure shows the actual formula because the criteria cells A13 and B13 are formatted for Text (**/R**ange **F**ormat **T**ext). If the criteria cells are not formatted for Text, 1-2-3 displays either a 1 or a 0 in the cells. 1-2-3 displays a 1 if the cell meets the criteria and a 0 if the cell doesn't meet the criteria.

You can have several AND conditions in the criteria range; this capability can be useful if you have a large database with many fields. In a client database, for example, you may have a State criterion TX, a City criterion Austin, and a Last Name criterion of S*. This search finds all people in a client database from Austin, Texas (TX), whose last name begins with the letter S.

Setting Up OR Conditions

Criteria placed on the same row have the effect of a logical AND; these criteria tell 1-2-3 to find or extract on this condition AND that one. Criteria placed on *different* rows have the effect of a logical OR; these criteria tell 1-2-3 to find or extract on this condition OR that one. You can set up a logical OR search on one or more fields.

Searching a single field for more than one condition is the simplest use of an OR condition. To extract the records where the STATE is TX or IN, for example, place TX in cell A13 and IN in cell A14 and expand the criteria range to include the additional row.

You also can specify a logical OR condition on two or more different fields. Suppose that you want to search for records where either the state isn't California or the units are greater than 6000. Figure 21.15 shows the OR criteria for this search and the results. After you enter the second criteria, adjust the criteria range to include the specified OR condition by expanding the criteria range down one row. After you issue the **E**xtract command, 1-2-3 copies five records to the output range.

Notice that the formula in cell B14 is formatted for Text; therefore, you see the actual formula.

Although Lombardis doesn't meet the condition of not being in California, this account does meet the condition of having greater than 6000 units and is, therefore, extracted to the output range along with the records for companies not in California. Only one condition OR the other needs to be met for 1-2-3 to extract a record to the output range.

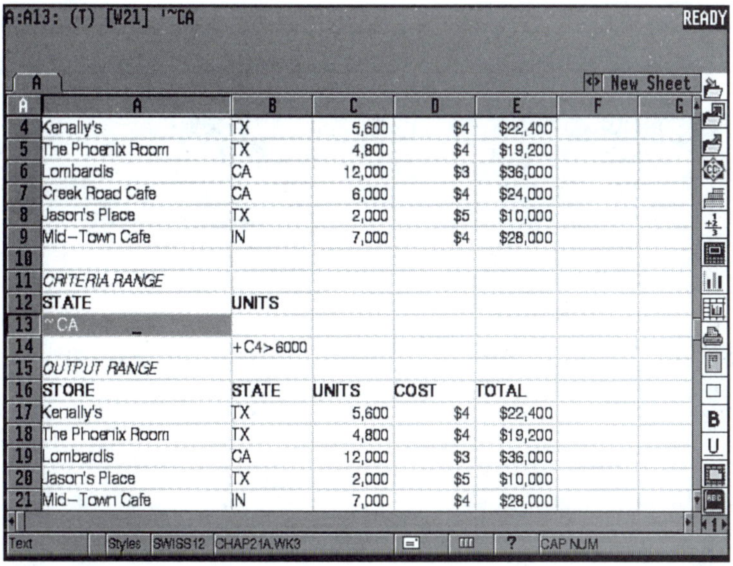

Fig. 21.15
Setting up a logical OR search on two fields.

> **Caution**
>
> Make sure that you expand the criteria range to include a new criterion. When working with 1-2-3 /**D**ata **Q**uery operations, a common mistake is to add a new criterion but forget to expand the criteria range.

To add more OR criteria, drop to a new row, type each new condition, and expand the criteria range. If you reduce the number of rows involved in an OR logical search, be sure that you contract the criteria range. Remember that a blank row in the criteria range matches all records in the database.

Although no technical reason prevents you from mixing AND and OR logical searches, you may find that correctly formulating this kind of mixed query is a difficult task. Follow the format of placing each AND condition in the row immediately below the criterion field-name row and each OR condition in a separate row below. Be careful, however, to ensure that each row in the criteria range specifies all AND conditions that apply.

Using String Searches

If you want to search on the partial contents of a field, you can use functions in a formula. Suppose that you can remember only the name *Phoenix* for a store name. You know the store name is more than just *Phoenix,* but you can't remember the rest of the name. You can use the formula shown in the

Tip
You should test the logic of the search conditions on a small sample database in which you can verify search results easily by scrolling through all records and noting which records should be extracted.

Fig. 21.16
A function condition used for a string search.

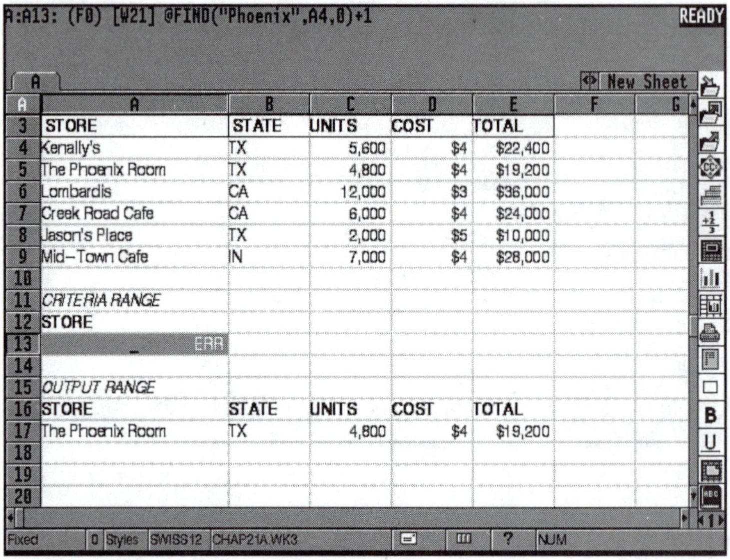

control panel of figure 21.16 as the search criterion in cell A13 (making certain, of course, to adjust the criteria range to include only cells A12 and A13).

Tip
You also can use the @LEFT and @RIGHT functions to find a portion of an entry. If you have a name field that includes first and last names, you can use @LEFT and @RIGHT to locate records by the first or last name. See Chapter 3, "Finding Solutions with Formulas and Functions," for more information.

Notice that, although 1-2-3 displays ERR in cell A13, the formula still works correctly when you issue the /Data Query Extract command. Remember that the @FIND function returns the starting position of the search string (Phoenix) in the string in which you are searching (the STORE field). If @FIND doesn't find the search string, this function returns ERR. Because Phoenix doesn't occur in the first record, the formula shows ERR. As each record is checked, however, 1-2-3 matches and returns a true value for the second record. In criteria formulas, 1-2-3 treats both ERR and zero as false and, therefore, as nonmatching values. (See Chapter 3, "Finding Solutions with Formulas and Functions," for a detailed discussion of 1-2-3 functions.)

Using Special Operators

To combine search conditions within a single field, use the special operators #AND# and #OR#. Use the special operator #NOT# to negate a search condition.

Use #AND# or #OR# to search on two or more conditions in the same field. Suppose that you want to extract all records with totals between 12,000 and 30,000. The formula shown in figure 21.17, +E4>12000#AND#E4<30000, matches the desired records. To meet the criteria, a number in the TOTAL column must be greater than 12,000 and less than 30,000.

Notice that the criteria formula in figure 21.17 is not formatted as Text. As previously described, the nonformatted formula evaluates to 1 if the criteria are true, or 0 if the criteria are false. In the example, cell E4 meets the criteria (true), and cell A13, therefore, displays the number 1.

◀ "Using the String Functions," p. 206

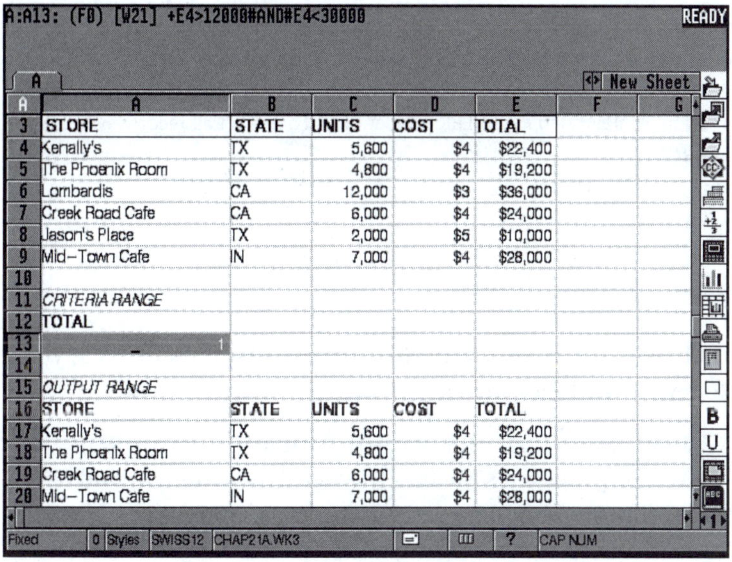

Fig. 21.17
Extracting records using the special operator #AND#.

Figure 21.18 shows an #OR# operation. Here, the #OR# condition is finding the records of California or Indiana companies.

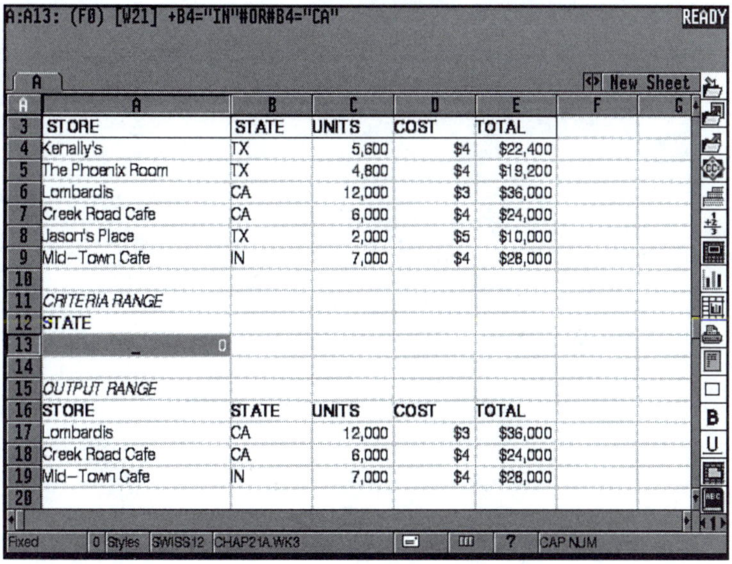

Fig. 21.18
Finding records of companies from either California or Indiana.

Use #NOT# at the beginning of a condition to negate this condition. #NOT#B4="TX" (where B4 is the first cell beneath the field name), for example, finds all companies not in Texas.

> **Note**
>
> Sometimes you need to enter **NA** into a cell to signify that the required data is "Not Available". Use **@NA** for this purpose. Then, to extract all records with NA, use **@ISNA(D4)** (where D4 is the first cell beneath the field name). At other times, certain formulas may calculate to ERR accidentally. To extract all records with ERR, use **@ISERR(D4)**.

From Here...

To learn how to use more advanced database techniques in 1-2-3, you may want to review the following chapters:

- Chapter 3, "Finding Solutions with Formulas and Functions," describes using string functions, such as the @FIND function, to find data in 1-2-3.

- Chapter 22, "High-Level Database Techniques," shows you how to create data tables and frequency distributions, perform regression analysis, and work with matrices.

Chapter 22

High-Level Database Techniques

The preceding chapters covered fundamental database operations, sorting, and querying. This chapter goes a step further to demonstrate the power available with 1-2-3's advanced data-management techniques. The definitions and examples in this chapter may help you understand how to apply these advanced concepts in your own applications.

This chapter shows you how to perform the following operations:

- Use data tables to perform what-if analysis

- Use advanced data-analysis features such as data distribution, data regression, and matrix manipulation

- Import text from ASCII files to use in your spreadsheet

Performing What-If Analysis with Data Tables

Often, you use worksheets to summarize and report on information from past events, such as last year's sales. In worksheets like this, all the information represents known quantities. Last year's sales summary, for example, deals with amounts whose exact values are known. The results of calculations performed with those values contain no uncertainties.

Other situations, however, involve variables whose exact values are not known. Worksheet models for financial projections often fall into this category. Next year's cash-flow projection, for example, depends on prevailing interest rates. Although you can make an educated guess about the interest rates, you cannot predict these variables exactly.

Data tables enable you to see the results of using different possible values for the variables in your worksheets. For example, you can use a data table to calculate what your monthly car payment will be for several different combinations of interest rate and loan period. This kind of analysis often is called *what-if* analysis. The **/D**ata **T**able commands in 1-2-3 provide a powerful, easy-to-use tool for performing what-if analysis.

Understanding Data-Table Terms and Concepts

Before you work with data tables, you must understand some terms and concepts:

- A *data table* is a table of information that 1-2-3 places in the worksheet when you choose one of the **/D**ata **T**able commands. The table includes information that you enter and information that 1-2-3 calculates when you choose the command.

- A *data-table range* is a worksheet range that contains a data table.

- A *variable* is a formula component whose value can change.

- An *input cell* is a worksheet cell that 1-2-3 uses for temporary storage during calculation of a data table. One input cell is required for each variable in the data-table formula. Each data-table formula should refer, directly or indirectly, to each input cell.

- An *input value* is a specific value that 1-2-3 uses for a variable during data-table calculations.

- The *results area* is the portion of a data table where 1-2-3 places calculation results. One result is generated for each combination of input values. The results area of a data table must be unprotected.

The formulas used in data tables can contain values, strings, cell addresses, and functions.

When you choose **/D**ata **T**able, the following menu appears:

1 2 3 Labeled **R**eset

The first four menu commands correspond to the four kinds of data tables that 1-2-3 can generate. The four table types differ in the number of formulas and variables the tables can contain. These table types are shown in the following table. The **R**eset menu option clears all table ranges and input cells for all data tables.

Command	Table Type
Data **T**able **1**	One variable, one or more formulas
Data **T**able **2**	Two variables, one formula
Data **T**able **3**	Three variables, one formula
Data **T**able **L**abeled	Unlimited variables and formulas

Creating a One-Variable Data Table

A data table created with the **/D**ata **T**able **1** command shows the effects that changing one variable has on the results of one or more formulas.

Before using this command, you must set up the data-table range and a single input cell. Then, when you choose the command, 1-2-3 fills in the table.

The input cell can be anywhere in the worksheet. The best practice is to identify the input cell by entering an appropriate label either above the input cell or to the left of the input cell.

The data-table range is a rectangular worksheet area that you can place in any empty worksheet location. The following list details the typical structure of a one-variable data-table range:

- The top row of the data-table range contains the formulas you want 1-2-3 to evaluate. Each formula must refer to the input cell.

- The left column of the data-table range contains values that you want 1-2-3 to substitute into the formulas.

- The top-left cell in the data-table range is not used. If you want, you can use this cell as the input cell.

- After the data table is calculated, each cell in the results range contains the result obtained by evaluating the formula at the top of that column with the input value at the left of that row.

◀ "Starting and Using Auditor," p. 529

Tip
To make sure that your formula cells refer to the input cell, use the Auditor to highlight the dependent formulas for the input cell. All your formulas should be highlighted.

Chapter 22—High-Level Database Techniques

Suppose that you plan to purchase a house with a 30-year mortgage in the $100,000-to-$150,000 range at a 10 percent or 11 percent interest rate. For each interest rate, you want to determine the monthly payment that results at each $5,000 interval in price, from $100,000 to $150,000.

Figure 22.1 shows a data table that will perform these calculations. In figure 22.1, cell B4 is the input cell. The formulas in cells A:C4 and A:D4 use the @PMT function to calculate the monthly payment at each interest rate.

Fig. 22.1
A one-variable table of loan-payment amounts ready to be filled in using /Data Table 1.

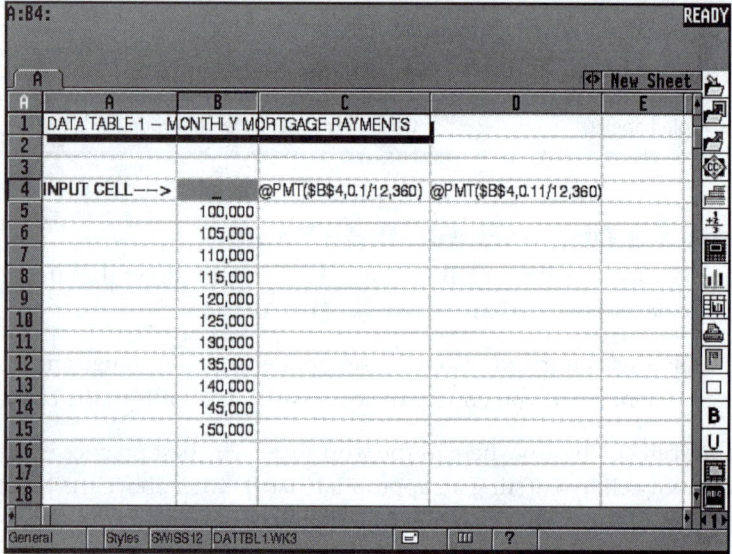

Troubleshooting

Every variable in my one-variable data table is the same.

Make sure that the formulas in the top row of the table refer to the input cell. You can use the Auditor to ensure that the formulas refer to the input cell. Another way to test this is to enter different values in the input cell. Make sure that the results of the formulas in the top row of the table change each time you change the value in the input cell.

My one-variable data table contains only zeros.

Make sure that you specified the table range correctly. The top row of the table must contain formulas that refer, directly or indirectly, to the input cell. The left column of the table must contain the values you want 1-2-3 to substitute into the input cell.

Cells B5 through B15 contain the principal amounts. To complete the table, choose **/D**ata **T**able **1**, specify B4..D15 as the table range, and type **B4** as the input cell. The resulting table, which calculates the mortgage payments on the different principal amounts at two different interest rates, is shown in figure 22.2.

Notice that cells C4 and D4 are formatted as Text so that you can see the formulas.

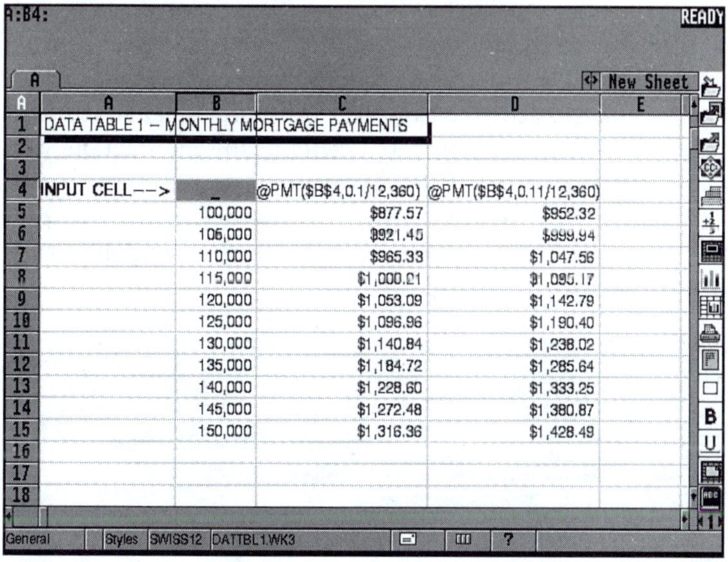

Fig. 22.2
The completed one-variable table of loan-payment amounts.

Creating a Two-Variable Data Table

A two-variable data table lets you evaluate a single formula based on changes in two variables. To use **/D**ata **T**able **2**, you need two input cells—one for each variable. You can use any cells in the worksheet as the input cells.

The size of the data-table range depends on the number of values you want to evaluate for each variable. The range is one column wider than the number of values of one variable and one row longer than the number of values of the other variable.

One difference between **/D**ata **T**able **1** and **/D**ata **T**able **2** is the location of the input values and formula(s) to be evaluated. In **/D**ata **T**able **1**, the input values are placed in the left column of the table, the formulas are placed along the top row of the table, and the top-left cell of the table is blank.

Tip
To help you remember which cells you used as the input cells, you can identify the input cells with an appropriate label in a cell next to or above each input cell.

In /Data Table 2, the input values for one variable are placed in the left column, the input values for the second variable are placed in the top row, and the top-left cell of the data table range contains the formula to be used. This formula should refer, directly or indirectly, to both input cells.

The cells below the formula in the left column of the table contain the values you want 1-2-3 to substitute into input cell 1. The cells to the right of the formula in the top row of the table contain the values you want 1-2-3 to substitute into input cell 2.

Tip
To make sure that your formula cell refers to the input cells, use the Auditor to highlight the precedent cells for the formula cell. Both input cells must be highlighted.

Suppose that you want to purchase a house for $100,000. You also are shopping for the best interest rate, and you have a budget to consider, so you need to choose terms for the loan that fit your needs and are within your budget limits. Before you approach the bank for a loan, you want a rough idea of the amount of the monthly payments. To determine this information, you create a data table that shows the monthly payments on a $100,000 loan at interest rates ranging from 7 percent to 12 percent, factored with four loan periods of 180, 240, 300, and 360 months. Figure 22.3 shows a two-variable data table that will perform these calculations.

Fig. 22.3
A two-variable data table ready to be filled in using /Data Table 2.

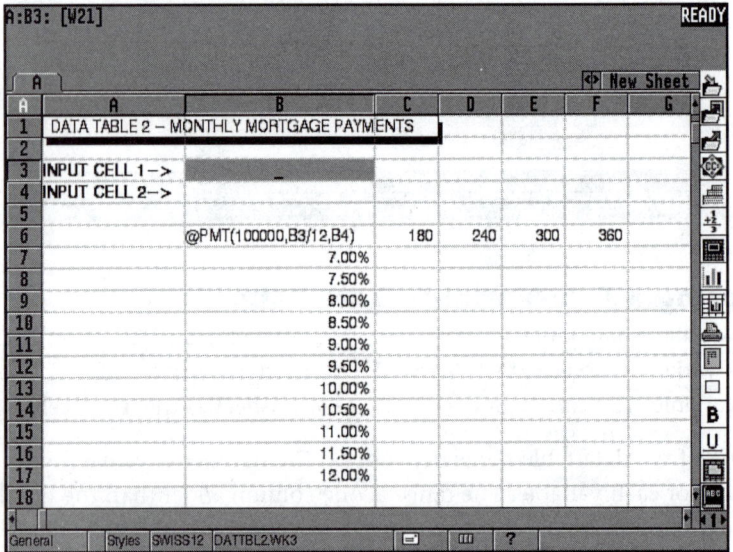

In figure 22.3, cells B3 and B4 are the input cells. The data-table range is B6..F17. The following formula, in cell B6, calculates the monthly payment of a loan based on an annual interest rate in cell B3 and a term, in months, in cell B4:

@PMT(100000,B3/12,B4)

The interest rates appear in B7..B17, and the four loan terms are in C6..F6.

Figure 22.4 shows the table that results from choosing **/D**ata **T**able **2** and specifying **B6..F17** as the table range, **B3** as input cell 1, and **B4** as input cell 2.

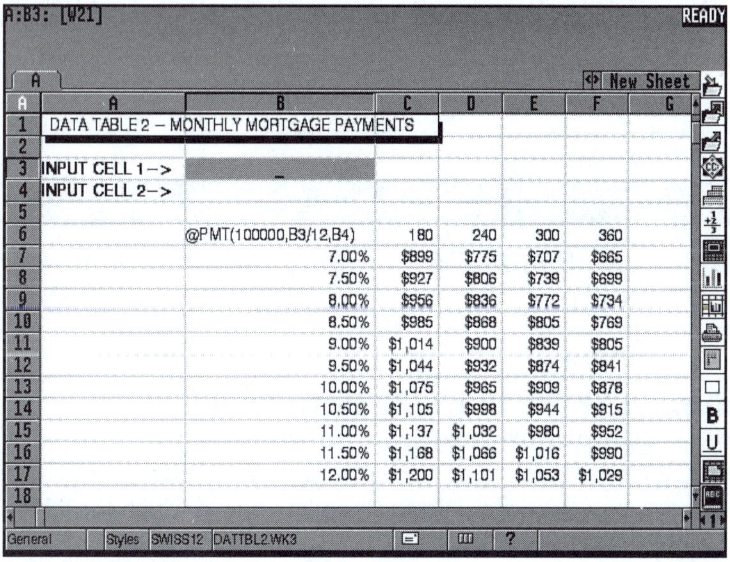

A:B3: [W21] READY

	A	B	C	D	E	F	G
1	DATA TABLE 2 – MONTHLY MORTGAGE PAYMENTS						
2							
3	INPUT CELL 1–>						
4	INPUT CELL 2–>						
5							
6		@PMT(100000,B3/12,B4)	180	240	300	360	
7		7.00%	$899	$775	$707	$665	
8		7.50%	$927	$806	$739	$699	
9		8.00%	$956	$836	$772	$734	
10		8.50%	$985	$868	$805	$769	
11		9.00%	$1,014	$900	$839	$805	
12		9.50%	$1,044	$932	$874	$841	
13		10.00%	$1,075	$965	$909	$878	
14		10.50%	$1,105	$998	$944	$915	
15		11.00%	$1,137	$1,032	$980	$952	
16		11.50%	$1,168	$1,066	$1,016	$990	
17		12.00%	$1,200	$1,101	$1,053	$1,029	
18							

General Styles SWISS12 DATTBL2.WK3

Fig. 22.4
The completed two-variable table of loan-payment amounts.

Troubleshooting

Every value in my two-variable data table is the same.

Make sure that the formula in the top-left cell of the table refers to both input cells. You can use the Auditor to ensure that the formula refers to the input cells. Another way to test this is to enter different values into the input cells. Make sure that the result of the formula in the top-left cell of the table changes each time you change the value in one of the input cells.

My two-variable data table contains only zeros.

Make sure that you specified the table range correctly. The top-left cell of the table must contain a formula that refers, directly or indirectly, to the input cells. The top row and left column of the table must contain the values you want 1-2-3 to substitute into the input cells.

(continues)

> (continued)
>
> *My two-variable data table contains values that don't make sense.*
>
> Make sure that you specified the input cells in the correct order. When 1-2-3 calculates the amounts to be placed in the data table, it substitutes the values in the left column of the table range into input cell 1 and the values in the top row into input cell 2. Reversing the input cells can cause incorrect results. One way to check this is to enter a value from the left column of the table in input cell 1 and a value from the top row in input cell 2. Make sure that the result of the formula in the top-left cell of the table is what you expect it to be.

> **Note**
>
> If you create a data table larger than the screen, you can use **/W**orksheet **T**itles to freeze the input values on the screen as you scroll through the results cells.

Creating a Three-Variable Data Table

A three-variable data table shows the effects of changing three variables in a single formula. The third dimension of a three-variable data table is represented by a *three-dimensional* worksheet range—one in which the table spans two or more worksheets.

The structure of a three-variable data table is an extension of the two-variable data-table structure, with the different values of variables 1 and 2 represented by different rows and columns. The third variable is located in the top-left corner of the data-table range; the different values of variable 3 are represented by different worksheets.

When you choose **/D**ata **T**able **3**, you define the table range as a three-dimensional range. In figure 22.5, the table range is A:C2..C:F5. The table range spans three worksheets. Notice that the tables in each worksheet must be in the same cell locations. The same cells (C2..F5) are used for the tables in each of the worksheets (A, B, and C).

You also need three input cells. As always, you can place these cells anywhere in any worksheet.

The formula evaluated in a three-variable data table should refer, directly or indirectly, to all three input cells. When you complete the command to create the table, 1-2-3 substitutes the values in the left column of the data-table range into input cell 1, the values in the top row into input cell 2, and the values in the top-left corner of the data-table range in each worksheet into input cell 3.

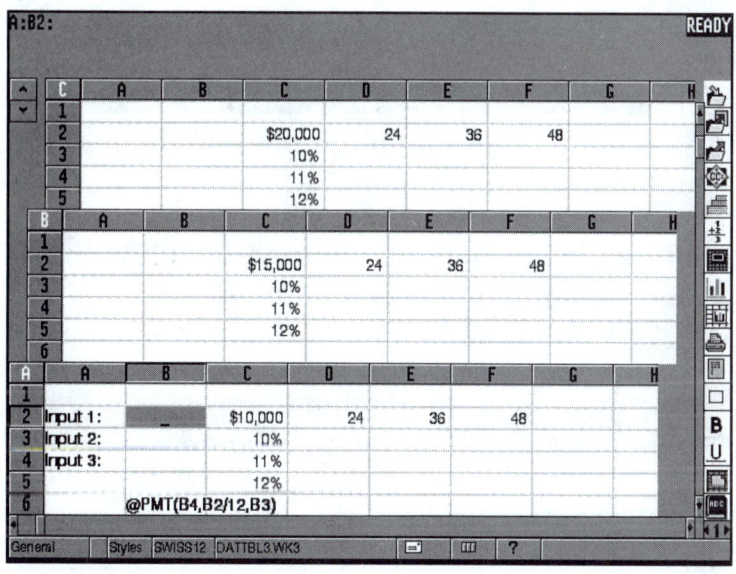

Fig. 22.5
A three-variable data table ready to be filled in using /**D**ata **T**able **3**.

Continuing the mortgage example, you can use a three-variable data table to calculate loan payments with a range of different values for each of three variables: principal amount, interest rate, and term.

In figure 22.18, the input cells are cells A:B2, A:B3, and A:B4. The data-table range is A:C2..C:F5. Because in a three-variable data table, the top-left cell of the table range is used for the values for input cell 3, you enter the formula outside the table range and specify the cell containing the formula when you choose the /**D**ata **T**able **3** command. In figure 22.18, the formula cell is cell A:B6, which contains the formula to calculate the monthly payment.

The left column of the table range in each worksheet contains the values you want 1-2-3 to substitute into input cell 1—in this case, interest rates. The top row contains the values for input cell 2—in this case, loan terms (in months). The top-left cell of the range in each worksheet contains the values for input cell 3—in this case, loan principal amounts.

Now choose /**D**ata **T**able **3**, and specify **A:C2..C:F5** as the table range, **A:B6** as the formula cell, **A:B2** as input cell 1, **A:B3** as input cell 2, and **A:B4** as input cell 3. Figure 22.6 shows the results.

Tip
When using three-variable tables, choose /**W**ork-sheet **W**indow **P**erspective to view all three active worksheets.

676   Chapter 22—High-Level Database Techniques

Fig. 22.6
The completed three-variable data table, showing loan-payment amounts for different interest rates, terms, and loan amounts.

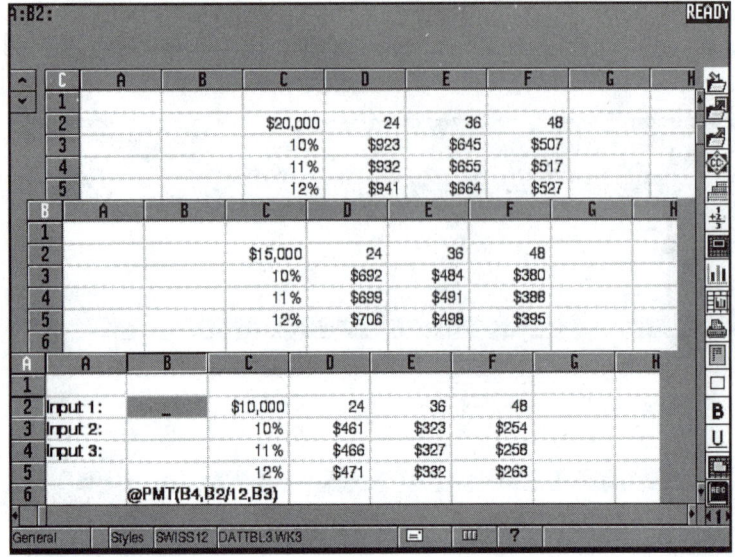

> **Troubleshooting**
>
> *Every value in my three-variable data table is the same.*
>
> Make sure that the formula in the formula cell of the table refers to all three input cells. You can use the Auditor to ensure that the formula refers to the input cells. Another way to test this is to enter different values into the input cells. Make sure that the result of the formula in the formula cell changes each time you change the value in one of the input cells.
>
> *My three-variable data table contains only zeros.*
>
> Make sure that you specified the table range correctly. The formula cell of the table must contain a formula that refers, directly or indirectly, to the input cells. The top row, left column, and top-left cell of the table in each worksheet must contain the values you want 1-2-3 to substitute into the input cells.
>
> *My three-variable data table contains values that don't make sense.*
>
> Make sure that you specified the input cells in the correct order. When 1-2-3 calculates the amounts to be placed in the data table, it substitutes the values in the left column of the table range in each sheet into input cell 1, the values in the top row in each sheet into input cell 2, and the values in the top-left cell in each sheet into input cell 3. Reversing the input cells can cause incorrect results. One way to check this is to enter a value from the left column of the table in input cell 1, a value from the top row in input cell 2, and a value from the top-left cell in input cell 3. Make sure that the result of the formula in the formula cell you specified is what you expect it to be.

Creating a Labeled Data Table

A *labeled data table*, which you create by using the **/D**ata **T**able **L**abeled command, is the most flexible kind of data table that 1-2-3 can create. With a labeled data table, you can perform any of the following procedures:

- Examine the effects of changing one or more variables in one or more formulas

- Include labels in the table to identify the table contents

- Use data in different worksheet areas as input for the data table

- Include in the table blank rows and text to improve the table's appearance

- Include in the data table formulas that perform calculations on the table results

Figure 22.7 shows the first worksheet of a two-worksheet table set up for use with **/D**ata **T**able **L**abeled. Figure 22.8 shows both worksheets of the completed table.

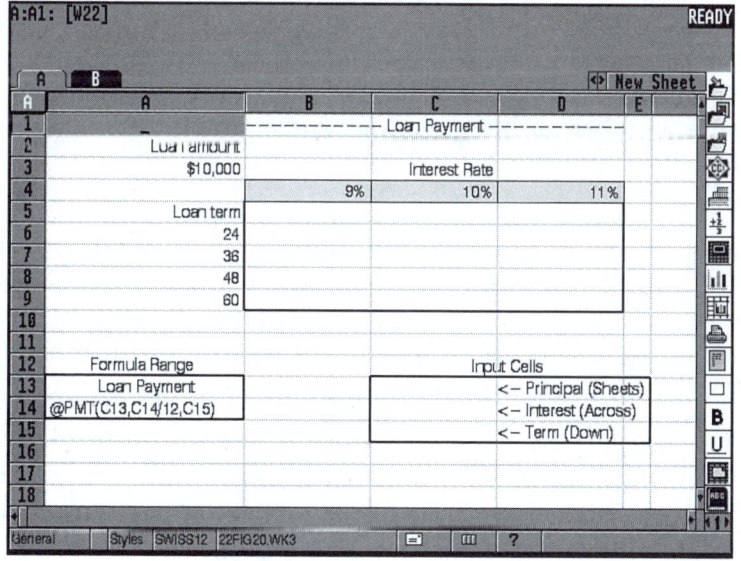

Fig. 22.7
The first worksheet in a two-worksheet table, ready to be filled in using **/D**ata **T**able **L**abeled.

Fig. 22.8
The completed two-worksheet table created with /**D**ata **T**able **L**abeled.

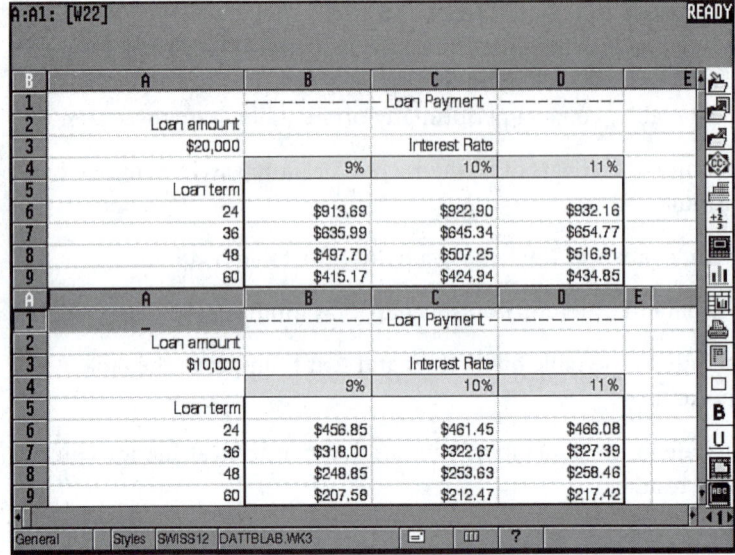

Understanding Labeled Data Table Terms and Concepts

The terms and explanations in this section are helpful when you create what-if scenarios using /**D**ata **T**able **L**abeled.

- The *formula range* is the worksheet range that contains the formula(s). The formulas calculate the data-table results; the formula range contains labels that identify each formula. In figure 22.7, A13..A14 is the formula range.

- The *formula-label range* contains copies of the labels in the formula range. The formula-label range also may contain blank cells, other labels, and values. The placement of labels in the formula-label range is used to determine which formula is used with the various input values of the data table and where the calculation results appear. In figure 22.7, B1..D1 is the formula-label range.

- A *row-variable range* is a region of the worksheet that contains rows of input values, organized by columns. A row-variable range may contain one or more columns, with each column containing a separate set of input variables. In figure 22.7, A6..A9 is the row-variable range.

- A *column-variable range* is a region of the worksheet that contains columns of input values, organized by rows. A column-variable range may contain one or more rows, with each row containing a separate set of input values. In figure 22.7, B4..D4 is the column-variable range.

- A *worksheet-variable range* is a three-dimensional region of the worksheet that contains one or more sets of input values. In figure 22.8, A:A3..B:A3 is the worksheet-variable range.

- The *input cells* in a labeled data table function just like the input cells used with other kinds of data tables. You need one input cell for each variable. In figure 22.7, C13..C15 are the input cells.

- **/D**ata **T**able **L**abeled doesn't require you to specify a data-table range. The location of the results area is determined by the locations of the input ranges.

- The specific variable ranges needed to create a labeled data table depend on the number of variables to be evaluated by the table formulas and on the layout of the results. A labeled data table that evaluates three variables, for example, can use all three kinds of variable ranges: column, row, and worksheet. You also can create a two-variable table by using any two of the three variable range types. A labeled data table that evaluates two variables can have any two variable ranges—a row-variable range and a column-variable range, for example, or a column-variable range and a worksheet-variable range.

Positioning the Results Area

The placement and structure of the variable ranges are important factors in determining the location and layout of the labeled data table. By changing the placement and structure of the variable ranges, you can control the location of the results area, and you can include blank rows, columns, and/or worksheets in the results area.

You can place the results of labeled data table calculations in the worksheet cells at the intersection of the row(s) that contain the nearest vertical range and the column(s) that contain the nearest horizontal range. (A *vertical range* is arranged in columns, such as a row-variable range. A *horizontal range* is arranged in rows, such as a column-variable range. A formula-label range can be either vertical or horizontal.)

To determine the placement of the results area, extend the rows that contain the row-variable range horizontally, both left and right, across the worksheet. Then extend the columns that contain the column-variable range, both up and down, along the worksheet. The cells where these *extended* rows and columns intersect are where 1-2-3 places the results area of the labeled data table.

680   Chapter 22—High-Level Database Techniques

In figure 22.7, no blank rows lie between the ranges and the results area. Figure 22.9 shows the same table with the locations of the row- and column-variable ranges changed. The results are placed at the intersection of the rows and columns that contain these variable ranges. This placement inserts blank rows and columns between the variable ranges and the results area.

Fig. 22.9
Blank rows (rows 5 through 7), included in the results area.

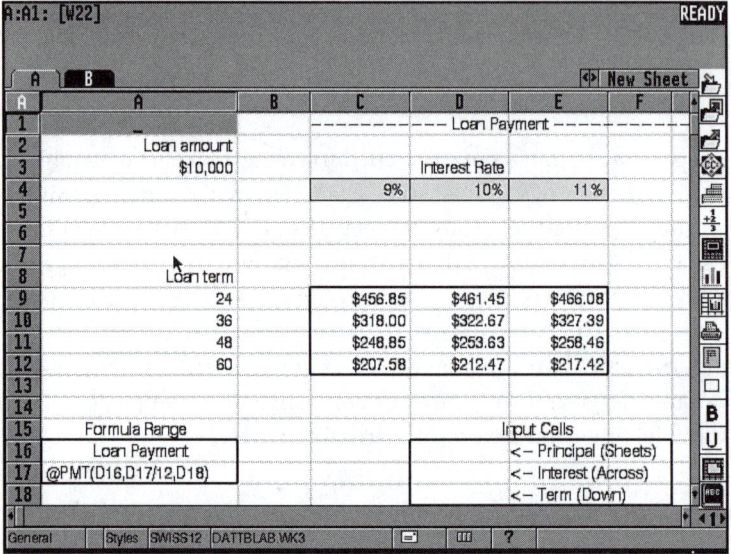

By placing the vertical and horizontal variable ranges adjacent to each other, you leave no space between the variable ranges and the results area. By placing the variable ranges in separate worksheet regions, you can leave blank rows and/or columns between the variable ranges and the results area.

The same principle applies when you are working in three dimensions (using a worksheet-variable range). The results area is placed at the intersection of the rows, columns, and worksheets that contain the variable ranges. By controlling the worksheets in which the variable ranges are placed, you can include blank worksheets between some of the variable ranges and the results area. In a four-worksheet file, for example, you can place the row- and column-variable ranges in worksheet D and the worksheet-variable range in worksheets A and B. 1-2-3 places the results in worksheets A and B only, leaving worksheet C blank.

Formatting the Results Area

The preceding section discussed controlling the blank space *between* the results area and the variable ranges. You also can control the placement of blank rows, columns, and worksheets *within* the results area. You achieve such control by including blank cells in the input ranges that you use to create the labeled data table.

For row- and column-variable ranges, the portion of the range closest to the results area is important. If the labeled data table includes a column-variable range, 1-2-3 checks the bottom row for blank cells. If the labeled data table includes a row-variable range, 1-2-3 checks the rightmost column for blank cells. If the formula-label range is the only vertical range or the only horizontal range in the labeled data table, 1-2-3 checks this range for blank cells. A blank cell or cells in any of these places causes the corresponding row(s) and/or column(s) of the results area to be blank.

Figure 22.10 shows an example of a labeled data table with blank rows in the results area.

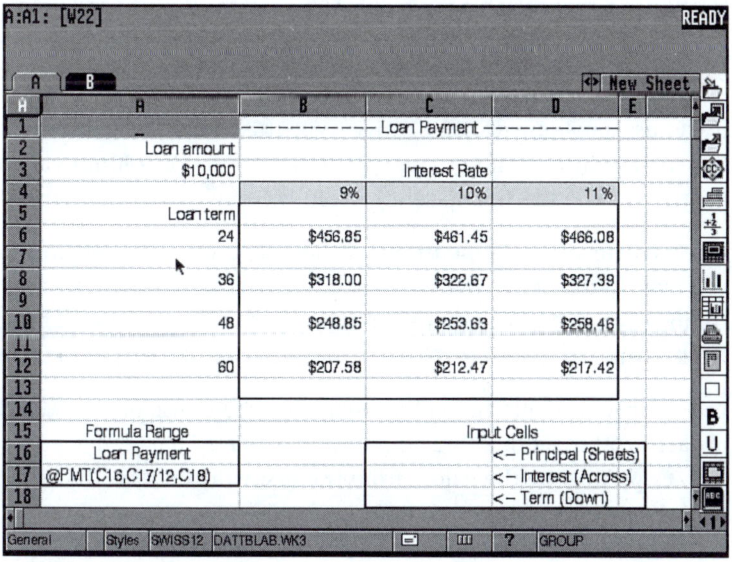

Fig. 22.10
Blank cells included in the row-variable range.

Creating a Sample Labeled Data Table

This section shows you how to create a labeled data table. You start by outlining the procedure for specifying the variable ranges. After you understand what to enter for each range, you can learn the steps to enter these ranges.

To specify variable ranges, follow these steps:

1. Select an empty location on the worksheet for the labeled data table.

The table's *minimum size* (rows by columns by worksheets) is determined by the number of values of each variable to be evaluated. The actual size of the results area depends on the specific formatting (inclusion, for example, of blank rows and/or columns).

2. Select a location for the input cell(s), and, if you want, identify the cells with labels typed in adjacent cells. You need one input cell for each variable to be analyzed.

3. Select a worksheet area to contain the formula range.

   The size of this range is two rows by as many columns as you have formulas. Enter the formula(s) in the second row of this range and the formula label(s) in the top row. The formula range must be outside the region that contains the results and the input values.

4. If you use a row-variable range, type this range either to the right or to the left of the results area. If you use more than one set of row input values, type these values in adjacent columns in the range.

5. If you use a column-variable range, type this range either above or below the results area. If you use more than one set of column-variable range, type the sets in adjacent rows in the range.

6. If you create a three-dimensional data table, each worksheet in which you want results to be placed must contain values in the row- and/or column-variable ranges. Type (or copy) these values in the additional worksheet(s) in the same relative positions as in the first worksheet.

   Because row-variable and column-variable values usually are identical in each worksheet of a three-dimensional labeled data table, you can use **/C**opy to copy the values from the first worksheet to the other worksheet(s).

7. If you use a worksheet-variable range, type one worksheet-variable value in the same cell of each worksheet.

   The worksheet-variable values form a *stack* that spans two or more worksheets. If you use more than one set of worksheet input values, each set should occupy a separate stack. These stacks must be adjacent.

8. Select a location for the formula-label range.

   You can place the formula-label range in a row above or below the column-variable range. If you use a column-variable range, the formula-label range must span the same number of columns as the column-variable range. If you have only one formula label and more than one column, type the formula and label-fill characters in the first cell of the formula-label range.

You also can place the formula-label range in a column to the left or right of the row-variable range or in a three-dimensional range between the worksheet-variable range and the results area. If the formula-label range doesn't span the same number of cells as the corresponding variable range, use the label-fill characters.

To create the payment schedule shown in figures 22.7 and 22.8, take the following steps:

1. First, set up worksheet A as shown in figure 22.7. (Notice that the entry in cell A:A14 is a formula; the cell is formatted with the Text format.)

2. Click the New Sheet button to insert a single worksheet (worksheet B) into the current file.

3. With the cell pointer in worksheet A, choose **/W**orksheet **G**lobal **G**roup **E**nable to apply all the formatting in worksheet A to the new worksheet.

4. Use the **/C**opy command to copy the range A:A1..A:D9 to cell B:B1.

5. Enter the value **20000** in cell B:A3.

6. If you want, choose **/W**orksheet **G**lobal **G**roup **D**isable to turn off GROUP mode; then use the **:F**ormat **L**ines **C**lear **A**ll command to clear the outlines from cells B:A13..B:E15.

Your worksheet A should look like figure 22.7. Your worksheet B should be identical to worksheet A from rows 1 through 9, except that cell A3 contains the value 10000 in worksheet A and 20000 in worksheet B.

Now you can start working with the **/D**ata **T**able commands to create the actual labeled data table. Choose **/D**ata **T**able **L**abeled. The following menu appears:

Formulas **D**own **A**cross **S**heets **I**nput-Cells **L**abel-Fill **G**o **Q**uit

Table 22.1 describes the functions of these commands.

Table 22.1 /Data Table Labeled Commands

Command	Description
Formulas	Specifies the formula range and the formula-label range
Down	Specifies the row-variable range and input cells
Across	Specifies the column-variable range and input cells
Sheets	Specifies the worksheet-variable range and input cells
Input-Cells	Verifies and/or edits the input cells specified with **D**own, **A**cross, or **S**heets
Label-Fill	Specifies the label-fill character
Go	Calculates the results and generates the labeled data table
Quit	Returns the worksheet to READY mode

To create the labeled data table, follow these steps:

1. Choose **/D**ata **T**able **L**abeled **F**ormulas, and type **A:A13.A:A14** as the formula range and **A:B1..A:D1** as the formula-label range.

2. Choose **D**own, and type **A:A6.A:A9** as the row-variable range. Press Enter to accept the highlighted range, then type **A:C15** as the corresponding input cell.

3. Choose **A**cross, and type **A:B4..A:D4** as the column-variable range. Press Enter to accept the highlighted range, then type **A:C14** as the corresponding input cell.

4. Choose **S**heets, and type **A:A3..B:A3** as the worksheet-variable range. Press Enter to accept the highlighted range, then type **A:C13** as the corresponding input cell.

5. If you want, choose **I**nput-Cells to verify and edit the addresses of variable ranges and input cells. 1-2-3 cycles through each set of variable ranges and input cells, displaying the addresses you initially entered. Press Enter to accept the original entries or specify new addresses.

6. If you are using label-fill characters but do not want to use the default hyphen (-), choose **L**abel-Fill and type the character you do want to use (for example, = or *).

7. Choose **G**o to have 1-2-3 calculate the table.

The resulting table should look like figure 22.8. 1-2-3 substitutes the input values from the various input ranges into the formula in the formula range, then places each result in the location defined by the intersection of the corresponding row, column, and worksheet.

You may have noticed that you can produce the same information by using **/D**ata **T**able **3**. By using a labeled data table, however, you have more flexibility, because you totally control where the various table ranges are placed. You can produce a table that is easier to format (and also easier to understand).

After creating a labeled data table, if you return to the **/D**ata **T**able **L**abeled menu and choose **D**own, **A**cross, or **S**heet, 1-2-3 remembers the variable range that you originally specified. If you accept the original variable range by pressing Enter, 1-2-3 *forgets* the input cell originally associated with that range, and you must respecify the input cell. As an alternative, you can specify another input cell referenced by the formulas used in another data table. This method lets you use the same sets of input values in different labeled data tables with only a few keystrokes.

Using More Than Three Variables

A labeled data table can calculate formulas based on values of more than three variables. **/D**ata **T**able **L**abeled can use only three kinds of variable ranges: column, row, and worksheet. To accommodate more than three kinds of variables, you must include more than one variable in a particular variable range.

The following section demonstrates how each kind of variable range can contain more than one part. A column-variable range, for example, can contain two or more rows. Each row is a separate variable with a separate input cell. A row-variable range can contain two or more columns. Each column is a separate variable with a separate input cell.

To set up a variable range that contains more than one variable, you must organize the values in a certain way. Remember the following guidelines for each of the three kinds of variable input ranges:

- In row-variable ranges, you must place in the far-right column the values that change with the greatest frequency.

- In column-variable ranges, you must place in the bottom row the values that change with the greatest frequency.

Chapter 22—High-Level Database Techniques

- In worksheet-variable ranges, the values that change with the greatest frequency must be in the bottom or rightmost group of cells, depending on the orientation of the range.

Figure 22.11 shows two row-variable ranges, each containing two variables. The row-variable range in B3..C11 is valid because the variable that changes most frequently (10,20,30) is in the column on the right. The values in F3..G11 don't constitute a valid row-variable range because the variable that changes most frequently is in the left column.

Fig. 22.11
Valid and invalid row-variable ranges.

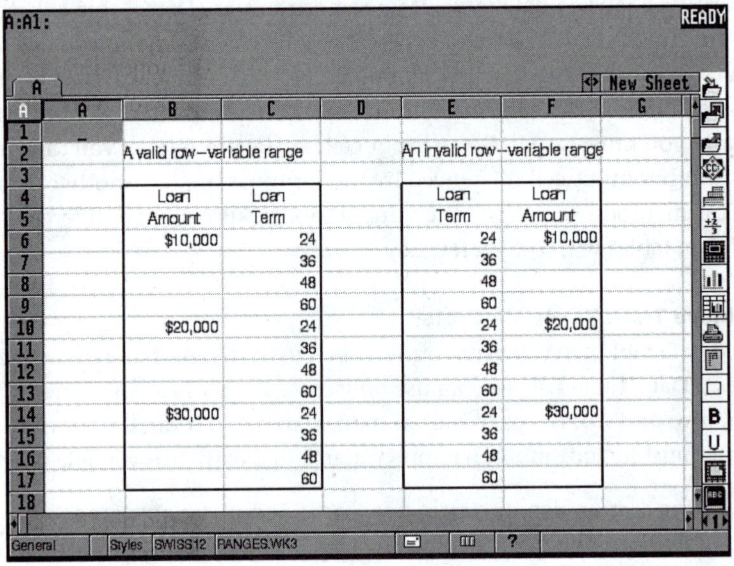

Figure 22.12 shows a labeled data table that uses one variable range containing two variables. This labeled data table provides the same information as the labeled data table in figure 22.8, but it does so in a single worksheet. Although this table contains only three variables, the principles easily can be extended to four or more variables.

In this worksheet, the row-variable range is C5..D13. The input cell for the first row variable, Loan Amount, is A16. The input cell for the second row variable, Loan Term, is A18. Cell A17, Input cell 1 is used for the column-row variable in this example.

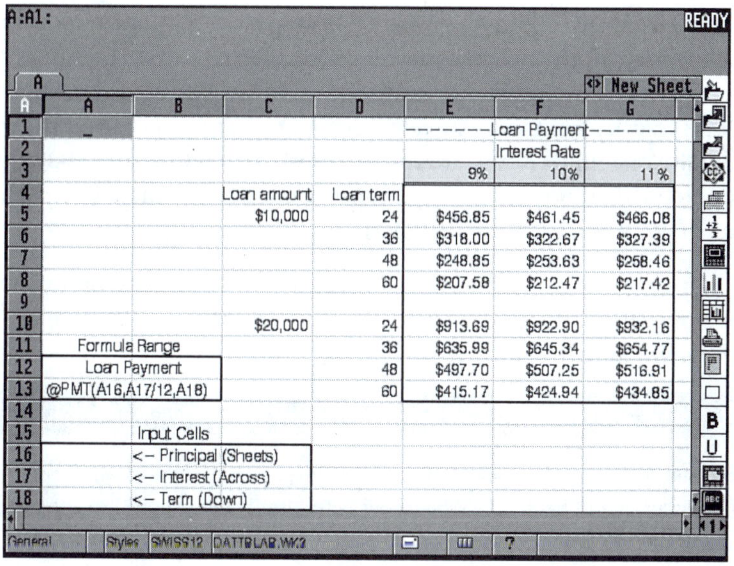

Fig. 22.12
A variable range that contains two variables, used to construct a three-variable labeled data table in a single worksheet.

Creating Frequency Distributions

The command for creating frequency distributions in 1-2-3 is **/D**ata **D**istribution. A *frequency distribution* describes the relationship between a set of classes and the frequency of occurrence of members of each class. A list of student exam scores illustrates the use of the **/D**ata **D**istribution command to produce a frequency distribution (see fig. 22.13).

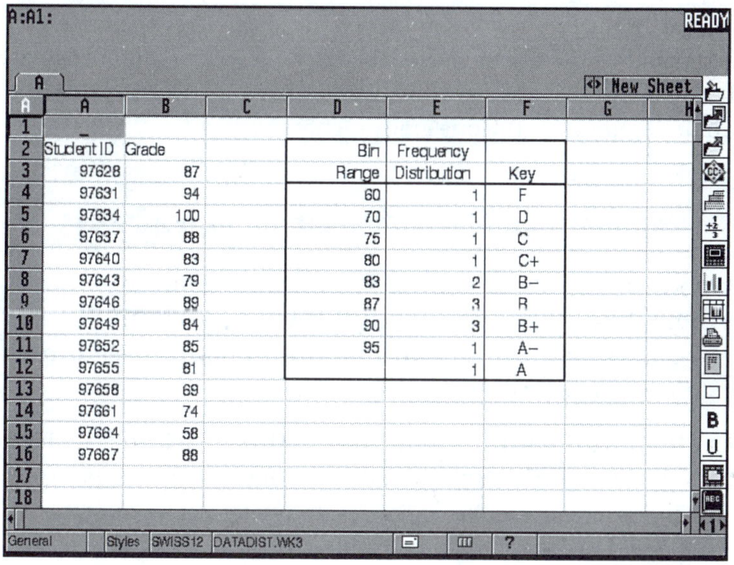

Fig. 22.13
A **/D**ata **D**istribution for exam scores.

To use the **/D**ata **D**istribution command, you must specify the *values range* and the *bin range* as the two parameters with which to work. The values range is the range that contains values (exam scores, in the example) for which you want 1-2-3 to calculate the frequency distribution. The bin range is the range that contains the limits of the groups, or "bins," that you want 1-2-3 to use in calculating the distribution. 1-2-3 prompts you to specify these two parameters when you choose **/D**ata **D**istribution.

The values range for this example—B3..B16, corresponds with the student ID numbers in cells A3..A16. After specifying B3..B16 for the values range, specify the bin range—D4..D11.

> **Note**
>
> If you want to use equal intervals in the bin range, you can use the **/D**ata **F**ill command (discussed in Chapter 2, "What Every 1-2-3 User Should Know") to enter the values for the bin range.

Tip

The **/D**ata **D**istribution command can help you summarize large quantities of numeric data. Using the **/G**raph command, you easily can graph the results of a data distribution.

When you choose **/D**ata **D**istribution and specify these ranges, 1-2-3 enters values in the results column (E4..E12) to the right of the bin range. The results column, which shows the frequency distribution, always appears in the column to the right of the bin range and extends one row farther down.

The values in the results column represent the frequency of distribution of the numbers in the values range for each interval. The first interval in the bin range is for values greater than zero and less than or equal to 60; the second interval is for values greater than 60 and less than or equal to 70; and so on. The last value in the results column (in cell E12, just below the corresponding column segment) shows the frequency of *leftover numbers*—numbers that don't fit into an interval classification. In the example, the last value in the results column represents the one grade higher than 95.

Performing a Regression Analysis

The **/D**ata **R**egression command gives you a multiple-regression-analysis package within 1-2-3. Although most people have no need for this advanced feature, 1-2-3 saves those who do need it the cost and inconvenience involved in buying a stand-alone statistical package.

Use **/D**ata **R**egression when you want to determine the relationship between one set of values (the dependent variables) and one or more other sets of values (the independent variables). The result usually is a set of numbers better represented in a graph than in a table.

Regression analysis has many uses in a business setting, including the following procedures:

- Relating sales to price, promotions, and other market factors
- Relating stock prices to earnings and interest rates
- Relating production costs to production levels

Consider linear regression to be a way to determine the *best-fit line* through a series of data points. (The best-fit line is the line for which the sum of the squares of the differences between the actual and predicted values for the dependent variable is the least. This is called the "least-squares" method for calculating a best-fit line. Depending on how well the best-fit line corresponds to the actual data, you may be able to use the best-fit line to explain or predict the relationship between the independent and dependent variables.) Multiple regression performs the same operation for several variables simultaneously, determining the best-fit line that relates the dependent variable to the set of independent variables.

► "Choosing an Appropriate Graph Type," p. 705

Consider a data sample that shows Annual Earnings vs. Age. Figure 22.14 shows this data; figure 22.15 shows the data plotted as an XY graph. (Use A4..A17 for the X-graph range and C4..C17 for the Y-graph range.)

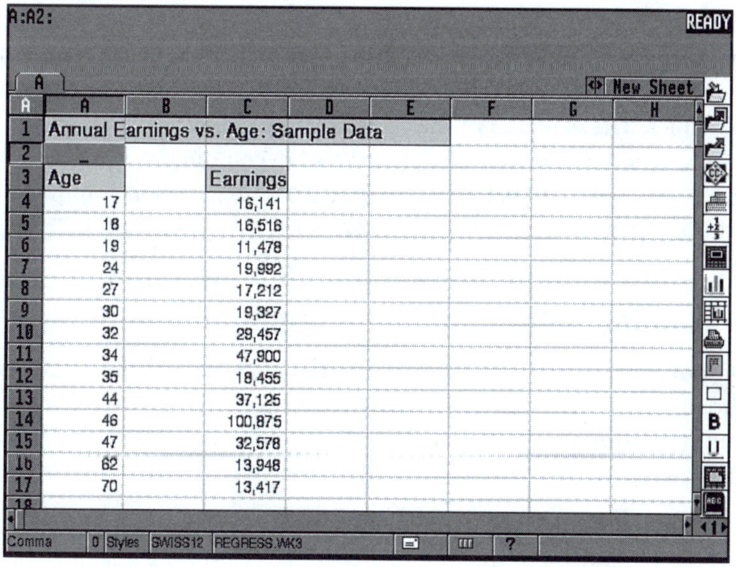

Annual Earnings vs. Age: Sample Data

Age		Earnings
17		16,141
18		16,516
19		11,478
24		19,992
27		17,212
30		19,327
32		29,457
34		47,900
35		18,455
44		37,125
46		100,875
47		32,578
62		13,948
70		13,417

Fig. 22.14 Annual Earnings vs. Age data.

Fig. 22.15
A graph of Annual Earnings vs. Age data.

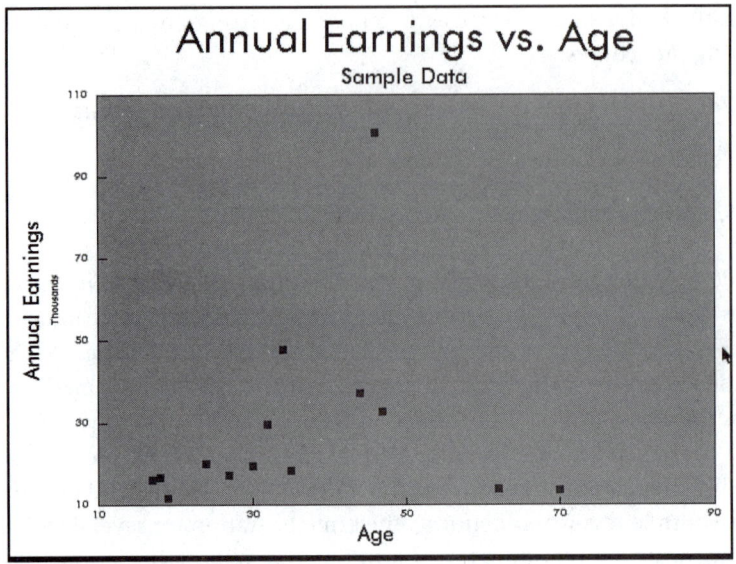

The **/D**ata **R**egression command can simultaneously determine how to draw a line through these data points and how well the line fits the data. When you choose the command, the following menu appears:

X-Range **Y**-Range **O**utput-Range **I**ntercept **R**eset **G**o **Q**uit

Use the **X**-Range command to select one or more independent variables for the regression. The **/D**ata **R**egression command can use up to 75 independent variables. The variables in the regression are columns of values, which means that you must convert all data in rows to columns by using the **/R**ange **T**rans command before issuing the **/D**ata **R**egression command. Here, the **X**-Range is specified as **A4..A17**.

The **Y**-Range command specifies the dependent variable. The **Y**-Range must be a single column; in this example, **C4..C17** is the **Y**-Range.

The **O**utput-Range command specifies the top-left corner of the results range. You should place this range in an unused section of the worksheet, because the output is written over all existing cell contents. Here, **E5** is specified as the output range.

The **I**ntercept command lets you specify whether the regression calculates the value of the y-intercept or uses a y-intercept of a constant value of zero. The two choices are Compute and Zero. In some applications, you always may need to use zero as the y-intercept.

Figure 22.16 shows the results of using the **/D**ata **R**egression **G**o command in the Annual Earnings vs. Age example. The results (in cells E5..H13) include the value of the constant and the coefficient of the single independent variable specified with the **X**-Range command. The results also include regression statistics that describe how well the regression line fits the data. In this case, the R-Squared value and the standard errors of the constant and the regression coefficient indicate that the regression line doesn't explain much of the variation in the dependent variable.

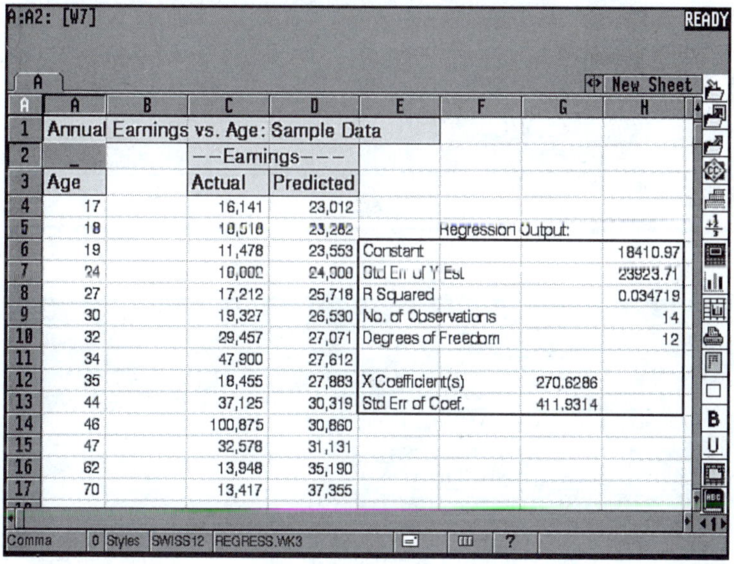

Fig. 22.16
/Data **R**egression results on the Annual Earnings vs. Age data.

The new data in column D is the computed regression line. These values consist of the constant plus the coefficient of the independent variable times its value in each row of the data. To calculate the regression line, type the formula **+$H$6+$G$12*A4** in cell D4. Then use the **/R**ange **F**ormat **,** (comma) **0** command to format the result. Finally, use **/C**opy from D4..D4 to D5..D17 to copy the formula to the other cells in column D. You can plot this line against the original data (as graph range B, formatted to display lines only), as shown in figure 22.17.

When you look at the Annual Earnings vs. Age plot, you notice that income appears to rise until age 47; then income begins to decline. You can use the **/D**ata **R**egression command to fit a line that describes this kind of relationship between Annual Earnings and Age. In figure 22.18, a column of data has been added (column B) to contain the square of the age in column A, and the regression has been recalculated to include the new column.

Fig. 22.17
A plot of Annual Earnings vs. Age data with a regression line.

	A	B	C	D	E	F	G	H
1	Annual Earnings vs. Age: Sample Data							
2			--Earnings---					
3	Age	Age^2	Actual	Predicted				
4	17	289	16,141	6,333				
5	18	324	16,516	8,978	Regression Output:			
6	19	361	11,478	11,526	Constant			-53593
7	24	576	19,992	22,799	Std Err of Y Est			20696.67
8	27	729	17,212	28,390	R Squared			0.33777
9	30	900	19,327	33,101	No. of Observations			14
10	32	1,024	29,457	35,754	Degrees of Freedom			11
11	34	1,156	47,900	38,015				
12	35	1,225	18,455	38,999	X Coefficient(s)		4355.73	-48.8638
13	44	1,936	37,125	43,459	Std Err of Coef.		1855.31	21.77899
14	46	2,116	100,875	43,375				
15	47	2,209	32,578	43,186				
16	62	3,844	13,948	28,630				
17	70	4,900	13,417	11,876				

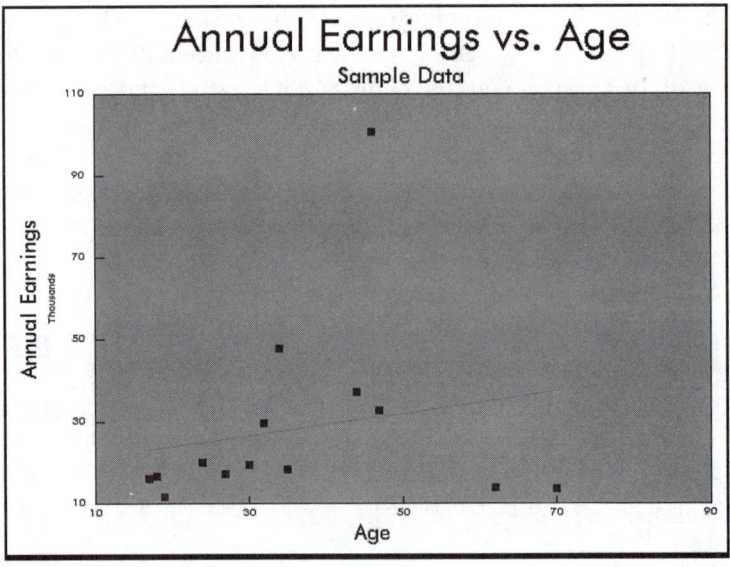

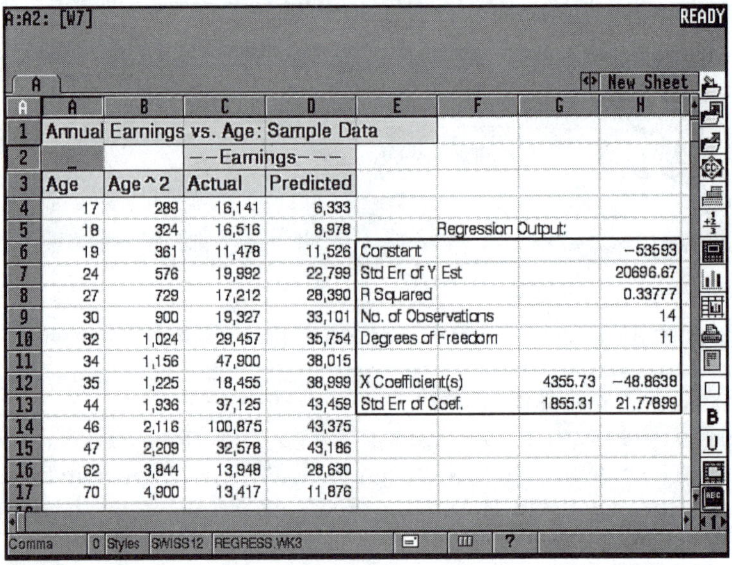

Fig. 22.18
Annual Earnings vs. Age Data and the square of Age.

To include this new column in the regression, specify the range A4..B17 for the **X**-Range, and recalculate the regression. Notice that the R Squared value in the regression statistics is much higher than in the regression of Annual Earnings vs. Age, which means that the combination of age and the square of age produces a line that fits the data more closely than the old one. (The R Squared value indicates that the regression only *explains* about one-third of the variation of the dependent variable.)

To graph the new line, adjust the formulas in column D by changing D4 to +$H$6+$G$12*A4+$H$12*B4, then copying the formula to D5..D17. This procedure adds the new regression coefficient to the equation that generates the regression line. Figure 22.19 shows the resulting graph. Notice that the regression line now is a parabola that rises until age 45, then declines. The regression line generated by a multiple regression may or may not be a straight line, depending on the independent variables used.

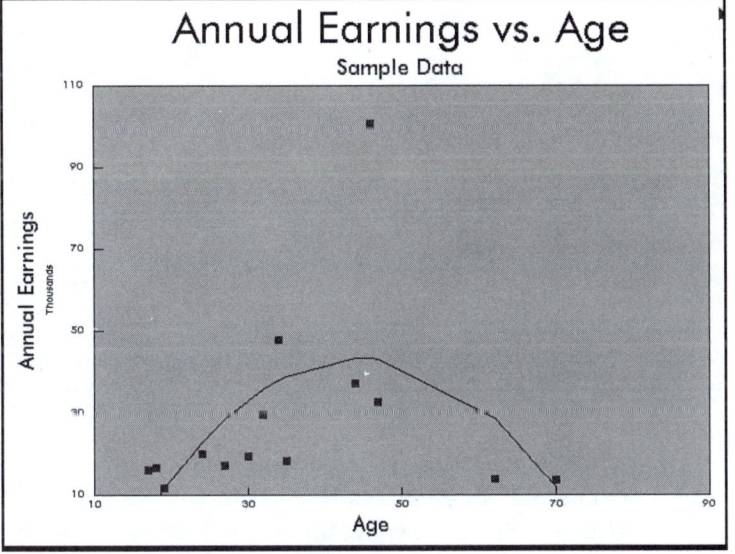

Fig. 22.19

A plot of Annual Earnings vs. Age data, with a revised regression line.

Working with Matrices

The **/D**ata **M**atrix command is a specialized mathematical command that lets you solve systems of simultaneous linear equations and manipulate the resulting solutions. This command is powerful but has limited application in a business setting. If you are using 1 2 3 for certain kinds of economic analysis or for scientific or engineering calculations, however, you may find this command valuable.

Chapter 22—High-Level Database Techniques

/Data Matrix generates a menu that contains two options: **Invert** and **Multiply**. **Invert** lets you invert a nonsingular square matrix of up to 80 rows and columns. Choose **Invert** and highlight the range you want to invert; then select an output range to hold the inverted solution matrix. You can place the output range anywhere in the worksheet, including on top of the matrix you are inverting. Figure 22.20 shows an inverted matrix.

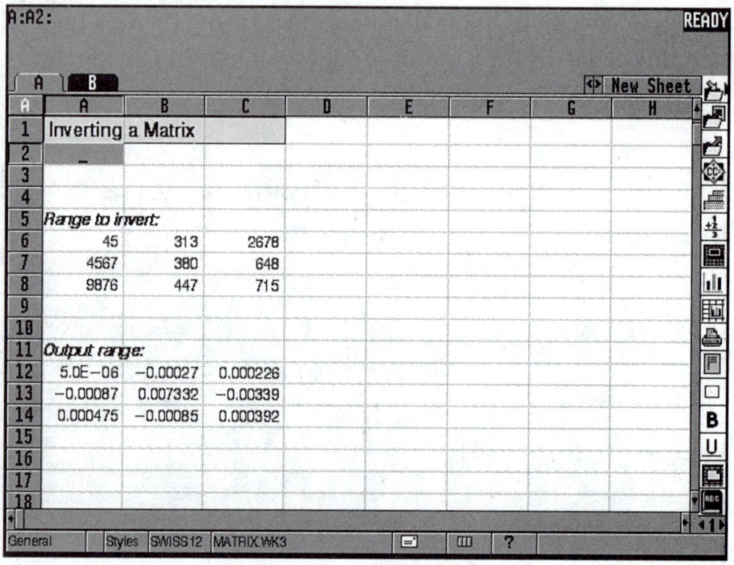

Fig. 22.20
An inverted matrix.

	A	B	C
1	Inverting a Matrix		
2			
3			
4			
5	Range to invert:		
6	45	313	2678
7	4567	380	648
8	9876	447	715
9			
10			
11	Output range:		
12	5.0E−06	−0.00027	0.000226
13	−0.00087	0.007332	−0.00339
14	0.000475	−0.00085	0.000392

Tip

If you want to use 1-2-3 to invert matrices and you don't have a math coprocessor or the equivalent, you may want to invest in a numeric coprocessor for your computer.

The time needed to invert a matrix is proportional to the cube of the number of rows and columns. A 25-by-25 matrix takes about 10 seconds to invert, and an 80-by-80 matrix takes almost five minutes to invert on a 16-MHz 80386 computer with no numeric coprocessor. Inverting a matrix on a 50-MHz 80486DX computer with a math coprocessor installed, however, takes only seconds.

The **/Data Matrix Multiply** command lets you multiply two rectangular matrices, according to the rules of matrix algebra. The number of columns in the first matrix must equal the number of rows in the second matrix. The result matrix has the same number of rows as the first matrix and the same number of columns as the second.

When you choose **/Data Matrix Multiply**, 1-2-3 prompts you for three ranges: the first matrix, the second matrix, and the output range. **Multiply** is fast compared with **Invert**, but it still may take some time if you multiply large matrices.

Figure 22.21 shows the result of multiplying two matrices.

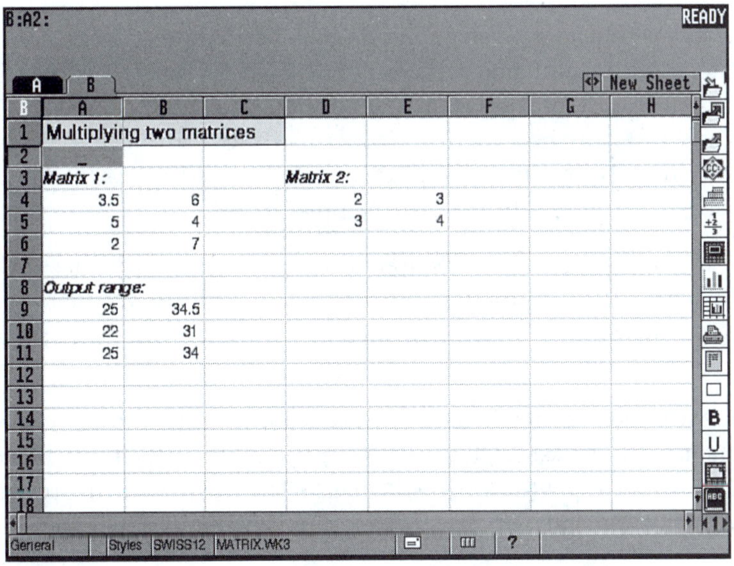

Fig. 22.21
The result of multiplying two matrices.

If you use the **/D**ata **M**atrix command with a three-dimensional input range, 1-2-3 performs inversions on a worksheet-by-worksheet basis. If you specify **A:B2..D:D4** as the input range and **A:F2** as the output range, for example, the following changes occur:

- A:B2..A:D4 is inverted and placed in A:F2..A:H4.

- B:B2..B:D4 is inverted and placed in B:F2..B:H4.

- C:B2..C:D4 is inverted and placed in C:F2..C:H4.

- D:B2..D:D4 is inverted and placed in D:F2..D:H4.

1-2-3 also performs multiplications on a worksheet-by-worksheet basis if you specify three-dimensional ranges.

Importing Data from Other Programs

1-2-3 provides several means of importing data from other applications. Options in the Translate utility can convert data directly to 1-2-3 worksheets from DIF, dBASE II, dBASE III, and dBASE III Plus files and also from other file formats. You then can access the data by using the **/F**ile **R**etrieve or **/F**ile **C**ombine command in the current worksheet. 1-2-3 Release 4 also can

◀ "Retrieving a 1-2-3 File," p. 138

◀ "Opening Files with the Viewer," p. 433

▶ "Understanding Macros," p. 830

▶ "Developing Programs with the Advanced Macro Commands," p. 866

translate WK3 (worksheet) files into the following formats: Enable, MultiPlan, and SuperCalc.

If you work with data from an application whose file format 1-2-3 cannot translate, or with mainframe data, you still can read your application's data into 1-2-3 Release 4, provided that your application can save data as ASCII text. Use the **/F**ile **I**mport command to read an ASCII text file into the current worksheet. Depending on the format, you can read an ASCII text file into a range of cells or into a single column of cells.

If your ASCII file contains *comma-delimited* data, in which a comma separates each item from the next and non-numeric data is enclosed in double-quotes, 1-2-3 can read the data directly to a range of worksheet cells, placing each item in its own cell.

If your ASCII file does not contain comma-delimited data, you still can read the data into the worksheet, but 1-2-3 places each line of the file in one cell as a long label. To split the individual items of data into cells, choose the **/D**ata **P**arse command.

You also can use functions to split data from long labels into cells, and you can use certain advanced macro commands to read and write an ASCII sequential file directly from a 1-2-3 macro.

The **/D**ata **P**arse command is a flexible and easy method of extracting numeric, string, and date data from long labels and placing this data in separate columns.

Suppose that you print a report containing sales data to a disk file in ASCII format. You want to load the ASCII file into a 1-2-3 worksheet and perform calculations on the data. To begin, choose **/F**ile **I**mport **T**ext to import the data into a worksheet. Because your data is not comma-delimited, 1-2-3 places each line of the report in a single cell as a long label. Before you can perform any calculations on the data, you need to split these long labels so that each data item is in its own cell. The **/D**ata **P**arse command performs this task.

The **/F**ile **I**mport **T**ext command loads the inventory data into range A3..A11. As you see in the control panel, which shows the contents of cell A4, all the data in that row is entered in cell A4 as a long label (see fig. 22.22).

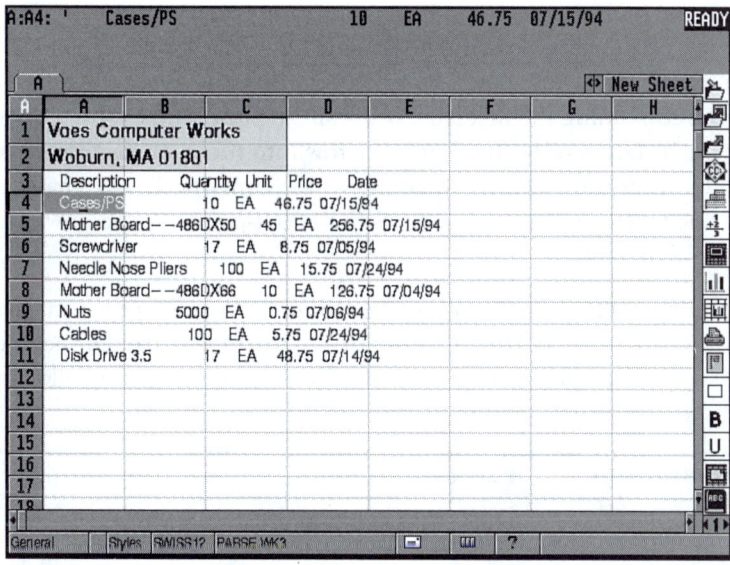

Fig. 22.22
The result of using the **/F**ile **I**mport **T**ext command.

To break the long labels into cells, use the **/D**ata **P**arse command. To begin, move the cell pointer to the first cell to be parsed, and choose **/D**ata **P**arse. The following menu appears:

Format-Line **I**nput-Column **O**utput-Range **R**eset **G**o **Q**uit

Use **F**ormat-Line to **C**reate or **E**dit a format line in the data to be parsed. A *format line* is a long label that specifies a pattern for splitting long labels into numbers, labels, and dates.

Use **I**nput-Column to specify the range of cells to be parsed. The input range, contained in just one column, consists of at least one cell that contains a format line and all cells that contain the long labels to be parsed.

Use **O**utput-Range to specify the worksheet range where 1-2-3 puts the parsed data. You can specify a rectangular range or the single cell at the top-left corner of the range. The output data has as many rows as it has long labels; the number of columns depends on the format line(s).

Use **R**eset to clear the previously set **I**nput-Column and **O**utput-Range.

Use **G**o to perform the parse, based on the specified **I**nput-Column, **F**ormat-Line, and **O**utput-Range.

Quit cancels the command and returns 1-2-3 to READY mode.

Chapter 22—High-Level Database Techniques

The first step in using the **/D**ata **P**arse command is creating one or more format lines. These lines specify the pattern 1-2-3 uses to split each long label into numbers, labels, and dates. To create a format line, place the cell pointer in the cell containing the first label you want to parse, and choose **/D**ata **P**arse **F**ormat-Line **C**reate. 1-2-3 inserts a row into the worksheet at the cell-pointer location and places a format line in the current cell. 1-2-3 bases the format line on the information it finds in the cell-pointer location when you begin the command.

A format line is a long label made up of certain letters and special characters. The letters denote the beginning position and the type of data in each field; special symbols define the length of a field and the spacing. The following table shows the letters and symbols used in format lines.

Letter/Symbol	Purpose
D	Marks the beginning of a Date field
L	Marks the beginning of a Label field
S	Marks the beginning of a Skip position
T	Marks the beginning of a Time field
V	Marks the beginning of a Value field
>	Defines the continuation of a field; use one > for each position in the field, excluding the first position
*	Defines blank spaces (in the data below the format line) that may be part of the block of data in the following cell

If the first row of your data contains field names or other labels and the other rows contain numeric data or dates, you may need to create more than one format line. In figure 22.22, for example, row 3 contains only field names; the subsequent rows contain labels, numbers, and dates. A format line that would correctly split the data in row 3 into labels would not work correctly for the data in rows 4 through 11.

Figure 22.23 shows the result of creating two format lines in the table of inventory data. The first format line, in cell A:A3, tells 1-2-3 to break the first line of data (the row of field names) into five labels. If you used this format line to parse all the data, 1-2-3 would interpret all the data as labels. Because some of the fields contain numbers and dates, you need to create a second format line, shown in cell A:A5. This second format line breaks each subsequent line of data into a label, a value, another label, another value, and a date.

Importing Data from Other Programs   **699**

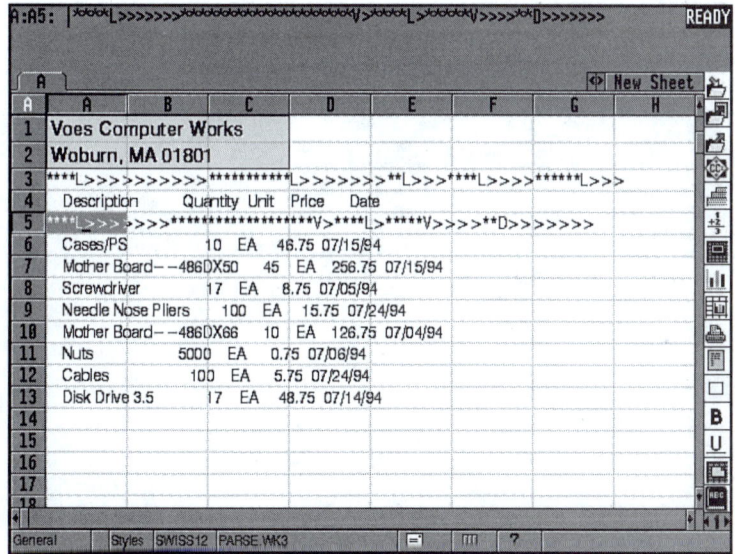

Fig. 22.23
Format lines created in a parse operation.

If necessary, you can edit a format line by choosing **/D**ata **P**arse **F**ormat-Line **E**dit.

Add as many format lines as you need in your data. To add more format lines, you must **Q**uit the **/D**ata **P**arse menu, move the cell pointer to the next row of data that you want to parse differently, and choose **/D**ata **P**arse **F**ormat-Line **C**reate in the new location.

After creating and editing your format lines as necessary, choose **I**nput-Column from the **P**arse menu, and specify the range that contains all the format lines and long labels to be parsed. In figure 22.23, you would specify the range **A3..A13**, which includes format lines, column headings, and data.

To specify the location where 1-2-3 is to place the parsed data, choose **O**utput-Range from the **P**arse menu, and specify an unused portion of the worksheet. To complete the operation, choose **G**o. Figure 22.24 shows the result of parsing the inventory data after specifying cell A:A18 as the top-left corner of the output range.

After parsing your data into individual cells, you may need to make formatting changes to make the data more presentable and usable. Figure 22.25 shows the final table of inventory data, which has been moved up to the top of the worksheet (replacing the long labels) and formatted.

Working with Databases

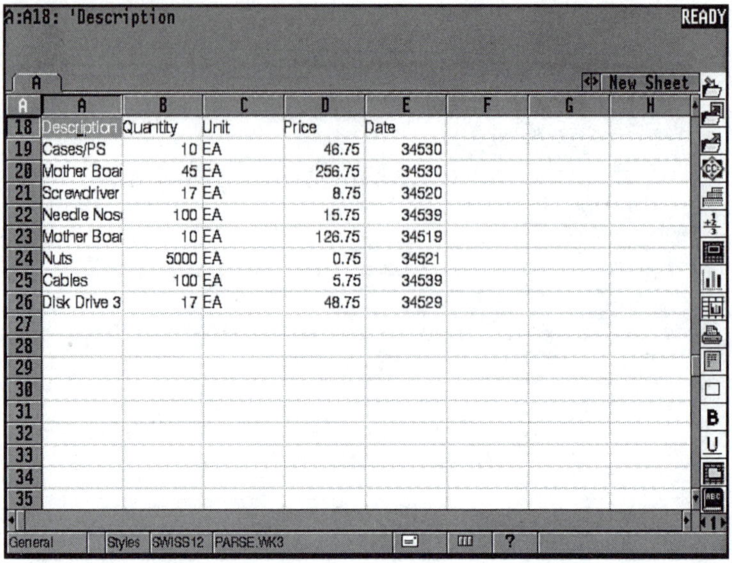

Fig. 22.24
The result of the **P**arse operation.

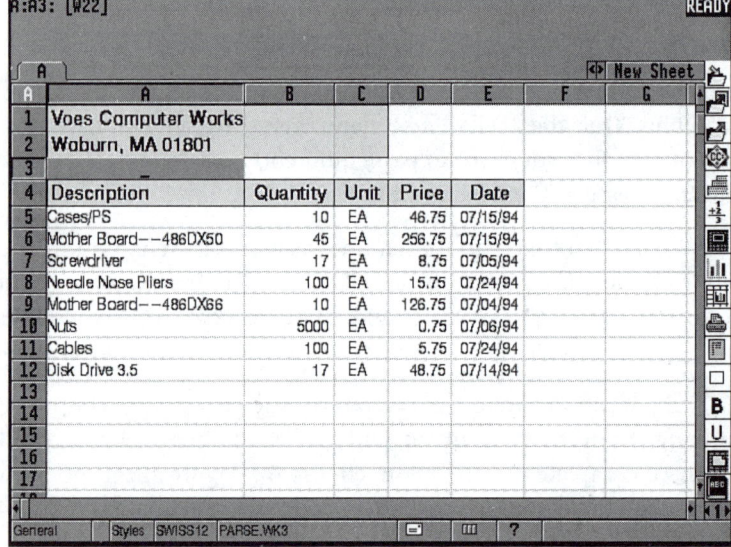

Fig. 22.25
The improved appearance of the parsed inventory data.

> **Caution**
> If your data contains labels of varying width, try to create a format line based on the longest label in each field. If you parse label data by using a format line based on shorter labels, 1-2-3 may break the labels into cells incorrectly. Field widths are less critical when you parse numeric data or dates. Make sure that the column widths specified in the format line are wide enough for the longest value or label in each field. To be safe, experiment with small amounts of data, editing your format lines as necessary until 1-2-3 parses the data correctly.

From Here...

For more information relating directly to advanced database techniques, you may want to review the following chapters of this book:

- Chapter 2, "What Every 1-2-3 User Should Know." This chapter shows you the easiest techniques for setting up a worksheet and introduces the basics of creating formulas.

- Chapter 3, "Finding Solutions with Formulas and Functions." This chapter gives you more information about creating and troubleshooting formulas and about using 1-2-3's built-in functions.

- Chapter 19, "Creating Databases." This chapter teaches you the basics of designing and setting up databases in 1-2-3.

- Chapter 21, "Finding Specific Data." This chapter teaches you how to use the **/D**ata **Q**uery commands to find and extract information from a 1-2-3 database.

- Chapter 30, "Sharing 1-2-3 Data with Databases." This chapter teaches you how to use the **/D**ata **E**xternal commands to link to data in other database programs.

Part VI
Graphing Your Data

23 Creating Effective Graphs

24 Creating Power Graphs

25 Developing Business Presentations

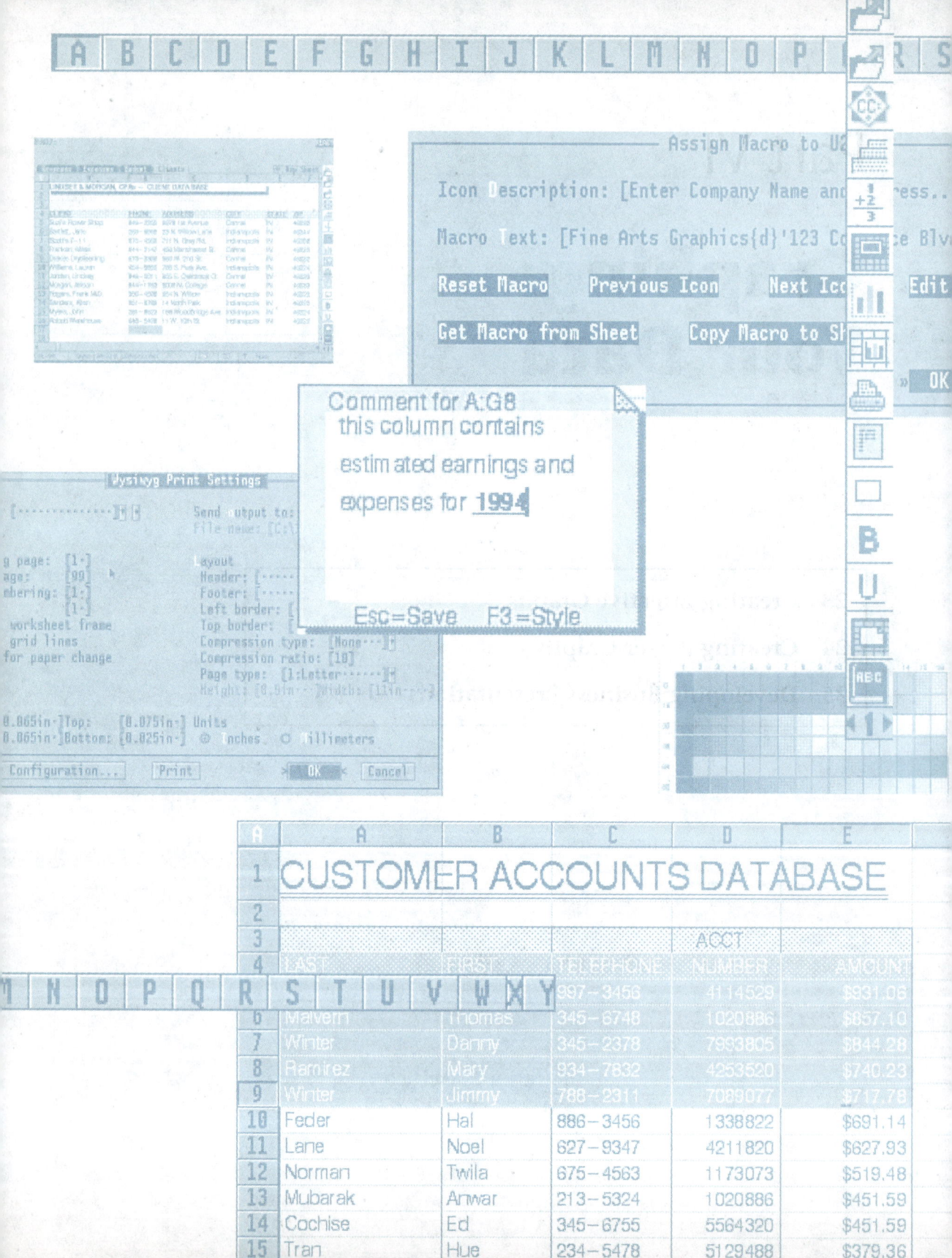

Chapter 23

Creating Effective Graphs

Graphs are an important tool for understanding and presenting trends and relationships among data series. Spotting a trend or analyzing data often is easier with a graph than with a sea of numbers. The business-graphics capabilities included in 1-2-3 are powerful yet easy-to-use tools that meet this important need. Chapter 2, "What Every 1-2-3 User Should Know," describes how to create a basic 1-2-3 graph. In this chapter, you learn how to make graphs more effective by choosing the best graph type for the data and by enhancing the graph with the additional 1-2-3 graph capabilities.

This chapter shows you how to perform the following tasks:

- Choose the appropriate graph type
- Add descriptive labels and numbers to graphs
- Customize the default graph display
- Specify graph colors and hatches
- View and save graphs
- Print graphs
- Include graphs in reports

Choosing an Appropriate Graph Type

You can use 1-2-3 to build eight types of graphs: line, bar, stacked-bar, area, mixed, pie, XY, and HLCO. In some cases, more than one graph type is appropriate for the data being graphed. Choosing the best graph for a given application sometimes is a matter of personal preference. A line, bar, or pie graph often is the best choice if you plan to graph only a single data range. At other times, however, only one graph type will do the job. HLCO graphs, for example, are specialized for presenting certain types of stock-market information. You may want to review the section "Creating Simple Graphs" in Chapter 2 before proceeding with this chapter.

The following table briefly summarizes each graph type and its purpose. This list isn't exhaustive, of course. Your creativity and ingenuity are the only real limiting factors when you apply the graph types to your data.

Type	Purpose
Line	Shows the trend of numeric data over time. Useful for comparing data ranges with a large number of data points (more than 20).
Bar	Compares related data at one point in time or shows the trend of numeric data over time. Best used with a small number of data points (fewer than 20).
XY	Shows the relationship between one numeric independent variable and one or more numeric dependent variables.
Stack-Bar	Shows two or more data ranges in terms of the proportion of the total contributed by each data point.
Pie	Graphs a single data series, showing what percentage of the total each data point contributes. (Don't use this type of graph if your data contains negative numbers.)
HLCO	Shows fluctuations in a stock's high-low-close-open prices over time. Other types of data with high, low, and average values (such as test scores and temperatures) also can be plotted as HLCO.
Mixed	Combines line and bar graphs to show (in a single graph) data best shown in bar format and data best shown in line format.
Area	Shows two or more data ranges in terms of the proportion of the total contributed by each data point by stacking and shading under the lines of a line chart. Useful for graphing more than 20 data points.

Building All Graph Types

This section focuses briefly on each of the graph types, giving an example and discussing any enhancements that apply particularly to that type. In this section, each example graph is based on the worksheet shown in figure 23.1.

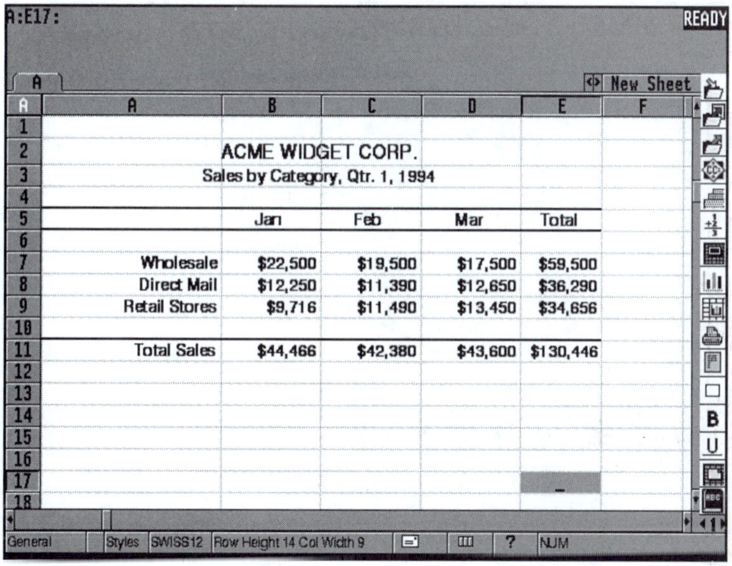

Fig. 23.1
A worksheet for examples of 1-2-3 graphs.

Line Graphs

Line graphs are useful for showing change over time. The line graph in figure 23.2 shows the steady increase in retail-store sales during the first quarter. Before you create this (or any other) graph, choose **/G**raph **R**eset **G**raph to reset any existing graph settings. Because **L**ine is the default graph type, you don't need to specify the graph type. Use the following command sequence to select the data ranges (press Enter after specifying the ranges and titles):

/Graph **A** **A:B9..A:D9**

Next, select the X data range:

X A:B5..A:D5

Finally, enter the graph titles:

Options **T**itles **F**irst **Acme Widget Corp.**

Titles **S**econd **Retail Stores**

When you press F10 (Graph), the line graph appears.

Fig. 23.2
A line graph depicting first-quarter retail sales.

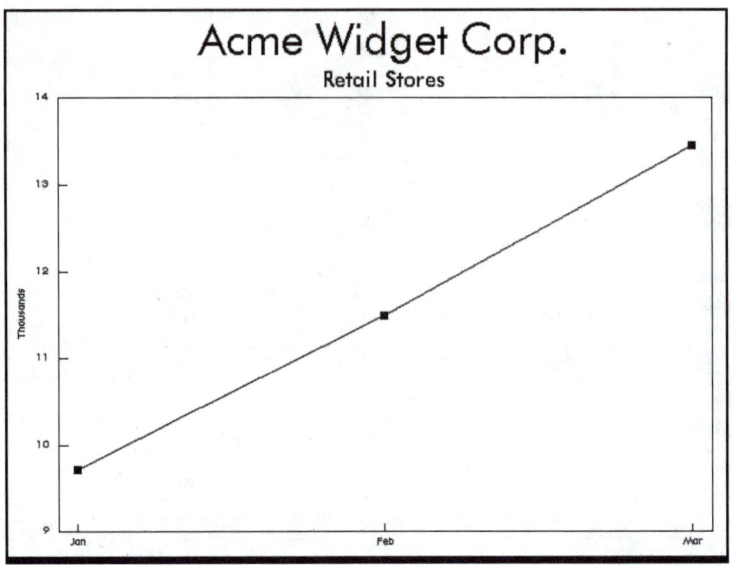

Bar Graphs

Bar graphs are frequently used to compare data over time. Suppose that you want to create a bar graph that shows each month's sales by category. A bar graph is appropriate for this data because the differences in sales figures can be clearly shown by the different bar heights.

To create the bar graph shown in figure 23.3, first choose **/G**raph **R**eset **G**raph to reset any existing graph settings. Then use the following command sequence to select the graph type and the data ranges (press Enter after specifying ranges and titles):

    /Graph **T**ype **B**ar

    A A:B7..A:D7

    B A:B8..A:D8

    C A:B9..A:D9

Next, select an X data range:

    X A:B5..A:D5

Continue with the following steps to add descriptive labels and legends to the graph. These and other commands are described more fully in "Adding

Descriptive Labels and Numbers" later in this chapter. Specify a range for data legends:

Options **L**egend **R**ange **A:A7..A:A9**

Finally, instead of typing the text for the titles, specify that the labels in cells A2 and A3 be used as graph titles (precede these cell references with a backslash):

Titles **F**irst **\A2**

Titles **S**econd **\A3**

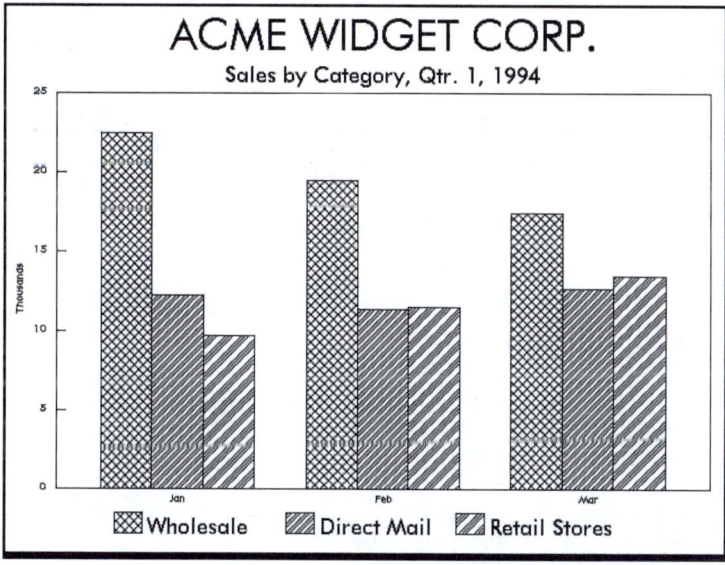

Fig. 23.3
Data from the worksheet in fig. 23.1, shown in a bar graph.

> **Note**
>
> The titles in figure 23.1 do not appear to be in cells A2 and A3 because they have been centered over the worksheet with the Wysiwyg **:T**ext **A**lign **C**enter command.

The resulting graph, shown in figure 23.3, clearly shows that Wholesale sales have been decreasing, Direct Mail sales have been holding about steady, and Retail Store sales have been increasing. In this graph, each of the three bars clustered around a tick mark on the x-axis represents sales from a certain category for that month. In each set of bars, the far left bar represents data

710 Chapter 23—Creating Effective Graphs

range A; the next, data range B; and the next, data range C. Monthly headings are centered under each bar cluster along the x-axis.

> **Note**
>
> Because you need this graph for later examples, assign it a name by choosing **/G**raph **N**ame **C**reate and entering **Q1SALES**. Now you can modify the graph in the following examples and recall it in its original form when needed.

Suppose you want to display this graph horizontally. Choose **T**ype **F**eatures **H**orizontal; the graph now is displayed as shown in figure 23.4. Horizontal display can be used with other graph types (except pie), but it is particularly appropriate for bar graphs. The choice between **V**ertical and **H**orizontal usually is a matter of personal preference.

Fig. 23.4
The graph from fig. 23.3, displayed horizontally.

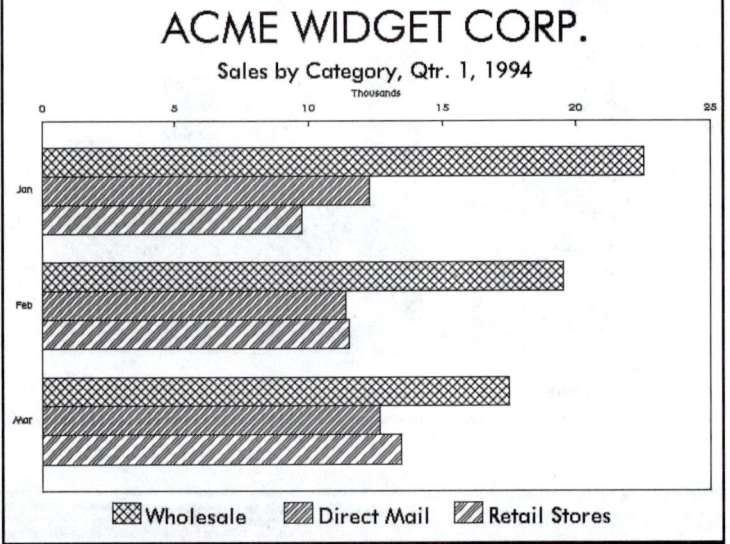

Stack-Bar Graphs

You may want to experiment with different graph types when you plot multiple time-series data. If the data ranges combine to produce a meaningful figure (for example, total monthly sales for Acme Widget Corp.), try using **S**tack-Bar as a graph type. These bars are plotted in the order A-B-C-D-E-F, with the A range closest to the x-axis. After entering the command sequences to create figure 23.4, you can create the stacked-bar graph shown in figure 23.5 by choosing **Type Features Vertical** to return to vertical graph display. Then choose **Type Stack-Bar** from the main **/Graph** menu, and choose **View** to display the graph on-screen.

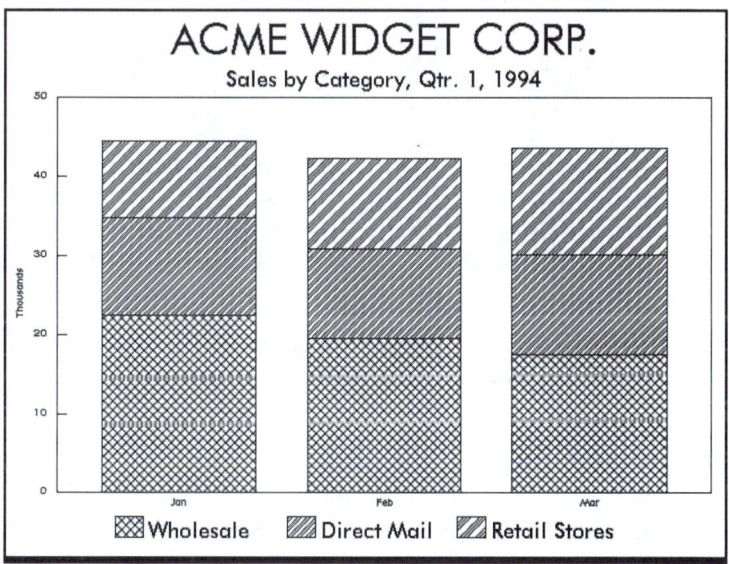

Fig. 23.5
The graph from fig. 23.3, displayed in stacked-bar format.

All the options you set to produce the bar graph in figure 23.3 are carried over to the new stacked-bar graph. 1-2-3 also automatically adjusts the upper and lower limits of the y-axis. In a stacked-bar graph, the lower limit always must be zero.

Area Graphs

If you have too much data to display clearly in a stacked-bar graph, consider using an area graph. Area graphs are stacked versions of line charts, showing the proportion of the total each of your data ranges represents. In addition, area charts shade or color the area under each line, hence the name *area chart*.

You can change the stacked-bar graph in the preceding section to an area chart simply by choosing **/Graph Type Area**. Figure 23.6 shows the resulting area graph.

Fig. 23.6
The graph from fig. 23.3, displayed as an area chart.

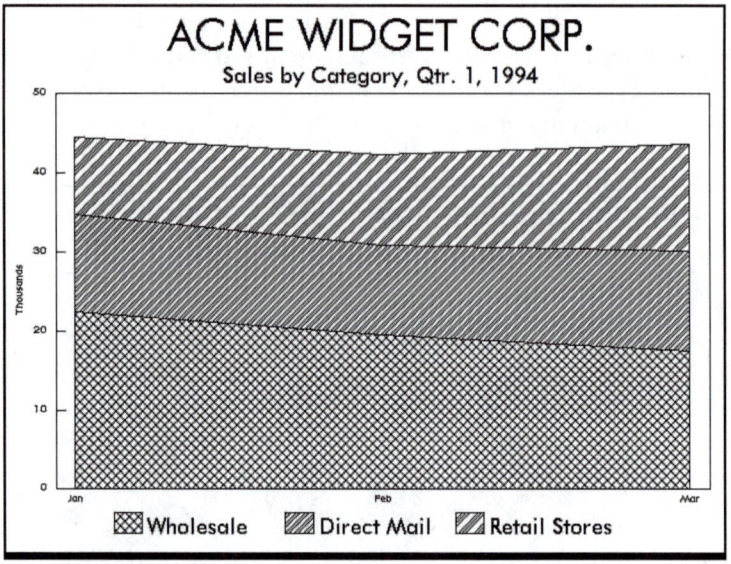

Mixed Graphs

A mixed graph is nothing more than a combination of the line and bar types. Data ranges A, B, and C are plotted as bars, and ranges D, E, and F are plotted as lines.

Suppose that you want to modify the graph in figure 23.3 to be a mixed graph, displaying individual sales categories as bars and total sales as a line. First, recall the settings (remember that you saved them as a named graph) by choosing **/G**raph **N**ame **U**se, highlighting Q1SALES, and pressing Enter. The graph is displayed as shown in figure 23.3. Return to the **/G**raph menu, choose **T**ype **M**ixed, and redisplay the graph. You may be surprised to see that it hasn't changed!

The graph didn't change because only the bar ranges, A through C, have been assigned. If no line ranges are assigned, a mixed graph displays just as a bar graph does. The opposite is true as well: if line ranges and no bar ranges are assigned, a mixed graph displays just like a line graph.

You can complete the mixed graph by entering the following commands from the main **/G**raph menu (press Enter after specifying the ranges):

D A:B11..A:D11

Options **L**egend **D** **\A11**

Quit **V**iew

The result is the graph shown in figure 23.7. The message of this graph is that although individual sales categories are changing, total sales remain relatively constant.

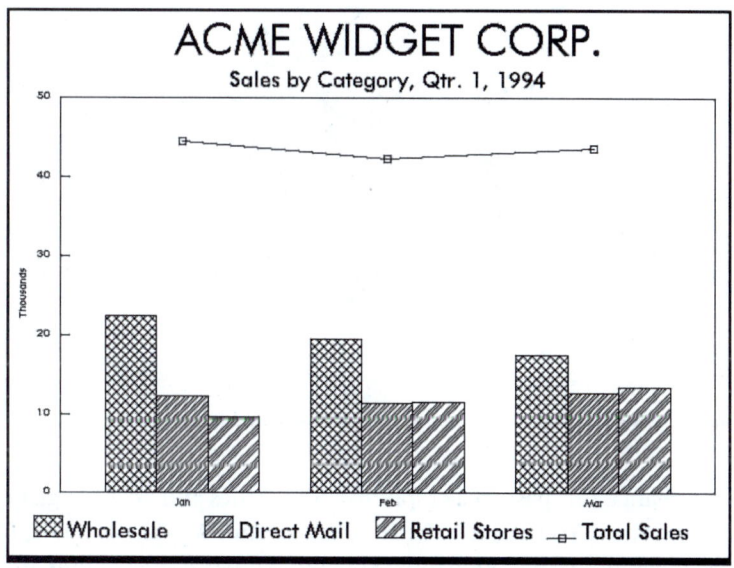

Fig. 23.7
A mixed graph.

Often, the data graphed as the line in a mixed graph is not in the same relative numerical range as the bars. Use the second y-axis option to graph this range so that it appears in the same relative region of the chart.

Pie Graphs

You use a pie graph to plot a single data range that contains only positive numbers. Many of the /**G**raph menu options, including those that deal with graph axes, don't apply to pie graphs.

▶ "Adding a Second Y-Scale," p. 759

Suppose that you want to construct a pie graph from the data shown in figure 23.1, and you want to graph the percentage of total sales in each category for the quarter. Start by choosing /**G**raph **R**eset **G**raph. Next, choose **T**ype **P**ie and specify **A:E7..A:E9** as data range **A**. When you display the graph, it appears as shown in figure 23.8.

1-2-3 automatically calculates and displays parenthetically the percentage of the whole represented by each pie slice. You can suppress these percentage values by using a C range, as described later in this section.

714   Chapter 23—Creating Effective Graphs

Fig. 23.8
A default pie graph.

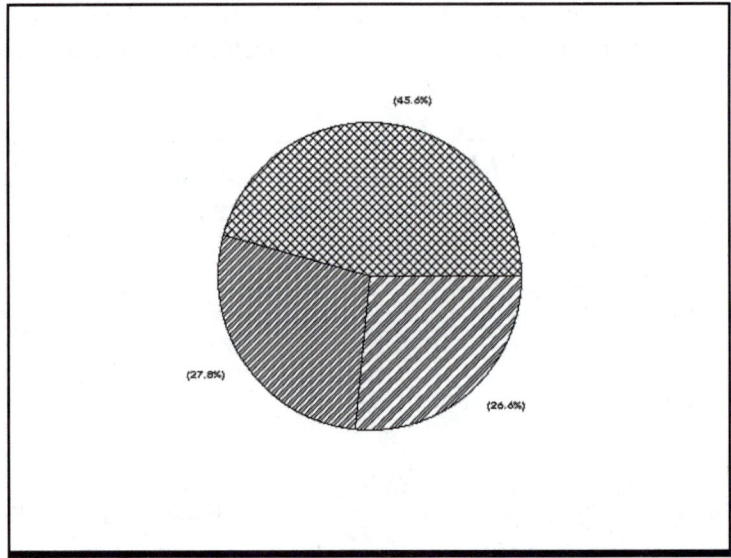

You can enhance this basic pie graph by adding titles and an X range of explanatory labels. You can use the labels in column A as the X range, for example, by entering the following command sequence (press Enter after specifying ranges and titles):

/Graph X   A:A7..A:A9

Options Titles First \A2

Titles Second **Total Sales by Category**

Quit View

Figure 23.9 shows the resulting graph.

Tip
Adding 100 to the numeric code in the B range results in an exploded pie slice.

To shade or explode pie slices in the sales-by-category worksheet graph, you must add a B range to the graph. Although the B range can be anywhere in the worksheet, place it adjacent to the A range for this example. In cells A:F7..A:F9, enter the values **4**, **5**, and **106**, in that order. (See "Specifying Colors, Hatches, Line Styles, and Symbols" later in this chapter for more information on using data values to control colors and shading.) From the /Graph menu, specify those three cells as the **B** range. Choosing **V**iew displays the graph shown in figure 23.10.

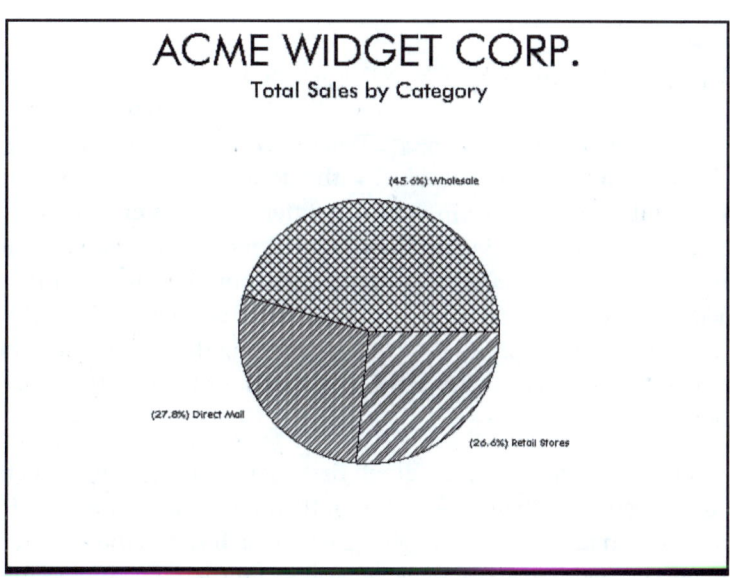

Fig. 23.9
A pie graph enhanced with titles and labels.

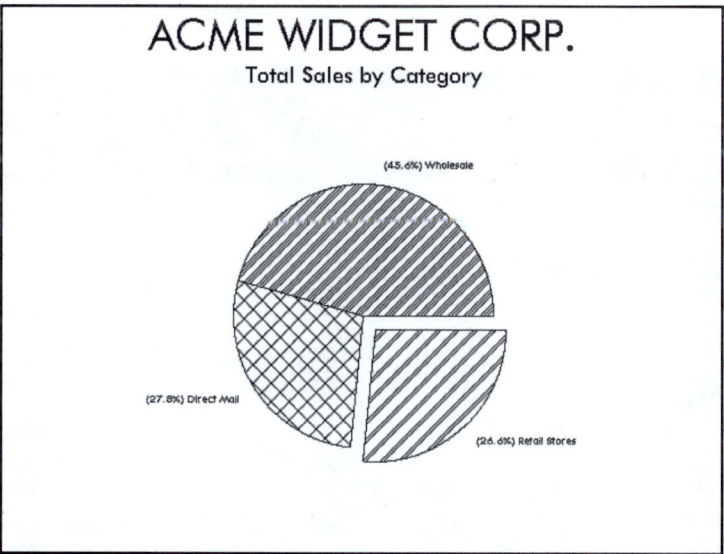

Fig. 23.10
An exploded pie graph.

To suppress the display of percentage values on the pie graph, assign a C range in the same manner as the B range. A value of 0 in a cell in the C range suppresses the percentage display for the corresponding pie slice. A blank cell retains the percentage display. You can have a C range with no B range.

XY Graphs

The XY graph, often called a *scatter plot,* is a unique variation of a line graph. In an XY graph, a data point's position on the x-axis is determined by a numeric value rather than by a category. Two or more data items from the same data range can have the same X value. Rather than show time-series data, XY graphs illustrate the relationships between different ranges of data items: age and income, for example, or educational achievements and salary. Think of one data item (X) as the *independent variable,* and consider the other item (Y) to be dependent on the first—that is, the *dependent variable.* Use the /**G**raph menu's **X** data range to specify the range containing the independent variable, and use one or more of the **A B C D E F** options to enter the dependent variable(s).

Suppose that you want to create a graph that shows the relationship between the amount spent on advertising each month and the sales generated. For the example, you can use the data in figure 23.11, which shows the advertising budget and sales by month for an entire year. A line graph would be an appropriate type for plotting sales as a function of month. For sales versus advertising budget, however, you must use an XY graph.

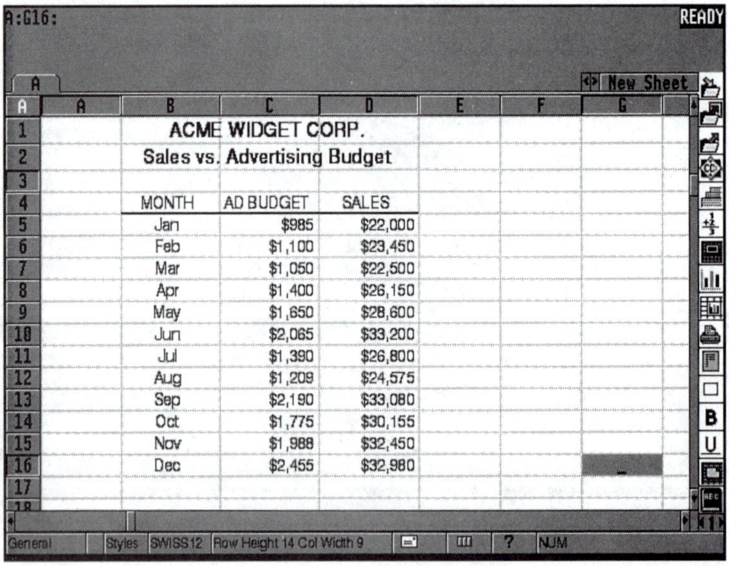

ACME WIDGET CORP.
Sales vs. Advertising Budget

MONTH	AD BUDGET	SALES
Jan	$985	$22,000
Feb	$1,100	$23,450
Mar	$1,050	$22,500
Apr	$1,400	$26,150
May	$1,650	$28,600
Jun	$2,065	$33,200
Jul	$1,390	$26,800
Aug	$1,209	$24,575
Sep	$2,190	$33,080
Oct	$1,775	$30,155
Nov	$1,988	$32,450
Dec	$2,455	$32,980

Fig. 23.11
Data to be plotted in an XY graph.

Tip
If you want to connect the points with a line, sort the X range with the /**D**ata **S**ort command or the Sort Ascending SmartIcon before graphing.

To create the XY graph, enter the following commands (press Enter after specifying ranges):

/**G**raph **T**ype **XY**

X A:C5..A:C16

A A:D5..A:D16

XY graphs usually are drawn without lines connecting the points. If the values aren't sorted, the lines can cross one another, creating a graph that is very difficult to read. For XY graphs, therefore, you usually set **F**ormat to **S**ymbols. Setting **F**ormat to **S**ymbols plots each data point as a symbol without lines connecting the symbols. Use the following **/G**raph commands to make that change and to add some other enhancements (press Enter after specifying the titles):

◄ "Sorting Database Records," p. 631

/Graph **O**ptions **F**ormat **G**raph **S**ymbols

Quit

Titles **F**irst **\A1**

Titles **S**econd **\A2**

Titles **X**-Axis **\C4**

Titles **Y**-Axis **\D4**

Figure 23.12 shows the resulting graph.

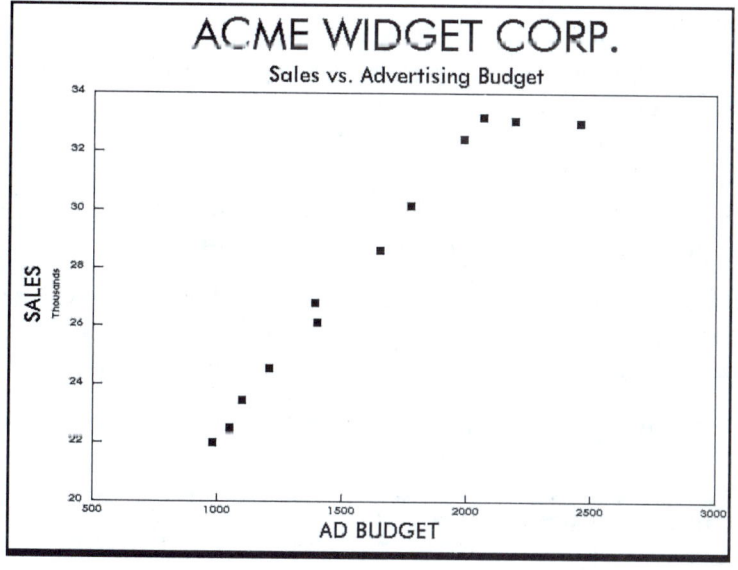

Fig. 23.12
An XY graph, showing the relationship between advertising and sales.

This graph clearly shows a trend between advertising expenditures and sales. As the advertising budget goes up, so do sales. Notice, however, that the plot flattens out at the top, suggesting that when advertising expenditures increase beyond $2,000 per month, they aren't having any additional effect on sales.

HLCO Graphs

HLCO stands for *high-low-close-open*. This graph is a special type used to graph data about the price of a stock over time. The following table lists the meanings of the values.

Value	Description
High	The stock's highest price in the given time period
Low	The stock's lowest price in the given time period
Close	The stock's price at the end (close) of the time period
Open	The stock's price at the start (open) of the time period

HLCO graphs are specialized for stock-market information, but you also can use HLCO graphs to track other kinds of fluctuating data over time, such as high, low, and average temperatures during the day or buy and sell rates for exchanging currencies.

Each set of data—four figures representing high, low, close, and open values—is represented in the graph as one vertical line. The vertical extent of the line (that is, the length) is from the low value to the high value. The close value is represented by a tick mark extending right from the line, and the open value is represented by a tick mark extending left. The total number of lines in the graph depends on the number of time periods included.

An HLCO graph also can include a set of bars and a line across the graph. The bars and line can be used for any quantity you want. In the financial world, the bars often are used to illustrate daily trading volume for a stock.

Data ranges for an HLCO graph are assigned as described in the following table.

Range	Values or Elements
A	High values
B	Low values

Range	Values or Elements
C	Closing values
D	Opening values
E	Bars
F	Line

You don't need to specify all these ranges; the minimum requirements are that the A and B ranges be specified, *or* the E range, *or* the F range. The graph in figure 23.13, for example, shows an HLCO plot of common-stock data for a fictional company. Graph enhancements have been added (an X range, titles, and axis labels).

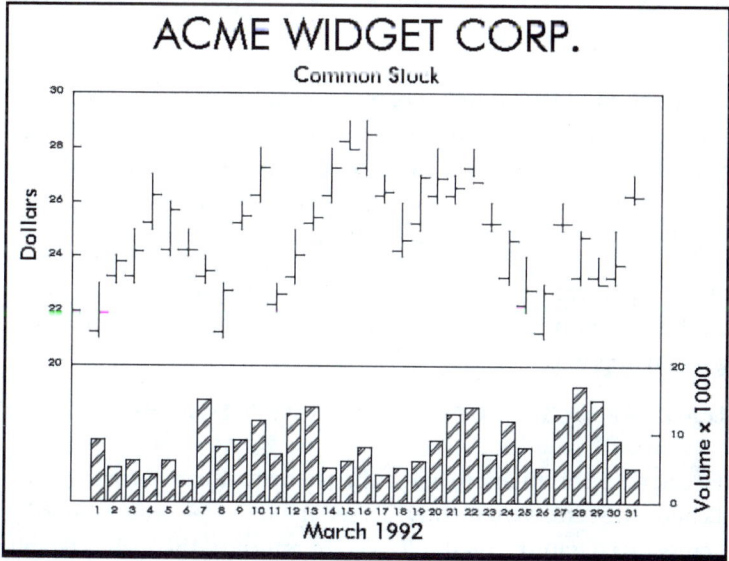

Fig. 23.13
An HLCO graph of stock-market information.

> **Note**
>
> Stock-market figures downloaded from on-line information services are usually text labels in the form '45 3/8. Use the @VALUE function (see Chapter 3, "Finding Solutions with Formulas and Functions") to change these labels to values that can be used in an HLCO graph.

Creating Graphs with the QuickGraph SmartIcon

The QuickGraph SmartIcon in 1-2-3 Release 4 provides an easy way to create a basic 1-2-3 graph. To use the QuickGraph SmartIcon, preselect the range of data for the graph and then click the QuickGraph SmartIcon. 1-2-3 displays the QuickGraph settings dialog box, preset for a columnwise bar graph. Columns in the range correspond to the X through F ranges. Use the mouse or the keyboard to change the graph type or options as necessary, or to select a rowwise graph. Click OK or press enter to display the graph. The graph appears in full-screen view as if you had selected **V**iew from the **/G**raph menu. Press any key to return to READY mode.

◀ "Creating Simple Graphs," p. 143

Adding Descriptive Labels and Numbers

1-2-3 Release 4 provides a number of ways to add descriptive labels and numbers to a graph. These labels include legends to describe the data ranges and the graph titles and notes. Some of these capabilities were used to provide additional explanations in the examples in the preceding section. This section describes these and additional 1-2-3 capabilities in detail.

Most of the 1-2-3 features for enhancing a graph's appearance are accessed through the **/G**raph **O**ptions menu. When you make this selection, the following menu appears:

    Legend **F**ormat **T**itles **G**rid **S**cale **C**olor **B**&**W** **D**ata-Labels **A**dvanced **Q**uit

As you work with this menu to add enhancements to your graphs, you should check the results frequently. To see the most recent version of your graph, press F10 (Graph); you don't need to return to the main **/G**raph menu to choose **V**iew. Press any key to exit the graph display and restore the **/G**raph menu to the screen. Alternatively, if you are working on a graph that has been placed over the worksheet, press F6 (Window) to hide the dialog box and display the underlying worksheet and graph. Depending on your video hardware, you also may be able to use the **/W**orksheet **W**indow **G**raph command to display the graph in a screen window (see "Viewing Graphs in a Screen Window" later in this chapter).

To add descriptive information to a graph, use the **T**itles, **D**ata-Labels, and **L**egend options in the **/G**raph **O**ptions menu. In addition, for all graph types except XY, you can use the **X** data-range option.

The **/G**raph **O**ptions **T**itles command positions the text in appropriate positions in the graph. You also can use the **:G**raph **E**dit command (described later) to add titles and text to the graph. The **:G**raph **E**dit commands allow greater flexibility but also require accurate placement by the user. For most graphs, the **/G**raph **O**ptions **T**itles command provides the best way to add descriptive titles to a graph.

Using the Titles Option

When you choose **/G**raph **O**ptions **T**itles, the following menu appears and the Graph Titles dialog box appears:

First **S**econd **X**-Axis **Y**-Axis **2**Y-Axis **N**ote **O**ther-Note

The **F**irst and **S**econd options center the titles you enter above the graph. The first title appears in larger type above the second title. After choosing **F**irst or **S**econd from the **/G**raph **O**ptions **T**itles menu, you can type the desired title in response to the prompt, or enter a backslash followed by the address or range name of the worksheet cell that contains the label or number to be used as the title.

The **X**-Axis, **Y**-Axis, and **2**Y-Axis options label the graph axes. **X**-Axis centers a horizontal label below the x-axis. **Y**-Axis places a vertical label to the left of the left y-axis. **2**Y-Axis places a vertical label to the right of the right y-axis. You can type the labels or enter a cell address or range name preceded by a backslash.

The **N**ote and **O**ther-Note options enter "footnotes" that appear in the lower left corner of the graph. **N**ote is the first line of a footnote, and **O**ther-Note is the second line. You can type the notes, or specify a cell address or range name.

Figure 23.14 shows the positions of the various titles as they appear in a graph.

Suppose that you want to enhance the basic line graph of the sales data amounts in figure 23.15. You can enter four titles by using cell references for two of the titles and typing new descriptions for the others.

Tip
Use the Wysiwyg **:G**raph **E**dit **A**dd **T**ext command to add text anywhere in a graph that has been placed in a worksheet.

Fig. 23.14
Graph positions of the seven **O**ptions **T**itles options.

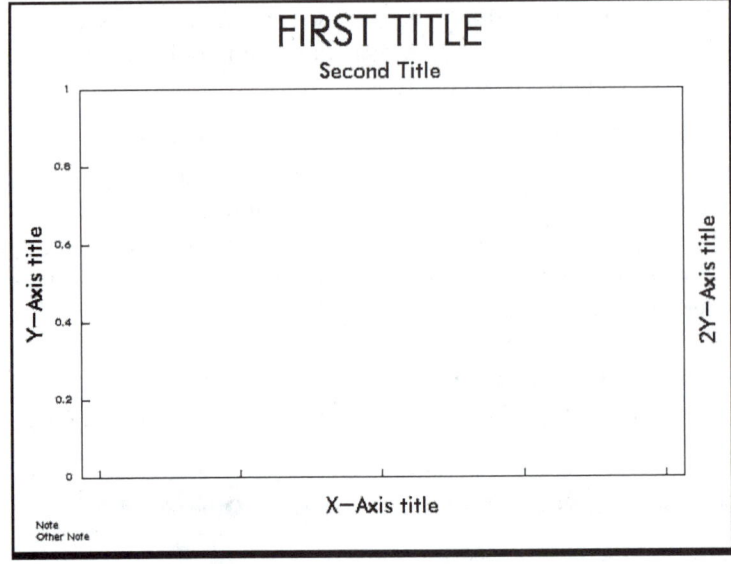

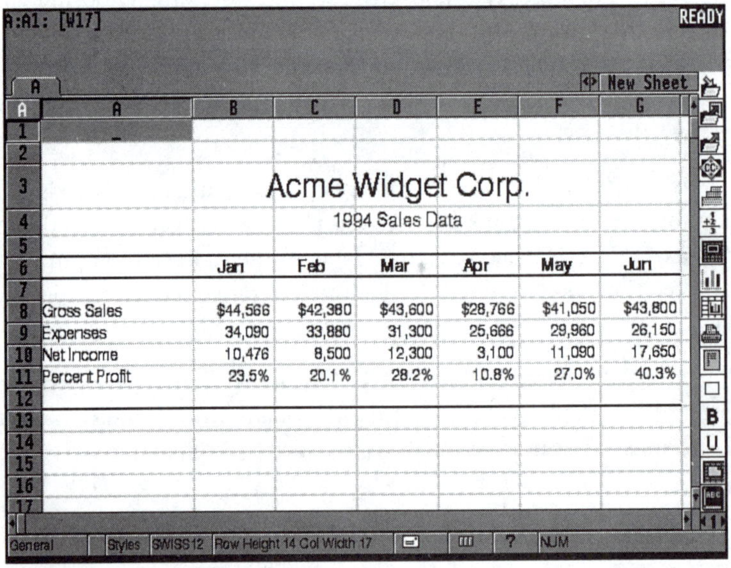

Fig. 23.15
The sales data worksheet.

Tip
When you use a backslash (\) to display formula data in a title, the formula information is updated in the graph every time the worksheet formula is recalculated.

Choose **/G**raph **O**ptions **T**itles to display the Graph Titles dialog box (see fig. 23.16). You can now use the menu command to set the titles or fill in the text boxes in the dialog box. To use the dialog box, click the box with the mouse and then click the input field for **F**irst. With the keyboard, press F2 (Edit) to use the dialog box. Type **\A3** to reference the cell containing

Adding Descriptive Labels and Numbers   **723**

Acme Widget Corp. Then use the mouse to select the **S**econd text box or press Tab. Enter **\A4** to make the label in cell A4 the second title centered above the graph.

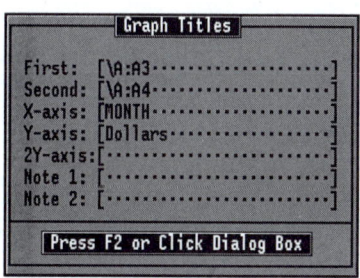

Fig. 23.16
The Graph Titles dialog box, showing the titles selected for a graph.

> **Note**
> The titles *appear* to be in cells B3 and C4 in figure 23.15, but these titles were entered in cells A3 and A4 and centered over the worksheet.

To label the x-axis, select or tab to the **X**-Axis text box and type **MONTH.** To enter the fourth title, select **Y**-Axis field and type **Dollars**. Figure 23.16 shows the completed Graph Titles dialog box.

Now, to check the graph, press F10 (Graph). Your graph should look like the enhanced graph shown in figure 23.17.

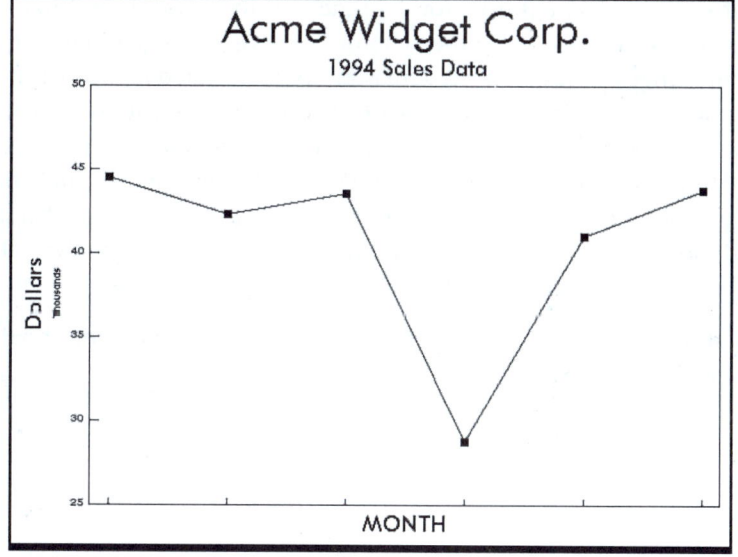

Fig. 23.17
The line graph with titles.

To edit a title, use the command sequence you used to create the title. The existing text, cell reference, or range name appears in the control panel, ready for you to edit. If you want to eliminate that title, press Esc and then press Enter.

Adding Data Labels to a Graph

Sometimes you may want to use labels in the graph to explain the data points. You can add these labels by choosing **D**ata-Labels from the **/G**raph **O**ptions menu. Following is the resulting menu:

    A B C D E F Group **Q**uit

From this menu, select the data range to which you are assigning data labels. Choose **G**roup if the data labels for multiple ranges are in adjacent columns. You cannot type the data labels, except with the **:G**raph **E**dit command; instead, you must specify a worksheet range containing the labels. You can specify the range by typing cell addresses, by pointing, or by entering a range name. After you specify the data-label range, the following menu appears:

    Center **L**eft **A**bove **R**ight **B**elow

The choice you make from this menu determines where each data label is displayed in relation to the corresponding data point. The labels (or numbers) in the data-label range are assigned to the graph data points in the order in which they are arranged in the worksheet.

Continue to enhance your sample line graph by entering as data labels the *Jan* through *Jun* headings from row 6 of the sales data worksheet. Choose **/G**raph **O**ptions **D**ata-Labels; then choose **A** to assign labels to the A range (the only range in the graph). To enter the six abbreviated monthly headings from row 6 of the worksheet, type **A:B6..A:G6** in response to the prompt for a label range and then press Enter. To specify a position for the labels, choose **A**bove from the following menu. Each set of data labels can have only one position; for example, you cannot position one cell within a data-label range *above* its associated data point and another cell within that same data-label range *below* its associated data point.

Now press F10 (Graph) to display the graph on-screen. Your graph should resemble figure 23.18.

Adding Descriptive Labels and Numbers   **725**

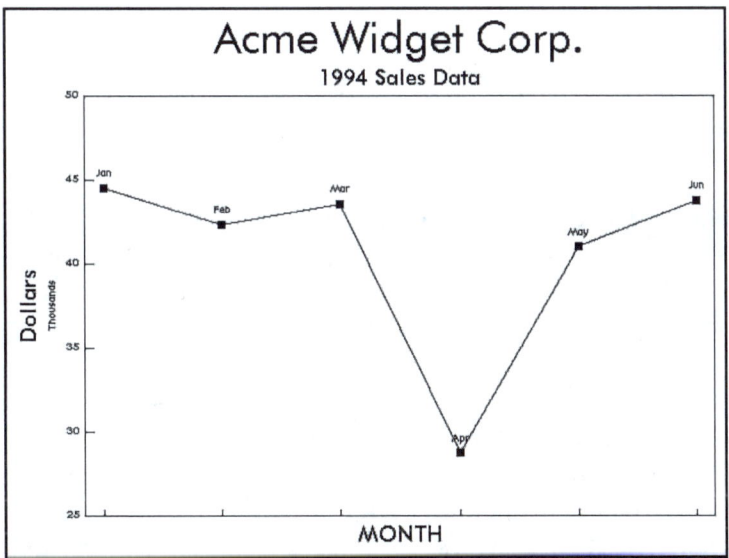

Fig. 23.18
A graph with data added as data labels.

> **Note**
>
> If you graph more than one data series, attach the data labels to the data range that includes the largest numeric values. Then choose **A**bove to position the data labels above the data points. These steps place the data labels as high as possible in the graph, where they don't obscure the data points.

The cells you specify for a data-label range can contain labels or values. If values, they are displayed in the graph with the same cell format as in the worksheet. If the values are formatted as **C**urrency with two decimal places in the worksheet, for example, they appear in Currency format in the graph.

To edit the range or position of the data labels, use the same command sequence you used to create the data labels. Then enter a different data-label range or specify a different position.

To remove data labels from a data range, follow the same steps you used to create the data labels, but specify a single empty cell as the data-label range. You cannot eliminate the existing range by pressing Esc, as you do to eliminate an unwanted title.

Caution

You can remove data labels by resetting the data range, but this method also removes the data range and any other associated options.

Note

Before reading the following section, delete the data labels that you created in the example in this section.

Entering Labels Below the X-Axis

Instead of placing descriptive information in a graph, you may prefer to enter label information along the x-axis. With all graph types except pie and XY, you can use the **/G**raph menu's **X** option to position labels below the x-axis.

To enter the *Jan* through *Jun* labels below the x-axis, choose **/G**raph **X** and enter the range containing the data labels: **A:B6..A:G6**. Then choose **V**iew. The labels *Jan* through *Jun* appear along the x-axis, as shown in figure 23.19.

Fig. 23.19
The sales data graph, with an X range showing dates.

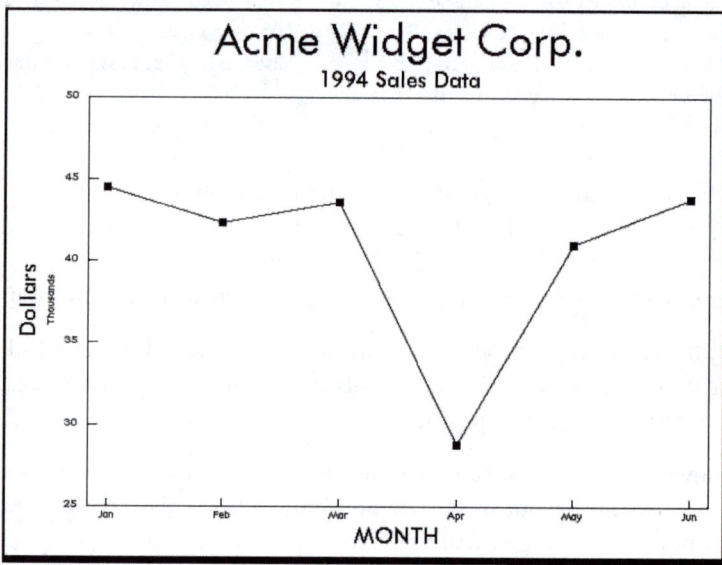

Using the Legend Option

A *data legend* is a key or label in the graph that explains the meaning of a symbol, line color, or hatch pattern. Data legends are particularly useful in graphs that include multiple data ranges.

When a graph contains more than one data range, you need to distinguish among the different ranges. If you are using a color monitor and you choose **C**olor from the **/G**raph **O**ptions menu, 1-2-3 differentiates data ranges with color. If the **B**&W (black and white) option is in effect, data ranges are marked with different symbols in line graphs and with different hatching patterns in other types of graphs. (Refer to table 2.5 in Chapter 2, "What Every 1-2-3 User Should Know," for a summary of the assignments that are specific to each data range.)

To add legends to a graph, choose **O**ptions **L**egend from the main **/G**raph menu. The following menu appears:

A B C D E F Range

Select the data range to which you are assigning a legend. Then, in response to the prompt, type the text for the legend, or enter a backslash followed by the address of the worksheet cell containing the legend text. Choose **R**ange to specify a worksheet range containing legend text for all the data ranges.

To illustrate the use of legends, you can add a second data range to the sales data line graph and then add legends to identify the two data ranges. Suppose that you want the graph to reflect two items: Gross Sales and Expenses. To add the second data range, choose **/G**raph **B** and then enter the range for the Expenses data: **A:B9..A:G9**. Next, choose **O**ptions **L**egend **A** to specify the legend for the first data range. Enter **Gross Sales** or type **\A8**. The program returns to the **O**ptions menu. To specify the legend for the second data range, choose **L**egend **B** and enter **Expenses** or **\A9**. Finally, press F10 (Graph) to display the graph. The modified graph should appear similar to the one shown in figure 23.20.

Tip
Using the **R**ange option ensures that the legends always reflect the data in the worksheet and that the labels are spelled as they are in the worksheet.

> **Note**
> For this example, the origin of the graph has been changed. See "Setting Minimum and Maximum Axis Values" in Chapter 24 for details on changing the graph scale.

Fig. 23.20
A graph with two data ranges and their legends.

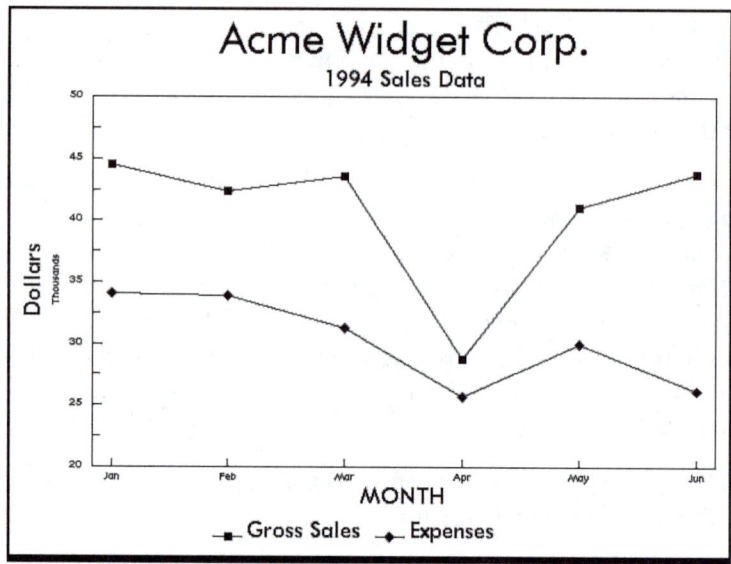

To edit a legend, use the same command sequence you used to create the legend. The existing text, cell reference, or range name appears in the control panel, ready for you to edit. To eliminate the legend, press Esc and then press Enter.

Legends are appropriate only for graphs that have two or more data series. You cannot use the **L**egend option for pie graphs, which have only one data series.

Altering the Default Graph Display

You can make graph enhancements beyond those discussed in the preceding sections by modifying the default settings 1-2-3 uses to create the basic graph. In this section, you learn how to enhance 1-2-3 graphs by changing the graph default settings.

Selecting the Format for Data in Graphs

The **/G**raph **O**ptions **F**ormat command enables you to specify the format of the lines in graphs that include lines: XY, mixed, line, and HLCO graphs. (The command affects only the line portions of mixed and HLCO graphs.) When you choose **F**ormat from the **O**ptions menu, the following menu appears:

    Graph A B C D E F Quit

Select the data range whose format you want to specify, or choose **G**raph to set the format for all data ranges. The following table describes the options in the menu that results from choosing **G**raph, **A**, **B**, **C**, **D**, **E**, or **F**.

Menu Item	Description
Lines	The data points are connected by lines, but no symbols are displayed.
Symbols	A symbol is displayed at each data point, but the symbols aren't connected by lines.
Both	Both symbols and connecting lines are displayed (the default setting).
Neither	Neither symbols nor lines are displayed. This option is used with centered data labels.
Area	The space between the indicated line and the line below it (or the x-axis) is filled with a color or hatch pattern. This choice also is available as a graph type.

Setting a Background Grid

Grid lines can help make your data-point values easier to read. 1-2-3 enables you to specify horizontal and/or vertical grid lines. The following table describes the options in the **/G**raph **O**ptions **G**rid menu.

Menu Item	Description
Horizontal	Draws a series of horizontal lines across the graph, spaced according to the tick marks on the y-axis.
Vertical	Draws a series of vertical lines across the graph, spaced according to the tick marks on the x-axis.
Both	Draws both horizontal and vertical lines.
Clear	Clears all grid lines from the graph.
Y-Axis	Determines whether horizontal grid lines are drawn according to tick marks on the left y-axis, the right y-axis, or both.
Secondary	Controls the drawing of the grid at intervals between the major grid lines.
Ticks	Adds tick marks at major or secondary intervals on the x- or y-axis.

1-2-3 Release 4 offers several new capabilities for controlling grid lines and tick marks. The graph shown in figure 23.21 includes horizontal grid lines and tick marks at the secondary intervals. Follow these steps to create this graph:

/**G**raph **O**ptions **G**rid **H**orizontal

Ticks **S**econdary **H**orizontal

Fig 23.21
A graph with a horizontal grid and secondary tick marks.

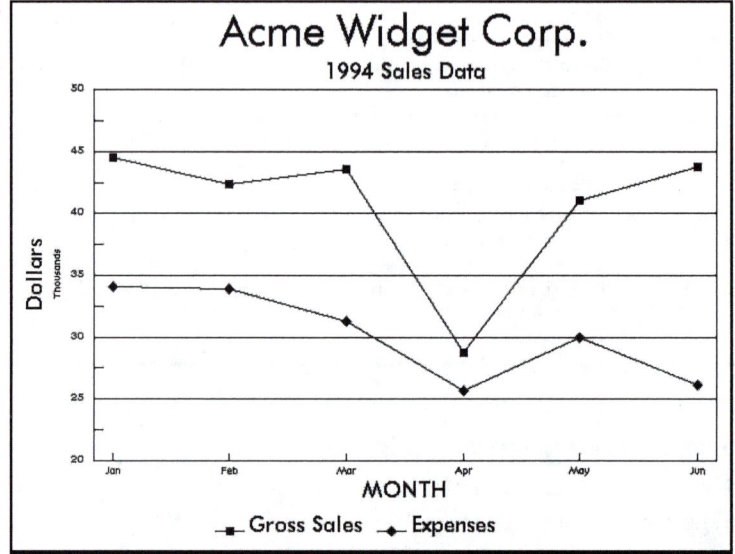

Experiment with different grid lines and tick marks, repeating the command sequence and specifying other options. You can add any combination of vertical and horizontal grid lines and tick marks. To eliminate the grid lines, choose /**G**raph **O**ptions **G**rid **C**lear. To eliminate secondary ticks, choose /**G**raph **O**ptions **G**rid **T**icks **C**lear.

Specifying Colors, Hatches, Line Styles, and Symbols

1-2-3 also enables you to select the color and hatching pattern for bars and shaded areas, and line styles and symbols for line graphs. Choosing **Ad**vanced from the /**G**raph **O**ptions menu takes you to the following menu:

Colors **T**ext **H**atches **S**ymbols **L**ines **Q**uit

You don't need to use any of the **A**dvanced options when you create a graph. The **A**dvanced options don't add any new data or information to a graph;

rather, they modify certain aspects of the way existing information in the graph is displayed and printed.

Specifying Colors

Choosing **/G**raph **O**ptions **A**dvanced **C**olors specifies the colors for the A-through-F data ranges and also enables you to hide one or more of the A-through-F ranges. The colors specified with this option are used in the graph display and during printing (if you have a color printer). When you choose **C**olors, the following menu appears:

A B C D E F Quit

Select the range whose color you want to specify. The following table describes the options in the resulting menu.

Menu Item	Description
1 through **8**	The color that corresponds to the selected number is used for all values in the specified data range. The particular colors that correspond to the numbers 1 through 8 depend on your graphics hardware and your printer.
Hide	The selected data range isn't displayed.
Range	Enables you to specify a worksheet range containing the color numbers to be assigned to individual values in the selected data range.

If you choose the **R**ange option, the color range must be the same size as the data range, and can contain values from 1 through 14. The color values are assigned, in order, to the values in the data range.

Although the **A**dvanced **C**olors menu provides only 8 colors, a color range enables you to specify 14 different colors. Display and printing of these 14 colors depend on your hardware.

By using a conditional function in the color range, you can display data points in a color that depends on their value. To display values above 10,000 in color 4 and values less than or equal to 10,000 in color 7, for example, follow these steps (assuming that the A data range is A:C4..A:C13):

1. Select a worksheet location for the color range—for example, A:D4..A:D13.

2. In cell A:D4, enter the formula **@IF(C4>10000,4,7)**, and then copy it to A:D4..A:D13.

3. Assign the color range by choosing **/G**raph **O**ptions **A**dvanced **C**olors **A** **R**ange and entering **A:D4..A:D13**.

By entering formulas in your color range, you can emphasize certain aspects of your data with colors.

◀ "Using the Logical Functions," p. 198

> **Note**
>
> The default colors for data ranges A through F are colors 2 through 7, respectively. When you use a color range, the first color in the range is used for the legend key (if any) for that data range. A negative value in the color range hides the corresponding value in the data range.

The **/G**raph **O**ptions **A**dvanced **C**olors **A** **R**ange setting is used for pie graphs only under certain conditions. If the graph display is set to **C**olor and colors haven't been specified with a B data range (in the next section "Specifying Hatches"), the **/G**raph **O**ptions **A**dvanced **C**olors **A** **R**ange setting controls the colors used to display a pie graph. Otherwise, 1-2-3 ignores the setting.

The **:G**raph **E**dit command also offers you ways to change the colors in your graph. To change the color of the area in which the titles print (the *background*), use the **:G**raph **E**dit **C**olor **B**ackground command. To change the color of each graph range, use **:G**raph **E**dit **C**olor **M**ap.

Specifying Hatches

The **H**atches option specifies the hatch patterns used for the bars in stacked-bar, mixed, bar, and HLCO graphs; the areas between lines in area graphs; and the slices in pie graphs. You use this option similarly to the way you use **/G**raph **O**ptions **A**dvanced **C**olors. Choose **/G**raph **O**ptions **A**dvanced **H**atches, and then select the desired data range (**A** through **F**). Next, choose one of the options described in the following table.

Menu Item	Description
1 through **8**	Assigns the corresponding hatch pattern to the selected data range. Displayed hatch patterns **1** through **8** are the same for all monitors, but printed hatch patterns may differ depending on your printer.
Range	Enables you to specify a worksheet *hatch range* that contains the hatch numbers to be assigned to individual values in the selected data range.

If you choose the **R**ange option, the hatch range must be the same size as the data range and can contain values from 1 through 14. The hatch values are assigned, in order, to the values in the data range.

Using a hatch range enables you to specify 14 different hatch patterns, although the **A**dvanced **H**atch menu provides only 8 patterns; the 6 additional selections are gray scales. Negative numbers in the hatch range hide the corresponding data values. The first hatch pattern in the hatch range is used for the legend key of the corresponding data range.

By using a conditional formula in the hatch range, you can display individual data values in different hatch patterns, depending on their value. The procedure is the same as for setting the color range (explained in the preceding section).

The **/G**raph **O**ptions **A**dvanced **H**atches **A R**ange setting controls pie-graph hatch patterns only when graph display is set to **C**olor or when graph display is set to **B**&W and hatch patterns aren't specified with a B range.

1-2-3 provides 14 different shading patterns for monochrome display and 14 colors for VGA color displays. Figure 23.22 shows the pie-graph shading patterns associated with each code number.

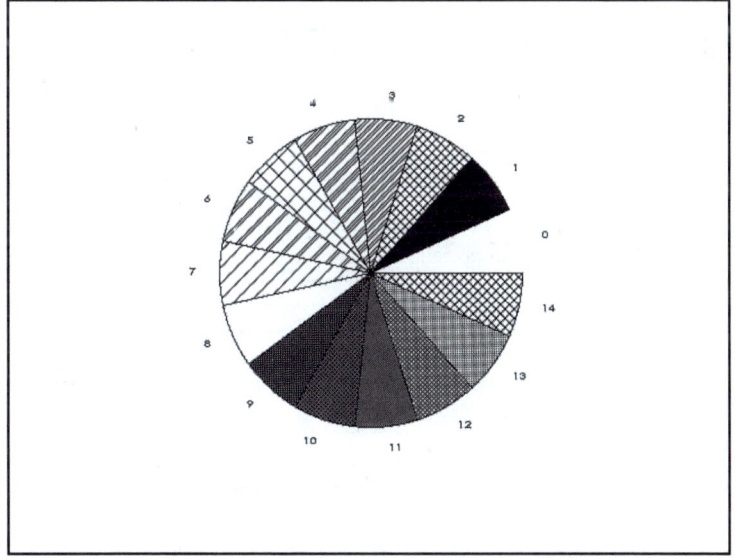

Fig. 23.22
The pie-graph hatch patterns associated with each pattern number.

1-2-3 automatically displays the pie slices in different colors or hatch patterns, depending on whether **O**ptions **B**&W or **O**ptions **C**olor is in effect. You can modify the assignment of colors or hatching and optionally *explode* individual pie slices for emphasis. To make these changes, use the B data range to enter codes for the pattern or colors for each pie slice. The B range can be any range of your worksheet that is the same size as the A data range being plotted as a pie graph. The codes for color *or* hatch pattern, depending on whether the graph is displayed in black and white or color, are listed in the following table.

Code	Meaning
0	Unshaded pie slice without an outer border
1 through 14	Specified hatch pattern or color
Negative value	Hidden slice

Specifying Line Styles

The **L**ines option specifies a line style for each line of the graph. You can choose any of seven styles, or hide the line entirely. The following table lists the styles.

Menu Choice	Line Style
1	Solid
2	Dotted
3	Dashed
4	Chain-dotted
5	Long-dotted
6	Long-dashed
7	Chain-dashed
8	Hidden

To change the line style for a range, use the **/G**raph **O**ptions **A**dvanced **L**ines command. Then select a range to modify and the desired line style. Figure 23.23 shows the line styles available in 1-2-3 Release 4. Solid and hidden are not shown but also are available.

Specifying Colors, Hatches, Line Styles, and Symbols   **735**

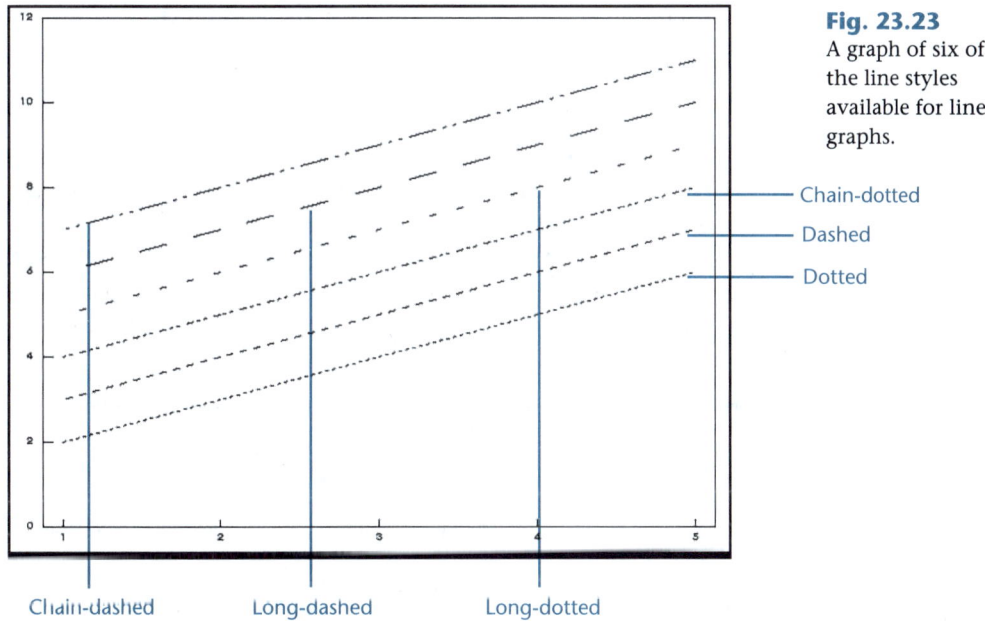

Fig. 23.23
A graph of six of the line styles available for line graphs.

Specifying Symbol Styles

The **S**ymbols option specifies a symbol style for each range in the graph. You can select from 12 different styles for symbols. The following table lists the available symbols.

Menu Choice	Symbol Style
1	Filled-in square
2	Filled-in diamond
3	Filled-in triangle
4	Hollow square
5	Hollow diamond
6	Hollow triangle
7	X symbol inside a hollow square
8	+ symbol inside a hollow diamond
9	Inverted Y symbol inside a hollow triangle
A	X symbol
B	+ symbol
C	Inverted Y symbol

To change the symbol style for a range, use the **/G**raph **O**ptions **A**dvanced **S**ymbols command. Then select a range to modify and the desired symbol style.

Setting Text Attributes

The **/G**raph **O**ptions **A**dvanced **T**ext command enables you to specify attributes for the text displayed and printed in graphs. (If you frequently change the attributes of graph text, consider taking advantage of the added flexibility of the **:G**raph **E**dit command. See "Using the Graphics Editor" in Chapter 24 for more information.) The following table describes the options in the **A**dvanced **T**ext menu.

Menu Item	Description
First	The first line of the graph title
Second	The second line of the graph title, the axis titles, and legend text
Third	The scale indicators, axis labels, data labels, and footnotes

After you specify the text group to be changed, the following menu appears:

    Color **F**ont **S**ize **Q**uit

The **C**olor option specifies the color to be used for the specified text group. The settings are displayed only when the graph display is set to **C**olor and is to be printed on a color printer. After choosing **C**olor, choose color **1** through **8** or **H**ide. As described earlier, the colors that correspond to the color numbers **1** through **8** depend on your graphics hardware and printer. **H**ide suppresses display of the selected text whether the display is set to **C**olor or to **B**&W.

The **F**ont option enables you to choose the font (type style) used for the specified text group. After choosing **A**dvanced **T**ext **F**ont, you choose the **F**irst, **S**econd, or **T**hird text group. You then can choose font **1** through **8** or **D**efault to use the default font for that text group. The defaults are font **1** for the first text group and font **3** for the second and third text groups.

The **S**ize option specifies the size of text to be used in the graph. Choose a size (**1** through **9**), or choose **D**efault to use the default size for that text group. The defaults are size **7** for the first text group, size **4** for the second text group, and size **2** for the third text group. Larger numbers correspond to larger type size.

> **Note**
> Although you can specify nine text sizes, 1-2-3 uses only three of them for screen display. Settings **1** through **3** display in the smallest text size, settings **4** through **6** in the medium size, and settings **7** through **9** in the largest size. The sizes available for printed graphs depend on your printer and on the font you chose with **/G**raph **O**ptions **A**dvanced **T**ext **F**ont.

If the text size you specify doesn't fit in the graph (both displayed and printed), 1-2-3 automatically reduces the text size (if a smaller size is available). If the text still doesn't fit, 1-2-3 truncates the text.

The **:G**raph **E**dit commands offer a way to magnify or reduce all the text in the graph. You can increase the text size by 50 percent, for example, by using the **:G**raph **E**dit **O**ptions **F**ont-Magnification command.

▶ "Using the Graphics Editor," p. 773

Viewing Graphs

Several options for viewing a graph on-screen are available in 1-2-3. You can view a graph from within the worksheet by using the entire screen to display the graph. If you have an EGA or VGA graphics adapter, you can display a graph in a screen window, leaving the worksheet visible in the remainder of the screen. Alternatively, you can place the graph in the worksheet with the **:G**raph **A**dd command (this command is discussed in Chapter 24, "Creating Power Graphs").

Viewing Graphs from the Worksheet

While working in a worksheet, you can view a graph in one of two ways: you can press F10 (Graph) or issue the **/G**raph **V**iew command. If a graph is currently defined, 1-2-3 clears the screen and displays the graph. If no graph is defined, 1-2-3 attempts to create an automatic graph (discussed in Chapter 2, "What Every 1-2-3 User Should Know"), based on the position of the cell pointer. If the cell pointer is in a valid automatic graph range, the automatic graph appears. If not, 1-2-3 beeps and displays a blank screen. Press Esc to return to the worksheet.

Viewing Graphs in a Screen Window

One useful feature of 1-2-3 is its capability to display a graph in a screen window. Choosing **/W**orksheet **W**indow **G**raph splits the screen vertically at the column to the right of the cell pointer. The current graph (if any) is displayed

Tip
After you define a graph, you can use F10 (Graph) and Esc to alternate quickly between the worksheet and the graph. Use this technique for what-if scenarios; as you modify worksheet data, you can quickly see the effects of the changes.

738   Chapter 23—Creating Effective Graphs

in the right window, and the worksheet remains displayed in the left window. Any changes made in the worksheet data or in the graph settings are reflected in the graph display immediately. Figure 23.24 shows a 1-2-3 screen with a graph displayed in a window.

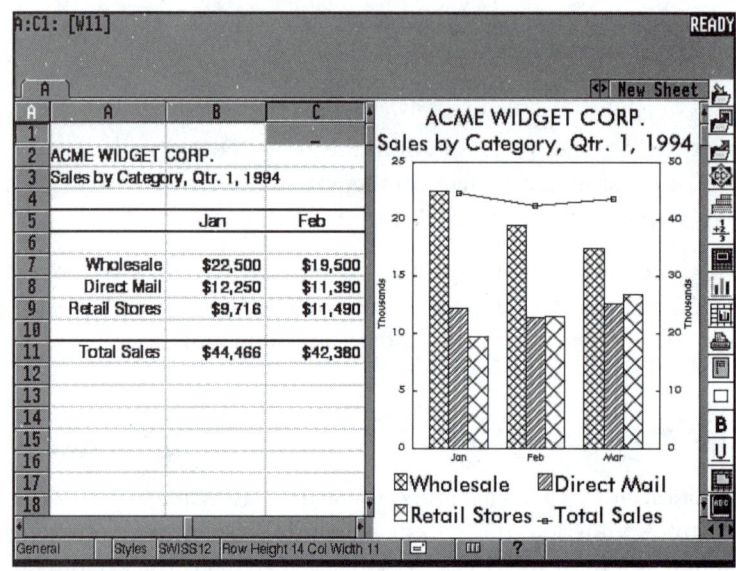

Fig. 23.24
The **/W**orksheet **W**indow **G**raph command displays the current graph in a screen window.

Tip
You can place a graph in the worksheet with the **:G**raph **A**dd command to achieve the same effect as displaying the graph in a window—with the added benefit of printing the worksheet exactly as it looks.

Displaying a graph in a window can be extremely useful during graph development. You can instantly see the effects of changes in data ranges, options, or graph types.

> **Note**
> **/W**orksheet **W**indow **G**raph doesn't work with all video hardware. With certain video adapters, you can display graphs full-screen but not in a window.

Tip
Using **:G**raph **A**dd to place a graph in the worksheet so that you can see both data and graph makes what-if graphing even easier.

Viewing Graphs in Wysiwyg

Wysiwyg offers yet another way to view your graphs. After defining the graph with 1-2-3's **/G**raph commands, you can insert it into a worksheet range with the **:G**raph **A**dd command. As with 1-2-3's graph window, you can simultaneously see your worksheet data and its graph. This capability is described in Chapter 24, "Creating Power Graphs."

Viewing a Graph in Color

The **C**olor and **B**&W (black and white) options in the **/G**raph **O**ptions menu determine whether graphs are displayed in monochrome or color. For color display, of course, you need a color monitor. You can choose **B**&W with a color or a monochrome monitor.

> **Note**
>
> When a graph is displayed in color, each data range is displayed in a different color. When displayed in monochrome, data ranges are differentiated by symbols, shapes, or shading patterns.

Saving Graphs and Graph Settings

You have learned how to create a basic graph and how to use options to enhance the display of that graph. This section shows you how to use **/G**raph **S**ave to save the graph for use by other programs. With **/G**raph **N**ame, you can save the graph settings for later use in the worksheet.

Saving Graphs on Disk

Unlike earlier versions, 1-2-3 Release 4 doesn't require you to save a graph to disk before printing. You can, however, save a graph in a disk file for later modification by other programs.

1-2-3 can save graphs in either of two file formats: *picture* or *metafile*. **P**icture (extension PIC) is the standard graph file format used in all versions of 1-2-3 and Symphony. **M**etafile (extension CGM) is a file format recognized by many other programs. Desktop publishing programs such as PageMaker and Ventura Publisher, for example, can import CGM files. Which format you use depends on the **/W**orksheet **G**lobal **D**efault **G**raph setting. To determine the current setting, choose **/W**orksheet **G**lobal **D**efault **S**tatus and look for the entry under `Graph save extension`. If `PIC` is listed, graphs are saved in picture file format. If `CGM` is displayed, metafile format is used. To change the setting, choose **/W**orksheet **G**lobal **D**efault **G**raph, and then choose **M**etafile or **P**IC.

To save a graph, choose **/G**raph **S**ave. 1-2-3 prompts you for the file name. You can use the arrow keys to highlight an existing name, or you can type a name one to eight characters long. 1-2-3 automatically supplies the PIC or CGM extension, depending on the format you selected. If a file with the specified name exists in the current directory, 1-2-3 displays a **C**ancel/**R**eplace menu similar to the one that appears when you try to save a worksheet file under an existing name. To overwrite the contents of the existing file, choose **R**eplace. To abort storage of the current graph, choose **C**ancel.

If you have set up directories for disk storage, you can store the graph to a directory other than the current directory without first issuing a **/F**ile **D**irectory command to change directories. To store the graph, choose **/G**raph **S**ave. Press Esc twice to remove all existing current-directory information. Then type the name of the directory in which you want to store the graph, followed by the file name of the graph.

Saving Graph Settings

◄ "Saving a 1-2-3 File," p. 136

Although using 1-2-3 to construct a graph from existing data in a worksheet is easy, rebuilding the graph whenever you wanted to print or display it onscreen would be tedious. Graphs saved to disk cannot be recalled into 1-2-3. You can save the settings for one or more graphs, however, and recall them later. These settings aren't saved in a separate file but are kept as part of the worksheet.

To save the current graph settings, you issue the **/G**raph **N**ame command. The following table describes the options in the **N**ame menu.

Menu Item	Description
Use	Displays a list of named graphs and makes current the one you select
Create	Saves the current graph setting under a user-specified name
Delete	Deletes a single named graph
Reset	Deletes all named graphs
Table	Creates a listing of all named graphs in the current worksheet

To use the **T**able option, move the cell pointer to the location where you want the listing to appear and press Enter. The listing occupies three columns and one row for each named graph. The listing gives the name, the type of graph (line, bar, and so on), and the first graph title. This list overwrites any existing worksheet data.

When you design multiple graphs, be sure to use the **C**reate option before you reset or change any settings for the next graph. If you forget, you may end up changing the previous graph's settings. Also, be sure to save the worksheet, even if the data hasn't changed.

Printing Graphs with the /Print Command

The first part of this chapter showed you how to create 1-2-3 graphs that are displayed on-screen. Screen graphs are fine as far as they go, but you often need to create printed copies that can be distributed to colleagues, used in business presentations, or filed for future reference.

If you have used earlier versions of 1-2-3, you may notice a major change in the way graphs are printed in Release 4. Rather than use a separate PrintGraph program, you now can print graphs from within the main 1-2-3 program.

Two main ways exist to print graphs from 1-2-3 Release 4: you can print the graphs from 1-2-3 with the **/P**rint command, or you can place a graph in the worksheet and print it with the **:P**rint command. The **/P**rint command prints graphs as they are created with the **/G**raph commands and doesn't print any enhancements added with the **:G**raph commands. Press F10 (Graph) to see how your graph will print with the **/P**rint command. Chapter 8, "Printing Reports," discusses both **P**rint commands.

This section covers the basics of printing a graph with the **/P**rint command. You also learn how to modify the quality, size, and orientation of printed graphs. In addition, you learn how to include one or more graphs in a printed report. The principles of background printing, print jobs, headers and footers, margins, and so on covered in Chapter 8 apply to graph printing as well. Before continuing with this chapter, you should be familiar with the material in Chapter 8.

Using the /Print Command

A graph (or a report containing a graph) can be sent directly to the printer or to an encoded disk file for later printing. To print immediately, choose **/P**rint **P**rinter. To send output to an encoded file, choose **/P**rint **E**ncoded and then enter the desired file name. To print the graph in the background, choose **/P**rint **B**ackground.

Note

You must run BPrint from DOS before using **/P**rint **B**ackground. See Chapter 8, "Printing Reports," for details.

Next, choose **I**mage and then **C**urrent or **N**amed-Graph. The **C**urrent option prints the current graph—that is, the graph that is displayed on-screen when you choose **/G**raph **V**iew or press F10 (Graph). The **N**amed-Graph option prints a graph you saved with **/G**raph **N**ame **C**reate. Highlight the desired name in the displayed list and press Enter. You can select any named graph from any active file.

After you specify the image to print, 1-2-3 returns to the **/P**rint [**P**,**E**] menu. Make sure that the printer is on-line, position the paper, choose **A**lign, and choose **G**o to start printing. You then can choose **Q**uit to return to your worksheet. The procedure for printing a graph is identical in many respects to printing a text-only report.

Using the /Print [P,E] Options' Advanced Image Command

Most aspects of a graph's appearance are decided when you design the graph for screen display. Colors, fonts, text size, and hatch patterns, for example, are specified as you create the graph on-screen. You cannot modify these features during printing. The final appearance of the printed graph may differ somewhat from its appearance on-screen, particularly with regard to fonts and colors (if you are using a color printer). The printed appearance of fonts and colors depends to a large extent on the specifics of your printer.

The default graph shape is a rectangle with a 4:3 (length:width) aspect ratio; the default size is a graph that fills the width of the page between the margins. By using the default page margin settings, you get a graph that is approximately 6 1/2 inches wide by 5 inches high.

Some aspects of a graph's appearance, such as the size and shape of the image, can be specified at print time. Choosing **O**ptions **A**dvanced **I**mage from the **/P**rint [**P**,**E**] menu displays the following menu options:

   Rotate **I**mage-Sz **D**ensity **Q**uit

The following sections describe these options.

Specifying the Size and Shape of the Graph

The **I**mage-Sz option specifies the size and shape of printed graphs. The following table describes the **I**mage-Sz options.

Menu Item	Description
Length-Fill	Enter a graph length in standard lines (6 per inch). 1-2-3 creates the largest possible graph using that length while maintaining the default 4:3 (length:width) ratio.

Menu Item	Description
Margin-Fill	1-2-3 creates a graph of the default shape that fills the page between the left and right margins (the default Image-Sz setting).
Reshape	Enter a graph length in standard lines (6 per inch) and a graph width in standard characters (10 per inch). 1-2-3 creates a graph of the specified size and shape.

> **Note**
>
> If the specified width or length exceeds the page size, 1-2-3 resizes the graph to fit on the page.

If you have printed a data range or another graph on part of the page, choose **/P**rint **P**rinter **P**age to have the next graph print on a new page. If you don't advance the paper to the next page and the graph doesn't fit on the remaining portion of the page, 1-2-3 automatically advances to the next page before starting the new graph.

To print the largest possible graph on a separate page, choose **R**eshape and then enter a length and width that exceed the dimensions of the page. 1-2-3 resizes the graph to the largest size that fits on the page.

When **L**ength-Fill or **R**eshape is selected and the graph length entered is longer than the page, 1-2-3 prints the largest possible graph, centering it vertically and horizontally on the page. With **M**argin-Fill, the graph is centered horizontally but not vertically.

Rotating the Graph

The **R**otate option determines whether the graph is printed upright (*portrait* format) or sideways (*landscape* format) on the page. **R**otate **N**o, the default setting, prints graphs upright on the page. Choose **R**otate **Y**es to print graphs rotated 90 degrees counterclockwise. If your printer cannot rotate graphs, choosing **Y**es has no effect.

When you rotate a graph, its size depends on the **I**mage-Sz settings. When you use the default **M**argin-Fill size, the graph's 4:3 (length:width) ratio doesn't change when the graph is rotated, but the right–left margin space is considered the length rather than the width. With the **L**ength-Fill size setting, the specified length is considered to be the width when the graph is rotated.

Rotate affects only graphs and doesn't affect the orientation used to print a data range. To rotate both data ranges and graphs, choose **/P**rint **[P,E] O**ptions **A**dvanced **L**ayout **O**rientation **L**andscape. This command sequence has an effect only if supported by your printer.

Choosing the Print Quality

The **D**ensity option offers you two choices: **D**raft or **F**inal. **D**raft produces a lower-density printout with an image that isn't as dark as **F**inal; however, on some printers, graphs in **D**raft density print significantly faster than those in **F**inal density. **D**raft density also puts less wear on printer ribbons and toner cartridges.

> **Tip**
> While you are experimenting to see how your graphs look on paper, use **D**raft density; then switch to **F**inal for the final printed copy.

> **Note**
> 1-2-3 supports only one density on some printers. In this case, the **I**mage **D**ensity selection has no effect.

Printing a Graph with Default Settings

Assuming that your printer is properly installed and connected, printing the current graph with the default settings is simple. Choose **/P**rint **P**rinter **I**mage **C**urrent **G**o; 1-2-3 prints your graph. Using the sample graph from earlier in this chapter, you get the printed result shown in figure 23.25.

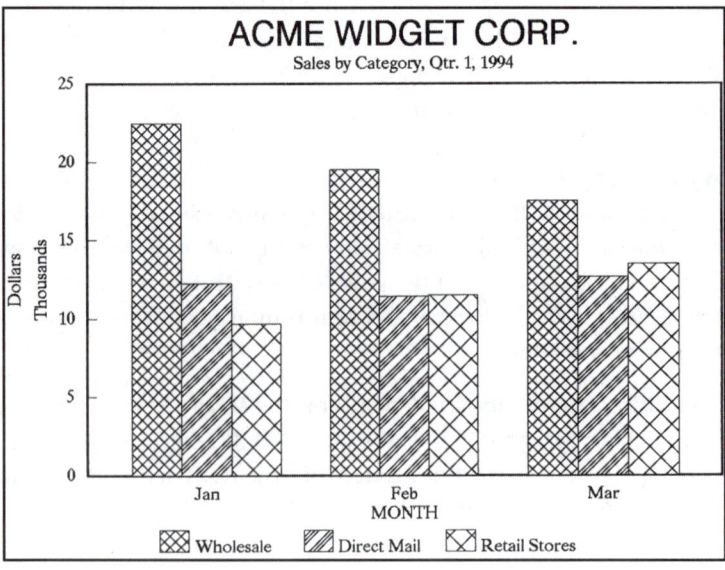

Fig. 23.25
A graph printed with the default **/P**rint **[P,E] O**ptions **A**dvanced **I**mage settings.

> **Note**
>
> With laser printers, you may need to choose **P**age before the graph will print.

To print a graph that isn't current but is a named graph, the procedure is only slightly different. Choose **/P**rint **P**rinter **I**mage **N**amed-Graph, highlight the name of the desired graph, and press Enter. Then choose **G**o **Q**uit.

Printing a Graph with Customized Print Settings

To see the effect of changing the graph size, choose **/P**rint **P**rinter **O**ptions **A**dvanced **I**mage **I**mage-Sz **R**eshape; in response to the prompts, enter **30** for width and **44** for length. Choose **Q**uit three times to return to the **/P**rint **[P,E]** menu, and then choose **G**o **Q**uit. You don't need to specify **I**mage again, because this image already is selected as the one to be printed. The printed graph now looks like the one shown in figure 23.26.

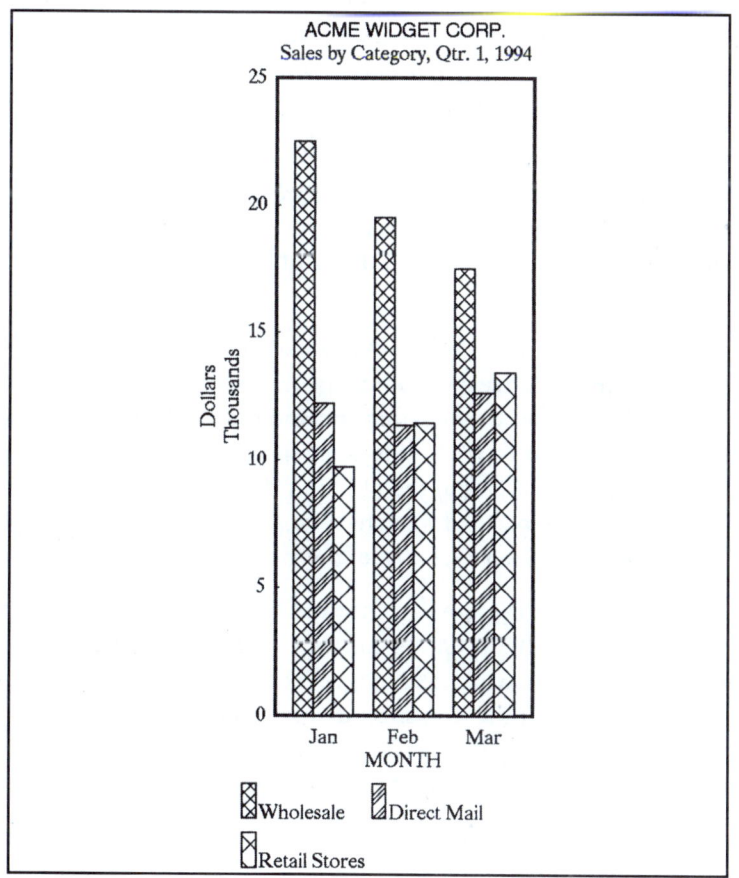

Fig. 23.26
The graph from fig. 23.25, printed with a width of 30 and a length of 44.

Saving Graph Print Settings

Keep in mind that graph size settings aren't saved with the graph. You can save them as a named print setting, however, as explained in Chapter 8, "Printing Reports." To save the print settings that produce figure 23.26, for example, choose **/P**rint [**P**,**E**] **O**ptions **N**ame **C**reate. 1-2-3 prompts you for a name to assign to the current print settings. Because these settings produce a tall, narrow graph, type **NARROW** and press Enter. The print settings are saved under that name when you save the worksheet with **/F**ile **S**ave.

The next time you want to print a graph with these settings, you can recall them by choosing **O**ptions **N**ame **U**se from the **/P**rint [**P**,**E**] menu, highlighting **NARROW,** and then pressing Enter.

Including Graphs in Reports

Printing your graphs on pages separate from the worksheet data and then collating them to produce a report is a simple matter. A more effective approach, however, is to place a graph and its supporting data on one page. If your graph size supports this arrangement, you can accomplish this objective easily with 1-2-3.

You can use either of two techniques to print worksheet data and graphs on a single page. In the first technique, you specify *both* the graph and the text as part of the same print job. This step is performed by including the name of the graph (preceded by an asterisk) in the print range. This method works with all types of printers.

To print a graph named DEFAULT with a worksheet range, type both ranges for the **/P**rint [**P**,**E**,**B**] **R**ange command. The range consists of the worksheet data range A1..E13 followed by a semicolon and the graph name preceded by an asterisk: **A1..E13;*DEFAULT**. This range specification tells 1-2-3 to print the worksheet range A1..E13 and then to print the graph DEFAULT (see fig. 23.27). Notice that the specified worksheet range should include a couple of blank lines at the end to separate it from the graph.

▶ "Adding a Graph," p. 768

◀ "Printing Data and Graphics on a Single Page," p. 368

A second technique you can use to print worksheet data and graphs on the same page is offered by the Wysiwyg add-in. Use the **:G**raph **A**dd command to insert the graph into a worksheet range. Then use the **:P**rint **R**ange **S**et command, and highlight the worksheet data and the graph. Figure 23.28 shows an example of printing worksheet data and a graph using the **:P**rint command. This technique and other graphics capabilities of the Wysiwyg add-in are described in Chapter 24, "Creating Power Graphs."

Including Graphs in Reports   **747**

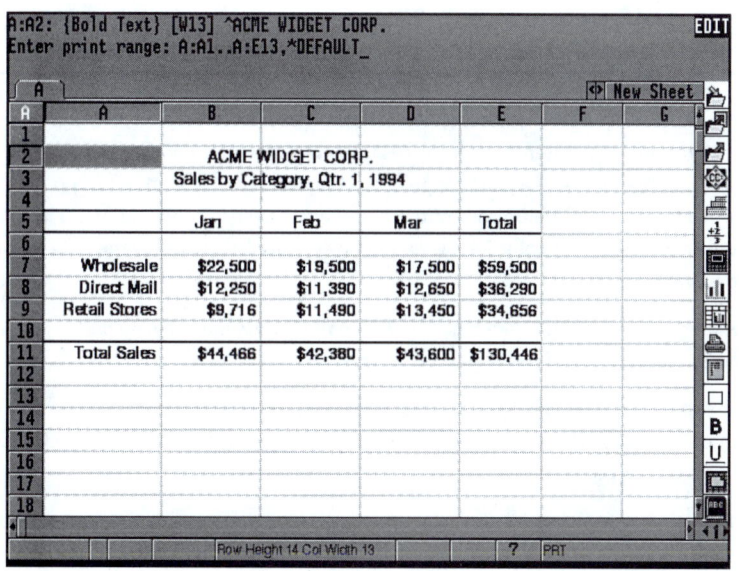

Fig. 23.27
A print range that includes worksheet data and a graph.

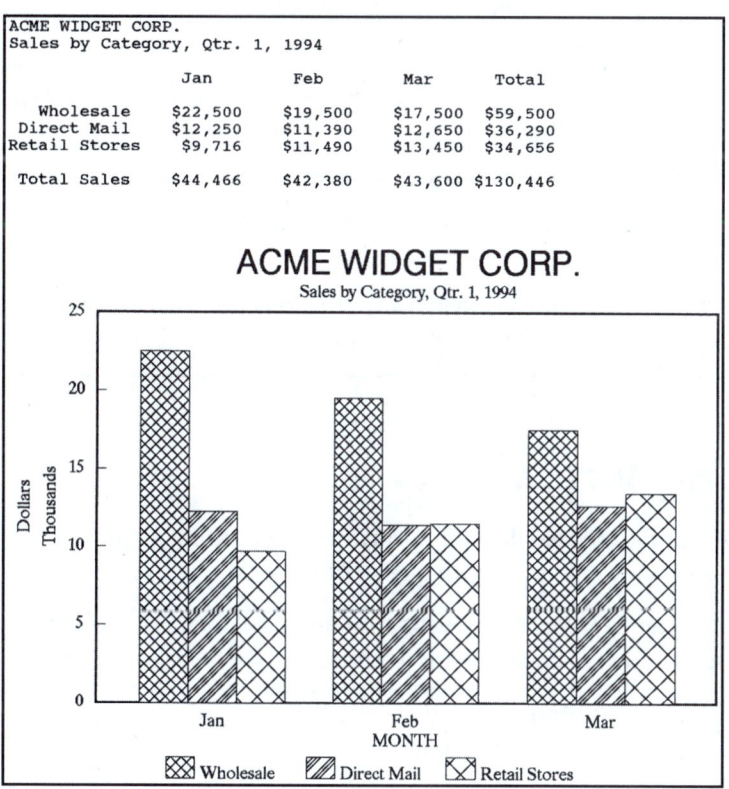

Fig. 23.28
A worksheet range and graph printed on the same page.

> **Troubleshooting**
>
> *A new range added to the graph doesn't appear when the graph is drawn.*
>
> Check the size of the numbers in the new data range in comparison to the other data being graphed. If the new data range is much smaller than the other ranges, the new line will be drawn at the bottom of the graph and may not be visible. Use a second y-axis (described in Chapter 24, "Creating Power Graphs") to show the data in the same graph.
>
> *The bars drawn in the graph are hard to tell apart because the hatching patterns for the different bars are very similar.*
>
> Sometimes, the hatching patterns that 1-2-3 chooses appear similar on-screen or in printouts. Use **/G**raph **O**ptions **A**dvanced **H**atches to choose a different hatch pattern for one of the ranges.
>
> *Named graphs no longer are available when I open the worksheet during a new 1-2-3 session.*
>
> Make sure that you're saving your worksheet file after naming the graph. The named graphs are saved as part of the file and are not written to disk unless you issue the **/F**ile **S**ave command.
>
> *The Graph Settings dialog box covers the information in the worksheet that will help define the graph.*
>
> Press the F6 (Window) key to hide the dialog box.
>
> *The line drawn in my XY graph goes all over the graph. How can I get it to go directly from point to point?*
>
> Your X and A ranges are not sorted in ascending order. Use the **/D**ata **S**ort command to sort all ranges, using the X range as the sort key.

From Here...

For information related directly to creating and printing graphs, you may want to review the following chapters of this book:

- Chapter 2, "What Every 1-2-3 User Should Know." This chapter describes how to create a basic 1-2-3 graph.

- Chapter 8, "Printing Reports." In this chapter, you learn how to use the **/P**rint and **:P**rint commands.

- Chapter 24, "Creating Power Graphs." This chapter describes how to use the advanced graph capabilities of 1-2-3 to make your graphs easier to understand.

- Chapter 25, "Developing Business Presentations." In this chapter, you learn how to use 1-2-3 to create business presentations.

Chapter 24

Creating Power Graphs

The basic 1-2-3 graph types meet your needs for many applications of 1-2-3, but you may want to use the additional capabilities offered by 1-2-3 to make your graphs clearer and easier to read. For example, you can use a second Y-axis to include absolute values and percentage changes in the same graph, or you may choose to draw attention to key information in your data by annotating your graphs with the Wysiwyg graphics editor. Using these capabilities can help you create graphs that make a more powerful statement than basic 1-2-3 graphs.

In this chapter, you learn to use the advanced graphics offered in 1-2-3 to create power graphs.

This chapter shows you how to use the following capabilities of 1-2-3 graphics:

- Modify the graph axes
- Add a second Y-scale to your graph
- Create graphs with special effects, including 100%, 3-D, and drop shadows
- Place a graph in a 1-2-3 worksheet
- Use the Wysiwyg graphics editor

Modifying the Graph Axes

The axes are an important part of your graph. They usually describe the data graphed through a label and a scale showing the numerical range the data spans. This section describes the ways you can modify the graph axes in 1-2-3

752   Chapter 24—Creating Power Graphs

to present your data more clearly. Graphs in this section are based on the worksheet shown in figure 24.1.

Fig. 24.1
The sales data worksheet.

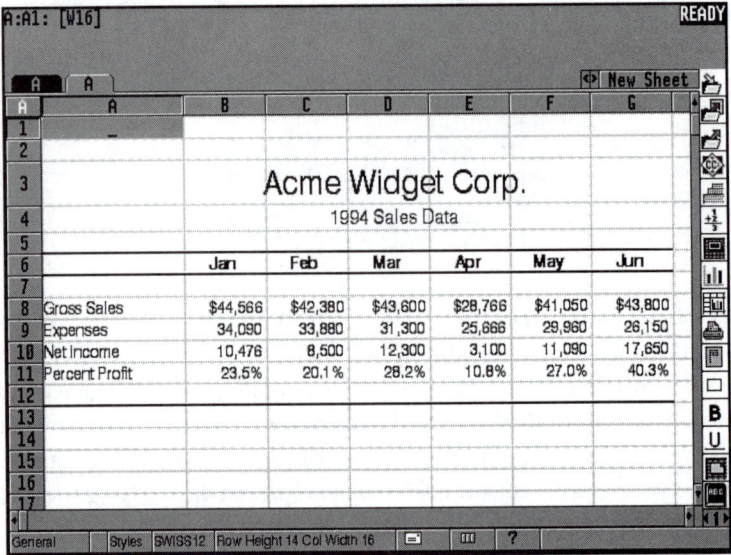

You may find it necessary to change the scale used on the x- or y-axis. For example, you may want to set smaller or larger ranges for the scale or to change the number of intervals marked on the axis. In addition, you may want to format the numbers displayed on the axis or to use a logarithmic scale. The /Graph Options Scale command enables you to make these changes to your graph.

The Scale option displays a series of menus that enable you to control how the graph's axes are displayed. When you choose /Graph Options Scale, the dialog box in figure 24.2 appears. This dialog box enables you to change all the scale options for each scale.

The following menu also appears:

   Y-Scale X-Scale Skip 2Y-Scale

If you choose Skip, you can specify that you want the graph to display only every *n*th data point in the X range. The *n* variable can range from 0 to 8,192, although you almost always will use low values, such as 2 or 5.

If you choose /Graph Options Scale Skip and enter a value of 2, the resulting graph looks similar to the one shown in figure 24.3. Notice that only *Jan*,

Mar, and *May* are displayed on the x-axis scale; *Feb, Apr*, and *Jun* have been skipped. In this case, using **S**kip doesn't improve the graph's appearance. If all the month names were spelled out, however, the x-axis would look too crowded; using **S**kip then would make the x-axis more legible.

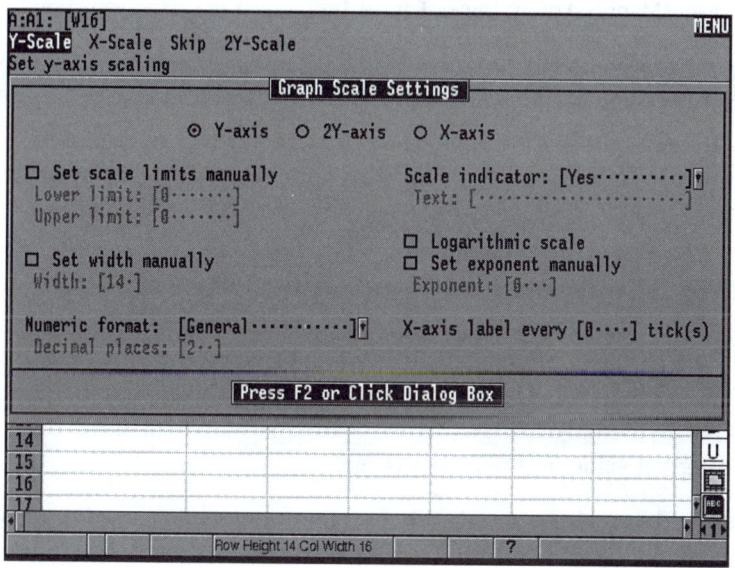

Fig. 24.2
The Graph Scale Settings dialog box, with the y-axis radio button selected.

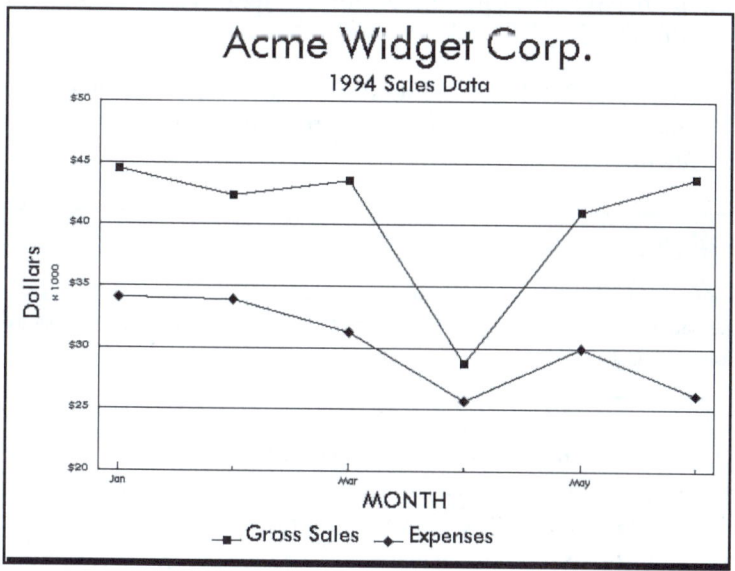

Fig. 24.3
The sales data graph with a horizontal grid and the x-axis **S**kip set to 2.

The other three options in this menu are for specifying which axis to change: the y-axis, the x-axis, or the second (right) y-axis. Whichever axis you select, the series of menus and options that appears after you select an axis is the same:

Automatic **M**anual **L**ower **U**pper **F**ormat **I**ndicator **T**ype **E**xponent **W**idth **Q**uit

> **Note**
>
> Any changes made from this menu apply only to the specific graph axis selected in the preceding menu.

Setting Minimum and Maximum Axis Values

When you create a graph with 1-2-3, the program automatically sets the *scale* (minimum to maximum range) of the y-axis based on the smallest and largest numbers in the data range(s) plotted. This method also applies to the second y-axis (when used). For XY graphs, 1-2-3 automatically establishes the x-axis scale based on values in the X data range.

Tip
You can control the display of primary and secondary tick marks. Use /**G**raph **O**ptions **G**rid **T**icks to control tick-mark display. See Chapter 23, "Creating Effective Graphs," for more information.

To change the scale and specify different minimum and/or maximum values, choose **M**anual, or check the `Set scale limits manually` setting, choose **L**ower, and enter the minimum axis value. Finally, choose **U**pper and enter the maximum axis value. Choosing **A**utomatic returns 1-2-3 to the default (automatic) scaling.

Although you can change the minimum and maximum axis values, you cannot determine the size of the tick-mark increment; 1-2-3 automatically sets this increment.

> **Caution**
>
> It's possible to set a scale range too small to include all the data points. In this case, some data points aren't plotted. 1-2-3 doesn't warn you if your changes cause this problem to occur.

Suppose that you want to change the y-axis origin in the sample graph. First, choose /**G**raph **O**ptions **G**rid **C**lear to get rid of the grid lines. Next, choose **S**cale **Y**-Scale **M**anual. Choose **L**ower, enter **0**, choose **U**pper, and enter **50000**. Figure 24.4 shows the new y-axis scale data.

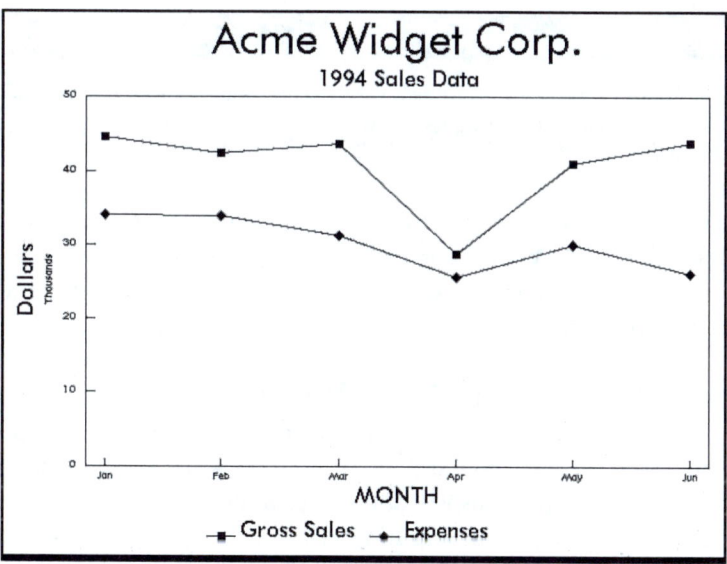

Fig. 24.4
The sales data graph with the y-axis scale set from 0 to 50000.

Notice how the perspective of the graph has changed. Earlier, with automatic scaling, the y-axis range was from 20000 to 50000. The April dip in sales appeared to be more severe than it was. With the scale set manually so that the y-axis origin is 0, the graph more accurately reflects the figures.

To return to automatic scaling, choose /Graph Options Scale Automatic or deselect the Set Scale limits manually setting in the dialog box.

Formatting the Axis Numbers

1-2-3's default setting is to display the axis scale values in **G**eneral format—the same format that is the default for the screen display of worksheet values. You can display axis scale values in any of 1-2-3's numeric formats. Choose **F**ormat from the /**G**raph **O**ptions **S**cale [**Y**-Axis, **X**-Axis, **2**Y-Axis] menu, and the following menu appears:

   Fixed **Sc**i **C**urrency , **G**eneral **+/–** **P**ercent **D**ate **T**ext **H**idden

You also can select a format by clicking the list control (down arrow) in the Graph Scale Settings dialog box. This displays a list of format options that is the same as those shown on the preceding menu.

Making a format choice here is exactly like selecting a format for a worksheet range with /**R**ange **F**ormat. This process includes specifying the number of decimal places and the particular **D**ate or **T**ime format desired.

Tip
If you have not yet made a selection in the dialog box, you may have to click the dialog box twice, once to enter the dialog box and then again to select an option.

756 Chapter 24—Creating Power Graphs

◄ "Setting Range and Worksheet Global Formats," p. 280

> **Note**
> /**G**raph **O**ptions **S**cale [**Y**, **X**, **2**] **F**ormat is a different command from /**G**raph **O**ptions **F**ormat, which controls the way lines are displayed.

Tip
To remove the x- or y-axis label, use the **H**idden format option.

For the sample graph, a currency format is appropriate for the y-axis. Choose /**G**raph **O**ptions **S**cale **Y**-Scale **F**ormat **C**urrency and enter **0** for the number of decimal places. Pressing F10 (Graph) displays the y-axis scale with the new format. (For an example, see the following section.)

Changing the Axis Scale Indicator

When axis scale values are some multiple of 10, 1-2-3 automatically displays a scale indicator, such as Thousands or Millions, between the axis and the axis title. You can suppress display of the scale indicator or enter your own scale-indicator text. After choosing **I**ndicator from the /**G**raph **O**ptions **S**cale [**Y**, **X**, **2**] menu or by clicking the list control for Scale indicator, you see three choices. **N**one suppresses display of the scale indicator. **M**anual enables you to define the indicator; you can type the scale-indicator text or specify a cell address preceded by a backslash. **Y**es restores the automatic indicator display.

To change the y-axis indicator in the sample graph, choose /**G**raph **O**ptions **S**cale **Y**-Scale **I**ndicator **M**anual and then enter **x 1000**. You also can specify a cell address or a range name for the indicator text, preceded by a backslash. If you press F10 (Graph), the graph appears, as shown in figure 24.5.

Fig. 24.5
The sales data graph with the y-axis scale set from 0 to 50000 and formatted as **C**urrency. The manual indicator also is set.

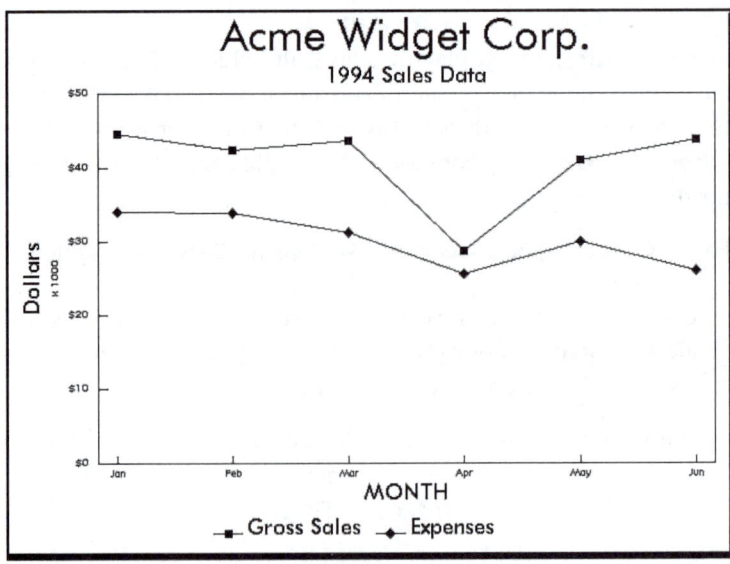

Specifying Axis Types

The **T**ype command in the **/G**raph **O**ptions **S**cale [**Y**, **X**, **2**] menu enables you to specify whether the graph axis will have a linear scale (the default) or a logarithmic scale. On a linear scale, equal distances on the axis correspond to linear increments in value: 10, 20, 30, and so on. On a logarithmic scale, equal distances on the axis correspond to logarithmic (base 10) increments in value: 10, 100, 1,000, and so on. Although you generally use linear scales, logarithmic scales are appropriate for graphing data that is logarithmic in nature or for graphing data sets that span a wide range of values when small fluctuations at the lower end of the data range must be visible.

Consider the exponential-growth data shown in figure 24.6. If you graph this data as a line graph with a linear Y scale, you get the graph shown in figure 24.7. Changing the y-axis to a logarithmic scale yields the graph shown in figure 24.8.

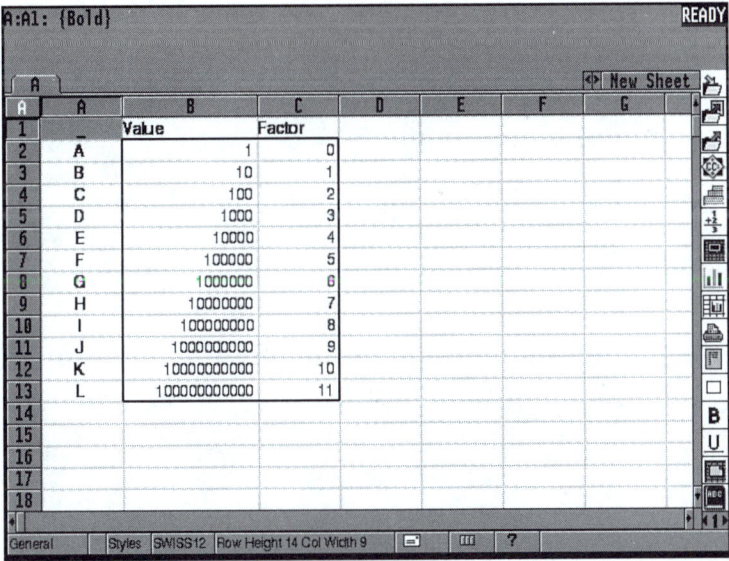

Fig. 24.6
Exponential-growth data appropriate for a log axis graph.

Fig. 24.7
The data graphed with a linear y-axis.

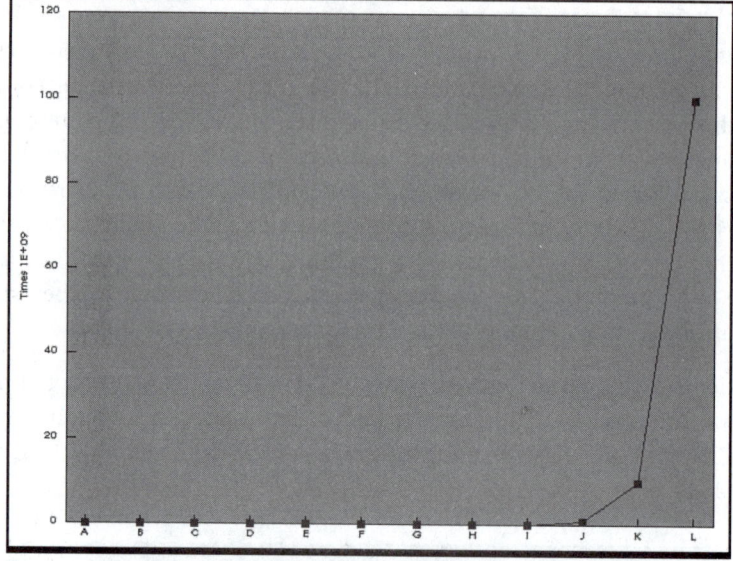

Fig. 24.8
The same data graphed with a logarithmic y-axis scale.

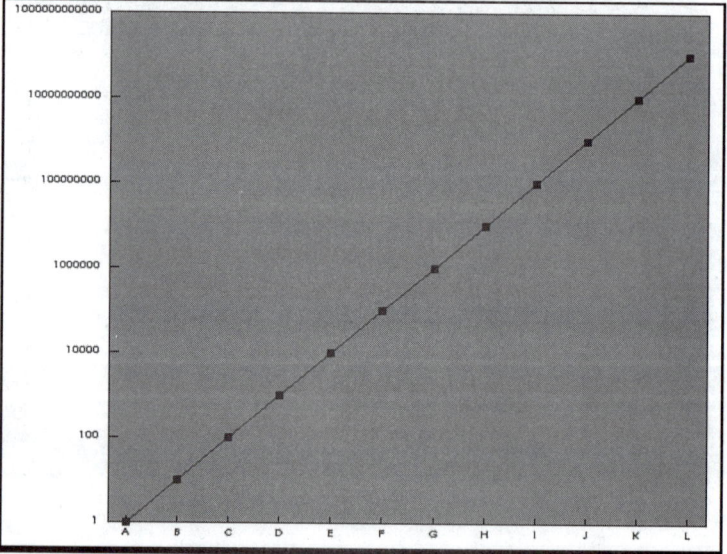

Setting the Scale Number Exponent

The *scale number exponent* is the power of 10 by which scale numbers must be multiplied to reflect the values in the graph. In the sample sales data graph, 1-2-3 has selected an exponent of 3. The scale values—for example, 30, 40, and 50—must be multiplied by 1,000 (10 to the third power) when you read the graph values. If you don't like 1-2-3's automatic selection, you can manually select a scale exponent—a value between –95 and 95.

To change the exponent in the sales data graph, choose **/G**raph **O**ptions **S**cale **Y**-Scale **E**xponent **M**anual and enter an exponent of **0**. You also need to choose **S**cale **Y**-Scale **I**ndicator **Y**es to remove the manual scale indicator (X 1000) that you entered earlier. The graph now should appear as shown in figure 24.9. (The skip factor has been set back to 0 to show all x-axis labels.)

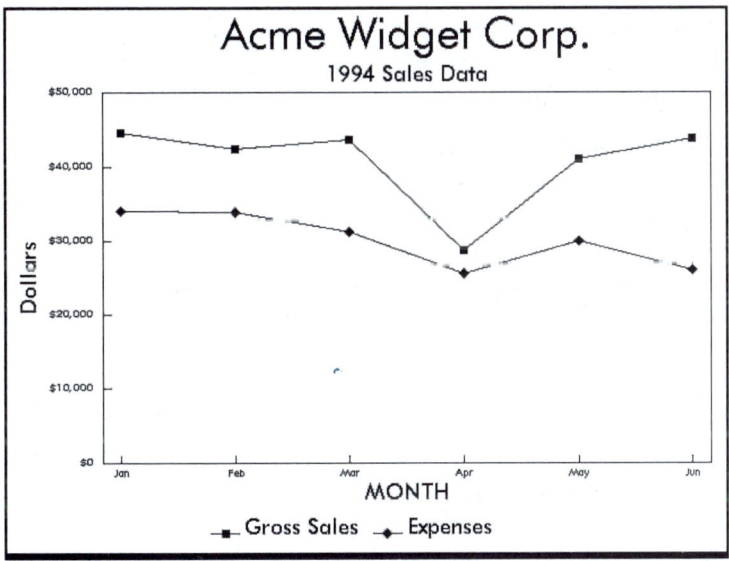

Fig. 24.9
The y-scale exponent set manually to 0.

Specifying Scale Number Width

When you choose **W**idth from the **/G**raph **O**ptions **S**cale [**Y**, **X**, **2**] menu, you have two choices for specifying the maximum width of the scale numbers displayed. Choose **A**utomatic (the default) to have 1-2-3 set the maximum width for scale numbers. Choose **M**anual to specify a maximum width between 0 and 50 (excluding 0). This option works much like setting column widths in a worksheet. If a scale number is longer than the maximum width minus 1, 1-2-3 displays asterisks instead of the number. You can use this option to provide additional space in the margin around the graph.

Adding a Second Y Scale

1-2-3 enables you to create graphs that have two separate y-axes with different scales. The second y-axis, called the *2Y-axis*, is displayed on the right side of the graph. By using dual y-axes, you can include in the same graph data sets that encompass widely different ranges of values. You can include in the same graph sales data and percentage growth of sales, for example, or data that is less than 1 and more than 24.

When you assign data ranges to graph ranges **A** through **F** in the **/G**raph menu, the ranges automatically are assigned to the first y-axis. To create a 2Y-axis, choose **/G**raph **T**ype **F**eatures. The following menu appears:

Vert **H**oriz **S**tacked **1**00% **2**Y-Ranges **Y**-Ranges **F**rame **D**rop-Shadow **3**D **T**able **Q**uit

The **2**Y-Ranges and **Y**-Ranges options are relevant to double-y-axis graphs. (The other menu options are covered in the following section.) Choose **2**Y-Ranges to display the following menu:

   Graph **A B C D E F Q**uit

Choosing **G**raph assigns all data ranges to the 2Y-axis. Choosing **A** through **F** assigns the indicated data range to the 2Y-axis. Notice that you don't enter data ranges here; you use the main **/G**raph menu to enter the data ranges. The choices you make in this menu only move existing ranges from the first to the second y-axis.

If you choose **Y**-Ranges from the **F**eatures menu, the menu appears the same as for the **2**Y-Ranges option:

   Graph **A B C D E F Q**uit

The options in this menu move data ranges back from the 2Y-axis to the y-axis.

To illustrate the advantages of having dual y-axes, you can modify the sample graph to display Gross Sales and Percent Profit. Choose **/G**raph **B**, press Esc or Backspace to cancel the current B range, and enter **A:B11..A:G11** as the B range. Next, choose **O**ptions **L**egend **B** and change the B legend to read **Percent Profit**. When you press F10 (Graph), the graph appears as shown in figure 24.10.

Where are the data points for Percent Profit? These data points are in the range .10 to .30, and the y-axis is scaled from 0 through 50000. The Percent Profit data points, therefore, are plotted almost on top of the x-axis.

To rectify this problem, return to the **/G**raph menu by pressing Esc. Then choose **T**ype **F**eatures **2**Y-Ranges **B** to assign the B data range (Percent Profits) to the 2Y-axis. Choose **Q**uit **Q**uit **O**ptions **S**cale **2**Y-Scale **F**ormat **P**ercent and enter **0** for the number of decimal places. Choose **M**anual **L**ower and enter **0**;

then choose **Upper** and enter **50%**. Choose **Q**uit **T**itles **2**Y-Axis and enter **% Profit**. Finally, press F10 (Graph). The graph shown in figure 24.11 appears. With dual y-axes, both the Gross Sales and the Percent Profit data ranges are displayed clearly.

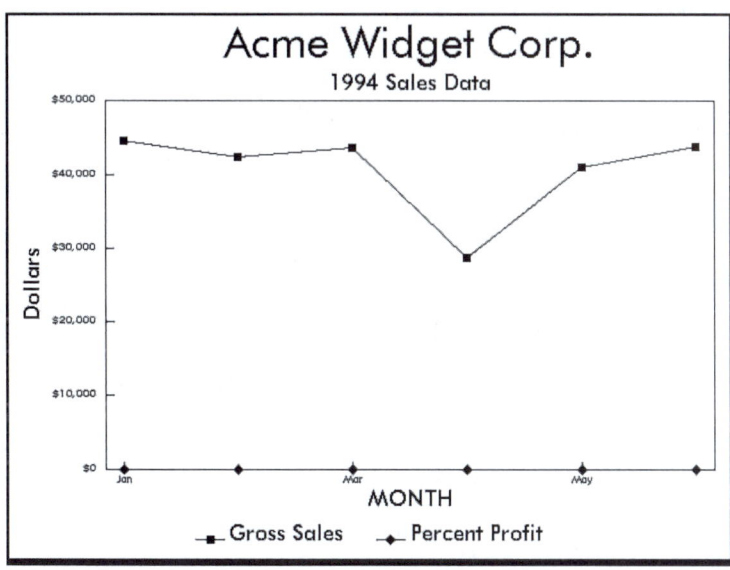

Fig. 24.10
Gross Sales and Percent Profit graphed on a single y-axis.

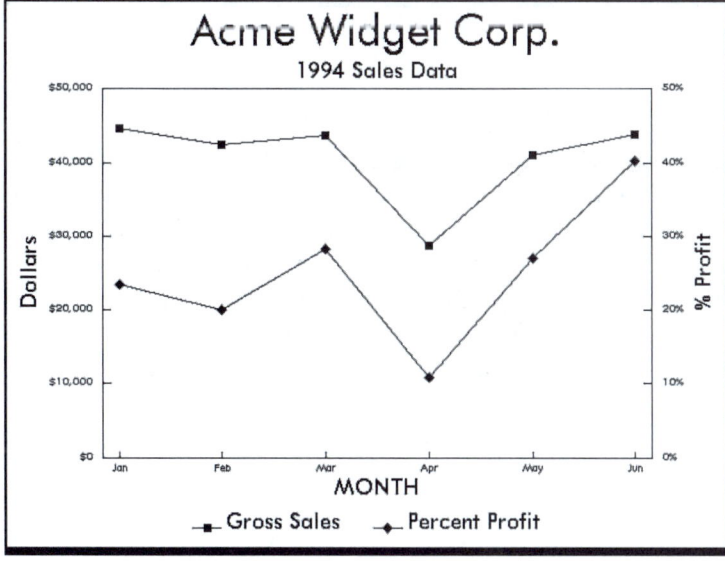

Fig. 24.11
Gross Sales and Percent Profit graphed on dual y-axes.

Using Other Features Menu Options

The **F**eatures menu contains options besides those that deal with 2Y-axes. The following table describes these options.

Menu Item	Description
Vert	Displays the graph upright (the default setting)
Horiz	Reverses the x- and y-axes
Stacked	Can be used with line, bar, mixed, and XY graphs that have two or more data ranges; the values in the data range are "stacked" on top of one another rather than plotted relative to the x-axis
100%	Applies to bar, line, mixed, stacked-bar, and XY graphs that include at least two data ranges; values in each data range are plotted as a percentage of the total value
Frame	Turns the sides of the box enclosing the graph data on and off
Drop-Shadow	Controls the display of a drop shadow or 3-D effect on graph bars and lines, or adds depth to a pie graph
3D	Creates a three-dimensional graph to display graph data ranges
Table	Displays a table of the graphed data below the graph

These features also are listed (in a different order) on the right side of the Graph Settings dialog box.

Figure 24.12 shows an example of a graph created without the **S**tacked option. The graph shows Expenses plotted as range A and Net Income plotted as range B, with **S**tacked (the default) turned off. To stack the data ranges in this graph, choose **T**ype **F**eatures **S**tacked **Y**es **Q**uit. The graph then appears as shown in figure 24.13. Notice that the B range, Net Income, is stacked on (added to) the A range. Because Net Profits plus Expenses equals Gross Sales, this graph actually is displaying three sets of information, even though Gross Sales isn't a selected data range.

Using Other Features Menu Options **763**

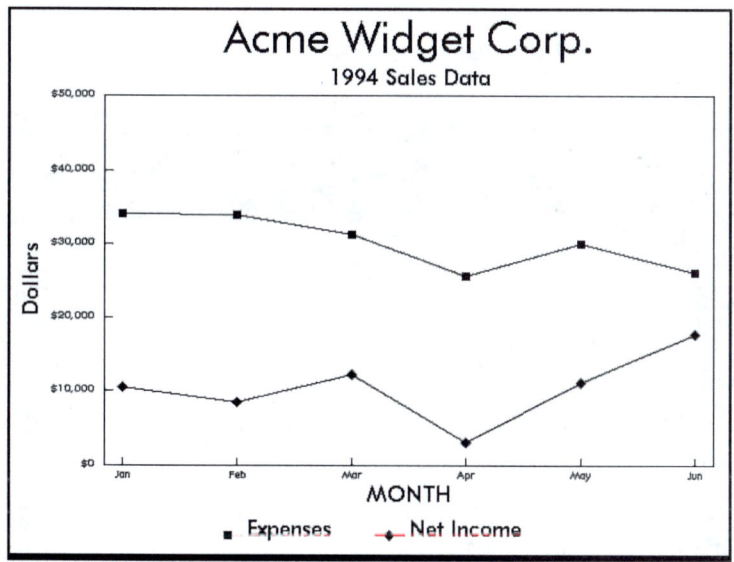

Fig. 24.12
The default graph with Expenses and Net Income unstacked.

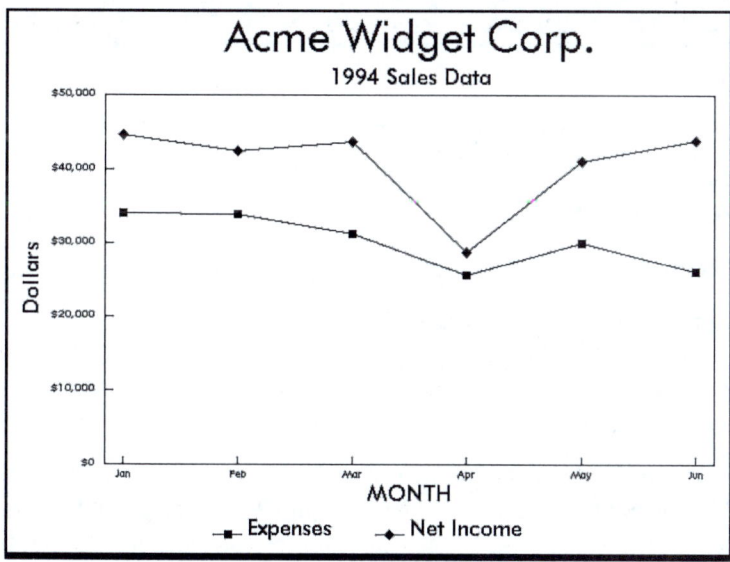

Fig. 24.13
Expenses and Net Income plotted on a stacked-line graph.

764 Chapter 24—Creating Power Graphs

To illustrate the type of graph produced with the **100%** option in the **Features** menu, consider the budget worksheet shown in figure 24.14.

Fig. 24.14
A three-month household-expenses worksheet.

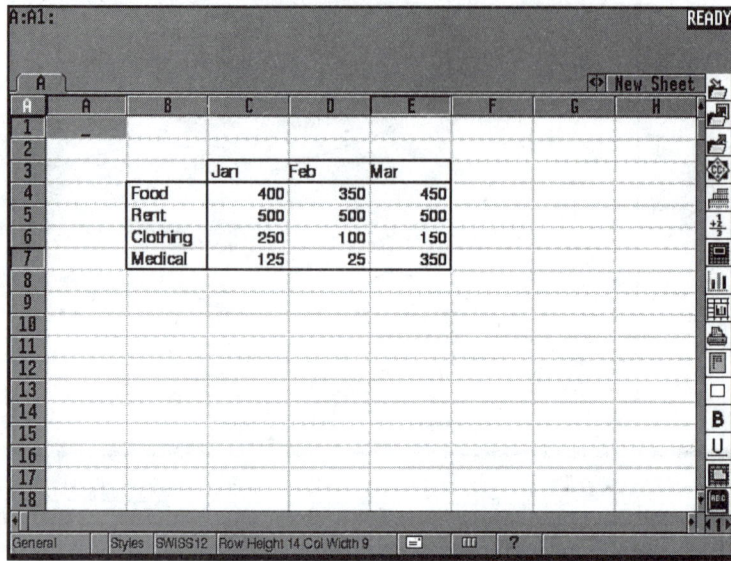

You can create a stacked-bar graph from the budget worksheet data by using the following command sequence:

/Graph **T**ype **S**tack-Bar

Group **A:C3..A:E7 R**owwise

Options **L**egend **R**ange **A:B4..A:B7**

The resulting graph, shown in figure 24.15, shows for each month the total dollar amount spent in each of the four categories.

Now return to the main **/G**raph menu, choose **T**ype **F**eatures **100% Y**es, and redisplay the graph. The result, shown in figure 24.16, is a graph that shows the *percentage* of each month's total expenses in each category. For certain types of data, such as sources of income or expense categories, a 100% graph can be quite useful.

Using Other Features Menu Options   **765**

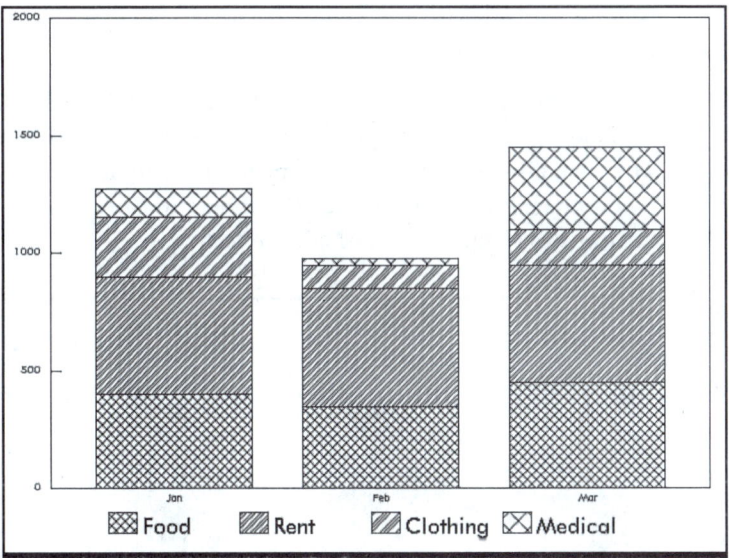

Fig. 24.15
The budget worksheet shown as a stacked-bar graph.

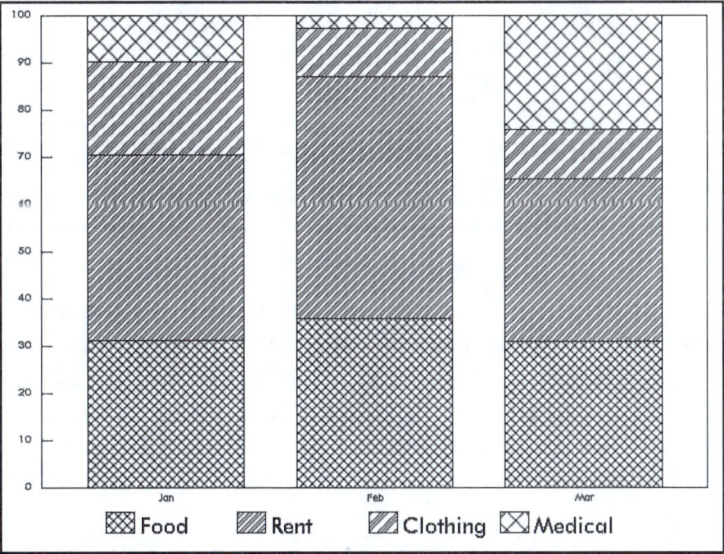

Fig. 24.16
The budget worksheet shown as a 100% stacked-bar graph.

The remaining choices (**F**rame, **D**rop-Shadow, **3**D, and **T**able) set options that change the appearance of the graph. The **F**rame command displays a menu of choices including **A**ll, **L**eft, **R**ight, **T**op, **B**ottom, **N**one, and **Q**uit. With these commands, you can display or hide the lines surrounding the graph area of all graphs except pie graphs (pie graphs don't have a frame). The

Drop-Shadow command adds depth to graph bars, lines, and pies. (The **3D** and **T**able options are described later in this section.)

In figure 24.17, the bars are drawn with a drop shadow, and the top and right frame lines are hidden. To set these options, choose **/G**raph **T**ype **F**eatures **F**rame **T**op, and then choose **F**rame **R**ight to turn off the right and top sides of the frame. Choose **Q**uit to return to the **/G**raph menu. Choose **T**ype **F**eatures **D**rop-Shadow **Y**es to set the drop-shadow effect.

Fig. 24.17
A bar graph with drop-shadow bars; the top and right frame sides are hidden.

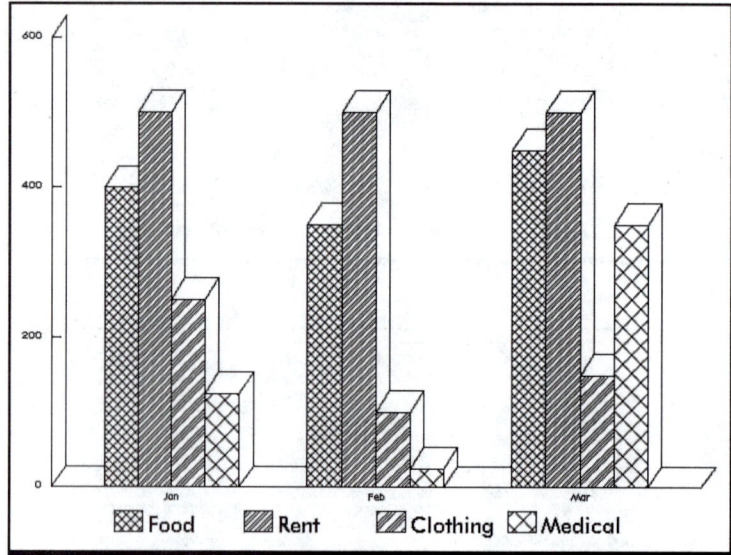

The **3D** command in the **F**eatures menu displays the sets of bars from front to back instead of side by side. The graph in figure 24.18 shows three data ranges graphed as bars. By choosing **T**ype **F**eatures **3D** from the menu, you cause the ranges to be graphed from front to back (see fig. 24.19). Notice that the order of the ranges has been changed so that the larger data doesn't obscure the smaller bars.

> **Caution**
>
> 3-D graphs can give a different perspective to your data. In many cases, however, 3-D graphs are more difficult to read, because large bars in the front can obscure smaller values that fall behind them. Use 3-D graphs with caution.

The final option in the **/G**raph **T**ype **F**eatures menu is **T**able. Choosing this option displays in the graph a table of the data values used for plotting the graph. Figure 24.20 shows the 3-D bar graph with the **T**able option selected.

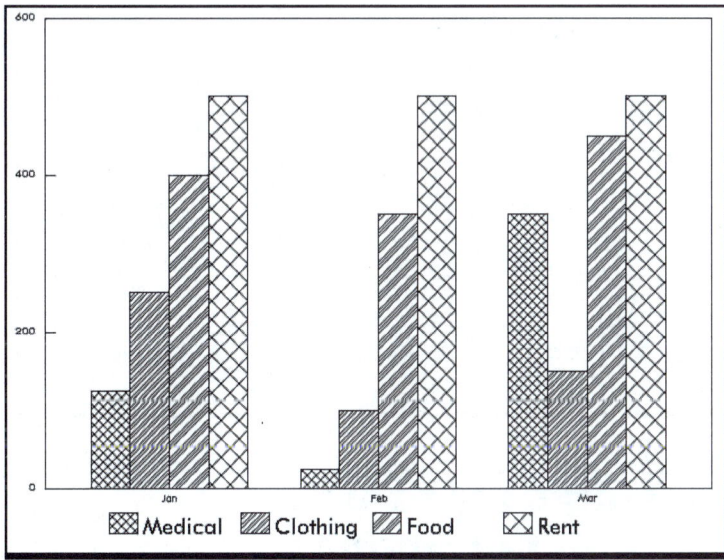

Fig. 24.18
A regular bar graph.

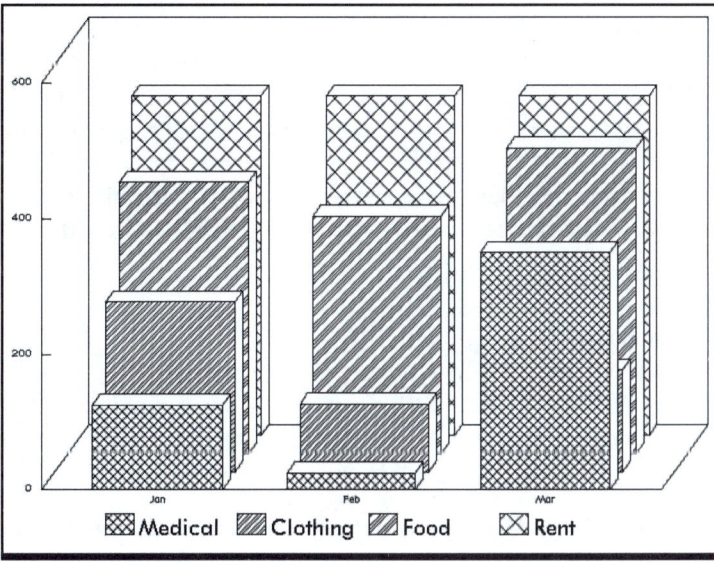

Fig. 24.19
The bar graph from figure 24.18, using the **3**D feature.

Fig. 24.20

The **T**able feature displays a table of data below the graph.

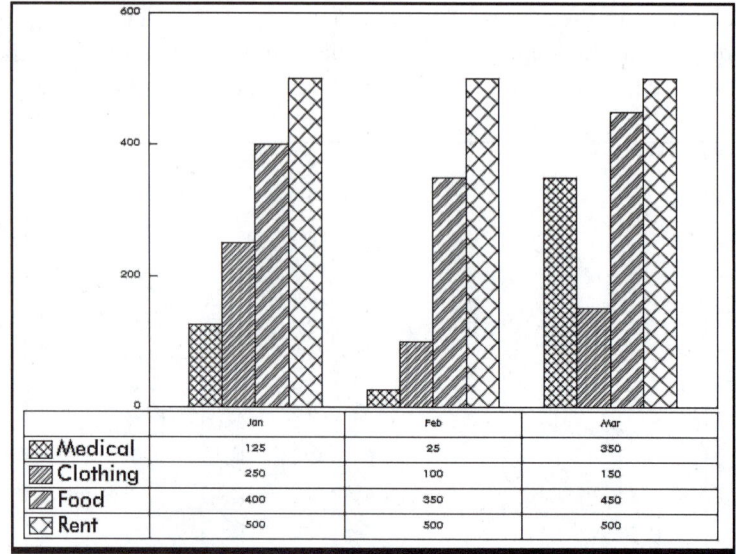

Enhancing Graphs with the :Graph Commands

In Chapter 23, "Creating Effective Graphs," and the first part of this chapter, you learned how to create and print graphs with 1-2-3's **/G**raph and **/P**rint commands. As you will see in the remainder of this chapter, the Wysiwyg add-in offers its own set of graphing commands in Release 4. The Wysiwyg **:G**raph commands aren't for creating graphs, however; they are primarily for annotating graphs created in 1-2-3 and other graphics programs. A graphics editor enables you to add geometric shapes, rotate and flip objects, and perform other advanced operations. You also can create drawings with the **:G**raph commands.

Adding a Graph

Before you can include a 1-2-3 graph in a formatted printed report, you must add the graph to the worksheet with the **:G**raph **A**dd command. With this command, you define the worksheet range in which you want the graph to appear, and 1-2-3 displays the graph in the worksheet.

 You also can add the current graph to the worksheet by clicking the Add Graph SmartIcon.

When you choose **:G**raph **A**dd, 1-2-3 displays the options described in the following table.

Menu Item	Description
Current	Inserts the current 1-2-3 graph (the one you see when you press F10)
Named	Inserts a 1-2-3 graph named with the **/G**raph **N**ame **C**reate command
PIC	Inserts a 1-2-3 graph created with the **/G**raph **S**ave command (any version of 1-2-3); the file has the extension PIC
Metafile	Inserts a graphic saved in metafile (CGM) format
Blank	Inserts an empty placeholder; use this option if you haven't created the graph yet but want to reserve space for it, or if you want to create your own graphic

> **Note**
>
> Graphics in metafile (CGM) format can be created by previous versions of the 1-2-3 line of products, an external graphics program such as Lotus Freelance, or commercial clip art. 1-2-3 Release 4 comes with a number of clip-art metafiles. To list the metafiles in 1-2-3 Release 4, issue the command **DIR *.CGM** at the DOS prompt while the 1-2-3 Release 4 directory is current.

Choose the **C**urrent option only if the worksheet contains a single graph. If your worksheet has multiple graphs, the graph in your worksheet is replaced with the new current graph every time you issue the **/G**raph **N**ame **U**se command. When your worksheet currently contains or may contain more than one graph, you should name the graph before adding it.

Depending on which **:G**raph **A**dd options you choose, 1-2-3 prompts you for information. If you choose **N**amed, for example, you must specify the name of the graph. If you choose **P**IC or **M**etafile, a list of PIC or CGM files in the current directory appears; select one of the names or choose a different directory. If you cannot remember which PIC or Metafile graph you want, cancel the **:G**raph **A**dd command (press Esc until you are back in READY mode) and then choose **:G**raph **V**iew to display the graphics files on-screen so that you can select the correct one.

Next, specify the range in which you want to paste the graph. The size and shape of the range you specify determines the size and shape of the graph when you print it. The graph is automatically scaled (down or up) to fit the specified range.

Chapter 24—Creating Power Graphs

> **Caution**
>
> To print the graph in the middle of a worksheet report, before you add the graph you should insert blank rows or columns where you want the graph to appear. If you don't, the graph overlays worksheet data. Be sure to insert enough rows and columns to make the graph the size you want.

Suppose that you want to paste the current 1-2-3 bar graph in the middle of a worksheet and then print the worksheet and graph. Figure 24.21 shows a sample worksheet with a graph added. Notice that the graph appears in the worksheet. This graph was added to the worksheet by choosing **:G**raph **A**dd **C**urrent and selecting the range A:B12..A:E22.

Fig. 24.21
A graph inserted into a worksheet range.

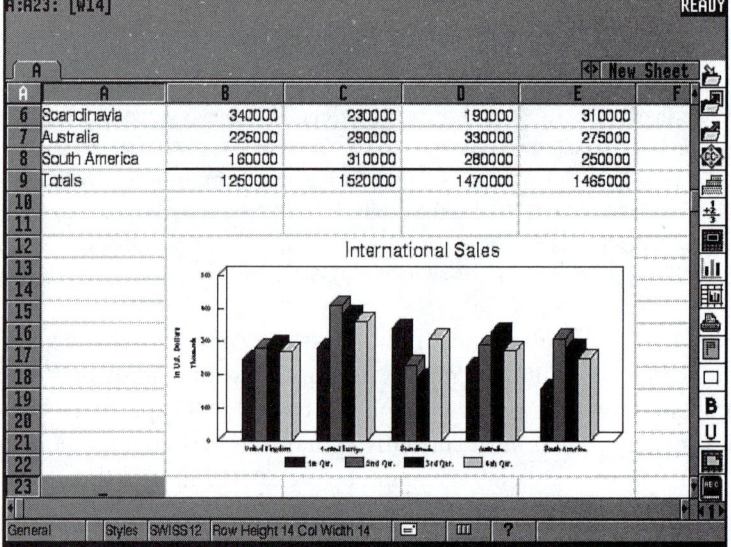

If you discover that you added the wrong graph, or if you later create a graph that you want to use in the same perfectly sized graph range, you can replace the existing graph with another. You don't have to remove one graph before adding another in the same location. Simply choose **:G**raph **S**ettings **G**raph and indicate the graph you want to replace by moving the cell pointer to one cell in the graph range. If the cell pointer isn't near the graph, you can press F3 (Name) and select the graph name from a list. Then answer some questions about the replacement graph. You must indicate the type of graph (**Cu**rrent, **N**amed, **P**IC, **M**etafile, or **B**lank) and specify the name, if prompted.

Any enhancements (such as annotations) that you added to the initial graph also appear in the new graph. If you don't want these enhancements in the new graph, don't use the **:G**raph **S**ettings **G**raph command. Instead, use **:G**raph **R**emove to delete the initial graph, and then insert the new graph with **:G**raph **A**dd.

Repositioning a Graph

After adding a graph, you may realize that the range isn't appropriate for your graph, or you may want to position the graph in a different area of the worksheet. The **:G**raph menu offers several commands for changing your graph's position. You can move, remove, or resize the graph.

If your worksheet is large or has many graphs, you can use the **:G**raph **G**oto command to move the cell pointer to a specific graph before repositioning the graph. After choosing **:G**raph **G**oto, select the name of the graph from the list or press F3 (Name) to see a full-screen list.

Moving a Graph

To move a graph from one worksheet location to another, use the **:G**raph **M**ove command. This command retains the graph's original size and shape (that is, the number of rows and columns), changing only the graph's position on the worksheet. When prompted to select the graph to be moved, you can place the cell pointer anywhere in the graph or press F3 (Name) to select the name of the graph from a list. After you press Enter, 1-2-3 prompts you for the target location. Place the cell pointer in the top left corner of the target range and press Enter. (You don't need to highlight the entire range.) The graph moves to its new location, retaining its original size and shape. If the new location has different row heights or column widths, the moved graph has a slightly different size and shape.

Resizing a Graph

After you add a graph, you may realize that the range you specified is too large or too small for the graph. The **:G**raph **S**ettings **R**ange command enables you to resize an existing graph.

After you select the graph to be resized, the current graph range is highlighted on-screen. Use the cell pointer to highlight a larger or smaller area. To specify a different range, press Esc or Backspace to cancel the old range before specifying the new one.

Removing a Graph

To delete a graph from the worksheet report, choose **:G**raph **R**emove. 1-2-3 prompts you for the graph to be removed. Move the cell pointer to the graph range, or press F3 (Name) and highlight the name of the graph you want to remove. Press Enter; the graph disappears. **:G**raph **R**emove doesn't delete the graph name or the graph's settings.

Copying a Graph

Graphs can be copied much like cells and ranges. Use the **:G**raph **D**uplicate command to copy a graph. 1-2-3 prompts you for the graph to be duplicated. Move the cell pointer to the graph range, or press F3 (Name) and highlight the name of the graph you want to copy. Press Enter, and then move the cell pointer to the top left corner of the position for the new copy of the graph. The **:G**raph **D**uplicate command copies the graph exactly as it appears in the worksheet, including all text and objects added with the Wysiwyg graphics editor.

Specifying Graph Settings

> **Tip**
> To turn on any **:G**raph **S**ettings option for all graphs in the worksheet, specify a range that includes all the graphs you added.

The preceding sections discussed two of the options in the **:G**raph **S**ettings menu (**G**raph and **R**ange). These two settings enable you to replace and resize a graph. The **:G**raph **S**ettings menu offers several more options, which are discussed in this section. You can apply these options to individual graphs.

The **:G**raph **S**ettings **D**isplay command controls whether you see the graphs that you add in the worksheet. By default, all graphs are displayed. Depending on your computer's speed, however, redrawing the screen can be slow when a graph is on-screen. If you set the **D**isplay option to **N**o, Wysiwyg displays a shaded rectangle in the graph range (see fig. 24.22). The rectangle is replaced with the actual graph when you print. Of course, you want to see the graph as you are editing and enhancing it, but when you finish, you may want to turn off display of the graph to speed redrawing of the screen.

> **Tip**
> After editing and enhancing a graph, you may want to turn off display of the graph to speed redrawing of the screen.

> **Note**
> When you choose **:G**raph **S**ettings **D**isplay **N**o, 1-2-3 asks you to specify the graphic(s) to be drawn or hidden.

The **:G**raph **S**ettings **S**ync command controls whether the graph is synchronized with your worksheet data. By default, every time you change a number in the worksheet, 1-2-3 redraws the graph to reflect the new values. This synchronization enables you to try what-if scenarios in your worksheet; enter different values, and the graph changes instantly.

Because redrawing the screen takes time, however, you may want to unsynchronize the graph and data. Choose :**G**raph **S**ettings **S**ync **N**o and point to a cell in the graph. Then, when the data changes, the graph remains static. To update the graph, choose :**G**raph **C**ompute or turn on synchronization with :**G**raph **S**ettings **S**ync **Y**es. The :**G**raph **C**ompute command redraws all graphs in the file. :**G**raph **S**ettings **S**ync **Y**es turns on synchronization for only the specified graphics.

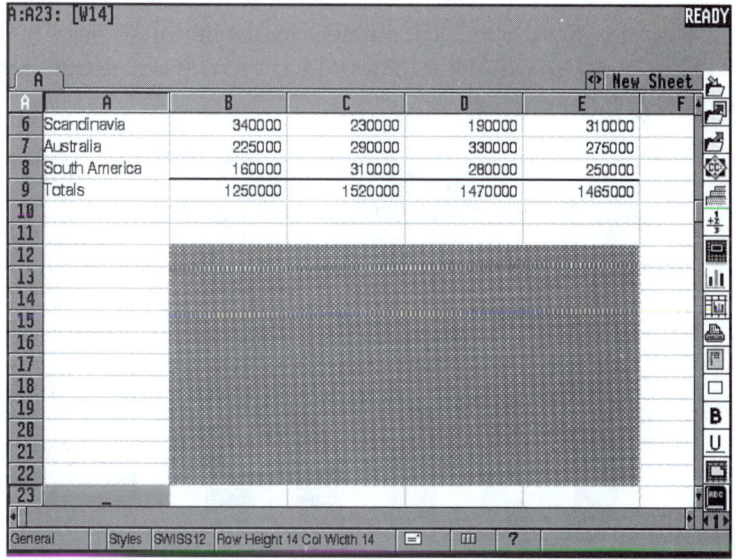

Fig. 24.22
A graph range with the graph display turned off.

The :**G**raph **S**ettings **O**paque command controls whether the graph hides any data typed in cells within the graph range. By default, the graph is opaque, and underlying data is hidden. To view the contents of the cells through the graph, choose :**G**raph **S**ettings **O**paque **N**o. Turning off the **O**paque setting is useful if you have entered in a cell of the graph range text that you want to appear as a note or label in the graph.

Using the Graphics Editor

The Wysiwyg add-in includes a graphics editor that enables you to add graphic objects to a graph and manipulate them. With the graphics editor, you can add text, arrows, boxes, and other geometric shapes. After you add these special objects, you can modify them, rearrange them, duplicate them, and transform them. The graphics editor doesn't require a mouse but is much easier to use with a mouse than with the keyboard alone.

Chapter 24—Creating Power Graphs

1-2-3 offers two ways to place a graph in the graphics editing window. You can choose **:G**raph **E**dit and then specify which graph you want to edit by placing the cell pointer anywhere in that graph's range. Alternatively, you can place the mouse pointer on the graph and double-click the mouse.

Figure 24.23 shows the graphics editing window with a graph in place. The graphics editing window is dedicated to graphic drawing. This window offers many specialized capabilities specifically designed for working with graphics. The editing menu always remains at the top of the screen and is active at all times; you cannot press Esc or click the right mouse button to clear the menu. The only way to exit the graphics editor is to choose the **Q**uit menu option or press Ctrl+Break.

Fig. 24.23
The graphics editing window.

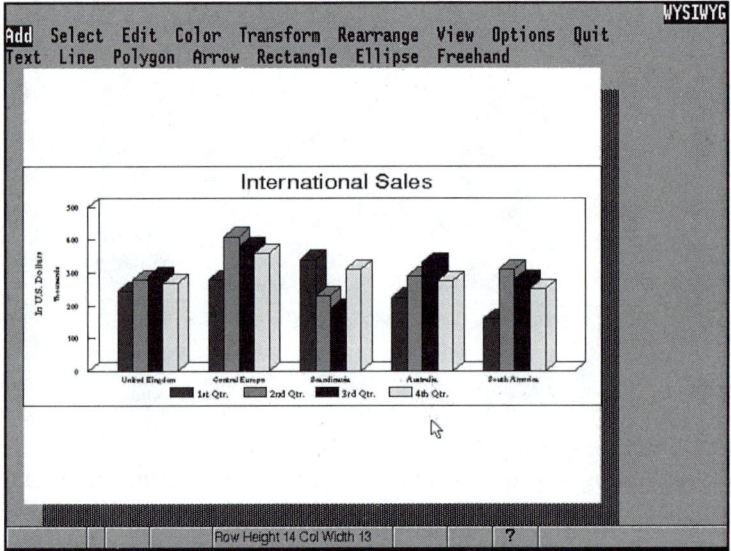

> **Note**
>
> The Undo feature doesn't work on single operations in the **:G**raph **E**dit menu; however, you can undo *all* activities in the current graph-editing session. Choose **Q**uit from the **:G**raph **E**dit menu, press Alt+F4 (Undo), and choose **Y**es. Undo undoes (resets) all changes you made to the graph between entering and leaving the graphics editor. This technique works only if Undo is enabled (choose **/W**orksheet **G**lobal **D**efault **O**ther **U**ndo **E**nable).

Adding Objects

The graphics editor enables you to add the following types of objects to your graphics: text, lines, polygons, arrows, rectangles, and ellipses. (You also can draw freehand.) These objects are designed to help you annotate your graphs; for example, you can add a brief explanation of why a data point is unusually high or low. Figure 24.24 shows how text, an arrow, and an ellipse can be used to point out a value in a graph.

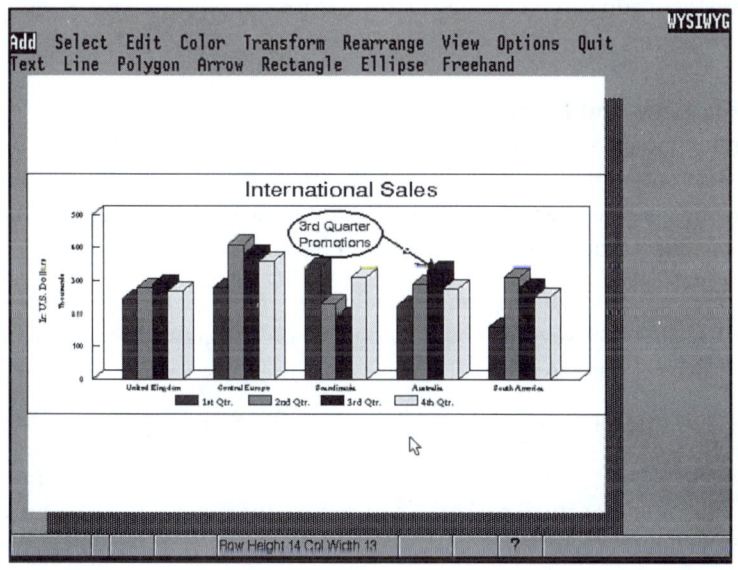

Fig. 24.24
A graph annotated with the graphics editor.

To create an object for your graph, choose **A**dd from the **:G**raph **E**dit menu and then specify the type of object you want to add. The following sections describe how to add each type of object.

Adding Text

With the **A**dd **T**ext command, you can insert titles or comments anywhere in the graph. To add text, choose **A**dd **T**ext from the **:G**raph **E**dit menu and type the text at the Text prompt at the top of the screen. The text can be up to 512 characters long. To insert the contents of a cell as text on a graph, type a backslash (\), followed by the cell coordinates or range name.

After you type the text and press Enter, indicate where you want to place the text. If you cannot see the phrase, press the down-arrow key or move the mouse until the text appears. Continue using the mouse or the direction keys to position the text in its final destination.

Tip
The direction keys, when pressed, move an object in small increments. Pressing and holding down a direction key, however, accelerates the speed of movement, making large movements much easier.

Chapter 24—Creating Power Graphs

To confirm the target location for the text, click the left mouse button or press Enter. Small solid squares, called *selection indicators*, surround the text. These boxes indicate that the object is selected and that you can perform another operation on it (move it, change the font, and so on). To change the font, use the **E**dit **F**ont command. To change the content of the text, use the **E**dit **T**ext command. These editing options are discussed in "Editing Objects" later in this chapter.

◀ "Applying Wysiwyg Formatting," p. 132

The text you add can include formatting (for example, boldface, italics, outline, and fonts).

Adding Lines and Arrows

Whether you draw lines or arrows, you use the process described in this section. The only difference is the result: the arrow has an arrowhead at one end of the line. Follow these basic steps to draw a line or arrow after you choose **L**ine or **A**rrow from the **:G**raph **E**dit **A**dd menu:

1. When 1-2-3 prompts you to Move to the first point, use the mouse or the direction keys to move the pointer on the graph to one end of the line you want to draw.

2. Click the left mouse button or press the space bar to anchor this point.

3. When 1-2-3 prompts you to Stretch the line to the next point, use the mouse or the direction keys to move the pointer to the other end of the line.

4. Double-click the mouse or press Enter to complete the line.

The line or arrow is drawn on-screen, and the selection indicator appears in the center of the line. If you are adding an arrow, the arrowhead appears at the second point you indicated. To switch the direction of the arrow, use the **:G**raph **E**dit **E**dit **A**rrowhead option. To change the line width, use the **:G**raph **E**dit **E**dit **W**idth option. For more information on these options, see "Editing Objects" later in this chapter.

You can connect several lines by repeating steps 2 and 3 of the preceding procedure. When you finish drawing a line, double-click the left mouse button or press Enter.

When drawing horizontal, vertical, or diagonal lines, you may notice that drawing straight lines is difficult; the lines end up being somewhat jagged. To prevent this jagged look, press and hold down the Shift key before you anchor the last point. The line segment automatically snaps to 45-degree angles, enabling you to draw perfectly straight lines.

Adding Polygons

A *polygon* is a multisided object; the object can have as many connecting lines as you want. You don't need to concern yourself about connecting the last side of the object with the first, because Wysiwyg automatically connects this segment for you. The steps for creating a polygon are similar to the ones you use for creating lines and arrows. Follow these steps:

1. Choose :**G**raph **E**dit **A**dd **P**olygon.

2. When 1-2-3 prompts you to Move to the first point, use the mouse or the direction keys to move the pointer to the first point of the polygon.

3. Press the left mouse button or the space bar to anchor this point.

4. When 1-2-3 prompts you to Stretch the line to the next point, use the mouse or the direction keys to move the pointer to mark the end of the line.

5. Press the left mouse button or the space bar to anchor this point.

6. Repeat steps 4 and 5 for each side of the polygon.

7. Double-click the mouse or press Enter to complete the polygon.

Adding Rectangles and Ellipses

Use rectangles and ellipses to enclose text and other objects in your graph. Figure 24.25 shows text with a rectangle drawn around it.

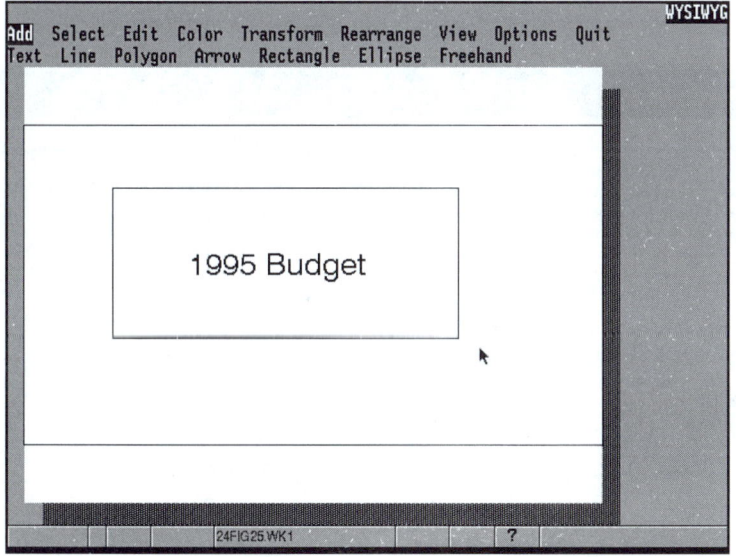

Fig. 24.25
Text enclosed within a rectangle.

Chapter 24—Creating Power Graphs

If you are drawing rectangles and ellipses with a mouse, use the click-and-drag method to define the shape. Press and hold down the left mouse button in the top left corner of the object; then drag the mouse to create the object in the desired size. Whether you are creating a rectangle or an ellipse, a rectangle appears on-screen until you release the mouse button (this rectangle is called the *bounding box*). As soon as you let go of the button, 1-2-3 draws the specified shape.

To draw rectangles and ellipses with the keyboard, follow these steps:

1. Choose **:G**raph **E**dit **A**dd; then choose **R**ectangle or **E**llipse.

2. Place the pointer on the top left corner of the range where you want the rectangle or ellipse to be located.

3. Press the space bar to anchor the corner.

4. Use the direction keys to stretch the bounding box to the desired size for the rectangle or ellipse.

5. Press Enter.

 You also can use the Circle Range SmartIcon to place an ellipse around a cell or range of cells. Select the range of cells in which you want to place the circle, and then click the Circle Range SmartIcon.

In the middle of each side of the rectangle or ellipse are selection indicators. To change the type of line (solid, dashed, or dotted) used in the rectangle or ellipse, use the **:G**raph **E**dit **E**dit **L**ine-Style command. This option is discussed in "Editing Objects" later in this chapter.

> **Note**
>
> To create a circle when you choose **E**llipse or a square when you choose **R**ectangle, press and hold down the Shift key before you set the object size. Although the object may not appear perfectly circular or square on-screen, it prints accurately.

Adding Objects Freehand

When you use the **:G**raph **E**dit **A**dd **F**reehand option, it's as if someone gave you a pencil and let you draw on the screen. Unless you have artistic ability, freehand drawing looks more like freehand scribbling; therefore, you may want to leave this option to the professionals (see fig. 24.26).

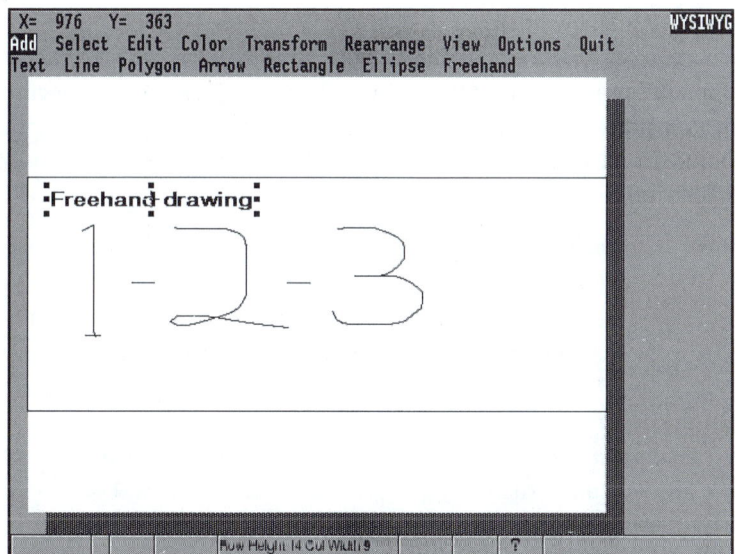

Fig. 24.26
A freehand drawing in the graphics editor.

You must have a mouse to draw freehand. Simply place the cursor where you want to begin drawing, press and hold down the left mouse button, and move the mouse to draw. Release the mouse button when you finish drawing a segment of the graphic. Each segment of the freehand drawing displays a selection indicator. To change the type of line (solid, dashed, or dotted), use the **:G**raph **E**dit **E**dit **L**ine-Style command. This option is discussed in "Editing Objects" on the following page.

Selecting Objects

You can make many changes to objects after you add them to a graph. You can change the line style and font, and you can move, delete, or copy the objects. Regardless of the operation you perform on the object, you must select the object or objects you want to change. If you just added the object, it's selected automatically. When an object is selected, selection indicators (small solid boxes) appear around the object.

Normally, you select the object or objects you want to change before you issue a command. If no object is selected, 1-2-3 prompts you to point to the object.

Mouse users have several selection techniques available (see the following section). Keyboard users use the **S**elect menu to select objects (see "Selecting with the Menu" on the following page).

Selecting with the Mouse

Mouse users can select a single object by clicking it. (You can select an object only when the main **:G**raph **E**dit menu is displayed.) Check the selection indicators to make sure that they surround the object you want to change. If two objects are close together, you may need to click several times until the correct object is selected.

Sometimes, you may want to select more than one object—to change the font of all the text you added, for example. To select multiple objects, press and hold down the Shift key as you click each object. If you accidentally select the wrong object, keep the Shift key down and click the object again.

Selecting with the Menu

To select a single object with the keyboard, use the **S**elect option and choose **O**ne. Wysiwyg displays the prompt Point to desired object. Use the direction keys to move the pointer to the object, and then press Enter. The selection indicators appear around the object.

> **Tip**
> Mouse users may want to use the **S**elect **C**ycle option if they are having trouble selecting an object that is close to another object.

Another way to select an object is with the **S**elect **C**ycle command. This option cycles through all the objects one at a time so that you can select one or more objects. Each time you press a direction key, a different object displays small boxes that look similar to selection indicators, except that these boxes are hollow. When an object you want to select (or deselect) displays the hollow selection boxes, press the space bar. Continue pressing the direction keys and/or the space bar until you have selected or deselected all the objects you want. When you finish, press Enter.

The **S**elect menu offers several other ways to select objects. The **A**ll option selects all objects you have added except the graph itself. The **N**one option deselects everything—the objects and the graph. **G**raph selects only the underlying graph. The **M**ore/Less option enables you to select an additional object or to deselect one of the currently selected objects. If you point to an object that isn't selected, 1-2-3 selects it; if the object is selected currently, the selection is removed.

Editing Objects

As mentioned throughout the "Adding Objects" section earlier in this chapter, the graphics editor provides ways to fine-tune the objects you add. Following is a list of the options you can change in your objects:

- Text content, alignment, and font
- Position of the arrowhead on an arrow

- Line style and width
- Sharpness of angles

The following sections examine each of the options in the **:G**raph **E**dit **E**dit menu. Remember to select the object or objects you want to edit before you issue a command.

Editing Text

The **T**ext option in the **:G**raph **E**dit **E**dit menu enables you to edit text you added with the **:G**raph **A**dd **T**ext command. You cannot edit text added with the **/G**raph commands (for example, titles and legends) or text that was part of a PIC or metafile graphic you added. When you choose **E**dit **T**ext, a copy of the text appears at the top of the screen. To correct or insert text, use the editing keys that you normally use in EDIT mode. (See Chapter 2, "What Every 1-2-3 User Should Know," for a list of editing keys.) Press Enter when you finish editing; the text is corrected.

> **Tip**
> An easy way to edit text is to select the text and then press F2 (Edit).

Centering Text

The **C**entering option aligns text with respect to the text's original location. If you choose **L**eft, the left edge of the text is aligned with the text's original center point. If you choose **R**ight, the right edge of the text is aligned with the original center. If you choose **C**enter, the center of the text is realigned with the text's original center.

Because of the way text is aligned, the **C**entering option isn't very useful. You may find it easier to position text with the **:G**raph **E**dit **R**earrange **M**ove command.

> **Tip**
> Press F4 to display the grid; this action makes lining up the text much easier. To remove the grid, press F4 again.

Changing Fonts

To change the font (typeface and size) of the text you added with the **:G**raph **E**dit **A**dd **T**ext command, use the **:G**raph **E**dit **E**dit **F**ont option. You cannot change the font of text that was part of the graph before you added it to your worksheet. To adjust the typeface and size of titles, labels, and legends added with the **/G**raph command, use the **/G**raph **O**ptions **A**dvanced **T**ext command.

When you choose **E**dit **F**ont, a list displays the eight fonts currently available in the worksheet. Choose the desired font number to change all the selected text. If the font you want to use isn't listed, exit the graphics editor by choosing **Q**uit. Then use the **:F**ormat **F**ont **R**eplace command to replace one of the existing eight fonts with the font you want to use.

Changing Line Styles

Using the **Line-Style** option, you can display different types of lines in your objects. Figure 24.27 shows examples of the six line styles. **S**olid is the default line style. You can also hide a line with the Hide menu command. You can change the line styles of lines, arrows, rectangles, polygons, ellipses, and freehand drawings.

Fig. 24.27
Examples of the six line styles.

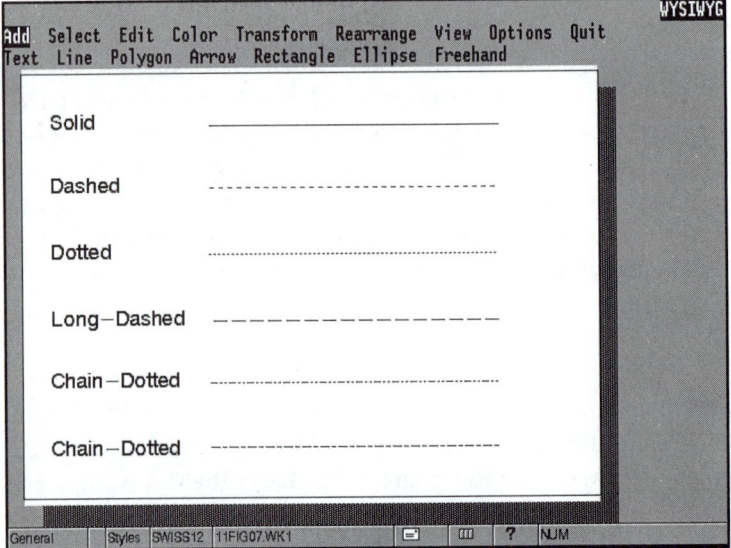

Changing Line Width

By default, line widths are quite thin. Use the **:G**raph **E**dit **E**dit **W**idth option to change the width of the lines in arrows, rectangles, polygons, ellipses, lines, and freehand drawings. Of course, only the lines in the selected object or objects are affected. Figure 24.28 shows examples of the five line widths.

Changing Arrowheads

When you draw arrows with the **A**dd **A**rrow option, the arrowhead automatically points from the line ending (the second point you indicated). Using the **:G**raph **E**dit **E**dit **A**rrowhead option, you can adjust arrowhead positioning. The following table describes the four arrowhead options.

Menu Item	Description
Switch	Moves the arrowhead to the opposite end of the line
One	Adds an arrowhead to a line (you can use this option to turn a line into an arrow)

Menu Item	Description
Two	Adds an arrowhead to each end of the line
None	Removes all arrowheads (you can use this option to turn an arrow into a line)

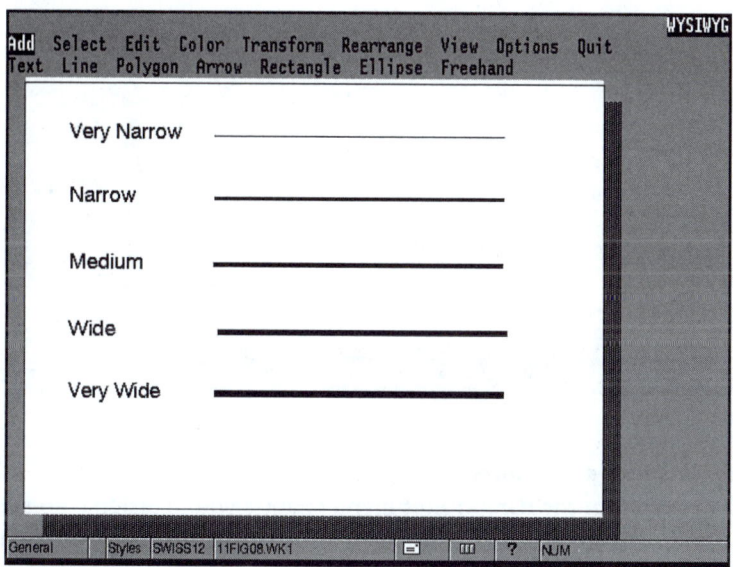

Fig. 24.28
Examples of the five line widths.

Smoothing Angles

By using the **S**moothing option, you can create smooth curves from sharp angles. You can smooth rectangles, polygons, freehand drawings, and connected line segments. The **E**dit **S**moothing menu displays the options listed in the following table.

Menu Item	Description
None	Returns a smoothed object to its original angles
Tight	Slightly smooths or rounds the object's angles
Medium	Provides the maximum smoothing available; smooths the angles to a greater degree than the **T**ight option

784 Chapter 24—Creating Power Graphs

Figure 24.29 shows a rectangle with **N**one, **T**ight, and **M**edium smoothing.

Fig. 24.29
The three types of smoothing.

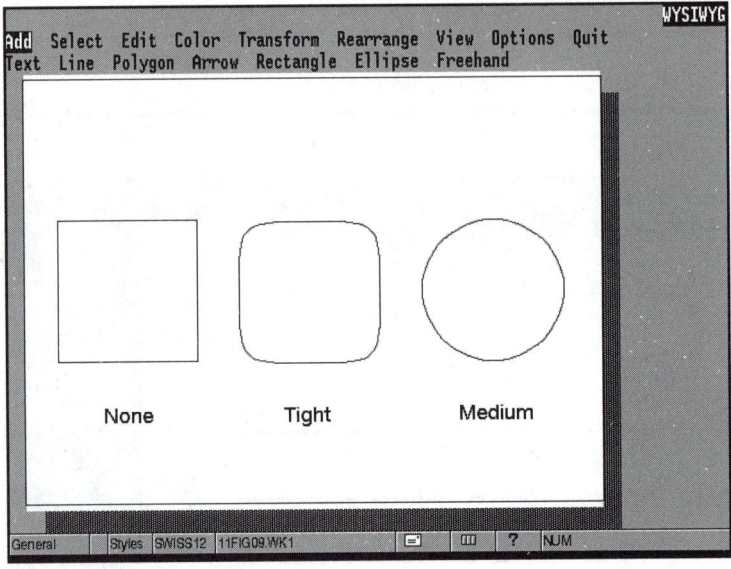

Adding Patterns and Colors

The **C**olor option in the **:G**raph **E**dit menu enables you to assign colors or patterns to your graphics. The following table describes the areas you can color or pattern with the **C**olor options.

Area	Description
Lines	Lines, arrows, and object outlines
Inside	The space inside a rectangle, ellipse, or polygon
Text	Text added with **:G**raph **E**dit **A**dd **T**ext (not legends or titles entered with **/G**raph commands)
Background	In the defined graph range, the area behind the graph (where the titles, legends, and scale indicators appear)

> **Note**
> The options listed in the preceding table don't apply to the underlying 1-2-3 graph.

To change the color or pattern of any element in the 1-2-3 graph, you can use color mapping (discussed later in this section) or the **/G**raph **O**ptions **A**dvanced command, described in Chapter 23, "Creating Effective Graphs."

To change a color, select the object(s) you want to modify and then choose **C**olors from the **:G**raph **E**dit menu. Specify the area in which you want to change the color (**L**ines, **I**nside, **T**ext, or **B**ackground). If you choose the **L**ines or **T**ext option, choose one of the following options from the menu:

Black **W**hite **R**ed **G**reen **D**ark-Blue **C**yan **Y**ellow **M**agenta **H**idden

If you choose the **I**nside or **B**ackground option, a color palette appears on-screen. If you have a monochrome monitor, the palette displays several patterns. Type the number that appears next to the desired color or pattern, or use the direction keys to move the box to the color or pattern you want and then press Enter. If you have a mouse, you can click the color or pattern.

The **:G**raph **E**dit **C**olor **M**ap option enables you to change the fill colors and patterns of the underlying graph. Suppose that you don't like the shade of green of the bars in a bar graph. You can use color mapping to adjust the shade, or you can use a different pattern.

◀ "Specifying Colors, Hatches, Line Styles, and Symbols," p. 730

> **Note**
>
> You cannot use the **C**olor **M**ap option to change the color of lines or text.

You can change the graphic with up to 16 different colors; the **M**ap menu indicates the 16 choices with the numbers 1 through 9 and the letters A through G. The numbers 1 through 7 correspond to 1-2-3 graph objects: **1** is the graph text, x-axis labels and frame; **2** is the A range; **3** is the B range; **4** is the C range; and so on. The remaining color choices refer to colors that may appear in other types of underlying graphics (for example, in a metafile graphic).

After you choose the color number or letter, the color palette appears. The current color or pattern is boxed. Select the color or pattern you want to use as a replacement by typing the number that appears next to the desired color or pattern, or by using the direction keys to move the box to the color or pattern and pressing Enter. Mouse users can click the color or pattern.

Suppose that you want to change the color of the A range. From the **C**olor **M**ap menu, choose **2**; the color palette displays a box around one of the colored squares. To choose a different color or pattern, use the direction keys to

Chapter 24—Creating Power Graphs

move the box to another colored square; then press Enter. The original A range color changes to the color or pattern you selected.

The procedure for changing the colors in a metafile-format graphic is a trial-and-error process. You must check the color palette for each of the numbers (1 through 7) and letters (A through G) until you find the color you want to change. Suppose that a metafile-format graphic contains a shade of yellow that you detest; you want to replace it with a shade of teal. From the **C**olor **M**ap menu, choose **1**, and look at the boxed shade in the color palette. If the color is yellow, you are in luck: you found the correct color number and now can highlight the teal shade you want to use. If color **1** isn't yellow, press Esc and continue choosing options from the **C**olor **M**ap menu until you see the yellow color boxed in the color palette.

If you have a color monitor but plan to print the graph on a black-and-white printer, you may want to view the graph in black-and-white before you print. Viewing the graph in black-and-white enables you to see how the colors translate into gray shades. Use the **:D**isplay **M**ode **B**&W command to change to a black-and-white display.

Changing the Display of the Graphics Editing Window

The graphics editor's **O**ptions and **V**iew menus provide ways to change the graphic editing window's display. The **O**ptions menu offers the following options: **G**rid, **C**ursor, and **F**ont-Magnification. The **V**iew menu enables you to size and reposition the contents of the editing window. The **V**iew menu offers the following options: **F**ull, **I**n, **P**an, +, –, **U**p, **D**own, **L**eft, and **R**ight. The following sections describe these options.

Modifying the Grid, Cursor, and Font-Magnification Settings

The **G**rid option in the **O**ptions menu enables you to display dotted lines to define the cells in the underlying worksheet. Grid lines can help you line up the objects you create with worksheet cells. The cell *coordinates* aren't displayed—only the cell outlines. Alternatively, you can press F4 to toggle the display of grid lines in the graphics editor.

> **Tip**
> Use the big cursor when you line up the edges of objects.

The **C**ursor option defines the size of the cursor: **B**ig or **S**mall. By default, the graphics editor's cursor is a small cross. The big cursor also is a cross, but its lines extend completely across the editing window. Figure 24.30 shows a rectangle being drawn with the big cursor. A large cursor simplifies lining up one edge of an object with another.

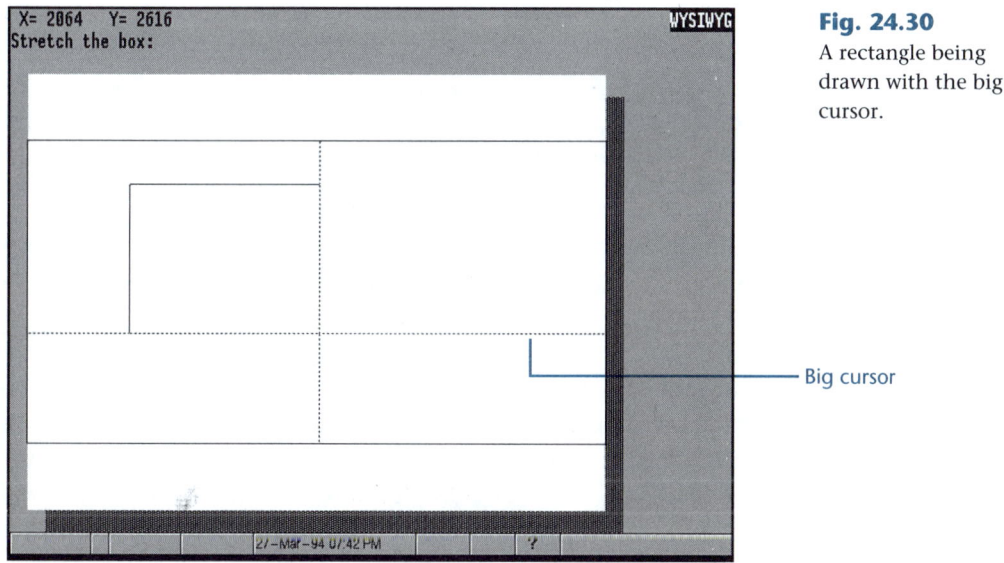

Fig. 24.30
A rectangle being drawn with the big cursor.

Using the **F**ont-Magnification option, you can scale the size of all text (up or down). This option applies to text inserted with **:G**raph **E**dit **A**dd **T**ext as well as the text in the underlying graph (that is, titles and legends). The **F**ont-Magnification option saves you from having to change the font size of each piece of text in your graph. If all your titles and legends are too large, you can use The **F**ont-Magnification to reduce them all at once, instead of using the **/G**raph **O**ptions **A**dvanced **T**ext command to change each element individually.

The font-magnification value is a percentage between 0 and 1,000. The default value is 100. To scale down the sizes, enter a value smaller than 100. To reduce the text to 80 percent of its current size, for example, type **80**. To magnify the text, enter a value larger than 100. To double the size of the text, for example, enter **200**. To display the text in its actual point size—instead of the scaled size chosen by the graphics editor—enter a font-magnification value of **0**.

Sizing and Repositioning the View

The options in the **:G**raph **E**dit **V**iew menu enable you to size and reposition the contents of the graphics editing window. You can use the options to concentrate on an area you are modifying. None of the **V**iew menu options changes the actual size of the graphic.

The **F**ull option restores the graphic to its normal full size after you resize or reposition it with the other **V**iew options.

Chapter 24—Creating Power Graphs

> **Note**
> Mouse users can use a second zooming method. From the **:G**raph **E**dit menu, press and hold down Ctrl while clicking-and-dragging a box around the area. To unzoom, press and hold down Ctrl, and click anywhere in the graphic.

The **In** option zooms in on a selected area of the graphic. Figure 24.31 shows a zoomed-in graphics window. When you choose this option, the prompt `Move to the first corner` appears. Indicate the area you want to zoom by drawing a box around the range. Mouse users should use the click-and-drag technique to stretch the box around the area. Keyboard users should use the direction keys to position the pointer on the first corner, press Enter, use the direction keys to stretch the box so that the area is surrounded, and then press Enter again.

Fig. 24.31
A zoomed-in graph.

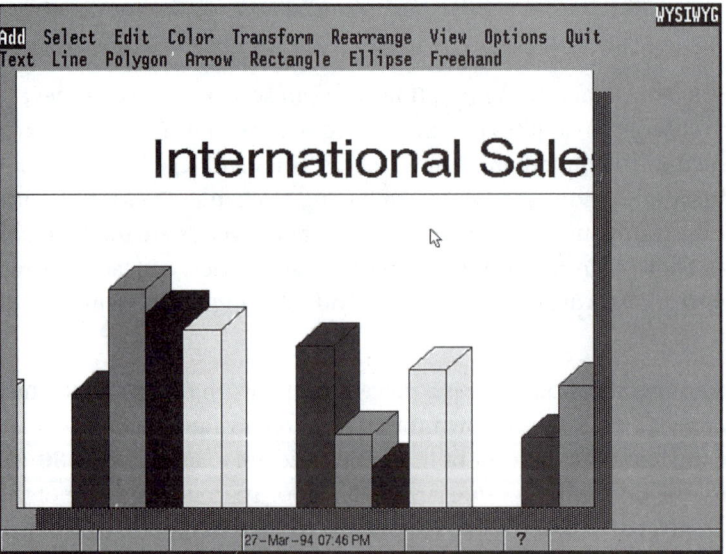

After you zoom an area, you may want to zoom even further or move the graph slightly in one direction. The remaining **V**iew options make these adjustments. Use the **+** option to zoom in further or the **−** option to unzoom. Each time you choose **+**, you zoom further. From the normal full size, you can zoom five times.

The **U**p, **D**own, **L**eft, and **R**ight options in the **V**iew menu enable you to see parts of a zoomed graphic that is not currently in the window. Each of these options moves the display one half-screen in the specified direction. To move the display up or down when you are at the **:G**raph **E**dit menu, press the up- or down-arrow key.

The **V**iew **P**an option is a way to zoom, unzoom, and move the display around all at once. **V**iew **P**an essentially is the **+**, **–**, **U**p, **D**own, **L**eft, and **R**ight options rolled into one. When you choose **V**iew **P**an, the following message explains what to do: Use cursor keys to move view, +/- to zoom, Enter to leave. Thus, you can press **+** to zoom, **–** to unzoom, and the direction keys to display a different part of the graph in the window. When you are satisfied with the window contents, press Enter. Choose **V**iew **F**ull to restore the screen to its original size and arrangement.

> **Tip**
> Actually, you don't even need to access the **V**iew menu to use the **+** and **–** options; you can press **+** and **–** at the main graphics editing menu.

Rearranging Objects

The **R**earrange option in the **:G**raph **E**dit menu enables you to delete, copy, and move the objects you added to your graphic with **:G**raph **E**dit **A**dd. Before you choose one of the **R**earrange options, select the object or objects you want to rearrange. For details on selecting objects with the mouse or the **:G**raph **E**dit **S**elect menu, refer to "Selecting Objects" earlier in this chapter.

Deleting and Restoring Objects

The **R**earrange **D**elete option removes the selected object(s) from the graph. Although Wysiwyg doesn't ask you to confirm your intention to delete, you can use the **R**earrange **R**estore command to retrieve the last deleted object or group of objects. Suppose that you select three objects at once and then choose **R**earrange **D**elete. All three objects are deleted. If you choose **R**earrange **R**estore, all three objects are retrieved in their original locations. But if you select and delete a line and then select and delete a rectangle, you cannot restore the deleted line; you can retrieve only the deleted rectangle.

As an alternative to using the **R**earrange **D**elete command, you can simply select the object(s) you want to delete and press Del. Press Ins to restore the most recently deleted object or group of objects.

> **Note**
>
> Make sure that no object is selected when you press Ins to restore a deleted object; when an object is selected and you press Ins, that object is copied.

Chapter 24—Creating Power Graphs

Tip

If you have a mouse, you don't need to use the **R**earrange **M**ove option; from the **:G**raph **E**dit menu, you can simply use the click-and-drag technique to reposition an object.

Moving Objects

To reposition an object, use the **R**earrange **M**ove option. If you haven't selected the object(s), 1-2-3 asks you to select the object(s) you want to move. Click the object, or use the direction keys to move the cursor to the object and then press Enter. (You must click the *outline* of the rectangle, ellipse, or polygon. If you click inside the object, you cancel the command.) After you make your selection, a copy of the object appears inside a bounding box. A hand icon also appears inside the bounding box, indicating that you are moving the object. Use the mouse or the direction keys to move the bounding box to the target location; then click the mouse or press Enter. Figure 24.32 shows a rectangle being moved.

Copying Objects

After you create an object, you may want to "clone" it. Using the **R**earrange **C**opy command ensures that two or more objects are the same size, with the same options. If you create a shaded rectangle with wide lines, for example, the copy of the rectangle also is shaded and has wide lines. When you copy an object, the following **:G**raph **E**dit options are copied along with the object:

- Edit options (**F**ont, **L**ine-Style, **W**idth, **A**rrowheads, **S**moothing)

- Color settings

- Transform options: **S**ize, **R**otate, **Q**uarter-Turn, **X**-Flip, **Y**-Flip, **H**orizontal, **V**ertical (for more information, see "Transforming Objects" later in this chapter)

If an object is selected when you choose the **R**earrange **C**opy command, 1-2-3 places a duplicate slightly to the right of and below the original object. If no object was selected when you chose **R**earrange **C**opy, 1-2-3 prompts you to select the objects to be copied. The **C**opy command doesn't prompt you for a target location; you must use the **R**earrange **M**ove command to put the object in place. Thus, copying is a two-step process.

Instead of using the **R**earrange **C**opy command, you can simply select the object and press the Ins key. Like the **R**earrange **C**opy command, Ins places the duplicated object next to the original; you must use the **R**earrange **M**ove command to put the object in position. If you don't have an object selected when you press Ins, the last deleted object is restored.

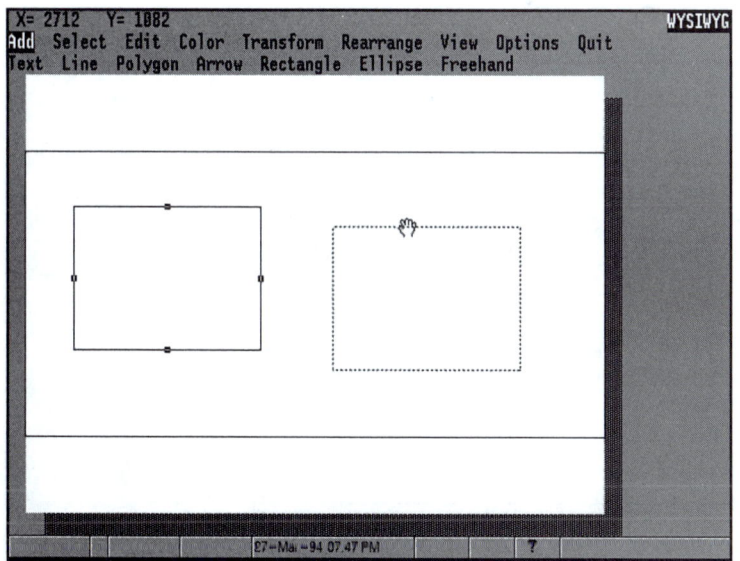

Fig. 24.32
Moving a rectangle with **R**earrange **M**ove.

Moving an Object to the Back or Front

When a colored or shaded object is positioned on top of an existing object, it may obscure the objects underneath it. Suppose that you add some text, draw an ellipse around it, and then add a pattern to the ellipse. After adding the pattern, you no longer can see the text because the ellipse is on top of the text (see the left ellipse in fig. 24.33). To see the text, you need to bring the text in front of the ellipse or to place the ellipse in back of the text. You can select the ellipse and choose **R**earrange **B**ack or select the text and choose **R**earrange **F**ront. The ellipse on the right side of figure 24.33 shows how the text reappears after the ellipse is moved to the back.

Locking an Object

After an object is the perfect size, in the perfect location, with the perfect options, you may want to use the **R**earrange **L**ock option to prevent it from being changed. When you lock an object, you cannot delete it, move it, transform it, color it, or edit it. You can copy it, but the duplicate isn't locked. If you later need to make a change to the locked object, use the **R**earrange **U**nlock option.

Tip
When objects seem to have disappeared mysteriously, they may be hidden by another object. Use the **R**earrange **F**ront and **B**ack options to find such missing objects.

Fig. 24.33
Using the **R**earrange **B**ack command.

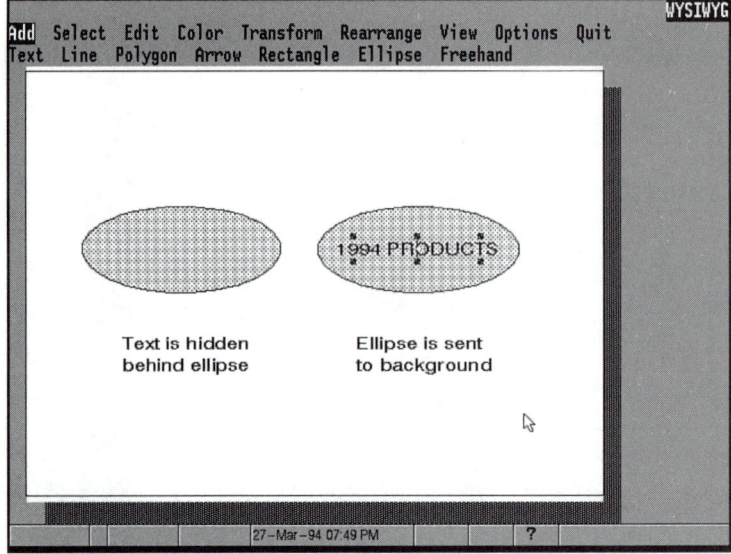

Transforming Objects

The commands in the **:G**raph **E**dit **T**ransform menu enable you to change geometric shapes that have been added with the **:G**raph **E**dit **A**dd command. With the **T**ransform command you can resize, rotate, flip, or slant the object vertically or horizontally. If you aren't happy with the transformed object, you can use **T**ransform **C**lear to clear all transformations made to the selected objects.

Sizing an Object

You can change the size (height and width) of any added objects, except text, with the **:G**raph **E**dit **T**ransform **S**ize command. (To change the text size, specify a different font with the **:G**raph **E**dit **E**dit **F**ont command.) When you choose the **T**ransform **S**ize command, the selected object is surrounded by a bounding box. The top left corner of the box is anchored, and the cursor is in the bottom right corner. Adjust the size of the object by pressing the direction keys or by moving the mouse until the bounding box is the desired size. Then press Enter or click the mouse to change to the new size.

Another way to adjust an object's size is with the **T**ransform **H**orizontal or **T**ransform **V**ertical option. These options also change the angles of the objects. For further information, see "Adjusting the Slant" later in this chapter.

Rotating an Object

The **T**ransform menu offers two ways to rotate an object. The **Q**uarter-Turn option rotates the selected object(s) in 90-degree increments in a counter-clockwise direction. Figure 24.34 shows an ellipse before and after a **Q**uarter-Turn rotation.

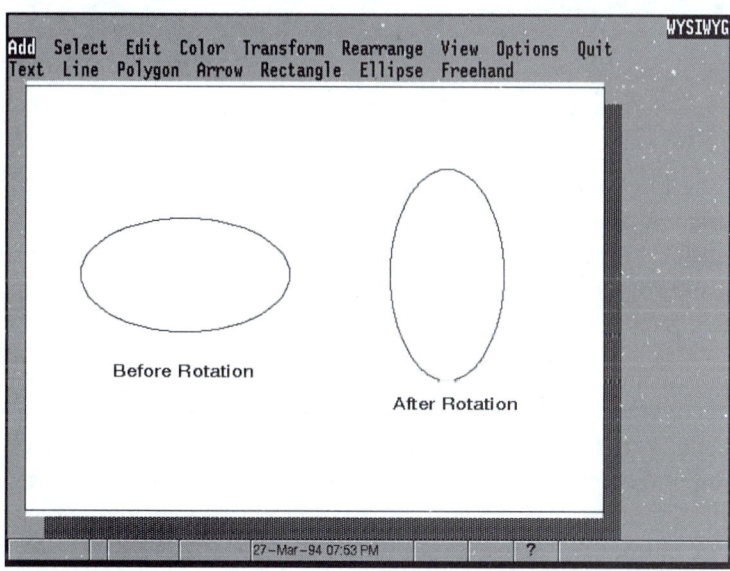

Fig. 24.34
An object before and after a quarter turn.

If you want to rotate an object in increments other than 90 degrees, use the **T**ransform **R**otate option; you can rotate the selected object or objects to any angle. An axis extends from the center of the object to the outside of the bounding box. Think of this axis as a handle that pulls the object in the direction you move the mouse or in the direction of the direction keys you press. As you rotate, the original object remains intact, and a copy of the object rotates. As soon as you press Enter or click the mouse, 1-2-3 moves the original object to the rotated angle, and the copy disappears.

> **Note**
> Some printers can print text rotated in 90-degree increments only. PostScript printers and the HP LaserJet Series II, III, and IV can print text at any angle.

Flipping an Object

Imagine that the selected object is a pancake and that the **X**-Flip and **Y**-Flip options are pancake turners. **X**-Flip flips the object over, positioning the original top left corner in the top right corner. **Y**-Flip turns the object upside down, positioning the top left corner in the bottom left corner. If you choose the wrong flip direction, you can reverse the action by choosing the same direction again. If you choose **X**-Flip, for example, and don't like the result, flip the object back to its original position by choosing **X**-Flip again.

> **Note**
>
> You don't notice any effect when you flip lines, rectangles, or ellipses that are in a 90-degree-angle position.

Adjusting the Slant

The **T**ransform **H**orizontal and **T**ransform **V**ertical options change the *slant* (angles) and size of the selected object(s). You even can flip the object in the same step.

In figure 24.35, the rectangle is being transformed horizontally. The top line is anchored; as you press the direction keys or move the mouse, you see the bounding box stretch freely in the direction in which you move the cursor. To flip the object, position the bounding box above the selected object. When the bounding box is the desired size and shape, press Enter or click the left mouse button. The object is moved into the position of the bounding box.

Fig. 24.35

Transforming a rectangle horizontally.

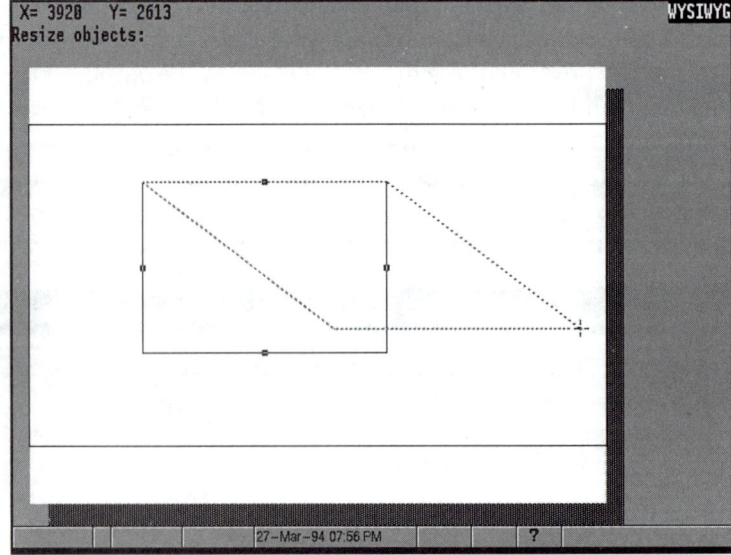

When you transform an object vertically, the left side of the object is anchored. To flip the object, position the bounding box to the left of the selected object.

Printing Graphics Created with the Graphics Editor

As mentioned in Chapter 23, "Creating Effective Graphs," the **/P**rint command prints graphs created with the **/G**raph command. You must use the **:P**rint command to print graphs added to a worksheet. The **:P**rint command also prints all annotations added in the graphics editor.

◀ " Using the **:P**rint Commands," p. 363

> **Troubleshooting**
>
> *Some graph ranges do not show up in the graph.*
>
> Compare the relative sizes of the graph ranges. The data in the ranges that don't appear may be so small that the ranges are plotted right next to the x-axis. If this is the case, try using a second y-axis for these ranges.
>
> *The data in the worksheet I used to create a graph is already in millions, so the thousands that 1-2-3 uses as a scale indicator is not accurate.*
>
> Use the **/G**raph **O**ptions **S**cale **Y**-Scale **I**ndicator **M**anual command to input an indicator that is appropriate for your data.
>
> *The graph I added to the worksheet obscures the data under it, which in this case should show through.*
>
> Graphs are opaque by default. Use the **:G**raph **S**ettings **O**paque **N**o command to make the graph transparent.
>
> *The latest object I added with the Wysiwyg graphics editor always appears on top, even when it should be behind other objects.*
>
> Use the **:G**raph **E**dit **R**earrange **B**ack command to move the object to the back of the stack of objects.

From Here...

For information related directly to creating power graphs, you may want to review the following chapters of this book:

- Chapter 2, "What Every 1-2-3 User Should Know," provides basic information on entering and editing data and on creating basic graphs.

- Chapter 6, "Making Your Worksheets Dazzle," provides information on 1-2-3 formatting options that also can apply to graph axes and Wysiwyg text.

- Chapter 8, "Printing Reports," provides information on printing worksheet ranges and graphs from 1-2-3.

- Chapter 23, "Creating Effective Graphs," provides information on using 1-2-3's graphics capabilities to create graphics that convey the meaning of your data.

Chapter 25

Developing Business Presentations

You can use the graphic and printing capabilities of 1-2-3 in many creative ways besides graphing and reporting worksheet data. This chapter discusses using the Wysiwyg capabilities available in 1-2-3 Release 4 to create high-quality presentation slides, overheads, and screen shows.

You can use black-and-white or color printers supported by 1-2-3 to print slides and graphics. With a color printer, you can print directly on transparent overhead projector film to create colorful, persuasive overhead presentations.

You also can use your computer for the slide show by projecting the PC screen image, much as you project the image of a transparency. This technique is often called a *computer screen show*. Screen show capabilities are often found in presentation graphics packages, but 1-2-3 provides many of the same capabilities and can create a visually interesting screen show.

You can display a slide show from your computer screen directly to an audience in several ways. The method you choose depends on the size of the audience and your budget. The easiest way to make a presentation to a moderate-size group (10 to 15) is to use a very large computer monitor. If you are presenting to a large group (50 or more), you may want to use a video projector. This projector is expensive to rent, however, and often is difficult to set up.

A newer device, called an *LCD projection panel*, enables you to project your PC screen with a standard overhead projector. This device fits directly on top of the overhead projector, is fairly inexpensive to buy or rent, and is easy to use. This device is often the best solution for making a presentation to a group of 20 to 100 people.

This chapter shows you how to accomplish the following tasks:

- Set up your worksheet for presentations
- Use 1-2-3 to convey a message
- Use color to emphasize main points
- Apply formats and use typefaces to design persuasive presentations
- Use a 3-D worksheet to organize your presentation
- Add graphs and graphics to your presentation
- Print your presentation
- Use macros to make screen shows easier

Setting Up Your Worksheet Area for Presentations

An important first step in using 1-2-3 for a presentation is setting up the work area for the presentation. The following sections first describe how you can use 1-2-3 for creating presentations and then provide many tips for projecting the presentation from the PC or printing it on overhead transparencies.

Using the Row-and-Column Structure To Assist with Layout

Creating a presentation in 1-2-3 is easy because of the row-and-column structure inherent in all worksheets. You can change the column widths and row heights of this row-and-column grid to customize presentations.

Creating slides in 1-2-3 is as easy as typing the text into worksheet cells. The first step is to organize your slide structure by using the rows and columns in the worksheet. Figure 25.1 shows how you can use 1-2-3 to set up a presentation template.

In this example, the column widths are shown in the first row of the worksheet. The key to creating the slide layout is setting up the appropriate column widths for text, bullets, and graphics. Organizing the columns in this manner enables you to easily indent bullets and other textual information. To add text, highlight the appropriate cell and type the new information. Long labels will display across the adjacent columns. The following table describes how the columns are used in figure 25.1.

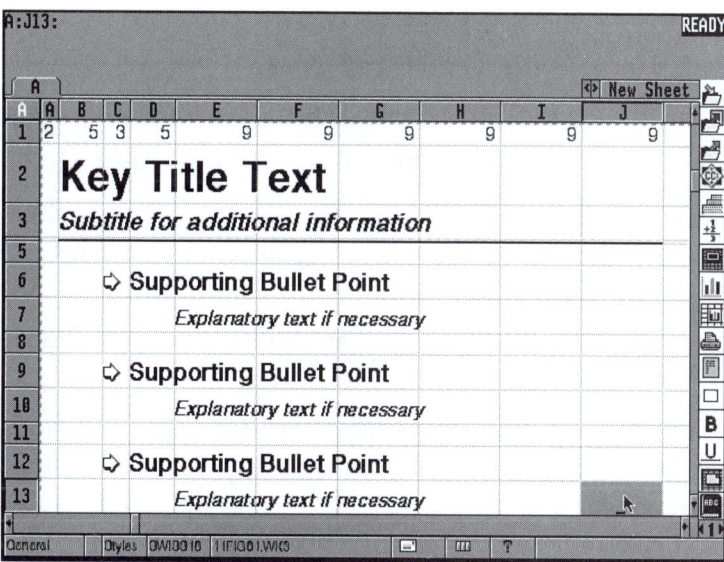

Fig. 25.1
A template for a slide layout in 1-2-3.

Column	Width	Description
A	2	Space to separate the overall slide contents from the page frame
B	5	Indentation for subtitles below the leader
C	3	Space for the bullet symbols
D	5	Indentation for text below bulleted items

Because row heights automatically change to fit the largest font in each row, you usually do not need to adjust row heights when creating a layout. Just skip rows between bullet points to provide space between the lines of text.

After you input the text, you can use the **:Format** commands or the live status bar to set attributes that make the text more readable. Larger typefaces and other attributes, such as bold, italics, and lines, make the information clearer for your audience.

◀ "Setting Column Widths," p. 121

Modifying the 1-2-3 Display for On-Screen Presentations

Although the standard 1-2-3 screen looks nothing like a presentation tool, giving 1-2-3 the appearance of a presentation graphics screen show is easy. You can create an effective screen show by using the **:D**isplay commands, which provide substantial flexibility for modifying the appearance of the screen display. To change the display of the 1-2-3 screen, follow these steps:

1. Select **:D**isplay **O**ptions **F**rame **N**one to turn off the worksheet frame.

2. Select **:D**isplay **O**ptions **G**rid **N**o to turn off the worksheet grid.

3. Select **:D**isplay **C**olors **C**ell-Pointer **W**hite to change the cell pointer to white (or choose the appropriate background color if the background is not white).

4. Select **/W**orksheet **G**lobal **D**efault **O**ther **C**lock **N**one to turn off the date-and-time indicator.

5. Select **/W**orksheet **G**lobal **D**efault **O**ther **D**isplay **S**croll-bars **N**o to turn off the scroll bars on the right and bottom of the worksheet area.

If you use a mouse, you can change the display options directly in the global setting dialog box.

At this point, only the mode indicator in the top right corner and the current cell information in the status bar remain on-screen. You must use a macro command to turn off the mode indicator. The INDICATE advanced macro command alters or turns off the mode indicator. To turn off the indicator, use the following within a macro:

    {INDICATE ""}

The null string, "", suppresses the indicator entirely; however, the null string retains the cell format and contents displayed in the control panel. You can cover the control panel with a solid bar by including 80 spaces inside the quotes of the INDICATE macro command.

> **Tip**
> To run this macro each time you load the worksheet file, name the macro \0 (backslash zero).

> ▶ "Naming and Running Macros," p. 852

The following macro combines all these steps to give the worksheet a presentation appearance:

```
:dofnqq                        Turn off the worksheet frame
:dccwqq                        Set the cell pointer to white
:dognqq                        Turn off the grid
/wgdocnq                       Turn off the clock indicator
/wgdodsnqq                     Turn off the scroll bars
{INDICATE @REPEAT(" ",80)}     Create a solid indicator bar
```

Developing Multiple-Page Presentations

Most presentations use more than one page or worksheet screen; 1-2-3 can accommodate presentations of almost any length. 1-2-3 Release 4 provides a three-dimensional (*multiple-page*) worksheet structure that makes organizing multiple-screen presentations easy.

Setting Up Your Worksheet Area for Presentations   **801**

With the 1-2-3 three-dimensional architecture, you can place each slide in its own worksheet. 1-2-3 Release 4 also provides tabs to enable you to easily move among worksheet pages. The tabs offer an easy way to change slides, especially if you do not move sequentially through the pages. Simply click the worksheet tab for the desired page. You can also press Ctrl+PgUp or Ctrl+PgDn to move between slides, or click the Next Worksheet or Previous Worksheet SmartIcons. Figure 25.2 shows a presentation using the worksheet tabs.

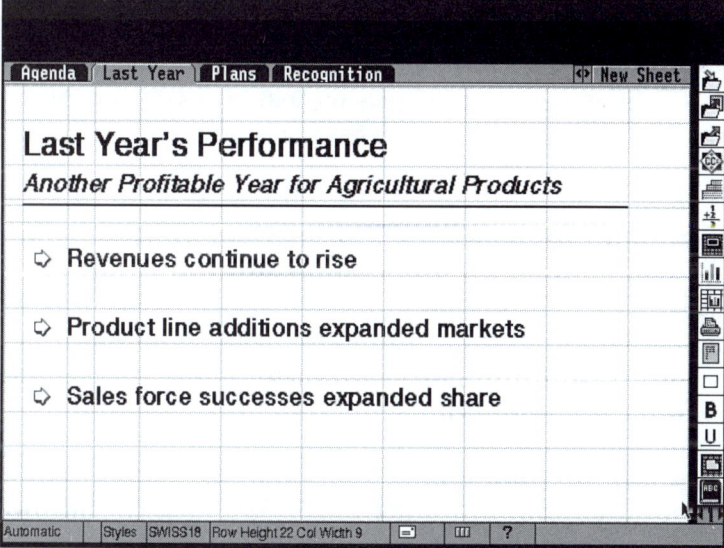

Fig. 25.2
Using the 1-2-3 worksheet tabs to organize slides on multiple pages.

> **Note**
>
> Tabs work best on shorter presentations. If you have too many tabs, or tabs with long names, you cannot display all the tabs along the top of the worksheet. Use the Tab Scroll buttons to display the hidden tabs or use Ctrl+PgUp or the Next Worksheet SmartIcon to move to later slides.

> **Note**
>
> 1-2-3 Release 4 also provides a GROUP mode feature, which enables you to use the format of one worksheet to format all the pages in multiple worksheets. The formats applied across the worksheets include column widths and Wysiwyg spreadsheet publishing formats. Use /**W**orksheet **G**lobal **G**roup **E**nable to enable GROUP mode.

◄ "Using Multiple-Worksheet Files," p. 458

The easiest way to use GROUP mode is to format one worksheet page and enable GROUP mode. Copy the formats throughout the entire worksheet file. Then disable GROUP mode because some worksheets may need to differ slightly from the master format.

Using 1-2-3 To Convey a Message

◄ "Formatting with the Wysiwyg Menu," p. 320

Although 1-2-3 provides many features to format printed pages and screen layouts, you shouldn't use all these capabilities at one time. Clear, persuasive, and successful presentations are created by following some simple rules and guidelines for style and format, and require simplicity in formatting and layout. Because an audience reads presentations from a distance, slides must be clear, in large type, and contain as few words as necessary to communicate your message to the audience.

Following Guidelines for Presenting Text

You can create persuasive slides by following some basic guidelines. 1-2-3 and Wysiwyg provide great flexibility for text size and font, colors, lines, and shading. The key to a successful presentation, however, is to use these elements in moderation. By following a few guidelines, you can create impressive and effective presentations.

Use Large Point Sizes for Text

You should use fonts that can be read from a distance. Titles should be a 24-point font or larger. Text used in presentations must never be smaller than 14 points.

Reduce Point Size for Subtitles and Bullets

Use type size to indicate the relative importance of text in a slide. To draw attention to the slide's key message, use the largest text for titles. Choose smaller type sizes for subtitles and bullets.

Limit the Number of Fonts on a Slide

Although Wysiwyg enables you to use up to eight different fonts on a page, the best slides use only one or two typefaces in three point sizes. Too many type styles make the slide difficult to read and reduce the impact of the slide's message.

Use a Sans Serif Typeface

You should format slide text in a sans serif typeface such as Swiss. Serif typefaces such as Dutch may be appropriate at times, but in general, sans serif text is easier to read.

Use Italics for Subtitles

A subtitle message usually supports or expands on the title message. Differentiate the subtitle from the title with a smaller point size and italics.

Use Boldface for All Titles and Bullets

Boldface makes the text on slides much easier to read and should be used for all titles, subtitles, and bullets. Be sure to apply the boldfacing consistently, however.

Emphasize the Title of the Slide

Slides convey information better when the title is easy to locate and read. You can use a solid or dotted line below the title to separate the title from the body of the slide (see figs. 25.3 and 25.4). Use the **:F**ormat **L**ines **W**ide **B**ottom command to place a solid line under the slide title.

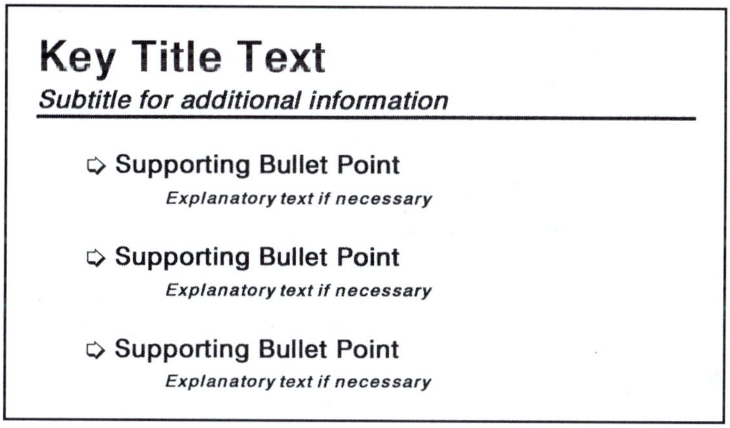

Fig. 25.3
A solid line emphasizing the slide title.

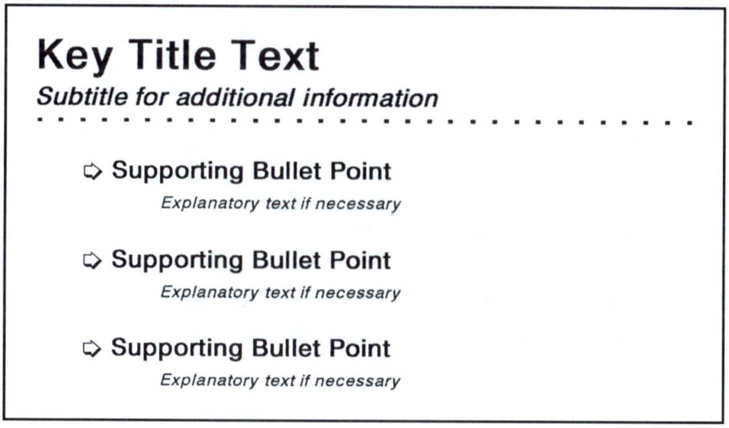

Fig. 25.4
A dotted line emphasizing the slide title.

Dotted lines also separate the title from the rest of the slide effectively. Dotted lines can be less jarring than a solid line and can give a softer tone to the slide. You can create a dotted line as a series of periods separated by spaces. To create a dotted line that spans the width of the screen, you need approximately 36 periods and spaces formatted with a 24-point Swiss font.

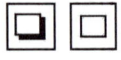

You also can emphasize a title by enclosing the text in an outline or colored box. In addition, you can use a drop-shadow effect to emphasize the title. Highlight the range and click the Shadow SmartIcon or the Outline SmartIcon. Figure 25.5 shows the same slide text with a title box that has a drop shadow.

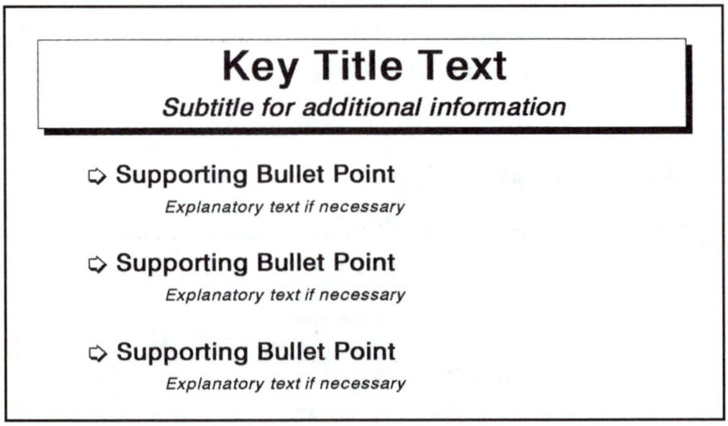

Fig. 25.5
An outline box with a drop shadow emphasizing the slide title.

Keep Slide Text to a Minimum

> **Tip**
> Adding another slide is always better than crowding too much information onto a single slide.

Slides should not be narratives of the entire presentation. Use the titles, subtitles, and bulleted items to present the essential points clearly. Rely on the spoken presentation to explain and elaborate on the basic information that the slides present.

Slides should contain a title and no more than four or five bulleted points. If the bullets require sub-bullets, your slide should contain no more than four main bullets. Limit the sub-bullets to two or three lines.

Use Parallel Grammatical Structure

All the bullets on a slide should use the same grammatical construction. Bullets can start with a noun or a verb of any tense, but all the bullets should use the same structure. A parallel construction creates a tighter presentation and conveys information more clearly. Figures 25.6 and 25.7 compare grammatical constructions that are parallel and are not parallel.

Fig. 25.6
Bullets that are parallel.

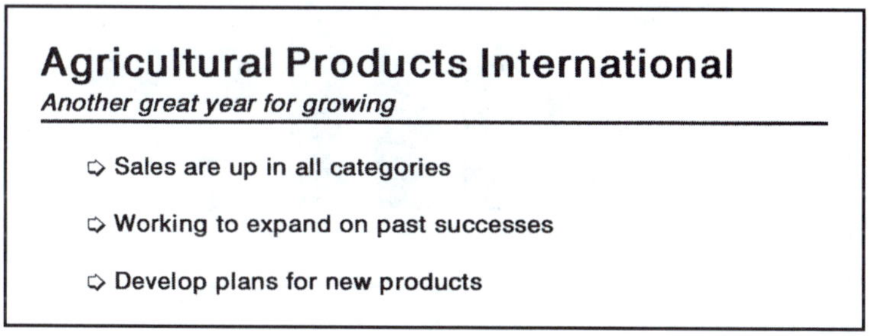

Fig. 25.7
Bullets that are not parallel.

Use Correct Spelling
Spelling or typographical errors detract from the content of a presentation and show a lack of attention to detail. Use the 1-2-3 command /**T**ools **S**pell **F**ile or click the Spell Check SmartIcon to check the spelling of all the text in the current presentation files.

◀ "Spell Checking Your Data," p. 284

Following Guidelines for Presenting Graphics
To make presentation slides more effective and persuasive, you can use graphic images. Like text, graphics are more effective when you follow certain guidelines.

Use Graphics To Explain the Key Point
A graphic can draw attention to the key point of the slide. You can use the **:G**raph **A**dd command to add a graphic to a worksheet. Do not include too many different thoughts, however, and do not present detailed information in a single graphic. The best graphics are clear, easy-to-read presentations of a single key point.

Use Text To Introduce and Explain the Graphic
Use titles to introduce the key message and to establish the context for the graphic. Effective graphics have a clear purpose. You can use bullets in your graphics to clarify or emphasize the points made by the text; however, do not

overload the page with information, as figure 25.8 illustrates. Figure 25.9 presents the same information clearly.

Fig. 25.8
A graphic containing too much information.

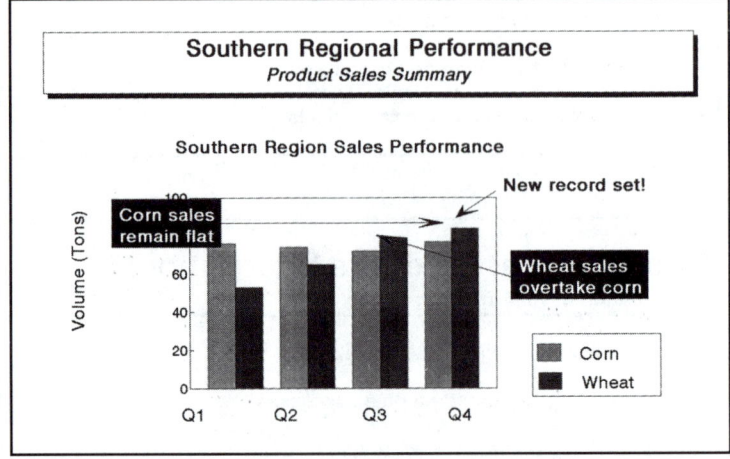

Fig. 25.9
Bullets explaining the chart and balancing it on the slide.

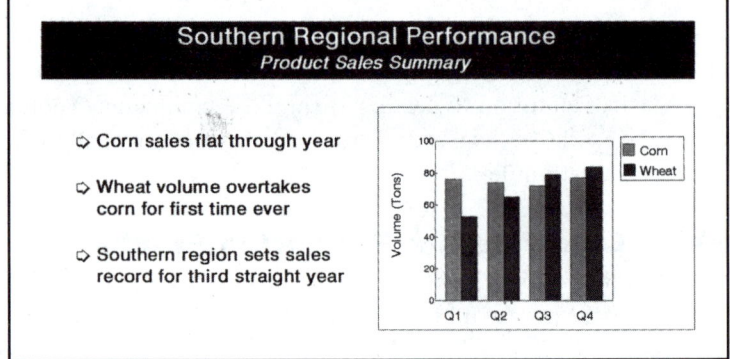

Position the Graphic To Balance the Page
Graphics add substance to a slide. You need to position a graphic to balance the page, however. Center a graphic if the slide contains little text; otherwise, position the graphic to the right or left to offset the weight of the other slide elements (refer to fig. 25.9).

Use a Single Graphic Per Slide
In most cases, a slide should contain only a single graphic. The key to an effective slide presentation is to present the key points with clear, simple illustrations.

Add Visual Interest with Clip Art

You can use commercially available clip art to make the presentation more interesting for the audience. Choose images that support your presentation's theme and are appropriate to the setting (see fig. 25.10).

◀ "Adding a Graph," p. 768

Fig. 25.10
Use clip art to liven up a presentation.

> **Note**
>
> 1-2-3 Release 4 includes a large number of clip art files with the CGM extension. These files are located in the \123R4D directory (or the default directory you specified when you installed 1-2-3).
>
> Lotus SmartPics is a collection of clip art sold by Lotus Selects. To order from Lotus Selects, call 1-800-635-6887. Be sure to order the CGM format that is compatible with DOS versions of 1-2-3.

Use Graphics To Represent Concepts

Use graphics of common objects to convey new ideas. Look at your environment for metaphors that effectively communicate your message. You can use building blocks, for example, to show the addition of new products over time. You can use pie graphs to show that a combination of the various parts make a whole (see fig. 25.11). A bridge can represent the joining of two separate entities.

Present Key Trends or Relationships

Use 1-2-3 graphs to illustrate key trends in data or to show the relationship among items. The graph in figure 25.9, for example, clearly shows the trends in product sales. Keep the graph simple by limiting the amount of information.

Fig. 25.11

A pie graph representing proportions.

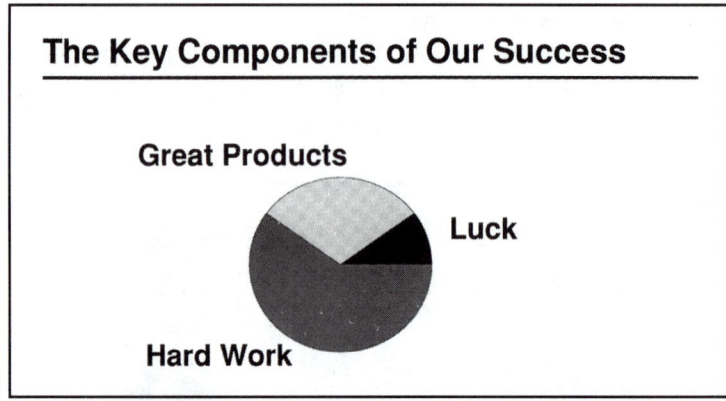

Tables of formatted data also can make great illustrations. You can draw attention to the trends and relationships among the data by using lines and arrows added with the graphics editor (see fig. 25.12). Chapter 24, "Creating Power Graphs," describes using the graphics editor in detail.

Fig. 25.12

A graph annotation pointing out key information in a worksheet table.

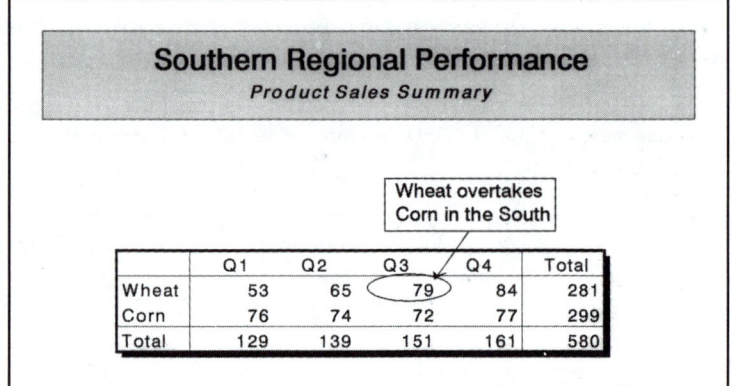

Using the Color Capabilities of 1-2-3

In addition to graphics, color enhances presentations. Color can add interest to the slides and highlight key data. Some colors, such as green and red, can add impact to the information presented.

> **Note**
>
> To present color, you must be able to print to a color printer or use a computer to give the presentation as a screen show. The colors, however, print on black-and-white printers as different shades of gray, which also can create a useful effect.

1-2-3 can format a worksheet with six colors for text and cell backgrounds. The default colors are dark blue, green, magenta, red, and yellow. The color gray is available and is used in place of cyan in the product. The graphics editor also provides 224 colors for shading graphic objects. By using the color capabilities, you can create appropriately colorful presentations.

Using Color To Highlight Presentation Elements

In a presentation, you can use colors in several ways. The most obvious method of adding color is to use a different color for the main point in the presentation. You can choose from several other common ways to use color, however.

Color can enhance the organizational structure of the presentation. Using a standard color layout makes the slides easy to understand and more interesting to read. Choose consistent colors for the different regions of the slide, such as blue text for the titles, red for the bullet symbols, and black for the bullet text. You also can use different background colors for different sections of the slide (see fig. 25.13).

Fig. 25.13
Using color to organize the slide layout.

Conveying Information with Selected Colors

Because many colors have common connotations, you can use color to convey meaning in a presentation. In business, for example, the color red represents a monetary loss or negative number, and black represents a profit or positive number.

Figure 25.14 shows a slide that could easily contain color. If the third bullet of the slide in figure 25.14 were red, for example, the viewer would immediately know that excessive expenses would result in a loss for the company.

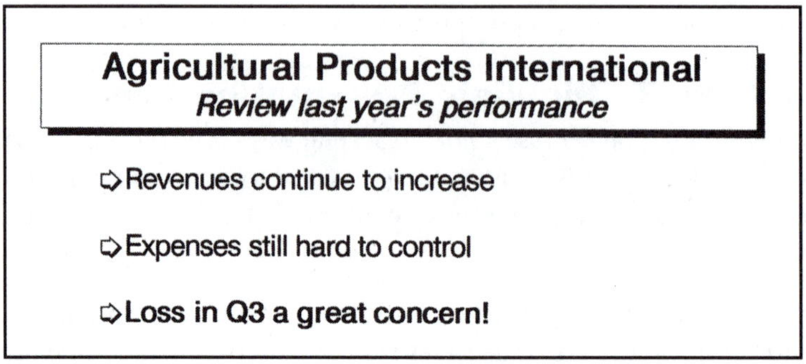

Fig. 25.14
Creating a slide that can use red to convey monetary loss.

```
┌─────────────────────────────────────────┐
│   Agricultural Products International   │
│       Review last year's performance    │
└─────────────────────────────────────────┘

   ▷ Revenues continue to increase

   ▷ Expenses still hard to control

   ▷ Loss in Q3 a great concern!
```

Red also can suggest danger. Blue is a peaceful and even soothing color. Green—the color of U.S. currency and the stoplight color for GO—can convey a message. Yellow often means caution, a message that also comes from traffic lights and road signs.

Creating Alternative Color Schemes

The standard Wysiwyg colors—the default colors—may not meet all your needs; they also can be overpowering if you use them extensively. You can, however, select from 64 different shades of these colors to create a more pleasing custom color scheme. The **:D**isplay **C**olors **R**eplace command replaces the default colors.

To replace the default colors, follow these steps:

1. Select **:D**isplay **C**olors **R**eplace.

2. With the cursor, highlight the color to replace but do *not* press Enter. Press the + or - keys to change the current color selection for the highlighted color.

    Alternatively, you can select the color to change by typing the first letter of the color or highlighting the color and pressing Enter. Then type a new color number and press Enter.

3. Select **Q**uit three times to return to READY mode.

You can experiment with the different shades to define your own color scheme. Table 25.1 lists the color numbers for color schemes with a softer set of colors.

Table 25.1 A Sample Wysiwyg Color Scheme

Color	Replacement Number	Default Color Number
Red	4	4
Green	42	18
Dark-Blue	33	1
Yellow	38	62
Magenta	21	5

You can replace the original color scheme with new defaults; however, a simple macro can set the colors for any purpose. The following macro sets the color scheme contained in table 25.1.

```
{PANELOFF}              Turn off control panel
:dcr                    Access :Display Colors Replace
menu
r4~                     Set Red to 4
g42~                    Set Green to 42
d33~                    Set Dark-Blue to 33
y38~                    Set Yellow to 38
m21~                    Set Magenta to 21
qqq                     Quit to READY mode
{PANELON}               Turn on control panel
```

Name this macro \0 so that it runs each time you load the presentation file. This macro ensures that you have the appropriate color scheme each time you use your PC to give a presentation.

Tip
Use the :Display Default Restore command to reset 1-2-3 to use the standard colors.

◄ "Setting Display Characteristics," p. 241

► "Naming and Running Macros," p. 852

> **Note**
>
> Do not replace the Cyan color choice. This color choice has been set to gray and is used for 1-2-3 Release 4 screen color design.

Selecting Color Schemes for Black-and-White Printing

Color schemes can be useful even if you plan to produce black-and-white presentations. With most printers, Wysiwyg prints different colors in different shades of gray.

You can see the gray scale representation on-screen with the black-and-white display mode. (Use the **:D**isplay **M**ode **B**&W command to switch to the black-and-white display mode.) Although useful, this display mode doesn't always show the gray scales on-screen exactly as they appear when printed.

Selecting Color for Background, Text, and Graphics

With 1-2-3, you can select the color of the cell background and the cell contents. This feature enables you to emphasize text or portions in the presentation file. Use the **:F**ormat **C**olor command to set the color.

The graphics editor also enables you to set colors in the worksheet and offers additional color choices designed for shading graphic objects. The **:G**raph **E**dit **C**olor **I**nside command colors the inside of any object in the graphics editing window.

◀ "Using the Graphics Editor," p. 773

By using blank graphs (described in Chapter 24, "Creating Power Graphs"), you can use all 224 colors for shading worksheet areas. First, select **:G**raph **A**dd **B**lank to create a blank graph over the worksheet area you intend to shade. If you want to shade the entire area, set the background color to the color derived with the **:G**raph **E**dit **C**olor **B**ackground command. To shade part of the graph range, select **:G**raph **E**dit **A**dd **R**ectangle to add a rectangle that fills the entire drawing area; shade the inside of the rectangle with the chosen color.

The only limitation of this technique is that the cell contents cannot show through the colors added in this manner. To display text over this color, add the text with the **:G**raph **E**dit **A**dd **T**ext command.

Using Color To Guide the Audience

◀ "Using Formatting Sequences," p. 333

Most presentations start with an agenda. You can tie a presentation together by repeating the agenda slide before switching to the next topic. This method is more effective if you also highlight the topic that follows. One way to highlight the topic is to use color. Figure 25.15 shows the slide you might choose to introduce the second topic (Define plan for upcoming growing season). In this example, the first and third bullets are shaded gray with the formatting sequence 3g (see the control panel). To enter this formatting sequence, press Ctrl+A; then type **3g** while in the EDIT mode.

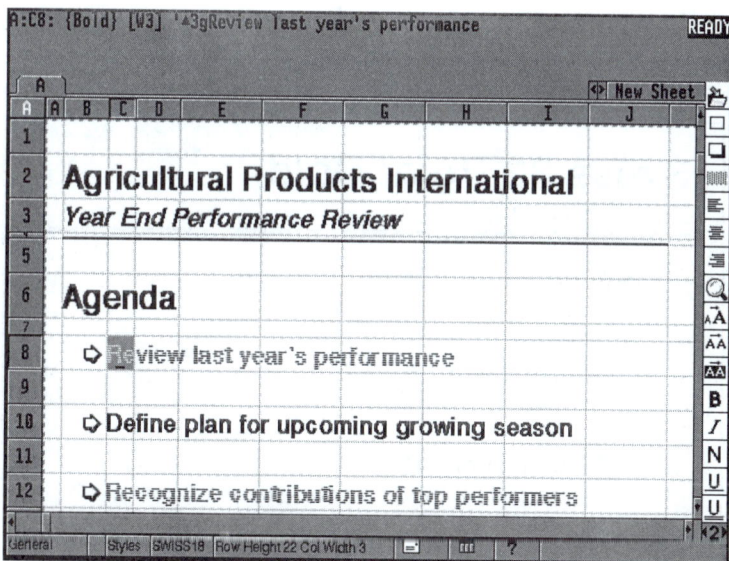

Fig. 25.15
Introducing the next topic by emphasizing a bulleted item.

Emphasizing Text or Graphic Elements

The Wysiwyg : menu in 1-2-3 provides several publishing options for formatting worksheets. You can use these capabilities to emphasize text and graphs and to make the content of the slide easier to read.

Selecting the Appropriate Font

Several factors affect the choice of fonts for presentations, including whether the presentation is for screen display or printing. If you plan only to print the presentation and have a PostScript printer, for example, you may want to choose from the PostScript printer fonts. If you will be presenting from the screen, however, you must limit your choice to the standard fonts (Swiss, Dutch, and so on) available in 1-2-3.

The beginning of this chapter discussed several guidelines for choosing fonts. Although these guidelines are not hard-and-fast rules, they are important to consider when you design a slide page.

◀ "Understanding Fonts," p. 321

You must use point sizes that are readable from a distance and typefaces that work together and balance the images on-screen. Figure 25.16 shows a slide with effective font selections. Figure 25.17, on the other hand, contains too many typefaces and type styles. The viewer is distracted by a multitude of fonts and loses the focus of the slide's message.

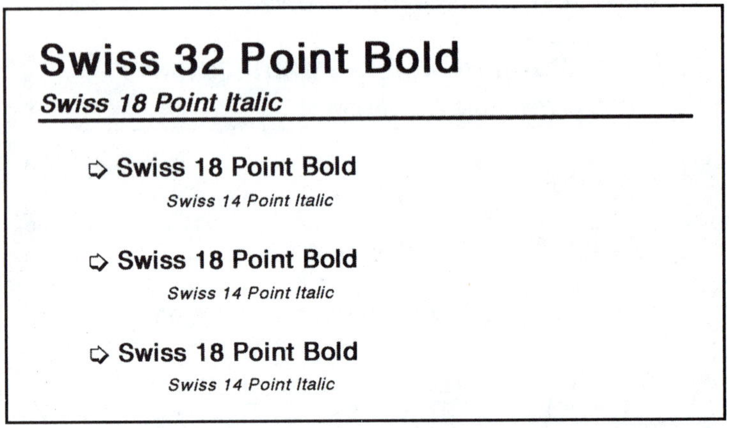

Fig. 25.16
Fonts that work together for clarity of presentation.

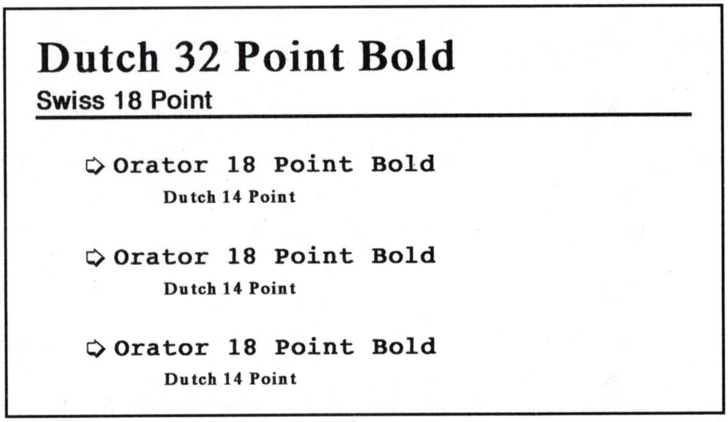

> **Swiss 32 Point Bold**
> *Swiss 18 Point Italic*
>
> ▷ **Swiss 18 Point Bold**
>   *Swiss 14 Point Italic*
>
> ▷ **Swiss 18 Point Bold**
>   *Swiss 14 Point Italic*
>
> ▷ **Swiss 18 Point Bold**
>   *Swiss 14 Point Italic*

Fig. 25.17
Fonts that make the slide difficult to read and understand.

> **Dutch 32 Point Bold**
> Swiss 18 Point
>
> ▷ `Orator 18 Point Bold`
>   Dutch 14 Point
>
> ▷ `Orator 18 Point Bold`
>   Dutch 14 Point
>
> ▷ `Orator 18 Point Bold`
>   Dutch 14 Point

Using Special Symbols

You can precede text items with special symbols, such as diamonds or arrows. These symbols are available with the Wysiwyg Xsymbol font. You can create the arrow symbol, for example, by placing the appropriate character in a cell and formatting the character with the Xsymbol font. The Xsymbol font point size should correspond to the adjacent text.

> **Note**
>
> Refer to the 1-2-3 Release 4 documentation for a listing of the characters that the Wysiwyg Xsymbol font offers.

Figure 25.18 shows the arrows on-screen. The control panel displays the character that creates the arrow symbol (*m* in this example).

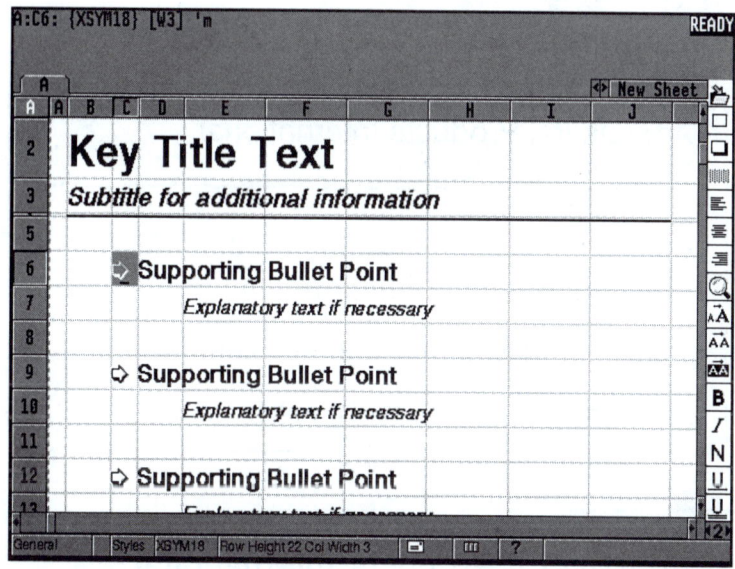

Fig. 25.18
Arrow symbols formatted with the Xsymbol font.

To add a bullet symbol to your text slide, follow these steps:

1. Decide which symbol to use.

2. Place the appropriate character in the cell next to the text.

   Type **m** for the arrow shown in figure 25.18, for example.

> **Note**
>
> From the keyboard, you cannot type the characters necessary for some symbols. For these symbols, use the ASCII number code for the character. In 1-2-3 Release 4, you can enter an ASCII code into a cell by pressing and holding the Alt key and typing the number on the numeric keypad. To enter ASCII character ú, for example, press Alt and type **163** on the number pad.

Using Boldface and Italics

Most audiences view slides from a distance. Because plain type tends to fade into the projection screen and become unreadable, you should use boldface for most text.

You also can use boldface to outline the structure of the slide; for example, you can reinforce the slide's structure by formatting symbols in boldface and leaving explanatory subtext plain. Figures 25.19 and 25.20 show a slide before and after adding boldface to the text.

Fig. 25.19
An organized slide with no boldface.

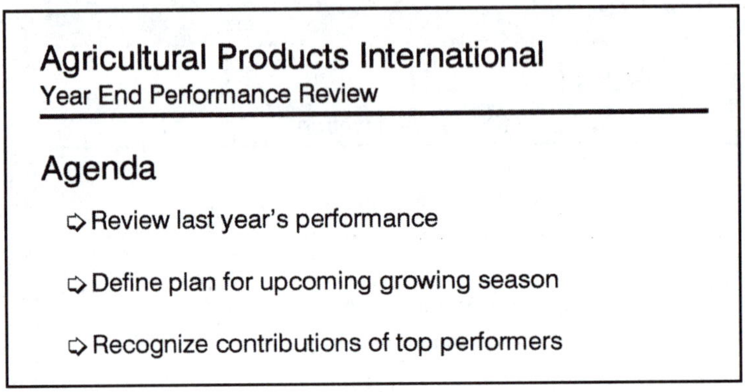

```
Agricultural Products International
Year End Performance Review
────────────────────────────────────

Agenda

  ▷ Review last year's performance

  ▷ Define plan for upcoming growing season

  ▷ Recognize contributions of top performers
```

Fig. 25.20
The same slide with boldface.

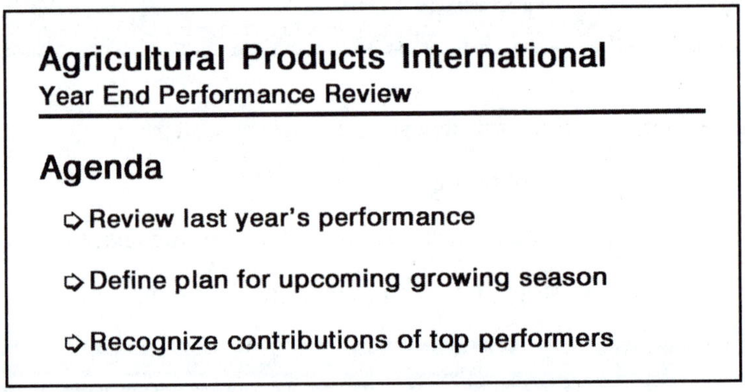

```
Agricultural Products International
Year End Performance Review
────────────────────────────────────

Agenda

  ▷ Review last year's performance

  ▷ Define plan for upcoming growing season

  ▷ Recognize contributions of top performers
```

You also can use italics to separate the parts of the slide and to show that text has special meaning. Italics are effective for emphasizing direct or indirect quotations, for example. If you use italic type, you should use boldfaced italic because italic text tends to be lighter than plain text and disappears into the page.

Figures 25.21 and 25.22 show different ways of using bold and italics to add emphasis and clarity to slides.

Emphasizing Text or Graphic Elements   **817**

Agricultural Products International
Year End Performance Review

Agenda

⇨ **Review last year's performance**
   Profits are up but at risk

⇨ **Define plan for upcoming growing season**
   It's never too early to plant the seeds for success

⇨ **Recognize contributions of top performers**
   Individual performance is still key to our success

Fig. 25.21
Boldface symbols with italic subtext.

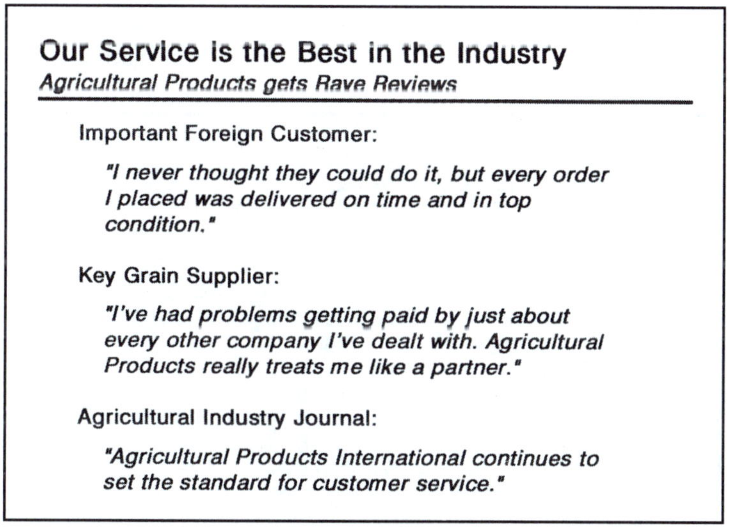

Our Service is the Best in the Industry
Agricultural Products gets Rave Reviews

Important Foreign Customer:

   "I never thought they could do it, but every order I placed was delivered on time and in top condition."

Key Grain Supplier:

   "I've had problems getting paid by just about every other company I've dealt with. Agricultural Products really treats me like a partner."

Agricultural Industry Journal:

   "Agricultural Products International continues to set the standard for customer service."

Fig. 25.22
A slide using boldface italics for quotations.

Using Lines, Boxes, and Shading

Lines, boxes, and shading offer an effective way to add structure and emphasis to a slide. By using these elements, you emphasize important text. You can use lines to emphasize slide titles, as described earlier, and to organize the slide. You can use text boxes to emphasize other text on the slide and to organize tables. Figure 25.23 shows a slide with a corporate mission statement placed in a shadow box.

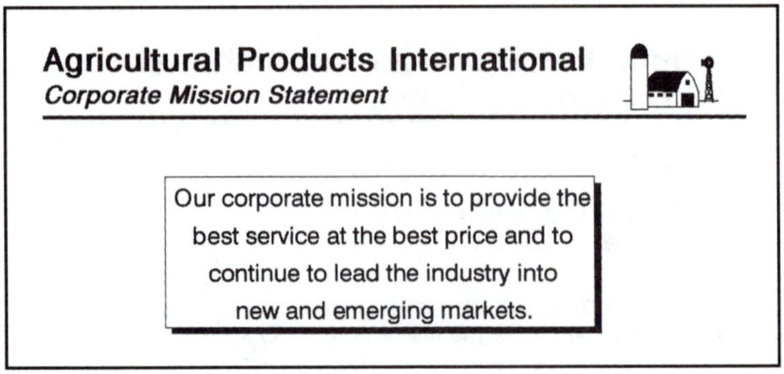

Fig. 25.23
A shadow box to emphasize key slide text.

Agricultural Products International
Corporate Mission Statement

> Our corporate mission is to provide the best service at the best price and to continue to lead the industry into new and emerging markets.

The row and column structure of the 1-2-3 worksheet enables you to include tables in presentations. Simple rows and columns of numbers and labels can be difficult to read, but you can add lines, borders, and shading to a table to increase the clarity of numbers and labels. Figure 25.24 shows an example of a table with little formatting; figure 25.25 shows a well-formatted table.

Fig. 25.24
A table with basic formatting.

Regional Performance Summary
Products Sold by Geographic Region

	Products			
Region	Wheat	Corn	Oats	Barley
U.S. North	405.1	408.8	412.4	416.1
U.S. South	405.7	409.4	NA	NA
U.S. Mid West	406.3	410.0	NA	NA
U.S. Far West	406.9	410.6	414.3	417.9
Europe	407.6	411.2	414.9	418.6
New Markets	408.2	411.8	NA	NA
Total	2439.8	2461.8	1241.6	1252.6

Fig. 25.25
A table organized with lines and shading.

Regional Performance Summary
Products Sold by Geographic Region

	Products			
Region	Wheat	Corn	Oats	Barley
North	405.1	408.8	412.4	416.1
South	405.7	409.4	NA	NA
Mid West	406.3	410.0	NA	NA
Far West	406.9	410.6	414.3	417.9
Total	1624.0	1638.8	826.7	834.0

The use of lines, boxes, and shading is essential to creating clear, organized slides. When used judiciously, these elements greatly enhance the effectiveness of any presentation.

◀ "Drawing Lines and Boxes," p. 330

Using the :Graph Commands To Add Impact

Graphic images can make slide presentations come alive. The **:G**raph commands provide a vast array of capabilities for adding 1-2-3 graphs, clip art, and freehand drawings to presentations. Graphs and graphic images can make slides easier to understand by presenting the information in pictures, relating the text to common images, or providing visually interesting breaks in the presentation.

Adding 1-2-3 Graphs

Tables of data are seldom effective in slide presentations and, in most cases, should be supplemented or replaced by graphs and charts. To create an effective slide that presents worksheet data, include important conclusions drawn from the data and a graph that supports these conclusions. Figure 25.26 shows such a slide.

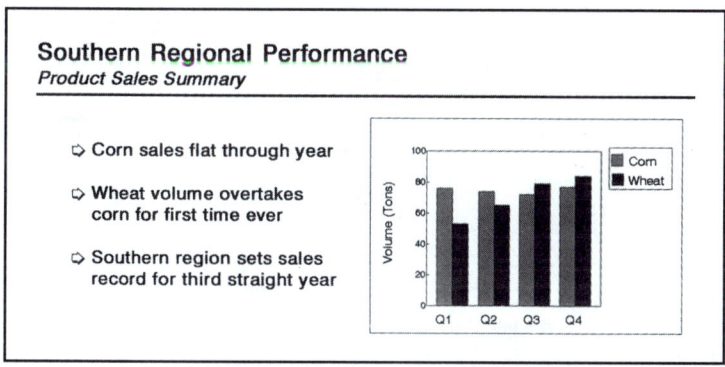

Fig. 25.26
Worksheet data with a graph presented in a slide.

You also can use 1-2-3 graphs as the basis for diagrams and other graphic images. Figure 25.27, for example, shows the expansion of Agricultural Products' product line. The bars do not represent specific quantities, but additional products. You can draw this chart with rectangles in the graphics editor, or you can draw the chart by placing equal values in a range of 1-2-3 worksheet cells and then using this range as your graph range.

Fig. 25.27
A chart based on a 1-2-3 graph.

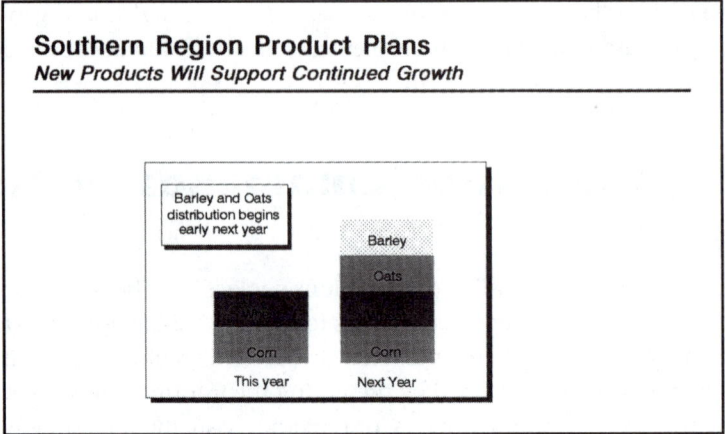

Adding Blank Graphs

◄ "Adding a Graph," p. 768

Blank graphs are drawing areas that can be placed anywhere in the worksheet. After you place a blank graph in the worksheet, you can use the graphics editor to draw virtually any type of free-form graphic. You can use blank graphs to explain difficult concepts or to illustrate key points presented on the slide. Figure 25.28 shows an example of an organizational chart created with a blank graph.

Fig. 25.28
A organizational chart drawn in a blank graph.

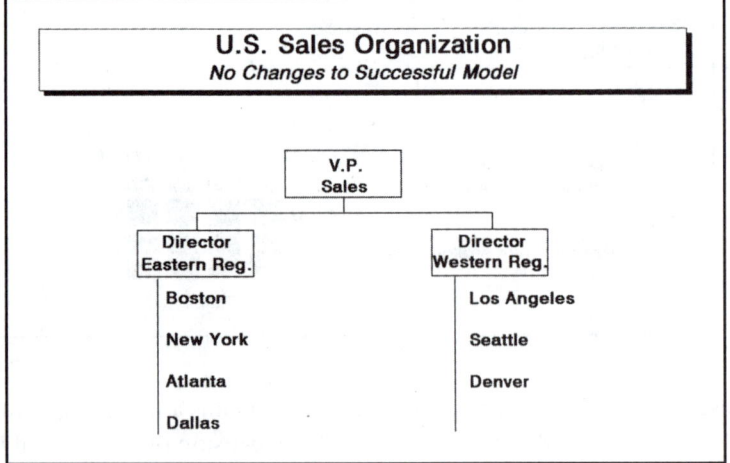

Using Clip Art

Virtually any image you want is available as clip art in the CGM (or metafile) format. 1-2-3 Release 4 includes a variety of clip art images that are copied into the \123R4D directory when you install the program. Clip art adds interest to the slide presentation and often can communicate key concepts. The graphics editor can annotate clip art, allowing you to adapt the image to the specific presentation. Figure 25.29 illustrates clip art used on slides.

Fig. 25.29
Adding clip art to a presentation.

Creating an Effective Background and Border for Presentations

The background and border for a slide can greatly enhance its readability. 1-2-3 has many options for creating backgrounds for slides. You can change the default background, white, by using the **:D**isplay **C**olors **B**ackground command. Changing the background in this way has no effect on the printing of the slides.

You also can use the **:F**ormat **C**olor **B**ackground command to select a background color for individual slides. Using this method, you can have a different color for each slide. Using a different color for each slide, however, can become distracting during the presentation; if you use different colors judiciously, you can create a striking impression. Unlike changing the default background color, the shaded background prints with the slide. When you select the color for a background, check that the text and graphic colors offer enough contrast to be readable from a distance.

You can use page borders to frame a slide on a page or a printout. One way to create a border is to frame the slide with a drop shadow (see fig. 25.30). Use the **:F**ormat **L**ines **O**utline and then the **:F**ormat **L**ines **S**hadow **S**et command to create a shadow box around the slide range, selecting the same range for both commands. To create the outline and drop shadow, select the range for the slide and click the Outline SmartIcon and then the Shadow SmartIcon.

Fig. 25.30
A slide framed by a drop shadow.

> **Agricultural Products International**
> *Today's Agenda*
>
> ▷ Increasing sales in all categories
> ▷ Working to expand on past successes
> ▷ Developing plans for new products

Printing Slides from 1-2-3

Most presentations ultimately are printed for distribution or duplication onto overhead transparencies. By using 1-2-3 and the Wysiwyg **:P**rint commands, you can print slides created on-screen.

You usually design slides to fit a landscape orientation. If you have a printer capable of printing landscape, use **:P**rint **C**onfig **O**rientation command to select the correct orientation.

You can use the **:W**orksheet **P**age **R**ow command to insert page breaks between slides so that each slide prints on its own page. This command places a horizontal page break in the worksheet. Place this break at the bottom of each slide. The page breaks appear on-screen.

◀ "Using the :Print Commands," p. 363

◀ "Using GROUP Mode To Change All the Work-sheets in a File," p. 471

If you have arranged your slides on multiple worksheets, place a page break at the bottom of each page by placing the cell pointer in the appropriate row and selecting **:W**orksheet **P**age **R**ow. To print all the slides, select a three-dimensional print range.

A slide formatted to fit the screen does not fill a printed page. You can enlarge the slide, however, by using the **:P**rint **L**ayout **C**ompression **M**anual command. A ratio of 125 percent enlarges the image to fit an 8 1/2-by-11-inch page. Before printing, use **:P**rint **P**review to verify that the slides fit correctly on the page.

Using Macros for Computer Presentations

Although many users print presentations created in 1-2-3, increasingly more users are delivering presentations directly from the computer. Delivering presentations directly from the computer enables you to use color and to create a "live" presentation environment.

1-2-3 macros can make computer slide shows easier to present and more interesting to view. With macros, for example, you can move automatically from slide to slide or simulate screen animation. You can use the macros described in the following sections to automate and animate your 1-2-3 slide shows.

A Macro for Changing Slides with the Enter Key

The simplest screen show macro pauses until you press the Enter key and then uses the {GOTO} key name to move to the next slide. To specify the worksheet letter as the range to go to, you type the worksheet letter followed by a colon for each slide. Figure 25.31 shows the macro in the worksheet.

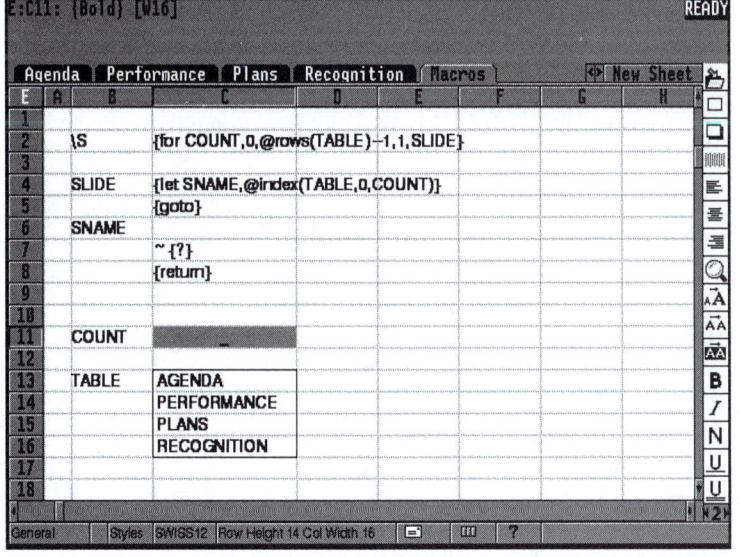

Fig. 25.31
A slide show macro.

The \s macro works for any number of slides. Build the table of slide names and use **/R**ange **N**ame **C**reate to name the range TABLE. The **/R**ange **N**ame **T**able command provides an easy way of listing the slide range names in the

824   Chapter 25—Developing Business Presentations

worksheet. You can use **/C**opy and **/M**ove to arrange the slides in the range TABLE without having to retype all the names.

A Macro for Timing Slide Changes

You can use a macro for timing the slide changes to enhance the preceding slide show macro. This macro establishes a predetermined delay before the screen moves to the next slide. You enter the number of seconds of delay in the column to the right of the slide name (see fig. 25.32). The range name TABLE must include both columns (columns F and G, in this example). If you press any key, the show moves to the next slide before the time elapses.

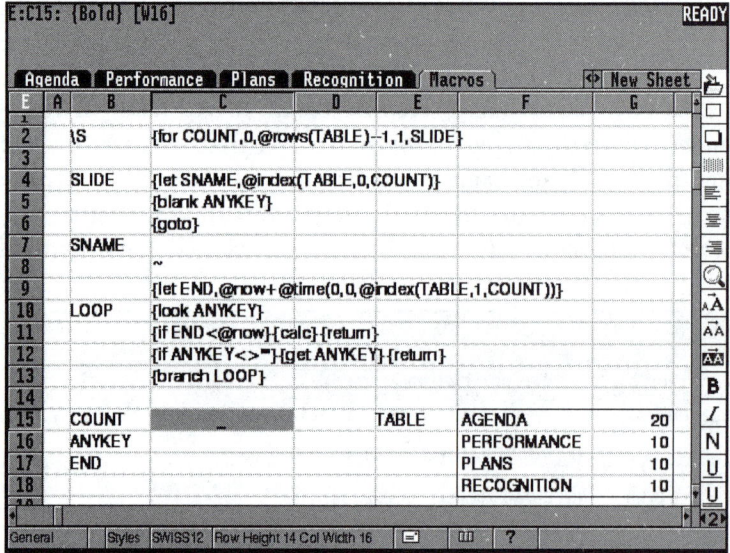

Fig. 25.32
An automatic screen show macro.

Troubleshooting

Clip art images placed in the worksheet obscure the underlying cells.

The default background for a CGM file is opaque. You can choose to allow cell information to display through the clip art image. Use the Wysiwyg command **:G**raph **S**ettings **O**paque **N**o to make the graph background transparent.

Presentation slides print either too large or too small for the page.

Use the Wysiwyg command **:P**rint **L**ayout **C**ompression to reduce or enlarge the size of your range on the printed page. Choose **A**utomatic to reduce it to fit on each page, or choose **M**anual to input a size to enlarge or reduce the range.

> *The colors in the CGM file placed in the worksheet are not the same as they are in the documentation.*
>
> Sometimes CGM colors are changed when the image is imported into 1-2-3. Use the Wysiwyg **:G**raph **E**dit **C**olor **M**ap command to change the colors used in the CGM image.

From Here...

For information relating directly to using 1-2-3 for presentations, you may want to review the following chapters of this book:

- Chapter 2, "What Every 1-2-3 User Should Know." This chapter provides an overview of the basic 1-2-3 capabilities, including using Wysiwyg formats, printing, and creating graphs.

- Chapter 4, "Controlling Your Worksheet Display." This chapter describes how to change the appearance of the 1-2-3 screen, including the commands necessary to set up 1-2-3 for screen shows.

- Chapter 8, "Printing Reports." This chapter explains how to use the **/P**rint and **:P**rint commands and when each is appropriate.

- Chapter 10, "Organizing Your Data with Multiple-Worksheet Files." In this chapter, you learn how to use the 3-D capabilities of 1-2-3 that are useful for organizing your presentation.

- Chapter 23, "Creating Effective Graphs." This chapter describes how to choose and create a graph that shows the information in your data.

- Chapter 24, "Creating Power Graphs." In this chapter, you learn how to use the more advanced graphic capabilities of 1-2-3 to make your graphs easier to understand.

- Chapter 26, "Short Macros To Make Your Life Easier." This chapter describes the basics you need to know to create the macros in this chapter.

Part VII
Automating with Macros

26 Short Macros To Make Your Life Easier

27 Advanced Macro Command Power Techniques

28 Controlling 1-2-3 with Macros

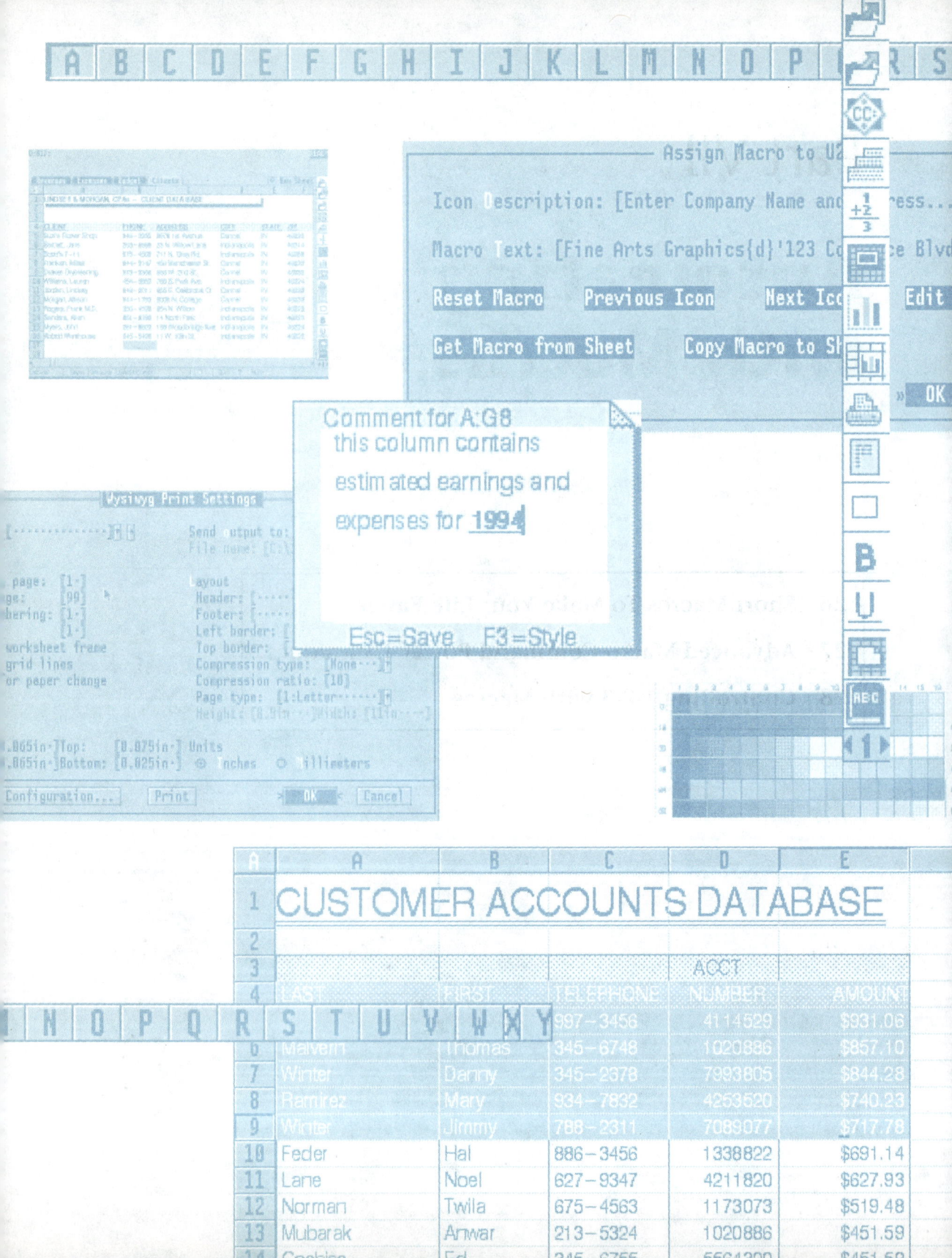

Chapter 26
Short Macros To Make Your Life Easier

At this point in *Using 1-2-3 Release 4 for DOS*, Special Edition, you have learned how 1-2-3's worksheet, database, and graphics features perform many useful functions in everyday business activities. Yet 1-2-3 has another feature that enhances the value of these functions: the macro capability. In its most basic form, a *macro* is a collection of keystrokes saved as a label in a worksheet range. Using 1-2-3 macros is a convenient way to automate the tasks you perform repeatedly, such as printing worksheets or changing global defaults, but macros can do much more for you. For example, with a more sophisticated macro, you can construct business applications that function in the same way as applications written in programming languages such as BASIC, C, and COBOL. This chapter lays the foundation of macro programming, using a number of short, simple examples.

1-2-3's macros consist of keystroke representations of the tasks you perform, plus special programming-language commands that have no direct equivalent in your everyday use of 1-2-3. For example, the macro equivalent of copying the contents of cell A1 to cell C1 is '/cA1~C1~, in which the tilde (~) represents the Enter key. These are almost exactly the keystrokes you use when you copy data, but to create a macro to accomplish this task, you enter **'/cA1~C1~** as a label in the spreadsheet. Because not all keystrokes can be represented in this simple manner, you also can use a collection of special macro key names. When you want a macro to move the cursor to cell A1, for example, you would enter the macro key name {HOME}.

This chapter introduces the macro recording feature. Macros that perform the equivalent of keystrokes you type can be recorded to minimize the chance of errors. This chapter also looks at some basic macro housekeeping, such as testing, debugging, and protecting your macros. Specifically, in this chapter, you learn how to accomplish the following tasks:

- Understand macro concepts
- Create macros with the record feature
- Name and run macros
- Test and debug macros
- Protect macros
- Assign macros to user SmartIcons

Understanding Macros

Macros are labels, and as such, you handle them in a similar manner. You can copy, edit, and move macros as you do other labels. The main function of macros is to provide a means of automating repetitive tasks. Consider the number of times you save and retrieve worksheet files, print reports, and perhaps set and reset worksheet formats. You perform each of these operations by pressing a sequence of keys—in some cases, quite a lengthy sequence. By using a macro, you can reduce any number of keystrokes to a simple two-keystroke process.

As an example, consider a simple macro that enters text. Suppose that your company's name is ABC Manufacturing Incorporated. Typing this name as an entry in the worksheet takes 31 keystrokes (if you count pressing the Enter key). Now suppose that you need to enter this text many times. You can type the entry's 31 keystrokes, copy the company name by using **/C**opy, or store the keystrokes in a macro. If you store the keystrokes in a macro, the next time you want to type the company's name, you can execute the 31 keystrokes by pressing just two keys.

In addition to saving you time by reducing the number of keystrokes you must press, macros save time because they execute tasks far faster than you can. One reason for this is that macros always execute as fast as possible; they don't have to pause to consider their next action. Furthermore, macros don't make mistakes, as users often do; hence, they don't waste even more time correcting their errors. Also, a macro doesn't need a coffee break; it runs without stopping until it is finished, while you take the coffee break. Finally, the way 1-2-3 handles the screen during macro execution is different and faster than during manual execution. All these factors combine to make macros valuable timesaving tools.

> **Note**
>
> When you run 1-2-3 manually, it must redraw the screen for every graphical dialog box. This process often is rather slow. When 1-2-3 runs a macro, however, it does not display the dialog boxes and therefore saves considerable time. This is an added incentive to create macros.

There are many reasons to consider using macros, including the following:

- Speeding your work
- Increasing accuracy
- Eliminating the boredom of long repetitive processes
- Simplifying complex tasks

Creating Some Sample Macros

The easiest way to understand macros is to create a few. The next two sections show you how to write two simple macros. The first macro enters text in a cell. The second macro executes a command specified in the macro.

Creating a Macro That Enters Text

In this section, you learn how to create a macro that can enter a company name (or any repetitive text) anywhere in a worksheet any number of times. The first step in creating a macro is planning. Before you begin creating a macro, you should determine what you want the macro to do and then identify the keystrokes that the macro will execute for you. In this example, you want the macro to enter some text: the company name. First, the macro must type the text and punctuation that makes up the company name. Then, as with any label, the macro must enter the typed characters in a cell by pressing the Enter key.

You start building a macro by storing the keystrokes as text in a worksheet cell. It is a good idea to store macros in sheets that don't contain other data. For this example, move the cell pointer to cell B6 of worksheet B and type the company name, **ABC Manufacturing Incorporated**, followed by a tilde (~). The tilde (~) is 1-2-3's special macro code, used to represent the Enter key. Cell B6 in figure 26.1 shows the sample macro.

Fig. 26.1
The \n macro with documentation. This macro automatically enters a label.

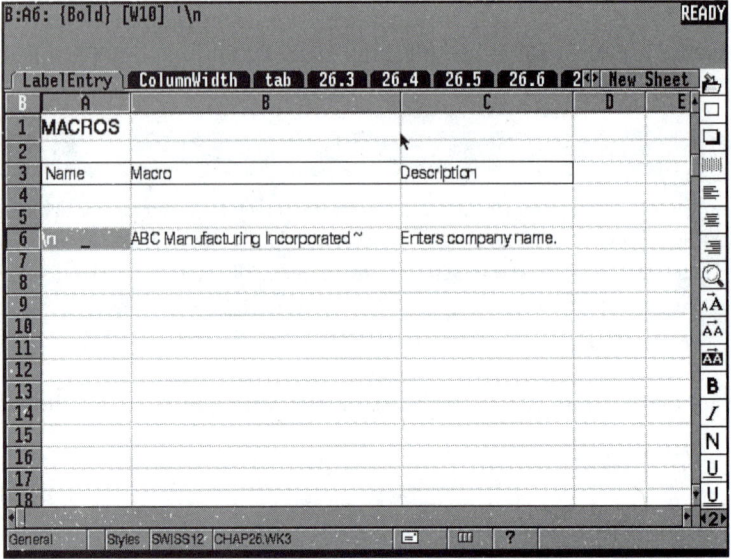

Note

If you forget to add the tilde at the end of the macro and run the macro, 1-2-3 displays the keystrokes in the control panel as if you had typed the keystrokes for a cell entry but hadn't pressed Enter. Forgetting the tilde is one of the most common mistakes that macro writers make.

After entering the text you want the macro to type, you can name this sequence of keystrokes as a macro. To name a macro, follow these steps:

1. Move to the cell containing the first line of the macro and choose the /**R**ange **N**ame **C**reate command.

2. At the Enter name to create prompt, type the name **\n** and press Enter. For macro names, the backslash (\) represents the Alt key (explained after these steps).

3. At the Enter range prompt, specify the cell containing the first line of the macro and press Enter.

4. Document the macro as shown in figure 26.1. Type the macro name (**\n**) in the cell to the left of the first line of the macro. Be sure to type an apostrophe before \n so that 1-2-3 enters this text as a label. Then enter a description of the purpose of the macro in the cell to the right

of the first line of the macro. For this example, enter the description
Enters company name. Documenting the macro in this way helps
you remember the macro's name and purpose.

> **Caution**
>
> A common mistake is to use the forward slash (/) instead of the backslash (\) when naming macros. 1-2-3 recognizes only the backslash as Alt. You can name ranges using the forward slash, but you cannot run them with a shortcut-key combination.

The most widely used structure for documenting macros in 1-2-3 involves placing the macro name in the cell to the left of the macro so that you can use the **/R**ange **N**ame **L**abels **R**ight command to apply the name to the macro. 1-2-3 doesn't require that you type the macro names in the worksheet; the names serve as documentation only.

To *execute* (run) this simple macro, move the cell pointer to the cell where you want to enter the company name and press Alt+N. 1-2-3 enters the title wherever the cursor is when you press Alt+N.

To use the macro in the future, save the file.

Writing a Simple Command Macro
In addition to macros that repeat text, you can write macros that execute commands. This section describes a simple macro that performs commands. To create and name the macro, you use the same steps you used to create and name the \n macro in the preceding section.

First, plan what you want the command macro to do. Suppose that you want to create a macro that changes the column width for the current column to 14. The keystrokes you use to enter this command are as follows:

1. Press / (forward slash) to display the 1-2-3 main menu.

2. Choose **W**orksheet.

3. Choose **C**olumn.

4. Choose **S**et-Width.

5. Enter the number for the desired column width (**14** in this example).

6. Press Enter.

834   Chapter 26—Short Macros To Make Your Life Easier

To create a macro that performs these operations, you can begin by entering the following text in an empty cell of column B of your macro sheet:

'/wcs14~

> **Note**
>
> You must type an apostrophe (') before the slash to indicate a label entry. If you don't type the apostrophe, pressing / accesses the 1-2-3 main menu.

Notice that each character of the macro is a keyboard character that you press to enter a command sequence. You must enter every macro as a label or as a formula that evaluates to a label.

Tip
When you document long macros, enter high-level documentation. Document lines of code that perform major tasks, not every line. If you try to document every line, you soon may find yourself not documenting any lines.

After you finish entering the macro, you should name and document it. You name the macro by typing the macro name (in this case, an Alt+*letter* combination) in the cell immediately to the left of the first line of the macro. Then you assign that name to the first line of the macro. Finally, you can document the macro by typing a description in the column to the right of the macro lines.

The **/R**ange **N**ame **C**reate command was used to name the first macro in this chapter. A second way to name cells is with the **/R**ange **N**ame **L**abels commands. Follow these steps to name and document a macro with the **/R**ange **N**ame **L**abels command:

Tip
When you are giving a macro an Alt+*letter* name, you can use only one letter, so try to pick descriptive letters. The name you choose for a simple macro should remind you of the macro's function.

1. In the cell to the left of the first line of your macro, enter the macro name (in this case, '\c).

2. With the cursor in the cell with the name, choose the **/R**ange **N**ame **L**abels **R**ight command and then press Enter. This command uses the label in current cell to name the cell to the right.

3. To document the macro further, move the cell pointer to the cell immediately to the right of the macro and enter a description of the macro's function (in this case, **Sets column width to 14.**).

Figure 26.2 shows the column-width macro with documentation.

After you name a macro, you should try the macro to make sure that it works. For this example, move the cell pointer to a column whose width you want to change and press Alt+C to run the macro. The macro changes the width of the column to 14.

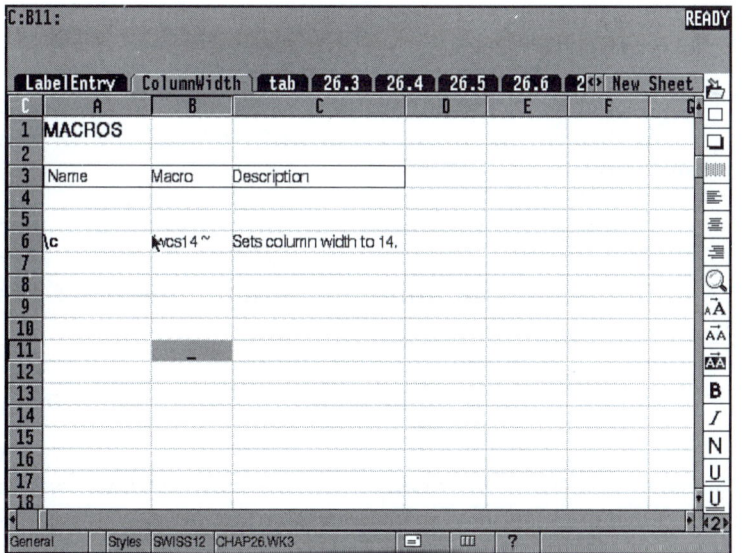

Fig. 26.2

The \c macro with documentation. This macro automatically changes a column's width.

Following Guidelines for Developing Macros

Following are the basic steps for creating any macro:

1. Plan what you want the macro to do.
2. Identify the keystrokes the macro must repeat.
3. Select an area of the worksheet for the macro.
4. Enter the keystrokes, keystroke equivalents, and commands for the macro.
5. Name the macro.
6. Document the macro.
7. Test and debug the macro.
8. Save the file containing the macro.

As your expertise increases and your macros become more complex, you continue to use the same basic steps to create a macro. Keep in mind that good planning is essential to creating smooth-running macros. Good documentation makes your macros easier for you and others to understand and to modify in the future.

836   Chapter 26—Short Macros To Make Your Life Easier

The following list describes the planning and actions required to execute the steps in creating your macros:

- *Planning macro objectives.* Outline the tasks you want the macro to perform, and then arrange the steps in the order in which the macro is to complete them.

- *Identifying keystrokes.* Keep in mind that basic macros are labels (text) that duplicate the keystrokes you want to replay. When you start creating macros, take the time to write down each keystroke and command that a macro must perform before you enter the macro in the worksheet. This deliberate approach saves time because you are less likely to miss a keystroke, which would lead to errors and the need for debugging.

> **Tip**
> If you put all your macros on one page, you can give that page's tab a descriptive name such as Macros.

- *Planning macro placement.* When you choose the area where you want to create a macro, be aware that a macro executes from its first cell down through every cell containing macro commands until it reaches a blank cell or a macro command that stops the execution. The macro ends when it reaches a blank cell, a numeric cell, a cell containing an ERR value, or an advanced macro command that terminates execution. To ensure that your macro stops executing after the last macro command, leave at least one blank cell below the last cell in the macro or, better yet, end the macro with the {QUIT} macro command. The {QUIT} macro command tells 1-2-3 to stop executing the macro, regardless of what follows it. This command is discussed in Chapter 27, "Advanced Macro Command Power Techniques."

For organizational and safety reasons, you should place your macros in a sheet of their own—probably the last sheet in the file. This practice reduces the chance of accidental changes to the macros and makes finding your macros easy.

- *Entering the macro.* When you type a macro in the worksheet, you must enter each cell of the macro as a label or as a formula that evaluates to a label. Certain keystrokes (such as numbers) cause 1-2-3 to change from READY mode to VALUE mode; other keystrokes (/ and <, for example) switch 1-2-3 to MENU mode. If you want to use a number (0 through 9) or any of the following characters as the first character in a macro cell, you first must type a label prefix, usually an apostrophe ('), but also a caret (^) or quotes ("):

    / + - @ # $. < (\ :

The apostrophe (') switches 1-2-3 from READY mode to LABEL mode. By using an apostrophe before numbers or any of the preceding characters, you ensure that 1-2-3 doesn't misinterpret your text entry. If any character not in this list is the first keystroke in the cell, 1-2-3 switches to LABEL mode and adds the apostrophe (') after you press Enter.

◀ "Creating Range Names," p. 88

- *Using cell addresses.* Generally, 1-2-3 doesn't update addresses in a macro when you make changes to the worksheet. As a consequence, any **/C**opy or **/M**ove operation, or any insertion or deletion of rows or columns, can cause a macro to use incorrect addresses. To eliminate this problem, use range names instead of addresses. Range names in a macro (like range names in formulas) use the update addresses when the macro runs.

- *Selecting the macro name.* You use the **/R**ange **N**ame **C**reate or the **/R**ange **N**ame **L**abels command to name the first cell containing the macro. You can name your macros with an Alt+*letter* name (such as \a), a descriptive name (such as PRINT_BUDGET), or the name \0 (backslash zero). A macro named \0 becomes an autoexec macro and runs every time the file containing it is retrieved or opened. Later sections in this chapter show you how to create and run a macro with each of these types of names. Macros that you want to run using the Alt+*letter* method must be named with the \ and one letter only. These are the only macros that can be run directly using the Alt+*letter* method.

- *Planning macro documentation.* Keep in mind that you document a macro to help you and others understand what the macro does and why. You can document macros in several ways. Using a descriptive name is one form of documentation. Another method is to enter documentation in the cells to the right of each line in the macro. The better you describe what the macro is doing, the easier the macro is to read and modify.

- *Testing and debugging.* New macros don't always perform exactly as you expect. You may need to make changes to the text of the macro (*debug* it) before it executes correctly. (This technique is described in "Testing and Debugging Macros" later in this chapter.) Because macros can affect your data, you always should test macros with dummy data before using them with real worksheet data that you need to preserve. It is even more important to always save your file before testing the macro. Macros can destroy not only the data in your file but also overwrite or erase the macro itself. If the macro causes damage, you can restore the original file from disk.

Tip
1-2-3 Release 4 has an Auto-Backup feature that can minimize data loss. (See Chapter 1, "What's New in Release 4 for DOS," for details.)

- *Saving macros.* Spending time creating macros and then losing them to a power loss or accidental deletion is wasteful. Frequently save the file containing your macros.

The following macro is developed with the preceding guidelines in mind. This macro saves the current file to two locations, thus providing you a one-keystroke procedure for making a backup. Most people know that they should make a backup copy on a different disk or drive as a safeguard against data loss, but they just can't seem to find the time to do it. Because saving your work is a common repetitive task, it's the perfect candidate for a macro.

Suppose that you want to save a file named BUDGET1.WK3 to the C:\LOTUS\DATA directory, and at the same time, you want to save a copy of this file to the F:\SHARE directory on your network. Use the following steps to create a macro that automatically saves your file and makes a backup copy on a second drive:

1. Move to an empty area of column B in your macro sheet.

2. Enter the following macro lines (replacing the drive, path, and file names with ones that are appropriate for you):

    '/fs{CE}C:\LOTUS\DATA\BUDGET1.WK3~r{ESC}

    '/fs{CE}F:\SHARE\BUDGET1.WK3~r{ESC}

3. Name the first cell of the macro '\s, using the **/R**ange **N**ame **C**reate command.

4. Type the name in the cell to the left of the macro's first line, and add additional documentation to the right of the macro.

This is an invaluable yet simple macro. The clear-entry command {CE} clears the default entry that 1-2-3 automatically displays in the edit line during commands such as **/F**ile **R**etrieve. The {ESC} command removes the r that would be in the edit line if this was the first time the file had been saved.

Using Macro Key Names

To identify certain keys and combinations of keys, 1-2-3 uses some special characters or words as *key names*—the special characters and words you use in macros to represent keystrokes that aren't alphanumeric characters. Many of the examples in this chapter use these key names, which are summarized in table 26.1. (See Chapter 2, "What Every 1-2-3 User Should Know," for explanations of the direction and function keys.)

> **Note**
>
> Some 1-2-3 keys, such as the tilde (~) and braces ({}), have special meanings in 1-2-3 macros. If you want to use these keys in a macro without invoking special meanings, enclose them in braces ({}). To have a macro enter a tilde as a character, for example (instead of interpreting the tilde as the Enter key), type **{~}** in the macro. To have a macro enter a brace (instead of interpreting the brace as the opening or closing brace of a macro command or subroutine), type **{{}** or **{}}** in the macro.

Table 26.1 Summary of Macro Key Names

Key Type	1-2-3 Key	Macro Key Name
Function Keys	Help (F1)	{HELP}
	Edit (F2)	{EDIT}
	Name (F3)	{NAME}
	Abs (F4)	{ABS}
	GoTo (F5)	{GOTO}
	Window (F6)	{WINDOW}
	Query (F7)	{QUERY}
	Table (F8)	{TABLE}
	Calc (F9)	{CALC}
	Graph (F10)	{GRAPH}
	App1 (Alt+F7)	{APP1}
	App2 (Alt+F8)	{APP2}
	App3 (Alt+F9)	{APP3}
	Addin (Alt+F10)	{ADDIN} or {APP4}
Direction Keys	↑	{UP} or {U}
	↓	{DOWN} or {D}
	←	{LEFT} or {L}
	→	{RIGHT} or {R}
	Shift+Tab or Ctrl+←	{BIGLEFT}
	Tab or Ctrl+→	{BIGRIGHT}
	PgUp	{PGUP}
	PgDn	{PGDN}
	Home	{HOME}

(continues)

Table 26.1 Continued

Key Type	1-2-3 Key	Macro Key Name
	End	{END}
	Enter	~
3D Direction Keys	First Cell (Ctrl+Home)	{FIRSTCELL} or {FC}
	Last Cell (End Ctrl+Home)	{LASTCELL} or {LC}
	Prev Sheet (Ctrl+PgDn)	{PREVSHEET} or {PS}
	Next Sheet (Ctrl+PgUp)	{NEXTSHEET} or {NS}
	File (Ctrl+End)	{FILE}
	Prev File (Ctrl+End Ctrl+PgDn)	{PREVFILE} or {PF} or {FILE}{PS}
	First File (Ctrl+End Home)	{FIRSTFILE} or {FF} or {FILE}{HOME}
	Last File (Ctrl+End End)	{LASTFILE} or {LF} or {FILE}{END}
	Next File (Ctrl+End Ctrl+PgUp)	{NEXTFILE} or {NF} or {FILE}{NS}
Editing Keys	Del	{DELETE} or {DEL}
	Ins	{INSERT} or {INS}
	Escape	{ESCAPE} or {ESC}
	Backspace	{BACKSPACE} or {BS}
Special Keys	Ctrl+Break (in MENU mode)	{BREAK}
	~	{~}
	{ (open brace)	{{}
	} (close brace)	{}}
	/ (slash) or < (less than)	/ or {MENU}

> **Note**
>
> Remember that the F4 {ABS} key has two functions: When you are entering a formula, the F4 key toggles between absolute and relative cell references. When you are in READY mode, F4 toggles to POINT mode, enabling you to anchor the cursor before a command.

You may notice that the table doesn't include the keys Caps Lock, Num Lock, Scroll Lock, Compose (Alt+F1), Record (Alt+F2), Run (Alt+F3), Undo (Alt+F4), PrtSc or Print Screen, and Shift. You cannot use these keystrokes in macros (although, as you learn in later sections, the Run command has a macro substitute).

When you use a key name in a macro, you must keep the entire key name in one cell. For example, you cannot split the key name {EDIT} into two cells: {ED in one cell and IT} in another. Also, be careful not to mix braces with parentheses. Avoid typing **(DOWN)**, for example.

You can repeat certain key names by including a repetition factor. A *repetition factor* tells 1-2-3 to repeat a command the specified number of times. Instead of typing **{LEFT}** three times, for example, you can type any of the following:

> {LEFT 3}
>
> {L 3}
>
> {LEFT @COLS(TABLE)} (when you are using a three-column table)
>
> {LEFT +B1} (where B1 contains the number 3)

When you use repetition factors, be sure to place one space between the key name and the number of repetitions.

One of the most common and repetitive spreadsheet tasks is printing. Following is a short print macro that demonstrates the use of several macro key-name commands. Suppose that you need to print two areas of your worksheet as two separate reports every week. From week to week, the number of lines to be printed changes, but you know that there always will be data in the entire first column and last row of both print ranges. Also, you need to print one report in landscape mode and the other in portrait mode, and each with different margins. Assume that you're printing using Wysiwyg. Follow these steps to create your print macro:

Tip
You cannot include the Compose (Alt+F1) key in a macro, but you can add LMBCS (Lotus Multibyte Character Set) characters to macro text or use the CHAR(n) function within your macros.

842   Chapter 26—Short Macros To Make Your Life Easier

1. Move to any empty area of your macro sheet, and enter the macro shown in figure 26.3.

Fig. 26.3
A macro for printing two ranges with different Wysiwyg settings.

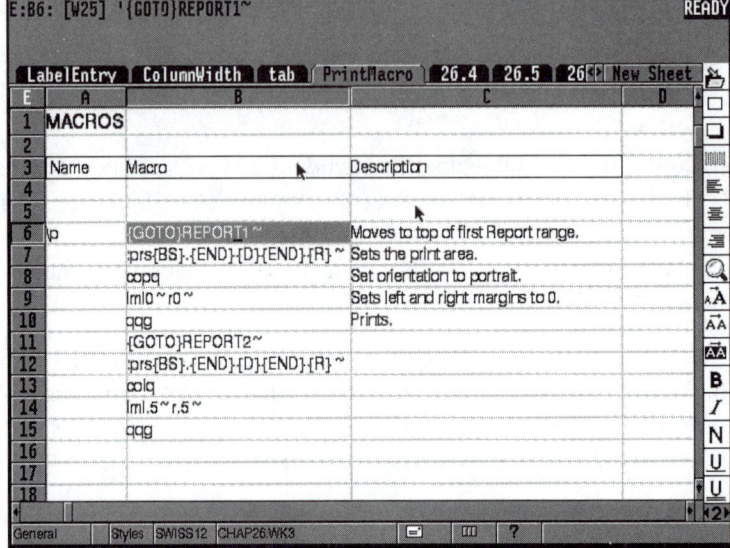

2. Add as much documentation as you feel is necessary.

3. Name the macro (in this case, '\p, because it is a print macro).

4. Name the top-left corners of your two print ranges, using the /**R**ange **N**ame **C**reate command. In this example, the ranges are REPORT1 and REPORT2.

Notice that the second five lines are virtually identical to the first five lines. This suggests that you could copy the first five lines and do a little editing to save time building the macro. Remember that macros are only labels. This macro used five of the key words from table 26.1: {GOTO}, {END}, {R}, {D}, and {BS}.

Planning the Macro Layout

Although you can enter up to 512 characters in one cell, a better practice is to break a long macro into a column of cells. By limiting each cell to a single task or a few simple tasks, you will find it easier to debug, modify, and document your macros.

Figure 26.4 shows two macros that execute the same sequence of keystrokes. These two macros are enhanced versions of the macro shown in figure 26.1. Both macros execute the following operations: enter the company name; move down one row; enter the address; move down one row; and enter the city, state, and ZIP code.

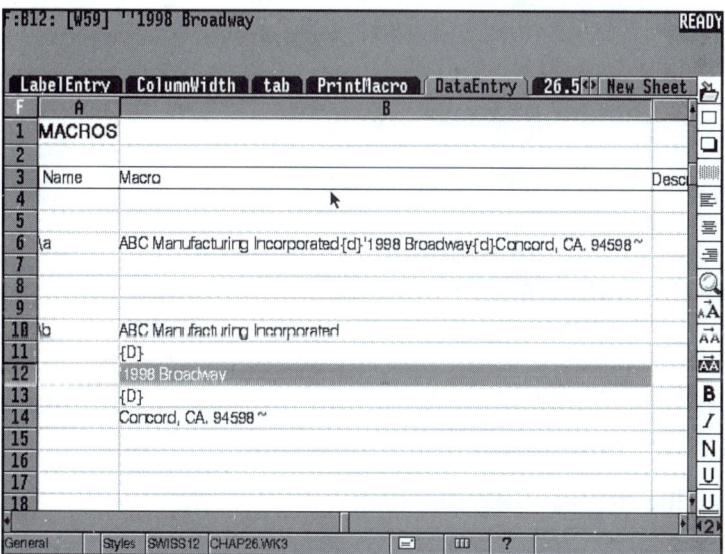

Fig. 26.4

Two macros to enter three lines of text. Breaking a macro into a number of lines can make it easier to read, document, and edit.

The \b macro works correctly whether you name just cell B10 or the range B10..B14. Remember that for simple keystroke macros as well as advanced macro command programs, 1-2-3 executes the keystrokes starting at the cell at the top of the range. After executing the keystrokes in B10, 1-2-3 moves down one cell and executes any keystrokes in that cell. Similarly, after completing those keystrokes, the program continues to move down and read until it encounters an empty cell, a cell containing a numeric value, an error, or an advanced macro command that explicitly stops the macro. (Chapter 27, "Advanced Macro Command Power Techniques," discusses these circumstances.)

> **Note**
>
> The entry in cell DataEntry:B12 of the \b macro contains an extra apostrophe at the beginning of the label (although only one apostrophe appears in that cell on-screen). The extra apostrophe ensures that 1-2-3 enters the text as a label when the macro is executed.

Although both macros perform the same functions, the \b macro is easier to read because it breaks the task into the following simple steps:

1. Type the company name.
2. Position the cell pointer.
3. Type the address.
4. Position the cell pointer.
5. Type the city, state, and ZIP code.

Macros are easier to read and understand if you separate keystrokes and key names into separate cells.

Documenting Macros

As mentioned earlier, you document your macros in the same way that you document other parts of a 1-2-3 worksheet. You can use some or all of the following documentation techniques:

- Use descriptive names as macro names
- Use the range-name note feature
- Include comments in the worksheet
- Use the new Tools Note feature
- Keep any external design notes

The following sections discuss these documentation techniques.

Using Descriptive Names

Some previous releases of 1-2-3 recognized only the backslash and a single letter as a macro name. Although easy to execute, these Alt+*letter* names aren't very descriptive. Using descriptive macro names helps you and other users remember the function of the macro. Use the Run key (Alt+F3) to execute macros with descriptive names. (See "Naming and Running Macros" later in this chapter.)

Attaching Notes to Range Names

Another 1-2-3 feature you can use to document your macros is range-name notes, created with the /**R**ange **N**ame **N**ote **C**reate command. This command attaches a note to a range name. If you have a print macro named \p, for example, you can document the macro with a range-name note that gives the description Prints the 1993 budget. This note gives you an idea of the purpose of the macro; you don't need to review the macro to discover its function. To list the range names, their cell references, and the attached notes, use /**R**ange **N**ame **N**ote **T**able.

◀ "Adding Notes About Ranges," p. 91

Including Comments in the Worksheet

For the simple macros shown thus far, documenting each line of the macro with descriptions isn't really necessary; identifying the tasks performed by these macros is fairly easy. With longer and more complex macros, however, documenting each major task of the macro is immensely helpful. Later, when you want to make changes to the macro, these internal comments provide information on the macro's purpose and its intended actions.

Documenting with the Notepad Feature

In Release 4, you can add notes to any cell with the /**T**ools **N**ote **A**dd command or the Notepad SmartIcon. This feature is discussed in Chapter 7, "Attaching Comments to Worksheet Cells."

Keeping External Design Notes

Be sure to retain important paperwork that you create as part of designing and constructing a macro. As with the other forms of macro documentation, this material eases the burden of trying to understand or modify a macro.

The most important piece of external documentation—one you must never neglect—is a hard-copy printout of the macro. Examples of other particularly valuable external documentation include notes on who requested a macro and why they requested it, who created a macro and who tested it, the underlying assumptions that determined the overall design, diagrams or outlines of macro operations or structure, and a copy of the worksheet.

Figure 26.5 shows a number of techniques used to document a macro. Is the documentation sufficient for you to interpret the macro?

Fig. 26.5
A date-stamp macro that demonstrates the use of several documentation techniques discussed in the preceding section.

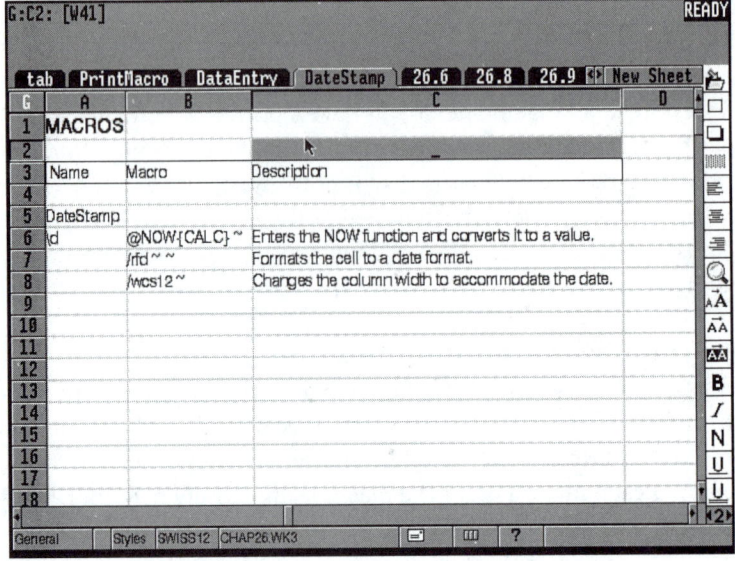

Creating Macros with the Record Feature

Tip
You can access the Macro menu quickly by pressing the Record (Alt+F2) key.

Tip
The Record feature helps you create better macros by eliminating forgotten keystrokes and the misspelling of key words.

1-2-3 Release 4 offers a simple way to create macros: the Record feature. The Record feature keeps a copy of your keystrokes in a macro buffer that you can use to create macros. To use Record to create a macro, choose the **/T**ools **M**acro **C**opy command, specify the keystrokes that will be part of the macro, and place the keystrokes in the location where you want to store the macro.

> **Caution**
>
> The Recorder records your errors as well as your correct keystrokes. This is not a problem; all you need to do is edit the final recording before or after you copy it into the worksheet.

Undo requires memory when it's enabled, so you may not always want it on. You can try the Record feature by creating a macro that enables the Undo feature. To issue this command manually, choose **/W**orksheet **G**lobal **D**efault **O**ther **U**ndo **E**nable **Q**uit. If you want to leave Undo on between sessions, you could add the **U**pdate command between the **E**nable and **Q**uit commands.

Creating Macros with the Record Feature

To record a macro, follow these steps:

1. Choose the **/T**ools **M**acro command, and then choose **E**rase from the Record menu (see fig. 26.6).

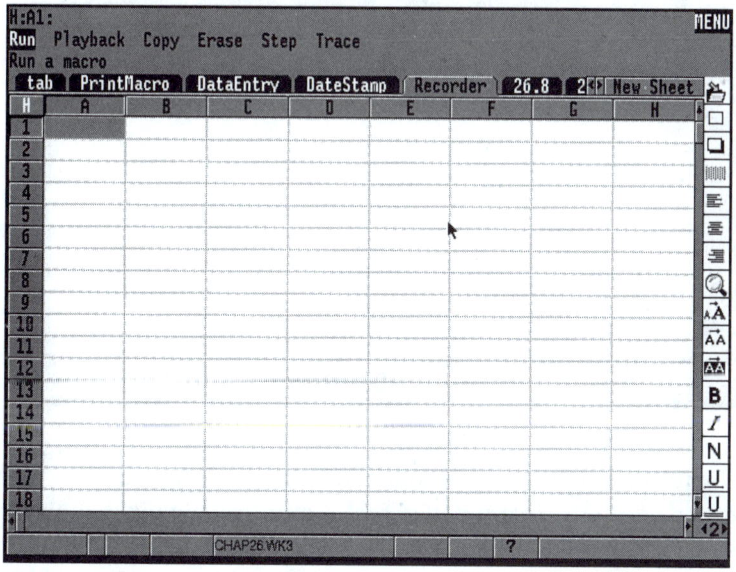

Fig. 26.6
The Record menu options are displayed when you press Alt+F2 or choose the /Tools Macro command.

You don't have to erase the buffer, but doing so helps you find the characters you need faster.

2. Type the keystrokes you want your macro to execute. For this example, type **/wgdoueuq**. The Recorder records your keystrokes in its buffer.

3. After you record the keystrokes of the macro, you must copy the keystrokes from the record buffer to the worksheet and give the macro a name. To copy the keystrokes from the record buffer to the worksheet, choose **/T**ools **M**acro, or press Alt+F2 (Record), and choose the **C**opy option from the Record menu. The keystrokes you typed since the beginning of the 1-2-3 session or since you last selected the **E**rase option appear in the control panel, as shown in figure 26.7.

4. In the control panel, move the cursor to the last character you want to copy to the worksheet. In this example, you don't need to move the cursor.

5. Press Tab to anchor the cursor. If you anchored the cursor in the wrong place, press Esc to unanchor it.

Fig. 26.7

The record buffer displays the keystrokes for the most recently executed commands, with some of the keystrokes highlighted.

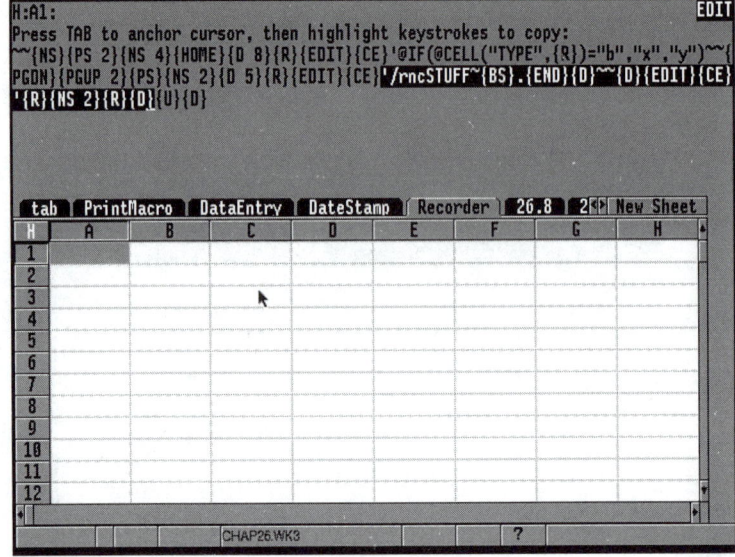

6. Use the direction keys to highlight the remaining keystrokes you want to copy from the record buffer. In this example, highlight all the keystrokes. You could press the Home key to quickly highlight everything when the cursor is anchored at the end of the desired selection. When all the desired keystrokes are highlighted, press Enter. The Select range to copy TO: prompt appears.

7. Move the cell pointer or type a cell address to specify the cell where you want to copy the characters, and then press Enter. 1-2-3 copies the keystrokes from the record buffer to the location you indicated.

8. Copy the macro you just placed in cell B6 down two lines to cell B8, and change the *e* to *d*. Remember that a macro is only a label, so you use 1-2-3's /Copy command to copy a macro that is already in the worksheet.

9. After you copy the keystrokes to the desired locations in the worksheet, finish the procedure by naming and documenting the macro (see fig. 26.8). The first macro is the result of copying keystrokes from the Recorder's buffer. The second is an edited copy of the first macro.

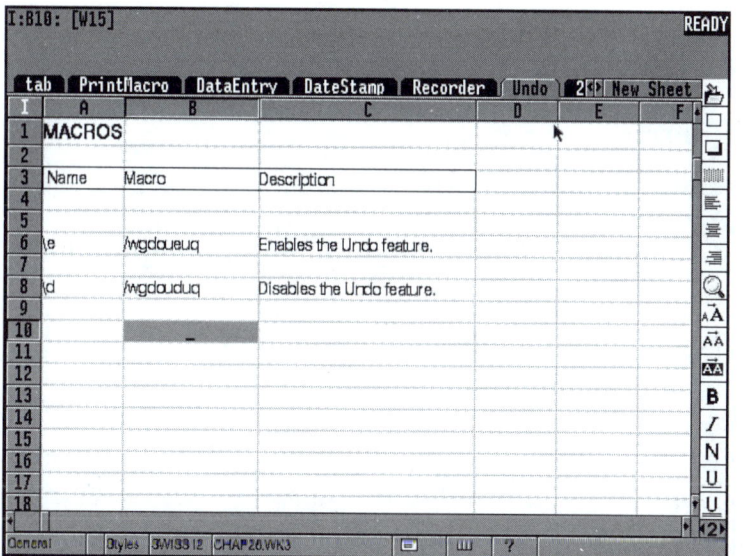

Fig. 26.8
Two macros that enable and disable the Undo feature.

> **Note**
>
> You can edit the keystrokes in the record buffer with the Backspace and Del keys or type new characters.

Do you ever need to put dates, such as months, across 12 consecutive columns? If you want a macro to do it for you, try to record a macro that fills a range of cells with a year's worth of months. The first date should be the current date, and each successive date should be a month later. Then have the macro format the resulting numbers to an appropriate date format and widen the columns sufficiently to display the dates correctly. Finally, name and document your macro.

Figure 26.9 shows a macro you could use to accomplish these tasks. Notice that when you copy from the record buffer, the macro lines may not be well organized. The macro in figure 26.9 was edited to make it more legible.

Tip
Always record as much of your macro as possible, even if you cannot record it in its entirety. The recorder does not misspell, it never uses incorrect syntax, and it never forgets a keystroke.

850   Chapter 26—Short Macros To Make Your Life Easier

Fig. 26.9
A macro recording of the /Data Fill command. This macro inserts a year's worth of monthly dates into a worksheet.

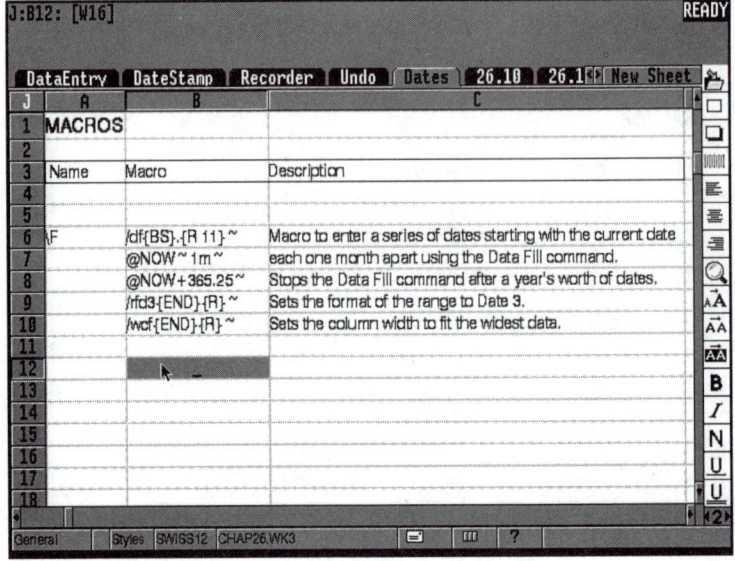

Following Guidelines for Using the Record Feature

You can use the Record feature to create long, complex macros. If you use Recorder to build large macros, however, keep the following information in mind:

- The record buffer is limited to 512 bytes (about 512 characters). When you type the 513th character, 1-2-3 "forgets" the first character—in effect removing the oldest characters from the record buffer to make room for the newest.

- Because some keys on your keyboard don't have character equivalents, 1-2-3 may combine several characters to represent a keystroke. The F5 key, for example, is represented by six characters: {GOTO}.

- The Record feature doesn't record all your keystrokes. Record doesn't record keys that have neither character symbols nor key names: Caps Lock, Num Lock, Scroll Lock, Compose (Alt+F1), Record (Alt+F2), Run (Alt+F3), Undo (Alt+F4), PrtSc or Print Screen, Shift, Ctrl+Break, and Ins.

- 1-2-3 uses shortcuts whenever possible. If you press the right-arrow key 10 times, the record buffer doesn't record the key name {RIGHT} 10 times. Instead, 1-2-3 uses a repetition factor and the most abbreviated form of the key name—in this case, {R 10}, using six keystrokes instead of the 10 you typed.

- If you execute an Alt+*letter* macro while recording, the name of the macro rather than the macro's keystrokes is recorded in the record buffer. If you execute a macro named \a, for example, the record buffer shows the keystrokes as {\a}.

- 1-2-3 uses as many rows as necessary to hold the characters you copy. If you directed 1-2-3 to copy the record buffer's contents to a range of cells too small to hold the copy, 1-2-3 uses additional cells below the range you specified. 1-2-3 overwrites any existing data in these cells with the contents of the record buffer.

- The column width of the range to which you copy the keystrokes affects the number of keystrokes that 1-2-3 copies to each cell. 1-2-3 doesn't split key names between cells; doing so creates a macro error. Although 1-2-3 may split keystrokes in the macro into illogical segments, the macro will work.

- If you use the direction keys to define a range while you are recording, 1-2-3 may replace the direction keys (End, Home, down-arrow, and so on) with the cell addresses of the range. When this situation occurs, you may need to edit the macro after using the Record feature.

> **Caution**
>
> The recorder will record some, but not all, mouse actions. Because of this, it probably is a good idea to use the keyboard when you are recording.

Using Playback To Repeat Keystrokes

One option in the Record menu enables you to *play back* the keystrokes in the record buffer. The steps you use to play back all (or some portion of) the keystrokes are similar to those you use to create the macro. You can play back a sequence of keystrokes as many times as you like. This feature can be useful when you want to repeat a sequence of keystrokes but don't need to create a macro for them.

Before you play back keystrokes, position the cell pointer in the location where you want 1-2-3 to repeat the keystrokes. Then follow these steps:

1. Press Alt+F2 (Record) or choose the **/T**ools **M**acro command, and then choose **P**layback from the Record menu. The record buffer displays the stored keystrokes.

2. Select the keystrokes you want to play back by positioning the cursor at the beginning or end of the sequence of keystrokes, pressing Tab to anchor the cursor, and then using the direction keys to highlight the range of keystrokes you want to play.

3. Press Enter. 1-2-3 plays back the keystrokes that you highlighted in the record buffer.

Naming and Running Macros

The technique you use to run a macro depends on how you name the macro. You run macros by using any of the following methods:

- Use the Alt+*letter* method for macros named with a backslash (\) and a single letter.

- Use the Run menu command (Alt+F3) to run any macro. If the macro has a name, select it and press Enter. Whether or not the macro has a name, you can run it by typing or selecting the address of its first cell and pressing Enter. To select a cell address, choose **R**un from the Record menu, press Esc, move the cursor to the cell containing the macro, and press Enter.

- Use the **/T**ools **M**acro **R**un command to run any macro. Use any of the selection techniques discussed in the preceding paragraph.

- You can click the Run Macro SmartIcon to run macros.

- 1-2-3 automatically runs a \0 macro when loading the worksheet. You also can run a \0 macro by using any of the techniques in this list.

The following sections describe the techniques for naming and running macros.

Tip
Because Alt+*letter* macros start with a backslash (\), you should consider starting all your macro names with \ so that you can differentiate macro names from other range names.

Using Alt+*letter* Macros

One way to name a macro is with the backslash key (\) and a letter. This type of macro is called an Alt+*letter* macro. To run this type of macro, you hold down the Alt key and press the letter. For example, to run the first macro in this chapter, (which was named \n), you could press Alt+N.

Because 1-2-3 doesn't differentiate between uppercase and lowercase letters in a macro name, you can use either. Both \a and \A are valid names for Alt+*letter* macros. But \a and \A are the same name as far as 1-2-3 is concerned, so you have only 26 shortcut names, not 52.

Alt+*letter* macro names are limiting. You can create only 26 macros (\a to \z) in one file. Single-letter names also are of little help when you are trying to identify a macro's purpose. Six months from now, you may have trouble remembering what the \c macro does: Does it *c*opy a cell, change a *c*olumn width, or type a *c*ompany name?

Using Macros with Descriptive Names

You can give a macro a descriptive name, as you would any range in the worksheet. These names can be up to 15 characters long and must obey 1-2-3's rules for range names. To run a macro with a long name, press Alt+F3 (Run), choose the /**T**ools **M**acro **R**un command, or click the Run Macro SmartIcon. 1-2-3 displays a list of all range names (including the Alt+*letter* macro names). Type or highlight the name of the macro you want to run, and then press Enter.

You have more flexibility when you use long names; you can create any number of macros and name them based on what they do. Instead of naming a macro \p because it prints a worksheet, for example, you can name the macro PRINT_BUDGET.

Tip
To see a full-screen list of range names, press F3 (Name) when the list of range names is displayed.

> **Caution**
> If you create a macro name with more than one word, such as PRINT_BUDGET, use an underscore (_) rather than a minus sign (–) to separate the words. 1-2-3 interprets a minus sign as subtraction and therefore interprets PRINT–BUDGET as the range PRINT minus the range BUDGET.

Avoid using macro names (such as CALC or RIGHT) that duplicate 1-2-3 keystroke equivalents or the advanced macro commands listed in Chapter 27. Using this type of macro name leads to unpredictable and often incorrect results. Also avoid using cell addresses (such as A1 or Q3) as macro names.

Tip
If you start all your macro names with a backslash (\), 1-2-3 groups the macros when it displays the list of ranges. For the print budget macro, for example, you can use the name \PRINT_BUDGET.

Using Macros That Execute Automatically

The third way to name a macro is to give it the name \0 (backslash zero). A macro with this name executes automatically when you load the worksheet. You use this type of macro to display data or execute commands as soon as the worksheet is opened. If you have a worksheet with payroll information and you want to limit the number of people who can view this information, for example, you can create an automatic macro that asks for a password before allowing the user to see the file's contents.

854   Chapter 26—Short Macros To Make Your Life Easier

Tip
For more control of an application, use the \0 macro in combination with an AUTO123 file. When you load 1-2-3, the program retrieves the AUTO123 file automatically and then executes the \0 macro immediately.

The \0 macros work automatically as long as the **/W**orksheet **G**lobal **D**efault Autoexec setting is **Y**es (the default setting). Any user can change the setting to **N**o, however, in which case \0 macros don't execute automatically when the file is retrieved.

Figure 26.10 shows an automatic macro that moves the cursor to a range called MESSAGE and then sets the working directory to D:\S\L4\DATA. In the next chapter, you see how you can add a password-protection system to your file with a \0 macro.

If you want the macro to be more flexible, you can have the macro ask the user to tell 1-2-3 where the user's files are located by replacing the macro line /fdD:\S\L4\DATA~ with /fd.

The three macros shown in figure 26.11 demonstrate many of the rules and conventions for naming and running macros. Here, the macros are used only to demonstrate the three ways to name and run a macro.

Fig. 26.10
An autoexec macro that moves to a given opening screen and then sets the working directory.

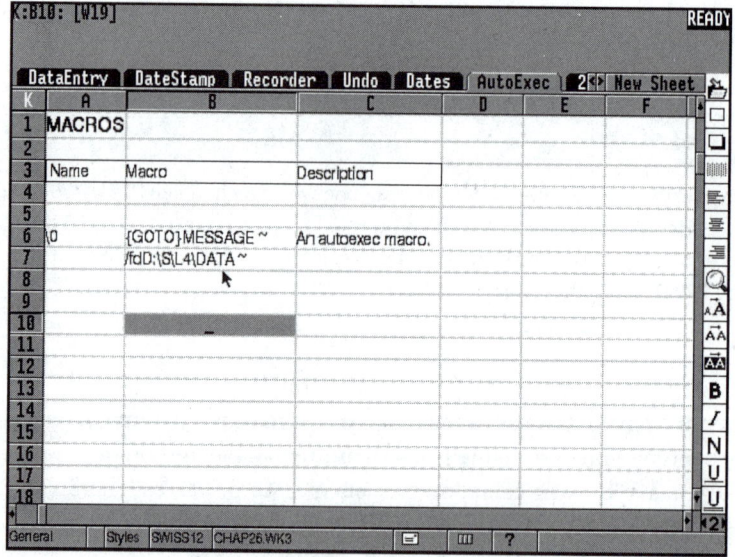

Tip
This autoexec macro is helpful if different people use the same computer. Save this file with the name AUTO123.WK3. At startup, 1-2-3 immediately asks for the drive where the user's files are located.

Before you run a macro, make sure that you position the cell pointer correctly or that the macro positions the cell pointer correctly for you. That is, make sure that the cell pointer is in the cell where you want the macro to insert text or start performing commands.

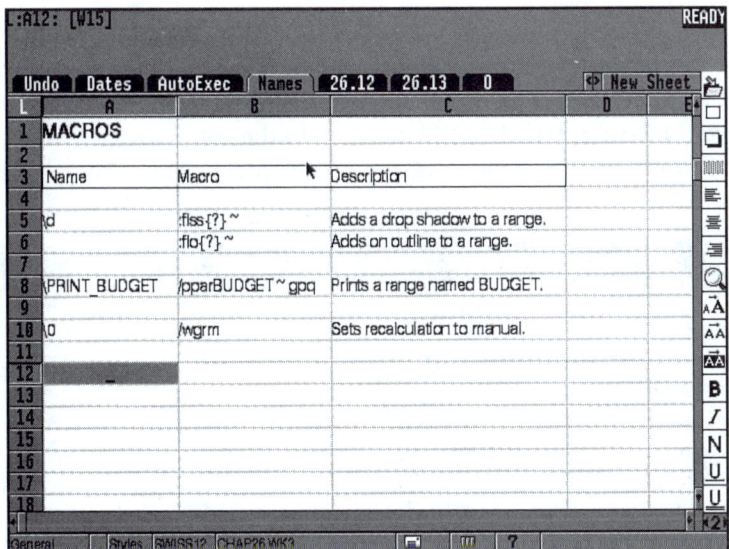

Fig. 26.11
Three macros that demonstrate common macro-naming conventions. The names are listed in column A.

Testing and Debugging Macros

No matter how carefully you construct macros, the first time you run a macro, you may encounter errors. Programmers call these errors *bugs* and the process of eliminating the errors *debugging*. The story goes that this term was introduced when the inventor of COBOL, Grace Hopper, discovered that a moth had shorted a circuit and crashed a computer. She removed the moth and announced that she had "debugged" the computer.

When you are testing and debugging long macros, you may find it useful to start the macro at some cell other than the first cell. To do this, choose the /**T**ools **M**acro **R**un command, type the address of the cell in the macro where you want 1-2-3 to begin, and press Enter.

> **Note**
> It is easiest to debug small macros or short portions of larger macros. You can break long macros into smaller pieces by inserting blank lines.

Using STEP and TRACE Modes

1-2-3's Step and Trace features are useful tools that make debugging fairly simple. When 1-2-3 is in STEP mode, a macro executes one *step* (keystroke) at a time. STEP mode gives you a chance to see, one step at a time, what the

Tip
While you test macros, split the screen with /Worksheet Window to see the macros and the data portion of the file.

◄ "Splitting the Screen," p. 234

856 Chapter 26—Short Macros To Make Your Life Easier

macro is doing. In TRACE mode, 1-2-3 displays each line of the macro in the bottom-left corner of the screen.

To turn on STEP mode, choose /**T**ools **M**acro **S**tep or click the STEP Mode SmartIcon. 1-2-3 displays the STEP indicator in the bottom-right corner of the screen. To turn on TRACE mode, choose /**T**ools **M**acro **T**race. Then test-run the macro.

Tip

Although you can use STEP mode without turning on the TRACE feature, debugging is much easier when you use STEP and TRACE together, because you see each step at the bottom of the screen.

> **Note**
>
> When you run a macro in STEP mode, the first keystroke doesn't execute until you press another key after pressing Enter. Notice also that you can press almost any key while you are stepping through a macro; 1-2-3 executes the next step every time you press a key. The only time the key you press becomes important is when the macro is expecting user input, such as a directory, path, or file name.

As soon as 1-2-3 executes the first keystroke of the macro, several things happen. 1-2-3 displays the macro cell address and the contents of that cell at the bottom of the screen. At the top of the screen, you see the actions you would see if you were executing the keystrokes by hand. If the keystroke works as you expected, press a key to tell 1-2-3 to execute the next keystroke in the macro.

By using the STEP and/or TRACE modes, you can pinpoint the error in your macro as it occurs. After you identify the error, exit the macro by pressing Ctrl+Break. (STEP and/or TRACE modes still are active, so the next time you try to run the macro, you will be in the STEP and/or TRACE modes. If you want to turn off either STEP or TRACE, choose the /**T**ools **M**acro **S**tep or the /**T**ools **M**acro **T**race command again.) Next, edit the macro cell to correct the error. Then rerun the macro to make sure that the error you found is the only one.

Figure 26.12 shows a macro that doesn't run properly. The macro was supposed to print only the rows of a print range that contained data (see fig. 26.13). A dummy column has been added to the left side of the print range, and the formula `@IF(@CELL("type",E13)="b","x","y")` was entered in cell D13 and copied to cells D14..D20. This approach is designed for 1-2-3's standard /**P**rint **P**rinter command. Remember that 1-2-3 won't print a row of a print range if the first cell of that row contains the pipe character (|).

Testing and Debugging Macros

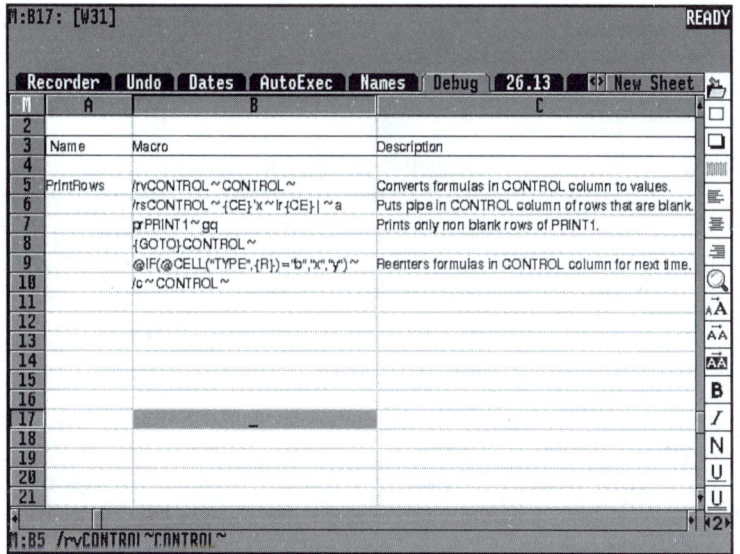

Fig. 26.12
A macro with a bug, running with TRACE and STEP on. Can you find the bug?

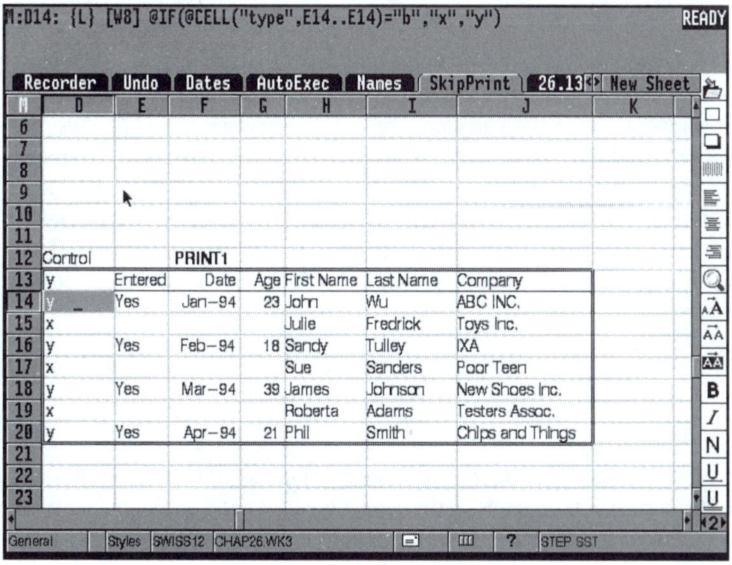

Fig. 26.13
The Print range for the Debug macro.

You might be able to study the macro and see the error. Even though the error is a very common mistake, it's easy to miss. When you run the macro in TRACE and STEP modes, you see that the macro fails at the **/P**rint **P**rinter command because the slash (/) is missing. This error would not have occurred if the macro had been recorded!

Troubleshooting

1-2-3 displays an error message indicating that my macro failed in cell D5, but there is no error in cell D5.

If 1-2-3 cannot execute a macro as written, the program displays an error message and the address of the cell in which the error is located. In most cases, this message points you to the error. Occasionally, however, the real error may precede the error identified in the error message—that is, 1-2-3 may have stopped executing keystrokes properly long before the error named in the message occurred.

My 1-2-3 macro stopped in the middle of a command, but there is nothing wrong with the command.

In the cell identified by the error message, check for common macro errors. If 1-2-3 stops during a command, you probably forgot to complete the command by including a tilde (~) to represent the Enter key. Or you may have forgotten to press **Q** to **Q**uit a menu level. Sometimes the macro must press **Q** more than once to **Q**uit several menu levels.

My macro completed what it was supposed to do, but it beeped or typed additional data after it should have stopped.

Even if 1-2-3 works all the way through a macro, the program may end with an error message or a beep. Remember that 1-2-3 continues to execute macro commands until the program encounters an empty cell, a cell with a numeric, ERR value, or a macro command that stops the macro. If 1-2-3 encounters data in the cell immediately below the last line of the macro, the program may consider that cell to be part of the macro. Don't put data in the cells directly below the last line of a macro; in other words, end your macros with a blank cell or the {QUIT} command. If you discover that the cell isn't empty, you may have identified one of the macro's problems.

When I run my macro, I get a message about an unrecognized macro key name or range name followed by a cell address, but the name looks correct.

Check to ensure that you correctly spelled the key names or range names in the macro. In addition, verify that you are using curly braces ({ }) rather than parentheses (( )) or brackets ([ ]); that you have the correct number and type of arguments for the key name; and that you don't have extra spaces in your macro, especially inside braces. Also make sure that there is a single space after a key name and its first argument — for example, {DOWN 15}, not {DOWN15}.

When I press Alt+N, 1-2-3 beeps and my macro doesn't run.

A common mistake is to incorrectly name the range containing the macro. When you run a macro, if you get a beep and nothing happens, the macro may be unnamed.

> To determine whether the range is named, press F5 (GoTo), type the macro name, and press Enter. If the range is named, the cell pointer goes to the cell containing the macro.
>
> *When I run my Alt+N macro, 1-2-3 enters NNNNNNN at the location of my cell pointer and doesn't execute the macro.*
>
> You may have named the wrong cell. This repeating label occurs because instead of naming the range where the macro is located, you named a range that included the macro name ('**\N**). When you ran the Alt+N macro, 1-2-3 used the keystrokes \N to create a repeating label. If the macro range is named incorrectly, use /**R**ange **N**ame **C**reate or /**R**ange **N**ame **L**abels command to rename the macro.

Protecting Macros

When you create worksheet applications that other people will use, you need to protect the applications' macros from accidental erasure or alteration. Unlike most programs, such as database management systems, 1-2-3 can store data and programs in the same file. Even if you put all your macros on a separate macro page, the macros remain accessible; so anyone who knows 1-2-3 can change them or get to the macro sheet and inadvertently modify something.

Most users store macros customized for a particular application in the file containing the application. To store macros in this way, place the macros together, but in a sheet containing other than those occupied by the data or models. Storing the macros together makes them easy to find and edit, and helps keep you from accidentally overwriting or erasing them.

◀ "Formatting a Multiple-Worksheet File," p. 471

A good strategy is to place the macros in a separate worksheet of the file containing the model. Place the data in worksheet A, for example, and the macros in worksheet B. If you use this storage approach, you can avoid some common problems. Suppose that you want to use 1-2-3 commands to insert or delete columns or rows. If the macros are in the same sheet as the data, you may delete rows or columns from your macros as well as the data.

> **Caution**
>
> Remember that if GROUP mode is on, commands that insert or delete rows or columns affect all worksheets, including any that contain macros. To disable GROUP mode, choose /**W**orksheet **G**lobal **G**roup **D**isable.

◄ "Hiding Worksheet Data," p. 516

> **Caution**
> If you store and run your macros in a different worksheet from the data, be sure that the macros position the cell pointer in the correct worksheet.

Tip
Inserting or deleting columns or rows can cause problems with cell addresses used in macros. To minimize this problem, use range names instead of cell addresses in macros.

Placing macros in a separate worksheet enables you to hide the macros. To hide an entire worksheet, use the **/W**orksheet **H**ide **E**nable command and specify the worksheet you want to hide.

You also can protect your macro files by saving them with passwords and by protecting the cells in which the macros are located. An additional type of protection you should consider is protection against changes to the worksheet on which the macro acts. This may mean adding cell protection or using range names.

Assigning a Macro to a User SmartIcon

◄ "Protecting Worksheet Data," p. 512

◄ "Protecting Files with Passwords," p. 519

◄ "Customizing SmartIcons," p. 261

One useful method you can use to make a macro available to any 1-2-3 Release 4 worksheet is to assign the macro to a user SmartIcon when using Wysiwyg. Twelve user SmartIcons are available, numbered U1 through U12. You can assign a single macro to each SmartIcon by using the Attach Macro to Icon SmartIcon. When you select the Attach Macro to Icon SmartIcon, the Assign Macro to U*n* dialog box appears. The *n* in the dialog box title indicates the number of the user SmartIcon you are editing or viewing.

To select the user SmartIcon to which you want to assign a macro, choose **P**revious Icon or **N**ext Icon until the desired number appears in the title of the dialog box. Next, choose Icon **D**escription, and type a description to appear when you choose the SmartIcon. This description may be up to 72 characters long. Then choose Macro **T**ext, and type the macro text (up to 512 characters) in the text box.

To copy the macro text from the worksheet, choose **G**et Macro from Sheet, specify the cell or range containing the macro, and then press Enter. To assign the macro to the user SmartIcon you selected, choose OK in the Assign

Macro to U*n* dialog box. 1-2-3 returns to READY mode. To clear the information in the text boxes of the Assign Macro to U*n* dialog box, choose **R**eset Macro. To cancel all changes you made in the Assign Macro to U*n* dialog box and return to READY mode, choose Cancel.

Figure 26.14 shows a macro to perform rank ordering on a column of data. Figure 26.15 shows part of the rank-order macro in the Assign Macro to U1 dialog box. The macro creates a column to the right of the data with the ranking of each data item. This macro requires that the user place the cursor in the first cell of the data to be rank-ordered.

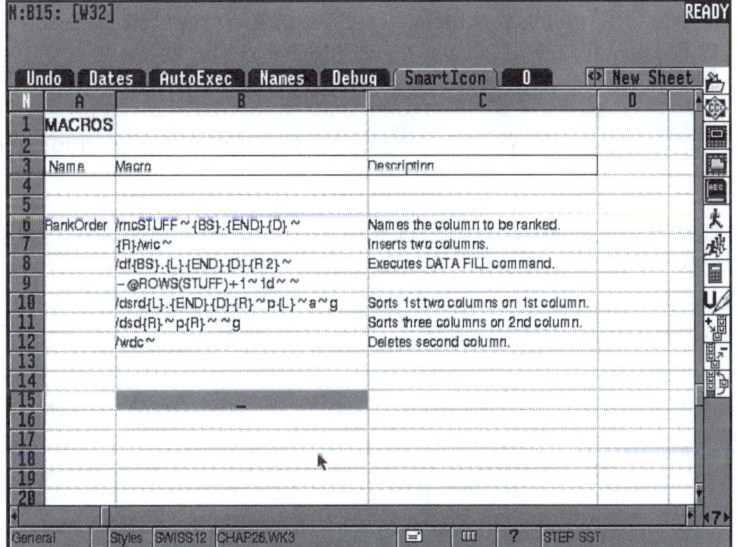

Fig. 26.14
A rank-ordering macro that is assigned to a user icon. The entire macro is visible in the worksheet.

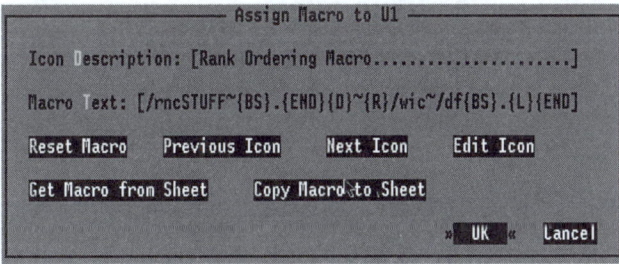

Fig. 26.15
The Assign Macro to U1 dialog box with the rank-ordering macro. Only part of the macro is directly visible in the dialog box.

From Here...

Because macros can automate virtually all aspects of worksheet work, every chapter in this book contains information that is relevant to your macro-programming efforts. Chapters that cover functions and additional macro commands and techniques should be of particular interest. These topics are covered in the following chapters:

- Chapter 3, "Finding Solutions with Formulas and Functions," discusses many of 1-2-3's built-in functions, all of which you can use in macros.

- Chapter 15, "Using Functions To Analyze Data," covers 1-2-3's database and lookup functions, which you also can incorporate into macros.

- Chapter 27, "Advanced Macro Command Power Techniques," introduces 1-2-3's *advanced macro commands* (a set of advanced programming commands) and helps you learn the functions and applications of those commands.

- Chapter 28, "Controlling 1-2-3 with Macros," develops an integrated application from scratch, illustrating how you can employ macros to automate information collection, analysis, and presentation in an effective manner.

Chapter 27

Advanced Macro Command Power Techniques

In addition to the keystroke macro capabilities discussed in Chapter 26, "Short Macros To Make Your Life Easier," 1-2-3 contains a set of advanced macro commands that offer many of the aspects of a full-featured programming language. You can use the advanced macro commands to customize and automate 1-2-3 for worksheet applications.

Chapter 26 shows you how to save time and streamline operations by using macros to automate keystrokes. However, after you learn the concepts and the advanced macro commands discussed in this chapter, you can develop programs that perform the following tasks:

- Create menu-driven worksheet models
- Accept and control input from a user
- Manipulate data in the worksheet
- Execute tasks a predetermined number of times
- Set up and print multiple reports

As you become more experienced with the advanced macro commands, you can take advantage of 1-2-3's full power to do the following:

- Disengage or redefine the function keys
- Develop a business accounting system
- Operate a 1-2-3 worksheet as a disk-based database

This chapter introduces you to the capabilities of programming with the advanced macro commands. If you use 1-2-3 and want to learn some of the advanced techniques of macro programming, you should enjoy this chapter. The techniques presented can help you become a 1-2-3 macro expert.

Why Use the Advanced Macro Commands?

Programs created with the advanced macro commands give you added control and flexibility in the use of 1-2-3 worksheets. You can develop a program, for example, that instructs and guides users as they enter data in a worksheet. With this program, you can ensure that different users enter data in the same way. Such a program is especially beneficial for novice users who aren't familiar with 1-2-3's commands and operations; novices can use program applications to update a worksheet, to check figures, or even to create graphs with ease.

If you want to take 1-2-3 to its practical limits, the set of advanced macro commands is the proper vehicle, and your creativity is the necessary fuel.

What Are the Advanced Macro Commands?

The 1-2-3 advanced macro commands are a set of invisible commands. These commands are called *invisible* because, unlike the function keys and 1-2-3 menu commands, the advanced macro commands cannot be invoked from the keyboard. You invoke advanced macro commands from within macro programs.

The \h macro in figure 27.1 is an example of a program written with the advanced macro commands. The program displays a help menu and shows a series of help screens.

The macro in figure 27.1 begins sending the current cell address to the range named HERE; in other words, the macro records the cell pointer's location so that it can return to it at the end of the program. The second line displays a custom help screen. The third line uses the MENUBRANCH command to display a menu with three options: select the next help screen, select the preceding help screen, and return to the original cell pointer position in the worksheet. The BRANCH command in the last lines of the **N**ext and **P**revious menu options (cells B18 and C18) causes the program to redisplay the menu so that the user can continue to move through the custom help screens.

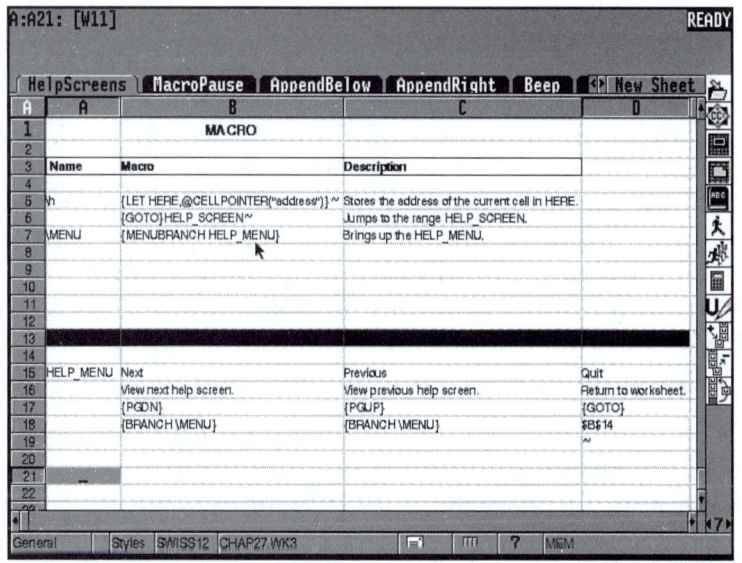

Fig. 27.1
A macro using advanced macro commands.

Notice that the program branches to range names rather than to cell addresses. A cell address would work; however, as discussed in Chapter 26, "Short Macros To Make Your Life Easier," you should follow the convention of using range names rather than cell addresses. Not only does this practice make the program easier to read, but as you rearrange your worksheet, 1-2-3 updates the range name addresses so that the macro continues to operate on the correct cells and ranges.

◀ "Following Guidelines for Developing Macros," p. 835

Understanding Advanced Macro Command Syntax

The examples in this chapter show you how to incorporate the advanced macro commands into macros to produce complete, efficient programs. Like the key names used in keystroke macros (discussed in Chapter 26), all advanced macro commands are enclosed in braces. Just as you must represent the right-arrow key in a macro as {RIGHT} or {R}, you also must enclose a command such as QUIT in braces: {QUIT}.

Like the {QUIT} command, some advanced macro commands are just a single command enclosed in braces. Many other commands, however, require additional arguments within the braces. An *argument* can consist of numbers, strings, cell addresses, range names, formulas, or functions. In Chapter 26, you saw that certain keystroke commands could have arguments, for example, {R 14} or {DOWN @ROWS(DATA)}.

Commands that take arguments have a syntax similar to that used with 1-2-3 functions. The general syntax of these commands is as follows:

{COMMAND *argument1,argument2,...,argumentN*}

A space separates the command name from the first argument. Commas (with no spaces) separate each argument (depending on your International punctuation setting). As you study the syntax for the specific commands described in this chapter, keep in mind the importance of following the rules for spacing and punctuation. The following example uses the BRANCH command to transfer program control to a specific location in the program:

{BRANCH \PRINT_ROUTINE}

The cell address or range name indicating where the program should branch must follow the command BRANCH. In this command, \PRINT_ROUTINE is the name of a range to which the BRANCH command will branch.

> **Note**
>
> If you aren't sure of the syntax or purpose of an advanced macro command, press the Help (F1) key. Choose Macro Command Index from the list of topics, and then choose from the four alphabetical groups. At this point, you see an alphabetic list of the valid commands and key names, such as {QUIT} and {CALC}. Use the direction keys or mouse to scroll through the list until you find the command you want to use. Highlight the command and press Enter. Help displays a description of the selected command, its syntax, and examples for its use. If you know the command but not the syntax, you can type the opening brace and the command, and press F1 (Help) or click the ? on the status line to go directly to the help screen for that command.

Developing Programs with the Advanced Macro Commands

Programming with the advanced macro commands begins, as with all programming, by defining the actions you want the program to perform and determining the sequence of those actions. Then you create the program, test it, debug it, and cross-check its results.

If you have created keystroke macros, you have a head start toward creating advanced macro command programs. These programs share many of the conventions used in simple keystroke macros. If you haven't experimented with 1-2-3 macros, review Chapter 26's simple keystroke macros before you try developing advanced macro command programs. Also, review Chapter 26's discussions of creating, using, and debugging macros; all of those concepts relate to advanced macro command programs.

As you do with keystroke macros, carefully plan and position the advanced macro command programs in the worksheet. The best practice is to store your macros in a separate worksheet or file. You can combine the macros you use with many worksheets into a single file. When the time comes to use the macros, select **/F**ile **O**pen to add the macro file to memory.

◀ "Following Guidelines for Developing Macros," p. 835

◀ "Testing and Debugging Macros," p. 855

Creating the Program

Creating programs with advanced macro commands follows all the same procedures discussed in Chapter 26. If you are new to macro programming, you should read that chapter before continuing with this chapter. Because advanced macro command programs usually are more complex than keystroke macros, documenting them is even more essential. A well-documented program such as the one shown in figure 27.1 is easier to understand, debug, and change than an undocumented program.

Naming and Running the Program

As described in Chapter 26, you have a choice of three types of names for a macro or an advanced macro command program. These name types are as follows:

- Alt+*letter*, such as \h (see fig. 27.1)
- Descriptive range name, such as \PRINT_BUDGET
- \0 (backslash zero), which runs when you retrieve the file containing the macro

Use the **/R**ange **N**ame **C**reate or **/R**ange **N**ame **L**abels command to give the program one of these three types of names. You also should enter the name of the macro in the cell to the left of the program's first line. 1-2-3 doesn't use this name; the name is only for documentation purposes.

> **Note**
>
> You can give a 1-2-3 range more than one name. You can give a frequently used macro a descriptive name as well as an Alt+*letter* name. By doing so, you take advantage of both the long, descriptive name, which is good for documentation, and the Alt+*letter* name, which is easy to use. Similarly, you may want to add a second Alt+*letter* name to a \0 macro so that you can run it using an Alt key combination even after the file has opened.

868 Chapter 27—Advanced Macro Command Power Techniques

> **Note**
>
> If you like your range names to be in all capitals, you do not need to enter the names in uppercase. If you use the **/R**ange **N**ame **L**abel commands, 1-2-3 converts the label names to uppercase. For example, if you have the name "hold" in cell A1 and you use **/R**ange **N**ame **L**abel **R**ight to name B1, when you move the cell pointer, the label in cell A1 changes to HOLD.

To run the macro program, use one of the following methods:

- Press Alt and *letter*, for macros with *letter* names

- Press the Run (Alt+F3) key

- Retrieve the file, and let 1-2-3 automatically run the \0 (backslash zero) macro

- Click the Run Macro SmartIcon for any macro

- Choose the **/T**ools **M**acro **R**un command

Debugging the Program

After you develop and run a program, you may need to debug it. Like keystroke macros, macro programs are subject to such problems as missing tildes (~) and misspelled key names and range names.

◄ "Specifying a Range with Range Names," p. 87

◄ "Testing and Debugging Macros," p. 855

To debug advanced macro command programs, use the STEP and TRACE modes in the same way that you use them for simple keystroke macros. Before you execute the program, choose the **/T**ools **M**acro command or press Record (Alt+F2) and select **S**tep, or click the STEP Mode SmartIcon to invoke STEP mode. Also, choose the **/T**ools **M**acro command or press Record (Alt+F2) and select **T**race to invoke TRACE mode. Then execute your advanced macro command program. Press the space bar to single-step through each instruction in the program. When you discover an error, press Ctrl+Break to stop the macro. Press Esc to clear the error message; then press F2 (Edit) to edit the program. Continue through the macro's execution again until all the errors are fixed and the program runs correctly.

Listing the Advanced Macro Commands

This section lists the advanced macro commands in alphabetical order. The list includes a description of each command, its syntax (showing the required arguments), and examples. The advanced macro commands can be grouped into six categories, according to use or function in a program. These categories are

- Input control
- Program control
- Decision making
- Data manipulation
- Program enhancement
- File manipulation

Table 27.1 shows the commands grouped by category, along with a brief description of the purpose of each command. Use this table to determine which command to use for a particular task. Then you can turn to the alphabetical listing for the command syntax, a complete description, and examples.

Table 27.1   Advanced Macro Commands by Category

Command	Description
Category: Input Control	
Uses: Creates prompts, performs edit checks on data input, modifies 1-2-3 interface	
{?}	Pauses macro execution for data entry from the user
{CE} or {CLEARENTRY}	Clears the default entry at a prompt such as a path or current range or setting
{FORM}	Interrupts macro execution for data entry into a form
{FORMBREAK}	Ends the FORM command, cancels the current form mode, and returns to the macro
{GET}	Records the user's next keystroke
{GETLABEL}	Accepts user input as a label

(continues)

Table 27.1 Continued

Command	Description
{GETNUMBER}	Accepts a number from the user
{LOOK}	Places the first character from a type-ahead buffer into a cell

Category: Program Control

Uses: Controls program execution, runs subroutines, specifies operating system commands

Command	Description
{BRANCH}	Continues execution at a new location in the program
{BREAKOFF}	Disables the Ctrl+Break key combination
{BREAKON}	Enables the Ctrl+Break key combination
{DEFINE}	Specifies cells to store contents of subroutine arguments
{DISPATCH}	Branches indirectly to a new location in the program
{MENUBRANCH}	Branches to and displays a menu in the control panel
{MENUCALL}	Similar to {MENUBRANCH}, except it returns to the statement after {MENUCALL}
{ONERROR}	Traps errors
{QUIT}	Ends program execution
{RESTART}	Cancels a subroutine
{RETURN}	Returns from a program subroutine or MENUCALL command
{*subroutine*}	Calls a subroutine
{ }	Moves execution through a macro cell without taking any action
{SYSTEM}	Executes an operating system command
{WAIT}	Waits a specified length of time

Category: Decision Making

Uses: Allows conditional tests and loop control

Command	Description
{FOR}	Executes a loop a specified number of times
{FORBREAK}	Ends a {FOR} loop

Command	Description
{IF}	Tests a condition and executes a different code a depending on the results of the test

Category: Data Manipulation
Uses: Enters or erases data in a worksheet

{APPENDBELOW}	Enters data below a range and expands the range to include the new data
{APPENDRIGHT}	Enters data to the right of the range and expands the range to include the new data
{BLANK}	Erases a cell or range
{CONTENTS}	Copies values to cells as labels
{LET}	Enters a number or label into a cell
{PUT}	Enters a number or label into a specified row/column offset within a range

Category: Program Enhancement
Uses: Controls screen display, program operation, and recalculation

{BEEP}	Sounds one of the computer's four tones
{FRAMEOFF}	Suppresses the display of the worksheet frame
{FRAMEON}	Displays the worksheet frame
{GRAPHOFF}	Removes a graph displayed by {GRAPHON}
{GRAPHON}	Displays the current graph and/or sets the named graph
{INDICATE}	Changes the control panel mode indicator
{PANELOFF}	Suppresses the display of control panel activity
{PANELON}	Reactivates the display of control panel actions
{RECALC}	Recalculates a portion of the worksheet, row by row
{RECALCCOL}	Recalculates a portion of the worksheet, column by column
{WINDOWSOFF}	Suppresses display of worksheet changes

(continues)

Table 27.1 Continued

Command	Description
{WINDOWSON}	Enables the display of worksheet changes

Category: File Manipulation
Uses: Opens, reads, writes, and closes text files

Command	Description
{CLOSE}	Closes a file opened with {OPEN}
{FILESIZE}	Records the size, in bytes, of an open file
{GETPOS}	Records a file pointer position
{OPEN}	Opens a file for reading, writing, or both
{READ}	Copies characters from an open file to a worksheet
{READLN}	Copies the next line from a file to a worksheet
{SETPOS}	Sets a new position for a file pointer
{WRITE}	Copies a string to an open file
{WRITELN}	Copies a string plus carriage-return-line-feed sequence to an open file

Tip
Use the INDICATE command to prompt when using {?}, as in the following example: {INDICATE Type Name}{?}~{INDICATE} The final INDICATE command returns control of the mode indicator to 1-2-3. Unless you do this, the last mode indicator set with the INDICATE command remains.

The ? Command

The ? command pauses the program so that the user can enter any type of information. During the pause, the control panel doesn't display a prompt; the user can move the cell pointer to direct the location of the input. The program continues executing after the user presses Enter. The format for the ? command is

    {?}

The following one-line program, for example, combines macro commands and this advanced macro command to create a file-retrieve program:

    /fr{NAME}{?}~

This program displays all files in the current drive and directory and then pauses to accept input from the user. The user can type the name of one of the displayed files or move the highlight to a file name and press Enter.

Even if you press Enter after typing an entry for the ? command, you still must include a tilde (~) after the ? command or move the cell pointer to another cell if you want 1-2-3 to accept your input.

The macro in figure 27.2 demonstrates the use of the ? command to stop and wait for user input. The macro pauses three times to allow the user to enter the three components of the DATE function. At each pause the macro prompts the user using the INDICATE command. Different prompt text is referenced by each INDICATE command. The user only needs to enter the year, month and day, pressing Enter between each one. The macro enters the DATE function and the commas between the arguments for the user and then converts the function to a value.

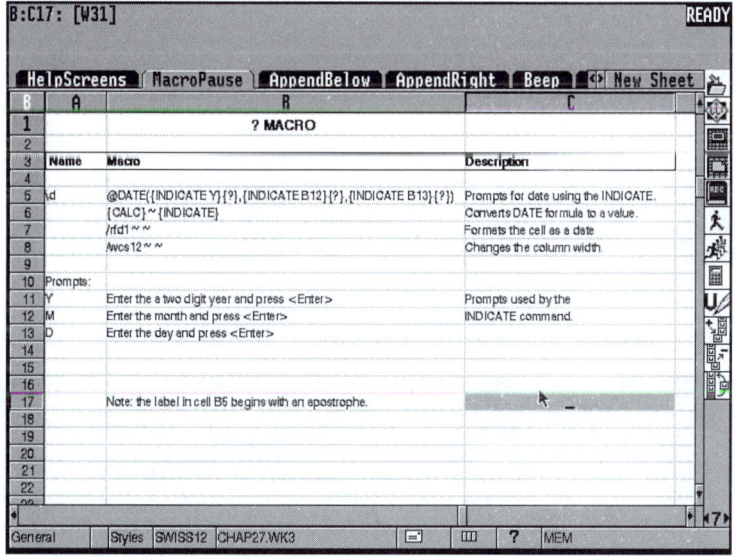

Fig. 27.2
Using {?} to pause a macro to get user input. This macro enters a date, as a value, using the DATE function.

The APPENDBELOW Command

The APPENDBELOW command copies the values from a range to the rows immediately below another range. As part of the copy operation, {APPENDBELOW} also expands the range to include the new data. Data is inserted but no new rows are added to the worksheet. The syntax of the APPENDBELOW command is

{APPENDBELOW *destination,source*}

The APPENDBELOW command copies the contents of *source* to *destination* and expands *destination* to include the new data. Figure 27.3 shows a simple

874 Chapter 27—Advanced Macro Command Power Techniques

example of a macro that uses {APPENDBELOW} to copy first-name and last-name information from the range called STUFF to the database range called TABLE2.

Fig. 27.3
A macro using the APPENDBELOW command to append data from a different file.

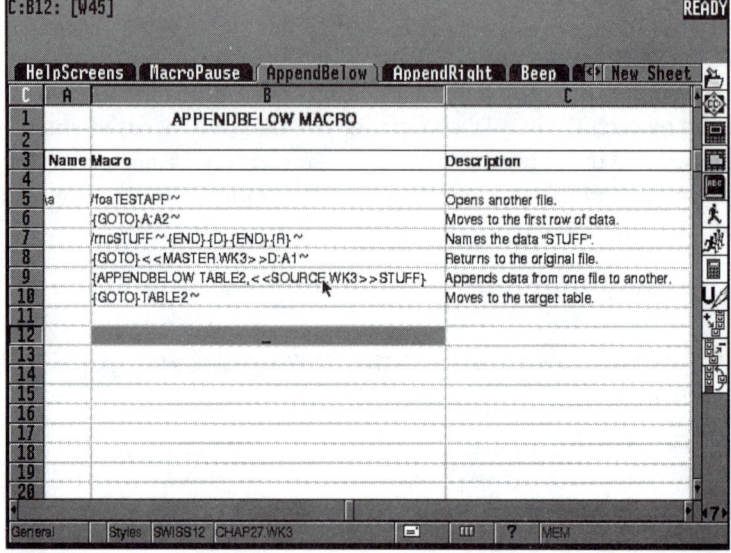

Notice the syntax necessary to move or append data between files.

> **Note**
>
> {APPENDBELOW} copies calculated values, not the actual formulas. In this respect, {APPENDBELOW} is similar to /**R**ange **V**alue.

The APPENDRIGHT Command

The APPENDRIGHT operation mirrors that of {APPENDBELOW}, with one exception: {APPENDRIGHT} copies the values of *source* to the right of *destination*. (The APPENDBELOW command copies the contents of *source* below *destination*.) The APPENDRIGHT command uses the following syntax:

{APPENDRIGHT *destination,source*}

{APPENDRIGHT} copies the contents of *source* to *destination* and expands *destination* to the right to include new data. Expanding the destination means that if the destination range has a range name, that name expands, and any formulas that referred to the original range now reference the new larger area.

{APPENDRIGHT} copies values, not formulas, to *destination*. {APPENDBELOW} and {APPENDRIGHT} are helpful companions to the FORM command. The two commands provide an easy way to copy data from an input form to a storage table or database range. Figure 27.4 shows the use of the FORM and APPENDRIGHT commands.

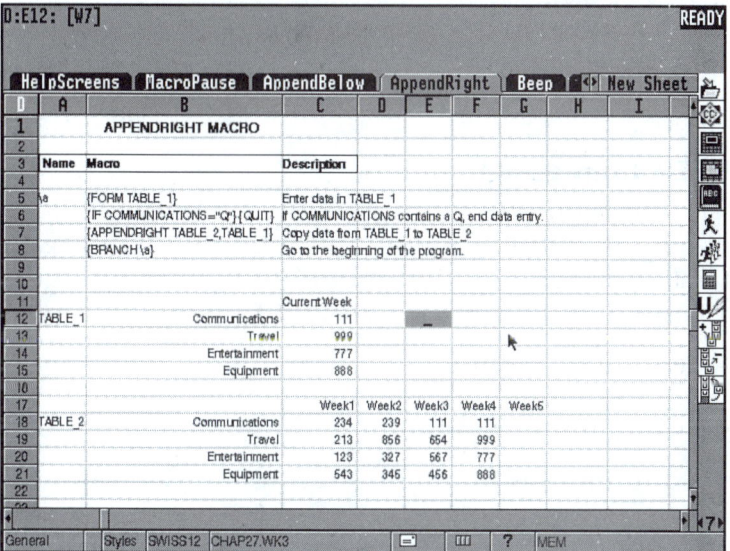

Fig. 27.4
A macro which adds weekly data to a cumulative table using the APPENDRIGHT command. Data from the input form area, TABLE_1, is copied to the ongoing database, TABLE_2.

Troubleshooting

1-2-3 beeps and displays a worksheet full *error message when running an append command macro.*

Most likely, the destination range has reached the bottom or the last column of the worksheet. For example, if the number of rows in the specified source exceeds the number of rows left in the worksheet below the specified destination, {APPENDBELOW} aborts. If only 100 rows are left in the worksheet, for example, you cannot copy 200 rows of information. Consider starting a new destination table.

1-2-3 beeps and displays a protected cell *error message.*

The destination cells to the right of or below the *destination* range are protected; turn off protection.

(continues)

> (continued)
>
> 1-2-3 beeps and displays a `Cannot write over data with APPEND commands` error message.
>
> Either append command fails if executing the command will destroy data in the *destination* range by overwriting it. This safety feature prevents the append commands from destroying data in the worksheet. Clear or move the information that is adjacent to the *destination* range.

The BEEP Command

The BEEP command activates the computer's speaker system to produce one of four tones. Each optional argument (*1* through *4*) produces a different tone. The BEEP command alerts the user to a specific condition in the program or gets the user's attention. The format of the BEEP command is

{BEEP [*number*]}

Consider the following {BEEP} statement:

`{IF A35>50}{BEEP 2}`

A useful place to use the BEEP command is within a long program. For example, you may want to be alerted when user input is needed or when the program comes to an end. You can also use a {BEEP} when the user has made an incorrect choice. Figure 27.5 shows the use of the BEEP command to warn users who have pressed Enter at a menu prompt too quickly. The first item on the menu acts to alert the careless user; if the user presses Enter while on this choice, 1-2-3 beeps and redisplays the menu. This macro also illustrates two approaches to return to the main menu, one using {BRANCH} and the other using {MENUBRANCH}.

> **Caution**
>
> If the setting for **/W**orksheet **G**lobal **D**efault **O**ther **B**eep is **N**o, {BEEP} doesn't sound.

> **Note**
>
> {BEEP} and {BEEP 1} produce the same tone. {BEEP 2}, {BEEP 3}, and {BEEP 4} produce different tones. Unlike other macro commands, the argument after BEEP (1, 2, 3, or 4) produces a different tone and does not repeat the command. To repeat a BEEP, you must use {BEEP} multiple times.

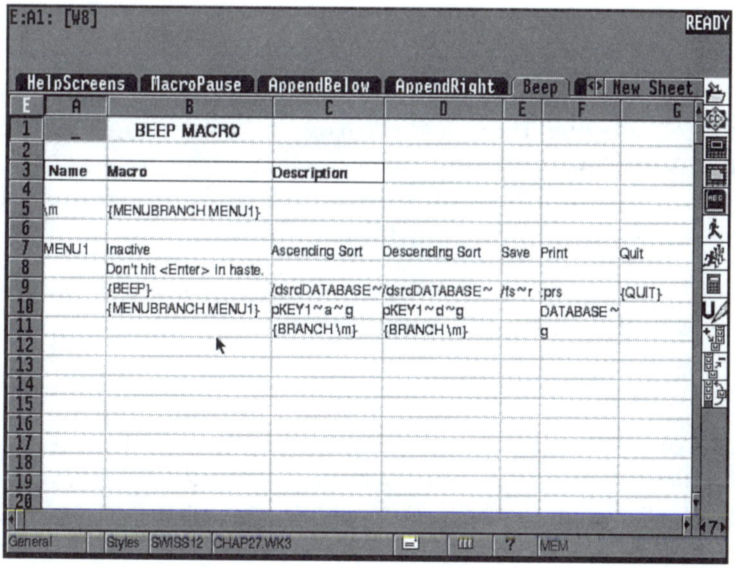

Fig. 27.5
A safety menu employing the BEEP command to alert the user to an incorrect choice.

The BLANK Command

The BLANK command erases a range of cells in the worksheet. This command works similarly to the **/R**ange **E**rase command, but using {BLANK} has an advantage over using **/R**ange **E**rase in advanced macro command programs. Because {BLANK} doesn't use menus, this command erases over four times faster than **/R**ange **E**rase. The syntax of the BLANK command is

{BLANK *location*}

{BLANK} erases the range defined by *location*. The statement {BLANK RANGE_1}, for example, erases RANGE_1.

The BRANCH Command

The BRANCH command causes program control to pass to the location indicated in the BRANCH statement. The program continues reading commands at the new location. Program control doesn't return to the original program from which it was passed unless directed to do so by another BRANCH statement. (If you want to branch back to the line below the original BRANCH statement, you should be using {*subroutine*}.) Use the following syntax for {BRANCH}:

{BRANCH *location*}

{BRANCH} continues program execution in the cell specified by *location*. The following example shows you how to use {BRANCH}.

Tip
Use {BLANK @CELLPOINTER("address")} to erase the contents of the current cell.

```
{GOTO}ENTRY~@COUNT(INVENTORY)~
{BRANCH \START}
```

The first line places the cell pointer in the cell named ENTRY and then enters the @COUNT function. The second line passes program control to the cell named \START, regardless of any commands that may follow the BRANCH command in the same cell location or in the cell below. 1-2-3 begins reading program commands in the cell with the range name \START.

{BRANCH} is an unconditional command unless it is preceded by an IF conditional statement, as in the following example:

```
{IF C22="alpha"}{BRANCH G24}
{GOTO}S101~
```

For the IF command to act as a conditional testing command, the IF command and the second command must be in the same cell. For more information, see the discussion on the IF command later in this chapter. Figure 27.6 shows a macro for generating factorials which employs the BRANCH command. Factorials are frequently used in statistics. 5 factorial, represented 5!, is equal to 5*4*3*2*1, which means multiply 5 times 4 times 3 times 2 times 1, which is equal to 120. This macro contains eight BRANCH commands and four tests. Because factorials must be positive whole numbers, and in 1-2-3, no larger than 69, there are tests and responses for each of these conditions. If you do not want these tests, you can simplify the macro by removing the macro commands from lines B6..B9 and B15..B21. Note that the entry in cell B10 is the label '+1~.

Fig. 27.6
A factorial macro demonstrating the use of the BRANCH command.

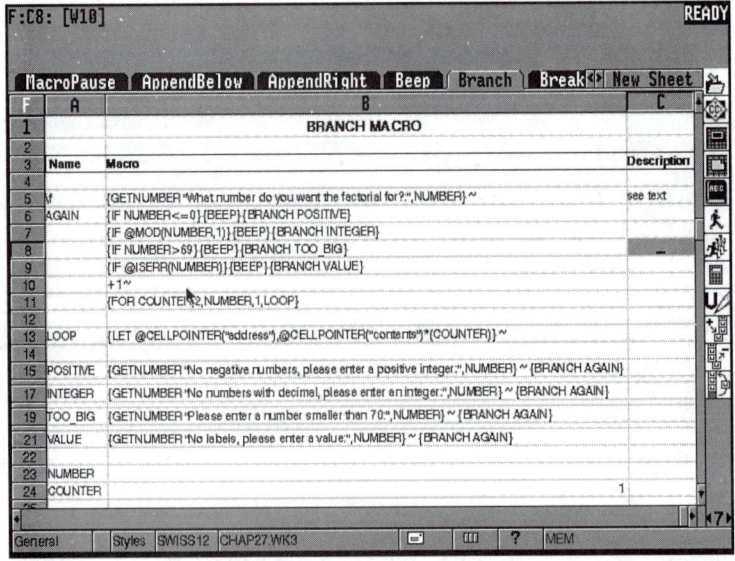

The BREAKOFF Command

The easiest way to stop a program is to press Ctrl+Break. Although you want to use Ctrl+Break when you debug programs, you may not want a user to use Ctrl+Break to stop macro program execution. To prevent Ctrl+Break from stopping the execution of a program, use the BREAKOFF command.

Before you use a BREAKOFF statement, make certain that you have fully debugged the program. You may need to use Ctrl+Break to halt the program and make a repair while you debug the program.

The syntax of the BREAKOFF command is

{BREAKOFF}

When the control panel contains a menu, you can halt program execution by pressing Esc, regardless of the presence of a BREAKOFF command.

Figure 27.7 shows a macro you can use to hide your work while you are away from your desk without having to close your worksheet, protecting sensitive information. When you press Alt+h the BREAKOFF command prevents a user from using Ctrl+Break to exit the macro. Then the cell pointer is sent to an empty area of the worksheet, in this case cell IV8192. Next the password prompt appears, the response to which is stored in the cell named PASSWORD. This response is compared with the item in the cell named SECRET using the @EXACT function, which is case sensitive, and if the response matches, the cell pointer is returned to cell A1 and the macro ends. If the response is incorrect the macro beeps and reprompts the user for the password. (Don't forget your password!)

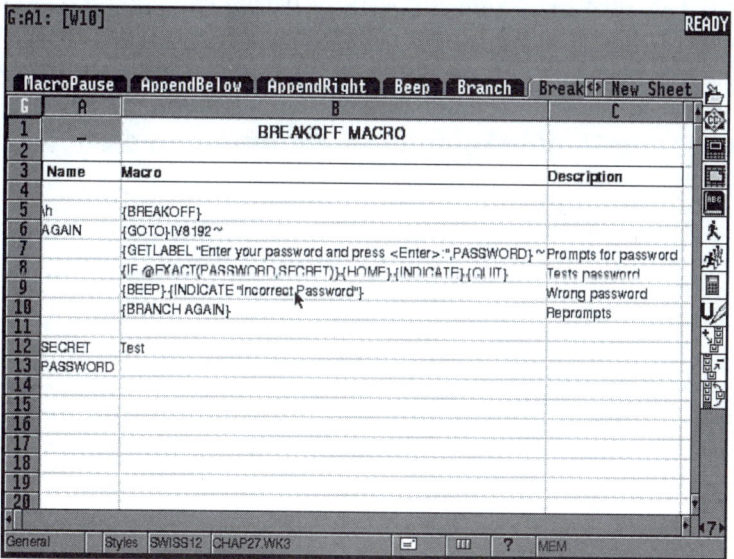

Fig. 27.7
A macro to hide sensitive data without closing your worksheet. This macro demonstrates a practical use of the BREAKOFF command.

The BREAKON Command

To restore the effect of Ctrl+Break, use the BREAKON command. The syntax of this command is

{BREAKON}

Because any Ctrl+Break commands in the keyboard buffer are executed as soon as the BREAKON command is executed, place {BREAKON} where the program can stop safely. {BREAKOFF} is canceled automatically when a macro ends, so it may not be necessary to add a BREAKON command to your macros.

> **Caution**
>
> You can possibly create an endless loop with no way out if you misplace the BREAKOFF and BREAKON commands. For example, in the following macro the BREAKOFF command is in cell A1:
>
>   {BREAKOFF}
>   {BRANCH A1}
>   {BREAKON}
>
> Because of this arrangement, the macro never executes the BREAKON command. First it turns off Break and immediately branches back to the BREAKOFF command. The only way out of an endless loop is to restart your computer, which means you lose any work you haven't saved.

The CE or CLEARENTRY Command

The CE or CLEARENTRY command clears the default entry on the edit line. You might want to clear the current path that appears when you choose the **/F**ile **O**pen or **/F**ile **S**ave commands, for example. Often, just pressing the Esc or Backspace key works fine; however, if you don't know how many times you need to press Esc or Backspace to clear the default entry on the edit line, CE is the best solution.

Suppose you want to save the current file to the C:\DATA directory but the current path is D:\USER\123\DATA. Your macro command would be

    '/fs{CE}C:\DATA\MYFILE~

The CLOSE Command

The CLOSE command closes an open ASCII file. If no file is open, the CLOSE command has no effect. The CLOSE command is particularly important for

ASCII files that you write or modify; if you don't close an ASCII file, you can lose the last data written to the file. Thus, the CLOSE command helps ensure that the data isn't damaged or lost. The syntax of the CLOSE command is

{CLOSE}

CLOSE doesn't take an argument.

{CLOSE} closes a file opened with {OPEN}. Under most circumstances, 1-2-3 automatically closes a file you don't close, but you should develop the habit of using {CLOSE} when you finish using any file opened with {OPEN}. Figure 27.8 shows the CLOSE command in use. Cell D4 shows the OPEN command that opens the file INPUT.TXT. The CLOSE command in cell D9 closes INPUT.TXT. Likewise, OUTPUT.TXT is opened in cells D13 and D14 and closed by the CLOSE command in cell D16. If no file is open, the CLOSE command does nothing.

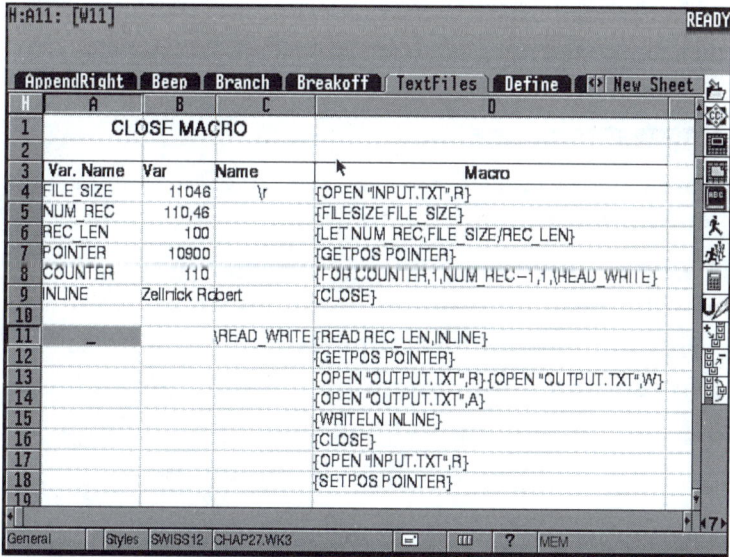

Fig. 27.8
A macro program that uses the CLOSE command.

The CONTENTS Command

The CONTENTS command copies the contents of one cell to another as a string. Optionally, CONTENTS also assigns a cell *width* or cell *format* to the cell containing the string. If you don't specify the width or number format, 1-2-3 uses the column width or number format of the source location to format the cell. The syntax of the CONTENTS command is

{CONTENTS *destination,source,[width],[format]*}

{CONTENTS} stores the contents of *source* in *destination* as a string. Suppose that you want to copy the number 123.456 from cell SOURCE_1 to cell DEST_1 and change the number to a string while you copy. The statement for this operation is

    {CONTENTS DEST_1,SOURCE_1}

The contents of cell DEST_1 are displayed as the string '123.456, with the left-align label-prefix character (apostrophe).

When {CONTENTS} makes a copy of the *source* number, the command also copies the way the number appears in the cell. If the source cell is formatted as **C**urrency with no decimal places, for example, the value 123.456 looks like $123, and CONTENTS copies the number to the destination cell as the string '$123. Similarly, if the source column width is 6 and the number is in the General format, the number appears as 123.4, and the destination cell will contain the string '123.4.

Suppose that you want to change the width of the string when you copy it. Rather than display the string as 123.456, you want to display it as 123.4. To get the result you want, change the statement to

    {CONTENTS DEST_2,SOURCE_1,6}

This statement uses a width of 6 to display the string. 1-2-3 truncates the least significant digits of the number to create the string.

Suppose that you want to change the string's display format while you copy the source cell contents and change the destination cell width. The following string changes the display format to **C**urrency **0**:

    {CONTENTS DEST_3,SOURCE_1,5,32}

The numbers to use for the format number in this statement are listed in Table 27.2. The result of the statement is the number $123.

Table 27.2 Numeric Format Codes for the CONTENTS Command

Code	Format of Destination String
0-15	**F**ixed, 0 to 15 decimal places
16-31	**S**cientific, 0 to 15 decimal places
32-47	**C**urrency, 0 to 15 decimal places
48-63	**P**ercent, 0 to 15 decimal places

Code	Format of Destination String
64-79	, (comma), 0 to 15 decimal places
112	+/ bar graph
113	**G**eneral format
114	**D1** (DD-MMM-YY)
115	**D2** (DD-MMM)
116	**D3** (MMM-YY)
117	**T**ext format
118	**H**idden format
119	**D6** (HH:MM:SS AM/PM time format)
120	**D7** (HH:MM AM/PM time format)
121	**D4** (Long International Date)
122	**D5** (Short International Date)
123	**D8** (Long International Time)
124	**D9** (Short International Time)
127	Current default display format

In the following examples of the CONTENTS command, the number in cell SOURCE_2 is 123.456, the width of the column that contains SOURCE_2 is 9, and the display format for cell SOURCE_2 is **F**ixed **2**.

The following command displays the label '123.46 in cell DEST_4, using the **F**ixed **2** format:

    {CONTENTS DEST_4,SOURCE_2}

The following command displays **** if a column has a width of 4, because a column width of 4 would be too narrow to display the number 123.46:

    {CONTENTS DEST_5,SOURCE_2,4}

The following command displays the label '123 in cell DEST_6, using the **F**ixed **0** format:

    {CONTENTS DEST_6,SOURCE_2,5,0}

> **Tip**
> Use numeric format code 117 (**T**ext format) to copy a formula and display it as text.

The CONTENTS command is somewhat specialized but is useful in situations that require converting numeric values to formatted strings. Using the **Text** format, {CONTENTS} can convert long numeric formulas to strings that are useful for debugging purposes.

The DEFINE Command

An important feature of 1-2-3's advanced macro commands is the capability of passing arguments to a subroutine. To tell 1-2-3 where in the worksheet to place the arguments, a subroutine that takes arguments must contain the DEFINE command as its first statement. The syntax of the DEFINE command is

{DEFINE *loc1*[:*Type1*],...,*locN*[:*TypeN*]}

{DEFINE} identifies the cells to contain the argument values; *loc1*, *loc2*, and so on are cells or ranges in which 1-2-3 stores the argument values for the called subroutine.

Type1 is *S* (or STRING) or *V* (or VALUE) and is optional; if not present, the default is STRING. If *loc1* is defined as type STRING, 1-2-3 places the argument from the subroutine call into *loc1* as a label.

If *loc* is defined as type VALUE, the corresponding argument in the subroutine call is treated as a formula, range name, or number; 1-2-3 places the value of the argument in *loc*. If the corresponding argument in the subroutine call isn't a valid number, string, or formula, 1-2-3 displays an error message. You don't have to enclose a string in quotation marks or use a leading plus sign (+) in a formula using cell references.

Consider the macro \d (see fig. 27.9). \d has a subroutine that creates a list of four dates, seven days apart, beginning with today. The subroutine takes one argument (@NOW). The DEFINE command stores the value of @NOW (today's date) in the cell called TODAY.

The rest of the program enters today's date in the current cell and the next three weekly dates in the cells to the right, and then formats the four cells as dates. The DEFINE command is only needed if you pass arguments within a subroutine call.

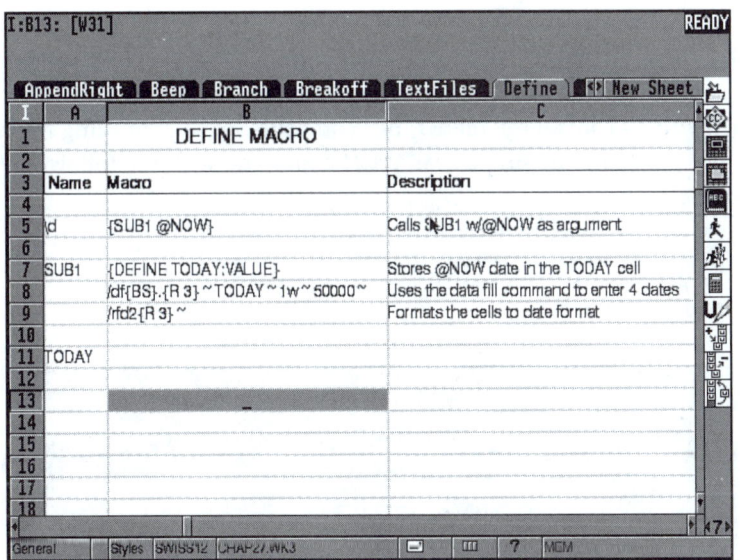

Fig. 27.9
An example of a macro that uses the DEFINE command to receive arguments from a subroutine call.

The DISPATCH Command

The DISPATCH command is similar to the BRANCH command, but the DISPATCH command branches indirectly to a cell address or range name contained in the *location* cell. This means that it is similar to the @@ function. The DISPATCH command could be used to replace multiple IF commands in your macro. The syntax of the command is

{DISPATCH *location*}

The *location* argument is a cell address or range name containing the destination of the {DISPATCH}. If the cell referenced by location doesn't contain a valid cell reference or range name, an error occurs and program execution either stops with an error message or continues at a location specified in an ONERROR command if one has been previously executed.

The *location* must contain a cell reference or range name that points to a single cell reference. If the *location* is a multiple-cell range or a range containing a single cell, the DISPATCH command acts like a BRANCH statement and transfers execution directly to the *location*.

In figure 27.10, the DISPATCH statement continues program execution at the location named by the ANSWER cell. In this example, ANSWER is daily, so

886 Chapter 27—Advanced Macro Command Power Techniques

the program execution goes to the cell named DAILY, which prints the range PRINT_DAILY. To appreciate the advantage of the DISPATCH command consider what the program in figure 27.10 would have required if you had used IF statements to control the branching. You could leave everything the same except for replacing the single DISPATCH command with the following lines:

```
{IF ANSWER=daily}{BRANCH DAILY}
{IF ANSWER=weekly}{BRANCH WEEKLY}
{IF ANSWER=monthly}{BRANCH MONTHLY}
{IF ANSWER=quarterly}{BRANCH QUARTERLY}
{BRANCH ANNUAL}
```

Fig. 27.10
An example of a macro that uses DISPATCH command to branch indirectly to a range name.

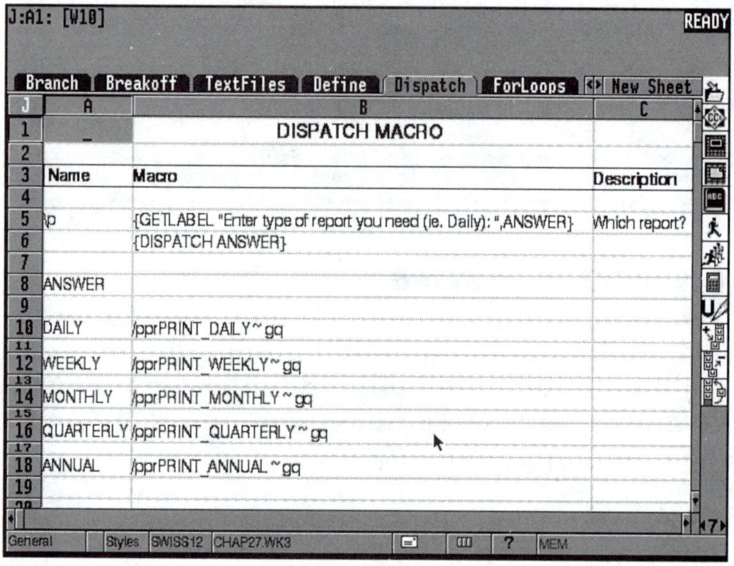

The FILESIZE Command

The FILESIZE command returns the size of a text file in bytes. The syntax of the command is

{FILESIZE *location*}

{FILESIZE} records the open file's size in *location*. The FILESIZE command determines the current length of the file and places this value in the cell referenced by *location*. Location can be a cell reference or a range name. For an example of the FILESIZE command, refer to figure 27.8.

The FOR and FORBREAK Commands

The FOR command provides 1-2-3 with loop capabilities. This command causes a subroutine to be executed a specified number of times. A subroutine executed more than once is called a *loop*. The syntax of the FOR command is

{FOR *counter,start,stop,step,routine*}

Counter is a cell you name that 1-2-3 uses to keep track of the number of times the subroutine has been executed in the loop. 1-2-3 replaces any existing value in *counter* with *start* and then increments *counter* by *step* until *stop* is reached. *Start* is the starting number for the counter, *stop* is the ending number, and *step* is the increment to add each time the subroutine runs. You specify values, range names, cell addresses or formulas for the *start*, *stop*, and *step* arguments. *Routine* is the name of the subroutine to execute and is a cell, range name, or formula returning a string.

If you use *nested loops* (one FOR loop inside another), you must complete the innermost loops before you complete the outer loop.

> **Caution**
>
> Although you can have multiple loops in FOR structures, make sure the flow from one loop to the next is logical.

The macro in figure 27.11 is an interesting illustration of a nested FOR loop. This macro finds and clears all cells containing '<Space>, that is, an apostrophe followed by a space. Many people clear cells by pressing the space bar; however, this does not clear a cell, instead it replaces the contents with an apostrophe followed by a space. Such invisible spaces can cause formulas such as AVERAGE to return incorrect answers, waste memory, and cause the END direction key combinations from operating as expected. This macro finds and clears these offending labels from the entire worksheet with just the press of a button. The macro step in cell B9 should be entered as a formula: **+"/rs{BS}.{HOME}~' ~lr~a{HOME}"**, with a space after the apostrophe. If you were to enter this line as a label the search command would modify this line of the macro, but since you make it a formula and have the search command only search labels, this line is not modified as the macro runs. In some versions of 1-2-3, you could use the **/R**ange **S**earch command to replace cells with space bar characters in them with nothing, but Release 4 replaces the apostrophe space with an apostrophe, which doesn't quite solve the problem.

Chapter 27—Advanced Macro Command Power Techniques

Fig. 27.11

This macro uses a nested FOR loop to control the movement of the cell pointer from row to row and from column to column.

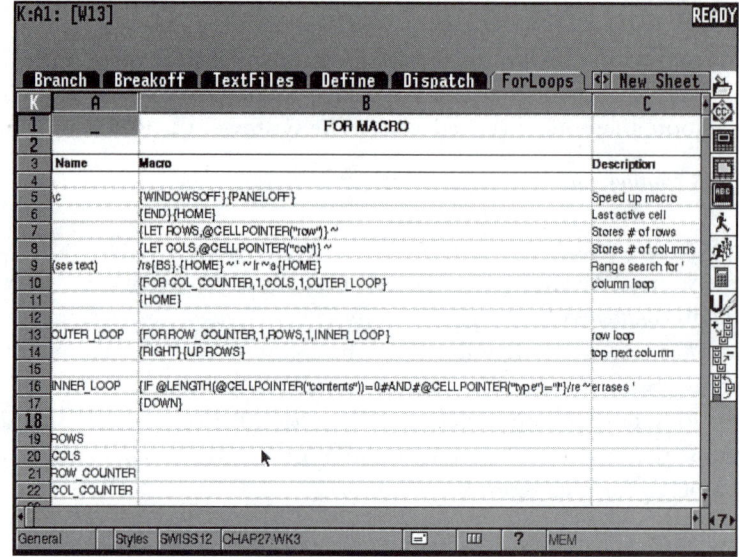

The FORBREAK command terminates a FOR command loop before the loop has completed its number of iterations. After {FORBREAK} the macro continues execution with the command following the FOR statement. For example, with the following line, 1-2-3 ends the loop as soon as the value in PREV_# exceeds 1,000:

    {IF PREV_#>1000}{FORBREAK}

Troubleshooting

Users keep breaking out of my macros before the macros finish running.

Use the BREAKOFF command, which prevents anyone from stopping the macros before they complete their execution.

My macro never stops until I use Ctrl+Break to stop it.

You've probably created an endless loop. Check the logical flow of your macro. In particular, look for BRANCH commands that branch back to an earlier part of your macro without ever letting the macro finish. Also check any IF commands that control the possible termination of your macro. For example, if you have a line such as {IF A1=100}{QUIT}, check to ensure that A1 will equal exactly 100 at some point during macro execution.

When I run my macro, I get the error "Invalid Range" at the cell with the FOR command.

> Check to make sure any range name arguments within the FOR command are really names in your spreadsheet.
>
> *My FOR loop never executes, but I get no error message.*
>
> Make sure you have not reversed the *start*, *stop*, or *step* arguments. For example, the following FOR command never executes: {FOR COUNTER,10,1,1,LOOP}
>
> *The FOR loop in my macro executes one too many times.*
>
> Make sure that the loop is not directly below the FOR command. If it is, the loop executes the proper number of times within the FOR command and then once more after it leaves the FOR command.

The FORM Command

The FORM command temporarily interrupts macro execution so the user can enter input into unprotected cells in a specified range. The FORM command, although similar to the **/R**ange **I**nput command, includes three additional options: branching to another line of advanced macro command instructions if the user enters certain keys; specifying a set of keystrokes as valid; and specifying a set of keystrokes as invalid. The syntax for the FORM command is

{FORM *input*,[*call-table*],[*include-keys*],[*exclude-keys*]}

{FORM} temporarily interrupts the macro so that a user can enter data into the *input* range—a worksheet range in which at least one cell has been unprotected with **/R**ange **U**nprot. The user enters data only in the unprotected cells.

> **Note**
>
> Worksheet protection does not need to be enabled for this command to work. It is the cell's protection status that is important, not the worksheet's protection status.

Without the last three arguments, which are optional, {FORM} functions exactly like **/R**ange **I**nput: you can use any keys to enter data into and move between the unprotected cells.

You can use the FORM command's three optional arguments (*call-table*, *include-keys*, and *exclude-keys*) individually or in combination.

Call-table is a two-column range in which the first column lists the names of keys on the keyboard, such as {CALC} or {GRAPH}, and the second column lists the commands to be executed when the key is pressed.

Include-keys is a range of all keystrokes accepted during execution of the FORM command. This list includes not only keystrokes used to enter data into the unprotected cells of the input range but also any other keys needed to operate the macro or to deal with an error condition.

Exclude-keys is a range listing all keystrokes not accepted during the execution of the FORM command. By specifying the unacceptable keys, you implicitly identify the acceptable keys; you probably will use the *include-keys* or the *exclude-keys* argument but not both.

To omit an optional argument, use one of the following command structures:

Structure	Purpose
{FORM *input*}	To omit all optional arguments
{FORM *input,call-table*}	To use only *call-table*
{FORM *input,,include-keys*}	To use only *include-keys*
{FORM *input,,,exclude-keys*}	To use only *exclude-keys*
{FORM *input,call-table,include-keys*}	To use *call-table* and *include-keys*
{FORM *input,call-table,,exclude-keys*}	To use *call-table* and *exclude-keys*

To complete execution of the FORM command, the user presses the key designated in the *call-table* or *include-keys* range to end the form. If the FORM command uses an *exclude-keys* range, the user presses Enter or Esc. 1-2-3 then continues execution of the macro program. When the user presses Enter or Esc, the cell pointer remains in its current position in the form.

Figure 27.12 shows an example of a form to accept data into the unprotected cells A19..D19 in the range INPUT. The *call-table* argument, CALL_TABLE (range B7..C8), specifies the additional keystrokes to execute if the user presses F1 (HELP) or Ins. If the user presses F1 (Help), the program beeps. If the user presses Ins, the program uses the FORMBREAK command to break out of the form.

This example doesn't have an *include-keys* argument but does have an *exclude-keys* argument. The range EXCLUDE (B10..B13) shows the excluded keystrokes.

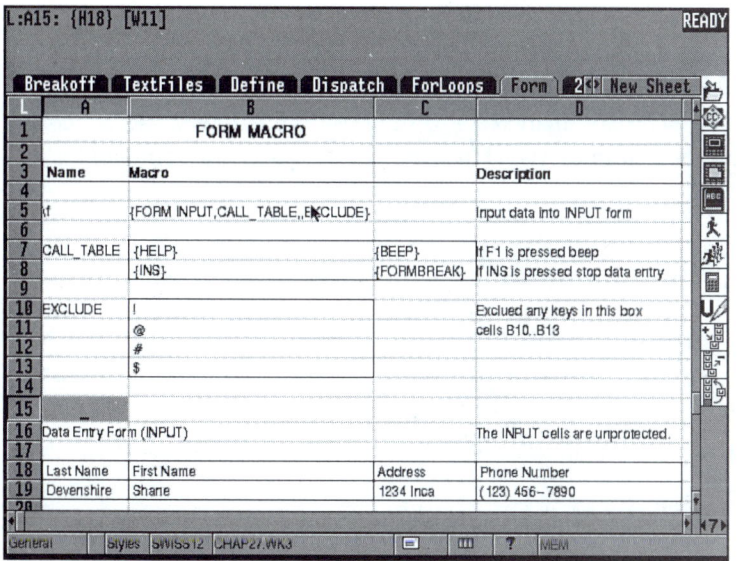

Fig. 27.12
The FORM command used to collect input with *call-table* and *exclude-key* ranges specified.

> **Note**
>
> All three optional arguments for {FORM} (*call-table*, *include-keys*, and *exclude-keys*) are case sensitive. If your *include-keys* argument lists an uppercase B but not a lowercase b, for example, only the uppercase B is accepted.

The FORMBREAK Command

The FORMBREAK command ends a FORM command and cancels the current form. The syntax of the command is

{FORMBREAK}

In addition to using {FORMBREAK} to end a FORM command and continue the macro on the line below the FORM command, you can use {FORMBREAK} with nested FORM commands. In this case, FORMBREAK ends the current form and returns to the preceding form. Suppose that you use the FORM command to create an order entry form with a Vendor field. If the user presses Ins in the Vendor field, the program displays a second form, which lists vendor names. The user chooses the name of the vendor or types a new name and presses Ins again. After the user presses Enter, the program issues a FORMBREAK command to return to the order entry form.

Refer to figure 27.12 for an example of the {FORMBREAK} command.

The FRAMEOFF Command

The FRAMEOFF command removes the column letters, worksheet letters, and row numbers from the 1-2-3 display. The syntax of the command is

{FRAMEOFF}

{FRAMEOFF} suppresses display of the worksheet frame, which can reduce distractions and sometimes provide a slight increase in the speed with which your macro executes. After you execute a FRAMEOFF command, 1-2-3 suppresses the worksheet frame display until the program encounters a FRAMEON command or is finished. 1-2-3 has a second command to accomplish this task, {BORDERSOFF}.

The FRAMEON Command

The FRAMEON command redisplays the column letters, worksheet letters, and row numbers suppressed by a FRAMEOFF command. The syntax for the FRAMEON command is

{FRAMEON}

{FRAMEON} redisplays the worksheet frame. The following sample program uses {FRAMEOFF} and {FRAMEON}:

```
{FRAMEOFF}{?}~
{DOWN 2}
{FRAMEON}{?}~
{RIGHT 3}
{FRAMEOFF}{?}~
```

Tip
{FRAMEOFF} and {FRAMEON} don't affect any of the special Wysiwyg frames, only the standard 1-2-3 frame. To display or suppress the Wysiwyg frames, use the Wysiwyg command :Display Options Frame and then choose the frame type you want.

The program initially suppresses display of the worksheet frame until you press a key, and then redisplays the worksheet frame until you press a key. Finally, the program again suppresses the worksheet frame until you press a key. If you construct this macro, notice that even though the last FRAMEOFF command doesn't have a matching FRAMEON command, the worksheet frame reappears when the macro program ends. 1-2-3 has a second command to accomplish this, {BORDERSON}.

The GET Command

The GET command suspends macro execution and waits for the user to press a key. When a key is pressed it is entered into a target cell as a left-aligned label. Then you can analyze or test the keystroke and, based on the result of the test, have the program take any appropriate action. The syntax of the GET command is

{GET *location*}

GET accepts a single keystroke into the range defined by *location*. The following example shows how you can use {GET}:

```
{GET CAPTURE}
{IF CAPTURE="q"}/fs~r
{GOTO}SALES~
```

In this program, the GET statement traps an individual keystroke in a cell named CAPTURE. The second line evaluates CAPTURE. If the keystroke in CAPTURE is the letter *q*, the file is saved automatically. If CAPTURE contains any other keystroke, /fs~r is ignored. In either case, control then passes to the third line of the program, which places the cell pointer in the cell with the range name SALES.

> **Note**
>
> The GET command returns the trapped keystroke value as soon as the user presses a single key. The GET command offers an advantage compared to the three other common input commands ({?}, {GETLABEL}, and {GETNUMBER}) in that the user doesn't have to press Enter after typing an entry.

Tip
If you want to use this command to capture more than one keystroke, use a series of GET commands, each of which sends the keystroke to a different *location*.

The GETLABEL Command

The GETLABEL command accepts any type of entry from the keyboard but stores the input as a label. The prompt, which may be a cell address, a range name, a calculation that evaluates to a string, or quoted or unquoted text, is displayed in the control panel. The syntax for the GETLABEL command is

{GETLABEL *prompt,location*}

{GETLABEL} places the entry in *location* as a label when the user presses Enter. The following example shows the use of the GETLABEL command:

```
{GETLABEL Enter order date (MM/DD/YY)   ,ORDER_DATE}
{LET ORDER_DATE,@DATEVALUE(ORDER_DATE)}
/rfd1ORDER_DATE~/wcfORDER_DATE~
```

The GETLABEL statement displays the prompt Enter order date (MM/DD/YY) and copies the user input as a label into the cell named ORDER_DATE. The second line converts the label in ORDER_DATE to a numeric date. The third line formats the cell ORDER_DATE as a date and sets its width to fit-widest.

Chapter 27—Advanced Macro Command Power Techniques

> **Caution**
>
> Though putting quotes around the prompt in a GETLABEL or GETNUMBER command isn't necessary, if the prompt contains a comma, colon, or semicolon, 1-2-3 assumes that it is an argument separator, so in those cases you will need the quotes around the prompt text. You can enter an unquoted prompt containing the comma, colon, or semicolon in a cell and then reference that cell in the *prompt* argument.

Figure 27.13 shows how to improve a macro by using {GETLABEL} with the IF, BRANCH, and BEEP commands to add error handling. If the user enters a label that cannot be converted to a date, the second {GETLABEL} displays an error message and prompts for a valid date. Also, notice the use of a cell address and a range name for the prompt arguments. This macro enters the date in the current cell rather than sending it to another cell as in the above example.

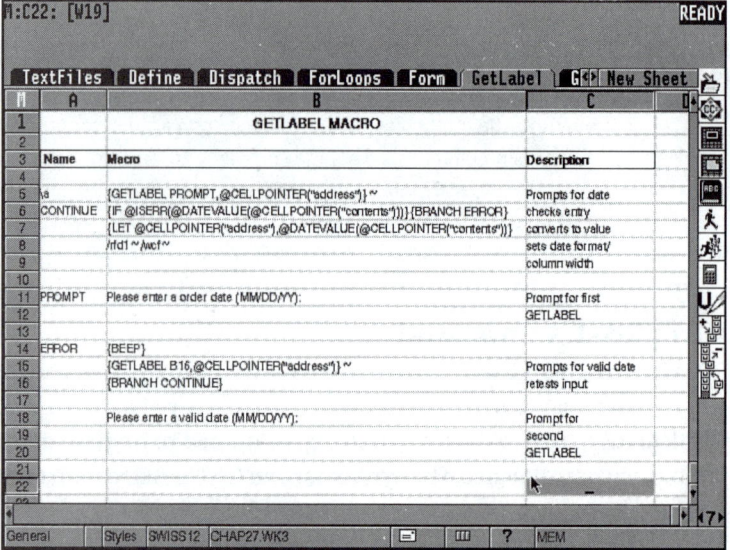

Fig. 27.13
A macro to accept a date as labels and convert it into numeric data. This macro demonstrates the use of the GETLABEL command.

The GETNUMBER Command

The GETNUMBER command accepts any number, function, or formula that evaluates to a value as input. The syntax for the GETNUMBER command is

{GETNUMBER *prompt,location*}

After the user types the input and presses Enter, 1-2-3 places the number in *location*. If the user presses Enter without having entered a number or tries to enter a label, 1-2-3 displays ERR in the *location* cell. *Prompt* is a string, cell address, range name, or calculation evaluating to text which may or may not be enclosed in quotation marks (see the discussion and caution for {GETLABEL} above). 1-2-3 displays the prompt in the control panel.

In the following example, the GETNUMBER statement displays a prompt and accepts a number in cell CLASS_CODE:

    {GETNUMBER "Classification code:",CLASS_CODE}

Figure 27.14 demonstrates the use of various types of prompts within a series of GETNUMBER commands. For example, the input to the prompt for height in inches is stored in the cell named HEIGHT. This value is tested for reasonableness. If it is unrealistically small, the fourth prompt appears. This prompt displays the user's incorrect response and reprompts for a correct response. This last prompt illustrates the fact that prompts, like most other macro command arguments, can be dynamic.

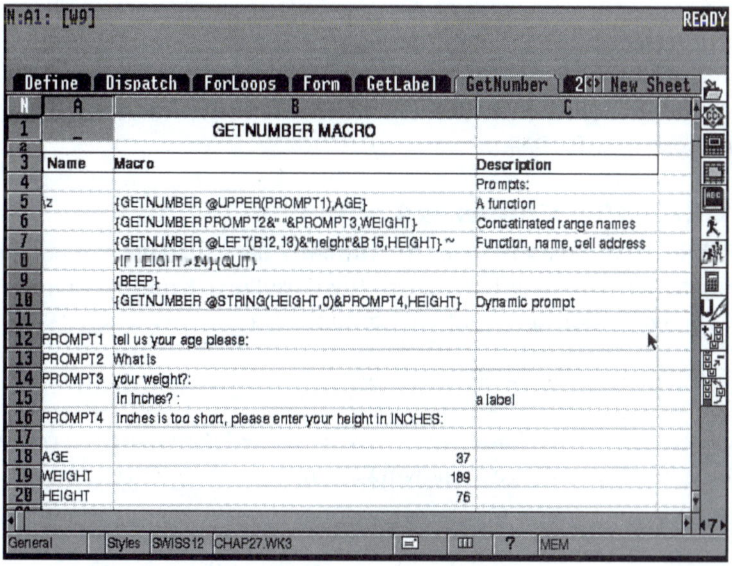

Fig. 27.14
The GETNUMBER command can accept numbers or formulas and functions which evaluate to numbers. Here they prompt the user for his or her age, weight, and height.

The GETPOS Command

The GETPOS command records the file pointer's current position. The syntax of this command is

    {GETPOS *location*}

{GETPOS} records a file pointer position in *location*. The current position of the file pointer is placed in the cell indicated by *location*, where *location* is either a cell or a range name.

The GETPOS command is useful for recording the file location of something you want to find again. You can use {GETPOS} to mark your current place in the file before you use {SETPOS} to move the file pointer to another position. You can use {GETPOS} to record the locations of important items in a quick-reference index. Refer to figure 27.8, which shows an example of how to use GETPOS.

> **Note**
>
> As figure 27.8 shows, you can use {GETPOS} to mark your position in one file before opening another ASCII file. Then you can use {SETPOS} to return to the same position in the first file.

The GRAPHOFF Command

The GRAPHOFF command removes the named graph from the display and redisplays the worksheet. The syntax for using the GRAPHOFF command is

{GRAPHOFF}

For more information about the GRAPHOFF command, read the following section about {GRAPHON}.

The GRAPHON Command

The GRAPHON command can set the currently named graph, display the currently named graph, or first set and then display the currently named graph. The syntax for the GRAPHON command is

{GRAPHON [*named-graph*],[nodisplay]}

To display a full-screen view of the currently named graph, use the command without arguments, as in the following example:

{GRAPHON}

To display a graph other than the current one, reset the currently named graph, and then redisplay it. If you have a graph setting named FIG_1, for example, use the following structure:

{GRAPHON FIG_1}

In either of the preceding cases, 1-2-3 continues to display a full-sized version of the graph until the macro program completes execution or encounters one of the following commands:

- {GRAPHOFF}
- {GRAPHON}
- {INDICATE}
- {?}
- Any command that displays a prompt or menu, such as {GETLABEL} or {MENUCALL}

To change the named graph but not display it, use the nodisplay argument. If you want the graph setting named FIG_1 to be the current graph setting, for example, but you don't want the graph displayed, use the following structure:

    {GRAPHON FIG_1,nodisplay}

Figure 27.15 uses the GRAPHON and GRAPHOFF commands to create a slide show. Between each graph you might choose to display a worksheet table of the data pertaining to the upcoming graph. If you don't want to see the worksheet between graphs, go directly from the WAIT command to the next GRAPHON command.

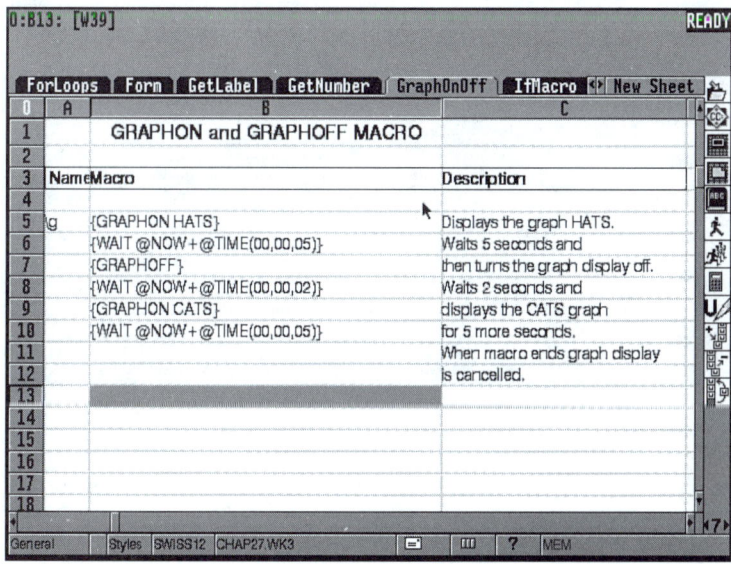

Fig. 27.15
A slide show macro using the GRAPHON and GRAPHOFF commands.

The IF Command

The IF statement performs a test, and based on the results of that test, executes the next command on the same line or the command on the following line. The syntax of the IF command is

{IF *test*}{*true*}

{*false*}

{IF} executes either the *true* or *false* statement based on the result of the *test*. Test is a logical expression, such as +B3>100. If *test* is true, 1-2-3 executes the remaining {*true*} commands on the same line as the IF command. Ordinarily the *true* command includes a QUIT or BRANCH command to skip the *false* statement. If *test* is false, 1-2-3 executes the next line in the macro, ignoring the *true* statements.

The IF statement can check for a variety of conditions including the position of the cell pointer, shows a specific numeric or string value. Figure 27.16 shows five IF commands to control a more complex macro.

Fig. 27.16
A macro that presents a choice list from which the macro eliminates items as the user types out his or her choice.

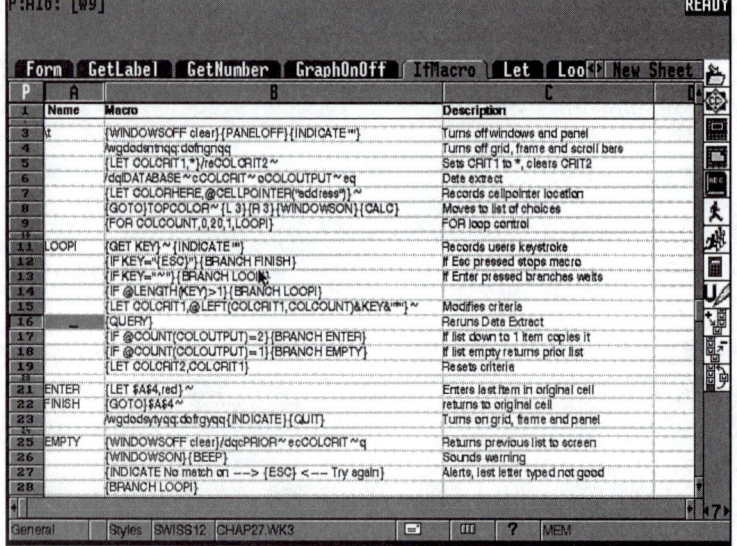

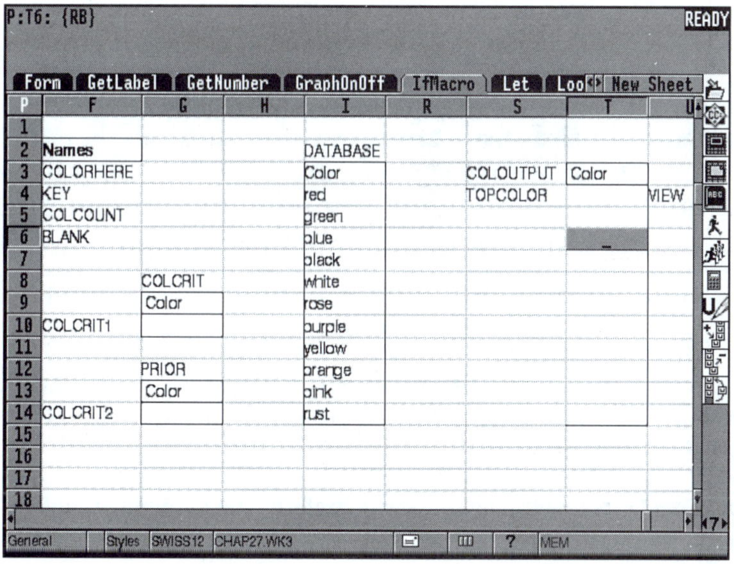

Fig. 27.17

A number of ranges needed for the macro in figure 27.16. Note the hidden columns.

When the user presses Alt+t, from anywhere in the worksheet, a list of choices is displayed. The user starts choosing from the list by typing the first letter of the item he or she wants. For example, if the user presses **r**, the macro reduces the displayed list to red and rose. If the user then types **o**, the word rose is placed in the cell that the cell pointer was in when the macro was activated because there are no other possibilities. If more than one word began with "ro" the list would shorten to show only those choices.

To set up this macro, follow these steps:

1. Enter all the text shown in figure 27.16 with the exception of cells B20, B21, and B26.

2. In cell B21, enter the following:

   ```
   +"{LET "&COLORHERE&","&TOPCOLOR&"}~"
   ```

3. In cell B22, enter

   ```
   +"{GOTO}"COLORHERE&"~"
   ```

4. In cell B27, enter

   ```
   +"{INDICATE No match on ----> "&KEY&" <---- Try again}"
   ```

5. Choose the **/R**ange **N**ame **L**abel **R**ight command to use the names in cells A3..A25 to name the adjacent cells of column B.

6. Enter all the text shown in figure 27.17. The text shown in columns R and S should be placed in some out-of-the-way place; here, a number of columns are hidden so that you can see both ranges in one figure.

7. Choose the /**R**ange **N**ame **L**abel **R**ight command to use the names in cells F3..F14 to name the adjacent cells of column G. Finally, name the ranges G9..G10, G13..G14, I3..I14, T4 and T3..T14 (COLCRIT, PRIOR, DATABASE, TOPCOLOR, and COLOUTPUT, respectively).

The macro uses the /**D**ATA **E**XTRACT command to create the list and to pare it down.

An IF statement is contained in a single cell. The *true* statement, which represents any commands that are in the same cell as the IF command, executes only if the result of the logical test is true.

The line directly below the IF statement contains the *false statement*, which executes if the result of the logical test in the IF statement is false or if the program statements in the *true* portion don't transfer to another part of the macro. For example, in figure 27.16, the IF statement on line B12 tests to see if the user has pressed the Esc key. If the Esc key has been pressed, the macro branches to the program FINISH, which returns the cell pointer to its original position, and redisplays the frame, scroll bars, and grid lines, and then ends.

The IF statement adds significant strength to 1-2-3's advanced macro commands. Just remember, if the code in the *true* clause doesn't branch or execute a QUIT command, the program continues its execution right through the *false* clause, which means your macro has executed both the *true* and *false* commands. This may be as you intend but make sure that this is not an error in your program.

The INDICATE Command

The INDICATE command alters the mode indicator in the upper right corner of the 1-2-3 screen. This command commonly is used to provide custom indicators. The INDICATE command accepts a *string* argument that can be as long as the control panel (typically 80 characters). This function is useful for sending messages to the user during macro execution. The syntax of the INDICATE command is

    {INDICATE [*string*]}

{INDICATE} resets the mode indicator to *string*. The following INDICATE command displays the message START in the upper right corner of the screen:

    {INDICATE START}

> **Note**
>
> In the preceding example, START is a string, but the INDICATE command also can use a range name, cell address, or expression that evaluates to a string for the *string* argument.

The program displays the START message until you exit 1-2-3, retrieve another file, select **/W**orksheet **E**rase **Y**es, or restore the indicator to 1-2-3's control using

    {INDICATE}

To blank the indicator completely, use

    {INDICATE ""}

If the *string* argument is a number, 1-2-3 displays an error message.

The LET Command

The LET command places a value or string in a target cell location without moving the cell pointer to that location. {LET} could be used to place criteria in a database criteria range, for example. The syntax of the LET command is

    {LET location,expression}

{LET} places the value of *expression* in *location*. The LET command can use numeric values, string values, or formulas. If the cells named FIRST and LAST contain the labels BOB and JONES, respectively, the following statement stores BOB JONES in the cell named NAME:

    {LET NAME,FIRST&" "&LAST}

Like the DEFINE command, the LET command enables you to specify whether the expression should be stored as a string or a value by using the arguments :STRING and :VALUE (or :S and :V) as a suffix after the expression argument. The :STRING suffix stores the text of the argument in *location*; the :VALUE suffix evaluates the argument as a string or numeric formula and places the result in *location*. When a suffix isn't specified, {LET} stores the argument's numeric or string value if the formula is valid; otherwise, the text of the argument is stored. The following statement, for example, stores BOB JONES in NAME:

    {LET NAME,FIRST&" "&LAST:VALUE}

The next statement, however, stores the string FIRST&" "&LAST in NAME:

    {LET NAME,FIRST&" "&LAST:STRING}

Tip
The *string* argument can be a string, a range name, or a cell address containing a string. You can also use a valid string formula such as {INDICATE @CELLPOINTER("address")}.

Chapter 27—Advanced Macro Command Power Techniques

When you want to right-align a label in 1-2-3, you precede it with a quote ("), however, this leaves a trailing space after the last letter. In Wysiwyg, you can use two quotes ("") to cause true-right alignment, but if you aren't using Wysiwyg, this trick doesn't work. Suppose you want to build a macro that will true-right align your labels. To make the label true-right align if you change column widths, you need to use a formula which is dynamic. Figure 27.18 shows a short macro that uses the LET command and builds a dynamic formula in the label's cell to cause the label to true-right align. Note the documentation below the macro, in particular observe the formula which is in cell B8 of the macro, it reads

```
+"@REPEAT("" "",@CELL(""width"","&HOLD1&")
-@LENGTH("""&HOLD&""")&""""&HOLD&"""~"
```

Notice the use of triple quotes. Triple quotes tell 1-2-3 to treat the second quotes as a literal, that is, don't use it to indicate text within a formula. For example, if you type +"Hi", 1-2-3 displays Hi. If you type +"""Hi""", 1-2-3 displays "Hi".

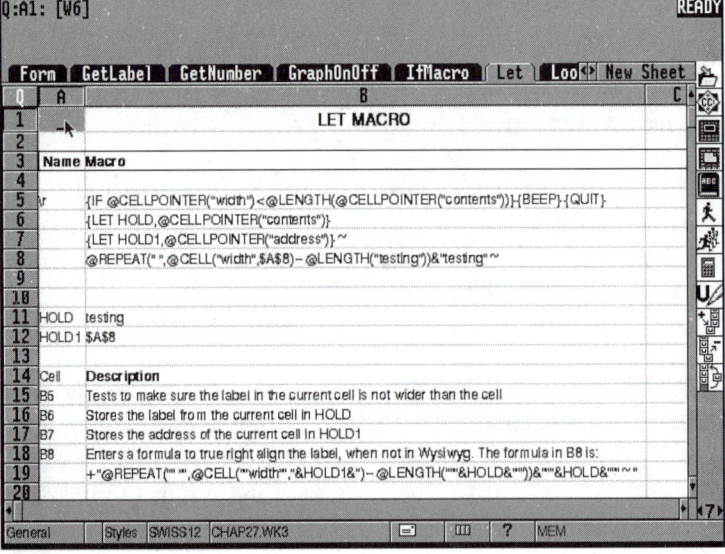

Fig. 27.18
This macro creates a formula to true-right align a label in a cell when the Wysiwyg display is off.

◀ "Finding solutions with Formulas and Functions," p. 157

Rather than use the LET command, you can move the cell pointer to the desired location with {GOTO} and enter the desired value into the cell. But the LET command has the major advantage of not disturbing the current location of the cell pointer. Furthermore, although you can enter numbers by using /**D**ata **F**ill, you cannot use this command to enter string values. Overall, the LET command is a convenient, useful, and fast way to set the value of a cell from within a program.

The LOOK Command

The LOOK command checks the type-ahead buffer for keystrokes. The syntax of the LOOK command is

{LOOK *location*}

{LOOK} places the first character from the type-ahead buffer into *location*. Location can be a cell address, a range, or a range name. You can use the LOOK command to interrupt macro processing when the user presses a key. To interrupt the macro, you have it check *location* to see what, if anything, the LOOK command put there. The macro can stop depending on what it finds in *location*.

> **Note**
>
> The type-ahead buffer is a small storage area in memory where DOS holds a few keystrokes until they are processed by an application, such as 1-2-3.

When you include the LOOK command in a program, the user can type a character at any time; the macro finds that single character when it executes the LOOK command. Because the character isn't removed from the type-ahead buffer, you must use the character or dispose of it before the program needs keyboard input or completes execution. One way to remove the first character from the type-ahead buffer is to use the GET commmand.

Although {LOOK} and {GET} are similar, they differ in an important way. {GET} pauses the macro until the user presses a key. Then {GET} places the keystroke into a cell, thus removing it from the type-ahead buffer. {LOOK}, however, places a copy of the keystroke into the cell specified by *location*, without pausing the macro or removing the keystroke from the buffer.

The \0 program uses the LOOK command (see fig. 27.19). This program starts by placing the time the macro starts in the cell named COUNTER. When the program encounters the LOOK command, 1-2-3 checks the keyboard type-ahead buffer and copies the first character found into the location called ANSWER.

In this example, an IF statement checks the contents of ANSWER and branches to the \CHECK_ANSWER macro if the user has typed a character. The IF command compares the contents of ANSWER to a null string. (A *null string* literally represents nothing.) You indicate a null string in a comparison test by placing two quotation marks side by side ("").

Fig. 27.19

The LOOK command is used to examine the type-ahead buffer and copy the first character from it.

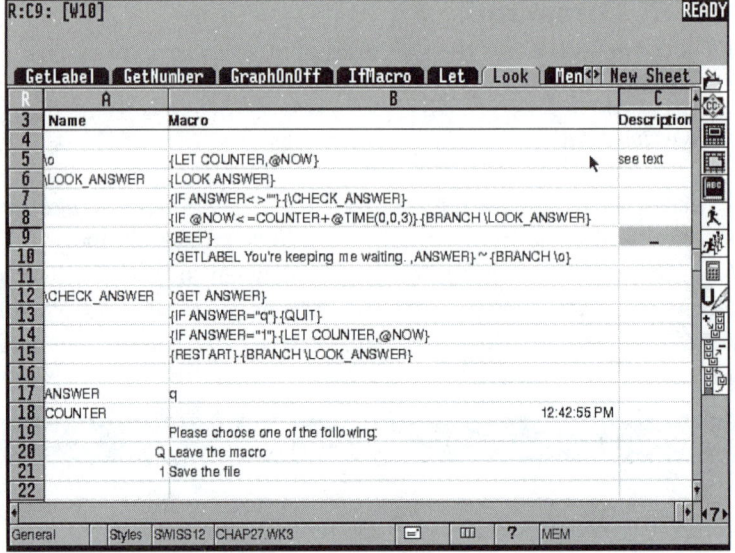

The GET command at the beginning of the \CHECK_ANSWER macro disposes of the keystroke that interrupted the loop. That is, {GET} removes the keystroke from the type-ahead buffer and places it in ANSWER.

The two IF statements in the \CHECK_ANSWER macro form a simple test of the user's menu selections (one of the selections resets the time stored in COUNTER). If the user doesn't type a character, 1-2-3 branches to cell B6, then executes the IF command in cell B7. This IF command tests whether the macro has waited more than 30 seconds for user input and, if it has, prompts the user.

This example demonstrates a powerful use of the LOOK command. By storing the time the macro starts, you can give the user a limited amount of time to make a selection. You can prompt the user if too much time elapses or have the macro make a default selection. You can produce a macro, for example, that continues after a specified time even if the user doesn't make a selection.

The LOOK command is most helpful when you have a long program to process and you want to be able to stop processing at certain points in the program. At several places in the program, you can enter a LOOK command followed by an IF statement (see fig. 27.19). Then, if the user presses a key, the program stops the next time a LOOK command executes. If no key is pressed, the program continues processing. In such cases, the LOOK command is preferable to the GET command, which always stops the program to wait for an entry.

The MENUBRANCH Command

The MENUBRANCH command defines a menu with as many as eight options and displays it in the control panel. You select options from this menu in the same way that you select options from a 1-2-3 menu. The syntax of the MENUBRANCH command is

{MENUBRANCH *location*}

{MENUBRANCH} executes a menu structure at *location*. Using from one to eight contiguous columns in the worksheet, you create the menu used by {MENUBRANCH}. Each column corresponds to one item in the menu. The upper left corner of the range named in a MENUBRANCH command must refer to the first menu item; otherwise, you receive the error message Invalid use of Menu macro command {MENUBRANCH}(S:B6) — Press F1(Help).

Each menu item consists of three or more rows in the same column. The first row is the name of the menu option. The option names can each be up to 512 characters long, but since you cannot view more than 80 character typically, there is no point in using longer names. Option names should begin with different letters, numbers, or characters. If two or more options begin with the same character and the user tries to use the first-letter technique to choose an option, 1-2-3 selects the first option with the specified letter.

The second row in the menu range contains optional descriptions of the menu items. When the cell pointer highlights the name of a menu option, the control panel displays the corresponding description under the menu option. Each description can contain as many as 80 characters of text. The description row must be present, even if it is blank.

When a choice is made from the menu, the macro executes commands under that choice beginning on the third row. Because control branches to the individual programs, program control must be directed by statements at the end of each individual program.

The menu items must be in contiguous columns (with no blank columns between them). A blank column in *location* signals the end of the menu structure.

The macro in figure 27.20 changes the case of text in the cell where the cell pointer is located. The part of the macro that converts text to propercase changes the first character of each word to uppercase. Normally, you would put the three macros in the third cell below the appropriate menu choice instead of using subroutines. Here they were arranged vertically in cells B12..B16 so that the individual commands of the macro are easier to read.

When converting to propercase, the macro checks to see if there are any apostrophes and branches accordingly. The range B18..B21 is named RANGE. The formulas for cells B18..B20 are shown in C18..C20; the formula for B21 is shown in B23. The only tricky formula is the one to deal with the apostrophe in a propercase situation, which is the formula in B21 and shown in cell B23.

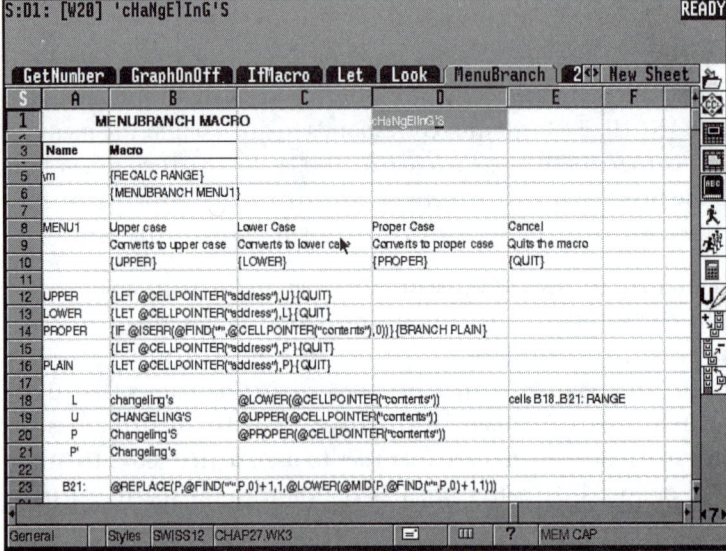

Fig. 27.20
This macro, which employs a MENUBRANCH command, changes the capitalization of labels to upper-, lower-, or propercase.

1-2-3's @PROPER function treats the letter following an apostrophe as the first letter of a new word and therefore capitalizes it. Therefore, propercase for *jane's* would be *Jane'S*. The formula in cell B21 finds the first character after the apostrophe and converts it back to lowercase.

> **Note**
>
> If you have a multilevel menu structure, you can make the Esc key function as it does in the 1-2-3 command menus (backing up to the menu preceding the current menu). If the user presses Esc instead of selecting a menu item, 1-2-3 stops displaying menu items and executes the next program command after the MENUBRANCH command. To make the program return to the preceding menu, add a {BRANCH} to transfer control back to the preceding MENUBRANCH command. Examples of this technique are shown in figure 27.5.

The MENUCALL Command

The MENUCALL command is similar to the MENUBRANCH command except that 1-2-3 executes the menu program as a subroutine. After executing an individual menu program, 1-2-3 continues executing the program at the cell immediately below the MENUCALL statement. The syntax of the MENUCALL command is

{MENUCALL *location*}

Figure 27.21 shows how to use a MENUCALL command to branch to a menu and then return to the macro's next line, which ends the macro.

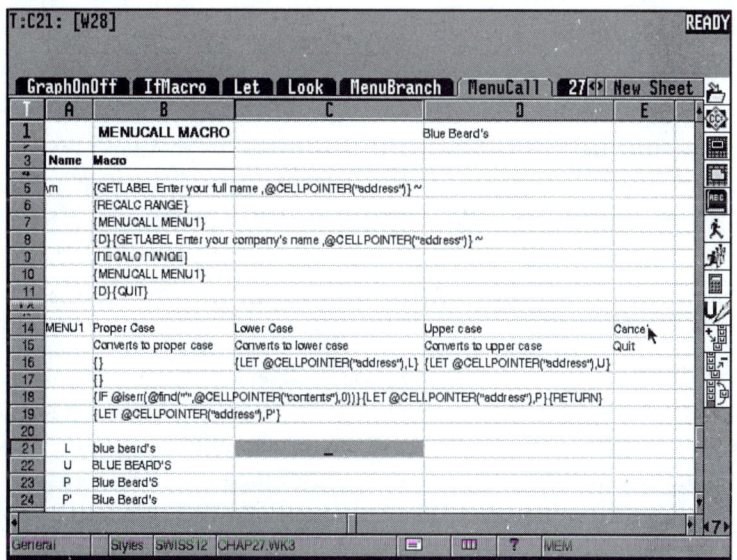

Fig. 27.21
The capitalization macro from figure 27.20 modified to demonstrate the use of the MENUCALL command to use the same menu system at more than one point in a macro.

When you use {MENUCALL}, 1-2-3 returns to the statement immediately following {MENUCALL} and continues executing until the program reads a blank cell or a RETURN command. In figure 27.21, 1-2-3 executes a call to the same menu structure twice in the same program. The formulas in cells B21..B24 are not shown but are identical to those in figure 27.20. Here the menu structure is laid out in a more typical fashion with each set of macro commands in the cells below their respective menu choices. The { } commands in cells B16..B17 are added to move the macro commands in cells B18..B19 down so that their full text is visible. The macro passes through any cells containing a { } command without taking any action.

The advantage of {MENUCALL} is that you can call the same menu from several places in a macro, return to the line after the calling point, and continue execution. This advantage is true of subroutines in general.

◀ "Using Functions To Analyze Data," p. 541

The ONERROR Command

Normally, a system error (such as an open disk drive door) during execution halts the execution of macro programs. The ONERROR command gives you a way to sidestep system errors that normally cause program termination. The general syntax of the ONERROR command is

{ONERROR branch,[message]}

{ONERROR} traps an error and passes program control to the cell indicated by *branch*. You can record the 1-2-3 error message in *message* (the optional second argument).

Because an ONERROR statement must be executed before it can trap an error, you may want to include an ONERROR statement near the start of your programs. Note that only one ONERROR statement can be in effect at a time. When you write your programs, make sure that the correct ONERROR is active when its specific error is most probable. A single ONERROR command will trap one error; if you want to trap more than one error, you need to have more than one ONERROR command in your macro.

The ONERROR statement shown in figure 27.22 acts as a safeguard against leaving drive A empty or not closing the drive door. If an error occurs, program control passes to the \CHECK_DRIVE macro, and 1-2-3's error message is placed in the cell named MESSAGE. The error message is incorporated into the prompt of the second GETLABEL command. The user responds by correcting the problem and pressing Enter. Then the macro branches back up to {RETRY} and attempts to save the file again.

Fig. 27.22
The ONERROR command used to prompt users to close the drive door.

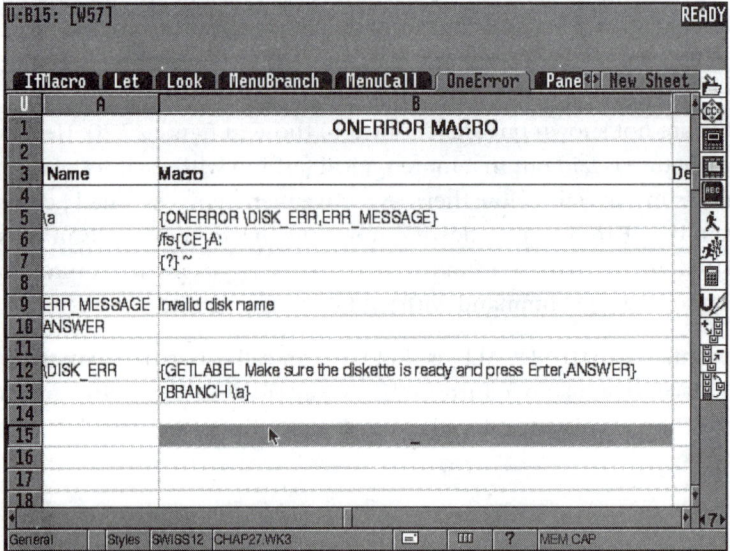

In addition to the simple example shown in figure 27.22, you can examine the error message from the ONERROR command and branch to a subroutine to correct the error.

> **Caution**
>
> The ONERROR command clears the subroutine stack, which may cause a macro to fail unexpectedly. 1-2-3 must keep track of the location of the macro command that calls a subroutine so that it knows where to return to when a subroutine has been completed. 1-2-3 keeps track of this information in a memory location that LOTUS calls a subroutine stack.

> **Troubleshooting**
>
> *My GETNUMBER command keeps entering ERR when I enter a date. Aren't dates numbers?*
>
> Dates may be numbers depending on what format you enter them in. For example, 1/1/93 is accepted as a date, but January 1, 1993 produces an ERR.
>
> *I get a* Syntax error in macro key/range *at the cell with my GETNUMBER and GETLABEL commands.*
>
> Check to see that there are no spaces after the prompt text or before the location argument.
>
> *The 1 2 3 mode indicator does not return after my macros finish executing.*
>
> You need to add the command {INDICATE}, without any argument, near the end of your macro.
>
> The ONERROR command is causing an *Unrecognized key/range name* error.
>
> Make sure you spelled this command as ONERROR not ONEERROR.
>
> *I have an ONERROR command in my macro, but the macro still crashes.*
>
> Your macro probably contains more than one error. You need one ONERROR command per possible error.

The OPEN Command

The OPEN command opens an ASCII file so that you can write to or read from that file. In the command's second argument, you can specify whether you want to read only, write only, or read from and write to the file.

1-2-3 accepts only one open ASCII file at a time. If you want to work with more than one ASCII file in your application, you must open each file before using it; 1-2-3 closes an open ASCII file before opening and using the next file.

The syntax of the OPEN command is

{OPEN *filename,access-mode*}

The *filename* argument can be a string, an expression with a string value, or a cell containing a string or a string expression. The string must be a valid operating system file name or path name. You can specify a file in the current directory by its name and extension. To specify a file in another directory, you may need to add a drive identification, a subdirectory path, or a complete operating system path to the file name and extension.

The *access-mode* argument is one of four characters (R, W, A, and M) that specify whether you want to read only, write only, or both read and write to the file, as explained in the following table.

Access-Mode Argument	Description
R	Read access opens an existing file and enables the READ and READLN commands. You cannot write to a file opened with Read access.
W	Write access opens a new file and enables the WRITE and WRITELN commands. Any existing file with the specified name is erased and replaced by the new file.
A	Append access opens an existing file and enables both the READ (or READLN) and WRITE (or WRITELN) commands. Append access places the byte pointer at the end of the file.
M	Modify access opens an existing file and enables both READ (or READLN) and WRITE (or WRITELN) commands. You cannot use Modify access to create a file. Modify access places the byte pointer at the beginning of the file.

The OPEN command succeeds if it can open the file with the access you request. If the OPEN command succeeds, program execution continues with the cell below the OPEN statement. Any commands after OPEN in the current cell are ignored.

The OPEN command fails with an error if the disk drive isn't ready. Use the ONERROR command to handle the possibility of such an error.

If you specify an access mode of READ, APPEND, or MODIFY but the file doesn't exist in the indicated directory, the OPEN command fails and program execution continues with the commands after the OPEN command in the current cell. To deal with the failure, you can place one or more commands in the cell after the OPEN command; for example, you can use a {BRANCH} or a subroutine call to a macro that deals with the failure.

The following statement opens the existing file named PASTDUE in the current directory for reading; if the file cannot be opened, the program branches to the routine \FIXIT:

    {OPEN "PASTDUE",R}{BRANCH \FIXIT}

The following statement opens the new file named CLIENTS.DAT in drive C, subdirectory DATA, for writing:

    {OPEN "C:\DATA\CLIENTS.DAT",W}

The following statement opens the file named in the cell FILE for Append access; if the file cannot be opened, the program branches to the routine \RETRY:

    {OPEN FILE,A}{BRANCH \RETRY}

In the following statement, 1-2-3 opens the file named in the cell FILE for Modify access; if the file cannot be opened, the program branches to the routine \RETRY:

    {OPEN FILE,M}{BRANCH \RETRY}

For an example that uses all the file commands except the READLN and WRITE commands (which are similar to the READ and WRITELN commands), refer to figure 27.8. In this example, the program named \r uses the OPEN command to open a file.

Figure 27.8 demonstrates the use of the file-manipulation commands to read data in 100-byte increments from one file (INPUT.TXT) and to write the same data to another file (OUTPUT.TXT) in lines that end with a carriage return and line feed.

As you look at the program in figure 27.8, take note of the following points:

- You must specify the value to use in REC_LEN before you execute the \r macro. This value determines the number of characters (bytes) to be read each time the READ_WRITE macro executes.

- The {OPEN "OUTPUT.TXT",R}{OPEN "OUTPUT.TXT",W} line creates OUTPUT.TXT if that file doesn't already exist. If the {OPEN} with Read access fails, {OPEN} with Write access creates the file. The subsequent {OPEN}, with an Append access statement, places the file pointer at the end of the file so that the WRITELN command extends the file.

■ {GETPOS} and {SETPOS} always refer to the currently open file (INPUT.TXT in this example). OUTPUT.TXT is closed when these commands are active.

The PANELOFF Command

The PANELOFF command freezes the control panel, suppressing the display of 1-2-3 commands in the control panel during macro execution. Note, however, that the advanced macro commands MENUBRANCH, MENUCALL, GETLABEL, GETNUMBER, and INDICATE override the PANELOFF command. The syntax of the PANELOFF command is

{PANELOFF [clear]}

The optional argument, clear, removes almost everything from the control panel and status line before freezing the control panel. Using {PANELOFF} helps speed up your macros.

In the following example, {PANELOFF} suppresses display in the control panel of the /Copy command in the second line of code:

```
{PANELOFF}
/cRANGE_1~RANGE_2~
```

> **Note**
>
> When the macro ends, 1-2-3 restores the panel display as soon as the user moves the cell pointer or issues a command.

Tip
Use {PANELON} at the end of a macro as a fast way to restore the control panel.

Figure 27.23 shows an example of a macro that uses {PANELOFF}. This macro executes menu commands before the loop to clear a range, create a new range name table, and rename the table range. Within the loop, the macro uses the menu command /Range Erase every time a range name, which has a cell address in sheet A:, is found. It is often a nuisance to get rid of dead range names; this macro does it for you automatically. Use the /Range Name Table command to list all your range names. Then, in the second column of the table, replace the cell addresses of any names you want deleted with an x. When you run the macro, all range names marked with an x are deleted.

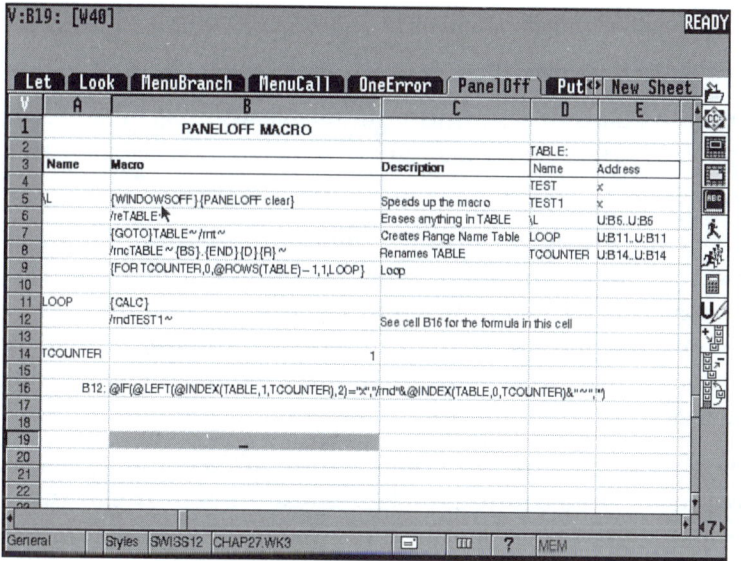

Fig. 27.23
A macro that automatically deletes unwanted range names. It runs faster because it uses the PANELOFF command.

The PANELON Command

The PANELON command unfreezes the control panel. The syntax of the PANELON command is

{PANELON}

{PANELON} reactivates the display in the control panel. In general you do not need to employ this command because 1-2-3 reactivates the panel as soon as the macro ends. In the following example, {PANELOFF} freezes the control panel display while RANGE_1 is copied to RANGE_2; then {PANELON} reactivates the control panel.

    {PANELOFF}
    /cRANGE_1~RANGE_2~
    {PANELON}

The PUT Command

The PUT command places a value within a range at the intersection of a specified row and a column. The syntax of the PUT command is

{PUT *range,col,row,value*}

{PUT} places *value* into the specified cell within *range*. *Range* is a range name or cell address to contain the value. *Col* is the column offset within the range; *row* defines the row offset within the range. *Value* is the value to place in the cell. *Col*, *row*, and *value* can be values, cells, or formulas.

914 Chapter 27—Advanced Macro Command Power Techniques

Consider the following PUT statement:

{PUT TABLE,COL,ROW,ARG4}

This statement places the contents of the cell named ARG4 in the range named TABLE at the intersection defined by the values in cells COL and ROW.

Keep in mind that the row and column offset numbers used with the PUT command follow the same conventions followed by functions (the first column is number 0; the second is number 1, and so on). Also, the row and column values must not specify a location outside the range. If this happens, the macro fails, and 1-2-3 informs you that the PUT statement contains an invalid range.

Figures 27.24 and 27.25 demonstrate a practical use of the PUT command. Suppose you receive a download of daily sales totals in two columns, as shown in the INPUT range of figure 27.24. You need to rearrange the data to put it in a layout similar to that shown in figure 27.25. In other words, the sales figures must be moved to the proper day of the appropriate month. This is not a pleasant job to do manually, but the PUT command can whirl right through it lickety-split. The incoming data may be in any date order, and there need not be data for every day.

Fig. 27.24

The incoming data and the macro used to distribute the data into the range TABLE shown in figure 27.25.

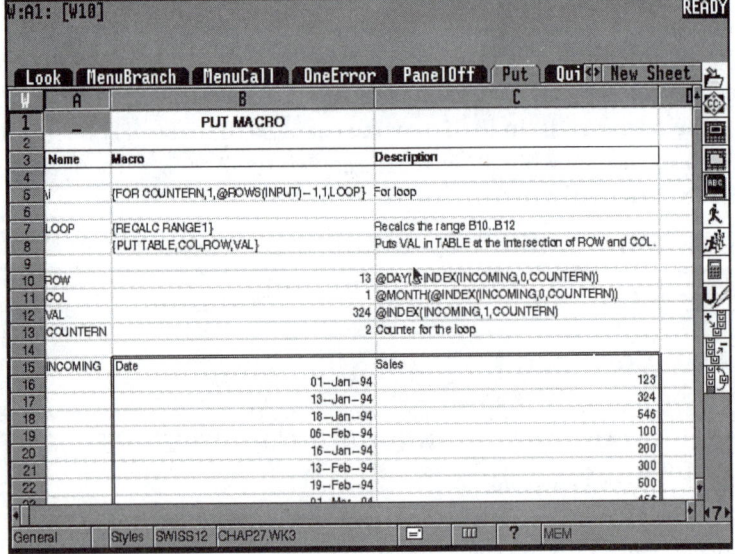

The short but effective macro shown in figure 27.24 rearranges the data at the press of a key. The PUT statement's arguments are the ROW, COL, and VAL ranges in cells B11, B12, and B13 which contain the three formulas shown in the corresponding range of column C.

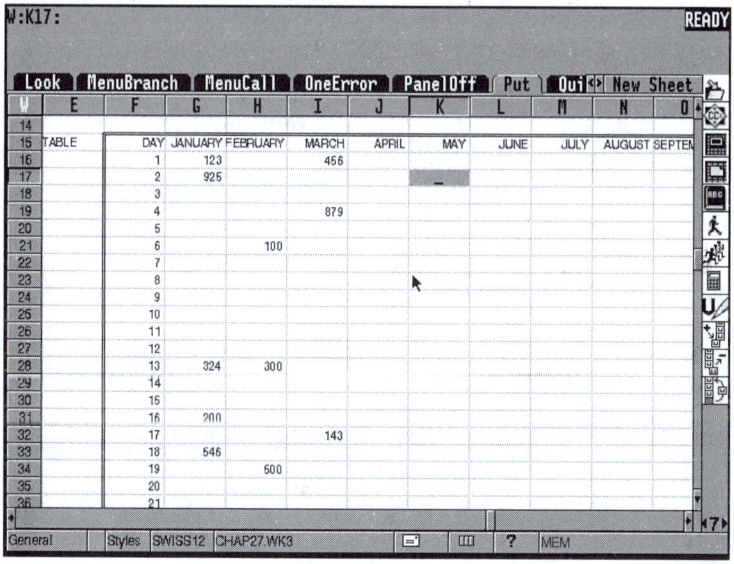

Fig. 27.25

The output range for the PUT command macro shown in figure 27.24.

The QUIT Command

The QUIT command forces the program to terminate unconditionally. Even without a QUIT command, the program terminates if it encounters a cell that is empty or that contains an entry other than a string (unless the program is a subroutine called by another program). Always include a QUIT statement in your program at the point at which you want execution to stop. (Conversely, don't put a QUIT command at the end of a program you intend to call as a subroutine.) The format of the QUIT command is

    {QUIT}

{QUIT} halts program execution. In the following example, the QUIT command forces the program sequence to terminate unconditionally

    {HOME}/fs~r{QUIT}

When {QUIT} is preceded by an IF command, as in the following example, the macro doesn't terminate unconditionally:

    {GETNUMBER "Enter a number: ",INPUT}
    {IF INPUT<1}{QUIT}

916 Chapter 27—Advanced Macro Command Power Techniques

Figure 27.26 shows a macro that goes down a column of data and boldfaces all the cells containing SUM functions. This macro demonstrates quite a number of useful techniques. The QUIT command after the test in cell B10 ends the macro if the test in that cell is true. The macro also uses two methods to determine where to terminate; first it moves the cell pointer to the last active cell in the worksheet with the {END} {HOME} combination and then sends that row's number to the cell MAX. Later this value is used in the FOR statement as the *stop* value for the loop. The second test to determine when the macro should stop is the {IF @CELLPOINTER("prefix")="\"} test that searches for the first cell with the repeat label prefix. You might need to use either one of these or another method to determine when a loop should end. With this macro your data can have a maximum of one repeat label prefix, and the prefix must be in the cell before the last total. A second point to notice is the use of four different CELLPOINTER functions.

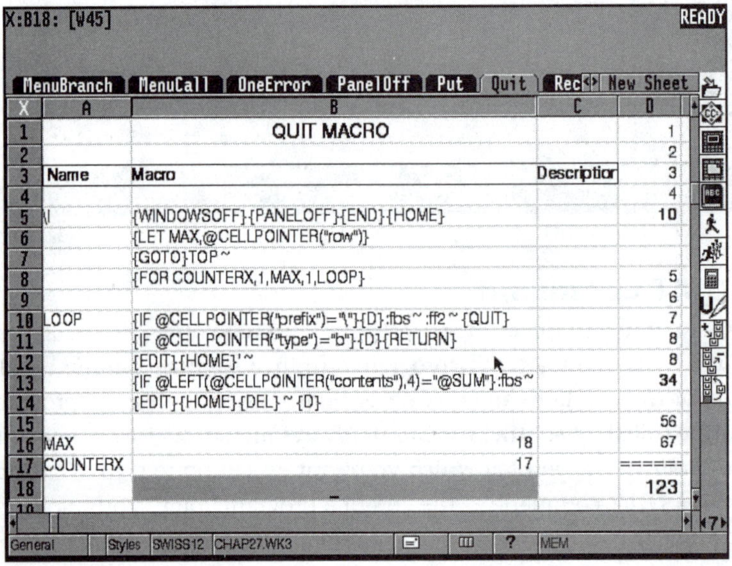

Fig. 27.26
A macro using a QUIT command. This macro moves down a column and boldfaces all the cells which contain the SUM function.

The READ Command

The READ command reads a specified number of characters from the currently open ASCII file, beginning at the present file pointer location. {READ} places the characters read from the ASCII file in the worksheet at the indicated cell location. The syntax of the READ command is

{READ *bytecount,location*}

{READ} copies the specified number of characters from a file to *location*. *Bytecount* is the number of bytes to read, starting at the current position of the file pointer. *Bytecount* can be any number between 0 and 511 (the maximum number of characters in a 1-2-3 label). *Location* is the cell or range to contain the characters from the file.

{READ} places the specified number of characters from the file into *location* as a label. If *bytecount* is greater than the number of characters remaining in the file, 1-2-3 reads the remaining characters into the specified *location*. After the READ command executes, the file pointer is positioned at the character following the last character read.

The following statement transfers information from the open file into the cell named INLINE.

    {READ REC_LEN,INLINE}

The amount of information transferred is determined by the contents of the cell named REC_LEN, which can contain either a value or a formula.

The READ command is useful when you want to read a specific number of characters into a location in the current worksheet. A data file that contains fixed-length records, for example, can be read conveniently by a READ command with the *bytecount* argument specified as the record length.

In ASCII text files from a word processing program or text editor, each line may end with a carriage-return-line-feed sequence, or the carriage-return-line-feed sequence may be only at the end of a paragraph. Often, ASCII text files with the carriage return and line feed at the end of each line can be read by using {READLN} (which reads a variable-length line) instead of {READ} (which reads a fixed number of characters).

The READLN Command

The READLN command reads one line of information (up to the next carriage return and line feed) from the currently open ASCII file, beginning at the file pointer's current position. The characters read are placed in the cell location in the current worksheet. You can use {READLN} instead of {READ} to read lines delimited by a carriage-return-line-feed combination. The READLN command syntax is

    {READLN *location*}

Starting at the current byte-pointer position in the ASCII file, {READLN} copies the remainder of the line from the ASCII file to *location*. In the following example, {READLN} copies a line from an open file into the cell named HERE.

    {READLN HERE}

Use {READLN} to read a line of text from a file whose lines are delimited by a carriage-return-line-feed combination. Use {READLN}, for example, to read the next line of an ASCII text file. ASCII text files (also referred to as print files) are created with 1-2-3's **/P**rint **F**ile command; 1-2-3 assigns the PRN file extension to these files.

If you attempt to read past the end of a file or if no file is open, 1-2-3 ignores the READ or READLN command and program execution continues with the next command. To handle the problem of an unexecuted READ or READLN statement, place a {BRANCH} or {*subroutine*} call after the READ or READLN command.

The RECALC and RECALCCOL Commands

You can use the RECALC and RECALCCOL macro commands to recalculate a portion of the worksheet. Being able to recalculate only a portion of the worksheet is useful for large worksheets in which recalculation time is long or for worksheets in which you need to recalculate certain values before proceeding to the next processing step. The syntax for the commands for partial recalculation are

    {RECALC *location*,[*condition*],[*iteration-number*]}

    {RECALCCOL *location*,[*condition*],[*iteration-number*]}

In both formats, *location* is a range or range name that specifies the cell containing the formulas to recalculate. *Condition* is either a logical expression or a reference to a cell. If you specify a cell for *condition*, the cell must be part of the recalculation range containing a logical expression. If you include the *condition* argument, 1-2-3 recalculates the range repeatedly until *condition* has a logical value of TRUE (<> 0). *Iteration-number* is the number of times to recalculate the formulas in *location*. If you include *iteration-number*, you must also include *condition* (use the value 0 to make *condition* always FALSE).

The *condition* and *iteration-number* arguments are optional. If *condition* is a reference to a cell outside the recalculation range, the value of *condition*—either TRUE (1) or FALSE (0)—doesn't change, and *condition* doesn't control the partial recalculation.

The RECALC and RECALCCOL commands differ in the order in which cells in the specified range are recalculated. RECALC calculates all the cells in the first row of the range, then all the cells in the second row, and so on. The RECALCCOL command calculates the cells in the first column of the range, then the cells in the second column, and so on. With either command, 1-2-3 recalculates only cells within the specified range.

> **Tip**
> Use {RECALC} if the formula to be recalculated is below and to the left of the cells on which it depends. Use {RECALCCOL} if the formula is above and to the right of the cells on which it depends.

> **Caution**
> You may have to use {CALC} if the formula to recalculate is above and to the left of cells on which it depends.

The formulas in the recalculation range can refer to values in cells outside the range; however, {RECALC} and {RECALCCOL} don't update those values. When the RECALC or RECALCCOL command is executed, the partial recalculation occurs immediately, although the results don't appear on-screen until the screen is redrawn. Meanwhile, 1 2 3 uses the recalculated numbers in calculations and conditional tests.

> **Tip**
> The CALC command recalculates in "natural order," but it affects the entire worksheet. To recalculate a smaller range in natural order, copy the range back onto itself.

Figure 27.27 shows an example of the use of the RECALC command. Assume you have a database, named DATA, containing many lines for each employee. One at a time you want to extract each employee's records to an output area which is part of a range you will print. You have a list of all the employee numbers in a range called EMPLOYEE, and because your worksheet contains many formulas, you have it set to manual recalculation, but you need to recalculate the criteria cell before each extract command.

The macro shown in figure 27.27 extracts records for each employee, one at a time, and prints them. Notice that the print, data input, criteria, and output ranges are defined before the loop is executed. Also, the type of query, an extract, is established before the loop executes. Because these commands are done outside the loop, each command is executed only once. If these commands were executed within the loop, they would be executed many times, slowing down the macro considerably.

The formula in cell B19, and shown in cell C19, controls the extraction process and is recalculated during each loop. This formula, which is part of the criteria range, determines the next employee number for the extract command.

Fig. 27.27
A macro using the RECALC command to control the generation of a report for each employee.

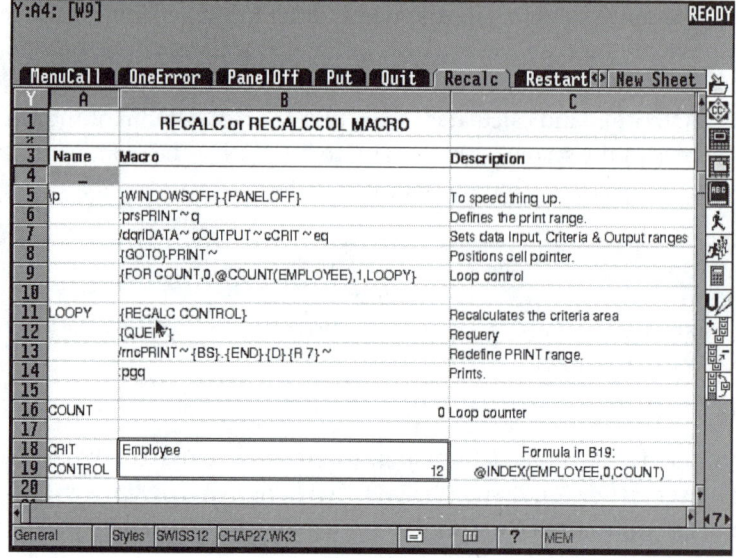

If the macro program ends and you want to be sure that the recalculated numbers are on-screen, use the PgUp and PgDn keys to move the window away from and back to the recalculated range. The act of moving away and back again updates the screen and displays the current values in the recalculated range.

In a program, you may need to use {CALC}, {RECALC}, or {RECALCCOL} after commands such as LET, GETNUMBER, and ? or after such 1-2-3 commands as **/R**ange **I**nput. You don't need to recalculate after invoking such 1-2-3 commands such as **/C**opy and **/M**ove; 1-2-3 automatically recalculates the affected ranges, even during program execution.

The RESTART Command

Just as the main program can call subroutines, one subroutine can call another. As 1-2-3 moves from one subroutine to the next, the program saves the addresses of where it has been. This technique is called *stacking* or *saving addresses on a stack*. By saving the addresses on a stack, 1-2-3 can trace its way back through the subroutine calls to the main program.

To prevent 1-2-3 from returning by the same path, you can eliminate the stack by using the RESTART command. {RESTART} enables you to cancel a subroutine at any time during execution. Although seldom used, {RESTART} can be quite helpful. 1-2-3's stack, for example, cannot exceed 32 nesting levels; if you attempt more than 32 calls, the macro terminates with an error.

You can clear the stack, however, by using {RESTART} before this problem occurs.

The RESTART command normally is used with an IF statement under a conditional testing evaluation. The syntax for this command is

{RESTART}

{RESTART} cancels a subroutine. For an example of how you can use the {RESTART} command to prevent a user from entering incorrect data in a database, see figure 27.28. In this example, the \b macro first prompts the user for his or her last name. Then the program makes a call to \SUB_1, which calls \SUB_2. \SUB_2, in turn, calls \SUB_3.

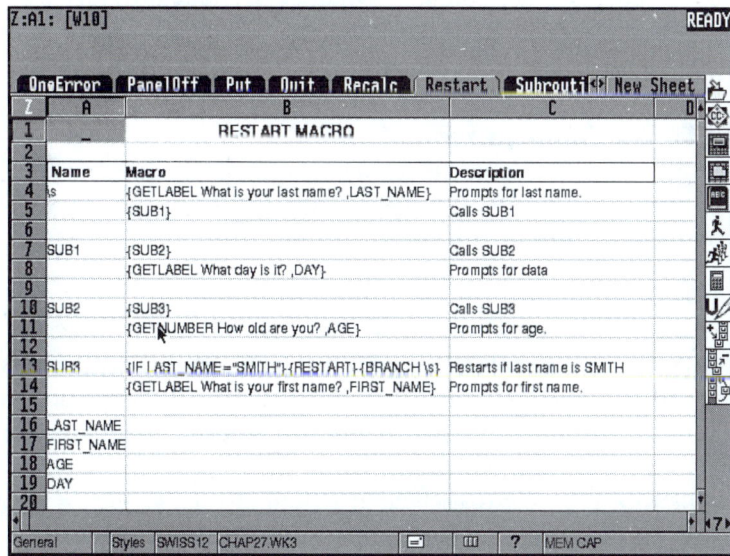

Fig. 27.28
A macro that uses the RESTART command to clear the subroutine stack.

The \SUB_3 program first checks to see whether the user entered SMITH as a LAST_NAME. If the user entered SMITH, the program doesn't accept the entry; the program executes a {RESTART} and then a {BRANCH} back to the \b macro. If the user entered anything other than SMITH, \SUB_3 prompts for the FIRST_NAME. When the user presses Enter, \SUB_3 ends, and control returns to the second line of \SUB_2, which displays the prompt How old are you? After the user enters something, \SUB_2 ends, and the second line of \SUB_1 executes.

The RETURN Command

The RETURN command indicates the end of subroutine execution and returns program control to the cell immediately below the cell that called the subroutine (or to other commands in the cell that contained the subroutine call). Don't confuse {RETURN} with {QUIT}, which ends the program completely. {RETURN} can be used with an IF statement to return conditionally from a subroutine. The syntax of this command is

{RETURN}

{RETURN} returns control from a subroutine or a subroutine loop back to the calling macro. Refer to figure 27.26 to see the use of the RETURN command. The IF statement in cell B11 checks to see if the current cell is blank, and if it is, the macro moves the cell pointer down one cell and returns to the loop without completing the remaining lines of the subroutine. After {RETURN}, the macro continues looping.

The SETPOS Command

The SETPOS command sets the file pointer to a specified position. {SETPOS} counts positions from the first character (position 0) to the last character in the ASCII file. The syntax of the command is

{SETPOS *file-position*}

SETPOS sets a new position for a file pointer. The *file-position* argument is a number or an expression resulting in a number specifying the character at which you want to position the file pointer. The first character in the file is at position 0, the second is at position 1, and so on. Suppose that you have a database file with 100 records, each 20 bytes long. To access the first record, you can use the following commands:

```
{SETPOS 0}
{READ 20,buffer}
```

To read the 15th record, use the following commands:

```
{SETPOS (15-1)*20}
{READ 20,buffer}
```

Nothing prevents you from setting the file pointer past the end of the file. If the file pointer is set at or past the end of the file and the program executes a READ or READLN command, the command does nothing; program execution continues with the next command on the same line as the {READ} or

{READLN}. If you set the file pointer at or past the end of the file and execute a WRITE or WRITELN command, 1-2-3 first extends the file to the length specified by the file pointer and then, starting at the file pointer, writes the characters.

> **Caution**
>
> If you inadvertently set the file pointer to a large number with {SETPOS} and then write to the file, 1-2-3 attempts to expand the file and write the text at the end of the file. If the file doesn't fit on the disk, the WRITE command does nothing; program execution continues with the next command on the same line as the WRITE command. If the file fits on the disk, however, 1-2-3 extends the file and writes the text at the end of the file.

If a file currently isn't open, {SETPOS} does nothing; execution continues with the next command on the same line as the SETPOS command. Otherwise, when the program completes the SETPOS command, execution continues on the next line of the program. You can place a BRANCH command or a subroutine call after the SETPOS command to handle the problem of an unexecuted statement. Refer to figure 27.8 for an example of the SETPOS command.

The {subroutine} Command

A *subroutine* is an independent program that can be run from within the main program. Calling a subroutine is as easy as enclosing the name of a routine in braces—for example, {\SUB}. To call a subroutine, you use the *{subroutine}* command. The syntax of this command is

{subroutine [argument1],[argument2],…,[argumentN]}

Subroutine is the name of the subroutine to call. You name a subroutine by using the **/R**ange **N**ame **C**reate command, just as you would any other range.

Argument1, *argument2*, and so on are optional arguments for the subroutine. These arguments are cells, range names, strings, formulas, or functions. If you want to pass arguments to a subroutine you must pair the arguments with arguments in a DEFINE command.

When 1-2-3 encounters a subroutine name in braces, the program passes control to the named routine. Then, when the routine is finished (when 1-2-3 encounters a blank cell or a RETURN command), program control passes to the next command in the cell containing the subroutine command or to the cell below.

By using subroutines, you can decrease macro-creation time. Rather than include the same macro lines to display a help screen in each advanced macro command program you create, you can type the macro lines once to create the help screen and then call those lines as a subroutine from each macro.

By using subroutines, you can easily isolate a problem. If you suspect that a subroutine is creating a problem, for example, you can replace the call to the subroutine with {BEEP}. Then run the macro. If the macro runs correctly, beeping when the subroutine should be called, you know that the problem is in the subroutine.

Subroutines are easy to enhance. If you decide to add new commands, you modify the subroutine once. All programs that call that subroutine reflect the new commands.

> **Caution**
>
> Because 1-2-3 has a limit of 32 nesting levels (subroutine levels) in its stack, the macro terminates with an error if you attempt more than 32 calls.

Figures 27.29 and 27.30 show a macro which employs a subroutine call to query and print multiple times. Suppose that every day, you need to generate a report listing the prior day's sales. Also, at the beginning of every month you need a report of all the prior month's transaction in addition to the daily report. And at the beginning of the year you need a list of all the prior year's transactions, the prior month's transaction, as well as the regular report for the previous day. The PRINT_REPORT subroutine is called three times when the annual report is run, twice when the monthly reports are run, and once daily. The **D**ata **Q**uery command is used to extract the appropriate records.

Figure 27.29 shows the macro while figure 27.30 shows a sample input area, the criteria and formula ranges. The ranges CRITERIA, CRIT_ROW, CRIT1, CRIT2, and FIRST_DATE are in cells D37..E38, D38..E38, D38, E38 and B46, respectively. Additionally, the ranges START_YEAR, END_YEAR, START_MONTH, and END_MONTH, in cells B30..B33, contain the criteria formulas, which are also displayed in cells C30..C33. Each of these formulas references the FIRST_DATE cell, which is the first date cell of the input range.

Listing the Advanced Macro Commands

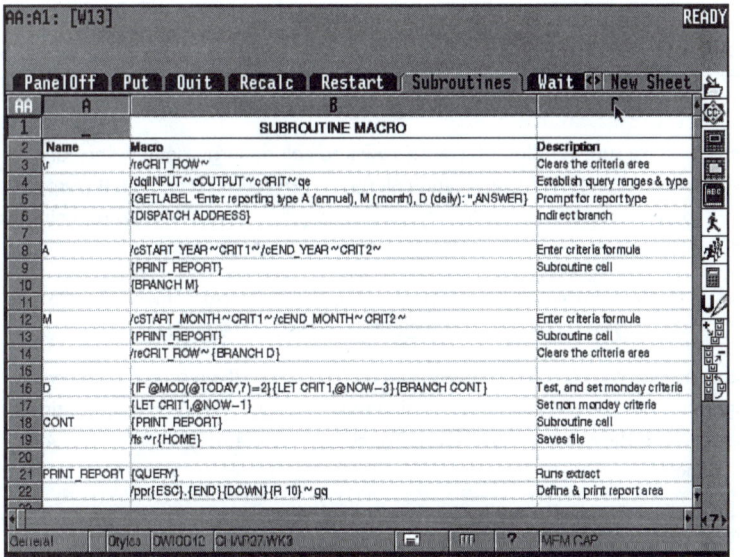

Fig. 27.29
A macro employing a subroutine command to repeatedly call a query and print routine.

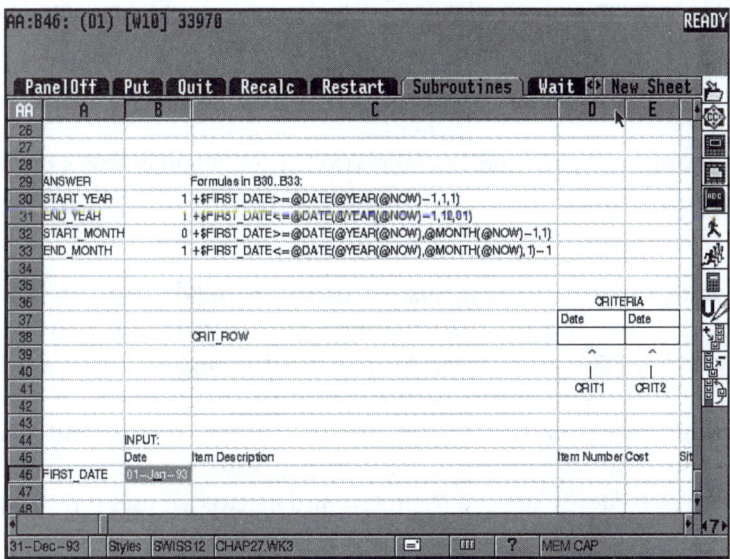

Fig. 27.30
A continuation of the macro in figure 27.29.

> **Troubleshooting**
>
> *The PUT command in my macro is causing an* `Invalid range` *error.*
>
> Check to make sure you don't have the row and column arguments reversed. Also, remember that the first row and column of your target range are 0 (zero), not 1. Therefore, your last row (or column) equals the number of rows (or columns) minus 1.
>
> *When I run a short macro in a small spreadsheet, the macro crashes with the message* `Memory full`. *I've checked everything, but I can't locate the problem.*
>
> Check to see if you have a nested subroutine (this is called a *recursive statement* in programming). For example, a subroutine that calls itself may fill the subroutine stack, causing the `memory full` error. To recover the memory, run the RESTART command.

The SYSTEM Command

The SYSTEM command executes any batch or operating system command and uses the following syntax:

{SYSTEM *command*}

The following example shows how the SYSTEM command executes the batch command PARK:

{SYSTEM PARK}

The operating system *command* that you execute with {SYSTEM} can be any operating system command or batch command. You can use as many as 127 characters to specify the *command*. Keep in mind a couple of warnings when you use {SYSTEM}. First, if you attempt to load a memory-resident program, you may not be able to resume 1-2-3. Second, some batch commands may prevent you from resuming 1-2-3. For these two reasons, be particularly careful to save your files before you begin testing a macro that uses {SYSTEM}.

The WAIT Command

The WAIT command causes the program to pause until an appointed time. The general syntax of the WAIT command is

{WAIT *argument*}

{WAIT} waits until the time or elapsed time specified by *argument*.

The *argument* in the WAIT command must contain a date plus a time. If you want the program to wait until 6:00 p.m. today to continue, use

    {WAIT @TODAY+@TIME(18,00,00)}

In this example, @TODAY returns the serial number for 12:00 a.m. on today's date. Then +@TIME(18,00,00) adds 18 hours (or .75 days) to the serial number, causing the WAIT statement to pause macro execution until 6:00 p.m. today. To make a program pause for 30 seconds, you can use either of the following expressions:

    {WAIT @NOW+@TIME(00,00,30)}

    {WAIT @NOW+.00035}

The macro in figure 27.31 uses this command to pause for 30 seconds between each print command, slowing the printing process down so that it doesn't overload the network print queue and crash the system. By allowing the printer enough time to print each invoice before sending the next one, the macro runs without crashing. The INDICATE command is used to keep the user informed as to the invoice being printed. The message for the INDICATE command is in cell B19, the formula for which is displayed in cell B20.

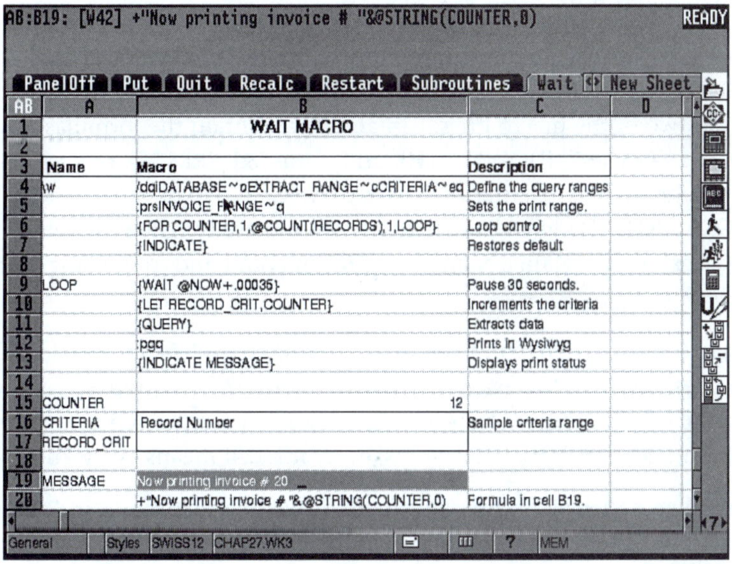

Fig. 27.31
A macro using the WAIT command to slow printing to a small print queue, thus preventing the system from crashing.

The WINDOWSOFF Command

The WINDOWSOFF command freezes the main part of the screen but does not affect the display of program commands in the control panel. The WINDOWSOFF command suppresses the current screen display, regardless of whether the program is executing.

{WINDOWSOFF} is useful when you are creating applications for beginning 1-2-3 users. {WINDOWSOFF} displays only the screen changes that the user must see; the command prevents the display of other changes that may confuse beginners. The syntax of the WINDOWSOFF command is

    {WINDOWSOFF}

In the following example, {WINDOWSOFF} suppresses the automatic screen-redrawing associated with the /Copy and /Calc commands.

    {WINDOWSOFF}
    /cRANGE_1~RANGE_2~{CALC}

The {WINDOWSOFF} and {PANELOFF} commands can have a significant effect on program execution time, in some cases reducing execution time by as much as 50 percent. Clearly, performance improvements depend on the particular application.

> **Tip**
> If an error occurs while {WINDOWSOFF} is in effect, normal updating of the worksheet window doesn't occur. Develop and test your programs without the WINDOWSOFF and WINDOWSON commands; then add these commands to the debugged and tested programs.

The macro in figure 27.32 illustrates how to use {WINDOWSOFF} and {PANELOFF} to eliminate screen redraws and reduce execution time. Note that two of the macro lines, B14 and B17, contain the formulas +"{GOTO}"&TEMP&"~{DOWN NTH}" and +"/m~"&HERE&"~", respectively. To complete the macro, enter the labels COUNTER, TEMP, TOP, HERE, BOTTOM, AND NTH in cells A26..A31 and use these to name the cells B26..B31 using the /Range Name Label Right command (these ranges are not shown in figure 27.32).

This macro sums up every *n*th cell in a column. To understand what this macro does, consider the example shown in figure 27.33. Suppose you want to sum the cells for Dept1. They are on every other row, which means you want to sum for n = 2. In other words, every *n*th cell means every 2nd cell.

The user places the cell pointer anywhere he wants the formula and then presses Alt+w. The macro prompts them for the top and bottom cells of the range and the value of n. Then it builds the formula.

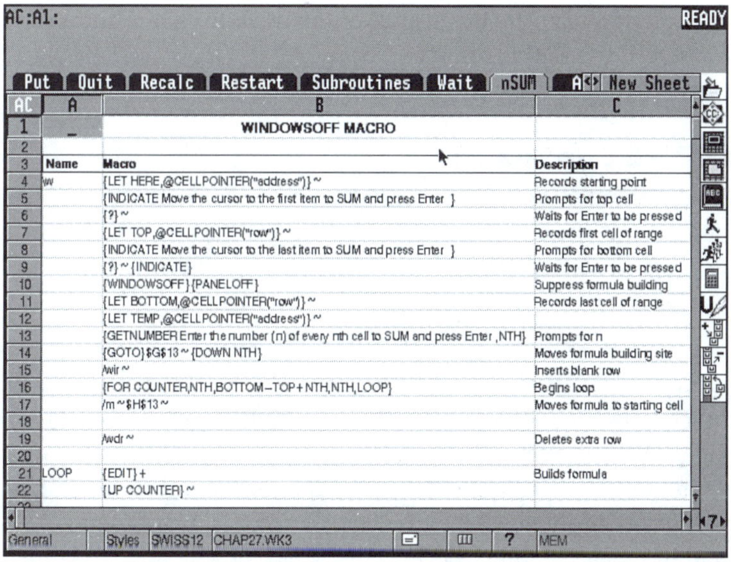

Listing the Advanced Macro Commands

Fig. 27.32
A macro to sum every *n*th cell of a range. Because there is considerable cell pointer movement during the execution of this macro, the screen display is suppressed by the WINDOWSOFF command.

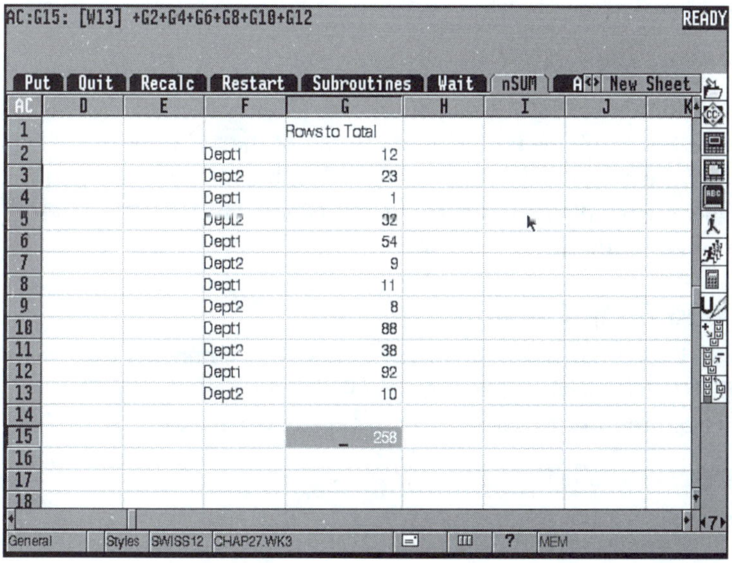

Fig. 27.33
An example using the WINDOWSOFF macro.

The WINDOWSON Command

The WINDOWSON command unfreezes the screen, enabling the display of worksheet changes. The syntax of the WINDOWSON command is

{WINDOWSON}

Unless you need to activate the display of the worksheet area during a macro, there is no need to use this command because 1-2-3 automatically reactivates the display when macro execution is terminated.

The WRITE Command

The WRITE command writes a string of text to the currently open ASCII file. The command syntax is

{WRITE *string*}

{WRITE} copies *string* to the open ASCII file. The *string* argument can be a literal string, a range name, a cell reference to a single cell containing a string or a string expression. Because {WRITE} doesn't place a carriage-return-line-feed sequence at the end of the string, you can use several WRITE statements to concatenate text on a single line. {WRITE} is well suited to creating or updating a file containing fixed-length database records. You can use the WRITE command in much the same way as the WRITELN command. To write the literal string PAID to an open ASCII file, for example, use the following command:

`{WRITE PAID}`

If the file pointer isn't at the end of the file, 1-2-3 overwrites existing characters in the file. If the file pointer is at the end of the ASCII file, 1-2-3 extends the file by the number of characters written. If the file pointer is past the end of the file (see the discussion of the SETPOS command), 1-2-3 extends the file by the length of the string.

The WRITELN Command

The WRITELN command is identical to the WRITE command except that {WRITELN} places a carriage-return-line-feed sequence after the last character written from the string. The WRITELN command syntax is

{WRITELN *string*}

{WRITELN} copies *string* (plus a carriage-return-line-feed sequence) to the open ASCII file. {WRITELN} is useful when the ASCII file being written or updated uses the carriage-return-line-feed sequence to mark the end of lines or records. Many applications use several WRITE statements to write a line to the ASCII file; then a {WRITELN} marks the end of the line. A WRITELN command is shown in figure 27.8.

The /x Commands

In addition to the advanced macro commands, 1-2-3 includes a set of eight /x commands. These commands were included in 1-2-3 Release 1A to provide a limited "programming" capability beyond simple keystroke macros. All eight /x commands have advanced macro command counterparts. The /x commands and their advanced macro command counterparts are described in the following table. Except in the rare instances in which /xn and /xl perform differently from their advanced macro command counterparts, the /x commands shouldn't be used in new programs developed in Release 4. The /x commands are useful, however, because they enable you to run Release 1A programs in Release 4.

/x Command	Description	Advanced Macro Command Alternative
/xc	Calls a subroutine	{subroutine}
/xg	Branches to a new location	{BRANCH}
/xi	Sets up an IF-THEN-ELSE condition	{IF}
/xl	Enters input as a label	{GETLABEL}
/xm	Branches to a menu	{MENUBRANCH}
/xn	Accepts input of numbers or formulas which return numbers	{GETNUMBER}
/xq	Quits execution	{QUIT}
/xr	Returns to the next line of the macro calling this subroutine	{RETURN}

Six of these commands (/xc, /xg, /xi, /xm, /xq, and /xr) work like their advanced macro command counterparts. /xq, for example, performs exactly like the advanced macro QUIT command. When inserted into a program, both commands produce the same result.

The other two /x commands (/xn and /xl) work a little differently from their advanced macro command counterparts ({GETNUMBER} and {GETLABEL}). The /xn and /xl commands prompt the user for text and numeric data respectively and then place the data in the current cell or the specified cell. For {GETNUMBER} and {GETLABEL} to place the entry in the current cell you must use @CELLPOINTER("address") as the location argument.

/xn, unlike {GETNUMBER}, doesn't accept alphabetic characters (except for range names and cell addresses), nor can the user press Enter in response to the prompt. With {GETNUMBER}, a blank entry or a text entry has a numeric value of ERR. With /xn, however, a blank entry or a text entry results in an error message, and the user is again prompted for a number. This difference can be useful in some applications. If you accidentally press Q (a letter) rather than *1*, for example, the /xn command returns an error message.

From Here...

For more information relating directly to the advanced macro commands, you may want to review the following chapters of this book:

- Chapter 3, "Finding Solutions with Formulas and Functions." Refer to this chapter to get more ideas of functions you might use to build more sophisticated macros.

- Chapter 15, "Using Functions To Analyze Data," discusses functions that you may choose to incorporate into your macros.

- Chapter 26, "Short Macros To Make Your Life Easier." Read this chapter to learn 1-2-3 macro key words and basic macro program techniques.

- Chapter 28, "Controlling 1-2-3 with Macros." Here you will develop an actual large macro application. Many useful techniques are demonstrated.

Chapter 28

Controlling 1-2-3 with Macros

Chapter 26, "Short Macros To Make Your Life Easier," introduced the basics of developing 1-2-3 macros. In Chapter 27, "Advanced Macro Command Power Techniques," you added 1-2-3's advanced macro commands to your repertoire, enhancing the tools with which you can build sophisticated applications. This chapter combines what you learned in the two preceding chapters to demonstrate the application development process, following the development of an application from inception to completion by using a real-world example. This chapter attempts to pull together the pieces of the programming puzzle.

You don't have to adhere to the approach presented here, but an organized and systematic method of some sort is strongly recommended. Otherwise, the task of programming can become extremely tedious and frustrating.

In this chapter, you learn to do the following:

- Understand the steps in application development
- Approach the design process
- Create complex applications
- Employ the modular programming style
- Apply debugging and documentation techniques

Reviewing the Steps for Application Development

It's always good to have a plan before you begin a task, and application development is no different. To make the application development process run smoothly, it is helpful to take an established approach to programming. You might consider the following steps in developing an application:

1. Develop a high-level overview.
2. Break the project into logical, manageable units.
3. Flesh out the detail of each unit.
4. Develop all necessary templates.
5. Write and record your program modules.
6. Test and debug each module.
7. Link the modules, retest, and debug.
8. Document the application.

Developing a High-Level Overview

The first thing you must do when you develop applications is determine what they are supposed to do. If you develop applications for yourself, this task is relatively easy, because you know what you want. When you develop applications for other people or at other people's direction, however, this step is not necessarily straightforward. It often is helpful to clarify what the input to the program will be and what the desired output should be. In management terminology, you want to know where you are and where you want to be so that you can determine how to get there.

Suppose that you are asked to develop a program that will generate a 1-2-3 slide show presenting cumulative daily sales totals by region and by product as compared with a set of budgeted numbers. After discussing the project with your manager, you determine that the data will come in daily from your company's 180 stores as PRN files.

You also decide that the output should consist of a chart for each product line and each region of the country. Each chart should display a month-to-date cumulative sales total for every working day of the current month. The charts also need to display the budgeted sales figures for the particular product line or sales region being presented. The slide show is to display each chart for a given length of time and then go on to the next chart. You are told that the users of the program know nothing about 1-2-3, so the entire process—from bringing in the PRN files to running the slide show—must be automatic.

This may seem simple enough on the first run-through, but as you begin to dig into the project, you discover undefined requirements, unforeseen constraints, and unexpected problems. Before you proceed further, therefore, you may want to get samples of the input and output.

After some thought, you request a copy of one of the input (PRN) files, a file containing the budgeted numbers and a sample of both the product and region charts. When you examine the PRN file, you determine that it contains five columns of data, only three of which you really need: region, product line, and cumulative daily sales totals. Your stores keep track of cumulative total sales by product for each day of the month, so each day's file contains yesterday's totals plus today's figures. When you receive the budgeted-numbers file, you discover that it is not a daily cumulative total, but instead has values for each product line by region by month. Figure 28.1 shows a portion of those numbers.

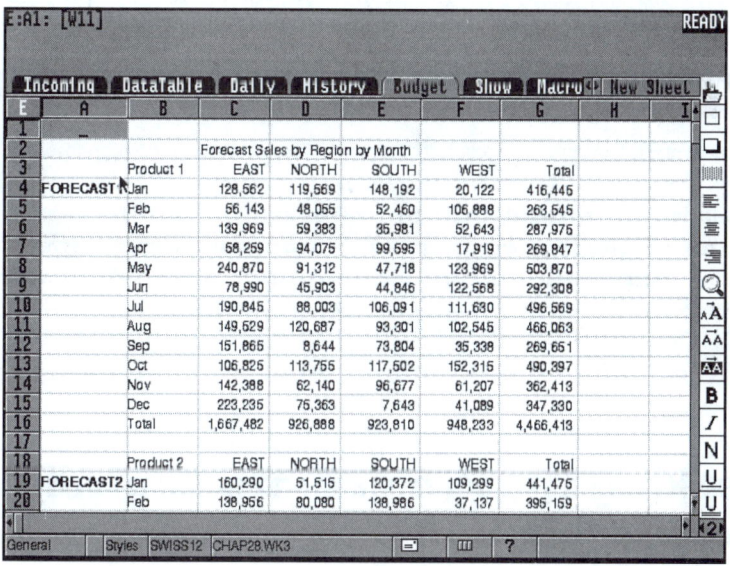

Fig. 28.1
Some of the input: a layout of the budgeted numbers, showing sales totals by product, month, and region.

Finally, your boss gives you a sample of what the charts should look like, indicating that the product-line and regional charts should be laid out identically. Figure 28.2 shows the sample chart.

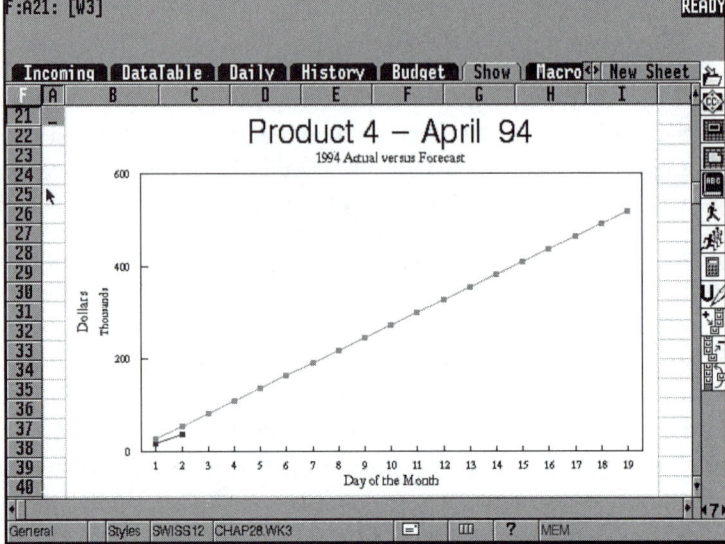

Fig. 28.2
A sample of the output: a chart of the cumulative sales figures for one product line by day for a given month.

With these initial pieces of the puzzle at hand, you are ready to proceed to the next step: outlining the overall project and breaking it into pieces.

> **Note**
>
> Applications are often developed in the wrong software. During the high-level project definition period, it may become apparent to you that the desired application should be developed within another type of software, such as a word processing package, a database program, or a graphics package. This is the stage of development at which it is most beneficial to voice your concerns. After a significant amount of time and energy has been invested, a major change of direction is less likely to be acceptable.

Breaking the Project into Logical, Manageable Units

The concept of breaking a large complex problem into smaller parts is not new. "Divide and conquer" is as good an adage in programming as in warfare. The process of dividing a program into smaller pieces suggests an approach called *modular programming*. The basic idea is to develop packets of code, called *modules*, that deal with individual tasks, and then to string these packets together. Organizing your programs in logical units not only encourages a modular programming style, but also makes it easier to develop, debug, maintain, and understand your programs. In addition, modularity can minimize the need for repetitive code through the use of subroutines. You will see that the use of subroutines is specifically designed to facilitate the process of modular programming, with its inherent benefits.

After studying the input and output, you decide that the project can be broken into the following major components:

- Importing the PRN files
- Parsing the PRN-file data
- Summarizing the data by region and product line
- Generating a data area of daily totals for each region and product line
- Generating a slide show

Be prepared to be flexible; don't be tied to your initial list. Sometimes, as you work on a module, you discover that it is becoming overwhelming; this suggests that the module itself should be broken into smaller pieces.

When you have established your basic outline or plan of attack, you can begin digging into the detail within each piece.

Fleshing Out the Detail for Each Module

The next step you should consider is an in-depth analysis of the actions of each module. It is said that good programmers spend 90 percent of their time analyzing and 10 percent programming. The process of detailing each module means determining exactly what each module will do and how it will do it. During this stage, you may want to take into consideration some of the following points:

- What 1-2-3 commands will be used?
- What system limitations may be encountered?
- What errors are likely to occur, and how will you handle them?

- What parts of the specifications need clarification?
- Would feedback to the user minimize future problems?

During this stage, you should determine the approach you intend to take to perform each task. The more detail, the better. The more detailed you become, the less work you will have to do at the coding stage and the more likely you will be to foresee problems. The following paragraphs address this issue, using the import module as a guide.

For the import module, you have examined one of the PRN files and determined that you can use the **/D**ata **P**arse command to put the data in a format that 1-2-3 can use. You also have learned that there are 180 stores sending files. The files will be stored in the directory D:\S\L4\INCOMING, and they will follow this naming convention: STORE###.PRN. The major issue for this module is how to have 1-2-3 open an unknown number of files that meet a predefined naming convention. You will see one answer to this problem later in this chapter, in the section "The Import Module."

As you work, the following questions might come to mind:

- Are any other PRN files located in this directory?
- Are preceding-day PRN files automatically cleared from the directory each day, or will your program need to deal with them?
- Does every store transmit a PRN file every business day?

You should always consider whether any software or hardware limitations may affect the project. Limitations to consider include available hard disk space, free RAM, and worksheet limitation, such as the 8,192-row maximum of 1-2-3.

For the import module, your major concerns revolve around the 180 PRN files. If each store sells 10 product lines and the incoming files contain one line for each product line, there are a maximum 1,800 lines, well within 1-2-3's 8,192-line limit. At this time, you also might consider what types of errors could occur during the import process and how you could deal with them. For example, you might ask the following questions:

- Can the directory be empty, and if so, what happens?
- What happens if a store does not send a file on a given day? Can the store send two files the next day?
- Could a PRN file have 0 bytes, and if so, would that affect the macro?

- What will happen if the PRN files have different structures from file to file?

> **Note**
>
> If you are developing a program for someone other than yourself, you should consider drawing up a detailed description of the project as you understand it. (This document is often called a *detail design*.) Within these program specifications, you can address all the concerns and questions that need to be resolved. You then can submit the specifications for user sign-off. This approach minimizes problems arising from misunderstandings.

Developing Templates

Before you begin programming, you should set up the worksheet with as much detail as possible. In Release 4, for example, you should consider how many sheets you will need and how they should be organized. You should set up areas for data storage, reports, tables, charts, and any other items that you deem appropriate. You also should enter any formulas that can be prepared in advance. By doing all this work ahead of time, you minimize the need to rewrite code to meet an unforeseen data layout, and you continue the process of clarifying the task requirements. For example, you may have been told that the imported files will contain four columns of data; however, when you import a test file you discover that there is an additional column containing data. Although you do not need this data, you must keep it in mind as you write the macro. You can easily plan your macro to address this somewhat different data layout. This layout of the data was unforeseen, but because you are aware of it prior to writing your macro, you will not need to waste time later modifying your macro.

In the model being considered here, you initially might decide to have separate pages for the imported data, the accumulation of summaries, the daily cumulative data, the budgeted figures, the charts, and the macro. For the module dealing with the importing of the PRN files, all you need is a title at the top of the page for each column. Because you have learned that the monthly data must be retained, you also decide to add a history page. Another area that you should lay out at this time is the budgeted figures. You also might choose to design one chart and to set up its data area to help you focus on layout considerations.

To set up the SALES file, follow these steps:

1. Open a new file.

2. Click the New Sheet button five times to add five more sheets.

3. Name the sheets A..G Incoming, DataTable, Daily, History, Budget, Show, and Macro, respectively.

4. Move to the Incoming sheet and enter the labels **Store #**, **State**, **Region**, **Line**, and **Sales** in cells A1..E1.

Writing and Recording Program Modules

The first rule to go by when you program in 1-2-3 is to record as much as possible. By recording as much of your program as possible, you save time and eliminate errors. If you type your macros, you need to spend time checking the syntax of commands. You also waste time finding errors and correcting them. If you can record the actions your macro will take, you eliminate these problems. As your macros become more sophisticated, however, many of the commands you will want to include cannot be recorded, so you cannot escape the syntax and debugging issues forever.

To make your programs easier to follow and easier to debug, you should consider following a standardized approach. Although some conventions are more widely accepted than others, the important thing is to be consistent. In the program described in this chapter, for example, all range names, keywords, function names, and cell addresses are entered in uppercase, and all menu commands are entered in lowercase.

Keep in mind that there are any number of ways to solve a programming problem. One programmer may be driven to write the most efficient code, whereas another strives for clarity and simplicity, and yet another hopes for anything that works. In the program used in this chapter, the goals are to strive for economy of code and to demonstrate some of the more sophisticated approaches available to the programmer.

Because you are going to take a modular approach to this program, you decide to call each module from a main program, which you can think of as the first module.

A modular approach also simplifies debugging. You will find it much easier to debug a small, self-contained module than to try to attack the entire macro program at once.

> **Caution**
>
> If you wait to debug an application until you complete it, a problem may surface in one module that requires rewriting code in many modules. You can reduce this situation by debugging as you go. The use of modular programming techniques tends to minimize the chance that problems in one module will affect another module, but this is not always the case. In this chapter, however, rather than have one debugging discussion with each module, and to help minimize the possible redundancy this could cause, the entire debugging discussion is done in the section entitled "Debugging the Application."

The Main Module

A main module should address any preparatory steps that are needed to safely and efficiently execute the entire macro. It is also common practice to have the main module call all of the supporting subroutines. In most programs, you should consider increasing the processing speed by adding the WINDOWSOFF and PANELOFF commands at the beginning of the macro.

A second issue you should consider is protecting yourself if the macro garbles the data during execution. Normally, you would avoid this problem by not saving the file. However, if you are not immediately aware of the problem, you might save the bad file. To minimize this problem, you can have 1-2-3 save a backup copy of your file before it makes any modifications. After these preparatory steps, you will have the main module call each of the supporting modules in succession. In this example, you intend to name the supporting modules IMPORT, PARSE, SUMMARY, DATA_WORKUP, and SLIDE_SHOW.

To begin the main module, follow these steps:

1. Enter the following macro lines in cells B1..B8 of the Macro sheet:

    ```
    {WINDOWSOFF}{PANELOFF}
    /fs{CE}D:\S\L4\DATA\BACKUP~r{ESC}
    /fs{CE}D:\S\L4\DATA\SALES~r{ESC}
    {IMPORT}
    {PARSE}
    {SUMMARY}
    {DATA_WORKUP}
    {SLIDE_SHOW}
    ```

2. Enter the labels **\m** and **\t** in cells A1..A2.

3. Choose the **/R**ange **N**ame **L**abels **R**ight command, and select the range A1..A2.

Tip
To make it easier to interpret your worksheets, it is helpful to display range names near their respective ranges and to format them as bold or some other format to distinguish them from other labels.

The reason for naming both cells B1 and B2 is to give you the option during development to bypass the first line of the macro so that you can see screen changes. When the program is up and running, you can remove the \t label and the associated range name. Notice that the macro first saves the file as BACKUP and then as SALES. This prevents the user from having to remember to change the file name back when saving the file manually. The inclusion of the ESC command at the end of both file-save lines addresses the situation that occurs when the named file is not in the specific directory; the command removes the ~r that would remain. The remainder of the main module calls each of five subroutines in succession. At this point, you should consider debugging the current module, although in this example there is little to debug. The debugging of the application is discussed in the section "Debugging the Application" later in this chapter.

> **Caution**
> If you consider using the BACKUP file as a backup in case of a system crash, you should save it to a different drive (not just a different directory) than the SALES file.

The Import Module

The import module imports each file in succession, placing it directly below the preceding file. You need to clear any preceding-day data from the import area before the import process begins. An alternative is to clear the import-data area of the current day's data later in the current run. By clearing the import-data area at the beginning of a new run, you make the old data available until the next time you run the macro.

The real challenge in this module is dealing with the fact that not all stores may transmit a file every day. How will the macro determine what files are in the specific directory and which ones to open? 1-2-3's file list is a wraparound window, so you have no way to determine when all the files were opened. 1-2-3 provides the **/F**ile **A**dmin **T**able command for bringing a listing of files in a directory into the worksheet. The macro puts this listing in an area that you name FTABLE. When you have a list in the worksheet, you can use the list to open one file at a time. Because you will have up to 180 files to open, a

FOR loop is an obvious approach. You want 1-2-3 to repeat the **/F**ile **I**mport **T**ext command one time for each file listed in the FTABLE. The code might be the following:

```
/fit{CE}D:\S\L4\DATA\
filename
```

You can get the file name from the FTABLE by using the INDEX(*range,column,row*) function. The file name is in the first (0) column of the FTABLE range. The row number is incremented one time for each loop, which means that you can use the FOR loop counter as the ROW argument in the INDEX command. Code often is easier to follow if one complete idea is on one line. In the preceding example, it would be helpful to combine both lines into one. The first line is text, however, and the second line is a function. You can solve this problem by using the concatenation operator & (ampersand) and building a self-adjusting formula.

After all the files have been imported, you want to parse the files and name the resulting range. As you consider this, you remember that although the layout of the files will be similar, there may be slight variations in the field lengths, which means that if you parse all the files based on the structure of the first file, problems may arise. An alternative is to parse each file as it is imported, in which case this command is needed within the FOR loop. The result of all these considerations is the module shown in figure 28.3.

> **Note**
> Although this is the first loop you have created in this program, it is named LOOP2 because of changes that will arise during later considerations.

If you want to test the macro when it's complete, you need a PRN file. If you don't have any PRN files handy, you can easily create as many dummy files as you want, for test purposes. To create a PRN file in 1-2-3, follow these steps:

1. Enter some dummy data in a blank area of a spreadsheet like that shown in figure 28.5.
2. Choose the command **/P**rint **F**ile, then enter the name of your dummy file and press Enter.
3. Choose **R**ange and highlight the data, without titles, and press Enter.
4. Choose **O**ptions **O**ther Unformatted, **O**ther **B**lank-Header **S**uppress, **M**argins **N**one, **Q**uit **G**o **Q**uit.

944 Chapter 28—Controlling 1-2-3 with Macros

Be careful. You should not create a dummy PRN file to use in place of a live sample file; doing so can lead to invalid assumptions, incorrect code, and a macro that will fail when used with live data.

Fig. 28.3
The code for the IMPORT_PARSE module.

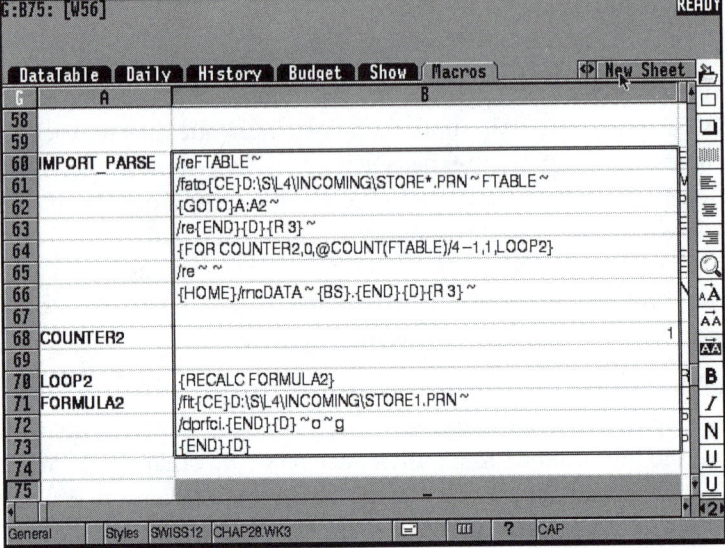

Now that you have a PRN file to use in testing, you can turn to the business of programming. To enter the macro shown in figure 28.3, follow these steps:

1. Enter the macro commands shown in cells B60..B73 of the Macro sheet, excluding cell B71.

2. Enter the labels shown in cells A60..A73.

3. Use the **/R**ange **N**ame **L**abels **R**ight command for the range A60..A71 to name the cells to the right.

4. Enter the following formula in cell B71:

    +"/fit{CE}D:\S\L4\INCOMING\"&@INDEX(FTABLE,0,COUNTER2)&"~"

5. Because you have incorporated the **/D**ata **P**arse command into the IMPORT macro, you no longer need separate subroutine calls for both PARSE and IMPORT. Replace the subroutine call in cell B4 with {IMPORT_PARSE}, and delete row 5.

Now examine each line of your code. The first line erases the range FTABLE in preparation for bringing in a list of all files in the given directory. 1-2-3's **/F**ile **A**dmin **T**able **O**ther command brings in a four-column list, with one line for each file with the designated name. For this example, the range L4..O204 on the Macro sheet was named FTABLE. Figure 28.4 shows a portion of the FTABLE range with titles added. Rows 6 and 7 show the data as 1-2-3 brings it in, whereas rows 4 and 5 have been formatted in date and time formats to show the data in a more useful manner.

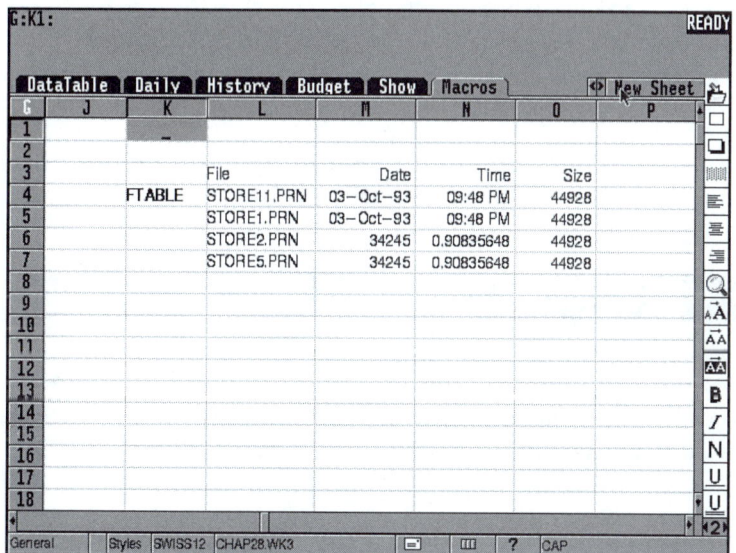

Fig. 28.4
A portion of FTABLE, the output range from the /**F**ile **A**dmin **T**able **O**ther command.

The second line of the module produces a list of all files in the given directory with the name STORE*.PRN and places the list in the range FTABLE. The third line of the macro places the cell pointer in cell A2 of the Import sheet, sheet A. The fourth line erases any data from the preceding import operation.

> **Note**
>
> Using the END command can cause problems if your data is not continuous. To minimize problems related to using the END command, use the cursor commands with an argument if you know how many rows or columns will be included. For example, it is safer to use {R 4} than to use {END}{RIGHT} if you know how many columns are to be included.

The FOR loop on the next line uses the range COUNTER2 to keep track of which loop is being executed. Zero (0) rather than one (1) was chosen as the starting value of the loop because the INDEX function considers the first row of FTABLE to be row 0. The ending value is the result of the calculation

COUNT(FTABLE)/4-1. Remember that FTABLE is four columns wide; hence, you divide by 4. Because the first row for the INDEX function is zero, the last row is one less than the number returned by the COUNT function.

When you write the macro, you probably will begin the loop with the formula shown in cell B71. When you test the module, you will discover that the formula does not update during the execution of the FOR loop. To force the formula to update, you can recalculate the worksheet with the CALC command, but the macro will run faster if you recalculate only the formula, using the RECALC command.

After a file is imported, the macro parses it with the **/D**ata **P**arse command shown in cell B72, and then moves to the last line of the data. The loop is incremented, and the process begins again for the next file.

> **Note**
>
> Because the output range for the parse command starts on the same row as the format line, the parsed data is copied up one row. This means that the last line of the unparsed data remains directly below the parsed data. When the next file is brought in, it is placed on this last, unparsed line, clearing the unwanted line.

After the FOR loop has completed all its actions, the macro executes lines B65..B66. The first line removes the last remaining unparsed line (see the preceding note). The second line names the parsed data and the titles on row 1 DATA.

When the module has completed its execution, it returns to the calling program, one line below the line that called it. Figure 28.5 shows a portion of the DATA range after the macro has parsed the data.

> **Note**
>
> The technique demonstrated here for opening all files in a given directory that meet a specific naming convention can be used in many situations. Suppose that you work on a network in which a hundred users use your template to analyze data. When the template is distributed and each user has saved a copy with his or her own data, making modifications to the file means modifying each copy of the file. This is not a pleasant prospect. If all the files are maintained in one directory and if the structure of the files is unaltered, you can use the preceding approach to design a macro that modifies all the files automatically. The macro would open each file, using the technique demonstrated in this section; make the necessary changes; and then save and close the file.

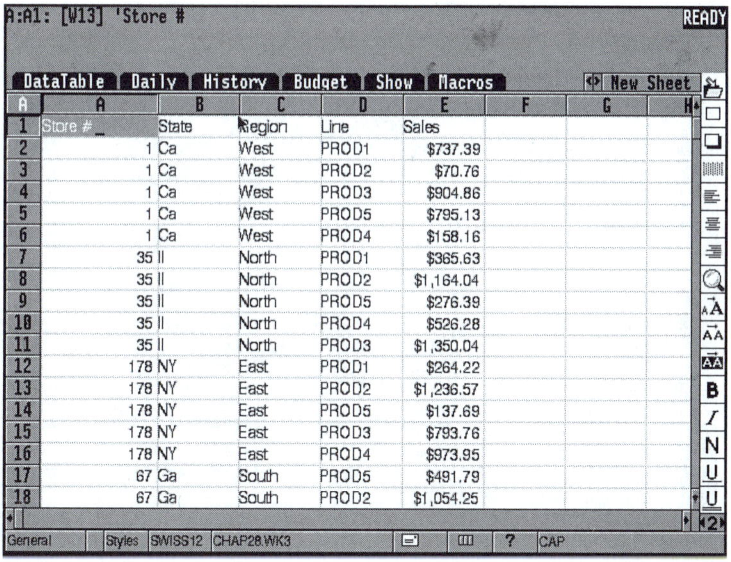

A	B	C	D	E
Store #	State	Region	Line	Sales
1	Ca	West	PROD1	$737.39
1	Ca	West	PROD2	$70.76
1	Ca	West	PROD3	$904.86
1	Ca	West	PROD5	$795.13
1	Ca	West	PROD4	$158.16
35	Il	North	PROD1	$365.63
35	Il	North	PROD2	$1,164.04
35	Il	North	PROD5	$276.39
35	Il	North	PROD4	$526.28
35	Il	North	PROD3	$1,350.04
178	NY	East	PROD1	$264.22
178	NY	East	PROD2	$1,236.57
178	NY	East	PROD5	$137.69
178	NY	East	PROD3	$793.76
178	NY	East	PROD4	$973.95
67	Ga	South	PROD5	$491.79
67	Ga	South	PROD2	$1,054.25

Fig. 28.5
A portion of the DATA range showing the results of the IMPORT_PARSE module.

Troubleshooting

The formula in cell B71 displays ERR.

If you have not named all the ranges in FTABLE and COUNTER2, the macro evaluates to ERR. If the FTABLE range is empty, the formula also evaluates to ERR. Finally, if the value in COUNTER2 is larger than the row number on which the last item in FTABLE is located, the formula returns ERR. The only one of these conditions that you must correct before running the macro is naming the ranges.

Only the first imported file is parsed.

Be sure that you include the *r* in cell B72. If you record the **/D**ata **P**arse command, you may forget to have it **R**eset before proceeding. In that case, the macro uses the previously parsed data in cell A2 to create the next format line, which results in unparsed data in all but the first file.

The DATA_WORKUP Module

The goal of the SUMMARY module is to total the sales figures for the current day by product line and sales region. To get a handle on this problem, you set up a table that illustrates how you want the summarized data to look. Figure 28.6 shows the summary area with some random data. In figure 28.6, only five product lines are shown for simplicity; however, you could easily address any number of product lines.

Fig. 28.6
The desired layout of the data summary area.

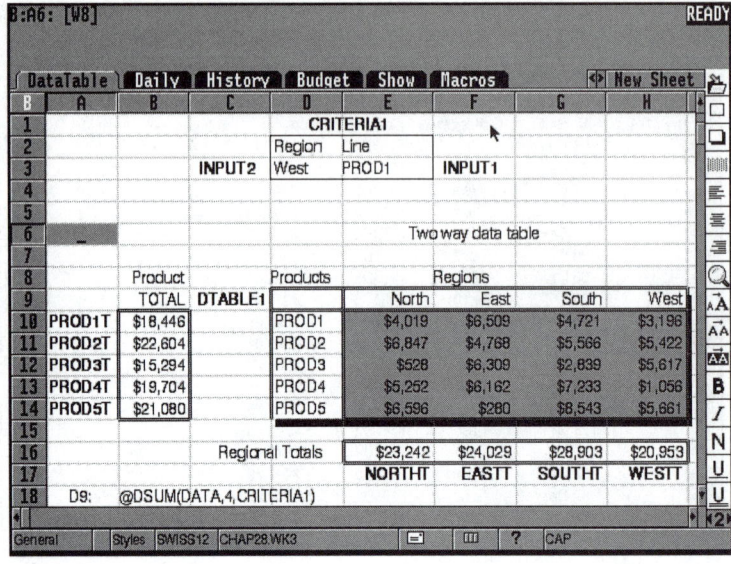

When you have set up this area as a template, its structure will give you a hint as to the approach to use to get the data into this final format. What you want is the sum of sales in each region for each product line. 1-2-3 has a set of data functions you can use in situations of this type. In this case, you want to use the @DSUM(*database,column,criteria*) function. For this example, the *database* argument is the range DATA, and the sales figures are in *column* 4. You need a two-column by two-row *criteria* range like the one shown in cells D2..E3 of figure 28.6.

Unfortunately, you need a separate *criteria* range for each DSUM formula. With 4 regions and 10 product lines, you would need 40 ranges; in addition, you would need to create 40 separate DSUM functions. Being aware of RAM limitations, you want to minimize the number of functions and criteria ranges, if possible. The table shown in figure 28.6 is in essence a crosstab table. The simplest way to create a crosstab table in 1-2-3 is to use the /**Data Table** command.

To set up the data table shown in figure 28.6, follow these steps:

1. Enter all the labels shown in the range A1..H17 in the DataTable sheet. Do not enter any of the values. (The special formatting is not necessary but can be useful as documentation.)

2. Enter the following formula in cell B10, and then copy it to the range B11..B14:

    ```
    @SUM(E10..H10)
    ```

3. Enter the following formula in cell E16, and then copy it to the range F16..H16:

    @SUM(E10..E14)

4. Enter the following formula in cell D9:

    @DSUM(DATA,4,CRITERIA1)

5. Choose the **/R**ange **N**ame **L**abels **R**ight command, and select the range A10..A14 to apply those names to the range B10..B14.

6. Choose the **/R**ange **N**ame **L**abels **U**p command, and select the range E17..H17 to apply those names to the range E16..H16.

7. Choose the **/R**ange **N**ame **C**reate command to name the ranges D2..E3, D3, E3, and D9..H14 CRITERIA1, INPUT2, INPUT1, and DTABLE1, respectively.

In figure 28.6, cell D9 has been formatted to Hidden. This has no effect on the program; it was done simply for appearance.

> **Note**
>
> The field names in a criteria range must match those in the database. There are two ways to ensure this: copy the titles from the database to the top of the criteria range, or enter formulas in the title line of the criteria range that reference the titles in the database. The second approach is a little more foolproof; if you change the titles of the columns of the database, the criteria table still works.

The **/D**ata **T**able **2** command uses the values in INPUT1 and INPUT2 to calculate the value of the DSUM formula in cell D9; the command then places that value in the table at the proper position. First, the **/D**ata **T**able command enters the column title in cell E9 of the TABLE range into the INPUT2 range and the row title in cell D10 into the INPUT1 range. Then the command copies the resulting value for the DSUM formula in cell D9 to cell E10. The command continues this process until it has calculated all the possible combinations.

The next step of the task is to enter the product-line totals and regional totals for the current day in a daily table for the entire month. To get a handle on this problem, you should set up the desired table as a template. Figure 28.7 shows a portion of the final table.

Fig. 28.7
A portion of the final layout. The range is set up to facilitate graphing.

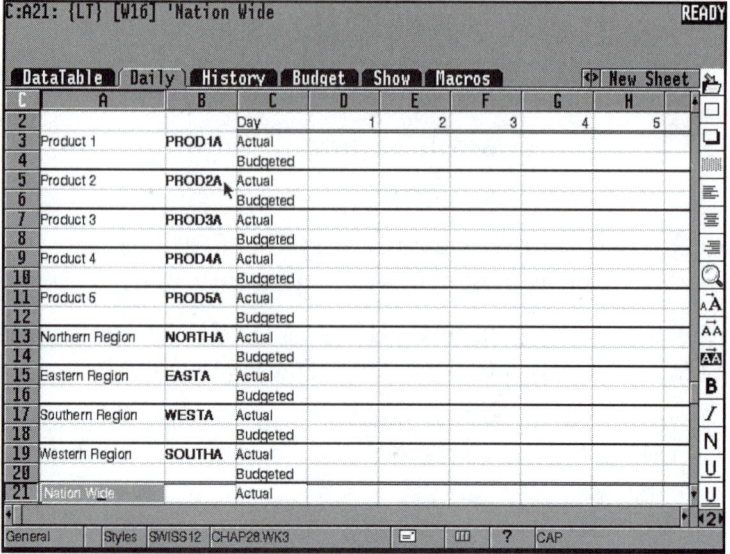

To set up the daily tracking table shown in figure 28.7, follow these steps:

1. Move to sheet C, Daily, and enter the labels shown in cells A2..C22.

2. Choose the **/D**ata **F**ill command to fill the range D2..Z2 with the numbers 1 to 23 (23 is the maximum number of work days in a given month for your company).

3. In cell D21, enter the following formula, and then copy the following formula to range D21..Z22:

    @IF(D19="","",D13+D15+D17+D19)

4. Choose the **/R**ange **N**ame **C**reate command to name the cells D3..Z3 with the name shown in cell B3, PROD1A. Repeat this step to name similar ranges in every other row from rows 5 to 19.

The formatting is added for clarity but is not necessary. Later, you will add formulas to calculate the forecast numbers.

With the data table solution, the SUMMARY module would be only one line long. Therefore, you decide to treat this one line as part of the DATA_WORKUP module and dispense with the SUMMARY module. Remember, the application development process should be dynamic, as this discussion illustrates.

With all the templates set up, you are ready to program the DATA_WORKUP module, shown in figure 28.8.

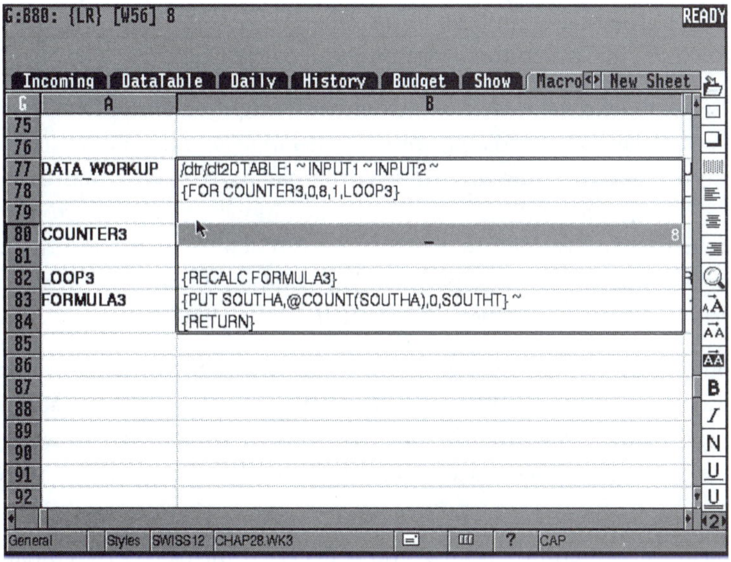

Fig. 28.8
The DATA_WORKUP module.

To create the module shown in figure 28.8, follow these steps:

1. Enter the macro commands shown in cells B77..B84 of the Macro sheet, excluding cell B83.

2. Enter the labels shown in cells A77..A83.

3. Use the **/R**ange **N**ame **L**abels **R**ight command for the range A77..A83 to name the cells to the right.

4. Enter the following formula in cell B83:

    +"{PUT "&@INDEX($PTABLE,0,COUNTER3)&" A,
    @COUNT(WESTA),0,"&@INDEX($PTABLE,0,COUNTER3)&"T}~"

5. Enter the following labels in cells D77..D86 of the Macro page: **PTABLE**, **PROD1**, **PROD2**, **PROD3**, **PROD4**, **PROD5**, **NORTH**, **EAST**, **SOUTH**, and **WEST**.

6. Choose the **/R**ange **N**ame **C**reate command to name the cell D78..D86 with the name in cell D77, PTABLE.

Now examine the code. The first line performs the **/D**ata **T**able command, using the previously named ranges TABLE1, INPUT1, and INPUT2. When the data table is created, you need a method of copying each of the nine total cells (ranges B10..B14 and E16..H16) to the appropriate cells of the table in the Daily page. For example, you want to copy the value in cell B10

(PROD1T) to the first empty cell in the range D3..Z3 (PROD1A). Then you want to copy PROD2T to the first empty cell of PROD2A.

The {PUT *location,column,row,value*} command might be useful here. This command places *value* into a position in the range *location* determined by the *row* and *column* offset numbers. In this example, the first PUT command is {PUT PROD1A,*column*,0,PROD1T}. The *column* in which you want to put the data is the first empty column, which 1-2-3 can determine by counting the number of items in the range PROD1A and subtracting one. This makes the first formula {PUT PROD1A,@COUNT(PROD1A)-1,0,PROD1T}.

You could make one copy of this formula for each of the product-line and region totals and then modify each copy to reflect a different product-line or region. To make it more interesting, however, you decide to create a loop with some dynamic code to accomplish the task. That is the formula in cell B83.

Looking at the preceding formula, you realize that the COUNT argument does not need to change; only the *location* and *value* arguments need to be dynamic. Further, the A and the T remain constant because of your well-chosen naming convention. This means that in each loop the macro needs to use the next item in the PTABLE that you entered in the range D78..D86. To cause the macro to do that, you use the INDEX function again. The INDEX function looks at PTABLE and checks row *n* of column 0 (where *n* is the row offset, which starts at 0). COUNTER3 is just what you need to increment the *row* argument.

The RECALC command serves the same purpose here as in the IMPORT_PARSE module. The last line's RETURN command is not necessary, but you might consider adding it if the command makes interpretation of the macro easier. When the FOR loop is complete, execution continues in the cell one line below the FOR command. Because the cell below the FOR command (B79) is empty, 1-2-3 interprets this as the end of the subroutine DATA_WORKUP and returns to the MAIN module.

> **Troubleshooting**
>
> *The DSUM formula is returning an incorrect value.*
>
> The *column* argument of DSUM starts with 0 as the first column. Also, make sure that the range named DATA includes the titles at the tops of the columns.
>
> *I typed the data table command in line B77, but the macro keeps bombing at that point.*

> You probably missed the second /. If you keystroke the command, you will find that 1-2-3 exits the **/D**ata **T**able command when you choose **R**eset. So you need to re-enter the **D**ata **T**able command.
>
> *The formula in cell B83 returns ERR.*
>
> See the discussion of the IMPORT_PARSE module in the preceding Troubleshooting section. Also check carefully to see whether you included all the quotation marks, ampersands, and commas. Finally, make sure that you did not enter letters (o) where digits (0) were needed.

The SLIDE_SHOW Module

The next module to address is the one that generates the slide show. Graph specifications require memory; therefore, the more graphs you have, the more memory you use. With 10 products and 4 regions, you would need graph specifications for 14 graphs. In addition, you would need to reset the graph ranges each day for every graph. Instead, you decide to create one graph area and one set of graph specifications. It would seem that you would need to copy the data for each graph into the graph area before displaying it; however, you come up with an ingenious method that eliminates the need to copy any data.

To remind yourself what the graphs will look like, refer to figure 28.2 earlier in this chapter.

The first area to set up is the OMNIGRAPH data area. You want to use a single range from which you will plot all your graphs. One approach would be to copy the data to the graph area before plotting each graph. But you have decided to use a formula approach to accomplish the same task. Part of the OMNIGRAPH data area and related documentation are shown in figure 29.9.

To set up the graph area shown in figure 28.9, follow these steps:

1. Move to the Show sheet and enter the labels shown in cells B2..B11.

2. Enter the labels in cells C9..C11.

3. Enter consecutive letters in cells C2..Y2, beginning with D.

4. Copy the day numbers from the range D2..Z2 of the Daily sheet to cell C3 of the Show sheet.

5. Enter the following formula in cell C4 and then copy it to the range D4..Y4:

    ```
    @@("C:"C$2&&@STRING(@CELLPOINTER("row"),0))
    ```

954   Chapter 28—Controlling 1-2-3 with Macros

6. Enter the following formula in cell C5 and then copy it to the range D5..Y5:

   @@("C:"C$2&@STRING(@CELLPOINTER("row")+1,0))

7. Enter the following formula in cell C8:

   @@("C:A"@STRING(@CELLPOINTER("row"),0))&" - "&
   @INDEX($DPM,0,$LAST_ROLL-1)&" "&@STRING(@YEAR(@NOW),0)

8. Choose the **/R**ange **N**ame **L**abels **R**ight command for the range B8..B11 to name the cells to the right.

9. Choose the **/R**ange **N**ame **C**reate command to name C3 DAY and the range C4..Y8 GRAPH_AREA.

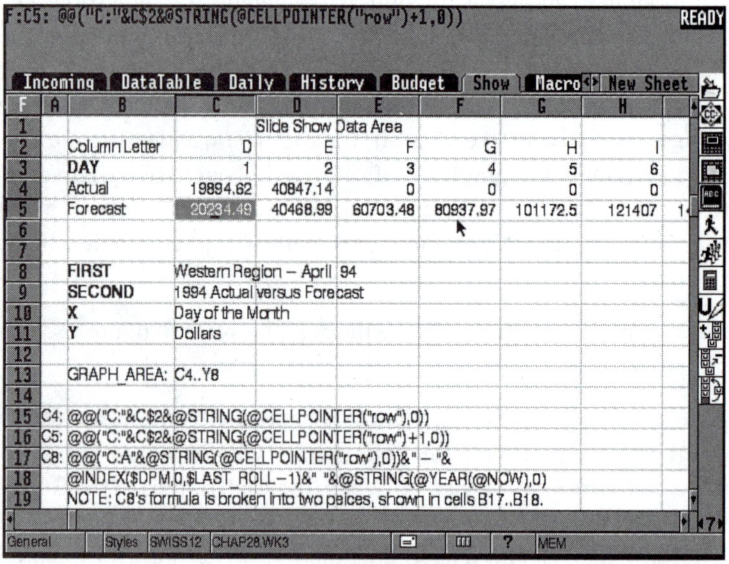

Fig. 28.9
The graph area in the Show sheet, containing formulas to make the OMNIGRAPH dynamic.

The tricky part of this page is the formulas. The CELLPOINTER("row") function returns the row number of the cell pointer. Referring to figure 28.7, imagine that your cell pointer is on cell C3 of the Daily sheet; this function would return 3. The STRING function converts the number 3 to the label 3 for use by the @@ function. The portion of the function that reads "C:"&C$2 concatenates the label in cell C2 of the Show sheet, "D," with the label C:. Thus the inner portion of the @@ function returns C:D3, a three-dimensional worksheet reference.

The @@ function returns the value in the cell C:D3, which is the "actual cumulative sales" for the first day of the current month for product 1. The formula in cell C5 works in an identical manner except that it references the cell one row below the cell pointer's location. In this case, it returns the budgeted value for the first product on the first day. Similarly, all the remaining formulas on rows 4 and 5 return the values for the first product.

Now consider what happens when you move the cell pointer down two rows on the Daily page and recalculate the worksheet. The formulas now return the values for Product 2. If you had set up the graph, you could press F10 and see the new chart.

The final formula in cell C8 returns the product-line title from the appropriate row of column A on the Daily sheet and then concatenates this with the month label as determined by the INDEX function, and further concatenates these with the current year. The INDEX function looks at a table called DPM (which you will construct in the following section) and returns the month label for the current month. The @STRING(@YEAR(@NOW),0) portion returns the year of the current date as a string.

To set up the OMNIGRAPH that will use the data area you just constructed, follow these steps:

1. Move to the Show sheet.
2. Choose the **/G**raph **T**ype **L**ine command.
3. Choose the **/O**ptions **T**itle **F**irst command, and enter **\FIRST**.
4. Repeat step 3, entering **\SECOND, \X,** and **\Y** for the **S**econd, **X**-axis, and **Y**-axis titles.
5. Choose the **/Q**uit **N**ame **C**reate command and name the graph OMNIGRAPH.
6. Choose **Q**uit.

The use of \FIRST for the title tells 1-2-3 to use the contents of the range named FIRST for the first title. There is no need to specify the x-axis or the A or B ranges, because the macro does it for you. The code for the SLIDE_SHOW module is relatively straightforward, so you enter it first. Then you set up your ingenious graph area.

956   Chapter 28—Controlling 1-2-3 with Macros

> **Note**
> There is an interesting variation of the use of a dynamic graphing range. If you embed a copy of OMNIGRAPH in your worksheet, you can watch it change as you move the cursor from line to line manually. All you need to do is position your cursor on the appropriate row and press F9 to have 1-2-3 recalculate the formulas and display a graph of the data on the current rows. With the formulas you used here, you do not even need to be on the same page as the data, just the correct row.

The next task is to enter the SLIDE_SHOW code shown in figure 28.10.

Fig. 28.10
The code for the SLIDE_SHOW module.

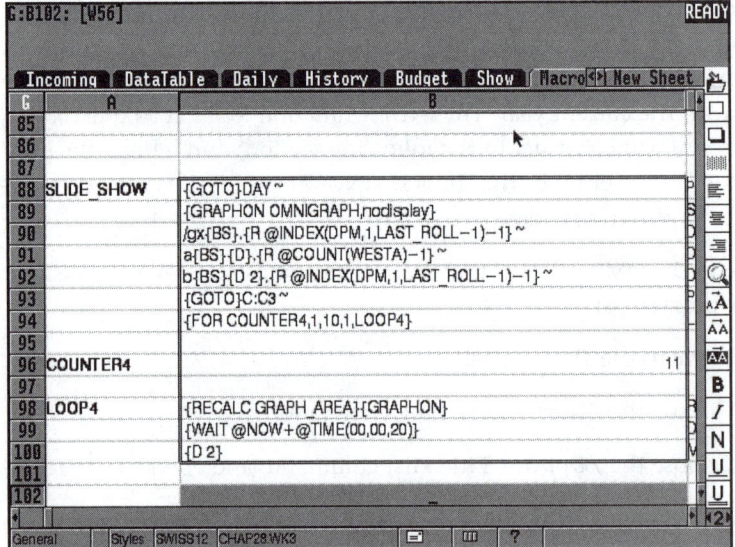

To enter the code shown in figure 28.10, follow these steps:

1. Enter the macro commands shown in cells B88..B100 of the Macro sheet.

2. Enter the labels shown in cells A88..A98.

3. Use the **/R**ange **N**ame **L**abels **R**ight command for the range A88..A98 to name the cells to the right.

4. Move to the Daily sheet and enter the two-column table shown in cells AB1..AC14 of figure 28.11.

5. Choose the **/R**ange **N**ame **C**reate command to name the range AB3..AC14 DPM. This is a table of the number of work days per month in your company.

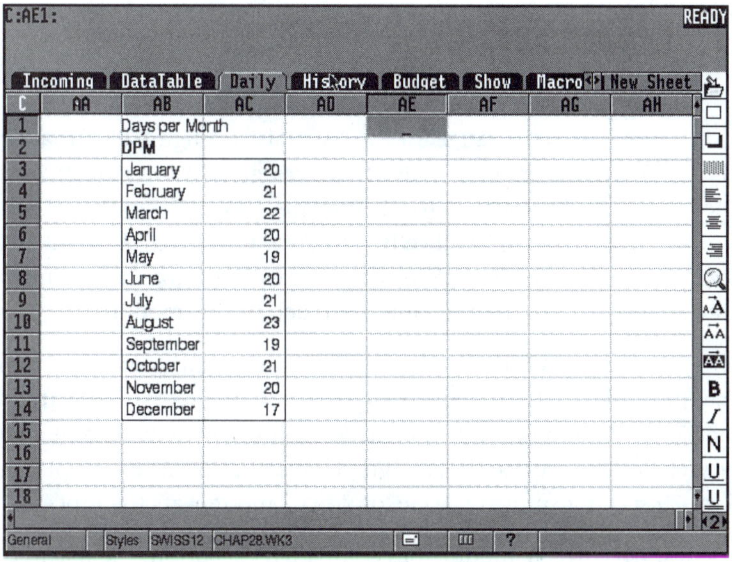

Fig. 28.11
A lookup table named DPM, showing the number of work days per month.

```
C:AE1:                                                        READY

 Incoming  DataTable  Daily   History  Budget  Show  Macro  New Sheet
 C    AA        AB        AC      AD      AE    AF     AG      AH
 1          Days per Month
 2          DPM
 3          January       20
 4          February      21
 5          March         22
 6          April         20
 7          May           19
 8          June          20
 9          July          21
10          August        23
11          September     19
12          October       21
13          November      20
14          December      17
15
16
17
18

General    Styles  SWISS12  CHAP28.WK3
```

When you program a module such as this, it is best to record as many keystrokes as possible and then modify them as necessary.

What does this macro do? First, it positions the cell pointer on the first cell of the x-axis data range. You will name that cell DAY later.

The {GRAPHON OMNIGRAPH,nodisplay} command makes a predefined graph named OMNIGRAPH the CURRENT graph but does not display it. The macro will display OMNIGRAPH once for each pass through LOOP4.

The third line selects the x-axis range by anchoring the cell pointer at the cell DAY and then moving to the right. Referring to figure 28.7, you need to highlight one number for each working day of the current month. You can determine the number of days in the month being graphed by using the DPM table in figure 28.11, assuming that you know what month is being graphed. For the time being, assume that the current month's number is being held in a cell called LAST_ROLL. (You see now that you will need to set up some mechanism to determine what month is being tracked. This is the kind of discovery that can arise in the middle of programming, introducing much additional labor.)

Knowing this, you can interpret {R @INDEX(DPM,1,LAST_ROLL-1)-1}. The INDEX function looks in the second column (1) of the range DPM and down to the row indicated by the value in LAST_ROLL. If you are plotting April, for example, LAST_ROLL contains the number 4. The INDEX function subtracts one from this value (because it counts the first row as 0) and returns 19, the fourth value in the second column of the range DPM. Finally, to select the range from day 1 out to day 19 (cells C3..U3), the macro must move right 18 times (19 minus 1).

The fourth line selects the range for the "Actuals" (in figure 28.9 that would be cells C4..D4), as the graph's A range. Referring again to figure 28.7, you see that the Actuals are located one row below the X-axis labels. The cell pointer must move right to highlight all cells with data. In the DATA-WORKUP module, you used the @COUNT(WESTA) function to determine how many cells contained data; you can use the same approach in this module.

The fifth line performs the same function for the B range (budgeted numbers) that the third line did for the x-axis labels. The next line positions the cell pointer. The FOR loop in cell B94 controls the display of one graph after another. The macro recalculates the graph area GRAPH_AREA, displays the graph for 20 seconds, moves the cursor down, and repeats the process.

When the SLIDE_SHOW module has completed execution, the macro returns to the main macro, and the program is done.

The ROLLOVER Module

As you developed your application, you discovered that a few items are missing. For example, at the end of each month, the macro needs to clear the Actuals out of the Daily page and to update the Budgeted numbers on that page. You have been asked to retain the monthly data for a year, so you need to store it somewhere. You also need to store the number of the month for which you currently are accumulating data. You need to perform all these steps once a month, but the date on which you must do these things varies, depending on when the last working day occurs.

You can take two approaches to dealing with the monthly rollover: you can have 1-2-3 determine when the rollover should occur and have it execute all the steps automatically, or you can let the user determine when the rollover should occur. Regardless of the approach you take, some of the code will be identical.

This section deals with the History sheet and the code that is common to both approaches.

Refer to figure 28.12 as you set up the History sheet.

To set up this sheet, follow these steps:

1. Move to the History sheet.

2. Enter the label **1** in cell A1 and the label **Jan** in cell A2.

3. Use the **/R**ange **N**ame **L**abels **R**ight command to use the label in A1 to name cell B1.

4. Repeat steps 2 and 3 every 25 lines down the page, but increment both the number label and the month name by one. Enter one set of labels for each of the 12 months (or for however long you need to retain the data).

5. Move to the Daily sheet and name the range A1..Z22 DAILYCUM.

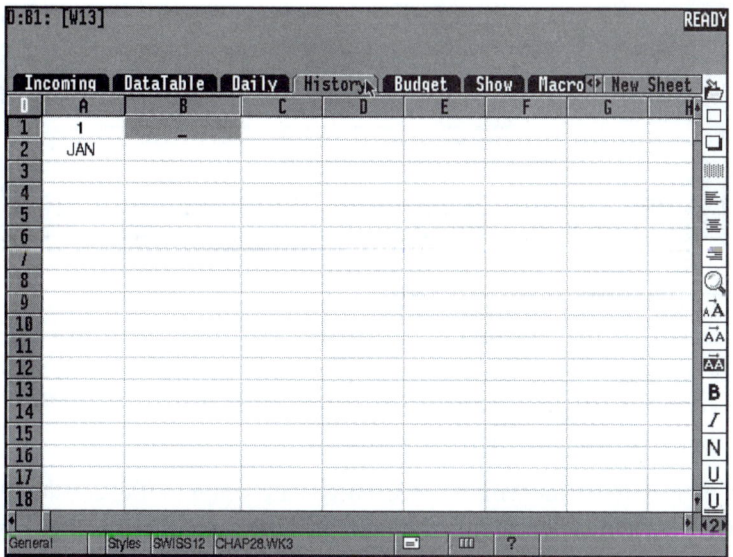

Fig. 28.12
A small portion of the History sheet, where the data from previous months will be stored.

With the history area set up, you now turn to the code. To set up the ROLLOVER module, refer to figure 28.13.

To set up this module, follow these steps:

1. Enter the macro commands shown in cells B32..B41 of the Macro sheet, excluding cells B33 and B40.

2. Enter the labels shown in cells A32..A43.

3. Use the **/R**ange **N**ame **L**abels **R**ight command for the range A32..A43 to name the cells to the right.

4. In cell B33, enter the following formula:

    +"/rvDAILYCUM~"&@STRING(@MONTH(@NOW)-1,0)&"~"

5. In cell B40, enter the following formula:

    +"{BLANK "&@INDEX(PTABLE,0,COUNTER1)&"A}~"

960   Chapter 28—Controlling 1-2-3 with Macros

Fig. 28.13

The common code for the ROLLOVER module, which handles the preparations for a new month.

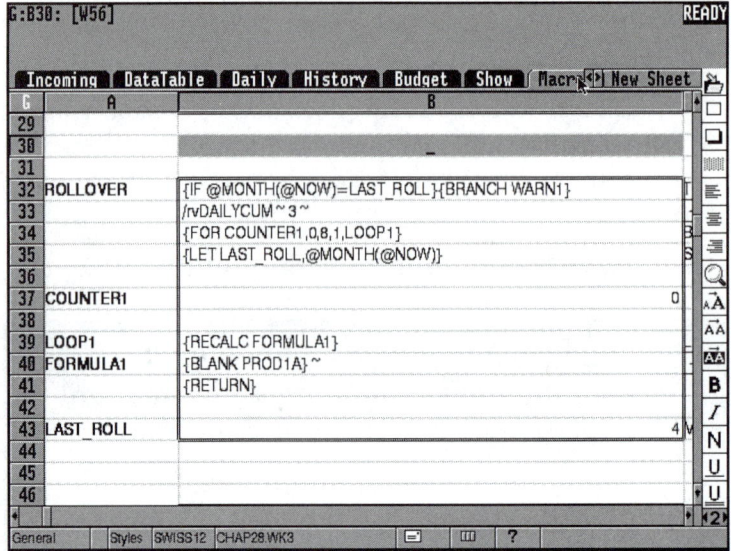

Line B32 is not common code for both approaches, but it has been included here because it is the only line of this module that you need to take out if you attempt to automate the entire rollover procedure. (If you take that approach, you need to remove line B32, move the label in A32 down one row, and name the cell to the right of it accordingly.)

Before you try to decide which approach you are going to use, consider the code for this module, excluding the first line. The code in cell B33 is a dynamic formula that uses the /**R**ange **V**alue command to copy the current month's Daily sheet figures to the appropriate range in the History sheet as values. Because the rollover cannot occur until the beginning of the new month, this formula concatenates the string value of the current month number minus one, with the rest of the /**R**ange **V**alue command.

The FOR loop on the next line controls the clearing of all the actuals from the Daily sheet. As in previous modules, the first command in the loop recalculates a formula, in this case located in the range named FORMULA1. The formula on the next line uses the same INDEX command as the FORMULA3 formula in the DATA_WORKUP module. Remember that each of the actual ranges in the Daily page are named PROD1A, PROD2A, and so on.

Suppose that you decide to automate the procedure. You first need to make the modification to line B32 as mentioned previously. Then you would replace the OPENING subroutine call in the Main module with the following line:

```
{IF @COUNT(PROD1A)=@INDEX(DPM,1,LAST_ROLL-1)}{ROLLOVER}
```

This line checks to see whether the Daily sheet is full for the current month. If so, the ROLLOVER subroutine is executed before any of the other modules.

To make this macro more interesting and to introduce a number of other techniques that are useful in programming, you choose the second approach, prompting for a user response. In this approach, the user must tell the macro whether today is the first day with data for the new month. All the steps for this approach are developed in the following section, "The OPENING Module."

Caution

The **/R**ange **E**rase command performs the same function as the BLANK command. Under some conditions, the BLANK command may not work; in that case, substitute the menu equivalent.

Troubleshooting

The macro keeps beeping and displaying the error message `Invalid cell or range address`.

You did not use labels to name the ranges in the History sheet. 1-2-3 will not name a cell 1 if you enter **1** in the adjacent cell and try to use the **/R**ange **N**ame **L**abels command. To use this command, you must enter the number 1 as a label.

The macro beeps and displays the error message `Unrecognized key/range name in cell B40`.

Make sure that you include a space between the keyword BLANK and the closing quotation marks that follow in the formula in cell B40 of the macro page. Also refer to the discussions in the Troubleshooting sections for the DATA_WORKUP module and the IMPORT_PARSE module.

The OPENING Module

In analyzing the requirements for the opening module, you note the following points. The macro should prompt the user to answer if the current day's data is the first day of the new month. Based on the response, the macro should proceed with the rollover or begin importing new data. If the user indicates that the current data is for the first day of the new month, the macro should check to see whether the rollover has been run previously during the current month. If the user indicates that the current data is not for

962 Chapter 28—Controlling 1-2-3 with Macros

the first day of the new month, the macro should check to see that data has not already been entered for all the days in the current month.

One of the decisions you must make when programming is how to interact with the user. For example, in this module you could prompt the user for input by using the GETLABEL, GETNUMBER, or GET command in combination with the INDICATE command. Alternatively you could develop a custom screen or custom menu system for the user. What you decide to use depends on your preferences, your programming skills, and the competence of your users.

As you set up the OPENING module, refer to figures 28.14 and 28.15.

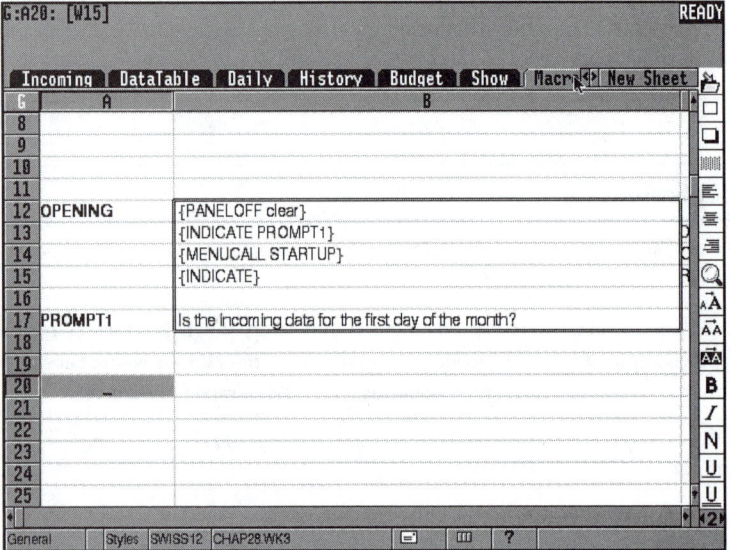

Fig. 28.14
The OPENING module's code from the Macro sheet.

To set up this module, follow these steps:

1. Enter the macro commands shown in cells B12..B17 of the Macro sheet, as shown in figure 28.14.

2. Enter the labels shown in cells A12..A17.

3. Choose the /**R**ange **N**ame **L**abels **R**ight command for the range A12..A17 to name the cells to the right.

4. Enter the menu definition area shown in range D12..G15 of figure 28.15. The complete labels for the range E13..G13 are shown in cells E17..E19.

5. Choose the **/R**ange **N**ame **L**abels **R**ight command to name the cells to the right of the label STARTUP.

6. Edit the labels in cells E12 and F12, adding about five trailing spaces to each. This helps space menu selections further apart when there are only a few choices.

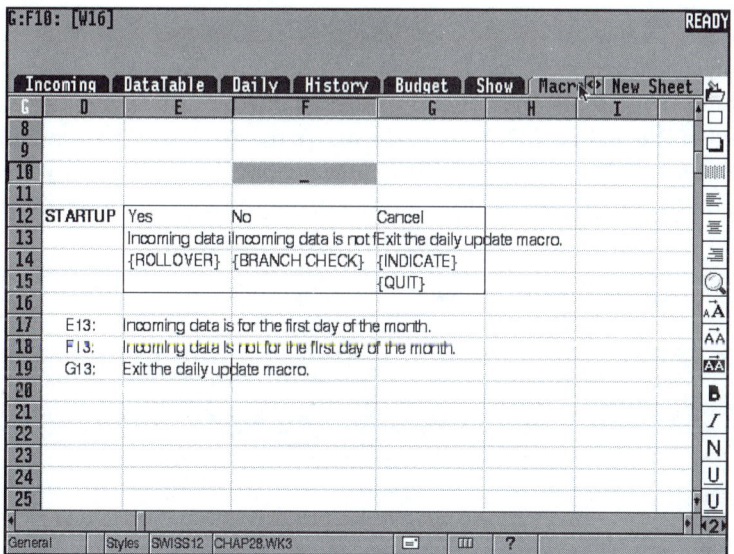

Fig. 28.15
The STARTUP menu's definition area on the Macro sheet.

First, this module turns off the panel and clears it of any distracting information. This is especially helpful with long prompts, which can run into other information on the same line of the screen. Then it displays the prompt from the range named PROMPT1. The next command calls the menu STARTUP. When the macro returns from the menucall, the INDICATE command restores 1-2-3's default indicator.

While the STARTUP menu is on-screen, the INDICATOR displays the question Is the incoming data for the first day of the month? If the user chooses Cancel, the macro resets the indicator and quits. This option gives the user a chance to exit the macro before much has occurred. If the user responds by choosing Yes, the macro calls the subroutine ROLLOVER. If the user responds No, the macro branches to the macro CHECK. In the following sections, you look at the error-handling methods used to check and respond to the user's choices.

Tip
If you use references to ranges whenever prompts are called for in macro functions, the prompts are easier to edit, more flexible, and safer.

The WARNING and CHECK Modules

If the user chooses Yes at the menu described in the preceding section, the macro calls the ROLLOVER subroutine, which was discussed in detail in the section "The ROLLOVER Module." At that time, the first line of the ROLLOVER module was left for later discussion. Following is the line of code that was passed over in the earlier discussion:

    {IF @MONTH(@NOW)=LAST_ROLL}{BRANCH WARN1}

This line checks to see whether the ROLLOVER routine has already been run this month; you don't want to run it twice in one month. Remember that at the end of the ROLLOVER routine, the macro records the current month in the cell LAST_ROLL. If the ROLLOVER routine has not executed, it will execute; on the other hand, if it has executed, the WARN1 module runs. In this section, you enter and examine that module.

As you set up the WARN1 module, refer to figure 28.16.

Fig. 28.16
The code for the WARN1 module, an error-handling subroutine.

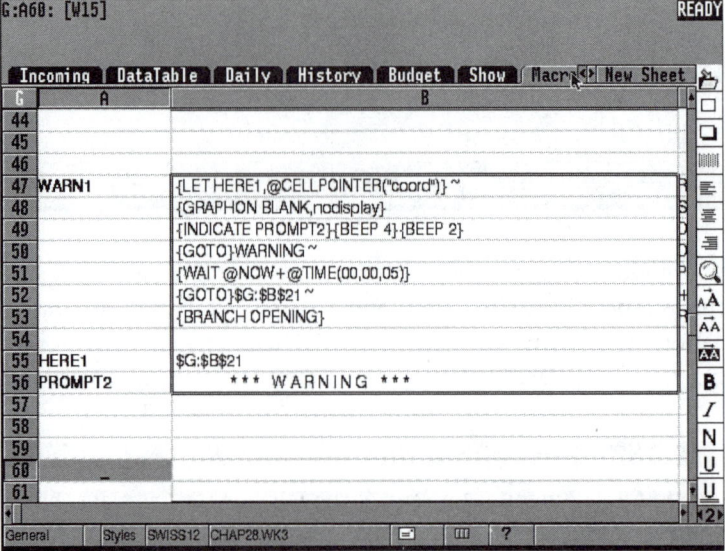

To set up this module, follow these steps:

1. Enter the macro commands shown in cells B47..B56 of the Macro sheet, excluding cell B52.

2. Enter the labels shown in cells A47..A56.

3. Choose the /**R**ange **N**ame **L**abels **R**ight command for the range A47..A56 to name the cells to the right.

4. In cell B52, enter the following formula:

    +"{GOTO}"&$HERE1&"~"

5. Move to an empty area of the Macro sheet, choose the **:F**ormat **C**olor **B**ackground **D**ark-Blue command, and color the range S4..X19. This area is where the warning screen will be located.

6. Add a drop shadow around this range, if you want, by choosing the **:F**ormat **L**ines **S**hadow **S**et command.

7. Choose the **/G**raph **R**eset **G**raph command; then choose the **N**ame **C**reate command and enter the name BLANK. Finish by choosing **Q**uit.

8. To add the blank graph on top of the colored range, choose the **:G**raph **A**dd **N**amed command and select BLANK. Then highlight the range T6..W17 and press Enter.

9. To color the graph, choose **:G**raph **E**dit and select any cell in the graph range T6..W17. Then choose **C**olor **B**ackground and select a light color.

10. Before exiting the **:G**raph **E**dit menu, add the text shown in figure 28.17 to the chart by choosing the **A**dd **T**ext command and typing the first line. When you have finished typing the first line, press Enter. Then position the cursor where you want the line to begin and press Enter a second time, to place the text. Repeat this process for the remaining lines, and make any font changes you desire. Then choose **Q**uit.

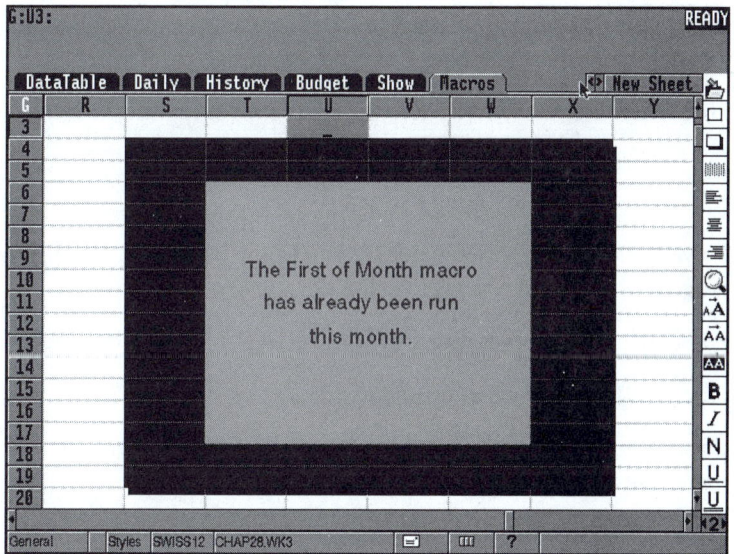

Fig. 28.17
A possible warning screen for your macro.

11. Choose the **/R**ange **N**ame **C**reate command to name the cell R3 WARNING.

This module is designed to warn the user if an error is detected by line B32 of the macro (see fig. 28.13). The macro alerts the user to the problem and returns to the STARTUP menu. During this routine, the macro beeps to attract the inattentive user and displays an explicit, colorful, full-screen warning.

> **Note**
>
> The label in PROMPT2 contains about 10 leading and trailing spaces; do not use the **/R**ange **L**abels **C**enter command to position it. Also, to make the label stand out, you can enter spaces between the letters.

The first line records the current three-dimensional position of the cell pointer in a range named HERE1, so that the macro can return the cell pointer to this location after execution. The second line of the macro makes the CURRENT graph the BLANK graph but does not display it. The third line of the macro displays the prompt located in the cell named PROMPT2 and then beeps twice. The cell pointer moves to the cell named WARNING and remains there for five seconds. Line B52 is a formula that concatenates the cell address in the cell named HERE1 with the GOTO command and a tilde. This line moves the cell pointer back to its original location. Finally, the macro branches back to the OPENING module and redisplays the STARTUP menu.

There are innumerable ways to warn users of errors; this method was used simply to demonstrate a number of useful techniques.

The CHECK module, shown in figure 28.18, is almost identical to the WARN1 module.

To enter this module, follow these steps:

1. Move to the macro sheet. Choose the **/C**opy command. Then select the range B47..B53 and copy it to cell B22.

2. Enter the macro command shown in cell B21 of the Macro sheet.

3. Enter the label shown in cell A21.

4. Choose the **/R**ange **N**ame **L**abels **R**ight command for the cell A21 to name the cells to the right.

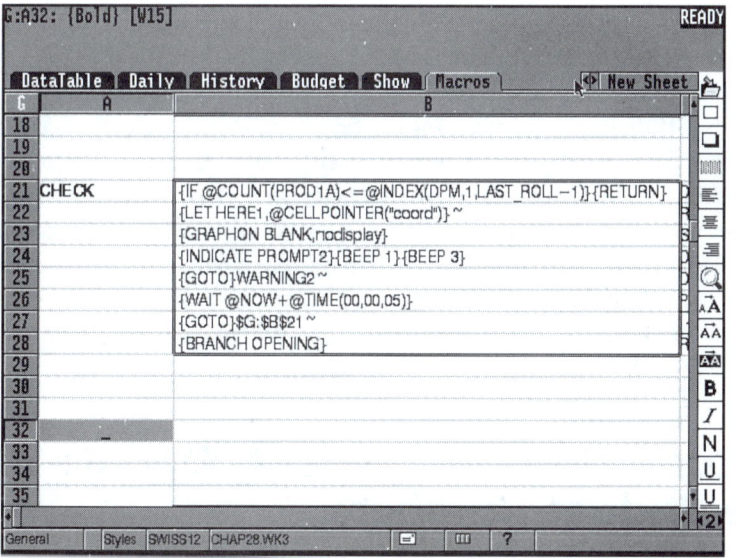

Fig. 28.18
The CHECK module, a second error-handling module.

5. The only modification you need to make to the code is to change WARNING to WARNING2 in cell B25. (This suggests that you could make this line of the WARN1 module a formula and use that code for both situations; see whether you can devise an approach that will enable you to replace lines B22..B28 with a call to WARN1.)

6. Refer to figure 28.19 and to the steps for setting up the WARNING screen to set up the WARNING2 screen.

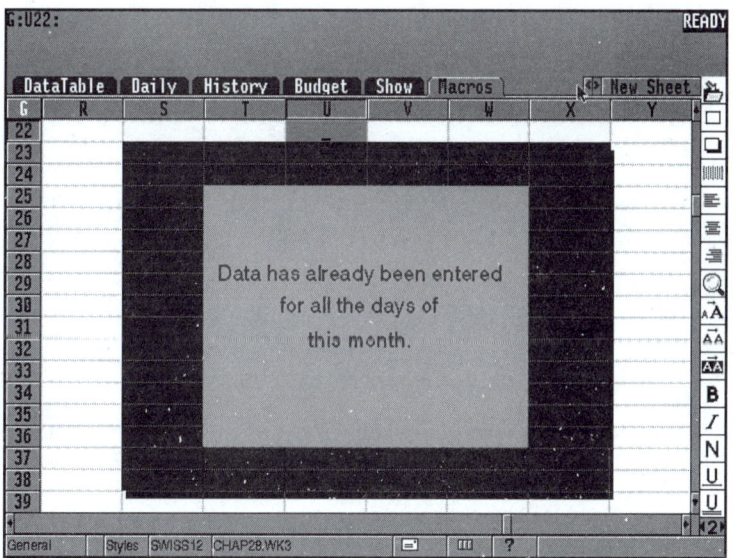

Fig. 28.19
The second warning screen.

The only line of this module that requires discussion is the first line in cell B21. Remember that this module is being executed when the user indicates that the current day's figures are not for the first day of the month. What happens if the incoming data is for the first day? This IF statement checks to see that at least one day of the current month needs data. The macro counts the number of items in the PROD1A range and checks to make sure that this number is less than the number of days in the current month, as determined by the INDEX function. If some days remain, the macro returns to the calling routine, which in this case means that it returns to the line after the OPENING call and begins bringing in the new data. If no days remain empty, the macro warns the user and returns to the STARTUP menu.

Automating the Monthly Update of the Budget Numbers

Now you need to develop the macro code that will update the budget figures in the Daily sheet at the beginning of each month. First, however, you should finish setting up the Budget sheet and then turn to the problem of updating the budget figures in the Daily page.

Figure 28.20 shows the desired layout of the Budget sheet. If you receive just the numbers by region by month and by product, you need to add the Total row shown in lines 16, 31, 46, 61, and 77, as well as the totaling column, such as the one shown in column G. Assuming that you already have these elements set up in your Budget sheet, you need only set up the formulas in the TOTALS, CUM, and YTD CUM ranges. The TOTALS range simply adds the corresponding ranges for the products. The CUM range must create running totals for each month of the year. The YTD CUM area should display the CUM numbers for the current month. To set up these formula areas, follow these steps:

1. Move to the Budget sheet and choose the **/C**opy command. Then select the range A48..G77 and copy it to cell A82.

2. Choose the **/R**ange **E**rase command to erase the data in the ranges C83..F94 and C99..F110.

3. Enter the labels shown in the range A81..A99.

4. Enter the following formula in cell C83, and then copy it to the range C83..F94:

    +C4+C19+C34+C49+C65

5. Enter the following formula in cell C99, and then copy it to the range C99..F110:

    +C83+C99

6. Enter the following formula in cell C112, and copy it to the range D112..G112:

    @INDEX($CUM,0,$LAST_ROLL-1)

7. Modify the formulas in cells D112..G112 by changing the column offset number for each formula from 0 to 1, 2, 3, and 4 respectively.

8. Choose the **/R**ange **N**ame **C**reate command to name the ranges C4..G16, C19..G31, C34..G46, C49..G61, C65..G77, C83..G95, C99..G110, and C112..F112. Name these ranges FORECAST1, FORECAST2, FORECAST3, FORECAST4, FORECAST5, TOTALS, CUM, and YTD_CUM, respectively.

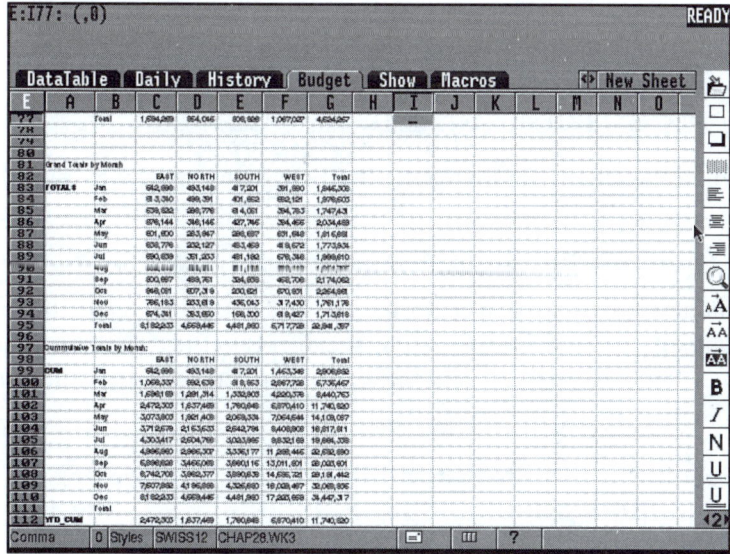

Fig. 28.20
The final layout of a portion of the Budget sheet.

This procedure sets up your Budget sheet. The only formulas to consider are those in the YTD_CUM range. These self-adjusting formulas use the month counter in LAST_ROLL as the row offset for the INDEX function. Therefore, the YTD_CUM range always reflects the year-to-date cumulative totals for the current month.

The next thing to do is consider what to do with the Daily sheet's budget numbers. First, note that you need daily cumulative budget numbers on the

Daily sheet, but that the Budget sheet contains only monthly cumulative numbers. What you need to do is spread the monthly numbers on the Daily sheet. The question is how to spread those numbers. You decide to assume that the budgeted numbers should be spread evenly over the month. After you develop some history, you can consider other ways to spread the numbers.

To modify the Daily sheet to reflect the budgeted numbers, follow these steps:

1. Move to the Daily sheet and enter the following formula in cell B1:

    @INDEX($DPM,1,LAST_ROLL)

2. Choose the /Range Name Create command to name B1 DCM (days in the current month).

3. Enter the following formula in cell B4, and then copy that formula to cells B6, B8, B10, and B12:

    @INDEX($FORECAST1,4,$LAST_ROLL-1)

4. Modify the formulas in cells B6, B8, B10, and B12 by changing FORECAST1 to FORECAST2 and so on.

5. Enter the following formula in cell B14 and then copy it to cells B16, B18, and B20:

    @INDEX($TOTALS,0,$LAST_ROLL-1)

6. Modify the formulas in cells B16, B18, and B20 by changing the column offset argument (the second argument) in the INDEX function to 1, 2, and 3 respectively. The formula in B16 should read as follows:

    @INDEX($TOTALS,1,$LAST_ROLL-1)

7. Enter the following formula in cell D4 and copy it to the range E4..Z4:

    @IF(D$2>$DCM," ",$B4*D$2/$DCM)

8. Copy the formulas in the range D4..Z4 to each of the Budget lines (D6, D8, and so on).

After you modify the Daily sheet, it looks something like figure 28.21.

These formulas automatically spread the current month's budgeted numbers in the Daily sheet; there is no need for a macro to accomplish this task.

Examine the formulas to see how they work. First, the formula in cell B1, @INDEX($DPM,1,LAST_ROLL), returns the number of work days in the

> **Tip**
> Although macros are powerful tools, you often can use worksheet functions to accomplish the same tasks more efficiently. Functions are not only automatic, but are also faster than macros.

current month. Next, look at the formula in cell B4, @INDEX($FORECAST1,4,$LAST_ROLL-1). This formula looks in the last column of the FORECAST1 range and returns the value from the LAST_ROLL-1 row, which is the current month's row. Finally, the formula in cell D4, @IF(D$2>$DCM,"",$B4*D$2/$DCM), checks to see whether the current day in cell D2 is greater than the number of days in the current month. If the current day is greater, the formula displays a blank; if not, the formula calculates the budget numbers as of that day. Study this formula to see how it makes these calculations.

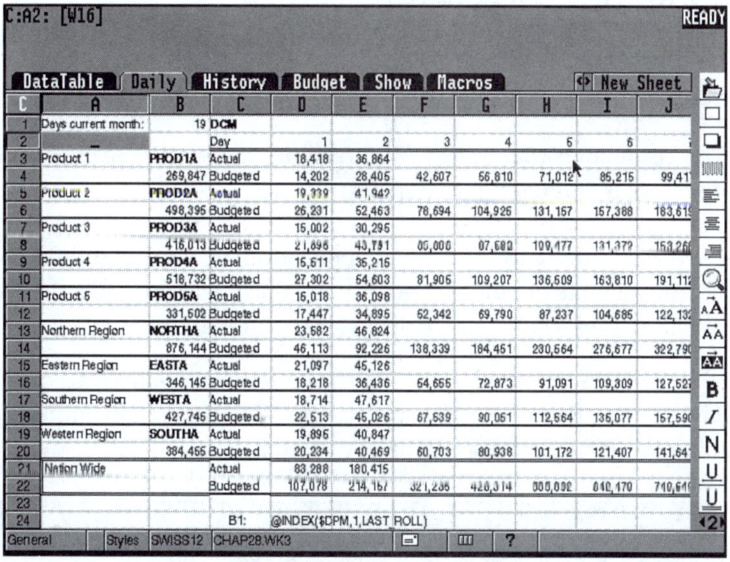

Fig. 28.21
The Daily sheet after adding formulas which update the budget numbers automatically.

Debugging the Application

The application is complete. Now it is time to test and debug the application, if you haven't been doing that as you developed each module. It generally is better to debug as you develop a module; at that point, everything is fresh in your mind, and solutions to any problems you discover may help you program the remaining modules.

◄ "Testing and Debugging Macros," p. 855

To improve the efficiency and success of the testing process, you can develop testing specifications. To develop testing specifications, you should consider the types of problems that your application could encounter. The procedure described in this section is similar to the procedure for error handling. You can develop a list of routine tests that you can run in all applications to which they are applicable.

While you develop testing specifications, consider the following points:

- Test numeric input with large positive values.
- Test numeric input with a value of zero (0).
- Test numeric input with negative values.
- Test numeric input with a label.
- Test numeric input with a blank.
- Test text input with a long label.
- Test text input with a value.
- Test text input with a blank.
- Test commands that work with directories to see what happens if the directory is empty or does not exist.

Because you have designed a modular application, debugging should be fairly easy. Creating a table of range names is good documentation practice, but it also is a handy tool when you are debugging your macros.

Figure 28.22 shows the range names in the current application. To create this table, choose the **/R**ange **N**ame **T**able command and select an empty two-column range where nothing will be overwritten.

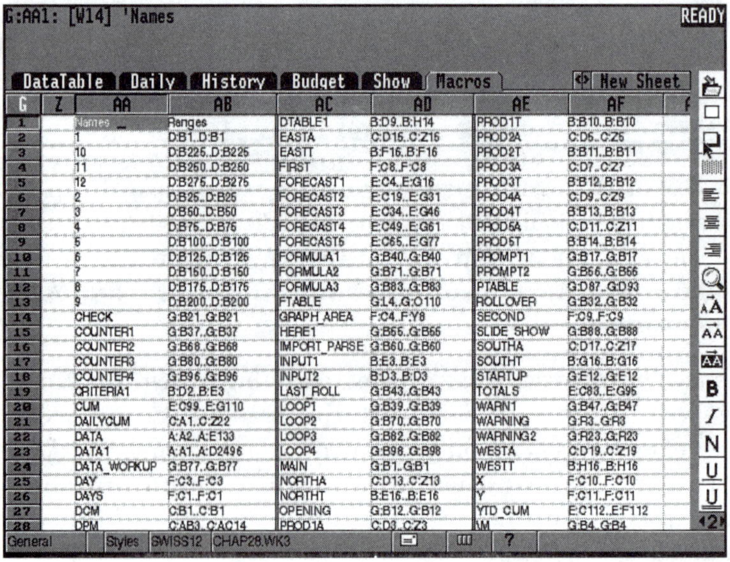

G	AA	AB	AC	AD	AE	AF
1	Names	Ranges	DTABLE1	B:D9..B:H14	PROD1T	B:B10..B:B10
2	1	D:B1..D:B1	EASTA	C:D15..C:Z15	PROD2A	C:D5..C:Z5
3	10	D:B225..D:B225	EASTT	B:F16..B:F16	PROD2T	B:B11..B:B11
4	11	D:B250..D:B250	FIRST	F:C8..F:C8	PROD3A	C:D7..C:Z7
5	12	D:B275..D:B275	FORECAST1	E:C4..E:G16	PROD3T	B:B12..B:B12
6	2	D:B25..D:B25	FORECAST2	E:C19..E:G31	PROD4A	C:D9..C:Z9
7	3	D:B50..D:B50	FORECAST3	E:C34..E:G46	PROD4T	B:B13..B:B13
8	4	D:B75..D:B75	FORECAST4	E:C49..E:G61	PROD5A	C:D11..C:Z11
9	5	D:B100..D:B100	FORECAST5	E:C65..E:G77	PROD5T	B:B14..B:B14
10	6	D:B125..D:B125	FORMULA1	G:B40..G:B40	PROMPT1	G:B17..G:B17
11	7	D:B150..D:B150	FORMULA2	G:B71..G:B71	PROMPT2	G:B56..G:B56
12	8	D:B175..D:B175	FORMULA3	G:B83..G:B83	PTABLE	G:D87..G:D93
13	9	D:B200..D:B200	FTABLE	G:L4..G:O110	ROLLOVER	G:B32..G:B32
14	CHECK	G:B21..G:B21	GRAPH_AREA	F:C4..F:Y8	SECOND	F:C9..F:C9
15	COUNTER1	G:B37..G:B37	HERE1	G:B55..G:B55	SLIDE_SHOW	G:B88..G:B88
16	COUNTER2	G:B68..G:B68	IMPORT_PARSE	G:B60..G:B60	SOUTHA	C:D17..C:Z17
17	COUNTER3	G:B80..G:B80	INPUT1	B:E3..B:E3	SOUTHT	B:G16..B:G16
18	COUNTER4	G:B96..G:B96	INPUT2	B:D3..B:D3	STARTUP	G:E12..G:E12
19	CRITERIA1	B:D2..B:E3	LAST_ROLL	G:B43..G:B43	TOTALS	E:C83..E:G95
20	CUM	E:C99..E:G110	LOOP1	G:B39..G:B39	WARN1	G:B47..G:B47
21	DAILYCUM	C:A1..C:Z22	LOOP2	G:B70..G:B70	WARNING	G:R3..G:R3
22	DATA	A:A2..A:E133	LOOP3	G:B82..G:B82	WARNING2	G:R23..G:R23
23	DATA1	A:A1..A:D2496	LOOP4	G:B98..G:B98	WESTA	C:D19..C:Z19
24	DATA_WORKUP	G:B77..G:B77	MAIN	G:B1..G:B1	WESTT	B:H16..B:H16
25	DAY	F:C3..F:C3	NORTHA	C:D13..C:Z13	X	F:C10..F:C10
26	DAYS	F:C1..F:C1	NORTHT	B:E16..B:E16	Y	F:C11..F:C11
27	DCM	C:B1..C:B1	OPENING	G:B12..G:B12	YTD_CUM	E:C112..E:F112
28	DPM	C:AB3..C:AC14	PROD1A	C:D3..C:Z3	\M	G:B4..G:B4

Fig. 28.22
A table of range names for your application. Normally, the table occupies only two columns; portions have been moved here to fit the complete table into one screen.

> **Note**
>
> You can add dynamic breakpoints to your macro by entering IF functions. You can set these breakpoints on or off at the touch of a key. Suppose that you want a breakpoint at line 24 on the Macro page. Replace the current label in cell B24 {INDICATE PROMPT2}{BEEP 1}{BEEP 3} with the following formula:
>
>   @IF(A4="","{INDICATE PROMPT2}{BEEP 1}{BEEP 3}","")
>
> When you want to turn this breakpoint on, you enter something in cell A4. Cell B24 then appears empty, and the macro halts. When cell A4 is empty, the macro text appears, and the macro runs normally. You can add a series of breakpoints that you can turn on or off just by changing the content of cell A4.

Documenting the Application

As you developed this application, you created various types of documentation. When you develop an application, consider using the following types of documentation:

◀ " Documenting Macros", p. 844

- Use range names.

- Enter range names near their respective ranges.

- Use a special format for range names (in this chapter, you used the bold format).

- Create a table of range names.

- Enter the names of your macro cells in the column to their left (as you did in this chapter).

- Enter detailed comments in the column to the right of your macro, here that is column C. Figures 28.24 through 28.28 show the complete documentation for the current application in column C of the Macro sheet.

- Enter copies of formulas as labels near the formulas, as you did in this application.

The first piece of documentation you need to include is the final version of the MAIN module. This is shown in figure 28.23.

Fig. 28.23
The final version of the MAIN module.

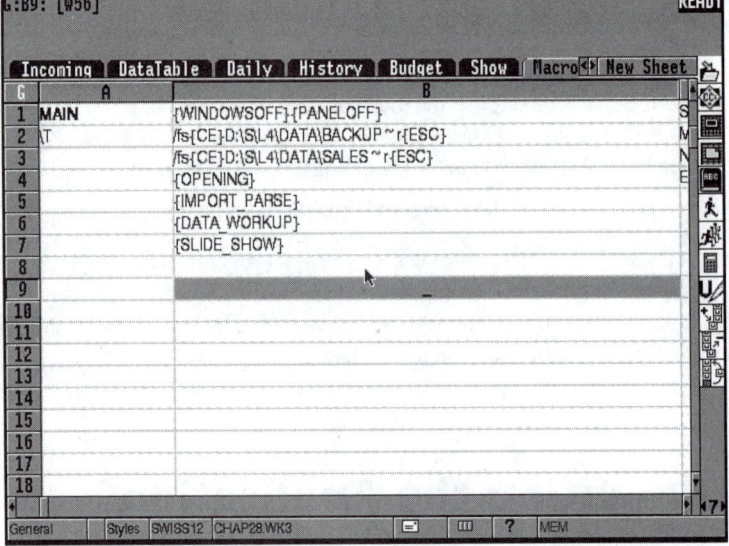

Fig. 28.24
The first page of documentation.

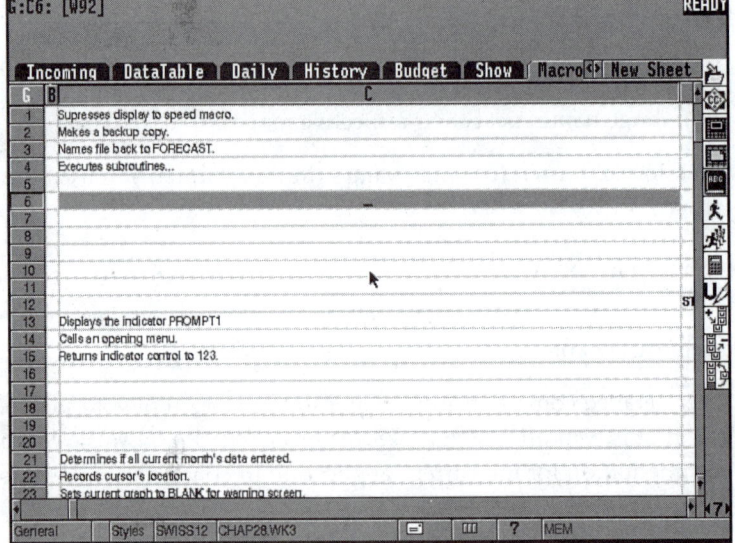

Documenting the Application **975**

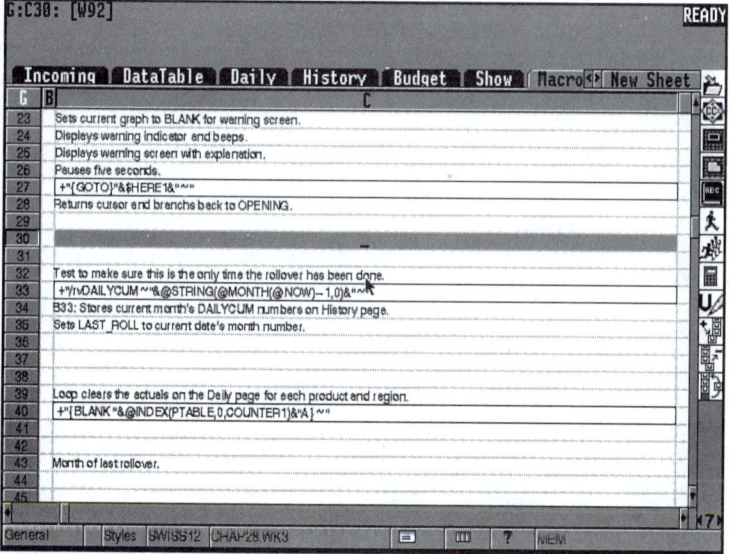

Fig. 28.25
The second page of documentation.

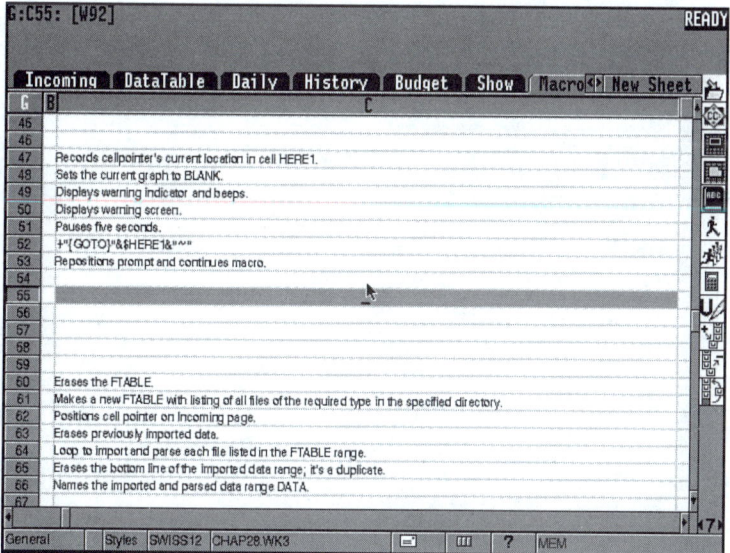

Fig. 28.26
Page three of the documentation.

976 Chapter 28—Controlling 1-2-3 with Macros

Fig. 28.27
The fourth page of documentation.

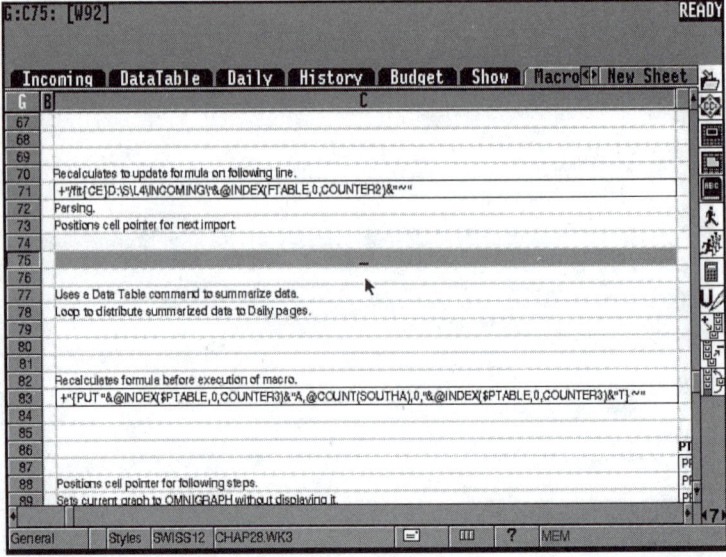

Fig. 28.28
The fifth page of documentation.

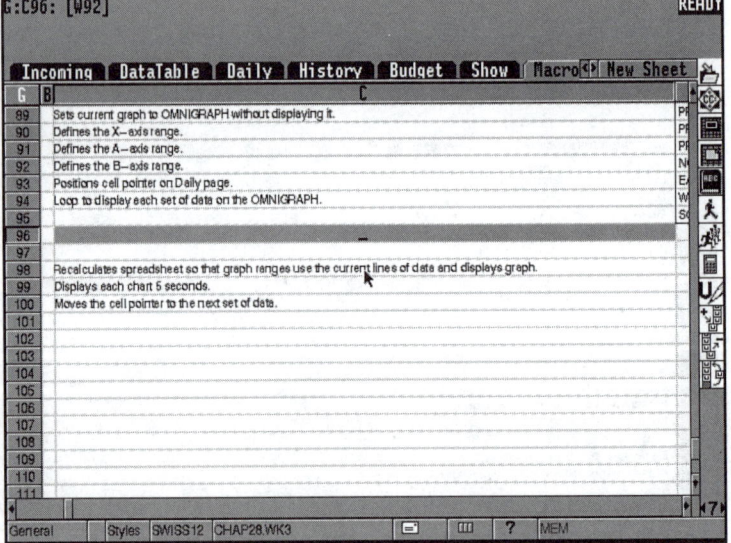

> **Troubleshooting**
>
> *I can't see the ranges in the table I created with the /**R**ange **N**ame **T**able command.*
>
> The /**R**ange **N**ame **T**able command does not create a dynamic table. Every time you add or delete range names, you need to update the table if you need a current copy.
>
> *I'm running my macro with step and trace on, but the macro actions are not displayed.*
>
> If your macro contains a WINDOWSOFF or PANELOFF command, take out that command temporarily.
>
> *I am getting various error messages and don't know what they mean.*
>
> Refer to the Troubleshooting sections earlier in this chapter. Also, when an error message appears, press F1 to have 1-2-3 explain the general meaning of the message.

From Here...

For more information related directly to controlling 1-2-3 with macros, you may want to review the following chapters of this book:

- Chapter 3, "Finding Solutions with Formulas and Functions." Refer to this chapter to get ideas of functions you might use to build more sophisticated macros.

- Chapter 15, "Using Functions To Analyze Data." This chapter also discusses functions that you may choose to incorporate into your macros.

- Chapter 26, "Short Macros To Make Your Life Easier." Read this chapter to learn 1-2-3 macro key names and basic macro programming techniques.

- Chapter 27, "Advanced Macro Command Power Techniques." This chapter presents all of 1-2-3's advanced macro commands with many practical examples.

Part VIII
Sharing Data

- 29 Sharing 1-2-3 Data with Windows Applications
- 30 Sharing 1-2-3 Data with Databases
- 31 Sharing 1-2-3 Data with DOS Word Processors

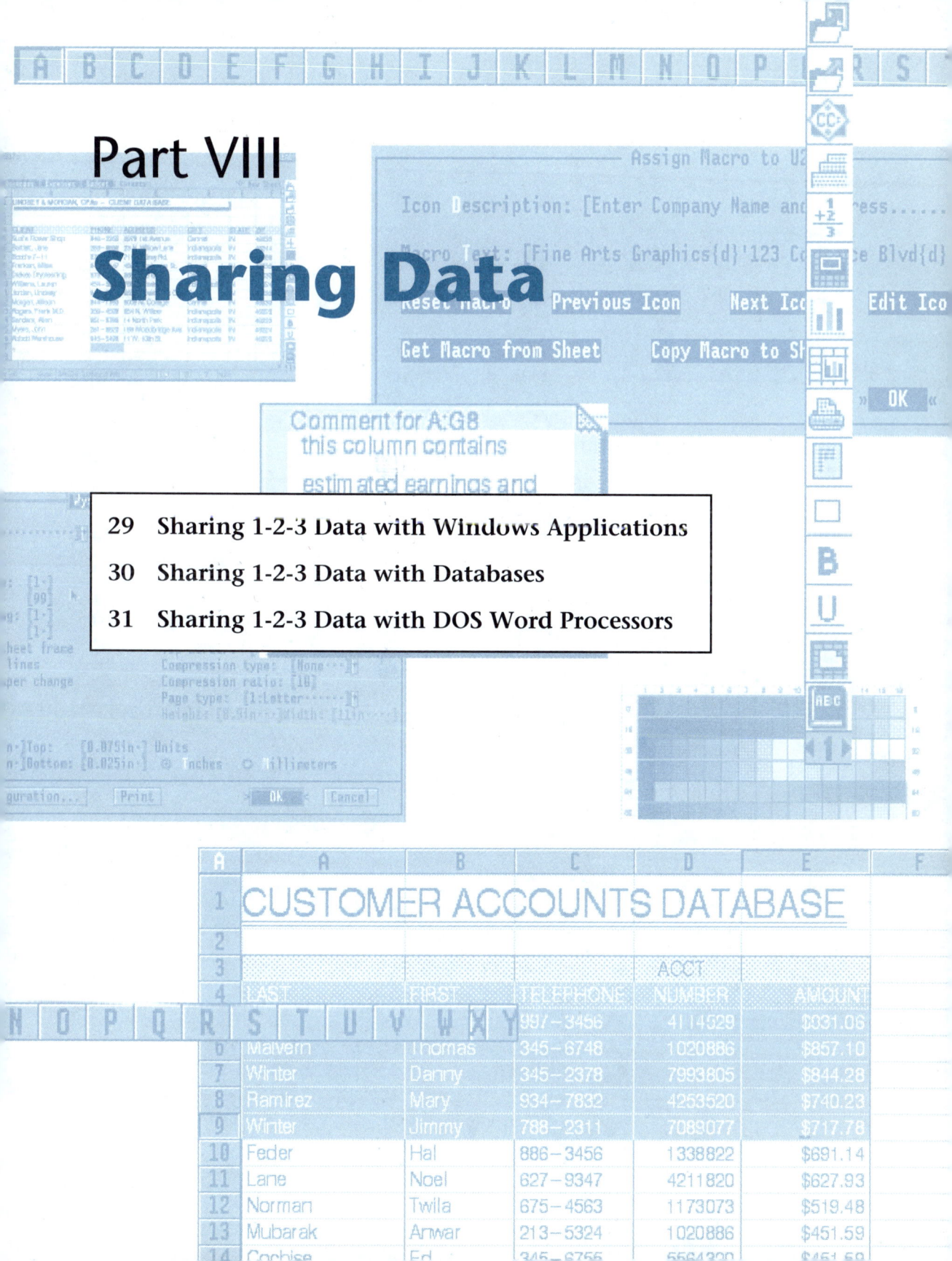

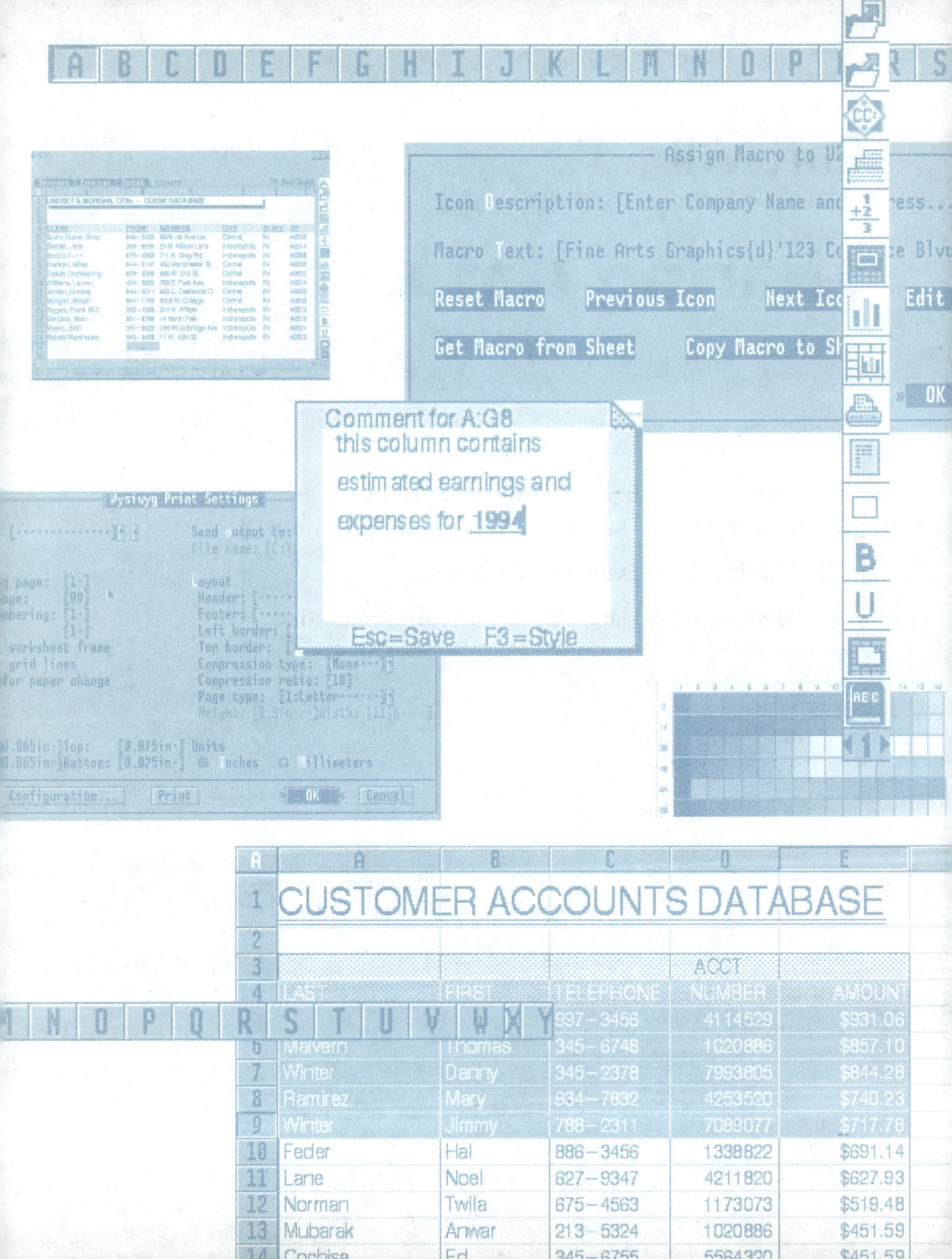

Chapter 29
Sharing 1-2-3 Data with Windows Applications

After you use Lotus 1-2-3 for a while, you may be in a situation where you want to use a portion of a worksheet in a word processing document, such as a letter, memo, or report. You may want to use a list of names and addresses as part of a mail merge. A graph that you created in 1-2-3 may work well in a newsletter article. Someone in the office who has another spreadsheet program may want to use your 1-2-3 data.

In each of these cases, you don't have to re-create your data in the new application; you can copy, import, or link your 1-2-3 information directly to the other application. If your other application is written for Microsoft Windows, you can transfer information from Lotus 1-2-3 in a number of ways. The new versions of Windows word processors (such as Microsoft Word 6, WordPerfect 6, and Lotus Ami Pro 3) and the new Windows spreadsheets (such as Lotus 1-2-3 Release 4 and Excel 5) are particularly suited to using data from Lotus 1-2-3 for DOS.

In this chapter, you learn how to use 1-2-3 for DOS data with the following programs:

- Microsoft Word for Windows
- WordPerfect for Windows
- Ami Pro
- 1-2-3 for Windows
- Microsoft Excel for Windows

Using 1-2-3 Release 4 with Microsoft Windows

Microsoft Windows (or *Windows*) is a popular operating environment for DOS. Windows enables you to start programs, manage directories and files, and run multiple programs at the same time in multiple windows on-screen. You can start and operate 1-2-3 Release 4 from the Windows environment. Although 1-2-3 Release 4 cannot take full advantage of Windows as can a program written specifically for Windows (such as 1-2-3 for Windows or Microsoft Excel), 1-2-3 Release 4 can transfer information to other programs while operating in Windows.

Microsoft Windows 3.1 operates in two modes. *Standard Mode* operates on a computer equipped with an 80286 microprocessor, such as an IBM AT or compatible. The other mode, which works on computers with an 80386 or better microprocessor, is *386-Enhanced Mode*. Although 1-2-3 Release 4 operates in either mode, it operates fastest in Standard Mode. In 386-Enhanced Mode, however, transferring information to other programs is more versatile. You also can operate multiple programs at the same time while in 386-Enhanced Mode.

Starting 1-2-3 from Microsoft Windows

◀ "Starting 1-2-3," p. 46

Although Lotus 1-2-3 Release 4 for DOS is not written specifically for Windows, you can start 1-2-3 for DOS through Windows and use the Clipboard to copy information; you can use the task-switching mechanisms of Windows and work with more than one program at a time. There are different ways you can start Lotus 1-2-3 within Windows:

- You can create a program icon for 1-2-3 and then double-click the icon each time you want to start 1-2-3. You can create the program icon for 1-2-3 and other DOS programs through a PIF file, described later in this section.

- You can launch 1-2-3 by going to the File Manager (located in the Main group), going to the drive and directory where 1-2-3 is installed, and double-clicking the 123.EXE or LOTUS.EXE file name.

- From the Program Manager or File Manager menu, you can choose **F**ile **R**un, type **C:\123R4D\123**, and choose OK. (If necessary, substitute the name of the drive and directory where 1-2-3 is installed.)

Using 1-2-3 Release 4 with Microsoft Windows 983

- You can double-click the MS-DOS Prompt icon (also located in the Main group) and then start 1-2-3 as you normally would from the DOS prompt by changing to the 1-2-3 directory and typing **123** or **Lotus**.

If you will use 1-2-3 within Windows often, you will want to create a program icon for 1-2-3. To create a program icon, you can use a file included with your 1-2-3 Release 4 for DOS disk. This is a special file called a *Program Information File* (PIF). You use PIF files because they contain information that Windows needs to run DOS programs such as 1-2-3. This information includes the amount of memory that 1-2-3 requires, whether 1-2-3 can run in a window, and whether 1-2-3 requires the entire screen.

> **Note**
>
> When you run 1-2-3 in *full-screen* mode, 1-2-3 occupies the entire screen. Although you may be able to use Wysiwyg in a 386-Enhanced Mode window, 1-2-3 will perform slowly. If you plan to use Wysiwyg in 386-Enhanced Mode, you should run 1-2-3 in full-screen format.

Lotus 1-2-3 Release 4 comes with a Windows icon that you can double-click to access 1-2-3 Release 4 from within Windows. To add this icon to a Windows program group, follow these steps:

1. Double-click the program group to open the group window where you want to place the icon.

   To place the 1-2-3 Release 4 icon in a program group called Non-Windows Applications, for example, double-click that program group.

2. From the Program Manager menu, choose **F**ile **N**ew. The New Program Object dialog box appears.

3. In the New Program Object dialog box, select Program **I**tem and then choose OK. The Program Item Properties dialog box appears.

4. In the **D**escription box, type **Lotus 1-2-3 Release 4**.

5. In the **C**ommand Line box, type the path to the 123R4.PIF file. If you installed 1-2-3 in the default drive and directory, for example, type **C:\123R4D\123R4.PIF** (see fig. 29.1).

Chapter 29—Sharing 1-2-3 Data with Windows Applications

> **Note**
>
> Windows automatically adds the directory where the PIF file is located—C:\123R4D, in this example—to the **W**orking Directory text box. If the 1-2-3 program files are in a different directory, type that directory's name in the **W**orking Directory text box.

Fig. 29.1
Complete the Program Item Properties dialog box with information required to launch 1-2-3.

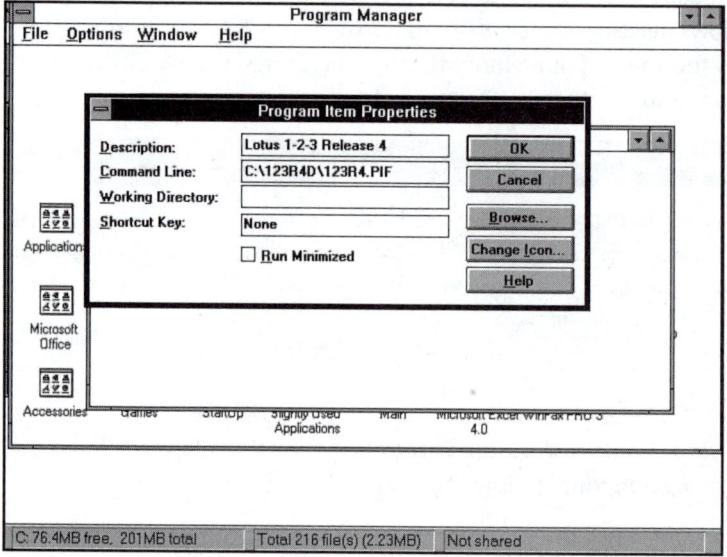

Tip
In the Program Item Properties and Change Icon dialog boxes, you can click the **B**rowse button to find program and icon files.

6. Click the Change **I**con button. (If an error message appears, choose OK to continue.) The Change Icon dialog box appears.

7. In the **F**ile Name box, type **C:\123R4D\123R4.ICO** (substitute another drive and directory, if applicable) and then choose OK. The 1-2-3 icon appears in the **C**urrent Icon box (see fig. 29.2).

8. Choose OK twice to accept this icon and return to the program group you selected in step 1. The icon now appears in the program group you selected.

In this example, the icon appears in the Non-Windows Applications program group (see fig. 29.3). To start 1-2-3 Release 4 from Windows, double-click this icon.

Fig. 29.2
Specify the file 123R4.ICO to locate the Lotus 1-2-3 icon.

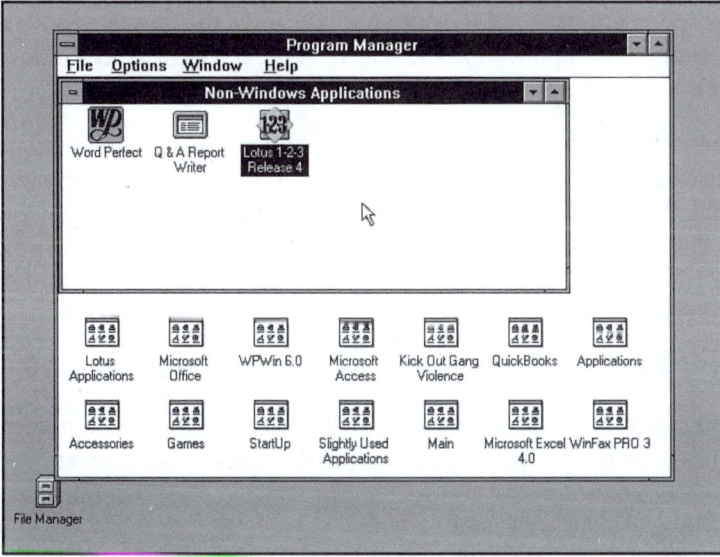

Fig. 29.3
The Lotus 1-2-3 Release 4 icon appears in the specified program group.

Operating 1-2-3 in Microsoft Windows

You can use the Alt+Tab key combination to switch from 1-2-3 Release 4 back to other Windows applications. When you switch back to another application, 1-2-3 stops whatever it is doing. When you switch back to 1-2-3, 1-2-3 continues where it left off.

Lotus 1-2-3 operates in Windows just as it does if you don't use Windows. A benefit of using Windows, however, is that you can easily switch between applications and transfer information between 1-2-3 and other applications.

While using 1-2-3 with Microsoft Windows, you can copy information from 1-2-3 to the Windows Clipboard. Using the Clipboard, you can paste the information to other applications, such as Word for Windows, WordPerfect for Windows, and Lotus Ami Pro.

Tip
If you have many programs running, it may be more convenient to press Ctrl+Esc to bring up the Task List and then double-click an application name.

Copying 1-2-3 Information to the Clipboard

The Windows Clipboard, a temporary location for copied data, is shared by most Windows applications. With a normal Windows application, to enter information into the Clipboard, you select the data or object and then choose **E**dit **C**opy or **E**dit **Cu**t. With a non-Windows application, you need to use the Control menu.

You can place a copy of the Lotus 1-2-3 screen in the Clipboard. If you want to copy the entire screen in full-screen mode, press the PrintScreen key. If you want to copy only a portion of the screen, you need to work in window mode to have access to the Control menu.

To access window mode, you have to run Windows in 386-Enhanced mode. To toggle back and forth between full-screen mode and window mode, press Alt+Enter. You will be able to copy only what you can view in a window, so after 1-2-3 is in window mode, you may need to increase the size of your window to see more of your worksheet. Click the Maximize button or drag a window border to increase the window's size.

To copy a portion of the 1-2-3 screen to the Clipboard, follow these steps:

1. You need to see on-screen all the data you want to copy. If necessary, move the cell pointer to position the data on the 1-2-3 screen.

   > **Note**
   >
   > The data in the 1-2-3 window can include text, values, formulas, Wysiwyg formatting, and charts.

2. Click the Control-menu box or press Alt+space bar. The drop-down Control menu appears (see fig. 29.4).

   > **Note**
   >
   > If you don't want the 1-2-3 menu to appear in the image, do not pass the mouse pointer over the control panel to get to the Control-menu box. Press Alt+space bar or move the mouse outside the 1-2-3 window.

Using 1-2-3 Release 4 with Microsoft Windows

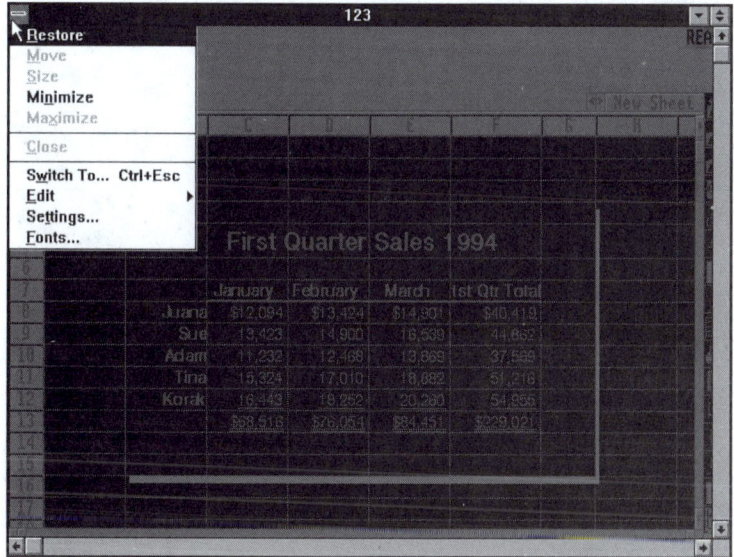

Fig. 29.4
Click the Control-menu box to display the Control menu.

3. Choose **E**dit Mar**k**. A blinking cursor appears in the top left corner of the 1-2-3 window.

4. Position the cursor where you want to start copying the screen.

5. Drag the mouse across the screen, or hold down the Shift key and press the direction keys, to highlight the portion of the screen you want to copy (see fig. 29.5).

6. When the screen is highlighted, press Enter.

Tip
You also can click the Control-menu box again and choose **E**dit **C**opy.

A picture of the screen is in the Clipboard. To use the picture, go to a Windows application (such as Word for Windows) and choose **E**dit **P**aste. The result in the document is a picture of the spreadsheet, as shown in figure 29.6—not the data itself. When you click the middle of the picture, the entire picture is selected, surrounded by black boxes called *handles*. You can delete the picture by pressing Del, move the picture by dragging it with the mouse, or change the size of the picture by dragging a handle. For more information, see your Windows and specific application documentation.

Fig. 29.5
Highlight the screen area to copy, and press Enter.

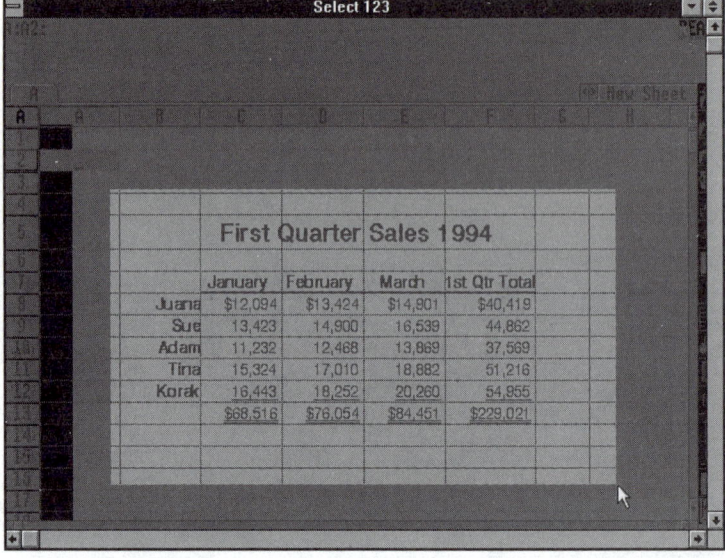

Fig. 29.6
Choose Edit Paste or click the Paste button to copy a spreadsheet area and graph from 1-2-3 into a Microsoft Word document.

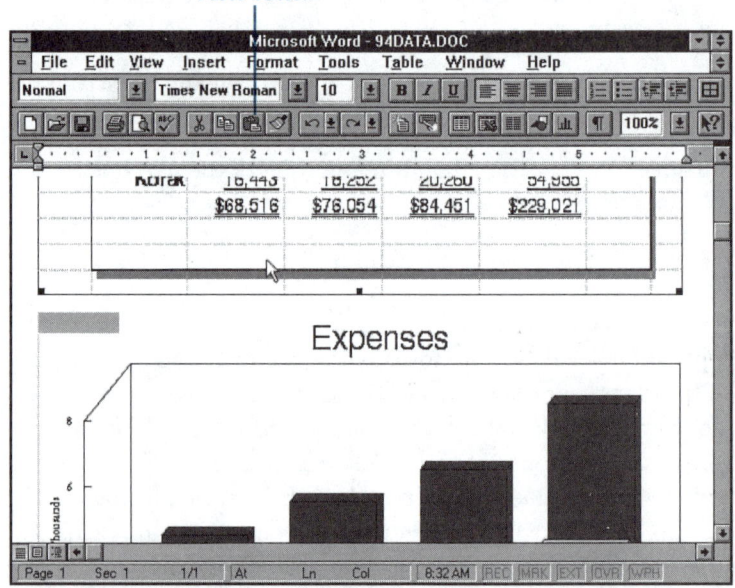

> **Note**
>
> The picture in the Windows application is pasted as a bit-map image. The resolution of the image depends on the resolution of your monitor.

Sharing Data with Windows Word Processors

Although copying the Lotus 1-2-3 screen to the Clipboard may be adequate for some uses, you will not be able to format or edit the 1-2-3 data within the application when you paste that data into the application. When you copy the Lotus 1-2-3 screen to the Clipboard, you also face a size limit, because you can copy only what can be displayed on-screen. If you want to use and edit Lotus 1-2-3 data in a word processing document as a table, as tabbed text, or in a merge operation, you must use alternative procedures.

Windows word processors such as Word for Windows, WordPerfect for Windows, and Ami Pro enable you to import Lotus 1-2-3 data in three ways:

- You can open a Lotus 1-2-3 file with **F**ile **O**pen.
- You can insert the data through an insert command.
- You can merge 1-2-3 data with a letter created in a word processing application.

Preparing the 1-2-3 Worksheet

To prepare the 1-2-3 worksheet, you may need to do different things, depending on the word processing application and the procedure you want to perform. Some word processing applications cannot read Lotus 1-2-3 Release 3 or 4 files; you may need to create one sheet and use **/F**ile **S**ave to save the file with a WK1 extension. Some word processors ask whether you want to use the entire worksheet or a range, and can accept range names; name the range you need by choosing **/R**ange **N**ame **C**reate. If your 1-2-3 data will be used in a merge operation, include in the range name the field-names row as well as the data in the worksheet.

If you want to use a 1-2-3 graph in another program, you can copy the graph to the Clipboard, as mentioned in "Sharing Data with Windows Word Processors" earlier in this chapter. You also may be able to use 1-2-3 graph files in a Windows application. Unless you have a color printer, you may need to experiment with the **/G**raph **O**ptions **B**&W and **/G**raph **O**ptions **C**olor settings to find the best output settings for your word processor. If you have more than one graph, make the graph active by choosing **/G**raph **N**ame **U**se; then choose **/G**raph **S**ave and type the name of the graph file. You can save the graph in either of two formats: PIC and CGM. The default format is CGM, but you can override the format by including the PIC extension in the file

◀ "Saving and Retrieving Your Work," p. 136

◀ "Specifying a Range with Range Names," p. 87

◀ "Designing a Database," p. 621

◀ "Creating Simple Graphs," p. 143

◀ "Saving Graphs and Graph Settings," p. 739

Tip
Save your graph twice, with CGM and PIC extensions. If your Windows application accepts both formats, import both versions of the file to test the output quality of the picture.

name. Check your Windows application documentation to see whether you can import either the PIC or CGM format.

If you are running 1-2-3 Release 4 under Windows, make sure that the worksheet you want to use is not in memory. In fact, after you save the file, the Windows process works faster if you exit 1-2-3 before you use the 1-2-3 files.

Sharing 1-2-3 Data with Microsoft Word 6.0 for Windows

As with any word processor, the procedure for importing 1-2-3 data to Microsoft Word for Windows depends on what you want to do with the imported data. If you want to import only a snapshot of a small amount of data, you may want to copy the screen to the Clipboard, as mentioned in "Sharing Data with Windows Word Processors." You may want to create tabbed columns of data from the worksheet or to create a table for the data in a Microsoft Word document. You also could use or create a graph from 1-2-3 data. Finally, you may want to use 1-2-3 data in a mail-merge operation to create personalized letters, envelopes, or mailing labels.

> **Note**
>
> To bring 1-2-3 data into Microsoft Word, you must have the appropriate translation program installed. This program is called *data filters*. If you try one of the procedures in this section and get an error message, the translation program may not be installed. If necessary, return to the installation program and choose Converters, Filters, and Data Access.
>
> If the procedure still does not work, you may need to get an additional converter for Lotus 1-2-3 Version 2.x and 3.x files from Microsoft. You can send for supplemental file-conversion disks by sending in the "Microsoft Word for Windows Supplemental Offers" coupon included in your Word for Windows package.
>
> You also can get these converters by downloading them from the Microsoft Download Service or from the MSWord Forum Files library on CompuServe. For more information on accessing these services, search for help information on the following topics in Word 6.0 for Windows: *Microsoft Download Service* and *Microsoft Forums on CompuServe*.

Creating a Word for Windows Table from 1-2-3 Data

If you want to convert your 1-2-3 data to a table, you have a choice of creating a new document or inserting the data into an existing document. Both commands work the same way; choose **F**ile **O**pen or **I**nsert F**i**le, and you see a dialog box that asks for the file name. If you want to see a list of your 1-2-3 files, you need to change the drive and directory and select All Files in the List Files of **T**ype drop-down list. After you indicate the name and location of the file, choose OK. The Open Spreadsheet dialog box appears (see fig. 29.7).

> **Note**
>
> If you open a 3-D worksheet or range, each sheet appears in a separate table in the Microsoft Word document. You cannot use sheet references when you import a 3-D worksheet, so use range names whenever you want to import ranges in sheets after sheet A.

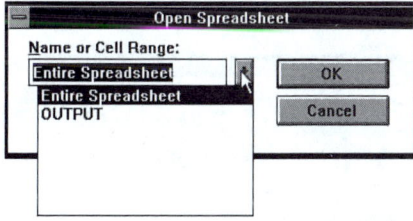

Fig. 29.7
In the Open Spreadsheet dialog box, click the drop-down arrow to display a list of ranges in the 1-2-3 file.

You have several options in the Open Spreadsheet dialog box:

- You can accept the default selection, Entire Spreadsheet, to import the entire worksheet.

- You can type range coordinates, such as A1..D5, or a range name in the **N**ame or Cell Range text box.

- You can click the pull-down arrow and make a selection from a list.

After you indicate the range, choose the OK command button. The spreadsheet data appears in your document in a table, as shown in figure 29.8.

After you import the data, edit and format the table as you would any other table in Microsoft Word. In the example shown in figure 29.8, you may want to change the font, merge the first-row cells with T**a**ble **M**erge Cells, delete the second row with T**a**ble **D**elete Rows, or choose among a list of formats with T**a**ble Table Auto**F**ormat, as shown in figure 29.9. When you finish editing and formatting your document, print and save the document as desired.

> **Tip**
>
> If you continually convert 1-2-3 data to Microsoft Word or another application that enables you to choose range names, use the same range name (such as OUTPUT) in all your files.

992 Chapter 29—Sharing 1-2-3 Data with Windows Applications

Fig. 29.8
The 1-2-3 data appears as a table in the Word document.

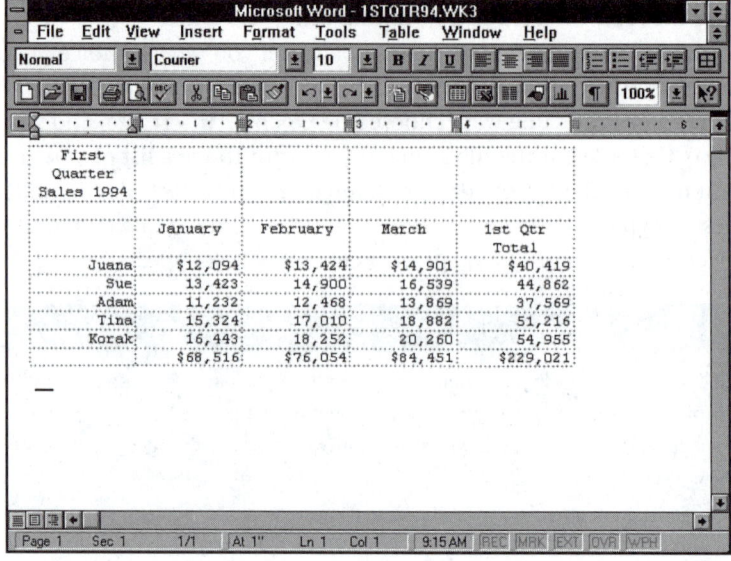

Fig. 29.9
Text was added, the font was changed, and Table AutoFormat was used to improve the table's appearance.

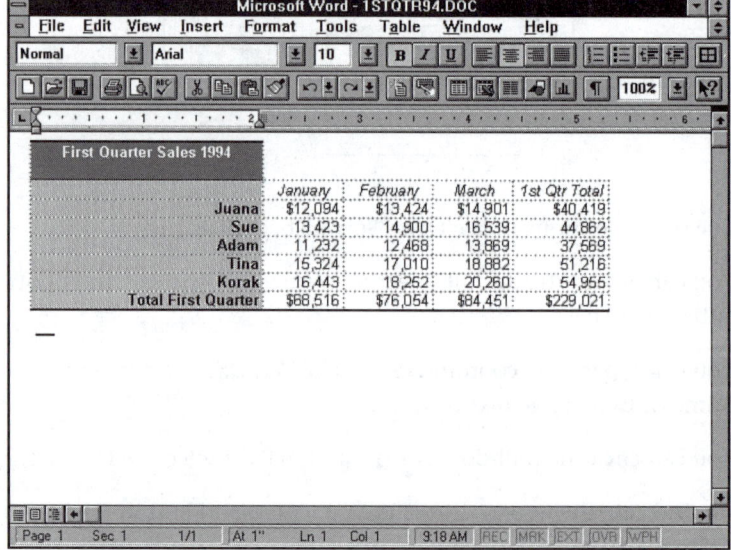

Caution

If you used **F**ile **O**pen to create a new document from your 1-2-3 data, make sure that you do not overwrite the 1-2-3 file when you save the document. Use **F**ile Save **A**s, delete the 1-2-3 file name (with a WK3 or WK1 extension), and type an appropriate name for a Word document (with a DOC extension). In the Save File as **T**ype pull-down list, select Word Document.

Inserting 1-2-3 Data as a Database

If you want more options for importing your data—such as choosing specific records and fields, sorting the data, and formatting your data—you can insert the 1-2-3 data as a database. Before you use the Microsoft Word procedure, the 1-2-3 file or named range must be in 1-2-3 database format, with the first row including field names and the subsequent rows including the records.

To begin the process and identify the 1-2-3 file, choose **I**nsert **D**atabase. The Database dialog box appears (see fig. 29.10). Choose the **G**et Data button. The Open Data Source dialog box that appears is like any other dialog box that requests a file name. Identify the file name, type, and location, and choose OK. As in the preceding section, "Creating a Word for Windows Table from 1-2-3 Data," fill out the Open Spreadsheet dialog box to identify the range or to use the entire spreadsheet.

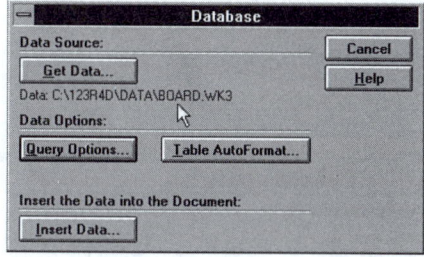

Fig. 29.10
After you choose the Get Data command button and select the 1-2-3 file, the name of the file (here, BOARD.WK3) appears below the button.

After you indicate the 1-2-3 file name and range, you return to the Database dialog box, in which you can select specific records, sort the database, and format the database.

To choose or sort records, choose the **Q**uery Options command button. A three-tab dialog box appears. To choose specific records based on field criteria, use the **F**ilter Records tab, shown in figure 29.11. In the Field column, click the pull-down arrow to display the field names (from the first row of your 1-2-3 worksheet or range). The Comparison column enables you to select options such as Equal To, Greater Than, and Is Blank. The Compare To column is where you enter values to be matched to the field.

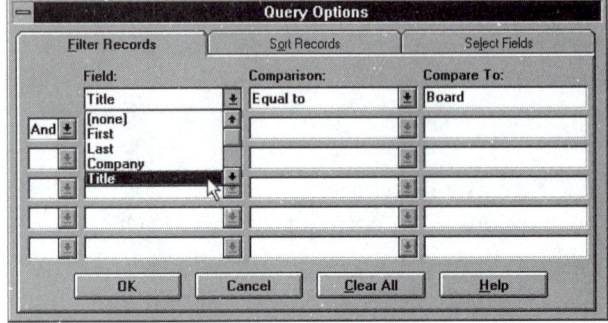

Fig. 29.11
Click the pull-down arrow to display a list of fields from the 1-2-3 database.

If you want to organize your database, choose the Query Options **S**ort Records tab and define how you want the database to be sorted. You can sort on up to three fields. Choose up to three fields in the **S**ort By, **T**hen By, and Then **B**y pull-down list boxes, and choose the Ascending or Descending option button for each of the fields. In figure 29.12, the records will first be sorted by last name. If any last names are duplicated, those records will be sorted by first name.

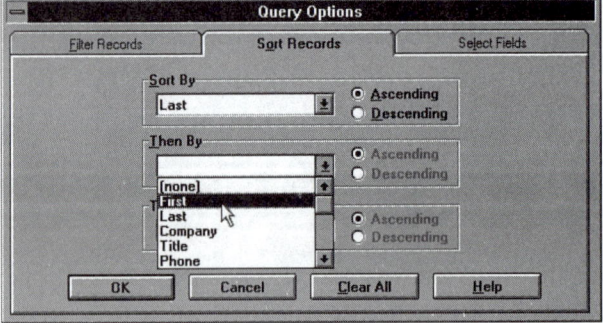

Fig. 29.12
Click the pull-down arrow to select a field name from the 1-2-3 database.

If you do not want to display all columns from the 1-2-3 worksheet or range, choose the Se**l**ect Fields tab in the Query Options dialog box (see fig. 29.13). One list box shows a list of the fields in the 1-2-3 file. The second list box shows a list of the fields you want to use in your Microsoft Word document. To remove a field from the Word document, highlight the field name and then choose the **R**emove command button.

Sharing Data with Windows Word Processors   **995**

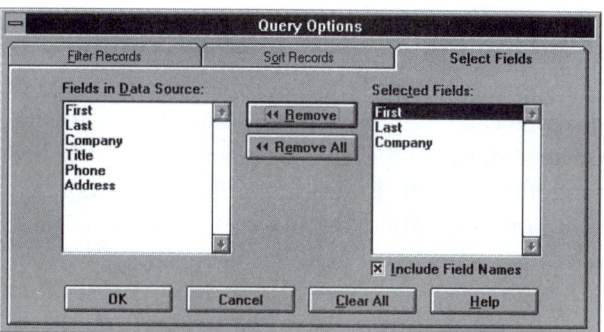

Fig. 29.13
In this example, only three (First, Last, and Company) of the six available fields will appear in the Microsoft Word document.

When you finish choosing query options, choose the OK command button in any of the three tabs to return to the Database dialog box.

If you want to select a format from a list of predefined formats, choose the **T**able AutoFormat button in the Database dialog box. In the Table AutoFormat dialog box, choose one of the options in the Forma**t**s list box, as shown in figure 29.14. Click any of the check boxes to specify which formats to apply to the portions of the database. The Preview area shows how the formatting will be applied. Choose OK to return to the Database dialog box.

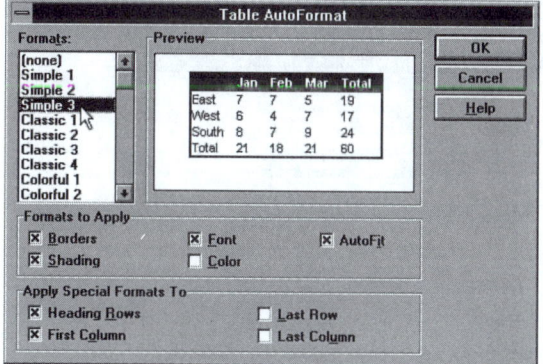

Fig. 29.14
Select one of the formats to use in your Microsoft Word table.

VIII

Sharing Data

> **Note**
>
> If you are going to insert a range of records from your 1-2-3 file, insert a blank column within 1-2-3 and use /**D**ata **F**ill to insert consecutive numbers, starting with 1 for the first record. You can use these record numbers in the Insert Records **F**rom and **T**o text boxes in the Microsoft Word Insert Data dialog box.

After you define the 1-2-3 file and apply any settings you want, you are ready to insert the 1-2-3 data into your document. Choose the **I**nsert Data command button to open the Insert Data dialog box, shown in figure 29.15. From this dialog box, you can insert all records in the database or only a range. If you plan to change the 1-2-3 file and want the changes to be updated in the Microsoft Word file, check the **I**nsert Data as Field check box. Choose OK to insert the 1-2-3 worksheet. After you choose OK, the 1-2-3 data appears in a table in your Word document, as shown in figure 29.16.

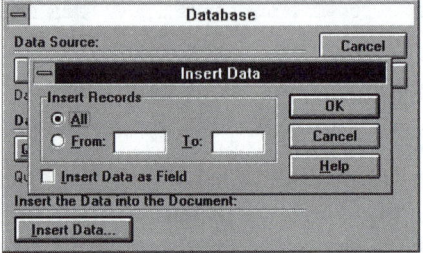

Fig. 29.15
To insert all records, accept the default All option and choose OK.

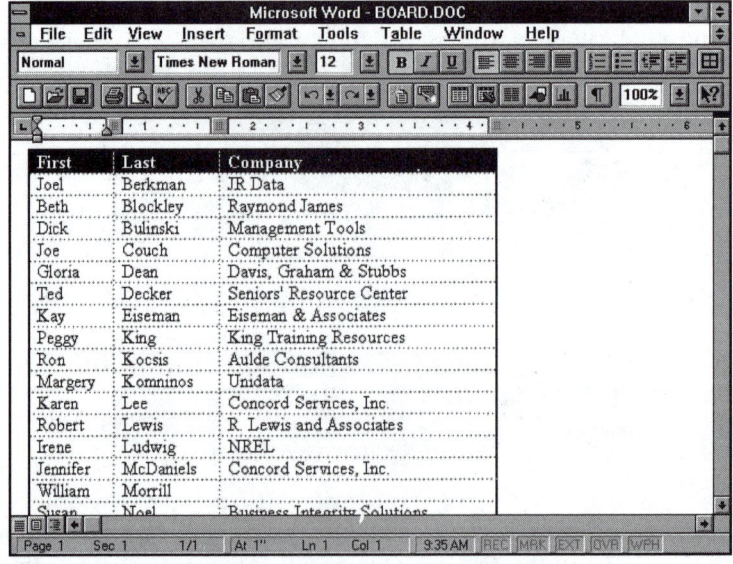

Fig. 29.16
The specific 1-2-3 data you selected through the Query Options and Insert Data dialog boxes appears as you formatted it with the Table AutoFormat dialog box.

Note

If you want your Microsoft Word document to be linked to your 1-2-3 worksheet, select the **I**nsert Data as Field option in the Insert Data dialog box before you import the worksheet. Save the Word document. After you make and save changes in the 1-2-3 worksheet, return to the Microsoft Word document. To display field codes, choose **T**ools **O**ptions. In the View tab, select the **F**ield Codes option and choose OK to return to the document. Move to the code that represents your table, and press F9 to update the changes. To see the changes, choose **T**ools **O**ptions; in the View tab, deselect the **F**ield Codes option and choose OK. If you don't update the links this way and try to press F9 with the table displayed rather than the code, Microsoft Word displays an error message indicating that it cannot convert the file and open the data source.

Importing a 1-2-3 Graph into a Word for Windows Document

If you want to import graphs into a Microsoft Word document, you have several options. You can copy the 1-2-3 graph into the Clipboard, as mentioned in "Copying 1-2-3 Information into the Clipboard" earlier in this chapter. Another option is to save the graph as a CGM file and use **I**nsert **P**icture to import the graph into your Word document.

◀ "Viewing Graphs," p. 737

Note

Although you can import the PIC format into Word, the titles and formatting do not import well. When you use CGM format, the graphs look better in the Word document.

Tip
You can edit the text and fonts in your graph by double-clicking the graph in the Word document.

In addition to importing the graph as a CGM file, you can use the Microsoft Graph applet and import your WK1 file. Microsoft Graph comes with Microsoft Word. To use this application, you need to save your 1-2-3 file with a WK1 extension; WK3 files do not work at this time.

To begin the process of inserting a graph, click the Insert Chart button in the standard toolbar or choose **I**nsert **O**bject and then choose Microsoft Graph 5.0. An example datasheet and graph appear on-screen, as shown in figure 29.17.

Fig. 29.17
The screen shows a window for the data (in a window called the datasheet) and a hatched pattern around the example graph.

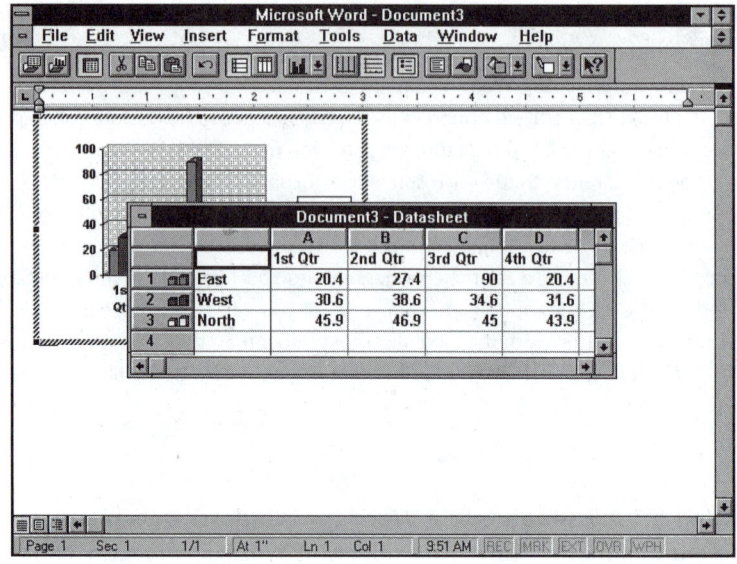

Position the insertion point in the cell you want to import. If your 1-2-3 range includes column and row labels, move to the first cell (above row 1 and to the left of column A). If the range includes only data, move to the first cell that contains data (A1). Your next step is to choose Edit Import Data. The Import Data dialog box appears (see fig. 29.18).

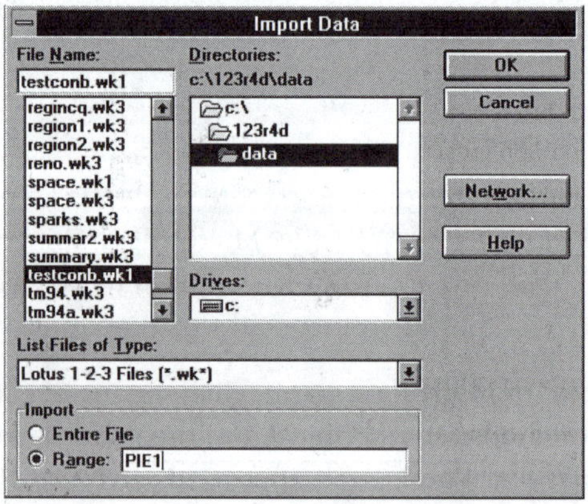

Fig. 29.18
Select a WK1 file and import the entire file or a range.

In the List Files of Type drop-down list, select Lotus 1-2-3 Files (*.WK*). Choose the name and location of the file. At the bottom of the dialog box is the Import section. Choose the Entire File option button, or choose Range and type the cell references or range name. Then choose OK. You see a message stating that import data will overwrite existing data (in this case, the sample data). Click OK. The new data appears in the datasheet. Edit or finish the chart's data, following the Microsoft Chart instructions. Double-click the datasheet's Control-menu box to close the datasheet and insert the chart into your Word document. When you return to the Word document, the chart is selected. Click outside the chart to unselect the chart and edit other portions of the Word document.

> **Note**
>
> If you have Microsoft Word loaded with Microsoft Graph, you can use Microsoft Graph with other Windows products. Look for Microsoft Graph under an Object choice in **I**nsert or **E**dit menus.

Merging Word for Windows Documents with 1-2-3 Data

You can use a 1-2-3 file as the source for names and addresses in a mail merge. You cannot use the 1-2-3 file directly, however; you must use the Lotus Translate utility to convert the file to an intermediate format. For this example, choose the dBASE format. Then, to merge the file, choose **T**ools Mail Me**r**ge and fill out the Mail Merge Helper dialog box as shown in your Microsoft Word documentation.

◀ "Transferring Files with the Translate Utility," p. 446

Sharing 1-2-3 Data with WordPerfect 6.0 for Windows

As with Microsoft Word, you can use 1-2-3 data in WordPerfect for Windows documents. You can use 1-2-3 data as a table within WordPerfect, create a graph in WordPerfect, or merge the 1-2-3 data into a letter, envelope, or mailing list.

Importing 1-2-3 Data into a WordPerfect for Windows Document

You have a few options for importing 1-2-3 data into a WordPerfect document. You can create a table from the 1-2-3 data, import the data with tabs separating each former 1-2-3 column, or import the data as information for a merge data file. In all cases, the process begins the same way.

If you want to start a new file with the 1-2-3 data, choose **F**ile **O**pen or click the Open PowerButton. If you want to insert 1-2-3 data into an existing document, you can choose **I**nsert Sp**r**eadsheet/Database **I**mport. Both procedures take you to the Import Data dialog box, shown in figure 29.19.

Fig. 29.19
The Import Data dialog box appears if you try to open a 1-2-3 worksheet or if you choose Insert Spreadsheet/Database.

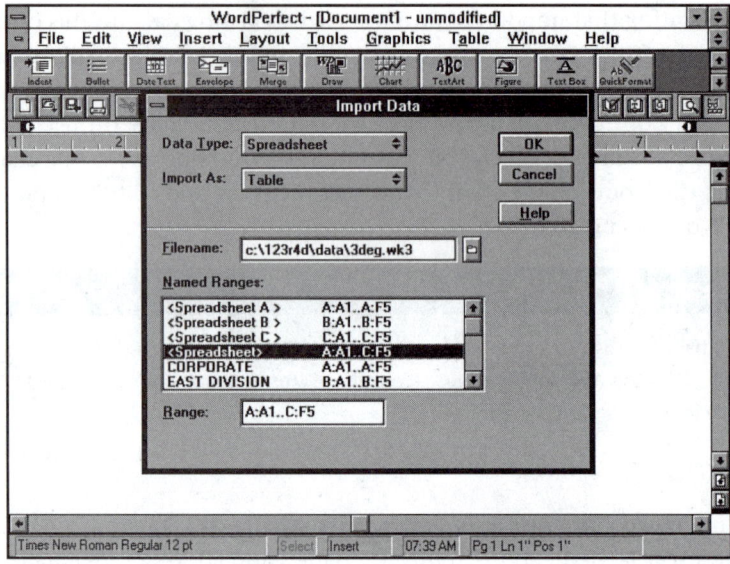

The word Spreadsheet should appear in the Data Type box. If you were importing a different type of file, such as a dBASE file, that program name should appear in the Data Type box.

The second box, Import As, gives you three options for using the 1-2-3 data in the document. Figure 29.20 shows a document in which the same file was imported with the three different options.

- Table (the default) makes each column and row of the 1-2-3 worksheet a column and row in a WordPerfect table.

- Text imports the 1-2-3 data with tabs separating columns and carriage returns separating rows.

- Merge Data File creates a file for merging. Information for each cell ends with ENDFIELD; information from each row ends with ENDRECORD.

Note

After you choose one Import As option, that option becomes the default for the next Import Data procedure.

Sharing Data with Windows Word Processors

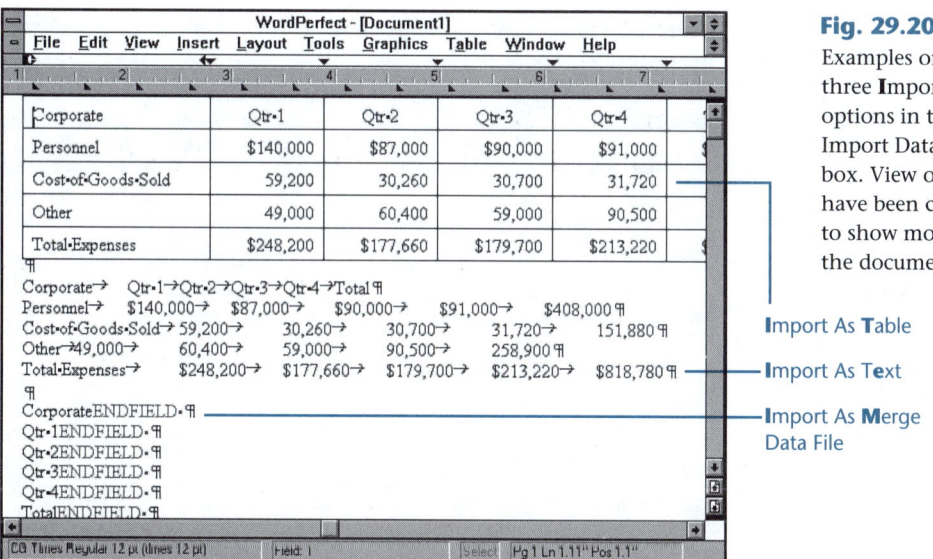

Fig. 29.20
Examples of the three **I**mport As options in the Import Data dialog box. View options have been changed to show more of the document.

In the **F**ilename text box, you can type the name and location of the file, or choose the file list button (the button next to the **F**ilename box) and browse your directories for the file. WordPerfect will enter the name of the last file you imported as the default name in the **F**ilename text box.

The **N**amed Ranges list box displays a separate entry for each worksheet in a multiple-sheet file, as well as a <Spreadsheet> entry that enables you to import the entire file and a list of named ranges. Select one of these items in the list, or type the range name or range coordinates in the **R**ange text box.

When you finish filling out the Import Data dialog box, choose OK; the 1-2-3 data is imported into your WordPerfect document, as shown in figure 29.21. Edit the document as you would any other WordPerfect document.

Tip
If you continually convert 1-2-3 data to WordPerfect or to another application in which you can specify ranges, use the same range name (such as OUTPUT) for all your files.

> **Caution**
>
> When you save the WordPerfect file, make sure that you do not overwrite the existing 1-2-3 worksheet. If you used **F**ile **O**pen to import the data, the default file name is the WK3 or WK1 file name. Choose **F**ile Save **A**s or press F3, and give the file a new name. You can delete the 1-2-3 extension and type the WordPerfect extension (WPD).

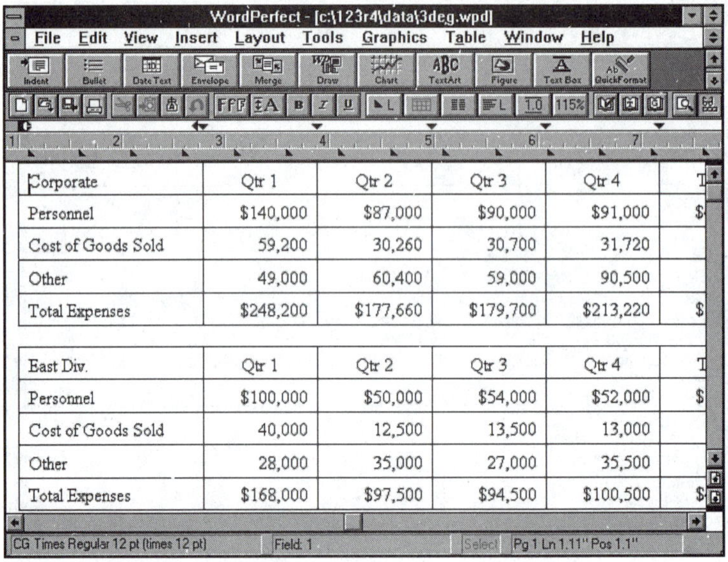

1002 Chapter 29—Sharing 1-2-3 Data with Windows Applications

Fig. 29.21
If you choose the Import As Table option for a 1-2-3 file that contains several worksheets, each worksheet becomes a separate table.

Creating a Link to Your 1-2-3 Data

◄ "Linking Files," p. 487

If you want the WordPerfect document to update automatically when you change the 1-2-3 file, you can link the WordPerfect document to the 1-2-3 file. Instead of following the procedure in the preceding section, choose **I**nsert Sp**r**eadsheet/Database **C**reate Link, as shown in figure 29.22. The Create Data Link dialog box is identical to the Import Data dialog box. Complete the Create Data Link dialog box as you would the Import Data dialog box.

Fig. 29.22
The Insert Spreadsheet/ Database menu also enables you to edit and update links.

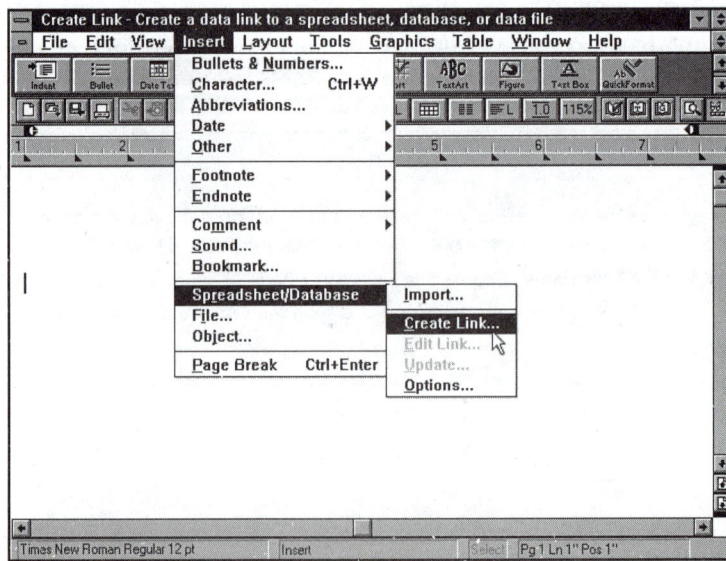

When you change and save the 1-2-3 file, you can choose to update the WordPerfect document on demand or to update the document automatically. To update the WordPerfect document on demand, choose **I**nsert Sp**r**eadsheet/Database **U**pdate Link and then choose Yes to update all links. If you want to change the linked range or worksheet, choose **I**nsert Sp**r**eadsheet/Database **E**dit Link. If you want links to update automatically whenever you retrieve the WordPerfect document, choose **I**nsert Sp**r**eadsheet/Database **O**ptions and then check the **U**pdate on Retrieve check box.

Merging WordPerfect for Windows Documents with 1-2-3 Data

You can use a 1-2-3 file as the source for names and addresses in a mail merge. You need to set up the 1-2-3 file as a database file, with the field names in row 1 and the records in the remaining rows. You can use a WK1 or WK3 file.

◀ "Designing a Database," p. 621

If you have an existing document that you want to use or convert to a merge form file, open the file, choose the Merge button, and then choose **T**ools **M**erge or press Shift+F9. The Merge dialog box appears (see fig. 29.23). Choose **F**orm to create a form letter, and choose Active Window to use the document that was on-screen when you began the merge. The Create Form File dialog box appears.

> **Note**
> If you want to create mailing labels, choose **L**ayout La**b**els in WordPerfect before you begin the merge process.

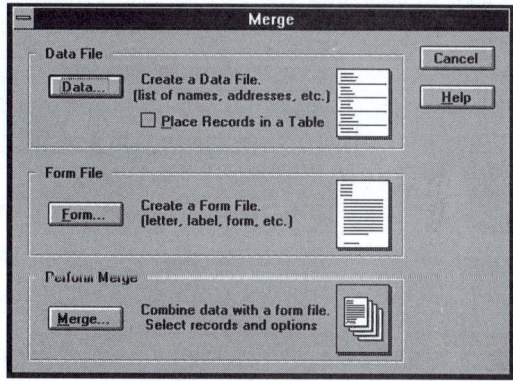

Fig. 29.23
To attach a 1-2-3 file, choose Form in the Merge dialog box and then choose Associate a Data File.

Choose **A**ssociate a Data File. Type the 1-2-3 file name, or choose the file selector button on the right side of the text box and browse for the file name. Choose OK to return to the WordPerfect window, which now displays the Merge Feature Bar.

Move to the place in your document where you want to insert a field-name placeholder. Choose the **I**nsert Field button in the Merge Feature Bar. The Insert Field Name or Number dialog box appears (see fig. 29.24). Select the field name and the **I**nsert command button. Add a space, carriage return, or other necessary character in the WordPerfect document; then select the next field name you need and choose **I**nsert. When you finish entering field names, choose **C**lose to return to the document.

> **Note**
>
> After you choose the **I**nsert Field button in the Merge Feature Bar, if you see a message saying that no field names or records were found, choose OK to exit the message and then choose Close in the Insert Field Name or Number dialog box. Choose the Go to Data button in the Merge Feature Bar to import the data to a separate file. After the data is imported, choose the Go to Form button and try again to insert the fields.

Fig. 29.24
Select the field names for which you want to create placeholders in your WordPerfect document.

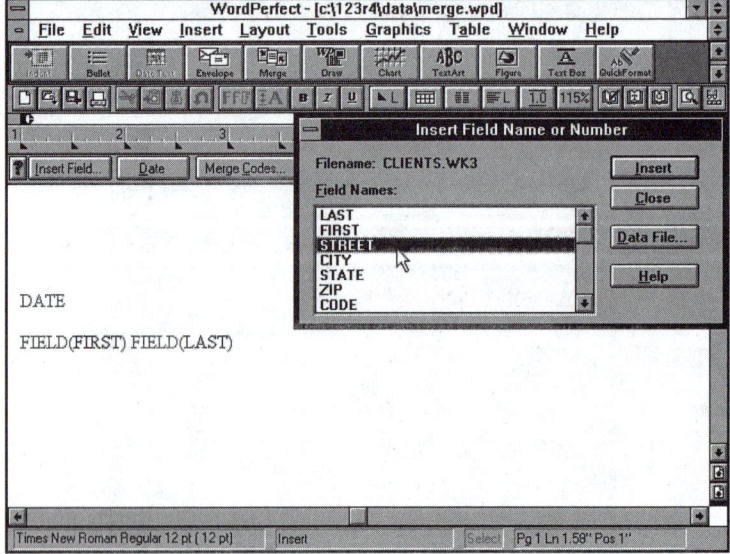

After you finish entering the field names and any text in your letter, click the
Merge button in the Merge Feature Bar. You return to the Merge dialog box
(refer to fig. 29.23). Choose the **M**erge button in the Merge dialog box. The
Perform Merge dialog box appears (see fig. 29.25).

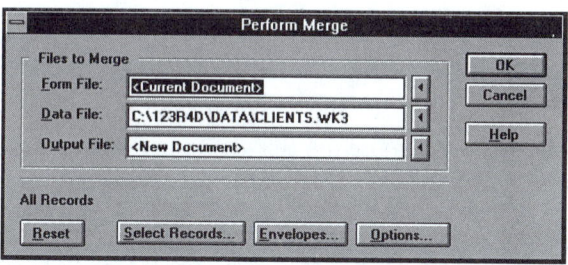

Fig. 29.25
The Perform Merge
dialog box should
show the name of
the document or
<Current
Document> in the
Form File box and
the name of your
1-2-3 file in the
Data File box.

To use specific records (not the entire 1-2-3 database), choose the **S**elect
Records button in the Perform Merge dialog box. The Select Records dialog
box appears (see fig. 29.26).

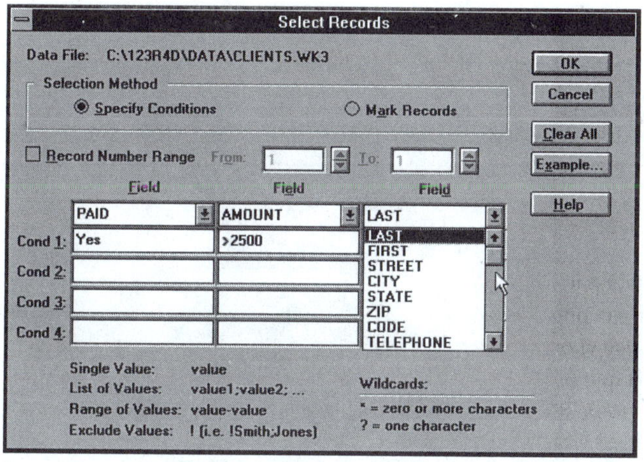

Fig. 29.26
If you select the
Specify Conditions
option, you can
use the pull-down
Field lists to
identify the field.

You can select records in this dialog box in three ways:

- To identify which records to use by record number, select the **R**ecord
  Number Range option, and type the first and last record of the range in
  the text boxes.

- Select the **S**pecify Conditions option, and in each Field column, select a field name from the pull-down list. In the Cond rows (1-4), type your criteria for finding the records, as shown in figure 29.26. (For more help, see the examples at the bottom of the dialog box or choose the E**x**ample button.)

- Select the M**a**rk Records option. The Select Records dialog box changes as shown in figure 29.27. If your 1-2-3 file contains many records, specify which records you want to display and the first field to be displayed. If necessary, choose the **U**pdate Record List button. In the Record **L**ist, check the check box of each record you want to use.

> **Note**
>
> If you are going to insert a range of records from your 1-2-3 file, insert a blank column within 1-2-3 and choose /**D**ata **F**ill to insert consecutive numbers, starting with 1 for the first record. You can use these record numbers in the **R**ecord Number Range in the WordPerfect Select Records dialog box.

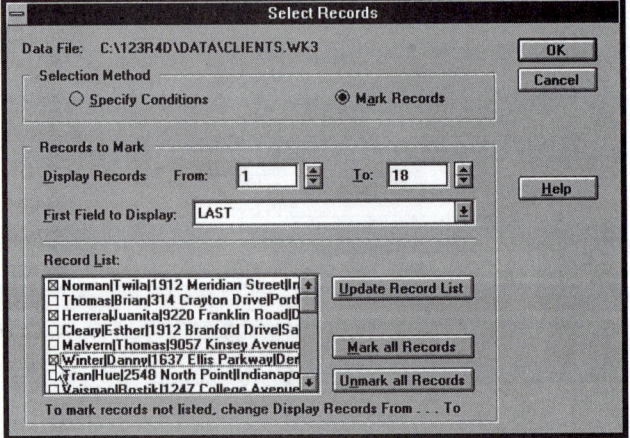

Fig. 29.27
The M**a**rk Records option enables you to specify each record.

After you choose one of the selection options, you return to the Perform Merge dialog box. If you want to create an envelope for each record you selected, choose the **E**nvelopes button. You can add your own mailing address. Place the insertion point in the **M**ailing Address text box, and choose the F**i**eld button for each of the fields to be entered in the mailing address. Make sure that you add spaces and carriage returns where necessary. Figure 29.28 shows a completed envelope.

Sharing Data with Windows Word Processors **1007**

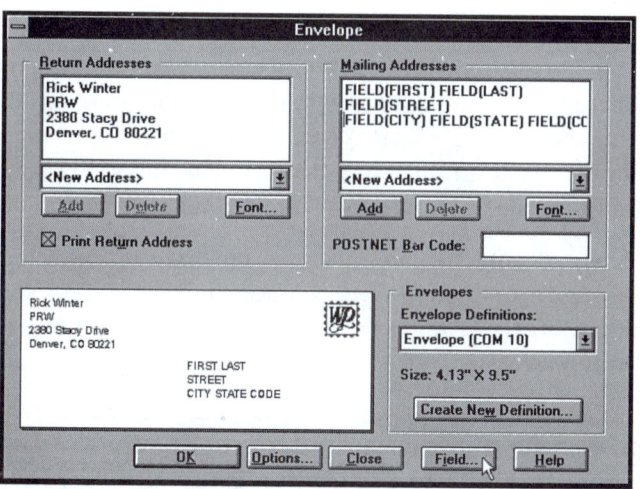

Fig. 29.28
Identify the fields from your 1-2-3 database by choosing the Field button in the Envelope dialog box.

When you finish creating the envelope, choose OK to return to the Perform Merge dialog box. When you are ready to perform the merge, choose OK. The merge appears in a new document. Each page is a separate record and will be a letter or envelope, depending on whether you defined the file as an envelope. Figure 29.29 shows a completed merge.

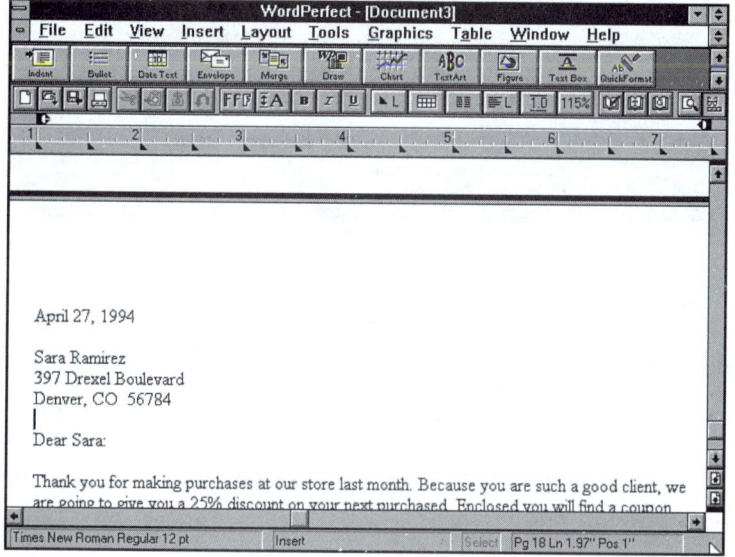

Fig. 29.29
In this example, 18 records were merged from the 1-2-3 data file and created 18 pages.

Importing a 1-2-3 Graph into a WordPerfect for Windows Document

If you want to import a graph into a WordPerfect document, you have several options. You can copy the 1-2-3 graph to the Clipboard (refer to "Copying 1-2-3 Information to the Clipboard" earlier in this chapter), or you can save the graph in PIC or CGM format in 1-2-3 and then choose **G**raphics **F**igure or click the Figure button to import the graph into the WordPerfect document.

After you choose **G**raphics **F**igure, you enter the Insert Image dialog box, shown in figure 29.30. Change to the directory and drive where your graphics file is located. In the List Files of **T**ype list, select Lotus PIC (*.PIC) or Computer Graphics Metafiles (*.CGM) to list the 1-2-3 graphics file.

Fig. 29.30
The default file type for inserting figures is WP Graphics (*.WPG). Change the file to Computer Graphics Metafiles (*.CGM) for Lotus 1-2-3 graphic files.

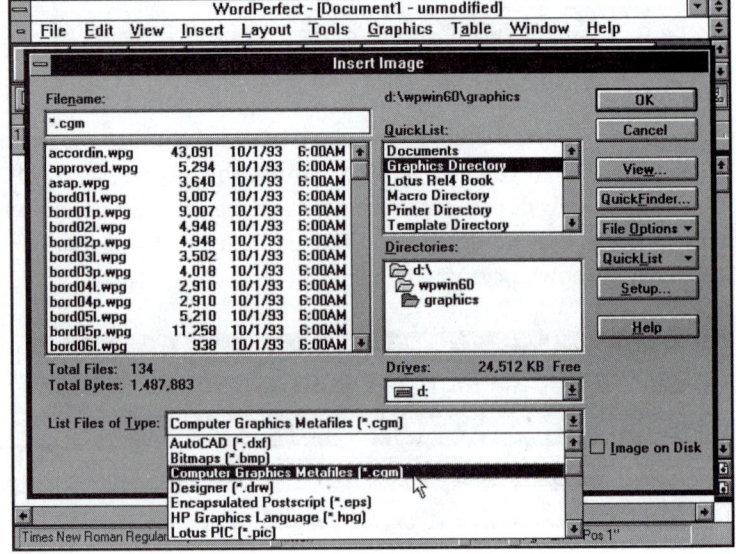

Tip
You can edit the text and fonts in your graph by double-clicking the graph in the WordPerfect document to enter the WP Draw applet.

After you insert the graph, you can edit, save, and print the document as you would any other WordPerfect document. See your WordPerfect documentation for more details.

You also can use the WP Draw applet that comes with WordPerfect for Windows to insert a graph. To begin the process, click the Chart button in the Button Bar or choose **G**raphics Cha**r**t. An example datasheet and graph appear on-screen, as shown in figure 29.31.

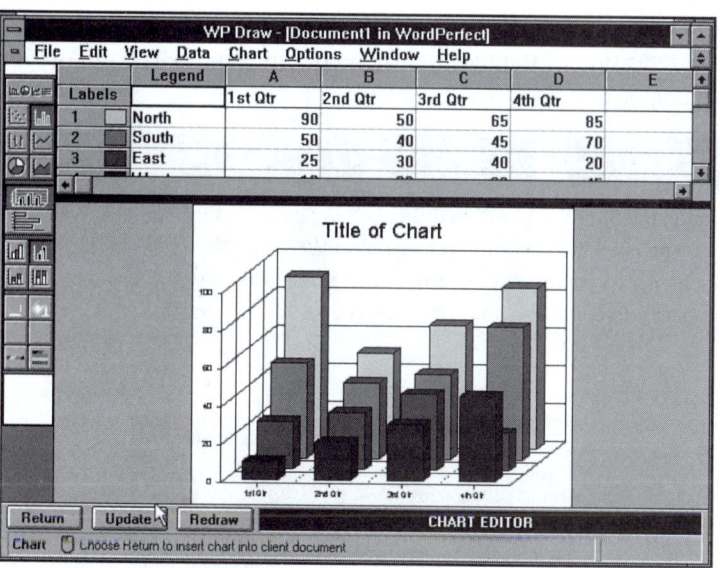

Fig. 29.31
The WP Draw Chart Editor shows a window for the datasheet and an example chart.

Position the insertion point in the cell you want to import. If your 1-2-3 range includes labels, move the first cell (above row 1 and to the left of column A). If the range contains only data, move to the first cell that contains data (A1). Your next step is to choose **F**ile **I**mport or press F4. The Import Chart Data dialog box appears (see fig. 29.32).

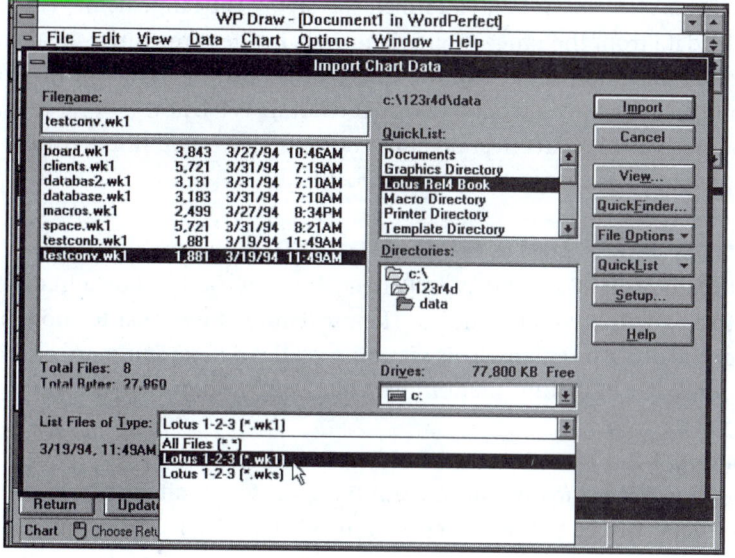

Fig. 29.32
Select a WK1 file and import the entire file or a range.

In the List Files of **T**ype drop-down list, select Lotus 1-2-3 (*.WK1). Select the name and location of the file, and then choose I**m**port. The Import Spreadsheet dialog box appears (see fig. 29.33).

> **Note**
>
> Although the Import Chart Data dialog box in figure 29.32 shows only WK1 and WKS Lotus 1-2-3 file options, you can import WK3 files. However, you must use range names to import data from worksheets other than sheet A. If you try to type worksheet references, the program displays an error message.

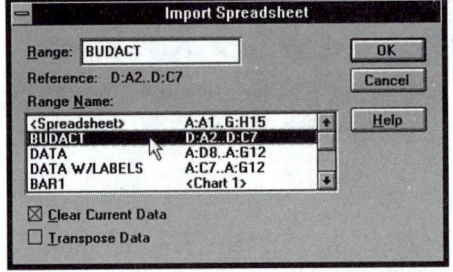

Fig. 29.33
The Import Spreadsheet dialog box enables you to select a range name or type the range of the graph.

In the Range **N**ame list, select a range name or a graph name. If you want to clear the data from the example graph, make sure that the **C**lear Current Data check box is checked. When you finish specifying the range name, choose OK. The data from the range or graph appears in the spreadsheet area, and a preview of the graph appears in the Chart Editor window. Change the chart type and legends as you would a normal chart in WP Draw. (For more information, see your WordPerfect documentation.) When you finish editing the graph, choose **F**ile E**x**it and Return to Document.

Sharing 1-2-3 Data with Ami Pro 3

As with Microsoft Word and WordPerfect, you can use 1-2-3 data in different ways to create Ami Pro documents. The procedures are similar to those in both of the other programs. This section provides a basic summary of the procedures. For more information, see your Ami Pro documentation.

Importing 1-2-3 Data into an Ami Pro Document

Unlike WordPerfect for Windows, Ami Pro gives you limited options for importing data. You can create a new document or insert 1-2-3 data into a document, but the data will go into the document only as tabbed data, with each column in the 1-2-3 file separated by tabs.

Sharing Data with Windows Word Processors **1011**

To import 1-2-3 data, choose **F**ile **O**pen, press Ctrl+O, or click the Open SmartIcon. The Open dialog box appears (see fig. 29.34). To list 1-2-3 Release 4 files, select 1-2-3 Rel 3 in the List Files of **T**ype pull-down list. Select the 1-2-3 file in the **F**iles list. To create a new document, choose the OK command button. Alternatively, to insert the 1-2-3 file into an existing document, choose the **I**nsert command button.

> **Note**
>
> If you want to import the 1-2-3 data as a table, first use Too**l**s Ta**b**les to create the table in Ami Pro, using the same number of columns and rows that your 1-2-3 file or range contains. After you create the table cells, choose **F**ile **O**pen and then choose the **I**nsert button to insert the 1-2-3 file into the table.

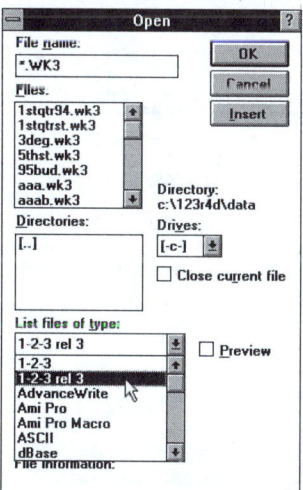

Fig. 29.34
The Ami Pro Open dialog box is similar to the Open dialog boxes in WordPerfect and Word, except that the Ami Pro version has an Insert command button.

After you choose OK or **I**nsert, the Import dialog box appears (see fig. 29.35). You can choose **E**ntire File to import the file, choose **A**ctive Worksheet to import the worksheet in which the cell pointer is located, or type a range name or range address in the **R**ange box.

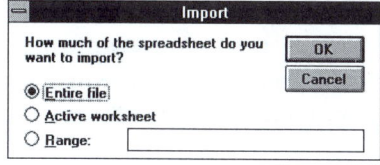

Fig. 29.35
The Import dialog box asks you for the range to import.

1012 Chapter 29—Sharing 1-2-3 Data with Windows Applications

After you choose OK, the Import Options dialog box appears, as shown in figure 29.36. Neither option in this dialog box affects your data or formatting in the worksheet. Select either option and choose OK. The data from the 1-2-3 file appears in your Ami Pro document, as shown in figure 29.37.

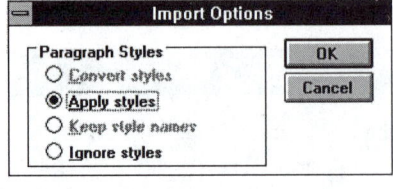

Fig. 29.36
The Import Options dialog box asks you about paragraph styles.

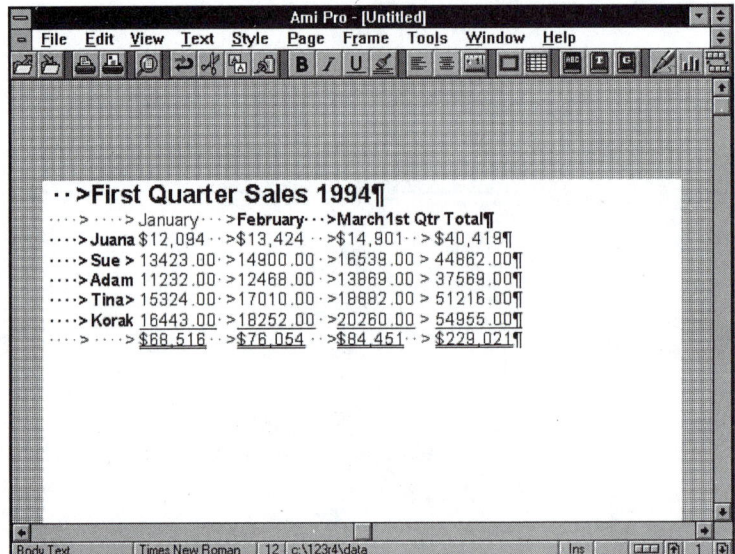

Fig. 29.37
The imported worksheet, with tabs and returns. To display tabs and returns, choose View View Preferences and mark the Tabs & Returns check box.

Importing a 1-2-3 Graph into an Ami Pro Document

If you want to import a graph into an Ami Pro document, you have several options. You can copy the 1-2-3 graph to the Clipboard (refer to "Copying 1-2-3 Information to the Clipboard" earlier in this chapter), or save the graph as a PIC or CGM format in 1-2-3 and then in Ami Pro choose **F**ile **I**mport Picture to import the graph into the Ami Pro document.

After you choose **F**ile **I**mport Picture, you enter the Import Picture dialog box. Change to the directory and drive where your graphics file is located. In the File **T**ype list, select Lotus PIC or CGM to list the Lotus graphic files; then choose OK. The Filter dialog box appears. For information on the options in this dialog box, choose the Help command button or see your Ami Pro manual. You may need to experiment with the various filter options to get the best output for your document and printer. Choose OK in the Filter dialog box to import the graph. The graph appears in a frame, as shown in figure 29.38. You can edit the graph as you would any other Ami Pro picture.

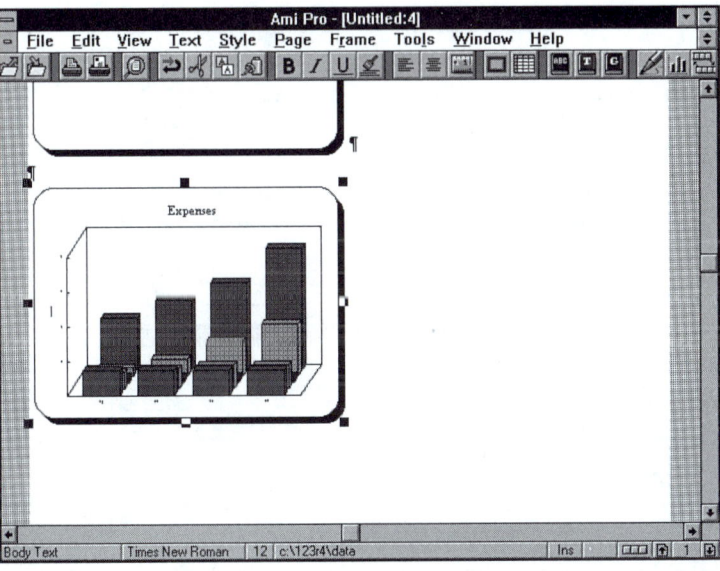

Fig. 29.38
When you choose **F**ile **I**mport Picture, the graph goes into an Ami Pro frame.

Merging Ami Pro Documents with 1-2-3 Data

As with Microsoft Word and WordPerfect, you can create letters in Ami Pro and merge them with 1-2-3 data. If you want to convert an existing letter to a merged document, open the letter and choose **F**ile Mer**g**e. The Welcome to Merge dialog box appears (see fig. 29.39).

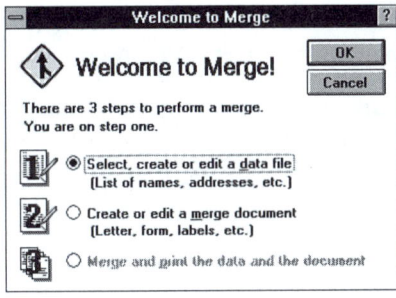

Fig. 29.39
The Welcome to Merge dialog box displays three steps.

Choose option 1 and the OK command button. You enter the Select Merge Data File dialog box, as shown in figure 29.40. Enter the name and location of the 1-2-3 file, and choose OK. The Merge Date File Fields dialog box appears (see fig. 29.41). If the first row of your data file includes field names, select Field Names in First Record of Data File. If your data does not include field names, you can use an Ami Pro (SAM) file.

Fig. 29.40

Identify the 1-2-3 file and location in the Select Merge Data File dialog box.

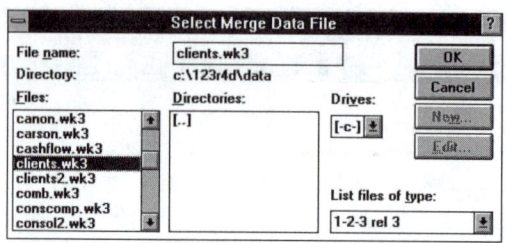

Fig. 29.41

The Merge Data File Fields dialog box asks you where the fields are located.

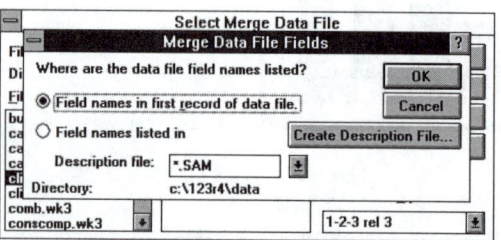

After you choose OK, you return to the Welcome to Merge dialog box, in which the second option is selected. Choose OK to create the form letter. Choose **Y**es in response to the next dialog box to use the current document. The Insert Merge Field dialog box appears in a corner of the screen (see fig. 29.42). Select a field and then click the Insert command button. You now are working in two places: the document and the Insert Merge Field dialog box. In the document, you can move the insertion point, add text, and format text (including the merge fields). Whenever you need another merge field, select it in the **F**ield Names list and click the Insert command button again.

When you finish inserting fields, choose the **C**ontinue Merge command button. You return to the Welcome to Merge dialog box, in which the third option is selected. Choose OK. The Merge dialog box appears (see fig. 29.43).

Sharing Data with Windows Word Processors **1015**

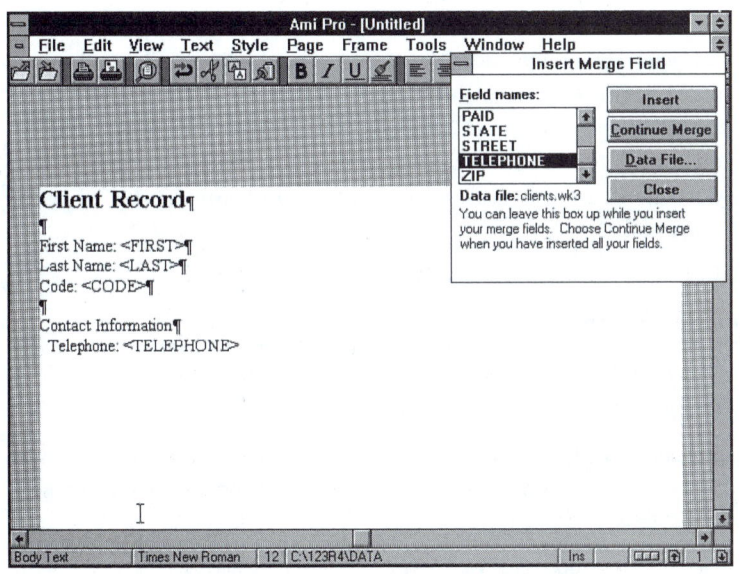

Fig. 29.42
Select each field name in the Insert Merge Field dialog box.

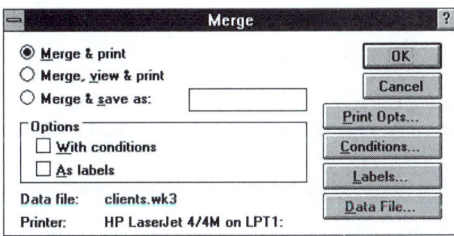

Fig. 29.43
The Merge dialog box enables you to specify where to merge the document and gives you other options for selecting and formatting data.

The following options appear in the Merge dialog box:

- **M**erge & Print enables you to send the merged document directly to the printer.

- Merge, **V**iew & Print enables you to merge to a new document. Choose **F**ile **P**rint to print the merged document.

- Merge & **S**ave As enables you to save the merged document with a file name so that you can edit and print the document later.

- The **P**rint Opts command button enables you to specify the number of copies, range of pages, and other options.

- The **C**onditions command button enables you to select records by showing field criteria. When you return to the Merge dialog box, make sure that the **W**ith Conditions check box is checked.

- The **L**abels command button enables you to specify how many labels you want on a page. When you return to the Merge dialog box, make sure that the **A**s Labels check box is checked.

After you complete the Merge dialog box, choose OK to start the merge. The merge documents appear on-screen, in a file, or on the printer, depending on the options you chose.

> **Troubleshooting**
>
> *I'm trying to use a 1-2-3 file in another application, and I get an error message saying that the file is in use.*
>
> You probably have the file open in 1-2-3. Press Ctrl+Esc to display the Task List, and double-click Lotus 1-2-3. Save your files, and choose **/W**orksheet **E**rase to close all open 1-2-3 files.
>
> If you are on a network, someone else may be using the file. Wait until that person is finished to continue the process.
>
> *When I try to bring a 1-2-3 worksheet or graph into Microsoft Word, I get an error message.*
>
> You may not have the file converter for 1-2-3 installed. See the note in "Sharing 1-2-3 Data with Microsoft Word 6.0 for Windows" earlier in this chapter.
>
> *When I try to merge a document, my names all run together.*
>
> When you insert fields for a merge, make sure that you include spaces and punctuation after field names as they would appear in the form letter, label, or envelope. Go back to the form letter, insert the necessary spaces and punctuation, and then run the merge again.
>
> *When I try to merge, the field names from 1-2-3 don't appear in the list.*
>
> Try to simplify the 1-2-3 file as much as possible. Row 1 should contain field names; the remaining rows should contain the data. Choose **/F**ile **S**ave and include a WK1 extension in the file name.
>
> If you still have problems, some programs enable you to create a data file when you import the data so that you don't have to create the data file during the merge process. In WordPerfect, for example, you can choose **F**ile **O**pen and select **I**mport As **M**erge Data File. Save this document as a WordPerfect document, and use this file as the data file.

I'm trying to import 1-2-3 data, but I get an error message saying that multiple worksheets are not valid.

Try using range names. If that doesn't work, create the data in one worksheet and choose **/F**ile **S**ave, including a WK1 extension in the file name.

I get lost in the merge process. I don't know where I am with the form letter or the data file.

Each application discussed in this section has a Merge Control Center dialog box that enables you to go to any of the three parts of the process. To access the Merge Control Center dialog box, do the following things:

Microsoft Word—Click the Mail Merge Helper button in the Merge toolbar or choose **T**ools Mail Me**r**ge.

WordPerfect—Click the Merge button in the Merge Feature Bar or in the Button Bar, choose **T**ools M**e**rge, or press Shift+F9.

Ami Pro—Choose **F**ile Mer**g**e

Note

If your application freezes while you're trying to work with 1-2-3 and Windows applications or you get General Protection Fault (GPF) messages, it may be because you have setup problems (and because you're dealing with new versions of applications). The problem seems to be exaggerated when you are switching between programs, copying and pasting data, and using graphics. The solution is not easy and often requires trial and error. Also, be careful—if you attempt to fix a problem and don't know what you're doing, the problem could get worse. If your application freezes or you get a GPF, exit all applications and Windows (if possible, or reboot your computer). Restart Windows and your applications.

If you generally have freezing and GPF problems, try doing some of the following before these problems occur: exit applications and documents you aren't using; increase available RAM; check your AUTOEXEC.BAT, CONFIG.SYS, and Windows INI files; reinstall your application with all the options you use; or get the latest interim release of the product with which you are working.

Sharing Data with Windows Spreadsheets

Sharing 1-2-3 data with Windows spreadsheet programs is much more straightforward than with word processors. Essentially, you open the 1-2-3 file, and the Windows spreadsheet program translates the 1-2-3 file for you. In almost all cases, the data translates with no problem. Most formatting and graphics (but not all) also translate. Macros are least likely to translate.

Lotus 1-2-3 is the undisputed leader in spreadsheet programs on the DOS side but has very strong competition from Microsoft Excel on the Windows side. Because the makers of most Windows spreadsheet programs want to convert 1-2-3 for DOS users to their applications, the migration to the Windows product is easy. Even in older versions of current programs, all you generally needed to do was choose **F**ile **O**pen and type the name of the 1-2-3 worksheet file. If the 1-2-3 file was in WK1 format, there essentially was no problem.

The complication arose when 1-2-3 went to three-dimensional spreadsheets in Release 3. The older Windows spreadsheet programs suggested either saving the file in WK1 format or importing each worksheet as a separate file. The new releases of Microsoft Excel and Quattro Pro, however, have multiple worksheets and can retrieve WK3 files.

Sharing Data with 1-2-3 Release 4 for Windows

◀ "Transferring Files," p. 443

As you would expect, when you import a 1-2-3 Release 4 for DOS file into 1-2-3 for Windows, the file translates better than in other programs. In 1-2-3 for Windows, choose **F**ile **O**pen or click the Open File SmartIcon. The default worksheet type is *.WK*, which lists all 1-2-3 Release 3 and 4 for DOS files, as shown in figure 29.44. Select the file name and choose OK. The file appears in 1-2-3 for Windows, as shown in figure 29.45.

Fig. 29.44
When you choose File Open, all Lotus 1-2-3 files are listed.

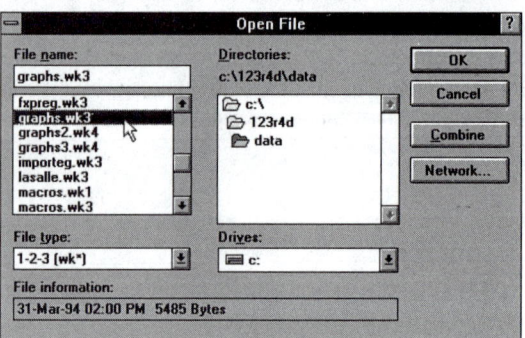

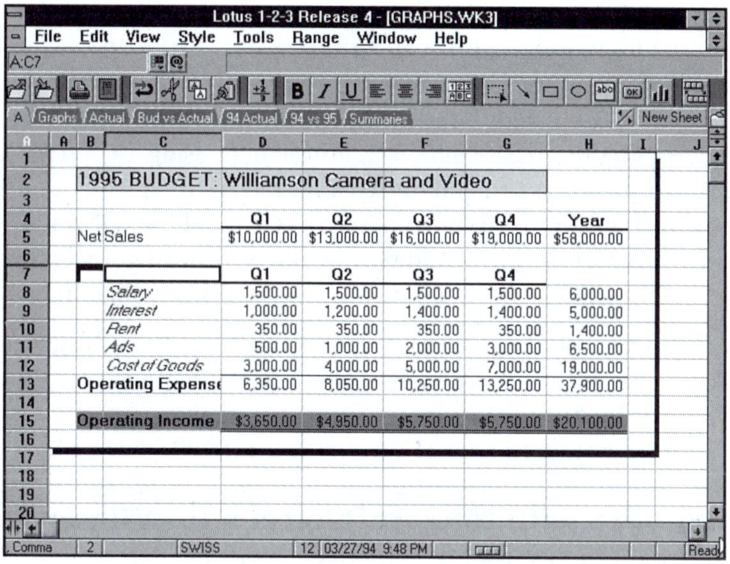

Fig. 29.45

The 1-2-3 file retains the DOS Wysiwyg formatting. Even the named tabs remain the same.

The 1-2-3 for DOS file retains almost all its formatting. Some of the graph information, however, may be lost if the graph types do not match. Figure 29.46 shows a worksheet with two imported graphs. Data is missing from one of the graphs.

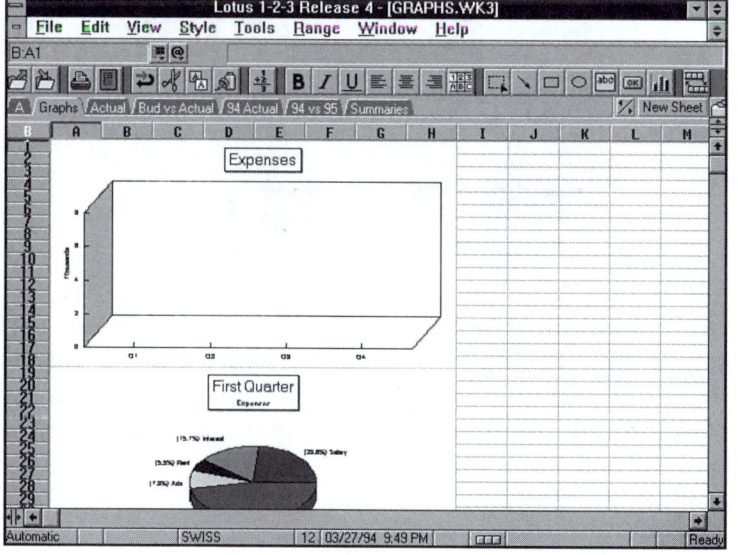

Fig. 29.46

Not all graph information translates from 1-2-3 Release 4 for DOS to 1-2-3 Release 4 for Windows.

Most of the forward-slash (/) and Wysiwyg colon (:) commands work the same in 1-2-3 for Windows as they do in 1-2-3 for DOS. 1-2-3 for Windows calls these two menus the Classic menu. Because these commands work, macros based on commands translate well between 1-2-3 for DOS and 1-2-3 for Windows. To run a macro, however, instead of pressing Alt and the letter for the macro, you press Ctrl and the letter for the macro. A few advanced macro commands from 1-2-3 for DOS (such as GETLABEL and FRAMEON) work differently in 1-2-3 for Windows or do not work at all in that program. For more information, see your 1-2-3 for Windows documentation.

Transferring a file from 1-2-3 Release 4 for Windows to 1-2-3 Release 4 for DOS is more difficult. You need to save the file in WK3 format or use the Lotus Translate utility. You lose more formatting, graphics, and macros in the process, as well as other features of 1-2-3 Release 4 for Windows.

Sharing Data with Microsoft Excel 5 for Windows

Unlike Microsoft Excel Version 4, Version 5 supports multiple-worksheet files. You can, therefore, open a WK3 file in Excel. Choose **F**ile **O**pen or click the Open button in the standard toolbar. In the Open dialog box, select Lotus 1-2-3 Files (*.WK*) to display 1-2-3 files, as shown in figure 29.47.

Fig. 29.47

To display a list of 1-2-3 files, select Lotus 1-2-3 Files in the List Files of **T**ype list.

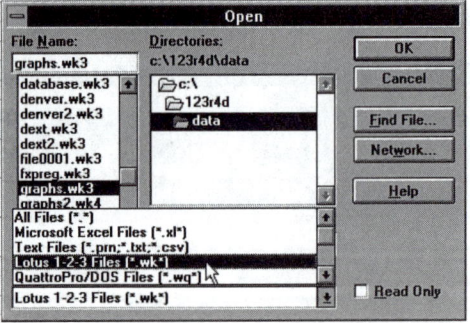

The data in 1-2-3 files translates well. You may need to edit some of the formatting, however, because it does not translate as well as it does between 1-2-3 programs. Figure 29.48 shows the file from figure 29.41 imported into Excel. Notice that the column widths are incorrect and that the worksheet tabs did not translate.

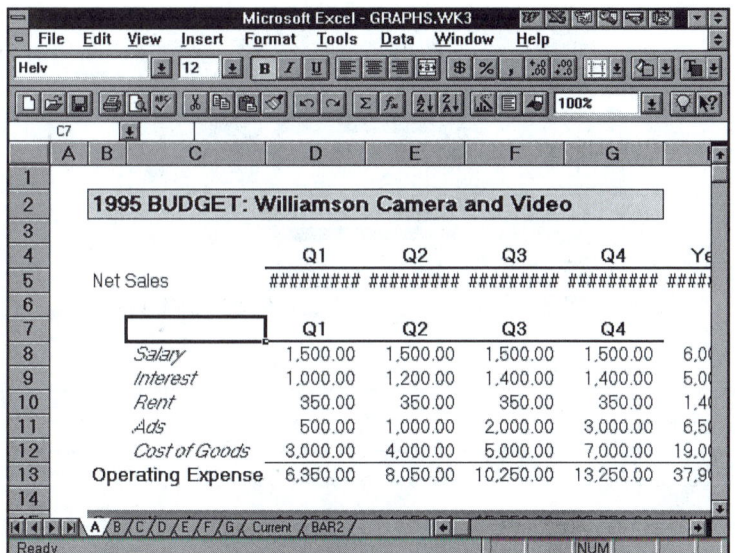

Fig. 29.48
The column widths need to be readjusted in Excel, as well as the worksheet tabs.

After you open a 1-2-3 file within Excel, you also run backslash macros by pressing Ctrl and the letter instead of Alt and the letter. Keystroke macros that use the forward-slash menus work, but Wysiwyg macros do not work at all. Excel's macro interpreter enables you to run macros that are compatible with 1-2-3 Release 2.01.

> **Note**
>
> Within Excel, you cannot create a macro range name that begins with a backslash. Therefore, you can run only existing macros in the 1-2-3 file. Microsoft Excel also has a translation assistant that enables you to translate 1-2-3 macros to Excel macros. From the File Manager, double-click the TRANS.EXE file in the Excel directory.

If you want to save an Excel worksheet as a 1-2-3 WK3 or WK1 worksheet, choose File Save As. Excel enables you to create the WK3 file as well as the FM3 file required for Wysiwyg formatting, as shown in figure 29.49. Unless you save the Excel worksheet this way, you cannot use the file in 1-2-3. The 1-2-3 Release 4 for DOS Translate utility does not enable you to translate Excel files to 1-2-3 files.

Fig. 29.49
Excel's Save As dialog box enables you to save in many different 1-2-3 formats.

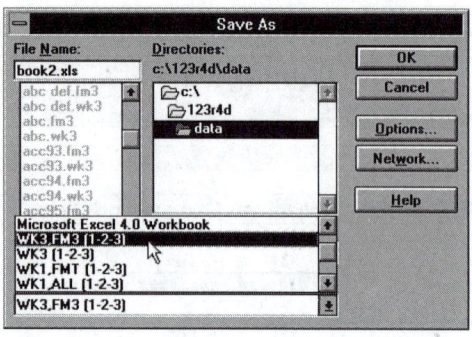

> **Troubleshooting**
>
> *I can't open a 1-2-3 Release 4 for Windows file in 1-2-3 Release 4 for DOS.*
>
> Even though both the Windows and DOS versions of the program are Release 4, you need to save the Windows file with a WK3 extension (the default is WK4).
>
> *I'm trying to use a 1-2-3 file in another application, and I get an error message saying that the file is in use.*
>
> You probably have the file open in 1-2-3 for DOS. Press Ctrl+Esc to display the Task List, and double-click Lotus 1-2-3. Save your files, and choose **/W**orksheet **E**rase to close all open 1-2-3 files.
>
> If you are on a network, someone else may be using the file. Wait until that person is finished to continue the process.
>
> *I'm trying to run my 1-2-3 backslash macros by pressing Alt and the letter, and I go to the Windows menu.*
>
> In Windows programs, the Alt key opens menus. (Alt+F, for example, opens the **F**ile menu.) In 1-2-3 for Windows and Microsoft Excel, you must press Ctrl rather than Alt to run backslash macros.

From Here...

In this chapter, you learned how to use 1-2-3 for DOS files in Windows applications. If you want to use 1-2-3 with other products, you may want to read the following chapters:

- Chapter 9, "Working with Files." This chapter discusses how to save, name, retrieve, and translate files.

- Chapter 30, "Sharing 1-2-3 Data with Databases." This chapter shows you how to use the **/D**ata **E**xternal command to link 1-2-3 files to database-management programs.

- Chapter 31, "Sharing 1-2-3 Data with DOS Word Processors." This chapter shows you how to use 1-2-3 files in word processing applications.

Chapter 30

Sharing 1-2-3 Data with Databases

Although 1-2-3 has its own database features that enable you to find and summarize data, these features are limited to the active file and do not include many advanced database commands. If you maintain a separate database in another program such as dBASE or FoxPro, you may want to avoid translating the file and instead use the existing database table in your 1-2-3 worksheets. With 1-2-3's **/D**ata **E**xternal feature, you can combine the best of 1-2-3 and your database-management program.

This chapter shows you how to link an external database, including

- External database terminology
- How to link to an external database table
- How to list database tables and fields
- How to remove a database table from the disk
- How to break the connection between 1-2-3 and the database

Working with External Databases

Figure 30.1 shows a 1-2-3 worksheet that is linked to a dBASE IV file through the **/D**ata **E**xternal command. None of the actual data was entered directly on the 1-2-3 worksheet. The cell contents line shows that the database function @DSUM is used. This worksheet also uses the **/D**ata **T**able command to create a summary of income by customer. Finally, a 1-2-3 graph is created to summarize the information.

VIII

Sharing Data

◀ "Creating Simple Graphs," p. 143

◀ "Analyzing Database Information," p. 541

◀ "Creating a One-Variable Data Table," p. 669

1026 Chapter 30—Sharing 1-2-3 Data with Databases

Fig. 30.1
A 1-2-3 file can use and summarize information from a dBASE III database file.

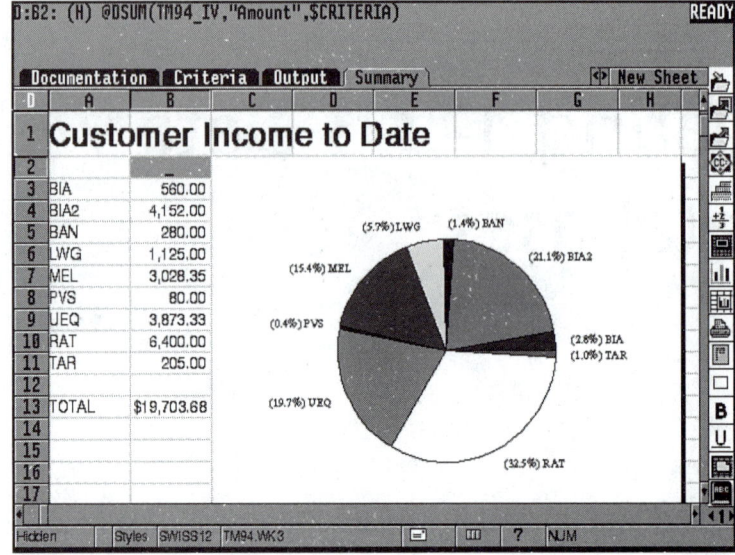

1-2-3's **/D**ata **E**xternal commands access data in tables within an *external database*. An *external table* is a file created and maintained by a database program other than 1-2-3, such as dBASE III, dBASE IV, FoxPro, Paradox, ORACLE, SQL Server, or another popular database product. After you establish a connection or link between 1-2-3 and an external table, you can perform the following tasks:

- Use **/D**ata **Q**uery commands to find and manipulate data in the external table and then work with that data in the worksheet

- Use formulas and database functions to perform calculations based on data in the external table

- Create a new external table that contains data from the worksheet or from an existing external table

When you choose **/D**ata **E**xternal, a menu with several options appears. These options are described in table 30.1.

Table 30.1 /Data External Commands	
Menu Item	**Description**
Use	Establishes a connection to an external table. (**U**se is the first step before using other **/D**ata **E**xternal commands.)

Menu Item	Description
List	Displays the names of the tables in an external database, or lists the names of the fields in an external table.
Create	Establishes a new table in an external database and copies data from a worksheet data table or another external table to the new table.
Delete	Deletes a table from an external database.
Other	Includes three functions: **R**efresh, which sets the interval for automatic updating of worksheet formulas that depend on an external table and for automatic re-execution of /**D**ata **Q**uery and /**D**ata **T**able commands; **C**ommand, which sends a command to a database-management program; and **T**ranslation, which permits translation of data created with foreign character sets.
Reset	Breaks the connection to an external table.
Quit	Returns the worksheet to READY mode.

Networks and database programs used on networks usually include controls to limit access to database files. These same controls apply when using 1-2-3 to access external database files. You may, for example, be prompted to type your user ID and password.

If prompted, type the ID and password, press Enter, and then continue with the 1-2-3 commands. You will have your usual access to the network files. If you encounter problems, contact the network administrator.

Understanding External Database Terminology

Data management in 1-2-3 is powerful and flexible because of Release 4's capability of using data from tables in external databases. Before you work with this feature, however, you need to become familiar with several terms.

A *database driver* is a program that serves as an interface between 1-2-3 and an external database; this driver enables 1-2-3 to transfer data to and from the external tables in the database. You need a separate database driver for each external database format you use. Lotus developed and uses the DataLens technology, and 1-2-3 Release 4 includes the following database drivers:

- dBASE IV—Compatible with the table format of dBASE IV, dBASE III Plus, and dBASE III files.

- **FoxPro**—Compatible with FoxPro 2.0 but does not support picture fields.

- **ORACLE**—Compatible with ORACLE Version 6.x databases.

- **ParaLens**—Compatible with the table format of Paradox Release 3.5 and 4.0.

- **SQL Server**—Compatible with Microsoft SQL Server and Sybase SQL Server.

An *external database* is the path where the external tables reside.

A *table name* identifies the external table with which you want to work. You must type the full table name before you can access the table from 1-2-3. The full table name consists of three or four parts, in the following order:

- The name of the database driver.

- The name of the external database file (including the path).

- An owner name or user ID, if required by the database program.

- The name of a table in the database, or a 1-2-3 range name assigned to the table.

Tip
1-2-3 Release 4 includes a worksheet file with 50 pages of database driver documentation. From the directory where 1-2-3 is installed (for example, C:\123R4D), retrieve the file DATALENS.WK3. This file has macros that allow you to view or print information on the available drivers.

A *table-creation string* contains information used by a database driver to create a new external table. After you create a new external table from within 1-2-3, you may need to specify a table-creation string, depending on the specific database driver in use. The provided sample driver requires no table-creation string. When in doubt, refer to the database driver documentation.

A *table definition* is a six-column worksheet range that contains information about a new external table. Information in a table definition always includes field names, data types, and field widths, and may include column labels, table-creation strings, and field descriptions.

Using an Existing External Table

Using the data in an external table doesn't differ much from using a worksheet database; you just need to establish a connection to the external table before you use the table, and then break the connection when you are finished. However, when you have a connection to an external table, you do not need to have the actual data in your 1-2-3 worksheet to manipulate the data in the table.

To use an existing external table, you first must set up the connection to the external table with the **/D**ata **E**xternal **U**se command. This command leads you through the components needed to define the full table name.

First, 1-2-3 displays a list of the available database drivers. After you select a driver (for example, dBASE IV), 1-2-3 lists the available external databases you can access with this driver. 1-2-3 then displays a list of the table names; each table name is preceded by an owner name, if appropriate. You can press the Name (F3) key to display a full-screen list for these components.

You choose a table name by typing or highlighting the name in the list provided and pressing Enter. After you establish a connection to an external table, 1-2-3 prompts you to assign to the table a range name. As a default, the table name is supplied for the range name. To use the default, press Enter. Otherwise, type the range name you want at the prompt and then press Enter. You use the range name to refer to the table as if the table were a worksheet database.

Notice that when you break the connection to an external table, the range name assigned to the table is lost. Formulas and functions that reference the range name become undefined when the connection is broken. You must respecify the range name every time you establish the connection. Be sure that you use the same range name each time if the worksheet contains formulas or functions that reference the range.

By using the range name assigned to the table, you can treat the external table as though this table is a worksheet database. You then can perform the following tasks:

- Copy some or all records from the external table to the worksheet with **/D**ata **Q**uery **E**xtract.

- Use **/D**ata **Q**uery **E**xtract to copy new records from the worksheet to the external table.

- Use formulas and database functions in the worksheet that reference data in the external table.

- Modify records in the external table with **/D**ata **Q**uery **M**odify (only if record modification is supported by the database driver in use).

- Use **/D**ata **E**xternal **O**ther to perform special database functions not available in 1-2-3.

- Terminate the connection to the external table with **/D**ata **E**xternal **R**eset.

Listing External Tables

You can use the **/D**ata **E**xternal **L**ist command to create a list, in your worksheet, of external tables. The **/D**ata **E**xternal **L**ist commands are described in the following table:

Menu Item	Description
Tables	Lists the names of all tables in an external database
Fields	Lists information about the structure of an external table to which you are connected (with **/D**ata **E**xternal **U**se)

A list of the tables in an external database file is useful if you forget the exact location of a particular table. To obtain such a list, choose **/D**ata **E**xternal **L**ist **T**ables. You are prompted to supply the database driver name and database name, just as you are for the **/D**ata **E**xternal **U**se command. After supplying the appropriate names, you are asked to provide an output range for the list.

This list consists of three columns and as many rows as tables in the database file. Because the list overwrites existing worksheet data, be sure that no important data is affected. Figure 30.2 shows a sample list (dBASE Database Tables). The first column of the list contains the table names. The second column contains the table descriptions, if used by the particular database, or NA (not applicable) if not used. The third column contains the table owner IDs, if used, or NA if not used. The sample dBASE III driver doesn't use table descriptions or table owner IDs.

> **Caution**
>
> An external table list overwrites existing worksheet data.

Tip
To review the contents of a particular table, use **/D**ata **E**xternal **L**ist **F**ields to list the structure.

You can use a list of a table's structure as a reminder of the contents of a particular external table. You also can use this list as the basis for creating a new table definition, as explained in the following section, "Creating a New External Table." To create this kind of list as shown in figure 30.2, choose **/D**ata **E**xternal **L**ist **F**ields. You are first prompted for the range name that identifies the external table, and then for the output range for the list.

The list consists of six columns and six rows as fields in the table. Again, this list overwrites existing worksheet data, so be careful. Each row in the list contains information about one field in the table. The contents of the columns are in the following list:

Column 1 Field name

Column 2 Field data type

Column 3 Field width, in characters

Column 4 Column label

Column 5 Field description

Column 6 Field-creation string

If the external table doesn't use column labels, field descriptions, or field-creation strings, these columns contain NA (see fig. 30.2). The SAMPLE dBASE III driver doesn't use these three fields.

> **Tip**
> If you are using the field names from your external table in a 1-2-3 criteria or output range, copy the names using /**D**ata External **L**ist **F**ields. Use /**R**ange **T**ranspose to copy the field names to a row. Then use /**D**ata Query **C**riteria and /**D**ata Query **O**utput to define the data query ranges.

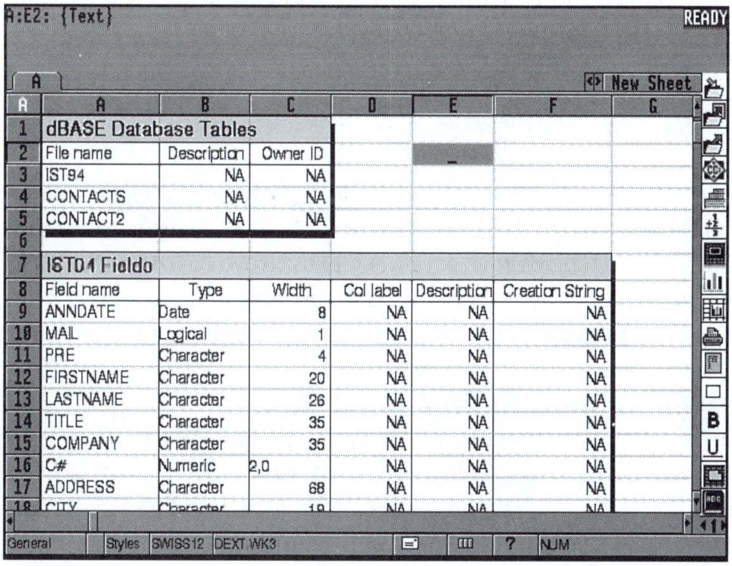

Fig. 30.2
This worksheet shows three data tables (files) from the results of /**D**ata External **L**ist **T**able. The fields from one of the data tables show as a result of /**D**ata External **L**ist **F**ields.

Creating a New External Table

You create a new external table by using the /**D**ata External **C**reate command. After you select this command, a menu with four options appears. Table 30.2 describes each of these options.

Table 30.2 /Data External Create Commands

Menu Item	Description
Name	Specifies the external database that contains the new table and specifies the table name.
Definition	Specifies the worksheet or external table used as a model for the structure of the new table; the two options are **C**reate-Definition, which creates a table definition based on a range in the model, and **U**se-Definition, which uses a table definition that already exists in the model.
Go	Creates the external table.
Quit	Returns the worksheet to READY mode.

The first step in creating an external table is to use the **/D**ata **E**xternal **C**reate **N**ame command to name the new external table. You are prompted to supply a name (including driver, path, and file name) for the new table, followed by a range name to access the table, as when you use the **/D**ata **E**xternal **U**se command. Next, you are prompted for a table-creation string. Because the sample driver doesn't support the table-creation string, just press Enter at this prompt.

To create a new external table, 1-2-3 must know the number, order, data types, and names of the fields in the new table. This information is provided in a *table definition*. If the new external table's structure is identical to an existing table's structure, 1-2-3 can create the table definition. If the new table has a unique structure, you must create and edit a table definition.

Duplicating an Existing Structure

You can duplicate the structure of either a worksheet database or an external table. To use a worksheet database, the worksheet must be in an active file and must contain a row of field names and at least one data record. After the **/D**ata **E**xternal **C**reate **D**efinition **C**reate-Definition command prompts you for an input range, you highlight the row of field names and the first data record row (see fig. 30.3). Next, the command prompts you for an output range for the table definition (see fig. 30.4). Remember that 1-2-3 overwrites existing data in this range. Figure 30.5 shows the resulting table definition.

To duplicate an external table structure, you first must establish a connection to the table and assign the table a 1-2-3 range name. Then you use **/D**ata **E**xternal **L**ist **F**ields to create the table definition.

Creating a New External Table **1033**

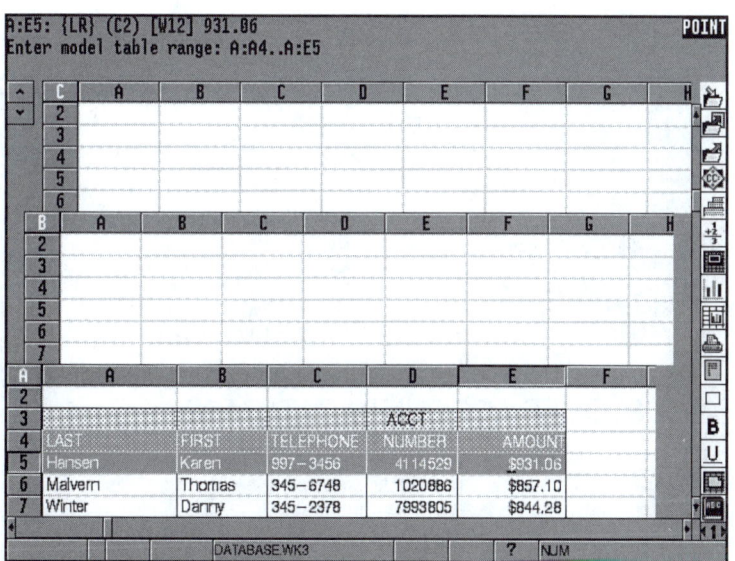

Fig. 30.3
Highlight the row of field names and a data record row at the prompt for the model table range.

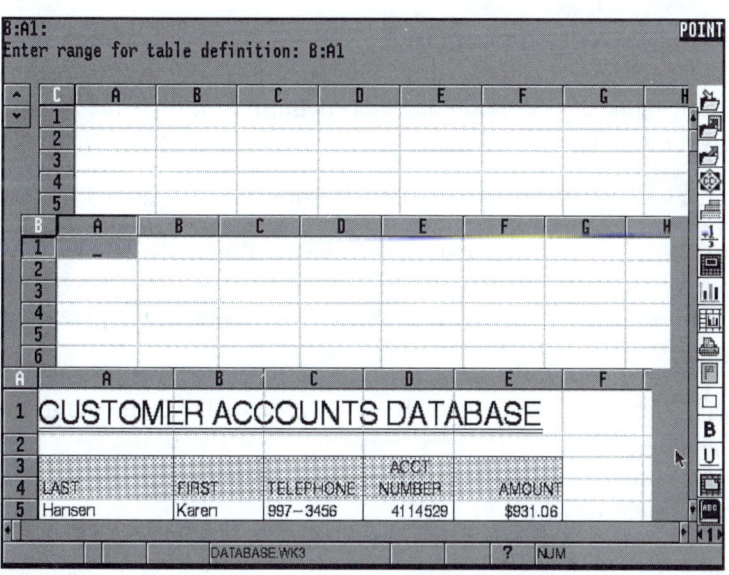

Fig. 30.4
Move the cell pointer to or type the range where you want to create the table definition.

Fig. 30.5
The resulting table definition appears on sheet B in this example. The field names are shaded on both the model table and the table definition to show how the names match.

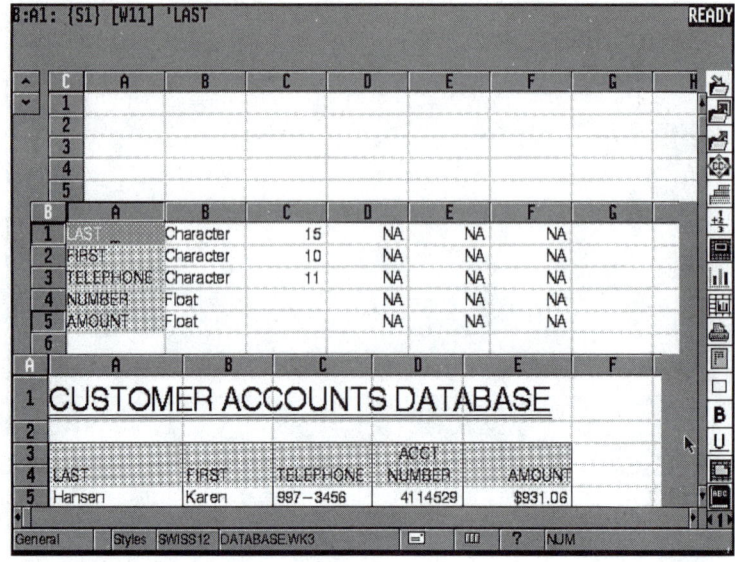

Creating a New Structure

To create a new external table with a new structure, you must set up a table definition. Figure 30.5 shows that a table definition contains six columns and one row for each field in the table.

Column 1 contains the field names; this information is required.

Column 2 contains the data type of each field. Although 1-2-3 has only two data types (value and label), some external tables have additional data types. Refer to the database driver documentation for information on the data types supported.

Column 3 specifies the width, in characters, assigned to each field in the external table. Fields that contain a label data type always require a width; fields that contain a value data type may or may not require a width, depending on the database driver in use.

Column 4 may contain column labels, again depending on the database driver in use. A *column label* is an alternative label for a database field; such a label provides additional identification of the field. These labels are particularly useful for fields that were assigned abbreviated field names. The column label *part number*, for example, is more informative than the field name *pnum*.

Column 5 may contain field descriptions, depending on the database driver in use. A *field description* is another version of a column label.

Finally, column 6 may contain field-creation strings if these strings are required by the database driver in use. A *field-creation string* contains information needed by some database drivers to create a field in a new table. If the database driver requires field-creation strings, the details are explained in the database driver documentation.

If the database driver that you use doesn't require a certain piece of information, the corresponding location in the table description contains *NA*. The dBASE IV driver provided with 1-2-3 does not use column labels, field descriptions, or field-creation strings. The corresponding locations in figure 30.5, therefore, contain *NA*.

Tip
Open the file DATALENS.WK3 for information on database driver requirements.

You can use one of two approaches in creating a new table definition range. First, you can copy a table definition from an existing external table and then edit the definition to reflect the structure for the new external table, which usually is the easier method. Second, you can type the table definition directly into a worksheet range. You use this method to create a new external table only if you know exactly what information is needed by the database driver in use.

If you want to copy and modify an existing table definition, you can use the **/D**ata **E**xternal **L**ist **F**ields command to list information about that table. (Listing external tables is described in the "Listing External Tables" section earlier in this chapter.) The information provided by this command is actually a complete table definition.

The next step is to edit this information to reflect the structure you want for the new external table. You edit the information as you edit other worksheet data. You may need to change field names, for example, or add or delete fields, change the order of the fields, change field widths and/or data types, add or modify column labels and field descriptions, or add field-creation strings.

After the table is named and the table definition is ready, you use the **/D**ata **E**xternal **C**reate **G**o command to create the external table and then use **Q**uit to return to READY mode. You can now use the **C**riteria, **E**xtract, **I**nput, and **O**utput commands on the **/D**ata **Q**uery menu to copy data from worksheet databases or other external tables to this new table.

◀ "Creating a Database," p. 622

◀ "Listing All Specified Records," p. 650

Using Other Data External Commands

In addition to using the **/D**ata **E**xternal commands already discussed, you can use additional commands to update the table, send commands to the external database program, and designate a different character set for use in the table. After you choose **/D**ata **E**xternal **O**ther, the following menu appears:

Refresh **C**ommand **T**ranslation

These menu commands are discussed in the following sections.

Controlling the External Database Updates

You use **/D**ata **E**xternal **O**ther **R**efresh to specify the time interval at which Release 4 updates the worksheet portions that depend on data in an external table. When you are connected to a network so that the external tables you are using can be modified by other users, you can use **/D**ata **E**xternal **O**ther **R**efresh to ensure that the information in your worksheet is up-to-date.

The **/D**ata **E**xternal **O**ther **R**efresh command offers the additional menu items described in the following table:

Menu Item	Description
Automatic	Updates the worksheet at a certain time interval.
Manual	Does not update the worksheet; updates must be performed by the user.
Interval	Specifies the time interval for **A**utomatic refresh, with the default set at 1 second; you can type any value from 0 through 3600 seconds (3600 seconds = 1 hour); the **I**nterval setting has no effect, however, if **R**efresh is set to **M**anual.

You can divide into two categories the worksheet components that depend on an external table: formulas and database functions that depend on recalculation, and **/D**ata **Q**uery and **/D**ata **T**able commands that don't depend on recalculation.

If you set **/D**ata **E**xternal **O**ther **R**efresh to **A**utomatic and also set worksheet recalculation to **A**utomatic, all components of the worksheet are updated at the specified time interval.

Using Other Data External Commands   **1037**

> **Caution**
>
> When you use automatic refresh, 1-2-3 continually goes out to the database on disk to get new data. This slows all 1-2-3 processes including typing, editing, and using menus. Because your speed is greatly affected, use the automatic refresh sparingly.

If you set **/D**ata **E**xternal **O**ther **R**efresh to **A**utomatic but set worksheet recalculation to **M**anual (by using **/W**orksheet **G**lobal **R**ecalc), the **/D**ata **Q**uery and **/D**ata **T**able commands are updated at the specified interval, but formulas and database functions are not. Formulas and database functions are updated only when F9 is pressed or a {CALC} or {RECALC} command is executed.

◀ "Analyzing Database Information," p. 541

◀ "Creating a One-Variable Data Table," p. 669

If you set **/D**ata **E**xternal **O**ther **R**efresh to **M**anual, you must manually update **/D**ata **Q**uery and **/D**ata **T**able commands by issuing the commands again. You must update formulas and database functions by issuing a Calc (F9) command.

1-2-3's background recalculation enables you to work during the recalculation process. If a recalculation cycle takes longer than the refresh interval, the next recalculation cycle begins immediately.

Tip
You can press F7 to update the last **/D**ata **Q**uery command and F8 to update the last **/D**ata **T**able command.

If you change the refresh interval with **/D**ata **E**xternal **O**ther **R**efresh **I**nterval, the new value is not saved with the worksheet. For the new value to take effect for future work sessions, choose **/W**orksheet **G**lobal **D**efault **U**pdate.

Sending Commands to the Database-Management Program

You use **/D**ata **E**xternal **O**ther **C**ommand to send commands to a database-management program, enabling you to perform database manipulations that are impossible to perform with 1-2-3 alone. To use this command, 1-2-3 must be connected to an external table of a database-management program that has a database driver which supports this command. Again, the SAMPLE driver supplied doesn't support this command.

The capabilities of the commands you issue with **/D**ata **E**xternal **O**ther **C**ommand (as well as the command syntax) depend on the database-management program—the commands have no relationship to 1-2-3's database-management commands. You must become familiar with the commands of the database program to which you want to send a command.

/Data **E**xternal **O**ther **C**ommand prompts you first for the external table name, including driver and database, and then for the database command. You can enter the database command either as a string or as the address of a cell that contains the command as a label. 1-2-3 sends the command and returns to READY mode.

Using /Data External Other Translation

When transferring information to and from external tables, 1-2-3 usually copies each character exactly as the character is found, with no modification. Occasionally, however, you may be working with a database created with a different character set from the one for which your computer hardware is configured. This may be true if your file came from a different country. With **/D**ata **E**xternal **O**ther **T**ranslation, you can instruct 1-2-3 to use a different character set to translate between the external table and the worksheet.

To determine whether a particular external table requires translation, use the **/D**ata **Q**uery commands to copy records from the external table to the worksheet. Examine the contents of the extracted records for strange-looking characters. If you find this kind of character, you may need to specify a translation character set. To translate an external table to which you are connected, supply the full table name to the **/D**ata **E**xternal **O**ther **T**ranslation command. The available character sets are displayed. After you select the character set, the translation takes place, and 1-2-3 returns to READY mode.

> **Note**
>
> The character set you use remains for use with all external tables for the particular database-management program (dBASE, FoxPro, and so on) until you quit 1-2-3 or choose another character set for the database program.

If only one character set is available, 1-2-3 selects this set. If more than one character set is available for the database in use, you may need to experiment to find the set that translates correctly. The selected character set is used to translate all data transferred to and from all tables in the specified database for the remainder of the current work session.

Deleting an External Table

You use the **/D**ata **E**xternal **D**elete command to delete external tables from the external database. Be careful with this command; using it deletes the file or a portion of it from the hard disk. Like the other **/D**ata **E**xternal commands, you must specify the database driver and database name and then highlight the external table to delete.

Disconnecting 1-2-3 and the External Table

/Data **E**xternal **R**eset breaks the connection between 1-2-3 and an external table. If only one external table is in use, choosing **/D**ata **E**xternal **R**eset ends the connection to this table. If more than one table is in use, you must specify the range name assigned to the database whose connection you want to break.

> **Caution**
>
> When you break a connection, you lose the table range name; all formulas or queries that use this name may produce errors.

After you break the connection, the range name of the table becomes undefined. Any worksheet formulas or queries that use this range name may produce errors.

> **Troubleshooting**
>
> *I have a database in a different directory. When I use the **/D**ata **E**xternal **U**se command, 1-2-3 gives me only one directory choice.*
>
> After you identify the database driver, 1-2-3 prompts you with any directories listed in a driver registration file. If no directories are listed, 1-2-3 uses only the current directory. Change your directory with **/F**ile **D**ir before you do the **/D**ata **E**xternal **U**se command or type the directory name when prompted.
>
> Your administrator can also modify the registration file to include more directory names. See the database drive documentation about modifying the LOTUS.BCF registration file.
>
> *I cannot access a dBASE file.*
>
> Make sure you have the correct path and file name. However, even if you have the correct file name, you will not be able to access the file if it is protected by a password. You will have to go into the dBASE program and remove the password.
>
> (continues)

> (continued)
>
> *Since I attached an external database to my 1-2-3 file, I get a WAIT mode indicator almost continually and it takes forever for me to do anything.*
>
> This happens when you use **/D**ata **E**xternal **O**ther **R**efresh **A**utomatic. Either change the refresh to manual or disconnect the external database from your worksheet with **/D**ata **E**xternal **R**eset.
>
> *My database formulas evaluate to ERR when I retrieve my file again.*
>
> When you retrieve a file that has links to an external database, you need to re-establish those links each time you retrieve the file with **/D**ata **E**xternal.
>
> You may want to create an automatic macro (\O) when you retrieve the file to automatically reattach the file's links to the external database.

From Here...

Because the **/D**ata **E**xternal command works so closely with other 1-2-3 database features, you may want to review the following chapters:

- Chapter 15, "Using Functions To Analyze Data," discusses database functions as well as other functions, such as @HLOOKUP and @VLOOKUP.

- Chapter 19, "Creating Databases," introduces you to database concepts including terminology, designing a database, and creating a database.

- Chapter 20, "Sorting Your Data," shows you how to organize your data alphabetically or numerically in a table.

- Chapter 21, "Finding Specific Data," shows you how to use **/D**ata **Q**uery commands to search for data.

- Chapter 22, "High-Level Database Techniques," shows you how to use data tables and other advanced database features.

Chapter 31

Sharing 1-2-3 Data with DOS Word Processors

Depending on how you want to use and edit 1-2-3 data in a word processing document (for example, as a table, as tabbed text, or in a merge), you need to choose a procedure in your word processing program that is compatible with your desired end result.

Word processors such as WordPerfect and Microsoft Word import 1-2-3 data in three ways:

- You can open a Lotus 1-2-3 file with the word processing file open or retrieve command.

- You can insert the data using an insert command.

- You can use the data on the spreadsheet as part of a merge process to merge with a letter created in a word processor.

This chapter shows you how to retrieve information from a 1-2-3 worksheet into a WordPerfect and Microsoft Word document. You will see how to create a document by opening the 1-2-3 file into a new document as well as inserting the 1-2-3 data into an existing document. If your 1-2-3 file contains information (such as name and address) that would be helpful in a merged word processing document, you will also see how to use the 1-2-3 data in the word processing merge process.

In this chapter, you learn to do the following:

- Create a table from 1-2-3 in WordPerfect and Microsoft Word
- Bring in 1-2-3 data with tabs separating the data
- Use 1-2-3 data as a merge-data file in WordPerfect and Microsoft Word
- Use 1-2-3 graphs in WordPerfect and Microsoft Word

Preparing the 1-2-3 Worksheet

◀ "Saving and Retrieving Your Work," p. 136

◀ "Specifying a Range with Range Names," p. 87

◀ "Designing a Database," p. 87

To prepare the 1-2-3 worksheet, you may need to do different things depending on the word processing application and the procedure you want to perform. Some word processing applications cannot read 1-2-3 Release 3.x or 4 files. Within 1-2-3 you may need to create one sheet and use /**F**ile **S**ave to save the file with a WK1 extension. Some word processors ask if you want to use the entire worksheet or a range and can accept range addresses or range names. Within 1-2-3, name the range you need with /**R**ange **N**ame **C**reate. If your 1-2-3 data is used as the data file in a merge, the first row of your spreadsheet should include the field names row. Start your data in row 2.

◀ "Creating Simple Graphs," p. 143

◀ "Saving Graphs and Graph Settings," p. 739

If you want to use a 1-2-3 graph in another program, you need to prepare and save the graph. Unless you have a color printer, you may need to experiment with 1-2-3's /**G**raph **O**ptions **B**&W or /**G**raph **O**ptions **C**olor settings to see the best output for your word processor. If you have more than one graph, make the graph active by using /**G**raph **N**ame **U**se, save the graph with /**G**raph **S**ave, and then type the name of the graph file. You can save the graph with two different formats, PIC and CGM. The default format is CGM, but you can override the default format by including the PIC extension. Check your word processing application documentation to see if you can import either the PIC or CGM format.

Sharing 1-2-3 Data with WordPerfect 6.0 for DOS

As with any word processor, the procedure for bringing in 1-2-3 data to WordPerfect depends on what you want to do with the data when it is in the word processor. You may want to create tabbed columns of data from the worksheet or create a table to show the data in a WordPerfect document. You may want to use the data from 1-2-3 during a mail-merge process to create personalized letters, envelopes, or mailing labels. Finally, you may want to include a graph from 1-2-3 in a WordPerfect graphic.

Importing 1-2-3 Data into a WordPerfect Document

You have a few options on how you can import your 1-2-3 data into a WordPerfect document. You can create a table, import the data with tabs separating each former 1-2-3 column, or import the data as information for a merge-data file. You can also choose whether to link the WordPerfect document to the 1-2-3 worksheet.

WordPerfect allows you to open or retrieve your 1-2-3 file. If you open the worksheet, you are not prompted for a range or whether you want the data in a table or tabbed format. For more options, see the upcoming section "Using Tools Spreadsheet To Import a 1-2-3 File."

Opening or Retrieving a 1-2-3 File

Because you cannot identify a range when you open a 1-2-3 document in WordPerfect, you first need to prepare the 1-2-3 file. Do not include blank rows or columns unless you want them in WordPerfect. Remove extra worksheets and documentation that you do not want in the WordPerfect table.

You can open a 1-2-3 file just as you do any WordPerfect document. You have several options depending on whether you want to have more than one document in memory and whether you remember the name of your file. Begin the process of retrieving your 1-2-3 spreadsheet by using one of the following WordPerfect commands:

- Choose **F**ile **O**pen or press Shift+F10 to create a new document window.

- Choose **F**ile **R**etrieve to insert the spreadsheet in the current document.

- If you don't remember the file name, click the File Mgr button or press F5 to show the list of files. Change the directory if necessary, and choose your 1-2-3 file. In the File Manager dialog box, choose **O**pen or **R**etrieve.

You can use either a WK1 or WK3 file for WordPerfect. After you identify your file, WordPerfect displays the File Format dialog box (see fig. 31.1) and indicates that the file you chose is not a WordPerfect 6.0 document. A list of file formats appears with the suggested format highlighted. If you saved your file with a WK1 extension, choose the Lotus 123 2.4 option. If you saved your file with a WK3 extension, choose the Lotus 123 3.1 option.

Tip
Save your graph twice, once with the CGM extension and once with the PIC extension. If your word processing application accepts both formats, import both versions of the file to test the output quality of the picture.

1044 Chapter 31—Sharing 1-2-3 Data with DOS Word Processors

> **Note**
> WordPerfect does not have a Lotus 1-2-3 Release 4 or 3.4 file format option. However, Release 3.1 works fine for WK3 files, and Release 2.4 works fine for WK1 files.

Fig. 31.1
The File Format dialog box shows Lotus 123 3.1 as the suggested choice for a WK3 file.

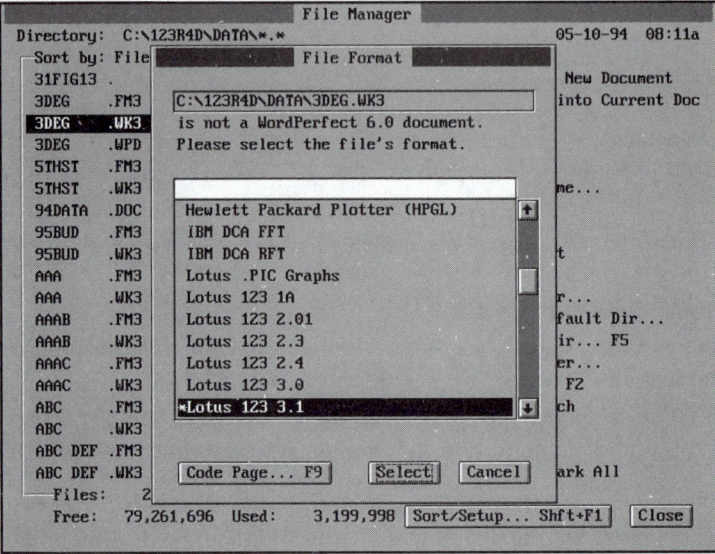

After you choose the file format, press Enter or choose the Select command button to retrieve the file. Each worksheet from your 1-2-3 file opens as a separate WordPerfect table in the WordPerfect document, as shown in figure 31.2.

> **Note**
> After you import the worksheets into WordPerfect, you may need to re-adjust the column widths as done with figure 31.2. Move into the column to change, press Alt+F11 or choose Layout Tables Edit, and press Ctrl+Right arrow to increase the column width. When finished in Table Edit mode, press F7 or choose Close to return to the document.

Importing a 1-2-3 File

When you use WordPerfect's Open or Retrieve command to import a spreadsheet, you have to retrieve all or none of the file. Also, if the spreadsheet changes, you have to repeat the procedure if you want the new values reflected in your WordPerfect document.

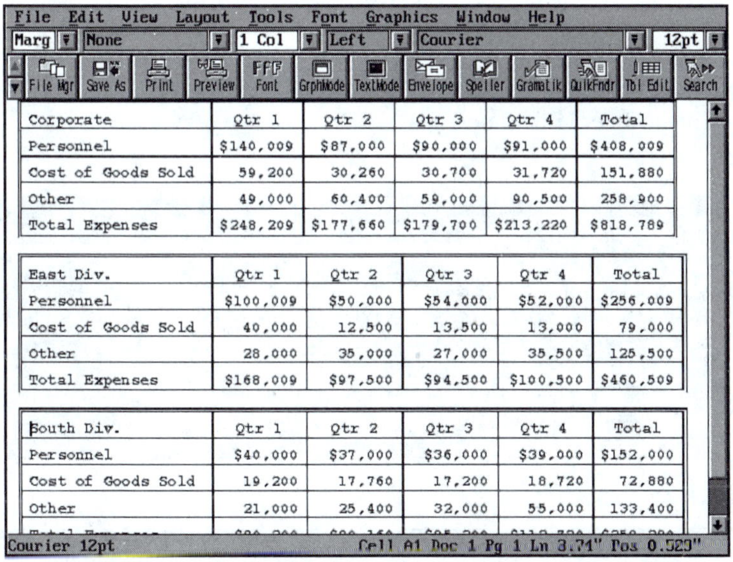

Fig. 31.2

This 1-2-3 file had three worksheets that turned into three WordPerfect tables.

You can use WordPerfect's **T**ools **S**preadsheet commands as an alternative to give you more options when importing 1-2-3 files into WordPerfect. Although you cannot create a new file from **T**ools **S**preadsheet, you can indicate a range and choose whether you want to link the 1-2-3 file to the WordPerfect document.

The first step you need to do is to open an existing WordPerfect document or start a new document and position your cursor in the WordPerfect document where you want to insert the 1-2-3 file data. Then choose **T**ools **S**preadsheet or press Alt+F7. A submenu appears with the following options:

- Choose **I**mport to bring a copy of the data into your WordPerfect document.

- Choose **C**reate Link to link the 1-2-3 file with the WordPerfect document. When you change the 1-2-3 file, the WordPerfect document can reflect the changes.

- Choose **E**dit Link to change the range or file name for an existing link.

- Choose **L**ink Options to update all links in the WordPerfect document or to have WordPerfect update the links automatically when you open the WordPerfect document. This option also allows you to see the link codes in your WordPerfect document.

1046 Chapter 31—Sharing 1-2-3 Data with DOS Word Processors

You need to choose **I**mport or **C**reate Link the first time you import your 1-2-3 file. Each of these two options gives you similar dialog boxes. Figure 31.3 shows the Import Spreadsheet dialog box, and figure 31.4 shows the Create Spreadsheet Link dialog box.

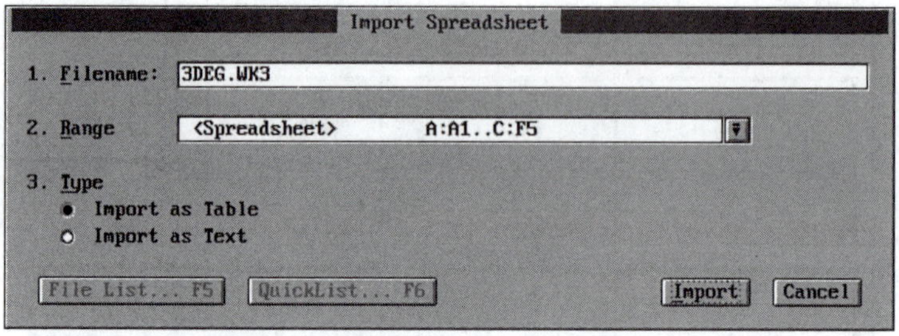

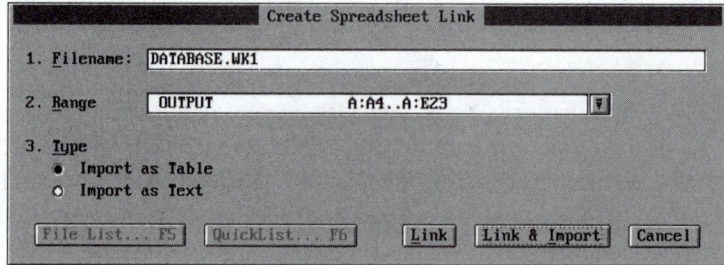

Fig. 31.3
The Import Spreadsheet dialog box allows you to choose the 1-2-3 file name, a range, and whether to import the 1-2-3 data as a table or as text.

Fig. 31.4
The Create Spreadsheet Link dialog box is identical to the Import Spreadsheet dialog box except that the Import button is replaced with the Link and Link & Import buttons.

To import or create a link, do the following when you get to either WordPerfect's Create Link or Import Spreadsheet dialog box:

1. In the **F**ilename text box, type the name of the 1-2-3 file, including the WK1 or WK3 extension and path if necessary.

2. If you don't remember the name of the file, choose the File List button or press F5, and choose the file name from the File Manager.

3. If you have your directories set up with QuickList, choose the QuickList button or press F6.

4. In the **R**ange text box, you can choose <Spreadsheet> to bring in the entire 1-2-3 file, you can type a range reference, you can type a range name, or you can use the drop-down arrow and choose from a list of the existing range names in the 1-2-3 file, as shown in figure 31.5.

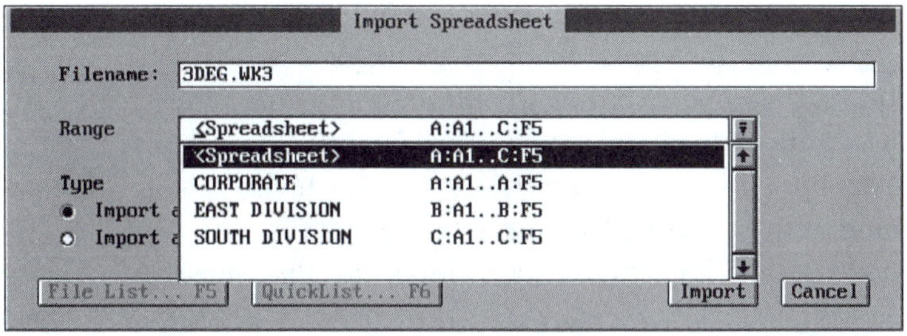

Fig. 31.5
When you click the Range drop-down arrow or choose Range and press the down-arrow key, you get a list of named ranges in the 1-2-3 file.

5. The **T**ype choice has two options. To import your 1-2-3 data as a table, choose Import as **T**able. To import your 1-2-3 data as text with tabs separating each column of information, choose Import as Te**x**t (see fig. 31.6). You may need to reset the tabs or change the format to display the data correctly. Compare figure 31.6 with figure 31.7, which shows the Import as Table option.

> **Note**
>
> WordPerfect does not show you hot keys (underlined letters) for items on dialog boxes until you make choices. For example, you will not see the underlined letters for the Items on the Create Spreadsheet Link dialog box while you are entering a name of the file in the Filename text box. Also, you will not see the hot keys for Import as **T**able or Import as Te**x**t until you choose **T**ype.

Tip
If you continually convert 1-2-3 data to WordPerfect or another application that allows you to choose range names, use the same range name (such as OUTPUT) in all your files.

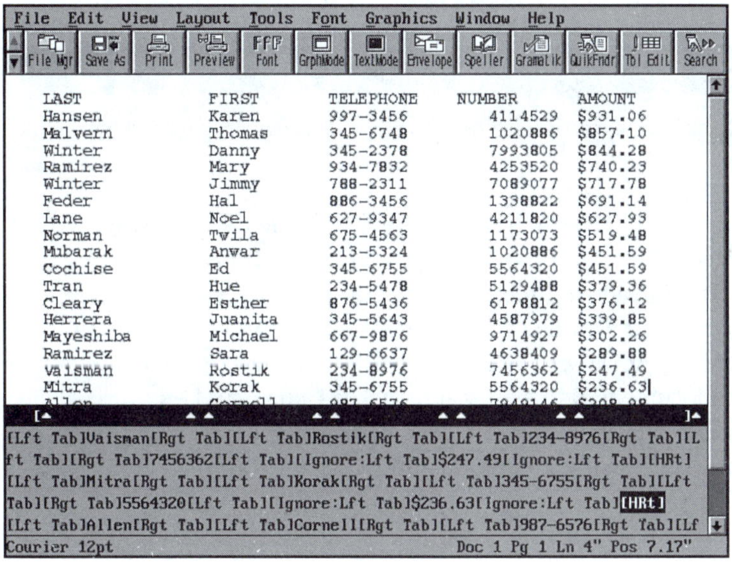

Fig. 31.6
The 1-2-3 data was imported as text. Reveal codes is on (Alt+F3) to show tabs separating the data.

1048 Chapter 31—Sharing 1-2-3 Data with DOS Word Processors

6. The final step is to choose one of the following command buttons: If you are in the **I**mport Spreadsheet dialog box, you have only one choice, the Import command button. If you are in the Create Spreadsheet Link dialog box, you have two choices. Choose Link to enter codes for a link but not get the data now. Choose Link & Import to bring in the codes for the link as well as get the data now. Figure 31.7 shows both a Link and a Link & Import for the same file.

Fig. 31.7
When you choose Link in the Create Spreadsheet Link dialog box, only codes appear in the document to identify where the spreadsheet data will go. When you choose Link & Import, you get the codes as well as the data.

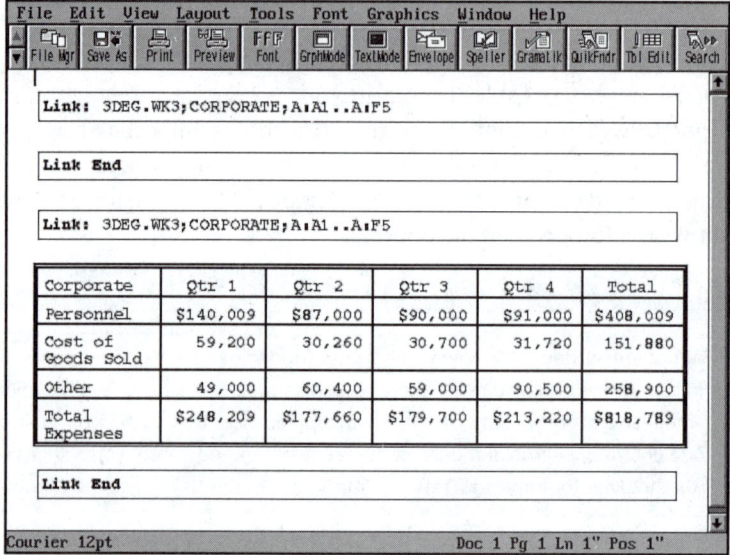

> **Note**
>
> You can see the link codes in Text mode and Graphics mode but not in Page mode.

Whether you choose Link or Link & Import, you can update the WordPerfect document when the 1-2-3 file changes. Choose **T**ools **S**preadsheet **L**ink Options. The Spreadsheet Link Options dialog box appears (see fig. 31.8). To update your WordPerfect document when you retrieve or open your WordPerfect document, choose Update on **R**etrieve. To update the WordPerfect document at this moment, choose **U**pdate All Links. If you choose either, the data appears in the document (whether you chose Link or Link & Import to establish your original link).

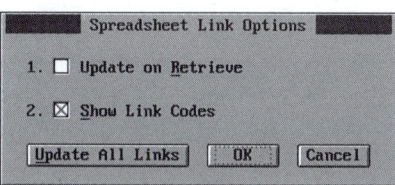

Fig. 31.8
Choose Update All Links to update your WordPerfect document with the latest information in your 1-2-3 files.

Merging WordPerfect Documents with 1-2-3 Data

You can use your 1-2-3 file as the source for names and addresses for a mail merge. Your 1-2-3 file needs to be set up as a database file with row 1 having the field names and rows 2 and down including the records for your data. You can use a WK1 or WK3 file, but the first worksheet has to include your database.

◀ "Designing a Database," p. 621

If you have an existing document you want to use or convert to a merge form file, open the file. To begin the merge, choose **T**ools **M**erge **D**efine or press Shift+F9. The Merge Codes dialog box appears (see fig. 31.9). This dialog box is the control center for your merge. From here, you can create the letter or the database information. In this example, you first create the form letter and then return to this dialog box to create the data.

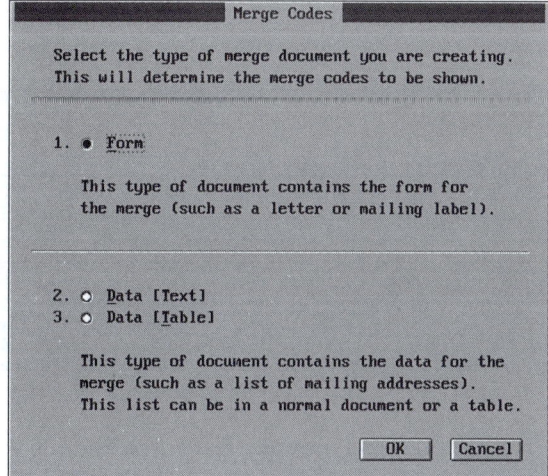

Fig. 31.9
To attach a 1-2-3 file and start your letter, choose **F**orm in the Merge Codes dialog box.

To create or update the form letter, do the following:

1. From the Merge Codes dialog box, choose **F**orm. The Merge Codes (Form File) File dialog box appears, as shown in figure 31.10.

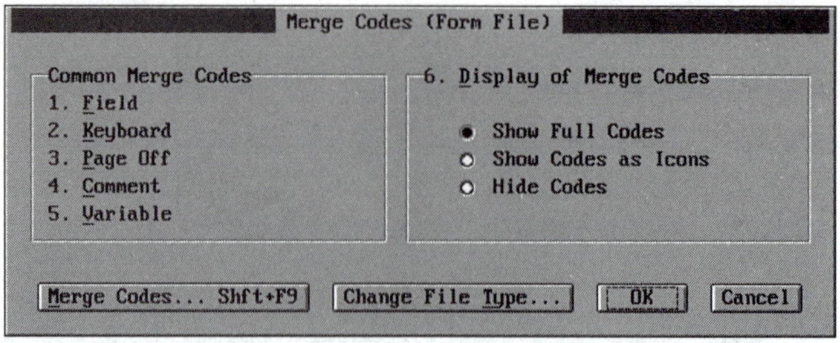

Fig. 31.10
The Merge Codes (Form File) dialog box allows you to identify data fields and insert other merge codes into the form letter.

2. Choose Field to identify the first field. The Parameter Entry dialog box appears, as shown in figure 31.11.

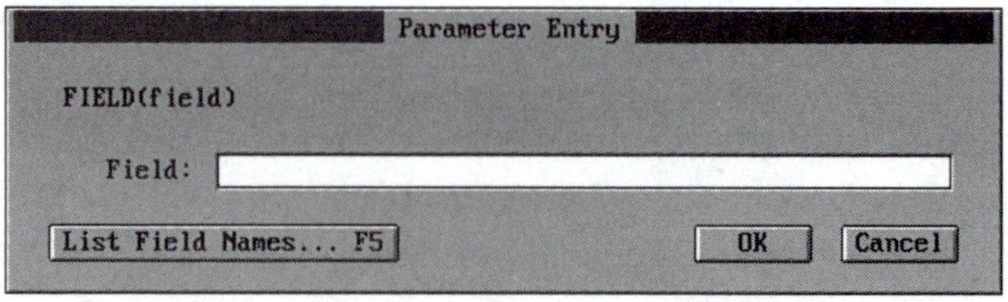

Fig. 31.11
If you know the names of the fields, type them; otherwise, choose List Field Names.

3. Choose List Field Names or press F5. The Select Data File For Field Names dialog box appears, as shown in figure 31.12.

Fig. 31.12
The Select Data File For Field Names dialog box appears when you select List Field Names.

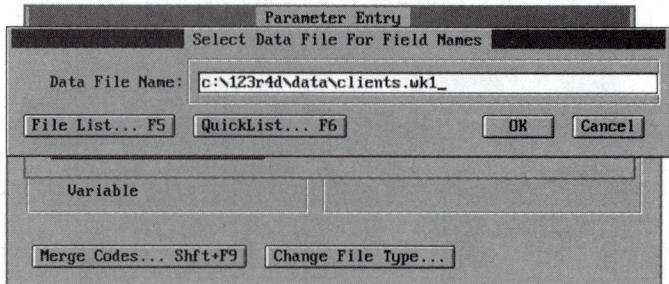

4. Enter the name of the 1-2-3 file and press Enter. The File Format dialog box appears.

5. You will be prompted to indicate the File Format of the 1-2-3 file. Identify Lotus 123 3.1 or other format. After you identify the file type, the List Field Names dialog box will appear, as shown in figure 31.13.

6. Choose the first field to appear in your form letter from the list of field names and press Enter. The field name code appears in your document. For example, the code for a 1-2-3 data file with a the data column labeled with "FIRST" appears as FIELD(FIRST) in your WordPerfect document.

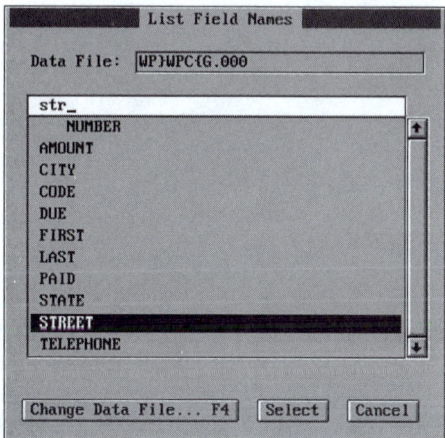

Fig. 31.13
In the List Field Names dialog box, you can type the first few letters of the desired field.

After you identify the 1-2-3 data file, the names appear each time you request to list field names. After you enter the first field name, move to the new location for a field and add the second field by pressing Shift+F9 (or **T**ools M**e**rge **D**efine). The Merge Codes (Form File) dialog box (shown in fig. 31.10) reappears. Choose **F**ield, and type the field name or choose from the list of field names shown in figure 31.13.

After you finish entering the field names (see fig. 31.14), you can continue typing your letter. When you finish typing and entering information, save the document.

To perform the merge, do the following:

1. Press Ctrl+F9 or choose **T**ools M**e**rge **R**un. The Run Merge dialog box appears, as shown in figure 31.15.

2. In the Run Merge dialog box, type the name of the WordPerfect document in the **F**orm File text box and the 1-2-3 file in the **D**ata File text box.

3. In the File Format dialog box, choose Lotus 123 2.4 or Lotus 123 3.1, as mentioned previously.

1052 Chapter 31—Sharing 1-2-3 Data with DOS Word Processors

Fig. 31.14
You can enter merge fields all in one place for the return address or throughout the letter.

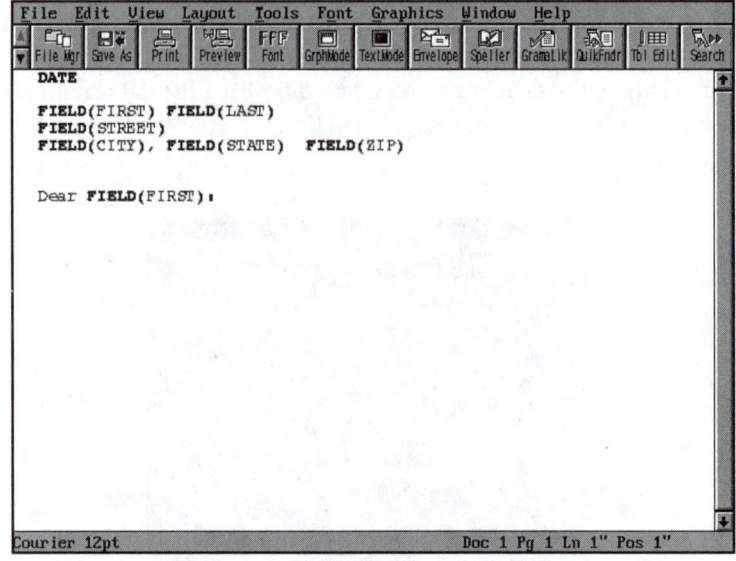

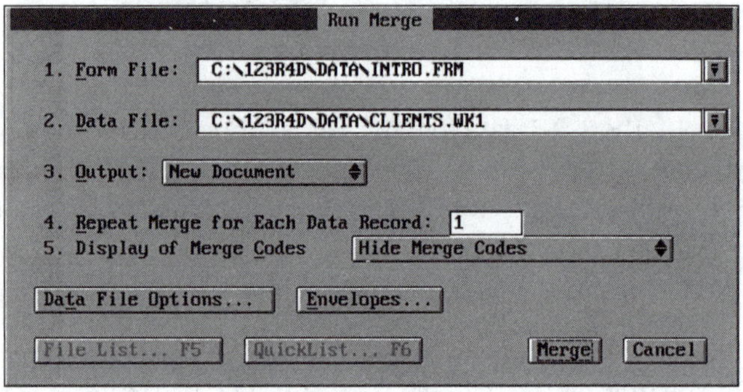

Fig. 31.15
The Data File Options button allows you to select records and generate envelopes for each data record.

4. If desired, change other options as shown in the following section, "Using Data File Options."

5. To begin the merge, choose the Merge button in the Run Merge dialog box.

Using Data File Options

When you click the Data File Options button, the Run Merge dialog box expands so that you can further customize the merge (see fig. 31.16). To choose specific records (not the entire 1-2-3 database), choose an option in the Data Record Selection area. There are four ways to select records from the Run Merge dialog box.

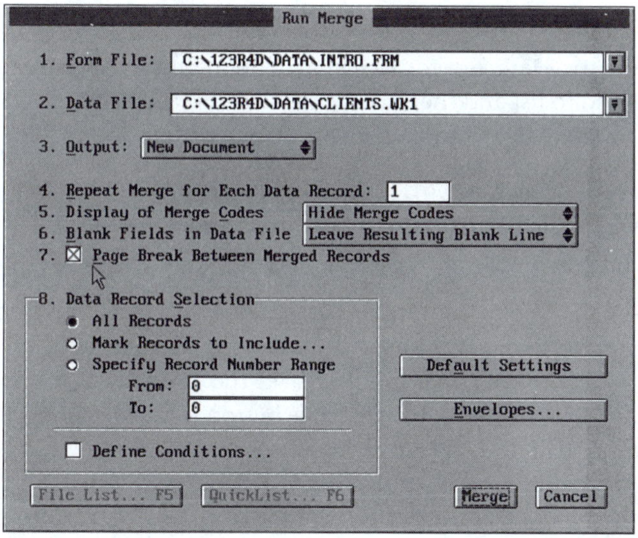

Sharing 1-2-3 Data with WordPerfect 6.0 for DOS **1053**

Fig. 31.16
The expanded Run Merge dialog box gives you additional options.

To select records, choose Data Record **S**election. The dialog box changes to show you the hot keys for this area of the Run Merge dialog box, as shown in figure 31.17. Select the records you want in one of the four ways:

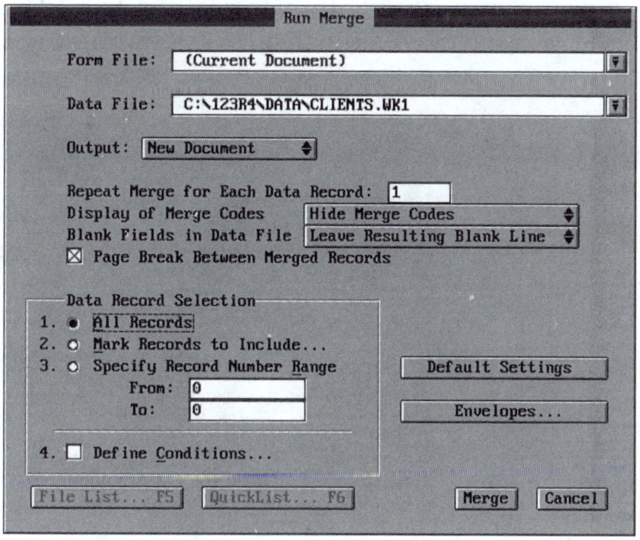

Fig. 31.17
You can use the numbers 1 to 4 or the hot keys to make a choice in the Data Record Selection area.

Tip

If you are going to insert a range of records from your 1-2-3 file, within 1-2-3 insert a blank column and use **/D**ata **F**ill to insert consecutive numbers starting with 1 for the first record. You can use these record numbers in the Specify Record Number **R**ange.

- To select the entire database, choose **A**ll Records.

- Choose the **M**ark Records to Include option button. WordPerfect asks for a field to list and then shows you a list of records starting with that field. Mark each record with an asterisk, and choose OK.

- To identify which records to use by record number, choose the Specify Record Number **R**ange and indicate the first and last record in the range.

- Choose the Define **C**onditions check box. The Define Conditions for Record Selection dialog box appears (see fig. 31.18). Define each condition with the field name and value. See the examples at the bottom of the dialog box, or click the E**x**ample button for help. Choose OK to return to the Run Merge dialog box.

After you choose one of the selection options, choose OK to return to the Run Merge dialog box. If you want to create an envelope for each record you choose, choose Generate an **E**nvelope for Each Data Record. The Envelope (Merge) dialog box appears; here, you can add your own mailing address and create envelopes from the 1-2-3 data file. Place the insertion point in the **M**ailing Address text box, and click the List Field Names button or press F5 for each of the fields to enter the mailing address. Make sure you add spaces and returns where necessary. Press F7 (Exit) to exit the Return Address and the Mailing Address text boxes. When you finish creating the envelope, click OK to return to the Run Merge dialog box.

> **Note**
>
> While you are in the Envelope (Merge) dialog box, the List Field Names button is dimmed until you enter the Return Address or Mailing Address text box.

When you are ready to perform the merge, click the Merge button at the bottom right of the Run Merge dialog box. The merge appears in a new document. Each page is a separate record and is a letter or envelope depending on which one you defined.

For more details on running the merge and selecting records, see your WordPerfect documentation.

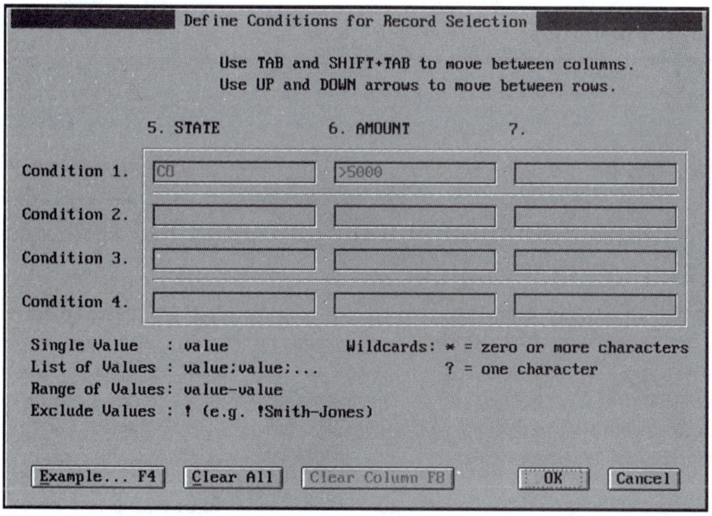

Fig. 31.18
These conditions indicate that all records from Colorado with amounts greater than 5000 will be printed.

Importing a 1-2-3 Graph into a WordPerfect Document

If you want to bring 1-2-3 graphs into your WordPerfect document, you need to save the graph as a PIC or CGM file format in Lotus 1-2-3 and use the WordPerfect **G**raphics **R**etrieve Image command to bring the graph into your WordPerfect document.

After you choose **G**raphics **R**etrieve Image, the Retrieve Image File dialog box appears (see fig. 31.19). You can enter the name of the file, choose File List, or press F5 to browse for the file. After you identify the file, you enter the File Format dialog box (refer to fig. 31.1). Choose Lotus PIC Graphs if your file has a PIC extension and CGM Graphics if your file has a CGM extension.

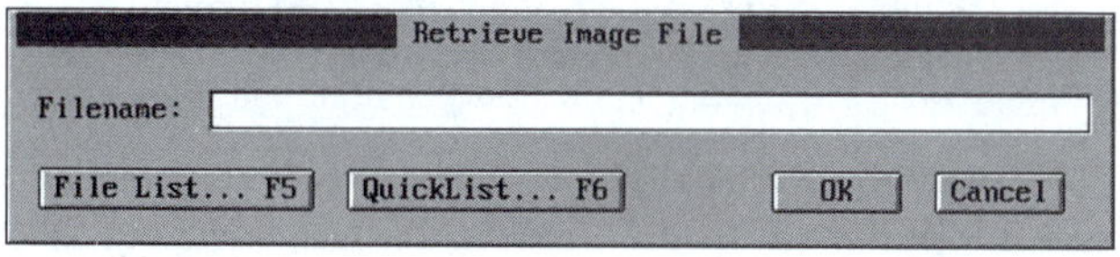

Tip
You can change the size of the graph by clicking in the graph and dragging the black handles surrounding the picture.

Fig. 31.19
The Retrieve Image File dialog box allows you to type a file name or list files.

After you insert the graph, edit, save, and print the document as you would any other in WordPerfect. See your WordPerfect documentation for more details.

Troubleshooting

I get lots of blank columns and rows when I try to insert a 1-2-3 file into my WordPerfect document.

You can delete the extra rows and columns within WordPerfect. Go to the table and press Alt+F11 or click the Table Edit button. Select one cell in each row or column and press Delete. From the Delete dialog box, choose whether to delete rows or columns.

It may be easier to return to 1-2-3 and change your spreadsheet. Delete any unnecessary rows and columns with **/W**orksheet **D**elete. Save your file, and return to WordPerfect.

When I'm trying to use a 1-2-3 file for a WordPerfect merge, the field names don't display when I try to list them.

To use a 1-2-3 file for a WordPerfect data file, the file has to be set up carefully. Remove any blank rows at the top of your worksheet. The first row must be a set of labels for field names. Make sure that you do not include spaces before the labels (Use **/R**ange **L**abel to center or right-justify the labels instead). The second row of the 1-2-3 file must begin your data.

If you have any blank lines in the file, you get blank forms during the WordPerfect merge. Use **/W**orksheet **D**elete **R**ow to get rid of blank lines in the 1-2-3 file.

The first sheet in the 1-2-3 file must also be your data. Delete any sheets before the data with **/W**orksheet **D**elete **S**heet.

My graphs don't look right when I try to bring them into my document.

You may need to experiment with the Graph Options. Choose **/G**raph **O**ptions **B**&**W** for most applications. If necessary, try a different graph type to simplify the graph. Three-dimensional graphs do not look good when the WordPerfect picture is small. In general, graphs in CGM format translate better than PIC format to WordPerfect documents. Use **/G**raph **S**ave to save the graph with a CGM format.

I run out of memory when I try to use the spreadsheet functions in WordPerfect.

Importing 1-2-3 spreadsheets seems to create memory conflicts more than many other processes in WordPerfect. Try doing some of the memory-saving options that WordPerfect recommends. Some include using **V**iew **T**ext Mode. Turn off the Button Bar and Ribbon. Make sure that you don't have any memory-resident programs running. For more information, see the "Memory" section, in the WordPerfect Version 6.0 DOS Reference Guide.

Sharing 1-2-3 Data with Microsoft Word 6.0 for DOS

As with WordPerfect, you can use 1-2-3 data in different ways to create Microsoft Word documents. You can use 1-2-3 data as a table within Word, create a graph in Word, or merge the 1-2-3 data into a letter.

Creating a Word Table from 1-2-3 Data

If you want to use your 1-2-3 data in a Word document, you have to insert the data into an existing document. In Word, you can choose **F**ile **N**ew and open a new document or **F**ile **O**pen and open an existing document. Position your cursor at the location in the document and choose **I**nsert **F**ile. The File dialog box appears.

If necessary, change the drive and directories in the **D**irectories area of the File dialog box. Type the name of the 1-2-3 file in the File **N**ame text box, or choose the file from the list in the **F**iles list box. After you choose the file name, you identify the range in the **R**ange drop-down list (see fig. 31.20). You can type a range name or range address, or choose the drop-down arrow and choose from a list.

Tip
If you continually convert 1-2-3 data to Microsoft Word or other applications that allow you to choose range names, use the same range name (such as OUTPUT) in all your files.

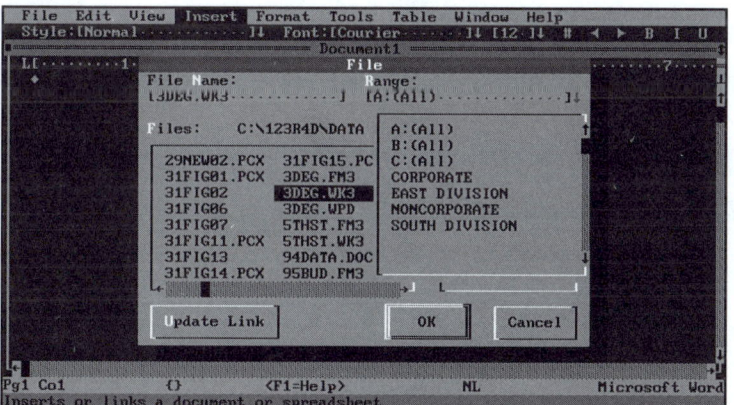

Fig. 31.20
The Range area in the File dialog box allows you to see a list of named ranges.

When you identify a file with more than one worksheet, Word allows you to import each sheet (identified with A:, B:, and C: in figure 31.20) or a range name. If you want a range smaller than a worksheet, you have to type the cell references or select a range name.

1058 Chapter 31—Sharing 1-2-3 Data with DOS Word Processors

If you attempt to import the entire file and the file is a three-dimensional worksheet or a range that includes more than one worksheet, Word prompts you to let you know that only the first sheet can be imported.

> **Note**
>
> If you want to import all worksheets on a multiple-sheet file, you need to do a separate **I**nsert **F**ile for each worksheet.

After you identify the file and the range to import, click the OK button in the File dialog box. Your 1-2-3 data becomes a table in your current Word document (see fig. 31.21).

> **Note**
>
> The default choice for inserting a spreadsheet file is to create a table. If you want your data to appear as columns separated by tabs, before you import the spreadsheet, choose **T**ools **Cu**stomize and unmark the last item in the Settings area, **I**nsert Spreadsheet as Table. Choose OK to return to your document and begin the import process.

Fig. 31.21
The 1-2-3 data appears as a table in the Word document.

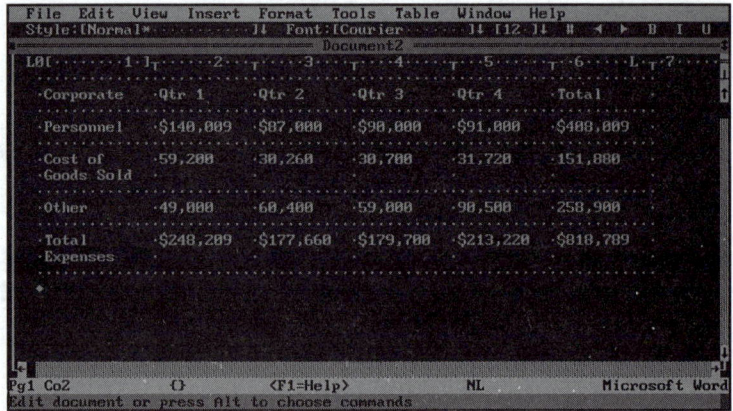

After you import the data, edit and format the table as you would any other table in Microsoft Word. In the example in figure 31.21, you may want to change the font and column widths (by dragging the column indicators on the ruler) or edit the table with items on the T**a**ble menu. To add lines around the table, use Forma**t B**order. After you finish editing and formatting your document, print and save the document as desired.

Creating a Link to Your 1-2-3 Data

If you want Word to update your document when changes appear in 1-2-3, choose **I**nsert **F**ile. Fill out the File dialog box as mentioned previously. However, mark the **L**ink check box (see fig. 31.22). When you want to update the link, choose **I**nsert **F**ile and then click the **U**pdate Link command button.

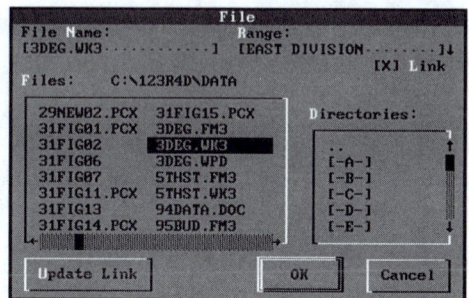

Fig. 31.22
Mark the Link checkbox to create a link between Word and the data from the 1-2-3 file.

Merging 1-2-3 Data with a Word Document

If you want to use 1-2-3 data as names and addresses for your data file, you need to first import the document as a table as mentioned previously. Save the table with a new document name. Then use the standard Merge procedure to create the letter form and merge it with the data file.

Importing a 1-2-3 Graph into a Word Document

Unlike WordPerfect, Microsoft Word supports only one of Lotus 1-2-3's two graphics file formats. While you are in 1-2-3, use **/G**raph **S**ave and save the graph with a PIC extension. Also, make sure that you use the **/G**raph **O**ptions **B**&W format before you save the graph.

◀ "Saving Graphs and Graph Settings," p. 739

When you want to bring graphs into your Microsoft Word document, choose **I**nsert **P**icture. The Picture dialog box appears (see fig. 31.23). You have the following options in the dialog box:

- Enter the file name in the Picture File **N**ame text box, or choose the file from the list in the **F**iles list box.

- Change the drive and directory in the **D**irectories list box.

- If you want to position the graph within the picture frame, choose **Al**ign in Frame and then Centered, Right, or Left.

- To change the size of the picture, change the **W**idth and **H**eight options in the Graphics Size area of the dialog box.

1060 Chapter 31—Sharing 1-2-3 Data with DOS Word Processors

- To change the white space around the graph, change **B**efore and **A**fter in the Space area of the dialog box.

- To look at how the page looks with the selected graph, choose the Pre**v**iew command button.

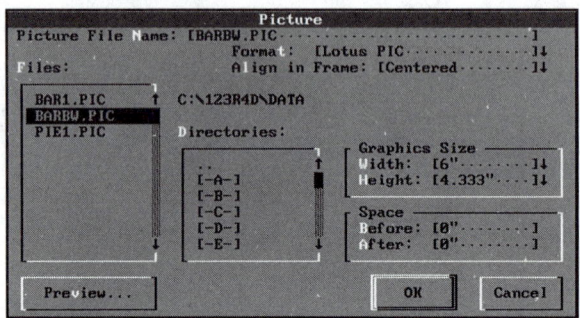

Fig. 31.23
Identify the name and location of the 1-2-3 graphic file in the Picture dialog box.

If you do not choose Pre**v**iew, choose OK to bring in the graph. When you return to the document, you see a code indicating the graph name, type, and size. You can edit this code and change the file name or location or change the width and length. For example, the code may appear as

    .G.C:\123R4\DATA\BAR1.PIC;6";4.333";Lotus PIC

You could change the 6" to 4" and the 4.333" to 2" to change the size of the picture. Save, preview, and print the document as you would any other Word document.

Troubleshooting

Many of the same problems occur in Microsoft Word as do in WordPerfect. See the Troubleshooting section after the WordPerfect section in this chapter. Here are some additional possibilities:

I want the 1-2-3 data to come in as tabs, or conversely, I want the 1-2-3 data to come in as tables.

Microsoft Word hid the option on the **T**ools C**u**stomize dialog box. Choose **In**sert Spreadsheet as Table to place spreadsheets as tables. Unmark this option to insert spreadsheets as tabs.

When I try to open a 1-2-3 file, I get a bunch of garbage in my Word document.

Unlike Word for Windows and WordPerfect for DOS or Windows, you cannot use the **F**ile **O**pen command to bring in a 1-2-3 document. Close the garbage document without saving it and use **I**nsert **F**ile instead.

From Here...

If you want to use 1-2-3 with products other than word processors, you may want to look at these other chapters:

- Chapter 9, "Working with Files," deals with how to save, name, retrieve, and translate files.

- Chapter 23, "Creating Effective Graphs," shows you how to choose graph types and change attributes.

- Chapter 29, "Sharing 1-2-3 Data with Windows Applications," shows you how to copy information within 1-2-3 files to the Windows Clipboard. You can also use 1-2-3 data and graphs in Windows word processing and spreadsheet applications.

- Chapter 30, "Sharing 1-2-3 Data with Databases," shows you how to use the **/D**ata **E**xternal feature to link your 1-2-3 files to database-management programs.

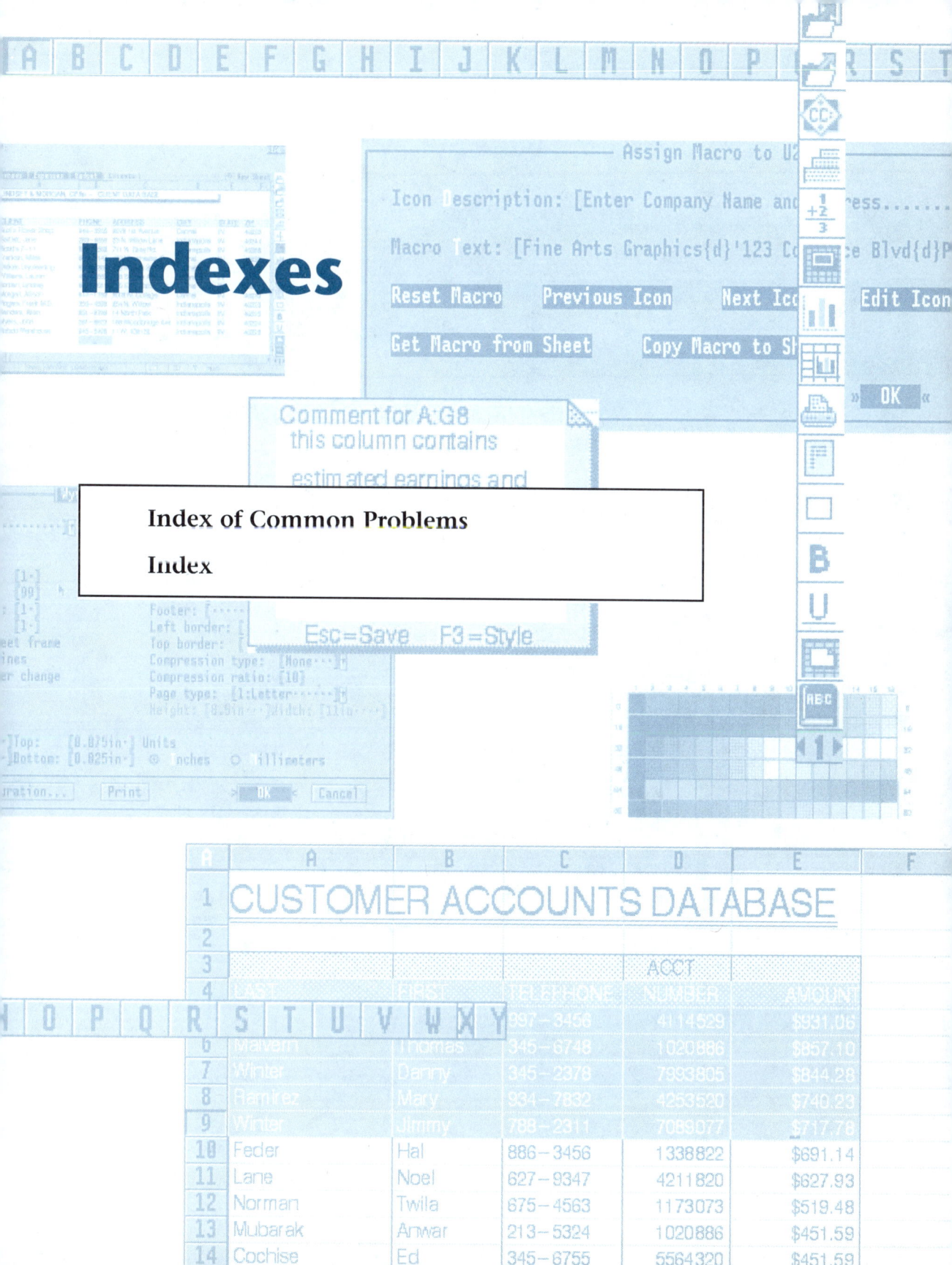

Indexes

Index of Common Problems

Index

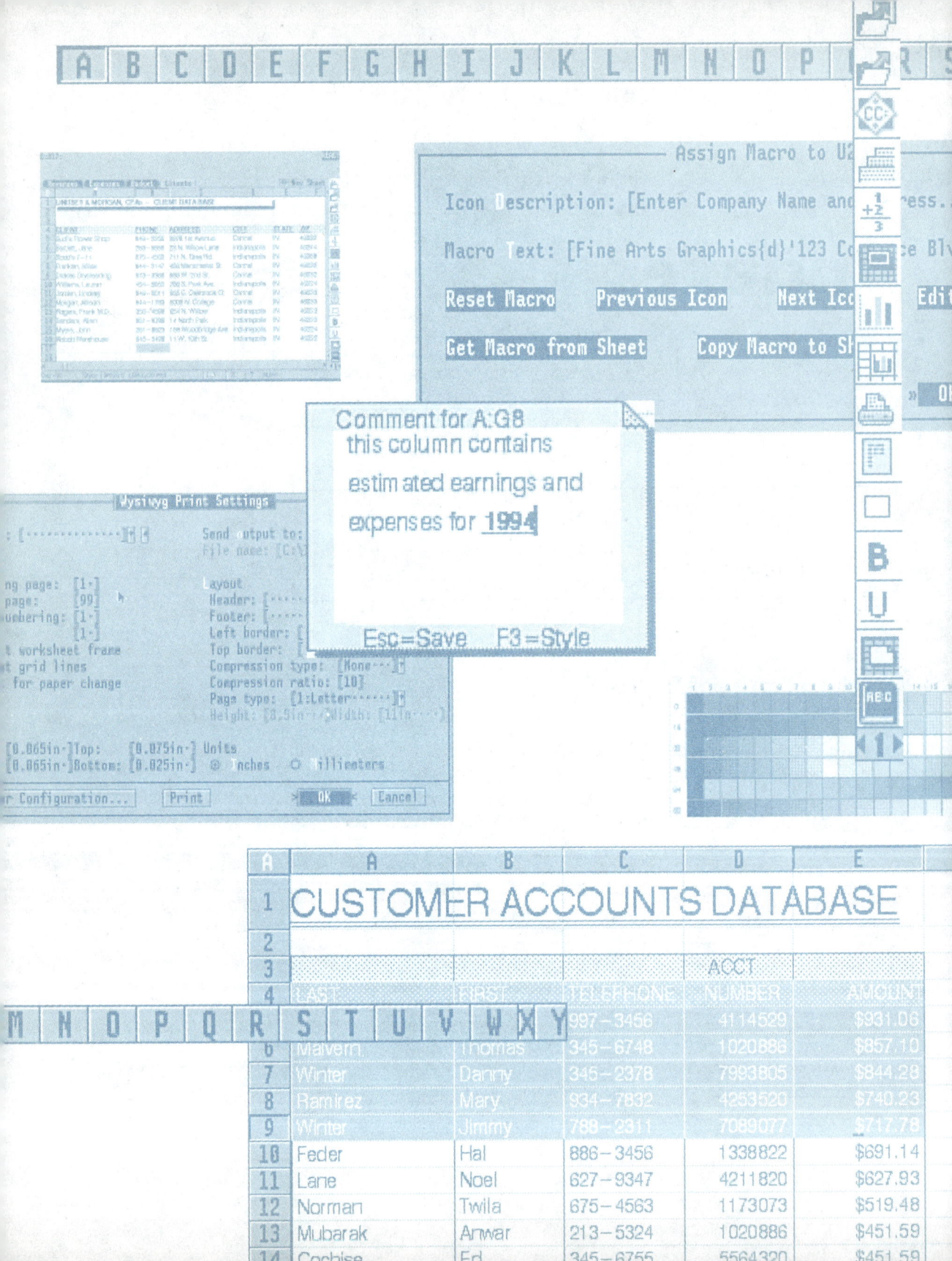

Index of Common Problems

1-2-3 Release 4 for DOS Basics

If you have this problem...	You'll find help here...
******* appears in a cell where a value should be	p. 80
1-2-3 beeps and the cell pointer doesn't move when you press the arrow keys	p. 56
Cell pointer doesn't move in the way you expect	p. 56
Dates: 1-2-3 converted a date to a number	p. 80
Decimals: 1-2-3 adds decimals to every value you enter in a cell	p. 81
Formula displays in a cell instead of the calculated results	p. 80
Formulas result in errors when you delete a row or column	p. 81
Functions: 1-2-3 displays text when a function is entered in a cell	p. 161
Functions: 1-2-3 will not enter a function into a cell	p. 161
Graph window is too narrow to interpret	p. 238
@MAX function returns a value of zero in a range that contains negative numbers	p. 194
@MIN function returns a value of zero in a range that does not contain zero	p. 194
New features of 1-2-3 Release 4 for DOS will not load	p. 44
QuickStart tutorial: Cannot locate on the 1-2-3 menu	p. 44

(continues)

1-2-3 Release 4 for DOS Basics, continued

If you have this problem...	You'll find help here...
SmartIcons: Original SmartIcons are missing from palette	p. 267
SmartIcons: User SmartIcon doesn't work correctly after editing a macro	p. 267
Split screen: 1-2-3 beeps when attempting to split the screen	p. 237
Undo feature doesn't work	p. 267

Formatting and Printing

If you have this problem...	You'll find help here...
Fonts: Using 1-2-3 Release 4 fonts with other 1-2-3 for DOS versions	p. 342
Header created with :Print Layout Titles contains page numbers, but they are not the correct numbers.	p. 403
Notepad displays text in a font that's too small to read.	p. 355
Notepad: Can't see existing notepads when you retrieve the file	p. 356
Notepad: Cannot access the /Tools Notepad menu	p. 355
Print borders appear twice in the printout.	p. 403
Print commands: /Worksheet Global Default Printer Name and Interface do not work in some worksheets	p. 362
Printing: When you issue a print command, nothing prints and you get an error message	p.403
Printing: When you use /Print to print a multiple-page report, gaps appear in the middle of the pages.	p. 403
Titles at the top of the worksheet never look centered	p. 342
Worksheet that someone else created looks different on your computer	p. 342
Wysiwyg enhancements don't print.	p. 403

Index of Common Problems

File Management

If you have this problem...	You'll find help here...
Combining: Accidentally chose /File Combine Copy rather than /File Combine Add and totals are wrong	p. 487
Combining: Accidentally repeated the last /File Combine Add twice	p. 487
Combining: Can't remember the cell references to combine or where you're at in the process	p. 486
Combining: Incorrect cell references result after you insert or delete rows	p. 487
Erased the wrong file and need it back	p. 439
GROUP Mode: Macros don't work after working in GROUP mode	p. 474
Linking files from Releases 2, 3, and 4	p. 491
Linking: ERR appears in cells that should be linked	p. 491
Linking: Program beeps when entering a long linking formula	p. 491
Multiple worksheets: An error results when you try to move to another worksheet in a multiple-worksheet file	p. 467
Multiple worksheets: Ctrl+PgUp and Ctrl+PgDn don't seem to work correctly	p. 467
Passwords: Can't retrieve a file with a password	p. 523
Perspective view doesn't work correctly	p. 467
Perspective view: Bottom two worksheets have no frame and are blank	p. 467
Protection: Nothing happens when you choose /Range Prot	p. 515
/Range Input causes problems with the screen display	p. 515
Retrieving: Cannot retrieve an existing file	p. 428
Retrieving: Don't remember the name of a file or its location	p. 427
Retrieving: File is not listed when you try to retrieve it	p. 427
Saving: Cannot save a file	p. 421
Saving: Try to save a file but receive a disk full message	p. 421
Templates: 1-2-3 beeps when you try to add data	p. 503

(continues)

File Management, continued

If you have this problem...	You'll find help here...
Templates: Accidentally save a worksheet using the template file name	p. 503
Templates: Can't print worksheet template because printer doesn't print in landscape	p. 503

Data Analysis

If you have this problem...	You'll find help here...
Backsolver reports an invalid formula cell	p. 599
Backsolver reports that it could not find a solution	p. 599
Database function (other than @DGET or @DQUERY) returns ERR	p. 547
Database function (other than @DQUERY) returns an incorrect or unexpected result other than ERR	p. 548
@DGET function returns ERR	p. 548
Solver finds fewer answers than you specified	p. 566
Solver finds more answers than you specified	p. 566
Solver reports a roundoff error	p. 566
Solver runs out of memory, or takes too long to solve a problem	p. 566, 588
Solver uses negative values for adjustable cells that shouldn't be negative	p. 566

Databases

If you have this problem...	You'll find help here...
Completed database is missing an important field	p. 626
Data tables: Every value in a three-variable data table is the same	p. 676
Data tables: Every value in a two-variable data table is the same	p. 673
Data tables: Every variable in a one-variable data table is the same	p. 670
Data tables: One-variable data table contains only zeros	p. 670
Data tables: Three-variable data table contains only zeros	p. 676
Data tables: Three-variable data table contains values that don't make sense	p. 676
Data tables: Two-variable data table contains only zeros	p. 673
Data tables: Two-variable data table contains values that don't make sense	p. 674
Database is out of order after adding new records	p. 638
Field highlighted in a record cannot be edited	p. 650
Field row scrolls off the screen	p. 626
Modified records are not replaced in the database	p. 654
Sorting: Field row shows up within the records after sorting	p. 638
Sorting: Records aren't sorted the way you intended	p. 638

Index of Common Problems

Graphs

If you have this problem...	You'll find help here...
Bars drawn in graph are hard to distinguish because hatching patterns are similar	p. 748
CGM file colors are not the same as they are in the documentation	p. 825
Clip art images placed in the worksheet obscure the underlying cells	p. 824
Graph added to the worksheet obscures data under it	p. 795
Graph ranges do not show up in the graph	p. 795
Graph Settings dialog box obstructs information in the worksheet	p. 748
Named graphs are no longer available when you open the worksheet in a new 1-2-3 session	p. 748
New range added to graph doesn't appear when graph is drawn	p. 748
Presentation slides print either too large or too small for the page	p. 824
Scale indicator in graph is not accurate	p. 795
Wysiwyg graphics editor always displays new objects on top, not behind other objects	p. 795
XY graph contains a line that goes all over the graph	p. 748

Macros

If you have this problem...	You'll find help here...
Error message appears, indicating that your macro failed in a certain cell	p. 858
Error message `Cannot write over data with APPEND commands` appears	p. 876
Error message `Invalid range` appears at the cell containing a FOR command	p. 888
Error message `Memory full` appears	p. 926
Error message `Protected cell` appears	p. 875
Error message `Syntax error in macro key/range` appears at the cell containing GETNUMBER or GETLABEL commands	p. 909

Index of Common Problems

If you have this problem...	You'll find help here...
Error message `Unrecognized key/range name` appears	p. 858
Error message `Worksheet full` appears when running an APPEND command macro	p. 875
FOR loop in a macro executes one too many times	p. 889
FOR loop in a macro never executes, but no error message appears	p. 889
GETNUMBER command keeps entering `ERR` when you enter a date	p. 909
Macro completed what it was supposed to do, but beeped or typed additional data after it should have stopped	p. 858
Macro crashes with ONERROR command	p. 909
Macro doesn't execute and 1-2-3 beeps when you try to run a macro	p. 858
Macro never stops until you use Ctrl+Break to stop it	p. 888
Macro stopped in the middle of a command, but there is nothing wrong with the command	p. 858
Macro users break out of a macro before the macro finishes running	p. 888
Mode indicator does not appear after macro finishes executing	p. 909
PUT command in macro causes an `Invalid range` error message	p. 926
Repeating data appears at the location of the cell pointer when you execute a macro	p. 859

Application Integration

If you have this problem...	You'll find help here...
1-2-3 Release 4 for Windows file won't open in 1-2-3 Release 4 for DOS	p. 1022
Cannot access a database in a different directory with /**D**ata **E**xternal **U**se	p. 1039
Cannot access a dBASE file	p. 1039
Database formulas evaluate to ERR when you retrieve a file	p. 1040
Error message appears when you bring a 1-2-3 worksheet or graph into Microsoft Word	p. 1016

(continues)

Index of Common Problems

Application Integration, continued

If you have this problem...	You'll find help here...
Error message `File is in use` appears when you try to use a 1-2-3 file in another application	p. 1022
Error message stating that multiple worksheets are not valid appears when you try to import 1-2-3 data	p. 1017
Menu appears when you use Alt+*letter* to execute a macro in a Windows program	p. 1022
Merge results in 1-2-3 field names not appearing in the list	p. 1016
Merging a document results in names that run together	p. 1016
WAIT mode indicator appears almost continually when accessing an external database	p. 1040

Index

Symbols

& (ampersand) for string concatenation, 77
' (apostrophe) in macros, 834
* (asterisk)
   as wildcard character, 424-425
   filling cells, 80
+/− format, 281, 302-303
? (question mark)
   as wildcard character, 424
   macro command, 872-873
@? function, 217
@@ function, 218
~ (tilde)
   as wildcard character, 657
   in macro code, 831
1-2-3 Release 4
   exiting, 49-50
   networks, 450-454
   new features, 31-44
   starting, 46-47, 982-984
   system requirements/options, 13-14
   Windows interaction, 982-988
   Windows version, 1018-1020
3-D graphs, 766
3-D ranges (multiple-worksheet files), 471
386-Enhanced Mode (Windows), 982

A

@ABS function, 162
absolute addresses, 80, 106-107
absolute value, 162
accessing DOS, 448-450
accounting functions, 178-189
@ACOS function, 168
active files, 408
Add Graph SmartIcon, 768
add-ins, 38
   functions, 217
   menu access, 48
   starting, 20
   see also individual add-ins
addition, 75
addresses (cells), 23
addressing cells (formulas), 79-81
adjustable cells (Solver), 558
advanced macro commands, 864-865
   Data Manipulation, 871
   Decision Making, 870-871
   File Management, 872
   Input Control, 869-870
   Program Control, 870
   Program Enhancement, 871-872
   programming, 866-868
   syntax, 865-866
   see also macros, commands
advancing paper (printers), 393-394
.AF3 files, 410
.AL3 files, 410
aligning
   cells, 65
   labels, 126-127
   paper (printer), 394
   text, 257
Allways files (.ALL), 341, 423
alphanumeric keys, 17-18
Alt+letter macros, 852-853
altering default graph, 728-730
Ami Pro, 989
Ami Pro 3
   graphs, 1012-1013
   importing 1-2-3 data, 1010-1012
   merging documents, 1013-1016
analyzing databases, 549-552
anchored cells, 83
AND conditions (queries), 661-662
#AND# operator, 664-666
annotating cells, 37
Answer reports (Solver), 578-579
answers (Solver), 563-566
APPENDBELOW command (macros), 873-874
appending
   graphs to presentations, 819
   graphs to worksheets, 252
   SmartIcons to Custom palette, 262
   SmartIcons to palettes, 257
APPENDRIGHT command (macros), 874-875
application development (macros), 931-936
   analyzing modules, 937-939
   debugging, 971-973
   documenting, 973-977
   modular approach, 936-937
   templates, 939-940
   updating formulas, 968-971

1074 application development (macros)

writing/recording modules
  CHECK module, 964-968
  DATA_WORKUP module, 947-952
  import module, 942-946
  main module, 941-942
  OPENING module, 961-963
  ROLLOVER module, 958-961
  SLIDE_SHOW module, 953-958
  WARNING module, 964-968
applying fonts, 253
arccosine, 167
arcsine, 167
arctangent, 167
area bar graphs, 711
area graphs, 148, 706
arguments (macros), 865
arrowheads (graphs), 782-783
arrows (graphs), 776
Ascending Sort SmartIcon, 261
ascending sorts, 253
ASCII files, 401-402
@ASIN function, 168
Assign Macro dialog box, 267
assigning macros to SmartIcons, 860-861
asterisk filled cells, 80
@ATAN function, 168
@ATAN2 function, 168
attaching
  macros to SmartIcons, 257, 264-269
  notepads to cells, 348-349
attaching notes to range names, 845
attempted answers (Solver), 565
attributes (text), 130
audit ranges, 531
Auditor, 529-539
  circular references, 229, 537-538
  commands, 530-531
  formulas, 534-535
  listing dependent formulas, 120
  modes, 532-533
  recalculation order, 536-537
  resetting options, 538
  setting audit range, 531
  starting, 529

auto-backup, 35
auto-executing macros, 505, 853-854
Automatic format, 281, 312-315
automatic graphs, 149
automatic recalculation, 227
automatically retrieving files, 424-426
@AVG function, 159, 189-192
axes (graphs), 751-759
  maximum/minimum values, 754-755
  scale indicator, 756
  scale number exponent, 758-759
  scale values, 755-756
  types, 757
  width, 759

B

background grids (graphs), 729-730
background printing
  loading BPrint utility, 399-400
  /Print command, 401
  :Print command (Wysiwyg), 401
background recalculation, 227
backgrounds (presentations), 821
Backsolver, 591-600
  multiple-variable changes, 596-599
    Solve option, 599
    specifying ranges, 597-598
    variables, 598
  single-variable changes, 591-596
    Solve option, 595-596
    specifying ranges, 593-594
    variables, 595
Backsolver add-in, 39
.BAK files, 138, 410
bar graphs, 147, 706-710
BEEP command (macros), 876
bin range (frequency distribution), 688
black-and-white presentations, 811-812

BLANK command (macros), 877, 961
blank graphs (presentations), 820
blank-header option (reports), 387
bold text
  presentations, 815-816
  worksheets, 133, 252
borders (presentations), 821
bounding boxes (graphs), 778
boxes (presentations), 817-819
boxes (Wysiwyg), 330-332
BPrint utility, 399-400
BRANCH command (macros), 877-878
BREAKOFF command (macros), 879
BREAKON command (macros), 880
browsing files (Viewer), 437
budgets (Solver example), 573-576
bugs (macros), 855
bullets
  bold text, 803
  presentations, 802, 815
Buy/Lease SmartSheet, 495-499
BUYLEASE.WK3 template, 38

C

CALC indicator, 26
canceling commands/macros
  commands, 21, 63, 136
  macros, 21
CAP indicator, 26
case conversion (strings), 211
cc:Mail, 454-455
CE command (macros), 880
@CELL function, 219-221
@CELLPOINTER function, 219-221
cell pointer (moving), 22, 51-53
cell references, 74-75
Cell-Pointer option (Wysiwyg), 246
cells
  * (asterisk) filled, 80
  absolute addresses, 80
  addresses, 23
  adjustable cells (Solver), 558

commands

aligning, 65
anchored, 83
annotating, 37
asterisk filled, 80
bold text, 252
center-aligning, 252
characteristics, 280
checking attributes, 219-221
checking values, 205-206
circling, 257
coloring, 253
column-width, 282
comments, 252, 346
constraint cells, 559
converting numbers to addresses, 221
copying, 98-101, 256
copying ranges, 255
data entry, 64-68
date/time formatting, 292
deleting, 255
drop shadows, 252
editing, 68-69
erasing, 116
filling, 70-74, 253
    dates/times, 72-74
    formulas, 71-72
    numbers, 70-71
find/replace operations, 112-116
formulas, 74-81
    addressing cells, 79-81
    errors, 78-79
    operators, 75-78
    types, 74
going to, 254
graphics mode, 282
inserting dates, 253
italic text, 253
justifying text, 318-320
kerning, 335
labels, 64-67, 130-132
left-aligning, 252
mixed addresses, 80
moving, 92-98
naming, 834
numeric data, 67-68, 290-317
optimal cells (Solver), 559-560, 571-572
printing, 252, 387-389
protecting, 512-513
range names, 59
referencing, 218
referencing in multiple-worksheets, 460
relative addressing, 79
restricting data entry, 514-515
right-aligning, 253
row height, 124-125
setting column width, 121-124
shading ranges, 252
summing, 251-253
supressing (reports), 380-381
text mode, 282
transposing data, 111
underlined, 252-253
values, 64
zero supression, 317
see also ranges

Cells Used reports (Solver), 586-587
center-aligning cells, 252
centering text (graphs), 781
CGA graphics, 234
CGM files, 410, 438, 769, 807, 997
@CHAR function, 216
character deletion, 21
CHECK module (application development), 964-968
checking cell attributes, 219-221
checking cell values, 205-206
checking for errors, 204
@CHOOSE function, 222
CIRC indicator, 26
Circle Range SmartIcon, 778
circling cells/ranges, 257
circular references, 228-230, 537-538
@CLEAN function, 215
CLEARENTRY command (macros), 880
clearing
    locked worksheet titles, 240
    macros from SmartIcons, 266-267
    print options, 397
click-and-drag operations (mouse), 16
clicking (mouse), 15
clip art, 807, 820-821
CLOSE command (macros), 880-881
CMD indicator, 26

@CODE function, 216
color
    graphs, 731-732, 739
    metafiles, 786
    presentations, 808-812
color format, 281, 316
coloring
    cells, 253
    graphs, 784-786
    reports, 393
    Wysiwyg presentations, 810-811
    ranges, 330
@COLS function, 223
column-variable ranges, 678
columns
    deleting, 119-121, 256
    fitting to widest entry, 35-36
    inserting, 117-118, 256
    labels, 1034
    width, 121-124, 282
combining worksheets, 481-487
    adding/subtracting data, 484-486
    copying data, 482-484
Comma format, 281, 297-299
comma formatting, 256, 291
comma-delimited, 696
commands
    Auditor menu, 530-531
    canceling, 21, 63, 136
    comparing print commands, 358-359
    /Copy, 98, 109
    /Data Distribution, 687-688
    /Data External, 447-448, 1025-1027
        Create, 1031
        Create Definition, 1032
        Create Go, 1035
        Delete, 1038
        List, 1030
        Other Command, 1037
        Other Refresh, 1036
        Other Translation, 1038
        Reset, 1039
        Use, 1029
    /Data Fill, 70-72
    /Data Matrix, 693
        Multiply, 694
    /Data Parse, 696-699, 938
    /Data Query, 644
        Extract, 548, 627, 650, 653

commands

Find, 548
Input, 645
Modify, 653
Output, 651
Unique, 655
/Data Regression, 688-693
/Data Sort, 631
    Data-Range, 633
    Primary-Key, 635
    Reset, 639
/Data Table, 948
    1, 669
    2, 671
    3, 674
    Labeled, 677
/File Admin
    Link-Refresh, 488
    Reservation Get, 453, 525
    Reservation Release, 453, 525
    Reservation Setting, 453
    Seal Disable, 524
    Seal File, 453, 523
    Seal Reservation-Settings, 453
    Table, 442, 942
    Table Linked, 490
/File Combine, 424, 434, 481, 695
    Add, 484-485
    Copy, 482
    Subtract, 484
/File Dir, 414-415, 425
/File Erase, 438
/File Import, 412, 424, 443-445
    Numbers, 437, 445
    Text, 437, 444, 696
/File List, 414, 440
    Linked, 490
/File New, 426, 459
    After, 426
/File Open, 138, 421, 424, 459
/File Retrieve, 138, 408, 414, 421, 424, 695
/File Save, 136, 416
/File View, 416, 428
    Link, 435, 489
    Open, 433
    Retrieve, 432
/File Xtract, 476-481
Find, 647-649
GoTo, 469
:Graph Add, 768

:Graph Duplicate, 772
:Graph Edit, 774
/Graph Features, 762-767
:Graph Goto, 771
/Graph Group, 152
:Graph Move, 771
/Graph Name, 740, 769
/Graph Options
    Advanced Colors, 731
    Advanced Hatches, 732, 748
    Advanced Lines, 734
    Advanced Symbols, 736
    Advanced Text, 736, 781
    Data-Labels, 724
    Scale, 752-755
    Titles, 721-724
/Graph Options Format, 728
:Graph Remove, 771-772
/Graph Reset, 707
/Graph Save, 739
:Graph Settings Display, 772
:Graph Settings Graph, 770
:Graph Settings Range, 771
:Graph Settings Sync, 772
/Graph Type, 760
/Graph View, 150, 737
:Graph View, 769
macros, 864-865
    ?, 872-873
    APPENDBELOW, 873-874
    APPENDRIGHT, 874-875
    BEEP, 876
    BLANK, 877, 961
    BRANCH, 877-878
    BREAKOFF, 879
    BREAKON, 880
    CE, 880
    CLEARENTRY, 880
    CLOSE, 880-881
    CONTENTS, 881-884
    Data Manipulation, 871
    Decision Making, 870-871
    DEFINE, 884
    DISPATCH, 885-886
    END, 945
    File Management, 872
    FILESIZE, 886
    FOR, 887-888
    FORBREAK, 888
    FORM, 889-891
    FORMBREAK, 891-892
    FRAMEOFF, 892
    FRAMEON, 892

    GET, 892-893
    GETLABEL, 893-894
    GETNUMBER, 894-895
    GETPOS, 895-896
    GRAPHOFF, 896
    GRAPHON, 896-897
    IF, 898-900
    INDICATE, 900-901
    Input Control, 869-870
    LET, 901-902
    LOOK, 903-904
    MENUBRANCH, 905-906
    MENUCALL, 906-907
    ONERROR, 908-909
    OPEN, 909-912
    PANELOFF, 912
    PANELON, 913
    Program Control, 870
    Program Enhancement, 871-872
    programming, 866-868
    PUT, 913-915
    QUIT, 915-916
    READ, 916-917
    READLN, 917-918
    RECALC, 918-920
    RECALCCOL, 918-920
    RESTART, 920-921
    RETURN, 922
    SETPOS, 922-923
    {subroutine}, 923-926
    syntax, 865-866
    SYSTEM, 926
    WAIT, 926-927
    WINDOWSOFF, 928
    WINDOWSON, 929-930
    WRITE, 930
    WRITELN, 930
    /x, 931-932
/Move, 92
pausing, 21
/Print, 381, 741-746
    background printing, 401
    default settings, 384-386
    menu options, 382-384
/Print Background, 741
/Print Cancel, 395-396
/Print Encoded, 398, 741
/Print File, 401, 443
/Print Printer, 357-359, 741
    Align, 394
    Clear, 397
    Hold, 394
    Image Current, 744

commands

Line, 393, 396
Options Advanced Wait, 395
Options Other Formatted, 402
Page, 393, 743
/Print Resume, 395
/Print Suspend, 395
/Quit, 408-409
/Range Erase, 116, 961
/Range Format
   +/−, 302
   Currency, 300
   Date, 303-304
   Date Time, 303, 307-308
   Hidden, 116, 311, 516
   Other Automatic, 72, 312
   Other Color, 316
   Other Label, 312
   Other Parentheses, 315
   Percent, 301
   Reset, 294, 516
   Sci, 302
   Text, 310
/Range Input, 514-515
/Range Justify, 128, 318-319
/Range Label, 126, 131
/Range Name
   Create, 88-90, 447, 602, 832
   Delete, 91
   Labels, 88-90, 834
   Notation Create, 91-92
   Note Table, 91
   Reset, 91
   Table, 91
/Range Search, 112
/Range Trans, 111
/Range Unprot, 512-515, 523
/Range Value, 110-111, 477
selecting, 16, 63
sending to database programs, 1037-1038
/Tools Analyze, 40
   Auditor, 529
   Backsolver, 592
   Solve Define, 561
/Tools Config-Addins, 40
/Tools DOS, 40, 439, 449-450
/Tools E-Mail, 40, 454
/Tools Macro, 40
   Copy, 846
   Run, 853

Step, 856
Trace, 856
/Tools Note, 37, 40, 845
/Tools Notepad, 347
   Add, 348
   Delete, 352
   Edit, 349
   Full Size, 350
   Hide, 351
   Icon, 349
   Table, 352
/Tools Spell, 40, 284-285
   Dictionary, 288
   File, 805
   Options menu, 285
/Tools Version, 40, 592, 603
   Create, 602, 605
   Delete, 609
   Manage-Scenario menu, 609
   Show, 608
   Update, 609
/Tools Wysiwyg, 40
Undo, 81, 134-136
Viewer menu, 430
/Worksheet Column, 121
   Column-Range Set-Width, 123
   Fit-Widest, 36, 122, 625
   Hide, 461, 517
   Set-Width, 80
/Worksheet Delete
   Column, 120, 628
   Delete, 464
   File, 408-409, 438, 442, 459
   Row, 119, 627
   Sheet, 459
/Worksheet Erase, 139, 408-409
/Worksheet Global, 473
   Col-Width, 123
   Default, 276-278
   Default Dir, 414
   Default Ext List, 412
   Default Ext Save, 413, 420
   Default Graph, 150, 739
   Default Graph PIC, 438
   Default Other Auto-Backup, 420
   Default Other Clock, 800
   Default Other Display Scroll-bars, 800

Default Other Display Tabs, 463
Default Other International Currency, 299
Default Other International Date, 304
Default Other International Negative Sign, 298
Default Other International Time, 307
Default Other Undo Enable, 134
Default Printer, 140, 384-385
Default Update, 134, 295, 298-343
Format Date Time, 303
Format Other Parentheses, 315
Group, 295
Group Disable, 472, 627
Group Enable, 459, 472
Label, 131
Prot Enable, 512-515, 523
Recalc, 536
Recalc Manual, 227
Zero, 317
Zero Label, 506
Zero Yes, 506
Format Date, 303
/Worksheet Hide
   Disable, 465
   Enable, 464, 519, 860
/Worksheet Insert, 461
   Column, 117, 628
   Row, 117, 626
   Sheet, 461
   Sheet After 1, 33
   Worksheet, 459
/Worksheet Titles, 239
   Clear, 240
   Horizontal, 240
   Vertical, 240
/Worksheet Window
   Clear, 236-237, 466
   Display 1, 234
   Display 2, 234
   Graph, 237, 720, 737
   Horizontal, 234
   Perspective, 236, 459, 466
   Sync, 235, 466
   Unsync, 235, 466
   Vertical, 234

1078 commands

Wysiwyg
  :Display Colors Background, 821-825
  :Display Colors Cell-Pointer, 800-825
  :Display Colors Replace, 810-825
  :Display Mode B&W, 786-795
  :Display Options Frame, 800-825
  :Display Options Grid, 800-825
  :Format Color Background, 821-825
  :Graph Add, 805-825
  :Graph Add Blank, 812-825
  :Graph Add Text, 781
  :Graph Edit Color Background, 812-825
  :Graph Edit Color Inside, 812-825
  :Graph Edit Color Map, 785-795
  :Graph Edit Edit Font, 781-795
  :Graph Edit Edit Width, 782-795
  :Graph Edit Transform, 792
  :Print Layout Compression, 822-825
  :Print Preview, 822-825
  :Print Range Set, 141
  :Text Align, 126
  :Text Clear, 128
  :Text Edit, 130-132
  :Text Reformat, 128
  :Text Set, 130
  :Worksheet Page Row, 822-825
  :Display Mode, 242
  :Display Zoom, 242
  :Format Bold Set command, 329
  :Format Color, 330
  :Format Font Library Erase command, 328
  :Format Font Library Retrieve command, 328
  :Format Font Library Save, 328
  :Format Font Replace, 327
  :Format Italics Set, 329
  :Format Lines, 330-331
  :Format Lines Bottom, 329
  :Format Shade, 332
  :Graph Add, 368
  :Graph Add command, 396
  :Graph Edit Color Background command, 732
  :Named-Style, 337
  :Print, 401, 357-359
  :Print Config menu, 362-363
  :Print Layout, 374
  :Print Layout Borders, 377
  :Print Layout Compression, 372
  :Print Layout Default command, 378
  :Print Layout Default Restore, 378
  :Print Layout Library, 378
  :Print Layout Margins, 375
  :Print Layout Page-Size, 375
  :Print Layout Titles, 375
  :Print menu, 363-365
  :Print Preview, 367
  :Print Range Set, 365, 373
  :Print Settings Frame, 377
  :Print Settings menu, 379-380
  :Special Copy, 336
  :Special Export, 341-342
  :Special Import, 340-341
  :Special Import Fonts command, 328
  :Special Move, 337
  :Text Reformat, 328
  see also SmartIcons
comments
  cells, 252, 346
  macros, 845
comparing strings, 211
complex operators, 201
composing international characters, 20
compound growth rates, 180
compounding investments, 185
compressing printouts, 372-373
computing string length, 211
concatenating strings, 76, 207
configuring printers, 362-363
consolidating worksheets, 475-476
  combining worksheets, 481-487
    adding/subtracting data, 484-486
    copying data, 482-484
  extracting data, 476-487
    formulas, 480-481
    values, 477-479
consolidations, 458
constraints (Solver), 559, 568-569
CONTENTS command (macros), 881-884
context-sensitive Help, 60
control panel, 22-25
controlling
  external database updates, 1036-1037
  printers, 393-397
    advancing paper, 393-394
    clearing options, 397
    holding print jobs, 394-395
    pausing, 395
    print settings, 397
    printer selection, 393
    printing graphs, 396
    stopping, 395-396
  recalculation, 226-230
convergence, 230
converting
  decimals to integers, 163
  files, 412, 446, 999
@COORD function, 221
/Copy command, 98, 109
copying
  cells, 98-101, 256
  formats (Wysiwyg), 336-337
  formulas
    absolute addressing, 106-107
    mixed addressing, 107-109
    relative addressing, 104-106
  graphs (Wysiwyg), 772
  notepads, 351-352

databases **1079**

objects (graphs), 790
ranges, 255
via Windows
    Clipboard, 986-988
    spreadsheets, 1018-1022
    word processor programs, 989-1017
Wysiwyg formatting, 257
correcting formula errors, 78-79
@COS function, 167
@COUNT function, 189, 192
criteria ranges (queries), 645-647, 657-666
    AND conditions, 661-662
    formulas, 658-660
    OR conditions, 662-663
    special operators, 664-666
    string searches, 663-664
    wildcards, 657-658
crosstab tables, 948
@CTERM function, 185
currency format, 256, 281, 299-300
cursor size, 786-787
Custom palette (SmartIcons), 261-264
customizing
    graphs, 720-728
        data labels, 724-726
        legends, 727-728
        printing, 745
        titles, 721-724
    SmartIcons, 261-270
        Custom palette, 261-264
        macros, 264-269
        picture changes, 269-270

D

@D360 function, 170
Daily Planner SmartSheet, 499-500
data analysis, 46
/Data Distribution command, 687-688
data entry, 64-68
/Data External commands
    Create, 1031
    Create Definition, 1032
    Create Go, 1035
    Delete, 1038
    List, 1030

Other Command, 1037
Other Refresh, 1036
Other Translation, 1038
Reset, 1039
Use, 1029
/Data External command, 447-448, 1025-1027
/Data Fill command, 70-72
data filters, 990
data labels (graphs), 724-726
Data Manipulation commands (macros), 871
/Data Matrix command, 693-694
/Data Parse command, 696-699, 938
/Data Query commands, 644
    Del, 656-657
    Extract, 548, 627, 650, 653
    Find, 548
    Input, 645
    Modify, 653
    Output, 651
    Unique, 655
data ranges (graphs), 149-154
/Data Regression command, 688-693
/Data Sort commands, 631
    Data-Range, 633
    Primary-Key, 635
    Reset, 639
/Data Table, 948
    1, 669
    2, 671
    3, 674
    Labeled, 677
data tables, 668-669
    labeled, 677-686
        formatting results area, 680-681
        multi-variable, 685-686
        payment schedule, 683
        positioning results area, 679-680
        terminology, 678-679
        variable ranges, 681-683
    one-variable, 669-671
    three-variable, 674-676
    two-variable, 671-674
data-management, 224
data-table ranges, 668
DATA_WORKUP module (application development), 947-952

database drivers, 1027
database functions, 158, 198
databases
    analyzing, 549-552
    calculating statistics, 543-546
    comma-delimited, 696
    creating, 622-628
    data entry, 624-626
    designing, 621-622
    deviations/variance, 546
    external, 1025-1027
        connecting, 1028-1029
        controlling updates, 1036-1037
        creating, 1031-1035
        deleting, 1038-1039
        disconnecting, 1039
        listing, 1030-1031
        sending commands, 1037-1038
        terminology, 1027-1028
        translating characters, 1038
    external, 548-549
    extracting records, 655-656
    extracting values/labels, 546
    fields, 620, 623-624
    frequency distribution, 687-688
    functions, 541-543
    importing data, 695-701
    inserting 1-2-3 data as, 993-997
    key fields, 620
    matrices, 693-695
    modifying, 626-628
    queries, 643
        criteria ranges, 657-666
        deleting records, 656-657
        extracting records, 653
        listing records, 650-655
        minimum requirements, 644-650
        modifying records, 653
        output range, 650-652
        unique records, 655-657
    records, 620
    regression-analysis, 688-693
    sorting records, 631-639
        extra-key method, 638
        restoring pre-sort order, 640-641
        single-key method, 633-637

1080 databases

sort order, 639-640
two-key method, 637-638
structure, 619-620
what-if analysis, 667-686
    labeled data tables, 677-686
    one-variable data tables, 669-671
    three-variable data tables, 674-676
    two-variable data tables, 671-674
date and time function, 158, 169-177
Date format, 281, 303-306
@DATE function, 170-172
date/time operations
    filling ranges, 72-74
    formatting, 292
    inserting in cells, 253
@DATEVALUE function, 172
@DAVG function, 542-544
@DAY function, 173
dBASE files, 447-448, 695
@DCOUNT function, 542-544
@DDB function, 186
debugging
    applications, 971-973
    macros, 837, 855
decimal conversion (integers), 163
Decision Making commands (macros), 870-871
Default Printer Settings dialog box, 140
default settings, 276
    directories, 414-415
    file names, 417
    /Printer command, 384-386
    printers, 359-363
        configuring, 362-363
        hardware-specific options, 361-362
        viewing, 360
    worksheets (global), 276-279
    Wysiwyg, 246
DEFINE command (macros), 884
defining page layout (reports), 375
defining problems (Solver), 561-562
deleting
    cells/ranges, 255
    characters, 21

columns, 119-121, 256
dictionary words (Spell Checker), 290
external databases, 1038-1039
graphs, 789
headers/footers (reports), 376
notepads, 352
records with queries, 656-657
rows, 119-121, 256
scenarios, 613-616
setup strings, 392
sheets (multiple-worksheets), 464
versions, 609
worksheets, 256
delimited files, 444-445
Density option (graphs), 744
dependents (Auditor), 535
depreciation, 185-189
Descending Sort SmartIcon, 261
descending sorts, 253
designing
    databases, 621-622
    data entry, 624-626
    fields, 623-624
    modifications, 626-628
    reports, 386-390
        blank-header option, 387
        headers/footers, 386-387
        page layout, 389-390
        printing cell contents, 387-389
        specifying output type, 387
detail designs (programs), 939
determining sort order (databases), 639-640
developing macros, 835-838
@DGET function, 542, 546-548
dialog boxes, 34
    Assign Macro, 267
    Default Printer Settings, 140
    Global Settings, 294
    Graph Scale Settings, 755
    Graph Settings, 144, 762
    Graph Titles, 722
    Icon Editor, 269
    Manage Scenarios, 610
    Modify Scenario, 613
    New Program Object, 983
    Personal Dictionary, 288-290
    Quick-Graph Settings, 154

QuickGraph, 251
QuickSort, 253, 635
Spell Check, 285-288
System Add-Ins, 48
dictionaries (Spell Checker), 288-290
Differences reports (Solver), 582-583
dimensions (ranges), 223
diminishing returns, 575
dingbats, 322
direction keys, 17, 53-59
directories, 414-416
    current, 415-416
    default, 414-415
    default settings, 276
    subdirectories, 425
directory paths, 414
disconnecting external databases, 1039
disk-based files, 408
disks
    directory changes, 414-416
    managing, 413-414
DISPATCH command (macros), 885-886
:Display Colors Background command, 821-825
:Display Colors Cell-Pointer command, 800-825
:Display Colors Replace command, 810-825
:Display Mode B&W command, 786-795
:Display Mode command, 242
display modifications (presentations), 799-800
:Display Options Frame command, 800-825
:Display Options Grid command, 800-825
display, see screen display
/Display Zoom command, 242
displaying
    graphics in worksheets, 237-238
    graphs, 20
    multiple-worksheet files, 465-467
    SmartIcon palette, 259
    versions, 608-609
    zeros, 317
division, 163
DLYPLNNR.WK3 template, 38
@DMAX function, 542-544
@DMIN function, 542-544

documenting
    applications, 973-977
    macros, 837, 844-845
DOS
    accessing, 448-450
    Shell, 450
double declining-balance depreciation, 186
@DQUERY function, 542, 548
Draft density (printing), 744
dragging (mouse), 16, 83
drop shadows, 252
@DSTD function, 542
@DSTDS function, 542
@DSUM function, 542-543
dual y-axis graphs, 759-761
duplicating external tables, 1032
@DVAR function, 542
@DVARS function, 542
dynamic graphing ranges, 956

E

e-mail, 42, 251, 454-455
edit line, 64
EDIT mode, 19, 24, 68-69
editing
    cells, 68-69
    graphs (Wysiwyg), 773-795
        arrowheads, 782-783
        bringing objects to front/rear, 791
        centering text, 781
        colors/patterns, 784-786
        copying objects, 790
        cursor, 786
        deleting/restoring objects, 789
        editing text, 781
        flipping objects, 793-794
        fonts, 781
        freehand drawings, 778-779
        Graphics Editor, 795
        grids, 786
        line styles, 782
        line styles/widths, 782
        lines/arrows, 776
        locking objects, 791
        moving objects, 790
        polygons, 777
        rectangles/ellipses, 777-778
        rotating objects, 793
        scaling fonts, 787
        selecting objects, 779-780
        sizing objects, 792
        slant, 794-795
        smoothing angles, 783-784
        text, 775-776
        view, 787-789
    macros, 267-269
    notepads, 349
EGA graphics, 234
electronic mail, *see* e-mail
ellipses (graphs), 777-778
EMS (expanded) memory, 35
.ENC files, 410
encapsulated PostScript files, *see* EPS files
encoded files, 398
END command (macros), 945
END indicator, 26
End key, 56-57
EPS files, 402-403
erasing
    cells, 116
    files, 437-440
    worksheets, 139
@ERR function, 223
error checking, 204
ERROR mode, 24
errors
    formulas, 78-79
    trapping, 203-204, 223-224
@EXACT function, 211
Excel, 1020-1021
executing macros, 833
exiting 1-2-3, 49-50
@EXP function, 166
Expense Report SmartSheet, 500-501
exponential notation, 68, 75
exporting formats (Wysiwyg), 341-342
EXPREPRT.WK3 template, 38
extensions (default), 409, 413
external databases, 448, 548-549, 1025-1027
    connecting, 1028-1029
    controlling updates, 1036-1037
    creating, 1031-1035
    deleting, 1038-1039
    disconnecting, 1039
    listing, 1030-1031
    sending commands, 1037-1038
    terminology, 1027-1028
    translating characters, 1038
Extra-Key (databases), 633
extra-key sorts (databases), 638
extracting
    records (databases), 653-656
    strings, 209-210
    worksheet data, 476-487
        formulas, 480-481
        values, 477-479

F

@FALSE function, 204
field descriptions, 1035
field-creation strings, 1035
fields (databases), 620, 623-624
/File Admin
    Link-Refresh, 488
    Reservation Get, 453, 525
    Reservation Release, 453, 525
    Reservation Setting, 453
    Seal Disable, 524
    Seal File, 453, 523
    Seal Reservation-Settings, 453
    Table, 442, 942
    Table Linked, 490
/File Combine, 424, 434, 481, 695
    Add, 484-485
    Copy, 482
    Subtract, 484
/File Dir command, 414-415, 425
/File Erase command, 438
file extensions, 409
/File Import, 412, 424, 443-445
    Numbers, 437, 445
    Text, 437, 444, 696
FILE indicator, 26
/File List command, 414, 440, 490
File Management commands (macros), 872
/File New, 426, 459
    After, 426
    Retrieve, 432

/File Open command, 138,
 421, 424, 459
/File Retrieve command, 138,
 408, 414, 421, 424, 695
/File Save command, 136, 416
file sharing (networks),
 450-451
/File View, 416, 428
 Link, 435, 489
 Open, 433
/File Xtract command,
 476-481
files
 .ALL format, 423
 ASCII files, 401-402
 automatic retrieval, 424
 .BAK extensions, 138
 cc:Mail, 454-455
 .CGM files, 438, 769,
  807, 997
 converting, 412, 446, 999
 dBASE format, 447-448, 695
 default extensions, 413
 disk-based, 408
 encoded files, 398
 .EPS files, 402-403
 erasing, 437-440
 .FMT format, 423
 linking, 487-491
  formulas, 488-490
  managing links, 490
  multiple worksheet file
   comparison, 490-491
 listing, 440-442
 managing, 408-409
 metafiles, 739, 769, 786
 multiple-worksheet files,
  457-474
   deleting sheets, 464
   displaying, 465-467
   formatting, 471-474
   formulas, 470
   hiding sheets, 464-465
   inserting sheets, 461-463
   naming sheets, 463
   navigating, 467-470
   referencing cells, 460
 naming, 409-413
 new, 426
 nonsharable, 450
 opening, 138, 421-428
  automatically, 425-426
  new, 426
  subdirectories, 425
  wildcards, 424-425

.PIC format, 997
picture format, 739
.PIF files, 983
previewing, 429
.PRN files, 943-944
RAM files, 408
replacing, 420
reserving (networks),
 452-453
saving, 136-138, 416-421
sealing, 453-454, 523-525
 full protection, 523-524
 reservations, 525
sharing (networks), 450-451
tables, 440-442
transferring, 443-448
 delimited files, 444-445
 external databases, 448
 pre-version 4 format, 448
 Translate utility, 446-447
 unstructured text files,
  444
translating, 448
updating links (networks),
 454
Viewer, 428-437
 browsing, 437
 commands, 430
 linking, 434-437
 multiple file operations,
  433-434
 navigating, 431-432
 retrieving files, 432-433
 sort order, 433
wildcards, 424-425
see also worksheets
FILES mode, 24
FILESIZE command (macros),
 886
filling
 cells, 253
 ranges
  dates/times, 72-74
  formulas, 71-72
  numbers, 70-71
Final density (printing), 744
financial and accounting
 function, 158
financial functions, 178-189
@FIND function, 208-209
FIND mode, 24
Find command, 647-649
Find/Replace operations, 255
finding
 cells, 112-116

dependents, 535
 formulas with Auditor, 534
 precedents, 534-535
fitting columns to widest
 entry, 35-36
Fixed format, 281, 297
fixed-space fonts, 322
flipping objects (graphs),
 793-794
floppy disks, 413
 directory changes, 414-416
 managing, 413-414
.FM3 files, 410
.FMB files, 410
.FMT files, 423
Font/Size SmartIcon, 324
fonts
 applying, 253
 dingbats, 322
 fixed-space, 322
 graphs, 736, 781
 Line Printer, 327
 points, 321
 presentations, 802, 813-814
 proportional, 322
 reports, 391
 sans serif, 322
 scaling (graphs), 787
 serif, 322
 soft fonts, 322
 Wysiwyg, 321-328
  libraries, 328
  replacing, 325-328
 Wysiwyg settings, 246
 XSymbol, 322
FOR command (macros),
 887-888
FORBREAK command
 (macros), 888
FORM command (macros),
 889-891
:Format Bold Set command,
 329
:Format Color Background
 command, 821-825
:Format Color command, 330
:Format Font Library Erase
 command, 328
:Format Font Library Retrieve
 command, 328
:Format Font Library Save
 command, 328
:Format Font Replace
 command, 327
:Format Italics Set command,
 329

functions

format lines, 697
:Format Lines Bottom
 command, 329
:Format Lines command,
 330-331
format selector, 292
:Format Shade command, 332
formatting, 275, 280-284
 +/- format, 302-303
 Automatic format, 312-315
 available formats, 280-283
 Color format, 316
 Comma format, 297-299
 copying (Wysiwyg), 257
 Currency format, 299-300
 Date format, 303-306
 Fixed format, 297
 General format, 296-297
 graph data, 728-729
 Hidden format, 311
 International format,
  316-317
 Label format, 312
 multiple-worksheet files,
  471-474
 notepad text, 353-356
 numeric data, 290-317
 Parentheses format, 315-316
 Percent format, 300-301
 results area (labeled data
  tables), 680-681
 Sci format, 301-302
 screen display, 233-234
 Text format, 309-310
 Time formats, 307-309
 versus content, 283-284
 Wysiwyg, 320-336
  copying, 336-337
  exporting formats,
   341-342
  fonts, 321-328
  formatting sequences,
   333-336
  importing formats,
   340-341
  lines/boxes, 330-332
  moving, 336-337
  named styles, 337-340
  options, 132-134
  range colors, 330
  sequences, 333-336
  shading, 332-333
  text attributes, 329
FORMBREAK command
 (macros), 891-892

formula ranges, 678
formula-label ranges, 678
formulas, 74-81, 157-159
 addressing cells, 79-81
 cell references, 74-75
 copying
  absolute addressing,
   106-107
  mixed addressing,
   107-109
  relative addressing,
   104-106
 database queries, 658-660
 dependents, 535
 errors, 78-79
 filling ranges, 71-72
 finding with Auditor, 534
 functions, 74
 linking files, 488-490
 logical formulas (Solver), 559
 multiple-worksheet files, 470
 operators
  logical formulas, 78
  numeric data, 75-76
  string data, 76-78
 precedents, 534-535
 recalculating, 257
 search and replace
  operations, 114-116
 types, 74
 see also functions
Frame display (Wysiwyg),
 244-245
FRAMEOFF command
 (macros), 892
FRAMEON command
 (macros), 892
freehand drawings, 778-779
freezing worksheet titles,
 238-241
frequency distribution,
 687-688
full-screen mode, 983
full-size notepads, 350-351
function keys, 17-20, 59-60
functions, 74, 157-159,
 541-553
 @?, 217
 @@, 218
 @ABS, 162
 accounting, 178
 @ACOS, 168
 add-ins, 217
 @ASIN, 168
 @ATAN, 168

@ATAN2, 168
@AVG, 159, 189-192
@CELL, 219-221
@CELLPOINTER, 219-221
@CHAR, 216
@CHOOSE, 222
@CLEAN, 215
@CODE, 216
@COLS, 223
@COORD, 221
@COS, 167
@COUNT, 189, 192
@CTERM, 185
@D360, 170
database, 158, 198
database functions, 541-543
@DATE, 170-172
date and time, 158, 169-177
@DATEVALUE, 172
@DAVG, 542-544
@DAY, 173
@DCOUNT, 542-544
@DDB, 186
@DGET, 542, 546-548
@DMAX, 542-544
@DMIN, 542-544
@DQUERY, 542, 548
@DSTD, 542
@DSTDS, 542
@DSUM, 542-543
@DVAR, 542
@DVARS, 542
entering, 159-161
@ERR, 223
@EXACT, 211
@EXP, 166
@FALSE, 204
financial and accounting,
 158, 178
@FIND, 208-209
@FV, 184
general mathematical, 158
@HLOOKUP, 549-551
@HOUR, 175
@IF, 199-203
@INDEX, 224, 551-552
@INFO, 225-226
@INT, 163
@IRR, 159, 179-180
@ISERR, 203
@ISNA, 203
@ISNUMBER, 205
@ISRANGE, 204
@ISSTRING, 205
@LEFT, 210

functions

@LENGTH, 211
@LN, 166
@LOG, 166
logarithmic, 158, 165-168
logical, 198-206
logical functions, 158
@LOWER, 211
mathematical, 161-168
@MAX, 189, 193-194
@MID, 209
@MIN, 189, 193-194
@MINUTE, 175
mixing data types, 208
@MOD, 163
@MONTH, 173
@N, 213
@NA, 223
@NOW, 176-177
@NPV, 182
@PI, 167
@PMT, 181-182
@PROPER, 212
@PV, 183
@RAND, 160, 165
@RATE, 180
@REPEAT, 212
@REPLACE, 210
@RIGHT, 210
@ROUND, 159, 164
@ROWS, 223
@S, 213
@SECOND, 175
@SHEETS, 223
@SIN, 167
@SLN, 185
@SOLVER, 588-589
Solver, 587-588
special, 159, 216-226
@SQRT, 165
statistical, 158, 189-198
@STD, 189, 194
@STDS, 189, 194
@STRING, 214
string, 159, 206-216
@SUM, 189, 196
@SUMPRODUCT, 189, 196-198
@SYD, 187
@TAN, 167
@TERM, 185
@TIME, 174
@TIMEVALUE, 175
@TODAY, 176-177
trigonometric, 158, 167-169
@TRIM, 213

troubleshooting, 161
@TRUE, 204
@UPPER, 211
@VALUE, 215, 719
@VAR, 189, 195
@VARS, 189, 195
@VDB, 187-189
@VLOOKUP, 549-551
@YEAR, 173
see also SmartIcons
future value calculations, 184
@FV function, 184

G

General format, 281, 296-297
general mathematical function, 158
generating random numbers, 165
GET command (macros), 892-893
GETLABEL command (macros), 893-894
GETNUMBER command (macros), 894-895
GETPOS command (macros), 895-896
global default settings (worksheets), 276-279
Global Settings dialog box, 294
going to cells/ranges, 254
GoTo command, 469
GoTo key, 59
grammar (presentations), 804
:Graph Add Blank command, 812-825
:Graph Add command, 368, 396, 768, 805-825
:Graph Add Text command, 781
:Graph Duplicate command, 772
:Graph Edit Color Background command, 732, 812-825
:Graph Edit Color Inside command, 812-825
:Graph Edit Color Map, 785-795
:Graph Edit command, 774
:Graph Edit Edit Font, 781-795
:Graph Edit Edit Width command, 782-795

:Graph Edit Transform, 792
/Graph Features commands, 762-767
:Graph Goto command, 771
/Graph Group command, 152
graph groups, 149
:Graph Move command, 771
/Graph Name, 740, 769
/Graph Options
  Advanced Colors, 731
  Advanced Hatches, 732, 748
  Advanced Lines, 734
  Advanced Symbols, 736
  Advanced Text, 736, 781
  Data-Labels, 724
  Scale, 752-755
  Scale Automatic, 755
  Titles, 721-724
/Graph Options Format command, 728
:Graph Remove command, 771-772
/Graph Reset command, 707
/Graph Save command, 739
Graph Scale Settings dialog box, 755
Graph Settings dialog box, 144, 762
:Graph Settings Display command, 772
:Graph Settings Graph command, 770
:Graph Settings Range command, 771
:Graph Settings Sync command, 772
Graph Titles dialog box, 722
/Graph Type command, 760
/Graph View command, 150, 737
:Graph View command, 769
graphics
  CGM files, 807
  clip art, 807
  indicating trends, 807
  Lotus SmartPics, 807
  number, 806
  positioning, 806
  presentations, 805-808
  strategies, 807
graphics mode, 282
GRAPHOFF command (macros), 896
GRAPHON command (macros), 896-897

graphs, 143-155, 705
   3D, 766
   appending, 252
   area bar graphs, 711
   axes, 751-759
      maximum/minimum values, 754-755
      scale indicator, 756
      scale number exponent, 758-759
      scale values, 755-756
      types, 757
      width, 759
   bar graphs, 708-710
   bounding boxes, 778
   color, 731-732, 739
   customizing, 720-728
      data labels, 724-726
      legends, 727-728
      titles, 721-724
   data ranges, 149-154
   default, 728-730
   default settings, 277
   displaying, 20, 237-238
   dual y-axis, 759-761
   Features menu commands, 762-767
   fonts, 736
   hatches, 732-734
   HLCO graphs, 718-719
   importing
      Ami Pro 3, 1012-1013
      Word for Windows, 997-999
      Word 6.0 for DOS, 1059-1060
      WordPerfect 6.0 for DOS, 1055
   line graphs, 155, 707
   line styles, 734
   metafiles, 769
   mixed bar graphs, 712-713
   pie graphs, 713-715
   presentations, 819-821
   printing, 396, 741-746
      custom settings, 745
      default settings, 744-745
      Density option, 744
      Image-Sz option, 742-743
      Rotate option, 743-744
      saving settings, 746
   QuickGraph feature, 154-155
   QuickGraph SmartIcon, 251, 720
   reports, 746-748
   saving, 739-740
   scatter plots, 716
   settings (saving), 740
   stack-bar graphs, 710-711
   symbol styles, 735-736
   text attributes, 736-737
   tick marks, 730
   types, 147-148, 705-706
   viewing, 256, 737-739
      color, 739
      windows, 737-738
      worksheets, 737
      Wysiwyg, 738
   Wysiwyg, 768-773
      adding, 768-771
      copying, 772
      moving, 771
      removing, 772
      repositioning, 771-772
      resizing, 771
      settings, 772-773
   XY graphs, 716-718
gray shades (presentations), 811
gridlines (Wysiwyg), 245, 730
grids (graphs), 786
GROUP indicator, 26
GROUP mode, 295, 801
   formatting multiple-worksheet files, 471-474
   macros, 859
guesses (Solver), 565

H

handles, 987
hard disks, 413
   directory changes, 414-416
   managing, 413-414
hardware-specific options (printers), 361-362
hatches (graphs), 732-734
headers/footers, 375-376, 386-387
Help, 60-62
   activating, 60-61
   keyboard shortcut, 19
   QuickStart, 62
HELP mode, 24
Hercules graphics, 234
Hidden format, 281, 311
hiding, 516-519
   notepads, 351

sheets (multiple-worksheets), 464-465
SmartIcon palette, 259
HIGHLIGHT mode (Auditor), 532
HLCO (high-low-close-open) graphs, 148, 706, 718-719
@HLOOKUP function, 549-551
holding print jobs, 394-395
home position (worksheets), 54
horizontal page breaks, 256, 370-371
horizontal ranges, 679
horizontal scroll bars, 33
horizontal scroll box, 53
@HOUR function, 175
How Solved reports (Solver), 579-580

I

Icon Editor dialog box, 269
icons
   attaching macros to, 257
   changing notepads into, 349-350
   see also SmartIcons
IF command (macros), 898-900
@IF function, 199-203
Image-Sz option (graphs), 742-743
import module (application development), 942-946
importing data, 695-701
   Ami Pro 3, 1010-1012
   delimited files, 444-445
   unstructured text files, 444
   Word for Windows, 997-999
   Word 6.0 for DOS, 1059-1060
   WordPerfect for Windows, 999-1001, 1008-1010
   WordPerfect 6.0 for DOS, 1043-1049
importing formats (Wysiwyg), 340 341
Impress FMT files, 341
Inconsistent Constraints reports (Solver), 583-585
@INDEX function, 224, 551-552

INDICATE command
  (macros), 800, 900-901
@INFO function, 225-226
input cells, 668, 679
Input Control commands
  (macros), 869-870
input range, 645
input values, 668
Insert Date SmartIcon, 305
Insert Worksheet SmartIcon,
  461
inserting
  columns, 117-118, 256
  dates in cells, 253
  rows, 117-118, 256
  sheets (multiple-worksheets),
    461-463
  worksheets, 256
@INT function, 163
intensity settings (Wysiwyg),
  246
interface enhancements, 31-34
internal line counters
  (printing), 394
internal rate of return,
  159, 179
international formatting
  options, 316-317
international settings
  currency type, 299
  date formats, 304
  time, 307
Investment Record
  SmartSheet, 502
investments, 185, 570-572
invoice templates, 508
INVSTREC.WK3 template, 38
@IRR function, 159, 179-180
@ISERR function, 203
@ISNA function, 203
@ISNUMBER function, 205
@ISRANGE function, 204
@ISSTRING function, 205
italics
  presentations, 803, 815-816
  worksheets, 253
iteration in circular
  references, 229-230

J-K

justifying text, 318-320

kerning, 335
key fields (databases), 620
key names (macros), 838-842
keyboard, 16-21
  direction keys, 53-59
  End key, 56-57
  GoTo key, 59
  moving cell pointer, 51
  navigating multiple-
    worksheet files, 468-469
  Scroll Lock key, 55-56
  selecting SmartIcons,
    258-259
  SmartIcon selection, 20

L

Label format, 281, 312
LABEL mode, 24
label prefixes, 65
labeled data tables, 677-686
  formatting results area,
    680-681
  multi-variable, 685-686
  payment schedule, 683
  positioning results area,
    679-680
  terminology, 678-679
  variable ranges, 681-683
labels, 46, 64
  aligning, 126-127
  cells, 64-67
  extracting from databases,
    546
  prefixes, 130-132
landscape orientation
  (printing), 743
layout settings (reports), 378
LCD projection panels, 797
@LEFT function, 210
left-aligning cells, 252
legends (graphs), 727-728
@LENGTH function, 211
LET command (macros),
  901-902
libraries (fonts), 328
line graphs, 147, 155, 706-707
Line Printer font, 327
line spacing (reports), 390
line styles (graphs), 734, 782
line styles/widths (graphs),
  782
lines
  adding to graphs, 776
  presentations, 817-819
lines (Wysiwyg), 330-332
linking files, 487-491
  formulas, 488-490
  managing links, 490
  multiple worksheet file
    comparison, 490-491
  Viewer, 434-437
  Word 6.0 for DOS, 1059
  WordPerfect for Windows,
    1002-1003
LIST mode (Auditor), 532-533
listing
  external tables, 1030-1031
  files, 440-442
  ranges, 91-93
  records (databases), 650-655
LMBCS, 216
LMBCS (Lotus Multibyte
  Character Set), 216, 299
@LN function, 166
loading
  BPrint utility, 399-400
  multiple files (Viewer),
    433-434
loan payments, 181-182
locating strings, 208-209
locking
  objects (graphs), 791
  worksheet titles, 238-241
@LOG function, 166
logarithmic function, 158,
  165-168
logical formulas, 74, 78, 559
logical functions, 158,
  198-206
logical operators, 78, 200-201
LOOK command (macros),
  903-904
Lotus 1-2-3, *see* 1-2-3
Lotus Multibyte Character Set,
  see LMBCS
Lotus SmartPics, 807
Lotus Translate, 412
@LOWER function, 211

M

macros, 829-845
  ' (apostrophe), 834
  ~ (tilde), 831
  advantages, 831
  Alt+letter type, 852-853
  application development,
    934-936
      analyzing modules,
        937-939

debugging, 971-973
documenting, 973-977
modular approach,
 936-937
modular programming,
 936-937
templates, 939-940
updating formulas,
 968-971
writing/recording
 modules, 940-968
arguments, 865
assigning to SmartIcons,
 860-861
attaching to icons, 257,
 264-269
auto-executing, 853-854
canceling, 21
clearing from SmartIcons,
 266-267
commands
 ?, 872-873
 APPENDBELOW, 873-874
 APPENDRIGHT, 874-875
 BEEP, 876
 BLANK, 877, 961
 BRANCH, 877-878
 BREAKOFF, 879
 BREAKON, 880
 CE, 880
 CLEARENTRY, 880
 CLOSE, 880-881
 CONTENTS, 881-884
 Data Manipulation, 871
 Decision Making,
  870-871
 DEFINE, 884
 DISPATCH, 885-886
 END, 945
 File Management, 872
 FILESIZE, 886
 FOR, 887-888
 FORBREAK, 888
 FORM, 889-891
 FORMBREAK, 891-892
 FRAMEOFF, 892
 FRAMEON, 892
 GET, 892-893
 GETLABEL, 893-894
 GETNUMBER, 894-895
 GETPOS, 895-896
 GRAPHOFF, 896
 GRAPHON, 896-897
 IF, 898-900
 INDICATE, 900-901

 Input Control, 869-870
 LET, 901-902
 LOOK, 903-904
 MENUBRANCH, 905-906
 MENUCALL, 906-907
 ONERROR, 908-909
 OPEN, 909-912
 PANELOFF, 912
 PANELON, 913
 Program Control, 870
 Program Enhancement,
  871-872
 programming, 866-868
 PUT, 913-915
 QUIT, 915-916
 READ, 916-917
 READLN, 917-918
 RECALC, 918-920
 RECALCCOL, 918-920
 RESTART, 920-921
 RETURN, 922
 SETPOS, 922-923
 {subroutine}, 923-926
 syntax, 865-866
 SYSTEM, 926
 WAIT, 926-927
 WINDOWSOFF, 928
 WINDOWSON, 929-930
 WRITE, 930
 WRITELN, 930
 /x, 931-932
debugging, 837, 855
developing, 835-838
documenting, 837, 844-845
DOS access, 449
editing, 267-269
executing, 833
GROUP mode, 859
INDICATE command, 800
key names, 838-842
layout, 842-844
naming, 837, 844
 Alt+letter type, 852-853
 descriptive names, 853
pausing, 21
playing back keystrokes,
 851-852
presentations, 823-825
print macro, 496
printing, 841
printouts, 845
PRN files, 943-944
protecting, 859-860
range-name notes, 845
recording, 829, 846-852

repetition factor, 841
running, 254
 Alt+letter type, 852
 descriptive names, 853
save macro, 495
saving, 838
Solver, 588-589
splitting screen, 235
STEP mode, 855-857
templates, 505
testing, 837, 855-859, 943
text entry, 831-833
Trace mode, 855-857
writing, 833-834
zoom macro, 496
**main module (application
 development), 941-942**
**Manage Scenarios dialog box,
 610**
managing
 disks, 413-414
 file links, 490
 files, 408-409
manual recalculation, 477
**mathematical function,
 161-168**
matrices, 693-695
@MAX function, 189, 193-194
**maximum values (axes),
 754-755**
MEM indicator, 26
memo templates, 507
memory models, 35
**memory-resident programs,
 449**
MENU mode, 24
menu pointer, 51
**MENUBRANCH command
 (macros), 905-906**
**MENUCALL command
 (macros), 906-932**
merging
 Ami Pro 3, 1013-1016
 Word 6.0 for DOS, 1059
 WordPerfect for Windows
  documents, 1003-1007
 WordPerfect 6.0 for DOS,
  1049-1054
metafiles, 739, 769, 786
**Microsoft Windows,
 see Windows**
Microsoft Word, *see* Word
@MID function, 209
@MIN function, 189, 193-194

minimum search
 requirements (databases),
 644-650
    criteria range, 645-647
    Find command, 647-649
    input range, 645
minimum values (axes),
 754-755
@MINUTE function, 175
mixed addressing (cells), 80,
 107-109
mixed bar graphs, 712-713
mixed graphs, 148, 706
mixing data types (functions),
 208
@MOD function, 163
mode indicators (control
 panel), 24-25
modes (Auditor), 532-533
Modify Scenario dialog box,
 613
modifying
    databases, 626-628
    records with queries, 653
    scenarios, 613
    SmartIcons, 267
modular programming,
 936-937
modulus, 163
@MONTH function, 173
mouse, 14-16
    dragging, 83
    moving cell pointer, 51-52
    pointer, 15
    selecting
        commands, 16
        objects, 780
        SmartIcons, 258
    terminology, 15-16
/Move command, 92
moving
    cells, 92-98
    formats (Wysiwyg), 336-337
    graphs (Wysiwyg), 771
    notepads, 351-352
    objects (graphs), 790
    ranges, 255
multi-page presentations,
 800-802
multi-variable database tables,
 685-686
multiple-author worksheets,
 615
multiple-page reports, 369-372
    horizontal page breaks,
     370-371
    vertical page breaks, 371-372
multiple-variable changes
 (Backsolver), 596-599
    Solve option, 599
    specifying ranges, 597-598
    variables, 598
multiple-worksheet files,
 457-474, 490-491
    deleting sheets, 464
    displaying, 465-467
    formatting, 471-474
    formulas, 470
    hiding sheets, 464-465
    inserting sheets, 461-463
    naming sheets, 463
    navigating, 467-470
    referencing cells, 460
    troubleshooting, 467

N

@N function, 213
@NA function, 223
named ranges, 602
named styles (Wysiwyg),
 337-340
:Named-Style command, 337
NAMES mode, 24
naming
    cells, 834
    fields (databases), 623-624
    files, 409-413
    macros, 837, 844
        Alt+letter type, 852-853
        descriptive names, 853
    print settings, 397
    ranges, 87-91
    sheets (multiple-worksheets),
     463
    templates, 504
natural order of recalculation,
 227
navigating
    multiple-worksheet files,
     467-470
    Viewer add-in, 431-432
    worksheets, 51-59
        direction keys, 53-59
        keyboard, 51
        mouse, 51-52
        scroll bars, 33, 52-53
        worksheet tabs, 32
negative numbers, 67
net present value, 182-183

Net Worth SmartSheet, 502
networks, 450-454
    cc:Mail, 454-455
    file sharing, 450-451
    passwords, 453-454
    reserving files, 452-453
    sealing files, 453-454
    updating links, 454
new features, 31-44
    auto-backup, 35
    cell annotation, 37
    e-mail, 42
    fitting columns to widest
     entry, 35-36
    interface enhancements,
     31-34
    memory, 35
    QuickStart, 43-44
    SmartSheet templates, 37-38
    Spell Checker, 43
    Tools menu, 38-40
    Version Manager, 40-41
New Program Object
 dialog box, 983
New Sheet button, 33
Next Worksheet SmartIcon,
 469, 801
nonsharable files, 450
#NOT# operator, 664-666
Notepad SmartIcon, 845
notepads, 346-356
    attaching to cells, 348-349
    changing to icons, 349-350
    copying, 351-352
    deleting, 352
    editing, 349
    formatting text, 353-356
    full-size, 350-351
    hiding, 351
    moving, 351-352
    tables, 352
    troubleshooting, 355-356
notes (ranges), 91-92
@NOW function, 176-177
@NPV function, 182
NUM indicator, 26
numeric data
    +/- format, 302-303
    absolute value, 162
    alignment, 282
    Automatic format, 312-315
    cell entry, 67-68
    Color format, 316
    Comma format, 291,
     297-299

comma formatting, 256
converting strings, 213-215
Currency format, 299-300
currency formatting, 256
Date formats, 303-306
Fixed format, 297
formatting, 290-317
General format, 296-297
Hidden format, 311
International format, 316-317
Label format, 312
Parentheses format, 315-316
percent (%) formatting, 256
Percent format, 300-301
random numbers, 160
rounding, 159, 164
rounding in cells, 68
Sci format, 301-302
scientific notation, 68
Text format, 309-310
Time format, 307-309
numeric keypad, 17-18
numeric keys, 17
numeric methods (Solver), 557

O

objects
　adding to graphs
　　freehand drawings, 778-779
　　lines/arrows, 776
　　polygons, 777
　　rectangles/ellipses, 777-778
　　text, 775-776
　selecting, 779-780
one-variable data tables, 669-671
ONERROR command (macros), 908-909
online Help
　activating, 60-61
　QuickStart, 62
OPEN command (macros), 909-912
opening
　files, 421-428
　　automatically, 425-426
　　new, 426
　　subdirectories, 425
　　wildcards, 424-425
　worksheets, 138, 251

OPENING module (application development), 961-963
operating system access, 448-450
operators
　complex operators, 201
　logical formulas, 78
　logical operators, 200-201
　numeric data, 75-76
　order of precedence, 75
　string data, 76-78
optimal answers (Solver), 565
optimal cells (Solver), 559-560, 571-572
optimal recalculation, 227
optimizing production (Solver example), 567-569
OR conditions (queries), 662-663
#OR# operator, 664-666
order of precedence (operators), 75
outline templates, 507
outlining ranges, 252
output ranges
　data regression, 690
　queries, 650-652
overriding operator precedence, 76
overtype mode, 21
OVR indicator, 26

P

page breaks, 245, 256, 822
page layout (reports), 389-390
page setup (printing), 374-378
palettes (SmartIcons), 250
　appending/removing SmartIcons, 257
　displaying/hiding, 259
　rearranging SmartIcons, 257
PANELOFF command (macros), 912
PANELON command (macros), 913
paper advance (printers), 393-394
paragraph formatting, 127-129
Parentheses format, 281, 315-316
password protection, 453-454, 519-523

paths, 414
patterns (graphs), 784-786
pausing print jobs, 395
payment schedule (labeled data tables), 683
percentage (%) formatting, 256, 281, 300-301
periodic payments (loans), 181
personal dictionary (Spell Checker), 288-290
Personal Dictionary dialog box, 288-290
perspective view, 251
@PI function, 167
.PIC files, 410, 997
picture changes (SmartIcons), 269-270
picture files, 739
pie graphs, 706, 713-715
.PIF files, 983
pitch (reports), 390
playing back keystrokes (macros), 851-852
@PMT function, 181-182
POINT mode, 25, 82
point size in presentations (text), 802
pointer (mouse), 15
points, 321
polygons (graphs), 777
portrait orientation (printing), 743
positioning
　graphics, 806
　results area (labeled data tables), 679-680
precedents (Auditor), 534-535
predicting outcomes, 41
prefixes (labels), 130-132
preselecting ranges, 86-87, 634
present value calculations, 182-183
presentations, 797-798
　backgrounds, 821
　black-and-white, 811-812
　bold type, 815-816
　borders, 821
　boxes, 817-819
　bullets, 802-803, 815
　clip art, 807, 820-821
　color, 808-812
　display modifications, 799-800
　fonts, 802, 813-814
　graphics, 805-808

presentations
graphs, 819-821
GROUP mode, 801
italics, 803, 815-816
LCD projection panels, 797
lines, 817-819
macros, 823-825
multi-page, 800-802
printing slides, 822
row-and-column structure, 798-799
sans serif typefaces, 802
screen shows, 797
shading, 817-819
slides, 798, 804
spelling, 805
subtitles, 802
symbols, 814-815
tabs, 801
text
  color, 812
  point size, 802
titles, 803-804
previewing
  files, 429
  print jobs, 141, 252, 367
Previous Worksheet SmartIcon, 467
Primary-Key (databases), 632
/Print Background, 741
print borders (reports), 377
/Print Cancel command, 395-396
/Print command, 381, 741-746
  background printing, 401
  default settings, 384-386
  menu options, 382-384
  Printer, 357-359
:Print command (Wysiwyg), 357-359, 401
:Print Config menu commands, 362-363
/Print Encoded command, 398, 741
/Print File command, 401, 443
:Print Layout commands (Wysiwyg), 374
  Borders command, 377
  Compression command, 372, 822-825
  Default command, 378
  Default Restore command, 378
  Library command, 378
  Margins commands, 375
  Page-Size command, 375
  Titles command, 375

print macro, 496
:Print menu commands, 363-365
print orientation (reports), 379-380
:Print Preview command, 367, 822-825
Print Preview SmartIcon, 367
/Print Printer commands, 741
  Align, 394
  Clear, 397
  Hold, 394
  Image Current, 744
  Line, 393, 396
  Options Advanced Wait, 395
  Options Other Formatted, 402
  Page, 393, 743
:Print Range Set command, 141, 365, 373
/Print Resume command, 395
:Print Settings command, 377-380
/Print Suspend command, 395
printer settings, 140
printing, 140-143
  ASCII files, 401-402
  background printing, 399-401
    loading BPrint utility, 399-400
    /Print command, 401
    :Print command (Wysiwyg), 401
  cell contents, 387-389
  cell ranges, 252
  command comparison, 358-359
  controlling printers
    advancing paper, 393-394
    clearing options, 397
    holding print jobs, 394-395
    pausing, 395
    print settings, 397
    printer selection, 393
    printing graphs, 396
    stopping, 395-396
  default print settings, 359-363
    hardware-specific options, 361-362
    troubleshooting, 362
    viewing, 360
  encoded files, 398

EPS files, 402-403
graphs, 396, 741-746
  custom settings, 745
  default settings, 744-745
  Density option, 744
  Image-Sz option, 742-743
  Rotate option, 743-744
  saving settings, 746
landscape orientation, 743
macros, 841
portrait orientation, 743
previewing print jobs, 141, 252
printer configuration, 362-363
printer defaults, 276
printer settings, 140
reports, 142-143, 357-403
  compressing output, 372-373
  defining page layout, 375
  headers/footers, 375-376
  horizontal page breaks, 370-371
  multiple ranges, 373-374
  multiple-page, 369-372
  page setup, 374-378
  previewing print jobs, 367
  print borders, 377
  :Print menu commands, 363-365
  print orientation, 379-380
  saving layout settings, 378
  single-page, 367-368
  specifying print range, 365-367
  supressing cells, 380-381
  three-dimensional ranges, 373
  vertical page breaks, 371-372
  worksheet frame, 377-378
screen display, 21
setup strings, 391-392
slides, 822
specifying print ranges, 141
text files on disk, 382
worksheets, 496
.PRN files, 410, 943-944
Program Control commands (macros), 870

Program Enhancement commands (macros), 871-872
Program Information Files, *see* PIF files
programming with macro commands, 866-868
programs
    mail enabled, 42
    memory-resident, 449
@PROPER function, 212
proportional fonts, 322
protecting
    macros, 859-860
    worksheets, 512-515
        cells/ranges, 512-513
        password protection, 519-523
        restricting data entry, 514-515
PRT indicator, 26
PUT command (macros), 913-915
@PV function, 183

Q

queries (databases), 643
    criteria ranges, 657-666
        AND conditions, 661-662
        formulas, 658-660
        OR conditions, 662-663
        special operators, 664-666
        string searches, 663-664
        wildcards, 657-658
    /Data Query Del command, 656-657
    deleting records, 656-657
    extracting records, 653
    listing records, 650-655
    minimum requirements, 644-650
        criteria range, 645-647
        Find command, 647-649
        input range, 645
    modifying records, 653
    output range, 650-652
    unique records, 655-657
Quick-Graph Settings dialog box, 154
QuickGraph dialog box, 251
QuickGraph feature, 154-155
QuickGraph SmartIcon, 720
QuickSort dialog box, 253, 635

QuickStart, 43-44, 62
/Quit command, 408-409
QUIT command (macros), 915-916

R

RAM files, 408
@RAND function, 165
random numbers, 165
/Range Erase command, 116, 961
/Range Format commands
    +/−, 302
    Currency, 300
    Date, 303, 304
    Date Time, 303, 307-308
    Hidden, 116, 311, 516
    Other Automatic, 72, 312
    Other Color, 316
    Other Label, 312
    Other Parentheses, 315
    Percent, 301
    Reset, 516
    Reset, 294
    Sci, 302
    Text, 310
/Range Input command, 514-515
/Range Justify command, 128, 318-319
/Range Label command, 126, 131
/Range Name
    Create, 88-90, 447, 602, 832
    Delete, 91
    Labels, 88-90, 834
    Notation Create, 91-92
    Note Table, 91
    Reset, 91
    Table, 91
range names, 59
/Range Search command, 112
/Range Trans command, 111
/Range Unprot command, 512-515, 523
/Range Value command, 110-111, 477
ranges (cells), 602
    attaching notes, 845
    circling, 257
    coloring (Wysiwyg), 330
    copying, 98-101, 255
    deleting, 255

dimensions, 223
drop shadows, 252
erasing, 116
filling
    dates/times, 72-74
    formulas, 71-72
    numbers, 70-71
formatting, 280-284
    available formats, 280-283
    numeric data, 290-317
    versus content, 283-284
going to, 254
listing, 91-93
moving, 92-98, 255
naming, 87-91
notes, 91
outlining, 252
preselecting, 634
printing, 252, 373-374
protecting, 512-513
scenarios, 601-603, 609-613
    creating, 611
    deleting, 613
    modifying, 613
selecting, 81-87
shading, 252
specifying print ranges, 365-367
supressing (reports), 380-381
transposing, 111
versions, 602-609
    creating, 605-608
    deleting, 609
    displaying, 608-609
    overlapping, 608
    updating, 609
see also cells
@RATE function, 180
READ command (macros), 916-917
READLN command (macros), 917-918
READY mode, 25
rearranging SmartIcons, 257, 263-264
RECALC command (macros), 918-920
RECALCCOL command (macros), 918-920
Recalculate SmartIcon, 227
recalculating
    formulas, 257
    pausing recalculation, 21

1092   recalculating

worksheets, 20, 226-230
  circular references, 228-230
  methods, 227-228
recalculation order, 536-537
recording
  macros, 829, 846-852
  program modules, 940-968
    CHECK module, 964-968
    DATA_WORKUP module, 947-952
    import module, 942-946
    main module, 941-942
    OPENING module, 961-963
    ROLLOVER module, 958-961
    SLIDE_SHOW module, 953-958
    WARNING module, 964-968
records (databases), 620
  see also databases
rectangles (graphs), 777-778
referencing cells, 218, 460
reformatting paragraphs, 127-129
regression-analysis, 688-693
relative addressing, 79, 104-106
removing
  graphs from worksheets, 237, 772
  nonprintable characters (strings), 215
  SmartIcons from Custom palette, 257, 262-263
  spaces from strings, 213
  text formatting (Wysiwyg), 253
  worksheet protection, 512
@REPEAT function, 212
repeating strings, 212
repetition factor (macros), 841
@REPLACE function, 210
replacing
  cell data, 112-116
  files, 420
  fonts (Wysiwyg), 325-328
  graphs (Wysiwyg), 770
reports
  background printing
    loading BPrint utility, 399-400
    /Print command, 401

:Print command (Wysiwyg), 401
color options, 393
compressing output, 372-373
default settings, 359-363
defining page layout, 375
designing, 386-390
  blank-header option, 387
  headers/footers, 386-387
  page layout, 389-390
  printing cell contents, 387-389
  specifying output type, 387
fonts, 391
graphs, 396, 746-748
headers/footers, 375-376
horizontal page breaks, 370-371
line spacing, 390
multiple ranges, 373-374
multiple-page, 369-372
page setup, 374-378
pitch, 390
previewing print jobs, 367
print borders, 377
print command comparison, 358-359
:Print menu commands, 363-365
print orientation, 379-380
printing, 142-143, 357-403
saving layout settings, 378
setup strings, 391-392
single-page, 367-368
Solver, 577-587
  Answer reports, 578-579
  Cells Used reports, 586-587
  Differences report, 582-583
  formats, 577
  How Solved reports, 579-580
  Inconsistent Constraints report, 583-585
  Unused Constraints reports, 585
  What-If reports, 580-581
specifying print range, 365-367
supressing cells, 380-381
three-dimensional ranges, 373
vertical page breaks, 371-372
worksheet frame, 377-378

repositioning graphs (Wysiwyg), 771-772
reserving files, 452-453
resetting Auditor options, 538
resizing graphs (Wysiwyg), 771
RESTART command (macros), 920-921
restoring
  objects, 789
  pre-sort order (databsases), 640-641
restricting data entry, 514-515
results area (data tables), 668
  formatting, 680-681
  positioning, 679-680
retrieving worksheets, 251, 421-428
  automatically, 425-426
  subdirectories, 425
  Viewer add-in, 432-433
  wildcards, 424-425
RETURN command (macros), 922
revising worksheets, 615
right-aligning cells, 253
@RIGHT function, 210
RO indicator, 26
ROLLOVER module (application development), 958-961
root names, 409
Rotate option, 743-744
rotating objects (graphs), 793
@RAND function, 160
@ROUND function, 159, 164
rounding off numeric data, 68
row-and-column structure (presentations), 798-799
row-variable ranges, 678
rows
  deleting, 119-121, 256
  height, 124-125
  inserting, 117-118, 256
  Wysiwyg display options, 246
@ROWS function, 223
running macros, 254
  Alt+ letter type, 852-853
  descriptive names, 853

S

@S function, 213
sans serif fonts, 322, 802
save macro, 495

Solver **1093**

saving
  files, 416-421
  graph settings, 746
  graphs, 739-740
  layout settings (reports), 378
  macros, 838
  print settings, 397
  templates, 495
  worksheets, 136-138, 251
scale indicator (axes), 756
scale number exponent (axes), 758-759
scale values (axes), 755-756
scaling fonts (graphs), 787
scatter plots, 716
scenarios (ranges), 601-603, 609-613
Sci format, 281, 301-302
scientific notation, 68
screen display, 22
  control panel, 22-25
  format changes, 233-234
  freezing titles, 238-241
  graphs, 237-238
  new elements, 32
  printing, 21
  splitting, 234-237
  standard, 233
  status bar, 25-27
  what-if analysis, 235
  worksheet area, 25
  Wysiwyg
    default settings, 246
    font directory settings, 246
    mode changes, 242
    options, 244-246
    row display options, 246
    zooming display, 242
screen shows, 797
scroll bars, 33, 52-53
SCROLL indicator, 26
Scroll Lock key, 55-56
scrolling
  windows, 21
  worksheets, 55-56
sealing files, 453-454
  full protection, 523-524
  reservations, 525
@SECOND function, 175
Secondary-Key (databases), 632
selecting
  answers (Solver), 565-566
  commands, 16, 63
  graph types, 147-148

printers, 393
ranges, 81-87
SmartIcons, 258-259
serif fonts, 322
session information, 225-226
SETPOS command (macros), 922-923
setting
  audit range, 531
  column width (cells), 121-124
setup strings (reports), 391-392
shading
  presentations, 817-819
  ranges, 252
  Wysiwyg, 332-333
sharing data (Version Manager), 614
@SHEETS function, 223
@SIN function, 167
single-key sorts (databases), 633-637
single-page reports, 367-368
single-variable changes (Backsolver), 591-596
  Solve option, 595-596
  specifying ranges, 593-594
  variables, 595
sizing objects (graphs), 792
slant (graphs), 794-795
SLIDE_SHOW module (application development), 953-958
slides, 798
  bullets, 815
  fonts, 802
  grammar, 804
  macros, 823-825
  page breaks, 822
  printing, 822
  text, 804
  titles, 803-804
@SLN function, 185
SmartIcons, 33, 249-271
  Add Graph, 768
  Align Text, 126
  appending to palettes, 257
  Ascending Sort, 635
  cc:Mail, 454
  Circle Range, 778
  clearing macros, 266-267
  customizing
    Custom palette, 261-264
    macros, 264-269
    picture changes, 269-270

  Delete, 116
  Delete Column, 628
  Delete Row, 119
  Descending Sort, 635
  descriptions, 265
  Font/Size, 324
  Insert Column, 117, 628
  Insert Date, 305
  Insert Row, 117, 626
  Insert Worksheet, 461
  listing, 251-258
  macro assignments, 860-861
  modifying, 267
  navigating worksheets, 54-55
  New File, 426
  Next Worksheet, 469, 801
  Notepad, 845
  palettes, 250, 259
  Previous Worksheet, 467
  Print, 143
  Print Preview, 367
  QuickGraph, 154, 720
  rearranging, 257
  Recalculate, 227
  removing from palettes, 257
  Retrieve File, 421
  Save File, 416
  Search, 112
  selecting, 20, 258-259
  Spell Check, 805
  STEP Mode, 856
  user SmartIcons, 860-861
  Version Manager, 260
  viewing descriptions, 250
SmartPics (Lotus), 807
SmartSheet templates, 37-38, 494-503
  Buy/Lease, 495-499
  Daily Planner, 499-500
  Expense Report, 500-501
  Investment Record, 502
  Net Worth, 502
  see also templates
smoothing angles (graphs), 783-784
soft fonts, 322
Solver, 39, 555-590
  adjustable cells, 558
  answers, 563-566
  applicability, 556
  budgets, 573-576
  constraints, 559, 568, 569
  defining problems, 561-562
  example problems, 567-576
  functions, 587-588
  investments, 570-572

logical formulas, 559
macros, 588-589
methods, 557
optimal cells, 559-560, 571-572
optimizing production, 567-569
reports
  Answer reports, 578-579
  Cells Used reports, 586-587
  Differences report, 582-583
  formats, 577
  How Solved reports, 579-580
  Inconsistent Constraints report, 583-585
  Unused Constraints reports, 585
  What-If reports, 580-581
selecting answers, 565-566
what-if analysis, 555
@SOLVER function, 588-589
sort order (Viewer), 433
sorting records (databases), 631-639
  ascending, 253
  descending, 253
  extra-key method, 638
  restoring pre-sort order, 640-641
  single-key method, 633-637
  sort order, 639-640
  two-key method, 637-638
:Special Copy command, 336
:Special Export command, 341-342
special functions, 159, 216-226
:Special Import command, 340-341
:Special Import Fonts command, 328
special keys, 17, 21-22
:Special Move command, 337
special operators (queries), 664-666
specifying
  output type (reports), 387
  print ranges, 141, 365-367
Spell Check SmartIcon, 805
Spell Checker, 43, 252, 284-290
  personal dictionary, 288-290

presentations, 805
Spell Check dialog box, 285-288
splitting screen display, 234-237
spreadsheets, 1018-1022
  1-2-3 for Windows, 1018-1020
  Excel, 1020-1021
square root calculations, 165
stack-bar graphs, 148, 706, 710-711
standard deviation, 194-195, 546
Standard Mode (Windows), 982
starting
  1-2-3, 46-47, 982-984
  add-ins, 20
  Auditor, 529
  Wysiwyg, 47-49
STAT mode, 25
statistical functions, 158, 189-198
status bar, 22, 25-27, 33
  format selector, 292
  Help button, 60
@STD function, 189, 194
@STDS function, 189, 194
STEP indicator, 26
STEP mode, 254, 855-857
step values, 70
STMTWRTH.WK3 template, 38
stop values, 70
stopping print jobs, 395-396
straight-line depreciation, 185-186
string formulas, 74
@STRING function, 214
string functions, 159, 206-216
string searches (queries), 663-664
strings, 76
  case conversion, 211
  comparing, 211
  computing length, 211
  computing LMBCS code, 216
  concatenating, 207
  converting to numeric data, 213-215
  extracting, 209-210
  locating, 208-209
  removing blank spaces, 213

removing nonprintable characters, 215
repeating, 212
replacing, 210
styles, *see* named styles
subdirectories, 425
{subroutine} command (macros), 923-926
subscripted text, 133
subtitles (presentations)
  italic text, 803
  point size, 802
@SUM function, 189, 196
sum-of-the-years'-digits depreciation, 187
summing cells, 251-253
@SUMPRODUCT function, 189, 196-198
superscripted text, 133
supressing
  cell ranges (reports), 380-381
  zeros, 317
@SYD function, 187
symbol styles (graphs), 735-736
symbolic methods (Solver), 557
symbols (presentations), 814-815
synchronized data scrolling, 235
synchronizing worksheets, 469
System Add-Ins dialog box, 48
SYSTEM command (macros), 926
system requirements/options, 13-14

T

table definitions, 1028, 1034-1035
table names, 1028
table-creation strings, 1028
tables (files), 224, 440-442
tabs in presentations, 801
@TAN function, 167
templates, 493-509
  application development, 939-940
  creating, 504
  examples, 507

troubleshooting **1095**

macros, 505
naming, 504
saving, 495
SmartSheets, 494-503
    Buy/Lease, 495-499
    Daily Planner, 499-500
    Expense Report, 500-501
    Investment Record, 502
    Net Worth, 502
see also SmartSheet templates
temporary files, 619
@TERM function, 185
testing macros, 837, 855-859, 943
text
    adding to graphs, 775-776
    aligning, 125-132, 257
    attributes, 130, 329
    boldface, 252, 815-816
    centering, 781
    color, 812
    editing, 781
    formatting notepad text, 353-356
    graphics, 805
    graphs (attributes), 736-737
    italics, 253, 815-816
    justifying, 318-320
    kerning, 335
    Label format, 312
    overtype mode, 21
    point size in presentations, 802
    points, 321
    reformatting paragraphs, 127-129
    removing formatting (Wysiwyg), 253
    sans serif typefaces (presentations), 802
    serif typefaces, 322
    slides, 804
    underlined, 252-253
    Wysiwyg formatting options, 132-134
:Text Align command, 126
:Text Clear, 128
:Text Edit command, 130-132
text entry macro, 831-833
text files
    delimited files, 444-445
    importing, 444
    printing to, 382
text format, 281, 309-310
Text mode, 282

:Text Reformat command, 128, 328
:Text Set command, 130
text-edit mode, 257
three-dimensional files
    see multiple-worksheet files
three-dimensional ranges, 373
three-variable data tables, 674-676
tick marks (graphs), 730
time formatting, 281, 307-309
@TIME function, 174
time, *see* date/time operations
@TIMEVALUE function, 175
titles
    freezing worksheet titles, 238-241
    graphs, 721-724
    presentations, 803-804
@TODAY function, 176-177
/Tools Analyze commands, 40
    Auditor, 529
    Backsolver, 592
    Solve Define, 561
/Tools Config-Addins command, 40
/Tools DOS command, 40, 439, 449-450
/Tools E-mail command, 40, 454
/Tools Macro commands, 40
    Copy, 846
    Run, 853
    Step, 856
    Trace, 856
Tools menu, 38-40
/Tools Note command, 37, 40, 845
/Tools Notepad commands, 347
    Add, 348
    Delete, 352
    Edit, 349
    Full-Size, 350
    Hide, 351
    Icon, 349
    Table, 352
/Tools Spell commands, 40, 284-285
    Dictionary, 288
    File, 805
    Options, 285
/Tools Version commands, 40, 592, 603
    Create, 602, 605
    Delete, 609

    Manage-Scenario menu, 609
    Show, 608
    Update, 609
/Tools Wysiwyg command, 40
totaling cells, 196
TRACE mode, 532-533, 855-857
transferring files, 443-448
    delimited files, 444-445
    external databases, 448
    pre-version 4.0 format, 448
    Translate utility, 446-447
    unstructured text files, 444
Translate utility, 446-447, 999
translating
    characters (external databases), 1038
    files, 448
transposing data, 111
trapping errors, 203-204, 223-224
trigonometric function, 158, 167-169
@TRIM function, 213
troubleshooting
    append macro commands, 875-876
    Backsolver, 599
    Buy/Lease SmartSheet, 497-503
    combining worksheets, 486-487
    database functions, 547-548
    databases, 626
    erasing files, 439-440
    formulas, 80-81
    functions, 161
    graphs, 748, 795
    GROUP mode, 474
    linking files, 491
    macros, 858-859
    multiple-worksheet files, 467
    notepads, 355-356
    one-variable data table, 670-671
    opening files, 427-428
    password protection, 523
    presentations, 824-825
    printer default settings, 362
    protecting files, 515
    queries, 654-655
    querying databases, 650
    QuickStart, 44
    saving files, 421
    Solver, 566, 588

sorting databases, 638
splitting screens, 237-238
templates, 503
three-variable data tables, 676
two-variable data tables, 673-674
@TRUE function, 204
tutorial (QuickStart), 43-44
two-key sorts (databases), 637-638
two-variable data tables, 671-674

U

underlined cells, 252-253
Undo command, 81, 134-136, 255
unique records (databases), 655-656
unstructured text files, 444
Unused Constraints reports (Solver), 585
updating
   file links, 454
   formulas (applications), 968-971
   versions, 609
@UPPER function, 211
user SmartIcons, 860-861

V

@VALUE function, 215, 719
VALUE mode, 25
values, 64
   extracting from databases, 546
   see also numeric data
values range (frequency distribution), 688
@VAR function, 189, 195
variable ranges (labeled data tables), 681-683
variable-rate declining-balance depreciation, 187
variables, 668
variance, 195-196
variation, 546
@VARS function, 189, 195

@VDB function, 187-189
Version Manager, 40-41, 601-616
   multiple-author worksheets, 615
   revising worksheets, 615
   scenarios, 609-613
      creating, 611
      deleting, 613
      modifying, 613
   sharing data, 614
   versions
      creating, 605-608
      deleting, 609
      displaying, 608-609
      updating, 609
   what-if analyses, 614-615
Version Manager SmartIcon, 260
versions (ranges), 602-609
vertical page breaks, 256, 371-372
vertical ranges, 679
vertical scroll bars, 33
vertical scroll box, 53
VGA graphics, 234
Viewer, 428-437
   browsing files, 437
   commands, 430
   linking files, 434-437
   multiple file operations, 433-434
   navigating, 431-432
   retrieving files, 432-433
   sort order, 433
viewing
   graphs, 256, 787-789
      color, 739
      windows, 737-738
      worksheets, 737
      Wysiwyg, 738
   printer settings, 360
   SmartIcon descriptions, 250
virtual memory, 35, 619
@VLOOKUP function, 549-551

W

WAIT command (macros), 926-927
WAIT mode, 25
WARNING module (application development), 964-968

what-if analysis, 41, 235, 555, 614-615, 667-686
   labeled data tables, 677-686
      formatting results area, 680-681
      multi-variable, 685-686
      payment schedule, 683
      positioning results area, 679-680
      terminology, 678-679
      variable ranges, 681-683
   one-variable data tables, 669-671
   reports (Solver), 580-581
   three-variable data tables, 674-676
   two-variable data tables, 671-674
wildcards, 424-425, 657-658
Windows, 982-988
   copying data
      Clipboard, 986-988
      spreadsheets, 1018-1022
      word processing programs, 989-1017
   starting 1-2-3 from, 982-984
windows
   scrolling, 21
   zooming, 237
WINDOWSOFF command (macros), 928
WINDOWSON command (macros), 929-930
.WK1 files, 411
.WK3 files, 409-410
.WKS files, 411
Word 6.0 for DOS
   importing graphs, 1059-1060
   linking, 1059
   merging documents, 1059
   tables, 1057-1058
Word for Windows, 989
   importing graphs, 997-999
   inserting data, 993-997
   merging documents, 999
   tables, 991-993
word processors, 989-1017, 1041-1060
   see also individual word processing applications
WordPerfect 6.0 for DOS, 1042-1056
   Data File Options, 1052-1054

importing, 1043-1056
merging documents, 1049-1056
retrieving 1-2-3 files, 1043-1044
WordPerfect for Windows, 989, 999-1010
  graphs, 1008-1010
  importing, 999-1001
  linking data, 1002-1003
  merging documents, 1003-1007
worksheet area, 22, 25
/Worksheet Column commands, 121
  Column-Range Set-Width, 123
  Fit-Widest, 36, 122, 625
  Hide, 461, 517
  Set-Width, 80
/Worksheet Delete
  Column, 120, 628
  Delete, 464
  File, 408-409, 438, 442, 459
  Row, 119, 627
  Sheet, 459
/Worksheet Erase command, 139, 408-409
worksheet frame, 22, 377-378
/Worksheet Global commands, 473
  Col-Width, 123
  Default, 276-278
  Default Dir, 414
  Default Ext List, 412
  Default Ext Save, 413, 420
  Default Graph, 150, 739
  Default Graph PIC, 438
  Default Other
    Auto-Backup, 420
    Clock, 800
    Display Scroll-bars, 800
    Display Tabs, 463
    International, 316
    International Currency, 299
    International Date, 304
    International Negative Sign, 298
    International Time, 307
    Undo Enable, 134
  Default Printer, 140, 384-385
  Default Update, 134, 295, 298
  Format Date, 303

Format Other Parentheses, 315
Group, 295
Group Disable, 472, 627
Group Enable, 459, 472
Label, 131
Prot Enable, 512-515, 523
Recalc, 536
Recalc Manual, 227
Zero, 317
Zero Label, 506
Zero Yes, 506
/Worksheet Hide commands
  Disable command, 465
  Enable, 519, 860
  Enable command, 464
/Worksheet Insert commands, 461
  Column, 117, 628
  Row, 117, 626
  Sheet After 1 command, 33
  Sheet command, 461
  Worksheet command, 459
:Worksheet Page Row command, 822-825
worksheet tabs, 22, 32
/Worksheet Titles commands, 239
  Clear, 240
  Horizontal, 240
  Vertical, 240
/Worksheet Window
  Clear, 236-237, 466
  Display 1, 234
  Display 2, 234
  Graph, 237, 720, 737
  Horizontal, 234
  Perspective, 236, 459, 466
  Sync, 235, 466
  Unsync, 235, 466
  Vertical, 234
worksheet-variable ranges, 679
worksheets, 22, 45
  appending graphs, 252
  auto-backup, 35
  automatic recalculation, 227
  background printing, 399-401
  background recalculation, 227
  circular references, 537-538
  clearing locked titles, 240
  comments, 345-356
  consolidating, 475-476

data entry, 64-68
default settings, 276-279
deleting, 256
editing, 68-69
erasing, 139
formatting
  available formats, 280-283
  versus content, 283-284
freezing titles, 238-241
graphs, 237-238
GROUP mode, 801
hiding data, 516-519
home position, 54
inserting, 256
labels, 64-67
multiple-author, 615
multiple-worksheet files, 457-474
navigating, 51-59
  direction keys, 53-59
  keyboard, 51
  mouse, 51-52
  scroll bars, 33, 52-53
  worksheet tabs, 32
new, 255
New Sheet button, 33
notepads, 346-356
  attaching to cells, 348-349
  changing to icons, 349-350
  copying, 351-352
  deleting, 352
  editing, 349
  formatting text, 353-356
  full-size, 350-351
  hiding, 351
  moving, 351-352
  tables, 352
numeric data, 67-68
opening, 138, 251
optimal recalculation, 227
password protection, 519-523
perspective view, 251
printing, 140-143, 496
protecting
  cells/ranges, 512-513
  restricting data entry, 514-515
range names, 59
recalculating, 20, 226-230
  circular references, 228-230
  methods, 227-228

1098 worksheets

recalculation order, 536-537
retrieving, 251
revising, 615
saving, 136-138, 251
scrolling, 55-56
Spell Checker, 284-290
    personal dictionary, 288-290
    Spell Check dialog box, 285-287
synchronized data scrolling, 235
synchronizing, 469
templates, 493-509
zero supression, 317
zooming, 253
see also files; presentations
.WR1 files, 411
WRITE command (macros), 930
WRITELN command (macros), 930
writing
    macros, 833-834
    program modules, 940-968
        CHECK module, 964-968
        DATA_WORKUP module, 947-952
        import module, 942-946
        main module, 941-942
        OPENING module, 961-963
        ROLLOVER module, 958-961
        SLIDE_SHOW module, 953-958
        WARNING module, 964-968
.WRK files, 411
Wysiwyg, 25, 241-246, 320-336
    aligning text, 125-132
    automatic startup, 48-49
    Cell-Pointer option, 246
    colors, 810-811
    commands
        :Display Colors Background, 821-825
        :Display Colors Cell-Pointer, 800-825
        :Display Colors Replace, 810-825
        :Display Mode, 242
        :Display Mode B&W, 786-795
        :Display Options Frame, 800-825
        :Display Options Grid, 800-825
        :Display Zoom, 242
        :Format Bold Set command, 329
        :Format Color, 330
        :Format Color Background, 821-825
        :Format Font Library Erase command, 328
        :Format Font Library Retrieve command, 328
        :Format Font Library Save, 328
        :Format Font Replace, 327
        :Format Italics Set, 329
        :Format Lines, 330-331
        :Format Lines Bottom, 329
        :Format Shade, 332
        :Graph Add, 368
        :Graph Add command, 396
        :Graph Add, 805-825
        :Graph Add Blank, 812-825
        :Graph Add Text, 781
        :Graph Edit Color Background, 732, 812-825
        :Graph Edit Color Inside, 812-825
        :Graph Edit Color Map, 785-795
        :Graph Edit Edit Font, 781-795
        :Graph Edit Edit Width, 782-795
        :Graph Edit Transform, 792
        :Named-Style, 337
        :Print, 401, 357-359, 363-365
        :Print Config menu, 362-363
        :Print Layout, 374
        :Print Layout Borders, 377
        :Print Layout Compression, 372, 822-825
        :Print Layout Default command, 378
        :Print Layout Default Restore, 378
        :Print Layout Library, 378
        :Print Layout Margins, 375
        :Print Layout Page-Size, 375
        :Print Layout Titles, 375
        :Print Preview, 367, 822-825
        :Print Range Set, 141, 365, 373
        :Print Settings Frame, 377
        :Print Settings menu, 379-380
        :Special Copy, 336
        :Special Export, 341-342
        :Special Import, 340-341
        :Special Import Fonts command, 328
        :Special Move, 337
        :Text Align, 126
        :Text Clear, 128
        :Text Edit, 130-132
        :Text Reformat, 128, 328
        :Text Set, 130
        :Worksheet Page Row, 822-825
    copying formatting, 257, 336-337
    default settings, 246
    drawing lines/boxes, 330-332
    editing graphs, 773-795
        arrowheads, 782-783
        bringing objects to front/rear, 791
        centering text, 781
        colors/patterns, 784-786
        copying objects, 790
        cursor, 786
        deleting/restoring objects, 789
        editing text, 781
        flipping objects, 793-794
        fonts, 781
        freehand drawings, 778-779
        Graphics Editor, 795
        grids, 786
        line styles, 782
        lines/arrows, 776

locking objects, 791
moving objects, 790
polygons, 777
rectangles/ellipses, 777-778
rotating objects, 793
scaling fonts, 787
selecting objects, 779-780
sizing objects, 792
slant, 794-795
smoothing angles, 783-784
text, 775-776
view, 787-789
exporting formats, 341-342
.FM3 files, 341
font directory settings, 246
fonts, 321-328
    libraries, 328
    replacing, 325-328
formatting options, 132-134
formatting sequences, 333-336
Frame display, 244-245
graphs, 768-773
    adding, 768-771
    copying, 772
    editing, 773-795
    moving, 771
    removing, 772
    repositioning, 771-772
    resizing, 771
    settings, 772-773
gridlines, 245
Help, 61
importing formats, 340-341
intensity settings, 246
manual startup, 48
mode changes, 242
moving formats, 336-337
named styles, 337-340
notepads, 346-356
options, 244-246
page breaks, 245
range colors, 330
removing text formatting, 253
replacing graphs, 770
row display options, 246
row height, 124-125
selecting
    commands, 63
    ranges, 86
shading, 332-333
starting, 47-49

text attributes, 329
viewing graphs, 738
Xsymbol font, 814
zooming display, 242

X–Y–Z

/x commands (macros), 931-932
X data-range option (graphs), 149
X-Range (data regression), 690
XMS (extended) memory, 35
XSymbol font, 322, 814
XY graphs, 147, 706, 716-718

y-axis (graphs), 759-761
y-intercept (data regression), 690
Y-Range (data regression), 690
@YEAR function, 173

zero supression, 317
ZOOM indicator, 26
zoom macro, 496
zooming
    windows, 237
    worksheets, 253
    Wysiwyg display, 242

GO AHEAD. PLUG YOURSELF INTO
MACMILLAN COMPUTER PUBLISHING.

Introducing the Macmillan Computer Publishing Forum on CompuServe®

Yes, it's true. Now, you can have CompuServe access to the same professional, friendly folks who have made computers easier for years. On the Macmillan Computer Publishing Forum, you'll find additional information on the topics covered by every Macmillan Computer Publishing imprint—including Que, Sams Publishing, New Riders Publishing, Alpha Books, Brady Books, Hayden Books, and Adobe Press. In addition, you'll be able to receive technical support and disk updates for the software produced by Que Software and Paramount Interactive, a division of the Paramount Technology Group. It's a great way to supplement the best information in the business.

WHAT CAN YOU DO ON THE MACMILLAN COMPUTER PUBLISHING FORUM?

Play an important role in the publishing process—and make our books better while you make your work easier:

- Leave messages and ask questions about Macmillan Computer Publishing books and software—you're guaranteed a response within 24 hours
- Download helpful tips and software to help you get the most out of your computer
- Contact authors of your favorite Macmillan Computer Publishing books through electronic mail
- Present your own book ideas
- Keep up to date on all the latest books available from each of Macmillan Computer Publishing's exciting imprints

JOIN NOW AND GET A FREE COMPUSERVE STARTER KIT!

To receive your free CompuServe Introductory Membership, call toll-free, **1-800-848-8199** and ask for representative **#597**. The Starter Kit Includes:

- Personal ID number and password
- $15 credit on the system
- Subscription to CompuServe Magazine

HERE'S HOW TO PLUG INTO MACMILLAN COMPUTER PUBLISHING:

Once on the CompuServe System, type any of these phrases to access the Macmillan Computer Publishing Forum:

GO MACMILLAN	**GO BRADY**
GO QUEBOOKS	**GO HAYDEN**
GO SAMS	**GO QUESOFT**
GO NEWRIDERS	**GO ALPHA**

Once you're on the CompuServe Information Service, be sure to take advantage of all of CompuServe's resources. CompuServe is home to more than 1,700 products and services—plus it has over 1.5 million members worldwide. You'll find valuable online reference materials, travel and investor services, electronic mail, weather updates, leisure-time games and hassle-free shopping (no jam-packed parking lots or crowded stores).

Seek out the hundreds of other forums that populate CompuServe. Covering diverse topics such as pet care, rock music, cooking, and political issues, you're sure to find others with the same concerns as you—and expand your knowledge at the same time.

Function Keys

Key	Description
F1 (Help)	Accesses the on-line Help utility.
F2 (Edit)	Switches 1-2-3 to EDIT mode to change the current cell. Activates a dialog box if one is displayed.
F3 (Name)	Displays a list of names if a command or formula accepts a range name or a file name. Displays a list of functions after an @ (at sign) appears in a formula. Displays a list of macro key names and advanced macro commands after a left brace ({) appears in a label.
F4 (Abs)	Changes a cell or range address from relative to absolute to mixed and back to relative. In READY mode, enables you to prespecify a range.
F5 (GoTo)	Moves the cell pointer to a specified cell, range, worksheet, or file.
F6 (Window)	On split screens, moves the cell pointer to another window or worksheet.
F7 (Query)	Repeats the last /Data Query command.
F8 (Table)	Repeats the last /Data Table command.
F9 (Calc)	In READY mode, recalculates all worksheets in memory. Converts to the current value a formula you are entering or editing.
F10 (Graph)	Displays the current graph, if one exists. If no current graph exists, creates and displays a graph of the data around the cell pointer.
Alt+F1 (Compose)	Creates international characters you cannot type from the keyboard.
Alt+F2 (Record)	Enables you to record and store up to the last 512 keystrokes in a cell or to repeat a series of commands.
Alt+F3 (Run)	Runs a macro.
Alt+F4 (Undo)	Reverses the last action.
Alt+F6 (Zoom)	Enlarges a split window to full size. Also removes Graph and Print Settings sheets from the screen so that you can see worksheet data when you select commands.
Alt+F7 (App1)	Starts an add-in program assigned to this key.
Alt+F8 (App2)	Starts an add-in program assigned to this key.
Alt+F9 (App3)	Starts an add-in program assigned to this key.
Alt+F10 (Addin)	Accesses the Add-In menu
Ctrl+F9 (Display Icons)	Hides and redisplays the SmartIcon palette.
Ctrl+F10 (Select Icons)	Enables you to select a SmartIcon with the keyboard.

The 1-2-3 Release 4 Screen

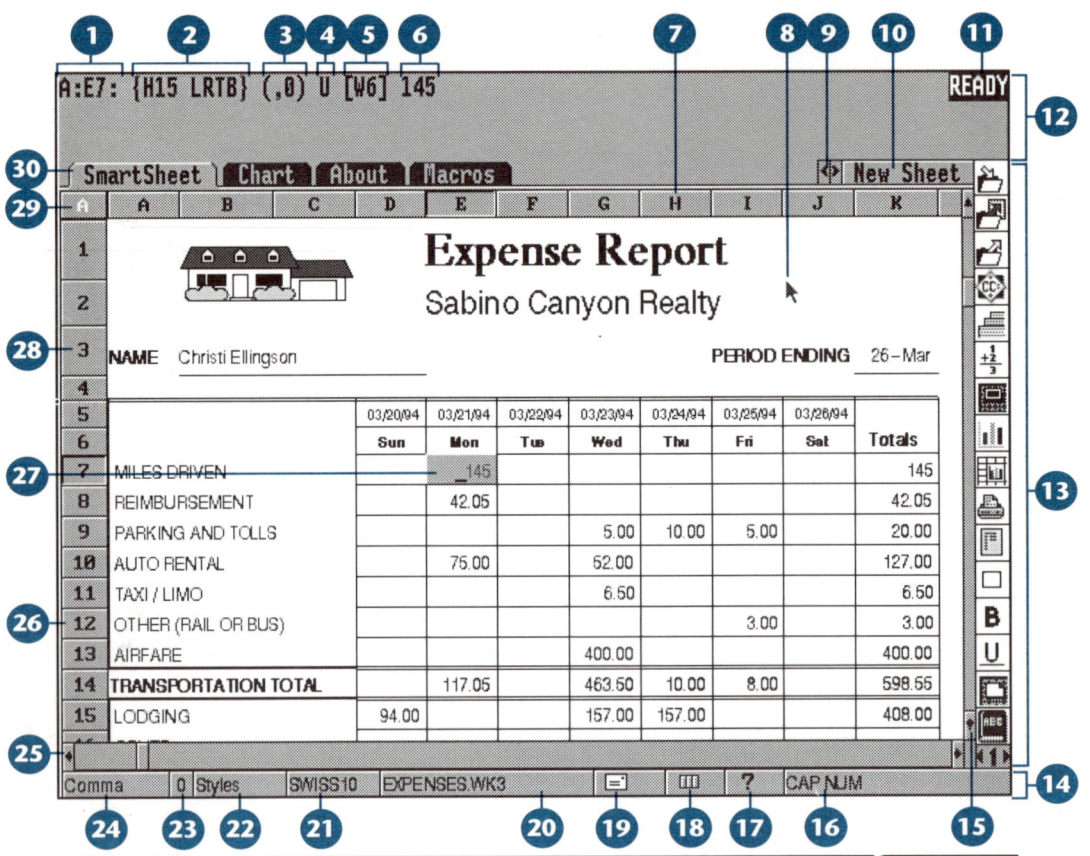

PARTS OF THE SCREEN

1. Cell address
2. Wysiwyg cell format
3. 1-2-3 cell format
4. Unprotected cell indicator
5. Column width
6. Cell contents
7. Column letters
8. Mouse pointer
9. Tab scrolling buttons
10. New Sheet button
11. Mode indicator
12. Control panel
13. SmartIcon palette
14. Status bar
15. Vertical scroll bar
16. Status indicators
17. Help button
18. SmartIcons selector
19. Mail button
20. File-and-clock indicator
21. Font selector
22. Named-style selector
23. Decimal selector
24. Format selector
25. Horizontal scroll bar
26. Worksheet frame
27. Cell pointer
28. Row numbers
29. Worksheet letter
30. Worksheet tabs